ENCYCLOPEDIA OF CONTEMPORARY BRITISH CULTURE

ENCYCLOPEDIA OF CONTEMPORARY BRITISH CULTURE

Edited by
Peter Childs and Mike Storry

London and New York

First published 1999
by Routledge
11 New Fetter Lane, London EC4P 4EE
Simultaneously published in the USA and Canada
by Routledge
29 West 35th Street, New York, NY 10001

Routledge is an imprint of the Taylor and Francis Group

© 1999 Routledge

Typeset in Baskerville and Optima by Routledge
Printed and bound in Great Britain by TJ International Ltd,
Padstow, Cornwall

British Library Cataloguing in Publication Data
A catalogue record for this book is available from the British Library

Library of Congress Cataloging in Publication Data
Encyclopedia of contemporary British culture / edited by Peter Childs and
Mike Storry.
p. cm.
Includes bibliographical information and index.
1. Great Britain – Civilization – 20th century – Encyclopedias.
2. Great Britain – History – Elizabeth II, 1952– – Encyclopedias.
I. Childs, Peter, 1962–   . II. Storry, Mike, 1943–   .
DA589.4.E53   1999   98–32205
306'.0941'0904–dc21   CIP

ISBN 0–415–14726–3

TO JO CROFT

Contents

Editorial team

General editors

Peter Childs
Cheltenham and Gloucester College of Higher Education

Mike Storry
Savannah College of Art and Design

Consultant editors

Andor Gomme
Keele University

Peter Bailey
John Moores University

Jo Croft
John Moores University

Margaret Marshment
John Moores University

Frank McDonough
John Moores University

Martin Dawber
John Moores University

Derrick Cameron
John Moores University

Sean Cubitt
John Moores University

Eugene Lange
John Moores University

Nicole Matthews
John Moores University

List of contributors

Louise Allen
Lancaster University

Neil Ankers
John Moores University

Carole Baldock

Jim Barnard

John Barry
Keele University

David Bateman
John Moores University

Cary Bazalgette
British Film Institute

David Bell
Staffordshire University

Alice Bennett
John Moores University

Kalwant Bhopal

Alison Bomber
Edinburgh University

Stuart Borthwick
John Moores University

Simon Bottom
University of Liverpool

Rachael Bradley

David Burrows
Wimbledon School of Art

Chris Byrne
Edinburgh College of Art

Dymphna Callery
John Moores University

Sarah Castell
Christ's College, Cambridge

Peter Childs
Cheltenham and Gloucester College of Higher
Education

Satinder Chohan

Paul Barry Clarke
University of Essex

Christopher Colby

Graham Connelly
University of Strathclyde

Helen Cooke

Simon Coppock

Sarah Corbett

John E. Cornwell

Nicky Coutts
Royal College of Art

Caroline Cox
London College of Fashion

David Croft

Jo Croft
John Moores University

Sean Cubitt
John Moores University

Edmund Cusick
John Moores University

Al Deakin
University of Westminster

John Deeney
University of Ulster at Coleraine

Kay Dickinson
University of Sussex

Mark Douglas
Falmouth College of Arts

Dave Egan
John Moores University

Jan Evans
John Moores University

Mark Evans
Coventry University

Fatima Fernandes
John Moores University

Rob Fillingham
St Helens College

Natalie Gale
Warwick University

Craig Gerrard
John Moores University

Claire Glossop
University of Leeds

Charlotte Goddard
Magdalene College, Cambridge

Barry Godfrey
University of Keele

Hilary J. Grainger
Staffordshire University

Michael Green
University of Birmingham

Steve Greenfield
University of Westminster

Matthew Grice

Trevor R. Griffiths
University of North London

Jim Hall
Falmouth College of Arts

George Hastings
Manchester University

Phil Hubbard
Coventry University

Eamonn Hughes
Queens University, Belfast

Jim Hunter

Lawrence Irvine Iles
British Labour Heritage

Dave Jackson
John Moores University

Sam Johnstone
Liverpool University

Chris Jones
National Resource Centre for Dance

Stephen C. Kenny
John Moores University

Steven Kerensky

Eugene Lange
John Moores University

Oliver Leaman
John Moores University

Graham Ley
University of Exeter

Alastair Lindsley

Jo Littler
Sussex University

Gerard Loughlin
University of Newcastle

Peter Lunt
University College London

Sophia Lycouris
Nottingham Trent University

Tom Maguire
Liverpool Hope University College

Jim Maloney
John Moores University

Andrea Martin
Royal Liverpool Philharmonic Orchestra

Nicole Matthews
John Moores University

Arthur McCullough
University of Ulster

Alexandra McGlynn
John Moores University

Clare McGlynn
University of Newcastle

Betty McLane-Iles
Truman State University

David McNeill
John Moores University

David Mellett
St Helens College

Bob Millington
Bolton Institute

Brett Mills
Canterbury Christ Church College

Miriam Mokal
John Moores University

Liz Moor
University College London

Joe Moran
John Moores University

Ron Moy
John Moores University

Jo Murphy-Lawless
University of Dublin

Rex Nash
University of Liverpool

Emma R. Norman

John Offer
University of Ulster

Joan Stewart Ormrod
Manchester Metropolitan University

Guy Osborn
University of Westminster

Rod Paterson
St Helens College

Jo Phoenix
Keele University

Robert Pulley
Falmouth College of Arts

Andrew Quicke
Regent University, Virginia

Lawrence Quill

Paul Rixon
Staffordshire University

Alice E. Sanger
University of Manchester

Pete Sheterline
Liverpool University

Svanborg Sigmarsdottir
University of Essex

Peter Simmons
Lancaster University

Jim Sinclair
Open Polytechnic of New Zealand

Darren Smale
John Moores University

David Smale
John Moores University

Christopher Smith
University of East Anglia

Tamsin Spargo
John Moores University

Helen Stoddart
Keele University

Elizabeth Storry
Queens University of Belfast

Mike Storry
Savannah College of Art and Design

Lucinda Towler
University of Warwick

Ryan S. Trimm
University of North Carolina

Mick Turner

Gordon Urquhart
University of Aberdeen

Jeanette Wardrop
South Bank University

Clare Whatling
University of Manchester

Colin Williams

John Williams
Sheffield Hallam University

Richard J. Williams
John Moores University

Brian Woolland
University of Reading

Roy Wormald
John Moores University

Introduction

British culture, like the proverbial elephant seized by several blindfolded persons, appears a very different beast depending on where you take hold of it. The entries in this encyclopedia are united by the term 'British' but separated by the stratifications of a 'culture' that has never been still and always been in a state of flux. Contemporary culture, like contemporary life, is changing faster than ever before, which means on the one hand that many of the traditional staple elements of 'British life' are no longer central to a definition of a contested national identity, and on the other hand, because the speed of movement is so great, a snapshot of current cultural practices is inevitably going to be blurred. So, assessing the contemporary is the hardest historical problem of all; but it is also the most exciting, perplexing, tantalizing and, we believe, the most fascinating. This book is an attempt to survey as much of contemporary British cultural practice as is possible without succumbing to the inevitable self-obsolescence that such a project brings with it.

The *Encyclopedia of Contemporary British Culture* brings together subjects which would probably never be found alongside each other in any other book. The entries vary in length from long assessments of changes in major cultural fields to short synopses of the careers of key individuals. The book is a compendium of many different and wide-ranging subject areas. Each area has a list of entries which has been designed in a particular way. This means that there are entries on many film directors, for example, but there are no entries on authors: the literature section is designed in terms of genre and market, not personality and industry. The *Encyclopedia* is arranged in alphabetical order so that unlikely bedfellows may

stimulate the browser or casual reader. Connections can also be traced by consulting the subject area classified contents list at the start and by looking up the cross-references signalled by the entries themselves. It is intended that this will enable several ways of approaching the material, for the general reader, the curious factfinder and the subject specialist.

In a selective enterprise such as this, the range of entries cannot be all-encompassing and the treatment of a subject like British culture cannot be exhaustive. In terms of temporal period, the book covers British life since the 1960s, though most entries are skewed towards the 1990s. In terms of scope, we attempted to cover in one way or another everything that has contributed more than ephemerally to British social life, but, to avoid a rapid proliferation of entries, we additionally decided to focus on people born in Britain (though some other nationals, either naturalized or resident in Britain, have also been included). The question of what is or is not 'British' was largely left up to contributors, and so no definitive position has been taken (and would raise more problems than it solved) beyond the political fact of any individual person's (or institution's) nationality. As editors, we have aimed for a certain amount of factual and stylistic consistency, but the dynamic of a subject such as national culture insists upon attitudinal variations and multiple perspectives. Contributors have been encouraged rather than discouraged to be opinionated and to raise contentious issues where appropriate.

The level of the book is such that it should be of interest both to the general reader and to the beginner seeking information on a specific topic. It also offers overviews and opinions for those already familiar with the content of the entries. We hope it will be of value to everyone involved in studying British culture, at all levels and in all countries. On longer entries, further reading, where available, has been recommended for anyone who wishes to study the subjects in greater depth.

Peter Childs
Mike Storry

Acknowledgements

We should like to thank all the editors and contributors for their help, plus everyone else who has put up with this project since 1995. Fiona Cairns, Samantha Parkinson, Mina Gera-Price and particularly Matthew Gale have been suppor- tive and ever resourceful editors on a project of several years upon which none but the brave should embark. Last and most of all, Peter would like to thank Childe Harold and Mike would like to thank Potiphar Gubbins.

How to use this book

The *Encyclopedia* contains over 900 alphabetically arranged, signed entries, ranging from concise, factual contributions to longer overview essays.

For readers with a particular interest, there is a thematic contents list which groups entries according to subject, e.g. music or the visual arts. In the body of each entry direct cross-references, indicated in bold type, lead to other relevant articles, while a 'see also' section at the end suggests related topics.

Biographical entries contain dates and places of birth and death, wherever the information is readily available, followed by the profession of the subject. Unless a country is indicated, the place of birth/death is in the United Kingdom. County names have been provided for some of the more obscure places

Suggestions for further reading are given where appropriate and where relevant texts are easily accessible.

Classified entry list

All of the entries in the *Encyclopedia* are categorized under the most appropriate subject heading(s). Some entries appear under more than one heading where relevant.

Architecture

agricultural buildings
Alsop, Will
Archigram
Architectural Association
Architectural Foundation
art galleries
Arup Associates
Birmingham Conference Centre
Byker Housing
Cardiff Bay Opera House
Chamberlain, Powell and Bon
Chipperfield, David
city redevelopment
Coates, Nigel
conservation groups
Crosby, Theo
Cullinan, Edward
Denys Lasdun and Partners
Dixon, Jeremy
Foster Associates
Gillespie, Kidd and Coia
green belts
Hammersmith Ark, London
high-tech
Hopkins, Michael
Horden, Richard
housing
industrial buildings
MacCormac, Richard
Martin, Leslie
Mather, Rick
modernism
municipal buildings

neo-classicism
new brutalism
new towns
Nicholas Grimshaw and Partners
office building
Outram, John
postmodernism
Powell and Moya
Prince of Wales's Institute
restaurants and bars
RIBA
Ritchie, Ian
Robert Maguire and Partners
Robert Matthew Johnson-Marshall and Partners
Rogers, Richard
shops
Smithson, Alison and Peter
Solar School, Wallasey
Spence, Basil
Stirling, James
St Ives
supermarkets and malls
Terry Farrell Partnership
town planning
university building
Wilkinson, Chris
Wilson, Colin St John
Yorke, Rosenberg and Mardall

Consumerism

advertising, influence of
appliances
auctions

Education and institutions

Ethnicity and belief

Fashion and design

Music

Labour Party
Labour Party black sections
libel, defamation and privacy
Liberal Democrats
lobby groups
Lonrho Affair
Maze Prison
Militant
military conflict
monetarism
Muslim Parliament
National Front
nationalist parties
nature
New Labour
North of England
nuclear and arms industries and protestors
pensioners
police
political consumerism
political publications
poll tax
poverty
prejudice
pressure groups
privacy
privatization and nationalization
recession
regulation
riots
SDP
secret services
serial killers
sex scandals
Sinn Féin
social welfare
Thatcherism
trade unions
tribalism
Ulster Unionists
violence
Westland Affair
Winter of Discontent
women in business
women in parliament

Sport

angling
athletics
badminton
betting shops
black sportsmen and women
boxing
cricket
cycling
FA Cup
football
golf
Grand National
Henley Regatta
Highland Games
hockey
horse racing
ice skating
long-distance runners
marathons
middle-distance runners
motor racing
racism in sport
rambling
rowing
rugby league
rugby union
sailing
showjumping
sport on television
sports stadia
sprinters
swimming
table tennis
tennis
University Boat Race
Wimbledon
women in sport
wrestling
yachting

Video and television

action series
advertising, television and video
animation
arts programming
Attenborough, David
audience research
BARB
BBC
black television
breakfast television

Visual and plastic arts

Youth and alternative culture

Abortion Acts

The Abortion Act of 1967, introduced by the Liberal MP David Steel, legalized in Britain. This Act came into force in April 1968 and applies to England, Wales and Scotland. The core provisions of the Act were that abortion was lawful in certain carefully defined circumstances. First, two registered medical practitioners had to be of the opinion that continuance of pregnancy would either risk the mother's mental or physical health or her children's health, or that there was a substantial risk that the child, if born, would suffer from serious mental or physical abnormalities. Second, and more contentiously, the mother's socio-economic circumstances and psychological health could be taken into consideration in reaching a decision.

The 1967 Act did not recognize a woman's right to an elective abortion. However, the social clause in the Act has been liberally interpreted to the extent that the right to abortion has been recognized in practice if not in law. Abortion under the provisions of the 1967 Act was initially set at twenty-eight weeks but this was reduced to twenty-four weeks in 1990. Approximately 84 percent of all abortions in Britain are conducted in the first trimester, so lowering the time limit has made little practical difference.

There have been various attempts to lower the time limit. The best known campaign was that of the Liberal MP David Alton, who sought to reduce the cut-off to eighteen weeks. The only major change to the law, however, has been in the course of the Human Fertilisation and Embryology Act (1990). The main provisions of this Act stemming from the **Warnock** report, were concerned with the moral issue arising from new reproductive technologies.

The 1990 Act, *inter alia*, amended the provisions of the 1967 Act by reducing the normal period of abortion to twenty-four weeks but permitting abortion after that period if the child was not going to be born alive or was to be born with a severe handicap. The 1990 Act therefore liberalized the law in some respects while tightening it in others. Until recently, the number of abortions stood more or less constant at just under 180,000 a year. However, the most recent figures show a marked increase of 8.3 percent from 1995. Increases in girls under 16 was 11.3 percent, with teenagers overall showing an increase of 15.2 percent.

It has long been the case that where the mother's life or well-being is threatened by the continuation of a pregnancy or birth, a doctor or midwife may take all reasonable measures to save that life, even if the cost is the destruction of the unborn child. In moral terms, this is covered by the doctrine of double effect: the intention is primarily to save the mother's life, the incidence is that the unborn life is sacrificed. There are some areas in which this principle still remains.

It is clearly and unequivocally the case that British law does not recognize the principle of a *de jure* right to abortion. However, in practice, providing some minimal requirements are met, an elective albeit often privately funded abortion will almost always be permitted. Such abortions can often be legally and medically processed quite quickly. For example, Marie Stopes International controversially offers 'lunch-time' abortions at several of its clinics. This regularly raises the question as to whether the law should be refined, to bring the *de jure* situation into line with factual conditions.

See also: age of consent; childbirth; family planning

Further reading

Morgan, D. and Lee, R.G. (1991) *Blackstone's Guide to the Human Fertilisation and Embryology Act 1990: Abortion and Embryo Research the New Law,* London: Blackstone Press.

PAUL BARRY CLARKE
SVANBORG SIGMARSDOTTIR

accessories

Mary **Quant** was at the forefront of the rising importance of fashion accessories in the 1960s. Quant introduced shiny plastic hipster belts with matching handbags and coloured tights which were all a fundamental part of the image for women. The nostalgic, wistful and romantic fashions of the 1970s were a reaction to the grim cultural scene and to the militant feminism of the time. Barbara Hulanicki, creator of **Biba**, had a marked effect on the accessories development. She was the first to sell soft skull caps with fringes of angelic curls framing the face. She was also responsible for popularising the pillbox hat with the small veil, which in the late 1970s became the most popular accessory for weddings (see **fashion, wedding**).

Punk, one of the biggest stories in fashion in the 1970s, provided a snarling response to conventional fashion. Born out of a relatively short lived anti-fashion street cult, it ended up representing some of the most pivotal ideas of its time through its notoriety, its similarity to tribal intimidation techniques and its anti-establishment political stance. In 1977 Malcolm McLaren and Vivienne **Westwood** opened their shop Sex on the Kings Road, London, and the key accessories consisted of a plethora of safety pins and metal chains, both for body piercing and for garment adornment. Punk anti-fashion filtered through not only to new wave street styles, but also to designers such as Zandra **Rhodes** and later in the 1980s to Jean-Paul Gaultier.

The market, rather than the medium, was the message in the 1980s, with wealth and the image of wealth a style attribute in itself. The Big Bang, with the greater accessibility to the stock markets, symbolized a return to the values of *laissez-faire* capitalism and a new breed of individual developed, the Yuppie. The smart accessories were Porsche cars, Filofaxes, Psion organizers, mobile phones and laptop computers.

In 1981 Roy Bishko, a South African lawyer, opened the first Tie Rack branch in Oxford Street, London, thus completely revolutionizing the notion of the fashion accessory. The company, whose key shops are located in airports, has been a phenomenal international success and has been instrumental in the appearance of countless other similar accessory-dedicated retailers.

The 1990s saw an enormous backlash against many of the values promoted in the 1980s. Environmentally friendly issues became increasingly influential and, despite the growing demand for new and exciting images, a heightened sensitivity to goods and the way to wear them became the most fashionable accessory.

See also: cosmetics; fashion (1980s); filofaxes; hats

Further reading

Mulvey, K. and Richards, M. (1998) *Decades of Beauty. The Changing Image of Women 1890s–1990s,* London: Hamlyn.

FATIMA FERNANDES

acronym groups

A pun on the word 'hippie', 'yuppie' is an acronym for Young Urban (or Upwardly mobile) Professional Person. The term was coined in the late 1970s and was followed in the 1980s by many similar acronyms: Guppie (a 'green' or environmentally conscious young professional); Buppie (a black yuppie); Yummie (a Muslim yuppie); Dinkie (a person in a couple with two incomes and no kids); Nimby (someone who is in favour of development generally but 'not in my back yard'); and Rumpie (a rural upwardly mobile professional, which is to say a city dweller who moves to large country houses, wears Barbour jackets, owns a 4-wheel drive, and commutes to a job in the city). The trend for such acronyms is part of a general increase in a fast-paced British society since the 1980s, towards abbreviations, buzzwords, localized acronyms and esoteric languages, which culminated in the joke usage TLA (three-letter acronym).

PETER CHILDS

action series

It is much easier to offer examples of programmes which can be described as 'action series' than it is to agree on a general definition. Most people would accept that, for example, *The Persuaders*, *Mission Impossible* and *The Fugitive* qualify, although they are all very different.

Equally, it is not easy to draw a clear distinction between genuine action series like *The Bill*, *London's Burning* or *Bugs* and more coy or zany ones such as *The Avengers* or *The Saint*, or even detective series such as *Morse*, hospital series such as *Casualty* or true-life programmes such as *Crimewatch*. There is action in all of these programmes, but it is not the predominant feature. One might say that programmes from all these other genres periodically take on aspects of the action series and vice versa: the simplified morality, the tied-up loose ends, the excitement, the lack of subtlety. An appropriate definition might then be: programmes where week by week there is formulaic violence and where good vanquishes evil.

Action series on television are watched by both sexes equally, and are almost as popular as soap operas and the news. To give an indication of viewing figures, 42.9 percent of adults watch *The Bill*, compared with the 45.4 percent who watch *Coronation Street*, the 35.3 percent who watch *EastEnders*, and the 43.5 percent who watch *News at Ten*. The programmes watched by most people tend to be British rather than imports. However,

the following American series are or have been popular with younger British audiences: *Superman*, *Robocop*, *Highlander*, *Airwolf*, *Team Nightrider* and *Xena: Warrior Princess*.

One of the factors that militate against showing more action series on television is that people are concerned about the potential copycat effects of watching television violence. This is exacerbated by the increasing numbers of channels on offer. A 1996 Sheffield University report found that eight out of the ten most violent programmes, measured in terms of violent acts, were action films shown on The Movie Channel or Sky Movies. The remaining two were cartoons. In a climate of fear partly induced by the case where the young boys who murdered toddler Jamie Bolger were allegedly influenced by a video they had seen, action films and series are under close surveillance. Even Tom and Jerry cartoons are considered potentially dangerous influences on young audiences.

See also: crime drama

MIKE STORRY

actors (female)

British cinema enjoyed a golden age in the 1960s, not only at home but abroad. For a film industry which was formed very much in the shadow of Hollywood, British actors provide a fascinating insight into the industry's self-perception in particular periods, and reflect cultural assumptions about Britishness. Thus, British actors were often invested with a patriotic imperative as bearers of British national culture. Filmgoing had a particular role in the social lives of young people, and the films of the 1960s shared and indeed helped to shape the concepts of youth which were characteristic of the social and political discourses of the time. The 1960s saw the emergence of new and challenging roles for female actors, reflecting the social and moral issues which impacted on young contemporary women. Films like *A Taste of Honey* (dir. Tony **Richardson**, 1961), and *Darling* (dir. John **Schlesinger**, 1965) introduced Rita Tushingham (b. 1940), and Julie Christie (b. 1940) in roles which contrasted sharply with the mature woman roles of 1950s films, played by actresses such as Diana Dors and Virginia McKenna. In the former film, the portrayal of Jo, a pregnant schoolgirl refusing to compromise, was consonant with the image of Rita Tushingham as a modern female star. *A Taste of Honey* portrays the emergence of specific discourses related to young women in 1960s society, suggesting that young women might be more powerful and more confident than before.

The 1960s girl was placed firmly within the context of consumption and with the sex scandal of the Profumo Affair (see **sex scandals**), which had at its heart a promiscuous young woman who had the power adversely to affect the Macmillan government, young women were very much seen in a new light. Similarly, in *Darling*, Diana, played by Christie, pushes yet further the representation and organization of female sexuality. Christie thus added sexual power and confidence to the honesty and unpredictability of Tushingham and created a figure which was to be carried through the British cinema into the late 1960s and beyond. Female actors like Christie and Tushingham, representing spontaneous and emotionally honest young women, showed cinema of the time to be working within a broader social context by reflecting contemporary attitudes to what was seen as a 1960s phenomenon. Such films also cultivated a new key audience, the youth market. In contrast to the candid depictions of the modern young woman, portrayed so convincingly by Tushingham and Christie, there was also the phenomenal success of Julie Andrews (b. 1935) in *The Sound of Music* (1965), a film which broke previous box office records. Although the film was American, Andrews's Britishness continued the tradition of upper middle-class respectability which stars like Anna Neagle had represented in previous decades.

After the period of stagnation in British cinema in the 1970s, predominantly caused by the withdrawal of American funding, there was a revival in the following decade and the heritage genre became extremely popular. One of the common stylistic and thematic features of the genre was the consistent use of specific actors, including Maggie **Smith** (b. 1934), Emma **Thompson** (b. 1959) and Helena Bonham-Carter (b. 1966). The superb Maggie Smith made her debut with the Oxford University Dramatic Society in a production of *Twelfth Night* in 1952, but is best remembered for

her remarkable performance in *The Prime of Jean Brodie* (dir. Ronald Neame, 1969), for which she won an Academy Award. Since the 1960s she has appeared in films, plays and television. Emma Thompson began performing as a member of the Cambridge Footlights and worked extensively in comedy before establishing her dramatic talents with diverse award winning roles. Specifically, in 1996 Thompson won two prestigious Golden Globe awards for screen writing and best dramatic film for her screenplay of Jane Austen's *Sense and Sensibility*. But perhaps it is Dame Peggy Ashcroft (1907–91), with her impressive work across theatre, film and television both in Britain and America, who best represents the outstanding quality and calibre of British female actors.

One of the many notable facets of British female actors is their refusal to constrain themselves to one sole medium and so have excelled in roles across theatre, television and cinema. The list of eclectic and multi-talented women who refuse to limit their performing arenas is too enormous to detail here, but joining the women already mentioned, the following are worthy of note: Dame Judi Dench (b. 1934), Glenda **Jackson** (b. 1936), Vanessa Redgrave (b. 1937), Jane Lapotaire (b. 1944) and Helen Mirren (b. 1946), who all began acting in the 1960s. Although some have argued that the notion of stardom has been seen as un-British and as a consequence has profoundly influenced the way British female actors have been marketed, this is merely conceding to a Hollywood mentality. Overall, and to their credit, British female actors have consistently valued their work above the trappings of stardom.

See also: actors (male); feminist theatre

Further reading

Geraghty, C. (1997) 'Women and Sixties British Cinema – The Development of the "Darling" Girl', in R. Murphy (ed.), *The British Cinema*, London: BFI.
Street, S. (1997) *British National Cinema*, London: Routledge.
Thumin, J. (1992) *Celluloid Sisters: Women and Popular Cinema*, London: Macmillan.

FATIMA FERNANDES

importance in which they are taken for Everyman
figures by the media – national barometers of
every issue. Actors' needs for publicity sit comfor-
tably with the media's hunger for occasionally
outrageous, professional, lively chat-show material,
iscussing work or relationships at length. Their
nge of backgrounds and wide variety of life
eriences apparently produce empathy with
vision audiences; hence the large number of
s who appear in quizzes, magazine pro-
mes and game shows. This exposure can
intense pressure on actors' private lives and
by some as professionally unhealthy. It has
d mockery of 'luvvies', an epithet referring
notional way in which actors sometimes
ch other and their work. Acting is a
demanding job, nerve-wracking and
draining, made worse by its chronic
d the destructiveness of critics, but,
many jobs, it is fulfilling and can be
e questions fired at actors might be
d to a writer, but writers are less
which leaves actors with a tight-
between surliness and over-

he theatre has brought a decline
age. The number of companies
Hull Truck, which bring fringe
al recognition, is tiny and the
argely taken over by musicals
and television drama (see
pportunities for new writers
d much of the writing
heatre continues to limit
al realism or musicals, it
ny of the ground lost to
line. There is evidence
d with television but
e theatre remains to
whether the decline
roduce a decline in
fine performers
and there are
lent or amateur
British acting is

Further reading

Callow, S. (1985) *Being an Actor*, London: Penguin
(thoughtful and witty survey of an actor's life).

STEPHEN KERENSKY

Actors Touring Company

Formed by John Retallack in 1978, Actors Touring
Company (ATC) is a small-scale theatre touring
company. With an avant-gardist verve, ATC
centralizes text and performance in vibrant and
intelligent contemporary reworkings of classic
dramatic, fictional and mythological narratives.
Past productions include Byron's *Don Juan*,
Goethe's *Tasso* and Jean Genet's *The Maids*.

Appointed artistic director in 1993, Nick
Philippou has continued ATC's valuable collaborations with other British and international companies, artists and writers like Kenneth McLeish and
Mark Ravenhill. Ravenhill's critically acclaimed
Faust (1997) and the Oscar Wilde-inspired *Handbag
(The Importance of Being Someone)* (1998) typify ATC's
pivotal role in creating a new theatre of dramatic
and historical intertextuality at the forefront of the
fringe (see **fringe theatre**).

SATINDER CHOHAN

adult education

Local authorities autonomously organize adult
education services. However, the Education Reform Act of 1988 makes it a duty of Local
Education Authorities (**LEAs**) to provide adequate
further education provision for mature students.
The main bodies working in the field are the
National Association of Educational Guidance
Services (which provides information and training
for those who wish to start or further a career, or
simply wish to learn); the National Institute for
Adult and Continuing Education (NIACE, which
runs short courses and publishes many books
including the *Year Book of Adult and Continuing
Education*); the Unit for the Development of Adult
and Continuing Education in England and Wales
(financed by the Department for Education and

actors (male)

The acting tradition in Britain stretches back to medieval mystery plays. For professionals, theatre is generally regarded as the greatest test although it is now difficult to earn a living on stage. Most actors therefore also do television or films unless, like Jim Dale, they star regularly on Broadway. Although cuts in arts budgets have led to many repertory companies disappearing and while the film industry is almost invisible, television fills the gap. There is no shortage of acting talent. But television has largely abandoned the literary plays that once gave theatre its cultural importance, replacing them with sensationalist drama, **action series**, sitcoms (see **situation comedy**) and **soap operas**, although some would dispute whether the latter's formlessness qualifies it as drama. Music hall traditions continue to exert an influence, primarily through stand-up comedy. Overall, the social revolution of the 1960s, combined with television's thirst for talent, have fostered a cohort of actors whose ability is often enlivened by concern for cultural and social issues.

From about 1970, with Peter O'Toole, Tom Courtney, Albert Finney, Michael Caine and Nicol Williamson established as international stars in sixties social realist films, British theatre and cinema declined. There are few famous liv stage playwrights. Television occupies the co sational place once held by theatre and is its own national stars. Actors such as Briers, Geoffrey Palmer, Rowan Atkins min Whitrow and Peter Sallis are partly through ability and partly b cers favour proven performers. B is identified with one type of rol can take Herculean efforts transfer successfully from genres.

Perennial favourites te billing initially and the actors are unpredic success in *I Didn't* wood's 1980s tel appeared in several quality plays and films. Da show was in 1968, but his first in the 1980s. Regulars range from

situation comedy, so the distinctions betwe film and television acting are blurred. and film were initially considered serious actors. Laurence Olivier w renouncing Hollywood to establ **National Theatre**. Actors such David Suchet and Alan Ric names working there or in **speare Company**. In the keep serious theatre alive of chasing what manage By contrast, commerc Conti utterly reject v of subsidized work

Modern acti motivation, b Olivier's advi on the set after a ru off-scree mand whic bli

The decline in in writing for the s like John Godber's productions to natio **West End** has been since the 1980s. Rad **radio drama**) make o but often only one required is formulaic. If itself to literal-minded soc seems unlikely to make up television and work will de that people are disenchant whether they will return to be seen, as does the question o of live theatre will eventually acting standards overall. Ma have sadly gone unmentione excellent performers even at st level, and at the turn of the century thriving.

See also: actors (female)

Enterprise to carry out research); the Scottish Institute of Adult and Continuing Education (which provides means of contact amongst adult and continuing educators); and the Workers Educational Association (WEA, a national organization with 900 branches which offer courses of different lengths on a wide range of subjects to interested adults and especially workers' movements). In addition to this there are the British branch of the University of the Third Age (founded in France in 1973, it reached the UK in 1983 and now has 100 British branches, primarily supporting voluntary self-help education for those over sixty) and the Open University (OU, founded in 1969 to offer distance-learning degrees, vocational training, short courses and summer schools). The OU has been a remarkable success. Originally named the 'University of the Air', it was established at Milton Keynes by a Labour government expressly to provide educational opportunities for part-time, mature students. Regular meetings with tutors are supplemented by radio broadcasts and television programmes, but the core of the learning process is the comprehensive package of course handbooks, the idea behind which has since been copied by many traditional **universities**. Overall, with the current emphasis on retraining, serial jobs and transferable skills, adult education is still an expanding market. Some university departments recruit mature students in excess of 50 percent of their total student population, and numbers are likely to increase.

See also: further education colleges

PETER CHILDS

advertising, influence of

Advertising is used for a variety of purposes: to attempt to persuade consumers to buy goods, change the image of a commodity or service, induce brand loyalty, encourage retailers to stock particular products, sell political ideas, or keep other goods out of a market. In its modern form, advertising has been dominated by and so defined as the paid-for promotion of commodities through mass media communication. Since the 1960s, advertising has moved from describing particular product features to placing greater emphasis on visual representation and associating products with a particular 'lifestyle'. As an increasingly visible practice graphically located between production and consumption, it has become a key site for analysis and debate in **media and cultural studies**.

On the Left in Britain in the 1950s and 1960s, advertising was interpreted as 'the handmaiden of capitalism', as obscuring the conditions of production and portraying idealized representations of consumption, but was rarely given sustained consideration. Many popular cultural critiques, most famously Vance Packard's *The Hidden Persuaders*, blended Cold War-derived conspiracy rhetoric with 'hyperdermic' communication models, in which the advertising industry's use of motivation research was described as having an insidious and immediate effect on an unwaveringly gullible populace. Anti-advertising discourses on both the Left and Right at this time tended to incorporate an elitist stance towards mass and youth culture, and to figure it as the prime example of American cultural colonization: as an unsightly boil on the fair face of 'authentic' British culture. Advertising was figured as pivotal to a society privileging 'the spectacle' or 'the image', and of visual over textual forms. In the 1970s, with the academic interest in semiology, ideology and psychoanalysis, structural analyses dismantled the signifying systems of adverts and provided more rigorous interpretations of the forms of symbolic gratification they offered. Judith Williamson's highly influential *Decoding Advertisements* linked Lacanian psychoanalysis to a feminist and ideological critique, asserting that 'advertisements are selling us something else besides consumer goods: in providing us with a structure in which we, and those goods, are interchangeable, they are selling us ourselves' (Williamson 1978: 13).

In the 1980s and 1990s, more attention was given to the social and symbolic relations of consumption, and the stark dichotomies between 'image' and 'reality', and the 'consumer-as-dupe' model so often evoked in previous studies were questioned. In particular it was recognized that by itself, advertising could not be held solely responsible for the social inequalities of capitalism, nor could it be divorced from other cultural discourses;

and that in this respect it had to a certain extent been 'demonized' (Nava *et al.* 1997: 4). Greater attention was given to how advertising might be read in relation to a wider landscape of 'promotional culture' (Wernick 1991) and as part of historically specific discursive formations.

Advertising both shapes and is shaped by the cultural forms it is part of, most obviously the media, manufacturing and service industries. During the 1950s and 1960s advertising expanded rapidly in Britain, as companies and manufacturers sought to exploit the increased spending power of workers made possible by full employment and the **welfare state**. The development of commercial television in 1955 was to a significant degree the result of lobbying from advertisers, who believed that sound and vision, direct entry into the home and immediate nationwide coverage would offer them an unprecedented and unbeatable form of promotional power. While advertising's overt influence on television came in the demarcated form of commercial breaks between programmes ('spot ads'), it also had a more integrated influence. Event sponsorship, game show prizes (see **game shows**) and bought-in feature films with **product placement**s provided cheaper routes of promotional visibility, ones incorporated into the programmes themselves. The dependency of commercial television on advertising revenue influenced the type of programmes produced; as advertisers in the 1960s and 1970s favoured large and stable mass audiences, this encouraged the series and programmes with a broad popular appeal, and discouraged those of a more experimental or controversial nature.

As advertising agencies grew alongside the mass media, advertising became split into two areas: promotional practices mainly in the mass media, for which agencies received commission (above the line) and all other activity, such as direct marketing (below the line). The competition to attract advertising revenue – which meant extra costs for media groups as they employed sales teams and marketing – took place across, as well as within, different media formats. National newspapers, for instance, did not manage to regain the amount of income they had received from advertising after television ('the blunt instrument') became the favoured form, but the regional press was able to differentiate itself and increase its profitability by carrying highly localized and **small ads**. Newspapers and magazines tailored service features to the advertising they encouraged and ran sponsored articles ('advertorials'). The relationship of print media to advertising has been similar to that of television in that the particular social groups or imagined constituencies valuable to advertisers – groups which are socially and historically mutable – are those presented with a wider range of publications. Historically, this has resulted in an unequal range of provision in terms of wealth, as more publications are targeted towards those with a high degree of disposable income, and in terms of interest (magazines about cookery have attracted more advertising interest, because of the wider range of associated commodities, than those about politics). New magazines have frequently begun their commodity-lives as proposals to advertisers to fill a perceived marketing niche.

While advertisement have been targeted towards specific social and cultural groups, advertising has been crucially important in the creation of these very categories. Demographic classifications of consumers, initially made in terms of occupational class, age, gender and region, were steadily expanded from the 1950s to include 'life cycle' variables (such as 'empty-nesters'). The consumer group most consistently produced and represented in advertising's cultural market has been women, since the business of purchasing, like consumption in general in the modern West, has overwhelmingly been gendered as female. The central character of advertisements in the 1950s and 1960s, the happy housewife and mother, continued her high visibility during the following decades and was joined and modified by the 'career woman' and the 'juggling' housewife. The extension of advertising aimed at men in the 1980s and 1990s, beyond that for work-related products and cars and into a greater emphasis on style and appearance, was marked in the Levis and Brylcreem ads and the rapidly expanding number of magazines primed for the **new man** and 'new lad'. These represented men engaging in a realm of consumption previously demarcated as female, and so played a crucial role in formulating and disseminating new codes of masculinity and in opening up new target markets.

In the 1980s, advertising gained a new cultural dominance in Britain. Deregulation of the media and advertising industries, expanding promotion of leisure and retail outlets and the extensive **privatization** of public services under **Thatcherism** meant an increase in the amount of space permitted to advertising, the range of products and services requiring it, and the shape it was allowed to take. The encouragement of free market enterprise in the public sector meant that a greater range of public services, such as **universities** and hospitals, adopted this distinct marketing ethos, and shares in newly privatized utilities like British Gas were heavily promoted in the media. The proliferation of these new forms of advertising became one of the more visible manifestations of enterprise culture.

The growing number of advertising agency mergers – which gathered momentum in the 1970s – paralleled the takeovers of the manufacturing companies and corporations employing them, increasing the consolidation and centralization of economic power in both spheres. Advertising costs soared as fewer and more powerful agencies gained control of big brand clients. As companies targeted consumers with greater precision and the market became increasingly segmented, smaller, more specialist and 'creative' agencies emerged. The conditions for British agencies were therefore extremely fertile, and they began to challenge American dominance of the industry. In 1986, London-based Saatchi & Saatchi became the biggest agency in the world, boosted by its intimacy with Thatcherism (it was widely credited for winning the 1979 election for the **Conservative Party** with the 'Labour isn't Working' campaign). The 'cult of the agency' was played out internally in the trade magazine *Campaign*, and 'advertising gurus' had a wider cultural resonance in film and television representations celebrating the creative businessman and his brother, the designer yuppie.

As more money was spent on advertising in the 1980s and the market became increasingly saturated, stylistic production values rose with many advertisements, such as those for Levis, becoming identifiably cinematic. This continued throughout the 1990s, and the use of drama (for example, Gold Blend's mini-soap opera) and controversy (such as Benetton and Wonderbra), as attempts to generate brand recognition and 'free' press publicity, became more widespread. The controversial ad was even cheaper if banned. In the 1990s, new legislation relaxed restrictions on 'parody ads', giving greater scope for ads to mock either their own genre or a competitor's tactics. This marked the enthusiastic interpellation by the advertising industry of more media-literate and cynical consumers, as well as an incorporation of criticism. All these developments were simultaneously a response to fears about new **viewing technologies** such as remote controls enabling zapping, video recorders which could cut out adverts, and the disruption of relatively stable markets by deregulation and by **cable and satellite** television. Many advertisers began to doubt the efficacy of television and either stopped using it or combined it with other forms of promotion (increasingly with Internet advertising in the 1990s). An exception was corporate programme sponsorship; after deregulation, sponsorship including 'bumper credits' on all commercial television productions except news, current affairs and controversial or political productions was permitted (for example, Cadbury's patronage of *Coronation Street*), and cable and satellite provided additional sponsorship space. Overall, by the early 1990s, the new technology, fragmented media market, effects of the recession and the threatened position of branded goods as they increasingly lost out to retailers' own labels resulted in a much-vaunted 'crisis' in the agencies, the collapse of the above the line and below the line distinctions in advertising, and use of a wider range of promotional forms.

Advertising continued to be used in the 1980s and 1990s by oligopolies and larger corporations to block the entrance of new products into a market, and to attempt to retain consumers and alter their behaviour (a Kellogg's campaign suggested that cornflakes should be eaten at night). Alliances between transnational media groups, 'mega agencies' and their multiple brand-owning clients became increasingly dominant. In the post-Fordist market, international product advertising mainly employs 'global but local' strategies, such as the references in McDonald's advertisements to British football, with relatively few advertisers (like Marlboro) adopting a singular worldwide campaign (see **globalization and consumerism**).

The debate around advertising's influence in the 1990s, as its influence on behavioural patterns was increasingly questioned by academic and advertising agency research, mainly revolved around the question of whether advertising was influential in persuading consumers to buy products at all, or whether the agencies' greatest achievement was in convincing companies of its necessity. While the public's increasing media literacy has been one contributing factor to the decline in traditional promotion techniques, advertising is increasingly used to secure commodity recognition in a cluttered marketplace, without which commodities face consignment to product oblivion. It is worth pointing out that the advertising industry disputes its own influence so as to avoid legislation curtailing its scope, and has successfully resisted external control by lobbying for its interests and establishing internally regulated bodies. Today, as at the beginning of the 1960s, it remains the case that more than nine out of ten of the most powerful corporations in the marketplace prefer it.

See also: advertising, television and video; commercial radio

Further reading

Brierly, S. (1995) *The Advertising Handbook*, London: Routledge.

Nava, M., Blake, A., MacRury, I. and Richards, B. (eds) (1997) *Buy This Book: Studies in Advertising and Consumption*, London: Routledge.

Wernick, A. (1991) *Promotional Culture: Advertising, Ideology and Symbolic Expression*, London: Sage Publications.

Williamson, J. (1978) *Decoding Advertisements: Ideology and Meaning in Advertising*, London: Marion Boyars.

JO LITTLER

advertising, television and video

Advertising is the means by which commercial values or messages are conveyed to the public. Two main broadcast forms exist: spot advertising and sponsorship. Spot advertising refers to the purchase of short slots between programmes while sponsor-ship focuses on programmes with which commercial concerns wish to become associated. Spot advertising is usually used to sell specific products, such as soap powder, while sponsorship is the preferred method for developing or creating a corporate's public persona. As national advertising rates are expensive, because of the large audiences delivered, huge importance is put on the placing and production of the advert. This often leads to a situation where the advert production costs per minute are more than those of the surrounding programmes.

While advertising is the regular means by which the US networks are funded, those in Europe have, until the 1990s, mostly relied on non-commercial means such as the television licence fee in Britain. Television advertising was first introduced into Britain in 1955 with ITV. Fears were initially expressed about the possible effect of advertisements on programme content. Advertising in a sponsored form was therefore prohibited in favour of spot advertising. This was seen as introducing a form of editorial policy into television, similar to newspapers, where the advertisements were kept separate from the content. The number of adverts, the content of adverts, their position and their separation from programmes was controlled and regulated by the ITA (forerunner of ITC).

In recent years in Britain more advertising-backed channels have appeared (**Channel 4**, **Channel 5** and **BSkyB**), which, providing new outlets for advertisers, have also fragmented the large audiences that broadcasting delivers. There has also been a change in regulation. Some prohibitions have gone while new ones have been introduced; for example, forms of sponsorship are now allowed, enabling Wella to 'bring you' *Friends*, while others, like tobacco sponsorship, have now been completely banned. Advertisers have also faced a 'revolt' by the viewer as they use new **viewing technologies**, such as remote controls, to miss out advertisements. Thus viewers can easily channel hop ('zapping'), when adverts are on, or can fast forward through adverts on video recordings ('zipping'). Advertisers have responded by making adverts more entertaining and interesting, often with an ongoing narrative. They have even made it possible to watch or 'scan' the advert viewed quickly on fast forward.

See also: ASA; National Viewers and Listeners Association; regulatory bodies

Further reading

Schudson, M. (1993) *Advertising: The Uneasy Persuasion*, London: Routledge.

PAUL RIXON

Afro-Caribbean communities

In the early period of postwar reconstruction, when Britain like all European countries was desperate for labour, there were too many jobs and too few workers. This gave rise to the Nationality Act of 1948, which granted United Kingdom citizenship to citizens of Britain's colonies and former colonies. Along with the ownership of a British passport came the right of lifelong residence in Britain.

Despite the demand for their services, and a legacy of colonial rule that had left large-scale unemployment in the British Caribbean, no dole or social security, and a cost of living that had almost doubled during the war, West Indians' response to Britain's invitation was slow. On 22 June 1948, 492 Jamaicans arrived at Tilbury in the ex-troopship *Empire Windrush*. Among them were singers, pianists, boxers and a complete dance band. Between thirty and forty of these first arrivals had already volunteered to work as miners. In October 1948, the *Orbita* brought 180 Afro-Caribbean workers to Liverpool, and three months later 39 Jamaicans, 15 of them women, arrived at Liverpool in the *Reina del Pacifico*. Next summer the *Georgic* brought 253 West Indians to Britain, 45 of them women. A few hundred came in 1950, about 1,000 in 1951, about 2,000 in 1952. Over the next four years larger numbers of Afro-Caribbean people arrived, including the wives and children of men settled in Britain. Ten years after the *Empire Windrush* there were in Britain about 125,000 Afro-Caribbean arrivals since the end of the war, and British industry gladly absorbed them.

In some industries, the demand for labour was so great that workers were actively recruited in their home countries. In April 1956, London Transport began recruiting staff in Barbados. They were lent their fares to Britain, and the loans were deducted weekly from their wages. Within twelve years, 3,787 Barbadians had been taken on. By 1966 London Transport had begun to recruit in Trinidad and Jamaica as well. The British Hotels and Restaurants Association recruited skilled workers in Barbados, and a Tory health minister, Enoch Powell, welcomed Afro-Caribbean nurses to Britain.

A great majority of the Afro-Caribbean settlers were in their twenties, with plenty to offer Britain. Of the men and women who came, a mere 13 percent had no skills; of the women, only 25 percent, one in four, were unskilled and half the women were non-manual workers. Almost half of the men, 46 percent, and over a quarter of the women, 27 percent, were skilled manual workers, but the newcomers found themselves in most cases being offered those jobs that local white people did not want: sweeping streets, general labouring or night shiftwork. In the 1950s, more than half the male Afro-Caribbean population of London held jobs with a lower status than their skills and experience fitted them for.

As a result of a colonial education system in which Britain was revered as the 'Mother Country', many of these new workers took their British citizenship seriously and saw themselves not as strangers, but as kinds of Englishmen. Disappointment and disillusionment of many kinds became part of the daily black experience of life in Britain. **Prejudice** against West Indian people was widespread. More than two-thirds of Britain's white population held a low opinion of black people or disapproved of them. Half of this prejudiced two-thirds were only mildly prejudiced. The other half were extremely antagonistic and their extreme prejudice meant that they resisted the idea of having any contact or communication with black people, objected vehemently to mixed marriages, would not work with black people in factories or offices, and generally felt that black people should not be allowed in Britain at all. In many industries, white trade unionists resisted the employment of black workers or insisted on a 'quota' system limiting them to a token handful, generally about 5 percent. Managements often had an understanding that the 'last in first out' rule should not apply to whites when black workers were employed, and that black workers should not be promoted over white. Most people viewed the plight of the Afro-Caribbean settlers with indifference and complacency.

Every encounter with white people presented a new set of problems. In the sphere of housing, racist discrimination operated by keeping blacks out of the housing market and herding them into bedsits in decaying inner city areas. Colour bars operated to keep black people out of pubs, clubs and dance halls where, ironically, black and black-inspired music was very popular. Churches and their congregations also displayed a plangent racism towards Afro-Caribbeans. Black workers began to meet in barbers' shops and cafes and on street corners. Here they began to set up their own clubs and churches and welfare associations. On occasions there were also efforts at collective action on the factory floor. Such action often took the form of petitions and appeals regarding working conditions, facilities, even wages; but, unsupported by their white fellow workers, these efforts were often ineffectual. In 1951, for instance, skilled Afro-Caribbean workers in an ordinance factory in Liverpool met secretly in the lavatories and wash-rooms to form a West Indian Association which would take up cases of discrimination. The Merseyside West Indian Association went through a period of vigorous political activity, taking up cases of unfair dismissal or treatment and the more general cause of colonial freedom. After being ousted from the workplace following discovery by employers, they switched headquarters to a bar-ber's shop; then, as membership outgrew the barber's, they moved into the white-owned Stanley House in Toxteth. This is an example of the way in which many associations became community based concerns. The response to the denial of decent housing led to the reliance on Jamaican 'pardner' or Trinidadian 'sou-sou' systems, whereby a group of people (often from the same parish or island) would pool their savings and lend out a lump sum to each individual in turn. Thus savings circulated among their own communities, and did not go into white banks or building societies. This was a sort of community banking system engendered by tradi-tion, but enforced by racial discrimination. The prices that black settlers had to pay for the houses and the interest rates charged by the sources that

were prepared to lend to them forced many people into overcrowding and multi-occupation, invoking further racial stereotyping and, in later years, the stringencies of the Public Health Act.

The postwar independence of India, and the impending loss of the West Indies and Africa, had spelled the end of the Empire and the decline of Britain as a great power. All that was left of the colonial enterprise was the ideology of white supremacy. The new settlers were seen by many white people as heathens who practised head-hunting, cannibalism, infanticide, polygamy and 'black magic'. Blacks were seen as backward, uncivilised and inherently inferior to Europeans, eating strange foods and carrying unpleasant diseases. The common belief was that most black settlers were ignorant, illiterate and lacked proper education.

Oswald Mosley's prewar British Union of Fascists was now revived as the Union Movement and was matched for its racist propaganda by a rash of other organizations: A.K. Chesterton's League of Empire Loyalists, Colin Jordan's White Defence League, John Bean's National Labour Party, and Andrew Fountaine's British National Party. In between these, together with various other organizations concerned with 'racial preservation', and the right wing of the Tory Party, white racism blossomed. Racial attacks became a regular part of the life of the Afro-Caribbean communities in Britain. In 1954, in a small street of terraced houses in Camden Town, London, Afro-Caribbeans were subjected to a spate of racial violence that lasted for two days, culminating in a petrol bomb attack on the house of an Afro-Caribbean settler. In August 1958, large-scale riots broke out in Nottingham where 2,500 Afro-Caribbeans and about 600 Asians were living. Following an attack on a black miner and his wife as they were leaving a cinema, there was fighting between blacks and whites for ninety minutes in St Ann's Well Road. Many attacks, and the clashes that often followed, were stimulated by fascist propaganda urging that black people be driven out of Britain. On weekend evenings in particular, gangs of 'teddy boys' cruised the streets over a wide area of London (armed with iron bars, sticks and knives) in a systematic and pitiless pursuit of isolated black victims. Many of these youth groups were directed by Mosleyites and the White Defence League, under the watchful eye of the police (the Notting Hill riot was a result of this). Many members of the Afro-Caribbean community in Britain talked seriously about going back home at this time. Others organized militant groups to defend their homes and their clubs.

Outside London, an identical pattern emerged in virtually every area of black settlement: cowardly hit-and-run attacks on individuals or houses, with an occasional eruption of mob violence such as the Middlesbrough riot of August 1961 when thousands of whites, chanting 'Let's get a wog', smashed the windows of black people's houses and set a black-owned café on fire. **Labour Party** chairman Tom Driberg told the Trades Union Congress: 'there are only 190,000 coloured people in our population of 50 million – that is, only four out of every 1,000. The real problem is not black skins, but white prejudice.'

Soon after the 1959 general election, a group of Tory MPs from Birmingham set up a lobbying organization for the introduction of immigration controls. Three years later, the first Commonwealth Immigrants Bill became law in 1962. This measure restricted the admission of Commonwealth settlers to those who had been issued with employment vouchers. This was a decisive political turning point in contemporary British race relations. Blackness was officially equated with second-class citizenship, and the status of 'undesirable immigrant' was given official approval. The 1962 Bill's 'unstated' and 'unrecognized' assumption was that black people were the source of the problem. Two years after the 1962 Act there came the next turning point when Peter Griffiths, Tory candidate for Smethwick, defeated a Labour minister with the slogan 'If you want a nigger for a neighbour vote Labour'. Racism was thus legitimated as the basis of an electoral appeal by the candidate of a major political party.

By the mid-1970s, two out of every five black people in Britain were born in the country. In the key areas of employment, housing and education, those born in Britain of Afro-Caribbean parents still faced a substantial amount of unfair discrimination, and the issue of police racism has become a major subject of debate. In 1966 Joseph A. Hunte's report to the West Indian Standing Conference on police brutality, 'Nigger Hunting in England', was

published with little reaction. By 1972, a select parliamentary committee on relations between black people and the police received a memorandum from the West Indian Standing Conference warning of the consequences if police racism was allowed to go unchecked. It was largely ignored, as was the work of sociologist Maureen Cain, whose book *Society and the Policemen's Role*, (1973), found that policemen generally believed that 'niggers' or 'nigs' were 'in the main ... pimps and layabouts, living off what we pay in taxes'. In 1979, a further, comprehensive account of police–black relations also fell on largely deaf ears. Beatings and forced confessions are part of what has been described by the British Black Panthers in 1970 as a deliberate campaign to intimidate, harass and imprison black people prepared to go out on the streets and demonstrate. Between 1976 and 1981, thirty-one black people in Britain were murdered by racists. In January 1981, thirteen young black people perished after a fire-bomb attack on a birthday party in Deptford. Three months later, 15,000 black people demonstrated. They protested against police handling of the inquiry, and demanded justice for black people. The police response, as seen by many members of the Afro-Caribbean community, was 'Swamp 81', the first part of a London-wide exercise known as 'Operation Star'. In six days, 120 plain clothes policemen stopped 943 people, 118 of whom were arrested.

After an entire decade of **police** harassment aimed at suppressing black resistance, black and white youth exploded together in the summer of 1981. The action started in Brixton, then spread to Southall and other parts of Britain. The unrest in Toxteth, Liverpool, lasted four days, during which 150 buildings were burnt down and 781 police put out of action. The popular backlash spread to Manchester, Leeds, Birmingham, Coventry, Wolverhampton, Stockport, Maidstone, Aldershot, Chester, Newcastle, Knaresborough, Derby, Edinburgh, Reading, Stoke, Gloucester, Halifax, Wood Green, Hackney, Bristol, Portsmouth, Luton, Walthamstow, Bedford, Hull, Nottingham, Birkenhead, Blackburn, Shrewsbury and elsewhere. This major uprising was followed by the Scarman Report, which investigated the possible causes of the disturbances. Unemployment and police brutality were outlined as two major causal factors, yet in 1991 Lord Gifford's report 'Loose The Shackles', based mainly on Liverpool, showed little if any alleviation of the problems outlined ten years earlier. The lessons to be learned from what happened in 1981 are to some extent still being digested, both by Britain's Afro-Caribbean communities and by the white population in general.

See also: Afro-Caribbean youth styles; Afrocentrists; Afropop and African music; Race Relations Acts

Further reading

Fryer, P. (1984) *Staying Power: The History of Black People In Britain*, London: Pluto (an invaluable resource, in terms of its volume of information, its primary sources and its perspective).

Lambeth City Council (1988) *Forty Winters On: Memories of Britain's Post-War Caribbean Immigrants*, London: Lambeth City Council (this is a commemorative book, with an introduction by Stuart Hall, marking the fortieth anniversary of the docking of the *Empire Windrush* with the first settlers).

Phillips, M. and Phillips, T. (1998) *Windrush: The Irresistible Rise of Multi-Racial Britain*, London: HarperCollins (a valuable history as well as a companion to the BBC television series of the same name).

EUGENE LANGE

Afro-Caribbean youth styles

Afro-Caribbean youth culture is largely based upon the mediation of black British urban experience by a heterogeneous fusion of Afro-diasporic influences. As a sub-cultural group, Afro-Caribbean youth have converted states of urban dislocation, socio-economic adversity and institutionalized racism to produce rearticulations of black British identity through musical, linguistic, sartorial and visual expressions.

Afro-Caribbean youth styles have metamorphosed through Caribbean-derived incarnations stemming from the Rudeboys of 1960s **ska** and rocksteady, the Rastafarians (see **Rastafarianism**) and **reggae** of the politicized 1970s to the Raggamuffins of the early 1990s. Diametrically opposed to Rastafarianism, Ragga music, fashion and dance celebrate an individualistic materialism, forthright sexuality and ostentatious attitude.

With later militant and Afrocentric variants (see **Afrocentrists**), the Fly-Girls and B-Boys of the 1980s, Afro-American **hip hop** culture created a unisex fashion consistent with the broader casual **sportswear** and casual trends among Afro-Caribbean youth in Britain. Trading in a common currency of style, designer tracksuits, expensive trainers and chunky gold accessories became signifiers of power and status in the reclaimed cultural terrain of the street.

Hip hop culture underlines the creative assemblage that defines Afro-Caribbean (and Asian) youth styles in Britain, whether through music (mixing, sampling or developing musical styles), dress (arranging assorted fake and real designer labels) or language. In 1981, Smiley Culture's chart hit 'Cockney Translation' signalled the black British blending of the Jamaican 'yardy' and the cockney 'geezer', delivering a distinctive dialect of rhyming cockney slang and fast-style Jamaican patois.

First widely practised by black-conscious youth during the 1970s, Jamaican patois and Afro-American street slang are linguistically employed to subvert forms of standard English. As with **graffiti** spray-painted on public property, Afro-Caribbean youth have reimagined linguistic and urban landscapes with non-conformist, self-affirming stylistic explosions of flowing and disrupted rhythms and colour. Institutional authorities, however, are inclined to view their occupation of such alternative subjective and leisure spaces as transgressive.

Afro-Caribbean youth have exerted a decisive stylistic influence on British youth and mainstream cultures as evidenced by the mod, skinhead, punk and dance (see **mods**; **skinheads**; **punk rock**; **dance music**) appropriation of aspects of Rudeboy, Rasta, hip hop and sound system culture. Soul II Soul perhaps ideally encapsulate the young, black and British cultural awakening of the mid-1980s with their unique synthesis of a black British attitude, music, fashion and philosophy (Tulloch 1992: 93).

See also: Afro-Caribbean communities; Afropop and African music; Asian youth styles

Further reading

Tulloch, C. (1992) 'Rebel Without A Pause: Black Streetstyle & Black Designers', in J. Ash and E. Wilson (eds), *Chic Thrills: A Fashion Reader*, London: Pandora Press (a brief but informative historical overview).

SATINDER CHOHAN

Afrocentrists

Afrocentrists see their culture as emanating from Africa. The two most visible groups are Rastafarians (see **Rastafarianism**), from broadly West Indian backgrounds, and blacks who foreground their African ancestry. Both groups see a recognition of African origins as crucial to the resolution of problems in and around their status as British subjects, redolent as it is of their history as colonial peoples. Their aim is the recognition and recovery of their lost history and culture. Afrocentrists fear that their distinctive culture will be submerged in a multicultural Britain and, partly taking their cue from Alex Haley's *Roots*, wish to celebrate their identity in clothing styles, music and dance rhythms. Important texts are *The Isis Papers* by Dr Frances Cress Welsing and the **Nation of Islam** speeches of Minister Louis Farrakhan. They celebrate an alternative to Christmas, called Kwaanza, in part centring on ancient Egyptian culture. Influences are Dr Ron Karenga and the American film director Spike Lee.

See also: Afro-Caribbean communities; Afro-Caribbean youth styles; Afropop and African music

MIKE STORRY

Afropop and African music

In the 1950s, Franco's Jazz in Zaire was one of the rare African bands to reach as far as Britain. In the 1960s, South African Abdullah Ibrahim, and the whole township Jazz scene, made a mark in the UK, as too did the legendary South African singer Miriam Makeba. Around the same time, the young Fela Kuti was inventing his Afro-beat sound in London. The 1970s saw the emergence of Afro-fusion band Osibisa, while Hugh Masekela and Dudu Pukwana made a splash in the world of Afro-jazz fusion. Manu Dbango's 'Soul Makossa' was a hit in the UK in 1973, and King Sunny Adé put his brand of Nigerian 'Ju-ju' music on the market. Today's current interest in popular African dance music started in the 1980s with Europeans bringing back music from their travels, and linking up with African musicians in bands like Jazira and The Ivory Coasters. London-based bands emerged, such as African Connexion, Hi-life International and Somo Somo, many of whom (like Taxi Pata Pata) were made up of expatriates from various African countries, ranging from Nigeria to Ghana, Zimbabwe, Zaire, South Africa, Tanzania and Kenya. Despite the prevalence of a sort of pan-African political correctness amongst many African musicians in the 1990s, the old colonial ties divide the new African music scene between two major spheres of influence: London and Paris.

The current UK movement took off in London in 1983, on the back of the Greater London Council's cultural policy, with a series of shows that launched now famous acts like Youssou N'Dour, Kanda Bongo Man, Sam Mangwana and Les Quatre Etoiles. In 1988, Mali's Mori Kanté hit the number one spot in several European charts with 'Yekke Yekke'. African musicians were finding a global market for their sound. Much of the music coming out of Africa since the 1980s has been categorized as 'world music'. Papa Wemba embraces the term 'world music' as a category that denotes his eclectic approach, which itself is part of the change that international attention has brought. Wemba plays for an international audience, but recognizes the need to plunge back into traditional music. In relation to African music at a **WOMAD** press conference he is quoted as saying: 'We are not a fashion. We are a continent.' Fellow Zairean Ray Lima also admits that he is not playing the Zairean music he would play at home. At the other end of the continuum, people like Thomas Mapfumo are rejecting the term 'world music' in order to emphasize cultural specificity. Both Mapfumo and master mbira player and fellow Zimbabwean Ephat Mujuru have contributed to the creation of the staunchly traditional 'chimerenga' music.

The diversity between artists who play traditional music, those who fuse and spice up the traditional, and artists who cross over completely to Western idioms is vast. Collaborating musically with Peter Gabriel put Senegal's Youssou N'Dour on the European map in much the same way that appearing on Paul Simon's 'Graceland' album made international figures of South African band Ladysmith Black Mambazo. While pioneering Senegalese 'mbalax' music, people like N'Dour are also taking it forward into the future, using European instruments to make their music more accessible to Western audiences. Despite the desire to cross over into the Western market, and the various efforts to conform to the marketing strategies of corporate entities like Peter Gabriel's Real World Records, many African musicians feel that there is a covert racism in operation in the Western press. It appears that while these new musical collaborations allow Peter Gabriel or Paul Simon to enrich their cultures, many critics feel that African musicians are compromising their own. Because a large proportion of up-and-coming African musicians are university educated, technologically aware and computer-literate, many want to break out of the closed cultural systems that they have been brought up in, making inevitable such fusions as Les Têtes Brulée's 'bikoutsi-rock' from Cameroon. But many people feel that, like Africa's raw materials in the past, its music is being plundered, manipulated and exploited to suit Western tastes. For example, Remi Ongala, Zairean-born Tanzanian superstar and UK favourite of the WOMAD festivals, radically changed his original line-up and the fundamental sound of his band after WOMAD, insisting on a more mainstream Zairean sound. Also worthy of mention, the Bhundu Boys play Zimbabwean 'jit jive', a very pan-African dance sound, like hi-life and soukous.

The Wassoulou Sound, a group of women singers from Mali, perform mainly traditional music, while Baaba Maal and Selif Keita blend traditional and Western forms very successfully. Ali Farka Touré plays a sort of African **blues**, while Angelique Kidjo from Benin, now a major force in Europe, plays a very funky Americanized form of her own traditional music. Jamaican **reggae** is also very popular throughout Africa: Alpha Blondy from Abidjan, like many Rasta-inspired bands, plays straight-up 'roots rock reggae', the only difference being that he sings in a combination of his own local dialect with French and some English. Blondy recorded a complete album with Jamaican band The Wailers, and his first album in 1983, *Jah Glory*, launched him as Africa's first reggae star. In the late 1990s, South Africa's Lucky Dube is set to steal Blondy's crown as the king of African reggae.

The debate surrounding the influence of the Western music industry on Afropop continues. On the continent of Africa itself, there are two big problems that hinder its continued growth. The first is the lack of recording studios and of the basic infrastructure that fosters a music industry. Due to this shortfall in resources, African musicians are plagued by piracy, lack of copyright protection and scarcity of the most basic tools of their trade, such as reeds and guitar strings, not to mention instruments themselves. With their first big earner, the Bhundu Boys returned to Zimbabwe, bringing with them only their country's second public address system; the government then impounded this because it was unhappy that the band did not bring hard currency back into the country.

This leads us to the second biggest problem facing African musicians: political turmoil. A number of African countries are experiencing democracy for the first time since independence. Ethnic and religious tensions remain strong in many regions. Many Algerian 'rai' stars have had to retire into exile in France because they have come under scrutiny by Islamic traditionalists, who claim they are playing debauched street music. Nigerian Fela Kuti's conflicts with the Nigerian government are legendary, and the inventor of the Afrobeat has been imprisoned once and continually harassed since the 1970s for his criticisms of his government and its military regimes. Yet, despite these hurdles, African music is becoming a major force in the world of popular music.

See also: Afro-Caribbean communities; Afro-Caribbean youth styles

Further reading

Bergman, B. (1985) *African Pop*, London: Cassell.
Ewens, G. (1991) *Africa Oye!: A Celebration of African Music*, Enfield: Guinness.

EUGENE LANGE

age of consent

The age of consent has been discussed from Plato, through Locke and into contemporary public policy. It covers a variety of different situations, from smoking, taking alcohol and watching X-rated movies to legal permission to engage in various forms of sexual intercourse. In Britain, the age of consent for smoking is sixteen years, and for taking alcohol is eighteen years. Ages of criminal responsibility vary widely according to the offence and are currently under review. Similarly, ages of civil contractual ability vary, but are generally set at sixteen or eighteen years. Until 1994, the age of consent between gay men was twenty-one years of age, after which it was lowered to eighteen. Between heterosexuals, the age of consent is sixteen years. This anomaly was challenged at the European Court of Human Rights in Strasbourg. In 1997, the incoming Labour government dropped the UK defence and sought an out of court settlement in which it would offer a free vote on the issue in the House of Commons. Subject to Parliamentary time, it is almost certain that the age of consent for same-sex relations will be reduced to sixteen (approved by the Commons vote in June 1998). At the same time, the government expressed a determination to increase the age of consent to smoking to eighteen. The apparent anomaly is explained by reducing gender inequality on the one hand and discouraging smoking, regardless of gender, on the other.

See also: armed forces and discrimination; family planning; gay liberation

PAUL BARRY CLARKE
SVANBORG SIGMARSDOTTIR

agitprop

Agitprop, a compression of agitational propaganda, can be considered as both a theatrical form and a distinctive function for artistic works (Szanto 1978). Evolved during the Russian Revolution, it was employed by socialist activists throughout Europe and the United States to raise the consciousness of the masses. It was revived in the 1960s in Britain in response to the demands of political campaigners, **pressure groups** and **trade unions** trying to communicate political analysis to popular audiences. The earliest company, formed in 1965, was Cartoon Archetypal Slogan Theatre (CAST). For CAST, rock and roll music was the main formative influence. Performances were characterized by direct audience address, swiftly interchanging sketches, documentary and music so that metaphors were created to explain the underlying politics of current events. An AgitProp collective was formed in London in 1968 which promoted a range of cultural political interventions, including street theatre. Other companies such as Red Ladder, Broadside Mobile Workers Theatre and Northwest Spanner developed similar short revue performances which were taken on to the street and to political meetings, working men's clubs and picket lines. More extended treatments were also possible, such as in Red Ladder's 'Strike While The Iron is Hot' (1974) addressing **equal pay** issues.

Three main factors reduced the use of agitprop as a political weapon over the course of the 1970s and 1980s. First, there was a loss of confidence in the relationships between left-wing theatres (see **left-wing theatre**), an increasingly fractured and ineffective political left, and popular audiences. Second, while the work was usually the product of collective creation, frustration at the perceived crudeness of analysis allowed by the form led writers like David Edgar into other dramatic modes. Third, following the 1979 election, the **Arts Council** progressively withdrew funding from left-wing theatre companies in England. In the absence of income, professional companies either split up or moved away from such polemic material. In Scotland, agitprop survived into the 1980s in the work of companies like 7:84 (Scotland), Wildcat Stage Productions and The Merry

Mac Fun Company. By the 1990s, however, professional agitprop had largely disappeared and the form reverted to its origins in the community activism of companies like Kirkby Response on Merseyside.

See also: avant-garde theatre; fringe theatre

Further reading

Itzin, C. (1980) *Stages in the Revolution: Political Theatre in Britain since 1968*, London: Eyre Methuen.
Szanto, G.H. (1978) *Theater and Propaganda*, Austin, TX: University of Texas Press.

TOM MAGUIRE

agricultural buildings

One of the major determining characteristics of Britain's landscapes is its agricultural buildings. Distinctive examples include Kentish oast houses, Yorkshire and Snowdonia stone barns, and Cotswolds byres and cowsheds. However, in the postwar period a decline in standards of aesthetic design has occurred. This has happened partly because agricultural holdings have been exempt from planning legislation and building control regulations, which apply generally but which are strictest in sensitive areas such as National Parks, where planning permissions are sparse and insist on stone cladding, slate roofs and so on. Consequently, Britain's rural landscape has become dominated by purely functional steel and breeze block constructions and north American type grain silos which, however efficient, make no attempt to blend in with their surroundings.

See also: industrial buildings; municipal buildings

MIKE STORRY

AIDS

AIDS, or Acquired Immune Deficiency Syndrome, is the generic term for a syndrome of opportunistic diseases that result from a weakened immune system. First identified in 1981 in Los Angeles and San Francisco, it was thought to be a consequence of drug abuse combined with high rates of male same-sex activity. That view, which still prevails in some places, was challenged by the view that a virus, HIV, triggered the syndrome.

High death rates, particularly among male same-sex partners in the US and the UK, have resulted in a culture of 'safe sex', that is, sex which either does not involve penetration or which involves only protected penetration among certain sections of the population. It has also led to a decline in needle sharing among intravenous drug users. Increased abortion rates indicate that the culture of safe sex is not fully established. There is some dispute about the precise source of AIDS and its mechanism of spread, but the decline of its incidence in those sectors of the population that have adopted practices of 'safe sex' and clean needles is significant. It seems to confirm that care counts and complacency is foolish.

See also: Clause 28; gay liberation

Further reading

Clarke, P.A.B. (1988) *Aids: Medicine Politics and Society*, London: LCAP.
Shilts, R. (1988) *And the Band Played On*, Harmondsworth: Penguin.

PAUL BARRY CLARKE

Akomfrah, John

b. 1957

Film-maker

John Akomfrah is best known for his two films, *Seven Songs for Malcolm X* (1993) and *Last Angel of History* (1995), made for **Black Audio Film Collective/Channel 4 Films**. The former combined documentary and narrative, and was offered in homage to the late African-American civil rights leader. It was a collection of testimonies of those who knew Malcolm X, including his widow Betty Shabazz and the film maker Spike Lee. It won the prize for Best Use of Archive Footage in a Documentary, at the 1993 Chicago Film Festival. The latter was an equally committed film and dealt with interpersonal relationships within the black community.

See also: Black Audio Film Collective; diasporan film-makers; Julien, Isaac

MIKE STORRY

Alsop, Will

b. 1947

Architect

Alsop has been Principal of Alsop Stormer Architects since 1981. He was educated at the **Architectural Association** and taught sculpture at St Martin's College, London. He collaborates with Bruce McLean (on architectural drawings), has worked with Cedric Price, and was formerly in practice with John Lyall. Major projects have been design work on the Cardiff barrage, planning on the rework of the De Lorean Belfast car factory, government buildings in Marseilles and design work on a ferry terminal in Hamburg. As long ago as 1975, Alsop notably defined conceptual architecture at a London ART Net conference as 'a limitless activity devoid of direction or dogma'. In other words, Alsop felt that the process and not the product was the chief goal of conceptual architecture.

See also: Architectural Association

PETER CHILDS

alternative comedy

Comedy in the 1980s and 1990s has been called 'the new rock and roll'. Certainly there has been a huge surge in audience figures for live comedy, and in response to the demand, new clubs and comedy venues have sprung up to provide an arena for comedy performers. When the Comedy Store, which now advertises itself as 'the unofficial National Theatre of comedy', opened in the summer of 1979 it was an isolated platform for comedy. By the mid-1990s, in London alone well over 100 shows could be found each week at dozens of venues.

The demographic of the expansion shows a clear increase in the middle-class audience in the south. A new wave of comedy has erupted out of the change of direction in stand-up comedy made by the so-called 'alternative' comedians of the early 1980s. The traditional act is joke-based or gag-based. Carefully constructed stories leading to a punchline or one-liners are formed around figures and structures – the mother-in-law, the fire-breathing wife, the meeting of an Englishman, an Irishman and a Scotsman – which are as fixed as the Punchinella and Columbine of medieval *commedia dell'arte*. Its home had been the working men's clubs of the north, with women often the stock figures positioned as the butt of the humour.

The change of direction initiated by the 'alternative' comedians was essentially towards the political, but also towards the politically correct. Commenting, as they largely did, from a left-wing or at least a liberal perspective, the alternative comedians opened up a younger, trendier and more affluent audience in the middle classes, and also created an arena which is more female and minority friendly. There was a genuine undercurrent of anger in the comedy of performers such as Ben Elton and Alexei Sayle, anger directed almost exclusively against the Establishment, the Conservative government, its policies and their perceived effects. The political diatribe attacking the Establishment is a direct descendant of the ground-breaking satire of the 1960s, a natural consequence of the irreverence shown for previously unassailable institutions by shows such as *That Was The Week That Was*.

As an extension of this political development, the stand-up routine naturally became more observational, pointing out and pointing up the oddities, irritations and absurdities of everyday British life, particularly from a political angle. This observational tack in turn led to routines which were less a series of unrelated jokes and more a stream of consciousness monologue of ideas. The burgeoning of the comedy circuit which has followed these alternative comics has seen these trends develop. The trains of thought and observations are no longer necessarily politically motivated, but may be absurd, surreal or more personal. Increasingly, performers are displaying their own personality, or that of the character they create as a mouthpiece. It is arguably this emphasis on individual personality which has led to the identification of comedy as the new rock and roll. Individuals stand out, audiences select favourites, stars are created; stars beget fans and so the industry expands.

The material of the new comedy may encourage a more politically correct atmosphere, a more demographically varied audience, but 'punters' are no easier to please. Rather than face alone the frequently hostile heckling which is now common at most new comedy venues, many performers, in accordance with the old adage that there is safety in numbers, choose to pursue a slightly different branch of comedy, working as part of a duo or team. The revue format is a university tradition; the Cambridge Footlights and the Oxford Revue have been in competition for decades. Again, it was in the 1960s that they came to the attention of a broader audience. The now legendary groups such as Dudley Moore, Peter Cook, Jonathan Miller and Alan Bennett in Beyond the Fringe, or the Monty Python team, combined members of both University revues and, largely through radio and television, broke through to a much larger audience.

Their legacy is seen in the sketch groups of today such as the Cheese Shop or Curried Goat. In addition, although a female stand-up is no longer such a rarity (the demographic changes apply to performers as well as audiences, and Jo Brand or Jenny Eclair can quell a heckler as well as any man), many women seem to work fruitfully within partnerships; French and Saunders forged the path which others such as Mel and Sue or the Girls with Big Jests are now following. These duos, like the sketch teams, base their acts upon short scenes and varied characters.

The revue format may mean that the sketches, skits and, occasionally, songs have a linking theme, but more usually the sketch show is simply a series of unconnected humorous situations presented dramatically, rather than just recounted as would be the case with a stand-up comic. This is the format most often translated to radio and television, as it is not as dependent as stand-up on having an audience to address because the members of the group can interact with one another. At its furthest extension, a team of comedians will improvise

scenes and dialogue. Improvisation is now the style favoured by the Comedy Store Players, hosts at the best-known of the London comedy venues.

Stand-up is the staple of most comedy clubs, but some offer more of a cabaret for an evening's entertainment. Stand-up acts may be featured, but they will be interspersed with sketches, singers or some of the many novelty acts who now ply their trade on the comedy circuit; groups such as Corky and the Juice Pigs, whose act is formed of comic songs and musical impressions, or perhaps the more circus-based antics of The Umbilical Brothers. Current British comedy has been revolutionized by the alternative movement of the late 1970s and early 1980s, and it now has a firm foothold in the television schedules with stars like Lee Evans, Jack Dee and Julian Clary who have their own shows.

See also: comedy on television; Comedy Store, The

Further reading

Double, O. (1988) *Stand Up*, London: Methuen.

ALISON BOMBER

alternative music

The label 'alternative music' was most prevalent during the mid- to late 1980s, and was often used as a synonym for 'indie music', the latter being seen by some commentators and fans as a misnomer, as many of the ostensibly independent labels were actually controlled by major record labels (see **indie pop**). For example, The Cure, one of the leading bands of the indie/alternative scene, were signed to Fiction, a small subsidiary of the Polygram empire. Furthermore, the term 'alternative' could also be applied to bands who sounded like indie bands but who recorded for major labels, such as Simple Minds (in their early years) who were signed first to Arista and then to Virgin.

Stylistically, alternative music was characterized primarily, but not exclusively, by guitar-based rock. Bands as diverse as Echo and The Bunnymen, with their 1960s-influenced sound, The Cult, who adopted a fairly straight take on heavy rock, and the Spacemen Three, who experimented with layering textures of sound over infrequently changing chords, were all encompassed within the 'alternative' tag. This broad stylistic range may be partially due to the fact that many of the bands who comprised the alternative scene either stemmed from or drew their inspiration from the post-punk movement, which in itself encompassed a wide range of sounds. Another, possibly more likely explanation is that the variety found within the alternative scene can be attributed to the fact that the term was used to describe any band that could not be neatly categorized as belonging to any of the established genres of the time.

It was perhaps this understanding of alternative music that led to the phrase becoming redundant. Alternative music was defined by what it was not, rather than by what it was. Most importantly, it was not mainstream chart music (a fact from which many alternative music fans took an elitist pleasure), so when an 'alternative' band such as The Smiths had a succession of top twenty singles, it became difficult to describe them as an alternative anymore. Similarly, alternative music was not dance music, but when groups such as Primal Scream began approaching dance **produ-cers** such as Andrew Weatherall to remix their songs, the distinction became blurred. Ultimately, the term alternative music ceased to have much meaning, and it fell out of common usage.

See also: indie pop; new wave; punk rock

Further reading

Savage, J. (1991) *England's Dreaming: Anarchy, Sex Pistols, Punk Rock and Beyond*, London: Faber & Faber.

SIMON BOTTOM

alternative poetry

The strongest 'alternative' tradition in contemporary British poetry is performance poetry, a form as varied as its practitioners. Often based on song-structures (such as repeated refrains) and the rhythms of popular music (including **jazz**, rock, **reggae** and **hip hop**), performance poetry is usually composed in the vernacular – often the dialect of specific regions or cultural groups – using devices (such as rhyme and alliteration) from oral rather than literary poetic traditions.

Inspired by the American Beat writers, in the late 1950s and early 1960s Christopher Logue's 'jazzetry' and Michael Horovitz's Poetry Olympics sought to recover poetry from the academic and literary establishment. Performances across the country by such poets as Adrian Mitchell, Jeff Nuttall, Libby Houston and Tom Pickard culminated with the Royal Albert Hall Poetry Olympics of 1965, attended by crowds of 8,000. The success of the **Mersey Poets**' pop-based writing of the late 1960s, and of John Cooper Clarke's punk poetry and the dub poetry of **black perfor-mance poets** in the 1970s, opened up new audiences through recordings (often with musical accompaniment) for independent **labels** and **local radio**. The dub and punk poets (also known as ranters) helped make protest poetry the dominant mode of performance poetry in the 1970s. The early 1980s saw comic poets like John Hegley and Seething Wells appear on the alternative cabaret circuit, and **new wave** performers like Attila the Stockbroker, Henry Normal and Joolz performed on the fringe at **rock festivals**. There was also a 1960s revival of Dada- and Surrealist-influenced experimental performance poetry: from Bob Cobbing and Edwin Morgan's sound poetry through to the spellbinding performances of profoundly deaf poet Aaron Williamson, the avant-garde used performed poetry to explore the boundaries between language and physical sound.

Despite critics' fears in the 1960s and 1970s that performance poetry would break literature into rival camps, conventional poets have shown an increasing interest in performing their works. As a BBC radio producer from 1973, the Group poet George MacBeth presented performances from new young poets to a wide non-specialist audience, and Tom Leonard, Liz Lochhead, Wendy Cope, Tony Harrison and Rita Ann Higgins are among the many poets to whom performance is as important as publication. By the 1990s, performance poetry was being taught on university courses and at workshops. **Poetry slams** regularly attracted large audiences, and poets performed with club DJs and in a variety of media, exploiting new video and recording technologies. The commercial potential of performance poetry was acknowledged by EMI's much hyped £1 million advance to Murray Lachlan Young in 1997.

See also: black performance poets; performance poetry; poetry slams

Further reading

Forbes, P. (ed.) (1997) *Poetry Review* 87(3) (special issue on performance poetry).

SIMON COPPOCK

ambient music

Drawing influence from artists such as Brian Eno, The Yellow Magic Orchestra and Tangerine Dream, ambient music contains soothing natural noises such as bird song, whale speech and other aquatic sounds, often laid over the top of a slow 'break beat' or **house** rhythm.

Ambient music was largely ignored by the mainstream until the **rave culture** boom of the late 1980s. While the main dancefloors of most raves and **clubs** invariably played acid house, it was in the 'chill-out rooms' of such clubs that ambient music could be found. Acclaimed records of this period included The KLF's *Chill Out* (1988), The Orb's *A Huge Ever Growing Pulsating Brain that Rules From the Centre of the Ultraworld* (1989) and an untitled album by Space, which was a collaboration between The KLF's Jimmy Cauty and The Orb's Alex Patterson, an ex-employee of EG, the record company that released Brian Eno's early ambient records. While some ambient music of this period was implicitly connected with **drug culture**, The Orb's record made this connection explicit, with its cover sleeve claim to be 'ambient house for the E generation'.

During the early 1990s ambient music's popularity broadened beyond rave culture, although it remained popular with fans of **dance music**, and was often listened to after a night spent at a club or rave. The natural calming sounds of The KLF (symbolized by the photograph of sheep on the cover of *Chill Out*) became increasingly popular,

and many ambient musicians recorded music that, like *Chill Out*, contained no beats at all.

The samples contained within this style led to criticisms that ambient music had become obsessed with 'new age' philosophy and green issues. Some artists began to reject the soporific nature of early ambient music in favour of a more abstract electronic sound. A good example of this move was The Aphex Twins' *Selected Ambient Works Volume Two* (1994), which eschewed the serenity of previous ambient music in favour of a minimal electronic darkness.

The career of the seminal ambient act The Future Sound of London can also be seen as following the three phases outlined above. While their first single 'Papua New Guinea' (1992) contained natural sounds combined with a house beat, their second single 'Cascade' (1993) was a more dreamy atmospheric sound, while their second album *ISDN* (1995) was an altogether more disturbing affair.

One sub-genre that has developed within ambient music is ambient dub, which combines the slow rhythm of dub **reggae** music with the natural and synthesized sounds characteristic of ambient. Again, The Orb have been at the forefront of this development with their track 'Towers of Dub'. Following on from this development has been the rise of a hybrid genre entitled ambient jungle. Ambient jungle takes on board the frenetic percussion of **jungle**, but avoids its aggressiveness through the creative use of strings, 'pads' and natural sounds. Artists working within this field include T-Power, LTJ Bukem, Alex Reece and Jacob's Optical Stairway.

STUART BORTHWICK

Amnesty International

Amnesty International was founded in 1961 by Peter Benenson. It is an independent worldwide voluntary movement, with a membership of 120,000 individuals in over 300 local groups throughout the UK. The organization's mandate calls for the release of all prisoners of conscience, fair and prompt trials for all political prisoners, and an end to torture and execution. As such, it is based on the United Nations Universal Declaration of Human Rights (1948).

Amnesty International UK has benefited from the growth in popularity of single-issue politics and pressure groups during the 1980s and 1990s. The cases of 'prisoners of conscience' such as the Beirut hostages, Nelson Mandela, and more recently Ken Saro-Wiwa, have hit the headlines.

See also: Friends of the Earth and Greenpeace

RACHAEL BRADLEY

Anderson, Lindsay

b. 1923, Bangalore (India); d. 1994, Dordogne (France)

Film-maker

Anderson's early career as an essayist and an exponent of experimental 'free cinema' developed a unique style which reflected upon the process of film making and the role of the individual in initiating social change. His first feature film, *This Sporting Life* (1963), was an intense drama of northern English working-class life. This was followed by a thematically linked trilogy. *If* (1969) offered the metaphor of the public school as the state of the nation. The sequel, *O Lucky Man* (1972), considered big business, civic corruption and the perversion of science and religion, but resisted easy conclusions. *Britannia Hospital* (1982) was less successful, using the ailing NHS as an analogue for a moribund Britain.

GORDON URQUHART

androgynous/unisex look

Androgynous looks have been produced under the various influences of politics, subcultures and musical styles. For men, embracing an androgynous style has meant the adoption of a decorative and sexualized style of clothing. Ironically, for women it has often involved the opposite, a desexualization and simplification of dress styles.

Music-related subcultures have had a major influence on men's embrace of unisex styles.

Swinging London and psychedelic styles, emerging in 1967 and 1968 from the mod look, took up bright colours and Op art designs in vivid and decorative clothing worn by men and women alike. The hippie subculture of the late 1960s and early 1970s allowed men to wear long hair, beads and headbands, a shift in style that was interpreted by contemporary commentators as accompanying a gentler style of masculinity and a more liberal approach to diverse sexual practices.

British **glam rock** took this emphasis on androgynous, sexualized style to a new limit in the early 1970s, with Marc Bolan and David Bowie adopting the glam personae of the Cosmic Crusader and Ziggy Stardust/Aladdin Sane, respectively. These characters from a genderless future emerged in prosperous circles in London, in contrast to the black **funk** style appearing simultaneously in the USA. Some **new romantics** of the early 1980s, especially Duran Duran, ABC and Culture Club, took up similar glamorous, androgynous male styles. Figures like Boy George showed the influence that gay subcultures had on these music-related styles, as does the origins of the word 'punk' as a term for a homosexual lover.

Musical trends also had an influence on women's adoption of androgynous styles. Jeans and t-shirts as unisex wear were popularized by the **hippies** and the **mods**, while jeans and dungarees were also embraced by the women's movement as comfortable, relatively unrestrictive clothing. Punk, too, offered a less feminine dress style for women, which has been more recently adapted by the Riot Grrrls. However, only in the 1980s did mainstream female musicians offer exemplars for androgynous style.

Grace Jones, who went on to appear in the Bond film *A View to a Kill* in the mid-1980s, adopted a punk-glam look of short sculptured hair and masculine tailoring. Jones's image showed the influence of high fashion through her collaboration with Jean-Paul Goude. Annie Lennox's adoption of the male suit in the earlier part of her career was a way of symbolizing control over her musical identity, and the adoption of the suit as a way of demonstrating a non-sexualized competence has persisted throughout the 1980s.

The women's movement, gay subcultures, lesbian 'butch' styles and peacenik hippie politics have all had an impact on androgynous styles. Nonetheless, there is considerable debate as to whether the popularity of unisex dress styles is connected to a liberalization of the distinction between genders or transformations in attitudes to gay and lesbian sexuality.

See also: bisexuality; 'gender benders'; transsexuals

Further reading

Garber, M. (1992) *Vested Interests: Crossdressing and Cultural Anxiety*, New York: Routledge

Polhemus, T. (1994) *Streetstyle: From Sidewalk to Catwalk*, London: Thames & Hudson.

NICOLE MATTHEWS

Anglican Church

Henry VIII's defence of the sacraments against Reformist tendencies led Pope Leo X in 1521 to bestow on him the title 'Defender of the Faith', which is still held by the British monarch. Just a few years later, failing to persuade Pope Clement VII to annul his marriage to Catharine of Aragon so that he could make Anne Boleyn his second wife and perhaps father an heir, he repudiated Roman authority over the Church in England and also gained control over the Church's possessions in England. Since the sixteenth century, the Church of England has steered an uncertain course between Catholic tendencies on the one hand (despite persistent preferences for national auton- omy) and Protestant attitudes on the other. Though asserting independence from papal authority, the Church of England claims to be part of the Catholic church, participating in the apostolic succession as direct inheritors of Christ's mandate to St Peter. Especially acute in Victorian times, the orientation of the Church of England remains a live issue today, for the Evangelical tradition has great strength, even though today's services, particularly the increasing emphasis on the Eu- charist, would have seemed distinctly ritualistic and Romish in previous centuries.

In terms of ecclesiastical administration, Eng- land is divided into two 'Provinces', with the **Archbishop of Canterbury** presiding over thirty sees (or dioceses), and the Archbishop of York presiding over fourteen sees in the north of the country. Sees are headed by diocesan bishops, increasingly with support from deputies called 'suffragan bishops'. Archdeacons oversee subdivi- sions of sees, with rural deans (not to be confused with the deans who head chapters of canons in cathedrals) leading groups of parish clergy. The traditional parish priest (whether called 'rector' or 'vicar' made little practical difference) caring for a parish, often for decades with scant guidance or interference, has become far less common. Today team ministries, often including women priests, generally look after a number of parishes.

The Church of England is not state-funded, but receives income from congregations and from endowments managed, not to universal approba- tion, by the Church Commissioners. It uses the money to pay and pension the clergy according to their place within the hierarchy and to maintain an expensive heritage of ancient and beautiful churches.

Though the Church of England is technically England's 'established church', the meaning of this status has undergone considerable change. It does not, as a state church, impose religious uniformity; from the earliest days, some variation in faith and practice was generally tolerated, and legal discri- mination against both Catholics and Protestant nonconformists effectively ended in 1829. The monarch, who under the 1701 Act of Settlement regulating succession to the throne must be Protestant, remains the 'supreme head' of the Church of England, vowing to defend it on accession and at coronation. But the powers of appointing the higher clergy secured by Henry VIII are, like other royal prerogatives, now exercised by the monarch on the advice of the Prime Minister, who only rarely rejects the recommendations he or she receives from Church of England bodies.

The Church of England retains certain consti- tutional privileges. Since the Middle Ages, when they represented a considerable 'estate' within the realm, senior churchmen have sat in the House of Lords as 'Lords Spiritual', originally outnumbering the 'Lords Temporal'. They currently comprise the two archbishops, the bishops of London, Winchester and Durham and twenty-one other diocesan bishops in order of seniority, these numbers being limited in Victorian times when additional bishoprics were created. The Lords Spiritual are in effect *ex officio* life peers for as long as they hold office. Particularly meritorious archbishops or bishops are then generally nominated as life peers on their retirement, meaning they continue to sit in the Lords. Peers who are in the clergy may sit in the House of Lords, but clergymen or women who are commoners, though entitled to vote in Parliamentary elections, cannot become MPs. Changes in the Church of England's representation in the House of Lords, mooted in Victorian times, will probably be included within wider reforms of the House of Lords being discussed at time of writing.

Historically, the foundations of worship in the Church of England have been the Book of Common Prayer, which took its definitive form in 1662 after more than a century of evolution from the Catholic service books, and the Authorised Version of the Bible (the King James Version), a translation dating from 1611 and also the product of prolonged development. Stylistically impressive, both were revered. But language changed, scholarship undermined interpretations, and the conviction grew that a renewal of the liturgy would make a wider appeal. Attempts to revise the Book of Common Prayer in the 1920s were voted down by MPs, many of whom were not Anglicans. Since then the Church of England has won greater control over its affairs. The General Synod, with representation for bishops, clergy and laity, introduced alternative services in 1980 and encouraged the use of, for instance, The New English Bible. Currently, worship in the Church of England appears highly eclectic as it has assumed a great variety in liturgical forms and styles, reflecting not only the tastes of different congregations and their clergy but also considerable diversity in doctrine within a generalized Christian outlook. The response is mixed. Some parishes and cathedrals attract large numbers, but the Church of England can no longer claim, even for baptisms and weddings, the loyalty of either the mass of the population or of the upper classes who were once its keenest supporters. The opinions of its leaders, though still widely reported, no longer command great respect in a multicultural, multi-faith country

where those who used to profess nominal allegiance to the Church of England are now generally indifferent.

The Empire and missionary endeavours have spread the doctrines, liturgy and organization of the Church of England far and wide. The Anglican Communion, as it is called, numbers some 70 million people. Its leaders come together once a decade in the Lambeth Conference, named after the Archbishop of Canterbury's London residence. As well as maintaining and developing Anglicanism, the Church places reunification with other churches and denominations high on its agenda.

See also: Archbishop of Canterbury; Protestant churches; women priests

Further reading

Baker, J. (1978) *The Church of England*, Exeter: Religious Education Press.

CHRISTOPHER SMITH

angling

There are 1,710 angling clubs, with 405,000 members, in Britain. Problems facing anglers include a decline in sponsorship, opposition from **animal rights** activists and the increase in numbers of seabirds flying inland to take fish (for which reason anglers would like cormorants to be taken off the protected list). Sea anglers also have experienced a decline in fish stocks. In the case of the declining stocks of sea trout, much of the blame is placed on salmon farms, which attract sea lice who attach themselves to the trout and eat them alive. Angling is also threatened with loss of sponsorship from tobacco companies and there has been some opposition to angling from animal rights activists, who regard it as a 'blood sport'. It has however become popular on television, where some of the angling is done abroad.

MIKE STORRY

animal rights

The issue of animal rights has theoretical and practical dimensions relating to the treatment of animals by humans. On the theoretical side, animal rights refers to the idea that animals ought to be ascribed rights to protect them from being abused and/or treated in particular ways. Animals are held to possess the capacities (such as sentience or consciousness) which make them deserving of rights in the same way that humans have rights on account of these capacities or properties. On the practical side, the animal rights movement in Britain is most usually associated with the more radical end of the 'animal welfare' movement. Those agitating for animal rights include **hunt saboteurs** and those seeking to end hunting foxes and deer with dogs, and others (such as the Animal Liberation Front) who oppose the use of animals for food, clothing, entertainment and medical experimentation.

JOHN BARRY

animation

With a long history in the United Kingdom, animation has developed along different lines to the much larger industry in North America. The lack of a large film distribution network meant a relative scarcity of work for animators in the postwar period. There was no market for syndicated cartoons, nor an equivalent of the large studio system employed by Walt Disney. At that time, the only real outlet for indigenous animators' talents was cinema advertising.

A handful of studios operated in London, the most notable being that of John Halas and Joy Batchelor. They produced the first British animated feature film, an adaptation of George Orwell's *Animal Farm* (1954). With its serious political allegory, this landmark production demonstrated the artists' commitment to animation for adults. The first ever cartoon opera, Joy Batchelor's *Ruddigore*, (1964), was further proof that animation was not solely intended as a novelty or for children.

The arrival of commercial television, and the resulting increase in work for advertising (see advertising, television and video), led to a rapid growth in the number of small studios in the UK. During the 1960s a number of animators began to operate independently. Perhaps tired of the mass production techniques necessary to work for television, animators began to assert more individual, expressive styles and tackle a wider range of subjects.

Influential in this shift was George Dunning, whose *The Flying Man* (1962) inspired others to push for greater artistic freedom. Dunning is perhaps best remembered for his work on the psychedelic Beatles epic *Yellow Submarine* (1968). Bob Godfrey worked anarchic humour into his parodies, many of which were concerned with sex; *Kama Sutra Rides Again* (1971) and *Dream Doll* (1979) are the most prominent examples. Godfrey's irreverent attitude has been compared to the **radio comedy** *The Goon Show.* A blend of surreal humour and Dada-inspired cutout graphics formed the basis for Terry Gilliam's animations for the television comedy show *Monty Python's Flying Circus* (1969–74).

Advertising and children's entertainment continued to provide the bulk of work for animators in the 1970s, representing opportunities to experiment with different techniques. Several feature-length animated films were produced for the cinema, largely adaptations of children's books such as Lee Mishkin's *Butterfly Ball* (1974), and Martin Rosen's *Watership Down* (1978). As the number of films produced increased, so independent animators found they could explore more personal subjects and vary their graphic styles. Geoff Dunbar's short film *Lautrec* (1974), based on the French artist's cancan drawings, won wide acclaim. *Ubu* (1979), derived from Alfred Jarry's play *Ubu Roi*, shocked many with its angry, grotesque characters. Alison de Vere's films use powerful symbolism to convey emotional and spiritual states. *Mr Pascal* (1979) deals with religious belief and transformation, and *The Black Dog* (1987) is a journey through a haunting dream landscape.

Certain artists began to move away from traditional techniques of two-dimensional cell animation in the Disney mould, and towards a more mixed media approach. In particular, stop-motion **photography** using real objects, people or puppets became popular. The Brothers Quay, influenced by Czech film maker Jan Svankmajer, started producing animated shorts using found objects such as dolls' heads, pieces of meat, hair and bones. Their dark, neo-Gothic style with its macabre air of decay is seen in *Epic Of Gilgamesh* (1981) and *Street of Crocodiles* (1986). Much of their commercial work has been made for music videos or television channel identifying graphics.

Aardman Animations, a studio started by Peter Lord and David Sproxton, specialized in plasticine animation. This technique was used throughout their Morph series for BBC children's television in the 1980s, and to great effect in the milestone music video for Peter Gabriel, *Sledgehammer* (1986). Aardman enjoyed international success with Nick **Park**'s *Creature Comforts* (1989) and *The Wrong Trousers* (1993), the second film featuring two enduring animated characters, Wallace and Grommit.

Animation has always been an area of the media industries more open to participation by women. Throughout the 1980s and 1990s they have taken an increasingly important role in the field in the UK. The role of **Channel 4** in funding much of this work has been widely recognized. The channel's remit to cater for niche audiences led to a separate commissioning department for animation for adults: many of the resulting films have been made by women.

Kayla Parker makes films that are experimental in form, with uncompromising subject matter. *Cage of Flame* (1992) celebrates menstruation and uses a combination of live action, stop-motion and scratching on the surface of the film to convey haunting, powerful imagery. *Sunset Strip* (1996) is a time-lapse film of drawings of sunsets made every evening over one year. The images are drawn directly onto the film using a variety of materials including nail varnish, magnolia petals, hair and net stockings.

Candy Guard examines everyday life through the eyes of her neurotic female characters in *Fatty Issues* (1990) and the series *Pond Life* (1996). Boyfriend trouble, shopping with Mum and weight watching all come under the microscope. The resulting mild misfortunes are played to hilarious effect.

Sarah Ann Kennedy works with more biting satire. Her *Crapston Villas* (1996) is a raucous parody of community values as represented by the East-enders soap opera. Kennedy playfully subverts the conventions of the soap genre, injecting an air of absurdity and desperation into her characters more reminiscent of a **situation comedy**. Coupled with outrageously scatological humour, the innovative animated series is a unique contribution to British culture.

These two long-running series (*Crapston Villas* and *Pond Life*) indicate a wider trend in television towards including animation in the wider field of entertainment programming. Popular American shows such as *Beavis and Butthead* and *The Simpsons* have influenced this move. While children's television (see **television, children's**) and the films of Disney still dominate the popular perception of animation, it seems that an approach more geared towards adults is here to stay.

See also: cartoons and puppetry

Further reading

Halas, J. (1987) *Masters of Animation*, London: BBC Books.

Pilling, J. (1992) *Women and Animation*, London: British Film Institute.

Russett, R. and Starr, C. (1976) *Experimental Animation*, New York: Da Capo Press.

CHRIS BYRNE

appliances

The terms 'black goods' and 'white goods' apply to audio, hi-fi and video equipment on the one hand, and washing machines, fridges and freezers on the other. These are catch-all terms which illustrate the retail industry's offering of discrete products to a mass consumer market. Ownership of possessions is connected with upward social mobility. Hence, twenty years ago, only members of higher social classes would own certain appliances such as videos, hi-fi equipment and dishwashers. Now, irrespective of need, members of all social classes will own such black appliances as videos and such white ones as dishwashers. Even people on social security benefits expect to own a television, a video and other 'non-essential' items.

MIKE STORRY

Arabic

With the advent of immigrants from countries in North Africa and the Middle East, the growth of Islam in Britain and a general awareness of the need for recognition of cultural diversity, there has been a revival of interest in the Arabic language. Such interest had hitherto been largely confined to such elite schools as London's School of Oriental and African Studies (SOAS), or to the writings of eccentric travellers like Sir Richard Burton, Wilfrid Thesiger and other 'Arabists'. Immigrant groups in Birmingham, Bradford and Leicester have set up weekend classes to teach their children Arabic. Also, expansion in higher education has meant that many more courses in spoken Arabic, as opposed to classical Arabic language are now taught.

See also: Baha'i; Islam

MIKE STORRY

Archbishop of Canterbury

The Archbishop of Canterbury and Primate of All England is the centre of Episcopalian Christian unity. The archbishopric was established in 601 AD when Pope Gregory I sent St Augustine to establish the authority of the Roman Catholic church in England. Augustine became the first Archbishop of Canterbury. By 1900 the archbishopric had become part of the axis of Church and State that forms part of the **Establishment**. It has also, from time to time, adopted a critical voice with respect to the state, particularly on matters of social justice.

William Temple (archbishop 1942–4) brought the Anglican Church national exposure and authority concerning unemployment and human rights. He supported the 1942 Beveridge Report on social security. The position of the Archbishop of Canterbury has become an increasingly political appointment made by the monarch on the advice of the Prime Minister of the day. These exercises of political patronage are increasingly seen as irrelevant, and sometimes even insulting, to the diverse views and cultures both within and without the United Kingdom.

Recent appointees have shown marked independence from their state patronage. Michael Ramsey (appointed 1961) is remembered primarily for his attempts to secure a rapprochement with Rome. Dr Donald Coggan succeeded Ramsey in 1974. Robert Runcie (appointed 1980) is perhaps the most well-known archbishop of recent years. His intellectual, learned and considered liberal approach was offset by Prime Minister Thatcher's appointment of an archbishop from the evangelical wing, Dr George Carey.

Carey became the 103rd archbishop of Canterbury in 1991. His indeterminate views against homosexuality and common law cohabitation have somewhat alienated him from both wings of the Church. The upshot is first, a putatively established church for which the pressures of disestablishment are great and second, a putatively established church which claims to represent the people as a whole but which commands almost no popular nor constitutionally safe and secure support. It now commands less than 5 percent of the active support of the population, and most of these are over 60 years of age.

In the long term, it must be doubted whether the Church can command popular support or justify its establishment. Structurally, and from the behaviour of its primates, it is far from clear if it is in its interest to be so tied to and so restricted by the State. So far, no Archbishop of Canterbury seems to be willing to grasp the issues involved. Without imaginative leadership in all these areas, it seems the Church is bound for difficult times.

See also: Anglican Church; women priests

Further reading

Hastings, A. (1991) *A History of English Christianity: 1920–90*, London: SCM Press Ltd.

PAUL BARRY CLARKE
EMMA R. NORMAN

Archigram

Formed in Hampstead in 1960 by Peter Cook, David Green and Michael Webb, Archigram was responsible for an eponymous journal, but almost no buildings. Inspired by the architect Buckminster Fuller and the critic Reyner Banham, it explored the application of technology to architecture, but was little concerned with its social effects. Archigram's highly exaggerated and ironic projects included Ron Herron's *Walking City* and Peter Cook's *Plug-In City*: fantastic, unfeasible structures which accommodated change by being themselves mobile or temporary. The group's main built project was the British Pavilion for Expo '70, but the clearest expression of their ideas may be the Centre Georges Pompidou, Paris by Renzo Piano and Richard **Rogers** (1975). Archigram disbanded in 1975.

RICHARD J. WILLIAMS

Architectural Association

In 1847, after much complaint in *The Builder* about the inadequacies of the training available for architects, the Architectural Association was founded in London, predominantly by younger practitioners who had not yet made their name. It was the successor of the Association of Architectural Draughtsmen, set up five years earlier. Its objectives combined the enhancement of the professional standing of its members through improved educational opportunities with the development of both the practical and aesthetic aspects of architecture. From relatively modest beginnings, the Architectural Association gained numbers and respect as it assumed responsibilities for teaching and examining and began to collect books and other material for its library. The Architectural Association retains its status in the training and education of architects and, for example, Will **Alsop**, David **Chipperfield** and Rick **Mather** have all studied and/or taught there.

CHRISTOPHER SMITH

Architectural Foundation

The Architectural Foundation is a London-based charity founded in 1847. It celebrates the achievements of modern architecture, showcases good design and encourages greater public involvement in the built environment. In 1997 it staged a digital exhibition of the capital's best modern buildings.

The display, called 'London Interactive', was opened by the Culture Secretary Chris Smith. Plans include an ambitious electronic future projection of the 'eCity', and also a 'virtual' retrospective where citizens of 2050 can revisit the city of today including seventy-four featured London developments built in the past decade. The sites range from the Oxo Tower restaurant, the ITN building and the Saatchi Gallery, to Piers Gough's public lavatories in Westbourne Grove, London.

MIKE STORRY

armed forces and discrimination

With the end of the Cold War, the armed forces' practices have come under scrutiny. Cases of sexual harassment and dismissal from the service for pregnancy have brought adverse court judgements. Complaints about pressure to have abortions have also generated bad publicity. Homosexuals who admit to being active are still barred from entry to the armed services on the grounds that they represent a security risk or that others will feel threatened by them. A number of cases of differential treatment of officers and enlisted men have occurred. For example, SAS soldiers have been prevented from publishing memoirs, while officers have been allowed to publish theirs.

See also: age of consent; armed forces and police; gay liberation

MIKE STORRY

armed forces and police

The armed forces encompasses the army, navy and air force. They protect the interests of the UK overseas. Since the Second World War, the forces have adapted to a new role. The standing armies of the Rhine and the Far East were withdrawn when Germany reunified and Hong Kong reverted to Chinese control. The forces are now envisaged as a rapid reaction force able to 'police' trouble spots on behalf of Britain, NATO or the United Nations. Recently, task forces were sent to the Falklands in

1982, the Persian Gulf in 1991 and Bosnia in 1993. The organization of the forces has also changed. Regiments have been merged in order to reduce personnel, and technological advances in military hardware have necessitated well-educated personnel. The forces have always recruited mainly from the working classes, and originally had a steady supply of conscripted men from National Service, which ended in 1957. The officer core, once provided by the public schools, now comes from bursary-funded graduates. However, despite high unemployment the armed forces now struggle to recruit high-calibre personnel. Some observers point to falling educational standards as the reason for this, while others cite the natural reluctance of youths to risk themselves in Northern Ireland; before the Irish 'troubles', few service people have died in combat since 1945, except in specific engagements such as those in Malaysia, Korea and the Falklands.

Since the foundation of the Metropolitan Police in 1829, the police have been likened to an army for the maintenance of order inside rather than outside Britain's shores. The police and armed forces are similar in many ways. Both recruit rank and file from the working classes and higher echelons (sergeants, commanders) from the educated middle classes, and both have struggled to recruit women and ethnic minorities because of ill-treatment and lack of promotion opportunities. Both also wield the coercive power of the State, and are the only legitimate users of violence. This aspect of police work and 'colonial' or 'paramilitary' policing is repeatedly criticized. For instance, the tactics used during large-scale demonstrations, the use of riot police 'snatch squads', CS gas and pepper spray have been attacked. However, despite persistent criticism from sections of the community, both agencies enjoy popular support, evidenced by the popularity of the detective genre and series such as *Soldier Soldier* on television. Despite this, most young people applauded the sentiment of anti-militarist films such as *The Deer Hunter* and *Apocalypse Now.*

See also: MI5 and MI6; police; secret services

Further reading

Dandeker, C. (1990) *Surveillance, Power and Modernity,* Cambridge: Polity Press.
Jefferson, T. (1990) *The Case Against Paramilitary Policing,* Milton Keynes: Open University Press.

BARRY GODFREY

aromatherapy

One of the most popular alternative therapies in Britain, aromatherapy is based on the use of essential oils, that is, those forming the odorous principles of plants. These are extracted and used to promote health and relaxation, to combat infection and to treat a range of ailments. Massage is one of several ways in which the oils can be effectively applied. Practitioners undergo a certified training course which includes the study of anatomy and physiology. Aromatherapy has its roots in ancient Egypt, but the twentieth-century promoter of its use was a French chemist, René Gattefosse, whose research into perfumery lead to the discovery of the therapeutic value of essential oils.

See also: holistic medicine; homeopathy

JAN EVANS

art galleries

Art galleries and museums, particularly after 1980, have formed some of the most exciting and controversial examples of postwar architecture in Britain. They form part of a global burgeoning of architecture commissioned to serve cultural purposes. The reasons for this expansion are complex and diverse, ranging from the changing functions and purposes of these institutions, the democratization of culture, the interest in heritage, tourism and changes in the funding mechanisms designed to support cultural activities. Diane Ghirardo (1996) identifies four types of museum – as shrine, as warehouse, as cultural shopping mall and as spectacle – in addition to other solutions. The Tate Gallery has provided some of the most interesting developments, beginning with the Clore Gallery

(1980–5), designed by Stirling Wilford Associates. The decision to decentralize its collections led to the Tate Gallery, Liverpool, (1988) by Stirling Wilford and the Tate Gallery, St Ives, (1991–3) by Evans and Shalev (see **Tate(s)**). Hertzog and De Meuron's designs to transform Bankside Power Station into the Museum of Modern Art are now well advanced. Similarly, the Design Museum (1987–9), designed by Conran Roche, forms part of the revitalization of the docklands area of London. The Sainsbury Wing of the National Gallery (1988–91), has proved to be one of the most controversial commissions, eliciting condemnation by the Prince of Wales as a 'monstrous carbuncle' on the face of a 'much loved friend'. The winning competition entry by Venturi, Scott Brown and Associates witnesses their belief that ambiguity and complexity in architecture are best suited to the contemporary context. Other extensions to museums and art galleries include the Sackler Galleries, Royal Academy, (1989–91) by **Foster Associates**, and the Entertainment Pavilion, Hayward Gallery, (1994) by Allies and Morrison. The Natural History Museum boasts the Ecology Gallery (1991) by Ian **Ritchie**, the Dinosaur Gallery (1992) by Heron Associates, and Imagination and Wonders at the National History Museum (1993), by David **Chipperfield**. There have also been developments in the provinces, notably the Museum of Science and Industry in Manchester, designed by BDP in 1986, The Henry Moore Institute, Leeds (1993) designed by Jeremy Dixon in association with BDP, The Pump House: People's History Museum, Manchester (1993) by OMI, and the Broadfield House Glass Museum, Glass Pavilion, Kingswinford, (1994) by Design Antenna.

See also: St Ives; Tate(s)

Further reading

Ghirardo, D. (1996) *Architecture After Modernism*, London: Thames & Hudson.

Papadakis, A.C. (1991) *New Museology, An Art and Design Profile*, London: Academy Editions.

HILARY GRAINGER

Arts Council

The Arts Council of Great Britain was established as an independent but government-funded public body by John Maynard Keynes at the end of the Second World War. Since 1994 there have been separate councils for England, Scotland, Wales and Northern Ireland. Gerry Robinson, the head of **Granada**, became chairman of the Arts Council of England in May 1998, when the membership was reduced from 22 people to 10. In 1998 the Arts Council of England shared out £187 million between 165 regularly-funded bodies including the **Royal Shakespeare Company** and the Royal Opera, and over 100 other schemes. It also had £250 million of **National Lottery** money to distribute. Following the removal of regional arts boards (RABs) members from the ruling Council, a process of devolution to the regions is currently in hand under Robinson, and the days of the Arts Council may be numbered.

See also: Crafts Council; Design Council

PETER CHILDS

arts programming

Coverage of the arts on television is part of the remit of both the **BBC** and the commercial stations. Those involved in 'the culture industry', complain that the arts are not taken seriously and general commentators talk of a dumbing down, and in 1997 the Independent Televison Commission (ITC) criticized ITV for its low provision of arts shows. However, compared with television in other countries, the arts are given considerable prominence in Britain. Dance, **opera** and orchestral music are all shown in prime time and serious attempts are made to cover culture which forms part of the fabric of British life. For example, during the Edinburgh Festival there is a nightly roundup on BBC2 called *Edinburgh Nights* and the annual Promenade Concerts from the Albert Hall, London, are broadcast every year.

Though the highest profile arts programme is ITV's *The South Bank Show*, hosted by Melvyn Bragg, the station with the strongest claim to broadcasting high culture is BBC2. While programmes like *The Late Show* and *Late Review* may cater to 'minority' interests, they are flagships for the BBC and indicate their commitment to quality programming.

Channel 4 has a reputation for showing the most innovative and specialized arts programmes, including contemporary dance. It has been responsible for screening much innovative drama. In his later years, Channel 4 was the preferred outlet for his plays by Dennis **Potter** (for example, *Cold Lazarus*). It was also the proving ground for Alan Bleasdale, who went on to promote new playwriting talent through his series of screenplays by new writers. Channel 4's reputation for supporting the arts declined slightly before the head of Channel 4, Michael Grade, announced he was leaving the industry in 1997. He was widely held responsible for the station's losing its creative edge in arts broadcasting.

Many commentators are fearful that the continual demand for high audience ratings figures will adversely affect broadcasting of the arts on television. They suggest that competition to terrestrial stations from cable and satellite television, which are now available in 25 percent of British homes, tends to jeopardize quality. However, there are many exceptions. For example, even the 'traditional' BBC is still very innovative. It is behind a risky project to produce *Comedy Nation*, a cross between BBC2's *Video Nation* and a traditional sketch show which is shot on hand-held cameras, and airs at midnight on Fridays. The rub may be that it costs £29,000 per episode to produce, compared with more than £200,000 per episode for shows like *The Fast Show.*

See also: performing arts on television

MIKE STORRY

Arup Associates

Born in Newcastle upon Tyne in 1895, Ove Arup studied philosophy, mathematics and then civil engineering. Director and chief engineer of the English engineering firm J.L. Kier and Company, from 1934 to 1938, he then founded the engineering and consulting firm Arup and Arup with his cousin. In 1946 he opened an independent engineering office, which operated from 1949 under the name Ove Arup and Partners. Finally, in 1963 the interdisciplinary and now internationally famous planning firm Arup Associates was launched.

In 1933 Arup was one of the founding members of the MARS group (Modern Architectural Research Group), indicating his early commitment to modern architecture. Acting as a consultant to the Russian architect Berthold Lubetkin and his Tecton Group, he was involved with High Point I flats (1933–5), the Finsbury Health Centre (1935–8) and the innovative buildings at London Zoo. Lubetkin and Arup were concerned to promote investigations into the employment of new materials and to establish an authentic technical base for modern architecture in Britain. Examples of their postwar engineering work include the school at Hunstanton, Norfolk (1949, 1952–4) by Alison and Peter **Smithson**, the Sydney Opera House (1956–74) by Utzon, the John Player Horizon factory at Nottingham (1968) with its integrated servicing and planning system, the multi-functional Bundesgartenschau Hall, Mannheim (1973–4), as well as the controversial structure for the Centre Pompidou in Paris (1971–7) by Piano and Rogers. Arup Associates have been involved in a number of university buildings; at Corpus Christi, Cambridge (1963), their precast concrete structure enhances the appearance of the architecture, while at Loughborough University of Technology (1967), their development of a regular planning module has allowed for considerable flexibility.

The dramatic footbridge linking the steep banks of the river Wear in Durham (1963), connecting the older precinct and the newer university development, Dunelm House (1964) is an example of Arup's personal design work. The height of the bridge exploits the dynamic of the diagonal slender struts. Recent work includes the overall planning of Stockley Park, (1984), a new breed of business park where the firm has contributed twelve flexible units, including the award winning headquarters for Haspro; and the design for Broadgate Square, with its ice rink in the heart of a tiered amphitheatre housing restaurants, bars and shops as part of Broadgate, London (1985–91).

Further reading

Brawne, M. (1985) *Arup Associates*, London: Hacker Art Books.

HILARY GRAINGER

ASA

Commercial advertisements were first transmitted on British television in 1955, and prior to 1962 regulation and control of advertising had been based on a number of voluntary codes. However, the system lacked any overall coherence. It was felt that some external regulation was necessary to preserve public confidence. The creation of the ASA (Advertising Standards Authority) was designed to remedy this and to ensure that non-broadcast advertisements are 'legal, decent, honest and truthful' by requiring that the rules contained in the British Codes of Advertising are followed by all advertisers (advertisements on television and cable programmes are regulated by the Independent Television Commission). Although the principle of self-regulation still applies – the Codes are drawn up by the advertising industry – there are numerous statutes which may affect advertisements. Following government criticism, the Code of Practice was strengthened in 1974 and the work of the ASA is now funded by a levy placed on display and direct mail advertising, collected by a separate body in order to preserve ASA independence.

There are an estimated 30 million advertisements published in the UK each year and these produce around 10,000 complaints to the ASA, of which some 25 percent are upheld. In addition to reacting to complaints, the ASA will also carry out its own checks to ensure compliance with the Codes. ASA powers include ordering adverts to be withdrawn overnight, temporarily removed or changed, with the potential ultimate penalty of a referral to the Office of Fair Trading and criminal proceedings. However, proceeding to court is used only as a last resort, as advertisers falling foul of the Codes of Practice will be subject to adverse publicity through the ASA's monthly report which is widely circulated through the industry.

Cigarette advertising has proved one of the most controversial areas, and a specific Code exists which strictly limits the content and context of such advertisements. Other specific categories of advertisements that are singled out include alcoholic drinks, health and beauty and medicines. The ASA may also be consulted in an advisory capacity by advertisers seeking to pre-empt potential problems. The ASA is a founder member of the European Advertising Standards Alliance, which includes all EU members, and a complaint made to ASA regarding an advertisement originating outside of the UK will be referred by the ASA to the national regulatory body in question.

See also: advertising, television and video; National Viewers and Listeners Association; regulatory bodies

GUY OSBORN
STEVE GREENFIELD

Ashley, Laura

b. 1925, Merthyr Tydfil; d. 1985

Fashion designer

Laura Ashley was one of the best-known names in British fashion. A self-taught designer, she started her own company in 1953, selling printed scarves, tea towels and aprons. In 1969 she developed a clothing range including smocks and dresses in traditional feminine shapes and simple floral prints, which epitomized her distinctive style and nostalgically evoked a lost world of pastoral England. From the late 1960s her stores in Britain and around the world were extraordinarily successful, and the company also developed soft furnishing and home decor ranges. The company's fortunes have been variable since her death, and the Laura Ashley style has been updated to fit more sophisticated modern trends.

TAMSIN SPARGO

Asian artists

As a loose grouping of largely migratory artists of Asian birth and British-born artists of Asian descent, Asian artists have counterpointed and hybridized Eastern and Western artistic styles and traditions to produce a culturally syncretic art which interrogates primary notions of identity, difference and representation within post-colonial contexts.

Between the mid-1950s and mid-1960s, Indian artists Francis Newton Souza and Avinash Chandra, and Pakistani artists Iqbal Geoffrey and Ahmed Parvez, rose to prominence in a British art scene intrigued by modernist expressions of 'otherness'. Against Chandra's more vivacious style, Souza's paintings subverted imperialist–colonial dialectics, engaging with religion and sexuality from the conflicted self-perspective of a Hindu heritage, Catholic and colonial upbringing. Parvez, as one of several 1950s Pakistani abstract expressionist painters pursuing their art in Britain, created a highly individualized style infused with properties of Muslim art, while Geoffrey's work was riddled with artistic contradictions and conceptualisms. Their influence however, subsided after an initial resounding impact. Fellow Pakistani Rasheed Araeen progressed from painting to minimalist, abstract sculptures inspired by the 1965 New Generation Sculpture to 1970s politicized art, before undertaking his visual art projects of subsequent decades.

The 1970s and 1980s produced sculptors like Avtarjeet Dhanjal, whose **organic art** exquisitely unifies nature and culture through contrasting materials, environments and traditions. Anish **Kapoor**'s sublime sculptures are imbued with transcendental and metaphysical dimensions. Dhruva Mistry's works reflect the craftsmanship and sensuous aestheticism of ancient Indian sculpture, while Juginder Lamba's sculptures similarly attempt to exteriorize inner emotional and spiritual lives.

The politicized 1980s and the 1990s witnessed the ascent of Asian female artists including Sutapa Biswas, Zarina Bhimji, Chila Kumari **Burman** and Perminder Kaur. Their varied artistic and performative approaches to race, gender, class, sexual politics and representation have elicited resolute challenges to established orthodoxies. Biswas's real and imagined reconstructions of migration, memory and history are deployed through mixed media, while Bhimji's sensory expressions of historical trauma, recovery and cross-cultural understanding through evocative art and materials are echoed in Perminder Kaur's subtle equivocations on themes of innocence and loss.

With British artists such as Burman, Keith Khan and photographer Roy Mehta (and even the fascinating epistemological enquiries into art and science of the late 'Young British Artist' Hamad Butt) provocatively exploring cultural multivocalities in diverse media, the once celebrated 'exotic' difference of Asian artists is being superseded by a generation reshaping the parameters of British art.

See also: painting; sculpture

Further reading

Araeen, Rasheed (1989) *The Other Story: Afro-Asian Artists in Post-war Britain*, London: South Bank Centre (essential documentation of black and Asian art).

SATINDER CHOHAN

Asian fashions

Asian fashions had an extensive impacted on British culture following postwar immigration and the 1960s counter-cultural mystification of the East, with the prejudicial British stereotypes initially associated with traditional Asian dress gradually shifting to Western mainstream appropriations of ethnic style and fashion.

Subject to subcontinental regional variations, Asian fashions are based around traditional gendered garments including women's casual *shalwar* (cotton pyjama trousers) and *kameez* (tunic top) with *dupatta* or *chunni* (chiffon head scarf) outfit. More intricately embroidered, classically or extravagantly designed versions of these *suits* are reserved for special social and religious occasions, as are the *lengha*, (a long heavy flaring skirt coupled with *kameez*-style tunic top) and *sari*. Bengali and Gujarati women don durable cotton *saris* as daily wear, with regionally diverse styles ranging from the hand-woven Bengali *jamdani* to silk South Indian *saris*.

Traditional male garments centre around the

men's *shalwar-kameez* or *kurta* (tunic top of slightly shorter length than the *kameez*) and *pyjama*, commonly worn by older Asian men or informally in the home. The pronounced religious influences of modest traditional dress are visible in the turbans and white caps worn by Sikh and Muslim men respectively (the different styles of turbans are indicative of regional and caste-based differences), and also Muslim women's *hijab*.

Asian fashions fluctuate between preserving traditions, Western appropriations as 'authentic' cultural markers and accommodating Western trends to produce a modified or hybridized look. Western appropriations which began with sandals, beads and *kurta* tops in the 1960s now include **accessories** and **body adornment** such as *mehndi*-decorated hands, other henna tattoos, facial markings, *bindis*, nose rings, bangles and weightier Indian gold accessories, once traditionally worn by married women only.

As Asian affluence grows, Bombay and Delhi-style fashion boutiques are becoming popular among the Westernized Asian middle classes, selling ready-made designer suits alongside more traditional fabric outlets. Economic stratification locates the continued practice of homemade fashion, based on classic and the latest imported subcontinental fashion designs, among ex-rural migrants in particular.

While traditional fashions are maintained among older Asians with social and religious aspects intact, **Asian youth styles** reflect the cross-cultural influences of recontextualized Asian fashions, although as Naseem Khan suggests, the conspicuous lack of an outstanding British Asian designer perhaps indicates the future of Asian fashions in Britain.

Further reading

Khan, N. (1992) 'Asian Women's Dress: From Burqah to Bloggs – Changing Clothes for Changing Times', in J. Ash and E. Wilson (eds), *Chic Thrills: A Fashion Reader*, London: Pandora Press (solid, informative introduction to (British) Asian fashions).

SATINDER CHOHAN

Asian theatre

British Asian **theatre** embraces the work of writers, performers and companies, with the involvement of musicians and choreographers such as Shobana Jeyasingh. Leading performers such as Saeed Jaffrey, Jamila Massey and Roshan Seth work in film, television and radio as well as in mainstream theatre, and the writer Ranjit Bolt primarily translates and adapts European classics. Writers such as Hanif Kureishi and Rukshana Ahmad (both in fiction as well as drama), Tanika Gupta, Parv Bancil and Ayub Khan Din have concerned themselves with issues of Asian identity; so too have the leading companies Tara Arts and Tamasha, and the independent director Indu Rubasingham. Diversity increased sharply during the 1990s, with multimedia presentations coming from companies such as Man Mela and Moti Roti.

Two independent British productions in 1970 involved the established performers Massey and Jaffrey in dramas about India: Dilip Hiro's *To Anchor a Cloud* and Partap Sharma's *A Touch of Brightness*, which engaged with the lives of prostitutes in Bombay. In 1974 Roshan Seth became an assistant director for *Cymbeline* for the Royal Shakespeare Company, and during the 1970s increasing pressure for integrated casting was put on the subsidized theatres by the Afro-Asian Committee of British Actors' Equity. Critical recognition was achieved by Hanif Kureishi, with his plays *The Mother Country* (1980), performed at the Riverside Studio, and *Borderline* (1981), devised with Joint Stock. The principle of integrated casting became more thoroughly established during the 1980s, with productions such as *Hedda in India* (1982), directed by Madhav Sharma, and Joint Stock's *The Great Celestial Cow* (1983) at the Royal Court. David Hare's *A Map of the World* (1983) at the National Theatre included an original role for an Asian actor, realized by Roshan Seth, and Seth also took the role of Lear's Fool in the National Theatre's *King Lear* (1986).

Of the British Asian theatre companies, Tara Arts staged its first production, Rabindranath Tagore's *The Sacrifice*, in 1977. Tara's artistic aims have been to examine the cultural position of Asians in Britain, and its artistic director, Jatinder Verma, stated that 'we need to be as critical of ourselves as we are of the society outside'. The company is based in London, and has a tradition of touring. It has also worked on co-productions with Contact Theatre (Manchester) and the Lyric Theatre (London), and has twice been invited to produce at the Royal National Theatre. The company has only ever had a small workshop space of its own, although funding allocated in the 1990s will see its facilities in Wandsworth enhanced.

Early plays such as *Inkalaab 1919* (1980) and *Lion's Raj* (1982) were devised, or scripted by Verma, and thematically they mediated between the historical experience of the Raj and contemporary society. In the 1980s Tara began to explore plays from the ancient Sanskrit tradition, such as *The Little Clay Cart*, and to develop the kind of theatre established in Indian performance, using the resources of dance, movement and music. With Buchner's *Danton's Death* (1989) Tara began an exploration of European classics, including Molière's *Tartuffe* and Gogol's *The Government Inspector* (1990), Sophocles's *Oedipus the King* (1991), Molière's *Le Bourgeois Gentilhomme* (1994), and Rostand's *Cyrano de Bergerac* (1995) in a version by Ranjit Bolt. Of these productions, *Tartuffe* was a major critical success which transposed Molière's hypocrite into a parasite in an Indian household, in a production which toured nationally. A further stage in this development was represented by productions of Shakespeare, featuring *Troilus and Cressida* (1993) and *A Midsummer Night's Dream* (1997). For the latter, Verma acknowledged influences from Beijing Opera, West African dance, Morris dancing, and Indian classical and folk dance, and Tara remains committed to what Verma calls 'the aesthetics of multiculturalism'.

Tamasha was founded in 1989 by Sudha Bhuchar and Kristine Landon-Smith to produce *Untouchable*, an adaptation of the novel by Mulk Raj Anand, which explored the treatment of India's lowest caste. Tamasha has produced plays on contemporary life in South Asia, and on the lives of Asians in Britain. Ruth Carter's *Women of the Dust* (1993) commemorated the fiftieth anniversary of the foundation of Oxfam by focusing on the lives of women construction workers in Delhi; the production was researched in India, and returned to India to tour. Abhijat Joshi's *A Shaft of Sunlight* (1994),

which examined the marriage between a Hindu and a Moslem in Ahmedabad, and Carter's *A Yearning* (1995), an adaptation of Lorca's *Yerma* to the Punjabi community in Britain, were co-produced with the Birmingham Rep, and concluded their tours in London. Ayub Khan-Din's *East is East* (1996 and 1997) looked at the history of a Pakistani immigrant in 1970s Salford, and the cultural clash experienced by the son of the family: the play came from a script workshop for British Asian writers held at the Royal Court. The company-devised production *A Tainted Dawn* (1997) commemorated the fiftieth anniversary of partition by drawing on the work of leading South Asian writers, examining the lives of ordinary people caught in the political events of 1947.

Independently of these companies, the director Indu Rubasingham has promoted multicultural casts and aesthetics in her productions of Kalidasa's *Shakuntala* (1997) and of two scripts by Tanika Gupta: *Voices on the Wind* (1995) and Gita Mehta's *A River Sutra* (1997), adapted by Gupta. Rukhsana Ahmad has written for theatre and radio: *Song for a Sanctuary*, on the loyalties and fears in a women's refuge, was produced at the Lyric Theatre (1991) and then on radio (1993), followed by the radio play *An Urnful of Ashes* (1995). Ahmad and Rita Wolf founded Kali Theatre in 1990, using workshops and rehearsed readings to support and develop the role of Asian women writers. Keith Khan and Ali Zaidi have explored visual and physical theatre with their company Moti Roti, and taken their work abroad to Canada, Pakistan and the USA. Man Mela, founded in 1993 and directed by Dominic Rai, has brought classical and contemporary music and dance together with contemporary Asian literature in multimedia events, and developed scripts on HIV and club culture.

See also: black theatre

Further reading

Ley, G. (1997) 'Theatre of Migration and the Search for a Multicultural Aesthetic: Twenty Years of Tara Arts', *New Theatre Quarterly* 52: 349–71.

Verma, J. (1996) 'The Challenge of Binglish:

Analysing Multicultural Productions', in P. Campbell (ed.), *Analysing Performance*, Manchester: Manchester University Press.

GRAHAM LEY

Asian underground

Since the 1980s, Asian musicians in Britain have been experimenting with **rap**, **dub** technology, **jungle** breakbeats, traditional Indian music and rock. In the mid- to late 1990s, Anglo-Asian artists with sitars, guitars and decks, such as Cornershop, Asian Dub Foundation, Fun-da-mental, Talvin Singh and Niwtin Sawhney, broke into the pop mainstream. Talvin Singh's Anokha played club nights at The Blue Note in London which attracted media stars, and Cornershop's 1997 album *When I Was Born for the Seventh Time* became a critical and commercial success (and included the number one single 'Brimful of Asha'). Though the bands vary in their political engagement, Asian Dub Foundation released their single 'Free Satpal Ram' in 1998 as a protest against the imprisonment of a Birmingham Asian who defended himself against racist attacks.

See also: bhangra

Further reading

Sharma, S., Hutnyk, J. and Sharma, A. (eds) (1996) *Dis-Orienting Rhythms: The Politics of the New Asian Dance Music*, London: Zed Books.

PETER CHILDS

Asian youth styles

Asian youth styles derive from the dualistic heritage bequeathed to second generation Asians in Britain. Spanning geographical, religious and caste divides, it is a heritage comprising the traditional Asian diasporic culture of their parents (who arrived as South Asian and African immigrants between the 1950s and 1970s) and the indigenous British culture of their birth and/or upbringing.

Afro-Caribbean youth styles comprise a third strongly discernible influence. During the 1970s and 1980s, the closely forged links between the second generation descendants of the largest British ethnic minority groups were fortified by the commonality of racism, their homogenized political categorizing as 'black', and working-class urban propinquity.

Fluidly manoeuvring themselves between white British and Afro-Caribbean cultures and their own culture, Asian youth have assimilated Western influences without relinquishing traditional ones. Late 1980s sampler and rave culture enabled **bhangra** to emerge from its sequins and synthesizer confines in crossover musical fusions with other dance styles such as **house** and **techno**, increasing its accessibility for 'British-Asian' youth. Daytime bhangra concerts were arranged, providing an alternative space for Asian youth to gather and dance without need of parental permission. Bhangra's fusion with ragga produced 'bhangramuffin' in the continued youth dialogue between Asian and Afro-Caribbean youth; Apache Indian embodies the bhangramuffin sound and style.

In 1996, the London-based emergence of an **Asian underground** identified another uniquely 'British-Asian' subculture integrating classical and popular Asian and Western musical and stylistic influences. Musical pioneers like Talvin Singh and Nitin Sawhney fused drum 'n' bass, frenetic breakbeats and experimental dance styles with classical Indian instrumentation (such as tablas, sitars, sarongis and bhajans), *quawwali* vocals and Bollywood samples by musical icons such as Nusrat Fateh Ali Khan, Lata Mangeshkar and Asha Bhosle. Asian underground youth combined traditional Indian dress like the *shalwar-kameez* (normally reserved for domestic and cultural occasions), Nehru tunics, *kurtha*, *sari* tops and *bindis* with trainers, club and combatwear (denoting a harder-edged, politically conscious musical-stylistic alliance exemplified by bands like Fun da Mental and Asian Dub Foundation).

Stereotypically regarded as a passive, alien group, resisting assimilation because of their cultural, religious and bilingual backgrounds, Asian youth have begun to hybridize their collective influences through a genuinely expressed British-Asian identity that confidently counter previous cultural displacements.

See also: Asian fashions

Further reading

Sharma, S., Hutnyk, J. and Sharma, A. (eds) (1996) *Dis-Orienting Rhythms: The Politics of the New Asian Dance Music*, London: Zed Books (an incisive examination of Asian dance music, providing a contextual grounding for Asian youth styles).

SATINDER CHOHAN

Associated Press

The Associated Press was a cooperative endeavour of six New York City newspapers, begun originally in 1840 to share the expense of sending a reporter to cover the Mexican War. It now gathers and distributes news from 150 cities throughout the world. Its impact in Britain has been both to supply world news to newspapers here and to provide an outlet for the work of many journalists working in Britain. Commentators worry that because news is controlled by three main agencies, Reuters, United Press International (UPI), and Associated Press (AP), (the last two being American) it tends to reflect a US world view. Others say such reporting is inevitable in the global village, and serves as a safeguard against the parochialism of British tabloid journalism.

MIKE STORRY

athletics

Britain has had a long and proud record in athletics, notably in running, but the 1980s and 1990s saw a decline in performance and public interest, sparking a debate about how best to train top athletes. Most observers accept that athletics requires serious work to remain one of Britain's top sports, and to make Britain a strong contender in international competition once more. A temporary boost to the sport was given by the British athletics team's topping (for the first time since 1950) of the European Championships medals table in 1998.

While British running's history in the 1980s and 1990s is impressive (Linford Christie, Colin Jackson, Steve Cram, Sebastian Coe, Steve Ovett, Sally Gunnell and Roger Black were the main stars of that period), the 1996 Atlanta Olympics performance was poor, with few track medals (and only a handful in field events), and Britain was outperformed by smaller and less wealthy countries which had invested considerably more over the years. This led to a fundamental debate about the nature and standard of British coaching and athletes, and the level of support given to the sport by the State.

The most widely accepted argument post-Atlanta was that not enough money has been invested in facilities and full-time coaches over the years, compared to countries such as France and Australia. Both of these spent heavily on training facilities and full-time coaches, and both did well in Atlanta. Britain has traditionally employed very few full-time coaches, so the time spent with athletes is shorter than is the case abroad. The training facilities are also not as good, as British-born long jumper Fiona May pointed out after winning a silver medal at Atlanta for her adopted Italy.

Two solutions have been suggested, both involving **National Lottery** funds. At the beginning, Lottery money could be used to build new sports centres, but not to pay coaches (a rule relaxed in 1996) or for competitors' preparation costs. Money is also expected to become available for a British Academy of Sports, to build excellence in young elite performers. Whether that can repair the damage of the 1980s, when schools sold off thousands of acres of sports fields to raise money, is another matter; changes to school curricula in the 1980s and early 1990s also mean that fewer teachers have the time and energy to take sports classes after hours, and the British Athletic Federation (BAF) has declared itself unlikely to use the Academy as a training base in any case.

The Federation, which runs the sport, itself suffered in the 1990s. The most disturbing event was the sacking of Andy Norman (largely responsible for the aggressive marketing of athletics) in 1994 after allegations were made about his role in the suicide of a respected journalist, and it soon became clear that Norman ran the BAF as a private fiefdom. Other problems include public rows with Linford Christie, Colin Jackson and

Tony Jarrett over appearance money, which dragged on through 1995, while the biggest issue remains drugs. Since drug testing became routine in the postwar period, Britain has suffered very few confirmed cases amongst its athletes, but even the suspicion of drug taking is enough to damage the sport; the most serious case, involving runner Diane Modahl in 1994 and 1995, alienated existing sponsors and put potential backers off altogether. Modahl was eventually cleared, but athletics has struggled for years to keep its sponsors, creating long-term uncertainty and making planning difficult.

The precarious financial position of athletics is clearly tied to the level of television coverage, which has long been crucial to sponsors. Meetings are no longer televised in Britain (some, including even big international meetings, were cancelled as a result), and the sport's media profile in the 1990s is generally low, a far cry from the heady days of the 1980s when Sebastian Coe and Steve Ovett dominated the headlines and generated huge public and media interest. The Olympics and Commonwealth Games obviously attract attention, but regular meetings around the country get little coverage, and are probably not the first choice of those stations that do screen them. With declining television and commercial interest, the BAF has struggled for years to finance its operations, even those limited contributions made to athletes and coaches. Over two financial years up to 1996, the BAF lost some £750,000 and made cuts in promotions and coaching as a result.

These payments to competitors are more vital than the public might think; athletes at the top end of the sport, like Christie and Gunnell, can make fortunes on and off the track but the average runner, jumper and thrower has never had any such security and struggles to make ends meet. Most have relied on help from family, the BAF and any sponsors who could be persuaded to fund their training. Two competitors at Atlanta even admitted to selling their official British team sweatshirts after the Games to raise money, such was their plight. Athletics has become increasingly heavily divided over the last two decades, with a few performers becoming very highly paid thanks to television and sponsorship, and a large mass of competitors below them earning far less. It is open to debate how this

has affected the use of drugs, and whether the athletes' union formed by Roger Black in 1995 will help redress the balance.

Athletics in the 1990s occupies a similar position to **tennis**, in that it struggles to build on the success of its regular major tournament in Britain. There are thousands of committed athletes and coaches, attending hundreds of meetings annually, but the sport remains short of money and facilities and is increasingly shorn of its established stars. Television and sponsors are only interested in telegenic, well-known stars to focus on, and the decline of existing household names leaves athletics struggling to attract and maintain television and sponsor interest. Money has long been the main problem (by the mid-1990s, this was even causing promising athletes and coaches to leave athletics for professional rugby union), but at least the BAF recognizes the importance of the questions hanging over the sport. The biggest issue might turn out to be 'who actually runs athletics in the 1990s: television, the promoters or the BAF?'

See also: long-distance runners; marathons; middle-distance runners; sprinters

REX NASH

Attenborough, David

b. 1926

Naturalist and broadcaster

David Attenborough, younger brother of actor-director Richard **Attenborough**, joined BBC television in 1952, fronting *Zoo Quest*, the programme which, between 1956 and 1965, transformed the teatime wildlife show from patronizing sentimentality into serious education children's programming. Attenborough then entered the BBC's administrative hierarchy, where he established both BBC2 and colour transmission. His catholic tastes and scheduling instincts brought shows as varied as snooker, 'The Forsyte Saga' and Jacob Bronowski's 'The Ascent of Man' to BBC2, establishing it as a widely appealing and innovative service. After fifteen years, however, Attenborough returned to broadcasting to complete the trilogy begun with 'Life on Earth', which was seen by an estimated 500 million people worldwide. Subsequent prestige series have made him perhaps the most universally popular, respected and influential broadcaster and ecologist on the planet.

SEAN CUBITT

Attenborough, Richard

b. 1923, Cambridge

Actor and film-maker

Richard Attenborough's distinguished and prolific career in film making began with supporting roles in dramas, war films and comedies, highlighted by his performance as the amoral gangster Pinky in *Brighton Rock* (1947). He soon combined acting with producing, making films such as *The Angry Silence* (1960), the powerful story of a trade union dispute, *Seance on a Wet Afternoon* (1964) and *10 Rillington Place* (1970), which demonstrated his capacity for studied, disturbing performances. Turning to directing in 1969 with *Oh! What a Lovely War*, Attenborough's perception of the film maker's role as that of a storyteller is borne out with his epics *Gandhi* (1982), *Cry Freedom* (1987) and *Chaplin* (1992). His versatility is confirmed by later acting roles, with appearances in Hollywood productions such as *Jurassic Park* (1993) and *Miracle on 34th Street* (1994).

ALICE E. SANGER

Attwood, David

b. 1952

Film-maker

David Attwood has directed films for television (often joint ventures with US/UK stations) aimed at a young avant-garde audience. *Wild West* (1992) was written by Harwant Bains, a 29-year-old of Punjabi extraction but born and raised in Southall. Attwood's film was likened to Stephen **Frears**' *My Beautiful Laundrette* (1985) (written by Hanif Kureishi), and dealt with the family relations of anarchic young Indian Londoners. His mini-series based on Daniel Defoe's novel, *The Fortunes and Misfortunes of Moll Flanders* (1996) was acclaimed. It treated farcically the life of someone who, though both prostitute (Moll) and thief (of Flanders lace) in the picaresque tradition, triumphed over her difficulties.

MIKE STORRY

auctions

The major auction houses in Britain are Sotheby's, Christie's, Bonham's and Philips. Scandals over the provenance of antiques in Italy and of the selling on of antiquities from the East have soured the reputation of Sotheby's. The popular television series *Lovejoy* thus reflects sceptical public attitudes to the higher echelons of the antique trade. Throughout Britain there are numerous smaller privately owned auction houses, dealing only occasionally in antiques and mainly in household goods from beds and living room furniture to electrical appliances. Many of these firms have followed the major firms' introduction of a so-called 'buyer's premium' of 10 percent of the purchase price as a means of boosting their typical commission rates of 17.5 percent on the first £100.

MIKE STORRY

audience research

Audience research has developed in two main interlinking strands: research by those working in the industry and research by academics. Industry research developed as a mechanism by which media producers and advertisers could both understand and shape media products for a knowable media audience. Such research has come to be dominated by a conception of the media user as part of homogeneous mass audience, one with similar uses, tastes, wants and desires that could be easily quantified. Those working in the more critical academic paradigm have come to problematize this notion, preferring instead a view of the media audience as heterogeneous and segmented. However, as the industry finds its notion of the mass audience questioned, the two strands have come closer together.

Industry research, either undertaken in-house or contracted out to independent research companies, is often coordinated by joint industry research boards, such as the Radio Joint Audience Research (RAJAR) for radio, Broadcasters' Audience Research Board (**BARB**) for television and Joint Industry Committee for Poster Audience Research (JICPAR) for posters. These produce audience data for their respective media, broken down into such divisions as social class, age, gender and geographical location. Such audience data is used by the industry, amongst other things, to improve the provision of its media output, to help fix advertising rates and to find the appropriate placing for advertisements. The methods used to collect such data tend to fall into two categories: random surveys of media users and ongoing panel surveys. While random surveys provide an instant snapshot of a media audience, panel surveys are able to offer a long term view by studying the same sample of media users.

Against these more quantitative approaches, many working in the academic strand (for example, David Morley's work on the family audience) have come to problematize the notion of a passive unsegregated audience. By using more qualitative styled approaches, attempts have been made to understand how different audiences understand and make use of the media. Thus, a more active view of a segmented audience has been obtained. Recent developments have seen a move away from studying the reception of the media by the viewer towards more ethnographic methods to study the way the media is used within a specific social-cultural context.

See also: BARB

Further reading

Ang, I. (1991) *Desperately Seeking the Audience*, London: Routledge (critical account of the experiences of European and American broadcasters to conceptualize the audience).

PAUL RIXON

autobiography

While critiques of intentionalism and representationalism may have pointed to the impossibility of unmediated self-expression, autobiography has proved a resilient genre in recent years, even emerging on the cutting edge of critical theory. These theoretical developments have been mirrored in fiction, where autobiography has been used both to question the nature and status of fiction and to show how the self is created rather than merely represented in narrative. Examples of this self-conscious blurring of the distinction between autobiography and fiction can be found, for example, in the novels of Jeanette Winterson, Julian Barnes and Martin Amis (see **novel**). In non-fiction writing, there has been a similar questioning of the self-containedness of autobiography as a genre, which is itself part of the general slipperiness of the boundaries between different genres and disciplines in recent years. Works published in the 1980s such as Ronald Fraser's *In Search of a Past*, Carolyn Steedman's *Landscape for a Good Woman* and Ann Oakley's *Taking it Like a Woman* seek to link sociological and psychoanalytical theory with personal experience, in order to both restore subjectivity to theoretical writing and to show how identity is culturally constructed.

The last two of these works also demonstrate the ways in which autobiography has been used to draw attention to unwritten histories marginalized by official discourses. A series of multi-authored collections, intersecting with the burgeoning field of oral history and life studies, similarly show how the normally individualistic genre of autobiography can be transformed into a collective process of resistance to dominant narratives. Examples include Liz Heron's Virago anthology, *Truth, Dare or Promise: Girls Growing up in the Fifties*, and *Between the Acts*, a series of moving testimonies edited by Kevin Porter and Jeffrey Weeks telling the story of British gay men in the period of the criminalization of homosexuality between 1885 and 1967. Working-class autobiographies produced by collaborative projects like the Federation of Worker Writers and Community Publishers since the 1970s have fulfilled a similar purpose. Whereas the traditional notion of autobiography might show the subject triumphantly transcending his or her immediate environment, these autobiographies reveal the subject as inextricably embedded in society and history.

See also: biography

Further reading

Marcus, L. (1994) *Auto/biographical Discourse: Theory, Criticism, Practice*, Manchester: Manchester University Press (the second half of this book examines autobiographical theory and writing of the last few decades, using predominantly British examples; an excellent synthesis of recent scholarship).

JOE MORAN

avant-garde cinema

The British avant-garde film movement surfaced in the late 1960s when it was stimulated by the London Film-Makers' Co-operative (LFMC) and by American influences such as Stan Brakhage, Kenneth Anger and Andy Warhol. Key figures in Britain included Steve Dwoskin, Andy Meyer, David Curtis, Peter Gidal, Malcolm Le Grice and Annabel Nicolson. Instead of using the term 'avant-garde', they chose labels such as structural, abstract, experimental, expanded or free. Their broadly structural and formal point of view quickly spread into disparate organizational, artistic and political currents, resulting in the evolution of a diffuse and variegated group.

British popular audiences had been left cold by earlier film movements, such as elitist avant-garde experiments, middle-class realism (**Anderson**, **Richardson**, **Reisz** and so on), critiques of the upper-class (as in **Losey**–Pinter films), and even the **Workshop Declaration**. For the most part they were absorbed by Hollywood films, and were often suspicious of political or avant-garde cinema in Europe. Ironically, the British avant-garde's practical foundations in structuralism and formalism enabled it to assimilate radical changes without engaging revolutionary ideologies. It cut away the visionary anti-Americanism that underlay American structuralists. Concentrating on material aspects of the medium, it forced subjective

existential choices and non-hierarchical mental activity on the viewer, as in Malcolm Le Grice's *Little Dog For Roger* (1967) and *Yes No Maybe Maybe Not* (1967), Peter Gidal's *Room* (1967), Roger Hammond's *Window Box* (1972), Mike Leggett's *Shepherd's Bush* (1971) and Steve Dwoskin's *Moment* (1969). Its intention was to challenge cinema's illusionism and voyeurism with its own formal image making.

This formula encouraged eclectic organization. As the LFMC's democratic workshop approach developed in a climate of anti-imperialist radicalism, beat poetry and Peoples' Shows, new film networks rapidly grew up around the British Film Institute (**BFI**), the Other Cinema and the Independent Film-Makers' Association. Many film-makers were located in the London art schools, and were supported by the **Arts Council** of Great Britain's Film and Video Artist's Subcommittee set up in 1977. By then the whole movement was saturated with the cultural politics and aesthetics of the late 1960s and 1970s.

The formalist canon was soon infiltrated by underground, anarchic, and gay critiques associated with film-makers such as Derek **Jarman**, James Mackay, John Maybury, Steve Chivers, Holly Warburton, Michael Kostiff, Cerith Wyn Evans and Isaac **Julien**. They frequently transgressed the film medium in the Super 8 festivals in Europe (1984–7), and innovatively fused video and film techniques (particularly Jarman and Peter **Greenaway**).

Academic critiques were mostly deconstructive and psychoanalytic, theorized in *Screen* and *Framework*. These reflected Gidal's structural/materialist focus on freeing the subject from the instrumental and reproductive power of the camera, and Laura Mulvey's negation of the voyeurism of narrative film. Peter Wollen, whose long-term goal was to synthesize formalism with the political aesthetic of the European avant-garde, combined with Mulvey to produce landmark films: *Penthesilea: Queen of the Amazons* (1974) mimes the play by Kleist, and interrogates the role and grounding of feminist images; and *Riddles of the Sphinx* (1977) explores the mother/child relationship in the encounter of Oedipus with the Sphinx, opening with mythic images of women and ending with an Egyptian sphinx with Greta Garbo's face. Whereas Gidal and Le Grice were interested in the material aspects of ideology, Mulvey and Wollen were moving towards a critique of ideology itself, and of mythologizing in the film medium.

Related works include Steve Dwoskin's *Girl* (1974), which films a naked woman who returns to the camera thus disturbing the audience's voyeuristic position, and Carola Klein's *Mirror Phase* (1978), which analyses home movies of her daughter's mirror recognition of herself. In *Telling Tales* (1978), Richard Woolley deconstructs British culture by examining film clichés of television soap serials like *Crossroads* and *Coronation Street*. William and Marilyn Rabin's *Black and Silver* (1981), based on Velasquez' painting *Las Meninas*, is an experimental narrative of Oscar Wilde's *The Birthday of the Infanta*, reflecting on the medium of film. Peter Watkins's work aims for reflexive critical practices that will more generally undermine the conventions of the medium.

Questions of narrative technique, subjectivity, documentary, and autobiography are worked consistently by feminist film-makers who broke with the LFMC to set up their own circles in East London. Sally **Potter**'s *Thriller* (1979) dissects popular narrative by using Mimi's return to *La Boheme* to investigate her own death as a conventional source of sentiment and drama. Potter's *The Gold Diggers* (1983) uses the gold rush for surrealist metaphors about the search for knowledge. Lis Rhodes's *Light Reading* (1978) investigates the formal aspects of film through autobiographical materials, developing earlier concerns of Le Grice's films about point of view and narrative space.

Most of these films are interested in the medium of film and its narrative codes and conventions. For the British avant-garde, form and content of the medium have always been a central part of the message. While Le Grice is currently involved in computer and electronic image making, others are interested in live reproductions of illusion, and correspondences of image and sound. The focus on film as material has always persisted.

The avant-garde has never since its structuralist beginnings reflected violent politics, but it has always been in line with radical groups such as the Leeds Animation Workshop, **Black Audio Film Collective** and Sankofa Film and Video Collective. Its strong point has been its ability to adapt to and successfully engage in a wide spectrum of audio-visual media, ranging from film and television through to video and **animation**.

See also: agitprop; avant-garde theatre; film, experimental

Further reading

MacDonald, S. (1993) *Avant-Garde Film: Motion Studies*, Cambridge: Cambridge University Press.
O'Prey, M. (ed.) (1996) *The British Avant-Garde Film 1926–1995*, Luton: University of Luton Press.

ARTHUR McCULLOUGH

avant-garde theatre

The term 'avant-garde' (derived from a French militaristic term meaning 'vanguard') in avant-garde theatre refers to the pioneering innovation in a progressive, experimentally-based anti-establishment theatre. Avant-garde theatre seeks to artistically and aesthetically surpass existing forms of dramatic performance and expression of a denormalizing, stimulating theatre of the imagination. Christopher Innes argues that along with 'anarchic primitivism', ' … anti-materialism and revolutionary politics, the hallmark of avant-garde drama is an aspiration to transcendence, to the spiritual in its widest sense.' (Innes 1993: 3)

Located in non-theatrical spaces, fringe and even popular or mainstream venues (for example, the **Royal Court**'s discontinued annual avant-garde season), avant-garde theatre explores the psychologies and physicalities of the self. Assimilating myth, symbolism, ritual and art forms from other cultures to deploying music, **mime**, mixed media, **performance art** and other sub-cultural and popular cultural art forms in site-specific and other spaces, avant-garde theatre functions as an exploratory reflection of the unconscious and modern human condition. It animatedly revitalizes imaginations through a 'theatre of mixed means' by trampling largely British realist and naturalistic theatrical traditions.

Preceding and flourishing during the late 1960s British fringe theatre explosions, specialist touring companies, small theatres and theatre laboratories emerged as places of artistic and technical experimentation including the freewheeling The People Show, Grotowskian-influenced Freehold, Charles Marowitz's Open Space Theatre and the Roy Hart Studio which explored voice through sound, emotion, psychology and technique. Marowitz's 1964 collaboration with Peter Brook on an Artaudian 'Theatre of Cruelty' season organically interrogated theatrical language through sublime physical performance, visceral atmosphere and abstract shock forms of verbal and non-verbal communication. The endless subjective–creative potentialities suggested by Brook's theorizations of the stage in *The Empty Space* (1968) were demonstrated by his continuing indefatigable avant-gardism.

Alongside other paradoxically established avant-gardist practitioners such as Stephen Berkoff and Lindsay Kemp, fringe venues like Battersea Arts Centre continue to feature anarchic experimentation by groups like the Empty Space Theatre Company's subversive classic performative theatre, Fecund Theatre or Perpetual Motion's energetic fusions of narrative, textual and live communicative forms. Yet the absence of a strongly avant-gardist tradition within a largely realist and naturalist British theatre is perhaps also attributable to the lack of extreme socio-political conditions necessary for such a theatre to thrive, with the future theatrical vanguard partly contingent upon cultural extremities to trigger their own imaginative extremes.

See also: agitprop; avant-garde cinema; fringe theatre

Further reading

Innes, C. (1993) *Avant-Garde Theatre 1892–1992*, London: Routledge (a foundational history of avant-garde theatre, albeit from a necessarily North American and European perspective).

SATINDER CHOHAN

Ayer, A.J.

b. 1910, London; d. 1988

Philosopher

A.J. Ayer's *Language, Truth and Logic* (1936) expounded the main themes of logical positivism, which has as its central tenet the 'verification principle', whereby verifiability is the criterion of meaning. Statements which can be verified neither by experience nor by deduction from a priori premises are literally meaningless. Ayer and others applied this principle to the analysis of ethical propositions such as 'x is good'. Such statements are neither true nor false, but merely expressions of emotion (the emotivist theory of ethics). While adhering to the verification principle, Ayer distinguished a mode of 'weak' verifiability whereby propositions may be considered meaningful if some conceivable method of verification can show them probable. Critics observe that the verification principle cannot itself be verified.

ROD PATERSON

B

baby boom

The term refers to the sharp increase in the rate of births in Europe and the US after 1945, when soldiers returned from the war. The boom continued almost uninterrupted to 1964, followed by a slump (or baby bust) in the mid-1960s. It is estimated that in 2030 there will be fewer than half as many children under five as there were in 1961 (3.5 million). The boom–slump cycle has led to a shift in the average age of the UK population, such that one person in three will be 60 or over in the year 2025. Economically, this has contributed to fears of a declining workforce, earners' ability to sustain pensions payments and surplus consumer goods. Meanwhile, baby boomers are currently responsible for running the country (for example, Tony Blair and William Hague) and producing its cultural output (hence the recycling in the 1990s of the fashions, celebrities and music of the 1960s and then the 1970s).

See also: childbirth; family planning

PETER CHILDS

Bacon, Francis

b. 1909, Dublin; d. 1992, London

Painter

Francis Bacon was the most prominent English painter of the twentieth century until his death in 1992. Major retrospectives were assembled by the Tate Gallery in 1962 and 1985 (see **Tate(s)**). A self-taught artist who worked against the current of mid-century painterly abstraction, Bacon experimented with the visceral and expressive dimensions of figuration. His aim, he famously suggested, was to 'hit the nervous system', and this desire to shock in part explains his concentration on the grotesque and exploration of violent and disturbing images. Bacon's first major painting, the triptych *Three Studies for Figures at the Base of a Crucifixion* (1944), exemplifies his distinctive counterpointing of brutally contorted biomorphic forms and the unadorned geometric settings which confine and isolate them. The harsh flatness of Bacon's early paintings and their traumatic iconography became points of cultural reference in postwar Europe.

Bacon radically reworked particular images from the tradition of European oil painting. In his well-known sequence of 'screaming popes' (1949–mid-1950s), he transformed the formal iconography of Velazquez's portrait of *Pope Innocent X* (1650) into a series of nightmarish studies in modern claustrophobia and isolation. Bacon's practice of serial image making was informed by his study of **photography**, and he used newspaper photographs, radiographic images and film stills as source materials. Bacon particularly admired Eadweard Muybridge's photographic motion studies of men wrestling (*c*.1885) and based an important series of male nude images on them. The motif of the male nude and copulating male bodies spans Bacon's career from *Two Figures* (1953) to *Triptych–Studies of the Human Body* (1979), and represents his most sustained and complex aesthetic exploration of homosexual desire.

In the 1960s–1970s, Bacon produced studies in the male nude, self-portraits and portraits of friends. In these works the mood is more personal and their style less distorted. Following the suicide of his lover and companion George Dyer in 1971, Bacon produced a series of memorial triptych paintings, including the poignant images of *Three Portraits–Triptych* (1973). In his late work, Bacon continued to explore uncanny images, as exemplified by the truncated male nude torso adorned in cricket pads in *Study of the Human Body* (1982). Bacon's influence can be traced in the work of David **Hockney** and more generally in the figurative revival associated with Neo-Expressionism.

See also: painting

Further reading

Sylvester, D. (1987) *The Brutality of Fact: Interviews with Francis Bacon*, London: Thames and Hudson (a series of definitive interviews).

MARK DOUGLAS

badminton

Badminton is played by a relatively large proportion of the British public, but it has long been in the shadow of **tennis** and lacks the latter's media profile, television coverage and finances. However, the sport remains optimistic about its future, and universities and colleges in particular have strong badminton traditions; the game is also very popular amongst people of minority backgrounds. In 1996, it was estimated that some 4 million people played badminton, or about 8 percent of the UK population.

But such relative popularity cannot hide the fact that British badminton has a low media profile, is short of finances and has a poor world standing. Of the top 50 women players in the world in 1996, only three were British, and only one of the top 50 men was British. This and the poor performances put in by the England side in the Sudirman Cup in Lausanne in 1995 prompted calls to end the historic underfunding of the sport. By comparison with Denmark, Indonesia, China and others,

badminton in Britain is financially weak, and this helps explain the difference in international performance between these countries and the UK.

That said, the Olympic status that badminton secured in 1985 (with full competition starting in Barcelona in 1992, after demonstration participation in 1988 in Seoul) has helped the financial situation, with total funding rising by 40 percent between 1992 and 1995. The top players get help direct from the British Olympic Association, leaving the national associations to focus their energies and resources on junior and upcoming talent.

Despite its problems, badminton is clearly determined to expand and revive its fortunes, as seen in the formation in 1995 of the first British circuit, the Grand Slam. But this must address the problem of top players withdrawing from tournaments to appear in lucrative European events, making the home circuit hard to publicize and market to spectators. Badminton could also hope to expand if calls for it to become part of the school curriculum were heeded. Many schools already offer badminton, but were it added to the curriculum itself, then the sport could conceivably enhance its potential source of future talent. In the meantime, badminton in England is forced to hope that appointments like that of the former European and Commonwealth champion, Steve Baddeley, as director of elite play will improve standards and results, with all the spin-offs that can generate.

Further reading

Badminton Association of England (1994) *Badminton*, London: Black.

REX NASH

BAFTA

BAFTA (the British Academy of Film and Television Arts) was formed in 1959 by the amalgamation of the Guild of Television Producers and Directors, dating from 1954, and the British Film Academy. The latter had been set up in 1946 by leading figures in British cinema as a non-profit-making organization with the object of improving standards and enhancing the status of British cinema and also to campaign for increased government recognition and financial support. It was a natural development to embrace the cognate arts of television; by the end of the 1950s television audiences had grown while cinema admissions were falling (though they have since picked up), and the overlap in personnel in the two media, which was already considerable, was to become even more marked as time passed. BAFTA, which has a preview theatre at its London premises at 195 Piccadilly, awards fellowships to distinguished practitioners in cinema and television. The concept of the Academy, along with its somewhat pretentious appellation, plainly owes something to the American Academy of Motion Picture Arts and Sciences, founded by Louis B. Mayer in 1929. Like its US counterpart, BAFTA is best known for annual awards that are presented at quite glittering occasions. Though sought after and respected, these have not as yet acquired anything like the same prestige – or box office clout – as the 'Oscars'. As well as giving awards for such categories as Best Film, Best Single Television Drama and Best Television Children's Programme (Factual), BAFTA, keen to promote the particular crafts within the wider sphere of film and television production, also singles out excellence in narrower fields such as Best Graphic Design, Best Television Make-Up and even Best (Film) Make-Up Hair. The important contribution of stalwarts to British film and television is commemorated by BAFTA in awards named after, for instance, Anthony Asquith, Alexander Korda, Michael Balcon and Richard Dimbleby.

BAFTA should not be confused with the **BFI** (British Film Institute) which was founded in 1933 and also seeks to promote interest in the moving image in cinema and on television, but does so by maintaining the National Film Archive, the National Film Theatre and the Museum of the Moving Image, and by publishing the *Monthly Film Bulletin* and the quarterly *Sight and Sound*.

See also: BFI; film awards

Further reading

Lee, Veronica (1997) 'The Curse of the Award Ceremonies Too Numerous to Mention', *Guardian*, 21 March (an informative, if rather jaundiced article).

CHRISTOPHER SMITH

Baha'i

The Baha'i (from the Farsi *Ar baha* (Allah)) faith was founded in nineteenth-century Iran by Bahā'u'llāh. Baha'is believe people need material and spiritual fulfilment. It is because the material and the spiritual aspects of life are not balanced in our world that people live in a state of anxiety. They seek to promote tolerance among all faiths and between the sexes. They want global unity and recognize the role of other religions' prophets, including Moses, Mohammed and Buddha, in securing it. Baha'i assemblies are dispersed throughout Britain and are organized regionally. They make extensive use of modern communications and maintain a website.

See also: Buddhism; Islam

MIKE STORRY

ballet

Only two ballets created in Britain in 1960 are still performed: Frederick Ashton's *La Fille mal gardeée* and Kenneth MacMillan's *The Invitation*, made for the **Royal Ballet** and its touring company, respectively. This is not surprising: Ashton and MacMillan are Britain's best-known choreographers, whose styles and reputations have cast long shadows. Their works are pillars of the repertoire of the Royal Ballet, the nation's flagship ballet company, which is mindful of keeping their legacy alive.

In 1960, Ashton was an established choreographer with thirty-four years' experience and several masterpieces behind him, entering his last decade of sustained creativity. Widely regarded as the greatest British choreographer, Ashton was a classicist, interested in the formal properties of the ballet vocabulary and using them to explore and express moods and emotions. Characterizations emerge from the steps rather than from an overlay of acting, as in *La Fille mal gardée*, which typically is also suffused with an affectionate regard for the characters' foibles and imbued with a sense of community. Known for his musicality, Ashton often dealt with romantic love in his ballets.

In 1960, MacMillan was an emerging choreographer with six professional ballets behind him, his most important works still to come. Dramatic and expressionistic, MacMillan's uncompromising ballets explore the dark sides of human behaviour and the psyche, requiring dancers with strong acting abilities. Often unsettling, his ballets brought gritty and harsh realities to the idealized world of ballet, as in *The Invitation* in which a young woman is raped. MacMillan's has always been a difficult talent to assess. His ballets still provoke debate over their choreographic craftsmanship, treatment of women, and subject matter, but there is no doubting their powerful theatricality and challenge to ballet's conventions – and audiences.

In the late 1950s and early 1960s, MacMillan was not alone in his desire to depict real people grappling with difficult situations. Peter Darrell at Western Theatre Ballet and Norman Morrice at Ballet Rambert, also influenced by new wave cinema and kitchen sink dramas, were making ballets about contemporary life, problems and relationships, thereby broadening the subjects ballet could address. Founded in Bristol in 1957, the small-scale Western Theatre Ballet performed predominantly short new works with a dramatic thrust. Darrell's subject matter ranged across betrayal and entrapment (*The Prisoners*, 1957), youth gangs (*Mods and Rockers*, 1963, set to Beatles songs) and mental illness (*Home*, 1965). Morrice emerged as Rambert's in-house choreographer in 1958 with *Two Brothers*, a love triangle centred on a James Dean-inspired loner. The women in his dance dramas never wore pointe shoes, ballet's distinguishing artifice.

The long-established companies absorbed this new trend while adhering to the typical three-pronged repertoire of the model ballet company: the three-act 'classics' from the nineteenth century; proven twentieth-century ballets from the Diaghilev era, foreign troupes' rosters and the company's own heritage; and new work. London Festival Ballet, which offered 'popular ballets at popular prices', continued to cater to the conservative

regional audiences' taste for foreign stars and easy-to-watch spectacle. Competing with it on the touring circuit were Ballet Rambert, with its core of Antony Tudor works and less hackneyed three-acts, and the Royal Ballet's second company, a training ground for young dancers and choreographers (such as MacMillan) that toured selections of the main company's repertoire.

At the Royal Opera House (**Covent Garden**), the Royal Ballet under Ashton's directorship (1963–70) carried on its three-pronged approach with new productions of the classics, the acquisition of masterworks from the 1920s and 1930s, and commissions from Tudor, Roland Petit and MacMillan (notably his first three-act ballet, *Romeo and Juliet*, in 1965). Ashton's new ballets during this decade continued his musings on romantic love (*The Two Pigeons*, 1961; *Marguerite and Armand*, 1963; *The Dream*, 1964; and *Enigma Variations*, 1968) and his essays in 'abstract' classicism (*Monotones*, 1965–6).

In the middle of the decade a new genre, American modern dance, took root in Britain (where it was called 'contemporary dance'), and the explosion of creativity experienced by this new art form into the 1970s underscores the distinct absence of promising new voices in ballet in this period. Ballet Rambert even bid farewell to ballet, at Morrice's suggestion, and embraced contemporary dance in 1966 when dwindling finances and audiences threatened its demise.

In a less radical move, the Royal dissolved its large-scale touring company in 1969 and formed the New Group to tour small ballets and more experimental pieces. American Glen Tetley, whose works merged the ballet and modern vocabularies, started the group off with *Field Figures* (1970), which was followed by acquisitions from Hans van Manen, a Dutch choreographer working in a similar vein. The new repertoire did not fare particularly well with the provincial audiences, however, and gradually the group grew to resemble its former self in size and repertoire, taking the name Sadler's Wells Royal Ballet (SWRB) in 1976.

Under MacMillan's directorship (1970–7), the Royal Ballet also imported examples of 'modern ballet' from the continent and updated the American slice of its repertoire with an influx of ballets by George Balanchine, Jerome Robbins and Tetley. The new works were predominantly by

MacMillan himself, including two full-evening ballets: *Anastasia* (1971), which explored the troubled past and psyche of the supposed surviving Romanov princess, and *Manon* (1974), which delved into the love and sex life of its materialistic heroine.

Meanwhile, regional ballet had firmly taken root. Western Theatre Ballet transferred to Glasgow in 1969 to become Scottish Theatre Ballet (now Scottish Ballet), directed by Darrell, whose output continued unabated (notably, *The Tales of Hoffmann*, 1972; *Mary, Queen of Scots*, 1976; *Five Rückert Songs*, 1978). Also in 1969, a new company, Northern Dance Theatre (now Northern Ballet Theatre), was founded in Manchester by Laverne Meyer, formerly Western's assistant director. In London, Festival Ballet under Beryl Grey acquired its first *Sleeping Beauty* (1890), staged by Rudolf Nureyev, who also choreographed his well-received *Romeo and Juliet* (1977) for the company.

After a marked scarcity of emerging choreographers, the 1980s at the two Royal companies percolated with a series of new works by young dancers. Quickly singled out was David Bintley, who produced an array of works for both companies, such as the classical *Galanteries* (1986) and the character-based '*Still Life' at the Penguin Café* (1988). More an upholder of tradition than an innovator, his style drawing on those of past masters, Bintley was initially a dancer and the resident choreographer at SWRB before moving to the main company in 1986 in the same capacities.

Less feted but more innovative, Ashley Page heralded his choreographic concerns in his first work for the Royal Ballet, *A Broken Set of Rules* (1984), which deconstructed ballet classicism. On the side, Page choreographed for contemporary dance companies and worked with postmodern dancers, and this exposure to other genres has informed his exploration of the ballet vocabulary and its conventions.

Although having handed over directorship of the Royal to Norman Morrice in 1977, MacMillan continued choreographing for the company, pushing balletic theatricality to breaking point with works such as *Mayerling* (1978), about the sordid life of the Habsburg Crown Prince Rudolf, and *Isadora* (1981), about the private life of modern dance pioneer Isadora Duncan. MacMillan had his quiet

moments: the lyrical *Gloria* (1980), a requiem for soldiers of the First World War, and the classical three-act *The Prince of the Pagodas* (1989). But his final ballet, *The Judas Tree* (1992), returned to form, echoing the controversial climax of *The Invitation*; only this time the woman is gang-raped.

Darrell's final years at Scottish Ballet were overshadowed by wranglings with the Scottish Arts Council, and his resignation in 1986 led to tentative appointments of artistic directors until Galina Samsova, a former ballerina at SWRB, took the helm in 1991. (She left six years later after further battles with the Arts Council.) Since his death in 1987, Scottish Ballet has largely ignored its Darrell repertoire.

The 1980s saw additional changes in directorship. Dancer Peter Schaufuss took over at Festival in 1984; dancer Anthony Dowell at the Royal in 1986; and dancer Christopher Gable at Northern Ballet Theatre (NBT) in 1987. Schaufuss's six-year directorship rekindled the flair and enthusiasm that Festival had been known for in the 1950s, after worries that it had become too close to the Royal Ballet mould under Grey and John Field (both former dancers at the Royal Ballet). Key events in his reign include rescuing Ashton's *Romeo and Juliet* (1955) from oblivion, appointing as resident choreographer Christopher Bruce, an alumni of Ballet Rambert in its modern dance guise, and renaming the company **English National Ballet** (ENB).

In 1990 Peter Wright, who had directed SWRB since its New Group days, guided the company's move to a permanent base in Birmingham. This engendered a new name, Birmingham Royal Ballet, and financial independence from the Royal Opera House. Known for his sure touch in producing the classics and in programming mixed bills that interested public and critics alike, Wright built a company that finally stepped out of the shadow of its older sister and became a significant rival. Upon Wright's retirement in 1995, Bintley became artistic director, having resigned from the Royal Ballet two years earlier.

Perhaps to counter criticisms over leaving the resident choreographer post vacant, in 1994 the Royal Ballet inaugurated its annual Dance Bites tour in which a small group of leading dancers take new short ballets by emerging choreographers to regional venues. As well as providing a training ground for young choreographers, Dance Bites is an outlet for seasoned practitioners, particularly Ashley Page.

With the economic necessity to fill theatres, artistic directors played it safe in the 1990s, programming mostly full-evening story ballets, which traditionally sell more tickets than mixed bills of short works. To sustain interest, productions of the classics resorted to startling redesigns, such as Maria Bjørnson's postmodern, skewed perspective set for the Royal's *Sleeping Beauty*; shock tactics, like Northern Ballet Theatre's reworking of *Swan Lake* (1995) in which all the swans are shot in a military coup; and spectacular gimmicks, such as ENB's *Swan Lake* in the round at the Royal Albert Hall, for seventy swans.

New full-evening works, aiming at popular appeal and accessibility, were based on familiar, usually literary storylines, and on the whole these ballets-as-entertainment were choreographically insubstantial. Northern Ballet Theatre's productions (in which Gable is billed as director alongside the choreographer) had the feel of musical shows, high on theatricality but low on memorable choreography (*A Christmas Carol*, 1992; *The Hunchback of Notre Dame*, 1998). ENB aimed at the children's market with *Alice in Wonderland* (1996) by Derek Deane, its director since 1993 and a former dancer and choreographer at the Royal Ballet. In Birmingham, Bintley followed up his 1989 hit *Hobson's Choice* with another crowd-pleasing drama, *Far From the Madding Crowd* (1996).

At the Royal Ballet, Dowell took a risk with *Mr Worldly Wise* (1995) by Twyla Tharp, an American postmodern choreographer, whose ballet challenged audiences to make their own reading of the narrative. As with Dowell's only other forays into the experimental – acquisitions from another postmodernist, William Forsythe of the Frankfurt Ballet – reactions were mixed.

As the twentieth century drew to a close, ballet was out of step with contemporary society on several levels. In an age of multiculturalism, ethnic minorities continued to be a rare sight on the ballet stage. In the post-feminist age, women had made only the odd transition from performing to artistic control, as directors (Grey at Festival and Samsova at Scottish) or as choreographers (Jennifer Jackson

and Susan Crow at SWRB in the 1980s). In the age of gay pride, homosexuality was rarely acknowledged, an exception being Bintley's *Edward II* (1995).

In the age of accountability, the Royal Ballet was tarnished by the financial and managerial scandals at the Royal Opera House, which caused an outcry over the level of government funding for 'elitist' pastimes. Hampered by the public image of ballet as the preserve of the very rich or the very young, artistic directors had to programme to entice the punters, leaving the knowledgeable dance-goer to wonder, 'whither ballet?' The deaths of Ashton (in 1988) and MacMillan (in 1992) marked an end of two overlapping eras in the artistic life of British ballet, which seemed to lie fallow, awaiting a new innovative classicist or audacious expressionist to make works that challenged and stretched their creator, the audiences and the art form.

See also: ballet music; choreography; modern dance

Further reading

Bland, A. (1981) *The Royal Ballet: The First 50 Years*, London: Threshold.

Goodwin, N. (1979) *A Ballet for Scotland: The First Ten Years of the Scottish Ballet*, Edinburgh: Canongate Publishing.

Vaughan, D. (1977) *Frederick Ashton and His Ballets*, London: A. & C. Black.

Woodcock, S. (1991) *The Sadler's Wells Royal Ballet, Now the Birmingham Royal Ballet*, London: Sinclair-Stevenson.

CHRIS JONES

ballet music

Tchaikovsky is by far the most well known **ballet** composer in 1990s Britain, and his ballet scores form a large part of most companies' repertory. Attending a performance of *The Nutcracker*, which has a seasonal story, has become a Christmas tradition for many. Audiences becoming familiar with ballet music in this way has assisted ballet's current popularity, ensuring that many pieces originally written for ballet productions have a life of their own away from the theatre, being performed live in orchestral concerts, recorded and used in advertising. Classical ballet's short, attractive movements are also suited to use as advertising jingles, and through these have reasserted their own popularity, drawing a new audience to the repertoire. This is clearly illustrated by Tchaikovsky's *Dance of the Mirlitons*, nicknamed 'Everyone's a Fruit and Nutcase' after being used in a television advertisement. Advertising's influence is perhaps most readily apparent in the compilations released of music popularized through commercials. Such 'bite-sized chunks' also found an eager audience in 1990s Britain through Classic FM's output of shorter pieces, such as Herold's Clog Dance from *La Fille mal gardée*.

Certain pieces are played as mainstream concert hall material more often than they are danced, with staged performances naturally requiring greater resources. Scores from Diaghilev's ballets such as Stravinsky's *The Rite of Spring* and *The Firebird* or Ravel's *Daphnis and Chloë* draw audiences into concert halls due to the strength of the music; they are powerful alone, though more so when danced. Conversely, scores are taken from concert hall to theatre and choreographed. Scottish Ballet's production of *A Midsummer Night's Dream* (1993) employed Mendelssohn's original music expanded into a full-length ballet score by Barrington Pheloung and choreographed by Robert Cohan, who also choreographed Vivaldi's *The Four Seasons* (1996) for the company.

Even composers of the stature of Tchaikovsky and Prokofiev were beholden to choreographers, **choreography** having a higher profile than composition. Christopher Gable, artistic director of Northern Ballet Theatre (NBT) maintains that this can prevent the composer from providing particular skilled input. NBT has worked in a more cooperative way with composers, with Gable himself collaborating with composer Carl Davis on *A Christmas Carol* (1992). NBT has developed its music provision from the use of recordings and occasional chamber ensembles, to having its own regular orchestra which performs and records in its own right.

See also: ballet

Further reading

Volkov, S. (1993) *Balanchine's Tchaikovsky*, London: Faber & Faber (choreographer on composer).

ANDREA MARTIN

Band Aid

The music industry's social conscience was thrust forcefully into the limelight with the formation of Band Aid in 1984. A coalition of musical artists as diverse as Boy George, Paul Weller, U2 and Sting was skilfully brought together by Bob Geldof (Boomtown Rats) and Midge Ure (Ultravox) with the aim of raising funds for Ethiopian famine relief. Band Aid produced one single, 'Do They Know It's Christmas?' which featured a plethora of artists, and also put together the 'global jukebox' that was Live Aid, with concerts held simultaneously in Philadelphia and London. The single twice reached number one, spending a total of twenty-six weeks in the charts. Overall, Band Aid raised over £100 million for Africa, and inspired spin-offs such as Sport Aid and Comic Relief.

See also: charities and charity shops

GUY OSBORN
STEVE GREENFIELD

Bandung File

Bandung File was a **Channel 4** programme which dealt with matters of concern to ethnic minorities. It was named after the Bandung Conference, a meeting of Asian and African states organized by Indonesia, Burma, Sri Lanka, India and Pakistan in Bandung, Indonesia, in 1955. The television programme offered a radical perspective on contemporary issues, such as the ethnic origins of western culture and issues surrounding racism and discrimination, as well as disputes on multiculturalism, 'political correctness' and Afrocentric curricula. Frequent contributors were Darcus Howe, Paul Boateng and Tariq Ali. A typical production was *Black Athena* (1991) on Martin Bernal's theories of the African origins of Greek civilization.

See also: black television

MIKE STORRY

Banks, Jeff

b. 1943, Ebbw Vale

Fashion designer

Banks, trained at St Martin's School of Art, is one of the most industrious designers and promoters of the British fashion industry. His Clobber boutique sold his own designs and those of other designers between 1964 and 1974, and in the mid-1970s he launched the highly successful Warehouse chain of high street stores selling his own affordable high fashion but wearable designs. He now has his own Jeff Banks label as well as design licenses for other companies. He was a presenter of early series of the **BBC** programme The Clothes Show, the first mainstream fashion programme on British television.

See also: Clothes Show, The; fashion (1980s); fashion (1990s)

TAMSIN SPARGO

BARB

The Broadcasting Audience Research Board (BARB) replaced the Joint Industry Committee for Television Audience Research (JICTAR) in 1981 to permit an industry standard for the collection of audience data. BARB, while jointly owned by the **BBC** and Independent Television Authority, includes on its committees representatives from other broadcasters and the advertising industry. BARB has contracts with AGB and RSMB Television Research (1991–7) for the collection of viewing information from a panel of 4,700 households. BARB compiles viewing information from Peoplemeters, attached to television sets, via telephone lines overnight, allowing the quick release of detailed audience data. Qualitative data, in terms of an Appreciative Index, is collected for BARB by the BBC's research department.

See also: audience research; National Viewers and Listeners Association

PAUL RIXON

Barbican Centre

The Barbican Centre was set up in 1982 to be both a national centre for the Arts and also to cater for the constituency of its immediate locality in the heart of London. It houses the largest of the City's lending libraries and its main Children's Library. The Royal Shakespeare Company has a full programme at the Barbican Theatre, while the Barbican Art Gallery has an outstanding programme of temporary exhibitions including photographs by George Rodger, Cecil Beaton, Karsch, Bill Brandt and the Hulton Deutsch Collection. It currently attracts over 150,000 visitors a year. The Barbican's two Exhibition Halls offer over 4,000 square metres of net exhibition space on two levels while the Barbican Hall seats 2,000 delegates, has three presentation cinemas, and numerous smaller conference suites.

See also: Chamberlain, Powell and Bon

MIKE STORRY

Barton, Derek

b. 1918, Gravesend; d. 1988, Texas

Chemist

Derek Barton was one of the pre-eminent chemists of the century. He won the Nobel Prize for chemistry (with Odd Hassel) for a four-page paper which revolutionized his field of organic chemistry. He graduated from London's Imperial College of Science and Technology in 1940 and continued to work in the same department for many years before posts at Harvard, Birkbeck, Glasgow, and then back to Birkbeck as Hofmann Professor of Chemistry until he retired at 60. He then worked in the USA and France, receiving many honours including a knighthood, the Légion d'honneur and the Japanese Order of the Rising Sun. His chief areas of contribution were conformational analysis, through which he changed the way chemists understand the shape and reactivity of molecules in three-dimensional space, steroids, natural product research and the significance of synthesis.

See also: science

MIKE STORRY

BBC

Postwar, the previous stability of the BBC belied its adaptations and responses to national and global cultural changes. The 1950s quiet Reithian conservatism did not last very long, as the BBC reacted to the cultural shifts of the early 1960s. Under Director-General Hugh Greene, the BBC engaged much more fully with the spirit of the time, with programmes like *That Was The Week That Was*, *Cathy Come Home*, *Till Death Do Us Part*, and Greene's parting shot to the BBC, *Monty Python's Flying Circus*, all of which received criticism and cause offence to both left-wing and right-wing commentators. Self-appointed 'moral' watchdogs such as Mary Whitehouse saw him and the BBC as dragging Britain into an amoral, anti-Christian, violent, crudely sexual mess. Such attacks have dogged the BBC ever since, with the Conservatives in the 1980s regularly accusing the BBC of left-wing bias and of not upholding 'British' standards, a confused phrase implying a lack of patriotism, particularly during the Falklands conflict in 1982.

The BBC long personified decency and stability since its inception in 1922, but the 1990s saw a painful and often controversial process of change. While much of the history of the BBC from 1945 was calm and unchanging, the 1990s saw uncharted waters of internal strife, job cuts, constant controversy and low morale as Thatcherite economics were brought to bear upon it. During John Birt's term as Director-General the BBC's structure was thoroughly overhauled; the creation of an internal market forced producers to buy in expertise rather than co-opting other departments. Birt claimed that this was more efficient in an age of tight public spending, but opponents have argued that the move simply claimed jobs, destroyed morale and generated an administrative paper mountain. It also meant the loss of expertise;

one result was the closing of the world famous Costume Department in 1996. Possibly the most damaging episode was the threat to the World Service in 1996, when BBC management seemed to fundamentally misunderstand the importance of the Service and were less than open about their plans for it.

But while the reforms were controversial, the BBC was at least thankful that the licence fee remained in place. The Broadcasting Bill of 1996 saw heated debates about the role of the BBC, and whether the fee should stay. The BBC won the battle, but the licence fee was deliberately kept below inflation for much of the 1990s, with the government claiming that there was scope for efficiency savings.

See also: Radio 1; Radio 2; Radio 3; Radio 4; Radio 5

Further reading

MacCabe, C. and Stewart, O. (eds) (1986) *The BBC and Public Service Broadcasting Editors*, Manchester: Manchester University Press.

SAM JOHNSTONE

Berlin, Isaiah

b. 1909, Riga (Latvia); d. 1997, Oxford

Philosopher

Isaiah Berlin was a philosopher and historian of ideas. He came to Britain from Riga, Latvia in 1920. He studied at Oxford and went on to became a fellow of All Souls (1932). During the Second World War he served at the British Embassy in Washington. He later became Chichele Professor of Social and Political Theory (1957–67), and Master of Wolfson College (1966–75). He was knighted in 1957. His works include: *Karl Marx* (1939); *Historical Inevitability* (1954), a criticism of determinism in history; and *The Crooked Timber of Humanity: Chapters in the History of Ideas* (1991). He maintained friendships with American academics and thinkers and was influential in affecting policy makers in the UK and USA.

See also: history; philosophy; politics

MIKE STORRY

betting shops

Betting shops appear on every British high street. The following companies operate shops: Ladbrokes (1,906 shops), William Hill, owned by Grand Metropolitan (1,510), Coral Racing, owned by Bass (833) and Stanley Racing (564). Fears of monopoly have led to the '440 yard' rule. Because most people walk to place a bet, when a merger of ownership is proposed between two shops within that distance, one must be sold to increase competition. It is generally assumed that betting shops receive the bulk of consumer spending on gambling; in fact casinos, at £2,461m, account for more than twice the amount spent in betting shops (£1,225m) and both bingo (£811m) and football pools (£823m) are close runners-up. Total betting shop revenue is about the same as the Government's Premium Bonds (£1,279m), though these do have an investment element.

There is no tax on 'on course' betting which accounts for an estimated 10 percent of the overall total, but the government takes 37.5 percent of stake money on **football pools**, 9 percent on general betting and 12 percent on the National Lottery.

Most bets are still on horse and greyhound racing, but in recent years betting shops have extended the range of bets they will take. Some are 'exotic', such as the likelihood of a human landing on Mars, but they are usually still sport-related: the outcome of games in the soccer World Cup, the half-time score of particular matches, the first player to score and so on.

Betting shops are traditionally an integral part of working-class life. They reflect a tradition of interest in horse racing, which is both upper and lower class and from which the middle class are by and large excluded. The puritanism of the latter in regard to gambling has been tempered only by government sponsored Premium Bonds and the **National Lottery**, and many middle-class people only bet on the **Grand National** and perhaps the Derby. Expenditure on betting and gaming by the average household has declined in real terms during the period 1983–96 by 32.3 percent, to 90 pence per week, but this is misleading because individual gamblers spend much larger sums and the National Lottery has taken up much of the slack.

Periodic claims are made that betting shops will be made more alluring to punters, through such measures as the serving of refreshments or providing comfortable chairs. In practice they remain largely male haunts, where, because of legal constraints, passers-by may not even see in through the windows and the family is excluded.

See also: Grand National; horse racing

MIKE STORRY

BFI

The British Film Institute (BFI) has operated to promote moving image culture in Britain since its establishment in 1933. The BFI was set in place following a Report on the Commission on Educational and Cultural Films in the late 1920s. This background continues to be reflected in its broad aim to establish the importance of recognizing film as a constitutive element of the cultural heritage. The emphasis upon the cultural significance of film and television is set out in a Royal Charter, which states the BFI's primary objective to nurture the understanding of film 'as a record of contemporary life and manners, to foster study and appreciation of it from these points of view'.

In practice, the BFI's services towards the promotion and development of the moving image are extremely wide-ranging. The BFI's complex on the South Bank combines the National Film Theatre (**NFT**), the Museum of the Moving Image (**MOMI**) and the administrative headquarters of the annual London Film Festival. It stands as a national centre for the appreciation of film and television in a cultural rather than commercial context.

The National Film and Television Archive was founded in 1935 and holds almost 300,000 film and television titles from 1895 to the present day. This resource is further supported by the Library and Information Services Division, which boasts the world's largest collection of documentation on film and television, with all material available for access through a national database (Source Information on Film and Television (SIFT)).

The BFI's Research and Education Division promotes **media education** through publishing, television production, the support of formal media education and the organization of events. These services take many forms, including the annual publication of the *BFI Film and Television Handbook*, the monthly publication of *Sight and Sound* magazine and the production of documentary television programmes (such as the *Century of Cinema* series).

The BFI also promotes the development of contemporary British cinema culture by supporting the distribution and exhibition of under-represented film genres through its association with thirty-five regional film theatres. In addition, it generates revenue for the production of innovative and otherwise commercially marginalized ventures.

Half of the BFI's funding comes from the government, with the rest from subscriptions from its 26,000 members, the provision of services, and sponsorship and donations. In recent years the BFI has been engaged in a political debate to ensure sufficient government funding to carry out its 'BFI 2000' programme, a strategy for its future survival. In July 1998 the Culture Secretary, Chris Smith, announced a new Film Council, which will bring together the BFI, British Screen, the British Film Commission and the films lottery department of the **Arts Council**.

See also: MOMI; NFT

Further reading

British Film Institute (1997) *BFI Film and Television Handbook 1997*, London: British Film Institute.

MATTHEW GRICE

bhangra

The term 'bhangra' describes the traditional agricultural folk music of the Punjab, but has come to be applied to all modern Asian pop music. It began in the UK in the late 1970s, but is still rooted in traditional folk songs. Its rhythms have been adapted to modern musical instruments with the traditional tumbi, dholkie and tabla providing the unique bhangra sounds. Groups like Heera, Alaap and Chirag Pechan dominate the scene, but individuals such as Apache Indian, Bally Sagoo and Johnny Zee have also become well known and have had a major impact on the mainstream music scene. Exceptions to the rule of all-male performers are Sangeeta, Najma Ahktar and Sabeena. Bhangra groups are much in demand for performance at weddings.

See also: Asian underground

Further reading

Sharma, S., Hutnyk, J. and Sharma, A. (eds) (1996) *Dis-Orienting Rhythms: The Politics of the New Asian Dance Music*, London: Zed Books.

MIKE STORRY

Biba

For many young women in Britain in the 1960s and 1970s, Biba was the epitome of style. The label was created by Polish-born designer Barbara Hulanicki and her husband Stephen Fitz-Simon. Biba started in 1963 as a mail order boutique, then moved to London shops of increasing size, culminating in the purchase of Derry and Toms department store in Kensington High Street in 1973. Hulanicki's designs combined the glamour of early Hollywood style with Art Deco pastiche, and the Biba store's complementary decor made it one of the most distinctive shops in London. The clothes included body-hugging dresses in muted colours at affordable prices, and glamorous accessories including 1920s and 1930s-style hats and feather boas. Biba's product range expanded rapidly to include cosmetics in adventurous colours, which were available in the company's stylish black and gold packaging. The Biba store closed in 1975 and the company's fortunes declined. The label was relaunched by a new company in 1996 and now features retro-styles which offer an updated Biba look for a new generation.

See also: designer labels; labels

TAMSIN SPARGO

bicycles

Whereas BMX (bicycle motocross) appealed primarily to teenagers, the arrival of the mountain bike in the early 1980s made cycling chic. Taking with them the rock outlaw image from the Californian hippies who prototyped them, the ease of handling, garish accessories and subcultural jargon captured the imagination of a generation who had previously thought cycling too staid or childlike. By the 1990s, as cyclists began to find mountain bikes too sluggish for everyday use, road bikes, for both racing and touring, flourished and nostalgia developed for classics like the Raleigh Chopper.

See also: cycling

GORDON URQUHART

big beat

An underground music scene which broke through in 1997 but had its origins earlier. Roots can be traced back to the Beastie Boys 1989 album *Paul's Boutique* or to the three *Give 'Em Enough Dope* 1990–1 compilations by Mark Jones. More recent sparks were generated by Wall of Sound, the Chemical Brothers' 1994 'Chemical Beats' track or the Propellerheads' 1996 'Take California'. Big beat is a dance music that moves on from **hip hop** and trip hop via **funk** and backbeat, fusing deep bass lines and big drum sounds. Turntable and **sampling** techniques are blended with lush strings and brash brass, and sometimes vocals, but also with traditional pop and rock songwriting skills. The release of the Propellerheads' first album *Decksandrumsandrockandroll* in January 1998 marked the mainstream arrival of big beat.

PETER CHILDS

Big Issue, The

Anita Roddick and John Bird founded *The Big Issue* in 1991 in response to the problems faced by the growing number of homeless people in Britain. In 1998 there were four independent companies. Vendors buy copies of the magazine at a minimal cost and sell it on the streets. Vendors make a living by keeping 60 percent of the cover price. In 1998, *The Big Issue* national sales reached 293,000 per week, with a readership of 1,213,000. Organizations such as *The Big Issue* became increasingly more important because Britain in the 1990s remained a divided society and the number of homeless people, from all walks of life, continued to grow at an alarming rate.

See also: homelessness; poverty, families and

FATIMA FERNANDES

bilingual communities

In Britain, bilingualism exists in those areas where linguistic minorities are present, usually as a result of historical and political changes. The Swann Report in 1985 revealed that there are at least twelve main languages in Britain, each involving over 100,000 speakers. However, because of the uniformity of the educational system in England and the existence of regulatory bodies which give an impression of linguistic harmony and order, the English language continues to represent and enhance a mythical unity within Britain. Therefore, it is important to paint a more accurate picture by identifying the silenced languages. There are many examples of indigenous and ethnic languages which challenge the pervasive power of the English language. For example, since the rise of Welsh nationalism in the 1970s, the popularity of the Welsh language has continued to grow. Britain has also had well-established black, Chinese and Indian communities since the nineteenth century; specifically in London and port areas such as Liverpool and Cardiff. Furthermore, since the 1950s and due to economic and political reasons, people from West Africa, the Caribbean, India, Pakistan and Hong Kong have settled in Britain. Languages are closely tied to notions of identity; thus, migrating people brought languages and cultures to Britain as a way of rebuilding or replacing lost countries and communities, as has happened in Chinatown in London and in Liverpool.

FATIMA FERNANDES

biography

The biography industry since 1960 has been remarkable in terms of its high quality, its continuity with past traditions, the distinctive nature of its topical variety and its sheer range of subjects. Standards and productivity have been high, despite the fact that the lavishly funded competition from abroad is fierce, even on what narrowly might be regarded as 'home turf' subjects (for which subsidised support is not so readily available to British researchers).

British biographers have also managed to achieve their singularity of appeal since 1960 by venturing abroad themselves, writing on topics that publishers of earlier decades tended to consider 'un-English'. That is, support has been extended to biographical studies of cultural icons of continental Europe and beyond. Examples of such successful projects are journalist Margaret Crosland's *Piaf* and Marianne Gray's *Depardieu: A Biography*. The quality of writing and the depth of insight in both portraits of the French 'artiste' are equal if not superior to French and American rival productions.

Moreover, although the new 'red brick' universities of the 1960s and the ex-polytechnics in the 1990s have tended not to shelve a separate library classification called 'biography', biographers have found that UK television, radio and the 'quality' press have consistently boosted their work supportively. The works of writers such as John Grigg and Peter Ackroyd, the biographers of Lloyd George and William Blake respectively, have been highlighted in features and documentaries by **BBC**2 and ITV's *The South Bank Show*.

Such biographers have challenged their overseas, generally academic rivals through their painstaking research, by the belief that period or contextuality often matters as much as subjectivity, and by their frequently magisterial but nevertheless empirical style. An example of this would be Margaret

Drabble's *Arnold Bennett: A Biography*. Drabble's work on Bennett was soundly researched but often far too cavalier and dismissive in her eccentric judgements of both her subject and his vital friends, such as literary editor Charles Masterman.

Continuity with pre-1960 British biographical traditions is strong and abundant, an enduring homage to the somewhat sceptical British reader's love of verisimilitude and factual veracity. Political biography of high quality most attests to this sense of continuity. It retains Lytton Strachey's rudely quizzical 'debunking' tradition on the one hand, and Sir Philip Magnus's reverential if mildly sceptical tradition on the other. In respect of the first, BBC and ITV (*Newsnight*, *World in Action*) reporter Donald McCormick authored a significant biography at the start of the 1960s in which he is acerbically critical of his left-wing subject (*The Mask of Merlin: A Critical Biography of David Lloyd George*). As regards the second tradition, Lord Roy Jenkins was awarded the Whitbread Prize for biography in the 1990s for his tome on Gladstone which embodies the opposite extreme of too much pompous centrist reverence for all but a few of its subject's rather sanctimonious 'grand old man's' priggish traits!

Yet, in the final analysis, the robustness of British biography since 1960 in terms of both insightfulness and commercial success is explained by this diversity and love of controversy, this refusal to be 'objective' and 'detached' or 'neutral,' even if in unspoken adherence to strong biographical continuity with either the satirical or hagiographical traditions. Personal familiarity with the subject, for instance, produces unique insights which bristle through the work of biographers of the 1970s, from Quentin Bell (*Virginia Woolf: A Biography*) to Christopher Sykes (*Nancy: The Life of Lady Astor*). As a result of each author's affectionate yet critical empathy with the subject, the reader arrives at a unique comprehension of the creative vitality of the former 'Bloomsbury' women's much over-psychoanalysed 'moods', in Woolf's case, and of the rather unhappy personal private life of Britain's first sitting woman MP, Astor, which explains her alleged 'hysteria' and supposed 'bad' temper, traits used unfairly against her until her death.

Some national cultures may well find the future of their own biographical traditions in academic canons; for instance, in the United States the University of Hawaii now publishes the world's only English language *Journal of Biography*. However, in Britain readers do seem to prefer non-institutionalized biography. Empathy, eccentricity and a traditionally critical spirit remain the preferred weapons of insight of British biographical writers.

See also: autobiography

Further reading

Hamilton, I. (1994) *Keepers of the Flame: Literary Estates and the Rise of Biography*, London: Faber & Faber (a useful discussion of the difficulties confronted by biographers).

LAWRENCE IRVINE ILES

Birmingham Conference Centre

Birmingham's International Conference Centre (1983–91), an investment by Birmingham City Council and the European Community, is the largest of its kind in the UK, providing a meeting facility for up to 3,000 people. Included in the complex is the acclaimed Symphony Hall. Eleven main conference halls and ten executive rooms are grouped around the spectacular Mall, which forms a route between Centenary Square and Canal Street. The architects' townscape study ensured commendable coherence in linking the complex with the city centre. While the nearby restored Victorian buildings and revived canal network reflect Birmingham's industrial past, the contemporary architecture of the ICC endorses Birmingham's claim to being a city with international facilities and aspirations.

HILARY GRAINGER

bisexuality

Bisexuality occupies an ambivalent position in contemporary British sexual culture, and continues to have an uneasy relationship with gay and lesbian culture on the one hand and heterosexual culture on the other. The presence of an increasingly politicized bisexual (or 'bi') community in Britain repeatedly brings these tensions to the fore, with debates around the inclusion of 'bisexual' in the title of Britain's annual Gay Pride festival and admitting bisexuals into lesbian and gay social spaces, for example, fuelling argument and precipitating both divisions and new alliances. The problematic adoption of the inclusive term 'queer' to define all sexual dissidents has also been the subject of widespread debate, at least in part reflecting the fragility of the relationship between bisexuality and homosexuality.

On a more positive note, the bi community in Britain has established a strong identity through a variety of self-run resources. These include a national magazine, *Bi Community News*, an annual conference, a telephone helpline and the development of a network of local and regional groups which hold meetings and events, liaise with local lesbian and gay groups and promote bi awareness in their locality. There also exists the Bi Academic Network, bringing together bisexual academics to discuss their work. In the academic arena, in fact, much important work has been done, exploring the position of bisexuality within contemporary culture.

Also significant to contemporary British bisexuality have been discourses within popular culture, and those surrounding HIV/**AIDS**. In the case of the former, there have been a number of high profile bisexuals 'coming out', including **Britpop** singer Brett Anderson (of Suede) and supermodel Rachel Williams, and coverage of bisexuality in the press, in films such as *Basic Instinct* and novels such as Dan Kavanagh's *Duffy* series. The HIV/AIDS discourses, on the other hand, have demonized bisexuality as the transmission route from the homosexual to the heterosexual community. Together these discourses and representations have often constructed bisexuals as promiscuous, libertarian and uncommitted. Against this tide, the British bi community has offered many alternative discourses, seeing bisexuality as challenging conventional sexual binaries (male/female, homosexual/heterosexual) and norms (such as monogamy and fixed sexual identity), and offering new possibilities for sex and gender relations within society.

See also: AIDS; gay liberation; 'gender benders'; outing

Further reading

Rose, S. (ed.) (1996) *Bisexual Horizons: Politics, Histories, Lives*, London: Lawrence & Wishart (written by members of the bisexual community, this provides a useful overview of key issues).

DAVID BELL

black art

Naseem Khan's 1976 survey of the cultural activities of ethnic minorities in Britain revealed that little financial support was provided by official bodies. This led to the establishment in London of the Minority Arts Advisory Service (MAAS) and its inter-cultural magazine *Artrage*. The term 'black art' most helpfully identifies work which draws upon the experience of black individuals and communities in Western societies, such as the 1977 mixed media performance by Rasheed Araeen called 'Paki Bastard – portrait of the artist as a black person'. However some 'black artists' object to the term, and to 'ethnic' or 'minority' art, on the grounds that it encourages ghettoizing and the frequent assumption that they will produce work that is both outside the mainstream and also redolent of their ethnic background. A large number of black artists in the 1970s and 1980s became familiar names in the art world, including Frank Bowling, Gavin Jantjes, Sokari Douglas Camp, Lubiana Himid, Marlene Smith, Sonia Boyce and Keith Piper. Several new magazines (such as *Black Phoenix* and *Black Arts in London*) were also founded at this time, and galleries opened (Black Arts Gallery and Creation for Liberation, both in 1983). Important initiatives in film were the **Black Audio Film Collective** and True Corner Productions, an independent black film company established by Rosemary Boateng, sister of the Labour MP Paul Boateng.

See also: black television; black theatre

PETER CHILDS

Black Audio Film Collective

The London-based Black Audio Film Collective emerged from the shared experience of British art schools, specifically Portsmouth, in the first years of the Thatcher government (1979–90). The Collective's first work, *Expeditions* (1983), an innovative and searching tape-slide production on colonial history and its legacies, received widespread critical interest and paved the way for their first major documentary, *Handsworth Songs* (1986), looking at the uprisings in Birmingham and London, with its slogan 'there are no stories in the riots, only the ghosts of other stories'. Handsworth took the Grierson prize for documentary, and has proved highly influential, despite controversy over its challenge to normative film language. The film had several influential features: a powerful sense of the spoken word as cinematic medium, a refusal to accept that black audiences required simple narration and positive images, and a devotion to the evolution of a new film language for the black experience.

The follow-up feature, *Testament* (1988), again directed by John **Akomfrah** and shot on location in Ghana, analyses in elliptical and poetic fragments 'the war zone of memories' of post-colonial struggle and the losses of exile. This theme would be reworked with Reece Auguiste in the director's chair in *Twilight City* (1989), an allusive, dense vision of London as a city of exile. Inspired by the work of Homi Bhabha, Paul Gilroy and Stuart Hall (who have appeared in several of their productions), the collective went on to analyse in *Who Needs a Heart* (1991) the histories of Black Power in the UK, again in characteristically elliptical form, and again with the disparities and juxtapositions welded into a whole by unique and inventive sound design by Trevor Matthison. The impact of films like Haile Gerima's *Harvest 3000* (1976), and Julie Dash's *Illusions* (1982), with their intimations of a film aesthetic as radically renewed as pop music had been by the emergence of **hip hop**, was transformed in these films, and in the series of television documentaries that have followed, perhaps the most impressive of which is *Mothership Connection* (a.k.a. The Last Angel of History), a history of science fiction imagery in diasporan music, distinguished by the intensity of its compositions and the dramatic use of digital effects. As with other **diasporan film-makers**, the current climate has proven inimical to innovation as much as to black culture. The only workshop to have survived the end of the **Workshop Declaration**, Black Audio Film Collective is one of the major centres of the emergent culture of contemporary Britain.

See also: diasporan film-makers

SEAN CUBITT

black Conservatives

Which major political party has been most accessible to people from ethnic minorities has been the subject of much debate. In 1987, four black Labour MPs became the first to be elected to Parliament for sixty years, despite the fact that more than 5 percent of Britain's population is black. The first black Conservative MP, Nirj Deva, was not elected to Parliament until 1992, but he did go on to become a minister before he lost his seat in May 1997. John Taylor, a barrister, was confronted with racist opposition in his attempts to be selected as candidate for Cheltenham in 1992. An embarrassed John Major elevated him to the House of Lords.

See also: black politics; Labour Party black sections

MIKE STORRY

black literature press

Black literary and arts presses and magazines include: Payback Press (re-releases key black texts such as Ben Sidran's *Black Talk*), X Press (London based publishers since 1992 of new and classic black fiction and especially pulp fiction such as Victor Headley's *Yardie*), Hansib (the oldest and largest black publishing house in Britain), Rutherford (imprint of Dangaroo press publishing black British literature), *The Voice* (Afro-Caribbean weekly), *Trends* (UK's most popular Muslim magazine), and *Artrage* (a long-standing black arts magazine). In the 1970s and 1980s, black presses

such as New Beacon Books, Peepal Tree and Bogle-L'Ouverture also started to make significant inroads into the poetry market. In the academic sphere, of most note is *Wasafiri*, a journal of literary criticism, imaginative writing, essays on the arts, events and resources related to Caribbean, African, Asian and associated literatures in English. Founded in 1984, it was originally published by The Association for the Teaching of Caribbean, African and Asian Literatures to foster multicultural debate and publish new writing.

See also: black press;   literature, African; literature, Caribbean

PETER CHILDS

black performance poets

Black performance poets have developed African and Caribbean oral traditions into a varied poetic language that is rooted in the speech of their communities, creating a powerful sense of black British identity through social documentary, the articulation of autonomous political thought and pure entertainment. Many poets have also developed sophisticated methods of transcription for their essentially oral work, so that the sound of the spoken voice is brought to the reading eye.

In 1976 Linton Kwesi **Johnson** coined the term 'dub poetry' for work that he and the Jamaicans Michael Smith, Mutabaruka and Oku Onuora were performing, inspired by the 'toasting' of **reggae** sound-system DJs U Roy and Big Youth, and the Last Poets' percussion-driven street poetry. Using Afro-Caribbean patois (following the example of the previous generation of writer/performers including James Berry, Edward Kamau Brathwaite and Louise Bennett), dub poetry uses speech- and reggae-rhythms (rather than the iambic pentameters that predominate in conventional English poetry) simultaneously to resist **received pronunciation** and to make their poetry familiar to audiences alienated by literary/academic writing. Much dub poetry deals with contemporary sociopolitical issues, but its variety is demonstrated by Jean Binta Breeze's love poetry and the playfulness of Benjamin Zephaniah.

Black performance poetry has taken many forms and subjects. Louise Bennett's investigations of folklore and dialect poems influenced John Agard's playful 'calypso poetry'. Merle Collins has drawn on the African tradition (often performing to Ghanaian high-life accompaniments played by African Dawn). Valerie Bloom, Scottish-born Jackie Kay and Grace Nichols have focused on the experiences of black women. A new generation of poets have relied on rap and **hip hop** rhythms, rather than on reggae (often explicitly titling poems 'raps'). Lemn Sissay has become a significant figure in the 1990s: in addition to his own work (including a collaboration with dance act Leftfield in 1995 on their 100,000-selling album *Leftism*) he has been active in promoting black and Asian performers through community publishing, workshops and visits to schools and libraries, in a tradition of community-based action exemplified from the 1970s by Linton Kwesi Johnson's involvement with the Race Today collective. Although still marginalized, black performance poetry has an increasing currency in the mainstream, signalled by Agard's appointment as first poet in residence at London's South Bank Centre, and Zephaniah's (unsuccessful) nomination for honorary chairs in poetry at both Oxford and Cambridge.

See also: alternative poetry; performance poetry; poetry slams

Further reading

Binta Breeze, J. (ed.) (1986) *Critical Quarterly* 38(4) ('Word Sound Power', a special edition on performance poetry).

Sissay, L. (ed.) (1997) *The Fire People: A Collection of Black British Poets*, Edinburgh: Payback Press.

SIMON COPPOCK

black politics

'Black' as a political construction derives from the protracted race struggles of the 1950s and 1960s onwards. A contentious term criticized for its simplistic reduction to an implicit ethnic dualism of black and white, 'black' has conversely functioned as a unifying term of empowerment among 'ethnic minority' groups to describe the commonality of their historical oppression, marginalization, personal and institutionalized racist experiences.

Black politics have been organized around the loosely successive phases of New Commonwealth immigration, settlement, protest and an active involvement in community and mainstream politics. The Commonwealth Immigration Bill (1962) and Race Relations Act (1965) (see **Race Relations Acts**) initiated the black immigration control and anti-discrimination legislation which has illustrated conflicting state attitudes to race. Government-sanctioned organizations like the Community Relations Councils (later the **Commission for Racial Equality**) coexisted alongside numerous politicized black welfare and cultural groups autonomously mobilized at an urban and grassroots level. Larger organizations such as the nationwide and left-wing Indian Workers Association (IWA) provided practical and legal support and advice for newly arrived and settled Indian migrants. The Campaign Against Racial Discrimination (1965) and Black People's Alliance (1968) enlisted the support of black representative groups in conglomerate fronts against racism.

During the racially polarized 1960s, Black Power groups like Black Unity and Michael X's Racial Adjustment Action Society (RAAS) offset Powellist politics and heralded the more confrontational tone of the 1970s. Industrial action protesting against exploitative migrant labour proliferated, while racist killings, conflict and the **National Front** led to the formation of the Anti-Nazi League (ANL) and youth organizations such as Southall Youth Movement (SYM). Riots including Notting Hill (1976), Southall (1979), St Paul's and Brixton (1981) and Broadwater Farm (1985) demonstrated the swollen social and political disaffection among black communities (see **riots and civil disobedience**).

The 1980s anti-racism and racial equality campaigns accompanied the election of four black Labour candidates to Parliament in 1987: Diane Abbot, Paul Boateng, Bernie Grant and Keith Vaz. However, the formation of the **Labour Party black sections** and the **black Conservatives** created controversy over their 'ghettoization' of black political interests, with the ascendancy of the ethnic right (such as the **Muslim Parliament**) also exposing the inadequate representation of black interests in mainstream politics. Yet from grassroots activism to its gradual integration into the racialized political mainstream, black political concerns are gradually emerging as an irrepressible force.

Further reading

Gilroy, P. (1987) *There Ain't No Black in the Union Jack*, London: Routledge (a classic cultural study conveying the complexities of race and nationhood).

SATINDER CHOHAN

black press

The emergence of the black press in Britain grew out of the demand for a representative voice, a voice that redresses the balance of the discriminatory mainstream media. Many black publications aim to address the social, cultural and political issues pertaining to their communities by supplying an alternative to the often negative stereotypes propagated by some mainstream news organs. The black press also provides employment opportunities for black people in the media professions.

By the end of the 1990s there were an estimated four hundred black newspapers and periodicals in Britain. This abundance has developed from the singularity of *The Letters of Ignatius Sancho* in 1782, published in letter form in periodicals of the day, up through the collective voices of Africans in the diaspora in prewar and mid-war era papers like *The Pan African*, the *African Telegraph* and *The Black Man*. Postwar papers like the *Jamaican Gleaner*, the *Caribbean Times* and the *West Indian Gazette* were unrelenting in their editorial attack on racial injustice. By the mid-1960s, most of these news organs had disappeared.

The period between 1960 and 1970 was a turning point for black publications, particularly as it saw the emergence of the journal *Race Today*, whose first editor was Darcus Howe (who actually started his career with a Notting Hill-based paper called *Hustler*). A number of pamphlets, newsletters, newspapers and journals appeared in the 1950s and 1960s, including *Black Voice*, *Grassroots*, *Freedom News*, *Frontline*, *Black Peoples Freedom Weekly*, *Black Workers Action Weekly*, *Black Liberator*, *Link*, *Carib*, *Anglo-Caribbean News*, *Tropic*, *Daylight International*, *West Indies Observer*, *Afro-Asian-Caribbean News* and *Magnet*.

More recently, the political journal *West Indian Digest*, the *Caribbean Times*, and *The Voice* appeared in the early 1980s. *Black Briton* and *Weekly Journal* both started publishing in the early 1990s. A wide range of glossy magazines including *Root*, *I-Conception*, *Chic*, *Origin* and *Black Beat International* all became available on the newsstands.

Some papers catered mostly for settlers interested in 'news from back home'. *The Voice* was the first paper to specifically target young blacks in Britain, which was unusual since most tabloids target social class rather than age. As a popular tabloid, it was expected to appeal to the average '*Mirror*' reader, and to have a core readership in the 18–39 age group.

The black glossy magazines have tended to target a broader economic band and age range. The magazines fall into several categories. There are women's magazines: *Pride*, *Black Beauty and Hair*, *Candace* and *Visions In Black*. There are special interest magazines, such as the political magazine *Race and Class*, the multicultural magazine *New Impact*, the literary journal *Wasafiri*, and the arts and entertainment magazines *Artrage* and *Flava*. There are also several religious magazines, *Trends*, *Muslimwise*, *The Crescent* and *Sufi*, to name but a few, as well as several sports magazines and a plethora of black music papers and magazines such as *Blues & Soul*, *Black Echoes*, *True*, *Hard Edge*, *Black Jazz* and *Hype*. Some of the latter are inter-racial initiatives.

See also: black literature press

Further reading

Benjamin, I. (1995) *The Black Press In Britain*, Stoke-on-Trent: Trentham Books (interesting in terms of its historical contextualization of black publishing in Britain).

EUGENE LANGE

black sportsmen and women

Britain boasts an impressive array of black sportsmen and women in the 1990s, with some of the problems they face having declined (albeit slowly) since their arrival in mainstream professional sport in the late 1970s. Since then, the England **football** team has picked a black captain and the England cricket side has featured many black players, as have rugby and **athletics**. There is also the heavy concentration of black competitors in **boxing**, though this might reflect the generally lower incomes of black people in Britain.

Most sports have come a long way since the late 1970s, but football has made particular progress. Here the trend setters were West Bromwich Albion, with their classy trio of Batson, Regis and Cunningham, but most clubs would not pick blacks until the 1980s. The first black England player was Viv Anderson in 1978, but this did not stop abuse from fans and team mates. John Barnes was told by right-wing fans in 1984 that goals by black players 'do not count'. Spectator racism has long been a problem in **cricket**, rugby league and football, with abuse from fans a regular part of the black performer's career.

Black sportswomen are less well known (sportswomen generally have a lower media profile), though many of the best British women athletes such as Ashia Hansen, Kelly Holmes and Diane Modahl are black. However, athletics is the one sport where black women have succeeded. Generally there are no, or very few, black competitors in British **golf**, **tennis**, **swimming** or **hockey**.

The situation has clearly improved since the offensive attitudes of the 1960s and 1970s, when many coaches believed black players could not perform in the cold, only had pace and power, and would upset dressing room harmony by not tolerating racist 'jokes' from colleagues. However, in the commercialized world of British sport in the 1980s and 1990s, the question of race became less important, and commercial opportunities in the 1990s are now open to black competitors if their sport's profile is high enough. Yet some sports still lack any top level black participants, and the 'genetic' abilities of black players are still sometimes questioned, as is their loyalty to their team. Black sportspeople are not yet treated like whites, but with the current generation proving so successful, and with high profile anti-racism campaigns getting backing from top black performers in the 1990s, the situation should improve further.

See also: athletics; sport, racism in

Further reading

Cashmore, E. (1982) *Black Sportsmen*, London: Routledge.

REX NASH

black television

The converging histories of Afro-Caribbean immigration and the mass expansion of television in 1950s Britain have belied their continuing divergence on a predominantly white broadcasting medium. Programmes targeted at **Afro-Caribbean communities** seek to redress the historical imbalance of black stereotyping, misrepresentation and mainstream marginalization on British television, addressing specific Afro-Caribbean cultural issues in various genres.

During the 1950s and 1960s, occasional dramas were produced against an impending national panic over race, immigration and an emergent racist politics which culminated in the speeches of Enoch Powell. John Elliot's *A Man From The Sun* (1956) dispelled colonial myths about the mother country from a working-class Afro-Caribbean perspective, while John Hopkins' *Fable* (1965) caused a political furore by depicting a British apartheid state based on black superiority. Theatrical adaptations confronted issues of interraciality in Ted Willis's *Hot Summer Night* (1952), and from positions of black interiority in Barry Reckford's *You in Your Small Corner* (1962).

In contrast, hugely popular shows including *The Black and White Minstrel Show* (1958–78), situation comedies '*Till Death Do Us Part* (1966–74), *Love Thy Neighbour* (1972–5), *Mixed Blessings* (1978), and even the all-black comedy *The Fosters* (1976), the black police drama *Wolcott* (1981) and 'explanatory' documentaries such as *Them and Us* (1970) have tended to reinforce racial stereotypes.

The first all-black soap *Empire Road* (1978–9), alongside the appearance of black professionals in *Black Silk* (1985) (and also John Elliot's black lawyer-based *Rainbow City* (1967)) and crime drama *South of the Border* (1988) positively challenged damaging black representations in traditionally white domains and genres.

Mainstream institutional bodies like the London Minorities Unit (LMU) established in 1980, and the BBC's Afro-Caribbean Programmes Unit (1989) and Multicultural Programmes Department (1990) were created to consider 'minority' audiences. The LMU's first production *Skin* (1980) introduced the current affairs magazine format adopted by *Ebony* (1982), Channel 4's *Black on Black* (1982) and its revised incarnations ***Bandung File*** and *Black Bag* (1991).

Channel 4's 1982 launch included a groundbreaking multicultural remit and, along with BBC2, the channel has broadcast numerous dramas such as *We the Ragamuffin* (1992), the inner city *Blazed* (1995) and Caryl Phillip's *The Final Passage* (1997). There have also been the black comedies *Desmonds* (1989) and *The Real McCoy* and documentaries like *Lest We Forget* (1990) and *Windrush* (1998).

The creative and institutional shift in black programming in the 1980s abandoned a troubled race relations paradigm to convey the pluralities of black experience. Nevertheless, segregationist aspects and a reluctance in broadcasting to risk alienating mainstream white audiences, particularly by commissioning cutting-edge programmes from more independent black production companies, continues to impede the development of black television.

Further reading

Ross, K. (1996) *Black and White Media: Black Images in Popular Film and Television*, Cambridge: Polity Press (includes a section robustly discussing multicultural programming).

SATINDER CHOHAN

black theatre

Black theatre occupies an interdisciplinary space which integrates an eclectic fusion of Afrodiasporic and black British literary-based dramatic text, music, song, dance, various media, linguistic forms, **live art** and **performance art**. By creating a diachronically and culturally resonant black vernacular inscribed with issues of identity, representation, tradition and history, black theatre dismantles the conventional structures of an exclusively white or Eurocentric theatre inclined to marginalize black experience.

A nascent black theatre involved Royal Court productions of Errol John's *Moon on a Rainbow Shawl* (1958), followed by a trilogy of Barry Reckord plays. During the 1960s and 1970s, other Caribbean-born dramatists such as Mustapha Matura, Alfred Fagon and Edgar White emerged to explore migrant identities, colonial legacies and conditions of exile, displacement and conflict between Caribbean and British culture.

In 1970, an Institute of Contemporary Arts (**ICA**) series of Black and White Power plays featured Mustapha Matura's first play *Black Pieces*, productions concerning the 1960s American civil rights and Black Power movements, and a general desire for cross-cultural articulations fortifying black artistic activity in Britain. The Dark and Light and Temba Theatre companies, along with fringe and specifically black venues like London's Keskidee Arts Centre and The Factory, produced myriad black plays during the politically inspired 1970s.

A subsequent generation of black British-born playwrights such as Tunde Ikoli and Caryl Phillips offered visceral dissections of cultural and intragenerational conflicts in plays like Phillips's *Strange Fruit* (1979). Their advancement of a predominantly male and politically based theatre which passionately responded to issues including racism, immigration, disenfranchised black youth and communities were soon diversified by the feminist concerns of 1980s black female dramatists like Jacqueline Rudet, Paulette Randall, Winsome Pinnock and Jackie Kay, whose black lesbian feminist choreopoem *Chiaroscuro* (1986) embraced kaleidoscopic performative techniques.

Amali Nepthali's *Ragamuffin* hybridized Caribbean popular traditions and black popular and political culture to collapse boundaries between its MC performers and audience. With an emphasis on communality and orature (for example, Benjamin Zephaniah's dub poetry plays), black theatre also demonstrates its polyphonic nature through revisionist adaptations of Western classics like Talawa Theatre Company's *King Lear* (1993) and *A Doll's House* (1996). Other companies such as Black Mime Theatre (1984) amplify continuing discussions about a British black theatre aesthetic. Alongside Talawa, however, the Black Theatre Cooperative (1979) is the only other fully funded British black theatre company, a serious infrastructural underfunding which threatens a vital British theatre dramatic narrative.

Further reading

Tompsett, A.R. (1996) *Black Theatre In Britain*, London: Harwood Academic Publishers (a valuable introduction to black theatre theory and practice).

SATINDER CHOHAN

'Black Women Talk' Collective

'Black Women Talk' is a collective of women of Asian and African descent living in Britain. It is concerned about the lack of outlets for black women's writing and accuse publishers of only publishing Afro-American women's writing in Britain because it is lucrative. The Collective is committed to publishing black British women's work because it feels that they have something distinctive to say, something which has been deliberately suppressed. It also seeks to make alternative material available to schools, libraries and other public information centres and to share skills cooperatively. It identifies its 'sister' presses as Kitchen Table, in the USA, and Third World Women Press in Delhi.

See also: black literature press; black women's movement

MIKE STORRY

black women's movement

The black women's movement emerged during the black and feminist consciousness-raising decades of the 1970s, drawing upon Black Power and anti-imperialist national liberation and women's liberation movements. The black women's movement gained momentum among black women during the late 1970s and 1980s through demonstrations of collective social and political activism.

Like the women's liberation movement, the black women's movement was not comprised of a single organizational unity, instead existing as a loosely structured network of black women's organizations, support and discussion groups mobilized at grassroots and community levels. The black women's movement unified Afro-Caribbean and Asian women through commonalities of race and gender, while simultaneously recognizing internal differentiations of class, cultural background, sexual orientation, politics, religion and language.

The terminology of 'black' and 'feminist' labels triggered self-defining and contentious debates within the black women's movement. A non-essentialized, politicized term, 'black' stressed both the foundational Afro-Asian unity of the black women's movement and the heterogeneity of black women everywhere. The term 'feminism' was often rejected for its implicit racism or reappropriated under the label 'black feminism', with the black women's movement primarily originating in response to the exclusionary nature of an ethnocentric and eurocentric feminism advocated by the largely white, middle-class women's liberation movement. The black women's movement questioned their universalist assumptions of female sexual and political oppression, exposing white feminism's emphasis on gender and personal politics through a privileged, predominantly separatist discourse which entirely negated black women's (and men's) experiences of racism, colonialism and imperialism. As Hazel Carby declared:

> Black feminists have been, and are still, demanding that the existence of racism must be acknowledged as a structuring feature of our relationships with white women. Both white

feminist theory and practice have to recognize that white women stand in a power relation as oppressors of black women. This compromises any feminist theory and practice founded on the notion of simple equality.

(Mirza 1997: 46)

The black women's movement enabled black women to assert themselves against a 'double invisibility' or 'double colonization' and to rally against oppressive forms of racism and sexism in all their personal and institutional guises. By recovering the marginalized narratives and voices of black women through a developing black and postcolonial feminism, the black women's movement confronted forces of cultural imperialism in hegemonic discourses, systems and practices, whether white feminism or the capitalist British state.

Black female academics like Carby and Pratibha Parmar critiqued white feminism and rejected its patronizing attitudes towards black women on issues relating to the family, class and sexuality. Commonly cited as a source of women's oppression, the family also offered a means of resistance for black women against racist and imperialist forces, for example, state immigration laws that divided black families, forced sterilizations and fuelled an abortion debate among black women. Black women objected to the cultural solopsism of white feminists, who denounced traditional practices such as purdah or arranged marriages through a misinformed understanding of the cultural complexities, simplistically imposing judgements shaped by their own ideological conditioning instead. Black feminists criticized their own misrepresentation and that of subaltern women by a 'First World' feminism constructing itself as a liberationist force for the oppressed victims of traditionalist cultures. Much early black feminist scholarship also sought to locate black women within their own subjective and critical spaces through processes of historical reclamation.

The black women's movement acknowledged its origins of struggle within a collective diasporic history of oppression through slavery, colonialism, Third World liberationist struggles, state racism and economic exploitation. Portrayed by white feminists, for example, as passive, docile females, black female migrant workers were often instigating agents and participants in industrial strikes and disputes, driven to activism by the race and employment issue. In a landmark 1977 dispute, Asian women led a high-profile strike against employers at the Grunswick Photoprocessing Plant, North London, against discriminatory terms and conditions of employment. In 1995, predominantly Asian female cleaners at Hillingdon Hospital, Middlesex, embarked on a continuing dispute following their sackings over rejected pay cuts.

In 1978, the socialist-based, non-hierarchical national black women's Organization of Women of African and Asian Descent (OWAAD) provided a discursive platform of exchange and network between black women and off-shoot black women's movement organizations. OWAAD held four conferences between 1978 and 1982, the first conference leading to the formation of women's groups nationwide, offering practical support for black women involved in protest campaigns, deportations, strikes, industrial disputes, domestic violence and for those with health, education or housing problems. For example, OWAAD staged a sit-in protest at Heathrow Airport to protest at the virginity tests conducted on Asian female immigrants to verify their claims of residency and marriage in Britain. The black women's movement exposed the tests as another demonstration of state racism intruding upon the personal and sexual lives of black immigrants. OWAAD eventually collapsed over structural deficiencies, internal wranglings over black sexualities and a unifying 'black' label which exposed its conflicting political perspectives, vying for OWAAD's prioritization in, for example, African liberationist struggles or British race issues.

OWAAD led to groups like Brixton Black Women's Group, the Asian Refuge Centre, Manchester Black Women's Cooperative and the championed Southall Black Sisters (SBS), supporting black women subjected to domestic and racial violence. SBS was involved in the historic overturning, on the grounds of severe psychological and physical abuse, of Kiranjit Ahluwalia's 1989 conviction for her husband's murder. Women Against Fundamentalism was also created to counter the patriarchal stance of religious fundamentalism within ethnic communities.

Despite its fragmentation during the 1980s and

1990s, the black women's movement has localized in instances of individual and collective 'black' activism and black British feminist agency. As Mirza emphasizes: 'Strategic multiplicity and contingency is a hallmark of black British feminism. If anything, what our struggles demonstrate is that you can have difference (polyvocality) within a conscious construction of sameness (i.e. black feminism)' (Mirza 1997: 21) The black women's movement made pioneering gains by introducing a myopic feminism to vital pluralisms, demonstrating the shortcomings of feminist theories which obviated factors of race and imperialism as power constructs. Importantly, it extended the post-colonial/postmodernist debate about women, race and imperialism in subjective, critical and political spaces from imposed positions of historical marginalization to one of empowered visibility in British institutional life and on its streets.

See also: 'Black Women Talk' Collective

Further reading

Amos, V., Lewis, G., Mama, A. and Parmar, P. (eds) (1984) 'Many Voices, One Chant: Black Feminist Perspectives', *Feminist Review* 17 (a formative black women's movement text which encapsulates nascent black feminist concerns).

Mirza, H.S. (1997) *Black British Feminism: A Reader*, London: Routledge (a definitive text of a developing post-colonial and postmodernist black feminism).

SATINDER CHOHAN

Blair, Les

b. 1941

Film-maker

Les Blair was at Salford Grammar school with Mike **Leigh** and Albert Finney. He produced (and Finney financed) Leigh's first film, *Bleak Moments*. He and Ken **Loach** are now partners in Parallax Films. As a director, he favours an improvisational style and has an optimistic outlook. His major films to date have been *Bad Behaviour* (1993) and *Jump the Gun* (1997). The former starred Sinead Cusack and

Stephen Rea and dealt sympathetically with middle-class love in Dublin. The latter is more political but still retains elements of domestic comedy. The film, which was well-received in South Africa, deals with relationships in a post-apartheid society where one of the new realities is a burgeoning sex industry.

MIKE STORRY

blues

The blues is a folk musical style evolved by rural southern African Americans around 1900. It speaks predominantly of their conditions in pre-Civil Rights America: disenfranchisement, alcoholism, migration, poverty and domestic strife.

Blues traditionally adheres to a rigid musical structure of twelve-bar groupings (three lines of four bars each), lyrically following an AAB rhyming pattern. Its scale, with its non-western 'blue notes', probably derives from Africa. Stylistic constraint, mirroring its performers' social subjugation, is countered by personalized vocal inflection and improvisation.

By the 1960s, African Americans began to dissociate themselves from its unproductive pessimism, while a new, mainly white fan base was developing through an appreciation of rare imported records in Britain. Blues artists' championing of underdog resistance appealed to the alienated teenagers of postwar Britain. Middle class and mainly living at home, they were caught between a desire for adult freedoms and strict parental regulation. Performing musicians of this age group increasingly turned to the blues for solace.

From the 1950s, American blues artists had been touring Britain. Enthusiastic but financially limited promoters flew over single performers to play with young British backing bands. Reverential white British audiences, although not untainted by racist tendencies, often treated them with more respect than the ingrained segregation at home allowed. The collaborations of the American and British performers involved, many of which were recorded, benefited both parties artistically.

Bands associated with and inspired by this

union, such as Graham Bond, Spencer Davis, The Animals, The Rolling Stones and The Yardbirds, gained popularity during the 1960s 'British Invasion' of the United States (along with extended worldwide acclaim). It is largely to their credit that the blues tradition, with its waning relevance to the African American community, was kept alive in its country of origin. It was they who first attracted a multi-racial audience to the genre, forged links that crossed prohibitive 'race' boundaries and brought performers out of obscurity.

British blues in the 1970s increasingly adopted western classical virtuosity, **jazz** improvisation and extended solo use. This acknowledged a sense of freedom and self-indulgence – both social and musical – that had evaded the early blues artists.

Despite major label disinterest in new bands, blues is still popular in British pubs and at specialist festivals. Famous artists such as Eric Clapton continue to voice their indebtedness to blues musicians.

Further reading

Brunning, B. (1995) *Blues in Britain, the History 1950 to the Present*, London: Blanford.

KAY DICKINSON

body adornment

Contemporary body adornment practices include tattooing and piercing (the two most common forms), scarification, branding, and, arguably, certain kinds of attire (especially cross-dressing and clothes which fetishize the body), make-up and body painting, hair styling, body building and other forms of 'body sculpting' (cosmetic surgery, transgender transformations, corsetting, plus other less common techniques of body-part modification, such as scrotal elongation by weighting). Mixing 'tribalism' or 'modern primitivism' (most commonly based around a blend of shamanistic, Native American, Oriental and Polynesian inspirations) with practices associated with sexual subcultures (fetish and **sadomasochism**) and, increasingly, cyberpunk aesthetics, the body adornment 'scene' has become a distinct and visible subculture in contemporary Britain. Simultaneously, its practices have proliferated, with tattooing and piercing enjoying prominence among assorted subcultures, including 'new age', 'queer', and music-based and style-based cultures such as **crusties** and punks. Although tattoos and certain forms of piercing (especially ear piercing) have long been popular, other forms of body adornment have also percolated into the mainstream (nose and navel piercing, for example), leading to debates about legislative regulation on health and age grounds.

Proponents of body alteration argue that the body is a primary means of self-expression, and that adornment is a form of resistance to powerlessness in modern life. Marking oneself as different is seen to challenge social norms. Pleasure is also evoked as a motive for adornment: both the pleasures of public shock or transgression, and the more private pleasures of heightened erotic possibility and sensation. These erotic aspects are commonly emphasized in cultural commentaries, and are especially central to the so-called 'fetish scene' which links adornment with other sexual practices such as bondage, submission-domination and sadomasochism (although there is no necessary co-existence between the two).

Cosmetic surgery and body building are in some ways distinct from piercing and tattooing, but deserve inclusion since both involve the purposeful alteration of the body for assorted motives, including pleasure. While these exist separately from other forms of adornment, there are significant crossovers. Similarly, cross-dressing and 'gender-bending' modifications warrant inclusion here, but cannot be understood solely in this context, for these too encompass a range of practices with quite distinct motives and meanings.

See also: 'gender benders'

Further reading

Polhemus, T. and Randall, H. (1996) *The Customized Body*, London: Serpent's Tail (lots of photographs, and useful overviews of many aspects of the body adornment scene).

DAVID BELL

body size

Fashion imagery operates around the display of an idealized body shape which, while continually changing, is always at variance with the general population. In the 1960s, Twiggy encapsulated the underdeveloped waif, which was to be revived in the 1990s in reaction to the aerobicized and worked-out body of the late 1970s and 1980s. In the 1990s, men have not escaped notions of the ideal with the stress on perfect pectorals and a muscular abdomen. The ideal body shape as perpetuated by the fashion industry met with criticism as a result of the critique provided by feminism in the late 1960s and 1970s. Feminism continues to question the viability of a fashionably ideal body to which women should aspire.

See also: eating disorders

CAROLINE COX

book marketing

Sophisticated forms of book marketing are a relatively recent phenomenon. The prevailing notion of publishing as a gentlemanly profession, in which the love of literature was more important than profit, and the widespread belief that books were all distinct products and therefore unmarketable anyway, contributed to the half-hearted and generally inefficient nature of book marketing up until the 1980s. However, book marketing has grown in significance in recent years, largely as a consequence of the increasing consolidation of the industry into the hands of commercially minded conglomerates.

Book marketing can be divided into direct and indirect forms. Direct forms are centred on books themselves and include paid advertising in mass media such as magazines, newspapers and television, special displays (or 'dump bins') in bookshops, and dustjacket blurbs and endorsements. More indirect forms of marketing are generally less expensive and are centred around arranging interviews for the author in the media, and appearances at bookshop signings or at literary festivals such as the annual events at Hay-on-Wye and Cheltenham. In some cases, the size of book contracts – like the

seven-figure advance received by first-time author Nicholas Evans for *The Horse Whisperer* in 1995 – can even be used as a source of free press publicity for the author. However, the most effective indirect form of book marketing remains the attempt to ensure that books are reviewed in the media, and publishers make strenuous attempts to do this by sending out proof copies and lobbying influential literary editors through networking. Since publishers generally only make serious efforts to publicize a small percentage of their list, and the gap between the so-called 'leads' and the 'midlist' is becoming wider, some observers have complained that the book industry is wielding a disproportionate influence in determining which books receive media attention.

The rise of major book chains like Waterstones and Dillons has recently added another major player to the area of book marketing, through their instigation of 'Books of the Month' and in-house magazines. Major publishers have also begun to create interactive bookstores on commercial on-line services such as Compuserve and Delphi or on the World Wide Web, through which readers can order copies either on-line or by telephone. It is anticipated that these bookstores will account for a significant proportion of the market in the future.

See also: publishing trends

Further reading

Baverstock, A. (1993) *Are Books Different? Marketing in the Book Trade*, London: Kogan Page.

JOE MORAN

Boorman, John

b. 1933

Film director

Boorman was head of documentaries at the **BBC** from 1960–4 before going on to direct his first feature, *Catch Us If You Can* (1965). His subsequent departure for the USA to direct *Point Blank*, a Hollywood-produced thriller with European sensibilities, was followed by trans-Atlantic projects involving dichotomous and mythic explorations of conflicted psychological, political and spiritual states of humanity. These included the surreal *Leo the Last* (1969), *Zardoz* (1973) and the allegorical quest narratives of *Deliverance* (1972), *Exorcist II: The Heretic* (1977), *Excalibur* (1981) and *The Emerald Forest* (1985). The autobiographical *Hope and Glory* (1987) and the factually based Irish gangster film *The General* (1988) consolidated Boorman's domestic (and international) reputation, celebrating an impassioned and determined directorial brilliance that has rarely wavered visually.

Further reading

Ciment, M. (1986) *John Boorman*, London: Faber.

SATINDER CHOHAN

boxing

World boxing has several 'governing bodies' (even after the 1998 merger of the World Boxing Association and the World Boxing Council), but British boxers who hold world titles at the time of writing include Lennox Lewis (heavyweight), Robin Read (super-middleweight), and 'Prince' Naseem Hamed (featherweight). Other prominent boxers who have become national figures and appear on talk shows include Chris Eubank, Joe Bugner and Frank Bruno.

Boxing in Britain has for many years been surrounded by negative publicity because of its health risks. With an influential official body like the British Medical Association campaigning for a government ban on the sport, it has been difficult to promote it, for example in schools. Attention focuses on periodic bouts where boxers are maimed or suffer brain damage. The latter has been associated, in American studies, with the effects of dehydration as boxers try desperately to get down to their weights immediately before a contest. In 1990, despite warnings, Nigel Benn was five pounds overweight forty-eight hours before the weigh-in for his fight with Chris Eubank. In May 1998, much adverse publicity was generated by the tragedy of Spencer Oliver, Young Boxer of the Year and defending European super-bantamweight champion, who sustained a blood clot at the Royal

Albert Hall in his fight with Ukrainian Sergei Devakov. Despite a public outcry, Tony Banks, the Sports Minister, rejected calls for a ban.

Interest in boxing as a spectator sport stems broadly speaking from the upper and lower classes, rather than the middle classes. At the National Sporting Club in London, the audience wear dinner suits and applaud only at the end of each round. At boxing matches around the country, on the other hand, audiences are largely male and working class.

Meanwhile, despite qualms about health and safety, women have been pushing to enter the sport. Britain's top woman boxer, Jane Couch, took the British Boxing Board of Control to a tribunal with a claim of sexual discrimination after it rejected her application for a licence to work as Britain's first professional woman boxer. The license was finally granted in June 1998, clearly marking a new era for British boxing.

The sport was also given a boost by Jim Sheridan's 1998 film *The Boxer*, in which Daniel **Day-Lewis**'s performance in the ring without an understudy achieved universal accolades. Day-Lewis was coached by Barry McGuigan, the former WBA featherweight champion, whose official biography was written by Sheridan.

See also: sport, racism in; wrestling

MIKE STORRY

Branagh, Kenneth

b. 1960, Belfast

Actor and director

Branagh graduated from RADA with the gold medal, garnering work immediately in the West End and with the RSC. In 1985 he decided to create a smaller scale company which could be truer to the principle of repertory, dividing roles fairly and allowing actors more influence. His Renaissance Theatre Company also gave established actors the opportunity to direct, amongst them Dame Judi Dench, Derek Jacobi and Geraldine McEwan. Following the success of the film version of Shakespeare's *Henry V* (1989), starring, adapted and directed by himself, Branagh shifted the main thrust of Renaissance towards cinema, releasing in quick succession between 1991 and 1995 *Dead Again*, *Peter's Friends*, *Much Ado About Nothing*, *Mary Shelley's Frankenstein* and *In the Bleak Midwinter*, followed by an acclaimed version of *Hamlet* (1997).

See also: Thompson, Emma

ALISON BOMBER

breakfast television

Breakfast television is older than most people imagine. It was first tried in the London ITV area in the late 1950s, and then in Yorkshire in the early 1970s. In the early 1980s, however, the IBA offered a separate breakfast franchise and **TV-am** duly began *Good Morning Britain* in February 1983, one month after the **BBC** had crept in with its rival broadcast *Breakfast Time*, with Frank Bough and Selina Scott. **Channel 4**'s bright, brash and home-based contribution, *The Big Breakfast*, started by Paula Yates and Bob Geldof, became a huge success and made a success of Chris Evans, a drag star of Lily Savage, and then a minor celebrity of Johnny Vaughan.

See also: daytime television

PETER CHILDS

British Black English

British Black English is used to describe the many strains of creole English spoken in Britain by immigrants from the Caribbean and their children. Particularly, it refers to the language used by the children of those who arrived in the 1950s and who have blended local varieties of English with the creole of their parents. Terms which cover similar areas are patois, creole and black English vernacular. Black youth culture, especially **Rastafarianism** and **reggae**, uses the mix as part of an aesthetic of black British identity, and there has also been a change wrought on 'English' literature to express black British experience. Many people switch from English to patois, and it is unclear whether these are separate speech systems or

whether there is a spectrum of varieties linking the two. British Black English is spoken primarily in London, but also in Birmingham, Leeds and other major cities. Patois has also entered the speech of some whites. Many poets also use British Black English, notably Grace Nichols and Fred D'Aguiar.

See also: black performance poets

Further reading

David Sutcliffe (1982) *British Black English*, Oxford: Blackwell.

PETER CHILDS

British Citizenship Acts

These Acts define who can live in Britain. Like all those before it, the British Nationality Act (1981) is contentious. It created a new British Dependent Territories citizenship, which does not give a right of abode in Britain. As people from both Gibraltar and the Falkland Islands were exempted from it, this has been seen as a racist measure. The government unwillingly gave 8,000 mainly Indian and Pakistani citizens of Hong Kong passports only because they would become 'stateless'. Discretionary treatment of certain high-profile individuals has laid various Home Secretaries open to charges of racism: Mohamed Al Fayed was denied, but John Paul Getty was accorded British citizenship by Michael Howard. The current Home Secretary, Jack Straw, has been pressured to introduce a more even-handed approach.

See also: Race Relations Acts

MIKE STORRY

British Council

Founded in 1934 and granted a charter in 1940, the British Council is an independent, non-political organization that receives government funding and generates fee income. Its mission is to promote worldwide knowledge of the English language and all aspects of British culture and the British 'way of life'. This it does by maintaining libraries and centres for language teaching and other studies in more than 200 towns and cities in more than a hundred countries. The British Council also commissions works of art of every sort from British writers, artists and composers, and mounts exhibitions in the United Kingdom and abroad.

See also: Arts Council

Further reading

Donaldson, F. (1984) *The British Council: The First Fifty Years*, London: Cape.

CHRISTOPHER SMITH

British film industry

The influence of the United States on British cinema is so overwhelming that the very existence of an indigenous British film industry is questionable. Leading British film critics Sarah Street, Geoffrey Nowell-Smith, John Hill, Duncan Petrie and John Caughie agree that it has become increasingly difficult to define any part of the industry as British rather than Anglo-American. Since 1980, no British company is involved in all aspects of the film business (as **Rank** and Associated British Picture Corporation once were). There seems only a British input into international (US) cinema. Intense international divisions of labour and huge expenditure on stars and publicity leave Britain to face American block booking, joint operation with American studios, and star drain to Hollywood. Hollywoodization appears an accomplished fact.

In this context, it makes little sense from a British point of view to think of the film industry as an integrated organization controlling its own production and distribution. Yet funding has been conducted as if an infrastructure for such an industry could be sustained in Britain. It is more meaningful to see the British position in relation to an International Film System (IFS). Indeed a major development occurred in the IFS in the early 1980s on the basis that the infrastructure was decisively occupied at an international level by the United States. Thereafter infrastructure policy in Britain

left an accumulating production bias, which as time went on became increasingly liable to US subversion.

Thus the Eady levy taken from cinemas and given to British film-makers failed as the Hollywood majors took more and more British studio space in order to qualify themselves for levy share. Quotas on cinemas having to screen a proportion of British features also failed as the number of films registered as British fell dramatically. As the high risk character of film investment intensified, the main funding body, the National Film Finance Corporation, had to be converted into a private company, British Screen Finance Limited. Even the most significant companies, **Goldcrest**, Thorn-EMI and Virgin, eventually had to stop production.

The underlying reason for these problems began in a phase of the IFS, lasting from the early 1960s to early 1980s. The crux was that Hollywood came to see Britain as a product of its own domestic and international role, compensating for its own anti-trust regulations, determined by competition at home, the strength of the dollar and the prospects of cultural hegemony in the international film industry. The USA's increasing domination in the IFS drew a series of national responses across Europe, such as new wave film movements, and a playing out of national and class film cultures versus Hollywood cultures.

In Britain there were two main reactions. One was located in cultural and studio-based organization, as at Shepperton Studios or **Pinewood Studios**, providing film genres such as British realism, **Hammer Horror**, James Bond, **Carry On films** and the cinema of 1960s Swinging London films. The other was a direct response to America implanting its film formulas and film making on British soil. The high costs and risks involved in hit-or-miss production encouraged erratic growth and exhaustion. At one point the problem was tackled by buying into exclusively American subjects, but for the most part this strategy flopped expensively, as with *The Jazz Singer* (1980), *Can't Stop the Music* (1980) and *Honky Tonk Freeway* (1981). Further efforts on the American market followed, as Petrie commented, in the wake of the disastrous *Raise the Titanic* (1980).

As Rank and Thorn-EMI were forced out of production in the mid-1980s, British production scattered to over 300 independent companies. There were still important film successes, like *Chariots of Fire* (1981), *Time Bandits* (1981), *Gandhi* (1982), *Nineteen Eighty-Four* (1984), *Company of Wolves* (1984) and *A Passage to India* (1985). These were mainly undertaken by Goldcrest, **Handmade Films**, **Merchant-Ivory Productions**, Palace Productions, Virgin Vision and **Working Title**. However, with the exceptions of Merchant-Ivory, Renaissance Films, Parallax, Recorded Pictures, Thin Man Films and PolyGram Filmed Entertainment, this period left little continuity in British film production, which declined in the early 1980s. Since then there has been a widespread tendency towards low-budget film making, with just a few companies making more than one film, as with HandMade Films, Metrodome Films, Recorded Picture Company, **Branagh**'s Renaissance Films, Parallax Pictures and Scala Productions. The only significant lasting company has been PolyGram (now 75 percent owned by the Dutch company Philips), as the sole inheritor of the mantle once shared by EMI, Rank, Goldcrest, Virgin and Palace.

The subsequent phase of the IFS dating from the early 1980s took shape with intensifying US and multinational control over box offices and film distribution, and with struggles for control in the media and communications industries, which exposed **cinemas** to new relationships in film consumption. Hence the USA increasingly gained the power to control both audio-visual markets and the wider aspects of international media property rights. Well over half of the revenue earned by most films now comes from the secondary markets of television and video. US domination of Europe in video distribution is even greater than in cinemas.

All this became apparent with the US campaign for complete deregulation of the EU's audio-visual industries during the 1993 negotiations over the General Agreements on Tariffs and Trade, and with European policies for supporting co-productions, distribution and training, and promoting culture and media industries as a means for regional development and economic regeneration. This is evident in the increasingly varied sources of financing available for UK film production, which include the European Script Fund, Eurimages, European Co-production Fund, European Media Programmes, British Screen Finance, British Film Institute (**BFI**), Glasgow Film Fund and Scottish Film Production Company, Northern Ireland Film Council, the **National Lottery**, **Channel 4 Films**, BBC Films and ITV.

Television played a key role in the transition from film industry studios to audio-visual systems, and continues to do so with the emergence of **BSkyB** as a major new source of investment funding through pre-investment and acquisition of pay-TV rights. This is paralleled by fragmentation, vertical de-integration and even casualization of the British film industry, though it has broadened the variety of film cultures and access to marginal producers, communities and workshops.

Although European television companies invest much more money in cinema than their British counterparts, British television has been one of the last remaining props for British film making. Channel Four developed its public service role through partnerships with British Screen and the BFI, and commissioned many critically important films including *The Draughtsman's Contract* (1982), *Angel* (1982), *The Ploughman's Lunch* (1983), *A Room With a View* (1985) *My Beautiful Launderette* (1985), *Letter to Brezhnev* (1985), *Caravaggio* (1986), *Mona Lisa* (1986), *Distant Voices, Still Lives* (1988), *Riff Raff* (1990), *Life is Sweet* (1990), *The Crying Game* (1992) and *Four Weddings and a Funeral* (1994).

The IFS has brought a new international division of labour to the British film industry, particularly in relation to Hollywood. In Hollywood there is an influx of British talent at every level of film making, including producers such as Sarah Radclyffe and Eric Fellner, directors like Stephen **Frears**, Alan **Parker**, Adrian Lyne and Mike Figgis, cinematographers like Douglas Slocombe and David Watkin, set designers, and a new international set of actors such as Gary Oldman, Miranda Richardson and Tim Roth. Among leading British earners in Hollywood are Sean **Connery**, Daniel **Day-Lewis**, Liam Neeson, Ralph Fiennes, Kenneth **Branagh**, Jeremy Irons, Anthony Hopkins, Hugh **Grant**, Gary Oldman and Ewan McGregor.

Within Britain, this division of labour takes the form of a service sector for international film making. Hollywood has increased its film making in Britain so that 121 feature films were produced or shot in 1996, compared to seventy-three in 1995 and ten in 1986. By 1995 the total production value of UK films reached £450 million, with the growth of Hollywood films bringing US investment here to £280 million, alongside a steady stream of European co-productions. Despite withdrawal from Eurimages at the end of 1995, twenty-eight UK–European co-productions were shot in 1996 (and twenty-six in 1995). At this point there were fourteen US–UK collaborations (the same as 1995), seven Canada–UK partnerships and nine UK combinations with Japan, South Africa or Australia.

After decline in the 1980s, it became difficult to maintain studio space anywhere in the UK. Despite this, **Pinewood Studios** saw a turning point with new US and US–UK productions in 1994. Elstree was re-opened in 1996 after scaling down three of its ten stages, and Ealing was bought by the National Film and Television School. New demand for space prompted a new studio, Leavesden, while Ridley and Tony **Scott** expanded Shepperton Studios to become the biggest post-production studio, with digital facilities to keep US post-production in Britain. Another notable development was Warner Brothers' search with United News and Media for a movie-themed amusement park.

On the periphery of this division of labour there is a small-scale independent British sector mostly formed by new production alliances. Fifty-three of the starts made in 1996 were completely UK funded (triple the 1995 total). Almost all were made for considerably less than £2 million. They include notable films such as Glasgow Film Fund's *Shallow Grave* (1994) (backed by the European Regional Development Fund), Merseyside Film Production Fund's *Butterfly Kiss* (1995), and Scottish Film Production Fund/BBC Scotland's *Franz Kafka's Its a Wonderful Life* (1995). On the other hand, many independents had to rely on major international studios for extra backing, and thus lost their own share of the profits. Britain's **Working Title**, without benefit (or restriction) of a major studio, made *Four Weddings and a Funeral* (1994), *Dead Man Walking* (1995) and *Fargo* (1996) for under £4 million each, financed at arm's length by PolyGram.

The difficulty for the independent sector is that its successes become embedded in the core processes of other audio-visual and television industries, or in distribution controlled by other corporations (as with *The English Patient* (1997)). A key problem is the need to retain rights and gain access to distribution channels; and not being in the core means the lack of an adequate legal regime for protecting property rights.

A worrying prospect is that the autonomy and low-budget talents of the small sector may be used to shore up the creative gaps in core production. Equally there are problems about the main service sector: while on paper 1996 and 1997 looked like great box office years for US studios in the UK market, in reality their profit margins narrowed dramatically as screen bottlenecks caused many films to underperform. Unless the US industry can save at least ten percent it will not come (as it showed in Ireland). Hollywood increasingly needs diversified leisure/consumer complexes tied to media strategies which integrate marketing and merchandising, along the lines of *101 Dalmations* (1997) or *Space Jam* (1997).

In policy terms, the Arts Council's plan for franchises with National Lottery funds to encourage new groups of distributors and producers appears to approach several of these problems. Many of the strongest bids for funding, however, have so far been coming from foreign-backed consortia of producers. Given the state of the contemporary IFS, a major question has to be whether it is wise to encourage such production at the expense of policies for new audio-visual organization and property rights, or cinemas or distributors, especially when the vast majority of British films cannot get screening in Britain. The intention that franchises promote shadow-like vertically integrated combines could have had a far more appropriate hearing in the previous phase of the IFS.

See also: BAFTA; BFI; cinemas

Further reading

Finney, A. (1996) *The State of European Cinema*, London: Cassell.

Friedman, L. (ed.) (1993) *British Cinema and*

Thatcherism: Fires Were Started, London: UCL Press.

McIntyre, S. (1996) 'Art and Industry: Regional Film and Video Policy in the UK', in A. Moran (ed.), *Film Policy: International, National and Regional Perspectives*, London: Routledge.

Street, S. (1997) *British National Cinema*, London: Routledge.

ARTHUR McCULLOUGH

BRITISH LIBRARY *see* Wilson, Colin St John

Britpop

Britpop was a label given to a number of British guitar-based groups who either emerged or achieved their first commercial success in the period 1993–4. The most well known Britpop groups were Blur, Pulp and Oasis. As with other generic terms, Britpop was partially a construction by the UK's weekly pop press. Unlike punk, there was no coherent set of values within Britpop, and the movement remained fundamentally musical rather than subcultural.

Despite the inevitable stylistic differences between the various groups, the vague term 'Britpop' does encompass certain common characteristics. Britpop tended to be traditional in terms of instrumentation and song structure. Great emphasis was placed upon songwriting craft, melody, harmony and lyrical content. Britpop's influences lie with earlier groups operating in a similar vein: The Beatles, The Kinks, The Small Faces, Slade, T. Rex and Madness. For the most part, Britpop placed the importance of the song and live performance above **dance music**'s values. Samplers and other computer-based modes of composition and performance had a very low priority. Britpop groups harked back to the somewhat mythical notion of a 'golden age' of pop when groups wrote well-crafted pop songs, performed them live and dealt with 'real' concerns and emotions in an authentic, 'honest' manner.

As noted, the term 'Britpop' was coined by the weekly music press – principally *Melody Maker* and *New Musical Express* (*NME*) – in early 1994. They

had been struggling to come to terms with the success of dance, particularly since the explosion of **rave culture** in 1988. Forms of dance music such as **techno** are largely DJ and club-based, rather than being reliant on live gigs and 'pop stars'. The weeklies, having a long history of championing music with a 'radical attitude', found themselves unable to deal with the more anonymous and blatantly escapist elements of dance music.

Grunge did fit many of the criteria for credibility to the weekly press, but chauvinistic elements needed to champion a new, home-grown guitar-based movement. During the late 1980s and early 1990s, a succession of these – Riot Grrll, Queercore, New Wave Of New Wave – were given extensive coverage, but all failed commercially. Throughout 1993 the weeklies continued to focus on grunge, but also covered new British groups such as Radiohead, and more particularly Suede, a key bridging band whose success did much to pave the way for Britpop.

Pulp and Blur were not new bands, but 1993 saw both begin the transition towards mainstream success. In November Pulp released their first single for a major label, 'Lipgloss', and Blur released their second album, *Modern Life Is Rubbish*. Both groups have a 'retro' sound and laid great stress on their 'Britishness' in terms of style, delivery and lyrical concerns. One of the main themes of Blur's album was an explicit critique of the Americanization of British life, and rock music in general. This was to remain an important aspect of Britpop.

In January 1994, an unnamed reviewer in *Melody Maker* touted Creation Records' new signing Oasis as having a big future. In a four-line feature, Oasis were said to 'plunder the vaults of golden Psychedelic Britpop with shameless glee'. Oasis were given their first major press coverage in the same week that Kurt Cobain died, effectively robbing Grunge of its only international figurehead.

By the time Oasis's first album, *Definitely Maybe*, was released in August, entering the British charts at number one, it was obvious that the combination of hype, chauvinism, the media-friendly frontmen of the most popular bands (Blur's Damon Albarn, Pulp's Jarvis Cocker and the Gallagher brothers of Oasis) and some pop songs in the classic vein would ensure that the Britpop movement had become a genuine phenomenon. Pulp's *His'n'Hers*, *Definitely Maybe* and Blur's hugely successful third album *Parklife* each spawned hit singles, and these three bands, alongside others drawn into the Britpop catchment area – Elastica, Supergrass and Sleeper – began to gain success worldwide, although the North American market proved the most resistant to the sounds of Britpop.

In the summer of 1995 the British media succeeded in their attempt to set up Blur versus Oasis as representatives in some kind of heavyweight boxing bout, with their assumed differences (self-conscious southern pop stars versus bluff northern rock realists) adding spice to the campaign. Although Blur won the battle to the top of the singles charts when 'Country House' and 'Roll With It' were simultaneously released, from this point onwards it was Oasis who gained the critical and commercial ascendancy. Their second album, *(What's The Story) Morning Glory*, was a huge international success, remaining in the bestseller lists for many months, while Blur's *The Great Escape* was a disappointment, such that they (ironically) turned to American music for inspiration on their next, self-titled album. Pulp's headlining appearance at the UK's premier festival – Glastonbury – in June was one of the musical highlights of the year, although the release of *Different Class* at the end of 1995 brought them good reviews but less commercial success than *His'n'Hers* (subsequently Pulp have done very well both critically and commercially).

By 1996, the sights and sounds of Britpop were an established worldwide phenomenon, with Oasis in particular topping the charts in all major music markets and selling out large outdoor venues in their hometown of Manchester in a matter of hours. Both the single 'Wonderwall' and their second album made the American top ten, and the band received the pop press's biggest accolade when they made the cover of *Rolling Stone* magazine in May.

There is little doubt that Britpop to a large degree defined the state of white British guitar pop in the mid- 1990s, with tracks such as Blur's 'Boys And Girls', Supergrass's 'Alright', Pulp's 'Common People' and Oasis's 'Live Forever' set to become the Karaoke staples of the next decade. However,

many would claim that despite the hype, the strong songs and the genuine star qualities of many of Britpop's best performers, the characteristic sounds and values behind the Britpop phenomenon were essentially conservative and reactionary. Nevertheless, in commercial terms Britpop provided a huge lift to the whole British music industry, boosting singles sales in an era of general decline, and increasing success for a variety of British bands throughout the world.

See also: pop and rock

Further reading

Leigh, S. (1996) *Halfway to Paradise: Britpop 1955– 62*, Folkestone: Finbar.

RON MOY

Broadcasting Acts

The 1980 and 1990 Broadcasting Acts are among the most important UK media legislation to date and have had significant effects, though not always as envisaged.

The 1980 Act created the framework for **Channel 4**, and its specific identity and remit. The station would serve a range of interests (notably minorities), innovate in programme design and production, and focus on education. Channel 4 would not produce programmes, but would commission them from independent producers. This fulfilled the government's desire to introduce competition to the industry, and so the Act mixed traditional public service concepts with Thatcherite competition. ITV would sell airtime for adverts on Channel, and Wales was allocated a channel, **S4C**.

The 1990 Act addressed the question of ITV network franchises. All commercial licences were now put out to tender, with two thresholds to be cleared; a 'quality' barrier (based on programme content) and the size of the bid (with the highest bidder expected to win).

The Act was amended, however, to allow the Independent Television Commission to look more carefully at the quality criteria and award licences to lower bids. This 'exceptional circumstances' clause partly explains why only seven of fifteen franchises awarded in 1991 went to the highest bidders. The Act also rejected calls to introduce subscriptions to fund the **BBC**, and switched Channel 4 from an IBA subsidiary to an institutional trust. A funding formula was established for Channel 4, so that if advertising revenue fell below a certain level, ITV companies would contribute some of the shortfall; conversely, any Channel 4 advertising surplus would be shared out among the ITV companies.

Both Acts have proved important. The 1980 legislation has worked well, with Channel 4 maintaining its market share at around 11 percent, pioneering innovative programmes and contributing strongly to British films. But the 1990 Act is more contentious, with complaints of declining quality and the loss of thousands of jobs. Certainly the regulatory bodies have warned some of the new companies about their output, while Channel 4's funding formula has worked in reverse, with the channel paying millions in advertising surpluses to ITV (although this rule was scrapped in 1996).

However, it is too early to say how tendering will work in the long term, and 1996 saw talk of privatizing Channel 4, a new challenge for commercial television alongside the 1997 arrival of **Channel 5** and cable, and **BSkyB**.

See also: Video Recordings Act

Further reading

Seymour-Ure, C. (1996) *The British Press and Broadcasting Since 1945*, Oxford: Blackwell, 2nd edn.

REX NASH

Brownlow, Kevin

b. 1938, Crowborough

Film-maker

Kevin Brownlow has devoted his life to film. He has been a film historian, a restorer and presenter of silent movies, and a writer. He has made films and television series about, for example, Abel Gance, Charlie Chaplin and Buster Keaton. He worked for Photoplay Productions, founded by his collaborator David Gill. In 1975, at the invitation of Jeremy **Isaacs**, he worked at Thames Television on a thirteen-part series about Hollywood in the era of silent films. David Gill had secured many old reels of Chaplin films, which he and Brownlow restored and made into a three-part series, *Unknown Chaplin*, which won an Emmy and a Peabody Award. He reconstructed *Ben Hur* (1926) and restored *The Four Horsemen of the Apocalypse* (1921).

MIKE STORRY

BSkyB

Sky TV was launched in Britain in 1988, and from very shaky foundations has become a key player in British broadcasting, and the unchallenged master of Britain's satellite industry. Owned by Rupert Murdoch's **News International**, about 20 percent of the British population subscribed to Sky in 1996, helping it to make a £250m profit. It is thus a very significant force (a position enhanced by News International's ownership of *The Times* and the *Sun*).

However, in the late 1980s this outcome was impossible to envisage; the fight between rivals British Satellite Broadcasting and Sky for the satellite market was only helping to destroy both, and the future looked bleak. Then Sky took over BSB in November 1990 (though officially it was a 'merger'), and although News International remained £4 billion in debt, BSkyB at least had some hope of survival. Ironically the deal that ultimately saved BSkyB (buying the rights to screen top flight English **football** in 1992) would have been impossible without the **BBC**. Had the BBC not joined forces with BSkyB in the bid, BSkyB could probably not have won.

Since then, BSkyB has grown both in size and market share, and offers a wide portfolio of new and classic movies, 24-hour news, lifestyle programmes, family viewing and three sports channels. It is clear that the sport stations are the key to BSkyB's success, hence the astronomical (and successful) £670m bid for the football deal in 1996; **rugby league**, **rugby union** and **cricket** were also snapped up in the mid-1990s.

However, BSkyB faces problems in its long-term future. Most seriously, the key football deal was placed under investigation by market regulators in both the EU and Britain in 1996. **Channel 5** came on air in the UK in 1997, cable television is growing in popularity (and is considerably cheaper than BSkyB), and some analysts argue that BSkyB cannot further expand its subscriber base. This means that either subscription rates rise considerably or BSkyB must start to shed some of its sports, either of which will damage market share and profitability. The question of media cross-ownership might also affect BSkyB, since if legislation restricting cross-ownership were introduced, the biggest casualty in Britain would be News International. Left untouched, BSkyB will remain very powerful, and has significant expansion plans in areas such as digital broadcasting and pay-per-view that could revolutionize the whole industry (this trend was exemplified by BSkyB's announced takeover of Manchester United football club in September 1998).

See also: cable and satellite

Further reading

Chippendale, J. and Franks, J. (1992) *Dished! The Rise and Fall of BSB*, London: Simon & Schuster.

REX NASH

Buddhism

Buddhism is a term popularly applied to the many and varied schools of thought which grew and developed from the teachings of the Buddha in India more than 2,500 years ago. Its influence has spread throughout the world and it has been an accepted part of British culture for some time. The various branches of the religion all emphasize the Buddha's teaching that individuals can gain liberation from an ongoing cycle of birth and death and the suffering contained therein. This is achieved by the cultivation of awareness and understanding gained through meditation, the goal of which is to attain *nirvana*, or enlightenment, a state which transcends this cycle. Perhaps it was the religion's lack of determinism and an emphasis on

individual free will which appealed to the population of 1960s Britain, particularly the 'hippie' youth (see **hippies**), in the prevailing mood of liberation in all areas of life. Freedom from postwar austerity gave people the chance to experiment with different lifestyles and there was a move away from established institutions. Meditation centres began to open around the country, and by the mid-1990s almost three hundred groups and centres were listed in the UK.

Prior to this, Buddhism already had a foundation in Britain with the Buddhist Society, founded in 1924 by the late Christmas Humphreys QC. The society provides information and instruction in all schools of Buddhism. Over the years the religion has moved away from its place on the fringes of the culture; most of those who now flock to the various centres for retreats and study tend to come from the educated middle class in the 'thirtysomething' age group. One of the most popular centres is the Kagyu Samye Ling Tibetan Centre in Dumfriesshire, established in the late 1960s by two young Tibetan monks who had fled to the East in 1959 in the wake of the Chinese invasion of their country. The Centre's twenty-fifth anniversary celebrations in 1993 were attended by the Dalai Lama, as well as by various British dignitaries including Sir David Steel MP (later Lord Steel). The Buddhapadipa temple in West London, staffed by missionary monks from Thailand, has also become a popular centre for study and traditional Theravada Buddhist practice. Established for many years, its present site was inaugurated in 1982 in the presence of HRH Princess Alexandra. The Buddhist Prison Chaplaincy Organisation and the Buddhist Hospice Trust enable a wider section of the population to have access to the religion.

See also: Hinduism; Islam; Jainism

JAN EVANS

bungee jumping

Bungee jumping is a controversial sport in which participants leap from bridges, cranes or other high spots, attached only by a long elastic rope secured to their ankles. It became popular in the 1980s, and in the 1990s a national organization was established in Britain to establish safety rules and standards. Many jumps have been prevented by local authorities on the grounds of dangerous activity. The term 'bungee' is itself taken from the children's word for a rubber, but it is also used for the elastic rope with hooks used by cyclists to secure belongings to their racks. A distant offshoot is bungee running in which participants are tied to the wall of a bar by an elastic cord and then required to run (sometimes for a drink) towards the other end of the room. Barfly jumping is stranger again: a participant in a velcro bodysuit jumps against a velcro covered wall in an attempt to stick to it as high up as possible.

See also: crazes

PETER CHILDS

Burman, Chila Kumari

b. 1957, Liverpool

Multimedia artist

Chila Kumari Burman works with, amongst other materials, collage, paint and video. Her images question racial and female stereotypes. In the 1980s she took prints from her own body, emphasizing the breasts or genital area by adding paint or glitter, to produce images of the female form which confront the viewer. In 1985 she took part in The Thin Black Line exhibition at the Institute of Contemporary Arts, creating an installation comprising of body prints overlaid with slogans which urged women to 'Reclaim Our Bodies'. In her 'auto-portraits' she adopts a number of Western and Asian identities, which examine the roles of women in both cultures, and she regularly includes autobiographical elements in her work.

LUCINDA TOWLER

Byker Housing

The Byker Housing project in Newcastle (1968) was a pioneering example of community architecture. It was designed by Ralph Erskine (b. 1914), a Swedish-based Scottish architect who believed that potential users of buildings should be consulted at the design stage. In order to establish direct contact with the future residents, Erskine established an office in the area earmarked for demolition and renewal. Local residents were encouraged to visit the design team during the sketch planning and detail design stages. Regular formal liaison and progress meetings between tenants and architects were also held. The project office effectively served as a local community centre. The new housing produced by this consultation process is uncompromisingly modern, mostly low-rise, informally planned, and built with traditional materials.

See also: housing

JIM HUNTER

C

cable and satellite

Since the early 1980s, the emergence of cable and satellite broadcasting has triggered a process of change in the structure of British broadcasting. As alternative programme distribution technologies to terrestrial broadcasting, cable and satellite have increasingly enabled transnational corporations to challenge the monopoly position traditionally held by Britain's existing public service television broadcasters.

The concept of the provision of broadcast services by cable and satellite is not new. Underground cable networks have existed in this country since the 1930s, later adapted for the delivery of television signals to areas with poor atmospheric reception. Satellites have been used for the exchange of live television broadcasts between nations since the USA launched the first commercial communications satellite in 1965. Both systems have undergone adaptive technological improvements since, gradually becoming economically viable alternatives to terrestrial broadcasting. In satellite broadcasting, signals are beamed from ground stations to geostationary communications satellites and reflected by them to receiving stations which relay the signals to receiving dishes or antennae. Cable or CATV (Community Aerial Television) involves the distribution of television signals to subscribers' homes from shared community satellite stations, as opposed to from the free-space radiation of signals. This involves the use of specialized low-loss coaxial and optical fibre cables which can carry high numbers of channels in multiplexed form.

It was not until the early 1980s that the British government began to investigate cable and satellite as a means of introducing competition to domestic broadcasting, a move symptomatic of the free enterprise ideology that characterized the simultaneous reform of other service industries, such as gas and electricity. In 1981 the Conservative government formed the Information Technology Advisory Panel (ITAP) to promote the development of cable networks throughout Britain, providing distribution services to be operated by private companies. The franchise for direct broadcasting by satellite (DBS) was granted in 1986. The race to secure programme transmission was finally won in 1990 by Rupert Murdoch's Sky, after a series of financial setbacks had forced its sole competitor, British Satellite Broadcasting (BSB), into a merger (see **BSkyB**).

The advance of cable and satellite in this country has been piecemeal, held up by a complex political debate centred upon issues of quality and choice. Projections of a fully commercialized communications marketplace remain polarized: it is seen on the one hand as facilitating consumer choice, and on the other as inevitably resulting in the destruction of television's social purpose to educate and inform as well as to entertain.

MATTHEW GRICE

Caine, Michael

b. Deptford, London, 1933

Actor

Michael Caine (born Maurice Micklewhite) is regarded as the most successful of the breed of

English film actors that came to prominence in the mid-1960s. The idea of working-class actors being major stars was new to the industry, and along with others such as Terence Stamp, David Hemmings and Albert Finney, Caine personified the shift in class cultures within the arts. Making his name in the films *Zulu* (1964), *The Ipcress File* (1965) and *Alfie* (1966), Caine moved to Hollywood, where he starred in numerous blockbusters. He received an Oscar for his role in Woody Allen's *Hannah and her Sisters* (1986), and has since returned to live in Britain.

SAM JOHNSTONE

Campaign for Press and Broadcasting Freedom

The CPBF was formed in 1979 as a broad-based organization that campaigns for a democratic and accountable media. The term is widely defined including the traditional press and broadcast media but also extending to **cable and satellite** and newer forms of information dissemination. It argues in favour of diversity and plurality rather than established concepts of impartiality and balance in broadcasting and objectivity in newspapers. At the heart of its programme in relation to broadcasting is a commitment to the concept of public service broadcasting, which the CPBF argues should be extended to all broadcast output. As an unfunded pressure group, it relies on subscriptions and donations from its members (approximately 1,500) and affiliated groups such as trade unions and other supportive groups. The CPBF have centred their campaign on the right to reply, media ownership and journalistic standards and ethics, although specific campaigns have also been launched in areas as diverse as racism and democracy. In addition to producing literature, books and other material, CPBF also publishes a bi-monthly magazine *Free Press* which provides excellent updates and commentary on related issues. As part of its campaign to monitor press coverage in election years, CPBF encourage members to take part in 'Electionwatch'. The Campaign's view is that the media should reflect diversity and not be dominated by any single party or view.

The upshot of much of the research and dissemination of information by the CPBF is to provoke debate and discussion, and it has achieved some success in this way via lobbying activities. Another crucial part of CPBF activities has been raising awareness by holding conferences on topical issues; for example a 1997 conference on racism in the media to tie in with the European Year against Racism. The Campaign is crucially aware of the importance of technological change to the distribution of material through the 'information superhighway', and it has produced a Media Manifesto, *21st Century Media: Shaping the Democratic Vision*.

See also: censorship; libel, defamation and privacy

Further reading

Williams, G. (1996) *Britain's Media: How They are Related* (available from CPBF, this provides an excellent analysis of 'the media revolution' and useful discussion on areas such as media control and ownership).

GUY OSBORN
STEVE GREENFIELD

campaigns

In the 1980s and 1990s, people who refuse to accept the entire agenda of a particular political party have focused instead on single issues. Organizations such as Greenpeace, Friends of the Earth and various campaigns to free those unjustly imprisoned (the Birmingham Six, the Guildford Four) have benefited from this trend. Lobbyists for particular campaigns have used sophisticated advertising methods, including t-shirts and narrowly targeted television and newspaper advertisements. Slogans like 'meat is murder' and 'furs are worn by beautiful animals and ugly people' placed on lapel badges and bumper stickers have created a climate of vegetarianism which has virtually eliminated the fur trade and produced 'vegetarian' (i.e. synthetic) Doc Martens boots.

See also: Band Aid

MIKE STORRY

car boot sales

Car boot sales, along with garage sales and attic sales, as forms of private selling are a phenomenon of recent years and reflect a number of economic and social trends and cultural practices. Jumble sales have traditionally been held in, for example, church halls and involved a recycling of clothes from the better-off to the less well-off. Proceeds were given to the owner or user of the premises: church, Scout or Guide group and so on. However, jumble sales, though very cheap (a bag may commonly be filled with clothes for 50 pence during the last hour), acquired a reputation as 'un-chic' affairs where one had to elbow aside competing purchasers and where a careful watch was kept for thieves. They thrived during periods of recession such as 1990–1, but are now less common than formerly.

With increasing affluence, people turned to 'attic' sales which were still held for charitable ends. People would pay £5 to a church or YMCA to rent a table in a hall. Proceeds of sales of general goods and bric-a-brac would be kept by the vendors, and the quality of goods on offer would be much higher than at jumble sales. They were a way for the middle classes to dispose of goods they would otherwise have to advertise or take to the tip. Garage sales tended to focus on the sale of household goods. They are the equivalent of US 'yard sales', but in Britain are nothing like as prevalent.

Car boot sales (akin to US 'flea markets') have become the predominant means of private selling. People rent space outdoors, often from a commercial provider, and sell household goods. At some huge regular car boot sales, a large turnover of money is involved and the police (at the behest of local retailers) have sought to intervene to prevent new goods from being sold. Local authorities have often banned regular car boot sales on the grounds that they cause parking problems and annoy local residents.

Supporters suggest that these sales form a cultural space, which is not so much about money as exchange. They fill a void on Sunday mornings which used to be taken up with churchgoing, and provide a forum for healthy socializing. Any attempts to control and regulate these events are seen as unhealthy and reflect an increasing tendency towards surveillance of the population at large, and are an attempt to criminalize gatherings which prior to the Criminal Justice Act (1994) would have been perfectly legal.

MIKE STORRY

Cardiff Bay Opera House

Planned as the centrepiece of the Cardiff Bay redevelopment, the Cardiff Opera House was the subject of an international design competition in 1994. Against competition from Norman Foster (see **Foster Associates**) of Britain and Rafael Moneo of Spain, amongst others, the Iraqi-born Zaha Hadid won. Her spectacular proposal, which she described as a 'crystal necklace', was a severe, modernist, largely glass structure overlooking the bay. The design was widely praised by the architectural profession, but a local media campaign against the building coupled with hesitant support from local government led to the rejection of the winning design in 1995, and the virtual collapse of the project. A 'millennium centre' by a different architect was later proposed for the site.

See also: modernism

RICHARD J. WILLIAMS

Carnaby Street

During the late 1950s and early 1960s, Carnaby Street, located in London's Soho district, was transformed when a group of 'youthquake' fashion designers, including John Stephen, Sally Tuffin and Marion Foale, were attracted there by the combination of low rents and West End location. Carnaby Street rapidly became both stage and centre for the image conscious **mods** and the growing metropolitan gay culture. Reciprocally, this combined spending power attracted increasing numbers of designer retailers, notably Ian Gray's Gear Boutique and John Michael's Mod Shop. By the mid-1960s Carnaby Street, now popularly named 'Peacock Alley', had become an internationally recognized symbol of 'swinging London'.

See also: fashion (1960s)

Further reading

Cohn, N. (1971) *Today There Are No Gentlemen*, London: George Weidenfeld & Nicholson.

MARK DOUGLAS

Carr, E.H.

b. 1892, London; d. 1982, Cambridge

Journalist and historian

Edward Hallett Carr was variously a historian, diplomat, journalist and essayist. After studying at Cambridge he worked in the Foreign Office from 1916 to 1936, when he took up a professorship at Aberystwyth. His major publication of this period was *The Twenty Years Crisis 1919–1939: An Introduction to the Study of International Relations* (1939), in which he rejected the 'harmony of interests' philosophy for the view that international diplomacy is a matter of hard bargaining over contrary interests. This was followed by a period (1941–6) as assistant editor of *The Times*, during which he advocated cooperation with the Soviet Union, which had by now been his major research interest for thirty years. His masterpiece was *A History of Soviet Russia*, published in fourteen volumes from 1950 to 1978. Most famously, he argued in *What is History?* (his 1961 Cambridge lectures) that history is the product of not the past but of historians, who are shaped by their own society. When he died he was part way through a history of the Communist International.

See also: history; Hobsbawm, Eric; Taylor, A.J.P.

MIKE STORRY

Carry On films

A series of thirty films, produced over five decades, the Carry On films were the brainchild of producer Peter Rogers and director Gerald Thomas. The films were essentially bawdy vignettes of English life, based around situations encompassing work, history or film parody.

The first in the series was *Carry On Sergeant*, which started life as a straight film adaptation of R.F. Delderfield's *The Bull Boys*. Thomas and Rogers were well acquainted with English cinematic humour; both were involved with the Doctor series of movies, adapted from the books by Richard Gordon. They adapted Delderfield's work in a similar fashion, and the Carry On series was born. Although not as ribald as later efforts, the film was so successful that the duo quickly embarked on producing a follow up, this time a humorous swipe at the National Health Service, called *Carry On Nurse*. The initial films owed much to the tradition of gentle British film **comedies**, and it was not until 1965 and the production of *Carry On Cleo* (a parody of the Burton/Taylor *Cleopatra* epic), that the series gained its saucy label. There followed twenty films of riotous slapstick, seaside postcard type jokes and definitive vulgar humour.

Appeals were made to the American market by filming in colour, and in the fourteenth film *Follow that Camel*, the use of Phil Silvers, the popular American comedian who played Sergeant Bilko. This, unfortunately for the production team, did not work, and the Carry On series still has only a cult following in the USA. The question of star names never bothered the producers again. The cast for each film was repertory based, with no star billing given to any of the main players. The series created star names, including Sid James, Kenneth Williams, Charles Hawtrey (all of whom were fairly well-known anyway) and Barbara Windsor, and these actors portrayed similar characters in all their appearances: James became the 'archetypal dirty old man', Williams a prissy know-all, Hawtrey a hapless, slightly camp innocent. The characters became associated with the actor, and it is no coincidence that in later films, the characters usually bore the actor's Christian name.

The final film in the series was *Carry on Columbus* (1992), a misguided attempt to recreate the heyday of the Carry Ons, but with the majority of the original cast dead, the film floundered, receiving terrible reviews. The death of Thomas in 1995 meant that no other Carry On films would be made.

See also: comedies; comedy on television; situation comedy

SAM JOHNSTONE

cars

Cars in Britain are not as culturally prized as in the USA. However, image and aspiration prevail over need. More four-wheel-drive vehicles are sold per capita in urban centres (where this capacity is least necessary) than in the country at large. Television advertisements use backgrounds which 'sell by association': Range Rovers are shown negotiating rugged terrain, Fiats drive round tortuous cobbled streets in small Continental towns. Often no other traffic is present. The advertisements sell an illusion of individual exploration and freedom, ignoring real-life traffic jams and the fact that the backdrops shown are usually under threat from motor vehicles. Friends of the Earth is virtually the only organization opposed to an unlimited increase in car ownership (see **Friends of the Earth and Greenpeace**).

See also: motor racing

MIKE STORRY

cartoons and puppetry

One of the great growth areas in television has been cartoons and puppetry. American television has clearly been influential, with *Sesame Street* and *The Simpsons*, especially as children and teenagers watch more television than adults and programme makers have been able to 'follow the age curve' by supplying new shows to growing audiences. Research from the Independent Television Commission in 1996 showed children watching ninety minutes more television per week than three years previously. Many of the ideas have originated in Britain: Jim Henson's *Muppet Show* was based in London, *Super Ted* started on **S4C**, and *Spitting Image* and Nick **Park**'s Wallace and Grommit are entirely home grown.

Puppetry developed from crude beginnings on television with *Bill and Ben the Flowerpot Men*, the

Woodentops, *Muffin the Mule* and Harry Corbett's *Sooty Show*. But none of these achieved the audience reached in the 1970s by Ivan Owen's Basil Brush. Twelve million viewers made him a national figure. The Queen, Princess Anne and James Callaghan, the prime minister, were said to be fans. He appeared regularly with Derek Fowlds (Sir Humphrey's sidekick in the situation comedy *Yes, Minister*) and with Sir Michael Hordern, breaking a convention that puppets and humans don't mix, and is set to reappear on satellite television.

One of the most successful puppet series of recent years has been *Spitting Image*. It is credited with destroying the political fortunes of the Liberal Party with its puppets of the two Davids, Owen and Steel, and its scathing representation of the monarchy has undoubtedly influenced as well as reflected popular opinion. *Teletubbies* would appear to be in the crude mode of *Bill and Ben*, but shrewd marketing has ensured its export and financial success.

Since 1992, three cartoon channels primarily aimed at children have been launched: The Cartoon Network, Nickelodeon and the Disney Channel. These can move markets: in 1996, British supermarket chains claimed that spinach sales in Britain doubled for two years in a row, due to a rerun of Popeye cartoons on the BBC. The Cartoon Network now commands 30 percent of all television watched by children aged between two and nine.

The most striking cartoon series have come to television via **animation**. Terry Gilliam's Monty Python animations have given way to those of Nick Park, who won Oscars for his works *The Wrong Trousers* and *A Close Shave* with the characters Wallace and Grommit. These cartoons are influenced by the (over)complex inventions of Heath Robinson.

See also: television, children's

MIKE STORRY

cash and carry

The changes in contemporary shopping, particularly for food, are not purely a matter of shifts from small retail units to supermarkets. The retail customer may select one of the major bulk buying outlets for cheap products, and most of the latter generally advertise a competitive price system of some form. This has led in some areas to the demise of local 'corner shops', which find it difficult to compete on price and range with their super-market rivals. A clear area where the small shop could previously outperform was in terms of their longer opening hours, but with the advent of late-night shopping and more lately the twenty-four-hour supermarket, this advantage has been largely lost. The small shops and indeed social clubs rely on 'cash and carry' businesses for supplies, where goods may be bought in bulk with little packaging or frills and at lower cost. The mark-up between the cash and carry price and subsequent retail price provided the element of profit for the small shopkeeper. The concept of cash and carry shopping has now spread into the retail market, with some major retail stores adopting a more Spartan approach to shelving and packaging in order to pass on price savings.

A significant further example of this phenom-enon has been the use by British daytrippers of the vast French hypermarkets which have sprung up close to the French ports. Because of differing national rates of duty on alcohol and a reassess-ment of duty-free allowances in the UK, British shoppers can enjoy extremely significant price savings over domestic purchases even on dis-counted prices at large retailers. Changes in domestic law have enabled purchases to be limited only by the notion that goods purchased must be for personal use; selling goods on remains unlawful, although there is much anecdotal evidence that this does in fact occur. This has not deterred the illicit trade in cheap alcohol and the emergence of 'booze cruises' designed to take advantage of the cheaper continental 'cash and carry' prices, a situation that is sure to continue with the advent of the Eurotunnel and an increase in the frequency of ferry channel crossings. The consequences for the British brewing and retail market in alcohol have been significant, with an increasing number of public house closures particularly in areas around ports. This also led to a legal challenge by one brewery over the Government's refusal to synchro-nize duty rates.

See also: cross-Channel shopping; supermarkets and malls

GUY OSBORN
STEVE GREENFIELD

catalogue shops

Argos is the leading catalogue store chain in Britain, and third in the world behind the American Best Products and Service Merchandise Groups. Argos has over 430 stores throughout Britain and the Republic of Ireland. It is estimated that around seven out of ten British households have a copy of the Argos catalogue. It is also the owner of Britain's leading **promotions** and incentive company, Argos Business Solutions. Argos was launched in 1973 by Richard Tompkins of the Green Shield Trading Stamp company, which he initiated in 1958. Tompkins recognized that trading stamps had a limited public appeal and launched Argos as a diversification, having imported the idea from the USA, where catalogue shopping was flourishing.

When Argos was launched, catalogue shopping referred to **mail order**. Argos offered the consumer all the benefits of browsing through a catalogue at home but coupled this with the immediacy of high street stores and instant purchasing. The Argos concept caught the nation's imagination. Even in a time of national inflation, a three-day week and a shortage of raw materials and finished goods, it became an immediate and phenomenal success. In 1979, partly as a result of the failing health of Tompkins, Argos was acquired by British and American Tobacco for £35million. Over the next eleven years the number of stores quickly increased from 91 to 251 and sales rose from £113 million in 1979 to £818 million by the end of 1989. Also, since it began, Argos has been noted for its innovative use of information technology. It is Britain's leading retailer in many product areas, such as toys and small electrical appliances, and has a significant market share in the sale of jewellery, sports equipment and do-it-yourself products. It has dominated the field since it first began and only one other company, Index Limited, which started trading in the late 1980s, has been successful in securing a share of the market. Ultimately, Argos and other similar catalogue shops are signifiers of the symptomatic immediate gratification which the late 1990s consumer demanded.

See also: mail order

FATIMA FERNANDES

Catholicism

The Second Vatican Council (1962–5) opened the Roman Catholic church to the modern world, in Britain as elsewhere. The liturgy was reformed, Latin was thrown out and the vernacular was introduced (fully from 1967). The laity was encouraged to participate in all aspects of church life, in worship and organization. Parish councils were set up and house masses introduced. (This involvement continues to increase as the number of priests and religious – friars, monks and nuns – decreases.) Of equal importance was a new openness to ecumenism, together with an ever-growing number of inter-marriages. These changes came at a time when the number of middle-class Catholics was increasing, with more of them entering higher education and the professions. As a result, British Catholics became more involved and influential in mainstream culture, and more knowledgeable and enquiring of their faith and church. The high point of these developments was the Liverpool National Pastoral Congress in 1980, which provided a model for a semi-democratic church, open to the possibility of married and women priests.

However, nothing came of the Congress, and from the mid-1960s the Catholic church, like other denominations, was in numerical decline. The reasons for this are complex, but a defining moment was Pope Paul VI's encyclical *Humanae Vitae* (1968), which extolled married life and accepted birth control, but condemned the use of artificial contraceptives. As a result of this and other social and cultural developments (increasing affluence, consumerism and the women's liberation movement), an ever-growing number of Catholics 'lapsed'; those that remained increasingly practised an internal dissent – in the bedroom and elsewhere. David Lodge provided the quintessential account of these changes in his novel *How Far Can You Go?* (1980).

Nevertheless, British Catholicism has not suffered the divisions between episcopacy and laity evident in other European countries, especially Germany and Holland. With the appointment of the Benedictine monk Basil Hume as Archbishop of Westminster in 1976, Catholicism became increasingly respected and respectable, and in the 1990s, even fashionable. It also became a refuge for Anglo-Catholics fleeing **women priests** in the **Anglican Church**. Catholic sensibilities have been evident in politics (Norman St John Stevas, Shirley Williams), literature (Anthony Burgess, Muriel Spark) and film (Terence **Davies**, Ken **Russell**).

Further reading

Hastings, A. (1991) *A History of English Christianity 1920–1990*, London: SCM Press (a readable and judicious account that situates Catholicism in the wider Christian world).

GERARD LOUGHLIN

Caton-Jones, Michael

b. 1958, Broxburn

Film-maker

Michael Caton-Jones has become known for his probing films about American life. His first film, *Scandal*, an account of the Profumo affair, an Establishment sexual imbroglio which pre-occupied courts and tabloids in the 1960s. The film featured John Hurt as Stephen Ward, osteopath to the Establishment, and Joanne Whalley-Kilmer as Christine Keeler, the eighteen-year-old at the centre of the affair. Ian McKellen, John Hurt, Leslie Phillips and Britt Ekland also appeared. His Scottish-American film, *Rob Roy* (1995), with Liam Neeson, Jessica Lange and John Hurt, showed his sure commercial touch through its appeal to an American audience. Other films are *This Boy's Life* (USA 1992) and *The Day of the Jackal* (1997).

MIKE STORRY

CBI

The CBI (Confederation of British Industry) was formed in 1965 by a merger of the three main employers' associations to represent business interests. It is financed by business, and in 1997 represented around 250,000 members. It acts as a pressure group for its members through the administration. It was particularly influential in the era of government planning in the economy, as the voice of industry on corporatist bodies. The chief executive of the CBI is the Director General, and the democratically elected Council is its governing body. The most pressing concerns facing the CBI in the 1990s were the proposed single European currency, to which it gave qualified support, and the European Social Chapter and working time directive, to which it was opposed.

See also: corporatism; corruption in the City; pressure groups; trade unions

COLIN WILLIAMS

Celtic tradition

The Celtic people probably migrated to the British Isles from a common Indo-European homeland somewhere in eastern Europe. The traditional Celtic nations are Alba (Scotland), Breizh (Brittany, or Gaul), Cymru (Wales), Eire (Ireland), Galatia (northern Spain), Kernow (Cornwall), Mannin (Isle of Man) and Britain. Celtic traditionalists are keen to reconnect or 'ground' themselves in history. Hence there has been a ready audience for the wealth of recent material produced from Celtic roots, such as Irish cultural products from musicians such as Enya and the Chieftains to films like Neil Jordan's *The Crying Game* and *The Commitments* and novels like Roddy Doyle's *Paddy Clark Ha Ha.* and Patrick McCabe's *The Butcher's Boy.*

See also: Irish communities

MIKE STORRY

censorship

To censor is to suppress communication that is deemed destructive of the common good. Thus censorship is usually associated with the exercise of authority over individuals. In Western society the term dates back to ancient Rome, where control over the moral character of the community was deemed an essential role of government. In conducting the census, the patrician censor excluded from public rights those whose beliefs did not meet the needs of the regime. In modern usage the concept has become rather more complex, seen as central to the well-being of the individual and the community but also synonymous with the abuse of power of governments over individuals.

There are two related sets of justifications which structure modern manifestations of censorship. The first set of concerns is embodied in legislation such as the UK Official Secrets Act, a mechanism for safeguarding not only military secrecy but also the everyday running of vital state services. Here the focus of censorship is political; it is a pre-emptive and punitive legislative framework designed to facilitate the everyday governance of the community, through the establishing of a set of proscribed rules and a framework for punishing those who contravene them.

Other forms are more educational in nature, and have to do with moulding the character and morality of people. This type of censorship takes many forms. For example, contemporary concerns regarding the role of the media are expressed in laws such as defamation, which prohibits speech or writing designed to injure or offend, and obscenity, which prohibits that which is likely to deprave or corrupt (especially children). Legislation of this kind gives rise to an additional form of censorship, namely self-censorship, the act of restraining one's expression for fear of external suppression.

The concept of censorship carries a negative charge, reflecting the centrality of the status of the individual in prevailing Western notions of liberal democracy. The premise of John Milton's *Areopagita*, a tract published in 1644 denouncing the insidious prohibition of press freedom by the state, is re-echoed in contemporary debates concerning free expression. The infamous *Spycatcher* case of 1987 marked a triumph of free speech over state censorship; a government injunction preventing the publication of sensitive material was overturned in the High Court. The emergence of new systems of communication and information distribution has further revived discussions of the proper role of censorship, with concerns focused upon the free exchange of data facilitated by new technologies.

See also: Campaign for Press and Broadcasting Freedom

Further reading

Kelly, S. (1978) *Access Denied*, Beverly Hills, CA: Sage.

MATTHEW GRICE

ceramics

The ceramics most people are familiar with is commercial and is therefore functional rather than aesthetic/sculptural. This industry is dominated by Staffordshire companies including Wedgwood. Although these are technologically innovative, advances in design are fewer than in the nineteenth century. For example, at Josiah Wedgwood's Etruria factory, modellers and artists created a series of fine figures and the firm produced outstanding wares in creamware, jasperware and Parian.

Contemporary 'non-commercial' craft ceramics, on the other hand, very often sees itself as a poor relation to the fine arts, in terms of its profile in education, its funding from government and its public esteem. It has gone through the doldrums, and there is a consensus that the 1980s were more dynamic than the 1990s. However, where exhibitors can provide the space, the interest is there. For example, in 1993 the Ceramic Contemporaries exhibition of work by art school students and recent graduates at the Victoria and Albert Museum (V&A) was visited by 12,000 people.

Arguably, the two major institutional influences on British ceramics are the V&A and the Craft Council, though the former is better known to the public than the latter. For generations, the V&A has been the place to visit for an overview of the history of ceramics from Britain and abroad.

Under its Chief Curator of Ceramics and Glass, Oliver Watson, the V&A Ceramics department has 70,000 objects in its care. However, despite its crucial responsibility, the V&A only has £12,000 a year to spend on acquisitions (aside from some private help) and this has to cover the fields of ceramics, glass, stained glass and plastic. Hence it will always be a record of ceramics from the past rather than a determinant of the direction of the contemporary.

The Crafts Council, on the other hand (which has an annual budget of £3.2m), attempts to fund individual potters working in the here and now. It disbursed £175,000 to individuals setting up as potters in 1996–7. By deft administrative manoeuvring, it has managed not to be subsumed into the **Arts Council**, but ceramists complain that it lacks the creative vision to supply leadership to the field of ceramics. Its current remit controversially includes the promotion of fashion.

As regards individual potters, perhaps the best known and most influential figure this century has been Bernard Leach. The major exhibition 'Bernard Leach – Potter and Artist' toured six Japanese museums and ended at the Craft Council in 1998. Leach studied at two art schools in London and went to Japan in 1911, and 'discovered' pottery as a medium capable of expressing universal values. On his return to England he established the Leach Pottery at St Ives, Cornwall. His essay 'Towards a Standard' and *A Potter's Book* were well regarded for the rigour and philosophical basis on which they sought to place ceramics, and they became highly influential. Practitioners became more aware of the philosophies behind the works they were producing. Leach applied Zen to the practice of the craft. History has not been kind to his ideas in the sense that the dispersal of the 'stable self' and 'grand narratives' has empowered the marginalized, and he can thus now sound patriarchal and authoritarian. However a potter like Terry Bell-Hughes who feels that his own work is about the reconciliation of conflicting ideas of modernism and contemporary rapid change (that is about the self-conscious rather than the un-self-conscious) nevertheless acknowledges Leach's influence and pays tribute to his opening up of British ceramics to an oriental vision. After some uncertainty about the Leach Pottery in St Ives following the death of Janet Leach in 1997, English Heritage has designated it as a site of historic interest.

A contrasting influential figure was the German immigrant Hans Coper, whose approach was intellectual and urban where Leach's valued the instinctive, rural and natural world. Coper's work was closer to that of the modernists Brancusi and Mies Van der Rohe. His friend Dame Lucie Rie, a Viennese refugee, produced colourful, urban and sophisticated new wave vases which now achieve the highest auction prices. The influential collector Liliana L. Epstein bought her work and that of the abstract, sculptural potters Gordon Baldwin (former head of ceramics at Eton College) and Ewen Henderson (who was taught by Rie at Camberwell). Baldwin and Henderson transcended the vessel shape at a time when, in the eyes of the art market, pots were pots and when the craft-versus-fine-art controversy seemed incapable of resolution.

There are some positive straws in the wind for ceramics. The University of Sunderland has launched a £16 million scheme to develop a glassmaking facility under Dan Klein, Professor of Glass. The project includes a National Glass Centre. An example of the kind of work likely to be produced is that of Anna Norberg. She made fifty-one glass chairs, one for each day of the 1998 Sunderland Glass Season exhibition. Titled: 'I Do Not Know What It Looks Like When Someone Dies: Electric Chair', a tiny, 10.5 inch tall chair consists of glass tubing containing a glowing electric filament. When the hot filament is turned off at the end of each day, the glass shatters and the chair dies. A heap of glass accumulates around the chair's plinth. Rising British glassmakers, in cast rather than blown glass, are Colin Reid, Peter Layton, Lucien Simon and Emma Woffenden. Ceramists include Joanna Constantinidis, Morgen Hall and Edmund de Waal.

An attempt has been made to replicate the kind of arrangement common in painting galleries where artists are 'tied' to the gallery. The Barrett Marsden Gallery in Islington, under its co-founder, Taijana Marsden, formerly director of the charitable crafts organization Contemporary Applied Arts (CAA) and now a ceramics consultant to Christie's, has taken the controversial step of making London-wide exclusivity agreements with

thirteen artists, including such established names as Alison Britton and Martin Smith, head of ceramics at the Royal College of Art.

Further reading

Ceramic Review, London: The Craft Potters Association of Great Britain (the most widely circulated and authoritative journal of ceramics).

MIKE STORRY

Chadha, Gurinder

In her two best films to date, *Bhaji on the Beach* (1993) for **Channel 4** and *Rich Deceiver* (1995) for the **BBC**, Chadha has explored questions of race, ethnicity, class and community. *Bhaji on the Beach* explores problems faced by Asian women squeezed between two cultures, and to an extent victimized by both their own cultural tenets and British Asian community standards. No easy resolutions are offered and Chadha does not flaunt a particular political line, but sympathizes with the pragmatic choices of today. Based on Gillian White's literary original, Chadha's film *Rich Deceiver* concentrates more on contemporary social problems (created by the windfall of winning the lottery) and male–female relations. It also examines the role of capitalism in determining personality.

See also: diasporan film-makers

MIKE STORRY

Chamberlain, Powell and Bon

The architectural firm of Chamberlain, Powell and Bon is a partnership founded in 1952 by Peter Chamberlain, Geoffrey Powell and Christof Bon. Their prize-winning scheme for high-density housing at Golden Lane, London (1953–7) rehearsed a controversial layout involving multiple ground levels, later embodied in their plan for the Barbican, London (1957) where the loose mixture of high-rise towers and slab blocks and separate traffic and pedestrian routes, gave architectural form to postwar socialism. At Vanbrugh Park,

Greenwich (1962) houses and flats form court-yards, squares and walkways. Educational build-ings include Bousfield Primary School, London (1954–6), Birmingham University Sports Centre and the Leeds University development plan (1958). A respect for the wider context of urban design is evident in their work.

See also: municipal buildings; town planning

HILARY GRAINGER

Channel 4

Launched in 1982 under the 1980 Broadcasting Act, Channel 4 (C4) has proved itself a viable, profitable and innovative channel, albeit one that attracts controversy. C4 was created with a specific purpose, to serve minority and alternative tastes and interests and to revolutionize programme production. It was also deliberately framed to bring market disciplines to the production industry, since C4 was not to produce its own programmes, but would commission them from independent companies. Thus, the new station would bring some competition to the industry, in line with Thatcherite economics. The channel would also concentrate on education.

In many ways, C4 has been a success. The station has built up a loyal base and distinctive identity and has kept its market share at around 11 percent. However, its minority remit has not been to everyone's liking, particularly under Michael Grade: seasons of programmes about sex (the 'Red Light Zone'), homosexuality, homelessness and other challenging subjects caused right-wing critic Paul Johnson to dub Grade 'Britain's pornogra-pher-in-chief'. *Brookside* also attracted considerable controversy (notably for a lesbian kiss in 1994), as did *Lipstick on your Collar*, *Eurotrash*, *The Girlie Show* and *The Word*. Perhaps such criticism is inevitable, however, since C4's remit is for material that would not find its way onto ITV and that reflects minority tastes.

Equally, C4 has made a significant contribution towards the British film industry, backing movies like *Four Weddings and a Funeral*, and showcasing other British films that would not appeal to ITV. In the mid-1990s, C4 has also been successful in importing several American soaps and dramas such as *Friends*, *ER* and *NYPD Blue*. But C4's success also forced changes to the funding formula created by the 1990 Broadcasting Act. It was argued that C4's advertising revenue was unstable, so any shortfall below a certain level would be underwritten by the various ITV companies. However, C4's strong portfolio since then has meant the station has been penalized by the formula, since any advertising surplus is shared out amongst the ITV companies. By 1996, this was running at £60m, which Grade called a 'sick joke'.

However, 1996 also saw C4 fighting the possibility of privatization. Grade argued that C4 served a distinctive purpose that a duty to share-holders would destroy or negate, and his deter-mined campaign won the day. Grade subsequently resigned as CEO in 1997, leaving the station in a very healthy situation.

See also: Channel 4 Films; Channel 5

Further reading

McRobbie, A. (ed.) (1982) *Four on 4*, Birmingham: Birmingham West Midlands Arts.

SAM JOHNSTONE

Channel 4 Films

Channel 4, which first began broadcasting in 1982, developed its public service role through partner-ships with British Screen and the **BFI**, and commissioned many critically important films of the 1980s and 1990s, including *The Draughtsman's Contract* (1982), *Angel* (1982), *The Ploughman's Lunch* (1983), *Another Time, Another Place* (1983), *A Room With a View* (1985), *Letter to Brezhnev* (1985), *Caravaggio* (1986), *Mona Lisa* (1986), *Distant Voices, Still Lives* (1988), *Riff Raff* (1990), *Life is Sweet* (1990), *The Crying Game* (1992) and *Four Weddings and a Funeral* (1994). Films made for Channel 4 are frequently characterized by a juxtaposition be-tween perceptions of the familiar and the foreign, the domestic and the exotic. They also tend to deal with less mainstream aspects to society (for example, homosexuality in *Another Country* (1984), *My Beautiful Launderette* (1985), *Maurice* (1987) and

Prick Up Your Ears (1987)) but in a soft-focus, traditionalist way that makes the subjects palatable to mainstream audiences. In this way, the films seem to fulfil the television station's remit and raise audience consciousness but also make a commercial profit.

See also: Channel 4; Euston Films

PETER CHILDS

Channel 5

Channel 5, television broadcasting's first new terrestrial station for ten years, was set up in 1997 after several false starts. Its advent had made existing stations apprehensive, but in the first two years they have not had much to worry about. Channel 5 is a free-to-air commercial station, whose start was delayed from January to Easter by technical problems which caused poor broadcast quality. Cartoonists joked that the snow on television screens was the Channel's identifying signal. These problems continue to dog the station in some regions.

An indication of its aims, ethos and youth orientation was given by its opening on Easter Sunday, serenaded by the Spice Girls. Critics accused the station of 'dumbing down' in its search for viewers. Its schedule originally contained many American imports and its programming was low budget. It screened a new soap opera, *Family Affairs*, made in Britain but by Grundy, makers of the Australian soap *Neighbours*. This offering was panned by critics, but did secure a small following.

The station's content has turned out to be nearer to that of Sky (see **BSkyB**) than of existing terrestrial stations. It is a tabloid version of Channel 4 which covers more mainstream concerns than the latter, but has similar documentaries on, for example, royalty, current affairs and endangered species. It has a snappy style in its presentation of news, placed at 8.30 pm to scoop the other networks. Kirsty Young and Ruth England are youthful solo presenters who, innovatively, are not seen sitting at desks or consoles but move around the studio. However the content of the actual news presented is as traditional as that of the other stations.

A reflection of Channel 5's youthful target audience is that there are pop music programmes like *The Pepsi Chart* and *Dr Fox's Chart Update*. It also shows re-runs of cult series like *Prisoner: Cell Block H* in the small hours. Channel 5 sport includes more imports from America: major league baseball, shown live, the *Asian Football Show* and its late-night sports magazine programme, *Live and Dangerous*.

The channel appears to have gained viewers more at the expense of the other commercial stations than of the BBC. However, partly because of its shaky start and partly because it has so far failed to find a suitable niche for itself, many critics feel it will have to be relaunched if it is to survive.

See also: Channel 4

MIKE STORRY

CHANNEL TUNNEL *see* Nicholas Grimshaw and Partners

Channel X

Channel X is a television company headed by the independent producer Alan Marke. He is perhaps best know for bringing Jonathan Ross and *The Last Resort* to television screens in 1987. The formats of both this show and the television channel are borrowed from the USA, particularly from *Late Night with David Letterman*. This is acknowledged and is seen regretfully in some quarters as a sign of creeping Americanization of British television. Programming at Channel X is likely to become more and more like American television in trying to fill airtime with cheap chat and game shows and even soft porn. Concepts of quality and a mission to raise the level of the audience are left out of consideration.

MIKE STORRY

chaos theory

Chaos theory is a mathematical theory which describes systems whose behaviour is apparently unpredictable, but which in fact conform to long-term repetitive patterns. Weather is an example of such a system, in that it may seem unpredictable, yet it operates through a continuum of established patterns of cloud types, cold fronts and regions of high and low pressure. The unpredictability of 'chaotic' systems comes from the existence of one or more events which can follow either one path or another (a 'bifurcation'), but where very small changes in the environment can influence which path is most likely to be taken. A popular metaphor for chaos has been the concept that storms and hurricanes in the Caribbean could have been initiated by the fluttering of the wings of a butterfly in China. Apparently insignificant local events can lead to very large consequences because elements within the system are poised at bifurcations and a number of small events taking one path can bring about major changes. Change is caused by an input of energy, such as heat from the sun. Patterns develop in the behaviour of the system because it contains a limited number of components; in the case of weather these include water, air and so on. These are affected by closely defined factors: the volume of the atmosphere, area of the oceans and so on, and the results are inevitable.

One of the first analysts of chaotic systems was Ilya Prigogine, who was awarded the Nobel Prize in 1977. He founded the 'Brussels School' of mathematical thought which focused on so-called 'dissipative' systems. Unlike closed systems, where the more classical chemical and physical concepts of stability, uniformity and equilibrium dominate, dissipative systems exchange energy and matter with their surroundings.

Through interdisciplinarity, chaos analyses, which have been used mainly in biology and chemistry are now applied to economic and political events where 'unpredictable' yet repetitive patterns of booms, recessions, crashes, revolutions and political shifts occur. Chaos theory and environmentalism have also influenced the new literary-critical field in British universities of eco-criticism, which challenges postmodernism and shifts discussion back from the artificial to the natural. Moreover, in an increasingly secular world where moral absolutes and the certainties of religion have been eroded, chaos theory appeals to thinkers in the 'new' fields of literary theory and cultural studies, such as Stuart Hall or Dick Hebdidge, who seek more complicated ways of explaining the complexity of cultural or social systems.

Further reading

Prigogine, I. and Stengers, I. (1984) *Order out of Chaos: Man's New Dialogue with Nature*, London: Flamingo.

PETE SHETERLINE

CHARING CROSS *see* Terry Farrell Partnership

charities and charity shops

Traditionally, indeed legally, the qualification for charity status has involved the patronage of one or more of four areas; the advancement of education, the relief of poverty, the advancement of religion, or other purposes beneficial to the community. These principles were set out in 1891 and, although it is now accepted that charitable objectives alter over time, these four basic areas remain the foundations of most charitable institutions. Recent moves have suggested a widening of the definition to embrace some small shops and post offices in order to provide the benefits of charitable status and preserve essential services for rural villages: 'The key to charity law is public benefit. ... If rural communities can demonstrate that village shops play a vital part in an area of social and economic deprivation, we would be willing to consider registration of the organization promoting the package as charity' (*Framework for the Review of the Register of Charities* 1998).

Charity has become linked with popular culture via a number of routes. Perhaps the most popular manifestation of 'charity consciousness' was seen with the **Band Aid** phenomenon, although this was followed by a number of other attempts to make pop stars/glitterati seem more compassionate by supporting charitable causes. Usually these have focused on responses to particular events such as the tragedies at Dunblane (a reworking of the Bob Dylan song 'Knockin' on Heaven's Door') and the Bradford City Football Ground fire (as a response to that disaster, 'Ferry Cross the Mersey', the most famous of all football anthems, was re-recorded by Gerry Marsden from Gerry and the Pacemakers, along with The Crowd, an all-star backing group). Perhaps the most successful example of this in terms of critical acclaim was the *Help* CD which was put out under the auspices of the Warchild charity. Warchild was set up by two film makers, Bill Leeson and David Wilson, after they witnessed the plight of children caught up in the war in former Yugoslavia and *Help* included works by artists including The Manic Street Preachers, Oasis, Blur, Paul McCartney, Brian Eno, Radiohead, Portishead and Massive Attack.

While many of these popular developments may have begun as a charitable response, increasingly they came to be seen by many as a more cynical exploitation of the public and charity became perceived by some as a means of selling product (see for example the response of Leeds anarchists Chumbawumba, who, twelve years before their Warholian fifteen minutes of fame on the back of 'Tubthumping' (1997), released an LP entitled *Pictures of Starving Children Sell Records*). Notwithstanding this, the popular music/charity crossovers and in particular the Band Aid phenomenon have undoubtedly increased public consciousness of the plight of charities at a time when successive governments have attempted to shift the burden of charitable donations away from the state and onto the whim of the individual.

Every high street now contains its share of charity shops offering mainly second-hand but also new goods. The benefits for charities are that shops provide an outlet for goods donated by the public and are staffed by volunteers; costs are thus minimized. A key factor in the rise of charity shops has been the availability of retail units in the high street, caused in part by the shift towards out-of-town shopping facilities. The revenue from such shops should not be underestimated. In 1993–4 the Oxfam shops raised over £17m, which amounted to more than 25 percent of the charity's total income. The original Oxfam shop was established in 1947, in Broad Street, Oxford, acting as a sorting centre for clothing donated for a national 'Appeal for Europe'. The spin-off was to establish a gift shop which resold the donated goods that were of no direct use to those overseas; in its first full financial year, the shop raised £650. In 1960 a second shop was opened, and in the following year the two shops raised a combined total of £38,695. By 1971 Oxfam had 310 shops operating, with the number rising to over 850 in the 1990s; there are now specialist furniture and book shops. A further approach has been to develop the sales of new products (such as nuts, jams, coffees, teas and hand-crafted goods such as baskets and ceramics) on the basis of the Fair Trade programme with Third World producers. Oxfam has clearly followed retailing and marketing trends, seeking to maintain its position as brand leader against increasing competition from other charities which have similarly sought to exploit the retail possibilities.

A further link between charity and popular culture can be seen in the way in which the perception of charity shops changed and became fashionable when pop music icons such as Morrissey (once of Mancunian legends The Smiths) and Jarvis Cocker (Pulp) flaunted the fact that they shopped for many of their clothes at charity shops, beginning what might be called an 'Oxfam chic' that was adopted by students and fashion victims throughout the country. This has now been exploited by the charity, which has started to extract the more sought-after clothes and sell these in a specialist outlet, following the examples of books and furniture.

See also: Band Aid

Further reading

Raphael, T. and Roll, J. (1984) *Carrying the Can: Charity and the Welfare State*, London: London Family Welfare Association.

GUY OSBORN
STEVE GREENFIELD

Charter 88

By the end of the 1980s, concern was growing over the perceived erosion of civil liberties under the Thatcher administration and the inadequacies of Britain's unwritten constitution. Consequently, Charter 88 was founded with the support of many prominent intellectuals in 1988, a date symbolically significant as the tricentennial of Britain's 'Glorious

Revolution'. This pressure group seeks a written constitution to redress the balance of power between the executive and the citizen. Charter 88 calls for a Bill of Rights to guarantee the civil liberties of the individual, freedom of information and open government, an electoral system of proportional representation and an independent, reformed judiciary. Executive dominance would be further constrained by distribution of power to local and regional levels and a democratic, reformed second chamber of government.

See also: democracy; pressure groups

COLIN WILLIAMS

Chelsom, Peter

b. 1956, Blackpool

Actor and film-maker

Peter Chelsom is an English actor and screenwriter as well as director. He first started acting in 1978 after studying at the Central School of Speech and Drama. His directorial debut was *Hear My Song* (1991), starring Adrian Dunbar and Tara Fitzgerald, followed by *Funny Bones* (1995), with Lee Evans and Jerry Lewis, both of which he co-wrote. His films are gentle comedies, rooted in music hall and popular entertainment, but distinctively filmed with an equal emphasis on slapstick and pathos. To some they seem nostalgic, but the films are perhaps unique in their dissection of continuities and influences across generations. His new Miramax film in 1998 was *The Mighty.*

PETER CHILDS

Child Support Agency

The Child Support Agency was established at six centres – Belfast, Birkenhead, Falkirk, Dudley, Hastings and Plymouth – in 1993. It aims to help single parents secure child maintenance payments from their (often absent) partners. There was widespread informed criticism of its approach: it was seen as government 'interference' in people's private lives, biased against men, unworkable

because of its mountainous caseload, and setting aside previously agreed court settlements. The agency went through turmoil under three directors in its first four years. In 1997 the National Audit Office refused to accept its annual accounts because of the high level of mistakes, and the Child Poverty Action Group said it was impoverishing families. In 1998, Labour proposed revisions that would give male parents who were not husbands similar rights, and also financial responsibilities, to fathers married to their children's mothers.

See also: poverty, families and; single parents

MIKE STORRY

childbirth

Childbirth and its management have been subject to radically different arguments since the 1960s, with one argument coming from the medical community and a second coming from women. The principal source of controversy has been the issue of defining what is best for women during childbirth, with, on the one hand, a medical view of the paramount need to establish maximum safety, and on the other hand, a contention about the need to secure circumstances for women that reflect the totality of physical, psychological and social aspects of childbirth. The dominant voice in the care of pregnant women, represented by the Royal College of Obstetricians and Gynaecologists, consistently argued before official review committees, from the Cranbrook Committee in 1959 to the Short Committee in 1984, that birth in hospital, especially birth in consultant-led units, would ensure the greatest safety for women and babies.

The counter-argument began with two women-led organizations, the Association for Improvements in Maternity Services (1960), a platform for exposing poor, unevaluated hospital care, and the National Childbirth Trust (1961), which focused on preparing women to enjoy childbearing, according to individual needs and expectations. Both promoted the value of a woman's control of her own birth situation. Their work was strengthened by Sheila Kitzinger, doyenne of the British childbirth movement, who emphasized in many books that the highly individual nature of birth was disrupted by a medical policy of increasing technological intervention.

The lack of a sound evaluative basis for the medical model of birth led to reconsiderations within the medical community. A 1987 report from the National Perinatal Epidemiological Unit challenged the notion that hospitalized birth was responsible for the drop in perinatal deaths. In 1992, the Winterton Parliamentary Committee concluded that the medical model of birth should no longer drive maternity services. The 1993 government publication, *Changing Childbirth*, accepted the need for unbiased information about maternity services and choice for women, in deciding their preferred maternity care and place of birth.

See also: family planning

Further reading

Department of Health (1993) *Changing Childbirth*, London: HMSO (current government policy on maternity care).

Kitzinger, Sheila (1987) *The Experience of Childbirth*, 5th edn, Harmondsworth: Penguin (remains the essential text for women).

JO MURPHY-LAWLESS

Chinese communities

Reliable and accurate numbers for ethnic Chinese living in the UK are notoriously difficult to come by, as the community is scattered and widely dispersed and contact with local government structures is low. However, most surveys, including the mid-1980s report on the British Chinese community by the Home Office, put the figure at over 100,000 with the heaviest concentrations in London, Manchester, Liverpool, Glasgow, Edinburgh, Birmingham and Cardiff. Despite the fact that this is one of the largest ethnic groups in the UK (fully one percent of the London population, for instance), the figure is small when one considers the size of the native Chinese population and the long colonial relationship between the two countries.

Chinese people first began to arrive in the UK in

the nineteenth century as seafarers (employed at a fraction of the cost of non-Chinese) on boats plying their trade mainly between the major port cities of southern China (Canton and Hong Kong) and London, Liverpool and Bristol. Many Chinese escaped the harsh conditions of life at sea by staying on at British ports when their ships sailed. Liverpool claims to have the oldest Chinatown in Europe following the founding, after the Opium Wars, of the Blue Funnel Line and the 'first direct steamship link between Britain and China'. Small numbers of Chinese settled in the South Docks area of Liverpool around Cleveland Square and Pitt Street and in the Limehouse area of London, and established small service businesses mainly for the transient Chinese seafaring population. Initially the immigrant Chinese were known for their candle-making, boarding houses and launderettes, which could be set up with little capital in terraced houses and run as a family business. Numbers fluctuated with political events in China and Britain and reached a peak during the Second World War.

Because they were concentrated around the docks, the Second World War wiped out much of the original Chinatowns in London, Liverpool and other major cities. In the postwar period the profile and location of Chinese communities began to change. Large numbers of people from the New Territories of Hong Kong (who currently make up about 90 percent of ethnic Chinese living in the UK) arrived and settled in the late 1950s and early 1960s after the collapse of agriculture there, and these communities were swollen by Malaysian, Singaporean and Vietnamese refugees over the next twenty years. London's Chinatown moved from Limehouse to Soho, Liverpool's from Cleveland Square to the Nelson Street area, Manchester became the second largest Chinatown in the country and much of the emphasis changed to catering and restaurants. These new Chinese helped, along with immigrants from the Indian sub-continent, to revolutionize the postwar eating habits of British people and the Chinese 'chippy' became a common sight in most of the country's city centres and suburban streets (there are over seventy Chinese restaurants in London's Soho alone). While the Cantonese (later Sichuan and Beijing) style of cooking food was imported, the sauces were made sharper and sweeter for British palates. Chinese immigrants also brought with them medical 'alternatives' – notably acupuncture – which have made significant inroads into mainstream medical practice in Britain.

Despite some second-generation Chinese entering professions like accountancy and law, the overwhelming concentration of Britain's Chinese population is in the catering trade (some 90 percent by most estimates). Their relative cultural isolation has been the subject of some speculation and is often ascribed to the cultural preferences of the Chinese themselves, in particular their reliance on their own family networks. For instance, the Runnymede Research Report, in its summary of the Home Office Committee Report on the Chinese community, stated:

> Chinese people from Hong Kong have been hardly anglicized at all in the century and a half since Hong Kong island became a colony. This can more easily be appreciated if one compares them with Caribbean people, of any sort of ethnic descent, or with people from India. ... But the Chinese are not especially interested in influencing other people nor do they readily accept non-Chinese influences on themselves.

However, Chinese people living in Britain have themselves challenged this account and pointed out that the profile of the Chinese population in other Western countries like the USA is quite different from the UK. These accounts blame a combination of factors for the isolation of the Chinese community, which include institutionalized racism and the 'restrictive system of immigration controls and work permit quotas' which has forced Chinese immigrants to fall back on family support structures. Britain has, according to the Chinese Information and Advice Centre, at best reluctantly accepted its obligations to its former colonial dependants and a succession of strict immigration controls since 1962 have left many Chinese in the UK in a kind of legal limbo which has been an important element in their lack of access to central services. This problem has been exacerbated by the state's policy of placing refugees (such as the 20,000 Chinese-Vietnamese who came here in the 1970s) in remote parts of Britain.

Britain's policy towards the Hong Kong handover to China in 1997 seemed to confirm this account. Most Hong Kong Chinese were refused British passports, and those who came to the UK mainly included members of the former Hong Kong police, army and colonial bureaucracy fleeing possible retribution by the communist government. Many of these new Chinese who did not find a home with Chinese already living in the UK settled in Milton Keynes.

Note: Thanks to David Tan, Chinese Liaison Officer for the City of Westminster, for his help with this survey.

See also: bilingual communities; Japanese communities

Further reading

Runnymede Research Report (1985) *The Chinese Community in Britain*, London: Runnymede Trust.

DAVID McNEILL

Chipperfield, David

b. 1953

Architect

David Chipperfield's influences are Western modernism and traditional Japanese architecture. He studied at Kingston Polytechnic and the **Architectural Association** before working for, among others, Richard Rogers and Partners and Foster Associates. He established David Chipperfield and Partners in 1984. The practice has worked on the Arnolfini Gallery in Bristol, Issey Miyake's **shops** in London, and the WG design and craft shop in Kensington. Chipperfield has predominantly worked in London and Tokyo, taught at the Royal College of Art and served as a director of the 9H gallery, London's only gallery devoted to contemporary international architecture.

PETER CHILDS

choreography

Originally referring to dance notation, by the beginning of the twentieth century the term came to mean the art of making dances as this is understood in the context of Western theatre dance forms. In the radical social, political and artistic climate of the 1960s the notion of choreography was deeply questioned, directly affecting subsequent dance production in both the American and British scenes.

In British ballet, new approaches to choreography became possible in direct relationship to major structural and administrative changes within the institutions involved, such as the **Royal Ballet**. In 1966, Ballet Rambert was transformed into a modern company with a focus on blending classical and modern tradition, and supporting work by both American (Glen Tetley) and British choreographers (Christopher Bruce and Richard Alston).

In 1966, the foundations of British modern dance were successfully laid. Robin Howard formed Contemporary Ballet Trust, an umbrella organization for the promotion of modern dance in Britain with particular emphasis on Graham technique, initially including a school and, a year later, a company (Contemporary Dance Group) under the artistic directorship of American dancer and choreographer Robert Cohan.

However, New Dance, an alternative dance movement born in the early 1970s, became the most radical British territory in which choreographic practices were reconsidered. In the American avant-garde dance of the 1960s, Yvonne Rainer, Trisha Brown, David Gordon, Steve Paxton, Lucinda Childs and Meredith Monk used pedestrian movement, chance procedures, **improvisation** and indeterminacy, speech and elements of popular culture in alternative choreography. Visiting New York in the early 1970s, the British choreographer Rosemary Butcher was inspired to develop a personal approach to choreography driven by her own questions about dance and a working method informed by visual art practices.

In 1973, American dancer and choreographer Mary Fulkerson was appointed head of dance at Dartington College of Arts in Devon to run a programme of alternative dance training. Fulkerson was also responsible for the organization of the Dartington Festivals (1978–87) which hosted the main manifestations of British experimental dance throughout the 1980s. The ADMA (Association of Dance and Mime Artists) Festivals of 1977 and 1978 in London had similar purposes but were less successful due to ineffective organization. In 1978, Dance Umbrella festival was also inaugurated in London under the initiative of Val Bourne and featured work by both American and British artists throughout the 1980s and 1990s. Rosemary Butcher, Miranda Tufnell, Laurie Booth, Yolande Snaith, Ian Spink, Gaby Agis, Sue Maclennan and Emilyn Claid are some of the key artists whose work shaped the identity of British alternative dance under the name New Dance.

The birth and consolidation of New Dance would not have been possible without the support of X6 collective, an artists' organization which safeguarded and promoted the philosophical, artistic and political principles of British alternative dance. In 1975, Emilyn Claid, Fergus Early, Maedée Duprès, Jacky Lansley and later Mary Prestidge formed X6 to face collectively the lack of space for training as well as rehearsing and performing alternative dance. They ran classes and workshops, mainly led by American dancers and teachers such as Mary Fulkerson, Steve Paxton and Lisa Nelson, and organized informal presentations of work. X6 also launched a quarterly publication under the name *New Dance* (1977–88). The role of X6 was highly and overtly political, in the sense that the collective was concerned with achieving specific social changes. This element becomes rather crucial when one attempts to explain the unique characteristics of British alternative dance from the 1970s onwards.

The agenda of X6 included issues of freedom and equality approached not only through choreographic work with specific meanings but also through the methods and policies adopted in the making. Dance was understood as a non-specialized activity, and as a space in which the personal could be expressed, encouraging in this way the subsequent development of both community dance and highly personalized professional choreography. Dance was expected to make people aware of social and political issues; hence an early interest in exploring women's issues, which soon became a strong enthusiasm for issue-based work.

British New Dance shared with American avant-garde dance of the 1960s and 1970s the use of pedestrian movement, non-trained performers, improvisation, collaboration, non-traditional performance spaces and the interest in alternative movement systems (release, contact improvisation), alternative approaches to the body (Alexander technique, Feldenkrais, body–mind centring), and non-Western movement techniques (martial arts, tai chi, capoeira).

During the 1980s some of the small independent British companies, such as Janet Smith and Dancers, Extemporary Dance Theatre and Second Stride, moved to middle scale, while the majority of independent choreographers became increasingly clearer in their aims. By the early 1990s British independent dance had become a vast arena of diverse statements choreographically manifested in a multiplicity of ways. The spectrum includes Emilyn Claid producing feminist and lesbian dance, Lloyd Newson and his company DV8 critiquing sexual stereotypes, Michael Clark exploring gay and camp work, Nigel Charnock blending movement and text in queer work, Wendy Houstoun bringing movement and text in cabaret style solo work, Shobana Jeyasingh and Nahid Siddiqui fusing classical Indian dance with Western contemporary dance elements, CandoCo Dance Company pioneering integrated dance work which brings together able and disabled bodies, Julyen Hamilton and Kirstie Simson working in improvisation, Liz Aggiss experimenting with movement, speech, singing, props, projections and elaborate costume to create an overall sense of image, Lea Anderson exploring the visuality of dance through a range of means including film, Jonathan Burrows and Russell Maliphant questioning their classical dance backgrounds through formal exploration of movement in relation to light, Matthew Bourne concentrating on highly subversive reworkings of the classics, Mark Baldwin introducing the use of computers to choreography, Wayne McGregor working on the threshold between live dance and virtual reality, Javier de Frutos interested in the uses of nudity, and company Ricochet celebrating the concept of a dancers-led company.

See also: ballet; English National Ballet; modern dance

Further reading

Mackrell, J. (1992) *Out of Line: The Story of British New Dance*, London: Dance Books.

White, J. (ed.) (1985) *20th Century Dance in Britain: A History of Five Dance Companies*, London: Dance Books.

SOPHIA LYCOURIS

Christian Science

Christian Science was founded in the USA in1879 by Mary Baker Eddy (1821–1910). About one-third of its 3,000 worldwide congregations are based outside the United States. It is popularly best known for its commitment to faith healing and its avoidance of conventional medicine, though this emphasis on healing has diminished in recent years. The definitive statement of the movement's teaching is contained in Eddy's book, *Science and Health with Key to the Scriptures*. The respected *Christian Science Monitor*, its daily newspaper published in Boston, promotes its teaching today. In Britain, Christian Science does not have a particularly high national profile, but the church's chain of Christian Science Reading Rooms in large and small towns throughout the country are a feature of provincial cultural life.

See also: Church of Scientology; evangelism

MIKE STORRY

Church of Scientology

Scientology is a religio-scientific movement developed in the USA in the 1950s by the science fiction author L. Ron Hubbard (1911–86). Its members, who include John Travolta, Tom Cruise and Priscilla Presley, believe that only through understanding themselves as spiritual beings can they come to understand the 'supreme being'. They practise psychotherapy via an electrical machine, in to which the subject speaks. Movements of a dial indicate whether or not the talker is suppressing emotion. The church claims 100,000 members in Britain, and has been allowed to advertise on television since 1996. It is better known by the general public for charges of false imprisonment made by former disillusioned members, who regard it as a cult.

See also: Christian Science; evangelism

MIKE STORRY

cinemas

British cinemas evolved from unsophisticated palaces for fantasy in the 1920s and 1930s, to more streamlined plush-carpeted and chromed viewing places in the postwar period, to multiplex sites designed for a new range of audience experiences in the 1980s and 1990s. They have seen concentration of buildings associated with proliferation of culture industries. Yet, while focusing on films with a widening range of consumer practices, cinemas have been conveying them to a narrowing band of the consuming public. British cinemas seem to be in the centre of a whirlpool of culture industries.

This is not only a matter of Americanization of the British cinema audience, although that is important: major US **film distributors** still determine the vast majority of decisions about what films will appear, when, and on how many screens in the UK. But there are also significant interactions between films and British culture industries, which mean that most successful films are those which express the logics of these industries, and cinema audiences are more likely to conform to the consumer mentalities implied by them.

Since the 1960s British films have responded to television, music, **heritage**, **fashion**, advertising and an array of culture industries that helped launch the styles of **Carnaby Street**, **mods** and **Sloane Rangers**, followed by youth/music fashions and **Britpop**. These trends were previewed in *Help* (1965), *Darling* (1965), *Alfie* (1965) and *Blow Up* (1966), as a new generation of British cinema-goers were disengaged from the cinematic style and tempo of Hollywood narrative films.

British television also helped change the viewing of mainstream audiences, giving birth to a new crossover viewer in the 1970s, with the attempted transfer to the big screen of successful television series such as *Steptoe and Son*, *On the Buses*, *George and Mildred*, *The Likely Lads*, *Dad's Army* and *Monty Python's Flying Circus*. By the 1980s television was modifying film-making genres, with series like *Jewel in the Crown* (1983) and *Brideshead Revisited* (1981), and with television backing for films such as *Maurice* (1987), *A Handful of Dust* (1987), *Chariots of Fire* (1981) and the **Merchant-Ivory Productions**' *Room With a View* (1985) and *Howards End* (1991).

Television enlivened **film music**, particularly through hit programmes such as *Top of the Pops* (the longest running British popular music show based on hits from the current week's top twenty or thirty, with studio guest artists miming their songs). Pop and rock films portrayed leading groups, as in Richard **Lester**'s *A Hard Day's Night* (1964), and John **Boorman**'s *Catch Us If You Can* (1985). Meanwhile the **music industry** entered cinema in a major way with EMI's takeover of Associated British Picture Corporation in 1969 (later Thorn-EMI Screen Entertainment).

By the time **Roeg** and Cammell's *Performance* (1970), starring Mick Jagger, was released it was clear that musical styles were destined to have a vital impact even in the most unlikely film genres (in this case, an underground film about a London protection racket). Avant-garde film-makers (see **avant-garde cinema**) influenced this pattern with Derek **Jarman** making a music video for the Pet Shop Boys, and Sophie Muller making a film promotion for the Eurythmics, called *Savage* (1987). **mods** and punk music (see **punk rock**) appeared with The Who in *Quadrophenia* (1979 re-released in 1997), and Hazel O'Connor in *Breaking Glass* (1980). The Sex Pistols played in *The Great Rock 'n' roll Swindle* (1980), while Sid Vicious was the subject of Alex **Cox**'s punk love story *Sid and Nancy* (1986). Alan **Parker** put Pink Floyd's entire album *The Wall* into a rock video in *Pink Floyd: The Wall* (1982). British music arrived inexorably with Ken **Russell**'s *Tommy* (1975), Michael Apted's *Stardust* (1974), Alan Parker's *The Commitments* (1991) and Iain Softley's *Backbeat* (1993), inciting a spate of films and **film music** extending from rock concerts to rave music (see **rave**).

The impact of such films has been made on a new audience generation. Over half come from the 15–35 age group (26 percent of the whole population), containing various multicultural groups interested in music consumption. But there are also signs of social class consumption, most clearly visible in the so-called heritage film. Film critics focus on heritage film because it highlights images of Britishness as commodities for consumption in the international market, and because it now accounts for up to 20 percent of current British film making. It sprang up with *Chariots of Fire* (1981), *A Room with a View* (1986) and *The Remains of the Day* (1993), and in 1995 five of the top ten British films in the USA were historic or literary adaptations. That year's output included *Sense and Sensibility, A Midsummer Night's Dream, The Wind in the Willows, The Woodlanders, Emma, Othello, The Portrait of a Lady, Richard III* and *Twelfth Night*.

Heritage films assist industries such as **fashion**, **theatre** and tourism. Tourist guides to film locations in Britain and Ireland recommend visitors to the sites of films by Kenneth **Branagh**, Hugh **Hudson**, Mike **Newell** and Merchant-Ivory. Even **book marketing** is boosted: at the height of the success of *Four Weddings and a Funeral* (1994) shops sold out of copies of the poems of W.H. Auden because 'Funeral Blues' was read at Simon Callow's funeral. The tourist perspective and encouragement of cultural artefacts hallmark British heritage films as culture industry vehicles. Their presumptions of historical reality and themes of romantic, non-exploitative relationships imply passive culture-confirming roles for film, cultural consumption for cinema audiences and commercial environments for film viewing.

These trends towards culture industry milieus are supported by other audience trends. The movie cathedrals that once showed spectacular epics and romances have given way to modern cinema outings which offer only the choice of more immediate consuming interactions over other film viewing sites. Two main consumer channels siphon film viewers into cinemas. One is Hollywood-ization of the British cinema environment, condensing audiences into urban service class spending environments. The other is the specific origin, content and process of film viewing, providing British cinemas with mainly Hollywood blockbuster movies, eating away at artistic and foreign language films and restricting British films, particularly specialist ones, to a paltry cinema existence.

Among major film-going countries, Britain has a uniquely high concentration of cinema ownership. Whereas in the USA no company owns more than 10 percent of the cinemas (with firms like Warner and Paramount owning less than 5 percent of all US cinemas), in Britain four of the five largest cinema owners are US-owned, and all major film distributors are closely related to them. Even so, the UK has fewer screens than any other major country, despite doubling its screens in the last decade. In 1995 the number of screens per million of population in Europe and the US was Sweden 138, US 100, France 77, Italy 65, Canada 64, Germany 61, Ireland 50 and the UK 33.

The doubling of British screens is almost entirely due to multiplex development, accounting for more than 40 percent of all admissions. In 1994, there were 75 multiplex sites having 650 screens, 90 percent of which were owned by the five major distributors (United Cinemas International, MGM, National Amusements, Warner and Odeon). By 1997, 800 screens out of a total of 2,000 were multiplex, built mostly in large cities. Warner and Virgin Cinemas plan megaplexes (5,000 seat, twenty-screen sites) in Sheffield, Glasgow, Bristol and Leeds, while American Multi Cinemas plans a twenty-six-screen site in Manchester.

A result of these developments has been the intensive organization of the international film system in Britain. The drive to monopolize cinema screens increases competition by conglomerate producers and distributors so that British film advertising and printing are exceptionally expensive. Advertising alone is an important source of consumer siphoning, sometimes being the sole attraction to cinemas, as opposed to personal or other forms of recommendation. More significant is the scope allowed for devolving property rights upon how films can be displayed, and where profits can be maximized. While British consumer spending on feature films rose steadily in the 1990s from £500 million to around £2,500 million, this breaks down into approximately one-third video retail, one-quarter movie channel subscription, one-fifth video rental, and only one-sixth cinema box office admissions.

An important indicator of this changing structure is the decline in foreign language films at the UK box office. Foreign language films take under

2 percent of total earnings, and UK audiences for foreign films dropped heavily from 1.94 million in 1993 to 0.25 million in 1995. In London, where borderline and subtitled films found the biggest audiences, most of the art house venues have gone. Since 1970 the Academyscreens, Berkeley, Cameo-Poly, Cinecenta, Continentale, Gala Royal, Paris Pullman, Venus, Times and various Classics have all closed. Not surprisingly, even the most spectacular European co-productions, such as Malle's *Damage* (1992), Polanski's *Bitter Moon* (1992), Annaud's *The Lover* (1992) and Scott's *1492*, with their formulas of European high culture, have been coolly received (or coolly distributed) in Britain.

Several new award-winning European films are unlikely to get any screening at all in the UK. Earnings of foreign language films at the UK box office compare dismally to English language films. Screen International's top ranking (1990–6) films in the English language are *Jurassic Park* (1993, US) £47.1 million; *Independence Day* (1996, US) £37.0 million; *Four Weddings and a Funeral* (1994, UK) £27.8 million; *Ghost* (1990, US) £23.3 million; and *The Lion King* (1994, US) £23.1 million. In foreign language the top films are *Cyrano de Bergerac* (1990, Fr) £2.4 million; *Il Postino* (1995, It/Fr) £1.3 million; *Delicatessen* (1990, Fr) £1.3 million; *Farewell My Concubine* (1993, Hong Kong/China) £1.0 million; and *Cinema Paradiso* (1988, It/Fr) £1.0 million.

British films are in a dangerously comparable position to non-English language films. Their earnings of between only 4 and 10 percent of the UK box office in the 1990s are by no means due to any lack of production. Far more British films are being produced than can be presently absorbed. Approximately half of all films made here never get released. Of those that do, many get a better showing elsewhere: *Secrets and Lies* (1996 Palme D'Or winner) made more in seven days in France than it did in nineteen weeks in the UK. Both British and foreign films appear to be unsustainable in the British cinematic complex.

The contrast with Hollywood blockbusters is arresting. Taking 1995 as a typical year, the top ten films shown in the UK took £125 million from a total box office of £380 million. In descending order the films were *Batman Forever* (US), *Casper* (US), *Goldeneye* (US/UK), *Apollo 13* (US), *Braveheart*

(US/UK), *Interview with the Vampire* (US/UK), *Pocohontas* (US), *Die Hard with a Vengeance* (US), *Stargate* (US) and *Dumb and Dumber* (US). By comparison, the top twenty films made in the UK took under £10 million altogether, the first three being *Shallow Grave* (£5 million), *The Englishman Who Went Up a Hill But Came Down a Mountain* (£2 million), and *Priest* (£1 million). This leaves about £2 million for the other main productions. (*The Madness of King George* (US/UK) took £5 million).

Any growth in screens has therefore only served to concentrate both the variety of films being seen and the range of audiences attending in Britain. It might have been expected that relationships with expanding cultural networks would extend cinema audiences, but this has patently not been the case. The majority of all cinema-going in the UK is now done by under 5 percent of the total population. The cinema audience in Britain seems to be converging in urban, multiplex, culture industry environments, into an increasingly coherent and exclusive social group.

See also: British film industry

Further reading

British Film Institute (1997) *BFI Film and Television Handbook 1997*, London: British Film Institute.

Friedman, L. (ed.) (1993) *British Cinema and Thatcherism: Fires Were Started*, London: UCL Press.

Higson, A. (1995) *Waving the Flag: Constructing a National Cinema in Britain*, Oxford: Clarendon Press.

ARTHUR McCULLOUGH

circus

In the course of the past two decades there have been two signal and connected developments within the reshaping of the circus in Britain. First, an ongoing public controversy about the training, performance and keeping of animals by circus companies has resulted in around 180 local authorities nationwide banning circuses with animal acts. The economic impact on traditional circuses such as Cottle's, Chipperfield's, Roberts' and Miller's has been severe, forcing them either to adapt in various ways or to supplement their tours with shows abroad. A major boon to these companies in the last decade, however, has been the exodus of highly skilled and state-trained performers from the former Soviet Union. Second, there has been a growing excitement of interest in what has been dubbed the 'New Circus'. Though there exist huge variations in both scale and style within the 'New Circus', what unites them all is their rejection of animal performers as well as a common genesis in the alternative arts of the 1970s, particularly street theatre and dance. Some of the performers, such as Pierrot Pillot-Bidon (founder of the French company Archaos), are the renegade children of the traditional circus families in circus schools such as Circus Space in London.

Two results of this broadening of the availability of skills have been that there is now more artistic interchange between circus and other performance-based arts so that circus skills are more in evidence within contemporary dance, **opera** and **theatre**, and at the same time the 'New Circus' is frequently more theatrical and narrative-based or theme-based than it has been since the early nineteenth century. Government funding for such training in the UK has been practically non-existent, so European and North American companies (for example Cirque du Soleil, The Big Apple Circus, Circus Baroque and Circus Oz) have tended to dominate the stage. From the outset, however, the circus (founded in London in 1768 by Philip Astley) quickly became identified for its internationalism and this is just as true for the 'New Circus'. Finally, the relationship between 'old' and 'new' circus in Britain is not necessarily an antagonistic one, as was demonstrated by Circus of Horrors, the commercially successful collaborative project between Archaos and Gerry Cottle.

See also: mime; physical theatre

HELEN STODDART

citizenship

Citizenship can refer to a political identity, a particular relation between state and individual, or a political activity. Strictly speaking, individuals in Britain are not citizens but subjects of the Crown, and British **democracy** rests not on the sovereignty of the people (as in most other democratic societies), but on the sovereignty of the 'crown in parliament'.

As a political identity, citizenship denotes membership of a particular polity; hence it is an exclusive identity, demarcating 'members' from 'non-members'. In this sense, citizenship is a political sense of identity and belonging to a particular political entity and community of fellow citizens. However, citizenship is often not commonly viewed or experienced as an exclusively 'political' identity, in that citizenship is often understood in terms of ethnic, racial or other terms. While it is most closely associated with the state, citizenship is more commonly associated with the 'nation'. On this view, citizenship implies belonging not just to a political entity (the state) but to a more nebulous and amorphous collectivity: the 'nation'. In Britain, this association of citizenship and nation has often expressed itself in racial or ethnic terms such that 'British citizenship' is not a freely chosen political relation or identity between individual and state, which means that anyone, any immigrant (in theory), can become a British citizen by being accepted by and in turn agreeing to obey the law of the land. There are those, mostly on the right-wing, nationalist side of the political spectrum, for whom citizenship does not automatically translate into 'full membership', since from this perspective, citizenship and belonging are a matter of blood or ethnic lineage and are not 'voluntary'. An example of this ethnic sense of British citizenship can be seen in the fascist British National Front slogan that 'There ain't no black in the Union Jack', which claims that one cannot be black and British. This minority view has increasingly been marginalized as Britain becomes a more multicultural society, and a less ethnic (i.e. white) sense of Britishness and citizenship has flourished.

As a relation between state and individual, citizenship connotes a set of rights and duties attached to the citizen. Citizen rights include the following: the right to be free from excessive interference by the state or its agencies, the right to a fair trial, the democratic rights of free association, voting and standing for office and freedom of religion and conscience. More recent 'social' rights, as a result of the creation of the postwar British welfare state, include the right to the services of the welfare state such as unemployment benefit, housing, education and health care. Citizen duties are obligations to the state and fellow citizens, and these include upholding and abiding by the law, being a jury member if selected and abiding by the instructions of state representatives.

As an activity, citizenship can mean either 'passive' or 'active' citizenship. By 'active citizenship' is meant the participation of citizens in political life and political decision making. Passive citizenship is how most people understand citizenship, voting in periodic national and local elections and electing representatives to govern, make laws and pass legislation.

See also: Charter 88

Further reading

Marshall, T.H. (1950) *Citizenship and Social Class*, Cambridge: Cambridge University Press.
Oliver, D. and Heater, D. (1994) *The Foundations of Citizenship*, Hemel Hempstead: Harvester Wheatsheaf.
Turner, B.S. (1993) *Citizenship and Social Theory*, London: Sage.

JOHN BARRY

city redevelopment

The spate of urban riots in Britain in 1981 helped induce the perceptions that state policy towards cities up to that point had failed, and that the cities themselves were in 'crisis'. The effect on public policy was probably greatest in the field of planning and urban development. There is more continuity than is generally realized between the policies of the postwar period and the policies of the post-1979 governments, but there is no doubt that the riots provoked a major reassessment at many levels.

A history of the field could be divided into three phases: a period in which the state assumed a key role, associated with postwar reconstruction; a period under the Thatcher administration in which the state's role was much reduced, in favour of a *laissez-faire* approach; and finally, the current

situation in which state controls have been strengthened again. In terms of the results that planning, or lack of it, has produced in Britain, it could be said that the models for the first and second phases have been American, while recent efforts at urban redevelopment have followed a continental European model, with sometimes striking results.

The postwar planning effort is described by a major piece of Parliamentary legislation, the Town and Country Planning Act of 1947. It enshrined the principle of securing 'a proper balance between competing demands for land', but it could be argued that its idea of 'balance' was one that was fundamentally biased against the European model of urban development. A central belief was that the cities were overpopulated, and that their 'overspill' populations should be removed from the centre (this idea was nothing new, and had been promoted since at least the 1840s). The means of doing this was the establishment of **new towns**, of which twelve were originally envisaged, eight around London, two in the Northeast, one in North-amptonshire and one in Wales; each was envisaged as a self-contained and balanced community. The New Towns provided a very high standard of housing for those on average incomes, and the policy has generally been regarded as a success: but it actually accounted for only 7 percent of the housing constructed since 1945. The rest was concentrated either in small private suburban developments, or in the public housing estates now surrounding most of Britain's major towns and cities.

The fracturing of the urban fabric was exaggerated by energetic slum clearance during the 1950s and 1960s, and the zoning of most major towns and cities, reducing the extent to which an area – particularly a central area – could have multiple uses. Physical manifestations of this included urban motorways, such as the Westway in London, or the Mancunian Way in Manchester, and enclosed shopping malls. By the middle 1960s most urban working-class populations had been removed to outlying estates, and the centres of most British cities had been given over to commercial, not residential, uses. As a result, they tend to resemble more North American cities than continental European ones.

These vast changes took place against an economic background of steady relative decline and, in the 1970s, crisis. Although planning had been strengthened during this time (with a new regional emphasis accompanying the establishment of the six big metropolitan counties in 1972), the cities continued to decline in terms of employment, and consequently in population. In some cases this was extremely striking: Greater London has lost 1.5 million people since its peak, Liverpool is down to 450,000 from a peak of more than a million, and Glasgow and Manchester have suffered comparable losses. Economic decline has been accompanied by social unrest, most strikingly in 1981.

It is at this point that British urban policy was marked by a dramatic change. Generally speaking this meant reducing the role of the state in urban policy (in practical terms this involved cutting funds for local planning departments), and the creation of 'enterprise zones' based on an American model, in which local taxation was reduced or deferred and planning restrictions all but abolished. In retrospect, this policy seems to have much in common with the 'non-plan' concept, proposed in a 1969 *New Society* article by, amongst others, Reyner Banham (1922–88), architectural critic and chief British apologist for Los Angeles.

The most spectacular work of the enterprise zone concept was the redevelopment of the Docklands area of London, managed by the London Docklands Development Corporation (LDDC) in the 1980s. Despite its proximity to the City of London, the area had profound employment problems, and attempts by the Greater London Council to revive it had stalled. The area of redevelopment was vast – some 2,050 hectares – making it at the time the largest redevelopment site in Europe. The LDDC, appointed by the government, was to oversee the development, but unlike the individual authorities for the creation of the New Towns, its powers were fundamentally limited. Primed by a government grant, it could acquire, own and assemble land for sale, but it was not responsible either for planning or for the provision of infrastructure.

The material achievements of the LDDC are impressive, and include the building of an airport, the development of Canary Wharf, a vast office development which at the time was Europe's tallest

building, the construction of a huge amount of new housing, much of it attractive, and the building of the London Arena. There is no doubt that London's centre of gravity has been shifted eastward, and it is significant that a large number of newspapers and magazines have chosen to relocate to Canary Wharf from their traditional home at Fleet Street. But Docklands is poorly integrated with the rest of London. It has, for example, provoked the resentment of the original residents of the area, who have seen the quality of their public infrastructure decline, while at the same time they have often been excluded from the new forms of employment that have appeared in the area. Also, with so much reliance on private finance, the development has been especially vulnerable to fluctuations in the economy.

There have also been criticisms of the architectural quality of the developments. An architectural development guide was produced in the early days of the project, but there were difficulties in adhering to this when there were no structures to enable it to be enforced. The appearance of the development is very mixed indeed, and the speed with which it was built has arguably led to buildings with a limited life.

The problems associated with Docklands were repeated in developments elsewhere, whether at Salford Quays, Manchester (much the largest outside Docklands), or the Albert Dock at Liverpool. A common problem has been the fact that the provision of an attractive, water-based environment does not in itself lead to the creation of a community. All the developments have been in some way successful – and more so than is generally agreed – but they have remained isolated from their surrounding communities, and the economic benefits have not generally affected their surroundings.

If vast waterside developments managed by Urban Development Corporations (UDCs) were an attempt to regenerate declining areas, the strong economic growth of the mid-1980s was better characterized by a different urban form. Out-of-town retail and business parks proliferated; hypermarkets appeared at major road junctions, while areas of the country such as the M4 motorway became in effect linear business parks. Such suburban growth was encouraged by successive

Conservative governments. Along with out-of-town commercial development, there was residential suburban development on a scale not seen since the 1960s, and it is this that gives the more accurate overall picture of urban policy during the 1980s. In spite of the high profile inner-city regeneration programmes managed by the UDCs, most British cities continued to register substantial population decline.

For all the benefits that 1980s-style developments brought, it became clear to the various groups involved that they were not sustainable. Land was not infinitely available for suburban development, especially in the densely populated southeast of the country where demand was greatest, and a consensus emerged that it was in nobody's interest that the cities should shrink further. Alternative developmental models began to be sought, and these tended to come from continental Europe. Much interest was shown in Spain, a country engaged in major urban reconstruction throughout the 1980s, culminating in a series of events in 1992 including the Barcelona Olympic Games. The reconstructed Spanish cities seemed to offer a model for successful urban living that could be translated to Britain. The main characteristics of the new model were the repopulation of the urban cores of cities, the fostering of development at a high population density, the encouraging of a mix of commercial, entertainment and residential uses, the retention of existing street plans, and the retention and reuse of older buildings where possible.

By 1996, government policy had only partially recognized these aims, so we cannot yet begin to speak of an official policy as is possible with the policies of the 1980s, and previously. However, the planning rules have changed nationally to prevent further out-of-town shopping malls (the guidance came too late to prevent the construction of five vast regional malls, which pose a threat to the retail cores of Bristol, Manchester and Glasgow, amongst other cities). However, public money has helped to fund a number of high-profile schemes which evidence the new thinking in practice.

The largest such scheme has probably been the redevelopment of Hulme, Manchester. Hulme, within walking distance of the centre of Manchester, was the city's most densely populated area in the 1930s, and counted a population of some 130,000. At this time it was designated a clearance area on account of the poor quality of the housing, and the area was comprehensively redeveloped in the 1960s. The dense grid of terraced housing was replaced with a mixture of point- and deck-access blocks, mainly prefabricated, and surrounded with plenty of open space; the original street pattern was largely obliterated. The population of the new Hulme was just 12,000, a tenth of what it had been in the 1930s.

Although designed to high standards, problems with the new buildings quickly became apparent, the external environment became degraded, and many of the properties became unlettable. By the mid-1980s it was clear that comprehensive redevelopment was necessary. Development of the area began again in 1994, and involved the reinstatement of some of the principal streets of the old Hulme, the replacement of the deck-access housing with more traditional forms, the development of mixed uses for each area of Hulme, the development of a variety of housing for different income groups, and finally, the reinstatement of physical links with the city centre. The overall framework for development draws on the positive aspects of the old community, but it also is explicitly an attempt to establish a continental European-style city quarter.

At the same time, there has been a striking amount of city-centre housing development in Glasgow, Manchester and London. Very often, this has involved the reuse of commercial buildings, particularly Victorian ones, and the process has in many cases been encouraged with public funding. While support for such schemes remains high – and urban councils are increasingly promoting their so-called 'night-time economies' – most city-centre housing has so far been built for urban professionals. It remains to be seen whether such policies can encourage the development of diverse communities, including families. While the populations of most major cities have now stabilized, the overall trend is still downwards, and despite recent planning efforts, the future looks suburban, not urban.

See also: town planning

Further reading

Esher, L. (1980) *A Broken Wave: The Rebuilding of England 1940–1980*, London: Allen Lane.

Middleton, M. (1991) *Cities in Transition*, London: Michael Joseph.

Rees, G. (1985) *Cities in Crisis*, London: Edward Arnold.

RICHARD J. WILLIAMS

civil service

The origin of the civil service goes back to Napoleon in practice, and to the works of Max Weber in principle. In Weber's ideal type, the civil service should be a rational model of decision making in which information flows up to the relevant level and decisions flow down. As not every decision can be made on a rational-legal basis, a political head would then make some decisions.

In principle, the civil service is a politically neutral body of people who, in true Weberian fashion, are politically neutral and committed to dealing with and implementing the instructions of the government of the day. Each country deals with this in a different way. In British culture, the service is hierarchically divided into a number of classes ranging from clerical to executive and administrative. Entry to each grade is by competition and while, in theory, it is possible to move upwards from one grade to another, in practice this is difficult. On the whole, recruitment tends to be directly into a particular class and, like British life in general, movement from one class to another is infrequent.

The most significant part of the civil service is the administrative grade. Entry to that grade is highly competitive and tends to be self-replicating in that the features already deemed successful from current post-holders are the characteristics sought in selection competitions. This makes the structure somewhat conservative. The conservatism is increased by a strong tendency to restrict entry to the administrative grade to candidates from Oxbridge. The end result is a high degree of ossification that reflects the still ossified **class system** of British culture and society.

The civil service is largely centred on London, but some deliberate movement out of London has taken place. Notable examples are taxation bodies and driver's licensing bodies. There have been numerous initiatives aimed at reducing the number of civil servants. These are almost always successful only by virtue of structural reorganization. Most significant in this and other respects, perhaps, has been the extraordinary growth of 'quangos' (quasi-autonomous governmental bodies) such as the Highways Authorities. These bodies, now numbering some 5,000, are responsible for a considerable amount of public expenditure and are largely unaccountable. Many of these are staffed by civil servants who are no longer bound by relations of trust. This generates a huge industry of checking on the activities of what would otherwise be perfectly trustworthy public servants.

It is hard to overestimate the damage done by the reduction of the culture of trust, and the incoming Labour government has, not surprisingly, politicized some areas of public service by making political rather than career appointments to crucial areas of policy and policy development. This politicization of the civil service may prove to be of the greatest moment in that it breaks both with Napoleonic and Weberian principles in favour of a presidential style of leadership that has, hitherto, been practised in Britain.

See also: Establishment, the

Further reading

Dowding, K. (1995) *The Civil Service*, London: Routledge.

PAUL BARRY CLARKE

Clarke, Arthur C.

b. 1917, Minehead

Writer

With a background in physics (having taken a degree from King's College, London), Clarke is best known as a science fiction writer. He has written more than seventy books, including *2001: A Space Odyssey* (for whose screenplay he was nominated for an Academy Award) and *Rendezvous with Rama*. He has lived in Sri Lanka for the past thirty years, where he is Chancellor of the University of Moratuwa, but he has retained his links with Britain (for example, as master of his old school, Richard Huish College in Taunton). He has made many appearances on radio and television, most notably with Walter Cronkite during the Apollo missions. His thirteen-part *Mysterious World* and *Strange Powers* television programmes have been seen worldwide.

See also: fantasy and science fiction; science; science fiction

MIKE STORRY

class system

Social class has been seen as the main divide in British politics. The characteristics which determine class include occupation, income, material possessions, family position, breeding, accent, education, appearance, lifestyle and power. Traditionally the British population has been separated into social classes which were assumed to have a common identity, and class consciousness and solidarity. Stratification in the capitalist system implies a hierarchical distribution of classes in ranked order. The Registrar General divides Britain into six classes on the basis of occupation: A, the established elite; B, the professions and lower management; C1, the skilled non-manual class; C2, the skilled manual class; D, semiskilled manual workers and E, unskilled. However, many sociologists consider this to be a rather dated approach.

Marxists believe there are two basic classes; the bourgeoisie and the proletariat, whose numbers increase with the development of industry but who can only bring about equality through revolution. Conservatives do not deny the existence of class divisions, but argue that this is inevitable and there is considerable mobility between classes which provides an incentive for effort. Socialists argue that social stratification is divisive and acts as a barrier to the motivation and recruitment of talent. They wish to reduce differences through direct taxation, welfare benefits, minimum wages and redistribution of wealth.

Class divisions have typically centred around the boundary between non-manual and manual work, but such dividing lines have blurred as the C1 group is said to have become proletarianized as much non-manual work is low paid, humdrum and repetitive compared to skilled manual work. Ivor Crewe entertains the idea of a divided working class: the traditional working class, whose numbers are shrinking, and a new working class who are more likely to live in the south, are homeowners, work in private industry and are less likely to vote for Labour on the basis of class. He believes there is a process of embourgeoisement, whereby manual workers are entering the middle classes and becoming less class-conscious and more individualistic. Others contend that there are no longer rigid class divisions, but that an underprivileged underclass exists comprising ethnic minorities, the unemployed, homeless and the mentally ill. This group lives beneath the poverty line and its numbers are growing with the welfare cuts of the 1980s and 1990s. The underclass may take a new form when the technology divide between haves and have-nots in British society grows greater.

See also: homelessness; poverty, families and; social welfare

Further reading

Crewe, I., Gosschalk, B. and Bartle, J. (eds) (1998) *Political Communications: Why Labour Won the General Election of 1997*, London: Frank Cass.

Haralambos, M. and Holborn, M. (1990) *Sociology: Themes and Perspectives*, London: HarperCollins (provides a detailed, modern view of the subject).

COLIN WILLIAMS

classical music

Classical music is one of the most important art forms in Britain, as it influences many other activities in addition to being a major industry and employer in its own right. The arts as a whole contribute a turnover of £5.5 billion to London's economy every year, employing 5 percent of the capital's workforce. Classical music is widely used for films, television and advertisements, and sells many soundtrack and theme tune recordings. The mass media have enabled more people to come into contact with music and also to discover more about those who make it. Interest in concerts increased from 1986–7 until 1995–6, when an estimated 12.7 percent of the adult population attended a classical music event.

The mass media have become the principal means by which most people encounter classical music. The popular, easygoing style of Classic FM, a national commercial radio station (see **commercial radio, national**) begun in 1992 which for much of its output plays shorter pieces or 'edited highlights', attracted many who may have considered **Radio 3** too highbrow. Radio 3 attempted to counter any such supposition by introducing lighter programming, for instance that of Brian Kay's Sunday morning programme, while maintaining its commitment to the more 'serious' end of the spectrum such as organizing and broadcasting the Proms season from the Royal Albert Hall, offering live opera, and supporting new music in commissions and broadcast concerts. Classic FM also sponsors many concerts and has adopted the Royal Philharmonic Orchestra (see **orchestras**) as its resident ensemble which, through a residency at the Royal Concert Hall in Nottingham, escapes some of London's orchestral squeeze.

Classical recordings are marketed, and their sales monitored, by similar methods to those of the pop **music industry**, with classical music having its own sales chart in addition to a 'classical crossover' chart (this title has caused debate over the pigeonholing of music and whether works have been placed in the 'right' chart). Certain classical pieces have become immensely popular as a result of links with sporting events, film, television and advertising, and such media have often introduced huge new audiences to classical music.

The 1990s saw heavy financial pressures put on the classical industry. The effect has been felt most by those earning least, but larger organizations are still feeling the pinch. An example of this was the 1993 enquiry into the future of the largest of London's orchestras headed by Lord Justice Hoffmann, in light of the threat by the Arts

Council to withdraw funding from them. Throughout the 1990s British musicians endured, along with other professions, their fair share of wage freezes, contract renegotiations and even pay cuts. Most arts organizations in Britain were extremely underfunded as the political climate was so unsupportive. **Local councils**, themselves under pressure through rate-capping and new demands on expenditure, were no longer able to contribute towards music funding as they once did. The **Arts Council** provided a certain amount, despite its own funding being cut (by about £17 million between 1994–6), and attempted to target more exciting and innovative projects. Extra funding which may have been expected from the **National Lottery** was initially subject to the rule that it could only be used for capital items such as building feasibility studies or instruments. Such grants, while welcomed, still left a shortfall to be made up. During the 1990s orchestras and opera companies had to devote resources to finding sponsorship in a very competitive market, with many establishing a staff department specifically for this task. There was necessarily a shift in management ethos towards dealing with these tight financial constraints, and budgets often became the first consideration in arts organizations when planning programmes, while a close eye was kept on the number of freelance personnel employed and the costs of projects.

As their employment situation is precarious, many classical musicians, and freelance performers in particular, develop their outside interests with a view to making earnings in addition to their performing and teaching activities. Professional associations supporting musicians include the Musicians' Union, Incorporated Society of Musicians, Musicians' Benevolent Fund, Royal Society of Musicians and British Performing Arts Medicine Trust. (On the one hand, an apparently slight injury can have a devastating effect on a musician's career. On the other hand, musicians are not highly regarded by the insurance industry; many companies will not offer them motor insurance).

Market research techniques are employed by most music organizations to determine the composition of audiences. There is concern over the perceived rise in average age of the audience for live classical music, and as a result moves are being made to attract younger people into concert halls. Most ensembles promote a series of childrens' concerts in addition to schools and other educational work. There is a feeling in many musical quarters that arts organizations should be a resource for the whole community and not just for those able to attend live performances. Most ensembles have outreach/education departments which provide opportunities for closer encounters with the workings of a professional music organization. Work in this field has been expanded through the 1980s and 1990s beyond school visits, and now typically spans a very broad audience including centres for the elderly and disabled, hospitals and prisons in addition to work with children, youth orchestras (several symphony orchestras run their own) and courses for teachers.

Throughout the industry, horizons have been necessarily widened: by concert hall managements expanding their brief to encourage outside lets from promoters of non-classical and non-musical events, and by artistic directors looking for ways to entice the public through their doors to enjoy more innovative events by established ensembles. London's Royal Albert Hall has for many years played host not only to the BBC's Proms concerts but also to pop concerts and **wrestling** matches, and Liverpool's Philharmonic Hall is now an established venue on pop and light music circuits in addition to the orchestral concerts and films it has always promoted. Carl Davis's performances of his scores to classic films by Chaplin and Lloyd, played live by the Royal Liverpool Philharmonic Orchestra (RLPO), were a particular success.

Organizers of music events have discovered new audiences away from the concert hall and there are many alternative venues being used for performances in festivals, particularly in summer when the marquees go up and the picnics come out. Many orchestras now offer 'pops' concerts, such as the RLPO's summer season by the River Mersey, and there are many summer outdoor concerts given all over the country, often at grand country mansions. These outdoor concerts often take their programming from the 'Last Night of the Proms' formula, including popular pieces such as Puccini's 'Nessun Dorma' (made famous by the 1990 football World Cup) and fireworks and cannons choreographed to Tchaikovsky's *1812 Overture*.

Such orchestral concerts are extremely popular. In the summer of 1996, a programme of popular classics given by Carl Davis with the RLPO and the Royal Artillery Band at Leeds Castle played to 16,000 people twice over. While concerts such as this cost a great deal to put on, with conductor, soloists, orchestra, band, stage and sound crew, fireworks and cannons to pay for, there is a good profit to be made if so many people can be enticed through the gates; the audience for one concert would fill most halls ten times over. It is suspected that many people come to such events but not to concerts through the year, and there is much speculation as to how they could be attracted to the concert halls.

Perhaps one such attraction could be the rumours of activities outlined in Jilly Cooper's racy novel *Appassionata* (1996), which has raised the profile of the music profession, albeit in light-hearted vein. It is set against the backdrop of a fictional regional orchestra, and while researching the book Cooper went on tour with the Royal Scottish National Orchestra.

The larger festivals, such as Edinburgh, the BBC Proms, the Three Choirs and Aldeburgh, are centred on events in concert halls and cathedrals but spill out into smaller venues and often onto the streets; Edinburgh's Fringe Festival (see **Edinburgh Festival and Fringe**) is as famous as the 'main event'. Smaller festivals can be more specialized in the events they offer, as in the examples of the York Early Music Festival, Huddersfield Contemporary Music Festival, Chard Festival of Women in Music, and Birkenhead Guitar Festival.

Chamber music is a vital part of Britain's musical life, with many 'homegrown' ensembles having played together for many years, such as the Chilingirian and Brodsky String Quartets. Chamber ensembles can perform in more intimate venues which are impractical for larger groups, and many are in residence at universities and other venues.

Britain has a strong and growing authentic music movement which has inspired much research and debate into period performance styles. The soloists, chamber groups and orchestras involved play music from medieval times up to the early twentieth century on period instruments or close copies, using performance techniques researched from the relevant period. Additionally, a thriving part of Britain's classical music scene is the tremendous amount of activity on the part of amateur musicians. The major catalyst for such activity is the National Federation of Music Societies (NFMS), which celebrated its diamond jubilee in 1996. Most towns and cities, whether or not they have a professional ensemble, can boast an amateur symphony orchestra, operatic society, chamber musicians and many other people who prefer to play or sing for their own pleasure. The NFMS also arranges concerts by professional players for music societies, and this enables a high standard of performance to be presented to audiences who may not easily gain access to live music.

Summer schools are an important focus for amateur and student musicians. Often linked to festivals, these typically provide opportunities for choral singers and orchestral players, with coaching available on an individual basis. One of the busiest is Dartington International Summer School, which offers a very diverse range of courses (Advanced Sonic Art, Madrigals and Lute Songs, Balinese Gamelan, and Week at the Knees on creating a music theatre piece) in addition to masterclasses and ensembles.

Such events are in addition to the many opportunities for childrens' music-making across Britain such as Saturday schools (where many professionals began their studies) and youth orchestra courses. Sadly, the political climate of the 1990s adversely affected music education; budgets were cut and instrumental teachers were either put on to reduced contracts or deprived of their jobs altogether. The ideal of access for all to instrumental teaching was lost through the introduction of charges.

There was controversy in the music press on the publication of Norman Lebrecht's book *When The Music Stops ... Managers, Maestros and the Corporate Murder of Classical Music*. Lebrecht argues that the music industry has been sold into the hands of multinational corporations and agents and that it is beholden to them rather than to artistic concerns. He outlines the history of the music business as opposed to the history of music as art, pointing out that this financial side of music has always been taboo. This book has been accused of citing a 'doomsday' scenario which may not exist, and of focusing merely on the economics of the profession. This is the first book to examine the links between music and business in such detail, and despite reservations held by some about its content, it has at least brought about debate on the future of the classical music industry.

See also: classical music, contemporary; classical soloists

Further reading

Carpenter, H. (1996) *The Envy of the World: 50 Years of the BBC Third Programme and Radio 3*, London: Weidenfeld & Nicholson.

Lebrecht, N. (1996) *When the Music Stops ... Managers, Maestros and the Corporate Murder of Classical Music*, London: Simon & Schuster (controversial and journalistic in style, the book divided opinion as to how gloomy the outlook really is).

ANDREA MARTIN

classical music, contemporary

During the 1980s and 1990s there appeared to be much diversification in the styles of music being produced by classical composers. Many who might previously have been identified as working in the western tradition explored different idioms, including **jazz**, rock and **folk music**, to a greater extent than before. Boundaries became blurred, leading to the identification of 'crossover' styles (a title not all were happy with), typified by the work of Django Bates, Frank Zappa and Elvis Costello with the Brodsky Quartet. Record labels such as ECM typified an across-the-board approach by recording meditative music by Arvo Pärt and Steve Reich through to jazz-influenced Pat Metheny. The rhythmic ideas generated by such as Americans Steve Reich and Philip Glass and the Dutch composer Louis Andriessen are mirrored by the work of British composers such as Graham Fitkin and Michael Nyman, whose **film music** attracts the attention of a wide public. Other successful film/television composers include George Fenton,

Carl Davis, Geoffrey Burgon and Barrington Pheloung.

Established composers who are still producing challenging works include Sir Peter Maxwell-Davies and Sir Harrison Birtwistle (of the 'Manchester School'); there was much media debate on the inclusion of Birtwistle's piece 'Panic' in the traditional Last Night of the Proms line-up in 1995.

Many composers of similar standing are not well publicized. The Society for the Promotion of New Music (SPNM) and the Huddersfield Festival of Contemporary Music ensure that they are heard and supported. Historically, composition was male-dominated, with women, including Judith Weir, Sally Beamish and Diana Burrell, only gaining wider recognition during the 1980s and 1990s. Many composers are 'in residence' with orchestras or education establishments, mutually beneficial schemes enabling the composition of new pieces.

Certain soloists and ensembles work especially hard to ensure a platform for new works. The London Sinfonietta and BBC Symphony Orchestra have for many years been performing and commissioning new pieces, as has soprano Jane Manning, whose ensemble Jane's Minstrels promotes contemporary British music. Contemporary Music Network (CMN) tours enable those further from London's 'hub' to experience new music.

Music improvised live and music generated from improvisations has had increased influence over many performers, mainly those working in chamber-sized groups. Bass player Barry Guy epitomizes a growing 'holistic' approach, having worked with performers as diverse as the Academy of Ancient Music and free improviser Evan Parker.

See also: classical music

Further reading

Morton, B. and Collins, P. (1992) *Contemporary Composers*, Chicago and London: St James Press (biographies/works of 500 composers).

ANDREA MARTIN

classical soloists

Certain soloists famous before 1960 endure in their popularity, inspiring reverence for the quality of their performances from fellow performers in particular; for example, violinists Yehudi Menuhin and Ida Haendel and cellist and conductor Msitslav Rostropovich attained legendary status worldwide. Similarly, Jean-Paul Tortelier (cello) and Glenn Gould (piano) inspired many players, while the early deaths of Dennis Brain (French horn) and Jacqueline du Pré (cello) were viewed as tragic losses to music. Du Pré's recordings continue to be popular long after her death in 1987.

A soloist's debut continues to be seen as a, if not the, crucial point in their career. Prestige is attached to a debut recital at London's Wigmore Hall, or a first appearance at the BBC's Proms, while successful performances and good reviews in the press generate interest and give performers useful publicity material.

Certain players gain a higher profile in the USA than Europe, and vice versa. Marketing has much to do with this, linking into record sales, though publicity varies between artists. While players such as Nigel Kennedy have been strongly advertised in Britain, more established figures such as pianists Murray Perahia and Maurizio Pollini continue to maintain their popularity and sell many recordings while keeping out of the limelight.

The amount of repertoire available for an instrument generally dictates how much solo exposure it receives, with violinists and pianists in the strongest positions. Certain players have expanded their instrument's repertoire by commissioning composers to write for them; for example, the flautist James Galway commissioned Rodrigo's Flute Concerto and orchestrated Poulenc's Flute Sonata. Performers playing instruments not generally regarded as soloistic have to be more enterprising, and many have consequently raised their instrument's profile. Evelyn Glennie has been a particular champion of new music for percussion, hitherto relatively unknown in a solo capacity, while Christian Lindberg, who became the world's first full-time classical trombonist in the 1980s, has premiered many new pieces including Jan Sanström's *Motorbike Concerto* (performed wearing full leathers) and created much interest in the instrument's solo potential. Pianist Joanna McGregor and saxophonist John Harle exemplify a growing movement towards embracing elements of music away from classical traditions, both performers also working with **jazz** musicians. Projects such as theirs, along with the Brodsky Quartet's collaboration with Elvis Costello, *The Juliet Letters*, have been given a much-resisted 'crossover' tag.

See also: classical music; classical music, contemporary; orchestras

ANDREA MARTIN

Clause 28

Clause 28 is the short name for a section in the Local Government Act of 1988 which made it illegal for local authorities to 'promote homosexuality'. The clause was widely opposed on marches, vigils and protests, and opponents developed a high-profile media support campaign from such figures as the actor Ian McKellen. The Clause appeared to be an attack on gay rights and civil liberties while also threatening subsidies for a huge range of cultural and educational activities. Aside from the backward step that the Clause in many ways represented, it also met with much opposition because its strictures were so loosely phrased and so could be tenuously applied to almost any event with which a gay or lesbian person or image was associated.

See also: gay liberation

PETER CHILDS

Clothes Show, The

The BBC launched *The Clothes Show*, the first mainstream television fashion show, in the 1988s, later allocating it a regular Sunday afternoon slot alongside the *Antiques Roadshow*. Presented by, amongst others, British designer and entrepreneur Jeff **Banks** and Caryn Franklin, the show included features on new fashion directions, both designer and high-street, and on aspects of the fashion industry. The show also featured extremely popular audience-participation slots such as 'Bride of the Year', 'make-overs' for members of the public and competitions to find new models and designers. The annual *Clothes Show Live* held in Birmingham is probably the most popular British fashion event open to the general public, and in the spring of 1988 the *Clothes Show Magazine* was launched for the programme's eight million viewers.

TAMSIN SPARGO

clubs

The main precursor to the contemporary club was the 1950s coffee bar. Invariably containing a jukebox full of rock 'n' roll records, the coffee bar became a meeting place for young people in the evenings and at weekends. The first 'proper' clubs drew upon a similar clientele. Containing little more than a simple record player, these clubs became the focus point for emergent youth subcultures such as **mods** and **teds**.

As the 'R&B' boom of the early 1960s gathered pace, the ballrooms of the previous generation became venues for dancing to **pop and rock** music. Of particular importance were those venues in the North of England that played the latest **soul** music imported from the USA. **Northern Soul** clubs such as The Wigan Casino and The Twisted Wheel in Manchester attracted a clientele who took their dancing very seriously. Often arriving with several changes of clothes, the dancers remained throughout the night until as late as 8 am. Legend has it that the air at The Wigan Casino was thick with the smell of liniment and talcum powder, the former used to prevent muscle-strain, and the latter used to prevent the floor from becoming sticky, enabling dancers to spin around at rapid speeds. Some establishment figures expressed concern at the burgeoning **drug culture** of the club scene in general, and there is certainly evidence to suggest that amphetamines and other stimulants were used to facilitate all-night dancing.

As pop and rock music became increasingly popular throughout the 1960s, so more clubs were developed. Of particular importance was the rise of the Tamla Motown label whose roster included

The Supremes, The Temptations and The Four Tops. It was during this period that a split developed between those venues that employed a band to provide a musical accompaniment to dancing, and those venues that merely played records. The former type of venue has developed into the modern rock venue of today, while the latter has developed into what we now generally consider to be a club: a place that plays records and is licensed for dancing. This split has developed into the divide between dance music and rock music that continues to this day.

The early 1970s saw the development of a specific style of club known as the disco. **Discos** subsequently became the dominant form of night-club in Britain, although specialist clubs that played music drawn from rock genres remained popular. Discos emphasized the other-worldly nature of the club experience, with their disorientating lights, elegant surroundings and a glamorous clientele. These clubs played soul and the emergent musical form of disco, a style of electronic dance music that emphasized its 'artificial' nature. It was during this period that the role of the club DJ became particularly important, with some DJs commanding considerable fees for their ability to transform recorded music through the usage of technology and through mixing two or three records together.

While the disco was the dominant form of club until the mid-1980s, there were exceptions to this rule. The **punk rock** explosion of the mid-1970s led to the opening of punk clubs in London such as The Roxy and The 100 Club. Spurred on by these developments, punk fans from other cities developed their own scenes. Clubs such as Eric's in Liverpool were the meeting point for the new generation of musicians who were to become the famous stars of the 1980s. As punk developed into **new wave**, the distinction between dance music and rock music was temporarily blurred by the experimental dance music of British bands such as The Human League, Depeche Mode and New Order.

The arrival of **house** music in Britain in 1987 led to the birth of the British club culture that we see today. In particular, the birth of acid house is seen as a defining moment. Legend has it that the British house club boom was started by a handful of working-class holiday-makers who had been clubbing in Ibiza and decided to attempt to replicate the experience during the winter of 1987–8. 'Balearic' clubs such as Shoom in London became increasingly popular. It was around this time that the drug ecstasy was first widely used in Britain.

Although initially centred on London, the acid house scene soon developed elsewhere in the country. Of pivotal importance was The Hacienda club in Manchester, with its resident DJs Mike Pickering and Graeme Park playing American house records to an enthusiastic crowd. As the acid house scene grew, it became apparent that a new type of nightclub was needed. The old discos were perceived to have lost their vitality, and the atmosphere in discos was often spoiled by alcohol-fuelled violence. In the search for new venues, acid house promoters began to use greenfield sites, disused warehouses and industrial buildings. This is the origin of contemporary **rave** culture.

As legislation was introduced to outlaw unlicensed raves, more and more venues were built to accommodate house culture's move back indoors. The important clubs of the early 1990s were Quadrant Park in Liverpool, Eclipse in Coventry (the first house club to obtain an all-night dancing licence), and Shelly's in Stoke-on-Trent. The early 1990s explosion in clubs has been fuelled by an explosion in dance music itself, with a bewildering array of sub-genres entering into the lexicon of contemporary youth culture.

Modern clubs are more popular than ever before. Containing a startling battery of sound and lighting technologies, they are perceived to be places where young people can escape from the harsh realities of contemporary life and spend a few hours dancing. Most modern clubs are connected to a specific style of dance music such as **techno** or **jungle**, and employ 'guest DJs', valued for their musical knowledge and technical skills, who can command thousands of pounds for a few hours work. Also central to the modern club is the resident DJ who can attract a regular clientele who will visit the club every week.

STUART BORTHWICK

Coates, Nigel

b. 1949

Architect

Born in 1949, Coates's extravagant humorous architecture first took off in Japan in the late 1980s, where he became the guru of club owners, retailers and restaurateurs. More British clients followed in the 1990s. Partnered since 1985 by Doug Branson in their Clerkenwell practice, Coates later seemed to become the architect of New Labour in 1997: he was invited to 10 Downing Street, asked to work on the Body Zone human figures in the Greenwich Millennium dome, and commissioned to design Britain's national exhibition at Expo 1998 in Lisbon. Known for his offbeat, largely anti-establishment 'narrative architecture' in the 1980s (for example, Jasper **Conran**'s (1985) and Katherine **Hamnett**'s (1987) **shops** in London), Coates was appointed Professor of Architecture at the Royal College of Art. In 1998 he has commissioned to design a temporary building to accommodate 'Powerhouse: UK', an exhibition of British creativity organized by the Department of Trade and Industry. A maverick of the ephemeral and inflatable, Coates's other projects include the organic, glass-clad domesticity of his Oyster House, presented at the Ideal Home Exhibition in 1998, and exhibitions at the Royal Academy's Living Bridges show, the Design Museum's Erotic Design, and the Sheffield pop centre.

See also: restaurants and bars

PETER CHILDS

Cockney

Theoretically the dialect of English spoken by those born within the sound of Bow Bells, Cockney is spoken much more widely. It is now known less for its rhyming slang ('apples and pears' for stairs) than for its links with 'Estuary English' ('hospi'ul' and 'wevva' for hospital and weather). The idea of the honest Cockney crippled by her accent was widely mythologized by Shaw's *Pygmalion* (1912, filmed as *My Fair Lady* in 1964). There, a Cockney flower girl is transformed into a 'lady' by the phonetician Professor Higgins. Michael **Caine** (followed by others such as Bob Hoskins) has conversely made Cockney 'legitimate'. Its more general current use signifies a wish to blur class boundaries and replace previous models where abandonment of Cockney was a stage in upward social mobility.

See also: dialect; Geordies; scouse

MIKE STORRY

comedies

British film comedy in the 1960s and early 1970s was dominated by sex comedies, such as *Percy* (1971) and *The Love Pill* (1971), inspired by farce and music hall and laden with double entendres and smutty jokes. The most famous of these are the **Carry On films**, produced by Peter Rogers and, beginning with the release of *Carry On Sergeant* in 1958, released at a rate of around two a year until the mid-1970s when the number slowed. *Carry On Columbus* (1992) revived the series with a cast drawn from 'alternative' comedy. Sex comedies, such as *Personal Services* (1987) and *Rita and Sue and Bob Too* (1987), continued to be produced.

Many of the British comedies of the 1970s and 1980s were connected to television sketch shows and sitcoms (see **situation comedy**). In the early 1970s, successful sitcoms spawned films like *Steptoe and Son* (1972), *Love Thy Neighbour* (1973) and *Porridge* (1979). More notable films have been produced by the comedians involved with sketch comedy.

The comics of *Monty Python's Flying Circus* employed a similar sketch-based, surrealistic style of humour in *And Now for Something Completely Different* (1973), *Monty Python and the Holy Grail* (1975), and *The Meaning of Life* (1983) while *Life of Brian* (1979) placed attacks on organized religion as well as left-wing cliquism in the context of a tighter plot. Members of the Python team, especially Terry Gilliam and John Cleese, have been involved in other successful comedies such as *Time Bandits* (1981), *Brazil* (1985), *Clockwise* (1985) and *A Fish Called Wanda* (1988). Eric Idle appeared along with Robbie Coltrane in the commercially successfully farce *Nuns on the Run* (1990). Similarly, *The Comic Strip*, in conjunction with director Peter Richardson, have been involved with the production of films like *The Bullshitters* (1984), *The Supergrass* (1985) and *Eat the Rich* (1988). Television comics Mel Smith and Griff Rhys-Jones also appeared in, amongst others, *Morons from Outer Space* (1985) and Smith has gone on to be a successful comedy director.

Many of the comedies of the 1980s and 1990s have character-based stories, employing drama as well as humour and addressing issues of racism, homophobia, poverty and political disillusionment. This is true of Stephen Frears and Hanif Kureishi's films *My Beautiful Laundrette* (1985) and *Sammy and Rosie Get Laid* (1988), Bruce **Robinson**'s *Withnail and I* (1986), Robert Smith's *The Love Child* (1987) and Gurinda **Chadha**'s *Bhaji on the Beach* (1993) as well as the films of Mike **Leigh**, including *Bleak Moments* (1971), *High Hopes* (1988), *Life is Sweet* (1990) and *Secrets and Lies* (1996). Character-based comedy also characterizes the films of Bill **Forsyth**, including *Gregory's Girl* (1981), *Local Hero* (1983) and *Comfort and Joy* (1984). Forsyth's *House-keeping* (1987) was funded by Hollywood, as are many other prominent British films such as *Educating Rita* (1983). Recently, animated comedy films have come to prominence, mainly due to the Oscar-winning success of Nick **Park**'s Wallace and Grommit films.

See also: comedy on television

Further reading

Walker, J. (1985) *The Once and Future Film*, London: Methuen.

NICOLE MATTHEWS

comedy on television

Comedy sketch shows are still one of the most popular forms of British television comedy. Earlier sketch shows, like those of Morecombe and Wise, Tommy Cooper, Benny Hill, Ronnie Barker and Ronnie Corbett drew on traditions of music hall and variety. Victoria Wood, one of the few women to break into this kind of comedy, similarly includes musical numbers along with sketches and mono-logues in her shows. Another tradition of comedy employed satire and the revue format in pro-grammes like *That Was the Week That Was* and *The Frost Report*. Satire has continued to appear on British comedy through the 1980s and 1990s with the political puppetry of *Spitting Image*, the politico-satirical impressions of *Rory Bremner – Who Else?* and the current affairs game show *Have I Got News for You*. Influential 'alternative' television sketch shows in the late 1960s and early 1970s included Dudley Moore and Peter Cook's *Not Only … But Also*, *Monty Python's Flying Circus* and Spike Milligan's numbered series of *Q*. These last two shows experimented with the form of the sketch show, abandoning punchlines in favour of surrealistic linking devices.

While play with the conventions of television could be found in the 1980s in Alexei Sayle's *Stuff*, *French and Saunders* and *A Bit of Fry and Laurie*, from this period 'alternative' comedy tended to focus more on anti-Tory, anti-racist and anti-sexist sentiments than experiments with the sketch form. This can be seen in programmes like *Saturday Live* with Ben Elton, *The Lenny Henry Show*, *The Real McCoy* and *The Mark Thomas Show*. Nonetheless, there has been resistance from many comedians to both the label of 'alternative' and the expectation of 'right-on' politics, despite, or perhaps because of, the under-representation of women and non-white performers in television sketch programmes. While the appearance of comics like Bob Monkhouse and Roy Castle as comperes has given British game-shows a comic flavour, more recently the hybrid genre of the comedy game show has become popular. Examples include the improvisation show *Whose Line is it Anyway?* and celebrity game shows like *Shooting Stars* and *They Think It's All Over*. *Sticky Moments* with Julian Clary showed the way that these shows can combine quite traditional kinds of British humour – in this case, Benny Hill-esque smutty double entendres – with a glamorous gay host, who disrupts the game show norms of heterosexuality and fair play. In the late 1990s, the sketches in sketch shows seemed to become ever shorter, to the extent that *The Fast Show* based itself upon a stream of thirty-second turns which, shorter than many television commercials, seemed ideally designed for an audience with a short attention span.

See also: Carry On films; comedies; situation comedy

Further reading

Wilmut, R. (1982) *From Fringe to Flying Circus: Celebrating a Unique Generation of Comedy 1960–1980*, London: Methuen.

Wilmut, R. and Rosengard, P. (1989), *Didn't You Kill My Mother-in-law? The Story of Alternative Comedy in Britain from The Comedy Store to Saturday Live*, London: Methuen.

NICOLE MATTHEWS

Comedy Store, The

The Comedy Store, based on a Los Angeles original, was founded by Peter Rosengard in 1979 in the Nell Gwynne strip club in Soho. It was compered first by Alexei Sayle (and later by Ben Elton), and twenty-five amateur comedians did stand-up routines. Bad performances were 'gonged' off. It was only on at midnight on Saturday and Sunday nights, and was one of the first 'one-nighter' clubs to revitalize London's nightlife. The ethos was anti-racist and anti-sexist. Double acts like Twentieth Century (Rik Mayall and Ade Edmondson) and The Outer Limits (Peter Richardson and Nigel Planer) got their start there. Audiences were diverse and members of the public could perform after the main acts.

See also: Carry On films; comedies; comedy on television; situation comedy

MIKE STORRY

comics

Comics have gone through a period of transformation in Britain in recent years. Circulation of mainstream titles fell after the 1960s and many folded altogether or merged with others. Despite the new fan-shop market, there was a steady decline in newsagent comic sales. Under hippie counterculture (see **hippies**), there were underground comics or 'comix', which remained so because of their anarchism and drug associations. However, they influenced and eventually were superseded by the mainstream. The latter borrowed their anti-authoritarianism, added a punk note of confrontation and aimed at an older audience.

In terms of quality, the industry produced three outstanding newsstand comics in the post-1960s period: *2000AD* (IPC/Fleetway, 1977), *Deadline* (Tom Astor, 1988) and *Viz* (House of Viz, 1979). Each of these comics was designed for a readership older than that for children's comics like the *Dandy* and *Beano*. Readers related to the punk movement with its distrust of authority, stress on working-class street credibility and fetishization of violence for its own sake.

2000AD was science-fiction based and designed to replace *Action*, which had fallen foul of censors nominally because of its violent bent, but also because of its anti-authoritarain stance borrowed from underground comics. *2000AD*'s best known character was Judge Dredd, an updated Dan Dare figure from the *Eagle* of the 1950s. *Judge Dredd Magazine* appeared in 1990, based on this character. The comic's layout was innovative – borrowing large eye-catching splash panels from US models – and its contributors particularly admired American Marvel comics. *Deadline*, with its emphasis on humour over adventure and its pop music features, was a cross between an adult humour comic and a music/style magazine. Its most successful character was Tank Girl, by Alan Martin and Jamie Hewlett. She was a shaven-headed outlaw in biker boots who became a mascot for feminist groups and later 'riot grrl' bands. A film based on Tank Girl did not do as well as was hoped.

Viz has been the most successful of all. Founded in Newcastle upon Tyne by brothers Chris and Simon Donald, its numerous controversial characters – Sid the Sexist, Fat Slags, Millie Tant – and its schoolboy humour were just what its target audience wanted. Its circulation at 3.3 million (1995) dwarfed that of its rivals.

See also: comics culture

Further reading

Sabin, R. (1993) *Adult Comics*, London: Routledge.

DAVE JACKSON

comics culture

By 1996 there were as many as 250 comics stores in the UK, compared with about 10 in 1977. Though this would seem to indicate a marked increase in the comic-buying public, it merely reflects a shift away from the traditional mainstream newsstand to the specialist shop. Actual comic sales have declined. Comics, traditionally thought of as children's literature, have gained a sort of adult respectability through the advent of graphic novels (long comics) and the 1980s boom in comic buying as financial speculation. Rare comics could be worth outrageous sums of money. Celebrity comic collectors included Jonathan Ross and Lenny Henry (who collaborated on *Neverwhere*, a television fantasy series with comic book creator Neil Gaiman). There are regular comic marts and conventions held in most major cities in the UK, the biggest being UKAC, which is held in London. The type of comics included in this phenomenon still tend to follow stereotypical science fiction or costumed superhero lines, although there are many exceptions.

Comics culture in the UK is dominated by US products, imported or reprinted under licence from American companies such as DC and Marvel. There have been several attempts to launch home grown comics in the UK, notably ***2000AD***, *Warrior, Deadline, Blast, Toxic* and *Revolver*. Of these, only *2000AD*, launched in 1977, still exists and although it has been Britain's most successful science fiction/superhero related title (Judge Dredd was recently made into a Hollywood movie) its popularity is dwindling. Most of Britain's more talented writers and artists have gone to work for American companies where the financial rewards are greater. Ironically, despite the higher profile of the adult comic-buying public, the UK market is still too small to support a home-grown comics industry. The comics fan, as opposed to the casual reader, buys his/her comics from specialist shops such as The Forbidden Planet rather than the traditional newsstand or newsagent. The Forbidden Planet chain of comic stores, owned by Nick Landau (also owner of Titan Books, Britain's biggest comic publisher) now have fifteen stores throughout the UK, having started off in 1977 with one shop in London's Denmark Street. Their newer London store is the biggest of its kind in the world. They stock science fiction and fantasy books, videos, film and television-related material, and trading cards; in fact, anything to do with 'trash culture'.

See also: comics

DAVE JACKSON

commercial radio

Since its inception in 1973, when the first two independent services (Capital and LBC) began broadcasting in London, commercial radio now accounts for nearly 50 percent of all listening in the UK. Apart from a period in the late 1970s, when the Labour administration restricted the numbers of new licences issued, there has been a steady and continuing growth, with over 200 stations on air in 1998. While the vast majority of these are regional or local services, the 1990 Broadcasting Act made provisions for national independent commercial radio stations. There are now three of these: Classic FM was the first to go on air in September 1992, followed by the rock station Virgin 1215 in 1993 and Talk Radio in 1995.

Many regional stations are also now broadcasting two distinct outputs, or 'split frequencies'. In addition to the main FM transmissions (with contemporary hit formats targeted at a young audience) these 'Gold' AM stations usually specialize in 'classic hits' from the 1960s to 1980s, and are used to increase their appeal for middle-aged listeners. However, despite these AM stations, older listeners seem to remain loyal to BBC radio.

From the late 1980s, large numbers of illegal **pirate radio** stations began broadcasting in and to major cities. A phenomenon of the growing rave scene (see **rave culture**), these focused almost exclusively on dance music. They rarely featured commercials for mainstream companies, with any advertising limited to the promotion of dance venues and club nights. However, the introduction of so-called 'incremental' licences allowed for specialized stations to broadcast legally in areas already covered by existing commercial services. London pirate stations such as Kiss FM and Choice FM successfully applied for licences, and began broadcasting legally in 1990. While their programming remains dance-oriented, they are now included in mainstream commercial media schedules. The increase in the numbers of stations on air, and the specific nature of their programming, provides advertisers with targeting opportunities not offered by terrestrial television. There are many specialist broadcasters, such as London Greek Radio and the Bradford-based Asian station Sunrise Radio, that cater for specific ethnic groups and languages. While commercials for local products and services are frequently produced at the radio stations from which they will be transmitted, national or larger budget campaigns are usually written and produced by the major (London-based) advertising agencies.

The impending introduction of the DAB (Digital Audio Broadcasting), in addition to improving audio and reception quality, will also radically increase the number of possible broadcasters, and revolutionize radio advertising in the next millennium.

See also: advertising, influence of; commercial radio, national

DAVID CROFT

commercial radio, national

National commercial radio stations were established in the UK in the early 1990s. Apart from the chance to cater for a sizeable youngish (18–35) leisured class, these stations were driven by a sympathetic commercial and competitive environment set in place by **Conservative governments** in the 1980s. Their success can be gauged by noting that, in early 1995, listeners to commercial radio exceeded BBC Radio's national audience for the first time (50.1 percent to 47.9 percent). Adding to the wide variety of radio experience now available in the UK, commercial radio contributes significantly to a generally buoyant market in this particularly intimate medium, a high profile which looks set to continue at least into the foreseeable future. Depending how one defines 'national', there are three or four stations, funded by advertising, which cover most of the UK.

Launched in September 1992, Classic FM was Britain's first national commercial station broadcasting 24 hours a day, seven days a week. Its aim is to 'bring classical music to the widest possible audience, reducing the aura of intimidation surrounding classical music'. It has a more populist approach than its seeming rival BBC **Radio 3**, but it has also attracted a fair portion of its listeners from middling **Radio 2**. National listening share is 3.1 percent (Radio 3, 1.0 percent), with an average weekly audience of 4.6m (Radio 3, 2.4m)

Virgin Radio started out in 1994 with the disadvantage of only being allowed to broadcast nationally on AM, though its London-only extension does have an FM slot. The station policy of adult rock attracts a sizeable weekly audience of around 3.2m (3 percent of the national figure). In 1998, control passed from Richard Branson to ex-*Big Breakfast* and **Radio 1** presenter Chris Evans.

Launched as a national non-music station in February 1995 on a policy of 'shock jocks', Talk Radio UK did not have an easy ride in its first eighteen months of broadcasting life, owing to public protests, rapid management turnover and financial difficulties. The more outrageous of the presenting jocks having been ousted, and there were signs of an increase in its national listening share in the late 1990s. This may well continue as the station finds the right commercial policy that will attract both listeners and advertisers in buoyant numbers (it currently attracts a 1.8 percent share of listeners).

Though not strictly a 'British' national radio station, since it broadcasts from Dublin, Atlantic 252 firmly targets the UK as its intended market, reaching the country north of a line from the Wash to Dorset. Its music policy is 'hot adult contemporary', playing top 40 hits to a youngish (15–30) audience. It has been particularly adroit at keeping its listeners happy by the use of very careful market research that determines which songs – using short snatches of current numbers – listeners want to hear more of. Thus by giving consumers what they really want, Atlantic has created a highly successful media product broadcasting on long wave only, so that listeners on the move never need to retune. Its average weekly reach is 2.2m (2.9 percent of share).

Note: All listening figures are from the second quarter of 1996 (source: RAJAR/RSL).

See also: commercial radio

Further reading

Scannell, P. (1991) *Broadcast Talk*, London: Sage.
Wilby, P. and Conroy, A. (1994) *The Radio Handbook*,
London: Routledge.

GEORGE HASTINGS

Commission for Racial Equality

The Commission for Racial Equality (CRE) is the
product of three Acts passed in the 1960s and
1970s. The Race Relations Act of 1965 established
the Race Relations Board to receive complaints of
unlawful discrimination and to have them investigated. The 1968 Race Relations Act enlarged the
Board and its scope, while the Community
Relations Commission was also established to
promote good race relations. A third Act in 1976
outlawed victimization and discrimination in
employment, industry and education, making it
an offence to incite racial hatred. The Act replaced
the Race Relations and Community Relations
Commission with the Commission for Racial
Equality, funded by the Home Office. The
Commission is credited with successfully fulfilling
its remit, particularly in its assistance of individuals
in unfair dismissal cases, where it has also
undoubtedly had a deterrent effect. Predictably,
tabloid newspapers and occasionally broadsheets
have attempted to pour ridicule on its attempts to
get to the heart of racism by policing language
which it sees as racist (such as 'black sheep' or
'black mark').

See also: Race Relations Acts

MIKE STORRY

Communist Party

The Communist Party of Great Britain was
formed in 1920 in response to an appeal by
Lenin. It was influential in the labour movement
until the onset of the Cold War, which prompted
long-term decline. The party was hampered by its

association with the Soviet Communist Party,
which provided a substantial secret subsidy
between 1958 and 1979. The party leadership
moved towards a more reformist, Eurocommunist
position in the 1970s causing a split with a
hardline faction centred around the *Morning Star*
newspaper. In 1991, following the collapse of the
Soviet Union, the Communist Party voted to
become the Democratic Left. In the 1990s they
gained publicity with instances of **direct action**
to support striking workers and protest against
local government cuts.

See also: Marxism; Militant; National Front;
trade unions

COLIN WILLIAMS

community politics

In the UK, community politics may be formal or
informal. The formal level provides a number of
opportunities in which community politics may
take place. These range from neighbourhood
watch schemes to parish councils and town
councils, district councils and county councils. In
the first case arrangements are informal but with
official back-up and training. In the second case
they have constitutional status and varying degrees
of power and budgetary control.

Constitutional changes resulting in formally
recognized devolved politics, in Wales and Scotland, are likely to result in an increase in regional
assemblies. It is also possible that this will result in
an increase in political interest at a lower level,
including informal political groupings.

Informal forms of community politics are often
generated by local objections to nationally proposed actions or to single-issue politics (often
instigated by new social movements). These 'grassroots' activities may be both parliamentary and
extra-parliamentary. Objections may be raised by
groups such as Greenpeace at inquiries to build
nuclear power stations, while direct action may be
mounted by others to prevent roads or runways
being built through special areas of natural or
scientific interest. If the formal objection fails,
extra-parliamentary activity may be invoked. This
usually takes the form of human obstruction to the

proposed construction, thus raising the political and financial cost.

The history of such communal objections has been increasingly successful. There are now several central government-sponsored projects (from train lines to bypasses) that have been thwarted by communal action. In the process, the value of community politics has been exhibited. By contrast, formal community politics has been increasingly devalued by declining powers, the growth of quangos (quasi non-governmental organizations) and centralization. In principle, membership of the European Union opens up a range of possibilities for community politics that have not yet been met in practice.

See also: democracy; pressure groups

Further reading

Smith, M.P. and Feagin, J. (eds) (1987) *The Capitalist City: Global Restructuring and Community Politics*, Oxford: Blackwell.

PAUL BARRY CLARKE
SVANBORG SIGMARSDOTTIR

community theatre

In the 1960s fringe companies, formed around political and cultural issues, began taking theatre into non-theatre venues. The most notable example was John **McGrath**'s 7:84 company, whose tour to the Scottish Highlands of *The Cheviot, The Stag and The Black, Black Oil* epitomized the notion of making live theatre available while promoting the ideology of a 'counterculture'. The community theatre movement grew out of the recognition of the needs of communities without theatre. It was generally populist in appeal, offering an aesthetic challenge to the style of establishment theatre and creating new venues and audiences; it also, by and large, retained an 'oppositional' stance grounded in a political idealism associated with ecological concerns and an acknowledgement of the oppressions of those outside the dominant class.

The idea that theatre could be made with communities began to take root. Welfare State International developed the concept of 'celebratory

protest' with their carnivalesque style of 'theatre-as-event', where audiences are in the thousands; Ann Jellicoe founded a new genre with the 'community play', involving hundreds of local people. Both have worked on the principle that art is a bonding agent for communities which have become fragmented. Direct participation has become the key element of community theatre, with professionals working as 'animateurs' to facilitate people in finding a voice and using theatre as a means of agitating for improvement, or as a way of animating (hidden) histories.

Whereas 'amateur' theatre groups still flourish as a hobby for the middle classes, who replicate the hierarchies of West End theatre, community theatre groups operate on democratic principles and are rooted in the concepts of accessibility, involvement and identification. There is cross-fertilization with other arts, as frequently community drama is allied with dance and music under the umbrella term 'community arts'.

Continued expansion of community theatre companies/groups in the 1960s testifies to the efficacy of this new branch of theatre practice. International theorists (Barba, Boal) have been influential in the move towards valorizing the 'process' of making community theatre, and of using drama as a cultural 'healing agent', as opposed to its product. The politics of those involved in the movement have diluted somewhat in the 1990s as the focus has shifted from the macro level of radical cultural intervention to the micro level of individual 'empowerment'.

See also: fringe theatre; improvisation; McGrath, John; theatre, regional

Further reading

Kershaw, B. (1992) *The Politics of Performance, Radical Theatre as Cultural Intervention*, London: Routledge.

DYMPHNA CALLERY

computer graphics and multimedia

Although artist-run organizations like London Video Access (now London Electronic Arts) had installed expensive paint systems by the mid-1980s, the advent of the Apple Macintosh was the key to the development of an artists' scene for multimedia in the UK. The DIY aesthetic of punk design, and the typographic revolt associated with Neville Brody, could both now be simulated on relatively cheap software packages, and the impact can be seen in the growth both of desktop published fanzines and the increasingly sophisticated use of photographic retouching programmes. Even the high-end video systems of the 1980s, like Harry and Paintbox, could now be reproduced on accessible machines.

The first artists to take advantage of this came out of the **video art** scene, notably artists with associations to the art schools of Sheffield and Dundee like Judith Goddard and Clive Gillman. Composited animations and finely honed moving graphics became a hallmark of a period of British electronic arts around 1990, when seminal works like Goddard's *Luminous Portrait*, Gillman's *NLV6 (Sublime)*, Keith Piper's *The Nation's Finest* and Steve Hawley's *Trout Descending a Staircase* began to circulate. However, video art faced a desperate struggle both with an entrenched conservatism in the gallery world and an almost closed distribution system in cinemas. The Liverpool-based Video Positive festival and the **Arts Council**-funded Film and Video Umbrella began to promote such work, and associated interactive installations by artists like Goddard, Piper and Simon Robertshaw, to a slowly widening public of afficionados and interested and active computer buffs.

William Latham's tenure of an IBM Fellowship between 1988 and 1993 introduced genetic algorithm or artificial life programming to the UK scene, and although critics like Cate Elwes deplored a certain 'toys for the boys' tendency, increasingly women artists, including Elwes, have been making exemplary and subtle use of the available technologies. New digital media have brought important works into publication: Gillman, Simon Biggs, Graham Harwood and Audio-ROM have made important CD-ROMs. Internet art is now widely discussed: two exemplary works are Jane Prophet's *Technosphere* and Heath Bunting's *irrational.org*. Major design practices like Amaze and Obsolete have grown swiftly in this climate, and an increasing number of art schools offer specialist degrees. An important new development is heralded by the work of Dispersed Data, a loose affiliation of black British multimedia artists and curators.

Further reading

Watt, A. (1993) *3D Computer Graphics*, 2nd edn, Wokingham: Addison-Wesley.

SEAN CUBITT

concert promoters

Concert promoters are responsible for hiring the venue, arranging the stages, the personal address systems, lighting, caterers, security and advertising, and coordinating ticket sales. The most influential and successful concert promoter in the UK is Harvey Goldsmith, who started out organizing university concerts. The Concert Promoters Association was formed in 1980, chaired by Goldsmith, to counteract the negative image of wheeler-dealer surrounding promoters. Many promoters also work the festival circuits, as well as the main rock venues. SJM are a massive organization, based in the north of England, but operating on a nationwide basis. Mean Fiddler promote the Phoenix and Reading festivals, as well as running their own venues and nationwide tours. Other main promoters are Metropolis, MCP and Riverman.

ALICE BENNETT

conductors

The conductor is the central figure in most orchestral performances and is the person with whom audiences generally identify. Certain conductors attain 'cult status' which even endures posthumously; examples include Herbert von Karajan and Leonard Bernstein, both powerful

musical personalities. Norman Lebrecht scruti-
nized the personality cult of the conductor in his
book *The Maestro Myth*, and there is debate as to the
extent to which a performance 'belongs' to the
conductor or to the orchestra. British conductors
rising to prominence during the 1980s and 1990s
included Sir Simon Rattle, who became synonymous with the City of Birmingham Symphony
Orchestra, and Richard Hickox, founder and close
associate of the City of London Sinfonia.

There is speculation as to why there appear to
be so few up-and-coming British conductors.
Conducting opportunities are scarce for students,
so for the most part they must study by observation
rather than practice. Many aim to work as
repetiteurs as a first step in a conducting career,
or set up groups of their own. Many British
orchestras and opera companies operate assistant
conductorships, usually aided by sponsorship.

There is also speculation about the lack of
women active in conducting – in the *British and
International Music Yearbook* there are fewer than
twenty female names in a total of 400 – though, as
in other professions, the balance is slowly tipping
towards equality, with the emergence of such
conductors as Jane Glover, Sian Edwards, Odaline
de la Martinez and Wasfi Kani.

Most holders of conducting posts with British
orchestras were born abroad. Many of these
simultaneously continue their international careers,
typically holding more than one orchestral post and
making guest appearances. For example, newcomers in 1996 to British conducting posts included
the Royal Philharmonic's music director, Daniele
Gatti, born in Milan; Frenchman Jean-Bernard
Pommier at the Northern Sinfonia; and American
Joseph Swensen, principal conductor of the Scottish
Chamber Orchestra. Many conductors from
abroad develop strong relationships with British
orchestras; for example, there is the close connection which has spanned a decade between Libor
Pešek, awarded the KBE for his services to British
interests, and the Royal Liverpool Philharmonic.

Conductors have also risen to especial prominence in the performance of authentic/period
music. Many, such as Roger Norrington and John
Eliot Gardiner, undertake careful study to ensure
performances are as close as possible to those of the
composer's time.

See also: classical music; classical soloists

Further reading

Lebrecht, N. (1992) *The Maestro Myth*, London:
Simon & Schuster.

ANDREA MARTIN

Connery, Sean

b. 1929, Edinburgh

Actor

One of the few British actors who can sell a film on
name alone, Sean Connery was born Thomas
Connery in Fountainbridge, a working-class suburb
of Edinburgh. Always identified with the role of
James Bond, his career began in British B-Movies
in the 1950s, and it was not until David Niven
refused the role of Bond in *Dr No* (1962) that
Connery, who took the role, became a household
name. His work in Hollywood includes *Marnie*
(1964), *Robin and Marion* (1976), *The Name of the Rose*
(1986) and *The Untouchables* (1987), for which he
won an Academy Award. Though living in Spain,
Connery remains passionate about Scotland, once
donating his fee from a Bond film to finance an
educational trust in the country.

SAM JOHNSTONE

Conran, Jasper

b. 1959, London

Fashion designer

Son of Terence **Conran**, whose impact on British
design and taste made him a household name, and
of writer Shirley Conran, Jasper Conran has
worked hard to carve his own niche in the world
of fashion and design. Born in 1960 and trained in
New York, he has a reputation for precision
tailoring and attention to detail. His first collection
was produced by Wallis in 1979, and he was named
British Designer of the Year in 1986. Although his
restrained, wearable classics make him a favourite
with the professional woman, he has recently

branched out into the more dramatic fields of **ballet** and theatre costume design.

TAMSIN SPARGO

Conran, Terence

b. 1931, Esher

Designer

Sir Terence Orby Conran has had an enormous influence on defining and indeed determining the design of shop and house interiors within Britain and Europe. His store Habitat, first opened in London in 1964, completely revolutionized notions of taste. Before Habitat, notions of good taste were almost exclusively conservative and elitist. Conran, having struggled for ten years to establish himself as a furniture designer and maker, redefined the world of retail and arguably transformed the idea of shopping into an enjoyable occasion rather than a necessary task. The cultural historian Christopher Frayling suggests that Conran has had more impact on design than the **Design Council** and the government put together.

Nicholas Ind's biography explains that part of the power of Habitat was its sensuality:

> the combination of touch, sight, sound and smell. In addition to the tactile displays, there were the pervasive odour of herbs and spices as well as the sound of modern jazz. Conran offered modern, affordable products in an uncluttered and elegant environment.
>
> (Ind 1995: 65)

His designs were an enormous success with the new affluent middle classes, and by 1980 there were forty-seven Habitat stores. Conran's entrepreneurial expertise gave rise to the merger of Habitat with other retailers such as Mothercare, Heal's and British Home Stores, forming the multi-million pound Storehouse Group; however, this failed to achieve the heights anticipated by Conran, predominantly because BHS was imbued with a culture that was resistant to his plans of bringing well-designed goods to the mass market.

As with Habitat's influence on shopping, Conran has also transformed and developed the landscape of eating out, with restaurants like Quaglino's, Bibendum and Pont de la Tour. It is important to stress that Conran has helped to transform society and its values, and he has made spending money a legitimate cultural practice. His diversity of interests as designer, restaurateur, retailer and writer have ensured him a permanent residency as arbiter of British taste.

See also: Conran, Jasper

Further reading

Ind, N. (1995) *Terence Conran: The Authorized Biography*, London: Sidgwick & Jackson.

FATIMA FERNANDES

conservation groups

Britain's major official national conservation agencies are English Heritage, Cadw (for Wales), Historic Scotland, and the Department of the Environment for Northern Ireland. The National Trust and The Landmark Trust are the highest profile national charities involved with conservation of buildings, but there are many lesser known bodies which identify historic buildings most at risk. They then lobby the official agencies responsible for listing and funding, and get them to supply the money. Examples of such organizations are The Georgian Group, the Victorian Society, the Ancient Monuments Society, the Society for the Protection of Ancient Buildings (SPAB) (founded by William Morris in 1877), and the newest amenity society, the Twentieth Century Society, which takes up the cause of buildings from 1914 to the present. More 'grassroots' organizations also contribute, such as the Campaign for the Preservation of Rural England and The Friends of Friendless Churches (set up to protect redundant Anglican churches in Wales).

Besides the above, there are numerous local voluntary organizations working to restore local landmarks or create wildlife refuges or city farms. These have the opportunity to apply for **National Lottery** funding, but this has become less easy since 1997.

The existence of these bodies and their distribution throughout Britain indicates a widespread interest in preserving and visiting Britain's historic buildings. For example in 1997, 2.9m people visited Historic Scotland's listed buildings, up 400,000 from the year before.

Listing of buildings contains a presumption against demolition, but it does not rule it out. In 1996 there were applications to demolish 266 listed buildings in England and Wales. Most were turned down or withdrawn, often in response to public feeling. Certainly in cities, people are now more aware of the depredations of previous redevelopers. Thus when the Church proposed restoring St Ethelburgha's Bishopsgate, destroyed by the 1993 IRA bomb, 'with a glazed facade', public opposition was voiced and a 'traditional' facing was chosen.

The change of government from Conservative to Labour in 1997 has meant less emphasis on conservation of buildings. There has been a shift in Lottery funds to education and 'community' projects and the amount going to historic buildings has been drastically reduced to £30m a year, when it was nearly double this a few years ago.

See also: heritage

Further reading

Isaacs, A. and Monk, J. (1993) *The Illustrated Dictionary of British Heritage*, Cambridge: Cambridge University Press.

MIKE STORRY

Conservative governments

The **Conservative Party** traditionally shuns the notions of ideology and abstract thought, and has established a practice of responding to particular circumstances in a manner which will preserve those institutions beneficial to the existing social and economic status quo. This approach has been tempered with a paternalistic concern for the less well-off, but only in so far as this facilitates the maintenance of established hierarchies. Some commentators have argued that the Thatcher government represented a discontinuity within

Conservative party history, that far from eschewing ideology Thatcher and her colleagues embraced it, even in the face of negative public opinion. Yet there is evidence of continuity within the Thatcher administrations, if not obviously within the economic sphere then certainly in the social policy of her governments.

The transfiguration within the Conservative party began in 1965 with the election of Edward Heath as leader. Heath's election was notable for two reasons. First, there was the manner in which he became leader. In late 1946 the selection process had been reformed at the instigation of Sir Alec Douglas Home into the now familiar three-stage voting process, allowing MPs to select their own leader from among their peers. Second, Heath was not of the same ilk as previous Conservative leaders. He was not an aristocrat, coming instead from a lower-middle class background.

Significantly, Heath was elected rather than his opponent Enoch Powell, who demonstrated a commitment to the *laissez-faire* ideals that were to grip the party within a decade. That is not to say that Heath rejected these ideals, but rather that he was more moderate in choosing a policy line that challenged **Labour Party** policy yet remained within the boundaries of the postwar consensus. This attitude can be attributed to Heath's distinctly conservative nature. He did not consider reducing state intervention out of a deep-seated ideological conviction, but because he felt it a practical approach to the problems of the time.

Under Heath, the Conservatives were defeated in the 1966 election. In the 1966 election manifesto, Heath sought to distance the Conservative Party from Labour. Heath chose to commit the Conservative party to the European community (in itself a commitment to free market principles), and promised reform of the **welfare state** and **trade unions**. These measures amounted to an attempt to forge public opinion rather than respond to it, which was a notably atypical line for a Conservative leader to adopt. It failed, and the Labour Party retained government.

The tone of the manifesto for the 1970 election, which the Conservatives won, was distinctly neo-liberal, tempered with Heath's pervading caution. Thus, although it talked of ending wage control policies and stressed a 'hands-off' approach to the economy, it did not specifically talk in monetarist terms or include privatization plans. The subsequent administration was marked by two distinct periods. In the first, immediately following the election, Heath threw off the Keynesian assumptions prevalent in politics at the time and pursued a deflationary non-statist approach to the economy. In the second, he renounced these ideas and went back to a Keynesian approach in 1971, a move known as the Heath U-turn. In the face of growing business failures and rising unemployment, Heath adopted a reflationary budget, instigated government support for ailing industries and businesses (such as Rolls-Royce) and created the interventionist Industrial Development Executive. Unfortunately, these measures coupled with a strict incomes policy were to bring about the demise of the Heath government. A large increase in the balance of payments deficit, rising inflation and strikes (leading to 'the **Winter of Discontent**') cost the Conservatives the next election.

Such failure indicated that it was time for a change of leadership. In the ensuing contest, Margaret Thatcher secured the leadership in the second ballot. From the outset it was clear that Thatcher did not share the common Conservative aversion to ideology, and it is arguably in this respect that it is most valid to view her administration as a watershed. Previously, the party had adopted the policy most appropriate to the time. Heath adopted anti-interventionist, monetarist ideals only as a response to the problems of the economy as he perceived them. Thatcher, however, adopted an individualistic, *laissez-faire* approach with passionate fervour. Monetarist economic policy was one such ideal.

Monetarist theory experienced a revival in the 1970s. Britain experienced the phenomenon of 'stagflation', increasing inflation and increasing unemployment. The Keynesian orthodoxy could not explain this, but monetarism could. The theory stated that the money supply needed to be controlled, because if the money supply exceeds the level of real output then inflation ensues. (The Labour Prime Minister, James Callaghan, had been forced to set financial targets as a condition of an IMF loan.) Thatcher warmed to monetarist theory very quickly, and, following her victory in the 1979 election, it was immediately used with the

objective of reducing inflation. The government published the Medium-Term Financial Strategy, detailing parameters of growth for the money supply up to 1984. The MTFS also contained plans for the Public Sector Borrowing Requirement (PSBR), the difference between government revenue and expenditure. The planned reduction in the PSBR was an idea antithetical to Keynesianism when there were already such high levels of unemployment. The result was clear: as inflation fell, unemployment rose drastically. However, contrary to monetarist theory the money supply (M3) actually grew as inflation fell. Strict control was not working. In 1982 with the revision of the MTFS, discretionary monetary policy was adopted. Aware of an upcoming election the government cut interest rates, in effect relaxing monetary policy. In 1984, economic circumstances forced Chancellor Nigel Lawson to suspend the monetary target range. Monetarist policy ceased to dictate Conservative economic policy. In a move which illustrates inconsistency within the Thatcher era, a period of reverse monetarism followed, during which time the principles of monetarism were abandoned.

The Thatcher government's radicalization of the economy was not limited to monetarism. There was also a strong commitment to altering the balance of the postwar mixed economy in favour of private ownership. A widespread programme of **privatization** was set in motion, a programme in line with the Thatcherite belief in the primacy of the market. Thatcher believed that state intervention caused inefficiency, that markets became distorted, and that industry became wasteful and lacklustre. The privatization of British Telecom (BT) was a signal event as the company maintained a (virtual) monopoly and as such was able to exploit the telecommunications market. Ever the champion of the consumer, the Conservative government drew up legislation and established a watchdog to monitor the industry, following a sequence of events which became common in subsequent privatizations. The programme of privatization was felt by some commentators to extend beyond sound economics into the grounds of an ideological obsession.

Nationalized industries were not the only barrier to the free market identified by the Thatcher government. The trade unions also stood in the way of an efficient capitalist economy, by seeking wage and productivity agreements. Through these actions, British industry lost competitiveness and the British economy suffered inflation and low growth. Widespread legislation was introduced to curb the power of the unions. Secondary picketing was banned, ballots prior to strike action became compulsory, and, most significantly, unions had to follow certain procedures before striking (if they did not they could be sued). Union membership dropped, and by 1993 stood at its lowest level since 1946.

The Thatcher administration was unique in the Conservative tradition for disregarding public opinion. Reforms of the National Health Service and social security system are good instances, but the most outstanding example was the community charge. Introduced in the Local Government Finance Act of 1988, it quickly became known as the **poll tax**. The level of popular opposition to the poll tax, thanks largely to the regressive nature of the tax, was overwhelming and, in addition to intra-party divisions over Europe, was to lead to Thatcher's political demise.

The liberal attitude towards the economy did not however extend into other areas of policy making. Thatcher's social policy was authoritarian in nature. Emphasis was given to the traditionally Conservative ideals of order and authority. Correspondingly, there was an extension in police powers and stiffer penalties for offenders. Far from encouraging liberal attitudes in society, as the government did in the economy, the Conservatives tried to reverse them.

The Thatcher era was of great political and economic significance. It altered the balance of the mixed economy through extensive privatization, while liberalization and deregulation opened up the British economy (for example, there was the removal of exchange controls in November 1979). The importance of the market became universally accepted. The trade unions and their influence was weakened (particularly the coal miners' union, the NUM, which was weakened by its defeat in the 1984–5 miners' strike). The structure of the British tax base was altered from domination by direct taxation to a strong emphasis upon indirect taxation. The rhetoric of the time was radical, but the policy outcomes were not always equally so. The size of the state did not shrink, nor did the money supply. Public expenditure levels have been maintained. With the decline of the traditional working class and increasing consumer affluence, the Conservative Party found that its ideals were not as unpopular as once they might have been. The Thatcher administration simply exploited this in setting the political agenda. In her pragmatic responses and authoritarian nature Thatcher reflected old Tory style, but in her ideological convictions she did not.

John Major was left with a set of difficult circumstances following his election as leader in November 1990. The economy was in the grip of **recession**, while Thatcher's dominant leadership style left Major looking weak rather than conciliatory or a unifying force. The internal tensions over Europe which contributed to Thatcher's ousting remained unresolved, an election loomed, and the Labour party were experiencing an upturn in fortunes compared to the barren days of the early 1980s. The Conservative Party rallied round their new leader in order to secure victory at the 1992 election. The party appealed to the public with reduced taxation and increased spending, resulting inevitably in an increasing PSBR. Major did well out of the Gulf War in 1991, experiencing a boost in personal ratings as a consequence. It was important for Major that he portrayed himself as different to Thatcher, but not too different. At the party conference in 1991 he gave a speech intended to illustrate this. He presented a more moderate path than Thatcher, yet still emphasized themes such as the right to choose and wealth creation. He aimed for compromise over Europe by securing opt-out clauses, and with the party behind him, led it to the 1992 election.

After winning the 1992 election, Major and the Party had mixed fortunes. The economy took a long time to recover from recession. The party were dogged by allegations of improper behaviour on the part of individual MPs, such as David Mellor, Michael Mates, Steven Norris, Graham Riddick and David Treddinick (over 'cash for questions'). The behaviour of the government was questioned by the Scott Inquiry and the Nolan Commission set up to investigate 'sleaze'. Major also suffered attacks from within his party, which remained fiercely divided over Europe, and he failed to satisfy the more right-wing elements within his party, who called for a return to the Thatcher era.

Major did not break with the ideas of the Thatcher administration; indeed, some of the most illiberal legislation on crime and punishment was passed under Major. In true Conservative tradition, he adapted Thatcherism to circumstances and his leadership style. He attempted to unify a divided party with a view to electoral success by subsuming ideology, but ultimately failed in the face of New Labour's promises of change and modernization.

See also: black Conservatives; fringe groups

Further reading

Evans, B. and Taylor, A. (1996) *From Salisbury To Major*, Manchester: Manchester University Press.

Gamble, A. (1991) 'The Thatcher Decade in Perspective' in G. Peele, A. Gamble and P. Dunleavy (eds), *Developments in British Politics 3*, London: Macmillan.

Hutton, W. (1996) *The State We're In*, London: Vintage.

ALASTAIR LINDSLEY

Conservative Party

The Conservative Party has been the most successful political force in Britain in the twentieth century. It has dominated government in the postwar period and their spell in office from 1979–97 was the longest of any party for almost two centuries. The Conservative Party is a hierarchical organization dominated by the party leader, who in turn have up until now been elected solely by Tory MPs. In the first ballot to decide a leader, the winner needs an overall majority and 15 percent more than the runner up. The second ballot requires a simple majority, and in a third contest only the two leading candidates participate in a head to head. In practice, the three stages are rarely needed. In 1990, Mrs Thatcher was opposed by Michael Heseltine and accrued 55 percent of the votes, just failing to attain the 15 percent lead.

She stood down and Heseltine, Douglas Hurd and John Major contested the second ballot. Major just failed to gain half the votes, but the other two candidates withdrew and Major became Prime Minister.

Outside of **parliament**, the Conservative Party is divided between Central Office and the National Association. The former is the professional, administrative wing of the party, responsible for the coordination and supervision of local organizations and the dissemination of policy initiatives. The Chairman and senior officials at Central Office are appointed by the party leader. The National Association is the federation of Conservative constituency associations and represents the mass membership of the party. Its officers are elected by the governing body, the Central Council, which consists of around 3,000 members and meets annually to discuss policy and internal matters. It is comprised of MPs and prospective candidates, constituency representatives, senior officials of Central Office and members of the Executive Committee of the National Association. The latter body meets every two months and its membership includes the party leader, officials and local representatives. It is advised by various policy committees from the Young Conservatives, local government and the parliamentary party.

Unlike its **Labour Party** counterpart, the annual Conservative Party conference is regarded as little more than a cosmetic exercise mounted to demonstrate party unity and support for the leader. There was, however, more genuine debate at conferences in the mid-1990s as party divisions on Europe became more apparent. Nevertheless, the conference has no policy-making functions, so party control remains decisively in the hands of the leader. Some Tory factions, specifically the Set the Party Free Group and the Charter Group, have criticized the undemocratic structure of the Conservative Party.

The membership of the party consists overwhelmingly of white, middle-class homeowners. In 1995, over half of the Conservative membership of half a million people was aged over sixty-five, but this was falling by 64,000 members a year. The party attracts most of its votes from the A, B and C1 social categories, but until 1997 also received a significant proportion of the working-class vote, attributed to the embourgeoisement of the working classes and populist Conservative policies on law and order, immigration and reducing direct taxation. The working-class vote reverted to Labour in 1997. Conservative Party candidates have predominantly upper or middle-class occupational backgrounds, many have attended **public schools** and most are graduates, usually from Oxbridge. This social exclusiveness is even more apparent in the Cabinet, where in 1992 only Major and Lord Wakeham had not been educated at a university. In the 1992 Parliament, the Conservatives had a lower proportion of women MPs than the two other major parties.

The Conservative Party has successfully evolved over time from the party of the landowning classes to the party of industry and big business. It has been able to move with change in order to win wider support, as witnessed by its attempts to attract working-class votes. Conservatives emphasize the concept of authority and the need for strong institutions of government. They are convinced of the merits of private ownership, as the sale of council houses and the **privatization** programme demonstrate. This also represents a political aim to attract voters, as council houses and public utilities were sold below their market value. Conservatives believe in equal opportunities, but argue against measures such as redistributing wealth as equality of outcome is inevitable, and indeed desirable to provide an incentive for effort. This explains their support for selective education, with Prime Minister Major proclaiming in 1996 his desire for a grammar school in every town.

The Conservative Party has been dominated by two ideologies throughout its history; the collectivist tradition and the libertarian tradition. The collectivist policy was prevalent in the twentieth century until Edward Heath's adoption of the neoliberal Selsdon Programme in 1970, and continued in the 1980s in the ideology of one-nation Conservatives, whom Thatcher labelled 'wets'. Major's Chancellor from 1993, Kenneth Clarke, is identified with this position. Collectivists accept the need for full employment and welfare provisions and for corporate decision making and state intervention in the economy to achieve growth and prosperity.

'Stagflation' in the late 1960s caused disillusionment with the achievements of the postwar consensus and gave renewed impetus to the party's libertarian wing. Margaret Thatcher's ideology was essentially libertarian, influenced by New Right writers such as Hayek and Friedman and by thinktanks. She believed that the state role in the economy should be limited to providing the conditions for a free market, and public expenditure should be cut. Welfare would ideally be provided by the family or the private sector, but not the 'nanny' state which created a dependency culture. Privatization would provide competition to bring about efficiency and consumer choice, the notion behind the internal market in the **NHS**. Thatcher advocated conviction politics, as opposed to the pluralist approach of one-nation Conservatism. This explains her attacks on the **trade unions**, local government and **pressure groups** whose vested interests she decided threatened the will of the people as expressed by their election of her as Prime Minister. Thatcher solved the ideological conflict in her party by systematically removing the 'wets' from her Cabinet and replacing them with ministers who shared her opinions. Vociferous appeals to nationalism, emphasis on the need for law and order, and a tough stance on crime and immigration were also elements of Thatcherism. These policies were attractive to much of the electorate, and have been termed 'authoritarian populism'.

John Major followed a similar agenda, despite policy initiatives like the Citizen's Charter, which were designed to improve public services by introducing more competition and choice, complaints procedures and better quality service to the citizen. His personal style was very different to his predecessor, however, amounting to 'Thatcherism with a human face' (according to Clarke). Reforms of government, the NHS and education continued under his premiership, as did privatizations and legislation against the unions. Major suffered due to the smallness of his majority in his second term, which was eventually eroded and he was forced to depend on the **Ulster Unionists** to support his minority government from 1996. This meant that rebellions over Europe could cause the government to lose crucial votes. Major's attempts to assert his authority included a confidence vote on the Social Chapter in 1993 and withdrawing the whip from eight 'Euro rebels' in 1994, only to reinstate it unconditionally after his defeat on a budget measure and resignation as Prime Minister in June 1995. He stood for re-election against the Eurosceptic John Redwood, on a European platform of 'no change', an election he won by 218 to 89 votes (with 20 abstentions).

The general election of 1979 was a watershed for the Conservative Party, which capitalized on Labour's failures in the **Winter of Discontent** and offered a clear alternative based on freedom from wage controls and lower taxation. They re-established themselves as the 'natural party of government' and were in office for eighteen consecutive years.

Margaret Thatcher was prime minister for eleven years, but in 1982 she was the most unpopular prime minister in history according to opinion polls, largely due to a rapid rise in unemployment. The turning point in her administration was the Falklands conflict, which restored her prestige in the eyes of the electorate. She gained successive victories in 1983 and 1987 with formidable Conservative majorities. Thatcher benefited in 1983 from a divided opposition with the emergence of the **SDP/Liberal Party** alliance and by the disarray of the Labour Party. In 1987, Conservative economic policies were seen to be working, the opposition remained divided, and a majority of white-collar workers and the changing geography of the vote resulted in more Conservative voters.

In her third term in office, criticism was levelled at Thatcher's leadership style as conviction politics came to appear like overbearing bossiness, a charge previously aimed at her during the **Westland Affair**. The introduction of the **poll tax** and her increasing intransigence in Europe made her unpopular with the public and amongst some of her own government. This resulted in the 1990 leadership contest, which ultimately brought her resignation. Although Thatcher's chosen successor was John Major, she soon publicly disagreed with him on certain policies, along with her Bruges Group and No Turning Back Group allies. This damaged Major's credibility as prime minister going into the 1992 election, when opinion polls predicted a narrow Labour victory.

In the event Major achieved a majority of twenty-two seats in 1992, a victory attributed to the strong media bias towards the Conservatives and the public's distrust of Labour to run the economy, in spite of the 1990s recession under the Conservatives. The party's divisions over Europe became more intractable from 1992, as witnessed by the appearance of Euro rebels over Exchange Rate Mechanism (ERM) membership, the Maastricht Treaty and the single currency. Sir James Goldsmith's creation of the Referendum Party also received the tacit support of some right-wing Eurosceptics. Major was derided in the press as a weak leader unable to control his party's warring factions. He suffered further due to Britain's undignified retreat from the ERM on Black Wednesday, and the consequent devaluation of the pound. Major as Chancellor had persuaded Thatcher to join the ERM just prior to her downfall, and the public identified him with this policy. This tarnished the Conservatives' reputation for astute running of the economy. Criticism was also directed at the largest increases in taxation since the Second World War, the state of the public services and 'sleaze'. The latter phenomenon destroyed Major's 'back to basics' campaign, intended to reduce crime and anti-social behaviour but associated in the press with the string of sexual and financial scandals concerning Conservative MPs in Major's second term.

The Labour Party's move to the right attracted many voters and some of the previously hostile tabloid press, notably the *Sun*, which claimed to have won the 1992 election for Major but backed Labour and Tony Blair in 1997. Eighteen years in opposition had forced Labour to review their policies and to impose tight discipline on the party and marginalize the radical left. Most privatized industries would remain in the private sector, trade unions would not regain their pre-1979 powers, and the free market would be accepted alongside social justice. In 1996, Blair committed a future Labour government to the Conservatives' spending targets in his attempt to woo the voters of middle England.

Despite evidence of economic recovery, the 1997 general election was a disaster for the Conservative Party, which received its lowest share of the vote since 1832. No Conservative seats were left in

Scotland or Wales, seven Cabinet members lost their seats and Conservative representation in the House of Commons slumped to 165. There was considerable evidence of tactical voting to oust the Conservatives, and Labour came to power with their best-ever majority of 179. The average swing against the Conservatives was 10.5 percent, though it was substantially greater in marginal constituencies. Amidst recriminations about who was to blame for the defeat, Major stood down and campaigning for the party leadership began, leading eventually to the accession of William Hague.

See also: black Conservatives; Conservative governments; fringe groups

Further reading

Cole, J. (1987) *The Thatcher Years: A Decade of Revolution in British Politics,* London: BBC Books.

Kavanagh, D. and Seldon, A. (eds) (1994) *The Major Effect,* London: Macmillan.

Ludlam, S. and Smith, M.J. (eds) (1996) *Contemporary British Conservatism,* London: Macmillan.

COLIN WILLIAMS

consumer language

The crucial element of consumer language is the relationship between the providers of goods and services and the users of such products, and how this relationship is described by the providers and others. Basically, new views of the producer–consumer relationship have led to a number of terms and ideas being created. These have taken a number of forms, but essentially these shifts in terminology with respect to consumers of goods and services have been part of a wider political realignment of the status of the providers of such goods. Whereas there was previously a sharp distinction between the private and public sectors, such lines have now become more blurred as the effects of privatization upon parts of the public sector has become more apparent. This has led to an altered view of the consumers of services, at least with respect to the terminology. Prime examples of such practices can be found within

sectors as diverse as higher education, where students have became consumers (a move likely to be exacerbated by the imposition of tuition fees in 1998), and the railways, where passengers have been redefined as clients or consumers of each rail service provider. This phenomenon is, however, not only predicated on the privatization policies of the Thatcher government. In areas such as football, spectators have changed from being 'fans' or supporters into a more ephemeral description of 'customers', with traditional values of fan loyalty being replaced by a more distinct emphasis on consumerism. This has been fuelled by a marketing boom which has sought to develop off-field sales (for example, Manchester United plc makes as much money from shop merchandise sales as from gate receipts).

The change in language has been most starkly seen with the election of the Labour government in 1997, where economic and social 'stakeholding' has emerged as a concept which may be applied through the private and public sectors and beyond. Consumers have a 'stake' in those businesses from which they buy goods and services, in tandem with the employees who work for the organization. However, in addition to this, the wider community is deemed to have a stake in the organization, thus emphasizing the tripartite nature of the economy. There is a cynical temptation to see this linguistic repackaging as being part of a tendency to 'put old wines in new bottles'.

See also: corporate identity; corporatism

GUY OSBORN
STEVE GREENFIELD

convenience stores

In the early 1960s, service was the key to successful selling. Therefore, unless the customer was in a position to make an expedition to **department stores**, local shops were still more convenient and were all that most people could afford. Independent retailers also reinforced their advantage by delivering goods to the customer. As time went on, however, the local convenience stores found it increasingly difficult to overcome the competitive prices and stock variety of the department stores and multiple chains.

In the 1970s, convenience stores enjoyed great success and quickly took over the high street, abandoned by department and chain stores due to lack of space. At the same time, President Idi Amin of Uganda expelled thousands of Ugandan Asians, many of whom came to England with nothing but their skills as shopkeepers and their willingness to stay open as long as there were customers. These arrivals had a marked effect on the British shopping scene. Furthermore, magazine publishers like IPC, in an attempt to revive flagging sales, offered to help in redesigning the traditional confectionery, tobacconist and newsagent shops, producing shops with floor-to-ceiling rows of magazines and tempting racks of sweets near the till.

The new-style corner shop once again provided the customer with the convenience of being able to call in at any hour of the night or day. Moreover, retailers quickly realized that consumers were less price-conscious when they shopped early or late. They appeared to accept that convenience stores were entitled to charge for the extra service they were providing. It was only in the 1990s that convenience stores began to face stiff competition from supermarkets with extended opening hours and cheaper goods.

See also: cash and carry; discount stores; street selling; supermarkets and malls

Further reading

Kay, W. (1987) *Battle For The High Street*, London: Piatkus Publishers.

FATIMA FERNANDES

corporate identity

It is only in the last fifteen years that multiple stores have established corporate identities which the public recognize. They have commissioned logos with distinctive colours and scripts, designed to encapsulate the values inherent in the company. These have become a form of shorthand which produces instant recognition on advertising hoardings, television ads, company reports, staff uniforms and so on. Assistants turn customers into mobile advertisements by giving them their purchases in distinctive carrier bags. On the positive side, homogeneity can lead to quality standards being set. Marks & Spencer and Sainsbury have been particularly successful in getting their names known in this way, and hence building brand loyalty which can be further developed by various store cards and supermarket banking.

See also: consumer language; corporatism

MIKE STORRY

corporatism

Corporatism describes the arrangement whereby government consults widely with relevant interest groups in order to formulate policies, especially in relation to economic planning. Corporatism was prevalent in the 1960s and 1970s after the establishment of the National Economic Development Council (NEDC) in 1962. This facilitated tripartite decision making between the British government, the TUC and the **CBI**. The New Right criticized corporatism for contributing to the nation's economic decline by hampering market forces and giving too much power to **pressure groups** and **trade unions**. Since 1979 the Conservative Party has been antagonistic towards corporatism, as exemplified by the adoption of conviction politics, hostility to the European Social Chapter with its emphasis on social partnership and worker consultation, and John Major's disbanding of the NEDC.

See also: consumer language; corporate identity

COLIN WILLIAMS

corruption in the City

In the late 1980s, a climate of greed encouraged a number of bank frauds including Bank of Credit and Commerce (BCCI), where thousands of Asian investors lost money. In other famous scandals, Nick Leeson is credited with bringing down the merchant bank Barings through unauthorized currency trading. Peter Young at Morgan Grenfell allowed conflicts of interest to lose money for unit trust holders. Many of the leaders of privatized former public utility companies were accused of enriching themselves by voting themselves hugely increased salaries to 'bring them into line with the private sector'; Cedric Brown, chairman of British Gas, became particularly notorious for this. Shareholders who believed they owned public utilities, both before and after they were sold, became disgruntled.

See also: CBI; financial crises

MIKE STORRY

cosmetics

In stark contrast to the ultra-sophisticated faces of the 1950s, the so-called 'dollybird' look of the 1960s placed the emphasis on looking young, even childlike, with eyes made up to be permanently agog. The 1960s also saw the development of customer beauty counters, where people could experiment. Furthermore, the marketing of cosmetics completely changed in the 1960s. Previously advertising had been earnest and dull, with lengthy descriptions of the quality of the product, very similar to the scientific information given in the mid- to late 1990s, however; in the 1960s cosmetics were publicized as sexual enhancers. Innuendoes flowed freely and explicit erotic images were employed to sell the apparent sexual advantages of make-up and perfume. The most important cosmetic item was eyeshadow, aimed at the younger consumer who had gained financial power in the 1960s. The Saturday morning shopper was a teenager, and **department stores** were concerned with gaining their custom, which was easily achieved with every new shade and fabulous packaging. Mary **Quant** was the key figure in revolutionizing cosmetics in the 1960s. False eyelashes and neon-frosted colours were a necessary part of the contemporary image. Quant continued to hold a dominant position, and in the late 1990s she headed a thriving make-up business and a string of retail outlets in Japan, where the young gave her cosmetics cult status. The 1960s also the emergence of age-oriented skin creams,

specifically Revlons Eterna 27 for the over-thirties market.

After the idealistic and ebullient 1960s came the limping and cynical 1970s. Make-up was often natural, but more frequently it was very colourful with heavily emphasized features and pencil-thin eyebrows. The face painting of the 1960s continued to some degree, heavily influenced by David Bowie. Cosmetic products went 'back to nature', seemingly including lemons, avocados or apples in every cosmetic recipe. There was also the aggressive war paint of the punk rocker (see **punk rock**). Advertisers relied heavily on the Belle Epoque for inspiration and many companies, like Yardley, often used reproductions of work by artists such as Klimt to enhance packaging.

The soft focus of the 1970s contrasted sharply with the vibrancy of 1980s make-up. There was also renewed interest in anti-ageing skin products, and many companies joined the race to develop the most beneficial anti-wrinkle cream. The 1980s was the era of power breakfasts, power walking and power dressing, and make-up had to be equally ostentatious. However, Anita Roddick, founder of The Body Shop, provided a welcome alternative to women who found the boom era make-up a trifle fussy. She was responsible for developing natural skin products and cosmetics, and has made a substantial difference to the production and marketing of cosmetics.

After the standardization of the groomed look in the 1980s, came the relief of experimentation and individuality in the 1990s. The 1990s consumer was far more sophisticated and educated in the techniques of cosmetics application. Products were expected to be environment and animal friendly, and the agenda was to enhance the individual's natural look without masking her own beauty or her personality.

See also: accessories; lesbian chic

Further reading

Mulvey, K. and Richards, M. (1998) *Decades of Beauty: The Changing Face of Women 1890s–1990s*, London: Hamlyn.

FATIMA FERNANDES

country music

Originally known as **folk music**, old time music, hillbilly or country and western, country music developed in the USA in the early 1920s. The folk music traditions of the UK were among the early influences of country music in the United States. The first country catalogue was issued in 1924 by Okeh in the USA. The music continued to follow two general strains. First, there was the traditional mountain music variety, which was responsible for the success of performers such as The Carter Family; in particular Maybelline Carter, whose influential guitar playing guaranteed her a regular spot at the Grand Ole Oprey for nearly two decades (1950–67). Maybelline's daughter eventually married Johnny Cash, after the family 'adopted' him when he was at a low point, just before the start of his successful career. The second strain of country music could be found in the more innovative style of Jimmie Rodgers, who popularized the combination of 12-bar blues with yodelling (a technique originally used by the blind guitarist Riley Puckett. Many see Puckett as the first major country singing star, having been the first to record a yodel at his first recording session in 1924).

Country music was adopted on a large scale by a Nashville radio station in the mid-1920s, and barn dances were held, first locally, then nationally. These events proved so successful that the barn dance evolved into what is known today as The Grand Ole Oprey. Nashville became the international centre of country music publishing in the 1940s, and then for recording in the 1950s. The success of Hank Williams as a recording artist established the Grand Ole Oprey for good. Country music has always carried the burden of being portrayed as having a tendency towards right-wing or 'redneck' beliefs, so the arrival of k.d. lang onto the American country music scene in the 1980s apparently caused a great upset among the regular Nashville set, who were uncomfortable with her androgynous appearance and her active promotion of vegetarianism and non-Christian beliefs. Her records were played on various radio stations, but only with a certain amount of reluctance on the part of disc jockeys, who would inevitably comment upon her appearance.

But with the appearance of k.d. lang there emerged a whole new appreciation of the country music scene. In the United Kingdom, a lesbian country and western scene was fast developing, of which k.d. lang's music was a central part. Country music was being appropriated by this new British scene in a number of recently formed women-only clubs. In the Nashville version of country fashion, female performers dressed as feminine counterparts to their men, in the traditional cowboy/cowgirl uniforms, but here, women were making a direct imitation of the male image in country music.

Prior to the popular chicness of k.d. lang, there had emerged another new strain of country in Great Britain in the late 1970s. It involved a gynaecologist from London called Hank Wangford and Wes McGee, a veteran pub rocker from the 1960s. Wangford was first introduced to country music after a meeting with Gram Parsons, who had been instrumental in turning American folk-rock group The Byrds into a very country-oriented band in the late 1960s. Parsons himself was considered too weird for the Nashville scene, but had made a huge impact on The Rolling Stones after he befriended Keith Richards, and the country influence is evident on the Rolling Stones albums *Sticky Fingers* and *Exile On Main Street*. Wangford's debut album for the Cow Pie label featured a host of top session musicians, notably Albert Lee, one of Britain's foremost country guitarists. Lee had previously played with Chet Atkins, a leading American country musician, and had been a member of Emmylou Harris's Hot Band. He had also played with Eric Clapton and the Everley Brothers. Albert Lee was also famous for writing the song *Country Boy*, which became a British country classic and was a hit for the American country star Ricky Skaggs. Wes McGee was a well-respected country player, both in Britain and America. He was the first British performer to be signed to a Nashville publishing company.

A surprise instalment in the history of British country music is that provided by Elvis Costello. Originally Costello, from Liverpool, was among the late 1970s new wave punks, with hits such as 'Oliver's Army' and 'I Can't Stand Up For Falling Down', but in the late 1980s he emerged with a cool country album called *Almost Blue*, which consisted of classic country covers and was recorded in Nashville. To promote the album, he held a concert at The Royal Albert Hall and hired The Royal Philharmonic Orchestra to perform, to wide acclaim. The Irish band U2 have also acknowledged the appeal of country music, inviting Wynona Judd of the American country duo The Judds to perform live on stage with them during their 1987 American tour of their *Joshua Tree* album. A mixing of various musical genres with country music has resulted in its popularity being carried through from 1920s America to 1990s Britain, with the emergence of styles such as cowpunk, alternative country, dark country and Irish country-folk-rock. The old timers co-exist alongside the new, bringing country music to the attention of the youth market and generating a whole new audience.

See also: jazz

Further reading

Vaughan, A. (1987) *Who's Who in New Country Music*, London: Omnibus (with a foreword by Ricky Skaggs, a clear guide to the country music scene, both in Britain and America).

ALICE BENNETT

Courtauld Institute

The Courtauld Institute takes its name from Samuel Courtauld. Born into a Huguenot family that had fled from France to England shortly after the Revocation of the Edict of Nantes (1685) and prospered, like many similar families, first as silversmiths and then as silk weavers, Courtauld became head of the textile firm bearing his name. His artistic interests were fostered by his wife, Elizabeth Kelsey, and he formed a considerable collection of Impressionist and Post-Impressionist works of art, a sympathy for things French perhaps helping him to recognize their merits earlier than others did. A gift of £50,000 to London's Tate Gallery in 1923 to help repair deficiencies in its holdings of French nineteenth-century paintings was followed eight years later by an even more significant act of patronage when, on the death of his wife, he endowed the Courtauld Institute. He

was joined in the enterprise by Viscount Lee of Fareham (1868–1947), who had served as Director of Food Production in Lloyd George's administration during the First World War, and by the lawyer Sir Robert Witt, who in 1903 had played an important part in the foundation of the National Art Collections Fund.

The mission of the Courtauld Institute is the provision, at undergraduate, graduate diploma, MA and research degree levels, of training and education in the history of Western European art. It also runs courses in museum studies and the preservation and restoration of works of art. The Courtauld Institute has a close relationship with the Warburg Institute, which after being founded in Hamburg by Aby Warburg, moved to London in 1933 and is devoted particularly to studying the survival and evolution of the classical tradition in art and thought. *The Journal of the Courtauld and Warburg Institute* is published annually. Granted the status of an institution within London University in 1944, the Courtauld Institute moved in 1989 into Somerset House, one of London's most impressive eighteenth-century buildings. There it has been possible to realize Courtauld's dream of ensuring that students studying art history do so in the proximity of his munificent bequest of pictures. The paintings, complemented not only by rich holdings of Old Master drawings but by a comprehensive library of books and an extensive collection of slides and other reproductions, make the Courtauld Institute with its four professors and many other specialists an exceptionally well-endowed centre for art history studies, and the public is admitted to the gallery.

See also: painting; Tate(s)

CHRISTOPHER SMITH

Covent Garden

In 1946 the present theatre, the third on this central London site, became home to the Covent Garden Opera (Royal Opera since 1968) and to the **Royal Ballet** (Sadler's Wells Ballet until 1956). Under musical directors like George Solti and Bernard Haitinck, Covent Garden became a major international opera house, and its **ballet** is also highly rated. However, criticism has been levelled at large subsidies, inconsistent standards, high ticket prices and, despite efforts to widen audience appeal, elitism. Winning substantial **National Lottery** funding, the Royal Opera House closed Covent Garden in 1997 for two years of redevelopment, planning to perform in the meantime at other venues in London.

See also: opera; opera singers

CHRISTOPHER SMITH

Cox, Alex

b. 1954

Film director

LA-based film-maker Cox achieved cult status with his debut *Repo Man* (1984), interspersing elements of bizarre Americana, punk subculture and popular music in a thriller fuelled by a vigorous imagination with a satirical edge. *Sid and Nancy* (1985) denoted his brief return to Britain, exemplifying in the extreme Cox's own fascination for protagonists trapped in environments of engulfing moral or physical degradation, corruption providing a thematic core of his attack on American imperialism in *Walker* (1987) and the naturalistic cult classic *Highway Patrolman* (1991). The seedy lowlife Las Vegas of *The Winner* (1998) underscores Cox's penchant for humorous, offbeat narratives, while the indulgent *Straight to Hell* (1986) typifies his excesses in a career noted for its glaring inconsistencies.

SATINDER CHOHAN

Crafts Council

Promoting not handicraft pastimes, but the high-grade skills, artistry and innovation of such 'hands-on' craftspersons as potters, metal workers, jewellers, bookbinders, weavers, knitters, quilters, embroiderers, stone masons, calligraphers, wood turners and furniture makers (rather than semi-industrial traditional specialized tradesmanship), the Crafts Council occupies a niche between the Arts Council on the one hand and the **Design Council**, with its remit to improve commercial design, on the other. The Arts and Crafts Movement had emerged as a force in British cultural life in the late nineteenth century, and voluntary efforts, both in London and in the provinces, to provide encouragement and attract official recognition through coordination in a sphere where individualism is always at a premium began before the Second World War, in the course of which some central organization developed. Progress for the Crafts Centre of Great Britain proved slow, however, grant aid was meagre, and frustration appears to have fuelled disputes over policy. Changing the name to the Crafts Council of Great Britain in 1964 was a bid for enhanced status.

Fortunes improved with the return of the Conservative government in 1970 when the Paymaster General, Lord Eccles, set up the Crafts Advisory Committee to make recommendations for meeting the needs of 'artistic craftsmen' and promote 'a nationwide interest' in their work. In 1979 the Crafts Advisory Council became the Crafts Council. A Royal Charter was granted in 1982, with revisions in 1993 to reflect the extension of the Council's responsibilities to Scotland. The Council fulfils its dual role of educating the public and supporting artist craftspersons by offering advice and commissions, collecting particularly fine examples of new work, mounting exhibitions, arranging lecture programmes, and publishing specialist catalogues and periodicals. Having first moved from rather unsatisfactory premises on Hay Hill (off Piccadilly) to Waterloo Place, the Craft Council's London base is now at 44a Pentonville Road, Islington, where the public can enjoy a succession of imaginative exhibitions.

Further reading

Harrod, T. (1994) *Factfile 3: The History of the Crafts Council*, London: Crafts Council.

CHRISTOPHER SMITH

crazes

British culture has witnessed a number of youth crazes such as the hula hoop in the 1950s and the Rubik's cube in the 1970s. The Rubik's cube (to take an example) was based around the solving of a cuboid puzzle with six different coloured sides with each side made up of nine separate coloured squares. These were jumbled and the puzzle involved reconstructing the cube to recreate the six sides of original colour. The puzzle spawned a playground culture of 'moves' and 'strategies' that was exacerbated by time considerations. Manufacturers built upon this fascination and adapted the concept to include different shapes and designs (such as spheres). Similar crazes arose around other desirable playground 'must haves' such as slime and silly putty.

In recent years crazes have tended to develop as multimedia events. Perhaps the best example of the early 1990s was the Teenage Mutant Ninja Turtle craze, where not only were the figures desirable artefacts but a whole merchandising machine was brought into play with a number of products built around the same theme. Many Disney films have produced merchandising spin-offs, and there has been a shift from the general craze towards specific marked designer goods.

The craze becomes more pronounced when the availability of the product is limited due to an unpredictability of demand. This is further fuelled when such (non) availability is immediately prior to times of conspicuous consumption, such as Christmas. Christmas 1997 was notable for example by the rush to obtain Teletubbies, small furry android creatures known by the individual names of Tinky-Winky, Dipsy, Laa-Laa and Po. The success of the television programme was not originally anticipated, and demand far outstripped supply with numerous newspaper reports of Telletubby auctions and violent parental encounters in the quest to obtain one. At the same time videos, books and children's cutlery were produced to fuel the demand for all things related to the Teletubbies. Some two months later, stocks were high and shops were overburdened illustrating once more the temporal nature of such crazes. A further prime example of the multimedia dimension to crazes is provided by the phenomenal Spice Girls. A manufactured all-girl band with six consecutive number one singles, the 'spice girl' brand quickly proliferated into many areas of product endorsement. Clothing and dolls were also produced and a successful film, *Spice World*, was released.

See also: bungee jumping

STEVE GREENFIELD
GUY OSBORN

credit cards

Though regarded as temptations to extravagance when introduced into the UK in the 1960s, credit cards soon became, at home or abroad (and for telephone orders as well as face-to-face purchases) an acceptable alternative to cash for all but the smallest payments for goods and services, and displaced cheques for many moderate-sized ones. By 1997, over one-quarter of shop and garage transactions were paid by credit card. Credit cards first emerged in the USA, where Diners Card and American Express began as a convenient means of paying travel and entertainment expenses. Banks and, more recently, building societies act as agents for such card providers as Visa and MasterCard, recruiting their customers as credit card holders. On paying a small annual fee and after a check on their creditworthiness, they receive a small plastic card personalized by both identification numbers and a magnetic strip or microchip. Instead of tendering cash or a cheque, purchasers present their card and sign a voucher on which details are recorded manually or electronically. The credit card provider then bills them monthly for all their credit card expenditure. Provided holders respect a previously agreed upper limit and clear their debt within the quite short period stipulated, no surcharge is levied for what is technically a revolving credit facility. Holders need not, however, pay off more than a relatively low percentage of their debt each month; this may ease temporary cash flow problems, but interest is charged at quite an expensive rate on any outstanding debt.

Retailers and service providers, whose profits probably rise with higher turnover without delays for cashing cheques, some of which may never be honoured, receive from the credit card provider prompt payment for all transactions, but a small percentage is deducted. This deduction, together with interest on uncleared debts, makes the enterprise profitable for credit card providers despite the cost of computers and administration. Marketed to more affluent members of the public, 'Gold' cards generally charge higher annual fees, but offer cheaper and longer credit for larger sums. Store cards do not seem very different to users; the disadvantage of their being acceptable only in a single store or chain is often offset by discounts on purchases that are justifiable because customer loyalty is maintained. Debit cards (such as Switch) operate virtually as electronic cheques.

See also: hire purchase; promotions; sales

Further reading

Sayer, P.E. (1988) *Credit Cards and the Law: An Introduction*, London: Fourmat (presents issues generally before discussing legal aspects).

CHRISTOPHER SMITH

Crick, Francis and Maurice Wilkins

Crick b. 1916, Northampton; Wilkins b. 1916, Pongeroa (New Zealand)

Scientists

Francis Crick and Maurice Wilkins, together with James Watson, can be said to have fundamentally advanced knowledge of the way in which heredity and biology affect the human body. In the early 1950s, Wilkins and Crick discovered that the basic building block of human life was to be found in deoxyribonucleic acid, a molecule taking the form of a double helix which underpins the protein structure necessary for life. This insight led to a basic understanding of human life. Combined with computerized methods of analysing each part of the human gene, it has led to the internationally supported human genome project. The aim of that project is to have a complete map of the genetic make-up of human life by the end of the millennium. The project has raised questions as

to whether knowledge about the basis of human life is patentable, and has reawakened the nature–nurture debate. Crick, in particular, has recently been reported as emphasizing genetic determinism, but it is far from clear that this is his final position.

See also: science

PAUL BARRY CLARKE

cricket

Cricket is a bat-and-ball summer game with elaborate 'laws' and terminology baffling to outsiders but very clear to initiates. It is played, under two 'umpires', by two teams of eleven on a level 'pitch' of closely mown turf twenty-two yards in length, in the middle of a grassed 'ground'. Ideally elliptical with a seventy-yard radius, grounds vary considerably in size and shape, which casts doubts on statistics of team and individual performances in reference books like *Wisden's Cricketers' Almanack* (annual since 1864). At the two ends of the pitch are 'wickets', three twenty-eight-inch wooden 'stumps' set to give an overall width of nine inches, with two wooden 'bails' resting in grooves across them. 'Creases' are marked out four feet in front of each wicket.

The captain winning the toss of a coin opts to 'bat' or 'field' first. In white trousers, shirt and pullover, wearing a cap (or visored helmet), padded gloves, leg-pads and other protection, and equipped with a willow bat four and one-half inches wide and thirty-eight inches long, including handle, the batsman 'opening the innings' takes his stance sideways on at the crease before one wicket; another batsmen, momentarily a virtual spectator, stands by the other. The batsman endeavours to score 'runs' by striking the ball at least far enough to allow him to run to the opposite wicket, as his partner runs to take his place. If time permits, more than one run can be scored from a single hit. Should the ball be hit over the boundary, six runs accrue; four are scored if the ball touches the ground on the way before going over the boundary.

The bowler, rotating his arm through an arc above his head, casts the hard leather-covered ball (three and one-half inches in diameter) down the pitch towards the wicket guarded by the batsman.

The bowler does not throw the ball: 'throwing', or jerking the arm while bowling, is outlawed. By delivering the ball at varying speeds (up to ninety miles per hour), and making it swerve in the air or turn to either side when landing on the pitch in front of the crease, bowlers aim to dismiss batsmen and prevent them scoring runs. On completion of an 'over' of six deliveries, the first bowler is replaced by another, who bowls from the opposite wicket at whichever batsman is then facing him. The alternation of ends is maintained throughout the innings. Selecting a suitable bowler at any particular juncture is a major responsibility for the captain.

A batsman is 'out' (and replaced by the next) if the ball penetrates his defence and topples the wicket (or strikes his leg-pad in front of it), or if, while trying to defend his wicket or hit a run, he strikes the ball into the air and it is caught before touching the ground by the wicket-keeper (who stands behind the wicket wearing pads and gloves) or any of the fielders, whom the captain has positioned, at his discretion, to prevent runs being scored and to hold catches. The batsman is also out 'stumped' or 'run out' if in trying to strike the ball or attempting a run, he quits the crease and any member of the fielding side breaks the wicket with the ball before the batsman runs back.

The batting side's innings continues until ten of its members are out or the captain, judging the score high enough, 'declares the innings closed'. Now the other side must try to score more runs. The new side wins the match provided it does. But, should it fail to do so, and if the side bowling second cannot dismiss all the other team's batsmen, then the match is not a win for the first side, but a 'draw'. A 'tie' results when scores are even. Ties are rare, but many matches end as draws, to the irritation of unsophisticated spectators.

Most matches are decided, often in a lengthy afternoon, on a single innings by each side. Matches at higher levels involve two innings by each side and last from two to five days. 'Tests' – internationals between countries like Australia and India, whose cricket dates back to imperial times – are generally held across a summer in 'series' of from three to six matches. This is a long time, and the tempo can occasionally appear leisurely, but tension mounts up surprisingly, often to the very last moment.

Cricket, an ancient game which underwent development in the eighteenth century, took its present form in the nineteenth century within the general evolution of sport for both spectators and participants, with the public schools playing a major role. Sometimes seen as character-forming – for example, 'that's just not cricket' became a byword for underhand conduct – cricket is played and discussed with great earnestness and rumours of cheating are taken very seriously.

In Test matches, England's recent record has been disappointing. The County Championship, for the eighteen English counties that have over the last century acquired 'first-class' status and play four-day matches, has not much public support; the lower-level Minor Counties Championship, with two-day matches, has even less. To revive interest, gain television coverage and make money, various sponsored one-innings championships have been introduced since 1963; only a limited number of overs are allowed for each innings, and the result depends simply on scores without the possibility of a draw. Crowds at grounds and high viewing figures prove there is a following for this rather more exciting form of cricket, though purists disapprove.

Traditional distinctions between 'gentlemen and players' (amateurs and professionals) were jettisoned in 1963, and though attempts by Australian media tycoon Kerry Packer to put the game on a different financial basis in the 1970s failed after causing disruption, pay has now improved. The Marylebone Cricket Club (MCC), founded in 1787, retains, like its famous Lord's Ground in London, something of its mystique, but has had to yield authority to the Cricket Council and the Test and County Cricket Board, and may have to cede further ground to the England and Wales Cricket Board. Reforms are regularly mooted, but often opposed. Local leagues of every variety flourish at lower levels, particularly in Yorkshire and Lancashire, but school cricket has declined, with implications for the future of the game. Cricket is, however, gaining popularity in countries outside the Test match ambit, such as Holland; and women's cricket, boasting a long history, has been steadily developing from a small base to impressive standards.

The quintessential English game, cricket has remained much the same for 200 years. However, this sense of stability and tradition has come under increasing threat from broadcasters, and their desire to secure and guarantee ratings, over the last twenty years. This is most clear in the growth of the one-day game, especially since the 1970s; county fixtures last four days, with drawn games common, but this is very much cricket for the purist, with the emphasis on classic technique and tactical thinking. One-day cricket is television-driven and has coloured kits. But while it has damaged levels of technique (except fielding), it is undeniably popular, since it only lasts one day, nearly always generates a result and brings considerable revenue into the game. It has long been a favourite of the television stations, and these games regularly sell out.

England's five-day Test matches against other countries have largely retained their popularity over the postwar period, with the Lord's Test always one of the great social and sporting occasions of the summer. Although still essentially an upper and middle-class sport, cricket success-fully spread its appeal to all classes (particularly via one-day matches), though some critics consider this more a problem than an achievement. It also has a strong cultural significance, reinforcing traditional images of England, like the old elites, the village green and church, fair play and other concepts of what it means to be English, a case argued by Prime Minister John Major, amongst others. It is no accident that Oxford and Cambridge Univer-sities still play first class fixtures against the counties.

The modern game comprises three one-day knockout competitions and the County Champion-ship, with the season lasting from April to September. Crowds are often low, especially in the dark and damp of April, because each day's play lasts until evening, and there are frequent lulls between periods of play. However, this just reinforces other cultural aspects of the game, with hampers and bottles of champagne common among spectators. BBC Radio 4's *Test Match Special* is one of Britain's longest running radio pro-grammes, and has carved out a place all of its own

in the traditional cultural imagery of 'England' (plans to drop it in the mid-1990s provoked a barrage of protest). Famous for its late presenter, Brian Johnston, typically eccentric commentators, genteel commentary and chocolate cakes sent in by listeners, *Test Match Special* (and by extension cricket in general) forms part of the core of Englishness and evokes images of a rural, pre-industrial England that for most people is no more.

The county championship is contested by counties from all over England, plus Glamorgan in Wales. Cricket is played in Scotland and Ireland but only at a very low level, and in Britain it is essentially an English sport. The most recent addition to the county scene, Durham, arrived with much fanfare in the early 1990s, but the team has struggled badly. Indeed the absence of a relegation system that saves Durham is cited as one reason for cricket's decline since the halcyon decades of the 1950s, in terms of attendances and playing standards. By the midway point in the season most counties have nothing to play for, and the lack of relegation means there is no reason to keep playing hard. Journalists have claimed for years that most players have no incentive to improve or entertain, to the detriment of the Test side and the sport overall.

However, after various experiments with differ-ent administrative systems, it was decided in 1996 to change the game's structure, with the creation of an England and Wales Cricket Board, though talk of introducing divisions into the championship (to sustain interest through the season) proved pre-mature. There has never been an organized transfer market, but the strict rules on the hiring of new players were clearly not working by the 1990s, and some counties want a formalized system of compensation when players change counties.

Kit sponsorship was only introduced in the early 1990s (usually attracting brewing companies), and cricket's ethos remains rather 'amateur', even though professionalism was introduced decades ago. But the pay structure has become increasingly unbalanced, with Test players earning very con-siderable sums, and the rest far below them (in 1995, the minimum wage for a capped county player was just £14,500). 'Benefit years' were introduced to reward the long-serving 'journey-man' professional who never makes a fortune from cricket, but increasingly in practice, benefits have only come to help established stars; some lesser names actually lost money.

But while football's commercial ethos has been absent, winning in cricket has always been very important, especially at Test level, where success and failure have regularly become common (if rather debatable) metaphors for the state and mood of the nation. The 1980s and 1990s saw England generally perform poorly, or not as well as expected, and more significantly, saw allegations of bowlers illegally doctoring the ball, on-field rows between captains and umpires, and a drugs episode (a Sussex player was banned in 1996 for nineteen months for taking cocaine). There have also been allegations of racism by top English players, and racist arguments about the 'loyalty' of non-English born players (England have picked naturalized players from South Africa, Zimbabwe, West Indies and New Zealand since the early 1980s).

Cricket is undoubtedly the English national summer sport, but it now has to face challenges from other sports (the football season encroaches a bit more on the cricket season every year), and from the demands of television. However, its very continuity and slow pace of change forms much of its appeal (the chairman of Glamorgan estimates that 1.4 million children play cricket each year, and 10.6 million people follow it), which represents an interesting problem for the authorities for the future.

Further reading

Green, B. (1988) *A History of Cricket*, London: Barrie & Jenkins.

Wynne-Thomas, P. (1987) *The History of Cricket*, Norwich: HMSO.

REX NASH
CHRISTOPHER SMITH

crime drama

Crime drama forms an important part of adult television viewing in Britain, and in the mid-1990s police and detective series dominated the mid-evening schedules. The vicarious pleasure enjoyed by viewers 'assisting' detectives in the crime investigation and putting the world to rights has been viewed by critics as inherently ideological and supporting the processes of cultural hegemony. In the 1960s, the realism of the **BBC**'s influential *Z-Cars* series, characteristically featuring police officers tackling juvenile and community crime in a northern town, was underpinned by the postwar democratic urge for social reform. By the 1970s such consensus views had broken down, and **Euston Films**' *The Sweeney*, which featured a maverick Flying Squad Inspector's tough, all-action response to armed robbery, acted out the populist authoritarian urge to hit back at crime, stirred up by the moral panic about 'mugging' in the right-wing press.

The search for up-market viewers in contemporary crime drama has led to an increasing emphasis on the detective's individualism – to focus on protagonists who stand apart from the rest of the team – and also to turn to characters already established in print. Both of these tendencies are exemplified in Central TV's prestigious *Inspector Morse* series. An ongoing trend in quality crime programmes such as *Taggart* (Border TV), *Morse*, *A Touch of Frost* (Yorkshire) and *Silent Witness* (BBC) is to use their greater narrative length to explore 'dark' crimes and to key into popular anxieties surrounding **serial killers**, sexual abuse and the occult. In particular, Granada's controversial *Cracker* series (acclaimed by critics but criticized by watchdog bodies) carries over something of the challenge formerly associated with serious television drama (see **drama on television**) in its uncompromising application of forensic psychology to violent crime.

In no area has crime drama been more visibly responsive to shifts in culture over the course of time than in its choice of police and detective protagonists. Following the pioneering success of *Juliet Bravo* (BBC) and *The Gentle Touch* (LWT) in the early 1980s, women detectives now head contemporary quality series such as *Silent Witness*, *Hetty Wainthrop Investigates* (BBC) and the excellent *Prime Suspect* series (Granada), which has continued to engage the institutionalized sexism of the police. The representation of ethnic minority groups is not yet so fully developed, but in series such as *The Bill* (Thames), *Thief Takers* (Central) and *Out of the Blue*

(BBC), black officers are regular members of the police team.

See also: thrillers, detective and spy writing

Further reading

Clarke, A. (1992) ' "You're nicked!": Television Police Series and the Fictional Representation of Law and Order', in D. Strinati and S. Wagg (eds), *Come on Down: Popular Media Culture in Post-War Britain*, London: Routledge, pp. 232–53.

BOB MILLINGTON

Crosby, Theo

b. 1925, Johannesburg (South Africa); d. 1994, London

Architect and designer

Born in South Africa, Crosby arrived in England in 1947. He worked on the influential Architectural Design and then went on to found Pentagram, a group which provides an extensive range of design services in many fields. Examples of their environmental design are Lewisham shopping centre and the **Arts Council** shop in London. Crosby is a great believer in visual complexity and compound symbolism. He considers the built environment the product of many complementary skills, not just or even primarily those of architects. Working with a team of designers at Pentagram, his remodelling of a section of Nash's Ulster Terrace in Regent's Park demonstrates Crosby's emphasis on fine detail and patterning. Pentagram have produced the signage for many notable buildings, from the British Library, the Victoria and Albert Museum and the Tate Galleries to the Barbican and Lloyd's.

PETER CHILDS

cross-Channel shopping

Cross-Channel shopping trips have become a British phenomenon since the UK joined the European Union. Coach and ferry companies encourage shoppers to take advantage of differ-

ential prices, particularly in relation to wines, spirits and tobacco, which have become much cheaper on the Continent than in the UK. Many shoppers only took advantage of the duty-free allowances available on cross-Channel ferries, but others drove vans to France to stock up in the hypermarkets. Purchases are ostensibly for private consumption, but in reality many are for resale. The EU has tried to homogenize tax rates and remove duty-free allowances on sales on airplanes and ferries between European countries, but has so far failed.

See also: cash and carry; discount stores; supermarkets and malls

MIKE STORRY

crusties

The term is applied predominantly to males, but also includes females. Crusties are young drop-outs who wear 'encrusted' dreadlocks or long matted hair and unfashionable nondescript baggy clothes (parkas, army trousers, fishermen's jumpers), usually of dark colours. Females wear long black 'granny' dresses and home-made bangles or possibly beaded hair. Crusties often have dogs (cross-bred Alsatians are popular) which they keep on leads made from a piece of string. Their bohemian lifestyle often involves living communally and the use of soft drugs. Crusties are evident in the high streets of many of Britain's towns, and are especially in evidence in Winchester, Glastonbury and other towns with a reputation for being havens for **hippies**.

MIKE STORRY

Cullinan, Edward

b. 1931, London

Architect

Educated at Cambridge and Berkeley, Cullinan established his own architectural practice, Edward Cullinan Architects, in 1965 after an eight-year period with Denys Lasdun. He has been a professor at London, Sheffield and Edinburgh

Universities, and has won many prizes including the 1991 Financial Times Architecture Award for the RMC International Headquarters work which he carried out in 1985–9. Significant building projects are Horder House, Hampshire (1960), Minster Lovell Mill, Oxfordshire (1972), Parish Church of St Mary, Barnes (1984), and the Visitor Centre at Fountains Abbey and Studley Royal (1992). Noted for what the *Architectural Review* christened 'romantic pragmatism', Cullinan's borrowings from the logical approach of modernism reconciled traditional materials, highly skilled craftwork and a sense of propriety.

PETER CHILDS

current affairs

Current affairs, news bulletins and documentary all employ actuality. While news can be seen as communicating daily events of note, or at least those events which are construed as properly belonging to the discourses of news, current affairs explores the issues that ground those events, the context of those issues and explanations for them. It rarely initiates public debate, usually responding to issues that have been brought into the public sphere through other discourses such as politics, scandal or economics. Accordingly, current affairs programming tends to comprise either a mixture of report, structured discussion and debate usually involving experts or extended reports unsupported by discussion.

Where there is discussion, especially where that takes the form of debate, it is led by a presenter. The role of the presenter is crucial in that he or she interprets or mediates both a range of facts around the issue and the way in which the experts present them, on behalf of the viewer or listener. The convention of the presenter or anchor-person as the linchpin around which the debate flows is compromised by the fact that the presenter negotiates both facts and defining questions, and orders or even selects the assembled experts.

The BBC World Service daily radio programme *The World*, for instance, structures discussion around issues of politics, arts, science and sport. The debate is conducted through the cross-examination of experts, usually by regular presenters who can be determining in any conclusion that is reached or how the debate is closed. The programme is anchored to the voices and personalities of the presenters, and its distinctive character is further stamped by the insertion of features, a quiz and listeners' views.

Television current affairs tends to locate the presenter behind a desk with occasional forays to a less formal area. While the desk infuses authority, the armchairs, while remaining resolutely unnatural, indicate an approach that is more leisured and discursive than the news. One of the walls of the studio will function as a screen for the back projection (chromokey) of reports and interviews with experts or correspondents who are not in the studio. The effect is to suppress any appearance of the means of production which might allow the premise or the authority of current affairs to be called into question.

See also: news, television; teletext

Further reading

Eldridge, J. (ed.) (1995) *Glasgow Media Group Reader*, vol. 1, *News, Content, Language and Visuals*, London: Routledge.

JIM HALL

cycling

Cycling is not a huge professional sport in the UK, despite high participation rates and the fact two million bicycles are sold in Britain annually, and the days when British teams could seriously challenge for top honours are just a memory. But individually, British cyclists have much to celebrate in the 1990s, and it is hoped that new facilities will raise the profile of cycling and performances.

The 1960s saw a strong British challenge for top honours, notably the Tour de France and the Tours of Italy and Spain, led by Tommy Simpson, but performances have since declined. In 1985 a British team did enter and complete the Tour de France (ANC-Halfords), but by the mid-1990s the chances of such a challenge happening again had become remote. However, this should not detract

from the individual performances of Chris Boardman, Max Schiandri and Graeme Obree, who
have won many important events during the 1990s.
Boardman is the best-known British cyclist, with
medals at the 1992 Olympics, a 1996 time trial and
prestigious world pursuit victories to his name.
Obree is best known for his technological
advances. The design of bicycles and of cycling
positions can be crucial, but Obree's innovations
have caused controversy, with some of his saddle
designs and cycling positions banned at international competition. Schiandri won the bronze
medal in the 1996 Olympic road race.

Boardman has argued that cycling must establish characters that people can relate to and
facilities to attract crowds, such as the £9m
National Cycling Centre, if it is to develop. Opened
in September 1994, the National Cycling Centre
was originally part of Manchester's bid to host the
Olympic games; it was built despite the failure of
that bid, going on to host national and international
events. By 1996 the Velodrome had a six-month
queue for bookings, and is considered a success.

However, cycling is short of money, a situation
not helped by the cancellation of top races: the
prestigious Milk Race was last held in 1993, and in
1995 sponsors declined to support the Tour of
Britain, which was likewise cancelled. The British
Cycling Federation (BCF) has itself faced internal
and media criticisms, struggling in 1996 to retain
its Sports Council grant of £400,000, and accused
of poor management, conflicts of interests and
inefficiency. An eleven-strong emergency committee was set up in late 1996 to address these issues.
There are fears that the future of cycling in the UK
rests on the BCF's ability to deal with these
questions.

See also: bicycles

REX NASH

D

dance music

Dance music evolved from the remnants of **disco** in the mid-1980s. Like disco music, its characteristic sound was that of repetition and was mainly studio produced. This heralded the changing nature of live performance, it being a rarity for live musicians to be involved in the actual recordings of a dance track due to the introduction of the digital sampler which could distort, edit or convert any pre-recorded sound. The mid-late 1980s saw the emergence of acts such as M/A/R/R/S with its seminal 'Pump up the Volume', Bomb The Bass with 'Beat Dis', S Express's 'Theme From S-Express' and Deelight's 'Groove Is In The Heart', along with the harder American styles of Eric B & Rakim's 'Paid In Full', and Public Enemy's 'Terminator X'. Like disco, dance has a distinct gay following. It addresses the listeners as dancers rather than thinkers, the emphasis being on bodily expression and movement without thought, its rhythm plugged straight into the body. The dancer experiences the comfort of repetition, abandoning personal power and becoming subject to the track's beats. This had large-scale appeal, including the rising notion of Gay Pride and the biggest re-emergence of youth drug culture since the 1960s. It also brought about the promotion of DJs on a large scale, with club mixes, twelve-inch mixes and dance mixes of original songs. DJs had their own in-house systems by now, and were producing specialized mixes from their respective clubs.

The evolution of dance music could be looked upon as a protest against the established music industry. Studios did not now need to accommodate musicians, just samplers, sequencers, turntables, tape machines, drum machines and synthesizers. An individual could now work from their own studio and produce a successful hit. Dance became the music of alienation and signified pop music's conversion to postmodernism, with its distance from the actual artist or musician; hence the crossover from 'song' to 'track'. The dance scene renounced its connection with disco as DJs started playing underground black American dance music, giving it more credibility and status. Clubs like the Hacienda in Manchester, Cream in Liverpool and London's Ministry of Sound emerged as main showcases for committed DJs. Dance became more innovative and experimental, and the skill to produce tracks using the latest equipment became an art in itself, but it also became too deanimated in reproduction, often burdening a track with its own accomplishments.

See also: clubs; hip hop; house; rave culture

Further reading

Potter, R.A. (1998) 'Not the Same: Race, Repetition and Difference in Hip-Hop and Dance Music', in T. Swiss, J. Sloop and A. Herman (eds), *Mapping The Beat: Popular Music and Contemporary Theory*, London: Blackwell.

ALICE BENNETT

Davies, Terence

b. 1945, Liverpool

Film-maker

Davies is a film-maker whose two themes are the violent foundations of a sense of place captured through a heightened nostalgia, and the relation of homosexuality to working-class culture and institutionalized Catholicism. In his trilogy (*Children* (1974), *Madonna and Child* (1980) and *Death and Transfiguration* (1983)) Davies, charting the central character from life to death, captured physical endurance and spiritual ferment through domestic hardship, sexual guilt and emotional repression. *Distant Voices, Still Lives* (1988) and *The Long Day Closes* (1992) evoke Davies's postwar childhood in Liverpool and, while still marked with a troubled haunting nostalgia for place and kinship, demonstrate a shift towards a more mainstream vision. Both films pointedly reflect the popular culture of the period.

GUY OSBORN
STEVE GREENFIELD

Dawkins, Richard

b. 1941, Nairobi (Kenya)

Biologist and writer

Dawkins is a biologist who has written on the scientific, religious and social implications of Darwinian evolution. He adopts an unconventional perspective in which genes are the fundamental targets of natural selection which may individually survive, mutate or become lost from the pool of genes depending upon their ability to make a successful organism. In *The Selfish Gene*, he considers social behaviour from this point of view, while in *The Blind Watchmaker* he details arguments that the evolution of complex living organisms requires only the cumulative selection (by the prevailing environment) of useful errors, or mutations, in genes and the laws of chemistry, but not the intervention of a deity. His lucid and compelling style has made evolution interesting to a wide audience.

See also: Hawking, Stephen; neo-Darwinism; science

PETE SHETERLINE

Day-Lewis, Daniel

b. 1958, London

Actor

The nephew of former poet laureate Cecil Day-Lewis and grandson of British film producer Sir Michael Balcon, Day-Lewis first came to prominence in the lauded Stephen **Frears** film *My Beautiful Laundrette* (1985). This was swiftly followed by the adaptation of E.M. Forster's novel *A Room with a View* (1985). In *My Left Foot* (1989), Day-Lewis played the Irish writer Christy Brown, gaining many critical plaudits for the manner in which he immersed himself in the role, spending time in a wheelchair to prepare himself. Never one to shy from contentious roles, he took the part of Gerry Conlon, wrongly convicted for IRA terrorism, in Jim Sheridan's *In the Name of the Father* (1993).

GUY OSBORN
STEVE GREENFIELD

daytime television

In the *Radio Times* in 1996, Polly Toynbee, the former social affairs editor of the BBC, derided the content of daytime television as 'stupidvision'. She called programmes on both BBC and ITV patronizing, and said that 'most of the presenters look like they have to pretend to be stupid because they think their audience is'. The stations claimed that their schedules were under review, but Toynbee's view was widely reported. This reflected a crisis in programming, as stations vied for the daytime audience consisting mainly of housewives, the unemployed, students, shift workers, the retired and the housebound. An index of the concern was that the *Pebble Mill* lunchtime chat show, presented by Alan Titchmarsh and Sarah Greene, was scrapped after twenty-three years on air.

The formats of programmes on different channels are often the same. Many, such as BBC's

Good Morning and ITV's *This Morning*, have a male and female host who try to create a cosy, friendly atmosphere in which items of news and general interest are presented for general discussion. Celebrities are often introduced and presenters try to recreate a chatty low-key 'elevenses'-style gathering that theoretically could be taking place around the kitchen table of any member of the home audience. That is, they are making up for the family and friends who are being missed by the viewer. This feeling of immediacy and close friendship from television (which for teenagers is deemed dangerously anonymous and alienating) is promoted by the use of coyly named presenters like 'Anne and Nick' or 'Richard and Judy', to suggest the boy and girl next door. It is a cynical formula which evidently works.

Other daytime programmes include discussion programmes involving studio audiences, such as *The Time, The Place* on ITV, and *Kilroy* on BBC1. Despite their presenters' bedside manners, they are cruder versions of the format perfected by Oprah Winfrey, whose show goes out later on Channel 4. *Can't Cook Won't Cook* is a popular programme on BBC1 which uses canned studio laughter while cooks, sometimes in a state of undress, prepare food and tell anecdotes. BBC2's *Ready, Steady Cook* differs only slightly. The other main staples of daytime television are endlessly recycled old films and quiz and **game shows**, such as *Fifteen to One* or *Supermarket Sweep*. 'Stupidvision' seems harsh, but arguably programming has become more populist due to pressure for ratings.

See also: breakfast television

MIKE STORRY

Deardon, Basil

b. 1911; d. 1971

Film director

Ensconced at Ealing Studios, Deardon co-directed comedies with Will Hay before *The Bells Go Down* (1943), his first film in an extensive and generically diverse cinematic opus. In 1949 he established a production company with Michael Relph, his designer and co-producer on several films. For many critics, Deardon captured the competent, restrained British quintessence of the Ealing films, but his commitment to the social problem film demonstrated a resolute engagement with controversial issues including the IRA in *The Gentle Gunman* (1952), British cinema's first interracial relationship in *Pool of London* (1952) and homosexuality in *Victim* (1961). *The Man Who Haunted Himself* (1970) was Deardon's last film before his death in 1971.

Further reading

Barr, C. (1993) *Ealing Studios*, London: Verso.

SATINDER CHOHAN

delicatessens

Britain's internationalism increased throughout the 1990s as people from all over the world have settled here. Foods which were unavailable in the 1950s, such as dry spaghetti and rice, are now commonplace. Supermarkets routinely stock hummus, halva, olives, nan bread and so on. Caught between a new cosmopolitan atmosphere and the fact that their cars are permanently stuck in traffic jams, urban dwellers, particularly Londoners, have turned to visiting delicatessens as a travel substitute; a sort of urban escapism focused on expensive 'exotic' food. Emphasis on the development of chic restaurants by owners like the Roux brothers and Terence **Conran** has also increased this focus on gastronomy, as have the numerous cuisines represented by street vendors selling kebabs, pizzas, shawermas and gyros.

See also: drink; food

MIKE STORRY

democracy

The word 'democracy' (derived from the Greek meaning 'rule by the people') established itself within British culture as a system of government, not by the people, but rather, for the people by representatives chosen by the people through elections held every four to five years. Using the 'Westminster model' of majority democracy, Britain is acknowledged as the birthplace of a bicameral system with a single party forming a government until the next election. This system has been replicated and altered to fit individual circumstances around the globe. The belief that England originated majority parliamentary democracy has in part defined the British concept of politics and aided the notion of a people united in democracy.

Central to the British concept of democracy is a respect for constitutionalism and the role of parliament. The belief that the constitution, albeit uncodified, will constrain the actions of parliamentarians and thus protect the interests of the people is clearly linked to the notion of respect for the legality of the British democratic system. The system is deemed to operate both above the state and above the individual and, while not perfect, is essentially incorruptible.

Supporting this belief in the legality of the system is the idea that each individual can contribute to the system simply by virtue of being part of society. The freedom of the individual is seen as sacrosanct, and each individual in the 'electorate' is free to choose whether to participate or not as well as which representative to vote for.

However, since the early 1970s, democracy has begun to lose its appeal to the people and its traditions have begun to be challenged. A new series of debates surrounding the contemporary cultural relevance of democracy has arisen. Of central importance are the call for constitutional reform or a Bill of Rights, expressed through **Charter 88**; the need for a change in the electoral system to one that works in the interests of all parties, not just the traditional two; and the rise of **pressure groups**.

See also: class system; Clause 28; general elections

Further reading

Madgwick, P. (1994) *A New Introduction To British Politics*, Cheltenham: Stanley Thomas (Publications) Ltd.

DARREN SMALE

Denys Lasdun and Partners

Born in London in 1914, Sir Denys Lasdun studied at the **Architectural Association** School, London. He was to occupy a unique position, practising in both the prewar and postwar periods. After initially working under Wells Coates (1935–7), he joined the Tecton group, founded by Berthold Lubetkin, until its dissolution in 1948 (from 1946 he was a partner). Here he gained valuable knowledge of influential modern movement buildings, including the flats at High Point I, the Finsbury Health Centre and buildings at London Zoo. In 1949–50 he and Lindsay Drake ran a London office; here in 1960 he founded Denys Lasdun and Partners, which continued since 1978 under the name Denys Lasdun, Redhouse and Softley. Greatly influenced by Le Corbusier, his early work included a house and studio in New Road, Paddington (1937). In spite of the experimental nature of his cluster blocks in Bethnal Green (1954), embodying Corbusian ideology, they managed to propose an alternative to the slab block in their desire to respect the local social and urban context. The luxury flats built in St James's Place in 1958 again mark a change from the somewhat uninspired 1950s British slab blocks imitative of continental examples. This carefully proportioned composition employed a 3:2 section to create ample living room views while still making the best of expensive city centre land. Despite its adoption of bold reinforced concrete horizontal bands, concern for massing and detail ensured that the block accords sensitively with its Palladian neighbour. Lasdun's work of the 1960s contrasted with the popular contemporary espousal of technological imagery. His concern for context became particularly apparent in his design for The Royal College of Physicians (1959–61), sited close to Nash's neo-classical terraces in Regent's Park. The composition, with its main white rectangular shell raised on piers above the lower sections, together with the purple brick auditorium is respectful of Nash but also invokes sculptural qualities of Nicholas Hawksmoor, so admired by Lasdun. His concern for context is manifest in designs for the University of East Anglia, Norwich (1962–8) where the stepped levels linking interior and exterior spaces wed the stratified spine to the landscape. Lasdun's 'urban landscape' philosophy is further evidenced at The National Theatre in London (1967–76), where the platforms, bridges and social spaces together with the auditoria allowed Lasdun to argue that 'the whole building could become a theatre'.

See also: new brutalism; Royal National Theatre

Further reading

Curtis, William J.R. (1994) *Denys Lasdun: Architecture, City, Landscape*, London: Phaidon.

HILARY GRAINGER

department stores

The Great Exhibition of 1851 was the inspiration for the development of department stores. William Whiteley built the first department store in London's Bayswater in 1863. The creation of department stores marked a crucial point in the development of mass marketing. The stores provided a manifest symbol of new possibilities, themselves dependent upon the development of mass advertising, a cheap, fast and effective transport network and new skills of accountancy, packaging and stock control. Although department stores should have prospered as living standards rose and the middle classes became the biggest part of the population, they failed to adapt with the times and successfully to negotiate the fierce competition from specialist chains. By the 1960s department stores, with their lack of parking and neglected shabby appearance, were of little interest to the new consumer. The new generation of consumers was paralleled by a new generation of retailers and manufacturers. Harrods, Britain's most famous department store, originally opened as a grocery store in 1849 by Charles Harrod, also found the 1960s enormously difficult. However, it is important to understand that Harrods is more than just another department store; in the 1990s it ranked with Buckingham Palace and the Tower of London as essential on any tourist's itinerary, to the extent that half of its £300 million annual turnover is secured from overseas customers. Harrods has

had a long and involved history of battles for ownership. Perhaps the most famous power struggle occurred in 1984, between the Egyptian Al Fayed brothers and Lonrho's Tiny Rowland.

See also: supermarkets and malls

Further reading

Benson, J. (1994) *The Rise of Consumer Society in Britain 1880–1980*, Harlow: Longman.

FATIMA FERNANDES

Design Council

An at times bland, traditionalist, and insipid organization established by the Board of Trade in 1944, the Design Council prior to 1972 was known as the Council of Industrial Design. The initial idea behind its inception was to encourage those working in industry and business to employ designers and so to raise the level of both visual marketing and corporate images alongside an increased public awareness of and appetite for sophisticated designs. The council has approved goods, handed out awards and publicized (via leaflets, conferences and exhibitions) both itself and its favoured companies. It started publication of its magazine *Design* in 1949 and built a permanent design space called the Design Centre in London's Haymarket in 1956. Directors of the Council have included Gordon Russell, Paul Reilly, Keith Grant and Ivor Owen.

See also: Arts Council; Crafts Council

PETER CHILDS

designer labels

Widespread designer label consciousness began in the late 1970s with the appearance of designer jeans, Gloria Vanderbilt and Calvin Klein being the key designers. Design and designer labels became retailing watchwords of the 1980s, transforming the appearance of the high street. Retailers quickly became aware of the selling power of designer-labelled products. They provided the retailers with the power to influence, seduce and manipulate the consumer into buying in a pattern and, frequently, contributing largely to the overall success of both retailer and designer. The boom times of the 1980s produced a new generation of highly affluent individuals, notably in the media and computer industries. Conspicuous consumption was the pervading theme, which in turn cultivated the insatiable desire for all designer labelled products. In the 1990s the overriding fashion element was individuality, and key designers played the most important role in fulfilling this desire. Consequently, the end result was not individuality but rather a homogeneous fashion look; so much so that the younger generation began rejecting designer label items like trainers, for example, because their parents had also adopted them, and opted instead for comfortable and traditional loafer designs. However, the obsession with designer labels continued and spread to products for the home, clothes for children and fashion **accessories**. This ethos became a form of religion for the 1990s consumer society and generally permeated all socio-economic groups.

See also: labels

FATIMA FERNANDES

devising

The main way in which devising differs from traditional **theatre** is that the latter is based on texts, whereas devising is based on specific stimuli that might include music, text, objects, paintings or movement. It is thus more transient, ephemeral and adventurous. It is often based in an alternative to conventional theatre space: in the community, outdoors, in schools or in hospitals (where Age Exchange Theatre Trust produces 'reminiscence theatre' for the elderly). Devisers, working in collaboration, decide in which direction they want the performance to go, instead of relying on the text of a particular author and simply interpreting it. They may create theatre for a particular audience, community or site-specific location.

Practitioners of devised theatre feel unsatisfied by the dominant literary theatre tradition which usually involves a hierarchical relationship between playwright and director. Under that regime there is little space for actors to make individual contributions other than through interpreting assigned roles. Devisers prefer a collective approach, where responsibility for the creation of art shifts from writer to creative artist (that is, to the actors themselves).

Devising was stimulated by the start of the theatre-in-education movement in 1965, in particular with the founding of the first British group at the Belgrade Theatre, Coventry. Working in schools meant that performers/devisers had to be much more versatile than mainstream actors, using skills from ballet, music, gymnastics, mime and magic as well as traditional ones. This enabled more personal input and commitment from actors, and encouraged more participation from audiences.

Theatre in the community around 1968 featured 'political' groups like Red Ladder Theatre Company or performance art groups like Welfare State International, whose often site-specific work produced celebratory spectacles using performance language that included non-verbal forms. Major Road produces large-scale events for local communities. The devised performance may involve a procession involving local participants, which is at once spectacle, celebration and event.

Technology is much more of a factor in devised theatre. Groups like The People Show structure themselves around visuals, with the additional use of lighting, sound, music and technical resources including slides and film clips. Forkbeard Fantasy is another collaborative artists' venture which makes interactive use of film and live performance and also performs abroad.

See also: community theatre; improvisation; theatre

Further reading

Oddey, A. (1996) *Devising Theatre: a Practical and Theoretical Handbook*, London: Routledge (an authoritative review of the practice).

MIKE STORRY

dialect

Dialect identifies groups within a language. Some people's speech displays features differentiating it from that used by members of other groups, although those belonging to either group can communicate with each other without excessive difficulty. When the problems in communicating become more severe, the boundary between different (albeit closely related) languages is crossed, as happens on linguistic frontiers. In the UK, dialect often makes it easy to spot a Scot, a Londoner or a Geordie, though all three can legitimately claim to be using English. Variations in the pronunciation of certain vowels and consonants often provide clear markers, as do intonation patterns and such characteristic speech elements as address forms. Differences in vocabulary also occur, but they appear to be less marked than formerly, before first urbanization and then education and the media contributed to the homogenization of English across the UK. As well as regional dialects English, like other languages, has social dialects. These reflect, in terms of accent, characteristic vocabulary and idioms, and even syntactic preferences, not so much the geographical origins of speakers as their education, trade or profession, age, sex and class.

Dialects provide philologists with evidence about historical developments in language, offering, for example, evidence about population shifts. They also attract attention as a cherished part of local culture. There has, however, been a tendency to confer prestige on certain varieties of English and to disparage others. In the earlier part of the twentieth century, command of **received pronunciation** and mastery of the pernickety distinctions between acceptable and incorrect English – codified in, for example, *Fowler's Modern English Usage* – came to be taken as proof of the intelligence and schooling indispensable for access to higher education and the learned professions. Exceptions were always made for certain regional accents (such as polite Edinburgh Scots), but generally anything smacking of provincialism was discouraged. The **BBC** used to act as a strong force for uniformity, allowing regional accents only within carefully defined contexts. Wider ethnic diversity has resulted in greater tolerance in linguistic matters, and as regionalism has grown as a socio-political force, the BBC has tended to a more pluralistic attitude even on national television. For better communication, out of courtesy or simply to ingratiate, most speakers deliberately or unconsciously practise 'accommodation', adjusting the balance between dialect and standard language according to their perceptions of the person they are addressing.

See also: Cockney; Geordies; scouse

Further reading

Trudgill, P. (1988) *Sociolinguistics*, Harmondsworth: Penguin.

CHRISTOPHER SMITH

diasporan film-makers

Lionel Ngakane's *Jemima and Johnnie* (1964), Frankie Lymon Jr's *Death May be Your Santa Claus* (1969) and Baldwin's *Nigger* (1968) are early examples of a still slow progress towards the expression of the black experience in film. The first black British director to complete a feature, and the first supported by a major funder (the British Film Institute), Horace Ove made a significant breakthrough with the important and still vibrant feature *Pressure* (1975), a coming-of-age drama set in the context of black radical politics in Notting Hill Gate. H.O. Nazareth, the leading documentarist whose *Talking History* (1983) brought together historians E.P. Thompson and C.L.R. James, Imruh Caesar, whose *Riots and Rumours of Riots* (1981) opened the door for a new documentary practice, and Menelik Shabazz, with his 1982 feature *Burning an Illusion*, gave important leads to younger film-makers beginning to train in the early 1980s. The arrival of **Channel 4** in 1981, with a specific area of its remit devoted to 'ethnic' television, allowed directors like Colin Prescod to work in film for broadcast, and younger creatives to gain a foothold in the industry. The success of Franco Rosso's dramatic feature *Babylon* (1980) demonstrated the box office potential of black themes, while the pressure for funding to kickstart black film-making in the UK was finally recognized in the aftermath of the urban uprisings of 1981.

The workshops that launched at this stage – Ceddo, Sankofa, Retake and **Black Audio Film Collective** – worked variously to produce training, shorts, documentaries and features, and crucially to offer screenings of African, Asian and African-American films by directors like Julie Dash, Anand Patwardhan and Haile Gerima. Retake's *Majdhar* (1984), Sankofa's *Territories* (1985) and *Passion of Remembrance* (1986), and Black Audio's *Handsworth Songs* (1986) defined a new, aggressively active and intelligent cinema, one that could move beyond the simple counter-propaganda model of positive images which had dominated earlier calls for black British film. This proved something of a bone of contention, notably when in January 1987, Salman Rushdie criticized *Handsworth Songs* in the pages of the *Guardian* for its complexity. That debate continues a decade later.

The workshops formed an important Association of Black Workshops, which helped promote their work, and to enable new groups to form in Liverpool, Leicester and other regional centres. The work itself became the subject of a flurry of important public events and publications in the UK and the USA. Some films, like Star Films' attempts to recreate the Hindi musical on shoestring budgets in London, received little critical support. Others, like the critically and commercially successful *My Beautiful Laundrette* (1985), scripted by novelist Hanif Kureishi, perhaps received more than they deserved. At the same time, both Kureishi's film and the workshop products did begin to work through and challenge a state of affairs which had become entirely oppressive, and which is caught deftly in a scene from *Passion of Remembrance* in which the failure of a black couple on television to answer an easy quiz question causes one of the characters to complain that every black face on film has to stand for the whole race. In the films of the mid-1980s and subsequently, diasporan film-makers insisted on the diversity and even the conflicts within black communities, conflicts over sexualities and gender, class and allegiance.

Ove's 1986 *Playing Away*, about a cricket match between a thoroughly traditional English village and a laid-back, partying Brixton XI, in some

respects a sentimental production, is able to undertake a more subtle analysis of attitudes within the Brixton team as result of this removal of the pressure for any black character to conform to idealized concepts of propriety and patience. Kureishi's second major script, *Sammy and Rosie Get Laid*, could portray its Indian protagonist as a villain. Nonetheless, one key problem remained, one which is common across the productions of the English independent cinema: the felt necessity of making every film as though it were your last. The result has been a number of films which suffer from being overburdened with themes and issues, perhaps the most disappointing of which was Isaac Julien's much-anticipated *Young Soul Rebels*, which placed extraordinary demands on its audience to follow major themes of racism, anti-racism, gay sexuality and even a reappraisal of 1970s soul music through an already complex plot.

In more recent years, the workshops have mostly broken up, as Channel 4 support for the workshop sector fell away in the late 1980s. Nonetheless, the networks still remain, and from them have arisen major directorial talents, not least among them women directors like Maureen Blackwood and Martine Attile, previously of Sankofa, and June Reid, previously of Ceddo. Meanwhile, new talents like Pratibha Parmar had emerged from the video scene, and a new wave of British Asian cineastes like Alnoor Dewshi and Alia Syed began to revivify the somewhat moribund avant-garde film tradition. The feature film area has been more difficult to work in, paradoxically, as costume dramas (in which the name of Ishmael Merchant is of course extremely prominent (see **Merchant-Ivory Productions**)) and other features have achieved remarkable success. Many of the 1980s generation now produce more work for gallery installations (see **installation art**), cinema shorts and television than for the features market. Notable exceptions have been the remarkably successful *Bhaji on the Beach* (1993), the first feature of director Gurinder **Chadha**, and *Wild West* (1992), David **Attwood**'s engaging and incisive story of an Asian country and western band, scripted by Harwant Bains. Only Hanif Kureishi's clichéd and unstructured directorial debut, *London Kills Me* (1991) disappointed.

There seems to be a major decline in the production of British Afro-Caribbean films in the 1990s, and a weakening of the excitement generated by new British Asian directors since the gains of the first years of the decade. Despite the importance of diasporan cultures to the formation of youth cultures in general in the UK, the cinema has failed to seize on this rich vein of talent in the years since 'riot money' flowed into the funding institutions and made black Britain a hot property.

See also: Black Audio Film Collective; Workshop Declaration

SEAN CUBITT

direct action

Direct action is the deliberate challenge to authority, usually the government, over a policy or policies, in a manner outside the conventional channels of parliamentary politics. It may be legal and institutionalized as with strikes, or extend to civil disobedience and violence. In the 1990s, direct action was associated with environmentalists, new age travellers, and political **fringe groups**. Mass demonstrations against the **poll tax** from 1989 were instrumental in its abandonment. Legislation such as the Public Order Act 1985 and the Criminal Justice Act 1994 were criticized as authoritarian attempts to stifle dissent. Nevertheless, prominent instances of direct action continued in the 1990s, including protests by the Green movement against live animal exports, the arms trade and nuclear weapons, and against environmental destruction.

See also: environmentalism; hunt saboteurs

COLIN WILLIAMS

directors

Contemporary directors reflect the multiplicity of approaches to making **theatre** that have informed the development of postwar theatre. Although they are accorded the status of the most powerful people in theatre, they are increasingly vulnerable to market forces as theatres, companies and productions are expected to make ends meet. The idea of pursuing a personal 'vision' is often sacrificed in order to be commercially viable. Joan Littlewood left Britain in disgust at the lack of state funding; Peter Brook also left after being unable to secure funding for his work in Britain.

Littlewood's legacy of ensemble practice and theatre as 'total experience', from her work with Theatre Workshop in the 1950s and early 1960s, survives, particularly in non-establishment forms such as **community theatre** and **physical theatre**. Her belief in maintaining a strong relationship between a theatre and its local community has also been practised, notably by Philip Hedley at Theatre Royal, Stratford East, and by Peter Cheeseman at Stoke-on-Trent.

George Devine at the **Royal Court** organized and taught **improvisation** classes for a shoal of new playwrights (including Keith Johnstone, Ann Jellicoe and Edward Bond) in addition to taking on a number of rebellious Oxbridge graduates (Lindsay **Anderson** and Bill Gaskill) who developed the legendary 'house style', a simple approach to design, acting and direction dedicated to serving the text. Rather more humanist than intellectual, and 'liberal' than 'left', this team encouraged actors to use their natural working-class accents – a revelation at the time – and nurtured a whole generation of dramatists.

Oxbridge's hold on the profession has continued with one or two exceptions, despite the fact that neither university offers specific courses or opportunities for would-be directors to study and work alongside actors. Consequently, British theatre is said to abound with directors who approach texts from an intellectual standpoint. Peter Brook is an exceptional case for, despite being a Cambridge graduate, he has increasingly focused attention on the somatic power of the actor. For Brook, theatre is a quest, a search for a simplicity of form and a richness of meaning which communicates on a universal level. His search has led him and his multi-ethnic company to Iran, Africa and India from his post-1970 base in Paris. He has been accused of cultural tourism; others view his attempts to create work which speaks on a universal level as a positive example of the benefits of artistic cross-fertilization in a global climate of increasing nationalism. Brook is immensely influential in British theatre, and is regarded as a guru by some.

Peter Hall is a director in a more traditional mould. Following his successes at the Royal Shakespeare Company, he became responsible for 'breaking in' the three stages at the National Theatre when it opened in 1973. His style is essentially 'director's theatre', in which the interpretative vision of the director is foregrounded. His all-male, masked production of *The Oresteia Trilogy* epitomized this approach, with an emphasis on spectacle. This production, together with Bill Bryden's *The Mysteries* (also translated by Tony Harrison in earthy northern dialect), which used the Cottesloe Theatre in promenade and placed God on top of scaffolding, also demonstrated a new boldness in reinterpreting the classics. Hall set up his own company at the Old Vic in 1995.

Alternative theatre in the 1970s produced a new breed of directors dedicated to creating accessible forms through which political meanings could be conveyed in the tradition of Littlewood, such as John **McGrath**. McGrath argues the case for viewing popular theatre forms as the most enduring and efficacious (*A Good Night Out*). At the Royal Court, Max Stafford-Clark took the reins after five years with Joint Stock, where he developed a distinctive workshop process, working with playwrights and actors together through improvisation on ideas and characters before the actual text was written. His significant work in this respect was with Caryl Churchill (*Cloud Nine, Serious Money*), and during his Court years he premiered many women writers (Dunbar, Daniels, Page and Wertenbaker among others). He continues the tradition of working with new writing into the late 1990s with his touring company Out of Joint.

Women began to make inroads into the profession. Some, like their male counterparts, created their own companies; examples are Yvonne Brewster (Talawa Theatre), who staged *The Importance of Being Ernest* with an all-black cast, and Deborah Warner (Kick Theatre), who graduated to the RSC and then the National (*King Lear*, 1990). An average of three to four women run regional theatres, including Jules Wright at the West Yorkshire Playhouse in Leeds; freelance women directors are more evident. Black directors

also tend to work freelance or set up companies, as did Jatinder Verma who directed an all-Asian version of *Tartuffe* (1990) at the National Theatre.

The 1980s was a decade when directors (often teamed with designers) rather than playwrights took the accolades in mainstream theatre. The Donnellan/Ormerod partnership (Cheek by Jowl) concentrates on revivals that carry the conviction of relevance through detailed and imaginative ensemble playing. Their all-male *As You Like It*, with a black Rosalind, was a commercial and artistic success. Other notables are Stephen Daldry (whose revisionary production of *An Inspector Calls* played the **West End** for three years), Katie Mitchell, Nicholas Hytner and Annie Castledine. Some of this generation of directors are being lured into the more financially rewarding fields of film.

Meanwhile, fringe and alternative theatre continues to produce exciting and inspiring work arrived at through collaborative methods where the director is a member of a creative team (Tim Etchells with Forced Entertainment, Simon McBurney with Theatre de Complicité). In such companies, actors are involved in the whole process from research to creative exploration, sometimes using their own experiences and histories as source material; there is no autonomous playwright, and the director's role becomes that of a 'theatre-wright' who oversees the making process. It is worth noting that in community theatre the term – and traditional job – 'director' is being replaced by that of 'enabler' or 'facilitator'.

See also: theatre

Further reading

Edwardes, J. (1994) 'Directors: The New Generation', in T. Shank (ed.), *Contemporary British Theatre*, London: Macmillan.

DYMPHNA CALLERY

disability

It is widely assumed that the term 'disability' refers to a biological or medical condition. However, since the late 1980s those involved in the campaign for civil rights for disabled people have stressed the difference between an impairment (lacking part or all of a limb or having a defective limb, organism or mechanism of the body) and a disability (the disadvantage or restriction of activity caused by a contemporary social situation, which takes no or little account of people who have physical impairments and thus excludes them from the mainstream of social activities). According to this definition, disability must be located within society rather than on or in the body of an individual. In the 1990s, the term has been widely employed by civil rights groups to attack discrimination against disabled people.

Impairment charities have been identified as central to the perpetuation of this discrimination, since most charity appeals represent disabled people as 'tragic but brave' individuals. Hevey (1990) has argued that this produces an understanding of disability as a personal rather than a socio-political problem. Typical examples of this are Mencap's use of the Dickensian Little Stephen character (encapsulating the idea that people with learning disablement are necessarily childlike and helpless) and the Multiple Sclerosis Society's campaign of the late 1980s which portrayed MS as a rip in an otherwise perfect body. Anger concerning these images has led large groups of disabled people to picket the sites of television charity 'spectaculars' such as the BBC's *Children in Need* and the ITV *Telethon*. In the mid-1990s, impairment charities such as SCOPE (formerly the Spastics Society) and Mencap have responded to this criticism by attempting to build more challenging imagery into their advertising.

In May 1994, the government blocked the Civil Rights (Disabled Persons) Bill which would have given disabled people full legal protection against discrimination in most areas of life. As a response to the demonstrations this provoked (including a mass rally in Trafalgar Square in July 1994) and the widespread support they received from the non-disabled public, the government drafted the Disability Discrimination Act, which became law in November 1995. This was heavily criticized for containing no commitment to civil rights, as the body it created – The National Disability Council – has no power to help a disabled person fight a case of discrimination. In this sense, the law concerning disabled people is considerably weaker than the laws which forbid discrimination on the grounds of race or gender.

Further reading

Oliver, M. (1990) *The Politics of Disablement*, London: Macmillan (a solid and accessible introduction).

Hevey, D. (1992) *The Creatures that Time Forgot*, London: Routledge (a lively and polemical discussion of visual images of disability).

AL DEAKIN

disco

For every generation of music listeners, there is always one trend that is felt to have brought about the death of 'real' music. So it was in the USA in the 1970s, where with the onslaught of the disco scene, musicians everywhere began retiring to the nearest cabaret circuit. Mainstream disco music was scorned, even during its commercial heyday.

'Disco' originates from the word 'discotheque', meaning 'record library'. Disco has three definitions: a type of music, a type of dancing, or a type of venue. The origins of the music itself can be traced back to late 1960s America, in clubs or taverns where youngsters would congregate to dance to records played on a jukebox. It was a shared social experience for poorer American youths. Disc jockeys were brought in to keep the dancers on the floor. In the predominantly gay and black clubs, Disc jockeys started to mix together various fast soul songs into one long track for prolonged dancing.

Discos were cheaper than live acts or musicians and the music was easy to reproduce on a mass scale. Successful British acts in the late 1970s and early 1980s were Kelly Marie, Liquid Gold, Leo Sayer, The Real Thing and Hazel Dean. The main message of the music was to shake your body to the rhythm, to 'get on down' with the beat. The lyrics themselves were a mere counter to the beat, reinforcing its rhythm, sexualizing young people everywhere; pulsating rhythms and throbbing beats aroused the listener, inspiring in them a desire to move. It was largely categorized as black or gay music, eroticizing black women who became known as 'disco divas', and vocalizing their capacity for sexual activity (for example, Donna Summer's 'Love To Love You Baby'). Key phrases in the disco repertoire were 'boogie', 'love', 'get down', 'funky', 'rhythm' and 'beat'. The 1980s saw a revival in the UK, thanks predominantly to gay artists like The Pet Shop Boys, Soft Cell and Bronski Beat, who continued their success into the 1990s while developing into more sophisticated performers. Its transition into **electro**-disco in fashionable clubs in the early 1980s was due to influences from abroad, such as Kraftwerk and Giorgio Moroder. Artists like Gary Numan and Ultravox realized the importance of the synthesizer and drum machine and produced introspective lyrics over electro-disco beats. Eventually, technological developments substituted musicians. Disco lost its original sensuality under mechanical studio conditions, but made an easy transition onto the **dance music** scene.

See also: clubs; discos; rave culture

Further reading

Blackford, A. (1979) *Disco Dancing Tonight*, London: Octopus.

ALICE BENNETT

discos

'Disco' is an abbreviation of 'discotheque', a word that combines the French terms for 'disc' and 'library'. Disco has its origins in the London mod clubs (see **mods**) and **Northern Soul** clubs of the early 1960s. However, by the late 1960s, popular music had moved away from its previous emphasis on the live performance as the 'authentic' musical medium. This move paralleled technological developments such as 'multitrack' recording, meaning that studio-produced music could not necessarily be replicated by a live band. As a consequence of these developments, the popular music of the early 1970s moved away from its previous emphasis on the 'traditional' guitar, bass, drums and vocals, towards a more synthesized form. Those clubs that had an emphasis on playing records, rather than a

live performance by a band, became increasingly popular.

Although the first British disco was The Discotheque in Wardour Street, London, probably the most influential British disco of the 1970s was The Embassy, also in London. A small 'members only' club with a capacity of around 400, The Embassy was one of the first venues to employ new lighting technologies such as the stroboscope, or 'strobe', and the ultraviolet bulb, which transformed the opulent surroundings of the building into a palace for dancing. Whereas the dominant musical genre of the early 1970s, **progressive rock**, was based upon a kind of cerebral intellectualism, the music played at discos placed an emphasis on rhythm and repetition in order to facilitate dancing.

As the culture of the disco in the 1970s became more popular, specific musical and clothing styles were developed. Both men and women wore outlandish costumes and danced for hours to the emergent **dance music** genre of disco itself. Possibly the most famous, and also the most influential, disco track is Donna Summer's 'I Feel Love' (1977). Musically revolutionary even by today's standards, this track set the blueprint for disco music for the next twenty years. Produced by Giorgio Moroder, 'I Feel Love' employed many of the experimental production techniques of the European pop avant-garde, and contained an incessant beat combined with synthesized electronic rhythms. Also popular with fans of disco is the film *Saturday Night Fever*, filmed entirely on location in and around the New York disco scene. The clothing, dance styles and particularly the soundtrack of this film, have remained influential.

Although **house**, **techno** and **jungle** are now the dominant forms of British dance music, the sound of disco remains influential. Very few contemporary clubs that play dance music continue to refer to themselves as discos, with most preferring the names 'nightclub' or 'dance club'. However, the phenomenon of the 'mobile disco' has survived. A mobile disco consists of a complete sound system including two turntables, an amplifier, speakers, a sound mixer and lighting show, available for hire and transportable by van. The convenience and portability of the mobile disco means that it will continue to be a staple feature of birthday parties, weddings and other small-scale private functions.

See also: clubs; disco; house

Further reading

Blackford, A. (1979) *Disco Dancing Tonight*, London: Octopus.

STUART BORTHWICK

discount stores

Particularly during the recession of 1990–1, shoppers in Britain became more price conscious. Tesco's 'pile 'em high and sell 'em cheap' philosophy had worked at the expense of the corner stores, which all but disappeared; but consumers' attitudes were now whetted and, leaving Tesco and Sainsbury to compete for the top of the market, they began to seek out even cheaper stores. These were supplied by Kwiksave and Asda, which deliberately targeted working-class consumers who were price-conscious through necessity. These stores employed advertising campaigns aimed at convincing consumers that they were being wise by shopping in such stores. Competition among discount stores increased again when Continental competitors such as Lidl and Aldi entered the market and operated using even greater economies of scale.

See also: cash and carry; convenience stores

MIKE STORRY

divorce law

Before 1857, marriage was 'for life' in the sense that a divorce could only be granted through Church courts and confirmed by a special act of Parliament. Divorce was for the rich and privileged, usually on the grounds of the husband's cruelty or the wife's adultery (no divorce was granted for a husband's adultery until 1801). After 1857, divorces were granted by secular courts and desertion was added as reasonable grounds (to be followed by 'unsoundness of mind' in 1938). More recently, in the 1969 Divorce Reform Act, the introduction of 'marital breakdown' as grounds for divorce has removed the elements of guilty and injured party, and since then the number of annual divorces has more than doubled. Divorce rates in Britain at the millennium are the highest in Europe, approaching 40 percent of first marriages, even though weddings are proving nearly as popular as ever.

See also: marriage; single parents

PETER CHILDS

Dixon, Jeremy

b. 1939

Dixon trained at the **Architectural Association** from 1958 to 1964. He established a private practice with his wife Fenella Dixon in 1973 after working for Peter and Alison **Smithson** among others. From 1983, Dixon worked with the Building Design Partnership on the extension to the Royal Opera House in London. He has become known as a city developer and worked on housing schemes in North Kensington, Maida Vale and the Isle of Dogs. Between 1981 and 1984 he also designed the London Tate Gallery restaurant and coffee shop (see **Tate(s)**). Dixon's blend of classicism with modernism has appealed to both his peers and to the Prince of Wales.

See also: Prince of Wales's Institute

PETER CHILDS

DJs

The role of the disc jockey (DJ) was specifically geared to the presenting of pop music shows on radio, but their role has changed dramatically over the years. Many DJs have expanded their job descriptions to include other media, notably television and record producing.

The birth of the DJ as personality came with the rise of **pirate radio** stations in the 1960s. DJs such as Tony Blackburn, Kenny Everett, John Peel and Dave Lee Travis all cut their teeth on pirate stations before the formation of BBC **Radio 1** in 1967. Working for the BBC opened up new vistas for these DJs, particularly within television. Beginning by hosting pop programmes such as *Top of the Pops* and *The Old Grey Whistle Test*, DJs went on to front many other entertainment programmes. Most notable within this category is Noel Edmonds, former Radio Luxembourg DJ and now the multi-millionaire owner of his own production company providing programmes for the BBC. Many of the presenters have been accused of owning an inflated ego, using their radio and television slots to put forward their opinions on events not linked to their job. This 'cult of the DJ' was satirized brilliantly by comedian Harry Enfield through his characters 'Smashie and Nicey', both of whom were heavy rock-loving, farm-owning, pipe-smoking caricatures of Radio 1 DJs Dave Lee Travis, Alan Freeman and Tony Blackburn. The accusations of presenters being out of touch with the new music scene led to a massive clear out of ageing DJs at Radio 1 in the early 1990s, the only exception being John Peel, long a champion of new music and the only presenter to have been with the station since its inception in 1967.

Outside broadcasting, many DJs became famous as recording artists, particularly after the **house** music explosion of the early 1990s. First involved in remixing current songs, DJs went on to become powerful figures in the music world, as producers and innovators. DJs who mixed live during club nights would develop reputations, leading to heavily oversubscribed club nights and the birth of the 'superclub', the best example of which is Cream in Liverpool. Names such as Mark Moore, Todd Terry and Jazzie B in the 1980s, and more recently Norman Cook, Sash and the Chemical Brothers, are examples of club DJs turned recording artists. The reverse has also occurred, with some established recording artists turning DJ, the best examples being Boy George (of Culture Club) and Bob Stanley (of St Etienne).

See also: Radio 2

SAM JOHNSTONE

documentary

Documentaries are broadcast regularly on British television, despite persistent fears about their diminution in a competitive climate. They are found in regular series slots on most channels, their objects of study continuing to include science, travel, wildlife, marginal groups and controversial social and political topics. Simultaneously, forms of documentary practice have become greatly diversified, so that sometimes their own workings rather than their subject matter attract public and academic discussion.

At the heart of documentary is a belief in evidence; in many programmes this is still delivered (despite various changes) by an apparently authoritative (or well-known 'name') presenter, in person or through voiceover. Explorations of such topics as nuclear waste, terrorism in Northern Ireland, or prison conditions continue to provoke public discussion and, at times, government hostility. Documentary subject matter (treated incisively, or not) now includes powerful groups and institutions as well as the disadvantaged.

Some observers and film-makers see such programmes as enriched but in part displaced by a dramatic rise in new ways of constructing documentaries. These include the dramatized documentary reconstruction of political or other events ('drama-doc'), and the regular documentary treatment of the life of a hospital or other institution on a continuing basis and with key 'personalities' ('docu-soap'). The availability of the lightweight camera has enabled the appearance of authored 'video diaries' and of the BBC's ambitious project *Video Nation* (broadcast in two minute, half hour and longer slots) recording the views and lives of 'ordinary British people', an approach which has been extended to Russian life and other subjects in parallel series.

Particularly controversial has been the evolution of the 'fly on the wall' documentary, drawing on extended on-site observation sometimes with 'authentically' rougher sound, jump-cutting and visible camera movements. The work of documentarists such as Molly Dineen, Roger Graef, Paul Watson and many others has embraced this kind of painstaking in-depth analysis, often through a series of institutions such as schools, the army, factories, police stations and the family. Later developments drew out the entertainment value of observing people and their foibles, so that documentaries on subjects such as shoplifting or learner car drivers began to draw very considerable audiences and even present the documentary as comedy. In the light of these innovations, much general debate continues to question the value, ethics and purpose of 'serious' documentary, together with its capacity to survive new ratings wars.

See also: current affairs; infotainment; news, television

Further reading

Macdonald, K. and Cousins, M. (1996) *Imagining the Real: The Faber Book of Documentary*, London: Faber & Faber.

MICHAEL GREEN

domestic violence

Domestic violence can include a number of violent acts towards or against women, such as rape, sexual assault and beatings. Radical feminists have argued that domestic violence is the basis of men's control over women. Others have indicated that the state perpetuates domestic violence against women: on the one hand, the welfare state does not provide women with enough economic resources to remain independent from violent men; on the other, the state rarely intervenes in cases of domestic violence. Feminists and others have made many attempts to assist women who are subjected to domestic violence and this has included organized support services for women as well as campaigns for changes in the way the state responds to women's complaints of violence.

See also: divorce law; marriage; WAVAW

KALWANT BHOPAL

Douglas, Bill

b. 1937; d. 1991

Film-maker

Douglas is a Scottish-born director who secured sponsorship from the British Film Institute in 1970 to set out to explore his roots on film. He produced a three-part 'documentary' series known as 'The Bill Douglas Trilogy'. In it he recreated his childhood and adolescence in a forsaken mining town. He used local actors and local extras, and took eight years to complete the three films: *My Childhood* (1972), *My Kin Folk* (1973) and *My Way Home* (1978). His film *Comrades* (1987) tells the story of the Tolpuddle Martyrs' struggle to form a union in the 1830s. It is historically accurate and respected actors Michael Hordern, Vanessa Redgrave and James Fox express their personal convictions by appearing in the film.

MIKE STORRY

Dr Martens

Dr Martens, known as Doc Martens or DMs, are the cult British-made air-sole shoes and steel-capped-toe boots that defined a decade of footloose rebellion in the 1970s. In 1992, R. Griggs Group, holders of the worldwide manufacturing rights to Dr Martens since 1959, merged with London avant-garde fashion firm, **Red or Dead**. Together, as Dr Martens Clothing, they sell a range of clothes and **accessories** aimed at the youth market. Previously associated with skinheads, hard men and 'bovver boys', DMs were adopted by feminists in the 1970s as both an anti-fashion and anti-femininity statement.

PETER CHILDS

drama on television

Drama has been associated with BBC television since before the Second World War and with ITV since 1955. The latter, on its opening night, screened excerpts from Oscar Wilde's *The Importance of Being Earnest*. Classic drama from playwrights such as Sheridan and Ibsen featured heavily in the early days. The BBC's Sunday plays (repeated midweek) had been broadcast since the 1930s. Drama has thus always been, for the BBC, a repository for middle-class values.

In the 1990s, the subject of television drama is much debated. Critics point to a golden age of productions such as *The Forsyte Saga* and *Brideshead Revisited* and identify a decline. Recent adaptations of *Emma* and *Pride and Prejudice* have offered a rebuttal. Others disparage contemporary television drama and see Alan Bleasdale and Willy Russell as no substitute for Dennis **Potter**. They view even the ubiquitous sitcoms as much beneath the standards set in the 1970s and 1980s by *Fawlty Towers* and *Yes Minister*. Others welcome the way drama has begun to reach a larger audience, even though it often deals with a less sophisticated range of issues.

In what might be seen as an adverse reflection on other television drama offerings, in 1997 *EastEnders* became the first soap opera to win the BAFTA award for best drama series. However, it may be that criteria for the awards have changed to reflect popular culture and public taste: television is about ratings, which may mean a move away from 'quality', as it had previously been defined. Thus the shows which attracted the largest audiences may not have matched Reithian standards, but did at least reflect ordinary people's lives. The final episode of *Only Fools and Horses*, starring David Jason as Del Boy, is a case in point. It was watched by a record 24.3m people at Christmas 1996. Given that there is plenty of competition, and that audiences have a choice, ratings do reflect script-writers' and producers' abilities to satisfy.

Television is accused of relying on reruns of previous drama series. These are always 'safe', and cheap, and this also suits a conservative audience who missed 'classic' programmes the first time round or who like to take nostalgia trips. Despite flops like the £10m *Rhodes* and *Nostromo*, there has been much innovative, genre-breaking drama on television. Jimmy McGovern's *Hillsborough* bridged documentary, drama and reportage and led, in real life, to the reopening of the inquiry into police conduct. *This Life*, with unknown actors, bucked a trend (for example, it was suggested that the only reason for *A Touch of Frost*'s 18m viewers was the presence of star David Jason) and became an unexpected success. All in all, the death of drama on television would seem to have been exaggerated, but most people still consider quality drama to be from the past: *The Forsyte Saga, Upstairs, Downstairs, Brideshead Revisited* or *The Jewel in the Crown*, for example. This was confirmed by a September 1998 *Radio Times* readers' poll, conducted to mark seventy-five years of the magazine, which found *I, Claudius* (1976) to be the 'best' period drama and Ken **Loach**'s *Cathy Come Home* (1966) the 'best' single television drama.

See also: crime drama; medical drama

MIKE STORRY

drink

Alcoholic beverages have existed in Britain for thousands of years and provisions relating to the use and misuse of alcohol reflect its historical importance. Distinctive features of the British brewing industry, such as the tied house system and judicial power to grant licences, are a legacy of the nineteenth century. **Licensing laws** are substantially unchanged since 1923. They exist to provide controlled conditions under which alcohol can be bought, sold and consumed to protect the public from anti-social behaviour related to alcohol consumption, and to prevent the sale of alcohol to children. Licences available include the full pub on licence for the sale of alcohol for consumption on or off the premises, off licences, restaurant and residential licences, and occasional licences. No licence is required for members clubs. Changes to licensing laws in 1995 allowed Sunday opening all day until 10.30 pm and off licence opening hours were also extended.

In Britain, a unit of alcohol is eight grammes of ethanol, the amount contained in half a pint of ordinary strength beer, a glass of wine or a measure of spirits. From 1996 the safe recommended limits were four daily units for men and three for women. The increase in awareness of health problems related to alcohol, alongside media pressure against 'lager louts' and drink-drivers, has led to a reduction in the amount of alcohol drunk. In 1984, the British Government signed the World

Health Declaration, with its commitment to reducing alcohol consumption by 25 percent before the year 2000. Significant advances have been made in the campaign against drinking and driving with the introduction of the breathalyzer in the late 1960s, as well as high-profile television advertising to discourage potential offenders. Home Office data in 1994 showed that despite the total number of tests having tripled since 1984, the number of people who were found positive or refused a test had fallen to 93,000 per annum.

The Brewers Society was founded in 1904 to represent the interests of the brewing industry. In 1995 it calculated that the industry employed half a million people and consisted of eighty established brewers, operating around 130 breweries and about ninety small wholesaling brewing units. There were 200,000 licensed premises. Beer remains the most popular drink in Britain and, in 1994, 28 million pints of beer were sold each day. The number of brewers has declined throughout the twentieth century, and the tendency towards mergers and acquisition continues. In 1995, five major brewers produced 91 percent of beer in Britain. The Campaign for Real Ale was formed in 1971 to safeguard the interests of small brewers, oppose takeovers, and promote improvements and individuality amongst British beers.

In 1990, a Monopoly and Mergers Commission Report was made as a result of claims that there was a monopoly in the brewing industry in the supply of beer. The Commission found that a complex monopoly existed against the public interest, and advocated restricting brewers to ownership of 2,000 pubs, allowing tenants able to sell 'guest beers' (that is, beers produced by brewers other than the pub owner) and increasing competition in order to widen consumer choice. The brewers lobbied intensively against the proposals, which were consequently diluted to the 1992 Beer Orders; these have nonetheless led to surplus brewing capacity and pub closures.

Pubs suffered a 13 percent decline in sales between 1990 and 1995. This is due to fewer young customers, cross-Channel shoppers making bulk beer purchases in France, drug taking, more competition for the 'leisure pound' and the growth of home entertainment. The provision of catering services is now considered very important to increase turnover and attract customers. The growth in the off sales market also adversely affects the pub. Prices of alcohol in off licences and supermarkets have continued to decrease relative to pub prices in the 1990s. The increase in beer off sales was attributed to innovations such as draught flow systems which improve beer quality, and large ranges of imported beers, while wine purchases have been encouraged by sampling promotions.

There is intense competition in the brewing industry, and several strategies have been adopted to encourage the public to choose particular brands. Sponsorship, particularly in sport, is seen as an effective method of self-promotion. Critics assert that drinking is incompatible with a healthy lifestyle and the practice should be discouraged. There are strict guidelines under the Independent Broadcasting Authority code for advertising alcohol. Nobody who is or appears to be under the age of twenty-five can advertise liquor and stimulant, and the intoxicating or sedative aspects of a drink cannot be emphasized. There should be no suggestion that drinking is masculine, daring or leads to sexual success. Drink cannot be connected with driving or operating machinery and should not be targeted at young people. The launch in Britain of alcoholic carbonates, commonly known as 'alcopops', in 1995 provoked the Portman Group, the regulatory body of the brewing industry (see **regulatory bodies**), to issue a code of practice on the marketing of alcoholic drinks to minors. Evidence in 1997 indicated that alcopops contributed to a growth in juvenile drunkenness.

In 1990 the annual per capita consumption of alcohol in Britain was 9.45 litres, and 94 percent of the population were customers of one or more of the alcohol producing industries. The long-term trend in the nation's drinking is the decline of spirits and, to a lesser extent, beer sales, coupled with an increased demand for wine, which by 1994 accounted for a quarter of Britain's expenditure on alcohol. As wine increases in popularity, brewers have taken steps to obtain a sizeable share in that market. The decline in the number of young people will adversely affect lager and vodka sales, while whisky sales will benefit most from an ageing population.

See also: food; licensing laws

Further reading

Mintel (1995) *Report on Pub Retailing*, London: Mintel International Group Limited.

COLIN WILLIAMS

drug culture

British drug culture has its origins in the youth subcultures of the 1950s and 1960s. While some aficionados of jazz smoked cannabis in order to enhance their enjoyment of music, it was the mod scene (**mods**) of the early 1960s that heralded the large-scale consumption of drugs. In particular, mods used a variety of legal and illegal drugs in order to facilitate all-night dancing at mod and **Northern Soul clubs**. While mainstream opinion suggested that drug usage led to dependence, many mods found that they could use drugs recreationally at weekends, with few side effects. However, many mods found themselves in difficulty due to the physically addictive nature of the 'uppers' that they consumed. This mirrored problems connected to many prescribed drugs at the time, in that doctors were prescribing amphetamine-based compounds for a variety of illnesses including narcolepsy, obesity and respiratory complaints. 'Amphetamine psychosis' and other unpleasant side effects led to a decrease in the popularity of these stimulants.

As the mod phenomenon declined in popularity, a new youth culture took its place. Within hippie culture (see **hippies**), drugs were a central element of the lifestyle. Whereas for mods the use of drugs was functional, in that it allowed them to dance for longer than they had previously been able to, the use of drugs by hippies was connected to their political values. Whereas mod culture was a culture of the 'weekender' and most mods held down steady jobs, hippies rejected what they perceived to be the materialism of western culture. In particular, hippies took hallucinogenics such as LSD as part of their rejection of the 'work ethic' central to mainstream British culture.

Although LSD does not lead to dependence in the same way as many stimulants, it is nevertheless a powerful drug that produces visual and other sensory distortions. In a sense the hippies created the first proper 'drug culture', in that the consumption of hallucinogenics was central to their everyday lifestyle. Many of the media texts spawned by hippie culture were connected to the consumption of LSD. In particular, The Beatles' album *Sergeant Pepper's Lonely Hearts Club Band* is said to have been influenced by John Lennon and Paul McCartney's experimentation with LSD. This connection is made explicit on the track 'Day in the Life' with its lyric of 'I'd love to turn you on'.

As with Mod culture, hippie culture suffered problems that were directly connected to drug usage. Although LSD has few physical side effects, it has a disturbing power to alter the mind. Many hippies never mentally recovered from their heavy LSD usage. There were some famous casualties; for instance the singer Syd Barrett left the band Pink Floyd as a result of psychiatric problems, and has never fully recovered.

As the hippie dream lost its potency, so British drug culture declined in popularity. The early 1970s are not connected with any specific drug. Although amphetamines, LSD, cannabis and increasingly heroin were used by many people, no culture sprang from their usage. Anecdotal evidence suggests that, at the time, many young people were opposed to drug usage, perceiving it to be 'old-fashioned' and connected to delinquency.

This changed with the **punk rock** explosion of the mid-1970s. The aggressive nature of many punks led them to take amphetamines at punk clubs and concerts. Amphetamine-based stimulants appeared to be the ideal drug for many punks. In particular, amphetamines led to aggression, perceived to be a desirable state of affairs by many punks. Central to the punk ethos was a desire for 'speed' and alertness, a violent opposition to 'the establishment', and a decadent rejection of mainstream values. This led many punks to be attracted to drug misuse. Again there were casualties. Solvent abuse in the form of glue sniffing took many young lives. Poly-drug use, the use of more than one drug at a time, led to other fatalities, including that of Sid Vicious, a leading punk musician with The Sex Pistols.

Towards the end of the 1970s, rising unemployment led to a widespread disillusionment within youth culture. With no likelihood of paid employment, and with right-wing attacks on 'benefit scroungers', many young people perceived themselves as having no place in British society. This led to an increase in heroin consumption in the early 1980s. Heroin is a different drug to cannabis, amphetamines and LSD in that it is very addictive, and users suffer severe withdrawal symptoms if they are unable to obtain the drug. Whereas amphetamines and, to a lesser extent LSD, can make the drug user outgoing and more communicative, heroin use leads to the individual withdrawing from the world around them. The heroin culture of the 1980s was particularly insular, while impurities in illegally imported heroin led to many fatalities.

The widespread drug culture of today has its roots in the shift in drug usage in the late 1980s. In particular **rave** culture has been credited with a general shift in drug culture away from physically addictive 'hard' drugs such as heroin towards the use of 'soft' drugs such as Ecstasy and cannabis. Whereas previously drug usage was perceived to be rebellious, anti-social and immoral, contemporary youth culture holds different views. Recent research has shown that up to 50 percent of young people in certain areas have tried an illegal drug at least once, and some figures suggest that up to 3 million young people use drugs such as ecstasy. Indeed, perhaps contemporary youth culture is not as different to mod culture as may initially appear. The use of ecstasy or cannabis is said to enhance music and to enable dancing for long periods of time, while not affecting the users' ability to maintain steady employment and function as a 'normal' member of society. However, these views are not held by the medical establishment, who suggest that the long-term effects of consuming amphetamines, ecstasy and cannabis are by no means clear. While some have predicted a softening in society's attitudes to drug consumption, these medical uncertainties mean that those drugs that are currently illegal will remain so.

STUART METCALFE

druids

Druids were a pre-Aryan group rather like a professional class whose work spanned the religious and the legal. They were the priestly caste of Celtic society and they presided at sacrifices, were responsible for medicine and rituals, and undertook the teaching of magic and tradition. They associated the oak and the mistletoe with their supreme deity. They conducted sacred rituals, performed sacrifices and arbitrated disputes within their jurisdiction. Heroes of Celtic mythology like the Irish Cuchullain, the Welsh Arianrhod and the Scottish queen Scathach, for whom Skye is named, were druids. Stonehenge and Glastonbury are examples of pre-Christian druidic sites which still exercise a strong spiritual pull especially on young people.

About a quarter of the 100,000 contemporary British pagans (who include shamanists, witches and Odinists) are druids. The present flowering of alternative spiritualities began in the 1960s. Druids emphasize poetry, divination, healing and pre-Christian mythology in their religious practice, often holding love of nature as a central belief. The Council of British Druid Orders was formed in 1988 to combat the ban on pagan celebrations at Stonehenge (which were resumed in 1998). The Council included the British Druid Order (pagan and goddess-oriented), the Order of Bards, Ovates and Druids (pagan and Christian mix), the Glastonbury Order of Druids and the London Druid Group, which practises magic. There are thirty-five druid groups in Britain, and over 300 throughout the world.

PETER CHILDS
MIKE STORRY

DTP

Typesetting and composition, along with most aspects of the print industry, have since the 1970s seen the replacement of mechanical and craft production by electronic systems such as photo-typesetting and laser printing technologies. These control how print looks on the page, its layout and any graphic elements. Simultaneously, word processing systems were developed which automated the manipulation of structures of content and the meaningful arrangements of sentences, paragraphs and chapters. Ultimately, photo-composition and word processing software converged in desktop publishing (DTP) software that could be employed on personal computers.

Typesetters and compositors use formatting software to specify the appearance of the page with great precision. DTP packages, on the other hand, can be used by non-specialists and hence are usually interactive (or 'wysiwyg': what you see is what you get), giving the user readily available options to move text and graphic elements around on that part of the computer screen which represents the printed page. The remainder of the screen is the desktop, where icons or graphic symbols representing tools and documents are kept. The desktop is the defining metaphor for the personal computer interface, and the DTP desktop includes icons for all the tools and processes used by compositors and graphic designers.

While word processing software brought text composition and printing to every computer user, DTP enabled the formatting and printing of complete documents including text, images and graphic design elements, not only to paper but, in the form of electronic publishing, to screen. Since most page printers now employ laser technology, DTP makes professional looking publication available to all computer users. The appearance of even quite informal written messages in both private and professional spheres has taken on the gravitas of published text. Computer users now incorporate the forms and symbols that were once reserved for publishers; columns, bullets, different typefaces and the whole range of graphic conventions appear in the most ephemeral of notes. This has general implications for readers' expectations of print and textual communications.

Traditional systems of writing and publishing insist upon content and form as quite separate matters. The writer edits content through a process of iteration, often inscribing ever more subtle distinctions into the text, while a more heuristic approach might be taken to the layout. DTP encompasses both processes in the same instant to produce a text that, while it is graphically informative and hence easier to read and understand, demands a new kind of literacy.

JIM HALL

dub

From Rock Steady onwards, many Jamaican 45s (singles) contained an alternative version on the B-side. This 'version' would be a 'dub' recording, a remix of the A-side with the main vocal dubbed out and treated with special effects. Early dub was recorded on a two-track machine with the vocals on one channel and the band on the other. Dub was invented by record cutter Osbourne Ruddock, who began to cut out the band right after the introduction (leaving the vocals *a capella*), and then abruptly cutting out the vocals while simultaneously dropping the music back in, sometimes chopping off words or letting the tail end of a sentence echo into the distance. By the mid-1970s, companies had begun to release sneak previews of coming releases in dub form on acetates. These rare gems became known as 'dub-plates'.

See also: black performance poets; Johnson, Linton Kwesi; reggae

EUGENE LANGE

E

Eagleton, Terry

b. 1943

Literary critic, playwright and academic

Terry Eagleton is a British Marxist literary critic and Oxford professor, enormously influential in the 1970s and 1980s. Eagleton developed his literary career with studies of Richardson's *Clarissa*, the Brontës, Shakespeare and modernism (in *Exiles and Émigrés*). He came to prominence with his slim overviews of left-wing theory and criticism, *Criticism and Ideology* (1976) and *Marxism and Literary Criticism* (1976). Eagleton's best-selling *Literary Theory* (1983) became the standard textbook introducing and critiquing the subject, while later works such as *The Ideology of the Aesthetic* (1990) have taken his career in new directions. Less influential in the 1990s, he has still become a youngish elder statesman of the British left, a key critic of postmodernism, and one of the few world-renowned British academics.

See also: Hall, Stuart; Marxism; Williams, Raymond

PETER CHILDS

eating disorders

The two commonest types of eating disorder are anorexia nervosa and bulimia. These conditions are characterized by serious disturbances in eating habits and appetitive disorders. Anorexia involves an intense fear of becoming obese. Patients can 'feel fat' when they are of normal weight, or even emaciated. The term 'anorexia' (loss of appetite) is misleading in the sense that, at the beginning, the patient is as hungry as anyone else who is starving themselves. Anorexia may start with dieting, which then becomes obsessive. Body weight may drop by one-half. The anorexic usually claims to be eating adequately and refuses to acknowledge the emaciation that is plain for others to see. Death from starvation occurs in about 10–15 percent of cases, despite the intervention of doctors.

The disorder often affects young women with 'perfectionist' personalities. The classic anorexic is young (mainly under 30, usually between 14–17), female (95 percent of cases) and from a middle or upper class family. However, the condition is also found in older women and men.

Bulimia (Greek for 'great hunger') is characterized by repeated episodes of 'bingeing', that is, eating a lot of high-calorie food followed by self-induced vomiting, or by laxative or amphetamine abuse. These periods are often associated with bouts of depression. Bulimia is frequently found in conjunction with, or as a phase of, anorexia nervosa. This regular gorging leads to guilt and the compulsive desire to be rid of the hated food. The bulimic, unlike the anorexic, functions relatively normally and rarely requires hospitalization, so the disease is not life-threatening. Bulimic behaviour arises from psychological difficulties involving a compulsive desire for perfection and may be exacerbated by poor self-image, stressful family relationships, or sometimes by leaving home. However, in many cases its cause is undoubtedly a purely physical one, more specifically the impaired secretion of a hormone, cholecystokinin (CCK), that normally induces a feeling of fullness after a meal.

In the case of both these illnesses it is tempting to feel that an 'epidemic' is under way: teenage girls seem to 'catch' it from one another. Estimates suggest that up to 1 percent of girls may become anorexic. However, as with previous such 'epidemics' (hysteria in the nineteenth century) there are often social or psychological causes which affect many people faced with similar circumstances. The illnesses have been given cult status by the fact that tabloid newspapers have suggested that both the Duchess of York and the Princess of Wales had suffered from them, and this may have made the diseases in a sense 'chic'. The reasons for suffering from them, though, are complex, specific and relate to individual circumstances.

Discussion of possible causes for these disorders has focused on women's position in society, influences from the media, family problems and rejection of adult sexuality. The Victorian 'separation of spheres' meant that while men concentrated on the public, the political and the business spheres of life, women were confined to the home and family. Thus they were by and large powerless to influence endemic structures which conditioned their lives. In those circumstances, the only asset over which a woman had a great degree of control was her own body. In such a situation of social powerlessness, distress may be unconsciously expressed in relation to food and body image.

Other suggestions have been that, as 'rules' have changed, women growing up feel free to seek their own identities. In denying herself, the woman can create a person she can admire, a person who appears to have no needs and no appetites. On the other hand, some adolescent girls resist the impetus to grow up. When anorexia begins in a girl who has just entered puberty, it is sometimes suggested that the illness represents an unconscious desire to remain a child.

It has become common on talk shows and in magazines, for example, to blame fashion, newspapers and television for the increase in eating disorders. Waif-like models such as Kate Moss are cited as representing impossibly desirable, almost 'heroin chic' images of beauty. Schoolchildren emulate these role models, seen constantly in advertisements, to the detriment of their own health. Young girls are also perhaps more susceptible to peer pressure, which forces them to diet and to become preoccupied with body image. This is evident in advice on anorexia or bulimia which, in response to readers' requests for help, has become a regular feature of many popular teenage magazine problem pages.

The number of older women admitting to having these disorders does not necessarily indicate that the diseases are being acknowledged because they are fashionable, but that women now live in a freer society where it is easier to speak out. They feel that, as women's roles change, they can deal with previously taboo subjects. The Princess of Wales admitted on a *Panorama* interview that she had suffered from bulimia. This revelation, in conjunction with that of her unhappy marriage, was used as evidence by psychologists who assert that a woman's social role is a contributory factor to this illness.

Anorexia nervosa is resistant to treatment. The principal aim must be to restore nutrition. The anorexic may be hospitalized and fed by stomach tube or through a vein. Because the illness is basically psychological, long-term psychotherapy for both mental and physical recovery is often necessary. However the majority of cases lead to spontaneous complete recovery.

See also: body size

Further reading

Eichenbaum, L. and Orbach, S. (1992) *Understanding Women*, Harmondsworth: Penguin.
Katzman, M. and Wooley, S. (eds) (1994) *Feminist Perspectives on Eating Disorders*, New York: Guilford.

ELIZABETH STORRY

Edinburgh Festival and Fringe

Every August, Edinburgh becomes a hive of artistic activity. Musicians, actors, comedians, artists, writers, film-makers, directors and producers descend upon the city to display a maelstrom of creativity. In addition to the International Festival and its unruly Fringe, Edinburgh in August is now also host to a film festival, television festival, book festival and a cornucopia of street performers who have not, as yet, formed themselves into an official festival.

The first Edinburgh International Festival took place in 1947. At that time it was regarded as a symbol of peace and unity in a world still recovering from war. This impulse was evident in the performance of Mahler's 'Lied von der Erde', sung by Kathleen Ferrier and Peter Pears, with Bruno Walter conducting the orchestra from which he had been parted since Hitler's invasion of Austria, the Vienna Philharmonic.

The Fringe of 1947 sprang up as a response to the under-representation of Scottish music and drama in the main Festival. This has been an issue for all subsequent Festival directors, addressed for instance under Frank Dunlop between 1984–91 when the Saltire Society regularly presented programmes of Scottish poetry and song as part of the Festival. With the magnificent Usher Hall and the beautiful new Festival theatre on offer as venues, Edinburgh continues to attract ground-breaking theatrical productions, musical premieres and major international artistes of the highest calibre.

The Fringe, on the other hand, has changed out of all recognition from its humble beginnings. In 1947, six theatre companies formed the unofficial Fringe; their aim, as already mentioned, being to redress the balance by providing a Scottish presence. In its fiftieth anniversary year, 1996, 646 groups from all over the world put on a total of 1,238 shows in over 200 venues. In the early years, as well as exploring Scottish drama absent from the main Festival, the Fringe lived up to its name – that which is on the edge – becoming an arena for innovative and experimental drama.

Fifty years on, things have changed drastically. Small-scale experimental drama must battle for its audiences against a comedy component which threatens to subsume the Fringe with its household names and television faces, a component which, to all intents and purposes, now forms a separate entity: a comedy festival, with audiences guaranteed only to those performing in the three major venues, the Assembly Rooms, the Pleasance and the Gilded Balloon.

ALISON BOMBER

Edzard, Christine

b. 1945

Film-maker

Christine Edzard has directed several acclaimed films including *Little Dorrit* (1988), *As You Like It* (1992) and the 3D film *The IMAX Nutcracker* (1997). She works with her husband, Richard Goodwin. *Little Dorrit* was a labour of love, for which she built sets, sewed costumes and made models at home to create a backdrop of Victorian London. Actors of the quality of Alec Guinness, Derek Jacobi, Cyril Cusack and Joan Greenwood appeared in a film that was made mostly out of love for Charles Dickens, and helped Edzard win an Academy Award. She protested that producers' cuts and re-shooting of *The IMAX Nutcracker* adversely affected the integrity of her work.

MIKE STORRY

electro

Electro was a musical genre which peaked in polarity around 1982–3. A sub-genre of **hip hop**, electro differed in using synthesized electronic music rather than samples of old **soul** or **funk** records. As well as hip hop, electro drew influences from electronic groups, both 'serious', such as Kraftwerk, and 'commercial', such as The Human League, fusing their sound with the more basic beeps, thuds and tinny melodies of early computer games. Those same computer games often provided imagery for electro songs (for example, The Jonzun Crew's 'PackJam' was originally called 'Pac Man'), while another influence was cartoons (for example, 'Smurf For What It's Worth' by The Smurfs), a thematic inheritance from P-Funk. This led to electro being primarily juvenile and escapist (not necessarily a bad thing), although there were powerful political electro records, such as 'No Sell Out', which mixed Keith LeBlanc's digital rhythms with extracts from recordings of Malcom X.

SIMON BOTTOM

electronic shopping

Electronic commerce has long been a feature of business transactions, but is now being extended to include transactions with consumers. Two main forms are being offered: digital television, where goods are displayed and can be bought through a hand-held keypad or remote control, and shopping on the **Internet**, where an enormous range of products and services can be purchased using the World Wide Web. Currently, large numbers of books, CDs and computer technologies are sold via the Internet, and it is widely assumed that these kinds of products, as well as those which are already successfully purchased via the telephone and mail order, will be the most popular goods for electronic shopping.

There are a number of important technical issues relating to electronic commerce. Restrictions on bandwidth pose a problem for the development of more sophisticated Internet commerce applications, and continuing expansion of the area is likely to depend upon resolving these in satisfactory ways. There are also a number of regulatory issues surrounding electronic commerce, in particular the need for globally agreed standards on taxation and consumer protection. Fears about the safety of sending personal information over the Internet are assumed by some to have been overblown, although clearly business has an interest in playing down any fears which may slow the development of this important growth area. It is for this reason that debates about encryption and 'digital signatures' are so critical, and that other innovations such as 'e-cash' (where small amounts of electronic credits can be used to purchase items) are being considered.

Extensive development of electronic commerce may change the relationship between producers and consumers, possibly giving more power to consumers, whose ability to research products, compare prices (through 'intelligent agents' and similar technologies) and shop abroad would be significantly extended. At the same time, Internet 'tracking' technologies will allow producers and retailers to gather extensive data about consumers' needs and tastes, enabling marketers to develop more sophisticated consumer models and to target advertising more precisely. Well-known brands may initially be more attractive to consumers, but there are also potential advantages for smaller organizations and specialist producers who will have the opportunity to expand their consumer base and marketing activities considerably. For both large and small producers, success in electronic commerce is likely to depend upon exploiting what is new and distinctive about the Internet, and creating new kinds of shopping opportunities.

LIZ MOOR
PETER LUNT

Elim

The Elim Fellowship began in America in 1933 as an informal association of churches, ministers and missionaries developing from those who trained at Elim Bible Institute and who were of 'Pentecostal conviction and Charismatic orientation'. Akin to American Baptist churches, it regards the Bible as 'the infallible Word of God and the supreme and final authority in all matters of faith and conduct'. It has benefited in Britain from increased recruitment to evangelical and fundamentalist Christian churches generally, and from some high-profile conversions including former SAS trooper Frank Collins, one of the team who stormed the Iranian Embassy, and the originator of Britain's chatlines, Nigel Holmes, who now works for the Elim magazine, *Direction*.

MIKE STORRY

EMAP Maclaren

EMAP Maclaren is one of the largest publishing concerns in the UK. It originated in a postwar merger of four newspaper publishers. East Midlands Allied Press (EMAP) moved into magazine publishing from the 1960s onward, and expanded greatly in the 1980s. It has been successful because it has been prepared to accept and promote innovative ideas and to seize opportunities in the youth culture market through publishing (magazines like *FHM* and *Empire*) and television at home and abroad. Its London base is EMAP Metro, which produces publications aimed at young people and was set up following the phenomenal success of a range of EMAP's youth publications including *Smash Hits*, *Just 17* and *Q*.

Smash Hits is the world's best-selling popular music magazine. It appears fortnightly and, in 1995, had a circulation of 274,005 with an estimated readership per edition of 899,000. The idea came from Nick Logan, former editor of *New Musical Express* (and later founder of *The Face*), in 1978. Its initial print run was 150,000 and its simple aim was to supply readers with the words to popular songs, and accompanying posters. It sold well from the start, partly because of its promotional giveaways of stickers and sticker albums, and it soon became a bi-weekly.

Just 17 was set up in 1983. Aimed at young girls, its 'preview' edition was given away free with *Smash Hits* (69 percent of whose readership were female). 'Jump-starting' it in this way gave it an initial circulation of 200,000, which by 1995 had become a weekly 242,603.

Metro published *Q* magazine in 1986. The editor and editorial director of *Smash Hits*, Mark Ellen and David Hepworth, were behind it. They had previously presented the BBC television rock programme *Whistle Test* and television coverage of the 1985 Live Aid concert. They and EMAP brought to *Q* a professionalism and quality finish – glossy paper, slick presentation – which were not then characteristic of the rest of the music press, which mainly consisted of looseleaf broadsheets unconcerned with style and finish. With *Q*, the editors felt that readers would want to keep the magazine rather than discard it as they would a newsprint/newspaper format. *Q*'s monthly circulation in 1995 was 174,995.

More recently, EMAP has expanded into local radio stations, such as London's Kiss FM, and has moved into Europe (in 1998 it was the third largest magazine publisher in France, with almost one-fifth of the market).

See also: music press; teen magazines; women's press

Further reading

Riley, S.G. (ed.) (1993) *Consumer Magazines of the British Isles*, Westport, CT: Greenwood Press (a useful compendium of essays on the provenance and personnel of magazines).

MIKE STORRY

English National Ballet

Despite a tortuous history punctuated by the potentially catastrophic financial crises typical of postwar policy for the arts generally and for dance in particular in the UK, the English National Ballet survives to delight audiences at London's Royal Festival Hall, usually during the early weeks of the year, before going on to tour the provinces. The company is associated above all with spectacular, even glamorous productions of full-length ballets performed in quite traditional styles. Though sometimes criticized for not generally being in the forefront of innovation, the ENB deserves credit for maintaining in repertory such romantic classics as *The Nutcracker* and *Cinderella*, thus attracting and satisfying a large if somewhat conventional public. It further contributes to dance in Britain by running a ballet school.

In 1950, anticipating the Festival of Britain by a year, the Festival Ballet emerged from the touring company headed by Anton Dolin (or, to give the Sussex-born dancer his English name, Sydney Healey-Kay) and Alicia Markova (Lillian Marks), who had both starred in Diaghilev's Ballets Russes and had teamed up on previous occasions. Markova left after two years and was replaced by Belinda Wright, but Dolin remained artistic director until handing over to John Gilpin in 1962. For the first fifteen years of its existence the manager was Dr Julian Braunsweg, an irrepressibly enterprising impresario. His policy was to provide, not only in the capital but also in provincial centres and even occasionally abroad, fine productions of popular ballets with international stars at affordable prices. That ought to have been a winning formula, especially as it combined the pursuit of excellence in its performances with an anti-elitist attitude towards its audiences. But, despite good houses, tickets sales could not meet ever-rising expenses, and the Festival Ballet, which lacked a permanent base, had to compete for funding with other companies that were considered more

adventurous in their programming. The consequence was repeated doubts about viability.

Whether successive names changes, first to the
London Festival Ballet, then to the English
National Ballet, have contributed to the maintenance of corporate identity and consistency of
artistic policy is a moot point as well. Despite its
difficulties the ENB has struggled through. Under
Peter Schaufuss, it strengthened its position as a
company specializing in the classics and contributing a vital strand to contemporary British dance
theatre.

See also: ballet; ballet music; Royal Ballet

Further reading

Braunsweg, Julian (1977) *Ballet Scandals*, 2nd edn,
London: Allen & Unwin.

CHRISTOPHER SMITH

entrepreneurs

These enterprise mavericks have come in many
guises, such as inventor Clive Sinclair, Anita
Roddick of the Body Shop and Laura **Ashley**.
Perhaps the most famous is Richard Branson (b.
1950), the Virgin boss who has diversified from a
music label and record shops into radio, airlines,
Internet provision, pensions, banking and more.
Branson started by importing cheaper goods from
France into the UK, opening a mail-order business,
and even distributing contraceptives in London in
the 1960s. In the 1990s he became something of a
media personality with his many attempts to
circumnavigate the globe in a succession of hot
air balloons. Entrepreneurs come and go, but
Branson's rise has appeared unstoppable; in a
survey of schoolchildren in the early 1990s, he was
voted the best contemporary British male role
model.

PETER CHILDS

environmentalism

Environmentalism has developed from the 1960s as
both an extensive body of thought and an
important cultural and political movement in
Britain. Philosophically, its roots can be traced to
aspects of eastern and Presocratic thought, while
medieval doctrines can be seen as an important
basis for many elements of contemporary 'green'
theory. There exists a spectrum of environmentalist
thought ranging from the 'deep' to the 'shallow',
with the former representing the most radical
strands of ecocentrism. Environmentalism has had
a significant impact on British and other (predominantly western) value systems, previously
premised upon technocentric and anthropocentric
assumptions and underpinned by cornucopian
images of the natural world as a source of great
riches to be freely exploited by humankind.

The impact of environmentalism on contemporary cultural movements in Britain and elsewhere is
apparent. The postmodernist movement (see **postmodernism**) has highlighted the significance of
New Age values and lifestyles and has incorporated
the concept of 'ecological crisis' into its critique of
the philosophy, social theory, art, architecture and
literature associated with the Enlightenment. In
addition, essentialist feminists have connected
ancient images of the earth as 'goddess' and giver
of life to current images of women and female
values as a counterposition to the aggressive,
competitive and destructive values associated with
men, militarism and the industrial age.

Beyond its philosophical and intellectual impact,
environmentalism has contributed to changes at
the level of cultural practice and symbolism. The
British Green movement encapsulates the full
spectrum of environmentalist thought ranging from
radical and often high-profile groups dealing in
'direct action' such as the 'sabs' (**hunt saboteurs**)
and other animal rights activists to the stereotypically 'middle-class' conservation groups such as
the Royal Society for the Protection of Birds
(RSPB) and a host of other such mainstream
organizations.

The British Green Party has had less of an
electoral impact than some of its sister parties in
continental **Europe**, although environmental pressure groups have played their part in the growth of

cause-oriented and often class-dealigned politics in Britain. **Green consumerism** has also been a very visible byproduct of the widespread impact of environmentalist ideas, representing an attempt to introduce the notion of sustainability into a changing marketplace. The current concern with 'sustainable cities' reflects the impact of environmentalism on the architectural and urban planning professions with a clear shift apparent in the form, aesthetic values and materials used in many major British cities.

Further reading

Pearce, D., Markandya, A. and Barbier, E.B. (1989) *Blueprint for a Green Economy*, London: Earthscan.

DAVE EGAN

equal pay

Early feminists such as Christabel Pankhurst argued that an important aspect of women's subordination was their economic dependence upon men. They insisted that all women be able to compete freely and equally in the labour market. Hence, 'equal pay for equal work' became a slogan for the Women's Party, which was founded in the early 1900s. Equal pay also became a predominant concern for contemporary feminists. In 1970, the Equal Pay Act was passed (and implemented in 1975). This Act specified that women were entitled to the same wage or salary if they were doing the same work as men. Recently, however, feminists have questioned how effective the legislation has been in opening further avenues of employment for women.

See also: women in business

KALWANT BHOPAL

Establishment, the

The Establishment embraces the hierarchy of institutions that combine to preserve the established order of society. The concept dates back to Edward I's Model Parliament (1295) where, for the first time, representatives from outside the high clergy and aristocracy were summoned to parliament. This parliament was generally thought to be the most immediate precursor of modern parliamentary government and included representatives from cities, shires and boroughs throughout England. The established church was incorporated into the English civil establishment after Henry VIII's institution of the Anglican Church was successful in its attempt to incite middle-class loyalty to the state.

More recently, the Establishment concerns the English constitution and the institutions engaged in its protection. At its centre is the relation between the institutions of church and state, and monarchy and parliament. The ancillary institutions are the civil service, the military, the public school system, the City and, latterly, major elements of the British media. All contribute in some way to the preservation of the established order of British social and political control and, to a large extent, continue to be based on upper-class interests. The new social movements of the 1960s and 1970s attempted to challenge the aristocratic and anti-democratic nature of the Establishment.

The conventions, traditions and institutions constituting the unwritten British constitution have permitted the endurance of a ruling class that continues to play an enormous role in shaping British public and political life. That role has little democratic foundation. The appointment and dismissal of notables within the Establishment has no recourse in public approval, election or even public visibility. As Lord Beaconsfield once remarked, 'the most powerful men are not public men. The public man is responsible, and the responsible man is a slave. It is private life that governs the world.' The accuracy of this description continues today.

The prime movers controlling the British Establishment constitute a very narrow group of less than five hundred individuals. Some, such as the monarch, the royal family, the Archbishops of Canterbury, York and notable bishops are public figures. Many of great influence are not. These comprise cabinet secretaries, senior civil servants, great families (such as the Salisburys), elder statesmen, the Governor of the Bank of England, the Director General of the BBC, the editor of

The Times, service chiefs and key officers from the secret services.

See also: civil service; public schools

Further reading

Hennessey, P. (1986) *The Great and the Good: An Inquiry into the British Establishment*, London: Policy Studies Institute.

PAUL BARRY CLARKE

EMMA R. NORMAN

Estuary English

Identified by D. Rosewarne in *The Times Educational Supplement* of 19 October 1984, Estuary English is the variety of English between Cockney and Southern Standard. It is spoken, particularly by young people, in areas around the Thames estuary (Kent, Essex and East London), and is spreading further afield thanks to radio and television. Marked phonetic features include replacing 't' with a glottal stop ('Ga'wic' for Gatwick), pronouncing th as v ('fevva' for feather), and dropping final consonants. 'Me and mi mate wasn' nevva goin' t' pay, no way', illustrates typical usage. Condemned by traditionalists as sloppy, Estuary English speakers are, in fact, whether deliberately or unconsciously, developing egalitarian speech habits that smooth over class or ethnic distinctions.

See also: Cockney; dialect

CHRISTOPHER SMITH

Europe

Born in the postwar era as a means of reconstruction and reconciliation, European union has developed into one of the most important political issues of the present day. Since its conception, the UK has been reluctant to participate, and this reluctance which has characterized British relationships with Europe.

The present day European Union, formalized with the ratification of the Maastricht Treaty (1992), started life as three different bodies: the European Coal and Steel Community (ECSC) established in 1951, the European Atomic Energy Community (EAEC or Euratom), and the European Economic Community (EEC), both established in 1957. These organizations were formed primarily under the auspices of France and Germany, in association with Italy and the Benelux nations. They merged in 1967, creating the European Community (EC) with headquarters in Brussels. Britain initially declined involvement and instead formed the European Free Trade Area (EFTA) in 1960 at the Stockholm Convention. The agenda of the European Community was of a more political nature than that of the members of the EFTA.

It was not until 1 January 1973, following two years of negotiations, that Britain joined the European Community. The decision was not without controversy. Harold Wilson's opposition government promised to renegotiate British EC membership and, following Labour's election in 1974, did so. The changes negotiated were minimal, but the process itself however added further to uncertainty as to whether Britain wished to continue its membership of the European Community. In June 1975, a national referendum was called upon the matter. Despite opposition from certain quarters, the British populace endorsed EC membership.

One element of EC membership which has caused dissension between Britain and the EC is the Common Agricultural Policy (CAP). For years the CAP was the central element of the EC budget, commanding 63 percent of expenditure as recently as 1981. If the CAP was unfair, the redistributional effects of the whole EC budget would also be unfair. Britain argued that, because of the CAP, the value of its contributions far outweighed the value of benefits received. The EC established two 'refunds' for Britain, first in 1980 and again at the Fontainbleau summit in 1984. Thus Britain continued its troubled relationship with the EC into the 1980s.

As time passed, the scope of the EC grew. By the time of the Fontainbleau summit Greece, Denmark and Ireland had joined, while Spain and Portugal joined in 1986. As the scope of the EC has increased, so too has its depth. Legislation of recent times has moved towards closer integration. For example, the passing of the Single European Act (1986) set out the guidelines for the completion of an internal market, and set the mood for future integration. Europe was to be much more than a customs union with a farm support policy, and a single internal market was to be established by 31 December 1992. To facilitate this, a legislative programme of some 300 acts to remove non-tariff barriers to trade was laid out. Monetary union became an EC goal, to be progressively realized. Issues of economic disparity between members of the union were to be addressed through the 'cohesion' policy. This was followed by the Maastricht Treaty (1992) which changed the European Community to the European Union. Other key elements of the treaty included further arrangements for economic and monetary union, including adoption of a single currency (the ecu), provisions for an independent European bank, and the development of a common defence and foreign policy. Both the Single European Act and The Maastricht treaty have meant closer economic and political ties.

Some sections of the media have argued that the level of economic and political integration discussed at present will change government and life in Britain. EC legislation on the content of British sausages is a good example. The process of deregulation which began with the creation of a customs union will have consequences for national sovereignty if taken to its fullest conclusion. Subsequent integration (such as adoption of a single currency) will mean the sacrifice of certain national economic tools (including control of the interest rate) and a degree of vulnerability to economic conditions in other countries. Those who take a negative view of European union will point out the Chancellor should be able to control the British economy from Westminster and that legislation which governs the British populace (for example, the legislation concerning the maximum length of the working week) should only originate from Parliament. The union will also benefit Britain, because the liberalization and deregulation of trade allows countries to exploit union markets more efficiently. An increased degree of economic stability should also be beneficial to industry.

As Britain moves closer to making a decision about possible inclusion within a single currency (at present the opt-out clause means Parliament's approval must be sought before such action can be taken), so opposition to European integration grows. Certain members of the **Conservative Party** (the so called Eurosceptics) have tried to split the party, and the 1997 election also featured members of Sir James Goldsmith's anti-Europe Referendum Party, the sole purpose of which was to call for a referendum on Europe. Britain's economic success appears to be tied to Europe, yet a reluctance to participate fully, which has always dogged the British relationship with Europe, is as strong as ever.

See also: Conservative governments

Further reading

Owen, R. and Dynes, M. (eds) (1993) *The Times Guide To The Single European Market*, London: Times Books.

ALASTAIR LINDSLEY

Euston Films

Euston films was founded as a subsidiary of **Thames TV** in March 1971. Its initial forays into television drama were one-hour plays, and it was one of these, *Regan* (1974), that led to the idea of full-length filmed serials. *Regan* became the basis for one of the 1970s' most loved and vilified television series, *The Sweeney*. Further popular shows followed, including *Minder, Out, Fox* and *Widows*. Euston soon gained a reputation as a producer of gritty drama, as well as pioneering the use of 16mm filming for television. Later series, such as *Reilly, Ace of Spies* and *The Flame Trees of Thika*, enhanced the company's reputation as one of the foremost British drama production teams.

See also: Channel 4 Films

SAM JOHNSTONE

euthanasia

Formerly called 'mercy killing', euthanasia means to facilitate someone else's death intentionally but also compassionately. It differs from assisted suicide in that euthanasia involves the other person performing some direct act to kill an individual. Euthanasia is illegal in Britain, but overseas, steps have been taken towards its legalization in The Netherlands, the US state of Oregon and the Australian Northern Territory. Debates over the ethics of euthanasia involve questions concerning a doctor's Hippocratic oath, parallels with abortion and suicide, religious beliefs, uncertainties over the motives of relatives, and the individual's right to an easy, painless death.

Advocates of euthanasia (from the Greek for 'good death') insist that the individual is entitled to opt for death as a release from suffering and undignified incapacity when medical science offers no hopes of restoration to health and predicts nothing better than more or less rapid terminal decline. While still capable of taking rational decisions, people are urged to contemplate the prospect of final illnesses, which, thanks to modern medicine, are becoming ever more protracted, often with a final phase of more or less vegetative helplessness, and to draw up 'living wills' directing their doctors to terminate their life once the point of no return is reached. Euthanasia is distinguished from suicide as coming only towards the very end of normal life and as being totally rational, not the action of one whose mind is unbalanced.

Orthodox religion condemns euthanasia as the unwarrantable curtailment of God-given life. The law does not accept euthanasia either. It denies the validity of 'living wills' and threatens with severe penalties (that are, however, rarely inflicted) those who assist their fellows in terminating their life, even when acting only on an explicit, formally recorded request. Fine distinctions are drawn, however, between euthanasia, interpreted as taking definite action to bring about death, and 'allowing nature to take its course', for instance, by switching off a life support system when it is recognized that the patient has no chance of recovery. Likewise, it appears generally accepted that there is justification in refraining from 'heroic endeavours': that is, taking extraordinary steps that might, because they cause further suffering for the individual or require an extravagant commitment of medical resources, be regarded as quite disproportionate to any potential prolongation of

a life that has by the time lost any quality making it worthwhile for the dying person, to the greater distress of her or his loved ones. Though hard evidence is not readily available, it seems that nowadays in Britain doctors are increasingly considered right in their unwillingness to allow their terminally ill patients to suffer unduly, even if, for example, prescribing larger doses of painkillers is likely to result in death somewhat sooner than might otherwise be the case. The euthanasia movement commands considerable support and will probably make further headway as Britain becomes an increasingly secularized society.

See also: Abortion Acts

Further reading

Keown, J. (1995) *Euthanasia Examined: Legal, Ethical and Clinical Perspectives*, Cambridge: Cambridge University Press.

CHRISTOPHER SMITH

evangelism

In the nineteenth century, evangelicals and Methodists were one and the same group, derived from the low church Protestantism of John Wesley. Evangelism is a branch of the Church of England which emphasizes that each person's salvation depends upon his or her own faith. The stress on belief and scripture eclipses that of ritual, good works or sacraments. The more recent outburst of evangelical activity in Britain was boosted by the visits of the American Billy Graham. There are now many charismatic leaders and small churches in the UK, and the more powerful appeal of evangelism alongside New Age religions is recognized as a considerable threat by the Church of England. Evangelism (spreading of the Gospel) has come to mean teaching the immutability of scripture, reflecting growth in religious conservatism worldwide. This view has made headway at the expense of all traditional UK Christian denominations. Evangelicals believe that changes in society will come about as the result of cumulative decisions on the part of individuals rather than by changes in social structures.

However, for some, a closer scrutiny of social and economic agendas has evolved (for example, David Sheppard, the recently retired Bishop of Liverpool and a former conventional evangelical, now heads the Church of England's Board of Social Responsibility).

See also: Anglican Church; Christian Science; Jehovah's Witnesses

MIKE STORRY

exegesis

Exegesis has turned from a conservative art to a radical process. Originally, it was the art of interpreting textual material, and its original source stems from the interpretation of biblical material. That material is always fragmented and therefore requires collation to produce a complete copy, known as a recension. In the twentieth century, exegesis, presented as interpretation, has been applied to cultural icons generally. This has resulted in a challenge to canonical writings and permitted a wide range of alternative writings to be treated with a seriousness otherwise denied them. The overall effect has been to provide so-called 'fringe' writing with a 'voice'. In extreme, the argument has been raised as to whether any writing can be regarded as superior to any other writing: 'all cultural products are equal'. The moderated contrasting argument is that good argument and quality can always be distinguished: 'all cultural products are equal but some are more equal than others'.

See also: literary theory

Further reading

'Deconstruction', in P.B. Clarke and A. Linzey (eds) (1996) *A Dictionary of Ethics, Theology and Society*, Routledge: London.

PAUL BARRY CLARKE

Express Group

Founded in 1900 to compete with the *Daily Mail*, the *Daily Express* became, between the two World Wars, a particularly influential popular newspaper that aggressively sought increased circulation. Under the leadership of the Canadian Max Aitken, Lord Beaverbrook, who became figuratively and literally a press baron and set out to influence contemporary events, it served the **Conservative Party** cause and promoted the values of the Empire. The paper's assertive self-confidence was given architectural expression in 1931 when its new offices in Fleet Street were built to what were regarded as daringly modern designs by Ellis and Clarke. Though the *Express* (as it is now called) is no longer the force that it was, it continues to occupy a significant place in what it argues is the 'middle', as opposed to the 'popular' segment of the market, a significant distinction for advertisers as well as editors. Respect for the readership is revealed in a layout which, though tabloid in format, tends to devote an entire page (apart from advertisements) to treating each story at some length in a style more restrained than that of, say, the *Sun*. Published now from Blackfriars and printed in Dockland, the *Express* currently sells about 1.2 million copies a day, or 8 percent of national daily paper sales. In the 'middle' sector, amounting to less than 25 percent of the total, it comes a poor second to its only middle-market rival, the *Mail*, which has nearly twice its circulation. Allowance must however be made for the half a million copies of the *Daily Star*, launched in 1978 as a 'popular' stablemate of the *Express*.

Founded in 1918, the *Express on Sunday*, now with its magazine *Boulevard*, sells nearly as well as the daily paper; the *Mail on Sunday*, however, is nearly twice as popular and appears to be winning more readers. Claiming in all 14 percent of the national market, the Express Group's recent corporate history has been complicated; since 1996 it has been owned by United News & Media, a company with wide interests in television and which also controls the *Yorkshire Post* and the *Lancashire Evening Post* under the umbrella of United Provincial Newspapers, reportedly up for sale in the spring of 1998. The chief executive of United News & Media is Lord Hollick, a life peer expected by many to reorient the Express Group away from the right wing while endeavouring to reverse falling circulation in a shrinking market.

See also: Guardian Group; Mirror Group; News International; Telegraph plc

CHRISTOPHER SMITH

Eysenck, Hans

b. 1916, Berlin (Germany)

Psychologist

Hans Eysenck is a well-known psychologist, based at the University of London. He developed his 'Eysenck Personality Inventory' which rates personality on the basis of characteristics such as extroversion–introversion, neuroticism and psychoticism. Directly opposed to and publicly critical of Freudian psychoanalysis, Eysenck has written on human intelligence and argued that genetic factors contribute more than environmental ones to intelligence. He became a controversial figure because his research on Irish people was used in the USA to substantiate a case for not educating black people. His public appearances at lectures in London and elsewhere were picketed as a result.

PETER CHILDS

F

FA Cup

Since its inaugural final of 1871, the FA Cup has firmly established itself within British cultural heritage. Recognized throughout the **football** world as the premier knockout competition for club sides, the FA Cup has grown from being of purely domestic interest, a chance for small teams to overcome their more illustrious rivals, to one that is televised in all corners of the globe, being shown live in over eighty countries each May. Arguably the most commercially successful British cultural export, the FA Cup has maintained its position as Britain's favourite sporting competition.

DARREN SMALE

facilities houses

Facilities houses are companies that offer various production facilities that can be hired by film and television production companies. In Britain, they tend to be clustered around the large television production centres of Leeds, Manchester and Soho in London. These facilities usually include an editing suite and sound mixing equipment, all backed up with trained personnel. The equipment is used either for on-line or off-line editing. Off-line editing is where a rough edit of a film is put together; on-line is when the finished edit is made. Editing can either be linear (in the sense that the editor has to find the correct place on the physical tape or film), or non-linear with digital editing

suites. In non-linear editing, images are stored digitally on computer disks and can be accessed at any point regardless of their position in the filmic flow. Such a shift towards digital editing is expensive, and costs are only retrieved if the machines are in constant use. Thus, one of the advantages of facilities houses for users is that the facility house bears the brunt of the capital outlay, while the user only pays for the time needed. Indeed, for large broadcasters there is not always any great advantage in having their own facilities, as these are often underused.

The number of facilities houses has increased in recent years, helped by the increases in independent television productions, corporate videos, advertisements and music video. Most companies undertaking corporate video, advert and music video work are independent companies without their own facilities. In the case of productions for broadcasting, the use of in-house facilities is declining. This is partly because some new broadcasters have no facilities (such as **Channel 4**) and rely instead on a large amount of commissioned material from independents, or because they are trying to introduce competition into their internal markets (such as the **BBC**). The BBC has a policy called 'producer choice', by which producers are allowed to use facilities or services from outside the BBC if they so wish. Indeed, some internal departments of large broadcasters, in an attempt to gain extra revenue, rent out part of their own premises and equipment just as facilities houses do.

Further reading

Tunstall, J. (1993) *Television Producers*, London: Routledge.

PAUL RIXON

family planning

Nature in every sphere of life is prodigal of reproductive capacity. Overpopulation in the animal and vegetable kingdoms is prevented by such factors as climate and shortages of food and water. Since human beings as a species are, however, remarkably adept in controlling their environment and organizing supplies of necessities, the population threatens to increase to danger point unless means are taken to limit excess reproductive capacities. These basic principles were stated by, for example, Thomas Malthus in his *Essay on Population* of 1798. In nineteenth-century Britain, however, material prosperity following industrialization and colonial expansion fostered a huge expansion in population, with improving public health countering the effects of industrial pollution and epidemics in slums. Though large families survived, they generally did so in comparative poverty. Eugenicist policies of trying to control the reproduction of the handicapped in order to obviate what they feared as racial degeneration were not taken up, but in the course of the twentieth century contraceptive practices, spreading from the bourgeoisie to the working classes, have become virtually universal, except among certain religious groups such as Roman Catholics, who are taught that these practices are sinful.

With these exceptions, prejudices that saw contraception as unmentionable and tainted with immorality have been overcome. The first steps were popularizing the notion of 'family planning', making contraception an element in 'responsible parenthood', on the grounds that the whole family, especially the mother, would benefit from limiting the number of children per couple and spacing pregnancies. Another stage was connected with the marked increase in female employment from the mid-twentieth century. Gradually, too, the opinion has spread that although sexual intercourse is natural and enjoyable, there is no reason why it should be inevitably and inexorably linked with procreation. The UK government has unobtrusively moved from a neutral attitude to willing assistance for those who want it. Contraception is usually by barrier methods (the vaginal pessary and the sheath or condom, the use of which has been officially encouraged to prevent the spread of AIDs), by inter-uterine device (IUD, or 'coil'), or by hormone pill. Surgical methods (male vasectomy and female sterilization), typically though not exclusively employed by older people who decide their families are 'complete', are more widely promoted in less developed countries alongside other forms of contraception, in efforts to avoid potentially devastating population explosions.

See also: Abortion Acts; childbirth

Further reading

Szarewski, A., and Guillbeaud, J. (1998) *Contraception: A User's Handbook*, 2nd edn, Oxford: Oxford University Press.

CHRISTOPHER SMITH

fantasy and science fiction

Both fantasy and science fiction exploit the sense of wonder to be gained from setting stories in distant times and places. As genres of **novel**, the forms are descended (along with horror) from the gothic novel (such as Mary Shelley's *Frankenstein*).

Many features of English-language fantasy, as with fairy tales, derive ultimately from medieval romances including Arthurian and Christian myths. Quests and grand good-versus-evil struggles are prominent in the works of C.S. Lewis and J.R.R. Tolkien, both of whom became immensely popular in the late 1960s, seeding a profusion of 'sword and sorcery' novels. More recently, Angela Carter has blended psychoanalytic and feminist perspectives, for example, giving a dark retelling of fairy tales in *The Bloody Chamber*, while Mary Gentle also uses elements of science fiction.

Where fantasy looks to the past for its Golden Ages, science fiction uses projections of current **science** and social issues, following a long tradition of utopian and dystopian fiction. Like H.G. Wells and Olaf Stapledon, John Wyndham placed his catastrophes and conflicts on a grand scale in time and space, and also touched on future human evolution. Arthur C. **Clarke** developed this latter theme, with near-mystic overtones, in the context of more favourable encounters with alien intelligence (*Childhood's End*, *2001*), while Doris Lessing used shifts between human and alien perspectives (*Shikasta*) to transcend more conventional political literature.

Both Brian Aldiss and J.G. Ballard extended the use of catastrophe, with Ballard exploring landscape and psyche in a manner comparable to Conrad and Greene. Ian Watson is an obvious successor to Ballard, but draws also on linguistics and mythology in his stories of psychological transformation in a context of alien encounters which are indirect and cryptic. Drug culture also had its effect, particularly through the multi-layered realities of Philip K. Dick, and in Michael Moorcock's fragmented narratives of Jerry Cornelius.

The comedy science fiction writing of Douglas Adams (the *Hitch-Hikers Guide to the Galaxy* series) and Rob Grant and Doug Naylor (*Red Dwarf*) shows a fondness for scientific paradox and twists, traceable to the Polish writer Stanislaw Lem and the American Robert Sheckley. Following Adams's lead, Terry Pratchett's approach to fantasy imaginatively exploits cliché to produce the bizarre but internally consistent Discworld, powered by magic and peopled by caricatures whose failings are very human, whatever their actual species. Cyberpunk writers such as Jeff Noon draw on the IT concept of virtual reality, effectively advancing the tradition of alternative realities which can be found in Lem, Dick, H.P. Lovecraft and even Lewis Carroll.

See also: science fiction

Further reading

Slusser, G.E. *et al.* (1983) *Coordinates: Placing Science Fiction and Fantasy*, Carbondale, IL: Southern Illinois University Press.

DAVID BATEMAN

fantasy football

Taken from an earlier American idea, fantasy football was introduced to Britain in 1992. The *Daily Telegraph* first ran a competition in 1993, allowing competitors to choose their own professional **football** team from any players within the English Premier League, within a certain spending limit. The competition's success led to similar games being introduced by nearly every other national newspaper. A new version of the game appeared on the World Wide Web in 1994, with **Radio 5** producing a show dedicated to the game and BBC2 providing a television version, hosted by comedians Frank Skinner and David Baddiel, in the same year. The programme ran for only three series, reflecting a decline in the popularity of fantasy football, but was revived by ITV for the 1998 World Cup.

See also: FA Cup; fanzines

SAM JOHNSTONE

fanzines

Independently produced magazines written by fans for fans, fanzines have come a long way from the 1970s cut 'n' paste publications. Today, fanzines are found mainly in sport and music. The first sports fanzines started in the 1970s, notably *Foul* (1972), a satirical **football** magazine largely inspired by *Private Eye*. Both then and now, fanzines locate themselves between the PR-filled club statements and the sensationalist hype of the mainstream media, and some have argued they represent cultural resistance by challenging dominant ideas. *Foul* was rather nostalgic, but its ideology is less important than its satire and independent spirit. That fans could write passionately and coherently about football was itself significant. *Foul* also provided a breeding ground for journalists who later became mainstream, like

Eamonn Dunphy and Peter Ball. It did not last beyond 1976, but it was the precursor of the articulate passionate male worldview later expressed by many club fanzines.

Nearly all football fanzines believe that football belongs to the ordinary fans, and that it must be saved (or reclaimed) from capitalist interests, politicians and media. The ordinary fan has football's interests at heart, and will defend it against exploitation by business concerns and politicians, and without these fans, it will decline inevitably. Thus, most fanzines have a political dimension, even if not in a party political sense, and many offer prescriptions for football's future and its organizations, as well as discussing the team, board, supporters and authorities.

However, fanzines also reflect wider cultural perspectives, reflecting musical tastes, fashion and styles. The 1980s Merseyside football/music magazine *The End* for instance had interminable debates about the origins of 'scally' dress sense and youth culture. All these elements to a greater or lesser degree are visible later in the wider fanzine movement. Often, regional identities (formed around politics, musical taste and genres, and various styles), were created, expressed and developed via fanzines.

All fanzines, whether they cover football or music, originate from the 1970s **punk rock** era, when messy sheets of badly Xeroxed A4 paper were distributed at concerts, complete with spelling mistakes. The flaws were not due to laziness or incompetence, but expressed the fundamental punk DIY ethic, and the fact that the fanzines were an antidote to mainstream magazines like *New Musical Express* and *Melody Maker*. The first punk fanzines had titles like *Sniffin' Glue* (started by Mark Perry), and *48 Thrills*, written by Adrian Thrills. Other important titles included a **new wave** magazine called *Jamming!* (by Tony Fletcher). The ethos of these fanzines is clear from one edition of *Sniffin' Glue*, where Perry printed a picture of three chords with the caption: 'Now go and form a band'.

These fanzines were outside the mainstream music press, and made no concessions to traditional sensibilities about language, expressing themselves in a very raw fashion; some see the early fanzines as both organic expressions of a scene in themselves, but also as a response to the way that the mainstream press were extremely slow to pick up on punk. Music fanzines are slightly different from football fanzines: by definition, they are about interpreting and discussing a cultural product, in this case records and songs. Football fanzines take an oppositional stance to their clubs (to the point where some have been sued and others banned from selling inside stadia), so they are situated as social actors inside the football world. Music fanzines sit outside the music world and comment upon it: they are more positive and celebratory, and act more as conduits of information than as conveyors of opinion and cultural positions. They will interview bands, discuss the records, lyrics and concerts, and act as a non-oppositional forum for fans.

Football fanzines usually argue that interviewing players is wasteful and defeats the publication's objective, which is to offer an independent site for fan expression. Moreover, the football fanzine world is more concentrated than the music fanzine world, since the central cultural product, football, is the same everywhere. Only perspectives and loyalties change. Music fanzines fragment into genres or individual bands, generating divisions and making the creation a sense of unity harder. The biggest, most mainstream football fanzine, *When Saturday Comes*, lists all the fanzines it knows about; there is no equivalent unifying forum for music fanzines.

The technology used by fanzines has also developed with the decades. The 1970s saw old typewriters and office Xerox machines, the 1980s had the personal computer revolution, and the 1990s witnessed some fanzines in existence only on the Internet or via electronic mail. This has led some theorists to accuse fanzines of hypocrisy (bemoaning modern trends while using the technological results of those trends to create their publications), while others have suggested fanzines are breaking down local and regional barriers, creating a global culture.

A common question is, who writes and reads fanzines? It is hard to say who reads them, since most surveys have not generated adequate samples, but most football fanzine editors are male, politically left-leaning, articulate, probably formally educated after age eighteen, and middle or lower-middle class. It is much harder to say who edits or reads music fanzines (though clearly far more women are actively involved), as there is no way of knowing the totality of the scene since it is so split into genre and band loyalties. However, the mid-1980s saw a clear tendency for people to become involved with music fanzines as a way into mainstream journalism: in 1997, the editor of *Loaded!* (a masculine culture magazine for the 'lads'), James Brown, began editing a Leeds music and style fanzine called *Attack on Bzag.*

For some, fanzines are simply ways for fans to indulge their unimportant opinions, shouting pointlessly amongst themselves, but it is clear that fanzines are also an important form of cultural expression. In a world where it is increasing difficult for alternative views to be heard, fanzines offer fans of football, style and music the chance to express themselves to their peers.

See also: fantasy football

Further reading

Redhead, S. (1991) *Football With Attitude*, Manchester: Wordsmith.

SAM JOHNSTONE

fashion (1960s)

The emergence of British fashion during the 1960s as a leading force in international style and design is linked with its decisive role in the development of pop culture. Early 1960s fashion emphasized the eminently modern values of visuality, immediacy, shock, change and novelty. The designs of Mary **Quant**, Tuffin and Foale, Ossie Clark, John Stephen and Barbara Hulanicki socially participated in the general transformations in British culture characteristic of the decade at large. The vibrantly pop-futurist designs of Quant and Clark self-consciously used the language of fashion and style to signify the birth of the new mood of affluence, the death of the old culture of class deference, and the utopian desire for youthful sexual freedom.

Mary Quant and her partners opened the celebrated boutique Bazaar on Kings Road,

Chelsea, in 1955. Quant was determined, in her own words, to develop an 'absolutely Twentieth Century fashion' and she played a central role in changing the economy and culture of London's fashion industry. Where postwar London fashion had continued to connote exclusivity, elegance and expense, the fashion values of the young designers accented inclusivity, experimentation and 'fun'. Quant saw the conservative fashion industry as outdated and irrelevant, and cultivated an insistently young and modern woman's fashion style. Her 'Chelsea look' made extensive use of synthetic materials such as plastic and PVC, and mixed spots, stripes and checks in self-conscious violation of traditional canons of good taste. Her design philosophy was summarized by the aphorism: 'good taste is death, vulgarity is life'. Quant is most famous for the design of the mini skirt and for promoting the concept of the 'total look' in which separates, coats, footwear, accessories and the short, angular 'bob' hair style (launched by Vidal Sassoon in 1963) were coordinated to produce a single aesthetic effect. The concept of the 'total look' was a defining motif of 1960s fashion, and was cultivated by important designers such as Barbara Hulanicki of the popular and low-priced **Biba** label.

Sally Tuffin and Marion Foale set up their design partnership in 1961 at a small showroom on **Carnaby Street**. Like most of the young designers, Tuffin and Foale were trained in the well-funded art schools and colleges of 1950s Britain. The influence of teachers of fashion such as Janey Ironside of the **Royal College of Art** was to prove enduring for their students. The Carnaby Street showroom of former RCA students Tuffin and Foale, much like Quant's Bazaar, represented a new development in fashion marketing. Fashion was integrated into the youth-coded environment of the boutique, a cultural space filled with pop music and poster images of pop stars and 1960s models (see **models, 1960s**). London's young designers also refused the elegant atmosphere of the classical couture show; instead, their fashion shows were 'happenings', alive with pop music and action, young models and media stars. Tuffin and Foale are best known for their innovative curtain lace dress suits, bicycle dresses, op art graphics and prints, and most famously of all, the trouser suit. The trouser suit broke with conventional forms of female dress, and predictably received derisive commentary in the mainstream press. However, Tuffin and Foale's bright, slim-fitted but soft jackets and matching hipster trousers were enormously successful and endlessly reproduced in inexpensive imitations.

Carnaby Street was also home to London's first menswear boutique, opened by John Stephen in 1957. Stephen modified the traditional masculine scheme of jacket, shirt and tie through the use of unorthodox and bright colours and close attention to contemporary tailoring and style. Recognizing that male interest in fashion was culturally coded as homosexual, Stephen deftly manipulated the hyper-masculine image of boxer Billy Walker in publicity campaigns designed to appeal to both gay and straight consumers. His pioneering strategy worked for two reasons: his clothes were inexpensive, and their youthful and sexualized urbanity appealed to the discriminating fashion consciousness of the **mods**. By 1966, Stephen operated nine menswear boutiques on the by now internationally famous Carnaby Street, and went on to design non-traditional, multi-coloured kaftan suits, calf and knee length 'furry' white coats, and other 'kooky' sartorial emblems of the mid-to-late 1960s psychedelic style.

Television was an important vector for the national proliferation of the styles and attitudes of mid-1960s 'swinging London'. New youth-targeted television shows, particularly *Ready, Steady, Go* hosted by fashion icon Cathy McGowan, were central to transmitting 'the look' across the UK. Barbara Hulanicki anecdotally recalls the affective value with which she and other designers invested McGowan's wardrobe on *Ready, Steady, Go*: 'Would Cathy wear a Biba dress or a Tuffin and Foale? ... I was green with envy when she chose "Tuffy Fluffies".' The fashion sensibility of the young designers, particularly their commitment to the 'total look' concept, was also reproduced in the stylized ensemble of sets and costumes in television pop series like *The Avengers*. In fact, the popularity of Honor Blackman as Cathy Gale and later Diana Rigg as Emma Peel owed much to their costuming, by Michael Whittaker and John Bates respectively. The impact of this mode of television programming combined with new systems of fashion distribution/retailing, including boutiques in provincial towns and cities and young fashion sections in department stores, to produce a mass teenage fashion culture in the UK.

By the end of the 1960s, the nostalgic and naturalist ideology of the **hippies**, and their preference for second-hand garments, non-western styles and all-natural fabrics challenged the futurism of 1960s pop fashion. Hippies rejected the urbanism and artificiality of pop fashion by appealing to the anti-commercial values and heterogeneous styles of the 'counterculture'. Hippie 'anti-fashion' was sartorially eclectic, and this point alone indicates that the design imperative of the 'total look' was in crisis.

See also: models, 1960s

Further reading

Hulanicki, B. (1983) *A to Biba and Back Again*, London: Comet (a case study in 1960s fashion and celebrity).

Quant, M. (1966) *Quant by Quant*, London: Cassell (Quant's vivid and detailed autobiography).

MARK DOUGLAS

fashion (1970s)

British fashion trends of the early 1970s reflected the diffusion of the 'total look' which had been cultivated by the celebrity designers of 1960s London. Where the designers of 'the look' had laid claim to the values of urbanism and pop, futurism and fun, the iconography of early 1970s fashion was more fragmented and the design imperatives less consistent. The decline in the prestige of the designer reflected social changes in attitude to fashion and the emergence of anti-fashion ideologies. The industry was criticized as exploitative of women by the emerging feminist movement, and dismissed for its artificiality and decadence from the anti-commercial, naturalist perspective of the **hippies**. Anti-fashion currents of 1970s youth style were to find their most spectacular expression in the image and attitude of punk, but the legacy of punk style was ironically the return of the designer to the centre of British fashion (see **punk rock**).

The key influences of hippie sartorial culture on 1970s style concepts were the rejection of the normative gender coding of European dress and introduction of the **retro** aesthetics of second-hand clothes consumption. Unable to capitalize on the second-hand market, the fashion industry concentrated on mainstreaming unisex clothing culture through the promotion of mass-produced denim wear. In the 1960s, blue jeans came to symbolize the generational mood of youthful nonconformity and the myth of the American West (freedom, individuality, adventure). By the early 1970s, the youthful denim image had ossified into a kind of cultural uniformity. In 1971 Levi-Strauss dominated the world jeans market, and that year received the prestigious USA Coty Fashion Critics Award. The fashion industry revised the basic jeans scheme by introducing a series of style innovations: embroidered jeans, for example, were tailored as bellbottoms or hip-huggers. The contemporary diversification of the jeans market can be dated from the mid-1970s with the introduction of 'designer' jeans from US companies such as Calvin Klein and Gloria Vanderbilt.

The simple blue jeans motif co-existed with other currents in early 1970s fashion, which exaggerated the futurism and artifice of 1960s pop. Hot pants made of velvet and velour and multi-coloured platform shoes typify the distortions of size and kitsch sensibility of early 1970s British pop fashion. **Glam** in particular explored the 'gender-bending' dimensions of pop chic. A gay-coded style formation of conspicuous outrageousness, glam spectacularly displayed themes of androgyny and transvestism. Glam star David Bowie was costumed in vibrantly coloured hair, vivid make-up, fluorescent space-age bodystockings and platform boots. Bowie's fetishistic image complemented the extraterrestrial and rock superstar fantasies of his songs as well as the sexually ambiguous pantomime of his shifting stage personae. By the mid-1970s, the tartan pop of the Bay City Rollers had reassembled elements of the glam image specifically for consumption by teenage girls. The sexualized dynamics of glam, however, also fed into punk style and later mutated into various post-punk fashions and trends.

Punk represents the most striking anti-fashion image of the 1970s, and is certainly the most critically discussed cultural formation of the era. In the UK, punk became a mass youth culture with distinctive regional variations and accents between 1976–8. Malcolm McLaren and Vivienne **Westwood** played major roles in the elaboration of London punk culture. McLaren and Westwood had been running a specialist boutique under various trading names at 430 Kings Road since 1971. In 1975 they began trading under the name SEX. Westwood designed S&M fetish and bondage wear as well as ripped t-shirts bearing insignia such as 'sex' or 'P-E-R-V' scripted in chicken bones. For Westwood, punk represented an anarchistic politics of sexual liberation and social change; the project was to transform fetish wear into street wear under the slogan 'out of the bedroom and into the streets!' McLaren formed the most famous British punk band, The Sex Pistols, who showcased Westwood's designs on stage and, before the notorious Bill Grundy interview, on television.

Punk fused elements of 'bottom-up' street attitude and alternative couture styling. In 1976, for example, style innovator Philip Sallon began constructing garments out of bin liners, and this cheap and disposable image was widely imitated. The key sartorial values of punk were shock, iconoclasm and fetishism; predictably, punk was greeted with public outrage and tabloid denunciation. Punk introduced the aesthetics of cut-ups and montage into street fashion. It combined the cult of self-laceration, taboo symbols (such as swastikas), crudely customized black leather jackets, bondage trousers, safety-pins, dog collars, day-glo coloured 'tribal' hair styles and extravagant make-up. Moreover, punk quoted and linked heterogeneous elements of older cultural styles including those of **teds**, **mods**, **skinheads** and rude boys. Leading designers Zandra **Rhodes** and Jean-Paul Gaultier reworked elements of punk stylistic experimentation in their 1977 couture collections, and by the following year, 'new wave' and 'savage' youth styles were diffusing into the mass market.

In 1978, the baroque dandyism of new romanticism (see **new romantics**) was emerging as a sartorial alternative to the aggressive and increasingly uniform stylistics of punk. Vivienne Westwood was joined by Helen Robinson of PX,

Stephen Jones and other designers for Demob, as well as Melissa Caplan and Steve Stewart of Body Map in the elaboration of new romantic style. Between 1978 and 1983 these designers produced flamboyant and glamorous clothes for such rising stars of the New Pop as Adam Ant, Boy George and Annie Lennox. New romanticism was a retro club aesthetic which revived styles ranging from the sartorial elegance of 1930s evening wear to Bowie's futuristic glam. It established the climate for the launch of a new mode of style magazine such as *The Face*, which would promote the postmodern fashion of the 1980s.

Further reading

Savage, J. (1991) *England's Dreaming: Anarchy, Sex Pistols, Punk Rock and Beyond*, London: Faber & Faber (the definitive history of Punk as cultural formation).

Thorne, T. (1993) *Fads, Fashions and Cults*, London: Bloomsbury (a stimulating popular study of postmodern culture).

MARK DOUGLAS

fashion (1980s)

Among the most striking features of the designer decade was the proliferation of a generalized postmodern aesthetics and stylistic sensibility (see **postmodernism**). Postmodern motifs of image, simulacrum, surface, spectacle, nostalgia, pastiche and play were ubiquitously relayed and circulated by the media and advertising industries. The fashion industry evolved new methods of clothing production and distribution, and acted as a catalyst for the development of 'lifestyle' targeted patterns of consumption. Televisual aesthetics dominated 1980s fashion as designers produced collections which accented display values for maximum television and video impact. International fashion shows became fantastic and dizzying spectacles, and fashion retail spaces were transformed into eclectic fantasies. For example, Nigel **Coates** redesigned shops for Katherine **Hamnett**, Jasper **Conran** and others, and described one of his schemes as 'Noah's Ark meets the Parthenon

during the Etruscan period with skyscrapers'. One effect of the successes of early 1980s fashion, and the industry's need structural for coordination, was that Norman Lamont, then parliamentary undersecretary at the Department of Trade and Industry, instituted a 'fashion think tank'. This led to the creation of the British Fashion Council, under the chair of Edward Rayne and including as members Terence **Conran**, Jean **Muir** and Beatrix Miller, editor of English **Vogue**.

Mainstream 1980s designers such as American Ralph Lauren marginalized the experimental currents of late 1970s British style innovation, especially punk aesthetic. Lauren revitalized masculine couture using the sexualized iconography of affluence and prestige, distinction and power. Magazines, including *GQ* and *Arena*, promoted male fashion and design by appeal to narcissistic and exhibitionist fantasies of class mobility, business acumen and sexual power. As such, mainstream 1980s fashion and design constituted a significant channel for the cultural diffusion of the values of **Thatcherism** and the economics of conspicuous consumption. The stylized urbanity of the yuppie's designer suit and 'power tie' ensemble and the broad-shouldered, **power dressing** profile of the businesswoman were models of the 1980s dress-for-success scheme and a celebration of the hegemony of 'enterprise culture'.

Another measure of the conservative turn in mainstream 1980s fashion was that Princess Diana's Sloane Ranger daytime wardrobe was endlessly reproduced by women in town and country (see **Sloane Rangers**), and the 1984 style guide *The Princess of Wales's Fashion Handbook* was a bestseller. Striking a similarly conservative note, Laura **Ashley**'s pastiche 1930s and 1940s tea dresses and interior designs drew upon the English rural imaginary to construct nostalgic images of domesticated femininity. By contrast, Katherine **Hamnett**'s 'protest design' struck an environmental and peace activist tone with her 1983/4 t-shirts printed with the slogans, 'stop Acid Rain' and '58 Per Cent Against Pershing'.

High street and shopping mall fashion underwent major restructuring in the 1980s as 'new wave' clothiers including Benneton, Next, Principles and Richard Shops sought to increase their share of the middle-income clothing market. The new wave clothiers used information technologies to integrate all stages of the design–production–advertising–retailing process into a single coordinated system. In-house designers and pattern cutters worked on computers, finished garments and accessories were merchandised through image coordinated franchise outlets, and computer-generated sales and stock reports were dispatched to corporate headquarters on a daily basis. In brief, new wave clothiers packaged and sold standardized middle-income fashion commodities and lifestyles in identity-rich settings, successfully tapping into the consumerist ethos of prosperity and pleasure that dominated the designer decade.

Pierre Bourdieu has shown how the field of fashion is governed by the logic of social distinction. This claim is historically appropriate to the 1980s in general and to the designer fetishism of the Casuals in particular. Emerging out of football terrace culture, the Casuals appropriated European designer **sportswear** including Lacoste, Fila and Ellesse to signify personal participation and success in the 1980s 'loadsamoney' economy. Ted Polhemus has suggested that by pulling 'themselves up by their bootstraps by dint of cunning enterprise, always flying the flag, giving short shrift to the liberals and moaning minnies, the Casuals gave Thatcherism its most literal interpretation'.

Fashioning alternatives to European sportswear and the conservative mood of mainstream style, postmodern designers Vivienne **Westwood**, Zandra **Rhodes**, Stephen Jones and John **Galliano** borrowed from the anarchic chic of London street style to produce witty, unorthodox and androgynous clothing for club celebrities and pop stars such as Boy George and Madonna. Boy George showcased a fex designed by Stephen Jones in the Culture Club video 'Do You Really Want to Hurt Me?' and this brought the designer international recognition and a contract to design **hats** for Jean-Paul Gaultier. Post-punk cult styles were the creative sources of the 1980s New Pop aesthetic. London style clubs, particularly Covent Garden's Blitz, were venues for the elite and ostentatious postmodern culture of the Posers. The Posers manipulated and juxtaposed elements of **retro** and contemporary style into playful and stylized collages, and their sartorial influences fed into the elaboration of new romanticism (see **new romantics**). Cult and club fashions were promoted in a new genre of style magazines including *The Face*, *i-D* and *Blitz*. In fact, the style press assumed a leading role in popularizing the New Pop and postmodern fashion, and in 1983 *The Face* was voted Magazine of the Year in the annual Magazine Publishing Awards.

During the late 1980s, gay 'high energy' dance culture combined with house styles to produce **rave** as the leading vector of British pop culture. Ravers developed regionally distinctive dress styles. The London rave scene combined a bright, loose fitting and dance-oriented fashion with a neo-hippie ideology and retro psychedelic garments, including smiley and tie-dyed t-shirts. The relatively autonomous development of northern 'scallydelic' rave culture, especially in Manchester and Liverpool, gave local designers such as Manchester's Joe Bloggs national publicity.

Further reading

Hebdige, D. (1988) *Hiding in the Light: On Images and Things*, London: Routledge (a critical discussion of postmodernism, including a study of 1980s style magazines and brief commentaries on Bourdieu).

Polhemus, T. (1994) *Street Style*, London: Thames & Hudson (an important illustrated guide to postwar British style formations).

MARK DOUGLAS

fashion (1990s)

The beginning of the 1990s was marked by the demise of the so-called yuppie and the concomitant hard, metropolitan chic and Thatcherite values embodied in **power dressing**. In its place came a new hegemony, a belief in a New Age and its associated spiritual values spurred on by the influential 1987 Mintel Report, *The Green Consumer*, which drew manufacturers' attention to a public actively seeking a respite from the 'I'm all right Jack' aesthetic of the 1980s. Apparently, consumers were becoming more inner-directed, and wanted products which could contribute to saving the planet. The first stirrings of this new aesthetic to greet the decade were from Rifat Ozbek, whose White Collection graced the catwalks in 1990. This look, which generated its own clichés when instantly adopted by high street chains such as Top Shop and Miss Selfridge, exemplified a quest for the spiritual over the material and was not ironic, despite the fact that the fashion industry operates alongside the notion of novelty for novelty's sake and would work against its own profit margins if advocating recycling. Accordingly, the fashion industry's response to the green movement took two forms: an appropriation on the metaphorical level, and a more serious attempt to promote real change within its modes of production. An image of 'greenness' was evoked by some designers such as Ozbek using white cotton – ironically, a cash crop responsible for much Third World pollution – but some British firms did attempt green modes of production. All went well until the concept became unfashionable and the next take was in opposition: that of the cyberpunk, who believes in technology rather than nature, and attempts to save the planet using computer terminals and the Internet rather than eco-friendly goods. However, Ozbek's look had not only acknowledged green consumerist tendencies (see **green consumerism**) but also nodded in the direction of the main influence on 1990s fashion. His separates based on sportswear items such as hooded sweatshirt tops and trainers exemplified the look which was to dominate the street. Crossovers appeared on fashion catwalks, and designers such as Nick Coleman and Michiko Koshino began to direct their creations at the clubber rather than the yuppie, acknowledging the tribalism of London nightlife.

London also became acknowledged once again as a centre for avant-garde fashion. It seemed as if the mythical Swinging Sixties were again being rerun in 1995 and 1996 when magazines such as *Time* and *Newsweek* in the USA produced features on London as the centre of a new style, recognizing the relationship between fashion and music encapsulated in guitar-based music such as **Brit-pop** and the concomitant reworking of 1960s and 1970s styles of dress by Johnsons La Rocka and Tm Gilbey.

The rise to power in Parisian couture houses of the designers John **Galliano** at Dior and Alexander **McQueen** at Givenchy showed that British fashion was being taking seriously by big business conglomerates such as LVMH, who effectively controlled Parisian couture. Galliano, known for his postmodernist plunderings of the history of style, a legacy of **Westwood**'s experiments in the 1980s and 1990s, was given the task of roping in a new generation of couture customers and lucrative licensing deals. In London, the New Generation of British designers garnered much publicity through the showcase of **London Fashion Week**, which became increasingly successful in the 1990s and introduced designers such as McQueen, Flyte and Ostell, Copperwheat Blundell, Pearce Fionda, Clements Ribeiro, Hussein Chalayan and **Red or Dead** to a bemused public.

The 1990s were also marked by the referencing of past styles from Vivienne Westwood's plundering of eighteenth and nineteenth century dress and 1950s couture, exemplified in collections such as the well-received Cafe Society Collection of 1994 which included long, sweeping skirts and softly tailored shirt-jackets emphasizing the bust, to Alexander McQueen's subversion of the minimalist designs of the 1960s Parisian ye ye couturiers adding his own postmodern reworkings to the repertoire of tailored suits for women. Paul **Smith** continued to reinvent male fashion, particularly the look of the natural predecessor of the 1990s man – the **mods** – using staples of masculine dress such as V-necked jumpers and biker jackets.

Attempts to demystify fashion were continued through the popularity of fashion-related programming on British television. *The Clothes Show*, with a mixture of the rag trade trained Jeff Banks and Caryn Franklin flying the flag for street chic, continued in popularity, followed by *Style Challenge* introducing the concept of the fashion makeover together with the role of the fashion stylist, who became an important figure within the magazine industry in the 1990s through photographic shoots in *The Face* and its younger counterparts *Don't Tell It, Dazed and Confused* and so on. Another staple part of the industry was acknowledged, that of public relations, which was sent up in the highly successful situation comedy *Absoloutely Fabulous*, which continued the mythology of the fashion business as one of champagne-guzzling harpies rather than being one of the biggest providers of revenue and employment in Britain.

However, the old guard were still going strong and companies still traded on the notion of 'Englishness' for tourist and home consumption. Hardy Amies' notion of 'evolution rather than revolution' was followed on in the production of companies like Hobbs and Mullberry who traded on an ineffable, timeless 'Englishness' of country houses, horses and herbaceous borders, and Laura Ashley whose pastiche of English heritage remained popular.

The traditions of English tailoring were brought more fully into the 1990s with designers such as Bella **Freud**, assistant in Vivienne Westwood's design studio for four years, shown in her signature tailored knitwear. She is typical of a new breed of young British designers emerging in the 1990s who have built up their businesses slowly, learning from the boom and bust which characterized many fashion firms in the 1980s.

Further reading

Martin, R. (ed.) (1995) *Contemporary Fashion Designers*, London, St James Press (a definitive overview of major fashion designers in the twentieth century).

CAROLINE COX

fashion, children's

Fashion reflects changes in any given society, and can be usefully used as a socio-economic barometer, especially as in times of hardship fashion and beauty are often the first to be affected. The study of the history of children's fashions sheds light on areas not covered by adult fashion. These include theories of childcare, the philosophy of education and the position of children within society.

The fashion for girls in the 1960s were a stark contrast to the national emblems used to decorate the printed rayon dresses and homemade knitwear of the 1950s, inspired by the marriage of Princess Elizabeth in 1947 and her coronation in 1953, which led to a tide of patriotism. The influence of American teenage styles, initially apparent in the late 1950s, continued to provide a model to which British girls aspired. By the early 1960s, goods as diverse as nylons and woollen garments, traditionally aimed at the adult market, were being directed at the youth market with advertisements showing teenage entertainments such as record parties. Also, the youth explosion within music and film provided radical new role models. Although there had been teenage singers and fashion models in the previous decade, they had always adopted an adult style of fashion.

An important role model was Twiggy, the seventeen-year-old model Lesley Hornby, who was named 'The Face of 1966' and also 'Woman of the Year'. Her undeveloped stick-like figure was ideally suited to the new mini skirt fashions designed by Mary **Quant**. The new dresses for girls remained as short as in previous decades, but far less detailed and less fitted. There was also the disposable dress made from non-woven material, later withdrawn because of concern for flammability, and the very popular crochet dress worn over a matching petticoat. However, these dress innovations coexisted with the more traditional dresses with full skirts and fitted bodices. Trousers, in the form of slacks or stretch ski pants became very fashionable, but were strongly forbidden for formal occasions. Boys' fashions in the 1960s were heavily influenced by the style of the British-based mod music and the Beatles. Denim fashions continued to be very popular and were made available in a variety of colours and styles.

A phenomenon of the 1970s was the entry of established clothes designers into the children's market. By the mid-1970s, fashions for girls and women had left behind the youthful and modern styles of the 1960s and had been replaced by fantasy and nostalgia-inspired designs, Also, denim fashions, influenced by old Hollywood Westerns and musicals, became very popular; examples include cowgirl skirts and checked shirts. There was also an abundance of flower-printed dresses and the revival of the sailor suit. Sportswear, previously confined to athletic meetings, began to appear in the high street and in discos. American films such as *Saturday Night Fever* (1977) also made an enormous impact. Furthermore, the marketing of clothes aimed at children developed sophisticated advertising strategies. Magazines aimed at pre-pubescent girls included countless fashion and beauty advice pages, training the young girl to be an active consumer.

In the 1980s the divide between the fashions of youths and adults disappeared, and very similar styles were worn by both groups. In the 1990s, in sharp contrast to the 1960s, children became even more fashion conscious than their parents. Products aimed at children and teenagers occupied an increasingly large place in national and family economics. In 1997, the advertising agency Saatchi and Saatchi carried out a research project to determine the extent to which British children under fifteen influenced family spending. It was discovered that a staggering £31 billion was spent to satisfy the needs of this most demanding consumer group. Close to £2 billion was directly devoted to clothes. Generally speaking, the parents of the late 1990s had very little say in what clothes their children should wear.

Further reading

Benson, J. (1994) 'The Creation of Youth Culture', in *The Rise of Consumer Society in Britain 1880–1980*, Essex: Longman.

Mulvey, K. and Richards, M. (1998) *Decades of Beauty: The Changing Image of Women 1890s–1990s*, London: Hamlyn.

Rose, C. (1989) *Children's Clothes Since 1750*, London: Batsford.

FATIMA FERNANDES

fashion, wedding

Weddings, with their lace, satin, tiaras and, especially, long white trailing gowns, traditionally symbolize the zenith of elegance and appearance for millions of women, yet historically only the elite wore white dresses. The wedding business grew in the 1950s, and despite the informal celebrity weddings since the 1960s and the fewer traditional church nuptials, vast amounts of money continued to be spent throughout the following decades in the ritual of tying the knot. The always changing face of fashion has had little effect on the style of wedding dresses. In the late 1990s, the majority of brides continued to opt for traditional white floor-length dresses with the essential veil. Men's wedding attire in the 1990s showed signs of change with more adventurous styles and colours, but traditional morning dress or classic suit and tie continued to be very popular.

The biggest style changes to emerge since the 1960s were in the areas of food, flowers, music and the venues. However, after the extravagant and boned wedding dresses of the 1950s, in the 1960s dresses became more simply designed and made in the latest fabric, nylon – which was later strongly rejected. The 1970s brought old-fashioned and homely designs, as epitomized by Laura **Ashley**. Generally speaking, natural fabrics, flowers and frills adorned everything and everyone.

The 1980s continued the re-feminization of brides, predominantly influenced by the romantic fairy tale wedding of Lady Diana Spencer to Prince Charles. Also, the boom years of the 1980s called for opulent dresses, extravagant hairstyles, big cars and elaborate receptions. The occasion became more significant than the wedding couple. Further, numerous people, principally women, formed bridal wear-related businesses. In the 1990s wedding fashions showed restraint and a simplicity which contrasted sharply with the 1980s. Although, brides generally wore white, much of the paraphernalia of previous decades was rejected without public humiliation.

See also: marriage

FATIMA FERNANDES

fashions, youth

The history of postwar British fashion and music formations reveals the collective ways in which non-elite groups and communities of young people have shaped distinctive cultures as 'particular ways of life'. Music and fashion have been used as common symbolic resources for the production of such sharply differentiated cultural identities as those of the **rockers**, **mods**, **skinheads** and punks (see **punk rock**). In this regard, Dick Hebdige persuasively argues that the succession of postwar youth styles can be structurally represented as a 'series of transformations of an initial set of items (clothes, dance, music, argot) unfolding through an internal set of polarities (mod v. rocker, skinhead v. greaser, skinhead v. hippie, punk v. hippie, ted v. punk, skinhead v. punk (see **hippies**; **teds**)) and defined against a parallel series of 'straight' transformations ('high'/mainstream fashion)'.

The rockers of the early to mid-1960s were heirs to the 'ton-up' motorbike subculture of the 1950s. The menacing biker image cultivated by the ton-up boys owed much to circulation of publicity shots and movie stills of Marlon Brando as the rebel outsider Johnny in *The Wild One* (1954), even though the film itself was banned in Britain. Ton-up boys dressed in austere black leather or PVC jackets, jeans and motorcycle boots, and their collective image and mobile subculture were demonized in the media as a delinquent and alien rock 'n' roll lifestyle. Rockers were also energized by the cults of speed and the motorcycle, but embellished the sartorial image they inherited. Rocker leather jackets were elaborately decorated with metal studs, badges, chains and painted emblems, while narrow and pointed 'winklepicker' shoes were optionally substituted for motorbike boots. Rockers, as their name implies, were culturally committed to the fast and uncompromising rock 'n' roll idiom of Billy Fury, Eddie Cochran and Gene Vincent, in opposition to both the mainstream sound of British pop and the rival fashion culture and preferred musical idiom of the mods. In 1964, tensions between mods and rockers broke out in a series of spectacular bank holiday battles in southern coastal towns.

The first generation of male working-class mods emerged in London during the mid- to late 1950s and constructed their cultural identity through the double appropriation of continental design and tailoring and the music of what Paul **Gilroy** has called the 'Black Atlantic'. Initially mods embraced be-bop and the cool currents in African-American **jazz**, while they were adorned in modernist, Italian-styled suits and rode chic Italian scooters. By the early 1960s, mods were dancing the steps of 'the ska' or 'the block' to the **ska** music of Prince Buster, the **soul** of James Brown, the rhythm and blues of John Lee Hooker and the Tamla Motown sound of Mary Wells. African-American R&B was an especially influential idiom and was imitated by

mod groups, including Georgie Fame and the Blue Flames. Meanwhile, a new and younger generation of mods championed the edgy 'Londonesque' sound of groups like The Who, whose song 'My Generation' (1965) gave articulation to their sense of distinctiveness and difference.

The skinheads rejected the fastidious style and narcissistic attitude of the mods and crafted an insistently chauvinist and proletarian 'hard mod' image consisting in tightly cropped hair, jeans, boots and braces. The early skins were overwhelmingly young, urban and white working-class males, although many 'crews' had black British members. Skins evolved out of the culture of the football terraces, but first gained media notoriety at the Rolling Stones free concert in Hyde Park in July 1969. Skinhead cults of violence and aggressive urban masculinity were the negation of the peace and love ideology and the naturalist ethic of hippie culture, and in practice this ideological dissonance did take the form of 'hippie bashing'. Moreover, skinhead violence assumed racist and homophobic forms in the rhetoric and practice of 'Paki bashing' and 'queer bashing'. Like the mods, skins appropriated Jamaican music, especially ska, rocksteady and **reggae** as well as the cool attitude of the rude boy. For example, Symarip's 'skinhead Moonstomp' became an anthem for skins while rude boy-styled mohair or 'tonic' suits, Ben Sherman shirts and loafer shoes became evening substitutes for collarless shirts and rolled-up jeans worn over 'bovver boots'. By the early 1970s, skinhead culture began to mutate into the variant 'white ethnic' styles of the suedeheads and smooths. The skinhead style and attitude was later to resurface as one as of a series of cultural responses to punk's cut-up bricolage, fetishistic iconography and provocative attitude.

Punk anti-fashion was an unstable constellation of various signifying elements and insignia derived from the repertoire of postwar British street styles. It was also decisively influenced by art school experimentation in fashion and design. Punk stylists like Johnny Rotten selected specific motifs and garments from the wardrobes of teds, rockers, mods, skinheads and **glam** rockers and combined them into iconoclastic and anarchic sartorial assemblages. Punk also drew attention to the body and alternative sexual lifestyles by means of sado-masochistic rubber wear, studded leather collars and practices of self-laceration and body piercing. The 'DIY' aesthetic of punk articulated a collective disaffection with and conspicuous rejection of mainstream fashion styles and generic Top 40 pop music. The punk rock of The Sex Pistols, The Buzzcocks or The Slits, for example, was characterized by a chaotic, furious and minimalist rock idiom, a defiantly coarse vocal style and lyric syntax, as well as an anarchic political message. Significantly, punk provided an alternative musical and cultural identity for women performers such as Siouxsie Sue or Polystyrene, and their example was important for the repositioning of women from the margins to the centre of British youth music and fashion cultures.

See also: Afro-Caribbean youth styles; Asian fashions; Asian youth styles; teenage and youth programming

Further reading

Chambers, I. (1985) *Urban Rhythms: Pop Music and Popular Culture*, London: Macmillan (a nuanced and well-researched account of postwar youth/music fashions).

Hebdige, D. (1979) *Subculture: The Meaning of Style*, London: Methuen (the classic semiotic analysis of subcultural style in the Birmingham CCCS tradition).

MARK DOUGLAS

faxes, modems and laptops

'Fax' is short for facsimile transmission. By the early 1980s, cheap fax machines (previously used by the police to transmit 'mug' shots) were being manufactured and their widespread availability led to the almost complete replacement of the old telex system for sending messages. 'Modem' is short for modulator/demodulator, an electronic device which, when attached to a phone line, can transmit data between remote computers. A modem box, or a modem card housed inside a computer, is essential for connection to the **Internet**. A 'laptop' or 'notebook' is a portable computer which can weigh as little as under three pounds, and is usually

carried in a nylon briefcase. They first appeared in 1984 and were used simply for word processing when on the move, away from a desktop computer. In the late 1990s, with a laptop and a modem and a mobile phone, it is possible to send a fax to Britain from the Kalahari desert.

See also: Internet

PETER CHILDS

feminist publishing houses

Feminist presses are not that new: the first, Victoria Press, was founded by Emily Faithfull in 1860. In terms of recent presses, Virago was established in 1978 by Carmen Callil, who had previously worked for several London publishers and who, in 1982, joined Chatto & Windus as publishing director and joint managing director, taking Virago with her. The aims of Virago were twofold: to recuperate good but out-of-print titles (mainly fiction) by women, and to promote new women's writing. Callil, an Australian, was in this respect capitalizing on and catering for the new markets engendered by the women's movement of the 1960s and 1970s (the establishment of the firm was celebrated/satirized in Fay Weldon's television script *Big Women*, which was made into a Channel 4 serial in 1998). Other major publishers have been Pandora (which closed in 1990) and The Women's Press, while Onlywomen Press and Sheba have published writing by working-class, black and lesbian women.

See also: feminist theatre; film, feminist; publishing trends

PETER CHILDS

feminist theatre

Theatre, like other branches of the arts and culture over the last thirty years, has progressively reflected the concerns of feminism. Within theatre there has been a spectrum of feminist approaches which involves re-readings of established texts, the recovery of neglected women's writing, and more 'political' theatre aimed at improving the situation of women.

Feminist playwrights question representations of the past, and unveil the mechanisms whereby women's lives have been obscured. Joan Littlewood founded her Theatre Workshop in the early 1950s, and her reworking of scripts gave an impetus to later feminist producers. Radical reinterpretations of Shakespeare plays, including a version of *Kiss Me Kate*, Cole Porter's musical version of *The Taming of the Shrew*, cast characters in reversed gender roles to subvert existing conventions. Reinterpreting texts has empowered actors, readers and spectators to bring about change rather than simply accept the value-system of the 'father' text. Roland Barthes's famous essay on 'The Death of the Author' (1968) also encouraged dramatists to re-think 'fixed' meanings.

Among 'lost' writers, the plays of Aphra Behn (1640–89) were given new productions, including university stagings of *The Rover* (1677), based on Behn's experience of male philandering in colonial Surinam and highlighting the limited choices open to women in the seventeenth century. Modern playwrights have dealt more often with relations between women. In Shelagh Delaney's *Taste of Honey* (1958) directed by Joan Littlewood, Helen and her daughter Jo have to share a squalid flat (and bed) in Salford and the play centres on questions around motherhood, female dependency on men for money, and Jo's attempt to start a different kind of life from that of her mother. Jo is seen as more responsible than her mother whose behaviour is still conditioned by her unsatisfactory relations with her own abusive mother.

Caryl Churchill initially addressed her plays to the predominantly female radio drama audience. She worked with Monstrous Regiment, (named after John Knox's sixteenth-century pamphlet 'The First Blast of the Trumpet Against the Monstrous Regiment of Women') to produce *Vinegar Tom* (1976). It deals with the sexism of Christian teaching, and makes a Brechtian attempt not just to enlighten but to enrage the audience into action. Her later plays have focused consistently on issues of gender in terms of history, male institutions and female agency.

Michelene Wandor worked with Gay Sweatshop and wrote *Care and Control* (1977) about the politics

surrounding child custody. Her full-length verse play *Aurora Leigh*, reworks the ending of Elizabeth Barrett Browning's poem. Instead of Aurora dominating Romney within a continuingly oppressive social structure, they both unite as a sign of the potential for renewal and constructive change in gender relations.

See also: feminist publishing houses; film, feminist

Further reading

Aston, E. (1995) *An Introduction to Feminism and Theatre*, London: Routledge.

Keyssar, H. (ed.) (1996) *Feminist Theatre and Theory*, Basingstoke: Macmillan.

MIKE STORRY

feminist theory

Feminism has made an important difference to British culture throughout the twentieth century as the struggle to change unequal gender relations has taken place in a range of contexts. Although women campaigned for change in the nineteenth century and earlier, the development of feminist theories of gender relations in what is known as Second Wave feminism marked a new and more concerted effort to understand the nature of oppression and to prioritize the struggle for change in the social, political and cultural position of women. Feminist theory is a term which encompasses a diversity of approaches and stances. Among the most influential strands are liberal, radical, Marxist, socialist and poststructuralist.

Liberal feminism developed from liberal political thought which championed the rights of an autonomous individual subject, claiming for women the rights and privileges which had been only afforded to men, and stressing the need for equality for women within the existing political and economic system. This includes campaigning for equal rights and opportunities, typified by struggles for the vote, for fairness in employment both in terms of pay, promotion opportunities and conditions, such as childcare provision, and for an end to legal, economic and social discrimination. While the achievements of liberal feminist campaigns in Britain have been undoubtedly beneficial to many women, the aim of this approach is to reform rather than radically change the system, and it tends to focus on the individual who, as in traditional liberal thought, often turns out to be white and middle class. Other feminists have argued that in order to achieve real change in the lives of all women we must overturn rather than reform the social, economic and political structures which sustain unequal gender relations.

Marxist feminists insist that social existence determines consciousness and that issues of sexual or gender difference and oppression cannot be separated from the context of capitalism. According to this view, women are positioned not only in terms of gender but also class, and their oppression is part of a wider system of economic and political exploitation which alienates all human beings. Marxist feminists have focused on women as workers, both paid and unpaid. One of the main criticisms of Marxist feminism is that it underestimates the extent to which women are oppressed by men, and it can allow gender to become a secondary issue to class. In direct contrast, radical feminism insists that the oppression of women is the oldest and most widespread form of oppression and that all areas of women's lives, and most notably their sexuality, have been governed by different forms of patriarchalist political and social institutions. Radical feminists have campaigned against these institutions and their effects, including marriage, pornography and the control of women's sexual and reproductive roles in medical and legal contexts, and have also insisted on celebrating female difference and on reclaiming an essentially female identity and culture in the arts, science and spirituality. In some instances, radical feminists have responded to the threat of patriarchy by calling for women to separate themselves from men and some radical feminists, particularly in the 1970s, argued for a political choice of lesbian feminism. Radical feminism, most popular in the USA, has been of limited influence in intellectual feminist circles in Britain, largely because of its insistence on an essential difference between men and women, which many feminists view as precluding the possibility of change just as liberal feminism with its stress on basic similarity limits the extent of change.

The most influential forms of feminist theory in Britain today are socialist and poststructuralist, although these labels are not always used. Socialist feminism developed from a dissatisfaction with the limitations of Marxist theories as the basis for analysing women's positions within the overlapping and intersecting structures of patriarchy and capitalism. Socialist feminist theorists such as Alison Jaggar have deployed a range of different theoretical approaches in their work, some of which derive from psychoanalytic theory, which earlier this century was condemned by many feminists as proscribing rather than describing an oppressive system of sexual difference. The debate between feminism and psychoanalysis has been fraught but productive, and is best seen as part of the development in Britain of a strand of feminist work influenced by poststructuralist critical and cultural theories of language and subjectivity. The vital difference between this and other approaches is its insistence that meanings, including the meaning of 'woman', are culturally constructed and as such are contingent, both historically and contextually, and open to change. Language is seen not to reflect but to produce reality, and also as being both a means of installing oppression within society and the individual and a site where feminists can intervene. There is, in this view, no such thing as an essential female identity, good or bad, any more than there is a universal human nature.

Poststructuralist feminist theory concentrates on gender in/and representation, and many of the best-known British exponents work in literary and cultural studies, including Catherine Belsey, Jacqueline Rose and Chris Weedon. Recent work has also focused on the intersection of gender with race, nationality and sexuality. In the context of a society which is seen as increasingly conservative, in which the gains made by liberal feminism seem threatened by recurrent calls for traditional family values, poststructuralist feminism has been accused by some of turning away from urgent social issues to questions of less practical relevance. But an increasing general awareness of the impact of cultural production on women's lives seems to support rather than undermine the case for the productiveness of this type of feminist analysis. Current feminist studies of the impact of scientific and technological developments such as the **Internet** indicate that this is a continually diversifying field.

See also: feminist publishing houses; feminist theatre; film, feminist; literary theory; post-structuralism

Further reading

Belsey, C. and Moore, J. (eds) (1989) *The Feminist Reader: Essays in Gender and the Politics of Literary Criticism*, Basingstoke: Macmillan (a coherent and representative collection).

Tong, R. (1992) *Feminist Thought: A Comprehensive Introduction*, London: Routledge (detailed and incisive but accessible throughout).

TAMSIN SPARGO

film, children's

The Cinematograph Films Act of 1957 guaranteed an annual grant to the Children's Film Foundation (CFF). With reduced fees to actors and directors, the CFF agreed in cooperation with the unions to subsidize production of low-budget features, shorts, and serials aimed at the 7–13 age group. This system was unique to Britain, and provided a non-profit-making organization funded by the Eady levy up to 1981. While based at Shepperton Studios, Ronald Spencer developed a production link with the CFF which became from 1982 the Children's Film and Television Foundation (CFTF). Shepperton productions for the CFTF include *The Young Detectives* (1964) by Gilbert Dunn, and *Project Z* (1968) and *The 'Copter Kids* (1975) by Spencer.

The CFTF brought several successful television and film partnerships to children's films, notably for the adaptation of Mary Norton's *The Borrowers* (**Working Title**/BBC Enterprises) which got ten million viewers and a British Academy award. Bob Godfrey Films received an award for *Henry's Cat* in 1994; Jim Henson Productions in London contributed to the *Muppet Shows*; and Siriol Productions, Cardiff, produced **animation** films for

children, such as *SuperTed*. Examples of the filming of classic children's fairy tales and stories are *The Princess and the Goblin* (1991), *The Water Babies* (1978) and *Watership Down* (1978).

The latter only partially reflect their authors. Indeed, authors such as J.M. Barrie, Roald Dahl and Beatrix Potter may be Britain's lasting international contribution to children's films. There is an unwillingness to confront modern cultures defined by *Star Wars* (1977, 1997) or *Home Alone* (1990), preferring (except **Parker**'s *Bugsy Malone* (1976)) the family viewing models of *The Railway Children* (1972), *The Amazing Mr Blundel* (1972), *Digby: the Biggest Dog in the World* (1973), *Tarka the Otter* (1978), or *Black Beauty* (1994). Some of this may be due to Lord Rank's early moralizing, or the club promises made at Oscar Deutsch's Odeon Saturday matinees.

An alternative is the Children's Film Unit, a registered Educational Charity set up in 1981 to encourage children in all aspects of film making. It has produced imaginative films with children on both sides of the camera, such as *Captain Stirrick* (1982), *Dark Enemy* (1984) and *Mister Skeeter* (1985). Its tenth feature, *Hard Road* (1989), is about two thirteen-year-olds who wind up the Children's Help Line, fake suicides, and drive a scarlet 1959 Ferrari into Sussex.

See also: literature, children's and teenage; television, children's

Further reading

Pym, J. (ed.) (1997) *TimeOut Film Guide*, London: Penguin Books.

ARTHUR McCULLOUGH

film, experimental

British experimental cinema has diverse origins and applications stemming from a diffuse avant-garde, involvements of film-makers in other arts, different kinds of support and a wide range of organizational networks. Many experimentalists came from art schools, such as the Slade School of Art (Steve Chivers, Lis Rhodes, David Curtis), the Royal College of Art (Peter Gidal, Cerith Wyn

Evans, Patrick Keiller), the fine art department at North East London Polytechnic, now the University of North London (David Parsons, and John Maybury), and St Martin's School of Art (Malcolm Le Grice, William Rabin, Isaac **Julien**, Kobena Mercer).

Experimental film has been identified with scientific approaches towards **painting** and arts, supported by the Artists' Film and Video Committee, set up by the **Arts Council** in 1972. However, ever since its origins in the 1920s with the Close Up circle and the British Documentary movement, experimentalism accumulated many influences from lyricism and surrealism to psychoanalysis and the American Underground. After 1974, it built loose organizational networks in the Independent Film-Makers Association (IFA) (formed to promote and coordinate the grant-aided sector, with collectives funded from the Regional Arts Associations), the Workshop Movement and **Channel 4**. The **Workshop Declaration** encouraged this by accrediting franchised workshops to different regional and collective ventures.

A cooperative tradition of distribution and exhibition spread through another key institution, the London Film Makers' Co-operative (LFMC), to groups such as Angry Arts, Polit-kino and The Other Cinema. The sheer variety of groups, such as Cinema Action, the Berwick Street Collective, Amber Films, London Women's Film Group, Leeds Animation Workshop, Sankofa, Ceddo and **Black Audio Film Collective**, often reflected difficulties in finding common ground, but this also stimulated diffusion of experimental influences into the industry generally.

This diffusion developed in films as varied as Richard **Lester**'s *The Knack* (1965), Lindsay **Anderson**'s *If* (1968), Karel **Reisz**'s *Morgan: A Suitable Case for Treatment* (1966), Stanley **Kubrick**'s *2001: A Space Odyssey* (1968), and **Roeg** and Cammell's *Performance* (1970). Publicity spread through magazines such as *Undercut* (set up in 1980 under the LFMC), *Framework*, *Screen* and *Sight and Sound*, and at London's National Film Theatre (**NFT**) and Institute of Contemporary Arts. Many famous and prolific British film-makers in the 1990s, such as **Greenaway**, **Potter**, Julien, **Davies** and **Jarman**, can be said to have important origins in experimental film.

See also: avant-garde cinema

Further reading

Curtis, D. (ed.) (1996) *A Directory of British Film and Video Artists*, London: Arts Council of England/ John Libbey Media.

ARTHUR McCULLOUGH

film, feminist

Feminist film is situated in ideological opposition to the patriarchal codes and conventions of dominant (or mainstream) cinema. It engages with issues of female identity, subjectivity, desire, sexuality, history and spectatorship, challenging the negative representations of women in film and their marginalization within the film industry itself.

Emerging concurrently with an ascendant women's movement during the early 1970s, the initial symbiosis between feminist film theory and film-making began to rupture by the late 1980s. While some feminist film-makers expressed continued support for a separatist deconstructive or countercinema, others advocated working simultaneously within and against mainstream conventions. They criticized the theoretical density, didacticism and white middle-class composition of feminist film that foreclosed its accessibility among socially, ethnically diverse and more mainstream audiences.

As a countercinema, feminist film has assimilated influences from socialist documentary and avant-garde film. A cinema vérité style allowed women to convey 'authentic' selves and experiences, rendering the personal as political in consciousness-raising films. 'Women-talking' documentaries include *Women of the Rhondda* (London Women's Film Group, 1972) and *Nightcleaners* (Berwick Street Collective, 1975), which preceded the Sheffield Film Co-op's more agitational socialist documentaries *A Woman Like You* (1976), *That's No Lady* (1977) and *Jobs For the Girls* (1979).

An avant-gardist experimentalism and aesthetic vigour infused films like *Riddles of the Sphinx* (Laura Mulvey and Peter Wollen, 1978), *Light Reading* (Lis Rhodes, 1978), *The Song of the Shirt* (Clayton and

Curling, 1979) and *Thriller* (Sally **Potter**, 1979). Their work (that of cine-theorist Mulvey in particular) exemplifies an interrelated feminist theory and practice, notably through the attempt to articulate a new 'feminine' cinematic syntax which disrupts conventional narrative, image and sound.

As transitional works, Lezli-Ann Barrett's *An Epic Poem* (1982) and Potter's *The Gold Diggers* (1983) were followed by *Business As Usual* (1987) and *Orlando* (1993) respectively, to demonstrate the viability of feminist concerns within a mainstream context. While 1990s feminist film making collapses boundaries between dominant and alternative cinemas, the explosion of black, lesbian and post-colonial theories has stimulated the presence of feminist film-makers in the independent and black workshop sectors. As film-makers of vitality and steadfast vision, their racial, sexual, cultural and diasporic explorations attest to the polyphonic nature of British feminist film making. They include Sankofa's Maureen Blackwood and Martina Attile, Ngozi Onwurah, Pratibha Parmar and Gurinder Chadha, whose *Bhaji on the Beach* (1994) signalled the stirrings of a black–Asian female foray into the mainstream.

See also: feminist publishing houses; feminist theatre

Further reading

Erens, P. (ed.) (1990) *Issues in Feminist Film Criticism*, Bloomington, IN: Indiana University Press (a comprehensive anthology of classic feminist film essays).

SATINDER CHOHAN

film awards

British awards are conferred by the British Academy of Film and Television Arts (BAFTA), British Film Institute Awards, Evening Standard British Film Awards, and London Film Critics Circle Awards. BAFTA awarded twenty of its top thirty awards (Best Film, Best Actress and Best Actor each year) to British talents in the 1990s.

Since 1960, Britain has obtained top awards at the three major film festivals, Cannes, Berlin and Venice. Awards at Cannes were Best Director in 1993 to Mike **Leigh** (*Naked*), the 1996 Palme D'Or for Leigh's *Secrets and Lies*, and in the same year Best Actress to Brenda Blethyn (also for *Secrets and Lies*). At Berlin, the 1994 Golden Bear went to *In the Name of the Father*, and the 1996 Golden Bear to *Sense and Sensibility*. At Venice, the Best Acress award in 1991 went to Tilda Swinton (*Edward II*). British directors receiving top awards at these festivals include Lindsay **Anderson**, Terence **Davies**, Isaac **Julien**, Neil **Jordan**, Carol **Reed**, Richard **Lester**, Ken **Loach**, Alan **Parker**, Tony **Richardson**, John **Schlesinger**, Ridley **Scott** and Peter Watkins.

Britain occupies second place (after the USA) in three of the most prestigious prizes (Oscars, New York Critics Awards and Cannes Festival), taking 25 percent of the awards in New York, 20 percent of the Oscars and 15 percent in Cannes since 1980. At the Oscars (awarded by the Academy of Motion Picture Arts and Sciences), the British tend to win in supporting roles and in American-made films. Yet, four of the fifteen people who have been most often nominated for Academy Awards are British: Richard Burton, Peter O'Toole, Deborah Kerr and Laurence Olivier. Three members of the **Redgrave family** have been nominated. During the period 1986–95, Emma **Thompson** had a record four nominations, seven people from Merchant-Ivory films received nominations, and *The Last Emperor* (UK/Italy 1987) won all nine Oscars for which it was nominated.

Oscar winners since 1960 include the following British films: *Darling* (1965), *The Lion in Winter* (1968), *Lawrence of Arabia* (1962), *Tom Jones* (1963), *A Man for All Seasons* (1966), *Oliver!* (1968), *Death on the Nile* (1978), *Chariots of Fire* (1981), *Gandhi* (1982, eight awards), *The Killing Fields* (1984), *A Room with a View* (1986), *The Mission* (1986), *My Left Foot* (1989), *The Crying Game* (1992), *Howard's End* (1992), *The Wrong Trousers* (1993), *Franz Kafka's It's a Wonderful Life* (1995) and *The English Patient* (1997, twelve nominations).

See also: BAFTA; film press

Further reading

Levy, E. (1991) *And The Winner Is ... : The History and Politics of the Oscar Awards*, New York: Continuum.

ARTHUR McCULLOUGH

film distributors

The Producers Alliance for Cinema and Television argued in the Mergers and Monopolies Report in 1994 that the concentrated structure of the British distribution market created bias against the distribution of non-US films. Film historian Ian Jarvie (1992: 122) showed that US companies abroad were originally distributors, not producers, operating a policy of wholly controlling distribution through foreign subsidiaries rather than local agents. Hence in Britain today, long after the collapse of the **Rank**/APBC duopoly, producers are almost totally at the mercy of American distributors.

Each of the five major distributors in the UK is affiliated to Hollywood studios, with the following accounting for over three-quarters of the UK industry: United International Pictures, Buena Vista International, Twentieth Century Fox Film Company, Warner Bros Distributors and Columbia Tristar Films. The 1995 report of the National Heritage Committee on the film industry notes these as primarily sales and marketing groups distributing films in the UK which have been made or acquired by their parent companies. They are involved in only one-third of films released, and earn three-quarters of the market from a limited number of blockbusters. Of the additional twenty-five independent companies, two or three (usually Rank Film Distributors, Entertainment Film Distributors, Polygram Filmed Entertainment or First Independent) account for most of the remaining quarter of the market. These smaller distributors circulate a wider range of films, including most of the British and Continental films, for a very small slice of the box office earnings. Artistic films are usually distributed by the British Film Institute (**BFI**), Institute of Contemporary Arts and Artificial Eye.

A Keynote report (1995) on British film shows that distributors make limited copies of most British films. For example, for Sally **Potter**'s *Orlando* (1992), ten copies were made for UK distributors, whereas in Italy forty copies were made. British Screen Finance remarked to the 1995 National Heritage Committee that the British cinema market is possibly one of the least hospitable in the world for British films, which are distributed mainly by the subsidiaries of their US competitors. One of the biggest problems facing all distributors is the cost of launching a new release (upwards of £1 million). As Julian Petley (1992: 78) points out, whereas the majors benefit from scale economies, most independents and smaller distributors do not. Independent producers who handle British or subtitled films face problems of limited distribution outlets as well as substantial costs of the new release. This helps to explain the demise of distributors such as Oasis and Enterprise.

Of all the world's major film markets, the UK has the greatest concentration of ownership and the greatest degree of integration between distributors and cinema exhibitors. John Hill (1992: 17) shows that from the mid-1980s, the gulf between production and distribution/exhibition deepened dramatically, while concentration in the distribution/exhibition sector tightened (often fatally for the independents). Although there is increasing competition amongst exhibitors, the majors have further concentrated their share by opening multiplex **cinemas**. Unfortunately, a rising number of screens does not necessarily mean that a wider variety or larger number of films is shown: long holdovers of popular films are common, and the multiplexes carve out core consumer sectors rather than creating new viewers.

One solution, suggested by Petley, is to encourage a British version of the EU scheme to enhance the distribution of low-budget films, or a quota for independent distribution and exhibition along the lines of the 25 percent ruling that was imposed on British television. Another, stemming from the Middleton Report and now in place through **National Lottery** funding, provides for a distribution-led studio approach towards a major film making and distribution company. The ultimate aim is for commercially viable films on which studios retain rights, thus enabling future productions.

Whether such approaches will succeed is difficult to judge. The underlying problems seem to be the increasingly volatile, risky nature of distribution, being heavily dependent on the success or failure of particular films. This makes distributors prefer to see the finished film before putting up any money, so that in abstaining from risk investment they ensure that British films remain small. In 1994, 46 percent of UK films had still not been released one year later, and the majority had poor box office receipts. In 1995, British films accounted for around 4 percent of the market share, compared to 2 percent for foreign language films. In 1996, over 120 British films were produced, yet just over 50 were released. Another problem is summed up by the fact that while the multiple Oscar-winner *The English Patient* (1997) was supposedly a British film, with an independent producer, the enormous box office takings still flowed to the USA.

The BFI *Handbook*'s Centenary Film Section pointed out that the British watched more than thirty films each in 1946 (when cinema was more popular in Britain than anywhere else in the world). Today the average person watches two films a year in the cinema, two films a week on television, and one film every three weeks on video: a film habit of more than 120 films a year. It may also be encouraging that almost 15 percent of the television networks' output in the UK is currently devoted to feature films. However, as interactions inevitably increase with the audio-visual industry, where film distribution is subject to wider media strategies of multinational companies, it is increasingly important for British film to concentrate on the development of property rights and distributive rights at the earliest possible stage.

See also: BFI; cinemas

Further reading

British Film Institute (1997) *BFI Film and Television Handbook 1997*, London: British Film Institute.

Hill, J. (1992) 'The Issue of National Cinema and British Film Production', in D. Petrie (ed.), *New Questions of British Cinema*, London: British Film Institute.

Jarvie, I. (1992) *Hollywood's Overseas Campaign: The North Atlantic Movie Trade, 1920–1950*, London: Cambridge University Press.

Petley, J. (1992) 'Independent Distribution in the UK: Problems and Proposals', in D. Petrie (ed.), *New Questions of British Cinema*, London: British Film Institute.

ARTHUR McCULLOUGH

film festivals

British film festivals are mostly small, specialized, non-competitive and unconnected with the commercial markets. There are six major international film festival markets, split into two tiers: the first tier comprises the American Film Market, Cannes and Milan, while the second comprises Venice, Toronto and Berlin. Since the 1960s Britain has a strong record of achievement in winning top **film awards** at Cannes, Berlin and Venice.

The main comparable event in Britain is the Edinburgh Film Festival, which since 1996 has taken the characteristics of a bustling film market. Otherwise, the London International Film Festival and Market, organized via the London Film Festival with support from West End cinemas and the Producers Alliance for Cinema and Television, has intentions to compete with Cannes, Berlin and Venice.

Major competitive international festivals favour large commercial over small artistic films. Smaller non-competitive festivals, not having the prestige and publicity that awards bring, tend to get local rather than international visitors. Moreover, due to the practices of **film distributors**, the scope for commercialization for British films through British festivals seems to be limited. Under 50 percent of UK films get released. Yet in terms of film projects, the UK has the highest number in Europe. In 1993, the comparative figures were UK (553 projects), France (366), Germany (260) and Italy (257). At this time, only 10 percent of UK film projects received financial backing, as opposed to 40 percent in France. This has serious consequences for film makers: whereas music can flourish in bars or garages, the only hope of breaking through for new film makers is often through the small range of minor film festivals.

Of the main thirty-five film festivals in Britain, fourteen are competitive. Most of the following are specialized: British Short Film Festival, London; Cinemagic – International Festival for Young People, Belfast; European Student Film Festival, London; International Celtic Film and Television Festival, Inverness; KinoFilm, Manchester; Manchester International Short Film and Video Festival (special categories in 1996 were Gay and Lesbian, Black Cinema, New Irish Cinema, New American Underground, Eastern European and Super 8); Wildscreen International Film and Symposium, Bristol; and the Edinburgh Film Festival.

Non-competitive festivals in London include the London Jewish Film Festival for films made by directors who are Jewish or concerned with issues relating to Jewish identity. (In 1996 its Lifetime Achievement Awards were given to Billy Wilder and Fred Zinneman). The London Lesbian and Gay Film Festival has non-competitive film and video. In 1994, it held the first national conference in Britain devoted to lesbian film making. Also non-competitive are London Children's Film Festival, London Latin American Film Festival and London International Environment Film Festival (Green Screen, which tours seven UK cities and seven foreign capitals).

Various other specialized festivals in Britain include Black Sunday – The British Genre Film, Manchester, dealing with horror, fantasy, film noir, **thrillers** and **science fiction** genres; The Comedy Film Festival, Southampton; Festival of Fantastic Films, for science fiction and fantasy; French Film Festival, Edinburgh; Italian Film Festival, Edinburgh; Raindance Film Showcase and Market, for independently produced features, shorts and documentaries, London; and Shots in the Dark – Crime, Mystery and Thriller Festival, Nottingham. The Welsh International Film Festival, Aberystwyth, includes films from Wales in Welsh and English; and the International Celtic Film and Television Festival, Penzance, celebrates work in minority languages, often community-based, in Scotland, Ireland, Wales, Cornwall and Brittany.

Among the larger festivals, Edinburgh Film Festival is the oldest continually running film festival in the world. In the 1960s, Edinburgh invented the idea of mounting retrospectives of film makers' work. It became a focus for women and film, psychoanalysis and cinema, **avant-garde cinema**, history/popular memory and Scottish film culture (Scotch Reels). Retrospectives include the work of Douglas Sirk, Roger Corman and Samuel Fuller. In 1993 it began premiering new British directors, with the work of Antonia Bird. In 1995 it launched a New British Expo showcase. Its golden anniversary included a retrospective of the year 1947, when *Black Narcissus* and *Odd Man Out* were released.

The London Film Festival (LFF) is a non-competitive festival showing films in November seen at other festivals during the year at the National Film Theatre and other London cinemas. At the 1996 fortieth LFF, British Film Institute (**BFI**) Fellowships were awarded to Ken **Loach** and Michael **Caine** (previous recipients include Orson Welles, Martin Scorsese, Michelangelo Antonio, Sir John Mills and Sir Dirk Bogarde). At the British Cinema Now strand there were twenty-one productions by UK-based film makers including *La Passione, Hard Men, Saint Ex, The Brylcreem Boys, Fetishes, Indian Story* and the BFI-production *Yin and Yang: Gender in Chinese Cinema*. In the 1970s, The London Film Festival under Derek Malcolm expanded its activities to include the independent Film-Makers Co-operative and the Institute of Contemporary Arts (ICA). At the same time the Hayward Gallery arranged festival settings for British and European avant-garde films, and experimental cinema was promoted by the Festival of Expanded Cinema at the ICA.

The Tenth Anniversary Leeds International Festival was celebrated in 1996 with sixteen days of premieres, galas, retrospectives, special guests and seminars. The twelfth Birmingham International Film and Television Festival in 1996 included New International Cinema, North American Showcase, Chinese focus, Lynda La Plante Retrospective and Real to Reel – The British Realist Tradition (featuring the works of Ken Loach, Humphrey Jennings, and Peter Watkins). Other main festivals include the Emirates Chelsea Film Festival (with Ridley **Scott** as President, set up in

1997 to support new film-making talent within the UK), the Cambridge Film Festival and the Sheffield International Documentary Festival.

See also: film awards; film press

Further reading

Caughie, J. and Rockett, K. (1996) *The Companion to British and Irish Cinema*, London: Cassell and BFI Publishing.

Roddick, N. (1996) *The Festival Business*, London: BFI Publishing.

ARTHUR McCULLOUGH

film music

Though the first cinema films had no sound track, the early picture palaces were not silent. To blot out noise from the projector and the audience and also to create atmosphere, a piano, organ or band, sometimes with many instrumentalists, nearly always provided music. The music was often extemporized or adapted from a stock repertory, but was sometimes composed specially for the film. Increasingly ingenious attempts to replace live players by mechanically reproduced sound led in 1928 to the first talkies. Their sound track carried not only speech but also the film's musical backing, though the orchestration had at first to make allowances for distortions inherent in early sound systems. By the mid-1930s, film music was developing as an essential part of cinematic art, not just in musicals and other films that more or less naturally called for music but also in productions of every sort from light comedy by way of the Westerns to heavy drama.

The vogue grew also for giving a film a 'theme tune', either a song or an instrumental motif that was given great prominence. In 1931–2 an Oscar was awarded for Best Sound Recording, but in 1934 there were Oscars for Best Song and Best Score. In Britain, Arthur Bliss composed the score for Korda's film of H.G. Wells' *Things to Come*; his example was followed by William Walton (*The First of the Few*, 1942, and *Henry V*, 1944). Ealing Studio's Ernest Irving regularly commissioned leading British composers, such as Vaughan Williams (*Scott*

of the Antarctic, 1948). Malcolm Arnold, with eighty film scores to his name, won an Oscar for his music for *The Bridge on the River Kwai* (1957). Particularly when not foregrounded but used rather to help create mood, film music offers the composer opportunities for experiment both in musical forms and orchestral coloration. Like nineteenth-century composers who quarried orchestral works out of their incidental music for the theatre (for example, Georges Bizet's Arlésienne suite (1872)), the earlier writers of film music often made concert arrangements of their scores. Today, CD versions of scores for successful films, such as John Horner's music for *Titanic*, sell well. The use of music in radio and television parallels developments of film music, though generally (despite exceptions like Benjamin Britten's score for a BBC adaptation of T.H. White's *The Sword in the Stone* in 1939), on a more modest level.

Further reading

Karlin, F. (1994) *Listening to Movies: The Film Lover's Guide to Film Music*, New York: Schirmer.

CHRISTOPHER SMITH

film policy

The **British film industry** has won many critical awards, but is hindered by a weak infrastructure and a lack of investment, despite relative stability in the 1990s and isolated successes such as *Four Weddings and a Funeral* (1994). The government has legislated with a view to avoiding economic dependence on subsidies or quotas while supporting non-commercial activities, and has encountered criticism for not providing sufficient support in an industry dominated by the USA.

Coinciding with British Film Year, the government reorganized the industry with the 1985 Film Act. This opened up the industry to market forces with measures such as the abolition of the Eady levy on cinema admissions and the phasing out of the 1979 capital allowances, policies which did little to curb the decline in production. This was designed to create an independent and competitive film industry, yet, due to the lack of investment in a high-risk industry, only support from television, especially **Channel 4 Films**, kept the industry alive. The issue was left until the 1990 Downing Street Seminar which examined ways of promoting British film abroad and making the industry more competitive.

Policy was finally reassessed with the June 1995 Policy Paper and the setting up of the Middleton Committee to advise on the financing of the film industry and how to encourage investment. The Committee recommended the creation of vertically integrated studios to improve distribution and spread the risks through a portfolio of films, the rejoining of Eurimages, a European production fund, and tax breaks, including the removal of the withholding tax on foreign artists. The subsequent government Policy Paper was criticized as being too little to relaunch the industry, with the lack of tax breaks proving a contentious issue given the success of such a policy in Ireland. Several new measures were introduced by the government. There was to be a London Film Commission to promote the capital, money to support initiatives for Cinema 100 and a feasibility study into a West End Showcase showing British Films. Money from the **National Lottery** was made available to compensate for the reduced government grant, subject to a successful application. These measures were meant to complement the government funding already in place through the British Film Institute (**BFI**), British Screen, the National Film and Television School (established in 1971), the British Film Commission, the European Co-Production Fund and other regional and media agencies.

CHRISTOPHER COLBY

film press

British film press has poor roots in the **British film industry**. In major film studios such as Elstree, Shepperton, **Pinewood Studios** and Ealing, communications were mostly confined to genres and stars, while in film distribution, in-house magazines almost entirely favoured their Hollywood base. The British Film Institute (**BFI**) *Handbook* lists over 150 film journals, magazines

and newspapers, but only a tiny proportion relates to industry: examples are *British Film* covering film making and broadcasting in the UK, *Scottish Film* on film making within Scotland, *In Camera* for cinematographers and technicians, *Screen International* for UK oriented trade, and *Producer* for independent producers.

The main roots of the film press are in British public opinion and related film values, and in new social identities, film collectives and culture industries. Films have been a staple of the British press both in quality and tabloid circulations, with articles and commentaries appearing in a dozen national, daily or weekly British newspapers with circulations ranging from 200,000 to over four million.

From 1960 to 1980, the social and political nature of film was an important concern in British public opinion, and film commentaries reflected the political orientations of their editors and film editors. One of the biggest controversies stemmed from Peter Watkins's film *The War Game* (1965) about a nuclear attack on Britain, which sections of the press considered propaganda for the Campaign for Nuclear Disarmament. Similarly the *Sunday Telegraph* and *Sunday Times* attacked the factual undertones of Ken **Loach**'s *Hidden Agenda* (1990) concerning a British shoot-to-kill policy in Northern Ireland.

These debates about realism and documentary fiction were covered by intellectual magazines like *Screen* up to 1994 (see **Screen and screen theory**). But by the 1970s, the serious film press had already been developing auteur criticism from the Continent. *Movie* transferred *Cahiers du Cinema* orientations to the British context, and became critical of the British new wave. The two magazines directly connected to the BFI – *Monthly Film Bulletin* and *Sight and Sound* – were developing new European and American as well as British styles and perspectives. Quality screen monthly magazines such as *Films and Filming* (which became *Film Review*) followed suit.

In the 1980s the serious film magazines (and an emerging fringe press) were affected by cultural studies and cultural movements in Britain. Some developed psychoanalysis, **feminist theory**, semiotics or **Marxism**, but many were directly influenced by social and political movements. For example, *Framework*, which began in 1968 as a university periodical assisted by the BFI was continued in the 1980s by the black film workshop Sankofa, emphasizing black, diasporan, feminist and gay film movements (see **diasporan film-makers**; **film, feminist**; **gay film**), while Leeds Animation Workshop was dubbed as women's eye propaganda for its feminist counter-propaganda to the cinematic debates over realism.

In 1983, *Artrage* announced a critical black presence in British cinema, and Ceddo Film/Video Workshop issued guerrilla press releases akin to the music of Bob Marley. Ten years later, *Screen* was including articles on popular Hindi cinema (for example, 'Images of Elvis in Indian Film'), while Ashish Rajadhyaksha and Paul Willeman were compiling an *Encyclopedia of Indian Cinema*. Britain's Asian press, Asian television and the ***Bandung File*** reflected the world's first mass video audience re-emerging in the mid- 1990s as big-screen Bollywood (Bombay Hindi cinema) audiences.

Yet the overarching influence on film press stems from Britain's role in an international film system which links films to wider media circuits and culture industries. British films represent less than 10 percent of British film markets, where audiences are controlled by loosely coupled multinational consumer organizations. The Sunday supplements' inclusion of films as part of a catch-all leisure net presaged more hybrid magazines like *Arena* and *The Face* covering film, literature, music and fashion, and the arrival in the late 1990s of magazines like *Uncut*, whose August 1998 (Take 15) issue includes articles on 'Nic **Roeg** on David Bowie', 'Music and Movie News', 'Canned Heat' (Cannes top 10 films), and 'Banned Aid' (British Board of Film Classification censorship). It is geared to highly marketed actors and directors such as Helena Bonham-Carter, Elizabeth Hurley, Kate Winslet, Kenneth **Branagh**, Emma **Thompson**, Peter **Greenaway** and Kristin Scott Thomas.

This might explain the unwillingness of British **film festivals** and film institutes to either have or develop effective World Wide Web sites, or it may be due to an amateurish approach. In the latter case there remains a variety of interesting publication. For example, *Film Dope*, *Film History* and *Vertigo* provide specialized research and debate for British film-makers and audiences; *Music From the Movies*

covers film music and its composers; *Picture House* is devoted to British cinema buildings of the past; and *Talking Pictures* has interviews and articles on all aspects of film culture in the UK. The first issue in 1998 of the annual *Journal of Popular British Cinema* reviews the subjects of genre and British cinema in **Carry On films**, 1950s war films, swinging London, crime films, British sexploitation, punk films and **Hammer Horror** films.

See also: film reviews

Further reading

Diawara, M. (1993) 'Power and Territory: The Emergence of Black British Film Collectives', in L. Friedman (ed.), *British Cinema and Thatcherism: Fires Were Started*, London: UCL Press.

Petley, J. (1997) 'Factual Fictions and Fictional Fallacies: Ken Loach's Documentary Dramas', in G. McKnight (ed.), *Agent of Challenge and Defiance: The Films of Ken Loach*, Trowbridge: Flicks Books.

ARTHUR McCULLOUGH

film reviews

British film reviewing was bestowed an ethos of social and moral responsibility by documentary realism, which formed an important part of British public opinion and its critical attitudes towards films. It is perhaps the last major film formula to survive into the 1970s, with perspectives on art, censorship, technique and other film issues.

The cinema advocated by reviewers emphasizes a serious purpose in film making in contrast to Hollywood dream movies, a quality cinema in contrast to mere entertainment, and an educated and independent attitude as opposed to either pure commercialism or art. Although the formula was damaged in the debates about 1960s progressive realism (for example, in the films of Peter Watkins and Ken **Loach**), its concerns about the social role of film were sustained in various ways by most of the established British reviewers.

From the 1960s until the end of the 1980s there has been an established circle of British film reviewers acting as key figures in **film festivals**, broadcasting, publishing and journalism. It has included Penelope Houston (editor of *Sight and Sound*), C.A. Lejeune and Philip French (film reviewers at the *Observer*), Dilys Powell and David Robinson (the *Sunday Times*), Richard Roud and Derek Malcolm (the *Guardian*), David Robinson (*The Times*), Alexander Walker (*Evening Standard*), and Barry **Norman** (television). It was sometimes controversially engaged by leading film-makers such as Lindsay **Anderson**, Alex **Cox**, Alan **Parker** and Ken Loach.

However, reviewers increasingly have to contend less with film making and cinema and more with new film cultures and film theories, new social movements and multicultural identities. Also, reviewing practices have begun to spread across a widening range of the **film press**, and increasingly in house commentary by the three hundred film societies listed under the British Federation of Film Societies. As an indicator of the changing scene, *Time Out*, a fortnightly broadsheet begun in 1968, grew rapidly in the 1980s to become the foremost weekly review of London film, theatre, music, clubs and dance. Many of its perspectives relate directly to the multicultural networks and culture industry circuits which connect cinema to new social identities and cultural interests groups.

Further reading

Pym, J. and Andrew, G. (1988) *The Time Out Film Guide*, London: Penguin (the first edition of an annual accumulated *Time Out Film Guide*, with an imposing array of British reviewers, and invaluable index of film subjects and categories).

ARTHUR McCULLOUGH

filofaxes

On sale in the UK since the 1920s, Filofax is a trade name for a personal organizer, which is a loose-leaf ring binder for carrying diaries, notes, address books, maps and anything else considered essential for day-to-day working and socializing. A style accessory of the 1980s, the Filofax became *de rigueur* among aspiring professionals or yuppies but became outmoded in the 1990s. Stealing Filofaxes (variously known as fax-napping or filo-napping)

for ransom purposes in the 1980s became common, as more and more well-off people came to rely upon these ever-growing, leather-clad life organizers. Electronic or palmtop organizers became more fashionable as the 1990s marched on and Filofax tried to broaden its market base away from simply the fashion-conscious.

See also: accessories; acronym groups; crazes; fashion (1980s)

PETER CHILDS

financial crises

The most famous recent financial crisis was 'Black Wednesday', 17 September 1992. The collapse in the pound following tensions between Norman Lamont, Chancellor of the Exchequer, and the German Bundesbank led the Bank of England to raise interest rates from 10 percent to 15 percent, and then to devalue the pound and pull out of the Exchange Rate Mechanism. The incident was a considerable embarrassment to John Major's Conservative government (see **Conservative governments**) and undermined Britain's presidency of the EC. Lamont resigned the following spring. Previous crises of different proportions were: the oil crisis of the mid-1970s, which followed from a threefold increase in the price of oil imposed by OPEC (Organization of Petroleum Exporting Countries) and led to the three-day week from January to March 1974. In 1979 there was the **Winter of Discontent**, marked by high levels of strikes and industrial unrest. Lastly, in 1986, there was the Big Bang on 27 October, the day the stock exchange was deregulated; this caused great financial upheaval both before and after, right up to Black Monday a year later, Britain's taste of a global financial crash.

PETER CHILDS

FINANCIAL TIMES PRINTING HOUSE *see* Nicholas Grimshaw and Partners

flying pickets

The term 'flying pickets' was first used in 1980 to describe the striking nurses who went to different hospitals to persuade other medical workers to join them. Similar pickets had been used by radical **trade unions** from the late 1960s as transport and communication links improved. The aim was to put pressure on companies and union members not directly involved in disputes to support strikers or to prevent 'blackleg' labour. The tactic was most successful in the 1972 miners strike, when mass secondary picketing on selected targets severely curtailed coal production and distribution. However, in 1980 the Conservative government implemented an Employment Act which restricted legal picketing to one's own place of work. The NUM still attempted to use flying pickets in the 1984–5 miners strike, but were deterred by police roadblocks.

COLIN WILLIAMS

folk music

Modern British folk music owes its character not just to the traditional music of people in the UK but also to the 'folk revival' of the 1950s and 1960s. A crucial figure in the movement was Ewan MacColl, who repopularized both traditional and contemporary folk songs through his series of 'Radio Ballads' during the 1950s. This music is still extremely influential in the 1990s. MacColl's more famous songs include 'The First Time Ever I Saw Your Face', 'Dirty Old Town' and 'The Manchester Rambler'.

There was a greater surge of interest in folk music in England in the 1960s. Martin Carthy, Norma Waterson and Roy Bailey were some of the better known folk artists to emerge, and all are still performing today. Towards the end of the decade the 'folk rock' bands began to appear with the formation of groups such as Fairport Convention, Steeleye Span and Lindisfarne. All these bands were headline performers in the 1990s.

The enduring popularity of the artists of the 1950s and 1960s indicates how little folk music has changed since then. Most new acts have much in common with their predecessors. 'Folk rock' has been continued by groups such as The Oyster Band and The Home Service. Protest singing, encapsulated by the work of Roy Bailey and Leon Rosselson, has been continued by the likes of Robb Johnson and Billy Bragg, as well as surfacing in other music genres such as **punk rock** and **reggae**. The mix of traditional and contemporary performance has been continued by Martin Carthy's daughter Eliza.

Despite the strong element of continuity, folk music has developed some new strands. The emergence of cajun and zydeco music has resulted in many English cajun bands as well as the performance of cajun numbers by many folk acts. Also, a successful fusion of English folk and reggae has been developed by Edward the Second, who will play 'Wild Mountain Thyme' to a reggae beat with accordion accompaniment, and the Red Hot Polkas, who feature traditional English lead instruments backed by an Afro-Caribbean rhythm section.

Essentially, folk music in the 1990s remained musically conservative but politically radical. The stereotype of the apolitical 'finger in the ear' folkie continues to circulate, but Ewan MacColl's seventieth birthday concert contained an address by Arthur Scargill and in 1998 Roy Bailey performed at the Royal Albert Hall alongside readings by Tony Benn. Folk music is still a place where radical songwriting finds a natural outlet, not least because of the importance it places on of lyrics and narrative.

Folk music continues to be especially popular at the many annual folk festivals throughout the country. Tens of thousands of people attend events such as those at Cambridge and Sidmouth. There are also flourishing folk clubs in many towns. The balanced age range at major festivals attests to folk's continued ability to attract new generations outside of the mainstream of popular culture.

Further reading

Brocken, M. (1997) 'The British Folk Revival', unpublished Ph.D. thesis, University of Liverpool.

JIM BARNARD

food

The history of any nation's diet is the history of the nation itself, with food fashions, fads and fancies mapping episodes of colonialism and migration, trade and exploration, cultural exchange and boundary marking. British food is no exception to this. Yet there is a fundamental contradiction in this food–nation equation. There is no essential national food: the food which we think of as characterizing a particular place always tells stories of movement and mixing. It is ironic, then, that those who claim to hate 'foreign food' and eat only 'plain old English fare' fail to realise there's no such thing; all there is is a menu of naturalized foods brought to these shores through the course of history, modified and mixed over time. Those most quintessentially British foodstuffs – potatoes, or tea, for example – are imports which contain (and often conceal) histories of colonial exploration and exploitation. Indeed, it is often suggested that the definitive British (or perhaps English) meal is no longer the Sunday roast, but the curry washed down with lager.

If we survey eating out in Britain today, we see a proliferation of so-called ethnic restaurants – Indian, Chinese, Thai, French, Italian and so on – many of which were originally opened to serve immigrant communities in Britain, but which have come to enjoy widespread popularity. Aside from these, probably the most remarked upon culinary import has been the very familiar American fast food outlet, which continues to be the source of anti-American sentiment for many who resent the Americanization of British eating. If we look at eating habits inside people's homes we see a similar picture of diversity, with pizzas and burgers and a whole global range of ready meals lying in fridges and freezers alongside British staples (which these 'foreign' foods themselves have most surely become). While this has been seen as a cause for concern among those who fear the erosion of traditional British food, it is celebrated by many people as opening up British culture to important outside influences. It is not always that straightforward – just because we eat 'foreign food' that does not necessarily imply tolerance and acceptance of other cultures – but the sheer breadth of foodstuffs consumed in Britain which have their origins outside the UK at least attests to some level of cultural co-mingling taking place at our tables. The rise of so-called 'foodie' culture in Britain has contributed to this culinary–cultural diversification, by placing emphasis on the benefits of an increasingly globalized consumer culture (see **globalization and consumerism**).

At the same time as this explosion in 'ethnic eating', there has been a consistent re-evaluation of British food itself, of what it comprises and how it is viewed both here and overseas. For a long time, British cooking has been seen as unimaginative, stodgy and traditional (in the worst sense of the word), with meat and two vegetables followed by pudding and custard symbolizing the average Briton's diet. While this denies the host of local and regional foodstuffs (which in themselves have never achieved the status of, for example, French or Italian regional cookery), the reputation of indigenous British cuisine has undergone something of a renaissance, with the rediscovery of lost traditions and the invention of new ways of cooking British foods. The resurgence of cooking with offal and the celebration of the cooking traditions of the English regions could be taken as emblematic of this turn.

What Britain eats is also the subject of close official scrutiny, with bodies such as the National Food Survey and reports such as the government's *The Nation's Diet* trying to quantify and analyse our dietary habits. Further, the nation's diet has also come under repeated scrutiny by the European government, which attempts to regulate and standardize agricultural production and markets across the very different nations that make up the European Community. Legislation coming from **Europe** concerning food and drink has become widespread in contemporary folklore, with stories of decrees from Brussels over the size of apples or the straightness of cucumbers fuelling British anti-European feeling. The image of the food mountain, built to stabilize markets and prices, has become a powerful symbolic landscape form for Europe. The huge furore around beef and bovine spongiform encephalopathy (a fatal brain disease believed to be passed from infected cattle to humans, where it causes a similarly fatal brain condition called Creutzfeld-Jakob Syndrome Variant), which led to a worldwide ban on British beef in the mid-1990s, also brought out the cultural politics of food production and consumption very starkly; especially so, perhaps, given the association of Britishness with beef. It thus provoked, in some Britons, the patriotic response of ignoring health warnings and continuing to eat British beef, mocking those overseas who are more cautious about their consumption habits.

Another interesting pop-cultural marker of the nation's culinary predilections is the publishing explosion in cookery books, together with the increasing range of cookery and food programmes on television. Food has come to take centre stage in popular culture, with chefs and critics becoming major media celebrities. No one person epitomizes this more than Delia Smith, a television cook who has achieved an incredible prominence within British culinary culture through a whole string of cookbooks and associated television series. Other prominent food celebrities who have championed British food include chef Gary Rhodes, whose *Rhodes Around Britain* books and television series took him all over the country in search of local and regional delicacies. The current star status of British chefs (and their restaurants), in fact, has helped change the image of the nation's cookery, putting a more progressive form of national pride back on many menus.

See also: drink; eating disorders

Further reading

Hardyment, C. (1995) *Slice of Life: The British Way of Eating since 1945*, London: BBC Books (based on a successful television series, and packed with fascinating historical detail).

Murcott, A. (ed.) (1983) *The Sociology of Food and Eating*, Aldershot: Gower (an excellent collection of papers on aspects of British culinary culture).

DAVID BELL

Foot, Michael

b. 1913, Plymouth

Politician

From a prominent political family, Foot entered Parliament in 1945 and for nine years (1948–52,

1955–60) was editor of the left-wing journal *Tribune*. In the Labour government of the 1970s, he served as Secretary for Employment (1974–6) and Lord President of the Council and Leader of the House of Commons (1976–9). He was elected leader of the Labour party to succeed James Callaghan in 1980, but resigned after Labour's defeat in the general election of 1983. Many in the Labour Party felt that his image was outmoded; he was regularly photographed shambling on Hampstead Heath with his dog and stick, and his literariness meant that he lacked the killer instinct necessary to lead a successful political party against the likes of Margaret Thatcher.

See also: Labour Party

MIKE STORRY

football

Recognized as Britain's national sport, football has had a chequered history since the Second World War. The war had limited the number of games, and with the end of hostilities, massive crowds precipitated the birth of what has become known as the 'golden era' of the game.

It was considered a 'golden era' because English first division clubs drew massive crowds, and yet the football was not overwhelmingly attractive. Facilities were poor, for players and spectators, and very little concern was paid to safety. This (amongst other reasons) led to the disaster at Bolton's ground in 1946, when thousands turned up to witness the return of one of football's most enduring legends, Sir Stanley Matthews. Starved of their weekly fix of football, 65,000 people crammed into Burnden Park, with another 20,000 still trying to get in. The inevitable crush killed thirty-three supporters, and injured over 500. It took forty-three years, and a similar disaster in Sheffield, before the football authorities and government looked seriously at the conditions faced by supporters.

English football had become isolated in the prewar period, with the refusal of the Football Association (FA) to join the world governing body FIFA. Few overseas internationals were played, and the English public believed that the country that had 'invented' and codified the game was still the elite nation in terms of practition. The 1950 World Cup in Brazil sowed the first seeds of doubt, following a humiliating exit against a part-time American team, but it was not until Hungary arrived to play England at Wembley that everyone realized the opposition was ahead in terms of tactics and fitness. Inspired by Ferenc Puskas, Hungary demolished the English facade of superiority by winning 6–3, the first occasion England had lost to an overseas side at home. A return game in Budapest a few months later saw an even worse defeat, 7–1, and the FA finally realized something needed to be done about the widening gap. The first division itself was fairly strong, but new methods of management, training and coaching were needed if the English could compete with overseas opposition. Managers such as Matt Busby (Manchester United), Alf Ramsey (Ipswich) and Bill Nicholson (Spurs) combined British hard work with continental training and coaching. Busby's United team of the late 1950s was considered the finest produced up to that time on home ground, and were one of the favourites to lift the new European Champions Cup inaugurated in 1956. A tragic plane crash in Munich put paid to those ambitions, and robbed British football of eight of its brightest prospects. Ramsey, meanwhile, had taken unfancied Ipswich to the First Division title in 1962, the year after promotion. His reward was the England manager's job in 1963, and the chance to prepare for the World Cup of 1966, to be held for the first time on home soil. England's victory in that year was based on Ramsey's forthright belief in his own systems, four outstanding players in Banks, Moore and the Charlton brothers, and the huge support from the home crowd. The victory would lead to English clubs competing brilliantly in European competitions over the next twenty years, with the likes of Manchester United (1968), Liverpool (1977, 1978, 1981, 1984), Nottingham Forest (1979, 1980) and Aston Villa (1982) winning the European Cup, and other sides such as Tottenham Hotspur, Everton, Arsenal and Manchester City winning other European trophies.

The popularity and the consequent financial success of the game during the 1960s led to the players union (the PFA) calling for an end to the maximum wage policy, which had been in operation since the advent of professionalism in the late nineteenth century. Although players were well paid in comparison with workers in manual occupations, clubs' profits were not being channelled back into the game, either via wages or ground improvements. A delegation led by PFA Chairman Jimmy Hill met with the FA at the Ministry of Labour in 1961, and following threat of strikes from the players, the FA backed down. A year later, following protracted negotiations and legal cases, players were granted freedom of contract. Previously, once a player had signed to a particular club, he was tied to it until they said he could leave. The PFA claimed this was a restraint of trade, and so illegal. The turning point came in 1964 when George Eastham, a Newcastle United player, took his club to court to allow him to make a lucrative move to Arsenal. Eastham won his case, ending the old contract system. Many players took advantage of the ruling to negotiate new contracts and, coupled with the ending of the maximum wage policy, a new breed of 'pop star' player was created by the media. These players were young, very well paid and gathered a following from teenagers second only to music stars. The finest example during the 1960s was George Best. Blessed with an extraordinary footballing talent, Best became just as well known on the front pages, with his playboy lifestyle making more headlines than his performances on the pitch.

Football's high times during this period were not reflected on the terraces. Money made from the game was routinely taken away from the clubs, and little was done to improve the infrastructure of stadia. Coupled with the growing problem of violence amongst supporters, the 1970s is remembered as a period of excellence on the pitch and severe problems off it. Organized groups of hooligans inspired much critical comment against the game and its governing bodies. Violent incidents involving fans at home and abroad dominated talk about football in the late 1970s and 1980s. Certain clubs became known for attracting hooligans, notably Leeds and Manchester United in the 1970s, and Millwall in the 1980s.

The year 1985 is widely seen as the watershed in the English game. Violence at Luton was followed by the death of one fan at Birmingham and then the deaths of fifty-six fans at Bradford City, when a wooden stand caught fire. The nadir followed at the end of May 1985 when fighting between Liverpool and Juventus fans before the European Cup final at Heysel in Brussels led to the deaths of thirty-nine Juventus supporters. British football was in tatters, with an awful reputation, and the Thatcher government decided to take on the task of reforming the game. Frustrated by what she saw as the inactivity and incompetence of the Football Association and Football League, particularly over the issue of hooliganism, Thatcher applied constant pressure on the game, leading to the passage of the Football Spectators Bill of 1988. Following on the example of Luton Town and their members scheme under Conservative MP David Evans, the Bill introduced a computerized membership scheme (dubbed an ID card by opponents) for all fans at all clubs, as the government sought to take control of the game. A popular campaign against the scheme was led by the new intermediaries in the cultural politics of football: Heysel led to the formation of the Football Supporters Association, a national non-club association of football fans, while a whole raft of **fanzines** were started across the country, leading the intellectual and media charge against the greed and disinterest of the football industry and the media. These forces ironically combined with the game's organizing bodies against Thatcher, and although it was ultimately the Hillsborough disaster that destroyed the ID cards system, the fans' revolt against the idea undoubtedly helped portray the Bill as ill-judged and badly framed.

Hillsborough is the second great breaking point in British football, and the catalyst for the transformation of the game in the 1990s. Ninety-six Liverpool fans were killed on the Leppings Lane terrace of Hillsborough, crushed against a steel fence, before an **FA Cup** tie against Nottingham Forest, after police failed to exercise proper crowd control outside and inside the ground. The disaster, caused by a combination of factors including mistakes by the South Yorkshire Police, the inadequacy of the Hillsborough ground, the poor safety facilities and lack of attention to basic detail, highlighted once more the poor state of the British game and its failure to develop a genuine relationship with supporters based on respect and dignity. It marked the lowest point in British football: within a week the fences were being removed, the

government remitted Lord Justice Taylor to investigate the disaster and its implications and announced its view that football should move to all-seater stadia. By January 1990, Taylor had produced two reports, the second of which was widely considered the blueprint for the future of the game. This radical document called for all-seater stadia, new safety measures and standards, and crucially, a new relationship between football and its fans. Backed by hundreds of millions of pounds of government money (raised by cutting duty on the pools and channelled through the Football Trust), the physical fabric of football was to be thoroughly 'modernized'. This period is thus one of direct government intervention in the game, on a number of different levels.

This process of redevelopment coincided with the explosion of the financial pressures that had been building up inside the game since the early 1980s, and the development of a much greater professionalization of the industry, notably including the ending of the traditional collectivized commercial arrangements of football. The mid-late 1980s had seen increasing pressure from top clubs to keep more of their revenue and to be given a greater share of television revenue, leading to numerous threats to split from the rest of the League, and ever growing television coverage of a very small number of clubs; this process inevitably culminated in the splitting off of the top clubs from the League in 1992, with the formation of the FA Premier League (FAPL), following a power struggle between the Football Association and the Football League for control of the game. The new division was to run its own affairs, and positively market football as hip and trendy: crucially, the money for the League was supplied by Rupert Murdoch's **BSkyB** satellite station, which paid £304m in 1992 for four years coverage. Fans would thus have to buy a satellite dish to see live coverage. This was a central part of the transformation of the game into a middle-class leisure experience based on conceptions of lifestyle and consumption, with an explosion of interest across non-traditional football fans and a massive expansion of the commercialization of the game, notably involving merchandise. The whole image of the game, its social meanings, its dominant values and the interaction between it and supporters were turned on their heads within a matter of years, with the Sky hype machine churning out ever more coverage. Football essentially realigned itself within aggressively capitalist Thatcherite free market doctrines, became a true business, and sought to appeal to the middle classes. The demography of the spectators changed as a result (as ticket prices soared). Some clubs floated on the stock market and international capital sought to take over plum clubs, although the finances of the game remained as poor as ever; only Manchester United made a profit in 1996–7, despite the second Sky deal signed in 1996 worth £670m over five years and the other millions pouring in from merchandise, sponsorship, advertising and other sources. Most of the new money was simply paid out to players in wages (some getting £50,000 per week), or in rapidly escalating transfer fees, particularly through the internationalization of the transfer market which led to the signing of players from all the world. Chelsea had over fifteen different nationalities represented in their 1998–9 squad alone.

Yet, despite the popularity of the league, the buoyancy of the crowds and the massive public interest in the game (reaching unprecedented levels post Euro96), the financial imperative and the consequences of the penetration of the game by international capital led to yet more pressure for further reform, most notably ideas for a European Super League regularly suggested in 1997 and 1998 by European media companies. Such plans would eliminate the risk inherent in existing competitions and hence offer greater financial stability, and could earn each club up to £100m.

Further radical change is likely over the next five years, notably including the creation of club television stations selling pay-per-view subscriptions for live games (following the introduction of digital broadcasting). However, the 1990s have in many ways been the most dramatic decade in the history of the game, with far-reaching changes to its constituency, its appeal and the way fans are attracted to clubs, and the complete and total dependence on football on television revenue and exposure (which culminated in the establishment in 1998 of Manchester United's own television station, no doubt the first of many).

See also: fantasy football; football pools

Further reading

Hornby, N. (1990) *Fever Pitch*, London: Methuen.

SAM JOHNSTONE

football pools

A system of sports betting based around the prediction of a football game's outcome. Although most professional football clubs now run their own pools companies, most gamblers place their stakes with one of three major companies: Littlewoods, Vernons and Zetters. Littlewoods is the oldest of these, and the formation of their business in 1923 became the cornerstone of the Littlewoods empire, which went on to encompass high street shops and **mail order** catalogues.

Littlewoods became pools innovators, being the first company to introduce a collector service in 1959, the Pools Panel (convened in January 1963 to compensate for the number of matches postponed due to bad weather) and the Australian pools in 1951. Dividends were at first rather small, the first million pound pools winners being a hospital syndicate in 1984, but payouts had been creeping up since the 1950s.

The pools companies banded together in 1973 to introduce a new game, 'spot-the-ball'. This competition paid lower dividends than the main pool, but 15 percent of the total raised was paid to the Football Trust, an organization set up by the government and the footballing authorities to fund the game at all levels. The pools funding came to an end in 1996, when the companies complained of lost earnings due to the introduction of the **National Lottery**.

The introduction of the Lottery affected the pools companies greatly. Unhindered by prohibitive betting laws, the Lottery soon took profits from the companies. Pleas were made to the Heritage Secretary in November 1994, and within two months the pools companies had won vital concessions: the minimum entry age was lowered to sixteen, promotion and advertising on television and radio was allowed for the first time, and first dividend payouts are allowed to 'roll-over', all in line with legislation relating to the National Lottery. Further inequalities were removed in 1995, when the pools betting duty was lowered from 37.5 percent to 32.5 percent. The pools companies still felt aggrieved, as the Lottery only paid a duty of 12 percent, but in November 1995 Kenneth Clarke, then Chancellor of the Exchequer, lowered the rate again to 27.5 percent, with a further decrease of 1 percent if the pools companies paid this further amount to both the Football Trust and the Foundation for Sport and the Arts. Half-time betting was added to the pools companies arsenal against the Lottery in 1996.

See also: fantasy football; football; National Lottery

SAM JOHNSTONE

Forbes, Bryan

b. 1926, London

Actor and film-maker

Bryan Forbes started as a supporting actor in dramas such as *An Inspector Calls* and *The Colditz Story* (1954). His career soon evolved to include screenwriting, directing and producing; in the early 1960s, amongst other projects he wrote the screenplay for *The Angry Silence*, and debuted as a director with *Whistle Down the Wind*. As screenwriter/director he maintained a commitment to low-key and bleak dramas with *The L-Shaped Room* and *Seance on a Wet Afternoon*. In the late 1960s, he became head of British production at EMI, but this opportunity did not have a particularly successful outcome. The fantastical *The Stepford Wives* (US, 1974) deviated from his favoured themes, and demonstrated the wider scope of his interests.

ALICE E. SANGER

Foreign Office

The Foreign Office, officially the Foreign and Commonwealth Office (FCO) since 1968, has traditionally been viewed as the most prestigious government department. Many famous names have held the Cabinet post of Foreign Secretary, including Castlereagh, Palmerston, Salisbury, Curzon, Eden and Bevin. In 1998 this seat was occupied by Robin Cook, the first Labour Foreign Secretary since 1979. The FCO is generally criticized by right-wing politicians for appearing to prefer appeasement, and by those on the Left for too much realpolitik. In truth, its mission is to protect British interests in the world, and therefore the insults of its political detractors are, in reality, commendations.

See also: civil service; Europe; MI5 and MI6

CRAIG GERRARD

formats

The introduction of the compact disc (CD) in 1982 was the latest of the new formats to rival the long-playing vinyl record. The tape cassette and the (short lived) eight-track cartridge had briefly threatened vinyl in the 1960s. Conceived jointly by Phillips and Sony, the CD was easy to market: it was unbreakable, unscratchable and small, and these plus points meant that CD quickly became a symbol of the yuppies. The **music industry** cashed in on the market for both new material and reissued old products. In recent years other digital-based formats, such as DCC (digital compact cassette), minidisc and DAT (digital audio tape) have been introduced with varying success. DAT has become the industry standard, replacing reel-to-reel tape in many recording studios, but the music-buying public has proved largely reluctant to buy their collections for a third time, having already replaced their vinyl with CDs over the last fifteen years. The introduction of minidisc in the early 1990s to rival CD was ultimately deemed a failure, due to the prohibitive cost of the hardware required, although it did have advantages over CD.

See also: music industry; music labels

SAM JOHNSTONE

Forsyth, Bill

b. 1947, Glasgow

Film-maker

After an acclaimed low-budget debut, *That Sinking Feeling* (1979), Forsyth came to prominence with *Gregory's Girl* (1981), a vigorously witty celebration of young love set in the Glasgow conurbation. As a writer and director, his eye for the unusual in incident and character became his trademark. He went on to make *Local Hero* (1983), featuring Burt Lancaster amongst a predominantly Scottish cast. It is informed by a Brigadoonish observation of the northwest of Scotland as 'the land that time forgot'. The myth proved its resilience: the film prospered on both sides of the Atlantic. The true story of Glasgow's ice cream gang wars formed a backdrop for *Comfort and Joy* (1984). Several American-based projects followed, with limited success.

GORDON URQUHART

Foster Associates

One of Britain's leading modern architects, often associated with **high-tech**, Foster studied at the University of Manchester (1956–61) and Yale University (1961–2), subsequently forming 'Team 4' in London in collaboration with his wife Wendy and Su and Richard **Rogers**. An early project was a house for Richard Rogers' parents. Foster Associates was founded in London 1967, and includes eight partners in addition to Norman and Wendy Foster (Loren Butt, Chubby S. Chabra, Spencer de Gray, Roy Fleetwood, Birkin Haward, James Meller, Graham Philllips and Mark Robertson). It has become an immensely successful practice with an international profile. Significant works include the controversial Reliance Controls Factory, Swindon (1966–7), the passenger terminal and administration building of Fred Olsen Lines in London (1971), and the celebrated headquarters of the Willis Faber Dumas offices in Ipswich (1974–5), whose curved glass facade reinforces the street boundaries and harmonizes with the urban environment. Two floors of office accommodation for 1,300 people are elevated and placed between amenity and support areas above and below, including a swimming pool and gymnasium on the ground floor and a restaurant pavilion set in the landscaped garden on the roof. Other important works include the Sainsbury Centre for the Visual Arts (1976–8) and Stansted Airport Terminal (1985–91), with its dramatic roof structure surmounting the vast open space of the main building. Such great 'neutral space envelopes' capable of accommodating differentiated functions are a feature of Foster's work. While being committed to the high-tech movement which celebrates the aesthetic of industrial production, Foster is also concerned with what he calls design 'development', evinced in the Hong Kong and Shanghai Bank (1979–85), described as the most expensive office building ever constructed. Here, all the main elements of the building, often prefabricated off-site, result from the close collaboration of architect and manufacturers ensuring high levels of craftsmanship and quality of detail. Stansted Airport Terminal witnesses a similar concern for detail, with the architect designing carpets, seating, check-out desks and retail outlets. More recent work includes a contribution to Stockley Park (1984) in Heathrow, Middlesex, a business park attracting international companies; the ITN Headquarters, London (1989); The Sackler Galleries, Royal Academy, London (1989–91); Riverside Offices and Apartments, London (1990), including Foster's own apartment; and the Library at Cranfield University (1993).

Further reading

Sudjic, D. (1986) *New Architecture: Foster, Rogers, Stirling*, London: Royal Academy of Arts.

HILARY GRAINGER

franchise auction

The idea of auctioning ITV franchises to the highest bidder was first mooted by the Peacock Committee in the mid-1980s. Previous to this, the Independent Broadcasting Authority (IBA) had taken account of an applicant's financial standing, managerial proposal and programme policy in the award of a franchise. The idea of allocating the franchises by auction, very much part of the Thatcherite philosophy of the 1980s, caused uproar both within and outside of the industry. Much of the criticism was levelled by the Campaign for Quality Television, which argued that the calibre of television would be harmed and that the Independent Television Commission (ITC), a reformatted IBA, should have more discretion in the awarding of franchises. The ensuing debate led to a modified auction process being introduced by the Broadcasting Act of 1990.

The Act required applicants initially to meet a quality hurdle before the highest bid rule would come into effect. The ITC was also granted an additional power that, in exceptional circumstances, meant they could award a franchise to a lower bid. The ITC's interpretation of the quality threshold took into account the quality of programmes proposed, the diversity of programmes to be offered and the degree of regional commitment. The diversity of programmes was to be judged against the amount of programmes to be offered in nine categories: drama, entertainment, sport, news, factual, educational, religious, arts and children's programming.

Guidelines for the auction were published in February 1991 and the awards were made in October 1991, with the new franchises coming into effect on 1 January 1993. Of the thirty-four applicants, fourteen failed to pass the quality threshold and the franchises were then allocated to those with the highest bids. The controversial 'exceptional circumstances clause' was never used. Four new broadcasters joined the ITV system: Carlton, Meridian, GM-TV and Westcountry replacing, respectively, **Thames TV**, TVS, **TV-am** and TSW. While some winning bids were extremely low (Central, for example, being unopposed, offered an annual payment of £2,000), others made large bids to secure a franchise (for example, Carlton's bid of £43m per year to displace Thames). Many of the franchise holders are now seeking a change in this arrangement, arguing that, apart from the discrepancy of the amounts paid by different franchise holders, money is draining out of the ITV system and so out of programming.

Further reading

O'Malley, T. (1994) *Closedown? The BBC and Government Broadcasting Policy 1979–92*, London: Pluto Press (critical overview of government policy at this time).

PAUL RIXON

franchising

Franchising is a system where companies sell their business formulas to applicants, who then operate independently. A percentage of profits is shared between franchiser and franchisee. There are several advantages to this system. For companies, franchising is a means of raising their (inter)national profiles. The franchisee buys a proven formula and receives support (for example, advertising costs are paid by the franchiser). UK examples are Hometune, Prontaprint Ltd, Co-op Travelcare and Body Shop International plc. Franchising is expected to increase from the current 24 percent of retail sales volume (1996) to 30 percent by the millennium. It appeals to some members of ethnic groups as a means of employing the whole family and, through virtual self-employment, retaining their own cultural identity.

See also: entrepreneurs

MIKE STORRY

Francis, Karl

b. 1943

Film-maker

After an apprenticeship with Hayden Pearce on *The Mouse and the Woman* (1981), Karl Francis directed some excellent films of his own. He has adopted a number of themes which deal with postcolonialism. He deals with the situation of the Welsh directly and by analogy with Irish issues in *Boy Soldier* (1986) (originally titled *Milwr Bychan*), where a young Welshman refuses to plead guilty to a murder charge when he had killed someone in self-defence in Northern Ireland. The film had a festival release in the USA in 1987. His other films include *Giro City* (1982), a thriller dealing with corporate corruption and starring Glenda Jackson and Jon Finch, and *Yr Alcoholig Lion* (1984).

MIKE STORRY

Frears, Stephen

b. 1941, Leicester

Film-maker

Stephen Frears began his career in theatre direction before moving to television drama in the 1970s. He made his name in cinema as assistant director to Lindsay **Anderson** on *If* (1968). *My Beautiful Laundrette* (1985), his third film as director, was met with critical acclaim and, ultimately, helped launch a career in Hollywood. Although *The Grifters* (1990) and *Dangerous Liaisons* (1988) both received Oscar nominations, Frears' proclivity towards 'difficult' social issues – reflected in earlier projects like *Sammy and Rosie Get Laid* (1987) and *Prick Up Your Ears* (1987) – has militated away from sustained commercial success in America. This emphasis on story over style has precipitated a return to less conspicuously mainstream ventures such as *The Snapper* (1993) and *The Van* (1996), both adapted from Roddy Doyle's Barrytown Trilogy.

MATTHEW GRICE

Freemasons

The Masonic Order – or Freemasonry – claims origins in Biblical times and an ancestry linking it with 'operative' masonry, the medieval guilds of masons who built the cathedrals. 'Speculative' Masonry apparently emerged in seventeenth-century England, as the crafts guilds disappeared. A decisive step in the development of modern Masonry was taken in 1717, when four London 'lodges' (or associations) of masons combined in a Grand Lodge under Anthony Sayer, who was given the title of Grand Master of England. Masonry soon spread across Western Europe and into the New World. Non-sectarian, yet revering a Supreme Being as artificer of the cosmos and reflecting contemporary ideals of the brotherhood of man in practical morality that put some stress on mutual aid, Masonry was suited to the Age of the Enlightenment, bringing intelligent men together without overmuch regard to class. Hostility from the Roman Church, while hardly impeding the movement's growth, tended to bring out its more radical aspects. One aspect of Masonry lies in its fondness for quite complex but fairly transparent symbolism embodied in initiation rites and other rituals, in robes, badges and regalia, and in hierarchical structures within which individual members occupy a particular place until climbing higher.

An air of mystery, even secrecy, veils Masonry. Doubtless attractive to members, this can cause unease in others, who feel excluded. Masons reply that though they have some secrets which they cherish, their attitudes and influence are wholly benign. That Masonry is not clandestine is evident in the sheer bulk of Freemasons' Hall in Long Acre, London, in the emblazoning of masonic symbols on their premises in many other towns, in the role royalty openly plays in the movement, and in its munificent charitable work. Similarities can be seen between Masonry and the friendly societies, which in the nineteenth century often invoked 'oriental' (that is, Egyptian or Israelite) or medieval traditions in style and ceremonies to add dimensions to mutual-aid programmes. Masonry, however, still attracts hostility, perhaps especially on account of its male orientations, and the mounting pressure to oblige masons to declare membership (for example, in 1998 all judges were asked officially whether they were Masons) reflects suspicions that for them mutual aid translates into the less reputable forms of networking, 'jobs for the boys' and 'closing ranks' when a brother Mason is in difficulties.

See also: Establishment, the

Further reading

Pick, F.L. and Knight, G.N. (1991) *A Pocket History of Freemasonry*, 8th edn, London: Muller.

CHRISTOPHER SMITH

freesheets

The boom in consumption and in advertising in the 1960s and 1970s prompted a 'newspaper revolution' in the provinces, pioneered by such mavericks as Eddie Shah, who later launched the *Today* newspaper, and Lionel Pickering. The result was that the number of weekly newspapers for which people had to pay halved between 1981 and 1991. Local papers were frequently home-delivered and free. In the 1990s, however, these freesheets came to be dominated by the older established companies. The Association of Free Newspapers subsequently had to be disbanded in the face of monopoly ownership.

PETER CHILDS

Freud, Bella

b. 1961

Fashion designer

Bella Freud worked in Vivienne **Westwood** and Malcom McLaren's famous 'seditionaries' shop before training in Rome and Milan. She returned to Britain and worked as Westwood's personal assistant before launching her own label in 1990. Her trademark designs are tailored suits and knitwear which wittily rework, update or parody British classics.

TAMSIN SPARGO

Freud, Lucian

b. 1922, Berlin (Germany)

Painter

For Freud, the expression is in the body. His early work seems naïve, linear and is meticulously drawn. From the 1950s, Freud began to explore the topography of his sitters' bodies in arresting detail; his handling became painterly, modelling the flesh with a great sense of physicality. Many of Freud's works have the ability to both captivate and unsettle the viewer. With haunted expressions, harsh lighting, angular poses and heavy impasto,

his figures are stripped of all sentiment. Viewers sense the vulnerability in *Night Portrait* (1977–8) and flinch at the emaciated *Two Women* (1992). As with *Naked Man, Back View* (1991–2), Freud is fascinated by bodies that exceed the boundaries.

See also: painting

NATALIE GALE

Friends of the Earth and Greenpeace

These two environmental groups established themselves in Britain in 1977 and 1971 respectively, with Friends of the Earth gaining instant media attention for its campaign against non-returnable bottles. Both organizations share a common environmental agenda (pollution control, nature preservation, wildlife/habitat preservation, anti-nuclear technology and nuclear arms), but what distinguishes them is strategy and political style. Membership of both organizations grew in the 1980s and 1990s. Studies estimate that about 8 percent of the British population (4.5 million) are members of some environmental group (Garner 1996: 64).

Greenpeace is the more 'radical' organization in terms of its campaigning style which includes direct action and publicity stunts, while Friends of the Earth adopts a traditional lobbying approach, seeking to influence government ministers, MPs and the public about its environmental agenda. Perhaps the most infamous example of Greenpeace's campaigning was its success in reversing a British government decision to dump the disused oil storage facility Brent Spar in 1995. Greenpeace is also associated in the public mind with having its flagship vessel *Rainbow Warrior* sunk by agents of the French secret service in July 1985 in the harbour at Auckland, New Zealand; one of its members was killed.

Greenpeace and Friends of the Earth have, according to McCormick (1991: 158) moved away from 'complaint and criticism, and towards research-based appeals to policy makers, industry and the public'. Indeed, such is the public disquiet and/or suspicion about 'official' science and information about environmental matters (from government or industry sources) that more people believe the scientific expertise of environmental groups such as Greenpeace and Friends of the Earth, which have a strong reputation for excellence and trustworthiness. The transition away from confrontational campaigning has been most notable with Friends of the Earth, with Greenpeace still retaining its radical, media-orientated style. These changes have meant that Friends of the Earth has moved towards being an 'insider' group, that is, accepted as part of the 'environment policy community' in the UK (though not as completely as other environmental organizations such as the National Trust and Council for the Protection of Rural England, which have more access to the policy-making process). On the other hand, Greenpeace has maintained its 'outsider' status, as a less compromising environmental organization.

See also: Amnesty International; animal rights; green consumerism; hunt saboteurs

Further reading

Garner, R. (1996) *Environmental Politics*, London: Prentice Hall/Harvester Wheatsheaf.
McCormick, J. (1991) *British Politics and the Environment*, London: Earthscan.

JOHN BARRY

fringe groups

In the postwar era of consensus politics it was difficult to locate distinctive and coherent major party fringe groups. Clearer ideological differences of opinion within the two dominant political parties emerged from the late 1960s, and factions developed despite leadership opposition.

The Tribune Group is the oldest surviving Labour faction. Founded in 1966, Tribune has traditionally been on the Left of the party, supporting trade unions, unilateral nuclear disarmament, high public spending and nationalization. Tribune was influential in the election of one of its members, Neil Kinnock, as Labour leader following the 1983 general election and moved towards the right with him. It has since been dubbed the 'soft left'. The 'hard left', or Campaign Group, split with Tribune following the acrimonious deputy leadership election of 1981 when the prominent left-winger Tony Benn failed to get elected.

The New Right tendency has been influential in the Conservative Party since Margaret Thatcher became Prime Minister. It is closely associated with right-wing think-tanks and supports free market economics, choice and competition, a reduced role for the state and freedom for the individual. The New Right advocated conviction politics and the need for a moral code of conduct. The traditional Tory right is represented by the Monday Club, which emphasizes authority, discipline, law and order and national sovereignty. It supports removal of trade union immunities and strict immigration policies.

The No Turning Back Group was founded in 1983 to support Mrs Thatcher's policies and to urge for continued **privatization**, dismantling of the **welfare state** bureaucracy, and cuts in public expenditure. The left of the party has had little influence since 1979. Thatcher labelled progressive Conservatives 'wets', and purged them from her Cabinets. They are represented by the Tory Reform Group, who support neo-corporatist measures to safeguard social welfare and criticize the 'hanging and flogging' element of the party.

In the 1990s, divisions in the Conservative Party over Europe were magnified by factional infighting. Conservative Eurosceptics were even refused the party whip after criticizing Major's policies concerning the Maastricht treaty. The Bruges Group, founded in 1988 after a Thatcher speech against European integration, is the principal Eurosceptic faction. Counter to this are pro-European factions such as the Positive European Group (1993) and the Action Centre for Europe (1994).

See also: black Conservatives; fringe parties; Labour Party black sections; lobby groups; Militant

Further reading

Garner, R. and Kelly, R. (1993) *British Political Parties Today*, Manchester: Manchester University Press.

COLIN WILLIAMS

fringe parties

Fringe groups, as their classification suggests, are those groups which lie on the periphery of the political spectrum. Britain's 'first past the post' electoral system encourages the main parties to accommodate a wide range of views, pushing radical groups to the fringe.

Extreme right groups, like the British National Party and the **National Front**, have pseudo-military organizations and are often explicitly racist. In the political climate of the late 1960s, these groups believed electoral success was possible due to the impact of immigration and Enoch Powell's infamous 'rivers of blood' speech, which predicted racial violence and raised invasion fears. Fighting elections gave the extreme right the appearance of offering democratic legitimacy and attracted members of the right-wing Conservative Monday Club faction. National Front support peaked at the February 1974 election, when it received 3.6 percent of the vote.

In response to National Front racist demonstrations, counter-protests have been organized by the extreme left, including the Anti Nazi League, a wing of the Leninist Socialist Workers Party (SWP). The SWP has some support amongst students, but its attempts to organize a return to class through building up rank and file trade union support (see **trade unions**) have failed.

Authoritarian Trotskyite groups such as the Revolutionary Socialist League, supporters of the **Militant** tendency, advocate a policy of entryism, whereby a revolutionary vanguard can infiltrate a host party. Militant succeeded in gaining positions on Labour's National Executive Committee, and at the 1983 elections Terry Fields and David Nellist, Militant adherents, gained Labour seats in Parliament. Militant were expelled from Labour in 1995 after their mishandling of Liverpool City Council's budget.

The British **Communist Party** has moved from a Stalinist to Eurocommunist position. In 1971 Communist shop stewards in the Upper Clyde shipbuilders inspired a memorable victory, obtaining the support of the entire labour movement to prevent Heath's government closing the shipyards. However, despite being able to dominate the National Union of Students for the 1970s and much of the 1980s, Communist Party membership has since suffered a dramatic decline.

A right-wing revival appears unlikely while Conservatives stay strong on nationalism and immigration, as the Asylum Bills in the 1980s and 1990s indicate. Although Labour has moved towards the centre, fringe group attempts to capture the left-wing vote and innovations such as Arthur Scargill's Socialist Labour Party have yielded little result.

See also: Communist Party; fringe groups; National Front

Further reading

Callaghan, J. (1987) *The Far Left in British Politics*, Oxford: Basil Blackwell.

Hainsworth, P. (ed.) (1992) *The Extreme Right in Europe and the USA*, London: Pinter Publishers.

COLIN WILLIAMS

fringe theatre

Fringe or alternative theatre defines itself against the mainstream subsidized and commercial theatre establishment, deriving its experimental and political incisiveness through its own active exclusion from the mainstream. It challenges dominant dramaturgical traditions by focusing on the development of new innovative forms of theatre.

The term 'fringe' theatre was originally coined to describe the theatrical events spontaneously staged on the 'fringes' of the Edinburgh Festival (see **Edinburgh Festival and Fringe**). Pervaded by the radicalism and revolutionary optimism of a younger generation, fringe theatre exploded during the late 1960s and early 1970s. Music, political ideology, performance and visual art contributed to extricating theatre from previously elitist confines. The fringe proliferated in non-traditional theatrical spaces such as pubs, clubs and warehouses, while the ensemble and touring group structures of early fringe formations (transporting theatre nationwide to unconventional audiences) were indicative of its originating ethos as a democratized theatre of resourceful collaboration.

An initial American impetus began with Jim Haynes's Traverse Theatre Club, Edinburgh (1963) and Arts Laboratory, London (1969), Charles Marowitz's Open Space Theatre (1968) and touring companies such as Inter-Action and Freehold. Pioneering early British groups included The People Show (1966), The Pip Simmons Group (1968–74) and Portable Theatre (1968–72). Eminent playwrights like Pam Gems, Howard Brenton and David Hare emerged from the left-wing inclined fringe.

From early fringe venues like Ambiance and the Almost Free, spaces including London's Waterman's Arts Centre, Gate and Bush fringe theatres and groups like Shared Experience (1975), Paines Plough (1975) and **Actors Touring Company** (1978) continue to nurture new talent (for example, Sarah Kane, Simon Bent and Enda Walsh). Selective **Arts Council** funding for small theatre companies during the Thatcherite 1980s strangled new creativity, the boundless energetic fervour of previous decades soundly dissipated in a creatively and financially spliced morass that created a specialized and institutionalized fringe.

With the fringe encompassing **agitprop**, **alternative comedy**, **improvisation**, **mime** and the cultural concerns of other specialized small theatres, companies like Tara Arts (1977), Sphinx (1974, formerly Women's Theatre Group) and Talawa (1986) have survived financial constraints to stage boundary-breaking plays in and beyond their respective **Asian theatre**, **feminist theatre** and **black theatre** moulds. The National Theatre production of Tara Arts' *Tartuffe* (1990) exemplifies the coalescing agendas and conceptions of fringe and mainstream theatre. Through a mutually beneficial interaction, a threatening mainstream appropriation of the fringe is conversely perceived as evincing a permanent fringe influence on British theatrical life.

Further reading

Rees, R. (1992) *Fringe First*, London: Oberon (an experiential insight into the early fringe through former touring company Foco Novo).

SATINDER CHOHAN

Frink, Elisabeth

b. 1930, Thurlow, Sussex; d. 1993, Woolland, Dorset

Sculptor

Born of widely-travelled parents with Dutch and French forebearers, the sculptor Elisabeth Frink spent her childhood in England. After training at Guildford and Chelsea, she taught at St Martin's College of Art. She enjoyed a formative period of her adolescence on the Continent, and also lived in France for some years. Her personal discovery of alternative traditions in other lands may have fortified her determination to go against the tide in the early 1960s when Anthony Caro at St Martin's became the main force in British **sculpture**. Rejecting his doctrine of Abstraction, she preferred more humane tendencies in sculpture, remaining true to a style that, though never literally realist, was always essentially figurative. For her, as for the Italian masters she had admired during a brief visit during her adolescence, and for Auguste Rodin (1840–1917), whose Symbolist sculpture had impressed her in Paris, living forms, especially the human body, remained the great source of inspiration. The male form particularly fascinated her; this may, as she suggested, be related to the fact that her father, who was often absent from home, was always a glamorous figure in her eyes.

Though Frink left quantities of drawings and sometimes carved stone, her favoured medium was plaster, which she build up on an armature to create forms. Others cast these in bronze afterwards, but she would then work over the surface and experiment with different forms of patination, seeking always to control the play of light and to add colour. Much of her work (for example, her *Heads with Goggles*) came in series. After doing all she could on a piece, she might decide that further changes would be abortive, so she would cease work on it and leave it as it stood. Then, after a pause, she would return to the subject with another essay – perhaps several – in the same series. In other words, Frink's work can, even more readily than that of most artists, be seen as a sequence of developments in a certain direction. Though only one of her works – an early one at that – was bought by the Tate Gallery during her lifetime,

Frink received honours such as the DBE as well as many commissions for work for prominent sites. A fine example is her *Horse and Rider* in Dover Street, London.

See also: Hepworth, Barbara; Moore, Henry; sculpture

Further reading

Lucie-Smith, E. and Frink, E. (1994) *Frink: A Portrait*, London: Bloomsbury.

CHRISTOPHER SMITH

funk

Funk began in the late 1960s, when soul music developed a fierce rhythmic drive. Drums and bass guitar came to the fore, playing short, repeated, eminently danceable riffs. The undisputed masters of this sound were James Brown and his band, the JBs, with songs such as 'Talkin' Loud & Sayin' Nothing' and 'I'm Payin' Taxes, What Am I Buyin'; the latter reflecting the fact that early funk music was often strongly politicized, due to the contemporaneity of the Black Power movement. At this time, while funk was itself still a fairly new musical form, its influence was beginning to be seen elsewhere. Jazz artists such as Miles Davis were incorporating funky elements in their work, while others, such as Herbie Hancock, fused the two forms to such an extent that a new genre, **jazz funk**, came into being.

As the 1970s progressed, funk became the major form of dance music and spread to Britain, with the funk flag being flown by Scottish group the Average White Band, whose 'Pick Up The Pieces' was a hit in both the UK and the USA in 1974. At around the same time, funk became less lyrically concerned with politics, and more with sex (the word 'funk' was originally African-American slang for the distinct smell associated with sexual activity); LaBelle's 'Lady Marmalade' and the Ohio Players' album *Honey* are good examples here. This overt sexuality was one of the elements that led to disco music growing out of funk in the mid-1970s.

With the rise of **disco**, funk become more extreme, with the leading groups of the time being Parliament and Funkadelic, or P-Funk, as they were collectively known (the personnel of both being almost identical). P-Funk was characterized by a complex, multi-layered sound wrapped in outlandish cartoon and sci-fi imagery, with characters such as Sir Nose D'Voidoffunk and Starchild adding to the sense of funk as being detached from the everyday world.

In the early 1980s, the complex P-Funk sound gave way to a more stripped down style, epitomized by groups such as Cameo and Zapp, while simultaneously the slick production values of bands like Mezzoforte and Level 42 led to a surge in popularity in jazz funk. Throughout of the 1980s and 1990s, the mainstay of funk has been in its strong influence on **rap** music, with all the varying styles of funk being much sampled by **hip hop** producers.

See also: jazz; soul

Further reading

Vincent, R. (1996) *Funk: The Music, the People, and the Rhythm of The One*, New York: St Martin's Griffin.

SIMON BOTTOM

furniture design

Absolute design values were widely rejected after the 1951 Festival of Britain (Seago 1995). A culturally determined, standardized style and ethos neither suited automated manufacture nor the approaches of a new generation of contemporary designers. The emergence of a pluralist attitude to furniture design in Britain reflected European and American developments in postmodernism and the avant-garde. Aspects of popular culture and technical innovation are clearly demonstrated in the collection of twentieth-century chairs at the Design Museum in London.

Antelope Chair (1951), designed by Ernest Race, is a typical example of the British Contemporary Style (Woodham 1997). Bent metal rod, manipulated into a fluid structural support for a plyformed seat, is more reminiscent of light aircraft production than traditional furniture manufacturing techniques of the 1950s. This new look shared influences with the work of influential European designers including Arne Jacobsen (*Ant Chair* for Fritz Hansen, 1953). As British designers continued to explore the possibilities provided by new production and material technologies during the 1960s, Robin Day's ubiquitous *Polypropylene Stacking Chair* for Hille (1962) demonstrated how an innovative manufacturer combined contemporary design with new technology (Garner 1980).

American architect Charles Eames was a major influence on the work of many British designers including Fred Scott. Scott's philosophy of restraint, informed by a careful study of ergonomics and a fluent knowledge of material and production technology, placed him at the centre of a new modernist movement. His *Supporto Chair* (1979) is widely acclaimed as a twentieth-century design classic.

Leading architects have helped to raise awareness of innovations related to contract furniture design; for example Norman Foster's *Nomos Conference Tables* for Tecno (1986) and Francis Duffy's expertise in office system design have informed many British manufacturers. However, the most important influence on the emergence of the British new wave is the interest and commitment of design entrepreneurs such as Zeev Aram, Terence **Conran** and Sheridan Coakley.

Terence Conran changed the complexion of British furniture when the King's Road Habitat store opened in 1964. Much new design came from Conran's studios, as many young designers aspired to work in his Covent Garden consultancy during the 1970s and 1980s. By example, he encouraged a new generation of designers to set up small workshops in London and other major cities.

An exhibition of Modern Chairs at the Whitechapel Art Gallery in 1970 featured over one hundred designs by an eclectic mix of international designers. Reyner Banham wrote: 'However you look at it, the area worst blighted by "furniturization" lies right under the human arse. Check the area under yours at the moment' (Glazebrook 1970). The exhibition paid little attention to the pop movement of the 1960s, as there was only one notable inclusion: the inflatable *Blow Chair* by Zanotta (1967). The Whitechapel exhibition raised

the profile of European furniture and, in 1971, British designers Jane and Charles Dillon pioneered a working relationship with the Milanese studio of Ettore Sotsass. It was his Memphis Studio that became the influential voice of postmodern design in the early 1980s (Sparke 1987).

Meanwhile, Ron Arad and colleagues at the **Architectural Association** (AA) rejected postmodern design as ephemeral (Sudjic 1989). Arad studied at the AA until 1979, in a time of experimentation and the pursuit of architectural ideas over technique. His *Rover Chair*, designed in 1981, utilizes car seats as 'creative salvage'. After working for leading European furniture manufacturers in the 1980s and 1990s, Arad was appointed by the **Royal College of Art** (RCA) as Professor of Furniture Design in 1988.

Many British manufacturers failed to meet the aspirations of young designers, and a rift opened between what architects prescribed and what manufacturers were producing. Spurred on by what was happening in Italy, enterprising designers such as Rodney Kinsman of OMK (Dormer 1987) began to compete for the attention of influential architects during the 1980s by organizing design and production. At the forefront of this movement were Peter Christian and Paul Chamberlain of Flux.

In the mid-1990s, London reclaimed its reputation as a leading centre for fashion and the arts, and a small number of furniture designers including Jasper Morrison, Matthew Hilton and Ross Lovegrove emerged as members of a European furniture design elite. Morrison's designs for batch production in the mid-1980s utilized manufacturing processes outside the mainstream British furniture industry. A typical example of this approach is the *Laundry Box Chair*. In 1986 he wrote: 'he (the designer) builds his own factory, not with bricks, but from the sprawling backstreets teeming with services and processes for materials both common and uncommon to his trade' (Dormer 1990).

Sheridan Coakley's patronage of Matthew Hilton and others helped to raise European awareness of young British design talent and in 1995, Hilton designed the *Orion Armchair* for the prestigious Aleph brand at Driade in Milan. By promoting a disparate group of individual furniture designers as 'the inventors of cult objects', Driade developed the reputation as a creative hothouse rather than a manufacturer of furniture. In 1997, Ross Lovegrove (highly regarded and recognized for his outstanding creativity in Europe and America) joined the Aleph group to design the *Spider, Spin and Bluebelle*. His new 'biomorphic' designs were made possible by the 'freedom to think about objects using advanced technology in a contemporary context'.

Few British furniture manufacturers have challenged the Italian 'dream factory' ethos. John Coleman's *Zupo Chairs* (1997) for Allermuir (Rich 1998) combine craft and design excellence in a uniquely British style. This successful partnership between design and manufacture in Britain is indicative of a newfound confidence.

Further reading

Dormer, P. (1987) *The New Furniture*, London: Thames & Hudson.

Garner, P. (1980) *Twentieth Century Furniture*, Oxford: Phaidon.

Glazebrook, M. (ed.) (1970) *Modern Chairs*, London: The Whitechapel Art Gallery.

Rich, T. (1998) 'Lancashire Hotshots', *Design Week* 22(5): 12–15.

Seago, A. (1995) *Burning the Box of Beautiful Things*, Oxford: Oxford University Press.

Sparke, P. (1987) *Design in Context*, London: Bloomsbury.

Sudjic, D. (1989) *Ron Arad: Restless Furniture*, London: Fourth Estate.

Woodham, J. (1997) *Twentieth Century Design*, Oxford: Oxford University Press.

BOB PULLEY

further education colleges

Further education (FE) colleges are part of the post-school education sector, providing courses in general education and in technical and vocational education. They have a long tradition, developing from the nineteenth-century Mechanics Institute movement, night schools and technical colleges. Expansion occurred after 1945 when the mainly evening provision was extended to a range of daytime, full-time and part-time courses. Many technical colleges were renamed FE colleges in the 1970s and 1980s to reflect a new breadth of academic, vocational and leisure provision. Some colleges styled themselves as community colleges to emphasize their concern with the particular social and economic needs of the neighbourhoods in which they were located.

Under the provisions of the Further and Higher Education Act (1992) and the Further and Higher Education (Scotland) Act (1992), FE colleges in England, Wales and Scotland were removed from local education authorities and 'incorporated' as independent institutions, managed by boards representing local industry, the business community and staff. Similar arrangements for colleges in Northern Ireland were introduced in 1998. Three particular trends have resulted from these changes: first, commercial activity by colleges, in marketing their facilities and courses and competing aggressively for students; second, mergers between institutions; and, third, increased provision of Higher National Certificate and Diploma courses, previously available almost exclusively in the higher education sector.

A feature of the FE expansion during the 1990s has been the recruitment of students in the over twenty-five age group (unemployed, seeking better-paid or more satisfying work, or supported by employers). Access courses prepare mature students for entry to university-level education (see **universities**). FE colleges are also regarded by the UK government as crucial partners in the Training Targets scheme to improve the qualifications and skills of young people and workers by the year 2000. The qualifications offered by FE colleges include academic 'A' Levels (or Scottish 'Highers') and General National/Scottish Vocational Qualifications (**GNVQ**s/GSVQs), based on standards set by industry, with assessment in the workplace or in simulated workplace conditions.

Current issues in the FE college sector include improving student guidance, counselling and childcare facilities, developing flexible study arrangements, opening up provision for older adults and those with special needs and making partnerships with universities so that college study can be credited towards a university degree.

See also: adult education

Further reading

McGinty, J. and Fish, J. (1993) *Further Education in the*

Market Place, London: Routledge (a review of developments post-1992).

GRAHAM CONNELLY

G

Gabor, Dennis

b. 1900, Budapest (Hungary); d. 1979

Physicist

Hungarian-born Dennis Gabor was working as an industrial research engineer in Germany when Hitler came to power. He moved to England in 1933, and later taught for twenty years at Imperial College, London, where he became professor of applied electronic physics. Although in 1948 he invented holography (a means of producing a three-dimensional photographic image without using a lens), he was not awarded the Nobel Prize for Physics for this discovery until 1971. Applications for his invention were not found until the development of lasers (lightwave amplification by stimulated emission of radiation) in the 1960s. In 1968 he was appointed staff scientist at CBS Laboratories in Stamford, Connecticut.

See also: science

MIKE STORRY

Gaelic

Gaelic (or Erse or Goidelic) is one of the Celtic family of Indo-European languages. The Celts invaded Ireland in the fourth century, and the languages that developed in the British Isles became known as Irish Gaelic, Manx (on the Isle of Man), Scottish Gaelic and Brythonic (encompassing Cornish, Welsh, Cumbric and Breton). Irish Gaelic is spoken by about one-sixth of the population of Ireland and has been promoted by the government and been taught in all Irish schools. Scottish Gaelic has no official status and is spoken by less then 2 percent of the population. Gaelic words in English include *glen*, *slogan*, *whiskey* and *galore*. Shelta is a jargon derived from Irish Gaelic and English. It is used by travellers and occasionally its words enter the common vocabulary as slang (for example 'monicker' is derived from *munik*, meaning name).

MIKE STORRY

Gaia hypothesis

The Gaia hypothesis provides a conceptual framework for enhancing understanding of the global environmental system. It was proposed by James Lovelock (1979) in his book *Gaia: A New Look at Life on Earth*, and based on the recognition that life on Earth has been maintained over the aeons by its ability to adapt to changing conditions. According to the Gaia model, life in the biosphere plays an active role in constantly maintaining the conditions necessary for the planet to support life. Such self-regulatory mechanisms ensure that the environment will remain essentially as it is in the future. The name 'Gaia' was recommended by the author William Golding, after the Greek earth goddess of that name.

See also: Friends of the Earth and Greenpeace; global warming; nature

ROY WORMALD

Galliano, John

b. 1960, Gibraltar

Fashion designer

John Galliano has become the most famous of all the younger British designers. A graduate of the old St Martins School of Art, he now works in Paris for Christian Dior. Since he started exhibiting his clothes in the mid-1980s, he has become known as one of the most innovative of contemporary fashion gurus, one who also seeks to learn from the past and is able to successfully blend modern sensibilities with historically influenced clothes. Galliano also favours glamour clothing and likes to shock, parading his models in satin knickers, feather boas and leather caps.

PETER CHILDS

game shows

Game shows are a staple of **daytime television**, and are more about filling up air time than raising the cultural awareness of viewers. Most formats originate in the USA, and deal with contestants winning prizes. They are based on a formula where a studio (and television) audience vicariously experiences the fortunes of individuals who are placed under pressure to perform. However, game shows vary in their degree of sophistication. Some are strictly informational, even academic; examples include *Mastermind*, presented by Magnus Magnusson or *University Challenge*, originally presented by Bamber Gascoigne and later revived with presenter Jeremy Paxman. Rapid-fire questions heighten the tension. The lights are lowered to focus concentration, and the studio audience registers the home audience's applause for them, in a sense acting like the chorus in a Greek drama.

Game shows tend to become associated with the presenters, who often make careers out of hosting 'their' programmes. Noel Edmonds's eponymous *Noel's House Party* is a case in point. *Gladiators* will always be associated with Ulrika Jonsson, *Blind Date* with Cilla Black, and *Countdown* with Richard Whitley and Carol Vorderman.

Some are clearly about the vicarious fulfilment of the audience's consumerist aspirations. In *The Price is Right*, the audience shouts advice to contestants about tackling further questions. In *Supermarket Sweep* (described as 'like shoppers on ecstasy'), contestants rush around with shopping trolleys to secure as many goods as they can within a specific time period.

Contestants also often reflect the audience constituency. That is, they are often couples, for example on *Mr and Mrs*, *The Generation Game* or Paul Daniels's *Every Second Counts*. Thus viewers of both sexes, and sometimes across generations, can identify with the action. Some programmes such as *The Crystal Maze* or *Ask the Family* use teams of workmates.

Some of the wittiest game shows have followed the lead of Radio 4's *The News Quiz* and the 'antidote to panel games', *I'm Sorry I Haven't A Clue*, by mocking the conventions within which they are meant to be operating. *Have I Got News For You*, with Angus Deayton, Ian Hislop and Paul Merton, takes this route and apart from having an avid following of intelligent viewers has politicians vying for the publicity afforded by being on the show. A spoof game show was offered to an intelligent audience by the surrealist comedians Vic Reeves and Bob Mortimer in their programme *Shooting Stars* (on which Ulrika Jonsson was a team captain). Game shows will continue to be popular with programmers because they are cheap, and with audiences because they are formulaic, comforting and escapist.

See also: talk shows

MIKE STORRY

gameboys

Gameboys are small hand-held electronic devices with screens. They use cartridges to enable people to play computer games. They were first produced by the Japanese company Nintendo in 1989, and are firmly established as an aspect of youth culture. Children of both sexes, from age seven to student years, play with them. Normally players play against themselves, but they can compete by linking machines together. The most popular games are the *Mario* and *Donkey Kong* series, and

Tetris, all of which can be played on the later, bulkier and more expensive Nintendo 64. Because of fears that these machines are 'isolating' young children, age limits have been imposed on some games

See also: crazes

MIKE STORRY

gay and lesbian writing

The increasing visibility and confidence of gay and lesbian culture in Britain in the postwar period has been matched by a growing body of explicitly gay and lesbian literature. Many high-street bookshops now have special sections devoted to gay and lesbian literature, and a significant number of gay writers and texts have acclaim in wider generic or mainstream markets.

The question of what makes a work of fiction gay or lesbian (the sexual orientation of its author, its subject matter, or a combination of both), is one that continues to engage critics and activists. This issue has been further complicated by the comparatively recent development of 'queer' politics and theory that contest binary divisions of gay/ straight and male/female and argue for more supple and subtle understandings of sexuality.

Many fictional texts which predate 'queer' theory, as well as those which are contemporaneous, have explored issues of sexuality and gender in ways that have exceeded the constraints of the explanatory models and taxonomies of their historical moments. In the 1960s, Brigid Brophy's *In Transit* (1969) featured a protagonist with no fixed gender, while the plays of Joe Orton, including *Entertaining Mr Sloane* (1964), *Loot* (1966) and *What the Butler Saw* (1967), foregrounded the chaotic pleasures of polymorphously perverse sexualities. While his plays shocked and delighted audiences, Orton himself achieved notoriety as an outrageous and iconoclastic personality, tragically murdered in 1967 by his lover Kenneth Halliwell.

Maureen Duffy's work, including plays, poetry and novels, notably *The Microcosm* (1966), portrays lesbian life. Duffy has been criticized for adhering to Freudian views on lesbianism and apparently endorsing butch–femme roles that some lesbians

have found unacceptable, but her work has been celebrated for exceeding the constraints of its theoretical framework and for its candour. The criticisms recall those levelled against the first British novel by a lesbian about lesbianism, Radclyffe Hall's *The Well of Loneliness* (1928). The novel, which was banned in England as an obscene publication, endorsed the view that lesbians should be socially accepted and provided a powerful lesbian role model in Stephen Gordon. Hall's adherence to the essentialist theory of 'congenital inversion', developed by late nineteenth-century sexologists, and the novel's tragic dimension have been criticized for undermining the positive representation of lesbianism. In the cases of both Duffy and Hall, the specific theoretical models of lesbian sexuality espoused by the writers have been seen as limiting their explorations of lesbianism, but both writers have been celebrated for depicting lesbian relationships as a vital part of everyday life.

The best-known lesbian writer in Britain today is Jeanette Winterson. Winterson's semi-autobiographical *Oranges Are Not the Only Fruit* (1985) presents a young girl's exploration of her lesbian sexuality by interweaving realist narrative and fairy-tale styles. The popular and critically acclaimed BBC television serial in 1990, based on the novel, made Winterson a household name and offered a rare opportunity to see a prime-time drama about lesbians. Winterson has continued to explore issues of different sexualities and of gender in other novels such as *The Passion* (1987), *Sexing the Cherry* (1989) and *Written on the Body* (1992), and in her short story collection *The World and Other Places* (1998), where she contrasts the intensity of some (gypsies, aviators, artists and sexual transgressors) with the mundanity of others ('mass man: parent, spouse, teacher, home owner, voter').

Other novels of note in the late 1980s and early 1990s were Alan Hollinghurst's critically acclaimed depiction of English gay life as seen through the eyes of its promiscuous aristocratic narrator *The Swimming Pool Library* (1988), which was followed by his Booker Prize-nominated *The Folding Star* (1994) and *The Spell* (1998), and Hanif Kureishi's *The Buddha of Suburbia* (1990) which explored the impact of the interrelationship of sexual and cultural differences on its young Anglo-Indian protagonist. Related concerns with post-colonial identities are evident in Patrick Gale's comic novel *Kansas in August* (1987), which, like his earlier and perhaps lighter novels *Ease* (1985) and *The Aerodynamics of Pork* (1985), features convoluted plotting and a wide range of characters searching for identity and love.

A strong feature of recent English lesbian fiction is the popular crime novel. The best-known works are by Val McDermid, including the girls' school mystery *Report for Murder* (1987) with 'cynical socialist lesbian feminist journalist' protagonist Lindsay Gordon, and a series featuring Manchester-based private detective Kate Brannigan, starting with *Dead Beat* (1992). Equally popular if less easy to categorize are Michael Carson's comic novels including *Sucking Sherbet Lemons* (1988), which explores the clash of Catholicism and gayness in an alternative coming of age novel and introduces his best-loved protagonist Martin Benson, whose further adventures are chronicled in later novels *Stripping Penguins Bare* (1991) and *Yanking Up the Yo-Yo* (1992). Other notable novels of the 1990s are Neil Bartlett's allusive love story *Ready to Catch Him Should He Fall* (1990) and Jonathan Neale's *The Laughter of Heroes* (1993), a bittersweet comic novel that was favourably compared with Armistead Maupin's *Tales of the City* series.

In the theatre, the most successful playwright dealing explicitly with gay issues has been American-born Martin Sherman, who lives in London. *Bent* (1979), his study of a young man's development from self-loathing to understanding and the discovery of love in a Nazi concentration camp, opened at London's Royal Court and was an immediate critical success. Its celebration of gay love in the face of oppression has made it a pertinent drama ever since, notably in the late 1980s when government legislation (specifically **Clause 28**) attempted to prohibit the promotion of homosexuality and threatened the funding of many gay and lesbian artists and writers. Jane Kirby's realist drama *Twice Over* (1988) explored the discovery by a teenage girl of her grandmother's unacknowledged lesbian relationship, and Peter Gill's *Mean Tears* (1987), a satirical drama about contemporary sexual mores, was produced at the National Theatre. This was unusual as most **gay theatre** has been produced in fringe venues and by groups such as Gay Sweatshop, who were at the forefront of gay and lesbian drama through the 1970s and 1980s.

Perhaps the most acclaimed figure in English gay writing is the poet Thom Gunn (b. 1929). Gunn's early verse celebrated heroic models of gay masculinity and often invited comparisons with the work of Auden and Isherwood. Gunn, like the earlier writers, moved to the United States and the impact impact of AIDS on his adopted San Francisco community is reflected in what is arguably his most acclaimed work, *The Man with Night Sweats* (1992). Against a background of homophobic denunciation of the gay community's apparent hedonism, Gunn explores the interrelationship of pleasure and pain in formal poetry that captures personal tragedy of public importance.

AIDS has been the spur and subject of much recent writing including *The Darker Proof: Stories from a Crisis* (1987) by Adam Mars-Jones and Edmund White, and Mars-Jones's *Monopolies of Loss* (1992). Mars-Jones, a film critic and writer who edited an influential collection of lesbian and gay fiction by British and American writers, *Mae West is Dead* (1983), started to write about AIDS after acting as 'buddy' to two AIDS patients. His novel *The Waters of Thirst* (1993) does not deal with AIDS but has been widely interpreted as a commentary on the effects of HIV on contemporary identities and relationships. AIDS was also a major theme in *A Matter of Life and Sex* (1991) by film critic and novelist Oscar Moore, whose own experiences of living with AIDS were movingly recounted in columns in the *Guardian* until his death in 1997.

See also: gay film; gay liberation

Further reading

Hobby, E. and White, C. (eds) (1991) *What Lesbians Do in Books*, London: Women's Press.

Summers, C.J. (ed.) (1997) *The Gay and Lesbian Literary Heritage*, London: Bloomsbury.

Woods, G. (1998) *A History of Gay Literature: The Male Tradition*, New Haven, CT: Yale University Press.

TAMSIN SPARGO

gay film

Gay subjects have appeared in British films in several forms: the new wave film movement in the 1960s, fascination with British gay personalities, oblique elements in mainstream films, ethnic film collectives, avant-garde film-making (see **avant-garde cinema**), and gay film-making and documentary films.

The British new wave acknowledged gayness as a part of realism in films such as *The L-Shaped Room* (1962) and *A Taste of Honey* (1961). In Basil **Dearden**'s *Victim* (1961), a gay married barrister has to confront a group of blackmailers who killed his former lover. Pointed gay subtexts appear in Joseph **Losey**'s *The Servant* (1963), in the relationship between a decadent aristocrat and an usurping servant (with a menacing screenplay by Harold Pinter), and *King and Country* (1964), in which an army officer's defence of a deserter reveals a strong underlying relationship.

Joe Orton's gay fame and writings gave rise to the films *Entertaining Mr Sloane* (1969), *Loot* (1972) and *Prick Up Your Ears* (1987); as did Quentin Crisp's witty autobiography to the film of *The Naked Civil Servant* (1980). David Hockney directed his semi-fictional autobiography in *A Bigger Splash* (1974). *The World of Gilbert and George* (1981) and *Francis Bacon* (1985) are documentary portrayals of the artists. The Cambridge homosexual spy scandal, which included Guy Burgess, Kim Philby, Anthony Blunt and Donald MacLean, was the subject of *An Englishman Abroad* (1985), *A Question of Attribution* (1992), and *Blunt: The Fourth Man* (1992).

Within mainstream films, Peter Finch played a troubled Jewish homosexual doctor in John **Schlesinger**'s *Sunday Bloody Sunday* (1971). Ken **Russell** presented D.H. Lawrence's sexual politics in *Women in Love* (1969), and the tortured homosexual artist in *The Music Lovers* (1970). In Antonia Bird's *Priest* (1994), a Liverpudlian priest struggles with morals and self-doubts before entering a gay bar. In *Hollow Reed* (1995), a court drama centres on gayness as the reason for a man's unfitness as a father. In Oshima's *Merry Christmas, Mr Lawrence* (1983) a Japanese commanding officer is smitten by his prisoner of war (David Bowie). Among the lightest mainstream treatments are Simon Callow's role in Mike **Newell**'s *Four Weddings and a Funeral* (1994),

and the fairy-tale romance of two teenage boys in a working-class housing project of southeast London in *Beautiful Thing* (1995).

Films about ethnic difference provide more substantial themes, particularly in the case of Isaac **Julien** of the Sankofa Collective, whose work situates the black gay man in punk, **rap** and **reggae** subcultures. Stephen **Frears**'s *My Beautiful Laundrette* (1985) (with screenplay by Hanif Kureishi) is a gay love story set in a London Asian community. Pratibha Parmar's *Khush* (1991) deals with the difficult experiences of Asian gay and lesbian cultures in Great Britain, North America and India, in which individual testimonies are intercut with dream and dance sequences and soundtrack. *The Colour of Britain* (1994) takes Asian artists (Anish Kapoor, Jatinder Verma and others), and redefines British culture and ethnicity, using the **post-colonial writing** and voices of Homi Bhabha, Paul **Gilroy** and Gilane Tawadros.

One of the two main influences on direct gay film-making sprang from the avant-garde in the 1980s around Derek **Jarman**, Cerith Wyn Evans and John Maybury, often using Super 8, and described by Jarman's biographer Michael O'Prey as having an inbuilt anti-professionalism, cheapness, and not least, in the hands of Jarman, celebration of gay eroticism. Their influences ranged from art schools, Benjamin Britten and David Hockney, to Malcolm McLaren and **punk rock**, with its anti-glamour and debunking of male technique.

By contrast, the second influence stems from individuals focusing intensely on gay concerns. The foremost of these is Terence **Davies**, whose partly autobiographical *Trilogy* (1976–83) charts the life of a lower middle-class Liverpudlian homosexual, tormented by conflicts of religion, guilt and frustration over his masochistic homosexuality. Davies's *Distant Voices, Still Lives* (1988), involving a psychic, traumatic life history, has been compared to the styles of Bergman and Bresson. Ron Peck's *Nighthawks* (1978) concerns a schoolteacher who cruises the discos and comes out via revelatory discussions with pupils; his *Strip Jack Naked: Nighthawks II* (1991) is an autobiographical documentary film history of British gay experience over the previous three decades. Christopher O'Hare's *Better Dead than Gay* (1955) traces the tortured history of Simon Harvey, who took his own life because he could not reconcile homosexuality with his religion and family. Constantine Giannaris's *North of Vortex* (1991) portrays a Kerouac landscape in which a gay poet picks up a bisexual sailor and a desperate waitress on the road. Guinnares's *Caught Looking* (1991), commissioned for **Channel 4**'s lesbian and gay series *Out*, invents a virtual reality game in which the player selects historical periods or locations, and chooses various gay action scenarios.

A key figure in gay cinema, Nigel Finch, died of **AIDS** while editing *Stonewall* (1995), which showed conditions for gays around 1969. Finch's *The Lost Language of Cranes* (1992) provides a London suburban setting for a troubled family's coming-out crisis. Peter MacKenzie's *To Die For (Heaven's a Drag)* (1994) was the first film to handle AIDS with a comic touch. The gay historian/documentarian, Stuart Marshall, made films about AIDS, gayness in the armed forces, and gay movements and organizations.

Awards to gay film-makers include the Chicago International Film Festival Bronze Hugo (1976, for part I), and Gold Hugo (1980, for part II) for Terence Davies's *Trilogy. Distant Voices, Still Lives* won the International Critics Prize at the Cannes Festival in 1988. Khush won various awards at festivals in Paris, Madrid and San Francisco. Giannares was voted Best Gay Film-maker of the Year 1992 by the British magazine *Gay Times*, and was awarded the Teddy Bear Prize for Best Gay Short (1992) at the Berlin Film Festival for *Caught Looking.*

See also: gay and lesbian writing; gay liberation; gay theatre

Further reading

Bourne, S. (1996) *Brief Encounters: Lesbians and Gays in British Cinema 1939–1971,* London: Cassell.

Howes, K. (1993) *Broadcasting It: An Encyclopedia of Homosexuality in Film, Radio and Television in the UK, 1923–93,* London: Cassell.

ARTHUR McCULLOUGH

gay liberation

To those born after the legalization of homosexuality in 1967 and still subject to harassment, it may seem ridiculous to claim that progress has been made. Deep-seated prejudices continue to block acceptance of homosexuals. Reasons advanced include the nature of homosexual sex, disapproval of making sexuality one's identity, and the false connection with paedophilia, all partially irrational. Gay liberation emerged to address issues arising from such prejudices, particularly anti-gay violence, police hostility and AIDS, as well as attempting to expunge any feelings of public shame attached to being gay.

Public ignorance is a problem, arising partly because discussion or dramatic representation of homosexuality before 1967 was virtually taboo. Filed under 'filth' in the eyes of the establishment, homosexuality was censored out of sight by the BBC, the Lord Chamberlain's department (theatre) and the British Board of Film Censors. Illustrations of their attitudes survive in Joe Orton's playscripts which list the Lord Chamberlain's cuts, and satires on radio's *Round the Horne* and television's *Monty Python*.

Gay liberation did not spring up immediately in 1967. Clubs opened and certain London pubs like the Colherne and the Salisbury were more or less taken over as gay culture began to establish itself openly. Occasional late discussions appeared on television and relevant books were reviewed in the Sunday broadsheets, but real activism only began in the early 1970s after many incidents of violence and police discrimination. The 1972 police attack on a Gay Liberation Front parade in New York mourning Judy Garland provided another spark.

In 1974 *Gay News* appeared, catering mainly for male homosexuals and continued until prosecution for blasphemy over a poem about Christ on the cross closed it, whereupon it re-emerged as *Gay Times*. This bizarre prosecution prompted a determined response. Stonewall arose from the Campaign for Homosexual Equality (CHE), with an intellectual membership base including many who campaigned for the Wolfenden Report that resulted in the 1967 Act. The movement was also galvanized by the fight against AIDS, news of which began to emerge in about 1978, police indifference to 'queerbashing', the age of consent, job discrimination and public behaviour issues. Further impetus was given by **Clause 28** of the Local Government Act (1988) which sought to prevent 'promoting' homosexuality in schools or public places. Outrage! was formed in 1990 with a more confrontational programme, including the 'outing' of bishops and MPs who conceal their sexuality and informed by ideas evolving from 'queer theory' in the USA.

See also: gay and lesbian writing; gay film; gay theatre

Further reading

Poulter, S.J. (1991) *Peers, Queers and Commons*, London: Routledge (telling account of how the gay liberation movement emerged).

STEPHEN KERENSKY

gay theatre

The **gay liberation** movement of the 1960s, the decriminalization of homosexual acts between adult males in 1967 and the removal of the Lord Chamberlain's theatrical censorship powers in 1968 combined to create fresh possibilities for the development of gay theatre. Central to these was the formation of Gay Sweatshop in 1975, a company devoted to producing gay and lesbian theatre by gay practitioners for gay audiences. While playwrights such as Joe Orton and John Osborne had made headway during the 1960s in dramatizing 'alternative sexualities', frequently portraying the homosexual as victim or vamp, the new gay theatre, not unlike **feminist theatre**, sought to dramatize sexual identity and oppression in its historical context, implicitly articulating the need for change – revolutionary or otherwise. Noel Greig's *As Time Goes By* (1977) explores gay male history in three sections – late Victorian England, Berlin in the 1930s and New York prior to the 1969 Stonewall riot – an epic form which combined in performance the traditions of 'drag' and 'camp', a political and celebratory theatre.

Martin Sherman's *Bent* (1979), about two homosexuals in a concentration camp, produced

by the 'flagship' **Royal Court** Theatre and subsequently receiving a **West End** run, indicated a change in attitudes in both producers and audiences. However, the impact of both the **AIDS** pandemic and **Clause 28**, a law forbidding the 'promotion' of homosexuality – resurgent homophobia while recasting the homosexual as victim – received an initially muted theatrical response. Significantly, it was the work of American playwrights Larry Kramer and Harvey Fierstein which received the greatest interest during the 1980s, an influence which culminated in the **Royal National Theatre** production of Tony Kushner's international hit *Angels in America* (1994).

Subsequently, critically and commercially successful playwrights such as Kevin Elyot, Jonathan Harvey and Mark Ravenhill demonstrated the benefits of a return to the 'well-made play', exploring themes of loss, 'coming out', sex and consumerism. More experimental theatre practice was to be found in the work of Neil Bartlett (Gloria Productions), in dance, **physical theatre** and **live art** (for example, DV8, Adventures in Motion Pictures).

In 1997, the **Arts Council** of England withdrew funding from Gay Sweatshop. Shifting attitudes have also led to the reappropriation of gay playwrights from the past such as Oscar Wilde, Noel Coward and Terence Rattigan. A 'gay theatre' was transformed into a 'queer theatre'.

See also: gay and lesbian writing; gay film; gay liberation

Further reading

de Jongh, N. (1992) *Not in Front of the Audience: Homosexuality on Stage*, London: Routledge (informed survey, particularly the final three chapters).

JOHN DEENEY

GCSEs

In 1984, the Department of Education and Science announced that from 1988 a new and unified system of examinations would be introduced in England and Wales (not Scotland) essentially for children in the 16-plus age group (that is, at the end of compulsory full-time education), although others could take it as well. Named the General Certificate of Secondary Education (GCSE), it was designed to replace the General Certificate of Education Ordinary level (GCE O-level) and the Certificate of Secondary Education (CSE). GCE O-level, dating from 1951, was designed for pupils in the top 20 percent of the ability range, who then were mainly at grammar schools with the intention of moving on through the sixth form to GCE Advanced level (A-level).

Though many secondary modern schools entered their abler students for GCE O-levels, the demand for examinations better suited to a wider range of capacities and aptitudes led in 1965 to the introduction of CSE. Results were graded on a five-point number scale, with grade 1 equivalent to grade C, regarded as 'pass' on the GCE five-letter scale from A down to E. The overlap was not entirely satisfactory, and CSE never acquired the prestige and acceptance of O-level even at the point of notional equivalence, let alone at lower levels. In comprehensive schools, running two examination systems caused difficulties. These, it was hoped, would be avoided by introducing GCSE for all students.

GCSE results are graded on a seven-letter scale from A to G, which incorporates ratings from both GCE and CSE. Like its predecessors, GCSE functions on the basis of a range of single-subject examinations, each assessed individually. Schools and pupils select subjects according to preference within the framework of the National Curriculum. The Department of Education and Science delegates the running of GCSE to regional examining boards and groups. Efforts have been made to devise appropriate syllabuses and marking schemes for the different subjects and to find objective criteria, so that instead of being graded on predetermined statistical norms, students are rewarded for positive achievements in examinations and course work (the proportion of which was regulated after complaints). GCSE seeks to involve teachers, under external moderation, in pupil assessment.

See also: National Curriculum; school examinations; school league tables; schools system

Further reading

Department of Education and Science (1985) *General Certificate of Secondary Education: A General Introduction*, London: HMSO.

Mobley, M. *et al.* (1986) *All About GCSE*, London: Heinemann.

CHRISTOPHER SMITH

'gender benders'

The term gender bender became commonplace in British culture around the early 1980s in being applied to a number of British pop stars with a penchant for cross-dressing, most notably Culture Club's Boy George and the singer Annie Lennox. These days the term can be attributed to any number of sex/gender performances, including gay male drag (popularly symbolized in *The Big Breakfast*'s Lily Savage); lesbian butch drag (such as the Daddy Boys, who 'pack' dildos, sport 'clone' moustaches and sometimes take male hormones in order to grow their own); and, an American import, the male to female transsexuals who, sporting penis and breasts, make an event of 'in-betweenism' at New York festival 'Wigstock' each September.

See also: androgynous/unisex look; bisexuality; sadomasochism

CLARE WHATLING

general elections

People eligible to vote in British general elections are British citizens and Irish citizens resident in the UK aged over eighteen years, provided they are not peers, imprisoned criminals, bankrupts or lunatics, or have been convicted of electoral malpractice over the previous five years. Around 7 percent of the population usually fail to get on the electoral roll, however. Unlike the fixed-term parliaments in most other Western democracies, the British Prime Minister can choose the date for a general election (unless s/he suffers a vote of no confidence) at any time during the five-year term, usually when it is politically expedient to do so.

The UK has 659 electoral constituencies, averaging around 65,000 eligible voters per single-member seat, although this hides significant variations. Constituency boundaries are decided every ten to fifteen years by a Boundary Commission appointed by the government. The Commission tries to prevent large discrepancies in constituency size and population, but usually also takes geographical and administrative factors into account. The **Labour Party** in opposition in 1983 and 1997 complained about the Commission's recommendations, alleging that gerrymandering had occurred in the redrawing of constituency boundaries.

The British Parliament is elected by a 'first past the post' electoral system. The advantage of this system is that it usually provides for strong majority government and does not give disproportionally large amounts of power to minor parties. However, it magnifies small national shifts between the two main parties, and disadvantages third parties and alternative parties. This was particularly evident in the 1983 and 1987 elections, when the **SDP/** Liberal Alliance gained around one-quarter of the votes but only one-thirtieth of the seats. In the 1992 election only sixty seats changed hands, and most seats are generally considered to be safe. Campaign resources are therefore directed at marginal constituencies.

The **Conservative Party** won an unprecedented four consecutive general elections from 1979 onward, and served eighteen years in office. The population favoured its tax-lowering agenda and the strong leadership provided by Margaret Thatcher until 1990. However, by the 1997 election the party had been damaged by divisions on Europe and allegations of 'sleaze'. Labour achieved a landslide victory, gaining their best-ever majority of 179, with 417 seats and 44 percent of the vote, while the Liberal Democrats increased their tally of seats to 46. There were 114 women MPs, more than ever before.

See also: Conservative governments; democracy

Further reading

Punnett, R.M. (1994) *British Government and Politics*, 6th edn, Aldershot: Dartmouth.

COLIN WILLIAMS

Generation X

'Generation X' is a term frequently used since Douglas Coupland's 1991 US novel of the same name to describe the slacker generation of the 1980s: a disaffected but well-educated, under-achieving, post-**baby boom** youth group who seemed to feel both concerned about global issues like the environment and the spread of multi-nationalism but also unable to make a political difference. Generation X were into grunge music, charity stores, the media, obscurism, postmodern superficiality and irony, as well as 'McJobs' for which they were overqualified. The following millennial group, Generation Y, are said to be into designer gear, self-advancement, business finance and clubbing, as well as both traditional lifestyles and risk taking.

PETER CHILDS

Geordies

'Geordies' is a term used to describe the population of Tyneside, but is also a nickname for anyone from the region. The word itself is a pet-name for 'George' and is said to have derived from George Stephenson's safety lamp for miners. The Geordie people and their strong, often high-pitched accents have been portrayed in numerous famous television programmes, such as *When the Boat Comes In*, *Auf Wiedersehen, Pet* and *Our Friends in the North*. Well-known Geordies include Paul Gascoigne and Jimmy Nail. Stereotypical Geordie culture is working class and very streetwise, supporting 'the Toon Army' (Newcastle United Football Club). The mythological stereotype associated with Geordies is macho male, as encapsulated in Reg Smythe's cartoon character Andy Capp: a work-shy, beer-swilling, rent-dodging pigeon fancier. This tough, misogynist image is particularly unpopular with local corporate bodies and feminist groups.

See also: Cockney; dialect; scouse

MIKE STORRY

Gillespie, Kidd and Coia

The architectural firm Gillespie, Kidd and Coia has its origins in an 1830 Glaswegian architectural practice. The firm's striking postwar achievements are largely attributable to the Isi Metzstein and Andrew MacMillan partnership. St Paul's, Glenrothes (1957) inaugurated a decade of innovative ecclesiastical architecture, yielding eighteen churches. Our Lady of Good Counsel, Dennistoun (1965) demonstrates their characteristic fascination with light, ingenious forms and spatial relationships in evincing traditional and modern aspects. Simultaneous secular work led to later projects at Hull, Oxford and Cambridge universities, but the fate of the demolished St Bride's campanile, St Benedict's, Drumchapel (demolished 1991) and the derelict St Peter's College, Cardross (1966) mirrored the firm's own. Its premature cessation followed the much lauded Robinson College, Cambridge (1980).

Further reading

Glendinning, M. (ed.) (1997) *Rebuilding Scotland: The Postwar Vision 1945–1975*, East Linton: Tucknell Press.

SATINDER CHOHAN

Gilroy, Paul

b. 1956, Bethnal Green, London

Academic

Gilroy, whose mother came from Guyana and was one of the first black headteachers in the UK, teaches at Goldsmiths' College in the University of London. He was one of the foremost black academics and cultural critics in Britain in the 1990s. He came to prominence as a contributor to the CCCS volume *The Empire Strikes Back*, an exploration of race and black experience in 1970s Britain. His own influential publications include *There Ain't No Black in the Union Jack* and *The Black Atlantic*, in which he describes a transnational culture linking blacks across America, Africa and Europe.

See also: Hall, Stuart

PETER CHILDS

giro culture

With the increase of joblessness in the early 1980s, the giro, an abbreviation for the girocheque method of welfare payment, became an icon of solidarity. Giro recipients maximized available resources. Leisure centres, cinemas and clubs offered discounts. The black and grey markets flourished, in both goods and jobs. With the 1990s, college and job creation schemes became vehicles to massage statistics, while maintaining **poverty**. Homelessness found a voice in the periodical *The Big Issue*. Alan Bleasdale's celebrated drama *The Boys from the Blackstuff* and the novels of James Kelman and Irvine Welsh offer portrayals of life on the dole. **Punk rock** and some later music, notably that of the Red Wedge confederation, displayed a politicization of the giro culture mentality.

See also: poverty, families and

GORDON URQUHART

glam

Taking both name and impetus from **glam rock**, glam was a short lived subculture in the early 1970s, based around an androgynous image. Many devotees of glam fashion aspired to the look of their pop star heroes, particularly Marc Bolan and David Bowie. As with most youth cultures, commercial interests tried to further the selling life of both the fashion and the music. The mid-1970s saw high-street fashion stores selling glittered flares, platform boots and other ephemera linked with glam, but by this point the main devotees had moved on to other images. Often viewed with hindsight as being slightly embarrassing, glam has nevertheless been linked as a direct descendant of other subcultures, in particular **new romantics**.

See also: disco

SAM JOHNSTONE

glam rock

The early 1970s saw the emergence of glam rock, so named because its concerns lay as much in an artist's appearance as in the music produced. In many ways, glam rock was both an extension and a rejection of the earlier hippie movement (indeed, many of the artists associated with the scene had earlier careers in bands associated with the hippies). The hippies' freedom of dress was adapted to the wearing of flamboyant clothes along with make-up and glitter. Gone, however, was most of the political involvement, as glam rock concerned itself almost entirely with the idea of simply having fun. However, one of the main proponents of the music, David Bowie, introduced an element of the politics of sexuality by stating, in a *Melody Maker* interview, that he was gay. For most artists, though, the extravagant dress and make-up had no overtones of sexuality.

Other leading figures in the glam scene included Gary Glitter, T-Rex, The Sweet and Slade. The music they made was largely simplistic, being a watered-down version of hard rock, usually based on a distorted guitar sound; songs had catchy choruses, often based on a chant (as in, for example Gary Glitter's 'Rock And Roll Part 2' or Slade's 'Cum On Feel The Noize'). This style was not exclusive, though, as can be evidenced in songs such as David Bowie's string-led ballad, 'Life On Mars' and Roxy Music's quietly menacing 'In Every Dream Home A Heartache'. For the most part, however, glam rock was an escape from the music of the late 1960s, which was perceived at the time as having been over-intellectualized. Noddy Holder, lead singer with Slade, summed up this attitude: '[Audiences] just wanted to be cool and sit down and dig the music and read deep things into it. But finally everybody got sick of that.'

It was, perhaps, this very simplicity that ensured glam rock's demise. By 1975, artists were either moving into other styles of music, as in the cases of Roxy Music and David Bowie (whose *Young Americans* album, with its Philly **soul** style marked the end of the glam rock era), or were simply fading towards obscurity and a career in small-scale revival nights as the (largely teenage) fans of the music grew up and found newer sounds to listen to.

See also: disco; glam; new romantics

Further reading

Hoskyns, B. (1998) *Glam! Bowie, Bolan and the Glitter Rock Revolution*, London: Faber.

SIMON BOTTOM

GLC

The GLC (Greater London Council) was established in 1965 as the successor to the London County Council. It had an administrative area of 610 square miles, responsibility for more than seven million people and, by 1977, 26,000 employees. Under the Conservative Sir Horace Cutler it devolved planning decisions to thirty-two local boroughs, but it remained an unwieldy bureaucracy. Its best-known leader was Labour left-winger Ken Livingstone, who antagonized the Conservative government by inviting members of the IRA for talks because he argued that the government was not protecting London. The GLC was abolished in 1986. Tony Blair's **New Labour** Party has not pledged to give London back its own governing body.

MIKE STORRY

global warming

Concerns about 'global warming' result from the observation that globally averaged temperatures have risen steadily by about $0.5°C$ over the last 100 years, and that some glaciers and the polar ice caps are retreating. Whether these data are conclusive remains contentious. It is proposed that global warming is caused by the increasing emissions of carbon dioxide and methane derived from the burning of fossil fuels by humankind. Sunlight absorbed by the earth warms it, but the average temperature is a result of the balance between heat absorbed and heat lost through the atmosphere. Carbon dioxide and methane reduce the loss of heat through the atmosphere, and so an increase in their concentration would be expected to give rise to an increase in average temperature (the greenhouse effect). An increase in temperature will decrease the amount of ice at the poles and thus lead to a rise in mean sea level. The possible extent of the rise predicted over the next century is sufficient to cause potential problems for low-lying cities like London and for whole countries like the Netherlands and Bangladesh.

See also: Gaia hypothesis; nature

PETE SHETERLINE

globalization and consumerism

Neither consumerism nor globalization are new phenomena. 'Consumer society' has been a common way of characterizing the experience of living in the advanced economies for much of the twentieth century, and a focus for critical study by theorists as diverse as American sociologist Thorstein Veblen, the journalist Vance Packard and the Frankfurt critical theorists Theodor Adorno and Max Horkheimer. Similarly, the 'general interdependence of world society', as Anthony Giddens characterizes globalization, was probably much more pronounced during the period before the collapse of the European colonial powers after the First World War. However, the notion that consumer tastes should be the guiding principle of social provision has coincided with a renewed period of globalization and has become an increasingly insistent theme in advanced economies since the 1970s and the rise of the Thatcherite New Right, with its aggressive, market-driven philosophy.

In Britain, the subsequent privatization of public services and utilities and the restructuring of the state's regulatory functions during the 1980s and 1990s has both increased the autonomous role of global capital and the transnational corporation, and lessened the state's ability to control them. While it has been pointed out that a number of these corporations now have business interests which dwarf the economies of many lesser nation states, theorists like Ohmae Kenichi celebrate the apparent decline of the state and the rise of a newly empowered 'global consumer'. It is within this context that recent critical debate has focused on the rearticulation of subjectivities and the disengagement from identity with national formations towards a more fragmented arena of individualized consumer identity increasingly oriented around the mass-marketing strategies of global corporations. The notion of consumption seems to have moved away from its negative connotations of wastefulness towards a more positive set of associations including an affirmation of the consumer as an active and resourceful subject.

Further reading

Waters, M. (1995) *Globalization*, London: Routledge.

DAVID McNEILL

Globe Theatre

Close to the site where Shakespeare's Globe playhouse once stood, a modern replica of the theatre has been erected, the first building with a thatched roof to be built in London since the Great Fire of 1666. The project, initiated by the late Sam Wanamaker to establish a 'living monument' to the Bard and recreate the authentic open-air performance dynamics of his plays, has been over twenty-five years in the making and has brought together scholars, educators, theatre professionals and the **heritage** industry. Surrounded by taller modern buildings the new Globe is less conspicuous than the original, but as a historical reconstruction, using traditional building materials and craftsmanship, it is still impressive. The replica may cause the tourist map of London to be redrawn.

See also: Royal Shakespeare Company; theatre

BOB MILLINGTON

GLYNDEBOURNE THEATRE *see* Hopkins, Michael

GNVQs

General National Vocational Qualifications (GNVQs), awarded by the National Council for Vocational Qualifications (NCVQ), and General Scottish Vocational Qualifications (GSVQs), awarded by the Scottish Qualifications Authority (SQA), are offered by schools and **further education colleges**. They are available at three levels, the lowest of which is a broadly-based vocational qualification; higher levels are awarded for skills demonstrated in occupational areas, such as business administration and care. GN/SVQs are made up of core skills in key areas of communication, numeracy, information technology and problem solving and also vocational competence, based on industry standards. Assessment of competence takes place either in the workplace during a student placement, or in simulated workplace conditions. The highest level is deemed equivalent to academic 'A' levels or 'Highers'.

See also: GCSEs; school examinations

GRAHAM CONNELLY

golf

Golf sees itself as having an image problem, which in turn causes an age problem. According to Mike Round at the Golf Foundation, fewer and fewer young people are taking up golf. The growth area is in the over-fifty-five age group. Accordingly the Golf Foundation has opened 223 'starter centres' where under-eighteens can be encouraged to learn the game. In 1998 under-sixteens were offered free entry to several major tournaments, and various other attempts are being made to attract youngsters who are motivated by fashion and see golf as stuffy and old-fashioned.

Golf also has an exclusivity problem: 79 percent of UK citizens have never played, and are intimidated by the financial and class barriers they perceive between them and entry to golf clubs (the average green fee alone is £15). To counter these perceptions, during National Golf Week the PGA pros give free lessons to 20,000 beginners at 400 facilities. This regime produced 12,000 new golfers in 1997, and has attracted a £300,000 three-year sponsorship from British Aerospace. The association with youth is also being promoted by broadcaster Chris Evans with a television programme about the game, *Tee Time*. Meanwhile within the sport itself, players like Nick Price and Nick Faldo complain about the performance of youngsters

who use big-headed drivers which allegedly mask their lack of skill; they want the clubs outlawed, saying that they 'overpower' courses.

Golf in Britain otherwise relies on the spread of its popularity from the USA. The profile of golf there was raised in several ways by the professional golfer Tiger Woods after his victory at the Masters in Augusta, Georgia in 1997. He became a role model for people of mixed race and for youth everywhere, but especially in Britain, where golf was seen as a sport for middle-aged, middle-class white people.

Television has tended to popularize golf, but numbers of people watching the last day of the Open on the BBC have declined from 4.8m in 1990 to 3.6m in 1997. However the number of hours shown on BSkyB has increased from 100 in 1991 to 2,100 in 1997 and the number of Sky viewers from 4.5m in 1996 to 7.2m in 1997. Colin Montgomerie is currently Britain's most successful golfer. New young hopefuls are Lee Westwood (a product of the golf 'starter' scheme) and Justin Rose.

Further reading

Scott, T. (ed.) (1977) *AA Guide to Golf in Britain*, London: Octopus.

MIKE STORRY

Gombrich, Ernest

b. 1909, Vienna (Austria)

Art historian

Gombrich moved from Vienna to Britain in 1936. He has spent most of his working life at the Warburg Institute, London. Gombrich's writings favour broad studies over narrow specialization. He acknowledges historically-located individual achievement, rather than the mechanisms of a suprahuman zeitgeist or an evolution towards perfect reproduction of an objective outside world. Works such as *Art and Illusion* (1960) analyse the relationship between representational art, scientific approaches, the psychology of perception and socio-historic context. He is best known for

The Story of Art (1950) which continues to be art history's best-selling book. It is as much a thoroughly approachable introduction as it is a recapitulation of a mainly male and Western canon.

See also: painting

KAY DICKINSON

Gormley, Antony

b. 1950, London

Sculptor

Antony Gormley creates introspective figures cast in lead from his own body. These forms are generalized to a type, broadly handled and devoid of any cultural or historical reference. At first his figures were implied, as in *Sleeping Place* (1974), or suggested by their absence, as in *Bed* (1981). Their actions evoke states of being and invite the spectator to contemplate human experience. *Three Places* recalls consciousness and *Three Calls* (1983–4) communication. His works encourage physical interaction; the terracotta installation of *Field* (1991) suggests the impact of overpopulation, while *Overlooking Bogside* (1987) acts as a symbol of reconciliation. Through the 1990s Gormley's works became more monumental, culminating in 1998 with the sixty-foot *Angel of the North*.

NATALIE GALE

gothic

The gothic subculture flourished in the early to mid 1980s, and took its impetus from the punk and post-punk movements. The anti-establishment attitude of the punks was replaced, however, with a romantic interest in all things macabre. Gothic style was characterized by the wearing of black clothing, elaborate jewellery and make up (often with faces deliberately paled in imitation of a vampiric look) and long, dyed, backcombed and spiked hair. This look was adapted from the icons of gothic, bands such as The Damned, Siouxsie and the Banshees, The Cure and the Sisters Of

Mercy. The subculture died out when many of its followers turned to 'grebo', a scruffier version of gothic, or to industrial rock.

SIMON BOTTOM

government inquiries

Any institution which possesses power and authority can abuse that position. Moreover, when a diverse collection of people constitute such an institution, they are able to abuse their positions in an individual manner. The British government is no exception, and has had its share of scandals and inquiries. These exist primarily on two levels. First, there have been individual abuses, some detrimental to democracy and the public interest, others just interesting headlines for the Sunday newspapers. Second, governmental abuses of power occur where there is evidence of a conspiratorial nature or of a cover-up. Both types represent a challenge to the efficient functioning of **democracy** within British society.

The 'cash for questions' episode illustrates clearly how individual MPs are able to abuse their positions to the detriment of democracy. Against a background of lingering suspicion, journalists from the *Sunday Times* somewhat insidiously offered both Conservative and Labour MPs £1,000 to ask specific questions in Parliament. Two of the Conservative MPs were interested enough for the paper to run a story claiming corruption at the highest level. The issue went to an inquiry and both MPs were fined for their actions. In addition, MP Tim Smith resigned over allegations concerning payments from Mohammed Al Fayed, the owner of Harrods. As the allegations continued, the opposition, the media and senior Conservatives put pressure on the government for a general inquiry. The resulting Nolan Inquiry, chaired by Lord Nolan, eventually recommended the establishment of a Parliamentary Commissioner for Standards, a ban on MPs working directly for lobbying companies, and a need for MPs to declare not only outside commitments but also their worth. This latter measure, and the establishment of a Commissioner, were approved by parliament.

The second form has recent cases also. Examples include the question of whether there was a 'shoot to kill' policy in Northern Ireland; the sinking of the Argentine warship *General Belgrano* during the Falklands crisis, in which the rules of engagement were changed at the last minute and actions were covered up; and the issue of whether the government made illegal (by breaching or changing guidelines) military sales to Iraq, which was the subject of the Scott inquiry.

The wider questions in all these cases are whether there should be more checks upon government and whether it is necessary to create a new regulatory body or extend the powers of those already in existence. The inquiries that have been undertaken have usually been as a result of media attention, not rigorous self-regulation.

See also: corruption in the City; Lonhro Affair; sex scandals

ALASTAIR LINDSLEY

graffiti

Graffiti (spray-painting in public spaces) has long been acknowledged as an art form (see the website at www.graffiti.org). However, in mainstream society it is still seen as an entirely deviant activity and 'offenders' are described as 'vandals'. It is seen as a crime against property and, significantly, legal sanctions against it are often applied more savagely than are those for offences against the person. A practitioner whose 'tag' or signature was 'Fisto' was jailed for five years (reduced to two on appeal) in 1996. Some styles of graffiti are copied from the USA, but many are indigenous. Nigel Rees has published collections of real or apocryphal examples in *Graffiti Lives OK* (1978) and *Graffiti 1* (1979).

See also: hip hop

MIKE STORRY

Granada

Granada Television is the ITV station for the northwest of England, and the producer of many well-known television shows. The station began broadcasting in 1956, and is the only survivor of the original ITV licensees.

Part of a much larger leisure group, Granada television was founded by Sidney Bernstein, the managing director of a company owning numerous theatres and cinemas around the North of England. Based in Manchester, the company vigorously campaigned for the Northern licence from the newly created ITA in 1954. The licence encouraged television companies to not only broadcast, but to create and produce innovative programming for transmission on the new ITV service. This Granada did, and has continued to do over the years. Its early programming reflected the local area, none more so than *Coronation Street*, Britain's first twice-weekly soap opera (see **soap operas**), and the world's longest running television drama programme. Started in 1960, the Street, as it is affectionately known, became Granada's flagship programme, quickly gaining a dedicated audience with viewing figures topping 19 million in the late 1980s. Other early programming included arts documentaries, one of which gave the Beatles their first television appearance in 1961.

Other innovative programming by Granada included the launch in 1963 of a weekly **current affairs** programme, *World in Action*, which has won over fifty awards for television journalism since its introduction. Adaptations from novels, such as *Brideshead Revisited* (1981), *A Kind of Loving* (1983) and *The Jewel in the Crown* (1984), also enhanced Granada as a quality programme maker, a fact underlined by *Channels* magazine (a US media publication) describing the firm as 'the best television company in the world'.

The ever-changing face of television broadcasting has meant that Granada has had to move with the times. The company introduced a new **cable and satellite** network in 1996, adding four more stations to their ever-expanding empire, which includes London Weekend Television (LWT), taken over by Granada in 1995. Programming for other networks, including *University Challenge* and *What the Papers Say* for the **BBC**, is also a major part of Granada's ethos, as is the production of feature films, upholding the belief that the **British film industry** can only survive with the financial backing of companies such as Granada and **Channel 4**. Determinedly populist but renowned for its quality, Granada has become both the most successful and the most powerful of all the independent television companies.

See also: Mersey Television; Thames TV; TV-am

Further reading

Nown, G. (1985) *Coronation Street 1960–85*, London: Ward Lock.

SAM JOHNSTONE

Grand National

The Grand National is an annual horse race held at Aintree, near Liverpool. It is the premier steeplechasing event in Britain. Among its famous jumps are Beecher's Brook, the Chair and the Canal Turn. These have had to be modified for reasons of animal welfare. The number of horses is also now limited to thirty. The Grand National is a British institution, and more money is bet on the National than on any other British horse race, partly because it has often been won by outsiders at a starting price of up to 150–1. Most people can remember a horse and the year in which it won. Jonathan Powell's successful film *Champions* (1983) was based on this race.

See also: betting shops; horse racing

MIKE STORRY

Grant, Hugh

b. 1960, London

Actor

Hugh Grant acted in his first film while still an undergraduate at Oxford, in the low-budget *Privileged* (1982). He had a gradual rise to stardom through television appearances and roles in films such as *Maurice* (1987), *Bitter Moon* (1992) and *The Remains of the Day* (1993). He became an international star through the lead role in the highly successful *Four Weddings and a Funeral* (1994). He followed this success with a string of films,

including *Sense and Sensibility* (1995) *Nine Months* (1995) and *Extreme Measures* (1996). He has become known for playing variations on the stereotype of a upper-class, repressed Englishman, although he has become as notable for his off-screen exploits and his self-effacing wit as for his acting.

See also: actors (male)

CHRISTOPHER COLBY

graphic design

Although it has been around for centuries in pageantry, stained glass windows and royal display, to name only a few examples, design's rise to the point of cultural saturation is arguably the defining example of art meeting late capitalism in the twentieth century. Creative artists have come to be routinely employed by everyone from small businesses and marketing departments to governments and multinational corporations. Following the impact of modernism on all understanding of art, the increase in the level of general awareness of the importance of design across Western culture since the Second World War is remarkable, as designers and then consumers have learned to manipulate and process all kinds of graphical language across the arts and in the media. Design operates at the border of different, sometimes contradictory aims: for example, it can be used simultaneously to clarify and to distort, as with the famous design of the London Underground map which bears little relation in terms of verisimilitude to the positions and distances between stations, but is much more comprehensible and useful than a literal, scaled rendering of the Tube lines would be.

Graphic design uses symbols, pictures, style and imagery for aesthetic, ideological and commercial reasons. It is driven by fashion and demand, but also creates fashions and desires.

Design in **photography** has drawn on the techniques of surrealist imagery and cubist collage. The importance of stark, startling geometric patterns also dates from this period, particularly from Russian communist propaganda posters. Design is also greatly affected by technology: the airbrush, new paint materials, computer graphics (see **computer graphics and multimedia**) and computer-aided design all allow new ways of either creating or executing designs. Since the 1980s, microchip technology has resulted in brash, multi-layered, easily manipulable imagery which mixes text, photographs and illustrations in a fragmentary but cluttered cyberworld of Quantel Paintbox design.

Typography has undergone several revolutions this century. It is now fashionable to eschew tradition, use precise geometrical shapes, avoid ornamentation, employ photographs for illustrative purposes and create contrast both through bright, primary colours and imagery. In Britain there is a strong tradition of typographical design. Edward Johnson designed the sans serif type for London Underground in 1916, Eric Gill produced the Gill Sans typeface for the Monotype Corporation in 1928, and, most influentially, Stanley Morrison (1889–1967) developed the now hegemonic Times New Roman typeface in 1932. Postwar Britain was largely conservative and took time to embrace the typographical strides taken in the USA, Germany and Switzerland. This was also a key time for the development of corporation logos (for example, the establishment of Henrion Design International in London in 1959), business heraldry and film posters, which fed off the International style of functional and aggressive designs which became somewhat predictable with their sharp lines and loud imagery. The reaction to this in the UK was **pop art**, the first British example of the world dreaming itself American: glossy, wealthy and sexy. The epitome of this style is Richard Hamilton's famous 1956 design, 'Just what is it that makes today's homes so different, so appealing?' One of the key realizations inherent in pop art, alongside the dominance of consumerism and popular culture, was the significance of mechanical reproduction: images were not unique one-off creations, but were to be replicated (hundreds of) thousands of times. This phenomenon led to a degree of sameness across the arts, as images circulated so widely that the knowledge of how to imitate successful styles and designs became commonplace.

In the 1960s, the cut-and-paste amateur collage style was also exemplified by *Private Eye*, a satirical magazine which always aimed to look rough and ready in terms of both its graphics and its photographs, in order to maintain an anti-

establishment, backroom-printing-press look. The other anti-establishment style was psychedelic art, which drew its inspiration from Art Nouveau for rock posters and underground magazines like *International Times*. In later decades, it was probably Neville Brody's bold designs for *The Face* magazine that were most praised in Britain. In the 1970s and 1980s, corporate design has also become increasingly important and contentious. Landor Associates' overhaul of British Airways imagery, from the Union Jack to a sober red, white and blue motif accompanied by a coat of arms, was as contentious in the early 1980s as the colourful and probably short-lived 'ethnic' redesign of their livery by BA in the late 1990s. In the late 1980s, the image of the London Metropolitan Police Force was re-promoted by Wolff Olins through a series of advertisements and billboards using **agitprop** designs.

In the 1990s, the ability to combine the technical work (typeface, composition, illustration, layout) of several people into one person's computer session via the proliferation of graphics software packages has revolutionized design craft and made it into a diverse and pervasive artistic practice predominantly based on desktop publishing. This has also brought the previously expensive power of graphic design into the smaller hands of micro-political pressure and lobby groups.

See also: DTP

Further reading

Dormer, P. (1993) *Design Since 1945*, London: Thames & Hudson.

PETER CHILDS

graphic novels

Graphic novels are comic books (see **comics**) of novel length published in hardback or paperback and unified by a main theme. They can be complete stories in comic book form, or serials collected into one book. Most graphic novels published in Britain are reprints of American and Japanese texts. However, many originators in America such as Alan Moore, Brian Bolland and Neil Gaiman are British. Main publishers and distributors for the British market are Titan Books, Boxtree, Penguin, Manga and Mandarin.

Although there have been graphic novels in America and Europe since the 1940s, mainstream popularity in Britain remained elusive until the 1980s. Promotion of graphic novels may have been a public relations exercise by the American comic book industry to gain a wider audience for their products.

In 1986–7, three key texts reworked traditional comic book genres. *The Dark Knight Returns*, by Frank Miller, and *Watchmen*, by Alan Moore and Dave Gibbons, interrogated costume, identity and power in the superhero. In *Maus*, Art Spiegelman described the Holocaust using 'funny animals': Jews were mice, Nazis were cats. The success of the Big Three led to a boom in sales. Graphic novels seemed to have achieved respectability by being stocked in public libraries, reviewed by the quality press and included in popular culture, art history and English academic courses. However, the hype surrounding the 'Big Three' and the notion that comics had grown up proved hollow when sales slumped in the early 1990s.

The graphic novel audience remains predominantly male, aged 16–30. In the past five years, readership has broadened and become younger. This may be due to easier accessibility through major book chainstores rather than only through specialist comic books shops. Globalization of mass media has led to a growth in syndicated texts. There is a increasing popularity of spin-off stories from American science fiction television shows and films such as *X Files*, *Star Trek* and *Aliens*. Interest in Japanese manga is fuelled by video games and animated films (*anime*). Some graphic novels have achieved mainstream recognition by crossing over into other media such as radio (*Death of Superman* and *Knightfall* were serialized on Radio 1), animation (*Spawn*, *Batman*) and film (*Tank Girl* (1996) and *Barb Wire* (1996)).

The potential for exploration of adult themes promised by the boom remains largely unfulfilled. Mainstream British audiences tend to perceive comic books as a children's medium. Some creators have produced books that explore mature themes. *Mr Punch* (Neil Gaiman, Dave McKean) and *The Tale of One Bad Rat* (Brian Talbot) deal with child abuse. *When the Wind Blows* (Raymond Briggs) explores the effects of nuclear war.

See also: comics; comics culture

Further reading

Sabin, R. (1993) *Adult Comics*, London: Routledge.

JOAN STEWART ORMROD

green belts

Green belts, as defined by planning legislation, are tracts of land surrounding urban areas where new development is largely prohibited. The legislation seeks to prevent the continuing outward growth of the conurbations, in order to retain the contrast between town and country and give the town-dweller easy access to the surrounding countryside.

In the interwar period (1918–39) the major British townships expanded rapidly. Improved public transport and the increasing use of private motor cars encouraged both public and private developers to build new 'overspill' housing estates on greenfield sites. Around London, the extension of the rail networks into the surrounding countryside saw a massive increase in 'dormitory' neighbourhoods providing homes for commuters working in central London.

Frederick J. Osborn, writing in *Green Belt Cities* (1964), set out the arguments for the 'garden city' idea, where townships of predetermined size would be surrounded by permanently protected green belts. Letchworth, in Hertfordshire, and Welwyn Garden City are early examples of moderate-sized towns in green surroundings. The concept of the green belt was enshrined in the Town and Country Planning Act (1947). Local planning authorities were henceforth given powers to prohibit new **housing** within designated green belts, unless it could be shown that the proposed development was limited to occupation by workers in agriculture, forestry or ancillary industries. The counties adjacent to the major towns had strongly opposed the outward expansion of the urban areas. The Green Belt Circular of 1955 strengthened their power: henceforth the green belts were to be seen as devices for limiting urban growth, with the landscape quality of the countryside clearly a secondary issue.

Since 1945, the growth of privately owned transport has led to massive pressure for development within the green belts. Housing developers prefer to build on greenfield sites: building costs are lower than for 'clearance' sites, and the new houses generally fetch better prices in their more salubrious surroundings. Local planning authorities are therefore constantly under pressure from commercial interests trying to undermine the green belt concept.

Proponents of green belts must continue to argue for the protection of the countryside against sprawl, and for new housing to be concentrated within the existing urban boundaries wherever possible. By retaining or increasing the density of the existing townships, civic amenities are strengthened, public transport is made more viable and the environmentally damaging reliance on the private motor car is reduced.

See also: city redevelopment; town planning

Further reading

Cullingworth, J.B. and Nadin, V. (1994) *Town and Country Planning in Britain*, London: Routledge (overview of British planning).

JIM HUNTER

green consumerism

The term 'green consumer' was first coined by environmental consultant John Elkington in 1986. Green consumerism was launched into the market place in September 1988 with Green Shopping Week and the publication of *The Green Consumer Guide*. The event had considerable media impact, and was followed up with another promotion in 1989 and other publications. The aim was to encourage consumers to be more aware of the environmental impact of the products that they bought and to mobilize consumer action to encourage manufacturers and retailers to provide 'environmentally friendly' alternatives. The campaign tapped a widespread feeling of public concern generated by a succession of environmen-

tal scares in the media, and seemed to empower ordinary people to take action.

Green consumerism has its antecedents in a long tradition of consumer boycotts and **political consumerism**. Where green consumerism differs is that it encourages consumers to buy products that are considered environmentally acceptable rather than simply to refuse those which are not. The idea is that business will respond more readily and creatively to positive market signals than to negative sanctions.

The philosophy underpinning green consumerism is that of consumer sovereignty, the idea that in the marketplace it is the consumer rather than the producer who says what goes. This is based on an analogy between the cash register and the ballot box, which is embodied in green consumerism through its linking of consumption and **citizenship**. The green consumer is encouraged to act simultaneously as a citizen, making political decisions and choices, and a consumer, engaging in the day-to-day activities of consumption. In theory this opens up possibilities for new forms of action, but in practice it often creates irreconcilable tensions for consumers attempting to balance 'saving the planet', by shopping for what are often premium-priced products, with practical and structural constraints. This produces feelings of guilt and disillusionment.

In the 1990s, green consumerism is no longer seen as a quick fix to the problems of consumption. Many environmentalists have criticized it for making only marginal changes while encouraging the continuation of unsustainably high levels of consumption. It has lost some of its appeal, as governments, businesses and consumers grapple with the complexities of changing patterns of consumption, but lives on as the rationale behind the European Union's eco-labelling scheme.

See also: Friends of the Earth and Greenpeace; Green Party

Further reading

Irvine, S. (1989) 'Consuming Fashions? The Limits of Green Consumerism', *The Ecologist* 19(3): 88–93.

PETER SIMMONS

Green Party

The party was originally founded in 1973 under the name 'People', to offer radical solutions to environmental problems. In 1975 it became the Ecology Party, and in 1985 the Green Party, in line with its Continental equivalents. From 1979, the party contested more seats in elections and gained increased publicity as a consequence. Nevertheless, the Greens in the 1990s continued to complain of a virtual media blackout, which further hampered electoral prospects already disadvantaged by the 'first past the post' voting system. In the 1989 European elections, the Green Party attracted its peak support of 2.25 million votes, yet failed to win a seat. By 1997 it still had no elected representation in Westminster or Brussels, though it had achieved limited success at local level.

The Green Party has attempted to stay in the public eye, along with the rest of the environmental movement, through high-profile campaigns. Protests in 1995–6 against the Newbury bypass and against the construction of a new runway at Manchester Airport in 1997 were widely reported. However, adverse press portrayal of the protesters depicted Green activists as hopelessly idealistic New Age Travellers and **hippies**, a stereotype reinforced by their hostility to the Criminal Justice Act of 1994. The party has also suffered through its reluctance to act like conventional parties, as in its unwillingness to choose a single leader. The Greens encouraged this alternative image in their 1997 General Election manifesto, which differentiates between 'grey' politicians and the Green Party.

The cornerstone of policy has always been the adoption of measures to preserve and protect the environment, but from the early 1980s efforts to expand the policy base became evident. The Greens favour interventionist economics and provisions to ensure universal rights to food, housing, warmth, education and recreation. They advocate extending civil liberties and reforming the British constitution along the lines of **Charter 88**. The Green Party's left-wing tendencies are revealed in its support for unilateral nuclear disarmament, withdrawal from NATO and the European Union, public ownership, union participation, solidarity action and picketing, and improved rights for women and minority groups.

Other policies include substantial tax reform, involving the abolition of National Insurance and new taxes on land, energy and raw materials, opposition to the market-based reforms of the **NHS**, and the decentralization of power to local communities.

See also: Friends of the Earth and Greenpeace; green consumerism

Further reading

Kemp, P. and Wall, D. (1990) *A Green Manifesto for the 1990s*, London: Penguin.

COLIN WILLIAMS

Greenaway, Peter

b. 1942

Film-maker

An art-school graduate, Greenaway directed a series of avant-garde shorts during the 1960s and 1970s. *The Draughtsman's Contract* (1982) introduced his self-reflexive, esoteric and opulent style, synchronizing text, sound. concept, image and visual technologies to enact a painterly cinema ideal within the architectonic structure of films such as *A Zed and Two Noughts* (1985), *The Belly of an Architect* (1987), *Drowning by Numbers* (1988), *Prospero's Books* (1991), *The Baby of Macon* (1993), *The Pillow Book* (1995) and the *Tulse Luper's Suitcases* (1998). Greenaway's films resonate with enigmatic, erudite musings on art, love, mortality, immortality and the baser human instincts in a cinema that has bewildered and bedazzled audiences in equal measure.

Further reading

Lawrence, A. (1997) *The Films of Peter Greenaway*, Cambridge: Cambridge University Press.

SATINDER CHOHAN

Greenham Common

Greenham Common in Berkshire, an RAF base during the Second World War, became a strategic base for United States Air Force B-47 nuclear bombers in the postwar period. In 1979, Greenham was selected as the future site for ninety-six US cruise missiles. In response to the missile deployment, the 'Women for Life on Earth' collective organized a protest march from Cardiff to Greenham in September 1981, establishing a women's peace camp on the perimeter of the base. The 'Greenham Women' staged various forms of protest, and their camp became a site of pilgrimage for many more women anti-nuclear protesters. Frequently evicted, they became an international symbol of resistance to nuclear arms and cold war bi-polarism.

See also: nuclear and arms industries and protesters

Further reading

Harford, B. and Hopkins, S. (eds) (1984) *Greenham Common: Women at the Wire*, London: The Women's Press.

MARK DOUGLAS

Greer, Germaine

b. 1939, Melbourne (Australia)

Writer and lecturer

An Australian feminist critic, writer and broadcaster, Germaine Greer has pursued her academic career at various institutions, including Warwick University as lecturer in English (1967–72). Her first publication, *The Female Eunuch* (1970), was an integral text of second-wave feminism. It enunciated Greer's polemical arguments about the patriarchal conditioning and control of Western women's lives, roles and representations alongside a rousing advocation of liberated female sexuality. Her numerous other works include *Sex and Destiny* (1984) and *The Change: Women, Ageing and The Menopause* (1991). She continues her studies of women's sexual existence, while her critical

explorations of triumphant and constrained female creativity among women painters in *The Obstacle Race* (1979) and poets in *Slipshod Sibyls* (1995) attest to her erudite and discerning outspokenness on literary and feminist issues.

SATINDER CHOHAN

Guardian Group

The *Manchester Guardian*, founded in 1821 and appearing as a daily newspaper since 1855, became under the editorship of C.P. Scott (from 1872 to 1929) the distinctive voice of intellectual liberalism not only in the Northwest but throughout Britain, although it depended on the *Manchester Evening News* for financial support. Shortening its title to the *Guardian* in 1959 was an assertion of its claim to be regarded as a national paper, and since 1961 it has been published in London. One of the 'quality' dailies in the characteristic 'broadsheet' format, the *Guardian* acquired a loyal readership. By the end of 1997 it was selling not far short of 400,000 copies a day (that is, a share of under 3 percent of the total national daily paper market, but around 14 percent of the 'quality' market) at a time when the *Daily Telegraph*'s circulation was 1.1 million and *The Times* had three-quarters of a million readers. Comparisons with the *Independent* are, however, perhaps more significant, as it was founded in 1986 to appeal to much the same readership as the *Guardian*; the latter outsells its rival by around 50 percent and appears to be forging further ahead.

As well as publishing the *Guardian*, Guardian Newspapers, part of the Guardian Media Group, also owns the *Observer*. Renowned as the world's oldest Sunday newspaper and with a reputation like that of the *Guardian* for sustaining over the years its critical radicalism on public issues and its nonconformist intellectual attitudes generally, the *Observer* underwent a number of disturbing changes in ownership, from the Astor family to the oil company Atlantic Richfield in 1976 and then, in 1981, being sold to R.W. ('Tiny') Rowland's Lonrho conglomerate, before being taken into the Guardian Group in 1993. This seemed an ideal marriage and, at least in retrospect, a perfectly natural one, and sharing a plant offered economies in production. The Group has, however, had to cope with somewhat disappointing results from the *Observer*, despite attempts to restore its old vigour. At the end of 1997, although it outsold the *Independent on Sunday*, its most direct rival, by about 150,000 copies, it achieved sales of only a little more than 400,000. Although this represented around 14 percent of the total circulation for 'quality' Sunday papers, the numbers were under a third of those of the *Sunday Times* and less than half those of the *Sunday Telegraph*, and the enterprise was imposing financial strain on Guardian Newspapers as a whole.

See also: Express Group; Mirror Group; News International; Telegraph plc

Further reading

Taylor, G. (1993) *Changing Faces: A History of 'The Guardian'*, London: Fourth Estate.

CHRISTOPHER SMITH

H

Hachette

Hachette is part of a French conglomerate Matra Hachette, which owns a number of businesses, including media ones, around the world. It is involved in defence and has contracts with government agencies internationally, including the UK Ministry of Defence. Matra launched the first minivan, the Espace, marketed by Renault in 1983. One of Hachette's owners was the international banking, property and business tycoon Baron Edmond de Rothschild, who, though a French citizen, was based in Switzerland and died in 1997. In June 1996 the company merged into Lagardère SCA, a company run from Paris by its managing partner, Jean-Luc Lagardère, who has controlled Hachette since 1981.

Hachette has a long and distinguished history in France, where the company is a household name, known for example as the publisher of France's top paperback imprint, Livres de Poche. Louis Hachette installed the first railway newsstands in stations along France's burgeoning railroad network in 1852, began publishing his *Dictionary of the French Language* in 1863, and in 1900 opened similar newsstands in the Paris metro system. Hachette's current main businesses in the media sector deal with book publishing, print media and distribution services. Possibly because of its conglomerate background, its approach to publishing decisions tends to be strictly commercial and thus in some quarters it is seen as ruthless.

Hachette-Carrère, the Paris publishing house, has a reputation of being 'quality but not stuffy', with an opportunistic eye to the commercial main chance. Thus in 1996 it published the 'memoirs' of President François Mitterrand's labrador dog Baltique in a book called *Aboitim 1*. The Paris publishing division was run for nine years by the Oxford-educated old Etonian David Campbell, who went on to buy and relaunch Everyman in 1991.

In UK publishing, the company collaborates with EMAP Magazines (see **EMAP Maclaren**) to publish monthlies such as *Elle* (first launched in 1945). It also produces a number of reference works which are at the cutting edge in that they are produced by integrating skills from the company's other areas of operation, and offer efficient sources of information. These make use of sophisticated computer databases and electronic information banks. Such publications include *Hachette Oxford Multimedia Dictionary*, the *Hachette Multimedia Dictionary*, the *Multimedia Atlas* and material presented on innovative CDs. This niche in reference publishing, created through expertise in technology, places the company in a influential global position regarding the dissemination of information, as illustrated for example by its ownership of Grolier.

MIKE STORRY

hairstyles

The bouffant or beehive was a standby for working-class women and continued to be so throughout the 1960s, resurfacing in the 1980s with the popularity of American soap operas such as *Dallas* and *Dynasty*. Women began to carefully tint, layer and backcomb their hair to sport a style colloquially referred to as 'big hair', which reflected their version of a fantasy American lifestyle. This helmet of hair as a signifier of female power, wealth and success was best seen in a modified form in the 1980s with the look of Margaret Thatcher.

In the early 1960s, helped by developments in the late 1950s in the USA when large mesh rollers were used for setting hair, increasing numbers of women began to dress their hair at home rather than attending a professional hairdressers for a shampoo and set, using hair rollers to create their own curls and waves. The introduction of hairspray also helped the beehive reach new heights. In response to this resistant consumerism, Vidal Sassoon and Leonard introduced geometrically styled haircuts which required an expert hairdresser and regular visits to the salon for their successful upkeep, as exemplified in the gamine look of Twiggy in the early 1960s.

Perhaps one of the most influential developments in hair for men was when the Beatles moptop was extended within counterculture into the long-haired hippie style in the late 1960s. Long hair became associated with freedom of speech, rebellion and a defiance of authority, and as such was severely criticized by the media, the implication being that the visual lines between the sexes were blurring and the whole concept of gender was in transition. A working-class revolt against the love and peace aesthetic espoused by the hippie was expressed in the peanut or skinhead look, which became conflated with violence on the football terraces and extreme right-wing movements in the 1970s and 1980s, but was cleverly subverted within gay culture with the Nero haircut. The gay man had appropriated the most 'masculine' of hairstyles.

Punk attacked the prevailing natural look in the mid-1970s, rejecting the sanitized blonde streaks held in place by Brut hairspray. The hair many women looked to was the traditional glamorous femininity expressed in the style of Farrah Fawcett-Majors, star of the US television programme *Charlie's Angels*. This rather orthodox version of femininity was rejected by the punk woman, who was deliberately artificial, rejecting society's judgements on what was deemed a correctly feminine appearance and supplanting it with a look

associated with pornographic, particularly fetishistic representation. Thus an area which traditionally signified woman's subordination had been reappropriated as subversion, seen in the use of bleached blonde hair with obviously dark roots to signal female rebellion. The punk style was exaggerated further in the 1980s with the Goth subculture, where a unisexual look of extreme backcombed, dyed black hair was popular amongst groups of young male and female adolescents, who listened to music put out on independent record labels by groups such as the Jesus and Mary Chain and the Cure (see **gothic**).

The introduction of Krazy Colour hair dye in the late 1970s made multicoloured hairstyles popular, seen to their most dramatic effect in the styles of the **new romantics** and pop stars such as Toyah. The New Dickensian look was introduced by Keith at Antennae, who invented hair extensions for white youth who wanted dreadlocks. Molten candle wax was dripped onto false hair pieces which were then entwined with the wearer's natural hair, the process reversed only by cutting it all off.

The appropriation of dreadlocks by white culture was ironic, as the debate surrounding the politics of the appearance of black hair had been in force since the 1960s. In the 1960s black hair was straightened, greased, backcombed and sprayed so that it did anything but look curly, using products like the Yvette Home Hair Straightening Kit. The influence of the Black Power movement in the USA led to the radical chic look and influenced white hairstyles to the extent that curly perms became popular and one could buy the Supreme Afro or Freedom wig from the back pages of the *New Musical Express* in 1975. The origins of the dreadlock were the tenets of Rastafarian religion, disseminated by the popularity of reggae through stars like Bob Marley and the Wailers, whose music crossed into white culture. The dreadlock, like the afro, was seen as a natural and thus more authentic form of black hair and spoke of black pride, while hair straightened smacked of a false consciousness. White youth created matted dreadlocks by deliberate mismanagement in the 1980s and 1990s, ornamented with bells and beads to show an allegiance to the New Age Traveller movement, and thus a rejection of consumerism and an espousal of a back to nature, New Age consciousness.

The 1990s were dominated by the New Age or Green movement where hair products became big business, especially if referencing ecological friendliness. At the same time, hairstyles entered a period of retrospection with heavily textured, early 1970s-inspired looks originally sported by stars such as Rod Stewart and the **glam rock** movement. The short, sharp hair cuts of the **mods** remained popular, as the style was a way for men to be fashionable without compromising their 'masculinity' by seeming too absorbed in their appearance; the style is particularly associated with **Britpop**. Women's styles varied from the shaven head of counterculture and the festival circuit as originally displayed by Sinead O'Connor, to the reverse perm of American soap star Jennifer Aniston from *Friends*.

Club life (see **clubs**) remains an important influence, from the soul boy wedge of the 1970s to the pageboy bob or Baldrick look introduced by male ravers in urban centres such as Manchester and Liverpool in the 1980s. Increasingly, wigs are being used in the late 1990s, reflecting the postmodern notion of a free-floating identity which can be put on or taken off at will and the transitory nature of style in the new millennium.

See also: hats

Further reading

Cox, C. (1999) *Good Hair Days: A History of Hairstyles*, London: Quarter Books.
De Courtais, G. (1988) *Women's Headdress and Hairstyles*, revised edn, London: Batsford.

CAROLINE COX

Hall, Stuart

b. 1932

A Rhodes Scholar at Oxford, Hall arrived in the UK from Jamaica in 1951 and has become arguably the leading cultural studies commentator in Britain. A radical sociologist in the 1960s and 1970s, he took over from Richard Hoggart as the head of the Birmingham CCCS, promoting a wide range of cultural and political analyses. He has been enormously influential in black studies in the UK, founded *New Left Review*, and helped introduce Continental philosophy in to Britain. His many seminal essays have attacked institutional white racism from Powell to Thatcher, and also helped to forge a black British aesthetic based on the idea of 'new ethnicities'.

See also: Gilroy, Paul

PETER CHILDS

Hammer Horror

In the 1960s, Hammer Films dominated the horror genre at home and abroad, achieving unparalleled economic success in the British film industry and generating a host of classic horror movies. The studio's most significant films represent a triumph of creativity and imagination over budget, and offer suspenseful plots complemented by vivid visual effects, atmospheric sets and strong casting.

Beginning as a 'B' movie company, Hammer's fortunes changed in the 1950s with *The Quatermass Experiment* (1955), a science-fiction thriller adapted from the successful television series. Having secured this foothold, the studio drew inspiration from the themes of Hollywood's 1930s horror films, and made Britain's first horror film in colour, *The Curse of Frankenstein* (1956). This venture united the talents of Hammer's most prolific director, Terence Fisher, with actors Peter Cushing (as Dr Frankenstein) and Christopher Lee (as the monster). The roles were the first of many which would come to define Lee and Cushing as Britain's leading horror stars. Hammer quickly confirmed its pre-eminence in horror with the release of the studio's most evocative and powerful film, *Dracula* (1958), directed by Fisher, and starring Lee (as the Count) and Cushing (as Van Helsing). With *The Mummy* released the following year, the studio's key prototypes were established. During the 1960s, when Hammer reached the peak of its commercial achievement, these assorted formulae were reworked in a succession of sequels. While standards varied and budgets remained small, innovation was sporadically offered in films such as *Taste of Fear*, a psychological thriller, *The Devil Rides Out*, a robust story of occultism and satanic worship, and *The Nanny*, with ageing silver screen actress Bette Davis as a psychopathic child minder.

Despite Hollywood's influential revitalization of the horror genre in the 1970s, with films like *The Exorcist* and *The Omen*, Hammer failed to respond to changing tastes and soon the cracks in their output began to show. The studio was still depending far too heavily on overused themes and the results were frequently poor: tired plots, histrionic performances and female stars cast with increasing gratuitousness. However, moving away from horror further precipitated the studio's demise, and film-making ended in 1979 with the remake of the thriller *The Lady Vanishes*.

Despite huge commercial success, Hammer rarely received critical acclaim. However, with the studio's popularity maintained by small screen exposure, new critical responses are beginning to emerge.

See also: science fiction; thrillers

Further reading

Maxford, H. (1996) *Hammer, House of Horror*, London: Batsford.

ALICE E. SANGER

Hammersmith Ark, London

The Ark, designed in 1991–2 by Ralph Erskine, is one of London's most unconventional and controversial landmark **office buildings**. Described as the 'swan-song of the commercial architecture of the Thatcher era', its curved and tiered copper and glass facade dominates the Hammersmith skyline. In an attempt to readdress the traditional form of office building, a working environment has been created in which companies can operate independently while at the same time contributing to the communal character of the central atrium. Designed with ecological ambitions to combat the blight of sick building syndrome, it combines natural lighting with sophisticated air conditioning and heating systems. Triple-glazing ensures reduc-

tion of heat loss and traffic noise from the nearby flyover.

HILARY GRAINGER

Hamnett, Katharine

b. 1948, Gravesend

Fashion designer

Katherine Hamnett founded her own company in London in 1979 after a decade of freelancing. Her menswear collection followed in 1982. She has become well-known for her allegiance to environmental and political issues, most famously noted in her introduction of slogan shirts in the 1980s, ranging from 'Choose Life' to '58 Per Cent Don't Want Pershing' (which she wore when meeting Margaret Thatcher, then Prime Minister, in 1984). Early collections made use of parachute silk, cotton jersey and drill, and highlighted her involvement with workwear and unisex styles, which have since been hugely imitated. She was nominated British Fashion Industry Designer of the Year in 1984, opened three more shops outside London in 1986, and launched her own short-lived magazine, *Tomorrow*, in 1985. Her influence declined in the 1990s.

PETER CHILDS

Handmade Films

During the 1980s, Handmade Films stood out as a rare phenomenon; it was an internationally renowned and consistently successful British film production company. It was established in 1978 by former Beatle George Harrison and financial consultant Denis O'Brien, initially to save *Monty Python's Life of Brian* after it had been shelved by its original US backers, EMI. Although the birth of Handmade was somewhat accidental (set up as an initiative to see through a single venture), *Life of Brian*'s international success alerted Harrison and O'Brien to the viability of a hitherto marginalized paradigm of cinema, characterized by modest budgets, innovation and flexibility, and a commitment to emerging British talent.

In the ten years after its inception Handmade completed twenty-two films, an impressively eclectic body of work which nevertheless retained a distinctive unifying character. Following the controversial comedy *Life of Brian*, a satirical (but not blasphemous) account of the birth of Christianity, came other projects associated with the Monty Python team, including Terry Gilliam's visionary science-fiction epic *Time Bandits* (1981) and the Michael Palin-scripted period comedy *The Missionary* (1981). A measure of its loyalty to participants in its early success is reflected also in Bob Hoskins's opportunity to direct *The Raggedy Rawney* in 1988, after he had appeared in earlier Handmade hits such as the violent British gangster movie *The Long Good Friday* (1980), *The Lonely Passion of Judith Hearne* (1987) and Neil **Jordan**'s successful thriller *Mona Lisa* (1986). The commitment to British acting, screenwriting and directing talent was reflected in other ventures, such as the black comedy *A Private Function* (1984), which was scripted by Alan Bennett, and Nicholas **Roeg**'s surreal oedipal thriller *Track 29* (1988), a collaboration with Dennis Potter. Bruce Robinson's inspired comedy *Withnail and I* (1987), which follows the fortunes of two unemployed actors at the end of the 1960s, is still hugely popular and represents many of Handmade's trademarks: its dedication to new directors, to narrative originality, its shoestring budget and not least its stream of humour and characterization that somehow is fundamentally 'British'.

Handmade's international recognition was achieved despite limited finances through inspired commissioning and pragmatic support. Despite surviving a number of financial setbacks – *Privates on Parade* (1982), *Water* (1984) and the 1986 Madonna vehicle *Shanghai Surprise* were box office disappointments – production was paralysed in 1989 by a series of protracted legal actions against US distributors in the face of faltering fortunes. In August 1994 Handmade was acquired by Paragon Entertainment Corporation, a Canadian giant geared towards bigger budget family entertainment films.

See also: Channel 4 Films; Euston Films

MATTHEW GRICE

Hare Krishna

Known in the west as 'ISKCON', (the International Society for Krishna Consciousness (1966)), the Hare Krishna religion originated 500 years ago in India. Based on the Bhagavad Gita, it teaches that of the four ages in a 4,300,000 year cycle, our present is the most degraded. Thus of the three means of restoring people to their original state of [Krishna] consciousness (mental speculation, meditation yoga and devotional service) only the latter is feasible: hence the chanting of the holy names of the Godhead, 'Hare Krishna, Hare Hare, Hare Rama'. The religion was popularized by Beatle George Harrison, and its shaven-headed adherents, in saffron-coloured robes, were a familiar sight in Britain's high streets in the 1960s and 1970s. More recently their visibility has declined.

See also: Buddhism; Hinduism; Jainism

MIKE STORRY

Harpers and Queen

Two long-established women's magazines, *The Queen* (begun in 1861) and *Harper's Bazaar* (1929), merged in 1970 to become *Harpers and Queen*. The hybrid is a monthly publication which specializes in fashion and articles covering the social calendar of the British upper classes. Most well-known of its columns has been 'Jennifer's Diary', a regular society review piece written by Betty Kenward for forty-seven years (to 1991) about parties and entertaining (the column had previously appeared in the *Tatler*). Other main subjects are property, education, antiques, the environment, travel, health and beauty. The magazine's subscription advertisements declare that '*Harpers and Queen* is the smartest, most elegant, and up-to-date magazine for the discerning reader.' Recent contributors have included Lloyd Grossman and Auberon Waugh. *Harpers and Queen* targets a wealthy upper-class female audience, and deals with haute couture, expensive travel and property. Its circulation has declined from 98,900 (1987) to 73,546 (1995), but advertising rates are sufficiently high to keep it viable.

See also: women's press

MIKE STORRY

HARVEY COURT, CAIUS COLLEGE, CAMBRIDGE *see* Leslie Martin, Colin St John Wilson

Harvey Nichols

Currently one of London's best-known fashion outlets, the Harvey Nichols store in Knightsbridge was founded in 1817. It has gained a growing reputation for offering collections by cutting-edge contemporary designers, and now has its own Harvey Nichols womenswear collection, heavily influenced by Hong Kong designers since the store was taken over by Dickson Concepts of Hong Kong in 1991. The store featured regularly as the favourite haunt of fashion victims Edina and Patsy in the popular BBC **situation comedy** *Absolutely Fabulous*, who were frequently seen laden with purchases from 'Harvey Nicks'.

TAMSIN SPARGO

hats

The postwar trend towards informal and youth-oriented fashions was marked by the decline of the hat as essential attire for the well-dressed woman or man. Throughout the 1950s, 1960s and 1970s, hats were increasingly reserved for an ever-diminishing range of special occasions such as weddings, formal public functions and events such as Ladies Day at the Ascot races. Although the latter provided newspapers and magazines with striking, and often ludicrous, images of the milliner's art (typified by the hats of self-taught hatmaker David Shilling, whose mother Gertrude appeared annually in one of his most ambitious creations), the survival of the hat in British fashion during this period can probably be ascribed to its role in street fashion. At different moments, berets, baseball caps and other workwear or sports headgear have remained popular with young people, who would rarely if ever wear the formal hats of an older generation.

One influential development in Britain in the 1990s was the trend for handmade soft fabric hats sold at music festivals and alternative events. These updated pastiches of the brightly coloured 'motley' of Elizabethan fools, including giant jester's hats, brightened the image of 'crusties' and other alternative groups.

The 1990s also saw the revival of more formal styles of dressing, and the growth of the British fashion industry has encouraged a resurgence of the milliner's art. The creations of designers such as Stephen Jones and the Irish-born, London-based Philip Treacy are not conventional final touches to an outfit (like many earlier models), but elaborate, often witty or outrageous creations which command attention in their own right. Hats featured in catwalk shows are often dramatic artworks, made of unconventional materials or covering half the model's body, and are designed for maximum visual impact rather than practicality, but their influence can be seen in more wearable designs available in the high street.

See also: hairstyles

TAMSIN SPARGO

Hawking, Stephen

b. 1942, Oxford

Physicist

Stephen Hawking's best-selling book on quantum physics, relativity, time and space was written from his wheelchair, to which he is confined by motor neurone disease. The book, *A Brief History of Time*, makes accessible some of the fundamental notions regarding space and time in an engaging and fascinating way. It also introduces rather controversial proposals, including the backward running of time and the anthropic principle, which proposes that only a deity could have so organized the fundamental properties of matter to allow life, and human beings in particular, to evolve. It became one of an increasing number of scientific books which have sold in large numbers to non-scientists.

See also: science

PETE SHETERLINE

health policies and the NHS

The National Health Service (**NHS**) was set up in 1948, as a bureaucratic, centrally controlled system whereby health care was available to all on the basis of need, free at the point of delivery and funded by taxation. The NHS was based on a tripartite structure with discrete functions for general practitioners (GPs), hospital doctors and local authority medical officers. Significant advancements in medical technology and an ageing population have meant that demand for health care has continued to rise, causing serious funding difficulties. Hence, the priority of the Department of Health has been to obtain value for money in health care spending.

By the late 1970s the NHS faced escalating costs and a growing sense of crisis, exacerbated by the industrial unrest and economic difficulties which characterized the period. The Thatcher government was committed to health service reform, highlighting the importance of primary care and the role of the voluntary and private sectors. In 1983, features of business management were adopted to improve NHS efficiency, including the creation of a supervisory board headed by the Minister of Health and the NHS Executive to oversee the running of the service. Further reforms in the 1980s included the deregulation of optical services and competitive tendering of catering, domestic and laundry services.

The most radical change to the workings of the NHS came with the 1990 NHS and Community Care Act, which created the internal market to promote competition between those supplying health services. Large public hospitals could become self-governing trusts and were able to raise income and capital and set pay scales for employees. The Act also gave wealthier GPs the option to become fundholders, paid on a cost per case basis. Any savings made by fundholders could be reinvested in their practices.

Widespread criticism continues to be levelled at the 1990 reforms, centred on the speed of change,

paucity of funds for start-up costs, lack of operational guidelines and reduced equity of access to similar services. Market mechanisms could not compensate for underfunding, and genuine competition did not exist between health authorities and trusts as patients were unwilling to travel long distances. In 1993 the NHS had almost one million people on waiting lists, and funding was one-quarter below the EU average. By the end of the 1997 financial year, two-thirds of NHS trusts were operating at a loss.

Further reading

Allsop, J. (1995) *Health Policy and the NHS Towards 2000*, 2nd edn, London: Longman.

COLIN WILLIAMS

heavy metal

The roots of heavy metal lie in the rhythm and blues movement of the 1960s. Gradually, the basic blues sound became 'heavier', with the distorted guitar coming to the forefront. By the early 1970s a distinct sound had evolved, with bands such as Black Sabbath, Led Zeppelin and Deep Purple leading the field. Examples of this first heavy metal sound can be found on albums such as Black Sabbath's *Paranoid* and Deep Purple *In Rock* (both 1970). Lyrically, heavy metal regularly retained the subject matter of its precursor – drinking and womanizing – but it also frequently concerned itself with the world of the mystical, and was occasionally accused of being satanic in nature; this image was enhanced by its being the music choice of biker gangs such as the **Hell's Angels**.

In the dress code of the bikers – denim jeans and denim or leather jackets – fans of heavy metal grew steadily in their numbers through the 1970s, and while the music never attained mass popularity (heavy metal singles rarely reached the charts), these fans proved to be steadfastly loyal to the music. By the early 1980s, a second generation of heavy metal bands had come into existence. These bands, christened the New Wave Of British Heavy Metal, or NWOBHM, by the music press, pushed the guitar further into the spotlight, with ever faster and more complex riffs coming to dominate the music. Chief among the NWOBHM bands were Gillan, Saxon and Iron Maiden. The latter's *The Number Of The Beast* album (1982) is perhaps the archetypal example of this sound.

At the same time as the NWOBHM was at the forefront of heavy metal, another style was developing which concentrated less on musicality and more on sheer speed and power. Bands such as Venom were the pioneers of this sound, which came to be variously known as black metal, death metal and, most popularly, thrash metal. While mainstream heavy metal had gained corporate acceptance, this new style was more underground, with small independent labels such as Neat Records and (later) Peaceville championing the scene. By the early 1990s, thrash metal was a major force within heavy metal and had widened the fanbase, drawing many ex-punks into the scene. The American 'grunge' movement has also influenced heavy metal in the 1990s, resulting in many bands turning away from speed and complexity and favouring instead a more traditional rock sound.

SIMON BOTTOM

Hell's Angels

Hell's Angels were US gangs of Harley Davidson motorcycle riders who wanted to continue the camaraderie of the Second World War. A London chapter was authorized from Oakland, California, in 1968. The original Angels inspired the film *The Wild One* with Marlon Brando, and the song 'Leader of the Pack' (1965). They practised violence, drug use and general anti-social behaviour. A more 'respectable' brand of independent, maverick Angel is based on the film *Easy Rider* with Peter Fonda, and a majority of British Angels follow this model. They have appeared in the media sporadically, usually in the context of a suburban nightmare: they were deemed the 'neighbours from hell' in a long running court case in Reading.

See also: heavy metal

MIKE STORRY

Henley Regatta

The Henley Royal Regatta, as it is formally known, was first held in 1839. As much a date on the social calendar as a sporting tournament, Henley still exudes a prewar upper-class charm, attracting non-participants who are eager just to be seen there. The popularity of the regatta has seen the tournament increase from an afternoon's **rowing** to fully two weeks of qualification and knockout competition. The regatta gained royal patronage in 1851 from the Prince Consort, and is still frequented by some members of the Royal Family. The sixteen competitive rowing events are all recognized formally by the sport's governing bodies, although Henley has the unique distinction of not being subject to any rowing federation rules.

SAM JOHNSTONE

Hepworth, Barbara

b. 1903, Wakefield; d. 1975, St Ives

Sculptor

Barbara Hepworth studied with Henry **Moore** at Leeds School of Art and later at the Royal College of Art in London. After completing her studies in 1924, she obtained a scholarship to travel and study in Italy for a year. During this period she was greatly influenced by the quality and power of light and its impact on colour and form (in much the same way as the impressionist painters before her), and by the sculptural forms of painters such as Masaccio.

During the period 1931–9, Hepworth and Moore were subject to similar influences, particularly the work produced by Gaudier and Epstein at the height of the Vorticist Movement, although some differences were already emerging. In 1931 Hepworth became a member of the 'Seven and Five Society', a group of seven painters and five sculptors including Moore. It was at around this time she met the painter Ben **Nicholson** (also a member), who, as well as later becoming her second husband, was also to be a major influence on her work.

It was in the early 1930s that her work took a real turn towards abstraction, perhaps best demonstrated by the sculpture *Pierced Form*, in which a hole was punched through a closed form. The use of the 'hole' was to be much further developed by both herself and Moore, and she appears to have been the first sculptor in England to use it. During the 1930s, working mainly in wood and stone, her work became increasingly abstract; after 1938 she began to move away from piercing forms with holes and began opening the holes out into different shapes and including strings and colour in her work. At the beginning of the war she moved to St Ives in Cornwall, where she drew inspiration from her observation and experience of the Cornish landscape.

In the early 1950s she parted from Ben Nicholson and began both working on a larger scale and experimenting in bronze, characteristics which marked the next phase of her work and which also bought international recognition. Subsequently she also worked in concrete and aluminium. She died on 21 May 1975 in a fire at Trewyn Studio (now reconditioned as a museum) in St Ives. Her work can be seen at locations in Britain, Europe and USA.

See also: sculpture; St Ives

Further reading

Curtis, P. (1998) *Barbara Hepworth*, St Ives Artists series, London: Tate Gallery Publishing.
Hammacher, A.M. (1987) *Barbara Hepworth*, revised edn, London: Thames & Hudson.

HELEN COOKE

heritage

The term 'heritage' is used to mean both the physical remains of Britain's past and the ideological use of that past in films, television, advertising and other media. The former sense often extends to the recent past (Paul McCartney's childhood home from the 1960s was acquired by the National Trust in 1998) and the latter has become the basis for Britain's 'heritage industry'.

A measure of how important certain buildings are is whether they are 'listed' by the Department of the Environment (which means they have restrictions placed on their alteration, refurbishment or demolition). Although Thatcherism opposed state intervention, during that era the number of listed buildings doubled and there are now 500,000 in England and Wales, as well as 42,000 in Scotland. Many twentieth-century buildings, such as Battersea Power Station, are now listed.

The launch in 1984 of English Heritage enabled the regeneration of projects such as Liverpool's Grade I-listed Albert Dock. Under the Labour government, English Heritage still receives over £100m annually, but its decisions, such as that to make one of its priorities 'the heritage of the future', encouraged government ministers to think it had lost its way; it is being forced to move from its London base to the regions. However, the establishment of a Department of National Heritage and of the Heritage Lottery Fund (with an income of £300m per year) has made the greatest impact on Britain's heritage of important buildings. Works like the restoration of the Albert Memorial would never have taken place without it.

Britain's great cathedrals, particularly the medieval ones – Chester, York, Winchester and Durham – were already ensuring their future through marketing themselves to tourists. However, heritage is used to sell products to other markets than tourists. Britons buy a version of themselves which is packaged in television series like *Inspector Morse* or *Heartbeat*, whose characters inhabit a world far removed from that of people who live in urban high-rise flats or semi-detached suburban houses. Films of the 1980s and 1990s, such as *The Remains of the Day* or *A Month in the Country* or Merchant-Ivory's oeuvre (see **Merchant-Ivory Productions**), are sold around the world as an image of an ideal Britain. Common elements of the aristocracy, venerable buildings and English eccentrics occur over and over in such films, offering a picture of a quaint, genteel and gentle England. They are eagerly consumed by Britons themselves as a kind of national myth.

See also: National Lottery

Further reading

Storry, M. and Childs, P. (1997) *British Cultural Identities*, London: Routledge, 1997.

MIKE STORRY

Hewish, Antony and Martin Ryle

Hewish b. 1924; Ryle b. 1918, Brighton; d. 1984, Cambridge

Astronomers

In 1959, Cambridge University appointed Martin Ryle to a new Chair of Radio Astronomy; in 1972 he was appointed Astronomer Royal. He and Antony Hewish worked under J.A. Ratcliffe at the Cavendish Laboratory, Cambridge. Ryle and Hewish were awarded the Nobel Prize for Physics in 1974 for their pioneering research in radio astrophysics: Ryle for his observations and inventions, in particular of the aperture synthesis technique and Hewish for his decisive role in the discovery of pulsars. Winning the Nobel Prize raised the international profile of British science, and also popularized it. Hewish contributed to the Royal Institution's well-known Christmas lectures, which were televised and became annual media events because of their accessibility, particularly to the young.

See also: science

MIKE STORRY

high-tech

The design style known as 'high-tech', associated with the work of architects Richard **Rogers**, Norman Foster (see **Foster Associates**), Nicholas Grimshaw and Michael **Hopkins**, was pioneered in Britain in the early 1970s. Although in the USA the term refers principally to an architectural style, in Britain high-tech points to a more rigorous approach in which advanced technology is acknowledged as representing the 'spirit of the age'. The aesthetics of industrial production and machine technology are celebrated and embodied in the methodology of design production. Industry is a source for both technology and imagery. Principally associated with factory and business applications, although now adopted for supermarkets, leisure centres, art galleries and modern offices in 'science parks', high-tech balances function and representation, engineering and architecture, at once symbolizing and representing technology rather than simply using it efficiently. The functional tradition of nineteenth-century architecture, together with important precursors, Sant'Elia, Mies van der Rohe, Mart Stam, Charles Eames, the Russian constuctivists, Buckminster Fuller, Archigram and the Japanese metabolises, all contributed to contemporary high-tech.

Distinguished by exposed steel structures and services, visible air conditioning ducts, renewable plug-in service pods and the characteristic use of metal and glass and suspension structures, high-tech buildings demonstrate the high priority placed on flexibility of use, witnessed particularly in the 'omniplatz', where internal and external spaces are conceived as serviced zones. The most distinctive example is the Pompidou Centre (1971–7), the six-storey 'cultural machine' designed by Piano and Rogers. Interpretations of high-tech vary, with Foster favouring a smooth exterior as at the Sainsbury Centre for the Visual Arts, Norwich (1977), and Rogers preferring to use more visceral compositions to dramatize function. Development can be traced from Foster and Rogers's Reliance Controls Factory in Swindon (1967) and the Pompidou Centre, to the Lloyd's Building, London (1978–86) by Rogers and the Shanghai Bank Building, Hong Kong by Foster (1989). Grimshaw argues, 'Our buildings are unusually economical and reflect the absolute necessity of conserving energy and saving resources', indicating significance beyond pristine metal-clad exteriors. Some early high-tech buildings are already deteriorating, which, as Diane Ghirardo points out, 'leads directly to a major problem of emphatically high-tech architecture: the strident application of technological appendages evinces a view of technology as aesthetic scenography rather than a type of architectural knowledge bound up within a broad and continuing research project'.

See also: Archigram; Foster Associates

Further reading

Davies, C. (1988) *High-Tech Architecture*, New York: Rizzoli.

HILARY GRAINGER

Highland Games

The Highland Games (or 'Heavy Events'), one of the most enduring images of Scotland today, help preserve forms of traditional Celtic sport and include events for men and women. The most famous event is tossing the caber, but others include throwing a weight for distance, the farmer's walk (carrying weights of 300 pounds), the Scottish hammer and putting the stone. Strength alone is not enough for these events, and good technique is essential. The Highland Games are steeped in important cultural imagery (with most competitors eligible to wear a kilt), sustaining traditional Scottish sporting culture, and they now represent sporting landlords, the ascendancy of the landed classes and a romanticized Scottish cultural identity.

Further reading

Jarvie, G. (1991) *Highland Games: The Making of the Myth*, Edinburgh: Edinburgh University Press.

REX NASH

HILLINGDON CIVIC CENTRE *see* Robert Matthew Johnson-Marshall and Partners

Hinduism

Ever since the British colonized the Indian subcontinent, Hindus have in their turn travelled to Britain, bringing with them the traditions and customs of a religion much older than Christianity. Hinduism, with its many gods and varied procedures of worship, is a religion of tremendous complexity, and in the process of its transplantation to Britain it has been adapted and redefined. Although there had been a steady migration of Indians to Britain after the Second World War, most tended to be from the Punjab and were therefore Sikhs.

In 1974, following General Idi Amin's order to all South Asian British passport-holders to quit Uganda, many Gujurati-speaking people sought refuge in Britain. The arrival of these Hindu refugees meant that Hindu religious institutions became firmly established in Britain. Hitherto, the religion had been propagated by various visiting holy men seeking British converts. A mission centre had been set up in London during the 1930s by a monk from the Ramakrishna mission, whose central office was in Calcutta. An English benefactor enabled the mission to purchase a property and establish a monastic community in North London, which provided Britain's first public place of worship for Hindus. By the late 1980s there were over a hundred Hindu temples in Britain, and the number is still increasing.

The religions of India caught the imagination of the general public in Britain, particularly that of disaffected youth, with the arrival on the scene of the Maharishi Mahesh Yogi in the 1960s. Interest was greatly enhanced by the devotion shown to the guru by the Beatles, particularly George Harrison, who made much publicized visits to the Indian holy man. The best-known branch of Hinduism in Britain is probably the International Society for Krishna Consciousness (ISKCON), founded by His Divine Grace A.C. Bhaktivedanta Swami Prabhupada. The movement arrived in Britain via the USA in the wake of the counterculture, bringing with it an appealing message of peace and harmony, and it continues to thrive. The best known ISKCON centre is probably Bhaktivedanta Manor in Letchmore Heath, Watford. Although 'Krishna Consciousness' is a modern term, the message it contains is definitely traditional and has its roots in a sixteenth-century movement associated with a Hindu saint. The regular gatherings at Bhaktivedanta Manor are attended by both Asian and British devotees and demonstrate how the religion has adapted within a Western milieu.

See also: Buddhism; Hare Krishna; Jainism

Further reading

Stutley, M. (1977) *A Dictionary of Hinduism*, London: Routledge & Kegan Paul.

JAN EVANS

hip hop

In 1979, when the Sugarhill Gang's 'Rapper's Delight' began with the words, 'I said a hip, hop, a hippit, a hippit to the hip hip hop, you don't stop the rock,' a name was found for the burgeoning street culture of urban New York. Hip hop culture is usually associated with rap music, but has in fact always expressed itself through four main artforms: MCing (rapping), DJing (providing the music to accompany the rap), breaking (breakdancing, an athletic form of dancing involving many acrobatic moves) and graf (**graffiti**). While the latter two are mainly associated with 'old school' (that is, early to mid-1980s) hip hop, there are still small but fiercely loyal groups of b-boys and b-girls who perform headspins to the music or spray their elaborate designs on trains and walls.

Hip hop spread to Britain quickly, and in the early 1980s it was fairly commonplace to see gangs of hip hop fans in shopping centres on Saturdays, breakdancing on pieces of linoleum, as much for their own pleasure as that of onlookers. It was the breakdancers who had the strongest effect on the clothing style associated with hip hop. The dancers needed clothes that were comfortable and allowed freedom of movement, along with footwear that provided traction and, once again, comfort. Hip hop style came therefore to be typified by loose-fitting clothes, tracksuits or baggy t-shirts and trousers worn with training shoes. The massive sports footwear industry owes its success to the hip hop fans of the 1980s, who sparked off the boom in sales and whose sometimes fanatical brand loyalty is reflected in the music. Run DMC immortalized their footwear in 'My Adidas', while KRS One used the line 'better stop wearing those wack Puma sneakers' to diss a rival. Both 'wack' (bad/of poor quality) and 'diss' (to show disrespect towards) are examples of the slang associated with hip hop culture. Much of this slang comes from American hip hop culture, but has been adopted by British

fans with few alterations. British magazine *Hip Hop Connection*, for example, runs a regular column entitled 'Creature From The Wack Lagoon'.

While hip hop culture has not been as immediately visible in the years since its early 1980s heyday, events such as the annual Fresh festival, held in London, testify to the fact that there are still many dedicated hip hop heads (as they are often called) around. It is of note that, although hip hop is usually (correctly) perceived as being a predominantly black cultural practice, it is not exclusively so. Hip hop's practitioners and fans (often one and the same; a comparatively high proportion of hip hop fans seem to want to be actively involved in the culture in some way) are generally accepting of anyone who shares their passion, regardless of race, seeing themselves as all being part of a kind of 'hip hop nation'.

See also: DJs; jungle; rave culture

SIMON BOTTOM

hippies

In the 1980s 'hippie convoys' of ramshackle buses and lorries were demonized as a threat to public order when they drove onto farmers' land. For many people, this was their first encounter with the term 'hippie', which had become an almost universally derogatory term associated with work-shy, unkempt, soft-drug users. Gradually however, they generated the sympathy of a public which was re-evaluating the hippie movement of the 1960s.

The original hippies were young and preached 'flower power', the lifestyle of San Francisco and non-violent protest. Some sought anarchy, em-braced the environment and rejected western materialism. They formed an anti-war, artistically prolific counterculture and used psychedelic drugs like LSD and marijuana. Their dreamy vision influenced fabric design, graphic art and music. They followed such bands as Love, the Grateful Dead, Jefferson Airplane and Pink Floyd; their gurus were Allen Ginsberg and Timothy Leary.

The movement was not just about lifestyle, but had a political dimension. On 17 March 1968, 25,000 demonstrators gathered in Trafalgar Square and marched to the American embassy protesting against the war in Vietnam. Speakers, including Vanessa Redgrave and Tariq Ali, denounced the complicity of Britain's Labour government. In the melée, 117 policemen and 45 demonstrators needed medical attention, and 246 people were arrested.

Hippies were denigrated by agencies whose outlooks they were arguably reflecting. For example, their message of non-violence, peace and love should have been welcomed by the Christian churches, but was not. Newspapers were scathing of their activities when both they and hippies were fighting against excessive state control over information. Journalists ridiculed hippies' lifestyles; ten years later they themselves were more casually dressed and were letting their hair grow. Hippies' 'civil disobedience' should have appealed to the radical university intellectuals who led the Campaign for Nuclear Disarmament, but again did not.

The movement has left a number of legacies. Very often, the children of people who dropped out and went to live in the West Country or Brighton rather than London could not get back to the urban centres fast enough. Some children complained about their parents' laxity and became themselves utterly strict. Others felt inadequate because their parents were not hippies.

Nostalgia is rehabilitating the movement. For example, the writers Arthur Matthews and Graham Linehan are working on a situation comedy for the BBC inspired by the Bruce **Robinson** cult film *Withnail and I*. Set in 1968, *A Bunch of Hippies* revolves around a radical underground paper loosely based on *Oz* magazine.

See also: crusties; mods; rockers

Further reading

Labin, S. (1972) *Hippies, Drugs and Promiscuity*, New York: Arlington House.

MIKE STORRY

hire purchase

Hire purchase, commonly abbreviated to HP (called 'instalment credit' in the USA, where the system emerged in the nineteenth century) plays an important but decreasing role in providing consumer credit, especially for poorer people, for the purchase of high-priced domestic goods such as carpets, furniture and electrical appliances and also, rather more generally, for cars. It is also quite extensively used by firms to ease cash flow problems when large items of equipment are needed. Instead of paying for the goods before taking them away or having them delivered, the purchaser is usually (though retailers can make arrangements for exceptions) required to pay immediately only an initial deposit, which is a percentage of the price. Thereafter the purchaser must pay off, generally in equal monthly instalments over a fixed term, usually of up to two years, the balance of the price and the total cost of interest over the period of the contract. Since interest is levied on the total cost of the goods throughout the period stipulated, HP can be quite expensive by comparison with other forms of credit (for example, personal loans and **credit cards**, which have tended to take the place of hire purchase) under which the charge for interest falls as and when the debt is reduced. There are, however, legal safeguards against extortionate rates of HP interest. Often purchasers are also encouraged to take out insurance against payment problems arising, for instance, from illness and unemployment; although such protection is valuable, it also increases costs.

Technically, the goods that HP customers are able to take and use remain the property of the sellers (or the finance house to which they have most likely sold on the debt) until all instalments have been paid. In the event of any default by the customer, they can be 'repossessed' (taken back) by the provider. In practice, however, some accommodation is often reached since part-used goods have very limited market value, even if the customer has scrupulously fulfilled the legal obligation taking reasonable care of them.

Legislation since the 1930s has been designed to protect customers from high-pressure salesmanship aimed at persuading them to take on excessive burdens at high interest rates. Postwar governments have also regulated HP, especially for cars, to curb credit during economic emergencies.

See also: cash and carry; credit cards; discount stores; mail order

Further reading

Goode, R.M. (1970) *Hire Purchase Law*, London: Butterworth.

CHRISTOPHER SMITH

history

Britain's contemporary historiography has, with some exceptions, its basis in the international community. Since the mid-1960s, history, like many other discourses, has been subject to the influence of two opposing forces: fragmentation and conjunction. The 'Great Men' school of political history has surrendered its dominance to a diversity of approaches. While most stress the democratic necessity for a description 'from below', there are a variety of techniques to enable that shift.

British Marxist history, for so long impenetrable to external influence, took on new developments in psychology, **structuralism** and **post-structuralism** and merged them with the base/superstructure model and class relations to create something more modern, with the focus on everyday life. After the Annales school in France, structuralism stressed the importance of the 'series' in the use of statistical methods. Taken up by the social and economic history discipline, and boosted by computer access, such approaches were seen to be empirically faultless, while still allowing the liberty of interpretation. Historical demography has been given the opportunity by this means to process large amounts of data to examine hidden trends. However, subsequently post-structuralism stressed the importance of the 'text' as the true instrument of evidence. Context became crucial to analysis, giving rise to a reawakened interest in historiography. Interdisciplinarity has enabled history to confront literature, in 'the new historicism'. Cultural history, having subsumed methodologies from anthropology, semiotics, psychohistory, literary and critical theory and other, more marginal techniques, lays claim to 'total history'. Intellectual history, the study of ideas, parries claims of elitism by evoking the 'trickle down effect' of the works of great thinkers. Similarly, the histories of medicine and science have increased attention to the social context of technical progress.

History has seen the reclamation of the voice for the muted: women, the sexually marginalized, minority ethnic groups, people with disabilities, the aged and the young. A growth of interest in local history has changed the focus away from the national to the regional, with Scottish, Welsh and Irish histories echoing the growing autonomy of those nations.

In conclusion, history, like all intellectual disciplines, is subject to the vagaries of fashion, both economic and cultural. The current postmodern hegemony of 'liberalism and the markets' ensures that history will speak with a pluralistic, democratic voice, legitimizing whomsoever is the paymaster.

See also: Carr, E.H.; Hobsbawm, Eric; Taylor, A.J.P.

Further reading

Burke, P. (ed.) (1991) *New Perspectives on Historical Writing*, London: Polity Press.

GORDON URQUHART

Hobsbawm, Eric

b. 1917, Alexandria (Egypt)

Historian

A British Marxist historian, Eric Hobsbawm concentrates not so much on political as social and economic change, emphasizing cultural shifts alongside alterations in class conditions. His specialist area is nineteenth and twentieth-century Europe, about which he has written the highly praised and popular quartet *The Age of Revolution, 1789–1848* (1975), *The Age of Capital, 1848–1875* (1962), *The Age of Empire, 1875–1914* (1987) and *Age of Extremes: The Short Twentieth Century, 1914–1991* (1994). A realist and pragmatist, Hobsbawm does not so much provide incisive insights as trace social themes across time. Among his other important books are *Labouring Men* (1964), *Industry and Empire* (1968) and *Revolutionaries* (1973).

See also: Carr, E.H.; history; Taylor, A.J.P.

PETER CHILDS

hockey

Hockey is a common sport for men and women in English-speaking countries, usually played on a grass field by two teams of eleven over two thirty-five minute periods. The name was only arrived at in the eighteenth or nineteenth centuries, though the sport itself dates back around 4,000 years to the earliest stick-and-ball games. Indoor hockey became more and more popular after the Second World War, a period which has also seen a continued rise in women's hockey (championed by the suffragettes at the start of the century). Britain boasts the oldest women's club in the world at Wimbledon (founded in 1889) and in many countries hockey is viewed primarily as a women's sport.

In Britain, hockey remains something of a Cinderella sport. Its image is that of a middle-class activity, played mainly by women, or possibly by well-mannered boys from the public schools. People remember Ronald Searle's cartoons or famous sequences from the St Trinian's films starring Alastair Sim and Joyce Grenfell with her catchphrase, 'jolly hockey-sticks'. Hockey comes well behind **football** and rugby (see **rugby league**; **rugby union**) in terms both of the number of practitioners and spectators, and is rarely televised. It has always been widely played in schools (more so by girls than by boys) and school coaches aim to make it more popular by introducing mini-hockey with fewer than the standard eleven players and by using smaller sticks and balls.

Hockey's rules were first formalized in 1886 in Britain by the Men's Hockey Association. At the local level, hockey is relatively healthy with 2,080 clubs and an estimated 87,000 regular players, but Britain today has lost at the international level any dominance that it once had. However the England team has benefited from the appointment of the Australian Barry Dancer as coach in January 1998. He played in two World Cups and has an Olympic silver medal from Montreal in 1976. He has brought on prominent players like Russell Garcia, the nation's most capped man, and the sole survivor from the 1988 gold medal-winning Olympics team, Calum Giles. Consequently England, whose previous best had been a silver medal in 1986, had a respectable performance at the 1998 World Cup, finishing in sixth place (just enough to satisfy the **National Lottery** funders, who put £1.6 m into the elite end of the sport).

England's women's team, by contrast, did not do so well. Under their coach Maggie Souyave, they could only manage ninth position in the World Cup, just ahead of Scotland. This World Cup (it is a quadrennial event) was held at Utrecht, The Netherlands, where, by contrast with hockey's status in Britain, it was the major sporting event of the year. Pakistan, the defending men's champions from 1994 were defeated, with the eventual winners being The Netherlands. Australia retained their position as world women's champions.

Some rule changes do not bode well for England. From July 1998, substitutions at penalty corners will be outlawed, bringing to a close the era of the penalty-corner specialist. This may prove difficult for Calum Giles, whose forte this has been. The advent of Lottery money should however revitalize the sport.

Further reading

Moore, C. (1988) *Discovering Hockey*, London: Partridge.

MIKE STORRY

Hockney, David

b. 1937, Bradford

Painter

David Hockney attended Bradford School of Art from 1953–9. His early scenes of domestic and urban realism were shaped by a traditional art school training and the influences of the Euston Road School and Kitchen Sink artists. An outstanding student at the Royal College of Art (1959–62), Hockney experimented with pure abstract **painting** before striving to incorporate its modernist tendencies within a more substantial figurative framework.

At the RCA, Hockney's fellow students included R.B. Kitaj, Derek Boushier and Peter Phillips, artists who participated in the 1961 Young Contemporaries Exhibition with Hockney and were identified as exponents of 1960s **pop art**. In a dawning age of celebrity and consumerism, Hockney's self-consciously stylistic, witty, graffitied and allusive art and eccentric public personality qualified him as a 'pop artist', a label he staunchly rejected. Early debates about Hockney's standing in a British arts tradition often stemmed from the apparent incompatibility of his roles as both serious artist and socialite, despite the strongly autobiographical vein in his work and his intimate friends and surroundings, homosexuality and lifestyle providing an expressive focus.

His first solo exhibition at Kasmin's Gallery, London in 1963 was soon followed by a formative trip to Los Angeles (Hockney eventually emigrated there in 1976). Homoerotic scenes were inspired by American physique magazines, the visual stimuli of his and others' photographic sources tellingly influential in his art. Showers, swimming pools and reflective surfaces appeared as frequent motifs in otherwise minimalist depictions of a selective Los Angeles landscape during a period which instigated flatter, more naturalistic, acrylic painted representations. During the 1970s, the restrictive effects of naturalism concentrated efforts on drawing and etching until 1977, when Hockney and Kitaj championed a return to representational art. Self-portraits, still-lifes, landscapes and characteristic large-scale double compositions continued to abound.

Hockney's early 1960s preoccupation with theatricality, artifice and spectatorship was later fulfilled through his stage design for productions like *Ubu Roi* (1966) and *Turandot* (1990). Hockney has repeatedly demonstrated an insatiable curiosity for exploring new styles and mediums through a subjective collage-like approach actualized in his later post-cubist fascination with perspectival art, involving photo-collages, fax, photocopier and computerized images. Despite his Los Angeles residency, Hockney arguably remains the most acclaimed British artist alive, his work perhaps criticized for its stylistic hollowness but celebrated for its inventive, fearless artistic explorations of contradictory preoccupations.

Further reading

Melia, P. (1995) *David Hockney*, Manchester: Man-chester University Press (critically incisive essays chronicling aspects of Hockney's oeuvre).

SATINDER CHOHAN

Hodgkin, Dorothy

b. 1910, Cairo (Egypt); d. 1994

Chemist

Hodgkin was a chemist who was little known until she won the 1964 Nobel Prize for Chemistry for her analysis of the most complex of the vitamins, B12. She began her academic career at Oxford and continued her analyses of complex biochemical substances at Cambridge from 1948 to 1956. She used X-rays to examine photographs of B12-related crystals. She also helped to conduct a large survey of the sterols (solid, mostly unsaturated, polycyclic alcohols such as cholesterol, derived from plants or animals). In 1961 she collaborated with the American crystallographer P. Galen Lenhert to complete the analysis of vitamin B12 in its natural occurrences. She also worked on the structure of penicillin and of many other important biochemicals.

See also: science

MIKE STORRY

holistic medicine

Holistic medicine is a term used to cover a spectrum of treatments available as an alternative to traditional allopathic medicine. Its practitioners diagnose and advise treatments from the perspective of the patient as an individual, rather than prescribing a remedy to cure the patient's symptoms. Holistic health centres offering a range of alternative therapies such as homeopathy, acupuncture and aromatherapy can be found in most towns and cities in the British Isles. Although the Royal Family had long been supporters of complementary medicine, a general upsurge of interest occurred during the early 1960s, caused in part by a disenchantment with traditional medicine following cases such as that of the drug thalidomide, which had been found to cause birth defects.

See also: homeopathy; NHS

JAN EVANS

homelessness

Three factors made homelessness a more visible feature of British society and culture in the 1990s. First, as a result of economic recession, family breakdown and poverty, increasing numbers of young people were found living on the streets of major cities for the first time. Second, under the Conservatives' 'Care in the Community' programme, people released from mental institutions ended up on the streets. Third, John Bird founded the magazine *The Big Issue* (based on a similar idea in New York), which is sold by homeless people who keep 60 percent of the proceeds. This brought homelessness into national focus. The Labour Party set up a Social Exclusion Unit, and in 1998 proposed that homeless people should be forced to accept places in hostels.

See also: poverty, families and

MIKE STORRY

homeopathy

Homeopathy is a system of medicine that aims to relieve suffering, to heal and to cure. It is based on a very simple natural principle: 'like cures like'. Hippocrates first referred to its principles in the fourth century BC, and the German physician Samuel Hahnemann rediscovered and made practical use of homeopathy in the nineteenth century. Since Hahnemann, it has waxed and waned in popularity. In the 1990s, following an extremely aggressive and stressful decade, holistic approaches became very popular and commercially sophisticated. Consequently, homeopathy was very much in vogue and gained credibility through the patronage of Prince Charles, filling the gap left by the growing disillusionment with modern-day conventional medicine.

See also: holistic medicine

FATIMA FERNANDES

Hopkins, Michael

b. 1935

Architect

Michael Hopkins is one of Britain's most prominent architects. Along with other award-winning architects such as Norman Foster (see **Foster Associates**) and Chris **Wilkinson**, Hopkins has been given a station on the new Jubilee Line extension to design. His style is often called 'friendly high-tech', as opposed to the uniquely British phenomenon of **high-tech** where buildings wear their insides on the outside, combining structure and function, a style owing more to the aircraft and space industries than to the organic or to human scale. His Lords Cricket Ground stand, designed with his wife Patty, and his new, enlarged Glyndebourne Festival Theatre, which preserved the countryside feel of its rural location, have both been well received.

MIKE STORRY

Horden, Richard

b. 1944

Architect

Richard Horden trained at the **Architectural Association** from 1964 to 1969 and worked for the Farrell Grimshaw Partnership (1971–2) and **Foster Associates** (1974–84), among others, before establishing Richard Horden Associates in 1985. Devoted to principles of logic and clarity, Horden has built distinctive houses by drawing on modern boat technology, and he has also designed dwellings for Dorset craft workers, yacht clubhouses and a marina control tower. From 1989 he worked on a major new office tower in Victoria, London. In the 1970s and 1980s he developed

high-tech projects such as the prestigious Sainsbury Centre for the Visual Arts (1978).

PETER CHILDS

horse racing

Horse racing in Britain takes place six days a week, fifty-two weeks a year, and is in fact increasing with all-weather flat racing throughout the winter months and summer steeplechase meetings. In addition, recent changes to betting laws (revenue from which funds the prize money for races) has allowed racing to take place on Sundays.

Horse racing enthusiasts are divided into two categories: those who follow flat racing, which takes place primarily during the summer, and those who support steeplechasing, most of which occurs during the winter months. The traditional seasons are arranged in this way as softer winter ground is less damaging for the steeplechase horses.

Major meetings in the steeplechase calendar include the Newbury Autumn Meeting, at which time the Hennessey Gold Cup is run. This meeting is generally accepted as the starting point for top-class steeplechasers, whose calendar will include the Kempton Christmas Meeting for the King George, in preparation for the Cheltenham Festival Meeting and the Champion Hurdle and Cheltenham Gold Cup, the winners of which are crowned as the leading steeplechase horses of the year. The three-day **Grand National** Meeting stages the most famous race in the calendar. This gruelling four and one-half mile marathon is the most watched annual sporting event in the world.

The major flat racing meetings echo the days when horse racing was a pursuit of the idle rich, taking place as they do over four days during mid-week. The Chester May Meeting with the Epsom Derby trial, and indeed the Epsom Derby Meeting in early June, play second fiddle to the splendour of Royal Ascot, Glorious Goodwood and York in August.

The British racecourse is divided along traditional class lines, with the members' enclosure being the most expensive to enter. Bookmakers are not allowed into the members' area and instead hang their boards over the rails (a coveted position giving rise to the distinction between rails bookmakers and bookmakers in the ring or areas where any bookmaker may buy a pitch) between the members' enclosure and Tattersalls, a less expensive enclosure housing the bookmakers themselves. The Silver Ring is the cheapest enclosure with the worst view, and is often at the centre of the course.

Modern racing is far less rigid and class-conscious than in the past, and efforts have been made towards a customer friendly approach. The night meetings under floodlights at Wolverhampton in particular are aimed towards a young audience.

See also: betting shops

Further reading

Blunt, N. (1977) *Horse Racing: An Inside Story*, London: Hamlyn.

JOHN E. CORNWELL

hostages

In the mid-1980s, after the collapse of law and order, extremist Shi'ite Muslims in Lebanon began taking Westerners prisoner in Beirut, including the Britons John McCarthy and Brian Keenan. As many as twenty-six were at one time held hostage by the Iranian-backed extremists, and though most were released after several years, three Britons died. The forced detention of these alleged 'spies' and 'subversives' led to a Syrian invasion, which attempted to restore authority but did not succeed in releasing the hostages. In the USA, the consequences were the Iran–Contra affair and its offshoot, the 'Arms for Hostages' scandal. In the UK, Terry Waite, the Archbishop of Canterbury's envoy, was despatched to Beirut to negotiate with the kidnappers but was himself taken hostage. By the late 1990s, all the surviving hostages had been released.

MIKE STORRY

house

House music was originally developed in the early 1980s by American musicians and **DJs** such as Frankie Knuckles, Farley Keith, DJ Pierre and Chip-E. Initially, house drew influence from up-tempo R&B and Salsoul. In particular, house DJs took records from these genres and 'remixed' them, re-editing them for the dancefloor and adding percussion from newly developed drum machines. In particular, the American gay scene championed house as 'its music', and **clubs** such as The Sound Factory in New York, and The Power Plant and The Gallery 21 in Chicago became focal points. The term 'house' is an abbreviation of the name of The Warehouse club in Chicago, and was used by local record shops to describe the music played there.

British dance culture imported house music in the late 1980s. Influenced by the style of house music played in Ibizan clubs during the summer of 1987, a generation of new DJs and musicians returned from their holidays and set about attempting to recreate the Ibiza club experience back in the United Kingdom. The clubs of the late 1980s that were playing house music included The Haçienda in Manchester, and Spectrum and Shoom in London.

As the influence of house music has spread, it has taken over from **disco** as the dominant form of British dance music. In musical terms, house can be described as an electronic dance music based on a strict 4/4 time signature, with a sequenced 'kick' drum on all four crotchets of each bar, at speeds of around 120–130 beats per minute. Melody and vocals are used to break up repetition.

Like contemporary **techno**, there are now a myriad of different styles of house. The subgenre of 'handbag house' appears to be particularly popular on British dancefloors. Dance culture's usage of the word 'handbag' started life as a derogatory term for clubs where women danced round their handbags. However, since 1993 it has been used to describe house music that has prominent female vocals, 'break downs' (where the kick drum stops, and the track 'breaks down', to be built up again), and a proliferation of piano 'stabs'. 'Hard house' is the term used to describe house music with a more aggressive feel to it, and some hard house of the mid-1990s is virtually indistinguishable from techno. Other subgenres popular on British dancefloors include the grand orchestral arrangements of 'epic house', the Latin rhythms of Italian house, and the vocal emphasis of 'garage house', named after the Paradise Garage club in New York.

Within dance culture, the DJs frequently become more famous than the musicians themselves. It has been suggested that British house DJs such as Sasha, Danny Rampling and Jeremy Healy are the 1990s equivalent to the rock star. House music fans also have affinities with particular clubs, and often travel hundreds of miles to visit their favourite club. Popular house clubs in Britain at the moment include The Ministry of Sound in London, Wobble in Birmingham, Cream in Liverpool, Rise in Sheffield and Slam in Glasgow.

See also: clubs; hip hop

STUART BORTHWICK

housing

Housing in Britain has increasingly been dominated by one type, the owner-occupied, single-family dwelling in a suburb, in marked contrast to practice elsewhere in Europe. It is not however the only form of British housing, and emphasizing it masks the fact that housing has, for most of the twentieth century, been an extremely contentious issue and has been subject to huge and frequent shifts of taste and public policy. For example, between 1945 and 1969, 59 percent of housing construction in Britain was public, a figure rarely matched in the then communist countries of Eastern Europe. The picture has changed radically since 1979, but the story of housing since the Second World War is in many ways the story of public housing, and responses to it.

Although the bulk of public housing (nearly two-thirds) built since the war was of a traditional form, that is a type of cottage, either terraced or semi-detached, the building form that has come to symbolize the reconstruction most is the modern tower block. It is also the form that had the greatest impact on existing street patterns, and the visual appearance of British towns and cities. Among the first examples built by the state were the Roehampton estate, designed by the then London County Council (LCC) in 1951, and the form of this estate established a pattern that would be followed elsewhere. The site was wooded, with some variation of level; the slim twelve-storey point blocks were arranged in groups, in a picturesque manner. They had balconies, and maximized the use of light and space; the land they occupied was open and available for public use. The pattern of multi-storey blocks in parkland was established here.

By the mid-1950s however, mainstream Modern Movement thinking, which had informed the production of LCC architects, was under pressure from a tendency generally known as the **new brutalism**. Its best-known adherents, Alison and Peter **Smithson**, argued for a re-evaluation of earlier built forms, and in particular they showed an interest in established forms of working-class housing. Their research resulted in designs for 'deck-access' blocks, in which layered 'streets in the sky' would aim to recreate in a modern form the sense of community found in working-class terraced housing. The pattern was evidenced in the Smithsons' own work at (for example) Robin Hood Lane, Tower Hamlets (begun 1968); the gigantic Park Hill complex in Sheffield also followed their example.

But if the new brutalism had led to a reassessment of LCC practice, outside of London the high point block was the most characteristic symbol of reconstruction, and designs from the early 1950s were the most common form in the larger cities such as Birmingham, Salford, and (spectacularly) Glasgow. In these cities, housing production was led by local politicians, such as David Gibson, and the quality of the buildings themselves was of secondary importance compared to their speed of production. The extraordinary cityscape on the outskirts of Glasgow is testament to the drive of local politicians.

If high point blocks were the most prominent housing type in the major provincial cities, a 1968 gas explosion at Ronan Point in the East End of London, causing its partial collapse and four deaths, was in many respects the downfall of the type, and the building of multi-storey blocks – of whichever type – declined sharply thereafter. In

their place came a variety of alternatives. In the late 1960s and early 1970s, Manchester built massive developments on the deck-access theme, most of which have since been demolished. In London there were various 1970s experiments on the theme of low-rise high density, in which features of more traditional forms of housing, such as individual enclosed gardens, made a return.

Since the 1960s, the major changes in housing have been political rather than formal. The Conservative government elected in 1979 carried out its promise of allowing council tenants to buy their own homes; shortly after, local government was forbidden from building any more public housing. The provision of low-cost accommodation has increasingly become the business of private housing associations such as the Guinness Trust or the North British Housing Association. Such organizations, using a mixture of private and public funding, have come to be the major institutional presence in many British inner cities, taking over the roles previously assumed by local government. With a few exceptions, however, the form of their building projects has been conventional, in marked contrast with the state housing projects they replaced.

Elsewhere in the inner cities, there have been many developments of high-income private housing since the late 1980s. The trend has been particularly marked in London, with areas close to the City most subject to redevelopment; elsewhere, there has been comparable development in areas such as Glasgow's Merchant City, Manchester's Whitworth Street corridor, Liverpool's Concert Square and Birmingham's Brindleyplace. In many cases, former warehouse or office buildings have been converted, sometimes to New York-style 'lofts', and where new building has taken place, it has often aped the style of these older buildings. Retail and leisure developments have frequently been a part of such schemes.

The visibility, and commercial success, of inner city private developments does not however indicate a decline in the popularity of traditional forms of suburban housing. The overall numbers of professional people living in city centres remains small, and the vast majority of the new housing has been built for single people, not families. While the inner cities might have been the site of major change, the overall pattern since the 1960s has been one of continuing suburbanization, with resultant pressures on areas designated as green belt. Whatever new developments, both private and public, there have been in the 1990s, 'housing' for most of the population continues to signify a single family dwelling in a suburb.

See also: city redevelopment; town planning

Further reading

Glendinning, M. and Muthesius, S. (1994) *Tower Block: Modern Public Housing in England, Scotland, Wales and Northern Ireland*, New Haven, CT, and London: Yale University Press.

RICHARD J. WILLIAMS

Hoyle, Fred

b. 1915, Bingley

Astronomer

Fred Hoyle held a number of academic posts at Cambridge and was professor of astronomy at the Royal Institution from 1969–72. His work on steady-state theory (the continuous creation of matter) was superseded by the discovery of background radiation, but his work on stars confirmed that hydrogen is there converted to helium. He is known by the general public for books aimed at popularizing science, including *Highlights in Astronomy* (1975), and for the fact that he also wrote science-fiction, notably *The Black Cloud* (1957). His autobiography, *The Small World of Fred Hoyle* appeared in 1986. Among his controversial hypotheses were the suggestions that life originated in interstellar dust and that flu epidemics are linked to sunspot outbreaks.

See also: science

MIKE STORRY

Hudson, Hugh

b. 1936

Film-maker

Hugh Hudson is a British film director who has become successful on both sides of the Atlantic. In 1975 he set up his own production company and directed *Chariots of Fire* (1981), a drama set against the background of the 1924 Summer Olympics. Partly funded by Dodi Fayed, it won an Academy Award as Best Picture of the year. The actress Andie McDowell made her debut in *Greystoke: The Legend of Tarzan, Lord of the Apes* (1984). In 1987 Hudson raised Labour's political vote through a personal profile dubbed 'Kinnock: The Movie'. *Lumière et Compagnie* (1995) entailed inviting other film makers to use a restored Lumiere camera. His latest movie, *World of Moss* (1998), directed for producer David Puttnam, was well received in America.

MIKE STORRY

hunt saboteurs

The Hunt Saboteurs Association (formed in 1963) is one of a number of groups spawned by the **animal rights** movement. The hunt saboteurs aim to disrupt ('sabb') hunting of stags and foxes with packs of hounds. They use 'direct action' (aniseed trails, misleading hunting horns) and are officially pledged to non-violent methods, although two saboteurs have been killed in recent years and many have been hospitalized. Members have been prosecuted for aggravated trespass under Section 68 of the Criminal Justice Act 1994. The HSA has numerous local branches throughout the UK, and popular support from a disparate range of people from **hippies** to professionals. Their principal opponents are the British Field Sports Society.

MIKE STORRY

hyperreality

Made famous by Umberto Eco's book *Travels in Hyperreality*, this term refers to the condition of modern living as theorized by the French post-modernist philosopher Jean Baudrillard. In brief, the hyperreal exists when imitations or representations become more 'real' than their originals, as when we prefer a sound recording to the original, or would rather see a film of the Grand Canyon than the Canyon itself. Disneyland is the most-discussed example of the hyperreal as it represents a perfect America (or jungle cruise, haunted house, or waterboat tour through scenes of Caribbean piracy) which is 'better' than the real life it supposedly copies. In Britain, the simulation environments of theme parks such as Camelot, or indeed the whole representation and marketing of Shakespeare in the tourist industry at Stratford, represents this production, acceleration and circulation of idealized signs and kitsch products for consumers to purchase in mock-real but distinctly authentic surroundings.

Increasingly, Euroamericans live in a world suffused with copies: simulations, recordings, prints, videos and so on. This is to the extent that we sometimes confuse the 'live' with the 'pre-recorded' (and so try to rewind a television programme we mistakenly think we are watching on video) or prefer the artificial to the natural (phone someone in the hope that their answer-phone will take the call). Ultimately, the hyperreal will have triumphed when we all prefer artificial human beings to real people (remember that Disneyland attractions use automatons and not actors).

See also: postmodernist theory

PETER CHILDS

I

ICA

The Institute of Contemporary Arts (ICA) was founded in 1948 to provide a conduit for the avant-garde within culture, and now is the foremost forum of its kind in the UK, promoting presentations, discourse and debate within contemporary art and culture. Prime movers in the formation of the ICA were the surrealist painter Sir Roland Penrose and the poet and critic Sir Herbert Read, who became the first President. The agenda was made clear when the first exhibition on '40 Years of Modern Art' opened in 1948, Herbert Read noting that 'such is our ideal – not another museum, another bleak exhibition gallery, another classical building in which insulated and classified specimens of a culture are displayed for instruction, but an adult play-centre, a workshop where work is a joy, a source of vitality and daring experiment'.

The ICA embraces a number of media including exhibitions, performance, experimental music, new bands, independent film and video, literary events and conferences on cultural and scientific issues. Located in an imposing John Nash designed Regency terrace on the Mall, the complex comprises two art galleries, a cinema, cinematheque and seminar rooms. The mission statement today is decidedly cutting edge and pluralistic, with the avowed aim of involving all people from all backgrounds in the exploration of new ideas (attempting to rebut claims of elitism); it also seeks to challenge orthodoxy in the arts, be a place of interaction, and above all provoke debate. Determined to increase its penetration, an attempt has been made to broaden its educative function. ICA Education was created in 1991 (now ICA Interaction), with student placements and internships and a series of discussions to develop new audiences and foster more audience participation. One of its great strengths is its constant self re-evaluation and a critical approach to its work; the ICA is constantly looking for different arenas and methods by which the aims of the ICA might be better served. Additional private funding through sponsorship is being secured and new areas and ideas are constantly being utilized. Confines of space have meant that a move from the Mall is being considered and new sites are being courted in order that the ICA can continue to fulfil its mission statement and maintain its reputation for originality, vitality and a 'spirit of discovery'.

See also: Arts Council; painting

GUY OSBORN
STEVE GREENFIELD

ice skating

There is prehistoric evidence for skating (with long bones for runners), and it is also known that the Vikings used iron skates. Known as a mode of winter travel in Britain since the early middle ages, skating started gaining social prestige in the late seventeenth century after being adopted by aristocratic refugees in the Low Countries, and skating races were attracting attention in the Fens by the 1760s. The modern sport, for both amateurs and professionals, emerged with the discovery in the

1870s of techniques for freezing water to create more or less permanent ice rinks indoors and out.

In speed skating, the competitors, whether men or women, race counter-clockwise around oval tracks over distances from 500 to 10,000 metres or, in 'short track' skating, on smaller tracks over distances up to 5,000 metres. In 1924 men's speed skating was included in the Winter Olympics; women's speed skating was admitted only in 1960. In figure skating, competitors, alone or in male–female pairs, must within a time limit perform a series of precisely defined compulsory exercises, and also show a range of prescribed skills in a 'free' programme of their own devising. Similar rules apply to ice dancing, for male–female pairs. Scoring, in terms of both technique and artistry, is carried out by a panel of judges whose individual marks are combined by complex formulae. The first world figure skating championship dates from 1896, and the sport was admitted to the Olympic Games in 1908. After the first ice dancing world championships in 1952, the discipline became an Olympic sport in 1976.

Ice-hockey, similar to **hockey** on grass or astro-turf, is played on an ice rink (maximum 60m × 30m) between two teams of six, including a particularly well-padded goalkeeper. A 'puck' – a composition disc three inches in diameter – is used instead of a ball. Fast and rough, the game, which is very popular at both amateur and professional level in Canada and is steadily gaining a following in the UK, has been an Olympic sport since 1920.

Thanks to Jayne Torvill and Christopher Dean, World and Olympic champions in 1984, ice dancing became popular on British television, and the couple, turning professional, also contributed to the already considerable popularity of spectacular shows on ice. At a recreational level, skating is still quite widely enjoyed in the UK all year round on indoor rinks in towns and on natural ice in the country in cold winters.

Further reading

Heller, M. (ed.) (1979) *The Illustrated Encyclopedia of Ice Skating*, New York: Paddington.

CHRISTOPHER SMITH

Illuminations

Illuminations is a multimedia company co-founded by John Wyver in 1983. It made its name in the arts area with such programmes as *K: Kenneth Clark 1903–1983*, and live coverage of the Turner Prize in 1993 and 1994. It addressed a new audience with *The Net*, which takes as its subject matter the new wave of digital communications, and has produced *The Mirror*, an online world that runs parallel with the series. In 1998, Illuminations won the Times Educational Supplement Resources Award for Mixed Media for *The Music Show*, a ten-part television series for **Channel 4** accompanied by a CD-ROM, teachers notes and music activity book for the classroom.

MIKE STORRY

imported television

Imported television refers to the flow of programmes into a nation's broadcasting system from other national systems. While this has traditionally meant the inward flow of individual programmes, the term can now be applied, with the advent of **cable and satellite** technologies, to the importation of complete television channels (for example, CNN). The importation of programmes by British broadcasters started in a small way before the Second World War, with short films and cartoons, but it was only with the arrival of ITV in 1955 that imported material, especially American programmes, found a major place on British television screens (for example, *Bonanza*, *Raw Hide* and *I Love Lucy*). Such well-made popular programmes, which could be sold cheaply as they had already covered production costs in the home market, were used both by **BBC** and ITV to attract and keep new audiences. Since the 1960s, ITV and the BBC have kept to a limit of 14 percent of foreign programming.

Those arguing in favour of importation point out that broadcasters and audiences in Britain benefit from the new forms of programming and different cultural outlooks, which also keep down the costs of providing a full schedule. For example, **Channel 4** has become infamous for using successful and popular American series to attract audiences and therefore advertisers, a strategy that has freed money up for domestic production. Others argue, in reference to the dominance of the commercial American product, that this 'Wall-to-Wall Dallas' is eroding and Americanizing the indigenous culture and identity.

As broadcasting enters the third age (the first was radio, the second was terrestrial television) with the appearance of satellite, cable and digital television, so the flow of programmes, both as discrete packages and in terms of television services, is becoming more international. With more channels coming on-stream, many without the resources or revenue of the established channels, there is an increased reliance on the cheaply sold popular American product (though other sources of supply do exist, such as Australia for soaps and Japan for cartoons). Likewise, the existing terrestrial broadcasters, trying to cut costs and compete with the new channels, also see imports as an important part of their strategy for survival. However, research suggests that domestically produced material is more popular than imports; for example, domestically made soaps constantly top the rating tables of most nations.

Further reading

Collins, R. (1990) *Television: Policy and Culture*, London: Unwin Hyman.

PAUL RIXON

improvisation

Improvisation has become an indispensable tool in postwar theatre. It is accepted as a valuable method for actors to explore both the 'inner truth' of a character and the world of the play when interpreting text-based drama. It is also increasingly recognized, and used, as a technique which actively produces innovative dramatic material. The concept of the rehearsal room as a creatively productive play-room has been legitimized during the postwar period. Improvisation workshops and **devising** are the basis of work in **community theatre** and **physical theatre**, and are also

considered an essential component of drama in education at all levels. Two manuals which have had a huge impact on the teaching and practice of drama are Keith Johnstone's *Impro* and Clive Barker's *Theatre Games*.

Following Theatre Workshop's *Oh What a Lovely War*, improvising around research materials has become the staple method of TIE (theatre in education) companies and those producing 'documentary drama' and 'heritage drama', where the play is evolved and is structured through the rehearsal process. In alternative theatre, Monstrous Regiment and Joint Stock developed influential methods of working with actors and playwrights together, where the issues and ideas of a play were explored first through improvisation before the writer shaped and structured a play-text (for example, Churchill's *Vinegar Tom* and *Cloud 9*, which are both remarkably unconventional in form).

Mike **Leigh** has refined a method of working in private improvisation with actors on his characters, before allowing them to meet and improvise situations which he eventually structures into a play. His work owes much to the 'naturalistic' tradition and the results are recognizable 'plays', which may be why his work transfers so well to the screen.

The 'collective commitment' that informs theatre produced through improvisation is indicative of the way the anti-star and anti-director system has evolved in alternative theatre, where ensemble practice in the cornerstone. A large number of companies work through collaborative methods rooted in improvisation to make their work, sometimes using a text as a springboard or starting point (Volcano's *Ibsenities*), incorporating autobiographical material (Forced Entertainment), or employing visual or design motifs (The People Show). This is not merely evidence of **postmodernism** in theatre but a move towards acknowledging the power of the actor as a creative initiator, and demonstrates a late twentieth-century shift in emphasis from the 'actor as interpreter' to the 'actor as creator'.

See also: community theatre; devising; physical theatre

Further reading

Frost, A. and Yarrow, R. (1990) *Improvisation in Drama*, London: Macmillan.

DYMPHNA CALLERY

INDEPENDENT, THE *see* Mirror Group

independent production

Until the early 1980s, the British broadcasting system was dominated by integrated broadcasting companies, the **BBC** and the ITV companies. Within these companies, all the functions of production, commissioning and scheduling were undertaken. However, with the creation of **Channel 4** in 1982, with no production base of its own and with a remit to encourage new voices, an independent production sector was born. This development was later reinforced with the requirement of the Broadcasting Act of 1990 for ITV and the BBC to use independent productions for 25 percent of their programmes. In the 1990s, a multifarious industrial structure appeared that included traditional broadcasters with their own in-house production facilities and independent production houses.

The appearance of Channel 4 signalled the arrival of the publisher–commissioner broadcaster, a broadcaster without any production base of its own. Instead, it commissions original programmes from either independent producers or production units of other broadcasters, with commissions including single programmes, series, serials or films. Internally, Channel 4 employs a number of editors responsible for commissioning programmes for different areas, such as documentary, drama and entertainment. Once programmes are commissioned, the independent producer hires the required personnel and equipment to undertake the production. While the commissioning director might oversee some aspects of the production, the production company has a high degree of autonomy.

In 1986, the Peacock Committee recommended that some competition should be introduced into BBC and ITV systems. This idea found political and ideological acceptance within the Conservative government of the time. The Broadcasting Act of 1990 introduced a requirement for 25 percent of the BBC and ITV programme output to be independent productions. In response, the BBC and ITV have introduced structural changes to allow access for independent producers to compete for commissions. Also with the ITV franchise round of 1992, four new broadcasters came into existence, all of which were publisher/commissioner broadcasters not unlike Channel 4.

Arguments have been put for and against more independent production. On one hand, it allows more voices into the system than previously, it allows greater autonomy and encourages creativity, and it is more competitive and therefore is efficient. Detractors argue that it has led to a casualization of labour and that the critical creative mass that underpinned the excellence of the old system is being dissipated.

See also: Channel 5; Channel X; IPPA, AIP and PACT

Further reading

Hood, S. (ed.) (1994) *Behind the Screens: The Structure of British Television in the Nineties*, London: Lawrence & Wishart.

PAUL RIXON

Indian communities

Like other migrant and diaspora communities, Indian communities have substantially redefined the cultural landscape of a post-imperial, post-colonial Britain of new ethnicities. Indian communities have undergone varying processes of hybridization, syncretization and transculturation, reconstructing parallel Indian social, economic, religious and linguistic structures in a British context without relinquishing their distinctive cultural heritages, individual and group identities and links to the homeland.

In the 1991 census of Great Britain, the 840,255 Indians comprised the largest single ethnic grouping, forming 27.7 percent of the ethnic minority population and approximately 1.5 percent of the

British population. Originating from the Indian subcontinent, Britain and as 'twice migrants' from East Africa, the intradiversity of identity and descent within Indian communities is further marked by axes of differentiation and cross-fertilization based on linguistic–regional, religious, caste, sectarian and kinship divisions. The Punjabi and East African Sikhs, East African, Gujarati and other Indian Hindus and Muslims have established British-inflected extensions of their Indian and East African linguistic–regional communities in Britain; for example, Punjabi Sikhs identify more easily with Punjabi Muslims than with East African Sikhs. Far from an homogenous grouping, loosely corresponding histories of migration, settlement and transculturation nevertheless conceal the variegation of Indian communities.

Despite a significant Indian presence in Britain from the sixteenth and seventeenth centuries onwards, the predominantly male pioneer migrants (ex-seamen, professionals, politicians and peddlars) of the pre-Second World War period established the foundations for Indian communities. The numbers of Indian migrants accelerated rapidly in the aftermath of the war. The permanent settlement of Indian communities was followed by the large-scale international migration of the 1950s and 1960s, partly triggered by the acute labour shortages of the postwar British economy. Failed British attempts to employ domestic and then European labour for mainly low-paid, unskilled and semi-skilled employment in the manufacturing, textile and engineering industries led to postwar labour recruitment drives in colonial and ex-colonial overseas territories. Localized considerations including the 1947 Partition of India and Pakistan, resultant land pressures, fragmented landholdings, migratory traditions within densely populated rural regions and affordable air travel coalesced with employment prospects and immediate social and economic amelioration for the joint family household to encourage mass voluntary Indian migration to Britain.

Arriving as 'temporary sojourners', Indian migrants sought to accumulate sufficient finance before returning to their homelands. The temporary framework suggested by a 'myth of return' enabled migrants both to assert their identities by maintaining cultural and value systems and to

psychologically resist assimilation and 'cultural contamination' so as to facilitate their eventual reintegration into India's rural communities; processes rendered easier by their negative reception in an often alien, prejudiced and racially exclusive British host culture. Gradually however, the 'temporary sojourners' became permanent settlers, the parallel community networks, material prosperity, employment and educational opportunities for future generations outweighing the advantages of return.

During the 1950s, active community organizations like the Indo-Pakistan Cultural Society (IPCS) and the nationwide Indian Workers Association (IWA) were established and, along with local *gurdwaras* (temples), began offering invaluable advice, practical and legal assistance (for example, on immigration, housing and employment), social and cultural activities to Indian members of the community. Early Indian communities settled primarily in Britain's metropolitan centres and industrial conurbations from the agriculturally prosperous, traditionally migratory regions of the Punjab and Gujarat in India and later from the urbanized, Westernized and professional milieus of East Africa. Among British Sikh communities, the majority descend from villages around the Punjabi Jullundhur Doaba and Hoshiapur regions, while the Gujarati migrants both from Gujarat and from East Africa comprise a Hindu majority and a Muslim minority. Punjabi (with written Gurmukhi as opposed to Urdu) is the most common language spoken among Sikhs, with Hindi, Gujarati and Urdu forming the other primary linguistic communities. More Hindus than Sikhs, however, originate as 'involuntary' or 'twice' East African migrants. Having migrated to East Africa from India during the earlier half of the century, they were expelled under systematic Africanization policies in Kenya in 1968 and in Uganda in 1972. While Indian migrants arrived as potential workers, East African Asians arrived in Britain as political refugees but as 'twice migrants' were better prepared for settlement.

Indian communities have settled in areas of specific industry-related labour and areas with strong localized migrant support networks, while socio-economic limitations including prejudice and racial discrimination in housing and employment have precluded settlement in other areas. The majority of Indians reside in the South East, London, the Midlands and Yorkshire, with clusters of Punjabi communities located in areas such as Wolverhampton, Leicester and Southall and Gujarati communities in Leicester and North London.

From low-paid, manual work in foundries, factories, bakeries, catering and textiles on their arrival, Indians have diversified into other fields of employment. Following an initial period of migration and settlement, politicized left-wing Indian communities confronted workplace and institutionalized racism in a number of high-profile industrial disputes. Community solidarity and significant political mobilization among Asian women have manifested themselves in disputes such as Woolf's (1965), Mansfield Hosiery (1972), Imperial Typewriters (1974) and Grunswick (1976), as Indian workers sought equal pay, equal treatment with white workers and union representation. Continuing disputes at Hillingdon Hospital during the 1990s illustrate the racial inequities suffered by Indian communities within the workplace.

Having initially confronted exploitative, low-paid manual employment, the burgeoning confidence of Indian communities is illustrated by the traditional status professions such as accountancy, law, medicine, dentistry and science-based occupations. Younger descendants have entered non-traditional professions such as the film, media and entertainment industries. An ethnic market sector was rapidly established as self-employed businesses and services catered for an Indian demographic, circumventing the racial discrimination experienced in standard employment, and now enjoys success in catering for a wider British market. Flourishing Asian restaurants, specialist shops, and Indian film industry and Asian press newspapers and weekly publications like *Des Pardes* and *Punjabi Times* enable first generation Indians to maintain communications with the subcontinent. Gujarati and East African Asians particularly demonstrated versatile entrepreneurial skills consistent with the merchant caste/commercial traditions of the Gujarat state and East African Asian involvement in African trade and industry affairs. Compared to Indian subcontinent rural migrants, East African Asians principally occupied the professional, educated middle-class echelons, hav-

ing worked within administrative, bureaucratic and commercial systems in urban East Africa. Disparities of wealth nevertheless manifest themselves among stratified Indian communities, low wages and high unemployment contrasting with thriving private economies.

The chain migration of male members of Indian families and village clans created initially male-dominated community clusters and migrant support networks. The 1962 Commonwealth Immigration Act and subsequent immigration laws ushered in a 'beat the ban' stream of female, younger filial and older parental dependants to reconstitute family and community structures in Britain. Effectively considered the preservers of social tradition and as the maintainers of extended familial relationships, Indian female migrants have enforced a domestic authority compounded by their growing economic independence as workers to redefine traditional roles.

The (agrarian-based) patrifocal joint household and extended family is paradigmatic among Indian communities, also functioning as a microcosm of the community itself. However, increasing Westernization, economic prosperity, moral, social and political factors have witnessed the individualization of kinship networks into nuclear and varied models of the joint/extended structure. Determinant factors of age and sex accord relative authority and respect, elder and male members traditionally wielding greater power within the family unit. While many generations cohabit, newly married couples continue to live in the husband's parents household both to inculcate the daughter-in-law with the family traditions and to transfer familial responsibilities to the son, both eventually caring for the elderly parents in a multi-generational household. Specific family roles accord certain values, expectations and responsibilities. Each family member is defined by their matrilineal and patrilineal relations through a complex use of kinship terminology which distinguishes their role and attendant responsibilities within the extended family: for example, while *masi* is the respectful appellation for a maternal aunt, *puah* is a paternal aunt.

Liberalized variations of the traditional arranged marriage, whereby parents undertook the selection of prospective marriage partners for their children have been gradually superseded by children exercising greater choice in the selection. The basic premise of marriage nevertheless remains the marriage of individuals synonymous with the marriage of families. Although 'love' marriages have increased, separation and divorce, once extreme taboos within the Indian community, are also rising as a consequence of the discordance between strictly traditional arrangements and correspondingly incompatible Western sensibilities and loosely fitting traditional roles.

Indian kinship structures are based upon the unspoken but inculcated code of *izzat* (honour, prestige) according to which the individual and family conduct themselves morally, socially and professionally and consolidate their position within family and community networks. A fluid term, *izzat* functions as the source of personal and familial honour which upholds the integrity of cultural systems, obviating moral dissolution and enforcing continued cultural conformity. It can also be considered as motivational factors for example, in migration, the pursuit of status-enhancing professions, ensuring a girl's chastity, selection of marriage partners or encouraging competition between individuals and families. While sometimes perceived as a restrictive code by girls and women particularly, Westernization and individualization are seen as threatening forces by older Indians, diminishing the tempering and respectful aspects of *izzat* by breeding a self-interested disregard for familial and broader structures through the primacy of individual wants and desires.

Indian communities cultivate strong notions of kinship, religious and caste (*jati*) identification and belonging among themselves. Hinduism and Sikhism, the majority religious groups, coexist alongside smaller Indian Muslim, Christian and Parsi communities. Similarly, caste endogamy is a prevalent consideration, particularly among first-generation Indians who strictly adhere to caste groupings in kinship and community networks and in cultural practices such as marriage and religious worship. The Hindu caste system provides a representative model for other complex and numerous caste systems, with the system of Brahmins (priests, religious teachers), Kshatriya (kings, aristocrats, warriors), Vaisya (merchants, traders), Sudra (servants) and Untouchables or people of the lowest

castes still exacting some resonance, but this is subject to regional interchange.

Despite scriptural doctrines which emphatically reject the Hindu caste system, Sikhs maintain their own endogamous caste system with hierarchical and occupationally-based divisions of agrarian descent. The Jats (farmers, landowners) are the highest caste followed by the Ramgharias (craftsmen) which also includes the Tarkhan and Lohar sub-castes. East African Asians constitute a large proportion of this group, their significant economic and social power elevating this middle-class group above traditionally lower caste confines. (Sanskritization describes this upward mobility of lower castes in Britain, economically or socially usurping higher castes in spite of the traditional caste hierarchies). Following the Ramgharias, the Ravidas or Valmik castes of Chuhre (sweepers) and Chumar (landless workers) hybridize elements of Sikhism and Hinduism but still suffer from existing intra-caste prejudices as exemplified by caste-segregated *gurdwaras* and religious committees. Although caste differences are subsumed beneath an encompassing Indian or Asian identity, closer analysis reveals caste as a continued source of affinity and exclusion among first-generation Indians in particular. Rather than a homogenous religious grouping which cultivates the notion of the Sikh *panth* (brotherhood), Sikhism exhibits caste and sectarian divisions, the latter characterized by pro- and anti-Khalistan (independent Sikh homeland) movements which surfaced during the turbulent Indira Gandhi years of the 1980s.

The Gujarati and East African Asians are comprised of an array of caste sub-divisions further compounded by Hindu sects such as the Vaishnava movements of Pushtimarg, Swaminarayan and Shaivites alongside myriad smaller sects and gurus, individually worshipped. Among the strongly mercantile Gujaratis in Britain, the Patidars (equitable descent from India and East Africa) and Lohanas (mainly East African migrants) are predominant alongside other Bani groups and smaller castes like Kanbis (labourers/farmers), Darjis (tailors), Suthars (carpenters), Prajapatis (potters) or Mochis (shoemakers). The Gujaratis also include Muslim, Jain and Parsi Zoroastrian minorities, the Parsis significantly constituting the first and oldest of Britain's Indian communities.

Like the *gurdwara* committees of the Sikhs and other regional Hindu groups, the Gujaratis have established caste, sectarian and politico-religious organizations such as the Swaminarayan Hindu Mission. Indian religious and sectarian diversity is exhaustive, the visible celebration of festivals like Holi, Diwali, Navratri, Eid and Vaisakhi illustrating their continuing importance for Britain's numerous Indian sub-communities.

Where a 'myth of return' has largely prevailed for first generation migrants, their Indian and British-born descendants lay claim to multiple identities and both Indian/East African and British heritages. While cultural conflicts between the first generation and their descendants exist, the former perceiving the latter as diluting integral cultural precepts and principles, the younger generation seek to negotiate a dialogue between Indian and Western cultures. However, the conflict 'between cultures' analysis of Asian youth (rather than specifically Indian; this generation is not as meticulous in highlighting internal cultural cleavages as their parents) is rejected in favour of highlighting the advantages of cross-cultural exchange. A fluid locationality between their own native, black and Western British culture is manifest in the developing dialogues of music, fashion, art, youth styles and cultural practices of an ascendant generation labelled as 'British Asian'. From the politicized 1970s, a decade of volatile race relations, the racist murder of Gurdip Singh Chaggar, localized riots and the subsequent formation of organizations like Southall Youth Movement, during the 1990s Indian youth are contributing to altered cultural landscapes as significantly as their parents in permanently settled Indian (British Asian) communities.

Further reading

Ballard, R. (ed.) (1994) *Desh Pardesh: The South Asian Presence in Britain*, London: Hurst and Company.

Britain's Black Population (1997) *Britain's Black Population: Social Change, Public Policy and Agenda*, Aldershot: Arena.

Modood, T. and Berthoud, R. (eds) (1997) *Ethnic Minorities in Britain: Diversity and Disadvantage*, London: Policy Studies Institute.

Robinson, V. (1986) *Transients, Settlers and Refugees: Asians in Britain*, Oxford: Clarendon Press.

SATINDER CHOHAN

Indian languages

Britain now has speakers of over a hundred different languages. Several of these languages are Indian, most notably Bengali, Hindi, Gujarati, Urdu and Panjabi, and are spoken especially in major cities such as London, Birmingham, Glasgow and Cardiff.

Bengali is one of the fifteen major languages of India and the official language of Bangladesh, with over 160 million speakers (the most famous Bengali writer was Rabindranath Tagore, winner of the Nobel Prize for Literature). Bengali and English have had links since the East India Company founded Calcutta in 1690. Gujarati is spoken by about twenty million people in Gujarat, Bombay and elsewhere in India, plus in East and South Africa, and Britain (many Gujurati-speaking people came to Britain in 1974, following General Idi Amin's order to all South Asian British passport holders to quit Uganda). Hindi has the fourth most common mother tongue with around 250 million, and is the most widely spoken Indian language. Panjabi is spoken by 12 million people in India and 40 million in Pakistan, and is the language of Sikhs. Urdu is associated with the Mughal Empire in India and is clearly related to Hindi. It is the national language of Pakistan, a first language of 30 million people and a second language of a further 100 million.

Indian languages have also contributed many familiar words to the English language, such as 'verandah' and 'juggernaut', as well as 'curry', 'pukka' and 'tiffin'. The well-known Victorian dictionary of Indian–English, entitled *Hobson–Jobson*, is still available today. Indian English is a hybrid language found all across India and also in Britain. It tends to be formal, lilting, sing-song and poetical. Writers such as G.V. Desani and Salman Rushdie have exploited its idiosyncracies to highly praised literary ends.

See also: Indian communities

PETER CHILDS

indie pop

Although independent record labels have a long history, the origins of indie music are to be found in the development of **punk rock** in the late 1970s. Part of the punk ethos was a reaction against control of the music industry by a handful of large multinational record companies. Punk bands, motivated by a 'DIY' approach to music production, began to produce and distribute their own records; hence the name 'indie', an abbreviation of 'independent'. As Punk gave way to **new wave**, a new generation of record labels were formed to promote new music, the pioneers being Rough Trade and Stiff in London, Postcard in Glasgow, Zoo in Liverpool, **two-tone** in Coventry and Factory in Manchester.

Indie scenes began to spring up around these particular labels. The Teardrop Explodes and Echo and the Bunnymen from Zoo Records produced music that was influenced by the **psychedelic rock** of The Doors and The Byrds from the 1960s. Artists on the Factory label such as Joy Division developed a dour industrial sound. Bands signed to Rough Trade and Postcard were distinctive in their search for a 'pure pop' form, while Madness, The Specials and The Selecter, all bands signed to the Two-Tone label, were particularly influenced by **ska** and were characterized by their multi-ethnic origins.

Many bands on indie labels shared a similar aesthetic, and as a result the phrase 'indie' began to be used to describe a particular generic sound, rather than merely the method of producing and distributing records. This aesthetic was based around a rejection of the excesses of progressive rock, with the preferred vinyl medium being the seven-inch single rather than the LP. As the 1980s continued, a whole array of indie bands and labels were formed. Bands on indie labels would release one or two singles that attracted the attention of the music media, and would then sign to a major label. Indie labels began to be seen as a breeding ground for new talent. Many internationally successful artists started their careers in this way.

Towards the end of the 1980s, as indie labels began to expand, many developed formal links with 'majors', multinational record companies such as Polygram and CBS. This sparked much debate within the indie scene as to the ethics of breaking away from the original DIY ethos. In particular many indie labels maintained control of the signing of new bands and the production of records, while forming distribution deals with major labels. This was compounded by the collapse of the Rough Trade and Factory labels. Since then the phrase indie is generally considered to refer to a musical genre. Bands such as Oasis, signed to Creation, who now have financial links with Sony, are considered to be indie bands despite their lack of 'independence'. Perhaps therefore the true indie bands of the 1990s are not the guitar-based groups with an indie 'sound', but those **techno**, **house** and **jungle** acts who continue to release and distribute their own records, without help from multinational companies.

See also: alternative music

Further reading

Savage, J. (1991) *England's Dreaming: Anarchy, Sex Pistols, Punk Rock and Beyond*, London: Faber & Faber.

STUART BORTHWICK

industrial buildings

The understanding that **high-tech** buildings were unsuitable (because of weather conditions and industrial wear and tear) for industry has resulted in a return to traditional cladding and construction. Jonathan Glancey writes that it is ironic 'that the components usually reflect the world of prewar engineering: split pins and tie-rods, drilled steel struts and crossbars' (1989: 148). Architects have also employed the past in predictable ways using bright, strikingly coloured doors and cladding, plus yards of glass. Some buildings reflect the products they house (for example, nuclear power stations are uniformly severe), while others embrace and express their owners' corporate image or ethos (for example, Richard Rogers's costly but very stylish Linn Products building in Glasgow). Many still require regular repainting, materials replacement (for example, of fabric), and maintenance while others have been made out of traditional materials (such as the return to brick for warehouses) because new materials such as plastic and aluminium are not tough or durable enough.

See also: agricultural buildings

Further reading

Glancey, J. (1989) *New British Architecture*, London: Thames and Hudson.

PETER CHILDS

industrial design

The primary catalyst to change in industrial design has been technology, which has allowed most mechanisms to become smaller, lighter and more stylish. Microchip technology, polymer science, foam plastics, composite materials and computer-aided design have all greatly affected design styles as well as production processes. Automated manufacturing has become commonplace, and 'expert systems' driven by computers can perfect production processes. Mass production has also changed to allow small modifications (often by reprogramming computer-driven tools) to products for a range of different consumers. Dominant postwar design features have been the penchant for 'clean lines', neat fixings and tidy casings, easy-to-use knobs and switches (functionalism as such has gone in and out of fashion), and ever smaller, more compact products.

See also: furniture design

PETER CHILDS

infotainment

Infotainment is a mixture of instructional and entertainment material. Multimedia encyclopedias or interactive CD-ROMs are sold as educational

material for children. Adults question the intellectual rigour in material deliberately aimed at catching the eye of the MTV generation, but many teachers defend it as 'appropriate packaging'. The term has also been applied disparagingly to material which purports to be authentic but is not. Stephen Spielberg's *Amistad* (1997) was accused of masquerading as 'the truth' when it was in reality both a sanitized and politicized version of history. Accompanying 'study packs' distributed free to schools were treated with scepticism because of their potential commercial agenda. However, many welcome infotainment as a means of rescuing a generation 'lost' to television.

See also: product placement; teletext

MIKE STORRY

installation art

The term 'installation art' has been in common use since at least the mid-1980s, and 'installations' have become familiar sights in British museums and galleries in the 1990s. The Turner Prize shortlists have increasingly included such work by British or British-based artists including Vong Phaophanit, Douglas Gordon and Rachel Whiteread.

The works to which the term 'installation art' refers are extremely diverse. If it is consistent at all, installation art is a hybrid form making use of techniques from sculpture, architecture, photography, film and video, and its artists are not identifiably 'installation artists' but sculptors or video artists who sometimes make installations. The work can often be physically entered by the viewer; it may be made for a specific site, whether a gallery or an outdoor site; it may damage or otherwise intervene in the space it occupies; it may be temporary; it may be apprehended in ways other than the visual. Precedents for the work can be found in some American art of the 1960s (for example Robert Smithson and Richard Serra) and the work of the British sculptor Richard Long.

Some better-known examples of installation art include *Neon Rice Field* (1993) by the British-based Vietnamese artist Vong Phaophanit. Varying in dimensions according to its site, the piece comprises a field of rice with peaks and troughs as if ploughed; the peaks are accentuated by a buried neon light running their whole length. The piece attracted considerable media attention on being shortlisted for the Turner Prize in 1993. Richard Wilson's work has made more extreme interventions: *Jamming Gears* (1996) made a variety of incisions and holes on the interior of the Serpentine Gallery, London, artistically vandalizing the space (fortunately before the gallery closed for renovation). Anya Gallacio has become known for filling galleries full of sensuous materials, sometimes flowers; in one case the walls of a Manchester gallery were smeared with chocolate. Mona Hatoum's work, based on the filming of her own body, has involved the creation of special spaces in which to view the footage, as has, in a different way the video artist Douglas Gordon. Other artists who have made installation art of note are Helen Chadwick, Nat Goodden and Gladstone Thompson. More sensuous than its 1960s antecedents, installation art has sometimes met with surprising popular success.

See also: organic art; sculpture

Further reading

de Oliveira, N. (1994) *Installation Art*, London: Thames & Hudson.

RICHARD J. WILLIAMS

International Broadcasting Trust

An independent, non-profit-making television production company, the International Broadcasting Trust (IBT) was established in 1982 as an educational charity to work with broadcasters, educationalists and film-makers worldwide. Its aim is to communicate global issues through television programmes about development, environmental and human rights issues for broadcast in the UK and also abroad. It was founded by seventy international organizations, including Oxfam, Amnesty International, Christian Aid and Friends of the Earth. IBT has been commissioned to make programmes, ranging from adult drama to schools programming, by all the major television companies and has made more than a hundred

programmes in the last decade (such as *Bitter Harvest*, *Battle for the Planet*, and *Young, British and Muslim*). The IBT is devoted to promoting international understanding through the media. They contend, for example, that there are only half as many documentaries about the rest of the world being shown in prime time at the end of the 1990s as there were at the beginning of the decade. If international coverage is left to news programmes, it will consist only of disasters and wars. Positive international cultural programming such as Madhur Jaffrey's *Taste of India* is the kind of thing the Trust prefers to see promoted, partly to counter latent British xenophobia. It also advocates the use of ethnic minority presenters for programmes about abroad, something distinctly lacking at present on British television.

MIKE STORRY

Internet

The Internet has taken time to become established as an integral aspect of British culture. The universities have been using 'the Net' as a source of information since it started. Academics are fascinated by the potential of the system and, for example, trivial things such as the website with the video camera trained on a coffee pot at Cambridge University is visited daily by thousands of 'surfers' from all over the world. Business users, on the other hand, have been slower to take up the opportunities supplied by the system. Thus, many large companies' websites are often crude 'front doors', with very little behind them.

Private subscribers tend to be the educated and financially secure middle class. Traditional service providers are Demon, Pipex, CompuServe and America Online, but now, in order to build up a valuable database of customers, companies such as Virgin and Tesco and organizations such as the Consumer Association (publishers of *Which?*) and Amnesty International are competing for subscribers. A conservatively estimated 350,000 people, excluding those who use cable, were connected in this way in 1998.

The Internet has had much social impact. After high-profile court cases, people have been jailed for downloading hardcore **pornography**. It is now common policy for companies to place time constraints on employees' surfing or accessing e-mail at work. Issues around the privacy of e-mails received there are hotly debated.

Commentators are divided about the long-term significance of the Internet. Some suggest that it is a truly 'democratic' phenomenon, where everyone has equal access to knowledge. Others suggest that it is a fad, rather like the glass and chromium Horn and Hardhart automated food dispensers popular in New York in the 1960s. One put coins in a slot and opened a flap to take a sandwich. They are now nowhere to be found.

For the Internet to be more fully integrated into grassroots culture and to involve more of the older generation, its technology will have to be made simpler. For example, it will have to be available through a television screen, using a remote control rather than a keyboard. Also the speed of transmission will have to increase beyond the capacity of existing ISDN cables. With the advent of digital television, Cable & Wireless Communications, Britain's biggest cable television and telecommunications group, intends to supply its 750,000 customers with the Internet, as well as up to 200 television channels.

See also: cable and satellite; electronic shopping

Further reading

Shields, R. (1996) *Cultures of Internet*, London: Sage.

MIKE STORRY

IPC Music Publishers

Derived from 'International Publishing Corporation', IPC Magazines is the UK's major publisher of consumer magazines. It is a division of Reed International PLC. Among others, it publishes *Classic Cars, Country Life, Golf Monthly, Horse and Hound, Ideal Home, Living, New Scientist, Shoot, Woman's Journal* and *Woman's Own*. The company has four divisions, including Southbank Publishing Group and Prospect Magazines.

In 1983, IPC launched *Number1* a weekly pop magazine, but its most important magazine in terms of popular culture is *New Musical Express*, universally known as *NME*. This broadsheet provided a formative influence in young people's lives right from the 1950s and gained respect as an authoritative commentary on popular music. It covered rock 'n' roll imports from America and other influences on the contemporary British scene. Its emphasis was regional and local, as well as national, and both it and *Melody Maker* wrote about people on the edge of the cult rock mainstream and tended to ignore established figures with more of a history. This allowed space for *Smash Hits* and the glossy EMAP Metro magazine *Q* (see **EMAP Maclaren**) to steal some of its readership. (Nick Logan, founder of *Smash Hits* and *The Face*, spent five years as editor of *NME*). In response, *NME* changed itself and introduced a regular rock column, and regained some of its readership.

As well as music, *NME* has supported general aspects of youth culture. For example it was enthusiastic about the comic *2000AD* and recommended it to readers. *NME* had itself been greatly influenced by the underground presses of the 1960s and early 1970s. It has always been regarded as a quality magazine and has taken its contributors from both 'low' and 'high' culture. So for example, cartoonist Ray Lowry came from the underground (*Cyclops*) and his work appeared in *NME* and *Private Eye*. Journalist Charles Shaar Murray's work appeared in *NME*, the *Observer* and the *Daily Telegraph*, and Julie Burchill has written for both the *NME* and the *Sunday Times*.

In 1995 the circulation of *NME* was a weekly 106,903. It is estimated that the magazine is read by 607,000 people per issue.

See also: music press

Further reading

Riley, S.G. (ed.) (1993) *Consumer Magazines of the British Isles*, Westport, CT: Greenwood Press.

MIKE STORRY

IPPA, AIP and PACT

The creation of a unified film and television trade body for independent producers, the Producers

Alliance for Cinema and Television (PACT), can be viewed as the result of the increasing closeness of film and television production and the increase in use of independent television producers. PACT was formed in 1991 when the Independent Programme Producers Association (IPPA) and The Producers' Association (TPA) merged. The IPPA formed in 1981 to fight initially for independent producers' rights in regard to **Channel 4** and later for more access to the **BBC** and ITV. The TPA itself was the result of a merger in 1990 of the Association of Independent Producers (AIP) and the British Film and Television Producers' Association (BFTA).

See also: independent production

PAUL RIXON

Ireland

'The Irish Question', first used in the latter part of the last century to refer to the long, difficult and often violent relationship between Ireland and Britain, has continued to be a permanent feature of British political and cultural life. Up until the creation of Saorstat Eireann (the Irish Free State) in 1922, made up of 26 of the 32 counties of Ireland (with six counties in what became Northern Ireland remaining part of the United Kingdom), Britain's answer to the Irish Question was some sort of Home Rule. In many respects, the 'unfinished business' of Britain's relationship with Ireland is at the heart of the problems of Northern Ireland, for while Home Rule was eventually seen as too little too late for the majority in Ireland, for the Unionist/Protestant minority in the northeast, 'home rule was Rome rule'.

Throughout its history as a British colony, Ireland had periodically revolted or rebelled against Britain, such as in the failed risings of 1798, 1848 and, most significantly, in the Easter Rising of 1916. Irish nationalist politics has always (like other nationalist politics) had both constitutional/democratic/non-violent and violent/terroristic aspects. Particularly in the latter half of the nineteenth century, the movement for Irish independence gained strength, especially when the political impetus for independence joined with the movement for the revival of Irish culture in the

1890s. An example of the deep impact of Britain's 'Irish problem' is that Irish nationalism was perceived to be such a threat that the London Metropolitan police force was created primarily to combat it.

The 'defining moment' of the Irish independence movement was the failed Easter Rising in 1916, when a small group of ill-equipped and badly-trained Irish nationalists led by Padraig Pearse took over by force of arms major key installations in Dublin and declared an independent Irish Republic. As Britain was at war, this rising was viewed as treason and British forces quickly and brutally suppressed the rebellion. While at first the rebellion did not have great public support in Ireland, public opinion quickly changed in favour of the rebels as a result of the decision to execute the leaders of the rebellion. As a result, in the next elections in 1918 **Sinn Féin** (the leading Irish nationalist party) won the overwhelming majority of Irish Westminster seats. However, in keeping with the practice of the contemporary Sinn Féin party, these Irish MPs refused to recognize the British Parliament and set up their own shadow Parliament (The Dáil). Efforts by the British government to quell this illegal parliament in Ireland and the movement for Irish independence led to the War of Independence (1919–21). Following a ceasefire in 1921, the British government agreed to talks and the result was the creation of the Irish Free State, which required the partition of Ireland and the creation of Northern Ireland. Northern Ireland, unlike the rest of Ireland, contained a majority of Protestants who did not wish to become part of an independent united Ireland which was seen as an exclusively authoritarian, Catholic and Gaelic entity. However, the new entity of Northern Ireland also contained a sizeable minority of Catholic Irish nationalists.

The creation of Northern Ireland led to the Stormont regime, which lasted from 1922 to 1972. Effectively, Northern Ireland became a statelet, with all the trappings of a state, and until the eruption of the 'troubles' in 1968, successive British governments simply ignored it and let the Protestant majority rule. In the words of one-time Prime Minster of Northern Ireland, William Craig, 'Northern Ireland is a Protestant state for a

Protestant people', a statement which graphically highlights the status of non-Protestants from the regime's point of view. While the amount, severity and degree of discrimination against Catholics in Northern Ireland is a fiercely disputed issue, it is fair to say that they were effectively second-class citizens. Catholics were denied job opportunities, were treated unequally in terms of housing and welfare and suffered discrimination in work, while, since most of them were also Irish nationalists, they were also viewed by the Stormont regime as 'the enemy within', seeking to destroy Northern Ireland and create a united Ireland.

In 1967 the Northern Ireland Civil Rights Association (NICRA) was formed to demand: equal citizenship for Catholics, the vote for everyone (and not just ratepayers in local elections), an end to gerrymandering (the practice of artificially drawing electoral boundaries to ensure a Unionist majority), fair allocation of public housing, and the scrapping of the hated 'B-Specials' security force. The Civil Rights movement led to a Protestant backlash, and throughout 1967 and 1968 Northern Ireland erupted into violence as loyalist extremists (including Ian Paisley) and the police attacked civil rights marches, leading to rioting in Belfast, Derry and other urban centres. Northern Ireland witnessed what we now call 'ethnic cleansing' as thousands of Catholics and Protestants were forced from their homes by **violence** or the threat of violence. In August 1969 the British government decided to send in British troops to restore law and order, and the 'troubles' were born.

The IRA (Irish Republican Army), which had long been a spent force, found a new lease of life as it defended Catholic ghettos in Belfast and Derry from attacks by Protestant mobs and the paramilitary B-Specials. At this stage, equal British citizenship within a reformed Northern Ireland, the original aims of the NICRA, was too little too late for many Catholics, who flocked to support or join the IRA and its political wing Sinn Féin. For the IRA, Northern Ireland was unreformable, a 'failed entity', and nothing short of British withdrawal from Northern Ireland and the creation of a united Ireland would do.

The 'Provos', or Provisional IRA (which split in 1970 from the more socialist 'Official IRA'), have become one of the most feared and successful terrorist organizations in the world, and synonymous with the 'troubles'. In the mid-1970s, the IRA began a series of terrorist campaigns both within Northern Ireland and on the mainland to try and force Britain to leave Northern Ireland. As a result of these bombing campaigns, the Prevention of Terrorism Act was hastily passed. Anti-Irish feeling in the wake of IRA atrocities such as the Birmingham and Guildford pub bombings of 1974 led to the wrongful convictions of the 'Birmingham Six' and the 'Guildford Four', both groups being eventually released from prison in the early 1990s. Other IRA atrocities included the murder of Earl Mountbatten and the car bomb in the Palace of Westminster which killed Conservative MP Airey Neave, both in 1979; the failed bombing of the Conservative party conference in Brighton in 1983; and a mortar attack on 10 Downing Street in 1991. Non-IRA atrocities include 'Bloody Sunday', when members of the British Parachute Regiment opened fire on innocent nationalist civilians in Derry in 1972, killing twelve, and the notorious 'Shankhill Butchers', a loyalist sectarian death squad which brutally tortured and murdered thirty Catholics in the mid-1970s.

Since the abolition of Stormont and the imposition of 'direct rule' in 1972, Northern Ireland has been governed from Westminster by the Northern Ireland Office. Millions of pounds have been spent in trying to reform, police and support Northern Ireland. Over 3,200 people have been killed in Northern Ireland as a result of the troubles. In reality, the 'troubles' in Northern Ireland amounted to an undeclared war which, while strenuously denied by the British government, characterized its military strategy in trying to defeat and contain republican and loyalist warring paramilitaries. For some, evidence that the troubles were viewed as a war can be seen in the British Army's 'shoot to kill' policy in the 1980s, and the alleged collusion between elements of the security forces in Northern Ireland and loyalist paramilitaries.

However, the devastating effects of the troubles go beyond those killed or injured and the millions of pounds worth of property destroyed, for they have affected political and everyday life in the Republic of Ireland, Britain and Northern Ireland. On the whole, with the exception of Scotland, for most of those on mainland Britain, Northern Ireland has always been a 'place apart' and radically different from the rest of Britain. A stark example of this is the statement in November 1990 by the then Secretary of State for Northern Ireland, Peter Brooke, who claimed that: 'The British government has no selfish strategic or economic interest in Northern Ireland: our role is to help, enable and encourage.' This admission of the conditional status of Northern Ireland as a part of the United Kingdom is something which would be unthinkable if the same were to be said of Cornwall or Cheshire. This is perhaps the paradox, irony and tragedy of Northern Ireland: while Unionists loudly proclaim their 'Britishness' and loyalty to the Crown, the overwhelming majority of Britons do not see them as 'fellow Britons', but as 'Irish' and having more in common with the nationalist community than with the mainstream of British society. A similar view can be said to characterize the attitude of those in the Republic of Ireland towards the Northern Ireland nationalists, and it is important to note that support for a United Ireland has been falling in the Republic over the last decade or so. Nevertheless, a majority support the aspiration to a United Ireland.

The ceasefire declared by the IRA in August 1994 (followed by a Loyalist cashier in October), and restored in May 1997, was the starting point of the 'peace process' which culminated in the 'Good Friday Agreement' of 10 April 1998. This multi-party agreement, the result of months of negotiation between all the major parties in Northern Ireland (with the exception of the Democratic Unionist Party), sets forth a new political settlement in Northern Ireland, and is an attempt at power-sharing. A similar attempt at a power-sharing arrangement in 1974, the Sunningdale Assembly, lasted from January to May until it was brought down by loyalist extremists, who called a general strike organized by the Ulster Worker's Council. According to the Good Friday Agreement, Northern Ireland is to have its own assembly, with proportional representation for the two communities. There is also provision for 'North–South' bodies between Northern Ireland and the Republic of Ireland, as well as 'East–West' bodies between Northern Ireland, Scotland, Wales, Westminster and Dublin. Elections to the new assembly took place in June 1998.

Oscar Wilde once said: 'The problem between England and Ireland is that the English cannot remember history while the Irish cannot forget it.' There is some truth in this claim, particularly when one looks at the reliving of history in the annual Orange marches celebrating the defeat of Catholic King James by Protestant William of Orange in 1690. Such traditions and the passion (and sometimes dogmatism) with which they are asserted strike many on the British mainland as singularly odd in their reliving of religious wars from over 300 years ago at the end of the twentieth century. Equally, the Irish republican perspective, which often sees the problems in Northern Ireland as stemming from the Ulster plantations of the early seventeenth century by Britain and sees Irish history as a series of glorious defeats at the hands of 'perfidious Albion', seems equally caught in letting the past guide the present and future.

However, it also needs to be pointed out that the relationship between Ireland (both North and South) and Britain has not been completely negative. Many of the greatest English-speaking writers of the twentieth century have been Irish, from W.B. Yeats, James Joyce, George Bernard Shaw and Samuel Beckett to the Nobel Prize-winning poet Seamus Heaney. Additionally, Irish culture has become increasingly popular in Britain and elsewhere. At the same time, what Britain and Ireland share is as (some would say more) important than what divides them, such as common cultural origins, a joint if tragic history, a common language, a long tradition of settling and living in both islands, and similar political cultures and institutions.

While it is always dangerous to predict events in Northern Ireland, it seems that the current peace process (which does not of course mean peace) has resulted in a truly historic opportunity of ending the troubles and marking a new, more positive relation between Britain and Ireland, one that is oriented towards the future rather than continually reliving the past.

See also: Irish communities; Sinn Féin; Ulster Unionists

Further reading

Aughey, A. and Morrow, D. (eds) (1996) *Northern Ireland Politics*, Harlow: Longman.

Catterall, P. and MacDougall, S. (eds) (1996) *The Northern Ireland Question in British Politics*, Basingstoke: Macmillan.

O'Leary, B. and McGarry, J. (1996) *The Politics of Antagonism: Understanding Northern Ireland*, 2nd edn, London: Athlone Press.

JOHN BARRY

Irish communities

The Irish community is the largest ethnic group in Britain. In the last population census, over 800,000 people described themselves as 'Irish'. Irish people and Irish affairs have a long and not always positive place in Britain and British history. Crucial to understanding the status of the Irish in Britain is the historical and current relationship between the two islands, especially the fact that Ireland was a colony of Britain until the creation of an independent Irish state in 1922.

Irish people have been coming to work and live in mainland Britain for over three hundred years, and their experience in many respects prefigured the experiences of other immigrants to Britain, in terms of discrimination, hostility and inferior treatment. A graphic illustration of this is the notices displayed in windows of some lodging houses in the 1950s which declared 'No Blacks, No Irish, No Dogs'.

While there has always been an Irish community in Britain, with the Great Irish Famine of 1845–8, a steady wave of emigration from Ireland to Britain began and continues to this day. Up until recently, those who came from Ireland worked in and were associated with particular professions such as the construction industry (Irish 'navvies' helping to build the infrastructure of Britain in the last century), nursing, domestic service, mining and agriculture. Recently this has changed, with Irish immigrants increasingly being young, educated professionals who have tended to find employment in the financial services sector, banking, management positions in British and foreign corporations and the education sector.

Historically, the Irish community has been concentrated in a number of cities such as London, Liverpool, Manchester, Birmingham and Glasgow. Victorian anti-Irish prejudice saw the Irish as feckless, untrustworthy, workshy drunkards and/or as amusing, entertaining but ultimately 'inferior' people. The attitude persists in various caricatures and shapes perceptions of the Irish in Britain in conjunction with the continuing 'troubles' in Northern Ireland. However, in recent years there has been a new confidence and vitality within the Irish community in Britain. 'Irishness' now has a new fashionable status, stemming from the current international appeal of everything Irish from traditional music and dance, such as the success of 'Riverdance', to the rock group U2 (one of the world's foremost bands). In contrast to the majority of its history and experience in Britain, the Irish community now is proud of its identity, traditions and culture. Evidence of this newfound confidence is its demands for inclusion on the population census and its increasing political organization in calling attention to the continuing problems faced by many within the Irish community, such as disproportionately high levels of mental illness, homelessness and ill health.

See also: Ireland

Further reading

Holohan, A. (1995) *Working Lives: The Irish in Britain*, Reading: Eastern Press.

Kearney, R. (ed.) (1990) *Migrations: The Irish at Home and Abroad*, Dublin: Wolfhound Press.

JOHN BARRY

IRN

Independent Radio News, a twenty-four-hour national and international news service, began broadcasting (first on LBC) when commercial radio was officially sanctioned in Britain in 1973. It was at first funded by the radio stations themselves, to whom information was transmitted by landline or teleprinter. Computer technology was installed in 1985, advertising became the source of funding in 1987, and distribution was changed to satellite in

1989. Unlike any other news broadcast organization in the world, IRN now pays its clients to take its services, giving it a market share and influence which is unrivalled in the UK.

PETER CHILDS

Isaacs, Jeremy

b. 1932, Glasgow

Sir Jeremy Isaacs has had a long and broadly successful career in various media positions, including head of **Channel 4**. However, his legacy will be overshadowed by Gerald Kaufman's highly critical Select Committee report on the running of the Royal Opera House where Isaacs was director from 1988–96. He allowed the company to become homeless during the refurbishment of its main premises, and his work came under scrutiny in the six-episode documentary *The House*, aired in 1996. The first fly-on-the-wall programme attracted a television audience of more than two million. The institution was shown as a shambles, and Isaacs was blamed by his successor for mismanaging financial and other aspects of the business.

MIKE STORRY

Islam

Islam is the religion of the Muslims, a monotheistic faith which regards itself as incorporating the final revelation in the message of the Qur'an from God to the Prophet Muhammad. This message ends the process of prophecy and completes the revelations of the Old and New Testaments. There are two main categories of Islam. The majority of believers adhere to Sunni Islam, which emphasizes dependence on the interpretation of religious texts by agreement between appropriate scholars. In the minority are followers of Shi'i Islam, which sees authority as residing more in particular individuals who serve as authorities themselves. The majority of British Muslims are Sunnis. Islam sets out principles of prayer, charity and pilgrimage for its adherents, and emphasizes study of the Qur'an. Men and women are given different roles within the religion, and there is often segregation during prayer and socially.

There are, at the end of the twentieth century, about two million Muslims in Britain. Around two-thirds come from South Asia, with the others from the Middle East, Cyprus and Iran. They are a very rapidly growing religious group, since the age structure of the population is comparatively young and Muslim families tend to have more children than the average. Although Muslims share a core of religious beliefs, there is not much unity among the Muslims in Britain. There has been a longstanding Muslim presence in Britain, but it is the recent large immigration from South Asia and East Africa which has led to the rapid growth of the Muslim population. Many Muslims came to work in the manufacturing industries of the North and Midlands, and the majority of the Pakistani community are based outside the Southeast and London. Given the change in economic structure from manufacturing to services, those Muslims have experienced high rates of unemployment, while other Muslim groups have managed to become successful in the self-employed sectors and the professions. This often has far more to do with their ethnic background than their religion, and there do seem to be different rates of success in education, employment and income between different ethnic groups, which often include Muslims. Islam is a religion and not the name of an ethnic group, so Muslims often cut across ethnic groups.

The Muslim community is largely based in the major British cities, especially London, Birmingham, Manchester, Bradford and Glasgow. As a fairly recent immigrant community, they have not enjoyed much success in British politics and culture, having managed to produce just one Muslim MP in the 1997 election, and without a major influence on cultural and commercial activities. Perhaps the most important group has been one of the smallest: the Arab community centred in London. London has become the centre of the Arabic press, and also a major financial centre for the oil economies of the Middle East, and the skill and learning of the Arab community has combined with their comparative wealth to dominate the intellectual life of the Islamic community. The notion of such a community should not be overstressed, however, since Muslims tend to divide up on ethnic grounds, and the attempts to link all facets of the community, such as the Muslim Parliament, are not widely supported. The community has had difficulties in representing itself with a common voice politically, and even in ensuring that the rules of *halal* (permitted) slaughter correctly apply to all such labelled meat. There has also been only limited support for the idea of Muslim schools, which so far have been rejected by the Department for Education as candidates for state support since they are invariably in areas of cities with too many school places already. Such rejection has led to suspicions about its precise motivation, of course, and has only served to increase the antagonism which some Muslims feel for the official institutions of the United Kingdom.

Islam is often regarded as a threatening and antagonistic force in Britain, especially given the activities of the anti-Rushdie book burnings in response to the publication of *The Satanic Verses*. The notion of Islamic fundamentalists who are determined to assert themselves has been perceived as a threat to liberal British culture, and there have certainly been a number of groups of Muslims who have insisted on their rights to a separate Islamic education and who have opposed the ethos of a multicultural approach to religion in the National Curriculum. There has also been a struggle between different organizations backed by Saudi and Iranian money to orientate the community in particular directions. Even those committed to a multicultural society have been disturbed by what seems to be a growth in Islamic exclusivism, especially among young British Muslims who have increasingly distanced themselves from their parents and challenged the traditional community and religious leadership. All this has taken place within a general cultural background which has replaced communism with Islam as the central threat internationally to the Western democracies, and it is hardly surprising that as a result British Muslims should feel under attack, and sometimes react vigorously. However, all the evidence suggests that very few British Muslims are attracted to fundamentalist ideas, which imply the necessity of a very distinct lifestyle for Muslims, and most Muslims continue to blend their religious principles with ordinary life in British society. An interesting question concerns the extent to which Muslims in Britain will be able to resist the forces of secularism, which have played such an important role in diminishing the role of religion in the lives of its nominal adherents. It is too early to answer this question, and it is worth emphasizing that the contemporary experience of Muslims in Britain is more affected by their ethnic background than by their religion.

See also: Indian communities; Pakistani communities

Further reading

Lewis, B. and Schnapper, D. (eds) (1994) *Muslims in Europe*, London: Pinter (an account of the British community compared with the situation in other European countries).

Lewis, P. (1994) *Islamic Britain: Religion, Politics and Identity among British Muslims*, London: I.B. Tauris (a very interesting account of a particular community, that in Bradford).

OLIVER LEAMAN

J

Jackson, Glenda

b. 1936, Birkenhead

Actress and politician

As an actress, Glenda Jackson was noted for her powerful stage and screen performances. Following success in the theatre, emphatic interpretation of her roles gained widespread attention on screen in the acclaimed adaptation of D.H. Lawrence's *Women in Love* (1969), directed by Ken **Russell**, for which she won an Oscar. In the 1970s she offered a forceful portrayal of Elizabeth I in *Mary, Queen of Scots* and showed an aptitude for comedy in *A Touch of Class*, for which she was awarded her second Oscar. Varied theatre and film appearances of the 1980s included involvement in further Ken Russell projects, including *Salomé's Last Dance* and *The Rainbow.* Jackson retired from acting in the 1990s to become a Labour Member of Parliament.

ALICE E. SANGER

Jainism

According to tradition, Mahavira, the founder of the Jain religion, was born in the state of Bihar in India in 599 BC. Jainism therefore has as great a claim to antiquity as Buddhism and there are similarities between the two religions. Jainism is an austere, non-theistic religion, its central tenet being non-violence, practised in an extremely comprehensive way by its monastic followers who are required to walk with extreme caution to avoid crushing insects and to wear masks and strain drinking water. A minority religion in India, it never became a missionary religion like Buddhism. Jainism found its way to Britain with members of the Indian merchant class who were, and remain, its chief adherents.

See also: Buddhism; Hinduism; Islam

JAN EVANS

Japanese communities

The modern relationship between Britain and Japan dates back to the nineteenth century. As the richest and most advanced industrial power, Britain was the obvious model for Japan's modernization programme following the Meiji Restoration of 1868; thousands of students and scholars were despatched by Japan's dirigiste government to learn from Britain's industrial, scientific, engineering and maritime successes. Many members of the future Japanese ruling class spent time mixing with and mimicking their British counterparts at universities in Britain; two of the current emperor's children studied at Oxford University. The Japanese novelist Natsume Soseki, who came to Britain in 1912 and spent most of that time holed up in his room, famously hated the place. Afterwards he wrote, 'The two years I spent in London were the most unpleasant years of my life. Among English gentlemen I lived in misery, like a poor dog that had strayed among a pack of wolves. I understand the population of London is about five million.

Frankly speaking, I felt as if I were a drop of water amid five million drops of oil.'

The short-lived Anglo-Japanese Alliance (1902–23) was interrupted by the clash of imperial ambitions which led ultimately to the Second World War; normal relations were restored again in the late 1940s. Despite this, however, the Japanese community in Britain was small throughout most of the postwar period (barely 1,000 people for most of the 1960s), and it is only really since the Japanese capital influx into Britain in the 1980s that the Japanese have become a significant economic and cultural force in this country. There are now over 50,000 students, company workers, government employees and their families registered as being resident in Britain, with almost half of these living in London and only 2,000 outside England. Many of these are attached to the UK arms of the banks, brokerage houses and electronics and automobile companies which have been established here from the late 1970s.

In addition there are thousands of tourists who come to visit the land of kings and queens, country estates, twee English villages, Wordsworth, Austen, Sherlock Holmes, Burns, Shakespeare and Beatrix Potter that they have read about in comics and books. A cultural map of Britain for many Japanese tourists would look like a jagged line running up the spine of the country and would include the major sights of London, Stratford, Wedgwood, the Lake District and Edinburgh. Brave souls who divert west to visit Beatle City in Liverpool are often shocked to find a scarred, de-industrialized landscape radically at odds with their misty-eyed cultural memories.

When not sightseeing, Japanese visitors crowd London's Regent Street and Camden Lock, and most British universities have many Japanese students studying English and other subjects. The relationship between Japanese and British universities is increasingly a reciprocal one. Japanese language and culture has become an important area of study, and about 500 young British undergraduates enrol in Japan's various public and private schemes every year to teach English.

Servicing the famously fussy and dedicated Japanese consumer in Britain are the many restaurants, shops and bars which have sprung up in the major cities and which have introduced Japanese cuisine including sushi, tempura and noodles to a generation of British people. Japanese pop culture too has arrived in Britain; manga comics, anime, karaoke, walkmans, video games and tamagochi have become ubiquitous cultural commodities during the 1980s and 1990s. Japanese generic design, with its eye for detail and its minimalist, superficial aesthetic in industry (cars and electronics) and fashion (Issey Miyake, Muji) has become a major influence on British culture. Popular music from Japan has a certain kitsch (shonen knife) or cult (Yellow Magic Orchestra) following in Britain but has never achieved mainstream success. There are some indications that a new generation of Japanese DJs and artists like Ken Ishii and Boom Boom Satellite, bringing with them so-called 'intelligent dance music' may be about to change this. Perhaps more significant than the influence of Japanese pop culture, however, are Japanese 'post-Fordist' management techniques and industrial strategies which have been imported and copied by British companies; 'just-in-time manufacturing', 'team-working' and 'total quality networks' have become part of the mainstream language of British management.

Despite the collapse of the bubble economy in Japan in the early 1990s and the longest recession in its postwar history, Japanese people still come to visit and live in the UK in large numbers. Indeed, notwithstanding the bitter legacy of the Second World War, there is every indication that the economic and cultural relationship between the two countries will deepen. Japanese capital has laid down firm roots here as a base for much of its European operations, and the many banks, car and electronic plants dotted around the country will not easily be uprooted.

See also: Chinese communities

Further reading

Insight Japan 5(4), February 1997, special issue *The Japanese in Britain*.

DAVID McNEILL

Jarman, Derek

b. 1942, Northwood; d. 1994, Dungeness

Painter and film-maker

Derek Jarman's protean career as artist, designer, film and video maker, writer, gardener, media celebrity and AIDS activist began with his first major painting exhibition at London's Liston Gallery in 1969. Jarman designed visually striking sets and costumes for theatre and cinema, notably for Ken **Russell**'s films *The Devils* and *The Savage Messiah*. While experimenting with Super 8 film-making techniques, Jarman completed his first feature film, *Sebastiane* (1975). He went on to direct an innovative and controversial oeuvre of gay cinema including *Jubilee*, *Caravaggio*, *The Last of England*, *The Garden*, *Edward II*, *Wittgenstein* and *Blue*. Jarman died of AIDS in 1994.

Further reading

O'Pray, M. (1995) *Derek Jarman: Dreams of England*, London: British Film Institute.

MARK DOUGLAS

jazz

London was considered a jazz city in the 1950s and 1960s. Gerrard Street, now Chinatown in London, saw the opening of countless jazz clubs, perhaps the most influential of which was Ronnie Scott's, founded in 1959. Ronnie Scott (b. 1927), a world-renowned tenor saxophonist, was the driving force behind securing a permanent home for jazz in Britain. Chris Barber (b. 1930) is recognized as one of the great pioneers of British jazz. He is best known for being a fine trombone player and bandleader, but started his musical studies as a violinist and soprano saxophonist. His biggest hit record was 'Petit Fleur' in 1959, which reached number three in the British chart and number five in the United States. 'Petit Fleur' made a significant impact on the trad jazz boom in Britain, and undoubtedly helped pave the way for trad musicians Kenny Ball (b. 1930), and Acker Bilk (b. 1929). Kenny Ball became a professional trumpeter in the mid-1950s and made his mark as an outstanding trad jazz performer. (Trad, an abbreviation of traditional jazz, was a peculiarly European form of deviant Dixieland, predominantly influenced and developed by British bands). His success continued in the 1960s but, due to the speedy invasion of **pop and rock** music he was forced to move into the cabaret scene and touring abroad. However, in 1968 he was back in London supporting Louis Armstrong, and during the 1970s he continued to tour jazz clubs and theatres in Europe and Britain. Due to his remarkable all-round talents and peak spots on television shows such as *Morecambe and Wise* and *Saturday Night at the Mill*, as well as regular appearances on Royal Variety Shows, he became a much loved and admired household name. In 1985, his band was the first to tour in the Soviet Union, where he was received with rapturous applause.

Acker Bilk, also a significant protagonist in Britain's trad boom, followed a similar career path and he too recorded commercial material. The key woman figure of this time was Cleo Laine (b. 1927), who made her first band appearance with Johnny Dankworth in the 1950s. Laine and Dankworth married and both enjoyed very successful careers. Laine's distinct delivery opened up opportunities in musical, theatre and acting.

The most significant development in the period 1950 to 1970 was the immense improvement in the standard of British jazz. Jim Godbolt argues that 'the history of jazz in Britain is a remarkable story of missionary zeal' (1989: 299). Numerous jazz jamborees and festivals were regularly held in London; many of these had been established in the 1930s, but were generally notable for having only a minimum of jazz content. However, by the late 1950s the Musicians Benevolent Fund, organizer of the jazz jamborees, belatedly realized that the musical content should be consistent with the title. Therefore in 1958, the bill included Johnny Dankworth and his Orchestra, Humphrey Lyttelton and his Band, the Jazz Couriers and Chris Barber. A unique feature of the British jazz scene was the number of musicians who were also writers, including Humphrey Lyttelton, George Melly, Sandy Brown, Ian Carr, Benny Green and John Chilton, amongst others. In 1972 John Chilton, through his own company Bloomsbury

Books, published his *Who's Who of Jazz*, a book that became a standard reference book. Shops devoted entirely to jazz and blues were mainly a postwar phenomenon. The first and most important was Dobells in London in the 1950s, which became a collectors' mecca and a dropping-in point for visiting musicians. Doug Dobell, the proprietor, continued to run the club until 31 December 1980, when representatives of Westminster City Council came to put padlocks on the door – the sounds of jazz were still defiantly issuing from inside, marking the sad end of an era.

Jazz within Britain has developed from the simple structures and harmonies of its beginnings to the sophistication and subtleties of the 1920s and 1930s, into the complexities of bebop and postbop music in the 1940s and 1950s. On entering the 1960s there was a proliferation of diverse jazz schools, with abstraction being very popular, and the term 'mainstream' was no longer applicable. The 1970s brought jazzrock fusion, influenced by Miles Davis, Charlie Mingus and John Coltrane. Also, the use of electric instruments and contemporary production techniques, including multi-track recording, became increasingly popular in the production of jazz music. With each successive decade the scope of the music expanded to such a degree that the term 'jazz' required regular reappraisals and redefinitions. Although jazz in the 1980s and 1990s continued to be considered a specialist music, it is important to recognize the enormous impact that it has had on twentieth century music in general. Also, the proliferation of jazz-dedicated radio stations, television shows and magazines helped it to reach a much wider audience, comparable with its popularity during the trad boom of the 1950s.

Courtney Pine, an outstanding saxophonist, was the first British-born black musician firmly to make his mark on the jazz scene in the 1980s, and his success led to unprecedented attention to jazz within Britain. Julian Joseph, Gay Crosby, Mark Mondesir, Orphy Robinson, Cheryl Alleyne, Steve Williamson, Kathy Stobart, Norma Winstone, Andy Sheppard and Tommy Smith were all significant figures in the emerging innovative jazz of the late 1980s and 1990s. Smith, perhaps the most diverse in approach, was the first British

musician to be signed up as a leader by the American-based Blue Note jazz label.

See also: funk; jazz funk; jazz soloists

Further reading

Carr, C. (1973) *Modern Jazz in Britain*, London: Latimer New Dimensions.

Cracker, C. (1994) *Get Into Jazz: A Comprehensive Beginners Guide*, New York: Bantam Books.

Godbolt, J. (1989) *A History of Jazz in Britain 1950–1970*, London: Quartet Books.

FATIMA FERNANDES

jazz funk

Jazz funk originated out of the process of mixing together sounds and rhythms from different sources, specifically the contemporary swing style of **jazz** in the 1950s and **funk**, a sort of high-energy black rock 'n' roll, which had emerged out of **soul** and rhythm and blues. Both jazz and funk can be considered to be meta-genres; they are each broader terms for a wider variety of associated musical styles. Jazz funk is often called fusion, because of the way it successfully blends the two styles. The jazz funk movement served to reinvigorate and heighten the jazz influence in pop music (see **pop and rock**). One of the most original exponents of jazz funk was George Clinton in the late 1960s, with his groups Parliament and Funkadelic. By the mid-1970s they had become an important force in black American music. Other American acts such as James Brown, Kool and the Gang and Earth Wind and Fire displayed considerable jazz funk tendencies. Jazz funk classics in the 1980s were Tom Browne's 'Funkin' For Jamaica' and Herbie Hancock's 'Rockit', in the same tradition as his 'Headhunters' album in the 1970s. In Great Britain in the early 1980s there was a revival of the jazz funk style, with bands such as Linx, Imagination and Shakatak bringing a slightly more **disco** feel to the music. Aiming to inspire in their listeners the notion of James Brown meets Charlie Parker, they took the theme of jazz funk fusion as a basis, and incorporated the New York avant-garde styles of James Chance and the

Contortions, and The Lounge Lizards, with the odd interspersions of African polyrhythms. The British revival was not altogether successful, lasting for perhaps a year, mainly due to the fact that it was considered to be a mere inventive version of disco pop.

More palatable bands followed, such as Rip, Rig and Panic, Maximum Joy, The Higsons and Pigbag, with their chart success 'Papa's Got a Brand New Pig Bag', a title borrowed from an earlier James Brown hit. Jazz funk was typified by its mixture of laid-back mellowness, the slapping technique employed by its bass players, and its groove factor, often backed by complicated percussion. Modern-day exponents of jazz funk in the UK are bands such as Level 42, Jamiroquai, Galliano and The Brand New Heavies.

See also: disco; jazz soloists

ALICE BENNETT

jazz soloists

Jazz, though cosmopolitan, is thoroughly integrated into British culture. Several overseas musicians work here, including Argentinian-born Lalo Schifrin and saxophonist Julian Arguelles. Colin Towns, who is best known for his scores for television dramas such as *Our Friends in the North*, has orchestrated many talented indigenous jazz soloists in his attempts to produce a synthesis of postwar orchestral jazz. He has devised concerts based on the work of musicians known for their work in Loose Tubes. Among soloists he has used are Nigel Hitchcock (flute), Pete King (saxophone), Mark Nightingale (trombone), Gerard Presencer (flugelhorn and trumpet) and Alan Skidmore (tenor sax). Other names well-known nationally are Winton Marsalis, Courtney Pine and Guy Barker.

See also: jazz funk

MIKE STORRY

Jehovah's Witnesses

The Jehovah's Witnesses are a religious sect that originated in the USA in 1872. They regard the return of Christ as imminent, after which the world will be theocratically governed and consist only of the 144,000 of the faithful; however, the elect will be chosen to reign with Christ in heaven.

Jehovah's Witnesses take a proselytizing view with regard to the faith and are active in door-to-door 'calls', but take a primarily fatalistic view about life and eschew interference with what God has decreed. Most spectacularly, this has resulted in the refusal to accept medical treatment that utilizes the blood of others. Such autonomous wishes are always respected, even if death is the outcome. Such wishes are not, however, extended to minors or to the guardians of minors; where guardians of minors refuse life-saving to those minors, the courts always overrule the refusal.

See also: Christian Science; evangelism

PAUL BARRY CLARKE

Jewish communities

Judaism is the religion of the Jewish people. It is a religion which prescribes rules for its followers, rules which are founded on interpretations of scripture and on universal moral principles. In modern times, the small Jewish population in Britain was swollen by large numbers of immigrants from Eastern Europe at the start of the century, and then by a more limited immigration from Nazi-occupied Europe before the start of the Second World War. The majority of British Jews follow Ashkenazi (European) rather than Sefardi (Oriental) rites and liturgies.

On the whole, the experience of the Jewish community in Britain has been a positive one, with many Jews reaching high positions in British political and cultural life and becoming successful in the commercial and professional spheres. This has enabled the community to move out of the poorer inner city areas which they first inhabited to the more prosperous suburbs, and to assimilate closely with the indigenous British population.

Judaism as a faith is based on the Torah, which can either refer to the first five books of the Bible, or to the whole of the Hebrew Bible, or even the body of Jewish law and practice. The Torah is based on the covenant which was established between God and Israel, and in its widest sense it has developed into an all-enveloping way of life. Jews take a variety of attitudes to their traditions. Almost half of the Jewish population in Britain are members of an orthodox community, which means that they generally adhere to a traditionalist ethos with respect to religion. They accept that the Torah is the direct revelation of the word of God and the divine will, and all the laws and regulations which have developed are representations of the way of life which God wants Jews to follow. This involves a strict set of rules concerning prayer, religious holidays and the sabbath, including rules about what sorts of food are kosher (holy or acceptable) and even what combinations of cloth are permissible for a Jew to wear. Within orthodoxy there is considerable variety of practice, extending to the Hasidim who wear clothes reminiscent of eighteenth-century Poland and live in self-contained communities, to the more modern orthodox Jew who is in appearance indistinguishable from anyone else in Britain, yet who nonetheless obeys a strict set of rules in his or her behaviour. The centre of religious life is both the home and the synagogue; as orthodox Jews are not supposed to take transport on Sabbath and festivals, so they need to live within walking distance of a synagogue. This has led to areas of some British cities becoming strongly Jewish, with several synagogues and families living in close proximity and with kosher butchers and other shops catering for the specific requirements of the Jewish community.

About 17 percent of the Jewish population are members of the Reform or Progressive movements, which regard divine revelation as changing and not something which can be captured perfectly within a system of legislation. The followers of these movements are less committed to traditional law and practice, and they pray not only in Hebrew but also in English. They tend to link their religion to the teachings of the prophets, which they interpret as coming close to modern forms of liberalism, and they do not discriminate between men and women with respect to religious roles.

Thirty-six percent of the Jewish population is not a member of any synagogue at all. If there is one issue which can be said to worry the whole community, it is that of assimilation. The Jewish population has shrunk quite dramatically since the end of the last war, from around 450,000 to 300,000. This is largely due to intermarriage, and ever-increasing numbers of Jews are marrying Gentiles. According to Jewish law, the child of a Jewish mother remains Jewish, but this is not the case if only the father is Jewish. In both cases, the children of such marriages are often not brought up within Judaism, and the parents may abandon such links as they have with their religion. In addition there are many Jews who are so assimilated into the local Gentile community that they follow few if any distinctive religious practices, and do not identify with the Jewish community or religion at all.

While in overall numbers the size of the community is shrinking rapidly, in wealth and power it remains very successful. Educational achievement and income levels remain above the average, and the proportion of Jewish parliamentarians and ministers far exceeds their share of the population as a whole. Anti-semitism has been a persistent strain in British culture, but it has not succeeded in restraining the advance of the Jewish community in society. During the Conservative government of Mrs Thatcher it was said that there were more Estonians in the Cabinet than Etonians, a reference to the high proportion of Jewish cabinet ministers. There are many influential Jewish politicians in all major political parties, in the media, in academic life and commerce. Although the Jewish community tends to identity itself with Israel and is solidly Zionist, there has only been limited migration to Israel. As the community has become wealthier and more established, there is evidence that its voting patterns have moved to the right. This was sometimes also a response to growing antagonism on the Left towards Israel.

The state of Israel is perhaps the strongest unifying factor in a very diverse community, but at other times there is often a great deal of internecine dispute, especially between the different religious organizations. The Chief Rabbi, for example, is only the head of the United Synagogue, not of the whole of the British Jewish community, and not even of the whole orthodox movement. Nonetheless, there is also often a strong feeling of belonging to a community, and as with many groups based on fairly recent immigration, considerable pride at the notable achievements of members of that community.

Further reading

Alderman, G. (1992) *Modern British Jewry*, Oxford: Oxford University Press (the standard discussion of the topic).

Rubinstein, W. (1996) *A History of the Jews in the English-Speaking World: Great Britain*, London: Macmillan (the best modern treatment of the topic).

OLIVER LEAMAN

Joffe, Roland

b. 1945, London

Film-maker

After working on television, Joffe went on to direct two unlikely 1980s blockbusters, *The Killing Fields* (1984) and *The Mission* (1985), for which he won Academy Award nominations and was hailed as the crest of the latest British wave to hit Hollywood. Up to, and arguably including, the egregious *The Scarlet Letter* (1995), Joffe had primarily made social conscience films (including *City of Joy* (1992), set in Calcutta) which had managed generally to combine sensitive subjects with box office success. His *Spongers* (1978), a television film about poverty in contemporary Britain, won the Prix Italia.

MIKE STORRY

Johnson, Linton Kwesi

b. 1952, Chapeltown (Jamaica)

Dub poet

After coming to Britain in 1963, Johnson took a sociology degree at Goldsmith's College in London. He has continued an early interest in music, literature, and politics through poetry performances, verse publications, writing for the *New Musical Express* and *Melody Maker*, and his involvement with the Race Today collective. His 1977 album *Dread Beat an' Blood* has been seen as the blueprint and catalyst for dub poetry with its combination of reggae rhythms (provided by Dennis Bovell) and Johnson's slow, careful and directly political lyrics. He is principally known for

tackling subjects such as the 1981 race riots, the arrest on suspicion laws, and white violence on blacks, particularly on *Forces of Victory* (1979), *Making History* (1984) and *Tings and Times* (1990).

See also: black performance poets; dub

PETER CHILDS

Jordan, Neil

b. 1950, County Sligo (Ireland)

Film-maker

Born in 1950, Jordan started as a writer moving on to script consultant on *Excalibur* (1981) before his directing debut, the impressive *Angel* (1982), a thriller set within the context of the troubles in Northern Ireland. Other films include *Company of Wolves* (1984) with its contemporary and adult treatment of a fairy tale, *Mona Lisa* (1986) and *We're No Angels* (1989). He returned to Irish-related issues in 1988 with *High Spirits*, *The Crying Game* (1992), a romantic thriller and the drama *The Miracle* (1991) although their treatment of his native Ireland was far less serious and more whimsical than either *Angel* or the controversial and critically acclaimed *Michael Collins* (1996) the romantic cinebiography of the legendary Irish leader.

GUY OSBORN
STEVE GREENFIELD

joyriding

The use of cars in criminal activity took on a new phase in the 1980s and 1990s as cars themselves became the focus of deviancy. Aside from conventional car theft, vehicles were stolen to be used by joyriders. Joyriding often involved the deliberate baiting of police patrols who would then be engaged in high-speed car chases through mainly urban areas. Prevalent activities amongst the youth of both neglected housing estates and the market town, they are considered as moments of dispossession and disenfranchisement from a fragmenting social order representing a form of escape. The subsequent 'moral panic' surrounding such activities was fuelled by television depiction and resulted in a number of legislative provisions to deal with the problem.

GUY OSBORN
STEVE GREENFIELD

Julien, Isaac

b. 1961

Film-maker

Isaac Julien lives in London where he works as a film director. He is one of the founding members of Sankofa Black Film Workshop, and the foremost of the new wave of black British independent film makers. He co-directed *The Passion of Remembrance* with Maureen Blackwood in 1986, and directed *This is Not an Aids Ad* in 1987. In 1989, he directed the prize-winning short film *Looking for Langston* (about US poet Langston Hughes). His full-length feature film, *Young Soul Rebels* (1991), made through the BFI Production Board with a budget of £1.2 million gained the International Critics Award at the Cannes Film Festival. His 1992 two-part documentary series *Black & White in Colour* for BBC television was shown in the New York Film Festival. In 1993 he made *The Attendant* for Channel 4 television.

See also: Black Audio Film Collective; diasporan film-makers

EUGENE LANGE

jungle

Jungle is a form of **dance music** characterized by the use of high-speed (usually around 160 beats per minute), highly syncopated drums and simple looped bass lines. Early jungle records often used a **reggae**/ragga 'toasting' style lead vocal, while the newer 'intelligent' style (a term invented by the dance music press which many jungle artists disown as being too elitist) is usually accompanied by ethereal strings and female vocals, often incorporating elements borrowed from **jazz**.

Jungle (sometimes also known as 'drum 'n' bass') developed from the hardcore **rave** scene when DJs realized that the breakbeats they were playing were approximately twice the speed of 1970s **dub** records, and that the bass lines from these tunes could be played over the drums. In these formative years, a major factor was the exclusivity of records, with tunes frequently being pressed only on a few 'dub plates' – white labelled twelve-inch singles – over which DJs would vie with each other, much as had happened in the early years of the **ska** scene. A development of this was a plethora of small, independent record labels, which often released only records made by one artist, as in the case of Photek's identically named imprint, or by a small, close-knit group of artists, as in, for example, the Good Looking/Looking Good label run by LTJ Bukem.

Another facet of the jungle scene is a widespread use of aliases, with artists changing their identity with each genre they cover. A prime example would have to be 4 Hero, who also record as Tek 9, Tom & Jerry, Nu Era and Jacob's Optical Stairway. As well as enabling more musical freedom, this tactic also allows artists to avoid being tied to any single record label, which means that jungle, perhaps more than any other style of music, is controlled by those who make it rather than being in the hands of the larger recording industry.

Sometimes called the British answer to **hip hop**, jungle was primarily associated with urban, predominantly black youth from its beginnings around 1992–3, until artists such as Goldie and Alex Reece achieved wider success in 1995. This led to some artists, including Reece and Photek, signing to major labels, with jungle subsequently moving towards mainstream acceptance. 1995 also saw the distinctive rhythms of the music beginning to appear on **techno** records, and by 1996 jungle backings could be heard in television advertising.

See also: clubs

SIMON BOTTOM

junk mail

Junk mail (alternatively known as direct mail) is sent unsolicited through the post. The availability of huge computer databases has enabled the direct mailing of millions of people. From the merchandisers' point of view, this is a cheap way of targeting customers. It can often pay its way with a response rate of less than 5 percent. Large privatized companies such as Southern Electric and United Utilities have come under fire from the Data Protection Registry for including with their bills promotional literature for insurance companies, motoring organizations and so on. In the year to March 1997, complaints from the public rose 32 percent to 3,897. Junk mail is also becoming a problem on fax machines, and in the late 1990s the Internet version of junk mail became known as 'spamming'.

MIKE STORRY

K

Kapoor, Anish

b. 1954

Sculptor

Winner of the Turner Prize in 1991, Anish Kapoor is best known for his biomorphic and geometric, sculpted shapes which he covers in brightly coloured pigments and displays in groups, developing relationships between each object which often suggest landscapes. Inspired by the mounds of intensely coloured powders which he saw on display in India, the artist tries to evoke something of his cultural heritage. The primary colours which he uses are often imbued with a symbolism which relates to Indian art and religion, while the shapes often imply fertility. He exhibited in the British Pavilion at the 1990 Venice Biennale, and an exhibition at the Hayward Gallery in 1998 saw Kapoor experimenting with the representation of absence.

See also: painting; sculpture

LUCINDA TOWLER

Kidron, Beeban

b. 1961

Film-maker

Beeban Kidron is a versatile director who has filmed both traditional and avant-garde stories. Her oeuvre includes a television adaptation of Jeannette Winterson's lesbian coming-of-age novel *Oranges Are Not the Only Fruit* (1989), plus the films *Antonia and Jane* (1991), *Used People* (1992) and *To Wong Foo, Thanks for Everything, Julie Newmar* (1995). The last named is the story (written by Douglas Carter Beane) of three drag queens en route to the Los Angeles gay pageant. They are marooned, and enliven a Mid-Western town with their 'theatricality – gay men celebrating their feminine side' (Kidron). Her period romance *Swept From The Sea* (1997) is based on Joseph Conrad's novella *Amy Foster*, and stars Vincent Perez, Rachel Weisz, Ian McKellen, Joss Ackland and Kathy Bates.

See also: film, feminist

MIKE STORRY

Knightsbridge

Knightsbridge is the fashionable area in London, between Chelsea and Kensington, where Harrods department store, designer shops and a very few expensive homes are located. Part of its mystique comes from the fact that the wealthy and powerful from all over the world are drawn to shop there; newspapers referred to the 'Knightsbridge trap' in the recent case of General Pinochet. Knightsbridge's epicentre is Sloane Square, an area inhabited by **Sloane Rangers** (well-to-do young women fashionably dressed with chic headscarves tied at the chin). Property developers, including The Prudential insurance company, have faced great opposition to their plans, particularly those for Knightsbridge Green opposite Harrods, because existing residents have strong support from West-minster Council.

See also: department stores

                                        MIKE STORRY

Kubrick, Stanley

b. 1928, New York (USA)

Film-maker

Though his early films were produced in Holly-wood, Kubrick's finest and most innovative work is British. He emigrated to the UK in 1961 and his first British film was an adaptation of Nabokov's *Lolita* (1962). This was followed by the classic anti-war satire, *Dr Strangelove* (1964). The success of these films led to Kubrick being the first director to take full artistic control over his work. *2001: A Space Odyssey* (1968) and *A Clockwork Orange* (1971) are testaments to his overall vision of film making, both visually intense and narratively confusing. Reaction to *A Clockwork Orange* made Kubrick rethink his artistic direction, and since 1971 he has made only three films: *Barry Lyndon* (1975), *The Shining* (1980) and *Full Metal Jacket* (1987). His first film for twelve years, *Eyes Wide Shut*, with Tom Cruise and Nicole Kidman, is due to be released in 1999.

                                        SAM JOHNSTONE

L

labels

The use of labelling on clothes has historically served a number of purposes. Essentially a badge of assured quality, the labels became for a time more a sign of conspicuous consumption. The switch towards more ostentatious advertising of names has been accompanied by the development of the cult of the individual designer. For a time, the fashion world dictated that t-shirts, belts, and clothes emblazoned with the name of the designer or producer were *de rigueur*, a trend developed by top designers such as Calvin Klein. This was a boon for counterfeiters, who were easily able to incorporate the fashionable look at little extra cost; it is the names and logos that identify the copied items for the pirate market. This was made even easier by the move towards more casual and sports clothing, which utilized materials that were more readily available to counterfeiters and correspondingly cheaper. A series of trade mark and intellectual property infringement cases were brought against offenders, but the problem is not easy to contain in a global market. While designers may not find much comfort in the notion that 'copying is the highest form of flattery', it is certainly true that a designer can be said to have arrived in the mass market when pirated versions of his or her designs begin to appear. As well as the issue of counterfeiting, a further attack on the exclusivity of designer clothing has been made by one of the giant supermarket retailers, Tesco. The company has sought to buy large quantities of designer products and sell them at greatly reduced prices. It became apparent that there was some resistance to this attempt to bring designer clothing into the mass market.

The concept of consumer goods identified with a particular designer extends beyond clothing and into other products such as spectacles and cosmetics. While some trendy designers have still embraced the idea of 'clothes as adverts' (notably Duffer of St George, which has evolved from a Camden market stall to a big-label business in little over ten years) and preppie designer Tommy Hilfiger still finds takers for clothes emblazoned in this way, there has been something of a backlash against this concept; more recently, the emphasis has been less on the conspicuous and more on the understated.

See also: designer labels

GUY OSBORN
STEVE GREENFIELD

labour migration

Since the recession of the early 1990s, labour has had to become more mobile. The Conservative cabinet minister Norman (later Lord) Tebbitt became notorious for his advice to the unemployed to 'get on your bike' (meaning to move house in search of work). Many unemployed gravitated from the north to the southeast of England, where the statistical rate of unemployment was lower by as much as 25 percent. In some cases these migrants were unable to find work, and were thus worse off than if they had stayed at home where they had the support of friends and family. Television reports of

homelessness on the streets of London and other major urban centres attributed blame for the problem to this advice.

See also: Big Issue, The; North of England

MIKE STORRY

Labour Party

Despite being one of the only two major parties in British politics, the Labour Party has suffered from a lack of electoral success, having won a clear governing majority only three times (1945, 1966 and 1997). It has long suffered from factional infighting, whether by committed Labour Party members who are divided along ideological lines, or by far-left groups who, through a process of entryism, have hijacked the party's popular support for their own ends (for example, the Revolutionary Socialist League). The moderate centrist factions of the Labour Party have had to contend with the challenges of the Left, to the apparent detriment of electoral success. This once self-professed socialist party has, since the 1980s, moved towards social democratic policies acknowledging the importance of the market. In the post-Thatcher era, the party has turned from what many saw as its founding tenets (such as a commitment to nationalized industries, or strong links with the **trade unions**) to present a pragmatic challenge to the long-standing incumbents.

During the 1970s the Labour Party swung to the left. The 1960s had seen the government of Harold Wilson (elected leader in 1963) fail both to run the economy successfully and to unite the party. Despite efforts to remedy the balance of payments deficit by reducing overseas expenditure and devaluing the pound in 1967, Wilson's economic success was limited. Labour lost the 1970 election and were in opposition again. The Left within the party formulated their own ideas, one of the best-known of which was the Alternative Economic Strategy (AES), as it became known. State intervention and control were central themes of the AES. In order to achieve their aims, the Left called for the creation of the National Enterprise Board which was to oversee this programme of widespread nationalization and planning. Recognizing

that the radical domestic agenda could not be addressed if the leadership's hands were tied by Brussels, they also called for withdrawal from **Europe**.

During this period, Tony Benn began to emerge as a leading light among the fundamentalist factions within the party. Popular amongst the ordinary party members, he was with, but not of, the leadership; despite his participation in the governments of Wilson (1964–70 and 1974–6) and Callaghan (1976–9), he rejected their social democratic agenda. Benn believed in class-based action and the need for the Labour party to move to the left.

As the economic situation worsened during the 1970s, so the Left continued their drive for influence of the leadership. The 1973 party conference adopted Labour's programme, which called for the creation of the aforementioned National Enterprise Board. The 1974 election manifesto was a compromise. Wilson, at odds with the Left and their programme, sought a social democratic path, and the tone of the manifesto was diluted, although it remained in keeping with the policies approved by conference.

The Labour Party was elected in February 1974 (with a minority administration until the October general election consolidated their position with a small majority). Once in power, the leadership sought to minimalize the Left's influence. Initially Wilson placated the Left; Tony Benn and Michael Foot, both doyens of the Left, received prominent government positions, Benn in Industry and Foot in Education. The 1975 Industry Act created the National Enterprise Board, but it was a pale imitation of what the Left had intended, having neither the scope nor funds to achieve the original aims. Benn was soon removed from the Department of Industry and sent to the much less important Department of Energy.

By the middle of the 1970s, events had overtaken the ideological battle within the Labour Party. Britain was experiencing a phenomenon known as stagflation, with high unemployment and high inflation. Keynesianism could not explain this, but **monetarism** could. The circumstances required action, and accordingly control of economic policy was wrested from the ideologues. The government was forced to adopt monetary discipline as a condition of an International Monetary Fund loan (necessitated by a run on sterling in 1976). A series of strikes in what was to become known as the **Winter of Discontent** finished any chance of a revival for Labour and, following a vote of no confidence, they were defeated at the 1979 election.

The 1980s were a turbulent time for the Labour Party, during which they were divided and electorally unsuccessful. The decade started well for the Left. When Callaghan stood down, Michael Foot replaced him as party leader (1980). In addition, constituency changes had favoured the Left. The party started to develop and adopt more overtly left-wing policies. By 1980, party conference support had been secured for unilateral nuclear disarmament, unconditional withdrawal from the European Community and the Alternative Economic Strategy, which involved increased nationalization. Labour's programme was revamped again in 1982. This time, however, the election manifesto of the following year (A New Hope For Britain) stuck closely to the policy document, much more closely than Wilson had done. The apparent failure of the Wilson/Callaghan government left social democracy open to its most fervent attack from the Left so far, and the result was a party split; in 1981 Roy Jenkins, David Owen, Shirley Williams and Bill Rodgers left Labour to form the Social Democratic Party (SDP), taking a number of Labour MPs with them. All four were revisionists and opposed the direction in which the fundamentalist Left wing was taking the party. The social democrats who remained within the party regrouped under the Labour Solidarity group banner and faced the 1983 election.

Labour suffered a crushing defeat, its worst since 1918. Foot stepped down immediately and was replaced by Neil Kinnock, who chose Roy Hattersley as his deputy. The Left were reeling. They finally had their chance to put their policies to the nation and had been rejected. They now became more isolated as new socialist thinkers found their voices within the party, men such as Bryan Gould, Robin Cook and Gordon Brown.

Kinnock was not able to proceed with a revisionist plan at any pace, not least for the reasons that he had the miners' strike and Militant

tendency to deal with. Kinnock rid the party of Militant, launching an attack at party conference (1985) and expelling members. He also condemned the tactics of Scargill during the 1984–5 miners' strike. Both actions illustrated Kinnock's commitment to a more moderate social democratic direction; but he moved slowly at first, aware that any radical change forced through in an expedite manner could further divide the party.

However, by the time of the 1987 election the manifesto was devoid of many of the Left's earlier promises. The radical agenda was diluted, as in the case of nationalization, or expunged, as in the case of the promise to leave the European Community. Kinnock stuck with the commitment to unilateral disarmament, but agreed to increased commitment to NATO. Further, Kinnock moved with the spirit of the time with regard to the economy, accepting the market and limiting his commitment to nationalization to key public areas. He talked of the social control of the economy, trying to coalesce social democracy with market-dominated economics. The process of change proceeded slowly during the period 1983–7 with Kinnock carefully laying important foundations period on which he was to build subsequently. Thus it was that Labour entered the 1987 election with a less radical agenda – and lost.

Following the 1987 election defeat, the pace of revisionist reform increased. A comprehensive policy review was instigated, which took two years to complete and culminated in the publication of the 70,000-word report, *Meet the Challenge, Make the Change*. The policy review set the trend for the Labour Party for the coming years. It was a practical response to Labour's lack of electoral success. It sought to increase the popularity of the party by moving away from unpopular policies such as nationalization and high taxation. In May 1990, a revised and slimmer version of the report, *Looking to the Future*, was published and formed the basis of Labour's 1992 election manifesto. The document had to contend with the fall of Keynesianism and move away from left-wing statist policies. Kinnock maintained that the review did not contradict the essence of the Party, although the commitment to the unions was weakened with an acceptance of many of Thatcher's restrictive reforms.

Kinnock managed to unite the party, and he altered the tone and direction of Labour policy. He offered a practical approach to making the party electable and led them to the 1992 election – only to suffer Labour's fourth consecutive defeat. He resigned, and John Smith, Kinnock's former shadow chancellor, succeeded him as leader of the Labour Party three months after the election. Smith was Labour Party leader until his untimely death in May 1994. He continued in the spirit of change if with his own style. Less antagonistic than Kinnock, he did not force the revisionist case so openly; yet he achieved monumental change. Significantly, he reformed the selection process for parliamentary candidates under the slogan 'One Member One Vote', weakening the power of the trade unions. Smith also came under pressure to reform Clause IV Part Four (viewed as Labour's commitment to nationalization and in essence the expression of the party's socialist commitment), most notably from Jack Straw, the shadow environment secretary. Clause IV had formed the essence of Labour Party policy for many years and although Smith was a modernizer he did not force the pace of change over this contentious issue. Cautiously and cleverly, he worked to further unite his party while continuing a programme of change.

Following John Smith's death, Tony Blair was elected leader. All early indications were that Blair would continue the work begun by his predecessors. Blair was clearly committed to a market economy and not afraid of making changes quickly. To Blair, socialism was not about a strong state controlling society but about society cooperating to the benefit of all; likewise in the economic sphere, he believed that government and industry should work in partnership. Soon after his election, Blair moved to alter the nature of the Labour Party and began by addressing the issue of Clause IV. In October 1994 he put forward a proposal to reform the constitution of the party, in his first platform speech as leader. This move received much press coverage and affirmed Blair's commitment to change. The new text of Clause IV was finally published in March 1995. Written principally by Blair, it set out Labour's commitment to the community and radically altered Labour's economic goals by detailing a belief in the market economy and the importance of both public and private ownership, thus giving up the commitment to common ownership and openly advocating a mixed economy. It also spoke of ensuring a just society and a caring community, in which the rights and interests of all are fairly represented. On 29 April 1995 Blair secured approval for the new proposal. In a short time, he had redefined the Party's aims as set out in its own constitution, creating what has become known as **New Labour**. As a consequence, the party secured a massive majority at the general election in May 1997.

Blair remains committed to change. His charismatic, almost presidential, leadership style stands as testament to this. He appears to have the support of his party in modernizing their organization and aims. Labour party policy continues to distance itself from previous left-wing ideals, leading some commentators to question where the process will end. Regardless of this, the Labour Party has undergone an extensive programme of modernization and reform. This change can be viewed partly as a response to changing social values, partly because of changing economic thought and partly due to a lack of electoral success.

See also: fringe groups; Labour Party black sections; Militant

Further reading

Jones, T. (1996) *Remaking The Labour Party,* London: Routledge.
Shaw, E. (1996) *The Labour Party Since 1945,* London: Blackwell.

ALASTAIR LINDSLEY

Labour Party black sections

Although more than 13 percent of the total Labour vote in 1983 came from ethnic minorities, there were no black MPs. Diane Abbott, Paul Boateng and Sharon Atkin promoted the idea of black sections within Labour to further minority representation and exercise some power within the party. The Labour leadership team of Neil Kinnock and Roy Hattersley, however, decided to stamp out black sections because they thought they were divisive and would prevent Labour from getting elected. Hence they deselected Atkin from a safe seat in Nottingham in 1987 when she said: 'I do not give a damn about Neil Kinnock and a racist Labour Party'. The idea of black sections then died.

See also: black Conservatives; black politics; fringe groups; New Labour

MIKE STORRY

'lads' and 'lager louts'

The terms 'lads' and 'lager louts' describe two different cultural phenomena. The lager lout first appeared as a conservative media target in the mid-1980s, the label encapsulating the leisure habits of nouveau riche working-class males who worked in City financial institutions, and their propensity for drinking imported bottled lager to excess and indulging in acts of violence. The 'lad' emerged in the early 1990s and was another media contrivance, set up in direct opposition to the politically correct male imagery that appeared at this time. The lad is seen as a beer-swilling, football-loving, girl-chasing caricature. Society was quick to acknowledge the lad: television shows, magazines, books and music all appeared to cater for the unreconstructed man.

See also: new man; tribalism

SAM JOHNSTONE

Laing, R.D.

b. 1927, Glasgow

Psychiatrist

Laing first came to public attention with the publication of his existentialist-inspired *The Divided Self* (1960) which challenged the orthodoxies of treatment. His influence declined steadily throughout the 1970s as clinical practice turned to new developments in drug therapy and away from the psycho-social nexus that Laing proffered. Now largely dismissed as an idealist, his emphasis on viewing the patient as a human being to be listened to remains influential, and represents a 'paradigm-shift' in thinking with regard to severe mental illness.

NEIL ANKERS

law courts

The historic public fascination with the proceedings of the criminal justice system remains undiminished, and is often fuelled by intense media activity. The courts, and specifically the image of the Central Criminal Court, The Old Bailey, remains a central dramatic forum in the narratives of everyday life. Recently, tensions between law and justice have appeared as the image of (in)justice has cast a shadow over a number of high profile miscarriage of justice cases (such as the Birmingham Six and the Bridgewater Four). To date, the English courts have resisted the intrusion of live television coverage that proved so controversial in the trials of O.J. Simpson and the Menendez brothers in the USA.

See also: government inquiries

GUY OSBORN
STEVE GREENFIELD

Lean, David

b. 1908, Croydon; d. 1991

Film-maker

Lean's career as a director was preceded by a long apprenticeship in film-making which ingrained in him a commitment to detail and quality. Despite the simplicity of *Brief Encounter* (1945), Lean established his ability to charge a narrative with powerful dramatic emphases. Versions of Charles Dickens's *Great Expectations* (1946) and *Oliver Twist* (1948), and later period dramas *Madeleine* (1950) and *Hobson's Choice* (1954), show an interest in conflicting social and moral codes more evident in his later films. The late 1950s and 1960s brought the larger scale projects for which Lean is best known, including *The Bridge on the River Kwai*, *Lawrence of Arabia* and *Doctor Zhivago*. While *A Passage to India* (1984) retained this sense of spectacle, his earliest works are arguably more assertive.

ALICE E. SANGER

LEAs

The golden era for Local Education Authorities (LEAs) in England and Wales was between the end of the Second World War and the 1974 reorganization of local government, when their position in a national system of education locally administered seemed assured. Reorganization ushered in a more corporate style of management and curbed the autonomy of Education Committees. LEAs now occupy a more ambiguous position in the education system, and are sometimes perceived within local government as a cuckoo in the nest, arousing envy and suspicion alike over the size of their budgets and their apparent need to do things differently from the rest of local government because of the nature of their clientele. Much of the ambiguity about their role and purpose stems from a stream of legislation that devolved a number of their responsibilities to schools, and also transferred greater powers to central government.

Government policy has veered between a preference for abolition and a recognition that LEAs were needed at least to carry out those responsibilities that private providers would find unattractive, most notably provision for children with special education needs. In the past ten years, LEAs have lost a number of responsibilities; for example, their role in both further and higher education and their pre-eminent position as a provider of adult education have been steadily eroded.

LEAs have also had to adjust to the reality of working with other organizations, including a variety of quangos, and to bidding for funds in order to secure services for their local population. The creation of grant-maintained schools (see **schools system**) was a halfway measure that was intended to lead to their demise; much other legislation has been destabilizing as it has left LEAs with responsibilities but with limited power to act. However, antipathy towards LEAs transcends party political lines and there is a perception, at least amongst some MPs, of bureaucracy, unresponsiveness and ineffectiveness at tackling underachievement.

In recent years there have been major changes in the way LEAs operate and, in a period of post-election consensus building, their position seems secure provided they can demonstrate effectiveness in delivering the government's agenda of raising achievement in schools. The inspection of LEAs will be an influence in this, but over the past ten years LEAs have become more diverse and it is not clear that they will have the resources with which to monitor, evaluate, advise and intervene effectively. While the cosy corporatism that once existed between officers, elected members and teacher unions has largely disappeared, amongst the challenges LEAs will face in the future is how to communicate their purpose to a wider public and how to become an effective advocate on behalf of parents while at the same time maintaining an overview of the needs of the whole local system. It is these kinds of pragmatic issues that will decide their fate, rather than an appeal for survival based on the preservation of local democracy.

In Scotland, the culture of governance has been different from England and Wales and the principle of Scottish Local Authorities (SLAs) working in partnership with the Scottish Office is one of the cornerstones of the education system that has been preserved. Many of the changes that have been introduced in England and Wales have been introduced in only a diluted form in Scotland without a substantial impact on the role of the SLAs. There was little or no interest in schools opting out of the SLA system, and devolved school management has been a much more limited initiative compared with the local management of schools in England and Wales. School boards in Scotland have few of the managerial responsibilities of their counterpart governing bodies south of the border. Much more significant has been the reorganization of local government, which broke up some very large authorities to create thirty-two smaller unitary authorities that have and will find difficulty in maintaining the level of service that schools have become used to.

The reforms in Northern Ireland have more closely followed those in England and Wales, including a similar approach to local management with devolved responsibilities given to school boards and a Northern Ireland national curriculum. The five Education and Libraries Boards (ELBs) are wholly responsible for the schools under their management, including the provision of a curriculum and advice service, but they have no powers to inspect the quality of education in their schools. Until the 1997 general election intervened, there were proposals to completely reorganize the ELBs and greatly reduce their responsibilities.

See also: schools system

Further reading

MacMahon, A. (1990) *A Handbook for LEAs*, London: Chapman.

JOHN WILLIAMS

Leavis, F.R.

b. 1895, Cambridge; d. 1978

Academic and critic

Frank Raymond Leavis was a teacher of English at Cambridge, whose mid-century authority derived from his co-editorship of the journal *Scrutiny* (1932–53) and numerous works of humanist literary and cultural criticism. A cultural conservative, Leavis valorized the 'great tradition' of English literature as the most organic, vital and morally serious use of the national language. He saw the task of criticism as the preservation and affirmation of the national language, literature and culture, against the disintegrating effects of capitalist modernity and mass media. Leavis's important works include *Revaluation* (1936) and *The Great Tradition* (1948).

See also: literary theory

MARK DOUGLAS

left-wing theatre

Although there has been a tradition of broadly left-wing theatrical ventures in Britain since the late nineteenth century, the pioneering work of the **Royal Court** theatre and Theatre Workshop in the 1950s provided a springboard for a remarkable flowering of politically committed theatre in the 1960s and 1970s. In the 1960s, socio-economic circumstances favoured the growth of a politically engaged theatre: central and local government support for theatre increased, and as the number of students in higher education rose, there was a growth in audiences prepared for a theatrical diet that encouraged a critical debate about political issues. In 1968, the abolition of the Lord Chamberlain's powers of stage censorship removed a powerful obstacle to attempts to stage political, religious and sexual issues. Touring companies devoted to raising political issues found support both from established theatrical venues and from groups of workers engaged in political action. Much of this new work was **agitprop**, aimed at issues of the day and utilizing stereotypes and cartoon-like action to make direct political points.

The success of what had been a very eclectic left-wing theatrical movement sparked off a series of new, more closely defined ventures for groups whose voices had been marginalized, focusing on issues of race, gender, sexual orientation and disability. However, after 1979 the Thatcher government initiated a slow process of pushing back the frontiers of political debate in the theatre, both directly, with legislation to abolish the Greater London Council (a staunch supporter of left-wing theatre) (see **GLC**) and to cut back funding of gay and lesbian theatre groups, and indirectly through reductions in subsidy that made it difficult to fund enough actors to tour large cast plays and for local government to support venues and companies alike. The **Arts Council** also chose to remove funding from theatre groups that might be seen as politically committed, such as 7:84 England, Foco Novo and Joint Stock (whose 1977 staging of David Hare's *Fanshen* about the Chinese revolution was highly influential), favouring instead dance and companies committed to exploring the classics. Although **alternative comedy** has sometimes offered a cheaper and less technically demanding medium for raising left wing issues and some Asian, black, community, feminist, gay and lesbian ventures survive, the broader umbrella has virtually disappeared.

See also: Asian theatre; avant-garde theatre; black theatre; community theatre; gay theatre

Further reading

Rees, R. (1992) *Fringe First*, London: Methuen (an important collection of interviews and recollections).

TREVOR R. GRIFFITHS

LEICESTER UNIVERSITY ENGINEERING BUILDING *see* Stirling, James

Leigh, Mike

b. 1943

Film-maker

Born in 1943, Leigh has been a writer and director for television, theatre and film. He trained at **RADA** and worked for a year as an assistant director at the **Royal Shakespeare Company**. He is noted for curiously light and bitter comedies of lower-middle and working-class manners and aspirations, in films such as *High Hopes* (1989), *Life is Sweet* (1990), *Naked* (1993), *Secrets and Lies* (1996) and *Career Girls* (1997). Leigh achieved celebrity in the 1970s with a series of television dramas, most famous of which was *Abigail's Party*, an excruciating and excoriating satire on upwardly mobile class pretensions, starring his then wife Alison Steadman.

PETER CHILDS

Leland, David

b. 1947

Playwright and film director

An occasional actor and playwright, Leland rose to prominence with a quartet of television plays examining the deficiencies of the British educational system. *Birth of a Nation, Flying in the Wind* and *RHINO* concluded with the powerful *Made in Britain* (1983). After co-writing the thriller *Mona Lisa*

(1986) and scripting *Personal Services* (1987), Leland continued his study of repressed sexual attitudes in the 1950s in his well-received first feature *Wish You Were Here* (1987). The hypochondria ridden *Checking Out* (1988) and the William McIlvanney adaptation *The Big Man* (1990) were followed by the Second World War sexualities of *The Land Girls* (1988). Leland's work exposes the insecurities and hypocrisies of sex and class inflected Britishness, his humour and incisive social realism occasionally susceptible to cliched sentimentality.

SATINDER CHOHAN

lesbian chic

The term 'lesbian chic' (often interchangeable with 'lipstick lesbianism' and 'new lesbianism'), used since at least the early 1990s, refers to a new fashion or style for lesbians which invariably involves the adoption of feminine accoutrements. The use of 'chic' implies 'high-class' rather than 'high-street' fashion, but from within lesbian culture, lesbian chic has come to denote the use of feminine fashion and styles as opposed to a more 'butch' look, and is thus not so class-specific. Elizabeth Wilson (1990) pinpoints a change to 'glamour' in British lesbian fashion in 1988.

Much like the lesbian sadomasochist movement which began some years earlier (though with less 'take-up' by the British media), the popularity of lesbian chic for lesbians is often connected to a rejection of anti-materialist and anti-patriarchal politics usually associated with lesbian feminism – itself often misrepresented as unitary and restrictive. Lesbian chic is not a rejuvenation of the lesbian butch/femme dyad popular in 1940s and 1950s cities; rather, masculine lesbian identities are seen to be decidedly unfashionable in the 'queer' 1990s, often by straights and 'queers' alike.

Perhaps the unfashionability of butch lesbian styles has been the impetus for the popularization of lesbian femininity in more mainstream media sites. Long-haired and lipsticked lesbian characters have appeared in British soap opera in the 1990s. The mainstream media also often represents lesbian chic through iconography which presents a white upper-class and often temporary lesbian identity, as a recent article in **Harpers and Queen** (June 1994) illustrates: here, straight women are reported playfully experimenting with lesbian sex. The instability of lesbian identity often intimated by such articles also connects lesbian chic to queer identity.

Criticisms of lesbian chic often concentrate on the way that the impetus for this style turns on an unfair dismissal of the political gains of the lesbian feminist movement in the 1970s and the 1980s, the demonization of masculine lesbian identities, and the way that the British media seem to have trivialized lesbian identity and culture in this representational context.

See also: accessories; bisexuality; gay liberation; 'gender benders'; sadomasochism

Further reading

Wilson, E. (1990) 'Deviant Dress', *Feminist Review* 35 (Summer): 67–74 (an excellent short history of lesbian fashion and quite specific to Britain).

LOUISE ALLEN

Lester, Richard

b. 1932, Philadelphia (USA)

Film-maker

Though born in America, Lester made his name directing quintessentially British 1960s films such as *A Hard Day's Night* (1964) and *The Knack* (1965). Along with the first, his second 'zany' Beatles movie, *Help* (1965), has become the model for pop movies right up to the Spice Girls' *Spiceworld: the Movie* in 1997. Always best when working on a small budget, Lester's early 'swinging London' films mixed the style of the Goons (with whom Lester had worked) with the attitudes of 1960s realist films and teenage culture.

MIKE STORRY

libel, defamation and privacy

Defamation (collectively, libel and slander) actions to protect reputations often provoke incessant tabloid newspaper interest, despite the fact that it is often these newspapers who are the defendants in such actions. In a demonstration of the increasingly litigious nature of the British, such actions are indicative of the continual struggle to erect barriers between the 'public' and the 'private' personality, and question the limits of concepts such as 'celebrity' status. In an era where there appears to be an insatiable desire to discover minutiae of detail concerning people in the public eye, there has been widespread debate concerning how far a person's private life can be interrogated. With no recognizable legal concept of a right to privacy, those suffering such an interrogation have little recourse to control the actions of writers and photographers. The problem has become even more pronounced as the tabloid press, in their worst excesses, try to achieve scoops at any cost; and their jobs are often made easier by the ready availability of 'high-tech' means of obtaining information. It is unsurprising that when serious mistakes are made in stories, the response of victims is often to sue for damage to their reputations. High-profile defamation cases have been brought by a number of television and sporting personalities such as Elton John and Ian Botham. Ironically, John's success against the *Sun* newspaper allowed it to create a front-page story featuring its apology to the singer.

Alongside this legal and media 'circus', there has been a long-standing debate regarding the extent of damages awarded by juries; unlike most civil actions, libel trials are generally still heard by juries. Throughout the late 1980s and early 1990s, initial large awards such as one million pounds to Elton John contributed to the Court of Appeal indicating that judges ought to advise juries on the appropriate level of compensation. The tightening of control was extended when the Court of Appeal was itself given power to substitute its own award when the original is deemed excessive.

The debate over the right to personal privacy has largely been in response to revelations concerning the personal lives of the Royal family, particularly the Duchess of York. This has led to a number of calls for legislation in this area, and has brought into sharp focus the divergence of the UK from other jurisdictions such as France.

See also: democracy; privacy

Further reading

Duncan, C. (1978) *Defamation*, London: Butterworth.

GUY OSBORN
STEVE GREENFIELD

Liberal Party

In the years following the Second World War, the Liberal Party went into a long-term decline. The Conservatives and Labour were firmly established as the two main parties of Britain, a position which was strengthened by the bipartisan nature of the House of Commons and the 'first past the post' electoral system. From the late 1950s, the Liberals have consistently achieved many by-election victories but have experienced little success at **general elections**.

In 1967, Jeremy Thorpe succeeded Joe Grimmond as party leader, rejuvenating the Liberal Party. The party managed to attract many young members who had radical views on international issues of the day. They developed organizations at grassroots level and performed well at local elections, benefiting from the widespread disillusionment with the bureaucracy and the **corporatism** of the 1960s and 1970s. In the February 1974 election, the Liberals obtained six million votes and returned fourteen MPs. Thorpe subsequently held what proved to be fruitless talks with Edward Heath about forming a coalition government.

David Steel became leader in 1976 after Thorpe's resignation in the wake of a sex scandal. Nevertheless, the Liberals were able to gain a consultative role in government from 1977–8 in the Lib–Lab pact, after Labour had lost its majority. With the government facing growing difficulties with the economy and the **trade unions**, the Liberals decided to leave the pact, but their election performance in 1979 was unimpressive and Mrs Thatcher's Conservatives swept to power.

The Liberal Party was soon linked in the centre of British politics with the **SDP**, Steel having negotiated with and encouraged the Gang of Four in their founding of a new party on the understanding that it would align itself with the Liberals at election times. The Liberal Party conference enthusiastically endorsed this proposition. In general the SDP/Liberal Alliance worked well, dominating the centre ground of British politics and enjoying the image of two parties working in harmony with each other, an impression which gave them the highest third party vote in the 1983 General Election for sixty years.

Despite the carefully nurtured image of unity, there was disagreement amongst members of both parties over policy and personality clashes between senior figures, particularly after David Owen replaced Roy Jenkins as SDP leader. Many Liberals and even prominent SDP politicians felt steamrollered into accepting the SDP leader's vision of the Alliance's future. The discord behind the united front of the Alliance became apparent in the highly charged post-election atmosphere following the decline of Alliance fortunes in 1987.

Owen and fellow SDP MPs Rosie Barnes and John Cartwright made it clear they would not join a merged party. Liberals Michael Meadowcroft and Tony Greaves declared their antagonism towards merger, the former even trying to continue the Liberal Party single-handedly. However, 88 percent of Liberals voted for merger along with 65 percent of SDP members. SDP MPs Robert MacLennan and Charles Kennedy joined the new party.

The choice of name and the constitution of the new party were the first obstacles to be overcome. The name Social and Liberal Democrats was eventually decided on, and this became the Liberal Democrats (often shortened to 'Lib Dems') following a membership ballot in October 1989. Steel and Maclennan were unsuccessful in their attempts to produce a constitution and policy document acceptable to Liberal MPs. A new policy document, evolved from policies already agreed between the two parties, and a constitution were ultimately hammered out; the latter had the concession to the SDP of an explicit commitment to NATO, in spite of opposition from Liberal unilateralists.

A leadership election for the new party was contested between two former Liberals, Paddy Ashdown and Alan Beith, in July 1988. Ashdown won with 70 percent of the vote. The new leader faced the difficult task of regaining public confidence and support and a drop of 50 percent in membership. Nevertheless Ashdown's popularity pushed up support for his party and under his leadership the Liberal Democrats gradually recovered and made three by-election gains from the Conservatives in 1990 and 1991. Since taking charge, Ashdown has consistently been the most popular leader with the public.

The revitalization of the Liberal Democrats fuelled media speculation that their support would be sufficient to force a hung parliament after the 1992 General Election. The Liberal Democrats offered a radical solution to Britain's economic ills by promising to create 600,000 extra jobs through government borrowing and to put a penny on income tax, to be spent on education. The possibility of a hung parliament meant that constitutional reform became a major election issue. Lib Dem leaders stipulated that their primary condition to guarantee Lib Dem support for a minority government would be the introduction of proportional representation. In the last week of campaigning Labour debated the merits of PR. Many Labour members regarded this as an error that cost Labour victory, given that it was a comparatively obscure issue compared with Labour's strongest campaign themes such as the state of the NHS. In the event the Conservatives won with a reduced majority and the Lib Dems picked up only 18 percent of the vote and twenty seats.

Since 1992, Liberal Democrat support has remained constant in the opinion polls at around the 20 percent mark. The party won four by-elections between 1993 and 1995. In the 1994 European elections the party obtained its first two MEPs, and in the local elections of May 1995 the Liberal Democrats became the second party of local government. In December 1995, the Lib Dems achieved a notable coup in attracting Conservative Emma Nicholson to cross the floor of the House of Commons and sit on the opposition benches as a Liberal Democrat MP. However the Lib Dems have found themselves squeezed as **New Labour** has continued to move to the right, adopting many of the policies of the former SDP.

Internally the Lib Dems have a constitutional structure which is largely a legacy of the SDP's centralized structure with its checks and balances to prevent too much power being concentrated in the hands of small cliques. This is combined with the Liberal's local party organization, which is reinforced by the Liberal Democrat federal structure with its state parties for England, Scotland and Wales, and England's twelve regional parties.

The Liberal Democrats continue to advocate the traditional Liberal Party positions supporting constitutional and electoral reform, close ties with Europe, environmental issues and individual rights and liberties. They now have a firmer commitment to the free market and support multilateral nuclear disarmament.

See also: fringe parties; sex scandals

Further reading

(1988) *Constitution of the Social and Liberal Democrats*, Hebden Bridge: Liberal Party Publications.

Cook, C. (1993) *A Short History of the Liberal Party, 1900–1988*, 3rd edn, Basingstoke: Macmillan.

COLIN WILLIAMS

Liberty

Liberty is one of London's most famous stores, founded in 1875 to sell clothing, fabrics, jewellery, ceramics and furniture. As well as importing goods like silk from the Empire, Liberty established links with designers from the Art Nouveau movement, including William Morris, Arthur Silver and Archibald Knox, who produced designs for the company. The company specialized in block-printed fabrics – lawns, woollens and linens – with distinctive designs which are known as 'Liberty prints'. The fabrics have featured in fashions by well-known designers, including Mary Quant in the 1960s, Zandra Rhodes in the 1970s and Joe Casely-Hayford in the 1990s.

TAMSIN SPARGO

licensing laws

British licensing laws cover areas as diverse as gaming, hygiene and landlord responsibility for behaviour on his/her premises. However there are essentially two central themes: the minimum age at which a person may buy alcohol, and hours during which they may do so on licensed premises.

Alcohol may not be purchased by anyone under the age of eighteen, nor may persons under eighteen consume alcohol on licensed premises. There is one exception; beer, porter, cider or perry can be served to someone between the ages of 16–18 if it is with a meal and if they are in a part of the building reserved for the service of meals, not a bar. Persons under fourteen must be accompanied on licensed premises, and are not allowed in any part of the establishment exclusively or mainly used for the sale of alcohol. Basic British opening hours for the sale of alcohol on licensed premises are 11am to 11pm weekdays and 12 noon to 10.30pm on Sundays and bank holidays. In Scotland these times are extended to 12 midnight on weekdays and Sundays, and to 1am on Saturdays. There is a drinking-up period of twenty minutes allowed at closing time, or thirty minutes if the alcohol is being consumed with a meal.

Off licenses may sell alcohol from 8am up until the terminal hour. There are a variety of circumstances under which extensions to these hours may be granted. One-off extensions can be obtained from the local licensing justices, provided the police are given fourteen days notice of the event. Special Hours Certificates may be granted to an establishment as long as licensing justices are satisfied that an entertainment's licence is in force, and that the relevant section of the premises is adapted adequately for the purpose of music, dancing and the sale of refreshments to which alcohol is ancillary. Licensees may apply for permission to open earlier (generally this would mean 10am). However, special dispensation can be made under certain conditions. The establishment might be close to a market, for example, or it might serve a fishing fleet. A licensee may also apply for an occasional license: this permits him or her to serve alcohol at a different venue, such as a cricket ground or a public hall. Finally, seasonal licenses can be granted to certain premises which only desire to sell alcohol at specific times of years, such as establishments connected with the tourist trade.

See also: drink

MICK TURNER

lingerie

The shapes and styles of lingerie and underwear have always been determined by the silhouettes dictated by outer fashion, but equally significant has been the revolution in the manufacture of fabrics. Nylon, the most important innovation in the history of underwear and lingerie, was widely used up until the 1970s. Lycra, introduced in 1959, together with stretch lace, knitted simplex, cotton polyester and other elastic fabrics, have encouraged new possibilities in design.

Lingerie and underwear enjoyed a complete revolution in the 1960s. Tights were being manufactured from 1960 onwards. Originally available for ballet dancers and sports people, the modern versions were much thinner, and Mary **Quant** also introduced tights in a variety of colours. However, older women continued to wear stockings, and it was only in 1976 that manufacturers finally stopped making removable suspenders for panty corselettes. Janet **Reger**, a major innovator in lingerie and underwear, established her company in 1967 and was successful into the mid-1980s. The general trend of foundations from the 1960s to the 1990s has been progressively towards increasingly natural shaping. Also, as feminism continued its onslaught on bounds of acceptability, underwear became outerwear; Jean-Paul Gaultier has been a key exponent of this new trend.

See also: body adornment; cosmetics

Further reading

McKenzie, J. (1997) *The Best in Lingerie Design*, London: Batsford.

FATIMA FERNANDES

literature, African

Africa has figured in English literature for several centuries. On the one hand, there are the well-known 'boys' own' stories of British adventure fiction, such as H. Rider Haggard's *King Solomon's Mines* (1885) and John Buchan's *Prester John* (1910). On the other hand, there are the few surviving accounts by Africans who travelled to Britain, such as the best-selling slave narrative *The Interesting Narrative of Olaudah Equiano, or Gustavus Vassa, the African, written by Himself* (1789). Other African writers of previous centuries were Ukawsaw Gronniosaw (an African prince christened James Albert), James Africanus Horton (the first African to graduate in medicine from Edinburgh University), Ignatius Sancho (born on a slave ship) and Mary Prince (from Bermuda), who gave the first female Afro-British account of Christian England in 1831. These and others are discussed in more detail by Edwards and Dabydeen (1991).

In terms of white African writing, canonical texts are Olive Schreiner's *The Story of an African Farm* (1883) and Doris Lessing's *The Grass is Singing* (1950), two stories of white alienation, female entrapment and black inequality (in these contexts, mention should also be made of Karen Blixen, Laurens van der Post, Nadine Gordimer and Elspeth Huxley). Key African novelists who have studied or lectured in Britain are Chinua Achebe and Ngugi wa Thiong'o (previously James Ngugi). Achebe engages with the disruption caused by British colonialism in his best-known books, *Things Fall Apart* (1958) and its sequel *No Longer at Ease* (1960), the latter focusing on political corruption. Ngugi, after writing several highly praised novels in English, such as *A Grain of Wheat* (1967) and *Weep Not, Child* (1964), turned against the 'language of the colonizers' in favour of his local language, Kikuyu. Achebe, however, has recommended English as a language in which the writer can speak to the world. Achebe, like Wole Soyinka, sees the writer as having an important role in forging a repository for the nation's history, figuring not as an individual voice (as in the West) but as a voice of the community.

There have not been many prominent African British writers in recent years, but special mention should be made of Diran Adebayo (whose parents and older siblings are from Nigeria), whose *Some Kind of Black* about Africans living in London won the Saga prize for new black writing in 1995. The most famous recent novelist is the Nigerian Ben Okri, who studied at the University of Essex. Okri has written several novels and is also a short story writer, but is best known for the social and magic realist novel *The Famished Road* (1991), which won the Booker Prize.

See also: literature, Caribbean; literature, Indian; post-colonial writing

Further reading

Edwards, P. and Dabydeen, D. (eds) (1991) *Black Writers in Britain 1760–1890*, Edinburgh: Edinburgh University Press.

PETER CHILDS

literature, Caribbean

Many Caribbean writers have moved to Britain, especially in the 1950s. V.S. Naipaul and Sam Selvon came from Trinidad, Wilson Harris from Guyana and George Lamming from Barbados. Others moved in the 1960s and 1970s such as Joan Riley (Jamaica), Caryl Phillips (St Kitts), and Grace Nichols (Guyana). Many of these writers show an acute abiding concern with the journey from the Caribbean to England and the differences between the two cultures, for example in Naipaul's *The Enigma of Arrival* (1987), Lamming's *The Emigrants* (1954), Riley's *The Unbelonging* (1985) and Phillips' *The Final Passage* (1985). In one of the early seminal texts of the period, *The Lonely Londoners* (1956), Sam Selvon uses the character and friends of Moses to explore the experience of alienation, racism and poverty that greeted Caribbean settlers in the 1950s. Moving from fiction to poetry, other writers have focused on the West Indian legacy of slavery, as in *Grace Nichols is a long memoried woman* and Edward Kamau Brathwaite's *Rights of Passage* (1967), *Masks* (1968) and *Islands* (1969). Such work is concerned to mesh past history with the present reality of Caribbean identity in relation to Europe.

In its reclamation of black history to rework present cultural identities, the Guyanese-born

David Dabydeen's poetry provides a good example. Respectively his three volumes, *Slave Song* (1984), *Coolie Odyssey* (1988) and *Turner* (1994), chronicle the domination and sadomasochism inherent in plantation life, rework the journey to the Caribbean of indentured Indians (who were 'employed' to replace slaves after emancipation in 1834) in a story of his mother's more recent journey to a cold, unwelcoming England looking for work, and the role of black experience in English art, particularly Turner's 1840 painting *Slavers Throwing Overboard the Dead and Dying*.

A further common theme is the role of women in Caribbean life, from Fred D'Aguiar's poetry collection *Mama Dot* (1985) about the pervasive matriarchal presence of his grandmother to Jamaica Kincaid's assertion of the unparalleled strength of motherhood in *Annie John* (1983). A final writer who should be mentioned is Jean Rhys, a novelist who resurfaced in 1966 after over thirty years of literary obscurity to publish *Wide Sargasso Sea*, a West Indian creole's response to reading the pro-colonial and patriarchal *Jane Eyre*. *Wide Sargasso Sea*, like many of the other books discussed here, has become a key text in **post-colonial writing**.

See also: literature, African; literature, Indian

Further reading

Dabydeen, D. and Wilson-Tagoe, N. (1988) *A Reader's Guide to West Indian and Black British Literature*, London: Hansib.

PETER CHILDS

literature, children's and teenage

The 1950s and 1960s are often described as a golden age of children's literature in Britain. This is ascribed to the breakdown of prewar ideologies and the absence of post-1970 **political correctness**. Fiction of this period fused the exciting narrative of adventure stories with the introspection, morality and magic of fantasy, showing a concern with the interaction of past and present. An outstanding example is *The Owl Service* by Alan Garner. More generally, children's fiction flourished as publishers began to attract writers of

literary merit. Historical novels by Rosemary Sutcliffe and Jill Paton Walsh coexisted alongside the historical fantasy of Joan Aiken and Penelope Lively.

Fantasy continued to be written throughout the 1970s, including Susan Cooper's epic battles between good and evil, and the 'psycho fantasy' of Penelope Farmer. However the main trend was the realistic 'teen' **novel**. This was influenced by American writers such as Robert Cormier and Judy Blume, but there was also an indigenous demand for authentic 'working-class' literature, showing urban children in realistic surroundings. These books (such as *Gumble's Yard* by John Rowe Townsend and *The Machine Gunners* by Robert Westall) developed into the so-called 'teen' novel which focused on issues affecting contemporary teenagers, including their struggle for cultural and sexual identity. No subject seemed taboo, including teenage sex, pregnancy, domestic violence or homosexuality. Many books tackled the problems of ethnic minorities, such as Jan Needle's *My Mate Shofiq* and the novels of Farrukh Dhondy. While the Children's Rights Workshop led the attack on racism and sexism in children's books and encouraged multi-ethnic literature, critics worried about political correctness, condemning 'case study' novels in which social realism seemed to take precedence over literary quality. Some of the most successful authors of the period concentrated on motivation and character rather than fashionable social problems, for example, Nina Bawden in *Carrie's War*, and Jill Paton Walsh in *Goldengrove* (1972) and *Unleaving* (1976). Also in the 1970s children's literature became an object of study in British universities, and in 1980 the Whitbread and Guardian prizes were set up, reflecting a desire to seek and reward quality writing for children.

The best-selling children's author of the 1970s and 1980s was Roald Dahl (1916–90). He has gained a dubious critical reputation, standing accused of oversimplification and sheer unpleasantness, but his grotesque and virtually amoral stories (such as *The B.F.G.*, *The Witches* and *Matilda*) are immensely popular with children all over the world. During the 1980s a number of children's books responded to Cold War fears with depictions of nuclear disaster (such as *Children of the Dust* by Louise Lawrence). Meanwhile Aidan Chambers throughout the 1980s and 1990s began to widen the boundaries of children's literature with such books as the sexually explicit and postmodernist *Breaktime*.

During the 1990s, Anne Finehas emerged as a major figure in children's literature, her humorous discussion of topics such as gender stereotyping and ecological worries twice winning her the Carnegie medal (for *Flour Babies* and *Goggle-eyes*). Children's authors have been influenced by contemporary events; *Gulf* by Robert Westall, links a young Iraqi soldier and a British boy, and *Wolf* by Gillian Cross combines an IRA thriller with psychological exploration. The struggle for cultural identity in a post-colonial world is charted in the works of Jamila Gavin, in books such as *Wheel of Surya*. Anthropomorphism survives into the 1990s in the popular animal stories of Brian Jacques and Robin Jarvis.

Concerns about children's literature in the 1990s focus on the fear that interactive electronic media may come to replace traditional books. Other worries include the increasing popularity of American formulaic 'series' books such as *Point Horror*, and fears that a National Curriculum in schools will result in a 'canon' of children's fiction, excluding new writers.

Ted Hughes and Charles Causley were the major figures of postwar children's poetry. The 1970s and 1980s saw the development of a colloquial tone, as poets began to focus on the everyday details of urban childhood. *Please Mrs Butler*, by Allan Ahlberg is a light and well-observed account of primary school life, but other comic poets such as Kit Wright and Michael Rosen reveal dark undercurrents beneath the everyday world. The poetry of the 1980s and 1990s tends to be demotic and best read aloud, such as the work of Brian Patten and Roger McGough. The rhythms of Anglo-Caribbean speech provide a rich source of contemporary children's poetry, for example in John Agard's *Laughter is an Egg*, Grace Nichol's *Come into my Tropical Garden* and James Berry's *When I Dance*.

By the 1960s, improvements in lithography allowed artists to work in full colour in many different media, and quality picture books became more common. This period saw the emergence of many artists who were to rise to prominence in the following decades, such as John Burningham and Raymond Briggs. In the late 1970s and 1980s the development of paper engineering led to an explosion in 'gimmicky' – or richly experimental, depending on your point of view – picture books. Led by Jan Pienkowski's *Haunted House*, these included pop-up and 'scratch and sniff' books. Standing out among the pile were Janet and Allan Ahlberg's *Postman*, books which contained removable letters in envelopes. The Ahlbergs' earlier work, *Each Peach Pear Plum* perfectly married word and picture, to the delight of critics who feared technological improvements privileged the illustration over the word. Picture books were put to the same service as teen novels during the 1980s, dealing with problems from potty training to the death of a parent. Gender roles were subverted in books like Robert Munsch's *The Paperbag Princess*. The 1990s have seen a postmodern trend amongst picture books, playing games with fiction and reality (for example, *The Book Mice* by Tony Knowles). There has also been a move towards more sumptuous illustration, particularly in retold fairy tale and legend, as can be seen in the jewel-like *Three Indian Princesses* (Jamila Gavin).

See also: film, children's; television, children's

Further reading

Berger, L.S. (ed.) (1995) *Twentieth-Century Children's Writers*, London: St. James's Press.

Hunt, P. (ed.) (1995) *Children's Literature, An Illustrated History*, Oxford: Oxford University Press.

CHARLOTTE GODDARD

literature, Indian

The somewhat reluctant granting of independence to India and Pakistan in 1947, and similar measures legally according national recognition and sovereignty to British Asian, Caribbean, and East African communities approximately a decade later, produced, if only through its very protracted clumsiness, a more complex and tortured sense of identity. Subsequently, maturing British Asian writers of the post-colonial period had the task of clarifying the complexity of their own identity, a task which was not straightforwardly apparent to a generation of readers who expected and desired from their fiction the affirmation of territorial loyalty and nationalism.

Sheer market pressure has since ensured a flourishing identity for British Asian fiction. Consequently, the London scene has tended to be dominated by a few great literary names. Arguably, even these figures continue to wrestle with the problem of what is entailed in adopting a 'brown' perspective or 'Eastern eye' in a Britain still resistantly occidental in the self-perception of its white majority. These writers are also preoccupied by familiar long-term problems in relation to their home countries, where race, caste, gender and religion are matters still painfully shaped by neocolonialist-bred clashes of privilege, city and rural economic poverty, and an unbowed human spirit.

From the start of the 1960s, the writings of the former Indian soldier Paul Scott (including *The Jewel in the Crown*) perpetuated a great deal of the enduring hold of the older Commonwealth 'neo-imperial' view of 'British' Asia and of Asian Britons, including long-time residents in Britain. Scott's work was further extended by a television version of Scott's *Raj Quartet* in the 1980s, which helped to launch the career of the British Asian actor Art Malik. Scott's writings and back-up interviews given before the end of his life are full of conviction, especially on religious differences, and they demonstrate a glorious eye for both class and caste hypocrisies. However, they tend to focus on the perspective of whites exhibiting English mores in the sub-continent.

Salman Rushdie, of wealthy Bombay Indian parents but British-educated and based now in London, has managed in one of his novels (*The Satanic Verses*) to move away from such 'English' parochialism. He has done this by showing readers how the secular and materialistic Asian middle classes, both in Britain and in the subcontinent, confront identity and cross-cultural alienation problems in their own right. However, he failed in another area, the attempt to reconcile Islam with the modern capitalist spirit of opportunism and liberated sensuality, to the extent of endangering his own personal safety. His earlier novels (written after being told at his English public school that he

would never make 'writer' status) were criticized, especially in Pakistan, for alleged betrayal and condescension towards genuine Asian values, although Rushdie himself (a respectful agnostic) has always denied any intention or desire to 'blaspheme'.

Born in Trinidad of Indian parents and now based in London, the novelist V.S. Naipaul has had an output as famous and widely appealing as Rushdie. However, his novels and occasional interviews reflect more confidence in the wider Asian diaspora, and a disgruntled affection for the bourgeoisie of all races. Also his characters show a profound irritation with 'Christian' or 'Western' secular criticism of a confident, modern Moslem perspective on life.

Similar optimism, even in the midst of some of the most appalling homophobic, racist and sexist Western inner-city environmental dereliction, is shown by two more tentatively established Asian British writers, whose London bases and left-wing views clearly shape their metropolitan sophisticated fiction. Ruth Prawer Jhabvala, who now lives in the USA, has written several key novels (as well as film scripts for **Merchant-Ivory Productions**) about the British experience and (mis)understanding of India, particularly *Esmond in India* and the Booker prize winner *Heat and Dust*. A similar perceptiveness about landscapes and prejudice, as well as 'time' and 'history' in more contemporary eras than those attempted by Scott, has been shown by Hanif Kureishi. His televised and filmed scripts (such as *My Beautiful Launderette*) have ensured that Asian gays/bisexuals, and anti-Thatcherite Asians, often in poverty-stricken South London, have voices and characters.

The myriad other Indian writers in English who have reached front ranks of literary status include Anita Desai, Arundhati Roy and Vikram Seth. English literature today would be as poor without Indian writing as it would have been in the first decades of the century without Irish writing.

See also: literature, African; literature, Caribbean; post-colonial writing; Rushdie Affair, the

Further reading

Nelson, E. (ed.) (1993) *Writers of the Indian Diaspora: A Bio-Bibliographical Critical Sourcebook*, Westport, CT: Greenwood Press (a collection of essays, excellent in overall sweep and very good on the new younger writers in London).

Paniker, A.K. (ed.) (1991) *Indian English Literature Since Independence*, New Delhi: Indian Association for English Studies (a collection of critiques favouring multicultural 'inheritance').

Williams, H.M. (1977) *Indo-Anglican Literature 1800–1970*, Bombay: Orient-Longman (clear and trenchant, providing the longer historical perspective without which even post-1960 fiction in Britain is incomprehensible).

LAWRENCE IRVINE ILES

literature, Northern Irish

While the identity politics central to the 'Troubles' which have dominated Northern Ireland since the mid-1960s are a major factor in the works of many writers, it should be remembered that the Troubles themselves are a response to broader changes, both inside and outside Northern Ireland. It is therefore better to see Northern Ireland as a place in which tradition and modernity, figured in locally nuanced ways, are in conflict.

As the 1960s opened, a generation of writers, already alert to change, was passing. These broadly leftist writers were born and raised before the Second World War, and brought an internationalist outlook to bear on Northern Ireland. Louis MacNeice's scepticism and emphasis on flux were a reaction against the bigoted certainties of Northern Ireland's enclosed political mindsets. W.R. Rodgers, an ex-Presbyterian clergyman whose poetry is marked by idiosyncracy and extravagance, though closer to official Unionism (see **Ulster Unionists**), shared MacNeice's openness about the divisions in Northern Irish society. Sam Hanna Bell's novels, a fictional history from below, engage with the radical politics associated with the dissenting Presbyterian tradition, an interest shared by the poet John Hewitt. Hewitt's treatment of Northern Ireland's numerous identities has been influential, and since his death he has

become a figurehead for a pluralist approach to Northern Ireland. Though not a part of this loose grouping, Janet McNeill can be mentioned alongside them, since her novels depict women who are defiant misfits in a stultified society.

The poet John Montague (who collaborated with Hewitt on *The Planter and the Gael* in 1970) and the novelists Benedict Kiely and Brian Moore are from Catholic backgrounds. Their treatment of repressive **Catholicism** and the theme of loss and dispossession leads to an interest in the relationship of the individual to communal and traditional structures. All three have produced work in which sexual liberation figures as an emblem of rebellion against puritanical Irish attitudes. Where Kiely's work turns nostalgically inward, Moore and Montague's work is increasingly internationalist, whether as a way of contextualizing Northern Ireland, dealing with exile from it or finding analogies for it.

The writers who emerged in the 1960s and after benefited from postwar expansionism, notably in educational opportunities. Of these, the most famous is Seamus Heaney (winner of the 1995 Nobel Prize for Literature). Heaney's work treats of the opposition between his rural childhood and the world opened to him by education. Under pressure to respond to the political situation, he turned to mythological and archaeological frameworks; accusations of essentialism are balanced by his sense of wonder in the everyday. Michael Longley's poetry works within coordinates formed by his botanical and increasingly ecologically sensitive awareness of the fragility of the natural world, and his allusions to war poetry from *The Odyssey* to Keith Douglas, and this has enabled him to write some of the most moving elegies of recent years. Derek Mahon's desire to escape from history into the aesthetic is undercut by an apocalyptic consciousness that order can be stifling. James Simmons's poetry is marked by the sexual liberationist attitude of the late 1960s and negotiates with popular cultural forms.

Among established novelists, Maurice Leitch (a counterpart to Brian Moore) details, in novels of great variety of style and setting, the experiences of Northern Irish Protestant life. John Morrow's robustly humorous approach to the Troubles represents an important aspect of Northern Irish culture absent from the more usual pietistic public commentary; Colin Bateman's comedy thrillers (many of which have been filmed) take their lead from Morrow. Jennifer Johnston's early novels dealt subtly with often destructive friendships across barriers of religion, class, gender and age, and while she has turned to considerations of the status of the female writer, her work is unified by a consistent attack on the traditional idea of the family. Bernard MacLaverty's fiction also centres on troubled relationships, but his variety of styles and settings ensures that each is troubled in a specific way.

A younger generation of poets has often been in reaction to Heaney. Ciaran Carson treats Belfast as both the place of the Troubles and as the ur-city – shape-shifting, restless, alienating – in a celebratory poetry influenced by contemporary American writing (notably C.K. Williams) and by traditional Irish music and storytelling; the improvisatory and digressive styles of the latter become a formal analogue of urban life. Medbh McGuckian's work combines *ecriture feminine*, in its disordered and intimate (never simply private) language, with pointedly political comments despite its gnomic appearance. Paul Muldoon, whose playfully cosmopolitan work is often a response to Heaney, combines references to both Irish and North American traditional tales and legends with influences from writers as diverse as Raymond Chandler and Bob Dylan, while being alert (some would say too alert) to contemporary theoretical writing. In Tom Paulin's, work the power and possibility of the dissenting tradition is thornily engaged, as he establishes a sense of the global reach of Protestant culture at odds with the siege mentality of Northern Irish Protestantism.

Novelists make up the most recent generation to come to prominence. Deirdre Madden's career started with a Troubles novel, but like many of her contemporaries, she is interested in the Troubles as simply one aspect of the socio-cultural context within which her characters move. Eoin McNamee's *Resurrection Man* (now filmed) is an exception to this rule in its attempt to find a language appropriate to the horrors of sectarian butchery. Glenn Patterson and Robert MacLiam Wilson are very much urban novelists for whom the Troubles are, again, only one part of the backdrop. Patterson has written about Belfast and about EuroDisney as a fantastical European city, while in *Eureka Street* Wilson sets the bomb-blasted Belfast of stereotype against a more luminous version of it as a paradisal place.

See also: literature, Scottish; literature, Welsh

Further reading

Corcoran, N. (ed.) (1992) *The Chosen Ground: Essays on the Contemporary Poetry of Northern Ireland*, Bridgend: Seren Books.

Kirkland, R. (1996) *Literature and Culture in Northern Ireland since 1965: Moments of Danger*, London: Longman.

EAMONN HUGHES

literature, Scottish

For many, James Kelman's Booker Prize victory in 1994 with *How Late It Was, How Late* and the popularity of Irvine Welsh's *Trainspotting* (published in 1993 and becoming a household name with the 1996 release of a film version) announced the arrival of Scottish literature. Their impact in the mid-1990s was in part due to the directness of their novels, frankly depicting disenfranchised urban Scottish communities at a time of political torpor at the end of a long period of Conservative rule in Britain. The use of urban vernacular gave their novels a raw authenticity, but this masked Kelman and Welsh's formal inventiveness; such as the unremitting precision of Kelman's 150-word 'Acid' (1983) or Welsh's typographical games in 'The Acid House' (1994) and *Marabou Stork Nightmares* (1995). By the mid-1990s, the Scottish novel was recognized for its combination of unsentimental working-class politics, accounts of urban degradation and violence, and black humour.

The recent history of Scottish literature is one of politically conscious innovation. The publication of Hugh MacDiarmid's modernist classic *A Drunk Man Looks at the Thistle* in 1926 had set the tone for much that followed. Writing in 'Lallans' (a literary language formed through careful and eclectic reappropriation of Scottish dialect words and archaisms as a self-conscious rejection of the linguistic dominance of English literature), Mac-Diarmid gave those who followed both a method and a political stance: he was at once a Scottish nationalist, Communist and modernist elitist. The use of Lallans (still viewed by some as the 'proper' language for Scottish literature) fell out of favour, though the lexical ingenuity and range of poets like W.N. Herbert and Robert Crawford in the 1980s can be seen a continuation of the tradition. From the 1960s, a keen sense of linguistic difference was demonstrated in a growing variety of experimental and vernacular modes of writing: Edwin Morgan's 'Instamatic' and sound poetry, Ian Hamilton Finlay's concrete poems, W.S. Graham and Norman MacCaig's development of Dylan Thomas's lyrical 'wordfloods', the explorations of their native Gaelic by Iain Crichton Smith, Sorley MacLean and Derick Thomson, and George Mackay Brown's evocations of his Orkney island community. Scottish writers also used 'standard' English to their own ends: a sense of the breadth of Scottish writing in English can be felt in the contrast between Muriel Spark's novel about a genteel Edinburgh girls' school (*The Prime of Miss Jean Brodie*, 1961) and the gothic violence of Iain Banks' *The Wasp Factory* (1984), or between Douglas Dunn's 1985 *Elegies* to his dead wife and Banks' science fiction (including *Consider Phlebas*, 1987). In effect, Scottish writers created a single literature of many languages: English, Gaelic, Lallans and, increasingly, 'urban phonetic dialect'.

The urban focus can be seen as early as 1962 in Edwin Morgan's *The Second Life*, but gained significant impetus from the weekly reading group set up by Philip Hobsbaum in Glasgow from 1971. There, writers like Alisdair Gray, Kelman, Tom Leonard and Liz Lochhead were able to meet and discuss their work; in the wake of the failed 1979 devolution referendum, Gray's postmodern epic novel *Lanark* (written and rewritten over some three decades) was finally published in 1981, Polygon produced Kelman's short-story collection *Not Not While the Giro* (1983), and in 1984 Leonard and Lochhead both published collected editions of their poetry (*Intimate Voices* and *Dreaming Frankenstein*). Leonard's work had promoted the suppressed voice of the urban working-classes as a literary language since the early 1970s, sustaining a subtle and relentless critique of class-based prejudices against non-standard English. Attacks on the hegemony of English were also made through satirical linguistic reversals, exemplified by Gray and Welsh's transcriptions of upper-class Oxbridge English or Cockney accents (pointing up the tacit assumption that the written word has a southern English accent) or Leonard's pointed poster-poem, 'An Oxford English Dictionary of an English Language' (1996, quoted here in full).

That the self-conscious privileging of specifically Scottish (rather than merely non-English) voices has not led to a stultifying parochialism is a testament to the internationalism of Scottish literature. Significantly, Gray's *Lanark* (the principal device of which is the pairing of a 'realist' working-class Glasgow with its fantastical mirror-image Unthank) includes a playful 'index of diffuse and imbedded Plagiarisms by Sidney Workman' which not only includes Hobsbaum, Kelman, Leonard and Lochhead, but cites a whole network of previous writers and thinkers (with Scots like Burns, Hume and Adam Smith listed alongside Ibsen, Freud, Blake and Kafka), effectively placing contemporary Scottish writing in a simultaneously Scottish and international context. Tom Scott's dialect versions of the French medieval poet François Villon, W.L. Lorimer's translation of the New Testament into Scots and Morgan's prolific translations from Italian, Russian, Spanish, German, Hungarian, French and Anglo-Saxon are examples of the wide-ranging literary influences that were brought into Scotland from abroad. Morgan also joined Finlay in introducing concrete poetry to the English-speaking world from Latin America in the 1960s, underlining a receptiveness to avant-garde and experimental approaches at that is at odds with the formal conservatism of mainstream English literature.

This openness to influence is helped by the proximity of many Scottish writers to their audience, partly through the maintenance of linguistic communities (notably for the Gaelic poets) but also through a commitment to performance, in many cases involving authors in writing for theatre (such as Liz Lochhead with *Mary Queen of Scots Got Her Head Chopped Off*, 1989). Social changes have also had an effect on the literary scene, once depicted as gathering of old men in an Edinburgh pub; increasing numbers of women writers have come to the fore since the 1960s. The poets Lochhead, Carol Ann Duffy, Kathleen Jamie and Jackie Kay, and prose writers Janice Galloway, A.L. Kennedy and Candia McWilliam are among the most prominent. Kay – daughter of a Nigerian father and Scottish mother, adopted by white Glaswegian parents – has also demonstrated the scope of contemporary Scottish literature, exploring notions of self- and gender-identity through the poems of *Adoption Papers* (1991) and the novel *Trumpet* (1997).

Further reading

Crawford, R. (1992) *Devolving English Literature*, Oxford: Oxford University Press.

Dunn, D. (ed.) (1992) *The Faber Book of Twentieth-Century Scottish Poetry*, London: Faber & Faber.

Kravitz, P. (ed.) (1997) *The Picador Book of Contemporary Scottish Fiction*, Basingstoke: Macmillan.

SIMON COPPOCK

literature, Welsh

The characteristics of Welsh literature of the twentieth century are its concern with place and landscape, language and nationhood, the individual within the community, industrial and economic decline, and the politics of identity: what it means to be Welsh and, more specifically, what it means to be a Welsh writer writing in English. Welsh writers see themselves as working from within a tradition which stretches back to Taliesin and the ancient bardic poets, and *The Mabinogion*, through to the writings of the present day.

Welsh poetry of the postwar period sweeps from the lyrical neo-romanticism of Dylan Thomas and Vernon Watkins, through the work of such poets as Idris Davis, Roland Mathias and David Jones, to Wales' second best-known poet, R.S. Thomas. Thomas's poetry speaks directly to the people and the landscape in his sparse and measured language, creating a moral universe shot through with the concerns of the modern Welsh nation. For Thomas, **poetry** is a vehicle for a kind of national remembrance, both a responsibility and a political act. The poetry of Danny Base epitomizes the dichotomy of national and personal identity. It displays a multi-dimensional vision, incorporating the topographies of the metropolis and the pastoral, the mystical and the physical, and the dilemmas of being Welsh/English, British/Jewish, poet/doctor. The younger Welsh poets writing today, for example, Gillian Clark and Tony Curtis, continue to be acutely aware of the need to confront their essential Welshness through their writing, and their role as Welsh poets in creating and invoking Wales.

In fiction, the short story has been a popular medium for the representation and expression of the Welsh way of life, with modern works taking their impetus from Glyn Jones's *The Blue Bed and Other Stories* (1937), a startling and poetic tale from the Wales of the Great Depression. Writers such as Kate Roberts recreated small corners of locality and lived experience, in stories and novels that dwelt on the lives of the people of the small communities, affected not only by internal economic decline but by the intrusion of wider concerns, for example in *Traed Mewn Cyffion* (Feet in Chains) (1936). More contemporary Welsh fiction has continued to explore the collapse of the traditional foundation of modern Wales, especially the mining industry, for example in Gwyn Jones's *Times Like These* (1979) and Gwyn Thomas's *Sorrow for My Sons* (1986), which remain resonant for our times.

See also: literature, Northern Irish; literature, Scottish; Welsh language; Welsh press

Further reading

Jarman, A.O.H. and Hughes, G.R. (eds) (1976) *A Guide to Welsh Literature*, Swansea: Davies.

SARAH CORBETT

literary magazines

The literary magazine has a British history that reaches back to the eighteenth century, and these early magazines prescribed a format which many of the magazines of the late twentieth century in Britain have largely held to: polemic critique, reviews of books and other cultural forms (embracing cinema by the 1930s and television by the 1960s), opinion pieces and original writing in different measures. Relative emphases and the qualities of writing have shifted: the *London Review of Books*' reportage pieces from, for example, Stephen Sackur on the Gulf War and reporting on the Balkans crises in the 1990s have been amongst the magazine's best writings in the last decade.

The frequency of publication of literary magazines has ranged from weekly, to twenty-four times a year, to monthly, to quarterly, to 'infrequently'. Some of the weekly magazines confine their literary and cultural writing to the second half of the magazine, as in the *New Statesman* and the *Spectator*. In these two cases there has been a more or less clearly signalled allegiance to the moderate left and to the libertarian right, respectively, which does not always survive in the literary ghetto of the back pages; although the 1980s saw a more rigid and uniform politico-literary regimentation, the *Spectator/Daily Telegraph* 'young fogey' nexus being a case in point. The weekly *Times Literary Supplement*'s position as the house journal of humanities academia was compromised when it became part of Rupert Murdoch's News International Corporation, and changes in the editorship seemed to signal a wish to conform to the right-wing hegemony of 1980s Britain. Nevertheless, it continues to stand at the centre of high literary cultural life in Britain. Odd as it may seem today, it was not until the late 1960s that the review articles – or any of the pieces published – were signed. What redirections in the editorial policy of the *TLS* have shown is how the breadth of interests has been extended by the changes in the formations of British cultural life. The literary magazine of the late 1990s is likely to give space in the same issue to reviewing a new biography of the young Wordsworth and to the drum 'n' bass compact disc by Roni Size.

Almost all of these journals have had long histories, with the *Spectator* tracing its origins back to the eighteenth century. Today, these are the venues where, along with the broadsheet daily and Sunday newspapers, 'the chattering classes' meet. While some of these publications might aspire to be mass circulation journals, none is read by more than a few thousand and yet each wants to claim for itself a kind of pre-eminence in its own part of

the forest of letters. However, there is also much following of fashions which change with the season: the analyses of the cultural impact of the life and death of the Princess of Wales are an example of this.

It is in the magazines that publish less frequently that culturally significant stances are more usually taken. These 'infrequent' publications have often had a relatively ephemeral life, but amongst significant names have been *Encounter*, *Stand*, the *Review*, the *New Review* and the *London Review of Books*. This last is distinguished by being, in form, a broadsheet newspaper that has clearly taken its design from the *New York Review of Books*.

Encounter, half political/cultural critique and half literary review, publishing original prose and poetry, reflected this dichotomy in its joint editorship – for example, that of Irving Kristol and Stephen Spender – with each editor having a cognate background. Its reputation was shaken by the revelation that it was in part financed by the CIA, as part of the US government's attempt to sustain a political and cultural climate of opinion supportive of Western democracies in the era of the Cold War.

The *Review* and the *New Review*, produced thanks to a relatively generous cultural largesse courtesy of the **Arts Council**, celebrated what they perceived as the centrality of Britain in the brightness and sharpness of the optimism of the third quarter of the century. There was a conscious 'smartness' about the *New Review*, edited with a dogmatic certainty and arrogantly aware of its cosmopolitan centrality, exploratory and innovative in its presentation of new forms of writing. However, it might be argued that its lasting achievement, inherited and maintained by Granta, was the rehabilitation of **travel writing** as a serious literary genre. This sense of centrality lasted little longer than the magazines themselves. The cultural and political landscape of the early 1980s caused them to cease publication. Their replacements, if the plural is accurate, have been marginal, trivially partisan and the culturally correct adornments of rich but capricious patrons.

Throughout its life, *Stand* has been a marked departure from these stereotypes in several important ways: it was the product of the determination of one person, the late Jon Silkin, and it was edited from the provinces, originally in Newcastle upon Tyne. It contained short prose fictions, poetry and reviews; it was healthily internationalist in the range of its contributors. Happily, it remains a model for beautifully produced, designed and edited literary magazines, always making a virtue of its eclecticism.

The *London Review of Books* is the most powerful cosmopolitan publication: it is adventurous in mixing reviews, reportage, diaries and poetry. It allows its writers space for long pieces, and attracts a readership that causes anyone becoming part of that group to question the meaning of the term 'literary'. It seems to espouse the renaissance idea that nothing should be beyond the interest of the person who wants to be a full participant in a world that sees 'culture' as wholly inclusive, and believes that good writing can encourage such participation.

See also: book marketing; publishing trends

JIM MALONEY

literary prizes

Although relatively small-scale awards such as the James Tait Black Memorial Prize and the Hawthornden Prize have existed since the end of the First World War, it is only in the 1980s and 1990s that literary prizes have become a significant part of British cultural life. This is partly because they are increasingly lucrative: there are now several prizes for which British authors are eligible with prize money in excess of £10,000. However, this money (usually provided by corporate sponsors) is still relatively small compared to international prizes like the Nobel Prize for Literature, and the real importance of the prizes lies in their potential for generating further promotion and book sales. Publishers are becoming increasingly astute at generating press coverage and bookshop displays for shortlisted and winning authors.

The most important of these accolades is the Booker Prize, established in 1968, which is open to full-length novels from Britain, the Commonwealth, Ireland, Pakistan and Bangladesh, and which carries an award of £20,000. Its predominance has increased in recent years as the prize ceremony has been televised annually, with a

discussion of the shortlisted novels preceding the announcement of the winner. The Whitbread Book of the Year, originating in 1971 as the Whitbread Literary Awards and boasting a total prize of £21,000, is second to the Booker in influence. Although there are a number of other up and coming prizes open to British authors – such as the Guardian Prize for Fiction, the Irish Times International Fiction Prize and the David Cohen British Literature Prize – at the moment only the Booker and the Whitbread can seriously affect sales. The 1993 Booker winner, Roddy Doyle, had achieved total sales of £6m for *Paddy Clarke Ha Ha Ha* by the end of the following year. The Booker can even make the reputations of relatively unknown authors, as happened with Salman Rushdie, who won for *Midnight's Children* in 1981, and A.S. Byatt, who won for *Possession* in 1990. However, the major literary prizes are certainly not essential to critical and commercial success, as the careers of authors like Martin Amis, Ian McEwan and Angela Carter testify. In turn, the experiences of Keri Hulme in 1985 and James Kelman in 1994 show that Booker wins cannot necessarily guarantee bigger sales or wider exposure. In some cases, as with Amis, authors can even achieve a certain notoriety for continually being omitted from shortlists. (The plot of Amis's novel *The Information* turns on the attempts of the central character, an unsuccessful author, to scupper the chances of a rival winning a lucrative international literary prize by accusing him of plagiarism).

Critics of the prizes maintain that they give the promotional hype of publishers and booksellers a veneer of cultural authority. Since most of the prizes are for 'literary' fiction – although some, like the Sunday Express Award and the W.H. Smith Literary Prize, make a point of being less 'elitist', and the Betty Trask awards explicitly exclude works of an 'experimental' nature – it can be argued that the prizes help to create a kind of major league of bankable literary names, contributing to a process of what Richard Todd calls 'contemporary literary canon-formation' (Todd 1996: 9). The prizes are therefore frequently accused of marginalizing particular writing and reading constituencies. The new £30,000 Orange Prize, which is only open to women authors, and the Saga Prize, for black authors born in Britain, for example, are both partly a response to the under-representation of these groups on other shortlists. The fact that the Booker Prize is often the subject of judging controversies (some Booker judges, like Nicholas Mosley in 1991 and Julia Neuberger in 1994, have resigned or openly expressed their displeasure at the choices of the rest of the jury) points to both the cultural significance of the prize and the subjectivity of its judgements. Since the majority of the new prizes are for novels, many claim that they take attention away from other genres like short story collections and poetry. This stipulation also creates problems of definition; for example, there was some controversy over the award of the Booker to Thomas Keneally's work of 'faction', *Schindler's Ark*, in 1982. The NCR Book Award is a highly lucrative prize for non-fiction, but the press attention it receives is significantly less than the fiction prizes. Some critics complain that, since the initial selection process for the prizes usually involves publishers nominating a set number of books from their lists to be considered by the juries, and the publishers tend to pick works by their established successful authors, it is hard for first novelists or less well-known authors to be short-listed. Other observers have criticized the ageism of several of the prizes; the Somerset Maugham and Eric Gregory awards and the Mail on Sunday/ John Llewellyn Rhys Prize, for instance, are only open to writers under thirty-five.

Supporters of the prizes maintain that they promote 'literary' fiction and other forms of 'serious' literature in an era when they are in danger of being squeezed out by the commercial imperatives of large publishers. They argue that the public arguments over the merits of the respective shortlists are both inevitable and healthy, and that these shortlists generally seek to represent English-language fiction in all its diversity. The Booker Prize in particular can certainly not be accused of little Englandism, since it has brought post-colonial fiction to a British readership through recent wins for authors such as Salman Rushdie (1981), J.M. Coetzee (1983), Peter Carey (1988) and Ben Okri (1991).

See also: novel; poetry; popular fiction

Further reading

Todd, R. (1996) *Consuming Fictions: The Booker Prize and Fiction in Britain Today*, London: Bloomsbury (the only full-length study of the new literary 'prize culture', this is a readable and largely positive account of the effects of the prizes on the consumption of literary fiction in the UK).

JOE MORAN

literary theory

Literary theory since the 1960s has sustained far more change than in the previous thirty years. After several decades of dominance by the New Critics and the close textual, practical readings recommended by the likes of F.R. **Leavis**, the 1960s saw a multiplying of critical approaches that has continued to the present, encompassing the following theoretical branches: formalist, structuralist, Marxist, feminist, post-structuralist, psychoanalytical, cultural materialist, phenomenological, reader-response, post-colonial and queer. Literary theory has therefore been overhauled by the influence of other disciplines, particularly **history**, linguistics, **philosophy**, anthropology, psychology, sociology and cultural studies. The shift can itself be described as a development from a modernist critical practice to a postmodernist plurality of theoretical reading.

Russian formalism developed around the time of the Russian Revolution in 1917. The detailed, technical, linguistic analysis of the formalists (for example, Shklovsky and Roman Jakobson) was based on the belief that literary language differed in key ways from other uses of language. The principal difference, they concluded, was that literary style hinged on 'defamiliarization' or 'making strange', the re-imagining of the world in unfamiliar terms in texts which are simultaneously aware of their own status as art (the quintessential novel was thus perhaps Sterne's *Tristram Shandy*).

Russian formalism had a great impact on structuralism, an approach less interested in individual works of literature than in systems or structures (linguistic, social, cultural, symbolic) that underlie a range of texts. Most important is the understanding that language is a self-sufficient system: it is not a mirror on the world but a plethora of signifiers (sounds or marks, or, loosely, words) which refer to signifieds (which are concepts not things). The literary critic is then concerned not with how the text refers to life but how it functions, how the signifiers (the words, textual components, or *parole*) relate to each other within the 'grammar' of the text and within the general system of language (*langue*).

Influenced by structuralist and then post-structuralist theories, Marxist criticism has changed greatly over the last few decades, but is still concerned to see the text in terms of an analysis of society and history. Since the advent of structuralism, Marxists (like Terry **Eagleton**) pay more attention to the ideology of the text, its gaps or repressions, and its contradictions. This ties up with feminist criticism (such as that of Kate **Millet** and Germaine **Greer**) because both are concerned with the political or social issues (the one with class and the other with gender) at stake in reading literature as well as in the texts themselves. For both theoretical positions, the main point is to reinterpret and change social understanding through analysis of the content (and sometimes the form) of the text.

Post-structuralist criticism encompasses and in particular develops from the work of the French theorists Jacques Derrida, Jacques Lacan and Michel Foucault who, from the perspectives of philosophy, psychoanalysis and social history respectively, have critiqued the systematic approach of structuralism and, while continuing structuralism's fascination with language, have focused on the ways in which discourse conditions all human relations of power or knowledge; that is, how everything is ultimately 'textual', made up of language.

Other theories are far more concerned with the internal workings of the text and the relation between language and mind. Psychoanalytical approaches employ the theories of Sigmund Freud, Carl Jung, Jacques Lacan, Julia Kristeva and others to go beneath the surface of the text to analyse its systems, repressions, contradictions or disturbances. Phenomenological criticism (stemming from the theories of Husserl) attempts to comprehend the author through the text: the critic should pay attention to nothing but the way in which the literary work embodies the author's consciousness. Reader-response criticism (for example, that of Stanley Fish, Wolfgang Iser or Hans Robert Jauss), by contrast, is more concerned with the activity and subject of reading than the author. It argues that meaning is generated in the act of reading and therefore criticism should focus on the process through which the reader, in a particular time and place, responds to the text, in dialogue with the words on the page.

Far closer to Marxism and feminism, other theories insist upon a 'return to history'. Cultural materialist (new historicist criticism is the US equivalent) approaches are most indebted to the work of the post-structuralist Michel Foucault (but the Marxist Raymond **Williams** is also key), and attempt to analyse culture through texts and vice versa. Grounding their analyses in historical sources, cultural materialists (like Jonathan Dollimore, Alan Sinfield or the American Stephen Greenblatt) often start outside the literary work with a discussion of contemporary non-literary texts and then use those intertextual reference points to analyse and often undermine (more conventional readings of) the play, poem or novel, paying close attention to marginalized figures and looking for signs of social change. Post-colonial criticism understands the literary canon in terms of the effects and legacies of (particularly the British) empire. It is also concerned to include in the literary curriculum writing from colonized cultures, aiming to study 'lost' texts by non-white writers just as feminism aims to recuperate neglected women's writing. Lastly, queer theory is concerned with the analysis of gender roles and sexuality. Greatly influenced by the work of Judith Butler, queer theory aims to destabilize conventional views of gender and sexual identity, particularly the binary system of sex differences that underpins patriarchal society and sustains a norm of heterosexism.

Literary studies appears always to be in crisis, concerned to contemplate its own future directions and possible demise. However, the analysis of (visual and written) texts will continue to generate new approaches and theories and will undoubtedly continue in one (post/inter)disciplinary form or another, reinvigorating and reinvigorated by other academic areas.

See also: feminist theory; Marxism; post-colonial writing; postmodernist theory; post-structuralism; structuralism

Further reading

Bradford, R. (ed.) (1996) *Studying Literature*, Hemel Hempstead: Harvester.

PETER CHILDS

live art

An elusive and uncircumscribed art form and practice, live art cross-fertilizes communicative and expressive elements from the visual arts, performance (theatre, dance, music), mass and mixed media, traditional, modern and technological cultures. Avant-gardist in approach and postmodern in nature, live art creates a culturally discursive space to disrupt, subvert and redefine existing relationships between art, the individual and the contemporary world in a perpetually transformatory process.

Live art derives from 1960s happenings and shares close affinities with **performance art**, with which it often overlaps. Like happenings, which also reject the permanence of art forms, live art is characterized by its impermanence and actuality within a temporally autonomous present, its transience rendering its inclusion in any art history repository problematic. Live art negates the past with no expectations of the future, and exists only as the lived memory of a unique personal and collective event exclusively shared by artist and 'audience' alike.

While performance art maintains boundaries between artist and audience, live art redefines its audience as participants, viewers or witnesses to the live event or spectacle. Their physical presence completes the transitory experience of the work, while its physical surroundings contextualize it within an acute social, political or cultural setting. Such transgressions lead, for example, from live art installations in organized artistic spaces to site-specific work, from abandoned or public areas to urban locations of thriving and underground club and music scenes.

Live art has featured in work by renowned artists like Gillian Wearing, Mark Wallinger, Heather Ackroyd and Daniel Harvey. Its free-flowing format has enabled black artists like David Medalla during the 1960s and 1970s and, later, Keith Khan, Lubaina Himid, Susan Lewis, SuAndi and Ronald Fraser Munro to produce culturally inflected manifestations of its personal, creative and political possibilities. For instance, Palestinian-born and cultural exile Mona Hatoum has engaged with universals of displacement, oppression, resistance and freedom through striking metamorphic processes involving the subjection and release of her physical self, in performance and video installation work.

Live art has conclusively entered the mainstream gallery space. Detractors emphasize its fleeting superficiality and pretension, but nevertheless, its urban deployment of vital, non-hierarchized cultural tools and its transgressive drive appear to inadvertently anticipate the artistic practices of a decolonized and postmodern immediate future.

See also: avant-garde theatre

Further reading

Childs, N. and Walwin, J. (eds) (1998) *A Split Second of Paradise*, London: Rivers Oram Press (fascinating articles about selected artists, capturing the essence of live, performance and installation art).

SATINDER CHOHAN

LLOYDS' BUILDING *see* Rogers, Richard

Loach, Ken

b. 1936, Nuneaton

Film-maker

Ken Loach is a left-wing film-maker who specializes in working-class realism and forms of resistance. In directing television drama (see **drama on television**), he pioneered the use of documentary film techniques and created a major social stir with *Cathy Come Home* (1966), the famous

drama-documentary on homelessness. His controversial series on socialism, *Days of Hope* (1975),
stimulated an influential theoretical debate on
realism in *Screen*. Increasingly censored by the
television establishment, Loach returned to low-
budget film features and *Hidden Agenda* (1990),
alleging 'shoot to kill' activities by the British Army
in **Ireland**, was acclaimed at the Cannes Festival.
More recent films such as *Riff-Raff* and *Land and
Freedom*, though critically highly regarded, are
regrettably screened more frequently in Europe
than Britain.

See also: *Screen* and screen theory

Further reading

McKnight, G. (ed.) (1995) *Agents of Challenge and Defiance: The Films of Ken Loach*, London: Flicks
Books.

BOB MILLINGTON

lobby groups

Lobbying is the political activity of influencing or
attempting to influence the political process in
general and policy-making in particular. It is an
activity widespread in politics where different
groups and interests seek to influence political
actors, such as policy makers, government ministers, MPs, members of political parties, the media
and so on. Lobbying can occur at every level of
politics, from local government and national
parliaments to supranational and international
political organizations such as the European Union
and the United Nations.

Lobbying is part and parcel of the realpolitik of
all modern political systems, and in liberal democracies is a highly professional activity which has not
always been the case. Whereas in the past lobbying
occurred through 'old boys' networks', informal, ad
hoc arrangements between political actors and
interest groups, in the modern political world there
are professional lobbying agencies who will, for a
fee, lobby on behalf of their clients. Very often these
professional lobbyists are ex-politicians, or are
closely connected with particular political parties.

For some, lobbying is not a problem for
democracies since all interests, groups and individuals can lobby or seek to lobby and influence
public policy. On this pluralist account of politics,
lobbying is simply another way to represent one's
interests alongside the formal voting mechanism.
For others, lobbying is inherently problematic,
since it is an attempt undemocratically to influence
democratically elected politicians, ministers and
governments, and lobbying is mostly used by
powerful interests and groups to amend government policy to suit themselves. Those that lobby
government are not usually the unemployed or
single mothers, but large corporations or well-
organized special interest groups such as farmers.

With the professionalization of lobbying in
recent years and its character as a paid-for service
has come the charge that lobbying introduces an
element of corruption into democratic politics.
Recent scandals in Britain, centred on the
unhealthy relationship between lobbyists and
elected politicians and ministers (from the disgraced former Conservative MPs Neil Hamilton
and Jonathan Aitken, to the more recent 1998
scandal surrounding the lobbyist Derek Draper
and the **New Labour** government) have demonstrated for some why lobbying is an inherently
undesirable (though inevitable) aspect of modern
democratic politics.

See also: democracy; pressure groups

JOHN BARRY

local councils

There are several levels of local councils, ranging
from parish councils to borough, district and
county councils. Generally, the turnout at local
elections is relatively low compared to national
parliamentary elections, and the results are often
determined by the national political struggle rather
than by local issues or personalities. Results of
elections are sometimes biased according to local
and personal factors, and sometimes according to
national factors.

Local councils provide services at the borough
level and are democratic institutions that allow
closer public scrutiny than is often the case with
national government. Local governments have

limited autonomy and can only exert power over matters granted by parliamentary legislation.

Local councils' largest source of income is in the form of grants from central government. The rest comes from local taxation, in particular the council tax, a property-based tax. Increasingly, central government has taken over many of the functions traditionally carried out by local governments, and other functions have been relegated to private enterprise. Local councils have lost control over gas, electricity, some healthcare areas, and public transport. Water, sewerage and drainage have now been privatized. Some local autonomy exists in educational structures, such as school curriculum and teaching methods, but with the 1988 Education Act and the Labour government's agenda to increase standards and inspect schools, this autonomy has been diminished in favour of increasing control by the central government of the school curriculum. Councils retain nominal control over some aspects of the local police, fire services, planning, social services and recreational matters but in practice, they are subservient to increasing central control in all these areas.

There are clear tensions in the relationship between local and central government and different views on how independent local councils should be from central government. Central government has made major changes in the infrastructure of local authorities. The primary shift has been a significant increase in centralization, a program of centrally declared standards, and a decline in local autonomy. These underlying principles have recently guided and continue to guide the relation between state and local councils. The present government's ostensible commitment to devolution and to the creation of an elected authority and mayor for London might have the side effect of increasing the relative autonomy of local government.

See also: GLC

Further reading

Elcock, H. (1994) *Local Government; Policy Management in Local Authorities*, 3rd edn, London: Routledge.

PAUL BARRY CLARKE
SVANBORG SIGMARSDOTTIR

local press

The most famous local newspaper, the Manchester *Guardian* eventually outgrew Lancashire to become a national daily. The *Scotsman* in Edinburgh counts as a national newspaper. Papers in Glasgow, Newcastle, Bristol, Cardiff, Liverpool, Leeds and Birmingham all have a considerable reputation and maintain generally high standards of journalism, but the majority, which represent smaller towns, tend to confine their activities to parochial matters. Local newspapers act as notice boards for events that frequently interest only the participants and their immediate families, and will rarely involve themselves in serious investigative journalism. There are many reasons for this, but the main one is the decline and disappearance of the independent publisher. Markets are much tighter now than thirty or forty years ago, and it is more important for publishers not to offend powerful local advertisers. This was always the case to some extent, but in the pre-television era some editors had more freedom to pursue local issues some of the time.

During the growth period of television, which has given more people more access to better entertainment and news services, the local press has fallen into the hands of fewer and fewer owners such as Reed Regional, London Independent and Guardian Gazette Newspapers. Combined with a greatly increased mobility in the labour market, the local paper has become less local in the sense that editors and journalists are less likely to be local people and more likely to be recent graduates beating a path to what was once Fleet Street. Life has been made additionally difficult for them by the **freesheets**, which carry mainly advertising with scraps of local news and sport tacked on. Like the national press until the 1997 election, most local papers tended to take an implicit right-wing stance on most issues, in line with the politics of their owners. Similarly, standards of journalism and literacy have declined in the local press just as they have in the tabloid press, which the former tend to echo albeit in a more low-key fashion.

Taken together, these developments have contributed to homogenization. Some papers will come out in one city and then appear with slight variations in half a dozen other local towns, as is the case in the areas around Canterbury and Leicester. Such is the dependence on advertising revenue that a major advertiser can exert pressure on the editor or the owner for favourable publicity. It is usually left to reporters from the national press or television to highlight serious wrongdoing at a local level.

See also: Northern Irish press; Scottish press; Welsh press

Further reading

Franklin, B. (1991) *What News? The Market, Politics and the Local Press*, London: Routledge & Kegan Paul.

STEPHEN KERENSKY

local radio

The first local radio service was set up by the BBC in Leicester in 1967. This was followed by stations in other centres of population, and the local radio movement became successful at creating a local identity and a community experience for its listeners. The potential success proved attractive to various interests starting up in the mid-1970s, who sought to combine the intimacy and extreme portability of the radio experience with the chance to bring freer commercial attitudes to a new market.

Both BBC and the commercial stations rely strongly on phone-ins as a way of involving their listeners and reinforcing the sense of local community. BBC stations often have daily two-hour or three-hour phone-in programmes on a variety of current national and local topics. Moreover, BBC stations tend to cater more for various local community groups, since these stations do not have the same commercial imperatives driving them as do their independent competitors, and they happily put on weekly thirty-minute programmes for local ethnic minorities. Only the London area could support a commercial enterprise like London Greek, which has a comparatively small but highly concentrated audience.

The commercial stations in general have a bigger share of local audience than the BBC

stations. Driven by market forces, they will try to maximize potential and often have an output on FM of standard chart material, while an AM sister channel will play 'golden oldies' to capture an older audience of equal interest to advertisers. Manchester's Piccadilly Radio follows this policy. The FM version (Key 103) has a 23.6 percent share of listeners, while its AM twin (1152 AM) claims 8.7 percent, with a sizeable 18.3 percent of the 35–44 age group. BBC GMR Talk's weekly share is 3.4 percent.

The popularity of local radio can be seen by the number of organizations wishing to apply for the very limited number of franchises becoming officially available from time to time. At time of writing, there are twenty-four special interest groups planning applications for the new London franchise over the crowded metropolitan airwaves, including a proposed Gay FM station with much high-profile support. This phenomenon is part of the general buoyancy of radio, owing as much to the very wide choice available as to the intimacy of the medium.

Indeed, the strength of interest in providing a local service for local people can also be gauged by the multiplicity of **pirate radio** stations, tending to operate clandestinely in inner city areas and generally providing a fare of local ethnic music. Because the government has a policy of allowing only very few licences, such stations are marginalized and *de facto* criminalized. On the whole, these stations would prefer to go legitimate and 'narrowcast' legally to their small but strongly defined local constituency, than be quasi-outlaws. This will need to be addressed as a fundamental issue in the next round of franchising.

See also: commercial radio; commercial radio, national

Further reading

Crisell, A. (1994) *Understanding Radio*, London: Methuen.

Scannell, P. (1991) *Broadcast Talk*, London: Sage.

GEORGE HASTINGS

London Fashion Week

Once a poor cousin to the Paris/Milan/New York shows, London Fashion Week has become a prestigious international event and not just an outing for minor talents at venues across the capital. There are now scouts out looking for the new John **Galliano**, Stella **McCartney** or Alexander **McQueen**, plus major celebrities seeking tickets for shows from the slightly less well-known such as Pearce Fionda, Bella **Freud**, Owen Gaster, Amanda Wakeley, Sonja Nuttall and Michiko Koshino. The 1998 catwalks showcased the latest new designers such as Tristan Webber, Deborah Milner, Julien MacDonald and Matthew Williamson, the star of the 1997 show. Additionally, the week provides opportunities for new models to develop a reputation, such as Cordelia, a sixteen-year-old Dorset schoolgirl tipped by *Vogue* in 1998 to become one of the top twenty models. The attempt to initiate a new Men's London Fashion Week in July 1998 met with only small success, as most of the top names such as Paul **Smith** and Katherine **Hamnett** elected to show abroad instead.

PETER CHILDS

Long, Richard

b. 1945, Bristol

Sculptor

Since 1965, Richard Long has refashioned the landscape around him, considering the transient nature of his surroundings. His earthworks concern the concepts of time, movement and place and are known by photographs, printed text and annotated maps. He has crossed each continent, creating sculptures of simple shapes from indigenous natural materials. Long's initial method of rearranging local materials can be seen in *A Line Made by Walking* (1967); this approach evolved into that expressed in *Bushwood Circle* (1977) and *River Avon Mud Hand Circles* (1984). His Ordinance Survey maps are annotated to provide additional information about his excursions, while his printed texts narrate his journey in pictorial form. His works are understated, non-representational and, in many cases, impermanent.

See also: sculpture

NATALIE GALE

long-distance runners

Britain has had a long and successful record of distance running, but the 1990s have seen poorer results, at least for the men, with the result that there have been calls for more financial backing. There remain a number of women who are world-class performers and have claimed numerous titles and victories. Ironically, interest for the women's sport was probably sparked by the controversial South African Zola Budd, who broke numerous British records and kept the sport's profile high. Since Budd, the brightest hope has been Paula Radcliffe (3000m, 5000m and mile distances), who won the world junior cross-country title in 1992; the intervening four years were blighted by injury, but Radcliffe has emerged once more, breaking Budd's 5000m record.

Other top female performers include marathon runner Marian Sutton, who won the Chicago race in 1996 after hovering on the edge of the elite for some time, and Yvonne Murray. Murray has had both many successes (European 3000m championship, world indoor 3000m championships, Commonwealth 10,000m), and a string of inglorious failures (as at three world championships and the 1992 Olympics). Probably the brightest star, however, is Liz McColgan, marathon, 10,000m and cross country runner.

The men have struggled to live down the successes of the 1980s by Moorcroft, Ovett and Cram, and Foster before them, and have less to celebrate than the women. In marathon, Richard Neurarkar (fifth at Atlanta in 1996) and Paul Evans (third in London in 1996 and winner in Chicago in 1996) are also joined by Eamonn Martin, who won London in 1993 and Chicago in 1995. In cross-country running, meanwhile, Britain has Andrew Pearson, who won a bronze at the 1995 European championships 9km race; the UK also took bronze in the team event. The track distances, though, have not seen success for Britain for some years.

Long-distance running has come to be dominated by Kenya and Ethiopia, amongst others, and the sport's profile is low in the UK. Of particular concern is the fact that most other countries pay their distance athletes, so allowing for full-time training. Marian Sutton complained that most of the women she ran against in Chicago were salaried, whereas she was forced to juggle a full-time job with her training schedule.

See also: athletics; marathons; middle-distance runners; sprinters

REX NASH

Lonrho Affair

The Lonhro Affair in 1973 was described by Edward Heath as 'the unpleasant and unacceptable face of capitalism'. Lonhro was an international mining and trading company accused of offering large financial 'incentives' to business contacts, including Duncan Sandys, an ex-Tory MP. Sandys was paid a tax-free sum in excess of £100,000 for leaving his consultancy job, a practice which was not in itself illegal, but which exposed a gaping hole in legislation. Subsequent scandals such as the 'cash for questions' inquiry into the 'purchase' of questions in the House of Commons in 1996, allegedly involving another prominent Tory MP, Neil Hamilton, have occurred sporadically.

See also: sex scandals; Westland Affair

PETER CHILDS

LORD'S STAND *see* Hopkins, Michael

Losey, Joseph

b. 1909, La Crosse, Wisconsin (USA); d. 1984

Film-maker

The son of an American lawyer, Joseph Losey abandoned a medical career for the stage, where his successful direction of Brecht's *Galileo, Galilei*

brought him an offer from RKO to direct his first feature. After establishing a reputation directing 'noir' thrillers, he fell foul of the Committee on Un-American Activities for refusing to abandon shooting *Stranger on the Prowl* in Italy, and was subsequently blacklisted. Moving to England, he made his best-known features, *The Criminal* (1960), *The Servant* (1963) and *The Go-Between* (1971). Ultimately a cineaste, his films reflected his passion for European cinema and the theatre. His career was long and highly productive; he directed over thirty features, culminating with an adaptation of Neil Dunn's play *Steaming*, released posthumously in 1985.

ROB FILLINGHAM

Lovell, Bernard

b. 1913, Oldham Common, Gloucestershire

Astrophysicist

Astrophysicist, author and cricket lover, Sir Bernard Lovell was a pioneer of radio astronomy in the period immediately following the Second World War. The building of the giant radio telescope at Jodrell Bank, Cheshire, followed initial success in the detection of meteor showers using radar. The financial difficulties encountered by the program did not stop the telescope, and it and Lovell became world famous. The successful tracking of the Soviet satellite Sputnik 1 in October 1957 earned Lovell a knighthood in 1961, and confirmed Britain's place at the forefront of radio astronomy.

A distinguished academic, contributing to numerous scientific journals, Lovell popularized astronomy by considering the broader theoretical issues posed by space exploration and modern cosmology. His books include *Radio Astronomy* (1951), *The Exploration of Outer Space* (1961) and *In The Centre of Immensities* (1978), the latter of which articulated his view of a compatibility between faith and science.

See also: science

PAUL BARRY CLARKE
LAWRENCE QUILL

MacCormac, Richard

b. 1938

Architect

Richard MacCormac trained at Cambridge and then University College before working for **Powell and Moya**, Lyons Israel Ellis and the London Borough of Merton. He founded MacCormac Jamieson in 1972, three years after starting in private practice. He is in essence a modernist, even though his buildings differ from the more brutal work of his contemporaries and employ natural and traditional materials. His principal work includes university buildings at Cambridge, Oxford and Bristol, housing projects at Duffryn, South Wales and Milton Keynes, and the redevelopment of Spitalfields Market in London. His latest highly praised building is the impressive Ruskin Library at Lancaster University, opened in mid-1998.

An architect of international standing, MacCormac has a keen interest in urban design and architectural theory. He has held a number of prominent positions including chairing architectural competitions such as The Sunday Times Building of the Year Award, and has been a member of the Royal Fine Art Commission and a Commissioner for English Heritage. In addition, he is a previous President of the Royal Institute of British Architects (**RIBA**), and was awarded the CBE in 1994.

MacCormac has been involved in a number of prestigious projects, including the Cable and Wireless College, Coventry (which won The Sunday Times Building of the Year award) and the Garden Quadrangle at St John's College Oxford (winner of the Independent on Sunday Building of the Year Award 1994). Other projects have included projected developments such as the Jubilee Line extension's Southwark Station, and the Coventry Phoenix initiative that aims to regenerate central public spaces and includes a public art events programme. MacCormac also designed the projected Tesco store at Ludlow in Shropshire which, rather than try to ape the surroundings, has attempted to draw upon the environs without resorting to some neo-architectural fancy by looking at how the town has developed and evolved, and then designing the new store to fit in with the landscape and to be sensitive to its ambience. A resident in the Spitalfields area of London, where much of his work is based, he has shown a keen awareness of social issues that need to be addressed within architecture, particularly in terms of (re)-creating communities and reclaiming spaces/places. MacCormac is a Fellow of the Royal Society of Arts and senior partner of MacCormac Jamieson and Pritchard. The firm is also responsible for designing the 'new' (it was first proposed in 1911) wing for London's Science Museum in South Kensington. This is to be known as the Wellcome Wing, as the Wellcome Trust have offered £16.5m funding, which will be supplemented by £23m from the Heritage Lottery Fund. The firm has had to pay careful attention to integrating its design so as not to adversely affect existing neighbours, including the Omani embassy.

GUY OSBORN
STEVE GREENFIELD

MacKenzie, John

b. 1932

Film-maker

An Edinburgh film-maker, John McKenzie produced television features in the early 1970s, and
made his name with *The Long Good Friday* (1980), a
crime film about a London East End gang. Set in
the 1930s American gangster tradition of *Scarface*
and *Little Caesar*, its cast included Bob Hoskins and
Helen Mirren. The film presaged Peter **Greenaway**'s *The Cook, The Thief, His Wife And Her Lover*
(1989). MacKenzie was best at documenting the
way tough, fearless working-class thugs could rise
and fall as infamous criminals. Others of his films
which achieved less critical and popular success
have been Graham Greene's *The Honorary Consul*
(1983), *The Fourth Protocol* (1987) and *The Last of the
Finest* (1990).

MIKE STORRY

magazines, satirical

The most influential humorous and satirical
magazines in Britain are *Private Eye, Viz* and the
revived *Punch*. The original *Punch*, founded in 1841,
became a national institution but then began to go
into decline. Alan Coren, editor from 1977–87,
though dubbed 'the funniest writer in Britain' by
the *Sunday Times* in 1976, failed to arrest its decline
and, despite the appointment of a young editor,
David Thomas, in 1989 with the brief of capturing
the yuppies, it eventually ceased publication in
1991. It was supplanted by *Private Eye*, which does
what Punch did when it was first published: attack
the Establishment. *Punch* was revived in 1996, but
with a much different format, a bland mixture of
topicality and humour.

The fortnightly magazine *Private Eye* was
founded in 1961 by Richard Ingrams, Christopher
Booker, Nicholas Luard and Willie Rushton. Its
humour was much more savage than that of *Punch*,
and it was not afraid of libel actions. It was nearly
closed on several occasions by successful libel suits,
notably from Sir James Goldsmith and Robert
Maxwell ('Sir Jams' and 'Cap'n Bob', as the *Eye*

called them). Ingrams appointed his own editorial
successor, Ian Hislop, then 26. In 1989 £250,000
was awarded against *Private Eye* for alleging that the
wife of the Yorkshire Ripper was paid for her story.
This again nearly led to closure. The circulation in
1995 had reached a healthy 183,216 copies, sold to
a readership which was 70 percent male and 30
percent female.

Viz came out of the punk movement in 1979. It
is aimed at a young male audience and consists
largely of 'schoolboy' humour about bodily functions. However, its humour is in many ways
genuinely iconoclastic and zany. Thus it has kept
a wider and more intelligent audience than its
remit would suggest. Part of its originality and
ethos may come from its Newcastle upon Tyne
base, away from the vogues of London. *Viz* has
been accused of sexism, but it has nearly half as
many women readers as, for example, *Good House-
keeping*. Its bi-monthly circulation in 1995 was
3,354,000 copies, with about 15 percent of its
readership being female.

Attempts were made to introduce magazines
which copied the *Viz* formula (such as *Zit, Poot, Gas*
and *Smut*), but they were of lower quality and
failed. *Oink* (1988) was of higher quality, but failed
because it was wrongly associated with the **top-
shelf magazines** among which it was sold.

See also: comics; comics culture

Further reading

Riley, S.G (ed.) (1993) *Consumer Magazines of the British Isles*, Westport, CT: Greenwood Press.

MIKE STORRY

Magnum

The photographic news agency Magnum was
formed as an international cooperative in 1947
by the Hungarian Robert Capa (a pseudonym of
Andre Friedman), the Frenchman Henri Cartier-
Bresson, the Swiss Werner Bischof and the
American David 'Chim' Seymour. The agency
supplied news photographs to publications around
the world. Eve Arnold joined the collective early on,
when the agency spotted one of her photographs in

London's *Picture Post*. The style the agency has tended to encourage is that of the original members: realistic, non-voyeuristic photojournalism, influenced by Walker Evans and Dorothea Lange, integrating personal drama with action in spontaneous yet carefully composed photos such as Capa's 'Moment of Death (of a Loyalist Soldier)' (1936).

See also: photography

MIKE STORRY

mail order

Around 5 percent of Britain's retail turnover is accounted for by mail order, but the importance of this segment is probably greater than the figures suggest. For though the percentage is currently not increasing, because of competition from high street shops and, more significantly, shopping malls, mail order is very important for those members of the public who are housebound on account of age, disability or family responsibilities, who live in remote areas, or who cannot for some other reason readily go shopping by public or private transport. For certain purchases, mail order also spares shoppers embarrassment or else offers a source of specialized goods not otherwise available. Mail order companies do not operate in expensive high streets or shopping centres but from semi-industrial premises, often in the Midlands or the Northwest where lower staff costs also help offset the costs of administration, packing and post. Serving a large customer base, they are able both to negotiate advantageous prices from manufacturers and wholesalers and to offer a remarkable choice of goods in a wider range of sizes than is available in many shops.

The basis of mail order is the advertising of goods, either in the press or, more typically, in an illustrated catalogue. The importance of the 'catalogue agent', usually a woman raising some extra cash by soliciting orders on the basis of the catalogue for a small commission, has diminished in recent years. Another crucial factor is good two-way communications. Customers, who generally pay when ordering or by credit card, although arrangements can usually also be made for payment by instalments, must be able to place their orders readily by post or, increasingly, telephone. An efficient service for meeting orders without errors and prompt delivery are essential if retailers are to maintain good relations with the public. They cannot survive either without an established reputation for acceptable quality, keen prices and readiness to honour their 'no quibble' guarantee to offer exchanges or refunds to dissatisfied purchasers. Computers have simplified the vital task of record-keeping, and improving quality control by suppliers also makes it easier to give customers the service they demand if they are to go on buying goods without inspecting them in advance of purchase.

Alongside the traditional catalogue names such as Littlewoods, Grattan's and Kay's, major mail order clothing companies working in the UK are Next Directory, Hawkshead, Racing Green, Land's End, La Redoute and, in a new move which may lead to market dominance, Marks & Spencer.

See also: catalogue shops; hire purchase

Further reading

Walsh, N. (1994) *The Good Mail Order Guide*, London: Macmillan.

CHRISTOPHER SMITH

marathons

Britain's main contribution to marathon races is obviously the London Marathon, the biggest such race in the world. The UK does host other races as well, as in Leeds, but London is the prestige event that attracts the most interest and the world's top competitors.

Held annually in April, the London race was founded in 1981 by runners Chris Brasher and John Disley, with Brasher acting as the head of London Marathon Ltd (who oversee the running of the race and arrange sponsorship deals) until 1995. In 1996 the organizers received 66,000 applications for a place in the race, of which only 38,500 were accepted. Over the first fifteen years of its existence some 300,000 people have taken part, most running for charities and dressed up in an array of costumes. Over that time, £60m has been raised for charity, of which £3m was specifically set aside for recreation sites in London. The race was always specifically designed not to be a financial burden on local taxpayers.

The race is so prestigious that the **BBC** broadcasts it live every year, offering blanket coverage of every step of the 26 miles and 385 yards course, and it attracts millions of viewers worldwide, including a peak of six million in Britain one year. It also attracts large general media coverage, and sponsors are very keen to get involved with the event. The biggest and latest deal saw food company Flora pay £6m for the sponsorship rights for three years, with the race costing £2.25m to stage annually. But despite these huge costs, the enormous interest from other sponsors means that the organizers can afford to pay top runners handsomely to appear, with British long-distance runner Liz McColgan being paid some £450,000 to run three times between 1993 and 1996; a total of £250,000 was available for appearance money in 1997's race. Some £100,000 made from the race is also annually spent on the UK long-distance running team.

Apart from London, there are races run annually in Leeds and on the south coast in April, and there are a number of shorter (twenty mile) and half-marathons held in Liskeard, Watford, Camberley and Reading, with some boasting their own dedicated sponsorship. Marathon races are clearly genuinely popular with people of all ages and from all backgrounds, and constitute one of the truly classless sports in the UK.

See also: athletics; long-distance runners; middle-distance runners; sprinters

REX NASH

marriage

It has been argued that marriage is becoming less popular in society, as fewer people are actually getting married. This is also evidenced by an increase in the number of marital breakdowns, which is reflected in the rising divorce rate. In Britain in 1971, one in eleven teenage women got married. By 1981, this figure had fallen to one in

twenty-four. Between 1981 and 1990, the marriage rate for all age groups fell from 7.1 per year per thousand of the eligible population to 6.8 (*General Household Survey, Social Trends*).

An alternative to marriage is co-habitation by couples who are not legally married. Data from the General Household Survey indicates the percentage of non-married women who were co-habiting more than doubled between 1979 and 1991, increasing from 11 percent to 23 percent. Another alternative to marriage is the increase in single-parent families. According to government statistics (Office of Population and Census Statistics), 2.5 percent of the population in 1961 lived in households with a lone parent and dependent children. By 1992 this figure had risen to 10.1 percent. Data from the General Household Survey indicates that between 1972 and 1991, the percentage of children living in single-parent families had increased from 8 percent to 18 percent. The General Household Survey also found that the majority of single parents were women. Ninety percent of single-parent families were headed by women.

Between 1971 and 1991, the proportion of single lone mothers who were divorced increased from 21 percent to 43 percent. The number of mothers who were single also increased from 16 percent to 34 percent. There has also been a significant increase in the divorce rate. In 1971 there were 6.0 persons divorcing per thousand married people; in 1991 this figure had more than doubled to 12.9. In 1991 there were 350,000 marriages, but 171,000 divorces, indicating there were nearly half as many divorces as marriages (*Social Trends* 1993).

The decline in the rate of marriage, an increase in co-habitation, an increase in single-parent families and an increase in marital breakdown all suggest that the institution of marriage is in decline in Britain.

See also: divorce law; domestic violence; single parents

Further reading

General Household Survey (1971, 1993).
Social Trends 23 (1993).

KALWANT BHOPAL

Martian Poets

With the publication of Craig Raine's *The Onion, Memory* (1978) and *A Martian Sends a Postcard Home* (1979), and Christopher Reid's *Arcadia* (1979), a brief and self-contained 'movement' in poetry was born. The 'Martians' were characterized by their attempt to look at the world from an alien perspective, loaded with the imagery of a topsy-turvy world. In the title poem from Raine's second collection, a Martian visitor writes home about the bizarre nature of the life he has found, forcing us as audience to re-examine what we take for granted in our world. Martian poetry injected a much needed dose of imagination, defamiliarization and inventiveness into British poetry, emerging from the more conservative poetry of the postwar period, epitomized by the Movement.

See also: poetry in the 1980s

SARAH CORBETT

Martin, Leslie

b. 1908, Manchester

Architect

Sir J. Leslie Martin achieved prominence as an academic as well as a practitioner. Educated at the School of Architecture, University of Manchester from 1927–30, he then lectured there from 1930 until taking up an appointment as Head of School of Architecture at the University of Hull, a post he held from 1934–9. Together with the painter Ben **Nicholson** and the sculptor Naum Gabo, he co-edited the short-lived constructivist magazines *Unit One* and *Circle* in 1937; these were one of the means by which Continental modernism was introduced to England. Principal assistant architect to the London, Midland and Scottish Railway from 1939 until 1948, he then moved to the architecture department of the London County Council. Martin's best-known early work, the Royal Festival Hall, London (1951, with Robert Matthew, Peter Moro and Edwin Williams) dates from this period and formed what William Curtis called 'the last mannered fanfare' of the modern movement. As Chief Architect of the LCC from 1953–6, Martin

established what was effectively a role as 'sponsor of design'. From 1956 Martin engaged in private practice in Cambridge and from 1959–72 he held the position of Professor and Head of the Department of Architecture, University of Cambridge. His work there includes the Harvey Court Residential Building at Gonville and Caius College (1957–62, with Colin St John **Wilson**) and the Stone Building at Peterhouse, Cambridge, also designed with Wilson in 1960–4. The Library Group, Oxford University (1963, with Colin St John Wilson, Patrick Hodgkinson and Douglas Lanham) comprises The Bodleian Law Library, The English Faculty Library and the Institute of Statistics Library, which are grouped together around an external public staircase and interlock to form a unified but free and picturesque composition.

In the 1960s, the critical reaction to 'mixed development', comprising towers and row houses, began to emerge in the form of 'low-rise high density' **housing**. Supported by Martin and Lionel March's research at Cambridge University into Fresnel Square and its application to housing, this solution, employed most notably by the London Borough of Camden, was sadly often as bleak as the tower blocks they sought to replace. Martin's ideas on perimeter planning were first employed at Pollard's Hill (1971) by the London Borough of Merton Architects Department. Martin's influential approach to comprehensive planning, and concerns for materials and constructional techniques continue to be promoted through The Martin Centre at Cambridge.

Further reading

Martin, L. (1983) *Buildings and Ideas 1933–83*, Cambridge: Cambridge University Press.

HILARY GRAINGER

Marxism

Debates on Marxist theory and practice are carried out in academic journals such as *New Left Review* and in the pages of magazines such as *Socialist Worker* and *Marxism Today*, as well as in the many political organizations influenced by Marxist thinking throughout the UK. Since the 1930s, Marxism and its rumoured follower post-Marxism have undergone a number of radical theoretical and ideological changes. The seminal intellectual figures in this revolution have rarely been British: they include Bertolt Brecht, Georg Lukács, Louis Althusser, Lucien Goldmann, Alain Touraine, Hannah Arendt, Antonio Gramsci, Walter Benjamin, Max Horkheimer and Theodor Adorno of the Frankfurt School. However, the influence of these Continental philosophers and theorists on British intellectual life since the 1960s has been considerable, and has impacted in many areas.

The Marxist historians Eric **Hobsbawm**, E.P. **Thompson** and A.J.P. **Taylor** have been amongst the most influential of their generation, and their overviews of modern British history are probably more widely known than any others. Since their first interventions in the 1970s and 1980s, Marxist history, which had previously been heavy going to all but the initiated, has responded to new developments in psychology and French critical theory, combining them with the traditional base/superstructure model to create a historiography which is both more aware of its own writing practice (in a metahistorical sense) and more attuned to everyday life.

The literary critic Terry **Eagleton** has been greatly influenced by the work of the French structuralist Louis Althusser on ideology (which is reproduced in cultural works) and, more recently, by the work of Walter Benjamin and the German social philosopher Jürgen Habermas. Eagleton took from Althusser the idea of Marxism as a scientific theory of human societies and of how to change them. Althusser in turn was greatly influenced by the theories of the Freudian psychoanalyst Jacques Lacan, and argued that ideology was not a consciously held set of beliefs but was the way in which individuals are defined as subjects within the social system; consequently, ideology works primarily at the level of the unconscious to recreate and maintain the existing relations of society. For his part, Eagleton uses such theories to analyse how history suffuses literary texts, which may themselves critique the ideologies of their times and in turn influence society.

The Welsh literary and cultural critic Raymond **Williams** was most influenced by the work of the Italian Antonio Gramsci. Williams, who had a problematic relationship with Marxism, argued that most Marxist criticism too easily separated economics from culture (which he discussed rather than ideology), dealing in generalities and masses at the expense of individuals. He also argued that conceptions of the literary and the artistic are determined by discourse and by vested material interests, not by timeless criteria. More generally, from the late 1950s onwards Williams proposed a broadly based study of not just literature but (popular) 'culture' (which he defined as 'lived experience') alongside society and politics. Williams himself greatly influenced the agenda of the Birmingham Centre for Contemporary Cultural Studies, which was led by the work of Richard Hoggart, Stuart **Hall** and Paul **Gilroy**.

In recent years, the attack of postmodernism on Marxism's totalizing drive to provide a grand narrative or complete explanation for social and economic life has resulted in, on the one hand, a backlash from critics such as Eagleton, and on the other hand, a shift towards the appropriation of only certain aspects of Marxist thought by critics such as Ernesto Laclau and Chantal Mouffe, leading to the creation of the term 'post-Marxism'. These critics aim less at the revolutionary overthrow of capitalist society than at the creation of ameliorating agendas for social change in conjunction with broad but temporary political coalitions. The key aspects here are agency, wide mobilization and demonstrable material change rather than a determinate economy or violent social transformation. Post-Marxists commonly advocate radical democracy.

See also: media and cultural studies; post-structuralism; structuralism

Further reading

Geras, N. (1985) 'Post-Marxism?' *New Left Review* 163 (May–June).

PETER CHILDS

Mather, Rick

b. 1937, Oregon (USA)

Architect

Rick Mather is known as an uncompromising new modernist. He studied from 1961 to 1967 at the **Architectural Association** in London before working on **housing** schemes for Lyons Israel Ellis and the London Borough of Southwark. He set up his own practice in 1972. His best-known works are the Peter Eaton bookshop in Holland Park (1974), the rebuilding of the Architectural Association (1977–82), a computer science building at the University of East Anglia (1981–5), and the Zen Chinese restaurants in Hampstead (1985) and Mayfair (1987).

See also: modernism

PETER CHILDS

Maze Prison

The Maze is a high-security prison complex built in the early 1970s. Situated southwest of Belfast, it was constructed to house Irish terrorists, both Republican and Loyalist. From 1976, new inmates were kept in the single-storey H-blocks for which the prison has become famous. Beginning in 1978, some inmates staged both a 'blanket' and a 'dirty' protest; this led ultimately to the hunger strikes of 1981, in which Bobby Sands, newly elected as an MP in the British Parliament, starved to death. The government refused to give in to demands for the reinstatement of the special or prisoner-of-war status accorded in the early 1970s, and there followed riots, more deaths and then a breakout of thirty-eight Republican prisoners, which embarrassed the authorities. The Maze's importance to the Republican cause was highlighted when, following the killing of Protestant paramilitary leader Billy Wright by Republican inmates, Northern Ireland Secretary Mo Mowlam came to the prison to negotiate with inmates to secure their participation in the peace process.

See also: Ireland

PETER CHILDS

McCartney, Stella

b. 1971

Fashion designer

Stella McCartney is a graduate of Central St Martin's College, and is one of the latest wave of young British fashion talents. She was appointed Chloé's new head designer in April 1997, after the departure of Karl Lagerfield. The youngest child of Paul and Linda McCartney (which suggests the roots of her refusal to use fur or leather in her collections) and close friend of model Kate Moss (who, with Naomi Campbell, appeared in her graduation show), she is well connected, and had developed only three commercial collections before landing the Chloé position. To date, she has been notable for her drawing from men's tailoring and for the design of slip dresses, lingerie tops, ribbon ties, long and drawstring skirts. She has worked for Christian Lacroix, Vogue, and the designer Betty Jackson. Under her own label she supplied the London store Tokio and Bergdorf-Goodman.

PETER CHILDS

McGrath, John

b. 1935, Birkenhead

Playwright and theatre director

John McGrath is a Scot who has worked as both playwright and director in the theatre. His work generally comes from a very left-of-centre perspective, and he is known for, among other plays, *A Satire of the Four Estates* which he wrote for and directed at the 1996 Edinburgh Festival. It was based on the well-known sixteenth-century Scottish morality play *Ane Pleasant Satyre of the Thrie Estaitis* by Sir David Lindsay. This latter play, in the mode of *Everyman*, attacked corruption in the church among other targets. McGrath transposed the setting to politics, where Margaret Thatcher, John Major and Rupert Murdoch ('Lord Merde') were demonized, and the idea of Scottish nationalism was promoted.

See also: community theatre

MIKE STORRY

McQueen, Alexander

b. London

Fashion designer

Still under thirty in 1998, the Cockney upstart McQueen has often intentionally courted the limits of taste in fashion by using animal pieces, rotting fruit and images of 'raped' highland women, although at the 1998 **London Fashion Week** his collection showcased an equally arresting but far less provocative Joan of Arc figure. McQueen puts pointy shoulder pads and flared cuffs on otherwise straight suits, and uses human hair, rhinestones and snakeskin as adornments. He is currently working for the French fashion house Givenchy. In 1998, after exhibiting his Paris collection, McQueen won the prestigious contract to clothe the latest big-name British star in Hollywood, Kate Winslet, for her appearance at the Academy Awards ceremony, where awards were heaped on her film *Titanic*.

PETER CHILDS

Medak, Peter

b. 1937, Budapest (Hungary)

Film-maker

Originally an associate producer on television series in Hollywood, Peter Medak's directing career commenced with *Negatives* (1968) and gathered acclaim with his satire of English aristocratic life, *The Ruling Class* (1972). His work in the 1980s received a mixed reception; his parody of the Zorro legend, *Zorro, the Gay Blade* (1981) was overshone by the disappointing *The Men's Club* (1986), described by Variety Movie Guide as a dated and distasteful piece of work. However his treatment of real life stories in the 1990s saw a welcome return to form. *The Krays* (1990), featuring the Kemp twins from the new romantic pop group Spandau Ballet, and *Let Him Have It* (1991), about the life and execution of Derek Bentley, were both shrewd observations of postwar Britain.

GUY OSBORN
STEVE GREENFIELD

Medawar, Peter

b. 1915, Rio de Janeiro (Brazil); d. 1987

Zoologist and immunologist

The immunologist Peter Medawar shared a Nobel Prize with MacFarlane Burnet in 1960, following their study of the way in which the body develops resistance to grafted tissue after infancy. His work, for which he was knighted in 1965, has been crucial in understanding post-transplant tissue rejection. He was director of the National Institute for Medical Research from 1962 to 1975, and was appointed professor of experimental medicine at the Royal Institution two years later.

PETER CHILDS

media and cultural studies

Cultural studies emerged during the late 1950s as a new field of knowledge production in British universities, and over subsequent decades has spread internationally, notably to the USA and Australia. In its first formation, cultural studies provided a forum in which culture, society and history were given full weight in the analysis of media texts, and where the symbolic, meaningful character of social relations could be explored. Contemporary cultural studies of the media represent a greatly expanded field of various research projects and diverse theoretical discourses ranging from **Marxism** and feminism, psychoanalysis and ethnography, to **post-structuralism** and **postmodernism**. While it is true to say that the academic study of media has a long history, especially in Europe and the United States, cultural studies approaches to media have shifted attention from 'media effects' and positivistic 'mass communications' debates to critical questions about the complex mediations which negotiate the encounter between media signifying practices and audience-decoding strategies.

One of the founding texts of British cultural studies, Richard Hoggart's *The Uses of Literacy* (1957) explores the terrain of communications and media from the perspective of culture conceptualized as part of the social experience of everyday life. Hoggart criticized postwar mass culture ('Americanization') as disintegrative of traditional working-class communality and solidarity. 'We are moving towards the creation of a mass culture', Hoggart claimed, and 'the remnants of what was at least in parts an urban culture "of the people" are being destroyed'. Hoggart's critique of the 'corrupt brightness ... improper appeals and moral evasions' of mass entertainment is set against an ethnographic mapping of residual forms of industrial working-class culture and their particular institutions. In fact, Hoggart develops the contrast between the 'older' and 'newer' cultures in Leavisite aesthetic and ethical terms (see **Leavis, F.R.**). The new commercial media are castigated as 'trivial' and 'anti-life', while the values of the older culture are said to embody values of 'the personal, the concrete, the local'.

Like Hoggart's work, Raymond **Williams**'s *The Long Revolution* (1961) places communications at the centre of 'common experience', proposing that:

> Since our way of seeing is literally our way of living, the process of communication is in fact the process of community: the sharing of common meanings, and thence common activities and purposes; the offering, reception and comparison of new meanings, leading to tensions and achievements of growth and change.
>
> (Williams 1965: 55)

Williams's theory of communications takes a dialectical and constructivist approach to culture: communities and social institutions in specific historical circumstances produce culture and negotiate social meanings. Specifically, Williams locates the media and the social production of meaning at the fulcrum of historical change. On the whole, Williams tends towards a more affirmative evaluation of the new media than Hoggart, and in part sees his project as an attempt to formulate criteria for aesthetic and moral discrimination between media products, between 'bad culture' such as 'the latest Tin-Pan drool' and the 'good living culture' of jazz (a 'real musical form') and the 'wonderful game' of football.

The formation of the Centre for Contemporary Cultural Studies (CCCS) in 1963 at the University of Birmingham under the directorship of Richard Hoggart, followed by Stuart **Hall** (1969–79),

represents a watershed in the development of the field of cultural studies. During the 1970s, the CCCS faculty and graduate students pursued the collective critical study of newly translated texts of Western Marxism (the Frankfurt School, Louis Althusser and Antonio Gramsci) in an effort to develop a theory of ideology structured by class categories and cognizant of the enlarged cultural power of the media. According to Hall, the vocation of the CCCS was 'to enable people to understand what is going on, and especially to provide ways of thinking, strategies for survival, and resources for resistance'. This vocation, together with the commitment to analysis of culture 'from below', resulted in the classic CCCS youth subculture studies, notably Dick Hebdige's *Subculture: The Meaning of Style* (1979), and the signature collective text *Policing the Crisis* (1978).

Using Gramsci's theory of hegemony and Althusser's conceptualization of media as an ideological state apparatus, *Policing the Crisis* is a 'conjunctural' analysis of media signifying practices in the context of economic decline, social conflict and the general crisis of authority in post-imperial Britain. Focusing on the exhaustion of 'spontaneous consent' to state authority in the 1970s and the media's role in constructing 'mugging' as a 'moral panic', the authors theorize that this moral panic signifies the political transition to an 'exceptional' form of 'coercive' state management of class conflict. In this account, the media are seen as 'a field of ideological struggle' and 'a key terrain where "consent" is won and lost'. Because the media legitimate through their 'own constructions and inflections' the definitions and interpretations of events as seen from the 'primary' perspective of the 'ruling class alliance', they are understood as central to the maintenance of its ideological authority. In their concrete analysis of street crime news reporting and the demonizing of young black British males as muggers, the authors argue that the media relied on government, police and judiciary sources as their 'primary definers'. Youth cultures and street crime were thereby discursively contextualized as parts of a general 'law and order' problem. The media's ideological amplification of this perspective resulted in popular support for 'the measures of control and containment which this version of social reality entails', particularly the passage of the notoriously racist stop-and-search or 'suss' law. Criticism has been made that this neo-Gramscian theory of media as 'a field of ideological struggle' and contested cultural meanings is not easily squared with the univocal implications of the claim that the media operate in a role of 'structured subordination' to the primary definitions of the ruling-class alliance.

It was partly in response to this ideological dilemma that Hall produced the classic treatise 'Encoding/Decoding' (1980). For Hall, media codes were to be critically analysed in terms of encoded 'preferred readings' and contextually situated decodings or productions of meaning by media audiences. Hall proposes that three major reading strategies structure the decoding process: dominant, negotiated and oppositional readings. Hall's theoretical intervention was complemented by Dave Morley's important empirical study *The 'Nationwide' Audience: Structure and Decoding* (1980). Morley redirected the community and communications focus of the early work of Hoggart and Williams to the ethnographic study of television audiences. He explored audience sense-making processes in relation to popular current affairs programming. He aimed to produce a typology of cultural responses to a budget day episode of *Nationwide* from twenty-nine audience discussion groups, including managers, trade unionists, students and Caribbean women. Morley found that particular audiences differed in their decoding practices, and explained these differences primarily through class factors. For example, the trade union group objected to the programme's content but accepted its style, while the managerial group did the opposite. Morley also found that participants in various groups were aware of the 'preferred' meaning of *Nationwide*, but that 'awareness of the construction by no means entails the rejection of what is being constructed'. Like Hall, Morley divided the range of audience responses into categories of dominant, negotiated and oppositional readings, and strongly critiqued the unilinear determinism implicit in the assumption that media texts determine audience response.

Hall's critical semiotics of encoding and decoding and Morley's empirical study of audience decoding practices heralded an ethnographic turn in cultural studies of the media to the qualitative audience research of the 1980s. In fact, this ethnographic work also interrupted the neo-Marxist class perspective of cultural studies of the media by introducing first, feminist analytics, and second, the politics of race and ethnicity. The latter interruption is best exemplified by the work of Paul **Gilroy**, while Dorothy Hobson's 1982 study of the mainly female viewership of the British soap opera *Crossroads* bears directly on questions of media. Hobson went to women's homes to watch and discuss *Crossroads* and found that it was incorporated into the everyday lives of its audience and was a shared source of pleasure and conversation among its female fans. Far from being passive in face of serial television production, female fans bring meaning to the programme by drawing on personal and community experience. For Hobson, soap opera 'is one of the most progressive forms of television because it is a form where the audience is in control', and therefore to 'try to say what *Crossroads* means to its audience is impossible for there is no single *Crossroads*, there are as many different *Crossroads* as there are viewers'.

Similarly, Ien Ang's important study, *Watching Dallas* (1985), investigated the reception of the world's most widely viewed television programme of the 1980s, the North American serial *Dallas*. Like Hobson, Ang designed her study of Dutch fan letters to explore how the popular appeal of the television serial for female fans 'is connected with our individual life histories, with the social situation we are in, with the aesthetic and cultural preferences we have developed and so on'. Developing a theory of the 'melodramatic imagination', Ang proposed that the soap operas are made up of 'an ensemble of textual devices for engaging the viewer at the level of fantasy'. The pleasures of the text occur as subjectively experienced 'structures of feeling' and hence to enjoy *Dallas* it is necessary to have learned a repertoire of 'cultural competencies' and appropriate decoding practices: 'the tragic structure of feeling suggested by *Dallas* will only make sense', Ang argues, 'if one can project oneself into, i.e. recognize, a melodramatic imagination'.

Cultural studies was also spreading overseas to Australia, and by the mid-1980s were fast becoming institutionalized in North American universities. In the USA, with some particular exceptions such as the Marxist Literary Group's annual Institute of Culture and Society, the Marxist politics and ambitions of British cultural studies were abandoned in favour of eclecticism in approaches to both theory building and cultural politics. Feminisms and sexuality studies, race and ethnicity research, poststructuralist and post-colonial theories and a wide variety of perspectives on popular culture and media characterize the main currents of North American cultural studies. Many cultural studies of the media in the late 1980s and 1990s incorporated currents of postmodern media theory and a mode of cultural populism, exemplified by John Fiske's *Television Culture* (1987) and *Understanding Popular Culture* (1989). Fiske's model of 'active' audiences who enact resistance to hegemony through subversive or oppositional readings and pleasurable appropriations of media texts stimulated a wave of 'new revisionist' studies concerned with the pleasures of popular culture and the resistant-decoding practices of postmodern media audiences. The overemphasis on audience agency and the neglect of the efficacy of social structure and power in this view has been extensively critiqued by cultural studies and media theorists. For example, Morley argues in *Television: Audience and Cultural Studies* (1992) that the challenge facing future cultural studies of television media will be the 'attempt to construct a model of television consumption that is sensitive to both the "vertical" dimensions of power and ideology and the "horizontal" dimension of television's insertion in, and articulation with, the context and practices of everyday life'. This call for the reinvigoration of a critical dimension in cultural studies of the media has been a shaping context for the work of Hall and others, including Paul Smith, in the 1990s.

Further reading

Ang, I. (1985) *Watching Dallas*, London: Routledge.

Brantlinger, P. (1990) *Crusoe's Footprints: Cultural Studies in Britain and America*, London: Routledge (a useful genealogy of cultural studies).

Fiske, J. (1987) *Television Culture*: London, Methuen.

—— (1989) *Understanding Popular Culture*, London: Unwin Hyman.

Hall, S. *et al.* (1978) *Policing the Crisis: Mugging, the State and Law and Order*, London: Macmillan.

—— (eds) (1980) *Culture, Media and Language*, London: Hutchinson (a good synoptic anthology of 1970s CCCS cultural studies and media theory).

Hoggart, R. (1957) *The Uses of Literacy*, Harmondsworth: Penguin.

Morley, D. (1980) *The 'Nationwide' Audience: Structure and Decoding*, London: BFI.

—— (1992) *Television: Audience and Cultural Studies*, London: Routledge.

Morley, D. and Chen, K.S. (eds) (1996) *Stuart Hall: Critical Dialogues in Cultural Studies*, London: Routledge (an important collection, including essays and interviews with Hall, discussing his intellectual project and its key place in development of cultural studies).

Williams, R. (1965) *The Long Revolution*, Harmondsworth, Pelican.

MARK DOUGLAS

media education

The first university courses in film studies, supported by critical debates in *Screen* and its offshoot *Screen Education*, were established in the 1970s. By the mid-1990s, some 30,000 young people annually opted for courses leading to public examinations in media studies at age sixteen or eighteen, and many thousands were applying each year for limited, but growing, numbers of university media courses.

The notion of media education as a general entitlement for all eight million UK schoolchildren began to emerge in the 1980s. By 1990, schools in all regions of the UK had some kind of curricular requirement (optional in Scotland, compulsory in the **National Curriculum** for England and Wales) to teach about the media. However, without concomitant resources and teacher training, fulfilment of these requirements is patchy and variable in quality.

Media education at any level typically involves critical study of a range of media, such as television, film, radio, the press, magazines and popular music. Media forms such as news, advertising and soap opera, which feature in more than one medium, are popular topics of study. Three different but overlapping approaches are commonly used to study media 'texts' (such as advertisements or films). Students look at how meanings are produced through close analysis of visual composition, soundtracks and so on; they find out about the institutional and financial background (for example, who produced it and why); and they consider who the audience is and what its responses and interpretations are likely to be. Some kind of practical production work usually forms part of the course.

Many older media students want to work in the media, but others regard their study simply as a useful preparation for the modern world. As digital technologies develop, media education is likely to change, becoming more practical and more commonly accepted as part of everyone's lifelong learning.

See also: MOMI; *Screen* and screen theory

Further reading

Buckingham, D. and Sefton-Green, J. (1996) *Cultural Studies Goes to School*, London: Taylor & Francis (detailed and usefully critical accounts of media education in practice).

CARY BAZALGETTE

medical drama

Medical drama is one of the most consistently popular and enduring forms of drama on British television. Conventionally set in hospitals (usually National Health Service ones), they concern the problems of both the patients who come to be treated and the medical staff who treat them. It is common for the staff to be the main characters, with patients appearing for single or multiple episodes. Dramatic tension arises out of life-and-death conflicts, and often concerns a variety of ethical and moral issues, exploring the effects of medical decisions on patients and the public. Because of this, medical drama is often criticized as a melodramatic form, concerned only with individualized, personal issues, and its similarities to **soap operas** are apparent.

Significant early British examples include *Emergency Ward 10* and *General Hospital*, in which the

standard genre conventions were already evident. *Dr Finlay's Casebook* was one of the first examples to be primarily situated outside of the hospital, and was instead concerned with a rural medical practice. The **BBC**'s most significant contributions are *Angels*, about a group of female trainee nurses, and *Casualty.* The latter has consistently been the BBC's most popular drama for many years, employing a variety of big name stars in cameo roles, launching the careers of a large number of actors and, in 1998, spawning a top 10 single.

The development of medical drama has seen a slow but definite movement away from the godlike, omniscient doctors of the 1950s towards an acceptance of the complexities of modern medicine. Issues such as **euthanasia** and **AIDS** have become commonplace dramatic fare, and characters are conventionally portrayed as multidimensional, flawed individuals, working within tight budget constraints and dealing with complex moral issues.

Medical drama has often been criticized by governments for its portrayal of the medical profession, particularly those dramas set within the National Health Service. This was especially true in the 1980s, when the Conservative government repeatedly lambasted *Casualty*'s portrayal of overworked staff and underfunded hospitals. The most extreme case of this resulted from the BBC's *Cardiac Arrest* in the mid-1990s, whose portrayal of a health service industry and staff in near-apocalyptic crisis shocked both the viewing public and professionals alike. The fact that the series was written by a practising NHS doctor (under an alias, for fear of reprisals) only strengthened the criticisms made by the programme.

See also: crime drama; documentary; drama on television; NHS

BRETT MILLS

Merchant-Ivory Productions

Merchant-Ivory is a film-making team comprising Ismail Merchant (producer), James Ivory (director) and Ruth Prawer Jhabvala (screenwriter), known particularly for historical dramas. Having first emerged in India, the partnership gained wider audiences with the British film *The Europeans* (1979), which set the tone for future projects. Further adaptations followed, particularly of works by E.M. Forster: *Maurice* (1987), *A Room With a View* (1985) and *Howard's End* (1992). This last, with its attention to detail, visual beauty, strong performances and tempered themes of class conflict and sexual identity, exemplifies the Merchant-Ivory style. While commercial and artistic success was sustained with *The Remains of the Day* (1993), the team has been criticized for lack of experimentation and for offering unchallenging interpretations of respected texts.

See also: heritage

ALICE E. SANGER

Mersey Poets

Also known as the Liverpool Poets, the Mersey Poets were Adrian Henri (1932–), Roger McGough (1937–) and Brian Patten (1946–). Writing during the 1960s, they published three collections as a group: *The Mersey Sound* (1967), *The Liverpool Scene* (1967) and *New Volume* (1983). Taking their style from both the American 'beat poets', and from the explosion of musical talent in Liverpool during the 1960s, they pioneered **performance poetry** in Britain. Their style was humorous and fitted in well with the tenets of pop art. All three have published poetry separately, and two have found careers within other media, Henri as an artist and art critic, McGough as a member of the satirical pop group *Scaffold*.

See also: poetry

SAM JOHNSTONE

Mersey Television

Mersey Television is the company set up and owned by Phil Redmond. Its output includes the realist soap opera *Brookside*, which since 1982 has provided **Channel 4** with its most highly-rated programme. In keeping with the channel's commitment to 'difference', *Brookside* has frequently presented an alternative image of family life, and storylines have been developed that engage serious social issues such as unemployment, heroin addiction and lesbianism. Mersey Television is Britain's largest **independent production** company, and its setting up in Liverpool not only provides much-needed jobs for the local work force but also challenges the metropolitan orientation of the television industry and extends the opportunities for television production and training in the regions.

See also: Granada; soap operas; Thames TV

BOB MILLINGTON

Methodists

'Methodist' was originally a term of abuse coined by Oxford undergraduates making fun of their fellow students who gathered around John Wesley and his younger brother Charles and attempted to follow their rule (or 'method') to deepen their religious life. John Wesley (1703–91) was the son of an Anglican clergyman. He himself took holy orders and never wished to break away from the Church of England, but he reacted against what he sensed as its spiritual aridity, and strove for evangelical revival. Returning from a missionary journey to the United States under the auspices of the Society for the Propagation of the Gospel, he found that his opinions were not welcomed by the Anglican church. He then took to preaching in the open air, soon attracting huge crowds who welcomed his Bible-based sermons with their stress on salvation for all through grace (Arminianism), personal commitment, and practical good works to alleviate suffering. His brother Charles added an invaluable dimension to the revivalist fervour with his hymns; these expounded simple doctrine in clear, vigorous language and were sung to catchy modern tunes. John Wesley was a tireless traveller, and his doctrines soon spread throughout Britain and North America, making a special appeal to the lowlier classes in society that Anglicanism tended to neglect. Disputes over the ordination of priests inevitably led to a breach with the Church of England, and squabbles about church organization and liturgy resulted in the division of Methodism into a number of more or less independent subgroups, each claiming it alone represented the genuine tradition. Reunion was achieved by the formation of the Methodist Church of Great Britain in 1932.

As currently constituted, the Methodist Church is characterized by a high degree of involvement of the laity in its work and organization, but the administration of communion is normally reserved to ministers. Though numbers are not buoyant, Methodism in Britain has some 400,000 full members, and more than a million people are more loosely connected; membership worldwide is around 26,000,000. Methodism has always had a strong social conscience, and in Wales in particular it has been a focus for political activism, especially trade unionism. There is truth in the saying that 'the Labour movement owes more to Methodism than to Marxism'. Methodism has also traditionally emphasized missionary work and children's education.

See also: Anglican Church; Elim

Further reading

The Methodist Church: Minutes of Conference and Directory, London: Methodist Church Conference Office, published annually.

CHRISTOPHER SMITH

MI5 and MI6

The names MI5 and MI6 are short forms of Military Intelligence, Section 5 and Section 6. The overall head of intelligence is the Chair of the Joint Intelligence Committee, to which post Pauline Neville-Jones was appointed in 1994. Section 5 is the counter-intelligence agency, until recently under the director-generalship of Stella Rimmington, appointed in 1992. Section 6 is the secret intelligence agency, which works primarily under Foreign Office control. It has operated under the direction of David Spedding since 1994. The peacetime existence of MI6 had previously been denied altogether. Though the base at GCHQ in Cheltenham had long been known, since 1991 greater information concerning the intelligence services has been released into the public domain

(it is now known, for example, that MI6 now occupies London's Vauxhall Cross (built 1989–92)). Most controversially, in the 1990s MI5 was deemed in breach of the European Convention on Human Rights because it carried out clandestine surveillance of campaigners for civil liberties.

See also: secret services

PETER CHILDS

middle-distance runners

The early 1980s saw a massive increase in interest in running in the UK, with large national events such as the Sunday Times National Fun Run and the London Marathon attracting tens of thousands of applicants. But away from the limelight, the growth of local competition on the roads and over countryside courses was equally spectacular. Inspired by British Olympic successes at the Moscow and Los Angeles Games (1980 and 1984) and celluloid celebrations of the 1924 Paris Olympiad (in David **Puttnam**'s Chariots of Fire), keen amateur club and independent runners competed en masse for often no more than a cheap commemorative medallion and the singular pleasure of finishing a race.

Despite a challenge from the sprints, perhaps the most commonly arranged and enthusiastically watched **athletics** events in Britain remain the middle-distance events. Ranging from 800 metres to 10,000 metres in length (but most commonly the classic 'shorter' distances of 1,500 metres and the mile), the middle-distance events formed the backbone of modern British track and field success. The tradition began with Roger Bannister's celebrated first sub-four-minute mile (3:59.4) on 6 May 1954, but reached a peak between 1979 and the mid-1980s when British athletes dominated the 800 metre, 1,000 metre, 1,500 metre and mile events.

Sebastian Coe and Steve Ovett, although rarely paired in competition outside of Olympic finals, cultivated a keen, albeit media-fuelled, rivalry which helped to make them both sporting celebrities and names to be feared in the athletics arena. Coe (now a Conservative MP) enjoyed a marvellous summer of running in 1979. In the space of just forty-one days, he broke three world records at 800 metres, 1,500 metres and the mile; the 800 metre record of 1 minute 39 seconds has now stood for over fifteen years. At the 1980 Olympics, Coe and Ovett stole the show in their battle for the major honours over the classic middle distances; in which Coe won gold at 1,500 metres and silver at 800, while Ovett took gold in the 800 and bronze in the 1,500.

In 1984 in Los Angeles, Coe retained his 1,500 metres Olympic title. But, despite the emergence of a third world-class British middle-distance runner, Steve Cram (who took silver behind Coe), the 'golden era' was waning. Ovett had a poor Olympics, troubled by illness and the heat, and never retained the form which once saw him unbeaten in forty-five successive races between 1977 and 1980. Coe too had peaked, but the special magic which these two athletes had brought to middle-distance running (Ovett once described their contests as akin to the Ali versus Frazier heavyweight boxing title fights), helped inspire confidence, interest and, most importantly, participation in British athletics at all levels.

See also: long-distance runners; marathons; sprinters

STEPHEN C. KENNY

Militant

The Militant tendency was a Trotskyist group within the British **Labour Party**. Though formally part of the party, the group had a distinct agenda and sought to use the more widespread support for the Labour Party to further its own ends. Militant succeeded in gaining control of several local Labour authorities, most infamously Merseyside. It did not, however, achieve widespread support, numbering around 5,000 members at its peak in the mid-1980s. Its political range was as limited as its support, focusing upon a few economic and class issues. Initially the Labour party spurned action against Militant members, but the style and tactics of the latter left them increasingly isolated and by 1985 Neil Kinnock attacked Militant openly. The movement was expunged from the party by 1992.

See also: Communist Party; fringe groups; Labour Party; lobby groups

ALASTAIR LINDSLEY

military clothing

The wearing of military clothing has been a fashion fad for both sexes since the early 1980s. Interest in grunge, nostalgia and recycling of fashions from the past have contributed to it. The male trend originated with **skinheads**, and was catered for by army surplus shops like Soldier of Fortune, which were trendier than the Army and Navy stores. The fashion may have originated for women when they adopted fishermen's hampers as a fashion accessory. Camouflaged military wear is often indistinguishable from fishing apparel. It is also a product of the search for cheap serviceable unisex clothing in the recessions of the 1980s and 1990s, which also spawned Doc Martens shoes and the 'uniform' wearing of jeans.

See also: Dr Martens

MIKE STORRY

military conflict

As Britain made the transition from a global to a regional power, the North Atlantic Treaty Organization (NATO) became the central focus of British security policy. The withdrawal from east of Suez in 1967 was the beginning of a major restructuring of the armed forces, which continued in the 1990s under the programme 'Options for Change'. This should be seen in the context of a rapidly changing technological environment, which has led to an increasing reliance on nuclear deterrence (for example, Polaris and Trident). However, British garrisons are still maintained in Gibraltar, Belize and the Falkland Islands (and in Hong Kong up to 1997). There is still a British UN presence in Cyprus, and troops have been active in Northern Ireland following the 1969 decision to send Army units to ensure the security of the province. The IRA's bombing campaign caused many casualties throughout the 1970s and 1980s.

The Falklands War in 1982 was an important event in the collective British psyche. Parliamentary criticism of government mishandling of the early stages of the Argentine invasion of the islands led to the resignation of the Foreign Secretary, Lord Carrington. But with her political survival at stake, Margaret Thatcher ordered a campaign to retake the islands, which received wide public support (although there was controversy over the sinking of the Argentine cruiser *General Belgrano*). The British task force succeeded, at a cost of 225 men killed and 777 wounded.

The involvement of considerable numbers of British troops in a conflict did not occur again until 1990, when 45,000 personnel took part in Operation Desert Storm against Iraq following the latter's invasion of Kuwait. British troops intervened as part of a UN-sponsored coalition of national forces.

From the late 1980s, Britain became more involved in UN peacekeeping operations. With the disintegration of the Cold War balance of power, there has been a proliferation of complex civil emergencies and a corresponding growth in UN solutions, often 'second generation' peacekeeping missions outside traditional parameters. For example, Britain has sent troops to Namibia (1989) and Cambodia (1992–3) to monitor and create elections, on observer missions in Iraq/Kuwait (1991–4), and humanitarian assistance and general peacekeeping duties in Rwanda (1994) and the former Yugoslavia (UNPROFOR 1992–5). The latter conflict, with its ethnic cleansing and attendant atrocities, has proved a gruelling challenge for British troops.

See also: Ireland

Further reading

Ovendale, R. (1994) *British Defence Policy since 1945*, Manchester: Manchester University Press.

RACHAEL BRADLEY

Millet, Kate

b. 1934, St Paul, Minnesota (USA)

Writer

An American feminist, Kate Millett became well known in the UK with the publication of her first book, *Sexual Politics* (1970) (her doctoral dissertation at Columbia). She argued that nearly all relations between men and women are determined by the male establishment's need to preserve its power over women. She claimed that assigning women to their traditional role of social work was akin to asking them to clean the Augean stable. They were thereby disabled from discovering and eliminating the structural inequities which guaranteed the inferior position of women in a patriarchal society. She is seen nowadays as not having taken a strong enough feminist line in her writing, and of not countenancing other forms of sexuality than the heterosexual.

See also: feminist theory

MIKE STORRY

mime

Since the 1970s, the term 'mime' has been applied to an increasingly varied field of theatrical activity, broadly characterized by a primary focus on physical expression. This activity draws together a number of historical strands, including the influence of several French mime teachers. British drama schools have tended to offer little training in mime, and have focused instead on acting that is voice/text based. The development of contemporary British mime reflects this marginalization, taking strength and identity from it.

Mime has typically seen itself in broad opposition to the text-based literary theatre of the **West End** and regional theatres (see **theatre, regional**). The 1970s and 1980s witnessed a growth in alternative theatre companies. These companies were often formed by young artists rejecting traditional ways of making theatre to devise and improvise work of their own. A contemporaneous revival of interest in street performance (for example, Covent Garden Piazza, Robotics and body popping) helped to provide a rich environment for a rapid development of mime and related activity. Initially in the 1970s, mime theatre relied on silent illusions and sketches. Critics accused this mime of being too formal, too technical and lacking in content. Later companies/artists sought to break down the formal restrictions of this earlier style, and performers such as Steven Berkoff, Moving Picture Mime Show and Théâtre de Complicité have since pointed the way for new physical-based theatre with a more popular voice and an increasingly strong sense of content.

Mime's accessibility, distinctiveness and physicality have made it attractive to a number of minority subcultures. In the 1990s, Black Mime Theatre developed a body of work distinctive in its focus on black issues and its exploration of a movement/mime 'voice' for black performers. Towards the end of the 1990s mime has reintegrated with dance, circus skills and acrobatics and provided a core of skills now being explored through new forms (such as Club performance, New Circus, **alternative comedy** and **physical theatre**), directly related to youth culture and subculture. Mime's growth, and its subsequent transformation into physical theatre, has coincided with an increasing willingness to accept the moving body as 'text'. The literal use of gesture as sign has developed into a more complex understanding of movement as a richly diverse and socially resonant vehicle for the making of meaning.

See also: improvisation; modern dance; theatre

Further reading

Leabhart, T. (1989) *Modern and Postmodern Mime*, Basingstoke: Macmillan Education Ltd (gives broad historical context).

MARK EVANS

Mirror Group

The Mirror Group – inevitably associated in the minds of many with the name of Robert Maxwell, who, in pursuit of his ambitious plans for a media empire, bought the *Daily Mirror* from Reed in 1984 and died in 1991 – is a major force in the British news media. Founded in 1903 with the specific intention of appealing to a female readership, the *Daily Mirror* has long been an important popular national tabloid newspaper. In 1997 The *Mirror*, as it had become, was Britain's second best-selling daily paper. With circulation figures of around 2.3 million, it claimed a share of nearly 17 percent in a total market of about 13.2 million copies (or 21 percent of the popular market). It was, however, outsold by the *Sun*, which sold 3.7 million copies (28 percent of the total, or 35 percent of the popular market) and appeared to be pulling even further ahead, stretching the lead by over half a million in five years.

Mirror Group is also strong in the popular Sunday paper market, with two papers that together are nearly as popular as the *News of the World*. The *Sunday Mirror* (the *Sunday Pictorial* until 1963) had a circulation in 1997 of a little more than two million copies (18 percent of the popular market), and the *Sunday People* sold about 1.8 million copies (another 15 percent).

See also: Express Group; Guardian Group; News International; Telegraph plc

CHRISTOPHER SMITH

Mitchell, Juliet

b. 1940

Psychoanalyst

Juliet Mitchell is a British psychoanalyst, who began publishing essays in the mid-1960s which fruitfully combined socialism and feminism. Her essay 'The Longest Revolution', published in *New Left Review* when she was only 26, used Marxist theory to explicate patriarchy and, together with her later 'Women's Liberation and the New Politics', helped to shape later feminist analyses. Her seminal *Psychoanalysis and Feminism* (1974) turned away from Reich and Laing to Freudian approaches in order to reveal deep-seated and ideological assumptions that underpinned women's oppression. Her work has been singularly important in discussions of the construction of femininity and in forging methodologies through which to subvert patriarchy. Her other books include

Women's Estate, Women: the Longest Revolution and, with Jacqueline Rose, *Feminine Sexuality.*

See also: feminist theory; Marxism

PETER CHILDS

models, 1960s

During the 1960s there emerged a new style of female model and fashion image: the model as pop cultural icon, star personality and sexualized 'child-woman' fetish object. The new models, particularly Jean Shrimpton and Twiggy (Lesley Hornby), refused the elegant and distanced anonymity of earlier couture models, even as they appropriated the youthful glamour of pop stars. The expanding British fashion, pop and advertising industries promoted the provocative, non-conventional and eroticized 'Youthquake' images constructed by the models and photographers. For example, the trend-setting television presenter Cathy McGowan modelled the innovative fashions of young British designers, including Tuffin and Foale and Barbara Hulanicki of Biba, each Friday night on the ground-breaking pop show *Ready, Steady, Go*. Pop singers Cilla Black and Sandie Shaw did likewise.

Jean Shrimpton personified the transition from the expense, sophistication and elegance of 1950s couture to the inexpensive and youthful pop fashion of the 1960s. She pioneered what Mary Quant called the 'Method School of Modelling'. Initially photographed by David Bailey in 1960 for **Vogue**, the published 'pin-ups' made Shrimpton an international sexual icon and fashion celebrity. Significantly, Shrimpton's classic English beauty type and her lithe figure contrasted sharply with that voluptuous mode of 1950s cinematic sexuality exemplified by Hollywood stars Marilyn Monroe or Jayne Mansfield. Central to the delineation of the fashionable child-woman 'look' were Shrimpton's shoulder length curtain of hair, her dramatic use of make-up and false eyelashes, and ever-shortening skirts. Furthermore, her non-traditional 'kinky' style and anti-establishment 'dolly' attitude was expressive of the cultural ideology of the **mods**.

Twiggy and her teenage manager-boyfriend Justin de Villeneuve (Nigel Davis) emerged in a blitz of media coverage in 1967. Twiggy's trademark prepubescent physique and androgynous boyish look (see **androgynous/unisex look**), combined with her London working-class accent, produced a fashion and media sensation on both sides of the Atlantic. Her career as fashion model and media celebrity translated into offers of film work and she starred in Ken **Russell**'s pastiche of the classic Hollywood musical, *The Boyfriend* (1971). However, controversy continues regarding the ways in which Twiggy's mode of ultra-thinness is associated with the social prevalence of image-related illnesses like anorexia, bulimia (see **eating disorders**) and other image-distortion syndromes in contemporary western girls and women.

See also: supermodels

Further reading

Quick, H. (1997) *Catwalking: A History of the Fashion Model*, London: Hamlyn (a popular, illustrated introduction).

MARK DOUGLAS

modern dance

The wide spectrum of modern and postmodern dance on offer in the UK at the end of the twentieth century had its genesis in the 1960s, when small groups of people dissatisfied with ballet began to look for a new way of moving, a new aesthetic, and new **choreography** more in tune with the contemporary climate. In 1963, the English philanthropist Robin Howard paid for a few British dancers to study at Martha Graham's school in New York. Howard had been captivated by Graham's modern dance company during its UK performances that year, and in 1954. He subsequently set up the Contemporary Dance Trust, which established the London School of Contemporary Dance (LSCD), founded London Contemporary Dance Theatre (LCDT), and opened The Place Theatre as a base for both. Led by Robert Cohan, a dancer from Graham's company, LCDT initially performed her work as well as Cohan's.

Concurrently, in 1966 the Ballet Rambert took the bold move of dropping its ballet repertory and embracing a new dance genre. Assistant director Norman Morrice, whose idea this was, modelled the scaled-down company on Nederlands Dans Theater's melding of balletic and modern techniques and invited Glen Tetley, an American choreographer working in this vein, to stage several pieces. Dancers were encouraged to choreograph, and the new repertory included work by Morrice, Christopher Bruce and John Chesworth, among others.

The 1970s saw the increasing acceptance and popularity of 'contemporary dance' among audiences, as well as reactions to it from dancers and choreographers who rejected the Graham technique and the move to the mainstream. In 1972, Richard Alston, a former LSCD student and occasional LCDT choreographer, formed his own company, Strider, which embraced different American techniques (Cunningham and release) and a low-key, formalist aesthetic. More radical departures were taken by the X6 Collective (for example, Jacky Lansley, Fergus Early and Emilyn Claid), who presented political works, and Rosemary Butcher, whose non-technical, non-theatrical movement reflected her studies with New York's Judson Church choreographers. Many of her dancers (such as Gaby Agis, Maedée Duprès, Sue MacLennan and Miranda Tufnell) later choreographed. Most of these alternative practitioners – who were grouped under the label 'new dance' – had contact with Mary Fulkerson, the American invited to head the Dartington College of Arts dance programme in 1973 and who introduced release technique and contact improvisation to Britain. In the mid-1970s, Chesworth took over Rambert's directorship, with Bruce as associate director and primary choreographer. At LCDT, while Cohan's work sustained the repertory, several dancers emerged as choreographers; two of these, Siobhan Davies and Robert North, were appointed associate choreographers in 1974.

In the late 1970s, festivals sprang up to showcase the range of dance, particularly 'new dance', being practised in the UK. The Dartington and ADMA festivals provided workshops as well as performances. Dance Umbrella, established by the Arts Council in 1978 (and still running), presented professional companies from the UK and abroad. By 1980, Cohan began talking of easing out of LCDT, resulting in a triumvirate directorship of himself, the company administrator, and first North and then Davies as the resident choreographer. North's tenure was short, as he was appointed director of Ballet Rambert in 1981; here his work joined that of Bruce and Alston as mainstays of the repertory.

Alston, meanwhile, was also making dances for Second Stride, formed in 1982 by Davies and Ian Spink (who eventually became the sole director). Spink's increasingly theatre-based, collaborative pieces were partially influenced by the German dance theatre of Pina Bausch, indicative of the European influences that began to be felt in British dance in the 1980s. Other new voices emerged in this decade. Michael Clark, dubbed the 'bad boy' of British dance, went for shock value, employing cross-dressing, outrageous costumes, fascist imagery and a live punk band. Janet Smith, with her witty, fluid pieces, chose accessibility. As director of Extemporary Dance Theatre, Emilyn Claid brought 'new dance' practices to mainstream audiences. Laurie Booth combined improvisation, release and contact work. Lloyd Newson's DV8 Physical Theatre explored relationships and sexuality in powerful pieces that drew on the performers' experiences. Yolande Snaith examined women's issues in increasingly surreal narratives. Postmodernist strategies were prevalent in the work of Lea Anderson, who formed the all-women group the Cholmondeleys in 1984 and later the all-male troupe the Featherstonehaughs.

The breadth and variety of dance in the 1990s defies generalization. Old labels no longer seem exact; new labels have not come to prominence (and debates rage over the term 'postmodern'). Named movement techniques have evolved, moulded to individuals' needs; new, unnamed ways of moving have emerged. Dance's boundaries with theatre and 'performance' have blurred. Because of the nature of public funding, few companies operate full-time and most choreographers work on a project basis, pulling together the money and the dancers to make a piece and tour it for a few months.

Several choreographers from the 1970s are still thriving. In 1986, Alston took over at Rambert, changing its name to Rambert Dance Company and bringing in a marked Cunningham flavour. But by the early 1990s, the board, questioning the audience appeal of his formalist work, replaced him with Bruce, who reintroduced accessible choreography. Alston was then invited to establish a new resident company at The Place, in the wake of LCDT's demise (in 1994). Davies, meanwhile, was associate choreographer of Alston's Rambert while leading her own company, through which she has explored the expressiveness of release technique. Their contemporary, Rosemary Butcher, has continued her minimalist work independently, holding a retrospective of twenty years' output in 1996.

Most choreographers from the 1980s are still going strong, joined by newcomers too numerous to mention. Shobana Jeyasingh fuses a classical Indian dance technique and modern British choreographic principles. Matthew Bourne's Adventures in Motion Pictures has made a speciality of reworking of the ballet classics in modern dance. Jonathan Burrows, Matthew Hawkins and Russell Maliphant have left behind their ballet training to explore new movement vocabularies. CandoCo explores the choreographic possibilities of using both dancers in wheelchairs and more traditional dancing bodies. Nigel Charnock and Javier de Frutos are interested in gay themes and icons. Fergus Early's Green Candle Dance Company is representative of the community and educational dance arena. The list of small-scale companies and independent choreographers is extensive, and growing.

See also: ballet; RADA

Further reading

Clarke, M. and Crisp, C. (1989) *London Contemporary Dance Theatre: The First 21 Years*, London: Dance Books.

Jordan, S. (1992) *Striding Out: Aspects of Contemporary and New Dance in Britain*, London: Dance Books.

Mackrell, J. (1992) *Out of Line: The Story of British New Dance*, London: Dance Books.

CHRIS JONES

modernism

Modernism, or the modern movement, in architecture is usually defined as a mode deriving from the work of the early Le Corbusier and of Walter Gropius and his colleagues at the Bauhaus in 1930s Germany, culminating in the work of Mies Van der Rohe in the 1950s and 1960s. Its formal characteristics could be described as the absence of decoration, the absence of façade, asymmetrical composition and the use of severe geometrical forms, often repeated over a large area. Entrances and exits tended to be left unemphasized, in favour of the sense that the building could be penetrated in multiple ways. Modernist construction favoured the concrete or steel frame over load-bearing masonry, and through the use of curtain-walling glass tended to become a structural element in its own right. The early conception of modernism was associated with certain utopian values, specifically that the provision of a planned architectural environment would lead to a better society.

Neither Le Corbusier, the Bauhaus architects, nor Mies ever built in Britain. Few examples of modern movement buildings exist in the country, and the majority date from the 1930s. The best-known are perhaps Berthold Lubetkin's Highpoint 1 apartments at Highgate, London, and Owen Williams's buildings for the *Daily Express* at London, Glasgow and Manchester. At the time, the modern movement was vigorously promoted by the *Architectural Review*, its photography of Williams's *Daily Express* building in Fleet Street being a fine example of its proselytizing tone. But the impact of the modern movement is arguably much stronger in terms of the indigenous responses to it, whether outright rejection or forms of adjustment.

The first widespread application of modern architecture in Britain came with the establishment of the **welfare state** in the period immediately after the Second World War. A style based on contemporary Swedish public architecture was adopted by London County Council architects, and spread to become the dominant mode for educational buildings until the late 1970s. Known as the 'contemporary style', or sometimes 'people's detailing', it employed a vernacular of gently pitched roofs, brick walls, exposed wood and picture windows. It was in other words a much softened version of the modern movement. For architects such as James **Stirling**, who admired Le Corbusier, the adoption of the Swedish model seemed to indicate a failure of nerve, as in its human scale and use of natural materials it seemed to evoke a pre-industrial time: Stirling once remarked, famously: 'Let's face it, William Morris was a Swede.'

If the architecture of the British welfare state adjusted modernism, British commercial architecture was also less modern than elsewhere; Mies Van der Rohe, prolific in the United States, was conspicuously absent in Britain. There was little commercial building until the late 1950s, when a vogue for high-rise office towers (along with other elements of urban design imported from the United States) became visible. If some of these, such as the Vickers Tower on the Embankment in London (1962) or the CIS Building at Manchester (1959), derived explicitly from the modern movement, many subjected the modern to considerable variation. Richard Siefert, for some time the most successful British commercial architect, designed Centre Point (1967), a thirty-five-storey tower at the junction of Charing Cross Road and Oxford Street, London; the arbitrary and decorative form of the windows alone identifies this structure as a far more frivolous piece of building than anything erected by Mies. Similarly, the vast Piccadilly Plaza (1965) complex in Manchester, comprising office towers, a hotel and a shopping centre, is an extraordinarily decorative structure incorporating stained glass, decorative tiling and coloured glass. In this aspect, and in the picturesque displacement of the various components of the structure, the complex in same ways better resembles the Victorian Gothic structures nearby than orthodox modern movement architecture.

In British public architecture, the dominant mode throughout the 1960s and 1970s was the so-called 'new brutalism', conceived of in opposition to all forms of the modern movement. Many of the major structures of this period, such as the Hayward Gallery (1968), the National Theatre (1972) and the Barbican Centre (1980), with their picturesque, informal composition, are best described in terms of **new brutalism**, not modernism. The modern movement was all but abandoned during this time. Richard **Rogers**

and Norman Foster (see **Foster Associates**), two architects who had in many respects kept the faith, built most of their early work abroad.

However, towards the end of the 1980s a reassessment of the modern began to emerge, and by the mid-1990s it was possible, for example, to describe a modernist group of architects working in the north of England. One indicator of this was the increasing visibility of the work of late modern architecture in Britain, a process perhaps begun with the completion of Rogers's Lloyds Building in the City of London in 1984, and continued with such structures as Foster's Stansted Airport (1992). These buildings, though far less restrained than early modernist works, nevertheless embodied modernist structural principles. At the same time, modernist details such as glass bricks and sunscreens began to reappear in commercial architecture.

However, it was not until the early 1990s that a revival of interest in modernism resulted in some new buildings, and this tendency has been particularly evident outside London. The work of the Manchester-based architects Stephen Hodder, Mills Beaumont Leavey Channon, Roger Stephenson and Ian Simpson is, in terms of composition, materials, placement and stylistic restraint, probably closer to the original principles of modernism than anything built in Britain since the 1930s. Hodder's uncompromising Centenary Building for Salford University (1996) received national recognition by winning the first James Stirling Prize for an educational building. The fact that it won suggests that modernism was finally acceptable as an architectural style; at the same time, the fact that such buildings look fresh is an indicator of the long isolation of British architecture from its European counterparts.

Further reading

Frampton, K. (1992) *Modern Architecture: A Critical History*, London: Thames & Hudson.

Lyall, S. (1980) *The State of British Architecture*, London: Architectural Press.

RICHARD J. WILLIAMS

mods

The term 'mods' refers to 'modernists', a bebop phrase that was used to describe a particular youth subculture of the early 1960s. Mods wore distinctive smart suits, listened to **ska** and other Caribbean music, and followed British bands such as The Who and The Small Faces. Many mods rode Italian scooters, and these mods attracted media attention when they fought with **rockers** at British seaside resorts. Many working-class mods became **skinheads**. There have been several revivals of the mod style, first in the late 1970s by fans of groups such as The Jam, and second in the mid-1990s by groups such as Blur.

See also: Britpop; pop and rock

STUART BORTHWICK

MOMI

The Museum of the Moving Image (MOMI) is situated within the **BFI**'s South Bank complex, promoting British film and television culture. Established in 1988, MOMI charts the development of moving images from pre-cinema experiments in photographic projection and optical illusion to today's industrialized and commercialized film and television production and exhibition systems. The chronological journey through history is supported with an impressive collection of memorabilia, artefacts, videotape clips and interactive working models. The museum also operates as a national centre for **media education**, with support and marketing services structured around the requirements of national curricula. It is also the location of special exhibitions and screenings in tandem with the neighbouring **NFT**, and includes a workshop dedicated to the development of animation.

See also: National Museum of Photography, Film and Television

MATTHEW GRICE

monarchy

In recent years, the monarchy has all but fallen into disrepute in Britain. It was the butt of sophisticated humour on television programmes such as *Spitting Image*, was lampooned in Sue Townsend's novel *The Queen and I* (1994) and became the subject of much tabloid treatment which ridiculed the affairs of Prince Charles, Prince Andrew and their wives. To compound such adverse publicity, Buckingham Palace has proved inept at handling the British media. Opponents of the Palace used the newspapers against them, publishing for example Prince Charles's conversations with his long-term lover Mrs Camilla Parker-Bowles. Broadcasts of this and other gaffes turned the royals into a beleaguered, if not endangered, institution.

Already, for many years the country had regarded those other than the immediate Royal Family as 'hangers-on' and questioned why they should pay for their support. But in the 1980s the Royal Family was hit by an avalanche of negative responses to rumours of the extra-marital affairs of the younger royals, none of whom had succeeded in contracting a marriage which endured. Princess Anne divorced Captain Mark Philips, Prince Andrew divorced Sarah Ferguson (Fergie) and Charles divorced Diana Spencer. Some people suggested that the royals should only contract arranged marriages with other royals. Conversely, supporters said they were only mirroring society at large.

In addition to problems with public relations and handling of the media, the monarchy made a number of other significant miscalculations of what the public would (under)stand. People might have tolerated the younger royals' peccadilloes if complaints had not been treated with lofty disdain, and if the monarchy had not chosen to ignore many crucial twentieth-century changes in society's outlook. For example, adherents of Margaret Thatcher's 1980s 'me' generation were unlikely to be as ready to continue to fund lifestyles which they themselves were never likely to emulate. A result of these miscalculations was that royalty lost more than it otherwise might have. For instance, conveniences like the Royal Train and the Royal Yacht *Britannia*, and more importantly the Queen's tax-free status, have gone. However, a number of royal palaces are still maintained.

The loss of tax-free status occurred after the Windsor Palace fire in the late 1980s, when the Queen thought she would be able simply to call on the government for help with the refurbishment costs. Instead, after an embarrassing public outcry, not only did she have to pay the £70m involved out of her own purse, but shortly thereafter had to pay income tax on her entire income.

An index of the worldwide interest in British royalty was the media coverage of the death of Diana, Princess of Wales. The Palace was seriously out of touch with the mood of the people when Diana was killed in a car crash in Paris in the summer of 1997. She was accompanied by Dodi Fayed, son of the Egyptian owner of Harrods department store, Mohammed Al Fayed, who had been denied British citizenship. Traditionalists feared that any offspring produced by this relationship would be in line to inherit the throne, and were thus seen as 'relieved' by the accident. Buckingham Palace appeared to think it could downplay the death of someone with whom it had had public quarrels, but people were well aware of the antipathy between the Palace and Diana (her early 1990s television interview with Martin Bashir drew 14 million viewers). There was thus a huge outpouring of public grief, and the Palace had both to lose face and to upgrade the funeral obsequies to three days of national mourning.

The Royal Family has always paradoxically drawn support from large segments of the working class, and no member has attracted affection more than the Queen Mother. Nearly a centenarian, at her every public appearance she is greeted with genuine affection possibly because of the gratitude which an older generation felt for a monarchy which chose to live in the heavily bombed city of London during the Second World War, and which insisted on carrying on construction of a cathedral at Liverpool, a 'futile' project at a time when bombs were dropping all around.

The monarchy continues to be much better received overseas than in Britain. Americans display much more interest in it than in their own 'aristocracy', and in Canada the young princes William and Harry received a rousing welcome to British Columbia in November 1998.

See also: Establishment, the; privacy

MARIANE SMITH

monetarism

This theory relates changes in inflation to the level of the money supply in relation to the level of real output. Monetarism is also used as a generic term for neo-liberal economic theories (such as liberalization and deregulation). A monetarist revival occurred in the 1970s as a result of a period of stagflation (simultaneous rising unemployment and rising inflation). Keynesian theories failed to provide an explanation for this, but monetarism did. Monetarism, adopted by the Callaghan administration in 1976, was continued with marked enthusiasm by the Thatcher administration. By the mid-1980s, monetarism had lost popular countenance and strict control of money supply ceased. However, successive Conservative administrations have continued to give primacy to the reduction of inflation and free market ideals.

See also: Conservative governments; Thatcherism

ALASTAIR LINDSLEY

Moore, Henry

b. 1898, Castleford; d. 1986, Perry Green, Hertfordshire

Sculptor

Henry Moore dominated British sculpture in the twentieth century. Rejecting the classicism of academic sculpture, Moore was influenced by the stylized figures of 'primitive art' (*Reclining Woman*, 1929, Leeds City Art Gallery) and modernist art from continental Europe. His most experimental work combines surrealism and the biomorphism of Picasso and Arp, with a commitment to 'truth to materials' and direct carving. The two central motifs of Moore's mature career date from the 1930s; the reclining female figure, often divided into two or more constituent parts and suggestive of landscape forms (*Four Piece Composition: Reclining*

Figure, 1934, Tate Gallery, London); and the pierced or hollowed form which explores the relationship between the interior and exterior space.

An official war artist, Moore's *Shelter Sketchbooks* heralded a more conservative approach to the figure (*Madonna and Child*, 1943–4, Church of St Matthew, Northampton). Success at the Venice Biennale in 1948 secured his international reputation and a worldwide market. Prestigious commissions followed, including the UNESCO headquarters in Paris (1956–8). Replacing stone carving with casting bronze editions, and using assistants, enabled Moore to increase production, with the majority of his 11,000 sculptures dating from the final half of his career.

Within Britain, Moore's audience grew through public commissions, open-air exhibitions in London parks, and John Read's films for the BBC. His modernist yet recognizably figurative style became the acceptable face of modern British art. Although Moore's popularity continued to grow, his artistic achievement is largely confined to his activities before the Second World War.

Moore's legacy continues through his charity. The Henry Moore Foundation (HMF) was established in 1977 'to advance the education of the public by the promotion of their appreciation of the fine arts and in particular the works of Henry Moore'. By the 1990s it was providing around £4 million per annum for the visual arts in Britain. Though Moore's work is promoted by the HMF, its broader objectives are devolved to other bodies; grants fund exhibitions and research around Britain. In Yorkshire, two organizations promote and exhibit sculpture of all periods and nationalities: the Henry Moore Centre for the Study of Sculpture, Leeds, which holds a sculpture collection, library and archive, and the Henry Moore Sculpture Trust, which organizes exhibitions at the Henry Moore Institute in Leeds and the Henry Moore Studio in Halifax.

See also: Hepworth, Barbara; sculpture

Further reading

Bowness, A., Read, H. and Sylvester, D. (1988) *Henry Moore: Complete Sculpture*, catalogue raisonné in six volumes, 5th edn, London: Lund Humphries.

CLAIRE GLOSSOP

Morris, Desmond

b. 1928

Anthropologist

Morris started as a zoologist at Birmingham and became an anthropologist at the University of Oxford. He examined interactional synchrony (people in a group moving in unison with, for example, a speaker) and postural congruence (adopting identical or mirror-image positions) He drew on his research into animal behaviour to produce a sociological critique of human behaviour, promulgated in his best-known work *The Naked Ape* (1967). His work, which includes *The Human Zoo* (1969), *Manwatching* (1977), *The Soccer Tribe* (1981), *Catwatching* and *Dogwatching* (both 1986), packages and popularizes science (he was head of Granada Television's Film Unit at London Zoo from 1956–9) and thus paved the way for books like Stephen **Hawking**'s *A Brief History of Time*.

MIKE STORRY

motor racing

Britain has played a major role in motor racing since the 1950s, when Jaguar sports cars regularly won the Le Mans Twenty-Four Hours race (this race still attracts some 50,000 British spectators annually). The motor racing industry has become a major high-tech employer and exporter. In Formula One (F1) racing, first Cooper and then Lotus cars revolutionized the sport, providing the vehicles for a string of British world champions: Graham Hill, Jim Clark, John Surtees (albeit in a Ferrari) and Jackie Stewart won eight of twelve championships between 1962 and 1973.

Traditionally, F1 cars raced in their national colour (such as British racing green), but since 1968 sponsorship has become an integral part of F1's success and cars now usually race in the sponsor's colours. One of the most striking examples is the successful Benetton team sponsored by the Italian clothing manufacturer. Tobacco manufacturers are also major investors in F1, since racing cars in their liveries offer a very important medium for circumventing increasingly restrictive television advertising regimes. The worldwide growth of interest in F1 is partly fuelled by its high-tech image (which encourages individual countries to wish to stage Grand Prix races), partly by the traditional male macho glamour of the world of fast cars, and partly by the desire to open up new markets to sponsors, particularly tobacco firms.

Formula One became a major television sport in Britain in the 1980s with the BBC's package of a distinctive Fleetwood Mac theme tune and presenter Murray Walker, a cult hero whose hectic commentary style found a perfect foil in the patrician insouciance of former world champion James Hunt. The entertainment potential of the sport's mixture of high-tech drama, business opportunities, noise and speed with individual drivers' psychologies is exemplified in the stormy history of the Williams team, who have regularly won world championships and, not quite as regularly, discarded the drivers who won them. Nigel Mansell won a Williams-mounted championship in 1992, after a career dogged by injury, accident and bad luck, and did not keep his seat but consolidated his popular reputation by winning the American Indycar championship the following season (in the face of the criticism of some commentators who appeared unable to forgive him his Midlands accent or for disproving their predictions about him). Similarly, Damon Hill, who won the 1996 championship in a Williams after what seemed like career-long battle with the ghost of his father Graham, was also dumped by the team.

TREVOR R. GRIFFITHS

MTV

Available in 25 percent of households worldwide, MTV (music television) boldly promotes itself as 'the global voice of youth culture'. Launched in the USA on 1 August 1981, MTV broadcasts music news, promotions, interviews, concert information and 'rockumentaries' as well as promotional music videos. MTV Europe was launched in London on 1 August 1987 as a '24 hours-a-day music and youth-oriented entertainment television channel'. In Europe, it broadcasts thirty-seven countries and over fifty-four million households through satellite, cable and terrestrial distribution, using the English language. The leading European consumer is France (fifteen million households), followed by Italy (eleven million); the UK has approximately four and one-half million viewing homes. Russia is a growing and important market with MTV accessible in some thirty million homes. Despite its American origins, some 90 percent of MTV Europe's programming is originated and produced in Europe. In addition, MTV broadcasts public service announcements on issues such as AIDS, racism, drugs and the environment.

MTV has been seen by some theorists as a fine example of postmodern culture (see **postmodernism**) with its frenzied and fragmented approach to scheduling. It is argued that this fragmented 'cut and paste' approach works on the level of parody and pastiche by merging high and low culture, much in the same way that the sampler has been seen as a postmodern musical magpie in terms of music production. Other have taken a contradictory line, arguing that far from the approach above, MTV increasingly conforms to established scheduling patterns, and that far from diversifying culture in the way outlined above by this 'pick and mix' approach, it may serve to maintain these lines of demarcation with most audiences being increasingly 'defined'. The international dimension to MTV makes it a very important player in the global **music industry**. It has the power to shift artists from their national marketplaces to not only the wider European and American markets but beyond into Asia, India, South America and Japan. It remains to be seen whether this cultural globalization will result in further standardization of product at the expense of traditional national and regional distinctions.

See also: pop television

Further reading

Banks, J. (1996) *Monopoly Television: MTV's Quest to Control the Music*, Boulder, CO: Westview Press.

GUY OSBORN
STEVE GREENFIELD

Muir, Jean

b. 1933, London; d. 1995

Fashion designer

Born in 1933, Muir trained in the fashion industry, working for **Liberty** and Jaeger until launching her own Jean Muir label in 1966. Her training as a dressmaker and tailor was reflected in the precision cutting of her elegant designs, whose apparent simplicity masked their impeccable tailoring. Muir's signature fabrics were soft jerseys and matt crepes in muted colours and navy blue, a colour which Muir made 'the new black'. Muir's designs brought her acclaim in the fashion media and a staunch following among women who wanted classic modern elegance rather than the shock of the new. The label has continued since her death in 1995.

See also: labels

TAMSIN SPARGO

municipal buildings

Postwar municipal building in Britain has continued the traditions of the nineteenth century in terms of the provision of civic centres and local government buildings, although other building types historically associated with local government, such as schools, libraries, swimming pools and leisure centres, are now often under the control of county councils. Hampshire County Council, led by the forward thinking Freddie Emery-Wallis, is acknowledged widely as a centre for excellence for public building. Visionary County Architect Colin Stansfield-Smith was appointed in 1974, and has orchestrated an innovative programme of public architecture.

One of the most celebrated examples of a civic centre is that of Newcastle upon Tyne, designed by the City Architect George Kenyon and built in two successive stages from 1960–3 and 1965–8. Occupying a central ten-acre site, the prominent feature of the composition is the council chamber. To the north is the reception suite, including the banqueting hall and Lord Mayor's and Sheriff's suites; to the south are committee rooms and administrative offices. Surmounting the complex is the familiar feature of the tall tower, with carillon, lantern and beacon and three golden castles from the City's coat of arms; the tower can be seen on the approach to and across the city, and forms a symbol of civic pride. Other examples of civic centres include Gravesend (1964) by H.T. Cadbury-Brown and Partners, and Sunderland (1968) by Basil **Spence**, Bonnington and Collins. Both provide cleverly articulated multi-functional complexes.

During the 1970s, many municipal buildings drew on the brutalist aesthetic, employing ubiquitous concrete; one of the most controversial examples was Birmingham Central Library (1974), designed by the John Madin Design Group. The Prince of Wales thought that it looked like 'a place where books are incinerated, not kept'.

Competitions for town halls have elicited some exciting responses, including the design for Northampton Town Hall, designed as a huge glass pyramid. This Platonic form was designed by Jeremy and Fenella Dixon in 1972, and positioned to relate to local ley lines. BDP's Town Hall, Tewkesbury (1977) together with Robert Matthew Johnson-Marshall's Civic Centre, Hillingdon, Middlesex (1977), established the popularity of normally domestic neo-vernacular as a viable style for civic building, and were described by the Prince of Wales as pioneering 'the departure from the nuclear-fallout-shelter look for public buildings'. However, one area of 'municipal' building which has fallen into decline in recent years is that of council housing, the prewar flagship of municipal aspiration.

See also: city redevelopment; town planning

HILARY GRAINGER

music colleges

Courses available at British music colleges generally include the more traditional performance-based conservatoire training which centres on the music of the Western European classical tradition, side by side with newer style courses covering disciplines as diverse as jazz, music therapy, early music, music technology and education.

Music colleges generally offer first degree/diploma courses of two kinds, either a more performance based course or a more academic Graduate or BA/BMus course. Skills typically covered include tuition in the student's principal instrument or voice, study of western European classical forms, harmony, orchestration, keyboard skills and ensemble playing. Entrance qualifications for undergraduates generally include a minimum performance standard of Grade 8, usually to be demonstrated in an audition, in addition to possible keyboard, aural and academic requirements. Music undergraduates are subject to the usual DFE funding arrangements, though funding for postgraduate courses can be hard to find: students are often obliged to make many approaches to charitable trusts though the colleges themselves can sometimes offer assistance from special trust funds. It is usually necessary for music students to work their way through college as they are obliged to provide themselves with instruments of sufficient quality to maintain a high performance standard, which often includes subsequent auditions for professional engagements.

There is an increasing awareness of the need for students to emerge from music training with the flexibility to move in new directions as the scope of professions in music expands. Consequently, music students are more often being encouraged to explore musical skills additional to that of their principal discipline, and to move away from European classical styles. An example of this more adventurous approach is the performance and communication skills course run by the Guildhall School of Music and Drama, both as a one-year postgraduate course and as a part of undergraduate training. Areas covered by this course include composition, theatre, workshop and presentation skills, t'ai chi and improvisation. A similar approach of artistic cross-fertilization is evident in the courses offered by the new Liverpool Institute for Performing Arts, which are aimed at contemporary performance styles.

Most music colleges offer facilities for external students including examinations, part-time courses and summer schools which cover subjects from early music to jazz and rock. Many colleges also run junior departments aimed at school age musicians, providing tuition and opportunities for ensemble playing.

See also: classical music; classical music, contemporary; classical soloists

Further reading

Rich, F. (ed.) *Music Education Yearbook*, London: Rhinegold, published annually.

ANDREA MARTIN

music industry

The market for rock and pop music is dominated by a handful of companies known as the Big Six: WEA, Sony, Polygram, CEMA, BMG and UNI. The global market remains under the power and influence of the Big Six because of their control over distribution.

In the USA, from the late 1930s onwards the major recording companies, Columbia (established in 1889), RCA (1929), Victor (1901) and Decca (1934), were competing over recording and reproducing techniques in order to gain a significant share of the market. In the 1930s, the standard record format was a ten-inch disc which rotated seventy-eight times per minute. After the war, Columbia were the first to introduce vinyl, and also the first to introduce the long-playing hi-fidelity record. They then went on to release the innovative twelve-inch $33\frac{1}{3}$ rpm long-player. RCA in turn developed a seven-inch record on vinyl which rotated forty-five times per minute. Because there was an appropriate market for each, each company decided to produce their records on both formats. The LP became the main outlet for classical music, and the 45 rpm seven-inch 'single' format was more convenient for popular music, which was played at radio stations and on juke-boxes. The seven-inch single format was much easier to distribute, and in this way, smaller record companies were able to promote their artists amongst radio stations cheaply and more effectively, giving rise to the development of independent national distribution companies. By 1948, the four main record companies were RCA, Columbia, Capitol and American Decca. Out of the top ten most successful records of that year, 81 percent were produced by these four major companies.

The music industry is a multi-layered organization, including not just the artists but also employees of the record companies from managing directors down to A&R (artistes and repertoire), recording studios, production and management companies, songwriting and music publishing houses (including film music and jingles for adverts as well as mainstream songs), the music press, manufacturing establishments (cutting and pressing rooms, blank tape and CD suppliers, makers and suppliers of instruments and PA systems), retail outlets (mail order catalogues, record stores), venues (from pubs to purpose-built complexes) and electronic media, from radio to the Internet. The music industry is not subsidized by the government, but regional councils will fund local events such as festivals or outdoor concerts. In the United Kingdom in 1996, retail sales exceeded £1bn, and the industry employed over 48,000 people. There is considerable revenue to be earned from the industry's various associated activities and products, such as tours and the merchandising which inevitably accompanies them, sponsorship deals, endorsement deals (of instruments and amplifiers, for example), royalties, and public appearances and interviews.

The international music industry is a multi-billion dollar enterprise, and is primarily articulated by the dynamics of market capitalism. It is historically located in the USA, but the United Kingdom has always played a significant artistic and commercial contribution. The music business follows the economy very closely, and tries to influence trends and consumer practices. The industry has been dominated by Western practices, not purely in terms of its products but also in its economic structures and its legal and political transactions. However, the Anglo-American hegemony has waned in recent years in the light of the emerging European market forces and the Japanese multimedia conglomerates, which have been instrumental in changing the identity of the industry.

The forces which can affect the structure of the industry range from customer behaviour through to competition from the smaller independent labels, the changes in technological reproduction and the creative process itself. The music and radio industries had always to a degree been interdependent, but in the United States during the period 1954–8 this interdependence underwent significant developments. Radio depended on the record industry as providers of material for its shows, and the record industry relied upon radio for the exposure and promotion of its products. Radio had started to become a medium in itself, and the number of radio stations was expanding rapidly. This inevitably led to the need for diversity and station identity, and thus radio became regional rather than national in focus. Stations were on the lookout for new or local talent, and were keen to offer air time to acts which belonged to the lesser known labels such as Sun, Atlantic and Coral. This created opportunities for the independent labels, enabling them to compete for a share in the national market.

Over the last two decades of the twentieth century there has been another substantial revolution within the framework and constitution of the industry, due to the external developments in mass media communications. Music in its commercial aspect was easily made into a commodity, and the systematic exploitation of consumers could be negotiated within the markets. The transformation of the media industry has led to a complete overhaul, with the ownership of media outlets belonging to a small number of corporate entities. In 1995, Seagram's Company bought 80 percent of MCA for $5.7 billion; Westinghouse took over CBS for $5.4 billion, and the Disney Corporation bought Capital Cities/ABC for $19 billion. In 1996, Time/Warner bought Turner Broadcasting, with its outlets in cable, film and sports organizations, for $7.56 billion, establishing the industry's role as a major player in other areas of media consumption. The music industry and its economy became integrated with the worldwide computerized infrastructure of telecommunications and media. This process of controlling both hardware and software markets and distributing products through a range of media types is called 'synergy', and it has created opportunities for crossover marketing strategies. Records could sell films, and vice versa; the film-to-video industry was booming, and computer games companies were now buying up rights for film and music. This was to be a complete monopolization of trans-global media, adopting the individual-as-consumer point of view.

Technology has always been a significant factor in shaping the development of the music industry. With the onslaught of technological advances in recording equipment and the introduction of new formats such as the compact disc (CD) and digital audio tape (DAT), new marketing strategies had to be developed, which in turn affected the consumption habits of the record-buying public. The CD offered a clarity of sound and a scope for longevity with which vinyl could not compete, bringing about its eventual decline. Also in decline was the sale of the seven-inch single. In 1980, before the rise of the CD, the gross annual worldwide turnover of singles was £550m, but in 1988 this had dropped to £375m. In the USA, cassette sales were on the increase, grossing $22.5m in 1988, and by the end of 1989, this figure had significantly risen to $32.5m. Vinyl had all but disappeared from the shelves of major record stores, but this in turn created an alternative market in the record collector, and jazz and blues connoisseurs still preferred the authenticity of vinyl.

A continuing problem faced by the industry is that of piracy. This can be in various forms, from the illegal recordings of live events (known as 'bootlegging'), to ticket-touting and forged merchandise (posters, t-shirts, programmes and so on). The pirate industry is estimated to have an international value of £3.7 billion, which totals 12 percent of the retail value of all legally sold recorded music. In the United Kingdom alone it is thought that music writers and publishers are losing about £40m annually, due to the upsurge in pirate CDs and cassettes. There is a current crisis in the music industry, with a catastrophic decline in sales, and the source of the blame lies in the increased tendency to visit the various music sites (of which there are more than 26,000) currently offering music free of charge on the Internet.

Music on the Internet is not yet covered by the various protecting bodies, such as the Mechanical Copyright Protection Society and the Performing Rights Society, and is offered without any authorization from, or payment to, the legal holders of the copyright. The Internet has therefore served to increase the threat of lost revenues for musicians. Customization on a mass scale is fast becoming the commercial pattern of the future. On visiting certain sites, the net user is invited to make a personal selection of desired tracks, which are then dispatched at a fraction of the price of a commercially produced CD.

Record companies need to maximize profits in order to create market stability, and within this need is the obligation to offer their customers a degree of change and innovation. The record industry is capable of establishing new and original ideas as standard in order to generate a market for them. This creates a cycle of innovation, whereby the next new act to come along has to be more diverse, or more original, in order to break through the now established norm.

During periods of a stabilized market, the major companies can exert some control over the growth of the smaller labels, which specialize in the more uncommercial genres or scenes, by buying them into their own conglomerates, or merging with them. This can often mean taking control of not just the performers, but also of their creative rights as artists (which led to a major court case involving George Michael). The independent record companies have risen in the international market stakes, and as they are swallowed up into the mainstream by the majors, others spring up in their wake. In the United States, industry power is located in three main areas, Los Angeles, New York City and Nashville, with the occasional 'scene' emerging on the peripheries, such as grunge in Seattle. In Britain, power has always been located in London, despite the phenomenal success of groups such as the Beatles, who were at the forefront of the idea of a regional sound in the 1960s; this 'Mersey' sound was resurrected in the 1980s by bands such as Echo and the Bunnymen, Wah, Teardrop Explodes and China Crisis, and again in the 1990s with The La's, Cast, Space and The Lightning Seeds. There was also the 'baggy' scene in 1980s Manchester with The

Stone Roses, The Inspiral Carpets and The Happy Mondays. National identity has become prominent in recent years; notable is the rise of the Welsh band with acts such as Catatonia, Super Furry Animals, 60ft Dolls and Park Trolley. Local labels are few and far between – Probe in Liverpool and Revolver in Wolverhampton are examples – and 99.9 percent of labels in Britain operate from London, which means that most bands have to migrate to the capital for the convenience of managers, agents and record label bosses.

There has been a rise in the consumption of independently produced and distributed artefacts, and the Big Six's dominance over the global market has declined in recent years. With the rise in popularity of world music (South American and Asian music's popularity is at an all-time high) the focus has shifted away from Anglo-America to Europe (especially in the light of the Ibiza 'rave' scene and the European quirky dance acts such as Whigfield, Aqua and Two Unlimited). The independent or alternative labels operate on a different basis to the major players, the difference being purely economic. The former deal with short-term contracts, sometimes without an advance to the artist, and production and distribution can be local rather than national. In the UK, Pinnacle are the main distributors of independent labels, while in the USA this role is filled by Jet Distribution. The desire for independent labels to produce innovative and quality work has to be matched with the necessity to work within economic boundaries, the main cost being that of promotion and marketing.

Nevertheless, the latter half of the twentieth century's rapidly developing technologies have made it possible for music to be both seen and heard far and wide, immortalizing musicians and their creative works in the process. Its omnipresence is guaranteed through radio, television, cable, satellite, vinyl, cassettes and CDs.

See also: pop and rock

Further reading

Shuker, R. (1994) *Understanding Popular Music*, London: Routledge.
—— (1998) *Key Concepts in Popular Music*, London:

Routledge (an excellent analysis of the music industry).

ALICE BENNETT

music labels

In the **music industry**, record labels fall into two categories, major and minor. The majors are those labels which are comprised of, or attached to, the main six record companies in the world (Sony, WEA, Polygram, CEMA, BMG and UNI). The minors are also known as indie labels, because they are independent from the major record companies, both in terms of artistry and finance. However, the independents often rely on the assistance of the majors for the distribution of their products, and adopt similar business practices in order to expand their market and establish the necessary industry contacts. Despite this, the independents consider themselves to be more flexible and innovative in their choice of signings. The main independent labels are Mute, 4AD and One Little Indian. The most successful British label is EMI (now a part of the Sony corporation), formed in March 1931. One of its subsidiaries was Parlophone, bought from Holland's Transoceanic Trading Company, and in the 1960s it also had a red label for novelty and comic acts. George Martin persuaded his bosses to release the Beatles's first two singles on this label, and with their success, Parlophone became an outlet for popular music. In 1979, EMI were in financial difficulties and were taken over by Thorn Electrical Industries becoming Thorn/EMI. Despite the takeover, EMI still maintained relative freedom, and went on to buy up Liberty, United Artists Records and the jazz label Blue Note.

Columbia is the oldest label still in existence, formed on 1 January 1889 by Edward Easton in the USA to sell musical recordings. By 1891 it was the biggest recording company in the world. In 1959, due to the success of rock 'n' roll, the independents were able to establish a niche for themselves, aiming to pioneer new sounds and style. The majors often overshadowed their attempts by buying up the smaller labels wholesale, artists included, so the process would begin all over again. Thus the majors had a decisive advantage over the independents, with a huge number of artists on their books covering each particular genre and able to satisfy every section of consumer trends.

With the rising popularity of the Internet, labels specializing in genres like **house**, **ambient music**, trip-hop and **techno** music take advantage of its ability for faster distribution. Instead of depending on sought-after airplay, the Internet can sell directly, one track at a time, to fans who visit the websites.

See also: record labels

Further reading

Burnett, R. (1996) *The Global Jukebox: The International Music Industry*, London: Routledge.

ALICE BENNETT

music press

The last decade has seen an increase in the academic research and analysis of popular music, largely due to the current trend of popular culture studies. The music press consists of a vast range of publications, the majority of which deal with popular music, and mainly that which is in, or is likely to be in, the UK Top 40 charts. The music press is largely based around so-called 'lifestyle' magazines, such as *Q* or *The Face*, which focus on the more avant-garde aspect of the culture of popular music; in the 1980s, they were commonly known as 'style Bibles'. Other publications of this genre, such as *Mojo* and *Vox*, have a similar format but are slightly less 'arty' and have a more general appeal. The most popular type of publication is what are known as 'the weeklies', including *Melody Maker* and *New Musical Express* (commonly known as *NME*); the general format consists of interviews with the latest big name, reviews of the latest album and single releases, reviews of live gigs, plenty of photos, plenty of adverts, a national gig guide and various chart listings. The youth or teenage market is catered for with publications such as *Smash Hits*, with its printed song lyrics of the latest chart hits and mini biographies of the latest pop sensation.

These types of magazines follow the trends rather than set them. The teen market is flooded with rather flimsy but glossy biographies of the latest pin-ups, consisting of lots of photos and little text, or small magazines which fold out into full-size posters. They are orientated towards the superstar status of the performer or band, rather than their musicianship. This type of publication is as accessible as the music it writes about. Image is the all-important factor. It is a rarity for a music paper or magazine to feature a picture of a record on its front cover.

There are also publications which cater specifically for the individual musician, such as *Modern Drummer* and *Guitar Weekly*. Trade magazines which cater more for musicians and technicians who wish to trade in or buy musical instruments or recording equipment are widely available. An indication of the changes in both availability and consumer trends of these publications is that until fairly recently, they were not to be located on the shelves of High Street newsagents, but had to be ordered through a newsagent or distributor; today, however, they are to be found at most major newsagents across the country.

There are also locally based magazines known as **fanzines**, the majority of which are produced by fans of a particular type of music or musician. Although usually rather unsophisticated, being mainly photocopies of self-produced material, they are of great value to the local music scene, promoting the regions, bands and venues which would otherwise not gain a mention in the national music press. Fanzines originated with the onset of punk in the 1970s. Following the do-it-yourself ethos of punk, they were non-commercial publications and therefore had more street credibility. The authorship was often anonymous. They help to define a local scene and identify with that community. Due to the absence of material, both published and recorded, of the more obscure artists, fanzines were a highly useful source of information. They often provided a springboard into mainstream journalism. More recently, fanzines have become a standard follow-up to most genres and types of artists. Their role has turned out to be of significant value as an ongoing source of information for the alternative genres that are constantly emerging within popular music. Some of them can even be found on the shelves of the local record store or newsagents.

Also to be found on the shelves in any major booksellers are biographies, autobiographies, rare record collecting magazines, books dedicated to the top 100 singles, histories of pop and rock music, genre-oriented books, era-oriented books and gender-oriented books. There is a considerable amount of literature being devoted to popular music. Catalogues have emerged in the last decade to keep up with the trend of musical textual analysis. There are many essays devoted to pop music and its varying genres in many cultural anthologies and journals.

The music industry is one of the biggest businesses in the world, and the music press plays a significant role within that industry. It is an essential marketing tool, playing a key role in the promotion of its products. The press will often play the role of 'gatekeeper', providing initial critical feedback on new releases.

The emergence of the **Internet** as a means of global communication has brought a new dimension to how popular music is promoted and received. There are now on-line music journals, with most major music magazines running websites; news and reviews are updated on a daily basis, and the information is accessible twenty-four hours a day. Another new format is the CD-ROM. A multimedia journal called *Nautilus CD* initiated the first CDRomagazine, published in the early 1990s, heralding a whole new genre called ROMags. These emulate the style of an authentic music magazine but with the added bonus of video footage and musical accompaniment of image and text. Images can be enhanced by the viewer, or additional music or text can be chosen. The potential of the media coverage of music is constantly being explored and extended, but as in pop music itself, the original format sits easily beside its modern counterpart.

See also: DJs; record labels

Further reading

Shuker, R. (1998) *Key Concepts in Popular Music*, London: Routledge (the most concise and comprehensive study of popular music).

ALICE BENNETT

Muslim Parliament

The 150-strong Muslim Parliament was established in London in 1992 by the late Islamic campaigner Dr Kalim Siddiqui (1933–96). Prior to its establishment, a statement of its aims appeared in the *Observer* (5 January 1991): 'This parliament must defend and promote the Muslim interest in Britain.' Dr Siddiqui's attempt to create an effective Islamic voice in Britain failed, mainly due to the fact that he bypassed the British Islamic establishment when setting up his parliament; hence he could not call on the network of local mosques to create interest in his cause. Also founded in 1989, the Islamic Party for Britain aims to represent British Muslims and to lobby for pro-Islamic legislation. Membership is over 1,000, and the Party contested five seats at the 1992 general election.

See also: black Conservatives; Islam; Labour Party black sections; Nation of Islam

EUGENE LANGE

N

Nation of Islam

The Nation of Islam is an American black Muslim anti-integrationist and black supremacist organization with origins in the 1960s civil rights movement. Well-known adherents have included Malcolm X and Muhammed Ali. Founding texts from the 1930s are W.D. Fard's *The Secret Rituals of the Nation of Islam* and *Teaching For the Lost Found Nation of Islam in a Mathematical Way*. Fard rejected white culture and Christianity, maintaining that American blacks should turn to Africa and Asia for comradeship and religion. Its British wing was established in 1995 and may have as many as 2,500 members. The Nation's leader in Britain is Michael Muhammad, while Leo X Chester and Wayne X run two of the organization's mosques; they also have two black-only schools which teach the Koran and African history, while a shop on Harlesden High Street called 'Respect for Life' sells Nation of Islam products.

See also: Islam; Muslim Parliament

PETER CHILDS

National Curriculum

A standard programme of education in England and Wales, the National Curriculum was introduced by the Education Reform Act of 1988. While politicians, the general public and commentators on education have welcomed the introduction of a standard programme, many teachers have opposed the uniformity and the restrictions which the National Curriculum has imposed. The Curriculum includes the core subjects of English, mathematics and science, plus foundation subjects of history, geography, technology, art, music and physical education (in January 1998 the Labour government placed a greater emphasis on core skills of literacy and numeracy). At secondary schools, a modern foreign language is also part of the programme. Attainment levels and assessment tests take place at key stages, which are at the ages of 7, 11, 14 and 16.

See also: school examinations; schools system

PETER CHILDS

National Front

The National Front was founded in 1967 through a merger of extreme right-wing groups. In the early 1970s the party gained prominence with its overtly racist attitude to large-scale coloured immigration from the New Commonwealth. In this period it attracted new members from the right-wing Conservative Monday Club faction, and enjoyed its greatest electoral successes. The National Front made strident appeals to British nationalism and captured the Union Jack as its symbol. The party's popularity faded with the right-wing programme of the Thatcher governments, as well as damaging splits in the 1980s. National Front membership and influence is now minimal, save in a few inner city areas.

See also: Communist Party; fringe parties

Further reading

Fielding, N. (1981) *The National Front*, London: Routledge & Kegan Paul.

COLIN WILLIAMS

National Lottery

Britain introduced a national lottery in November 1994, the last country in Europe to do so. The private company Camelot was given a seven-year licence to run the lottery. Tickets are sold through newsagents and post offices. The lottery's revenues were originally estimated at £14–35m per week but have far exceeded that, reaching around £85m per week (plus £17m from 'Instants' scratch cards), and nine out of ten adults are claimed to buy tickets occasionally. The highest win to date was £22.5m, but the odds of winning the jackpot are astronomically poor, at 14 million to one. The bookmakers Ladbrokes have likened the odds to those of Elvis landing a UFO on the Loch Ness Monster. However, the smaller prizes are more winnable. Of the money subscribed, 50 percent goes in prize money, 12 percent in tax, 5 percent to the retailer, 5 percent to Camelot and 28 percent to 'good causes'. 'Good causes' has come to mean the arts, charities, **heritage** and sport.

The draw takes place twice weekly, on Wednesday and Saturday. The lottery is arguably popular because it offers the possibility of social change. However, its inception has highlighted potential for social upheaval and division. Predictably, some people have not been able to cope with huge winnings, and many legal cases have centred on breaches of trust among workmates, within families and between friends.

Complaints against the lottery have come from Church leaders, charities whose revenues have fallen and the **football pools**, among others. It is argued that people are spending money they cannot afford, that revenues are being diverted from the poor to the rich, and that money is being given to undeserving causes. Partly to assuage these concerns, the government has made some changes, including introducing a sixth 'good cause' called the New Opportunities Fund, which concentrates on health and education projects, and creating NESTA (National Endowment for Science and the Arts) to foster arts and science creativity. However, many people feel that these areas should be covered already by core government spending. The government has also introduced a watchdog committee to monitor the spending of lottery money. This was largely prompted by high-profile mismanagement at the Royal Opera House, the subject of the television documentary series *The House*. Undoubtedly, lottery funds have made a huge impact on the organizations that have received them, at both local and national level, and have in many cases replaced years of underfunding or no funding at all.

See also: betting shops

Further reading

Fitzhurst, L. and Rhoades, L. (1997) *The National Lottery Yearbook*, London: Directory of Social Change.

MIKE STORRY

National Museum of Photography, Film and Television

Based in Bradford, the National Museum of Photography, Film and Television (NMPFT) opened in 1983 to explore the history, aesthetics, art and science of the visual medium in photography, film and television. Its rare archives, renowned collections, interactive displays and special exhibitions examine still and moving images and their relationship to developing technologies. For instance, while the cinematography collection charts the historical processes of film production with early optical apparatus such as the praxinscope and the magic lantern, the museum's own Pictureville cinema and IMAX cinema screen (at $52' \times 64'$, the largest in Britain) illustrate their evolution in the modern era. In 1998, the Imaging Frontiers programme prepared an expanded NMPFT for the digital and multimedia communications age.

SATINDER CHOHAN

National Viewers and Listeners Association

Formed by Mary Whitehouse in 1964 as the 'Clean-up TV Campaign' to combat increasing television liberalization, the National Viewers and Listeners Association (NVLA) is the foremost watchdog on 'standards' in British television. It opposes sex, violence and irreligiosity on television, theatre, video and film, and conducted prosecutions against *Monty Python's Life of Brian* and Scorsese's *Last Temptation of Christ*. The NVLA firmly believe that the media cause crime and violence, and has formed links with Christian MPs who lobby for changes to laws on video and television output. Often accused of Puritanism, the NVLA claims to represent the decency of ordinary people, counteracting the trendy left-wing intelligentsia and their liberalizing 1960s ideas.

See also: censorship

Further reading

Matthews, T.D. (1994) *Censored*, London: Chatto & Windus.

REX NASH

nationalist parties

The Scottish National Party (SNP) was founded in 1934 by supporters of self-government for Scotland. Support grew from the late 1960s, thanks to public dissatisfaction with the two-party system and the failings of the postwar consensus. The SNP benefited from the protest vote, and popularity was boosted with the discovery of North Sea oil in 1970. This increased the economic viability of an independent Scottish state, with the SNP claiming, 'It's Scotland's Oil'. Support peaked in the October 1974 general election when the party won eleven seats and 800,000 votes.

Plaid Cymru, literally 'the Party of Wales', was formed in 1925 and, like the SNP, experienced its greatest electoral popularity in October 1974 when it gained three seats and 170,000 votes. It stresses the importance of the Welsh language and culture, and seeks self-government for Wales within the European Union. Independence for Wales is seen as more difficult to achieve than Scottish independence, as Wales has fewer natural resources and no administrative apparatus separate from England. Nevertheless, Plaid Cymru is angered by Labour's 1997 manifesto proposals for a devolved Scottish Parliament with legislative powers when a Welsh assembly would not have a similar capacity.

Both nationalist parties have a left-of-centre political orientation. Plaid Cymru has an explicit commitment to 'decentralized socialism', and both parties advocate increasing income tax for higher earners, an economic priority of full employment, increased welfare spending, unilateral nuclear disarmament and constitutional and electoral change along the lines proposed by **Charter 88**. In Parliament, the SNP and Plaid Cymru have an alliance and undertook joint initiatives in the 1997 general election campaign.

Nationalist popularity declined following the failure of the 1979 referenda for devolution to Scotland and Wales under Callaghan's minority Labour administration. Only 20 percent of Welsh voters supported devolution, and although 52 percent of Scottish voters wanted the measure, 42 percent of the Scottish population had to vote for devolution to change Scotland's constitutional status and only 33 percent did so. The 1990s witnessed a resurgence in nationalist support. Both parties increased their share of the vote in the 1992 general election and became the second parties of local government behind Labour in their respective countries during Major's second term. At the 1997 general election the SNP won six seats, and Plaid Cymru four.

See also: Scottish language; S4C; Welsh language

Further reading

Davies, C.A. (1989) *Welsh Nationalism and the Modern State*, New York: Praeger.

Marr, A. (1992) *The Battle for Scotland*, Harmondsworth: Penguin.

COLIN WILLIAMS

nationalized and privatized industries

After its 1945 victory, Clement Attlee's Labour government immediately began bringing transport (most notably the railways) and key industries such as coal mining, gas and electricity into public ownership. Developing the ancient state monopoly of the Post Office (extended to telecommunications in 1912) and the municipal ownership of many utilities, the programme was carried through all the more readily because state control had applied throughout the Second World War and because private finance was unavailable for postwar reconstruction. Labour thinking was based on socialist convictions. Consumers and workers alike would, it was argued, benefit from the replacement of capitalist exploitation by public ownership dedicated to ensuring that the means of production and transport operated for the good of all within a planned economy. The various nationalized industries' day-to-day operations were entrusted to quasi-independent boards. These, however, were required to work within financial guidelines laid down by government.

Apart from the steel industry, whose status changed with successive governments, nationalization went forward steadily until reversed by Margaret Thatcher's Conservative government after 1979. Arguments for **privatization**, as denationalization was soon called, were that lack of competition bred inefficiency in nationalized industries, especially those hampered because the state had difficulties funding them and yet persisted, despite its scant business experience, in interfering with management; this in turn impeded responses to market forces. Ideals of employees' identification with whichever nationalized industry they worked for had not been borne out by experience and were contrasted with the benefits of wider share ownership. The proceeds of selling nationalized industries and cutting subsidies and other payments would also reduce public spending, resulting in tax cuts.

When shares in privatized industries were offered to the public, sales were brisk, even hectic, leading to accusations that prices were pitched too low. Complex regulatory machinery was set up to prevent abuse of monopolies, promote competition and ensure standards of service. Complaints were voiced about corrupt 'fat cats', directors and managers in the new companies who paid themselves excessive salaries (see **corruption in the City**). Though controversial, the privatization programme was carried through. The **Labour Party** accepted its irreversibility when, before the 1997 election, it was persuaded by its leadership to abandon 'Clause 4', its traditional pledge to strive for nationalization. Since 1979 many other countries have followed the UK and embarked on privatization programmes.

See also: CBI; Conservative governments

Further reading

Neuberger, J. (ed.) (1987) *Privatisation: Fair Shares for All or Selling the Family Silver?* London: Macmillan (three essays presenting opposing views).

CHRISTOPHER SMITH

nature

The distinction between nature and convention goes back to Anaximander, is well noted by Aristotle, and is the source of much social and political theory. It was not, however, until the romanticization of nature in the early modern period that nature came to be seen as an object of distinction and beauty that could be both interacted with and appreciated. Rousseau, Byron and Wordsworth exemplified this latter view.

Changes in attitude in contemporary times, while built on an earlier romanticism, coincided with the first photographs of the Earth from space in the 1960s. These pictures conveyed the immeasurable beauty of the globe, and its finitude. For the first time, the boundaries of the planet were clearly visible. Consequently, it was recognized that the Earth is a fragile totality composed of a precarious balance of interdependent ecosystems, and that human survival depended upon preserving this balance. Contemporary public and media interest in nature and conservation emerged from this background of romanticization, spatial/global images and the increasing knowledge of the variety of species. That background produced knowledge of, and images of, particularity on the one hand and the globe as a universality on the other.

These poles have been dealt with in and through unprecedented media interest, ranging from the highly scientific journals such as *Nature* and *National Geographic* to more amateur expressions such as *Bird Watching* and *Country Walking*. British television broadcasts on nature are internationally renowned; the most popular series have been *Survival* and *Life on Earth*. In the mid-1990s, increasing public interest in the natural world led to the introduction of the satellite channel Discovery; a large part of this documentary channel is devoted to topics concerning nature. As well as passive reception, active reception of media on Nature is now available via the Internet. This interactive medium offers a variety of possible interfaces. *Earth Kids*, for example, teaches children about ecological concerns.

Ecological groups have merged with political concerns, as in the case of **Friends of the Earth and Greenpeace**. Such groups have attempted to draw attention to the value of the natural habitat and have used the media to great effect in their objections to government-backed activity, from the building of nuclear power plants to airport runways. Two thousand years ago, Horace wrote that, 'You may drive out nature with a pitchfork, yet shall be constantly running back', the implication being that, if the planet is to escape ecological disaster, public recognition of its fragility is clearly necessary.

See also: Gaia hypothesis; green consumerism

Further reading

Attenborough, D. (1980) *Life on Earth*, London: Book Club Associates.

PAUL BARRY CLARKE
EMMA R. NORMAN

neo-classicism

Neo-classicism, a term generally associated with nineteenth-century architecture, has marked an attempt on the part of twentieth-century architects to resist the modern movement in its determination to develop a definitive style. Postwar architects including Philip Johnson, Charles Moore, Robert Venturi and Frank Gehry began to consider architecture in historical terms. They were followed by architectural critics, notably Colin Rowe, Michael Graves (architect and writer) and Allan Greenberg, who maintained that certain elements of modern architecture owe a debt to historical antecedents. During the 1960s the reductivist consistency of 1950s **modernism** was challenged, and by the late 1970s, **postmodernism** had emerged. Resonances of classicism can be felt in many postwar architectural productions, particularly in the work of American architects during the late 1970s and 1980s. Luxembourg-born Leon Krier has been more explicit in his adoption of early nineteenth-century neo-classicism, as in his design for the Royal Mint Square Project, London (1974). British architects Terry Farrell, James **Stirling**, John **Outram** and Robert Adam both respond to and undermine classicism.

Described by Robert A.M. Stern as a 'canonical classicist', Raymond Erith (1904–73) quietly followed the classical ideal during the period of postwar **new brutalism**. Wivenhoe New Park, Essex (1963) remains one of his most characteristic buildings. Erith's protégé and architectural partner Quinlan Terry emerged in the early 1970s to lead Britain's classical revival, commanding a range of variations of classicism. Beginning with a series of small country houses, it was Frog Meadow, Dedham, Essex (1979) and a country house, Waverton, near Moreton-in-Marsh, Glouctershire (1977–9) that established his reputation. Dufours Place, London (1981–3), containing offices and residential apartments, shows an interest in the picturesque manipulation of classicism further exploited at the larger Richmond Riverside Development (1983–8) where a range of classical forms from the sixteenth to the early nineteenth century were rehearsed. Terry's most explicitly neo-classical commission was for Downing College, Cambridge, where he designed the Howard Building (1983–7), located within a context of nineteenth and twentieth-century buildings including the chaste West Lodge by William Wilkins (1807–21), additional work by Edward Barry (1830–80) and the North Range (1930) by Sir Herbert Baker

(1862–1945). Arrol and Snell and Siddel Gibson have produced neo-classical works in the provinces.

Further reading

Stern, R.A.M. (1988) *Modern Classicism*, New York: Rizzoli.

HILARY GRAINGER

neo-Darwinism

Charles Darwin knew nothing of the mechanism of heredity when he proposed his theory of evolution, even though this was some forty years after Mendel had initiated the study of genetics through his work on pea heredity. Neo-Darwinism is the assimilation of genetics into Darwinian evolutionary theory; the term is given to the paradigm which emerged from the synthesis of the key tenets of Darwin's theory of evolution by natural selection and of Mendel's discovery of the units of heredity, subsequently understood as genes. Neo-Darwinian theory was initially proposed by J.B.S. Haldane and R.A. Fisher, among others, and states that evolution of diversity proceeds by the progressive selection of organisms which are different by virtue of mutations which occur randomly in their genes.

While key elements of basic neo-Darwinian theory remain within current views of evolution, subsequent evidence has suggested that many different processes and events have played and will continue to play an important part in the evolution of the diversity of organisms in the biosphere. Many more may yet remain to be discovered. Many processes contribute to the rate of evolution of diversity in addition to simple mutations, including: (1) the symbiotic theory of evolution which proposes that the consolidation over time of collaborations (symbioses) between different types of simpler cells (bacteria) gave rise (and may yet give rise) to more complex cells (the eukaryotic cells of plants and animals); (2) the knowledge that extracellular agents like viruses can transport genetic material (genes) between cells; (3) the relatively recent discovery that genes are divided into segments of coding and non-coding DNA which might lead to rather large changes in the structure of gene products from a single mutation at a segment boundary; and (4) that simple mutations in genes which play key orchestrating roles in embryogenic development can lead to rather large changes in the overall structure of the adult organism.

While these various mechanisms for altering gene structure provide the engine for evolution, the process of diversification requires also the range of environmental conditions which exist in different geographical locations and at different times (for example, the ice ages). These are the environments which will favour or penalize organisms with particular characteristics and perhaps initiate divergent lineages of organisms which are more successful than average in those environments.

See also: Dawkins, Richard

Further reading

Ho, M. (1984) *Beyond Neo Darwinism*, London: Academic Press.

PETE SHETERLINE

new age music

The new age movement is largely rooted in the 1980s, but its actual origins can be found in the mid-1970s in America. New age music grew out of the remains of the art-rock movement, primarily a British scene, with artists such as Brian Eno and Peter Gabriel. In 1976, a label called Windham Hill was formed by Will Ackerman, a guitarist, who wanted to distribute his album *In Search of the Turtle's Navel*. He sold his records through bookshops, health stores and by word of mouth. By 1984, sales had reached $20m. The term 'new age music' was first widely applied to Ackerman's label and its products, but Ackerman stated that this term bore no relation to his label or his music. At about the same time in New York City, a company called Vital Body Marketing were themselves producing a 'New Age Music Catalogue', which contained a list of hundreds of LPs of 'listenable music that touches the spirit'.

New age music is a blend of acoustic with soft rock, a hint of white **jazz**, updated by using the latest studio technology. It is often defined as mood music, and in this respect can be regarded as a reaction against the loudness and aggression of the **pop and rock** genres. New age music is technically slick. It soothes the listener with its cascading string sections reminiscent of earlier times, and introduces the modern elements of minimalism and improvisation. Its concerned lyrics, if lyrics exist at all in the compositions, tend towards the ecological and environmental. The music is characterized by its technically accomplished lush orchestral scores, often depicted as thoughtful, listenable beautiful chamber music. It keys in to the new age philosophy of getting back to nature and transcending everyday troubles. It is also known for its pretentious presentations, such that its defining feature is not how it sounds but how it looks. The elaborate style of its record covers established new age music's identity as an essentially visual musical genre. New age composers such as Deuter, Kitaro, Harold Budd and Hans-Joachim Roedelius were all inspired by Eastern music, and combined this with the floatiness of classical Indian music. There has evolved a whole scene in the UK with artists such as Banco De Gaia, Zion Train and Transglobal Underground, with Planet Dog being the main promoter and label.

See also: classical music, contemporary

Further reading

Bergman, B. and Horn, R. (1985) *Experimental Pop: Frontiers of the Rock Era*, Dorset: Blandford Press.

ALICE BENNETT

new brutalism

'New brutalism' was a term coined in Britain in 1954 to characterize an architecture which provided a conscious embodiment of a mood widespread among younger architects of the 1950s. Frustrated by the lack of opportunities for building in postwar Britain and by an increasing dissatisfaction with the aesthetic compromises entered into by establishment architects, they were prompted to offer a new response.

Stripped neo-Georgian or the so-called contemporary style, based on Scandinavian modifications of modernism, were the forms favoured for the comprehensive social building programmes initiated by the welfare state, intended as a setting for postwar 'New Britain'. These suave and undemanding, humanized versions of the modern movement, supported by the architects of the London County Council and promulgated by individuals including J.M. Richards and Nikolas Pevsner in the editorial pages of the *Architectural Review*, became known as 'the new humanism' or 'the new empiricism'. These forms were unacceptable to a growing number, who proposed 'new brutalism' as an alternative architectural morality. This was a structural, spatial, organizational and material concept, attuned to the given and necessary conditions of buildings. Alison and Peter **Smithson**, supported by the critic Reyner Banham and other members of the '20th Century Group' in London, were united in their desire to convey the realities of modern urban life by means of a new art. They sought to introduce a vein of social realism referencing the socio-anthropological roots of popular culture and informed by an interest in Continental existentialism. The Smithsons ideas for 'urban reidentification' brought them into contact with the sculptor Eduardo Paolozzi, the photographer Nigel Henderson and Dubuffet's anti-'polite' art cult of *art brut*. These ideas found crystallization in the London exhibitions 'Parallel of Life and Art' at the Institute of Contemporary Arts, 1953 and 'This is Tomorrow', 1956 at the Whitechapel Art Gallery.

Early examples of a conscious brutalist sensibility showed an admiration for the uncompromising intellectual qualities and roots in tradition of Mies van der Rohe and Le Corbusier. Palladian clarity and restraint, the heroic scale of architecture by Vanbrugh and Hawksmoor and the uncompromising forms of nineteenth-century engineering structures were all embraced. The Smithson's Hunstanton School, Norfolk (1949–54), invokes the elegant steel-frame vocabulary of Mies's Illinois Institute of Technology, and reflects his honest use of materials and structure. However, their sprawling plans for the Golden Lane Housing Project, London (1952) show a move away from this Miesian expression, towards an aesthetic of change. By the mid-1950s, the rather puritanical and hermetic British brutalism was extended to embrace an international movement which espoused a brutalism of form. Le Corbusier's *béton brut*, exhibited at the Unité d'Habitation, Marseilles (1947–52), Chandigargh, India (1951–64) and the Maison Jaoul (1955), influenced the formulation of the aesthetic aimed at expressing complete honesty in form described by Reyner Banham as 'a unique and memorable image'. A developing concern for honesty in expressing functional spaces and their interrelationships is reflected in the Smithson's scheme for the *Economist* offices, St James's, London (1959–64), which solve the problem of adapting a modern building type to the requirements of a particular place. At Park Hill, Sheffield (1961) by Jack Lynn and Ivor Smith, rationalism has been abandoned in favour of a brutalist composition based on the topography of the site and the planning of communications within the **housing** complex. The arrangement of Robin Hood Gardens, London (1966–72), with street decks intended to express and embody the ideal community, was a further demonstration of the Smithson's housing theories.

A series of late brutalist 'monuments' by James **Stirling** and James Gowan show the final integration of the formal and populist aspects of the British brutalist aesthetic with a glass and brick 'vernacular' drawn from nineteenth-century industrial structures. In these university buildings, formal and functional concerns are combined with citations of the canonical forms of the modern movement. The dormitory project for Selwyn College, Cambridge (1959) and the Engineering Building for Leicester University (1959) formed the basis of their personal style, based on a syntax of glass and brick, invoking a heroic engineering romanticism. Stirling's History Faculty Building, Cambridge University (1964), continues this trend, with the teaching and library spaces being integrated by means of a radial plan in which the diagonal becomes a major organizing axis. The vocabulary of Leicester is fully exploited and extended in the almost overwhelming prominence of glass. The Florey Building, a student residence at Queen's College, Oxford (1966–71), with its reminders of Le Corbusier's Pavillon Suisse and

Aalto's Baker House, at once acknowledges and denies the modern movement.

See also: ICA; modernism

Further reading

Banham, R. (1966) *The New Brutalism: Ethic or Aesthetic*, New York.

HILARY GRAINGER

New Labour

In the context of opposition to the **Conservative governments** of Margaret Thatcher and John Major between 1979 and 1997, and particularly after their 1987 election defeat, the **Labour Party** began to articulate an ideology and rhetoric of 'new realism'. A modernising ideology, new realism recognized that Thatcherism had changed the agenda of British politics and, as a consequence, proposed that the Labour party rethink its project and objectives. This perspective informed the Policy Review process of the late 1980s and, by the early 1990s, the party was retreating from such policies as unilateral nuclear disarmament and the denationalization of primary industries. The political ascendancy of the modernising tendency was confirmed in 1994 when, following the death of John Smith, Tony Blair assumed party leadership. Blair promoted the centrist social democratic programme of 'social-ism' under the slogan New Labour and led the party to its largest Parliamentary majority ever at the General Election of 1st May 1997 with 418 Labour MPs elected.

New Labour 'social-ism' rejects the socialist currents which helped shape the party's postwar political agenda, and advances a pragmatic programme of political modernization, constitutional reform, 'stakeholding' democracy, social inclusion and community development. Symbolically important was the 1995 revision of Clause Four of the Party's constitution, when the language of social opportunity 'for the many and not the few' was substituted for the socialist principle of 'the common ownership of the means of production'. In practice, New Labour's 'Iron Chancellor' Gordon Brown has insisted on fiscal discipline and reoriented the party's macroeconomic policy from Keynesian economic management to the neo-liberal strategy of renewal spending on infrastructure, training, education and job creation. New Labour has also articulated a proactive vision of Britain's role in Europe, but, compromising with the late 1990s mood of Euro-scepticism, opted out of the launch of the euro in the year 2000.

The most significant achievements of the early New Labour government were in constitutional reform. Referendums in September 1997 established the Scottish Parliament and Welsh Assembly, and significant progress was made in Northern Ireland with the signing of the multi-party peace declaration in April 1998. However, critics have charged that New Labour's strict party discipline and soundbite approach to politics has been bought at the cost of the suppression of left-wing dissent.

See also: Militant

Further reading

Shaw, E. (1996) *The Labour Party Since 1945*, London: Blackwell (an illuminating modern history of the party).

MARK DOUGLAS

new man

The 'new man' is seen by some as challenging traditional masculinity by embracing, variously, emotional openness, an interest in physical grooming and traditionally female tasks like child-rearing, as well as rejecting machismo. New age spirituality is less commonly linked to the British 'new man' than to the US men's movement. Others see 'the new man' as a response by left-wing men to feminism and the gay liberation movement in the 1970s and 1980s. However, there is little evidence of large numbers of men taking on greater childcare and domestic tasks. Others see 'the new man' as a media creation for the marketing of cosmetic and body improvement products, and do not link a male concern with personal appearance with any other, pro-feminist changes in dominant forms of masculinity.

See also: 'lads' and 'lager louts'

NICOLE MATTHEWS

new romantics

An elite youth subculture and a genre of music confined to the early 1980s. Conceived almost simultaneously in both London and Birmingham, the scene produced bands such as Duran Duran, Spandau Ballet and Visage. Concerned as much with image as musical prowess, new romantic bands dominated both the charts and the nation's bedroom walls from 1981 to 1984, although only Duran Duran garnered critical praise. Taking their musical direction from **glam rock** and European synth-pop, the new romantics saw themselves as serious, glamorous artists. The **music press**, however, did not agree, and there were long debates over 'content versus style' in the pages of *NME* and *Melody Maker*. A new romantic revival (called 'Romo') threatened to break out in 1996, but the groups spearheading the movement largely sank without trace.

See also: new wave

SAM JOHNSTONE

new towns

The modern British 'new town' emerged in the formative years of reconstruction after the Second World War. The national mood favoured a centralist policy to influence the creation of new towns intended to relieve the overcrowding of the great metropolitan centres such as London and Glasgow. Design principles, considering the location of industry and housing with convenient transportation while at the same time preserving the countryside, ensured planned neighbourhoods with social and other facilities in spacious and amenable surroundings. The social composition of the new communities was also a matter for attention with regard to popular concepts of egalitarianism. Directly descended from the proposals put forward by Ebenezer Howard at the end of the nineteenth century, the new town policy evolved gradually from the first garden cities at Letchworth (1903) and Welwyn (1920), and through the propagandist activities of individuals, notably F.J. Osborn, and organizations such as the Town and Country Planning Association. Final endorsement was secured through Sir Patrick Abercrombie's plans for London in 1943 and 1944, which were to form the basis for urban and regional planning for twenty years.

The New Towns Act (1946) set out government procedure for a national policy of town design, specifying the choice of agency for building a town, the legislation required and the principles on which the town should be designed and the plan implemented. Initially, a total of twenty-six new towns were envisaged: thirteen for London, seven for the rest of England and six for Scotland, with populations of between 30,000 and 50,000 people, on sites varying in size from 5,500 to 11,000 acres. Between 1946 and 1949 eight new towns were designated, intended to absorb excess population from the Greater London area. Critics of the new towns drew attention to their totalitarian form, and the consultation process surrounding the designation of the first, Stevenage (1946), was both acrimonious and disputatious. The other towns forming the 'London ring' were Crawley (1947), Hemel Hempstead (1947), Harlow (1947), Welwyn Garden City (1948), Hatfield (1948), Basildon (1949) and Bracknell (1949). Others were designed to serve the special needs (social and industrial) of their areas, including Newton Aycliffe (1947), Peterlee (1948) and Corby (1950). In Scotland and Wales, East Kilbride, Glenrothes and Cwmbran, Monmouthshire, were designated in 1947, 1948 and 1949 respectively. These Mark I new towns are characterized by fairly low densities, and as a central concept adopted subdivision of the towns into almost self-contained neighbourhood units planned around school and community facilities, involving strict land zoning. Based on an American concept from the 1920s, this planning device has fallen into disrepute in recent years.

Cumbernauld (1956), Skelmersdale (1961), Runcorn (1964), Dawley (1964, renamed Telford in 1968), Redditch (1964), Washington (1968), Livingstone (1962) and West Lothian, (1962) were all Mark II new towns designed to meet overspill needs. Proposals for Northern Ireland stemmed from the Belfast Regional Survey and Plan (1962) and included Craigavon (1965), Antrim (1966), Ballymena (1967) and Londonderry (1969). Mark II plans, for higher populations, are more centralized and have to consider the effects of the growing rise of the motor car, either by providing appropriate roads or by the creation of effective public transport facilities. Mark III new towns, including Central Lancashire (1970) and Milton Keynes (1967), were intended for larger populations of 500,000 and 250,000 respectively. They involve the incorporation of several existing large communities and evidence a much greater incidence of private development.

Advocates, including Frank Schaffer, a former official from the Ministry of Town and Country Planning, were resolutely optimistic in their belief in the new towns as a social panacea, but 'new town blues' were reported in the 1950s. Cullingworth's official history (1979) argues that despite their becoming social and planning models for other local authorities to emulate, the new towns did not fulfil expectations in a number of ways. In 1972 they formed a very small percentage of postwar housing. As Gordon Cherry contends, industry does not relocate as readily as people, and the building of dormitory areas in the vicinity of existing manufacturing centres tended significantly to outweigh the building in new towns, so reducing the intended effect on overcrowded cities. Furthermore, new towns are not necessarily meeting, directly, the social need for which they were intended because only a proportion of the residents are drawn from the overcrowded conurbations they were meant to relieve.

See also: town planning

Further reading

Cherry, G.E. (1996) *Town Planning in Britain since 1900, The Rise and Fall of the Planning Ideal*, Oxford: Blackwell.

Cullingworth, J.B. (1979) *Environmental Planning*, vol. III, *New Towns Policy*, London: HMSO.

Schaffer, F. (1970) *The New Town Story*, London: MacGibbon & Kee.

HILARY GRAINGER

new wave

Taking its name from a movement in French literature and film of the 1950s (*nouvelle vague*), new wave was a term used to describe a pop music style which evolved in the late 1970s, parallel to **punk rock**. New wave was for some people a sanitized, more commercially defined form of punk, although it was at one point used as a general term for the stripped down back-to-basics style which included punk. For instance, Phonogram released an LP in 1977 entitled *New Wave* which featured mostly American acts such as The Ramones (pioneers of the American punk sound), Richard Hell and the Voidoids (whose singer first sported the ripped t-shirt and spiky hair style which defined the look adopted by British punks) and Talking Heads alongside British and Irish acts The Damned and The Boomtown Rats (both of whom were seen as punks).

Very quickly, however, the term underwent a transition from a loose description of the latest thing (which in many ways defined itself more by what it was not – that is, old, progressive or **heavy metal** rock, adult-orientated pop, or **disco**) to a commercially defined genre which was a less outrageous, more musically competent version of punk. In America, acts such as Blondie, Tom Petty and the Heartbreakers, Mink Deville and Talking Heads were defined as new wave. In Britain, XTC, Elvis Costello, The Records, Squeeze and The Motors were joined by ex-punks The Boomtown Rats in an assault on the nation's pop sensibilities under the banner of new wave. In both countries, new wave began to infiltrate the mainstream of popular culture and displace some of the older acts, where punk for all its initial impact had failed. Eventually the term fell into disuse because it became too general, taking in any new acts in the early 1980s except heavy metal. Ironically, the early 1980s saw bands such as Def Leppard and Iron Maiden promoted as a new wave of British heavy metal, claiming to replace ageing rock superstars with a lean and hungry, younger variety. In the post-grunge 1990s there was a music paper-based campaign to promote a 'new wave of new wave' with British bands such as Elastica, Smash and others wearing punk and new wave influences on their sleeves, including The Clash, Wire,

Blondie, The Stranglers and so on. This movement was eclipsed by **Britpop**.

See also: alternative music; indie pop

Further reading

Savage, J. (1991) *England's Dreaming: Anarchy, Sex Pistols, Punk Rock and Beyond*, London: Faber & Faber.

DAVE JACKSON

Newell, Mike

b. 1942

Film-maker

Mike Newell is a film director whose first major film, *The Awakening* (1980), was a horror story loosely based on Bram Stoker's *The Jewel of the Seven Stars*. His *Dance with a Stranger* (1985), based on the true story of Ruth Ellis, the last woman to be hanged in Britain, helped form his reputation. *The Good Father* (1987) starred Anthony Hopkins as a man coming to terms with a post-feminist landscape, while *Soursweet* (1989) concerned a Chinese family adapting to cultural and economic life in London. Following *Enchanted April* (1991), a comedy of manners originally made for **BBC**, was the Irish-set 'western' *Into the West* (1992). His most successful film to date is *Four Weddings and a Funeral* (1994), which starred Hugh **Grant**.

GUY OSBORN

news, television

In the UK, news scheduling defines each television station. The **BBC** have claimed the *Nine O'Clock News* slot, leaving ITV to broadcast *News at Ten*. Similarly, the BBC's decision to broadcast half an hour of early evening national news at 6 pm (followed by local news), has led Channel 4 to schedule an hour of more in-depth news at 7 pm. BBC2 has continued to offer news discussion later in the evening and *Newsnight* has become one of its flagship programmes. Television stations are also defined by their newsreaders, who are considered national icons of British identity and authority: the BBC's introduction of the first woman newsreader, Angela Rippon, in the 1970s was therefore in several senses a milestone. So too was the rise of Trevor MacDonald, a black newsreader who has become a figurehead for the preservation of 'correct' English, in the 1980s. Since the early 1980s, BBC and ITV have broadcast early morning news magazine programmes to rival **Radio 4**'s *Today* programme and the daily papers, which people have less time to read than in the days of family breakfasts. In the 1990s, the genre has been successfully spoofed in the award-winning **Channel 4** series *Drop the Dead Donkey*.

See also: breakfast television; current affairs

PETER CHILDS

News International

Part of Australian tycoon Rupert Murdoch's global News Corporation, News International is the biggest and most influential media conglomerate in the UK, and inspires strong opinions and controversy. Currently, its most significant British components are the *Sun*, *The Times*, and the Sky satellite channel (see **BSkyB**). This gives News International a formidable position in the British media industry, a situation that has prompted calls for restrictions on cross-media ownership, notably from the **Labour Party**.

While News International titles staunchly backed the **Conservative governments** over the last twenty years (with accusations that Murdoch has interfered in editorial decisions), both *The Times* and the *Sun* offered grudging acceptances of Labour Party leader Tony Blair. He responded in kind, and Labour's position on cross-ownership was diluted in 1995. This effectively removed the biggest threat to News International in Britain.

But while critics can point to News International's over-dominant market position, there is also no doubting the financial and media acumen of those running it. The *Sun* was ailing badly when News International acquired it in 1971, but it has been the biggest selling UK daily since the

mid-1980s, and is the model followed by other tabloids. *The Times* was equally in decline in the mid-1980s, but News International managers recognized the editorial and policy errors that created that problem, and the paper steadily clawed back both its circulation and reputation. Undoubtedly much of this is due to the backing these papers get; both can survive price wars better than any other paper because they can call on News International's huge resources to back them up, unlike their competitors.

Another significant decision was the controversial move in 1986 from Fleet Street to Wapping in London's East End. This led to a violent and bitter dispute between management and workers, but in the end Murdoch won, and now nearly every national paper operates out of the East End or Docklands, using the revolutionary computer technology that News International installed during the move to Wapping.

News International will continue to generate controversy while it maintains its dominant market position, and rightly so. It will certainly be interesting to see whether a new government introduces stricter laws on cross-ownership, but for many, News International represents a story of true entrepreneurial ability, risk-taking and innovation. The company currently has a wide range of significant plans for future development.

See also: Guardian Group; Express Group; Mirror Group; Telegraph plc

Further reading

Seymour-Ure, C. (1996) *The British Press and Broadcasting Since 1945*, 2nd edn, London: Blackwell.

REX NASH

newsstands and newsagents

Newspapers are still sold from newsstands by street vendors in cities, but the newspaper business in Britain is dominated by W.H. Smith, who control distribution and have their own retail shops. There are a few other national chains including John Menzies, Martin and Forbuoys. Magazines and comics are their other staple sources of income and sales of **National Lottery** tickets (from which they take 5 percent commission). The growth of specialist **comics** shops such as The Forbidden Planet means that fewer comics are bought at traditional mainstream newsstands and newsagents. Recently supermarkets have started selling newspapers and magazines, and this would seem to accelerate the trend away from newsstands and specialist newsagents.

See also: football pools

MIKE STORRY

NFT

After its founding in 1933, the British Film Institute (**BFI**) began to screen programmes throughout the UK for the purposes of education and study. However, these events were of necessity limited and unthematic, and it became important that if the BFI were to be of importance to the wider public, then a dedicated forum was needed. The National Film Theatre provided this focus and fulcrum when it arrived on 23 October 1952; BFI membership immediately rose from some 2,000 to nearly 15,000 by the end of the year. The NFT was originally housed in the Telekinema, a temporary building on London's South Bank that sat 400 people, built as part of the Festival of Britain in 1951. The BFI suggested that the Telekinema be spared demolition and given over for use as a National Film Theatre.

First programmes at the NFT included Norman McLaren's stereoscopic **animation** films and a revival of *Pygmalion*, but a programming policy which sought to balance screen masterpieces, thematic and contemporary trends and highlighting the new and experimental was subject to criticism as its objectives were not always fully realized. This indeed has underpinned the NFT's own quandary/position – the tension between being a theatre for everyone, yet upholding the highest cinematic standards – a tension between high and low art, between art and commerce. The original Telekinema was unable to keep up with the technical advances that were being made, and in 1957 the present theatre under Waterloo Bridge

was opened, to be followed by a second house in 1970. In the late 1980s this was complemented by the arrival of the Museum of the Modern Image (**MOMI**) and the opportunity of observing the workings of the cinema to the public.

Further reading

Forty Years 1952–1992 (NFT Pamphlet).

GUY OSBORN
STEVE GREENFIELD

NHS

The NHS (National Health Service) was among the greatest reforms made by Clement Attlee's Labour government following the Second World War. The Beveridge Report (Sir William Beveridge's 1942 Report on Social Insurance and Allied Services) recommended the introduction of universal comprehensive lifelong cover, replacing the various provisions for public health dating from Victorian times and for personal health insurance and social security introduced by the Liberal government early in the twentieth century, as well as many voluntary and self-help schemes. Labour prioritized these health policy proposals. Under health minister Aneurin Bevan, the National Health Services Act of 1946 took effect in 1948. All UK residents became entitled to medical, dental, optical and related services, and also to medicines, dentures, spectacles and so on, as needed without charge or reference to a contributions record (unlike various social security benefits). Integrating general practitioners (GPs) into the new system caused difficulties, and although most came into the NHS from the start, they retain some contractual independence. Administratively, the NHS is divided into regions, under the Ministry of Health in England and elsewhere under the Secretaries of State for Scotland, Wales and Northern Ireland. The public, apparently not identifying with its health region despite indirect local representation, focuses on its GPs and the nearest hospitals, or on the NHS centrally. A vast organization, the NHS employs one million workers of every category. There are 32,000 GPs,

19,000 dentists and 300 district hospitals. Funding, which Beveridge underestimated, has escalated. Charges for prescriptions were introduced in 1951 by Gaitskell, but 80 percent of patients are exempt, including the young, pregnant women, the unemployed, the chronically sick and pensioners. Attempts to reduce costs – by allocating to GPs certain funds to manage, creating an 'internal market' to promote efficiency through competition between providers of medical services and making hospitals self-governing trusts – were not marked successes. The Patient's Charter (1992) brought scant benefits. Waiting lists for non-emergency hospital treatment remain lengthy. Bevan, foreseeing ever-increasing demands for health services, if not the soaring costs of high-tech medicine, predicted that the NHS would always need more cash, but pioneers like him failed to emphasize that although the NHS would provide treatment free at point of use, taxpayers would have to pay up in the end. Costing £1,700 per household a year (17 percent of government expenditure or 5 percent of GDP), the NHS claims huge resources, but is not expensive by international standards, and its contribution to the nation's health and the relief of suffering is inestimable.

See also: health policies and the NHS

Further reading

Ranade, W. (1994) *A Future for the NHS*, London: Longmans.

CHRISTOPHER SMITH

Nicholas Grimshaw and Partners

A 1965 graduate of the **Architectural Association** and a contemporary of Richard **Rogers** and Norman Foster (see **Foster Associates**), Nicholas Grimshaw created his present firm in 1980. A practitioner of the **high-tech** style, his numerous factory structures include those for Herman Miller in Bath (1976), BMW at Bracknell (1980), Vitra at Weil am Rhein, Germany (1981) and for the *Financial Times* in London (1988). His involvements in high-profile projects include the energy saving British Pavilion at the Expo '92 in Seville, built out

of glass with canvas sides and a water cascade down one elevation. His additions to Waterloo Station (1990–3) show a move away from surface articulation towards a more profound interest in enclosing space.

HILARY GRAINGER

Nicholson, Ben

b. 1894, Denham, Buckinghamshire; d. 1982

Painter

The son of the Victorian painter William Nicholson, Ben Nicholson was one of the best-known British painters of the twentieth century and a pioneer of abstract art. His early work concentrated on still lifes and landscapes, often in a cubist style. In the 1930s he spent much time in Paris, where he met Mondrian, under whose influence Nicholson began to specialize in painted reliefs. This uncompromising and 'unBritish' new work, such as the 1935 *White Relief* in the Tate, used only right angles and circles. Such arrangements put him in the vanguard of the British abstract movement, and he was a member of the influential artists' group Unit One as well as an editor, with Leslie **Martin**, of the constructivist manifesto *Circle*. He later moved on to serene painted abstracts with solid blocks of colour. His first wife, Winifred Nicholson, was also a distinguished painter, and his second wife was the famous sculptor Barbara **Hepworth**, with whom Nicholson lived at **St Ives** in the 1940s and began the local art movement centred there.

See also: Moore, Henry; painting; sculpture

PETER CHILDS

Norman, Barry

b. 1933, London

Film critic

Barry Norman is a witty, popular and sometimes populist British cinema critic, the son of film producer-director Leslie Norman. He is best known for the BBC movie review programme *Film*. Aside from a brief detour during his wilderness years as presenter of *Omnibus* (1982), Norman has stuck to what he seems to enjoy best: writing and talking about movies, through television (for example, *The Hollywood Greats* (1978–9)) and books (*Barry Norman's 100 Greatest Movies* (1995)). Broadcast since 1972, *Film*'s mainstream selection of big hitters and Norman's avuncular presentational style continue to draw steady audiences despite challenges from brash and livelier review shows, and Norman was never usurped as he coasted home in his autumn years to retirement from the BBC in 1998 and a move to satellite.

See also: film reviews

DAVID McNEILL

North of England

The North of England exists by virtue of a North–South Divide. This is often regarded as a variable construct, but the division does have deep historical roots. It was taken by the Romans to be along a line from the Humber on the east to the Mersey on the west, a division that still stands for most purposes. The area to the north was referred to as Britannia Inferior and that to the south as Britannia Superior. Lifestyle, life chances and culture vary remarkably between North and South. The economic base of the distinction is built primarily on heavy versus light industry. The post-Fordist decline of heavy industry has left high unemployment levels in the North. Diet differences, a higher rate of smoking, and a lower degree of general attention to preventive medicine have led to inferior life expectancy and markedly poorer life chances. That said, the North has produced a distinctive popular culture, ranging from the Beatles to Jimmy Connolly. A droll and dry humour, combined with a more communitarian life style, distinguishes the North. These factors, among others, differentiate North and South. In itself, difference and diversity in liberal societies is laudable, but when such difference affects life chances it is a source of some concern. There have

been several centralized initiatives to attempt to even out these differences in life chances.

See also: class system

PAUL BARRY CLARKE

Northern Irish press

The daily newspaper market in Northern Ireland is dominated by the *Belfast Telegraph* (circulation around 130,000), the *Irish News* (47,000), and the *Belfast Newsletter* (32,000), although local versions of British tabloids like the *Mirror* and the *Sun* have made some inroads into urban working-class readerships in recent years. Northern Ireland manages to produce only two Sunday papers: the *Sunday Life* (104,000) and the Northern edition of the Southern-based *Sunday World* (71,000). There are approximately twenty-four weekly regional newspapers and a number of free weeklies, based mainly in the urban centres east of the river Bann. Also worthy of mention are political organs like *An Phoblacht*, the newspaper of Sinn Féin and the *Andersonstown News*, both weeklies which sell in large numbers but do not appear on official industry circulation lists.

The usual readership profiles based on occupation, class and income are complicated in Northern Ireland by political and sectarian allegiances, which colour editorial positions and coverage of everyday Northern Irish life. Thus, the broadsheet *Irish News* has an almost exclusively Catholic/Nationalist readership, and the tabloid *Belfast Newsletter* an exclusively Protestant/Unionist audience. The broadsheet *Belfast Telegraph*, while editorially a 'Unionist newspaper', has a traditionally more moderate perspective on contentious issues like parades and demonstrations than the *Newsletter*, and sells in significant numbers to Catholics. Regional newspapers too, depending on ownership and local readership, often have sharply defined political positions. The *Derry Journal*, for instance, the largest-selling regional newspaper (over 50,000 in two weekly editions) is read by Derry's majority Nationalist population, while the *Londonderry Sentinel*, as the title might suggest, caters mainly for local Protestants.

See also: Scottish press; Welsh press

DAVID McNEILL

Northern Soul

Nothern Soul is better described as a subculture rather than a musical genre. Based around clubs such as the Wigan Casino and the Torch in Stoke-on-Trent, the first flowerings of the scene began in the late 1960s, when clubs in the north of England would hold 'all-nighters' with the DJs playing obscure American rockabilly and R&B records. With the popularity of the Tamla Motown and Stax record labels came a shift in the playlists to a purely 'soul' sound, hence the name. Unknown in the south of the country, Northern Soul clubs quickly gained cult status in the 1970s and 1980s, and gave rise to the enduring popularity of artists such as Jackie Wilson, James Brown and Wilson Pickett.

See also: DJs; soul

SAM JOHNSTONE

Notting Hill Carnival

The Notting Hill Carnival is an annual street carnival held on August Bank Holiday in Notting Hill, a London district with a large black population. Since its inception in 1966, the event has grown enormously from a local celebration of the Caribbean in London to become Britain's largest carnival, attracting one and one-half million people. It attracts all kinds of people, but still retains a West Indian feel. Recent carnivals, especially in the 1980s, have been marred by racial attacks, and have also attracted a heavy **police** presence which has resulted in clashes between police and participants. Politicians vie with each other to claim a media-friendly position alongside the crowds, and in 1997 the new Conservative Party leader, William Hague, declared the carnival the most important cultural event in Britain.

See also: Afro-Caribbean communities

PETER CHILDS

novel

Postwar fiction of the 1950s and early 1960s was characterized by novels of class mobility, sexual adventure and realist aesthetics. Women were still under-represented in publishers' prestigious fiction lists, but influential texts appeared from writers as culturally varied as Anthony Powell, Angus Wilson, Kingsley Amis, George Lamming, Colin MacInnes, Alan Sillitoe, John Braine and David Storey. Their novels displayed a greater interest in culture and society, and concentrated on such issues as class, education, the north/south divide, politics and race. To this extent, in contrast to the prewar modernist writers, they were less concerned with pushing at the boundaries of art and the medium of prose than with exploring the material relations of contemporary social experience. This emphasis is consonant with a social and formal shift in the concerns of the theatre (the kitchen sink dramas of John Osborne or Shelagh Delaney), poetry (Philip Larkin and 'the Movement'), and cinema (the 'gritty northern realism' films of English working-class life, such as *Billy Liar, Room at the Top* and *A Kind of Loving*, all based on recent novels). The 1950s also saw a notable rash of fantasy novels, with the completion of Mervyn Peake's *Gormenghast* trilogy, the start of C.S. Lewis's Narnia chronicles, and the appearance of Tolkein's epic *The Lord of the Rings*: these novels, which were in many ways Christian parables, and their popularity have been seen as a response to and retreat from the war, a subject which has been said to have produced no great British novel (unlike *Catch-22* or *The Naked and the Dead* in the USA).

In the 1960s, experimentalist writers such as Lawrence Durrell were still preoccupied with form (the composition of *The Alexandria Quartet* is based on the four dimensions of space/time) while realist novelists such as Margaret Drabble wrote variously about the 'promiscuous generation' or the national malaise. Other writers such as Anthony Burgess and Iris Murdoch sit between these two trends: Burgess because a novel such as *A Clockwork Orange* experiments in a radical way with both language and social trends, and Murdoch because her novels, in their plots and characterizations, contain both a concern with (at first existentialist) philosophy and a strong narrative drive. Murdoch, the first widely and consistently lauded postwar British woman writer, was at first placed by critics with the 'angry young men' of the 1950s, an indication of how a dominant trend can assimilate other voices. The 1960s also saw the first examples of post-modernist British novels, by John Fowles (*The French Lieutenant's Woman*), Christine Brooke-Rose (*Such*), B.S. Johnson (*Alberto Angelo*), Eva Figes (*Winter Journey*), Andrew Sinclair (*Gog*) and Muriel Spark (*The Driver's Seat*): self-conscious fictions which experiment with previous genres, toy with literary theory, question traditional character representations of a stable personal identity, and complicate organizations of narrative space and time, expressing the liberatory impulse of the decade in prose techniques.

A different group of writers emerged in the 1970s, many of whom now constitute the established names of the 1990s. These were novelists who had not experienced the war, the eclipse of the British Empire or the struggles for teenage identity in the mid-1950s, but had grown up instead with high and popular culture, with the literary tradition and television, rock music, the welfare state and the Cold War. Martin Amis's early novels, such as *Dead Babies*, marked a new ethos for a younger generation: drugs, parties, money, hedonism, consumer culture and a sometimes morbid treatment of sexuality, which was even more apparent in the first short fictions of Ian McEwan. An alternative fantastic, ornate and erotic prose became the recognizable style of Angela Carter in novels such as *The Passion of New Eve*, an allegory of the rebirth and self-fashioning of the women's movement in the 1970s, and *The Bloody Chamber and Other Stories*, a series of macabre, lush, sexualized versions of traditional fairy tales.

Carter combined writing fiction with university teaching and critical writing. This is also the case with David Lodge and Malcolm Bradbury, who produced different varieties of the 'campus novel' in the 1970s. Bradbury's *The History Man* satirized the sexual politics of redbrick universities, while Lodge's *Small World* and *Changing Places* poked fun at literary theory, the international conference scene and transatlantic differences between the glamorous academic world of Euphoria State, California and the low-budget drabness of Rummidge, England. The dominant themes of novels in the decade reflected in alternative ways the postwar shift in social attitudes, sexual mores, religious consciousness and youth movements, together with the growing Americanization of British culture.

Politically, these novels sprang out of the collapse of the liberal consensus in the 1960s. Also from this perspective, Doris Lessing's *The Golden Notebook* and *Children of Violence* quintet combined an intense interest in socialist politics with an investigation into the forces that shaped women's emotional and social lives since the war, while others of her novels appraised her own and South Africa's post-colonial predicament. Also trying to assess the failure of liberalism, Paul Scott dissected the end of Empire in the *Raj Quartet*, a sustained attempt to deal with the colonial legacy that most writers, with the exception of Lessing, J.G. Farrell and Anthony Burgess seemed to want to ignore. Lessing also published allegorical fantasy and science fiction in the 1970s, from *Briefing on a Descent into Hell* to her *Canopus in Argus: Archives* series. Since then, other more popular **science fiction** writers (such as Brian Aldiss, Michael Moorcock, and J.G. Ballard) and fantasy writers (such as Iain Banks, Douglas Adams, Clive Barker and Terry Pratchett) have pushed their genres into different realms of philosophical and psychological extremity, while retaining undercurrents of social comment, and gained cult status alongside the growth of horror movies and science fiction television series, products of the mainstream mass consumer culture which was widely and wrongly anticipated to bring about the commercial failure of the novel.

Fiction in the 1980s, including Graham Swift's *Waterland*, Alasdair Gray's *Lanark*, and Julian Barnes's *A History of the World in 10½ Chapters*, showed a postmodernist concern with history and its narrative construction (discussed as historiographic metafiction) which suggested that analysts of historiography needed to pay attention to the same prose effects as literary critics. Discourse, metaphor, fantasy, narration (different but related explorations in chronology, history and loss came in Martin Amis's *Time's Arrow*, Marina Warner's *The Lost Father* and Ian McEwan's *The Child in Time*). Barnes's earlier novel, *Flaubert's Parrot*, described by John Fowles as 'too good to win the Booker Prize', played similar tricks with **biography**, as did

D.M. Thomas's *The White Hotel* and Peter Ackroyd's *The Last Will and Testament of Oscar Wilde*. Ackroyd has gone on in the 1990s, with his studies of Charles Dickens and William Blake, to contest the boundary between biography and fiction from the other side, introducing overt rhetorical or literary techniques into his life stories. The comic social novel, along the lines of Evelyn Waugh and Kingsley Amis, continues in the work of writers as varied as William Boyd, Beryl Bainbridge and Tom Sharpe. A.S. Byatt, in her tour de force *Possession*, brought together satirical slants on post-structuralist theory, the academic novel, detective fiction, the late Victorian romance and biography. Most significantly, Byatt succeeded in blending the social perspective of the liberal realist novel with a dissection of history, identity, and language more typical of postmodernist writing.

The explicit treatment of heterosexual sex had ceased to be taboo following the Lady Chatterley trial in 1960. Also, from the momentum gained by an increasingly militant movement in the 1970s, **gay and lesbian writing** broke into the mainstream in the 1980s with such authors as Jeanette Winterson, Alan Hollinghurst and Maureen Duffy. Gender theory, body politics, queer theory and media interest in 'hysterical illnesses' all led to increased emphasis on sexuality and identity. Also, a number of new women's presses (see **women's press**) were founded in the 1970s and 1980s after the success of Virago in 1973. Emma Tennant, Fay Weldon and Pat Barker produced assertive but questioning novels that confronted chauvinism, patriarchy and male violence, while a lighter and more lyrical and romantic style of writing was admired in the work of Anita Brookner, Barbara Pym and Penelope Lively. More recent feminist novelists like Zoë Fairbairns and Sarah Dunant have remodelled masculinist genres such as the science fiction novel, detective fiction and crime thrillers. Fairbairns also founded the very productive Feminist Writers group with Sara Maitland, Michelene Wandor and Michèle Roberts.

Britain's only Nobel Prize-winning novelist since the war is William Golding (1983), whose continued concern with the interlocking of the material and spiritual planes was apparent in his trilogy *To the Ends of the Earth*, which began with *Rites of Passage* in 1980. Echoes of this sea-tale are found in Barry Unsworth's Booker Prize-winning novel *Sacred Hunger*, a powerful condemnation of the eighteenth-century slave trade that exemplified the recent shift to a concern with reclaimed histories, colonialism, the black Atlantic, and racial, ethnic and religious differences. The most controversial work of fiction in the 1980s was Salman Rushdie's fourth novel, *The Satanic Verses*, which brought book-burning to Britain's streets and the *fatwa* from Iran. Rushdie's earlier excoriation of Pakistan's history since independence, *Shame*, had been banned in several countries and brought him many enemies, but *The Satanic Verses*, a novel of migrants and post-colonial reinscriptions mainly set in Ellowen Deeowen (London), provoked greater controversy on religious rather than political grounds. A defining moment in itself, the **Rushdie Affair** became the backdrop to Hanif Kureishi's 1995 novel of racial tension and multicultural failure, *The Black Album*. Kureishi also, like Rushdie, considered the meeting of East and West in *The Buddha of Suburbia*, a portmanteau of trends of the 1970s that explored sexuality and politics, glam and punk rock, and suburban and metropolitan attitudes against a hybrid background of ambition and mysticism in Britain's appropriation of India's 'spirituality' but rejection of the transnationals it had actively recruited from the Commonwealth since the 1950s. Kazuo Ishiguro also provided an understated but probing examination of British values in *The Remains of the Day*, a novel which took the formality and traditional hierarchies of his earlier stories set in Japan and transferred them to an analysis of class and nostalgia in England, where repression and master–slave relationships were shown to have infected and stultified both emotional and political action.

Alasdair Gray, Scotland's most experimental contemporary novelist, has been followed by such writers as James Kelman, Janice Galloway, William McIlvanney and Agnes Owen. The most well-known recent Anglo-Welsh novelists are Alice Thomas Ellis and Bernice Rubens, while Northern Ireland has produced one of the most consistently excellent British writers in Brian Moore, whose novel *Black Robe* approaches the Troubles imaginatively and tangentially through a story of settlers and natives in seventeenth-century Canada.

However, the contemporary period is most readily characterized in terms of decolonization and diaspora. For example, Indian fiction in English, concerned with migrant identity and colonial relationships, has revealed some of the most exciting writers of the last fifteen years: Vikram Seth, Ruth Prawer Jhabvala, Kamala Markandaya, Amit Chaudhuri, Shashi Tharoor and Sunetra Gupta. While Steven Connor argues that amid these cultural cross-currents, transnational tensions and international writings, 'it is now hard to be sure of what "the British novel" may be said to consist' (Connor 1996: 27), its examples are constantly being promoted and good fiction is appearing from the likes of Jane Gardam, Adam Thorpe, Jane Rogers, David Wilson, Jane Smiley, Sebastian Faulks and Joan Riley.

See also: popular fiction; readership

Further reading

Connor, S. (1996) *The English Novel in History 1950–95*, London: Routledge (an incisive and wide-ranging appraisal with some excellent short analyses).

Stevenson, R. (1986) *The British Novel Since the Thirties*, London: Batsford (now a little dated, but an immensely readable introduction all the same).

Taylor, D.J. (1993) *After the War: The Novel and England Since 1945*, London: Chatto & Windus (a highly selective account, from an author with an axe to grind about the state of the novel, in the tradition of liberal criticism).

Waugh, P. (1995) *Harvest of the Sixties*, Oxford: Opus (a comprehensive and authoritative review of literature since the 1960s).

PETER CHILDS

nuclear and arms industries and protestors

There have been a number of both general and specific campaigns and protest against the arms industry and particularly nuclear weapons. These have at times focused on individual sites where nuclear weapons have been located. A prime example of this was the women's peace camp established at **Greenham Common** in Newbury, Berkshire, outside a United States airbase where cruise missiles were located. The women-only nature of the camp provided a focus not only for the protest against nuclear weapons but as a positive element of the feminist movement. Other camps were sited at other bases in Great Britain, emphasizing that positive action outside of the mainstream pressure groups could raise and maintain the debate over nuclear weapons.

Organizations such as the longstanding Campaign for Nuclear Disarmament (CND) and Greenpeace have campaigned against the nuclear threat. CND was founded in 1958 and organized an annual Easter march to the weapons research establishment at Aldermaston in Berkshire. Greenpeace have organized numerous campaigns to highlight threats to the environment, including nuclear tests carried out by France in the South Pacific. During this campaign, the Greenpeace vessel *Rainbow Warrior* was sunk by French agents and a crew member was killed.

Other arms protests have concentrated on companies who manufacture and supply weapons, both generally and to particular regimes that have been seen as oppressive. Such action has been taken at company annual general meetings where protestors can, through the purchase of a small shareholding, gain access and ask difficult questions. In terms of popular cultural representations, the issue of nuclear war was memorably raised by Raymond Briggs in *When the Wind Blows* and has also been a focus for popular music and protest. The music festival organized by Michael Eavis at his farm in Glastonbury has for many years donated profits to CND along with other charitable organizations, and there have in the past been a number of artists who have been broadly aligned with this cause including Billy Bragg and Paul Weller. While in the Style Council, as well as playing benefit concerts, Paul Weller included a number of exhortations to join CND on LP sleeves, along with the following quote from a Greenham Common woman which perhaps summarizes the issue: 'We are concerned with the preservation of all life. How dare the government presume the right to kill others in our names?'

See also: Friends of the Earth and Greenpeace

Further reading

Minnion, J. (1983) *The CND Story*, London: Alison & Busby.

GUY OSBORN
STEVE GREENFIELD

NUJ

Originating out of 'chapels' in Fleet Street in the late nineteenth century, the National Union of Journalists (NUJ) is the world's largest journalists' union with over 20,000 members in the UK.

During the 1980s and 1990s the union was faced with a variety of problems, caused largely by the introduction of new technology which irrevocably altered the traditional demarcation lines between journalists and printers and led to several major industrial confrontations. The union also had to counter attempts to shift from collective agreements to personal contracts and ultimately union de-recognition. In addition to the usual union services, the NUJ has also produced a code of conduct which outlines the ethical and professional standards that journalists should seek to maintain.

See also: News International; trade unions

GUY OSBORN
STEVE GREENFIELD

O

office buildings

Office building in the 1960s was characterized by the tall, thin skyscraper, perhaps the most famous of which being CentrePoint at the end of London's Oxford Street. By the 1980s, such buildings were both unpopular and unfashionable (though many were salvaged by remodelling, such as John **Outram**'s conversion of the Harp Central Heating buildings in Kent in 1984). One of the most famous of recent London buildings, Lloyd's high-tech Gothic headquarters developed by Richard **Rogers**, continued the modernist idea of the building as machine and rivalled the best-known American office towers. However, the 1980s saw a large influx of American office architects (such as Skidmore, Owings and Merrill and John Burgee Architects) who could design and construct a steel-framed building together, thus quickening the whole process. The major functional change over the period has been the revolution in technology which means deep-floor plans and high floor-to-ceiling depths.

The 1980s saw a large expansion in office buildings, especially after the deregulation of the London Stock Market in 1986. New offices were required quickly, and had to be of a new kind to convey the right image of the banks and trading houses and to house their computer equipment. An early example is Arup Associates' stern glass and steel building at 1 Finsbury Avenue (1984), which won several major awards, and was built around the increasingly common feature of a central covered courtyard. Elegant modernist (as in David Chipperfield's Brownloe Mews in Clerkenwell) and classical (as in Erith and Terry's Dufours Place in Soho) buildings now sit alongside each other and attempt to relieve the drabness of the 1960s blocks which still dominate many skylines.

In the late 1990s, it has been argued that the new office space has become somewhere to interact and relax as much as work (in the traditional sense). New management ideas means new buildings, and the 1990s emphasis on communication and information sharing requires 'streets', 'hubs', 'oases' and 'clubs' rather than corridors and rooms. A good example is Ralph Erskine's Seagram building, the **Hammersmith Ark**, in West London, full of scenic views, terraces, walkways, towers and penthouses.

See also: art galleries; restaurants and bars; shops

Further reading

Glancey, J. (1989) *New British Architecture*, London: Thames & Hudson.

PETER CHILDS

official secrets and D-Notices

Control of sensitive information relating to national security is governed by the Official Secrets Acts, the first of which was passed entirely in one Parliamentary day in 1911 in response to scare stories concerning German spies. Shortly after this a committee, the Defence Press and Broadcasting Committee, was established to give advice and guidance to publishers. The Committee contains representatives of both the armed forces and the media. It may issue 'Private and Confidential Notices' on specific matters, although these have no independent legal force. The impotence of the government in containing 'sensitive' information was illustrated by the farcical and unsuccessful attempts to suppress the book *Spycatcher*, the memoirs of former British secret agent Peter Wright.

See also: censorship; libel, defamation and privacy

GUY OSBORN
STEVE GREENFIELD

oi

Oi refers to a type of music, closely affiliated to **punk rock**, that was briefly popular at the start of the 1980s. Designed to appeal to disaffected unemployed youth, oi music was fast and aggressive with lyrics that emphasized dissatisfaction with British society. Bands such as the 4 Skins attracted a violent skinhead following (see **skinheads**). Many oi bands drew influence from **ska** and **reggae** and stressed their multicultural origins, although a minority flirted with fascist imagery and became members of right-wing groups such as the **National Front**. These bands, such as Skrewdriver, became known as 'white noise' bands, and developed links with European Nazis.

STUART BORTHWICK

Oldfield, Bruce

b. 1950, London

Fashion designer

Raised in a Dr Barnardo's children's home, Oldfield was fostered and trained by a tailor and dressmaker, Violet Masters, and became one of Britain's most famous designers of evening wear. After designing for Bendel's store in New York and selling sketches to Yves Saint Laurent, he launched his own ready-to-wear collection in 1975 and a

couture line in 1978. His glamorous, ultra-feminine ball gowns and party dresses have made him a consistently popular choice with celebrities, and his 'rags to riches' story made him an obvious role model for many in the 1980s. Famous enough to have appeared as a castaway on *Desert Island Discs*, the London-born Oldfield has become a popular designer with royalty, aristocracy and the showbusiness elite. In 1990 he was awarded an OBE.

TAMSIN SPARGO

opera

During the 1980s and 1990s, opera became popular with a much wider public, probably due to both the activities of organizations promoting opera and the increasing use of operatic themes for films, advertising and sporting events. There remains, however, a dichotomy between the ideas of availability of opera for all by such means as cheap tickets, rehearsal passes and community/education programmes, and the idea that by its very expensive nature opera is only for the few who can afford it. The latter is cited as an argument against the subsidy of opera by the public purse, as opera is not cheap and only a limited number of people can be accommodated at any one performance.

In June 1995, the Royal Opera House (ROH) was successful in its bid for £55m from the Arts Council's **National Lottery** board towards its controversial £213m redevelopment scheme. The ROH made efforts to reach a wider public, including relays to screens in **Covent Garden**'s piazza, which deflected attention away from its need for large sums of money. Along with most arts organizations, it had suffered real-terms cuts in government funding during the 1980s and 1990s.

The ROH was the subject of the BBC2 documentary *The House*, screened in February 1996. The programme generated much interest: '... critics thought it extraordinary that the ROH had let the camera crews in ... by the end of the series, Jeremy Isaacs was thought of as shrewd for doing so' (*Guardian*, 22 June 1996). Doubtless many viewers were surprised by the amount of work behind opera and **ballet** productions and the complexity of the ROH.

Debate continues as to whether opera should be performed in its original language or translated for reasons of immediacy to its audience. The ROH performs in original languages, using subtitles in English. However, the English National Opera (ENO) (which grew from the English Opera Group begun by Benjamin Britten and Peter Pears's circle in 1947 to encourage the development of a repertory of English operas) performs in English, and mounts many contemporary British operas. ENO has along with other companies run advertising campaigns selling opera on its bloodthirsty and seductive elements: one such campaign in 1990 featured suggestive and evocative photographs of percussionist John Harrod and soprano Lesley Garrett. Along with other opera singers, Garrett has brought more widespread publicity to opera through her solo career and media appearances, including a television programme of her own.

Away from London, regional opera companies similarly fought for their survival along with the new breed of smaller companies. Anthony Freud, general director of Welsh National Opera (WNO), commented that, 'Trimming is no longer an option, we've trimmed as much as we can. ... What we can't provide is the ultimate miracle: to exist without the means to exist' (*Classical Music*, 6 July 1996). WNO also goes on tour away from its home in Cardiff: 'We are the provider, and in many cases the sole provider, of opera in the cities we visit' (*Classical Music*, 13 April 1996). The opera began most of its 1990s productions in Cardiff's New Theatre, a venue viewed by musical director Carlo Rizzi as 'terrible'. Much comment was made in the press about plans to build the new **Cardiff Bay Opera House**, and a controversial design by Zaha Hadid, original winner of the international competition. Competition for Millennium Commission funding was perceived from the proposed National Stadium development at Cardiff Arms Park, though eventually a lottery award was made in summer 1996 to Cardiff Bay Development Corporation to fund a feasibility study for a 'millennium centre for the arts' to include a new opera house. Perceived tensions between opera and sport brought about by the various announcements of plans highlighted the differing attitudes towards them amongst commentators and public. Once again, the argument arose that opera is 'elitist'.

Other important opera organizations include Leeds based Opera North, Scottish Opera, Glyndebourne, the D'Oyly Carte (specializing in Gilbert and Sullivan and aspiring to be the nation's light opera company) and Garsington Opera, in addition to the many smaller companies, both professional and amateur.

A movement away from the 'elitist' tag has been made by the now numerous small companies presenting productions in imaginative ways, often in 'miniature', such as those of Travelling Opera, begun by baritone Peter Knapp in 1986. As Knapp said, 'I ... felt that there were many things about the way opera was presented that conspired to keep people away, including the language issue, the scale and the cost, so I wanted to find a way of making it more attractive to a new audience' (*Classical Music*, 6 January 1996). Travelling Opera manages without public subsidy: 'It remains incredibly difficult for us to mount opera at the level we achieve without public money, and revolves around me calling on peoples' goodwill for every show.' For touring performances, special orchestrations are used which only employ a dozen players, and singers double up for choruses. Besides performing in Travelling Opera shows, Knapp has done everything from driving the company van and building the sets to rehearsing the cast: 'If I had been told twenty years ago that within the space of a week I would attend festival performances of two of Mozart's greatest operas, one in an Oxfordshire manor house garden and the other in a Lancashire village church I should have suspected a hoax. ... The growth of enterprising small summer festivals in Britain has been remarkable' (M. Kennedy, 'Opera Reviews', *Sunday Telegraph*, 7 July 1996).

See also: opera singers

Further reading

Adam, N. (ed.) (1993) *Who's Who in British Opera*, Aldershot: Scolar Press.

Boyden, M. (1997) *The Rough Guide to Opera*, London: Rough Guides Ltd.

Milnes, R. (ed.) *Opera*, Wickford: DSB (fortnightly publication).

Sutcliffe, T. (1996) *Believing in Opera*, London: Faber & Faber.

ANDREA MARTIN

opera singers

Singers catch the public's imagination, a phenomenon which is exploited by those marketing them, and singers' photographs often feature on promotional material. Owing to the proliferation of mass media during the late twentieth century, singers in particular amongst musicians have benefited from access to a greatly increased audience. For the big names, this has meant international fame and fortunes. The Three Tenors (Carreras, Domingo and Pavarotti) are probably the best known classical singers in the world following the publicity generated by their 1990 concert linked to the football World Cup.

Classically trained singers move in various directions (musicals, early or contemporary music), although the mainstream career path is opera, oratorio or recital work. The idea of the diva or prima donna, often taken to mean a temperamental but brilliant female opera star, continues and certain singers are given the respect of royalty. Maria Callas is seen by many as a legendary figure, and her recordings are still released and promoted posthumously. Similarly revered are Kirsten Flagstad, Birgit Nilsson, Joan Sutherland and Elisabeth Schwarzkopf, along with younger names Jessye Norman, Kathleen Battle and Kiri Te Kanawa, who became a household name in Britain following her appearance at the wedding of Prince Charles and Lady Diana Spencer in 1981.

The success during the 1980s of boy treble Aled Jones, famous for 'Walking in the Air' from the animated film of Raymond Briggs' *The Snowman*, preceded that of treble Anthony Way in the 1990s with music featured in the television adaptation of Joanna Trollope's *The Choir*. Both productions attracted interest from a new audience for this principally sacred repertoire.

The 'crossover' phenomenon had an impact on singers from the 1980s onward, examples being Malcolm McLaren's use of Puccini's *Madam Butterfly*, and Montserrat Caballé's collaboration with rock group Queen on the single 'Barcelona'. Soprano Lesley Garrett, a star of English National Opera, was involved in several ventures aimed at popularizing operatic repertoire including a CD, *Diva, A Soprano at the Movies* (featuring classical vocal repertoire used in films), and her own television programme. Baritone Bryn Terfel's career took off during the 1990s, including a CD of Rogers and Hammerstein songs amongst more traditional operatic and recital work. He has a strong following who travel overseas to hear him, and like many singers he has his own website.

See also: opera

Further reading

Matheopoulos, H. (1998) *Diva: The New Generation*, London: Little, Brown & Co.

ANDREA MARTIN

orchestras

Britain's orchestras are world-renowned for their high standard of performance, and also their ability to perform well on little rehearsal time. Continental orchestras often have generous rehearsal time in which to perfect pieces, but, through financial necessity, the British must be able to produce a high standard of performance quickly (hence the emphasis on sight-reading in auditions).

Britain has six symphony orchestras in London and eleven regional contract orchestras. The 1993 Hoffmann report investigated the question of dividing scarce Arts Council funds between London's major orchestras, throwing them unwillingly into competition with each other. Arts Council funding in Britain is comparatively low compared to that on the Continent, and the situation affected orchestras such as the London Philharmonic Orchestra, whose members took a clawback/pay cut as a result.

Most of Britain's orchestras are in a difficult financial position, reliant on the generosity of private individuals, corporate sponsors and bank support. They have a firm bedrock of support from numerous friends' organizations which raise money for smaller outgoings, but the principal concern is core funding for day-to-day running expenses. The shortfall has not to date been made available from **National Lottery** sources, as these funds were limited in the early 1990s to capital expenditure. Sponsorship has become vital, and partnerships have developed such as that of the BT Scottish Ensemble with British Telecom. Orchestral concerts and tours can be mutually beneficial to orchestra and sponsor, with both parties gaining publicity and prestige.

The format of orchestral performances has changed little this century. Mainstream concerts generally follow the overture/concerto/interval/symphony pattern, with conductor and players in formal dress. Programme planners try to balance mainstream repertoire (Beethoven, Brahms) with more adventurous contemporary works, although audiences can be nervous of unfamiliar names of composers on programmes. There have been accusations of elitism levelled at the orchestral establishment, despite strenuous efforts by way of community events, 'pops' concerts, pre-concert talks and an increasing amount of education work by musicians.

In spite of the desperate financial climate, several concert halls were built or refurbished in the early 1990s. These include Manchester's £42m Bridgewater Hall (with European and city council funding), Birmingham's Symphony Hall and Liverpool's Philharmonic Hall.

See also: classical music; classical soloists

Further reading

Stern, I. (chair) (1990) *The Evolution of the Symphony Orchestra, History, Problems and Agendas*, London: Weidenfeld & Nicolson (report on the Wheatland Foundation conference).

ANDREA MARTIN

organic art

Despite its seemingly trendy and up-to-the-minute image, the comparison of a work of art to an organism dates back to classical antiquity. In *Phaedrus*, for example, Plato states that a successful oration must adhere to a coherent principle of composition which should determine the order and relation of its parts. Further to this, Plato maintains that in its construction a good oration should be constructed like a living creature, and it must not lack any organ or limb that would cause it to differ from a living form.

In modern times, organic art conjures up visions of fashionable, wholesome, politically correct works of art. It is a term that, alongside organic farming and organic gardening, has returned to carve out its cultural and political niche in the latter decades of the twentieth century. Either rejecting or criticizing post-industrial scientific advances and the manipulation of the natural world, organic art occupies territory that is devoted to a re-enchantment with natural materials and processes.

A close relation to organic art is organic architecture, of which the leading exponent was Frank Lloyd Wright. Organic architecture lays special stress on close relationships between building and landscape. It was an aim that buildings should seem to grow out of the landscape rather than have the appearance of being perched on alien terrain.

Three artists adhering to this cooperative approach to working practice are Andy Goldsworthy, Richard **Long** and David Nash. Goldsworthy has made work using ice and plant matter, Long is renowned for his works that involve the arrangement of stones, while Nash makes carvings from found wood. In all three cases, an important factor is an awareness intrinsic to the work, of ways in which materials taken originally from the environment will continue to interact and relate to the environments in which they are subsequently placed.

Although Goldsworthy, Long and Nash have many contemporaries who share a call of sympathy with a beleaguered natural world, a new generation of artists are also concerned with organic principles. However, unlike their predecessors, artists such as Susan Derges and Daro Montag use what could be perceived as contrary technological references to, for example, photography in order to elude to natural systems and forces at work within the environment. Common to all derivations of organic art, however, are qualities of truth to life and a positive, at times almost reverent, relationship to the natural world.

See also: pop art; sculpture

NICKY COUTTS

Orthodox Christianity

The various Orthodox Churches, whose name etymologically constitutes a claim to doctrinal correctness that is not universally accepted, have over 150 million adherents. Though with only about half as many members as the Protestant churches, who themselves are outnumbered more than three to one by Roman Catholics, they form the third largest branch of the Christian church. The Orthodox Churches developed from Byzantine Christianity, which was centred on Constantinople, the capital of the Eastern Empire, and gradually became detached from Roman Catholicism by disputes over papal authority and differences over theology (particularly the so-called 'filioque' dispute on the question whether the Holy Spirit came solely from God the Father or also from God the Son). Attempts at reunification, at the Councils of Lyons (1274) and of Florence (1438), were abortive. After Constantinople fell to the Turks in 1453, the Orthodox Church in Russia, a country where great missionary efforts had been made since the eighth century, became the largest and most influential congregation. Other Orthodox Churches evolved in Bulgaria and in Greece, whence came the term 'Greek Orthodox', which is commonly used in England. Though discouraged under communism, Orthodox Christianity survived in Russia and Eastern Europe, emerging with renewed vigour under more liberal regimes.

Served by priests who are usually married men, Orthodox Christians revere the sacraments as sacred mysteries. The liturgy is generally conducted in the congregation's own language, though sometimes in archaic versions. Icons – pictures of Christ, the Blessed Virgin or various saints – occupy an important place in Orthodox devotion.

In Britain Orthodox Christianity has long had a presence. The Victorian Bishop Benson derived the popular 'Nine Lessons and Carols' Christmas service from Byzantine sources, mystic hymns from the liturgy were included in *The English Hymnal* (1906), and the Orthodox Church was recognized as being 'in communion' with Anglicanism. Though Archbishop Makarios's role in the Enosis Movement for the union of Cyprus with Greece from 1950 provoked some to wonder whether his political activity was compatible with his calling, criticism died down quite quickly. After the partition of Cyprus following the Turkish invasion, many Cypriots emigrated to Britain, swelling the Greek Orthodox congregations. Numbering under 20,000 in 1975, these had risen to an impressive 88,000 in 1994.

See also: Anglican Church; Catholicism; Jewish communities

Further reading

Doak, M. (1978) *The Orthodox Church*, Exeter: Religious Education Press.

CHRISTOPHER SMITH

out-of-town shopping

Patterns of retailing have been changing in Britain over the last three or four decades. Although convenience stores offering limited ranges of food and domestic products and, particularly, newsagents that also sell tobacco and confectionery still retain significant (though relatively low volume) trade, traditional high streets with their stores under local ownership and others belonging to national chains have lost business virtually everywhere to shopping centres (known as 'malls' when in urban situations). To accommodate a range of shops ranging from large 'anchor' stores (such as Debenhams, House of Fraser and Marks & Spencer), a major food retailer (such as Tesco or Sainsbury), chemist (such as Boots), banks and a variety of smaller specialist shops down to a post office, dry-cleaning outlets and newspaper kiosks, shopping centres require huge premises and, despite efforts (notably at Gateshead's Metro Centre) to promote public transport, they also need vast car parks for customers who often come from quite long distances and hope to return with their car boots laden with purchases. Generally located out of town on greenfield sites (such as Lakeside, at Thurrock in Essex), shopping centres sometimes also participate in large-scale schemes for urban and suburban renewal, on occasion taking over redundant premises and adapting them for new purposes.

Shopping centres develop the supermarkets' concept of one-stop shopping by offering customers facilities for making all their purchases, from the week's food, clothing and footwear to durables such as carpets, furniture and electrical goods, during a single trip to one site, often all under one roof. Customers buy snacks or more substantial meals at a 'food hall' in the course of what is often a half-day visit. Huge crowds and ever-climbing turnover, especially at peak times (for example, the pre-Christmas period) and during sales, demonstrate that people generally like to drive, often in a family group, to a shopping centre; once the car is parked, they can stroll around safely in a cheerful environment viewing a wide choice of goods. Retailers, together with companies that carry out development and lease the premises, such as Capital Shopping Centres, achieve outstanding results.

Doubts have, however, been raised. As declining local retailing has social implications, and in order to protect **green belts** around conurbations, official planning guidance since the mid-1990s has discouraged further out-of-town shopping centres.

See also: supermarkets and malls; town planning

Further reading

Gayler, H.J. (1984) *Retail Innovation in Britain*, Norwich: Geo.

CHRISTOPHER SMITH

outing

Outing, revealing the homosexuality of closeted gay public figures, is a concept that rose from within the American gay movement in the late 1980s in New York and was soon exported to Britain. Thus argues Michelangelo Signorile in his preface to the British edition to his 1993 outing manifesto, *Queer in America*. Both Signorile and

Gabriel Rotello, editor of the now defunct gay lifestyle magazine *Outweek*, are fierce exponents of the strategy, and in the early 1990s the magazine was at the forefront of its defence. Initially, outing was a strategy directed at US politicians who were known or reputed to be gay but who lent support to homophobic political agendas. It was, however, quickly extended to any public figure reputed to be lesbian, gay or bisexual, and keeping quiet about it. For most people, outing came to the fore in 1991 when the anonymous US activist group Outpost flyposted images of stars around New York under the heading ABSOLUTELY QUEER. Most notable amongst these was the Hollywood film actress Jodie Foster, who was later 'outed' by lesbian and gay activists from US groups ACTUP, Queer Nation and the Gay and Lesbian Alliance Against Defamation (GLAAD) at the 1992 Academy Awards, ostensibly for lending her support to *The Silence of the Lambs*, a film which these groups condemned as homophobic for its portrayal of serial killer Jame Gumb.

The pros and cons of outing reached British through a series of debates in the newspapers, on television and in pubs across the nation. No major British star was outed. The hypocrisy of the British press was however exposed by gay Australian duo Faggots Rooting Out Closets (FROCS). Vociferously against outing as the expression of lesbian and gay activism, but only too happy to cast innuendo over stars in order to sell their papers, the British tabloids visibly salivated at FROCS promise to out a selection of British MPs and media figures. Having collected the media together, FROCS revealed their cunning expose – a series of posters with faces filled with the media print of the past few weeks.

See also: armed forces and discrimination; gay liberation

CLARE WHATLING

Outram, John

b. 1934

Architect

John Outram is an original and articulate architect,

trained at the Polytechnic of Central London and at the **Architectural Association**, where he studied before doing apprentice housing and town planning work with the Greater London Council. After toying with **high-tech**, he set up in business for himself in 1973, since when he has developed a number of warehouses at Poyle, Middlesex (1976), Kensall Road, London (1982) and Aztec West, Bristol (1987). Other buildings include the Harp Central Heating headquarters in Kent (1984), a Sussex country house at Wadhurst (1986), and a pumping station for the London Docklands Corporation on the Isle of Dogs (1988).

PETER CHILDS

P

painting

A number of factors make discussion of postwar British painting difficult. The number of different, co-existing styles of painting is one problem. Another, perhaps more serious problem is the fact that painting has not been dominated by an avant-garde at any one time, as has certainly been true of painting in the United States. There has also been resistance to the idea of the avant-garde from some of painting's major figures, notably David **Hockney**. British painting, in common with other forms of art making, is a centralized business, with the London institutions tending to dominate. However, painting is arguably less centralized than **sculpture**, and has competitions such as the biennial John Moores prize (at Liverpool) and Northern Young Contemporaries (at Manchester) having managed to focus attention outside London. There has also been vigorous promotion of Scottish painting since the 1980s, and the Glasgow Museum of Modern Art, which opened in 1996, has deliberately focused on such work.

Two important tendencies in painting can nevertheless be described, defining collectively the practice of painting in the 1960s, and it is against this that current practice should be seen. On the one hand, the term **School of London** has been used to describe a generation of painters who emerged in the 1950s, including Frank Auerbach, Francis **Bacon**, Lucian **Freud** and Leon Kossoff. Diffuse both in terms of style and the institutions with which the artists were associated, the 'school' can however be defined as deriving inspiration from expressionism, as opposed to the focus on the

surfaces of domestic life evidenced by the so-called 'kitchen sink' realist such as John Bratby. Of the four artists mentioned, only one (Kossoff) was born in London, and his background was a Jewish immigrant family in the East End of London. It has often been argued that the distance these artists had from mainstream British culture was partly responsible for the alieneated appearance of their painting.

Bacon's work is probably the best-known: his *Three Studies for Figures at the Base of a Crucifixion* (1944) is regarded as the beginning of his career (the artist in fact destroyed most of the work he made prior to this), and the work in effect functions as a manifesto for the following forty-eight years' work. The paintings usually describe what is in effect a stage, on which a figure, or figures, are shown; the disjunction in treatment between the figure and ground is often striking, the latter being dealt with in a matter-of-fact way while the former is often apparently subject to impressionistic violence. The original subjects frequently derive from old master sources. *Study from Portrait of Pope Innocent X* (1965) is a good example of these characteristics; the original source is the portrait by the Spanish seventeenth-century painter Velásquez.

The work of Auerbach and Kossoff is technically similar, involving the use of heavy impasto (exaggerated in the case of Auerbach), thick, expressionistic brushmarks and strong colour. Their subjects differ, however: Auerbach's work is basically expressionistic London cityscapes, worked up in the studio from numerous sketches, while Kossoff's work focuses on the human figure, although the setting is often made extremely precise. A well-known painting of Kossoff's, depicting a sea of children in a pool, bears the title *Children's Swimming Pool, 11 O'clock, Saturday Morning, August 1969* (1969).

Freud's work, although it has been described in terms of the School of London, is superficially quite different. The subject is the human figure (Freud's models, including the late performance artist Leigh Bowery, have sometimes become celebrities in their own right), but the treatment is extremely precise, with only a little formal exaggeration.

Contemporary with the emergence of the so-called School of London was **pop art**. This tendency in Britain developed out of discussions at the Independent Group at the Institute for Contemporary Arts in the early 1950s. The discussions were explicitly interdisciplinary, but the painter Richard Hamilton played an important part and helped organize the exhibitions *This is Tomorrow* and *Man, Machine and Motion*. His own painting in the late 1950s and early 1960s evidenced a collage technique, in which disparate elements would be juxtaposed. *Hommage á Chrysler Corp* (1957) is one of the better-known examples. Juxtaposing the headlamp assembly of a Chrysler car with Marilyn Monroe's lips and a schematic brassière cup, it is an overt critique of the language of contemporary advertising. Hamilton's work, in contrast to that of American pop artists, often had an overtly political edge: a grotesque portrait of Hugh Gaitskell 'as a famous monster of filmland' was made in response to the Labour party's softening line on nuclear disarmament in the 1960s.

A less critical approach is evidenced by Peter Blake, a student at the Royal College of Art and Hamilton's contemporary. His *Got A Girl* (1962) incorporates already nostalgic photographs of Elvis Presley and the disc that gives the title to the picture above a schematic, but faded stripe pattern. The collaged material is already nostalgic, and the painted part is slightly distressed in appearance, giving a worn look: the piece in other words appears to have a history, an idea at odds with the fresh appearance of other pop art, a comparison especially striking if made with American work of the same period. A work from the same time, *Self Portrait with Badges*, continues this theme, showing

the artists as an enthusiastic consumer of popular – specifically American – culture.

A later generation of artists at the Royal College of Art included Patrick Caulfield, David Hockney, Allen Jones and Richard Smith. None of this work was as politically engaged as (for example) Hamilton's work had been, but it evidenced a much more explicit sexuality than had previously been possible. While still at the RCA, Hockney had painted *We Two Boys Clinging Together* (1961), in which the artist had fantasized that a newspaper headline 'Two Boys Cling To Cliff all Night' referred to the singer Cliff Richard; the image itself is childish and ambiguous, although the homo-erotic content is clear enough. But Hockney's later work, made on the artist's removal to Los Angeles in 1963, is much more explicitly homoerotic: the images of naked men in Californian swimming pools derive from homosexual soft pornography as much as from direct observation.

Hockney encouraged Allen Jones to make use of commercially available fetishistic imagery, which resulted in a notorious series of furniture pieces involving female mannequins. There were also numerous paintings on the same theme, often using airbrushing and other techniques of commercial art. Richard Smith's paintings could initially resemble American colour field painting in their size and soft geometrical forms, but their titles (or example *Product* (1962)) suggested otherwise. Closer examination of the works revealed the source of their imagery in **graphic design**, particularly cigarette packets. Patrick Caulfield, another con-temporary at the RCA, made more explicit references to art history. His *Portrait of Juan Gris* (1963) places the Spanish artist against a yellow background, surrounded by abstract linear forms that seem to refer back to vorticism or constructi-vism. The work is highly ironic: the image of the artist is cartoon-like, shadowless and outlined in black, while the background yellow, applied uni-formly, is a commercially available house paint.

Working outside either of the traditions of pop or the School of London is Bridget **Riley**, whose so-called 'op art' canvases composed of regular patterns of lines produce a highly physical, often disorientating effect on the spectator. Her work had particular success in New York in the mid-1960s, and she won the International Prize for Painting at the Venice Biennale in 1968.

During the later 1960s, and for much of the 1970s, British art production was dominated by sculpture and conceptual art, in common with most parts of the United States and Europe. The painters who came to prominence in the 1960s continued to produce, exhibit and sell work – Hockney might be singled out as having been particularly successful during the 1970s – but little sense remained of painting as a potential avant-garde. However, a reassessment of painting could be said to have occurred at the beginning of the 1980s. There was renewed critical and commercial interest in Auerbach, Kossof, Freud and Bacon, accompanied by the international revival of interest in figurative painting, especially with narrative content, represented by exhibitions such as *A New Spirit in Painting at the Hayward Gallery*, London in 1981. The exhibition featured work by Auerbach and Bacon, as well as new work by Frank Stella, Andy Warhol and Julian Schnabel. At the same time, painters of the same chronological generation were promoted as exemplars of a new style of painting that accepted the conventional limits of the practice, and was generally figurative and sometimes full of literary allusions. Such painters included John Hoyland, Howard Hodgkin, Ken Kiff, Stephen McKenna and John Walker, all of whom were exhibited at the British Art Show in 1984. A new movement in painting was therefore construed around artists who were at mature stages of their careers.

A younger generation of Scottish-based painters, including Stephen Campbell, Jock McFadyen and Adrian Wiszniewski, worked in a similar way, and were often exhibited together with the older artists. Campbell's work is a good example. His large canvases, painted using an eclectic mixture of styles, quote from art historical sources; like much of the painting of the 1980s, the works appear to set up narratives which are then deliberately frustrated. What remains is a play of surfaces, a manner of operation that compares with the novels of Gabriel García Marquez or Umberto Eco, to give examples of two authors who were popular at the time.

If the painting of the 1980s – in common with the sculpture of the same period – had generally accepted the technical and institutional limits of painting, in order to work within it, towards the end of the decade a new type of painting began to emerge which seemed to reopen a type of epistemological inquiry. Goldsmith's College has in recent years been popularly associated with a reconfigured form of conceptual art during the late 1980s, and also produced a number of outstanding painters, among them Ian Davenport and Gary Hume. Davenport's large abstract canvases seem to reconfigure the process-oriented painting of American artists such as Jackson Pollock and, particularly, Morris Louis. A canvas typically comprises a series of parallel stripes made by pouring; the process recalls Louis, and it is no accident that Davenport has frequently been photographed, paint-splattered, in his studio in a manner that deliberately recalls the famous photographs of Pollock taken by Hans Namuth in the 1950s. However the materials (commercial gloss paint, often in garish colours) suggests that the work reads abstract expressionism ironically. Davenport's work seems to reconfigure abstract expressionism for a much cooler, better-informed audience.

Gary Hume's work makes more explicit use of historical sources, so *After Petrus Christus* (1994), included in the British Art Show IV, starts from a fifteenth-century portrait, obliterating detail with crudely-applied gloss paint in garish colours. The graffiti-like marks effectively vandalize the image. A comparable vandalism of painting could be said to be achieved by Chris Ofili, whose works on the theme of a childhood visit to Africa, also included in the British Art show, were stuck with elephant dung.

But these artists, who would identify themselves as painters, are now in some respects atypical. For many prominent artists of the same generation, painting has simply become one mode of operation amongst many. Damien Hirst, better known for monumental installations involving preserved dead animals, has also produced painting, as has Mark Wallinger. British art schools continue to produce painters, especially outside of London, but in the mid-1990s, critical attention seemed to be focused elsewhere. Whether painting will revive as a discrete practice is unclear.

See also: Royal Academy; Tate(s)

Further reading

Arts Council of Great Britain (1995) *British Art Show 4*, London: Arts Council.

Hayward Gallery (1981) *A New Spirit in Painting*, London: Hayward Gallery.

Royal Academy of Arts (1987) *British Art in the Twentieth Century*, Munich: Prestel.

RICHARD J. WILLIAMS

Pakistani communities

Pakistani communities began settling in Britain following the New Commonwealth immigration of the 1950s and 1960s. As migrants from the Islamic nation state of Pakistan (itself shaped by migrant experiences following the 1947 India–Pakistan Partition and the 1972 cessation of East Pakistan (Bangladesh)), Pakistanis comprise a complex transnational religious and political grouping in Britain. Sharing close affinities with other South Asian communities, particularly **Indian communities**, Pakistani communities demonstrate among other characteristics, an intracultural heterogeneity according to rural–urban, regional, caste and sectarian divisions.

Pakistani communities were partly established by pioneer migrants who fought in the British Indian army and navy during the First and Second World Wars. Like other overseas ex-colonial subjects, Pakistanis were lured by the employment, economic and social opportunities presented by severe labour shortages in Britain, while other localized factors such as partition, population and land pressure and the Mangla Dam construction also influenced migration. The 1950s and 1960s 'beat the ban' influx of Pakistani immigrants, encouraged by immigration legislation like the Commonwealth Immigrants Act (1962) and ironically, the work voucher system (designed to regulate the immigrant flow) continued the chain migration instigated by pioneer migrants to consolidate these developing communities. The 'myth of return' was ultimately dispelled for many as temporary sojourners became permanent settlers.

With Urdu employed as the oral and literary language of the Pakistani communities, other familial languages are based on linguistic-regional descent. The majority of Pakistanis descended from regions with migratory traditions such as primarily rural but also urban Punjab, the Mirpur district of Azad (Free) Kashmir (some of whom identify themselves as Kashmiri) and the North-West Frontier. Others included smaller numbers from other regions such as Sind and Baluchistan and Muhajirs (Indian refugees). Pakistani communities settled in largely unskilled labour-specific areas like the Midlands, the engineering and industrial north, and the textile regions of West Yorkshire, Lancashire and Greater Manchester, while other significant communities have formed in Bradford, Birmingham and dispersed parts of London.

Migrant support networks and intricate kinship structures underpinned processes of chain migration among Pakistani communities. Migrants relied on the patronage of other Pakistani migrant relatives and friends to facilitate their arrival in Britain. Initial all-male settlements were gradually superseded by family reunions with wives, children and parents and then the addition of British-born dependants which accelerated concentrated parallel reconstructions of traditional Pakistani culture in Britain.

Pakistani communities are effectively based on the binding but definitionally flexible structural notion of the *biraderi* (fraternity, brotherhood), existing simultaneously as consanguineous kinship systems and socially endogamous networks (in and between) Britain and Pakistan. The *biraderi* is a collective and mutually dependant unit bound by kinship, social, religious or political links, extended through arranged marriages, often with first cousins or other distantly related family members to fortify its endogamous structure. Pakistani families function around the joint household and categorized notions of the extended family which traditionally demonstrate a patrifocal emphasis and patrilineal line of descent. While older and male members exercise superior authority and command greater respect, women have modified their traditional household roles, becoming as inclined as their male counterparts to seek self-employment or employment outside their domestic domain. Customary traditions like purdah and the wearing of the *burqah* and *hijab* are sporadically maintained. *Izzat* (honour, prestige) is the foundational attitudinal and behavioural principal in all social interactions, enacted through a group conscious *biraderi*, a motivating force for achievement and advancement inextricably linked to culturally integral notions of social status and material wealth.

Despite the rejection of *zat* or caste distinctions in **Islam**, some Pakistani communities loosely equate social status through the caste considerations of rural village life and hierarchical divisions of *ashrafs* (nobles), *zamindar* (landowners) and *kammi* (craftsmen and artisans). *Zat* also functions in determining acceptability between prospective marriage partners. Westernization and Ashrafization are seen as potential forces of respective upward socio-economic and religious mobility. Westernization, however, is often posited as a deleterious and morally corrupting power against assertions of a trans-ethnic Islamic identity.

Sectarian factions highlight the majority Sunni and minority Shi'a sects among British Muslims, yet further divisions occur according to followers of, for example, the exegetically and theologically opposed reformist Deobandi, traditional Barelwi, Ahymadiyyahs and other modernist movements. Politics and religion have combined to preserve Pakistani Muslim traditions, the **Rushdie Affair** signifying a pivotal moment in the birth of British Muslim history.

As a Muslim grouping, Pakistanis have acutely experienced the British/Western distortions of Islam and Islamic fundamentalism, although the politico-religious foundations of their communities remain strongly enforced. From the early supportive and advisory role provided for newly-arrived immigrants and settled Pakistanis by the 1957 established Pakistani Welfare Association to the 1963 formation of a National Federation of Pakistani Associations in Great Britain encompassing smaller grassroots organizations, community solidarity has soldered over internal divisions and wranglings among individual leaders to enforce notions of the *biraderi* on a broader community level. Concurrent religious developments have sought to fulfil objectives of cultural preservation, building mosques and creating local Muslim organizations, councils and after-school weekly Islamic educational groups to maintain an active involvement from all sections of the community. The Rushdie Affair led to the formation of the

Muslim Parliament and increased political activity among Muslims intent on asserting their identities against a perceived hostile, exclusionary British state. While many of the largely British-born descendants of Pakistani migrants are redefining their Pakistani identities and traditional heritages within British contexts in realms including family, marriage and career (particularly among young women), some 'British Muslim' youth are reasserting their Islamic heritage in rejection of culturally imperialistic Western influences.

Pakistanis have endured disadvantageous exclusionisms in the social sector especially, for example in employment and housing. Engaged in different accelerations of social mobility and being less economically established than their Indian neighbours on arrival, they have still determinedly negotiated their own social, political and cultural standing in a British context through emphatic kinship, regional/nationalistic and religious roots, whether retaining or rejecting traditionalisms in creating a clearly defined middle ground.

See also: Indian communities

Further reading

Anwar, M. (1979) *The Myth of Return*, London: Heinemann (a pivotal, if somewhat dated text on Pakistani culture).

Shaw, A. (1994) 'The Pakistani Community in Oxford', in R. Ballard (ed.), *Desh Pardesh – The South Asian Presence in Britain*, London: Hurst and Company (a thorough microcosmic study of a Pakistani community in Britain).

SATINDER CHOHAN

Paolozzi, Eduardo

b. 1924

Sculptor

Eduardo Paolozzi influenced the development of **pop art** in Britain during the mid-1950s with his collages made of juxtaposed images taken from magazines and advertisements, which were inspired by dada and surrealism. As a sculptor, he was commissioned to produce a fountain for the

Festival of Britain in 1951. During the 1960s he created large, robot-like, bronze figures whose surfaces were covered in casts taken from mechanical gadgetry. Among his public commissions are the mosaic decorations for the Tottenham Court Underground Station, London, the installation of which was completed in 1985, and the twelve-foot-high bronze sculpture inspired by William Blake's image of Isaac Newton, situated in the piazza of the new British Library which opened in 1998.

See also: sculpture

LUCINDA TOWLER

Park, Nick

b. 1958

Film-maker

Nick Park is the twice Oscar-winning film animator who created Wallace and Grommit, the plasticine man and dog stars of *A Grand Day Out* (1989), *The Wrong Trousers* (1993) and *A Close Shave* (1995). In each film, Wallace's love of gadgetry and enterprise set the loveable duo off on a comic adventure in which northern domestic common sense must overcome the threat of cyber-culture. The detailed attention to cinematics, the wealth of intertextuality and the superb parody of action adventure films provide some of the distinctive features of the animator's engaging postmodern style. The films, supported by strong video sales and merchandising, have demonstrated international appeal across all age groups, and have sold in over seventy countries.

See also: animation

BOB MILLINGTON

Parker, Alan

b. 1944, London

Film-maker

Alan Parker began his career directing commercials such as the famous Joan Collins 'Cinzano' advertisements. In 1977 he made his first mainstream film, *Bugsy Malone*, a 1930s children's gangster movie, after which he directed a range of films which have only their style in common: from *Midnight Express* (1978) through *Fame, Angel Heart, The Wall, Mississippi Burning* and *Birdy* to *The Road to Wellville* (1994) and *Evita* (1996). Parker has been accused of abandoning Britain for Hollywood in the 1980s but with *The Commitments* (1991) he made a praised and profitable film outside the USA. Parker has arguably been the most commercially successful British director over the last twenty years: a critic of British realism, he makes films that are technically impressive but often melodramatic and sensationalist. To general astonishment, in 1998 he became chairman of the **BFI** and was widely tipped to take over the Labour government's new Film Council.

PETER CHILDS

parliament

The British parliament has its origins in the thirteenth-century baronial councils. It is now a bicameral chamber that includes the monarch or the monarch's representative. Currently its full name is 'The Queen in Parliament', and it is a sovereign body that covers England, Wales, Scotland (since 1707) and Northern Ireland (since 1922). Under a variety of treaties, some of its powers have been ceded to the European Union. Some of its prerogatives have also been ceded through international treaties such as the United Nations Declaration on Human Rights.

The House of Commons is the primary democratic chamber. It is composed of 651 directly elected representatives who must seek re-election at not more than five-year intervals. The House of Commons is presided over by the Speaker, whose responsibility it is to make certain that the conduct of business in the House is in accordance with its own conventions and rules.

The second chamber is the House of Lords. This is composed of approximately 1,200 peers, both life and hereditary. In addition, the two archbishops (Canterbury and York) and twenty-four bishops sit, as do the Law Lords. The House is presided over by the Lord Chancellor. The House of Lords can amend and delay bills that have been passed in the House of Commons. By convention, it will not delay the Finance Bill or any bill that was included in the manifesto of the governing party in the House of Commons. Should the House of Lords delay any bill (as with the lowering of the age of consent for homosexual sex to sixteen in 1998), the Commons can ultimately reject this delay.

There have been many calls to abolish the House of Lords. Hitherto such calls have been rejected, as there is a clear democratic advantage in having a revising chamber. It is likely that the constitutional reform currently under discussion will retain the second chamber while removing the voting rights of hereditary peers. It is unlikely that any reform will significantly strengthen the legitimacy of the second chamber, as that would weaken the House of Commons, a move that is likely to be politically and culturally unacceptable.

See also: Conservative governments; democracy

Further reading

Punnett, R.M. (1994) *British Government and Politics*, 6th edn, Dartmouth: Aldershot.

PAUL BARRY CLARKE
SVANBORG SIGMARSDOTTIR

Penrose, Roger

b. 1931, Colchester

Mathematician

Roger Penrose is a mathematician with radical views about the relationship between quantum physics and consciousness. He, like **Dawkins** and **Hawking**, has been able to interest and influence a wide audience through his lucid and compelling style. In his widely read books, *The Emperor's New Mind* and *Shadows of the Mind*, he examines consciousness and the human mind from the perspective of the laws of physics and binary computers, and concludes that classical computers lack some fundamental aspect of function found in human and other animal brains. His views are contentious amongst the artificial intelligence (AI) community, whose major paradigm is that increasing complexity of computers can or will lead to consciousness.

PETE SHETERLINE

pensioners

The state pension is paid to anyone who has made enough National Insurance contributions in the course of their working life. Retirement age in the UK is still 65 for men and 60 for women, although in 1990 the European Court of Justice ruled that there should be no discrimination between men and women with regard to pension schemes (in the UK, a common retirement age of 65 is being phased in). There is additionally a perceived lack of cultural discussion of retired people's lives, which figure little in mainstream television programmes. This led Richard Ingrams to found *The Oldie* magazine in the late 1980s, and others have mounted their own protests. For example, in January 1998 near South Kensington underground station, the artist Melanie Manchot displayed five six-by-three-metre posters of her 66-year-old mother in her underwear with the caption 'Look at you loving me', to counter the marginalization of older people. Unlike the USA, Britain has no anti-age discrimination law, yet one-third of the population will be over 60 by the year 2000, and many are both able and wanting to work (as witnessed by the success of stores like B&Q and Sainsbury, which have actively recruited people over retirement age).

See also: baby boom

PETER CHILDS

performance art

As a category, performance art is hard to define, as it has referred to an extremely wide range of practices. If most have involved artists acting in real time and space in a planned event, there has been enormous variation in the duration of the event, choice of site, number of participants, ancillary equipment and intent.

The widespread use of the term in Britain dates

from the early 1970s, and the general acceptance of live performance in art schools, museums and galleries dates from the same time. If British performance art was late to develop, it has nevertheless gone on to have an international impact, and it continues to do so. However its audience is small, in comparison with New York, where performance art has enjoyed genuine popularity.

A well-known early work of British performance art is *Underneath the Arches* by Gilbert and George (1969), in which the pair, their faces painted gold and dressed in their trademark identical suits, one carrying a walking stick, the other a glove, stood on a table and moved around stiffly to a recording of the Flanagan and Alan song of the same title. The piece was performed a number of times internationally. The early 1970s saw considerable activity in the field. Bruce McLean and the Nice Style Pose Band (1972–5) developed 999 proposals for 'poses', performed by the group at assorted locations over the three years of its existence. Meanwhile Stuart Brisley was staging far more confrontational works, including *And For Today, Nothing* in which Brisley spent two weeks motionless in a detritus-filled bathtub. Other important artists of the 1970s include the Ting Theatre of Mistakes, and Genesis P. Orridge and Cosi Fanni Tutti, who alternated between performances as COUM Transmissions, and the punk band Throbbing Gristle.

Since the 1970s, performances have often featured the artist motionless in a gallery or museum, in work sometimes known as live art. Examples include Stephen Taylor Woodrow's *Living Paintings* (1986), Tilda Swinton's *Matilda Swinton (1960–)* (1996), the latter presenting the sleeping artist in a glass case for the duration of an exhibition. By contrast, the group Index have staged events which recall New York happenings in their manipulation of the general public and the urban environment. Performance art remains an important strand of British art, if somewhat overshadowed by **painting** and **sculpture**.

See also: ballet; modern dance; opera; performing arts on television; physical theatre

Further reading

Goldberg, R. (1979) *Performance Art*, London: Thames & Hudson.

RICHARD J. WILLIAMS

performance poetry

Broadly, performance poetry is any poetry delivered effectively in performance; narrowly, it is poetry composed specifically for performance rather than for the page. With the spread of literacy, Britain had lost any earlier tradition of poetry performance, and modern, essentially urban, performance poetry began in Britain in the late 1950s. Influenced by US jazz and beat poets such as Allen Ginsberg, mostly young poets began to perform their work at jazz clubs and cafes, both with and between the jazz. From this unlikely initial setting, pop poetry grew to become a major part of 1960s counterculture. Adrian Mitchell (b. 1932) became an important political voice, speaking poems with a directness, outrage and musicality that drew on Brechtian drama as well as rock 'n' roll.

Meanwhile in Liverpool, during the rise of Merseybeat, Adrian Henri (b. 1932) was bringing together the existing poetry scene with multi-arts events. These events, more accessible than the arts 'happenings' in the USA, led poetry performances to incorporate elements of drama, satire, comedy and music as well as the visual arts. Roger McGough (b. 1937) delivered his funny-sad poems with sharp satirical wit, performing both solo and with The Scaffold, while Henri formed the poetry-and-music band The Liverpool Scene, and Brian Patten's (b. 1946) lilting hypnotic delivery brought a particular emotional intensity to his lyrical poetry. Henri, McGough and Patten performed widely with the poetry–music–comedy roadshow Grimms into the early 1970s, and still command a wide audience.

With the rise of **punk rock**, **new wave** and **reggae** music in the mid-to-late 1970s came new styles of performance poetry, mostly with a fresh political emphasis. John Cooper Clarke mixed high-speed wit and scorn with frequently surreal imagery. Joolz delivered aggressive urban poetry to the music of New Model Army. Of the reggae and dub poets, Linton Kwesi **Johnson** (b. 1952) first achieved prominence in the late 1970s, followed in the 1980s by Benjamin Zephaniah and Levi Tafari.

During the 1980s and 1990s, the initial flourishing of alternative cabaret and comedy venues prompted more comedic and dramatic approaches. John Hegley combines the roles of poet, singer and comedian; Henry Normal and Lemn Sissay both use comedy, and Ian McMillan blends surrealism with satire. The group Atomic Lip frequently act out their poetry and interweave their four voices, a development of the vocal blending used by rap crews since the original 'rapid poetry' of The Last Poets. 1990s performance poetry promoters include Apples & Snakes (London), the Dead Good Poets Society (Liverpool), Morden Tower (Newcastle), and the Edinburgh Writers Association.

See also: black performance poets; Johnson, Linton Kwesi; poetry slams

Further reading

Forbes, P. (ed.) (1997) *Poetry Review* 87(3), special issue on performance poetry.

DAVID BATEMAN

performing arts on television

Television coverage of performing arts is varied. The **BBC** is far more likely than independent television companies to screen ballet, opera or classical music, and BBC2 is its preferred channel for these programmes. Some avant-garde work is produced on **Channel 4**. Other stations' 'high culture' presentations extend only as far as good quality made-for-television drama (Jane Austen/George Eliot) and arts programmes such as *The Late Show*. Populist stage shows like *Riverdance* are televised, and *Later With Jools Holland* contains a varied and impressive mix of live music. Regional channels of the BBC and ITV (especially Welsh ones) and also **S4C** often have operatic and orchestral company performances. The annual Eisteddfod has full coverage on S4C. Satellite television presents very little in these programme areas, though there is an arts channel on cable television.

Such ballet as appears on television is confined to BBC2 and Channel 4. The latter tends to deal more with contemporary dance, showcasing such companies as Spiral Dance and offering ten-minute dance slots, but BBC2 also shows original work. For example, in prime time in 1998 it screened *Urban Clan* by Aboriginal choreographer Stephen Page, performed by the Bangarra Dance Theatre of Sydney, and Maguy Marin's interpretation of *Coppelia*.

One of the most notorious television interventions into the world of opera occurred with the showing of *The House: Inside the Royal Opera House Covent Garden* in 1995. This fly-on-the-wall six-part documentary was made by Double Exposure for BBC2, with the permission of the then director Jeremy **Isaacs**. Critics felt he had been naive in allowing this to happen, as it exposed the inefficiencies and internal wranglings of a bastion of high culture at a time when it was under attack for its supposed elitism and blithe disregard for commercial considerations.

Glyndebourne, by contrast, was thriving, and unlike the homeless Royal Opera House it rebuilt its auditorium on time, to budget and without government subsidy. Channel 4 under Michael Grade televised the acclaimed production of Janáček's *The Makropoulos Case* from there in 1996. Wagner's *Ring Cycle* was also shown in 1997.

As regards **classical music**, events like the Young Musician of the Year and the Leeds Piano Competition are always covered on television, and a staple of BBC1 programming is the Promenade Concerts televised from the Albert Hall, London, hosted in 1998 by James Naughtie. The annual broadcast of the Last Night of the Proms, with its staple fare including 'Jerusalem', 'Rule Britannia' and 'Land of Hope and Glory', is one of the rare occasions when high popular culture and television coincide.

See also: ballet; modern dance; opera; physical theatre

MIKE STORRY

philosophy

Philosophy (from the Greek *philo* (love) and *sophia* (wisdom)) in British culture has undergone a series of revolutionary changes since 1960. Until recently, English language philosophy was dominated by analytic and linguistic philosophy based on works by Bertrand **Russell**, G.E. Moore, Wittgenstein and the ordinary language philosophy of Austin. The early logical positivist tradition rejected metaphysics as a genuine line of philosophical enquiry, arguing that its findings were speculative, inconclusive, unverifiable and, thus, meaningless. Instead, philosophy was allied with empirical science. Its task was identified as simply to derive meaning through the logical analysis of concepts and the language we use to express, apprehend and classify them. Oxford linguistic philosophy, spearheaded by Gilbert **Ryle**, A.J. **Ayer** and J.L. Austin, was ascendant in Britain until the mid-1960s.

Before the second half of the century, this analytic approach shared almost no intersection with continental philosophy. The principle strands of continental thought concerned existentialism (Kierkegaard, Sartre), phenomenology (Husserl, Heidegger, Merleau-Ponty), **structuralism** (Saussure, Levi-Strauss, Chomsky) and critical theory (Lukacs, Adorno, Marcuse). While radically divergent, such continental philosophers generally emphasized contextual relations of interdependence and the consequent requirement of apprehending the structures of the world in their totality. These approaches, while far removed from the formal, abstract, atomistic methods of English language philosophy, challenged that model by introducing global context and the 'linguistic turn': the view that the world might be shaped by rather than make language.

In consequence, Anglo-American philosophy is no longer restricted to mere conceptual analysis. Its convergence with continental philosophy has resounded throughout all the disciplines of social science in an attempt to come to terms with the particularity, complexity and undecidability of the many and varied social contexts in which we live. This constitutes a serious challenge to canonical philosophers such as Plato, Aristotle, Hobbes or Locke, for the death of universalism has injected the particularistic fringes of philosophy with new vitality while leaving mainstream philosophical disciplines such as metaphysics and epistemology either discredited, irrelevant or incredulous.

The linguistic turn revolutionized the way in which we view the world and the place of philosophy within it. Most significantly, social and cultural worlds are no longer seen as external, real and analytically objective objects, but as something in which we participate. Philosophy is now regarded as part of our cultural enterprise rather than a mere examination of that culture.

Engagement in philosophy no longer requires an ivory tower retreat and is part of any thoughtful, world-engaging enterprise. If philosophy dwells in the world itself, it asks only that we engage in the world, that we immerse ourselves in our particular culture, and that we perceive the meanings, values and possibilities in a multiplicity of diverse ways of life. This permits radical and intriguing questions from cultural fringes to have a legitimacy and a voice that was hitherto excluded or silenced.

Further reading

Bunnin, N. and Tsui-James, E.P. (1996) *The Blackwell Companion to Philosophy*, Oxford: Blackwell.

PAUL BARRY CLARKE
EMMA R. NORMAN

phone-ins and chat shows

Chat shows involve a regular presenter interviewing various celebrities in a consistent format. Though guests appear to promote products, the interview focuses upon a gentle, entertaining revelation of their humanity. The successful host skilfully mediates between naturalistic conversation and a genuine search for personal insight. On radio, Wilfred Pickles interviewed guests informally (*Have A Go*, 1948), but it was Michael Parkinson who popularized the chat show as a television genre, succeeded by Terry Wogan, whose eponymous show ran for fifteen years. *Desert Island Discs* (**Radio 4**) is the longest running radio chat show, probably due to the flexible interest of its invariable question. Current daytime chat shows (such as *This Morning ... With Richard and Judy*, ITV) foreground friendliness and do not attempt unpleasantly personal questions. However, some hosts entertain by exploiting the genre's pseudo-revelatory nature to ask truly difficult questions, and it is then that the format segues into television comedy. Clive Anderson displays his quick wit at his guests' expense (*Clive Anderson Talks Back*, 1990), and Edna Everage's guests are foils to her comic routine. Caroline Aherne's *Mrs Merton* (1995) is the most recent in this tradition. Steve Coogan invents fictional guests to heighten the incapability of Alan Partridge, his creation (*Knowing Me, Knowing You*, 1995).

Phone-ins also rely upon the creation of a familiar register. A radio or television presenter invites the audience to contribute live to a programme. *Call Nick Ross* on **Radio 4** debated more cerebral issues, but in the entertainment sector of the phone-in, callers pose questions to celebrities or answer questions themselves for prizes; on other programmes those with emotional problems are encouraged to phone, the anonymity of the exercise allowing voyeuristic discussion of personal trauma. On local radio, this inexpensive genre is continually popular. Public interest in the private lives of both celebrities and nonentities means that chat show and phone-in techniques now define many presenter-led shows; *Kilroy!* and *Vanessa* combine public discussion of social and personal problems with chat show style interviews, as does *The Time … The Place*, a live studio debate (ITV). The division between viewer and presenter is becoming deliberately blurred to promote a contemporary, spontaneous image. This seems particularly true of **breakfast television** and radio. Chris Evans incorporated an open phone and fax line into his shows (*Radio One Breakfast Show* and *The Big Breakfast*, **Channel 4**) rather than setting aside a particular time for phone-ins.

See also: daytime television; talk shows

SARAH CASTELL

photography

The postwar euphoria of victory combined with an ongoing austerity of rationing in Britain gave way to a new optimism for the children of what was to become known as the baby-boomer years (see **baby boom**). In its attempts to both rebuild and present itself as a modern nation, British culture was to undergo a revolution of American origins, which found its expression not only in the more traditional arts of **painting** and **sculpture** but within design, architecture, photography and publishing and the new media industry of television. At the beginning of the 1960s the new global communications were just beginning; but by 1969, NASA had landed men on the moon, who photographically recorded the event and sent video images back to earth via a satellite link.

Photographers of the 1960s may be linked, but not exclusively, with four main consumer growth areas of the 1960s: fashion (for example, David Bailey, Terence Donovan and Brian Duffy); **pop and rock** music (Robert Freeman's pictures of the Beatles); photo journalism (Tony Ray-Jones, Don McCullin, Larry Burrows, Tim Page); and portraiture (Jane Bown, Bill Brandt, Lord Snowdon).

A central theme of photojournalism and portraiture in the 1960s included social life from both the successful, wealthier end of society and the less fortunate, poorer members of British society. For example, the growing royal family and the Queen's visits to the British colonies was a popular theme amongst most daily newspapers and journals. The Queen's brother-in-law, Lord Snowdon (previously Anthony Armstrong-Jones), became a court photographer as well as maintaining a career of more general portraiture and magazine work. Other photographers like Don McCullin specialized in photojournalism which was confrontational and often included images of destitution and dereliction. This included photographs of one of the poorest parts of London in McCullin's 1961 series *East of Aldgate*, used by director Michaelangelo Antonioni in his film *Blow Up*, although paradoxically, the character of the photographer in the film, Thomas, was based on the personality of David Bailey. Bailey was interviewed in 1964 by Francis Wyndham, and Antonioni used the text as the base for the part of Thomas.

Photography was about to undergo an important status shift coinciding with the birth of the *Sunday Times Magazine* in 1962 and the overhaul of *Queen* magazine. Previously, as Cecil Beaton remarked, the photographer had been regarded as 'a sort of inferior tradesman'. The publishing houses and magazines were owned by Oxbridge graduates, but the new photographers were bridging traditional class boundaries; many of them, like David Bailey, were from working-class east London backgrounds. Also, artists such as Richard Hamilton began using photomontage techniques as part of their work, thus challenging the traditions of both painting and photography and often as a critique of fashion magazines and advertising. The exception to the encroaching use of colour in photography was within landscape and documentary photography, where black and white was used as a specific formal composition (for example, by Bill Brandt), or was to be connoted with realism within the documentary tradition.

The fighting that had begun in Northern Ireland between Loyalist Protestants and Republicans in 1969 at first went largely unreported. However, when the first British soldier was killed on 31 October 1970, this made headline news in Britain. The public, through newspaper reports and photographs, had suddenly been made aware that the situation in Northern Ireland was in fact war. Similarly, when the Vietnam war ended in 1975, the *Daily Mail*'s headline on Wednesday 30 April 1975 was 'THE END', with a photograph captioned: 'Americans and refugees clamber to an airlift helicopter'. Tim Page, one of many British photographers to record the war in Vietnam, left home at fifteen and did not return until twenty years later. He was later to publish his experiences in detail in *Tim Page's Nam* and *Page After Page*.

Changing attitudes to photography were also expressed by advertising agencies. In the late 1970s, cigarette manufacturers like Gallaher began to consider the image itself – without a caption – as a means to selling Benson and Hedges Gold and Silk Cut cigarettes. The adverts used a rhetorical language of metaphor, rebus and metonomy, incorporating a strong use of colour, such as cut purple silk or gold dust. The first of these new adverts appeared in 1978, using the photographs of Adrian Flowers.

By 1973, the young photographer Martin Parr was beginning to have his work seen and published. This was classified as 'new documentary' photography. 'New' referred to the use of colour and a sense of humour. His photographs examined the eccentricities of the class system and British obsessions with leisure time, hobbies and DIY. In contrast, old monochrome documentary (for example, that of Chris Killip and Graham Smith) reaffirmed themes of formal concerns together with a mythology of the British northerner.

A topical concern for the environment in the 1970s was reflected in landscape photography. The exhibition *The Land* was presented at the Victoria and Albert Museum in 1975, and the 1970s also saw the publication of the work of John Davies, Paul Hill and Fay Godwin. John Davies's work sought to revive the tradition of landscape photography, both rural and urban. The work of both Paul Hill and Fay Godwin attempted to describe and preserve a specific place, and also draw attention to the encroaching legal and illegal restrictions of access by landowners. These included farmers, the Defence Department, new water schemes and government road-building operations.

Photography education was also starting to change. In the mid-1970s, the conceptual artist Victor Burgin was appointed to the photography degree course at the Polytechnic of Central London (PCL, now the University of Westminster). His enthusiasm for reading as well as photographing established a new way of teaching photography based on the writings, amongst others, of the semiologist Roland Barthes, the psychoanalyst Sigmund Freud and feminist writing. Students on the course were encouraged to analyse photographs within a structure of context and meaning. Graduates from this course in the 1980s included Jo Spence (one of the founder members of Camerawork), Olivier Richon, Mitra Tabrizian and Karen Knorr. In 1980, Victor Burgin edited *Thinking Photography*, which included essays by himself, John Tagg, Umberto Eco and others.

An enlightenment within photography characterized the 1980s, reflecting the new teaching at PCL and other colleges. Slowly decreasing were galleries that only showed white, male documentary photographers; instead, these were being replaced by more radical venues that attempted to encourage a wider representation of photographers previously neglected by traditional photo galleries (for example women, gays and lesbians, ethnic minorities and the disabled). A new audience was also sought and from a broader section of the population.

Family album photography began to be taken seriously partly resulting from the work of Jo Spence (1934–92) and her autobiographical analysis of childhood and adolescence using family album photographs. She also pioneered what became known as 'photo therapy' with Rosy Martin, photographing staged memories from their family histories as a way of confronting labelled identities. In 1982, Jo Spence was diagnosed with breast cancer and was concerned about the existing attitudes and treatments. After consultation with alternative therapists, she decided to take responsibility for the treatment of her illness, including the use of photo therapy. Her book *Putting Myself in the Picture* was published in 1986 (her later work *Family Snaps* was published in 1991).

Other photographers, writers and artists also began exploring issues relating to bodily representation including sexual identity and its stereotyping, **pornography**, erotic photography, the ageing or sick body, sexual fantasy and desire, and voyeurism and fetishism. Helen Chadwick's (1953–96) work from the 1980s asked questions of identity, sensuality, endurance and perhaps most poignantly, transience: she was to die suddenly, aged 43. Her work incorporated large, photocopied images of herself and photographic references to meat, intestines and laboratory samples of her own bodily tissue. She was shortlisted for the Turner Prize in 1987 after her exhibition *Of Mutability* at the Institute of Contemporary Arts (ICA) in 1986. Her book *Enfleshings* was published in 1989.

In 1988, Aperture published *British Photography: Towards a Bigger Picture*. This contained work by photographers already mentioned plus Keith Arnatt, Hannah Collins, Anna Fox, Paul Graham, Tim Head, Susan Trangmar and others.

Gradually women, gay and ethnic minority artists were also finding publishers for their work. The **Arts Council** realized the dearth of published material from these photographers and attempted to correct the under-representation. Black photographers like David A. Bailey, Sunil Gupta, Ingrid Pollard, Maud Sulter and others saw the desperate need for better and broader representation of black arts in Britain and began curating their own shows. The *Essential Black Art* exhibition in 1988 included the work of photographer Zarina Bhimji. *The Other Story* was first shown at a major public arts venue, the Hayward Gallery, London in 1989; it contained the work of painters, sculptors, video makers and photographers.

The war in Northern Ireland, or the 'Troubles', as it became known, continued into the 1980s and 1990s. The photographer and artist Willie Doherty's work explores issues of cultural difference in Northern Ireland. His photographs often refer to surveillance, borders, invasion and the dialogue of misinformation from both sides. Some photographs incorporate text printed onto the surface. His exhibition *Unknown Depths* began at the Ffotogallery, Cardiff in 1990 and then toured to Glasgow, Derry and London. Another work, *Same Old Story*, was exhibited at Matt's Gallery, London in 1997.

The interest in the family and the photographing of children (including issues of child pornography), was to continue into the 1990s including the exhibition *Whose Looking at the Family*, curated by Val Williams at the Barbican Gallery, London in 1993. The photographers Nick Waplington and Richard Billingham were both to produce work which recorded life in three very different families. Nick Waplington began photographing two families on a council estate near Nottingham in 1987. In 1991, some of the photographs were published and exhibited as *Living Room*. He said in 1994:

When I began the project, I'd seen pictures of housing estates, black and white pictures of the old school. The people in them looked like victims, and I wanted to show that they're not. They're not being beaten. These people are fighting back.

His intention was to portray a more positive and caring attitude to family life, the results being often gently humorous, but within an overwhelming subtext of **poverty**.

Richard Billingham's work *Ray's a Laugh* was also published in 1996 as a book. The explicit snap shots of his immediate family, including his father Ray, are taken inside his alcoholic parents' flat. They also include pictures of the family dog and cat and his brother. They were originally intended as references for paintings when he was at art college and still living at the family home. Since then, he says he continues to photograph 'as an attempt to comprehend myself and them more fully'.

In 1993, Hannah Collins was shortlisted for the Turner Prize. By the mid-1990s noticeable numbers of women art and photography graduates were both showing and selling their work in photography venues and public or commercial art galleries. In London this was typified by Goldsmith's College graduates. Artists such as Jane and Louise Wilson, Bridget Smith, Gillian Wearing, Catherine Yass, Tacita Dean, Sarah Jones and Virginia Nimarkoh were already meeting dealers and getting attention from curators and critics before leaving college. This defied the usual system of graduating students (especially women) having to wait passively for curators and dealers to become interested in them. Their work, especially Gillian Wearing's, possessed a raw vibrancy coupled with an attitude which insisted the work be noticed. In 1997 the shortlist for the Turner Prize was all women, including that year's winner, Gillian Wearing.

Further reading

Design Council (1987) *Best of British: Design and Photography*, Geneva: Rotovision.

ALEXANDRA McGLYNN

physical theatre

Physical theatre focuses on the visceral qualities of theatre, and is characterized by an emphasis on the actor's body as the primary sign; it is rooted in the belief that the actor is the 'total resource' for 'total theatre'. Physical theatre is a broad church which includes hybridized forms previously labelled 'visual theatre' (The People Show), 'dance-drama' (DV8), 'mask theatre' (Trickster), which demonstrate the mutations and cross-pollination which have impacted on theatre since 1960. It has strong relationships with **mime**, **circus** and commedia styles, elements which figure in training and praxis. Design is frequently an integral force, with actors involved in creating environments with and without 'props'.

Many contemporary practitioners have trained with Jacques Lecoq, and more have been influenced by him via workshops conducted by his alumni. Training is handed down through this *ad hoc* oral and experiential process, although skills sharing and self-teaching are crucial factors, which may account for the multiplicity of styles under the umbrella term 'physical theatre'. Two key concepts underpin the process by which somatic creativity is harnessed in Lecoq's training, which aims to promote creative autonomy: the notion of individual 'neutrality' where actors aspire to a 'state of readiness' in which they are physically alert, mentally open and imaginatively charged, ready for any stimulus to provoke a spontaneous creative response; and the importance of imaginative 'play', or 'le jeu', an open-ended approach to **improvisation** where actors develop *complicité*, a shared belief and understanding which is the crux of ensemble practice.

The term *complicité* is also used to describe the relationship struck between actors and audience in physical theatre, where no fourth wall exists and the intention is to keep open that invisible loop which enables an imaginative collusion to operate between stage and spectator. There is a tendency towards the comic, an acknowledgement perhaps that the concept of the 'hero' has been replaced by the grotesque clown: some teaching concentrates on discovering the 'clown within' and 'bouffon clowning'.

Physical theatre techniques are applied to 'serious' texts (for example, Kaos Theatre). Steven Berkoff has developed his own distinctive brand of physical theatre, forging texts in powerful brawny language which act in counterpoint to a heightened gestural style. He, like most practitioners, is confined to the margins, although the National Theatre has twice invited Theatre de Complicité to work there, firstly with the devised *Street of Crocodiles*, then with *Caucasian Chalk Circle*.

See also: modern dance

DYMPHNA CALLERY

Pinewood Studios

Located twenty miles west of London and named after the pine trees in the grounds, Pinewood has been at the heart of both British and international film production. The property, Heatherden Hall, was bought by Charles Boot in 1934, and he and J. Arthur **Rank** became partners in the project to build the studios. Pinewood proved groundbreaking in its use of the 'unit system' that allowed more than one film to be made at a time, and this enabled Pinewood to achieve the highest output of any studio in the world. The first film to be completed at Pinewood was *Talk of the Devil* (1939, Reed) while the immediate postwar period (Pinewood had been requisitioned and hosted the Army Film Production Unit during the Second World War) saw six major productions including the acclaimed *Oliver Twist* (1948, **Lean**) and *The Red Shoes* (1948, **Powell** and Pressburger), a landmark film in British cinematography for its bold and expressive use of colour.

The 1950s saw numerous productions including the Doctor series, medical farces which were the predecessors to the **Carry On films**; the series commenced with *Doctor in the House* (1954, Thomas) and led to a further six films. Other notable films of the 1950s era include the *Prince and the Showgirl* (1957, Olivier) starring Marilyn Monroe, *Reach for the Sky* (1956, Gilbert), *Carve Her Name with Pride* (1958, Gilbert), *North West Frontier* (1959, Thompson) and *The Thirty-Nine Steps* (1959, Thomas). This latter film was a reworking of John Buchan's novel, originally filmed by Hitchcock in 1939. Because of its innovation and expertise, American production companies flocked to Pinewood and a major reinvestment was required. During the 1960s, four new stages were built to accommodate every aspect of film and television production. This period also saw the start of the association between Pinewood and the James Bond series, which commenced in 1962 with *Dr No* (Young). The studios have continued to produce imaginative and technically challenging material, such as *Superman* (1978, Donner), *Superman II* (1980, Lester), *Superman III* (1983, Lester), *Superman IV: The Quest for Peace* (1987, Furie), *Adventures of Baron Munchausen* (1988, Gilliam) and *Batman* (1989, Burton). It has been heavily involved with notable television productions such as *The Camomile Lawn*, *Jeeves and Wooster* and the *Minder* series. Today it boasts the world's largest silent stage and Europe's biggest exterior tank, and is carrying on the commitment to modernization.

See also: British film industry; cinemas

GUY OSBORN

pirate radio

'Pirate radio', as we know it, began at sea in 1958 with Radio Mercur broadcasting to Denmark from the ship *Cheeta*. Piracy hit Britain from Radio Veronica's ship when the Commercial Neutral Broadcasting Company made its first ever sea pirate broadcast in 1961. Ronan O'Rahilly hoisted the jolly roger from a converted ferry situated in the Irish port of Greenore, to launch Radio Caroline on Good Friday 1964; DJ Simon Dee opened the station officially on Easter Sunday. Within a few months, Radio Caroline was attracting seven million listeners. New stations appeared and disappeared within the next nine months, including Radio Atlanta, Radio 207, Caroline North, Radio Scotland and 370.

The Marine Offences Act laid down tight control in 1967, in the same year that the BBC restructured its services (from which emerged **Radio 1**). The first voice heard on Radio 1 was that of ex-Radio Luxembourg and pirate DJ Tony Blackburn. In this year the BBC also launched the first of their local radio stations, Radio Leicester (there are now thirty-five local stations).

Piracy on the high seas saw its heyday from 1968 to 1970. Stations were raided, disappeared and only sporadically reappeared. Radio Geronimo, a survivor of the earlier raids, claimed over two million listeners; Radio Veronica survived until September 1972. Radio Jackie, a new station, appeared in 1969 and broadcast twenty-four hours a day during 1970, and Radio North Sea International came on the air.

1983 and 1984 marked the return of large-scale sea piracy in the form of Radio Laser and Radio Caroline, both transmitting from the North Sea. Land-based pirates emerged, at first transmitting taped music and then later live programmes in high-quality stereo, twenty-four hours a day, seven days a week. As a result of this, the Telecommunications Act was passed in July 1984 to tighten up any loopholes that pirates operating on land might slip through.

Of the many land-based pirates to have emerged, Radio Invicta, London Weekend Radio (LWR) and Dread Broadcasting Station (DBC), are the three most noteworthy. Radio Invicta led the way in black music pirates in 1970, as the first **soul** pirate station. Started by soul enthusiast Tony Johns, it lasted fourteen years. The station played live for forty-eight hours over Christmas and New Year in 1976, and received a summons and a fine for it. At the same time, Robbie Vincent was given a soul show on Radio 1. LWR's Tim Westwood did for **hip hop** what Johns did for soul. On LWR you could hear mix tapes from local crews running side by side with their New York counterparts. In September 1984, Tim Westwood held a GLC-backed hip hop festival on the south bank in London that drew in a crowd of thirty thousand people. He now hosts Radio 1's Hip Hop show. Dread Broadcasting Corporation emerged around 1981 to play **reggae** presented by Rastas. DBC used echoes, sirens and all the sound effects used by sound systems in the bluesdance. In 1984, DBC disappeared off the airwaves; DBC's Miss P was recruited as a Radio 1 DJ. Globe FM's DJ Jack-Undercover, operating in Nottingham, 1996, points out how Radio 1's strategy for survival in the 1990s is to poach new talent and audiences from the pirates: he cites the recruitment of ex-pirates Lisa L'Anson and Steve Edwards as evidence.

See also: commercial radio; DJs; Radio 1

Further reading

Hind, J. and Mosco, S. (1985) *Rebel Radio: The Full Story of British Pirate Radio*, London: Pluto.

EUGENE LANGE

playwrights

A middle-class enclave in the early 1950s, theatre began to broaden towards the end of the decade thanks to a crop of new playwrights, and also

began to attract fresh audiences. Middle-brow plays by Terence Rattigan (*The Winslow Boy* (1946), *Separate Tables* (1955)) or Agatha Christie (*The Mousetrap* (1953)) gave way to plays located in ordinary settings rather than smart drawing rooms. The watershed is generally seen as John Osborne's play *Look Back in Anger* (1956), which railed against the **Establishment** and signalled the advent of the Angry Young Man movement, where playwrights sought not so much to entertain as to outrage their audiences. *Look Back in Anger* was set in a bedsit. An ironing board was a stage prop, and the abusive central character Jimmy Porter browbeat his wife Alison for her class origins and her implication in the imperialist project of Britain's past (her father had been in the British army in India), neither of which she could do anything about. Osborne boasted that the most pleasing thing to him about the premiere of his play was the sound of the seats flipping up, as audience members left incensed by Jimmy Porter's diatribes against his mother-in-law. One can detect the influence of Brecht's alienation effect here, given a twist to attack the British **class system**.

Osborne enabled the advent of writers like Joe Orton (*Loot* (1967), *Entertaining Mr Sloane* (1964)) and even Willy Russell (*Educating Rita*, *Blood Brothers*, *Shirley Valentine*), as the theatre became for a time a carnivalesque place where all social classes might mix. Orton's plays were iconoclastic and outrageous, especially in the context of the homophobic times in which they appeared, and ironically in the 1990s, productions of them are well attended by groups of black-leather-clad homosexuals, for whom they have attained cult status. Arnold Wesker arguably could also never have found an audience for his so-called 'kitchen sink' dramas without *Look Back in Anger*, although in practice he was helped by the fact that the Royal Court theatre was state-subsidized to encourage new work. His plays *Roots* (1959), *The Kitchen* (1961) and *Chips with Everything* (1962) were acclaimed at the time and are still regularly revived, because they deal with and continue to relate to the problems and experience of ordinary people's lives.

Some critics suggest that the revival in British theatre actually came from abroad. They cite the visit to Britain in 1951 of Bertolt Brecht's Berliner Ensemble, and it is undeniable that Britain has often looked overseas for its dramatic influences. It has always had an almost exaggerated respect for the European 'greats'. So, university groups will automatically stage Alfred Jarry's *Ubu Roi* (1896), Brecht's *Caucasian Chalk Circle* (1948) or *Mother Courage* (1941). Brecht's influence and reputation are now undoubtedly on the wane, but they have been very powerful. He stated himself that he thought his future as a dramatist depended on the survival of socialism, and it may be possible to map a shared decline. Botho Strauss suggested that a film like Alfred Hitchcock's *The Birds* (1963) would outlast *Mother Courage* because it is mythic while the latter is instructive.

Ibsen and Strindberg are still studied in drama schools, although the latter is seldom performed in commercial theatres (an exception being *There Are Crimes and Crimes* (1900) at The Haymarket, Leicester in April 1998). Productions of Ibsen's *Doll's House* (1879), however, enjoyed a vogue during the second wave of feminism. Revivals of works by Arthur Miller or Tennessee Williams are also always popular, though less of an influence on British playwrights. However, the playwrighting force which has really dominated British theatre in the last ten years has been Irish.

Irish playwrights from Sheridan, Congreve and Goldsmith to Wilde, Synge and Shaw for long blazed a trail in British theatre. In much later times Samuel Beckett's work, though less frequently performed at main 'box office' theatres, has become a very powerful influence on British theatre in general. *Waiting for Godot* (1952) has developed into a standard college work for both study and production. *Happy Days* (1961) and *Endgame* (1958) are staples of college syllabuses. *Not I* with Billie Whitelaw was first screened on BBC2 in 1977. Harold Pinter's works *The Birthday Party* (1958) and *The Homecoming* (1965), with their enigmatic silences and their questioning of the possibilities of communication perhaps owe most to the influence of Beckett. But even productions like that of Kingsley Amis's *The Old Devils* at Theatr Clwyd in 1989 posed the same nihilistic questions as Beckett, through the use of stage props. For example, as actors (including the seventy-one-year-old lead) first appeared on stage, suspended above them was a spotlighted publicity photo of them in their golden youth smilingly eagerly when they

were full of hope and promise. The audience was left to make cruel comparisons between the past and the present and to draw its own conclusions about the ravages of age and the meaning of life.

Other influential Irish writers in recent years include Brendan Behan. His *The Hostage* (1958) has regularly been staged in London. All of Brian Friel's works, including *Philadelphia Here I Come* (1964), *The Faith Healer* (1979), *Translations* (1980) and *Dancing at Lughnasa* (1990), have played to enthusiastic audiences in Britain. Indeed, for a time it has seemed as though there was a total eclipse for British dramatists, with few exceptions.

There has been a strong trend in political drama spearheaded by David Hare (for example, *The Secret Rapture* (1989), about Thatcher's Britain in the 1980s), Howard Brenton (*Pravda*, co-written with Hare (1985) about Rupert Murdoch's rise with **News International**), David Edgar (*Destiny* (1976) about the National Front) and Trevor Griffiths (*The Gulf Between Us* (1998) about the Gulf War). Other British playwrights whose work has featured prominently in British theatre in the last two decades include Tom Stoppard, Alan Ayckbourn, Caryl Churchill, Alan Bleasdale, Willy Russell, Dennis **Potter**, Michael Frayn and Alan Bennett.

Stoppard's writing has been prolific and, after critics' initial critical reservations (Kenneth Tynan described *Travesties* (1974) as 'a triple-decker bus, that isn't going anywhere') has dominated the London stage. He deals with witty, linguistically astute explorations of cross-purposes, existential questions, and moral dilemmas in plays such as *Rosencrantz and Guildenstern are Dead* (1966), *Jumpers* (1972) and *Arcadia* (1993). His play *Professional Foul* (1977), an attack on the repressive Czech regime, premiered on television and combined black humour with serious ideological discussion in its treatment of the moral dilemmas facing a football-mad professor on a freebie to a conference in Prague. He has to decide whether or not to flout his hosts' hospitality by smuggling out of the country a manuscript given to him by a former student.

Alan Ayckbourn is a popular and perceptive playwright who has based himself at his own theatre in Scarborough. There he has staged a string of successful productions, including *Absurd*

Person Singular (1972), in which a desperate woman repeatedly tries and fails to commit suicide while those around her remain entirely oblivious.

Caryl Churchill's feminist work always relates to contemporary themes. She is best-known perhaps for her two commercially successful plays, *Top Girls* (1982) and *Serious Money* (1987). The latter is set in the greed-oriented City, when yuppies were in vogue.

Alan Bleasdale's work has mainly been seen on television, but he originated as a playwright for the theatre in Liverpool and took charge of Channel 4's programme to encourage young writing talent. His work includes *Boys from the Blackstuff*, an acclaimed series which, though set in Liverpool, articulated the misery being experienced by those on the dole throughout Thatcher's Britain. The catchphrases 'gizzajob' and 'I can do that', repeated by a character in the play called Yosser Hughes, became commonplace around the country. Bleasdale's play *GBH*, about the right-wing takeover of a city council, also earned him national accolades and was compulsive watching on television.

The multi-talented Willy Russell was heavily involved with the film of his acclaimed play *Shirley Valentine*, the story of a whimsical fancy which turns into a flight for freedom for the eponymous heroine to a new life on a Greek island. A measure of his success as a dramatist is the fact that for this film, audiences – predominantly of housewives (or 'Shirley Valentines') – queued round the block at local cinema venues throughout Britain. His play *Educating Rita* struck a chord with women everywhere, dealing as it did with the educational aspirations of a working-class Liverpool woman whose chauvinist husband seeks to thwart them in order to keep her as his own possession. It performed a necessary attack on the male chauvinism of working class values, from within the class rather than from outside. It has been translated into numerous languages and made into a successful film (set in Trinity College Dublin) with Michael Caine and Julie Walters.

The most recent 'invader' of British theatre has been another young Irish writer, Sebastian Barry. He is one of the astonishing new wave of Irish playwrights – others include Billy Roche and Conor McPherson – who have revitalized British theatre over the past decade. Barry's *The Steward of*

Christendom is reminiscent of Brian Friel's *Faith Healer*, and its favourable reception was only eclipsed by that of *Our Lady of Sligo*, which played at the National Theatre from April 1998 to rave reviews.

However, there is much home-grown talent which is reversing the trends referred to above, and many contemporary British dramatists are now exporting their work. Some writers, including Malcolm Bradbury, see a revival in UK theatre at the moment. Bradbury premiered his first play for the theatre for thirty years, *Inside Trading*, at the new Playhouse in Norwich in 1998.

Mark Ravenhill's play *Shopping and Fucking* was wildly popular at the Berlin Festival in 1998. He has also written *Handbag or The Importance of Being Someone*, a witty but harrowing sequel to Oscar Wilde's *The Importance of Being Earnest* (1895). Other names to look out for are Jim Cartwright, who wrote *I Licked a Slag's Deodorant*, Patrick Marber, Sarah Kane, Jez Butterworth, David Harrower, Ed Thomas and Rebecca Pritchard. The last named is one of the Royal Court's young prodigies. She has a gift for sharp dialogue, ribald humour and sudden moments of pathos. These are evidenced in *Yard Gal*, a co-production between the Royal Court and Clean Break, a company that works with women offenders both inside and outside prison. Two girls, one black one white, reminisce hilariously about their misspent lives, but when the audience think the play is about to become homiletic (abusive father; bad experience in children's home) they are forced to see and remember instead how much the two girls look out for one another.

Another notable young contemporary playwright is Ben Brown whose play *All Things Considered* was staged at the Hampstead Theatre in 1997, when he was twenty-seven. It takes up the theme of Ayckbourn's *Absurd Person Singular* mentioned above, and in it an Oxbridge professor of philosophy decides to commit suicide, but is prevented from doing so by a succession of visitors who bring their own problems to him for solution. Critics found it derivative (Simon Gray's *Butley* and Christopher Hampton's *The Philanthropist*), but it built well on these initial influences and eschewed a tendency among young contemporary writers to deal with inner city despair and presented instead boulevard comedy: the play opens with the suicidal don wearing a plastic bag on his head like an absurd hat. Sarah Kane is another very talented female playwright, whose *Cleansed* played at the Royal Court in 1977. Her talent is to create a hermetic world of obsessive misery and horror, and she does not so much prescribe solutions to social problems as enable the audience to understand the lives of others. It can thus fairly be said that the theatre as a medium, and the playwrights who write for it, are still handling both the problems of day-to-day life and questions of existentialism.

See also: actors (female); actors (male); directors; theatre

Further reading

Chambers, C. and Prior, M. (1987) *Playwright's Progress: Patterns of Postwar British Drama*, Oxford: Amber Lane Press.

MIKE STORRY

poetry

It is a commonly acknowledged truism that reading and writing poetry are both valued and difficult exercises. Poetry has an important cultural position because it is often manifestly difficult, made so by the apparent obscurity of its allusiveness and the disruption of syntax and narrative direction. Its complications require that the reader must learn new rules and recognize patterns that are embedded and hidden in a text that is observably different in its lexis and form from that of prose; it possesses explicitly and implicitly the constituents of high art. Its nature has been characterized as being something that we have to be taught, as in dancing, as opposed to that which we learned, walking; and yet in its use of patterns of rhythm, rhyme (sometimes) and metrics it invokes the prevocal and corporeal which lie beneath and come before language. If it is possible to characterize a 'British' poem of the second half of the century, it would be the lyric narrative, borrowing from the poet's life – often using a first person narrative voice – and not moving far from the kinds

of metrics that the preceding years and poets had given them.

The best illustration of this relative stasis in form, voice and aspect is to be found in the way that two collections of poems may be said to stand for the beginning and end of the century: Thomas Hardy's *Poems* of 1912–13 and Ted Hughes's *Birthday Letters* are both collections written after the death of a wife, the first immediately after and the second apparently nearly thirty-five years after the deaths of the women in question. They are both awkwardly passionate, haunted by guilt and lost love, and oddly similar in their metrical elaboration. Unconsciously, they enclose the century in a circle of theme and form.

W.B. Yeats (1865–1939) wrote a poem in which he listed in a wittily rhythmic pattern the names of his contemporaries, a form mimicked equally wittily by Anthony Thwaite in a 1975 poem. It would be tempting to list the poets published in the British Isles in the latter half of the twentieth century in alphabetical order, but such a list would extend far beyond he limits of this entry. It is perhaps more useful, then, to consider the issues which have relevance and significance to the writing, publishing and reading of poetry in the latter half of the twentieth century in Britain.

The first consideration is that poetry, as it is generally conceived, perceived and published, is a product of high culture and art: not all publishing houses in the British Isles have had a poetry list. Faber & Faber, the Oxford University Press, Jonathan Cape and, more recently, Bloodaxe and Carcanet have been amongst the strongest publishers of poetry. The older publishers have used other parts of their lists to subsidize poetry, while regional and national arts' funding bodies have supported the newer houses.

Reading poetry, or listening to its reading, is considered a reflective, thoughtful, profound, even at times somewhat sombre activity. Performance poetry, which calls for rhythmic participation from its audience and sometimes even laughter, is seen, perhaps wrongly, as a surrender to levity. Despite all the attempts to demonstrate that poetry's motto is 'make it new', it is an indication of a pervasive conservatism that the favourite poem of the British people, as recorded in a poll in 1995, was Rudyard Kipling's 'If'. However, a 1996 BBC television telephone poll for the favourite poem written since 1945 gave the prize to Jenny Joseph's 'Warning', a sharply witty poem that anticipates the pleasures of a woman's wildness in her old age. It may merely reveal how unrepresentative telephone polls can be.

If the reader now looks back to the beginning of the 1960s and the poetry appearing in original texts and anthologies, poetry seemed in large measure to be the creative second job of male university teachers of literature. There were eccentrics and primitives, but they were often given the same status as primitive painters: subjects for an almost anthropological study rather than critical evaluation and enjoyment. Women, if they appeared in those anthologies, were either safe because they were not going to embarrass any reader by being, as Jeni Couzyn has pointed out, 'too female', or because they were, as Alfred Alvarez claimed for Sylvia Plath, '[steering] clear of feminine charm, deliciousness, gentility, supersensitivity, the act of being a poet.' There were even anthologizers who thought that there were no women poets who were worth including in their selections.

The anthologizers and critics have regularly over these years celebrated newness, vividness, originality and a strongly empiricist stance on the part of the poet under scrutiny; anything much of a metaphysics or a veering towards transcendentalism are not things that are valued or celebrated. The most famous photograph of a British poet from the 1950s and 1960s might well be Philip Larkin in a belted gabardine fawn raincoat, wheeling a bicycle through an overgrown churchyard; the picture serendipitously gathers in two of his best-known poems, 'Church Going' and the later 'Whitsun Weddings' The rather shallow readings of his poems led to a sloppy christening of him as 'the laureate of the suburbs'. Ironically, the two poems actually explore the possibility of forms of transcendental experience by way of denial and frustrated desire.

Out of the anthologizers' lists of 'approved' poets and the genteel publicists' celebrations of the daringly safe and the safely daring, a kind of hierarchy emerged. The poets whose work first achieved eminence were Ted Hughes, Thom Gunn and Philip Larkin. It is worth looking at how, in achieving this distinction, their work effaces that of those who are their near contemporaries or who predate them. As examples, Thomas Hardy, Edward Thomas and John Betjeman are seen as Larkin's poetic antecedents; it is a kind of influence spotting that ignores the more important recognition of, for example, Larkin's consciousness of his poetry's relationship to Wordsworth's in the use of meditative stances (Larkin's 'The Old Fools' (1974) is a transumption of Wordsworth's 'Intimations of Immortality'). Further, such a creation of a hierarchy can mean that powerful and important poets become excluded or at best marginalized until rescued by partisan conviction and advocacy: Basil Bunting's work serves as an example of this tendency. 'Briggflatts' is one of the best long poems of this century, but his poetry has struggled to take its place in the consciousness of the poetry reading public. There is now a Basil Bunting Archive at the University of Durham; although he was an internationalist, cosmopolitan thinker and writer, financial exigency forced him to become a subeditor on the regional newspapers published in the city of Newcastle upon Tyne.

In an essay first written in 1974 but published in his 1980 collection of essays, *Preoccupations*, Seamus Heaney names the poets he thinks constitute a joint linguistic and thematic hierarchy at the forefront of British poetry. He names first Ted Hughes for his choosing a language and, increasingly, themes which reached back into Norse and Germanic linguistic roots and mythology; second comes Geoffrey Hill, for his latinate language that explores a medieval world and its renaissance continuance; finally, in Larkin's work he finds a summation and incorporation of all of these cullings from the past and his own wider historical sense into the most potent and redolent language and subject matter. Was it because Thom Gunn had by then moved to California that he had been replaced in the triumvirate? By a further irony, Seamus Heaney has become the central poet of 'British' experience in the years since he wrote of those others, a process that culminated in his being awarded the Nobel Prize for Literature in 1995.

This universal recogntion of the worth of Heaney's poetry points to the way in which poetry has moved in the latter part of this century. The central themes which transcend and subsume the names of individual poets and which trace the course of poetry's route to the present have been a questioning of those previously held canonical assumptions which created inclusions and exclusions in poetry publishers' lists and anthologizers' choices. There has been a concomitant setting up of powerful publishing houses outside the cultural metropolis, a place not too far culturally or topographically from Bloomsbury. It has meant a moving to what some have seen as the margins from that cosmopolitan centre. At its best, this has meant a confrontation with the real and terrible; at its worst, an unearned and unworthy posturing. The poetry of Heaney, Michael Longley, U.A. Fanthorpe, Geoffrey Hill and Adrian Mitchell provide examples from the whole of this spectrum of responses.

In the best poetry there has been a necessary re-engagement with the grinding pains of recent history. Adrian Mitchell is quoted as saying that nobody is interested in poetry because poetry isn't interested in anything; a claim his own poetry attempted to challenge when he wrote about the West's involvement in Vietnam in the 1960s and early 1970s. The most powerful poetry in the British Isles takes on personal, regional and national histories that reflect the consequences of class, racial, political and gendered experience. The emergence of poets who wrote about being out on the margins, in whatever way, meant that they drew those margins to the centre of their readers' attention. It is no accident that the long torment of the north of Ireland has produced from Ireland the most powerful poetry of the last half-century, though hardly ever as a directly polemical or crudely partisan intervention.

These poetries of engagement have revealed unexplored territories: poets have come to Britain out of the long shadow of an imperial and colonial past to remind us of what that experience meant and of how change has been quicker and more fundamental than Britain has sometimes realized or seemed to want. Poets as various as Peter Porter, Benjamin Zephaniah, Fred D'Aguiar, James Berry, Beverley Brown, Jackie Kay and Derek Walcott (an earlier Nobel laureate) remind Britain of their and its otherness, where the one was an indictment and the other could be an indifference that sometimes touched contempt.

Themes from the margins have crowded in upon Britain, and there is one other that has enormous significance: the European experience of the Holocaust and of totalitarian oppression. This has produced a literature which some might argue we have been fortunate to avoid, but which puts into perspective the concerns of much British poetry: still introspective, lyrical in mode and self-conscious in its representation of disregard of that wider, darker world (although Ireland's long agony has made that unfortunate difference for British poetry). It is worth remembering that the totalitarian regimes of Eastern Europe thought poets were important enough to imprison or to be sent into internal exile and deprived of the right to earn a living.

The writing and reading of poetry has remained a mark of high cultural achievement: poetry texts are often regarded as difficult in a paradoxical way. Very rarely, unless the poet is Christopher Reid, is the vocabulary obscure or recondite, but the structural density of the text, the complexity of allusion and the definitive recourse to figuration mean that reading poetry calls for an armoury of critical and cultural weaponry, tactical sprightliness in line-by-line reading, and a consciously chosen strategy of interpretation. Critical and theoretical writing have been taken up with the exploration and combative critique of the strategies for reading poetry and of the place of poetry within the widest of critical contexts. At the same time, poetry has often been ignored in that its cultural exclusivity has meant that it does not impinge on the lives of many except in a formal, formulaic, even ritualistic way, as suggested by the choice of 'If' as an enduring favourite poem. It remains remarkable that the most often-used poetry appears in the 'Deaths' and 'In Memoriam' columns of British regional and local newspapers, where anonymously composed, sentimental elegiac couplets, supplied by the newspapers from catalogued lists, commemorate the deceased loved ones of those who have paid for the insertion of the entries.

See also: Martian Poets; Mersey Poets; performance poetry; poetry anthologies

Further reading

Childs, P. (1998) *The Twentieth Century in Poetry*, London: Routledge.

O'Brien, S. (1998) *The Deregulated Muse*, Newcastle: Bloodaxe.

JIM MALONEY

poetry anthologies

For many, their first meeting with poetry is the anthology, as school reader, GCSE or A-level set text. The selection principle in anthologies is rarely made explicit. Nevertheless this is how, unnoticing, readers begin to regard literature's worth and value canonically. It is therefore important to interrogate the process of selection and justification. Further, some politicians, who have responsibility for curriculum direction, believe that encouraging or directing curriculum managers to prescribe their contents can promote an 'approved' poetic culture.

A wide spectrum of anthologizing agendas exists: gendered, chronological, regional and national are all present. The reader must not only examine the selection of poets but the editorial principles expressed by the anthologizers' introductions. For example, the almost total omission of women poets in earlier anthologies seems inexplicable, were it not in some cases deliberately and insultingly 'justified'. There is, however, an important line of collections with claims to the term 'key anthology'. It runs at least from Robert Conquest's *New Lines* (1956) through Alfred Alvarez's *The New Poetry* (1962) and Edward Lucie-Smith's *British Poetry Since 1945* (1970, revised 1985), to Blake Morrison and Andrew Motion's *Penguin Book of Contemporary British Poetry* (1982), and on to Jeni Couzyn's *Bloodaxe Book of Contemporary Women Poets* (1985) and *The New British Poetry* (1988), edited by Eric Mottram, Gillian Allnutt, Fred D'Aguiar and Ken Edwards. The latest is Bloodaxe's *The New Poetry Anthology* (1993), edited by Michael Hulse, David Morley and David Kennedy. 'New' is the key word as each struggles to claim power and relevance for its anthologized poets.

The anthologists reveal their desire to shock and surprise, claiming relevance and centrality. In the same paragraph of promotional comment, one anthology praises itself as, 'the most controversial event in the poetry world for many years ... ', and ends, 'it has been taken up as a set text for many school and university courses'. In their confrontation with past and contemporary foes, anthology editors claim their selection's victory.

Nevertheless, the most worthwhile development has been the geographical spread of poetry presses with quirky anthologizing principles; almost every British region possesses at least one publisher of poetry. Bloodaxe in Newcastle upon Tyne and Carcanet in Manchester serve as exemplary models for many others.

See also: poetry; poetry in the 1970s; poetry in the 1980s; poetry in the 1990s

Further reading

Longley, E. (1996) 'Signposting the Century', *Poetry Review* 86(1): 8–12.

JIM MALONEY

poetry in the 1970s

The 1970s mark a point of transition in poetry. In 1974, Philip Larkin published his last collection of poems, *High Windows*. The poets, mainly men, whose work had been published for twenty or thirty years or even more, continued to be published, but for many the end of their creative lives was approaching. The most powerful influences were Thomas Hardy (1840–1928) and, more covertly, Edward Thomas (1878–1917). There was a lack of influence in the poetry of the time, and in earlier decades, of the work of the more obviously modernist poetry of Ezra Pound (1885–1972), T.S. Eliot (1888–1965) or even W.H. Auden (1907–73).

This decade saw the poetry of the powerful writers emerge from the jostling mob into the permanent critical memory, gathering regard and judicious admiration. Tony Harrison, Douglas Dunn, Geoffrey Hill, Seamus Heaney, Ruth Pitter and U.A. Fanthorpe are amongst a host of those worth reading. The influence of poetry being written in other countries seems minimal: especially lacking is the sprightliness, speed and power of intellectual control and emotional dynamics found in European and American poetry. Even in the most challenging British poetry there is a sense of the prepared 'set piece' in which all the movements are rigidly mapped. A partial breakout might have existed in the work of Craig Raine, where a deracinated metaphysical style reworked the ordinary into the fantastic with flip-flopping, metaphoric trickery. The signature poem, 'A Martian Sends A Postcard Home', gave a name to the manner and drew a line under the Martian 'movement' (see **Martian Poets**).

At the same time a multitude of poetic voices that were to break the cosmopolitan and centralizing hegemony of the London-based 'academic' poetry emerged. Black Afro-Caribbean, women's and regional poetic voices that were seen not as remarkable primitifs but as authentic and variant voices were published. They often took their richness from the coming together of poets in regional centres: the Morden Tower readings, organized by Tom Pickard in Newcastle-upon-Tyne, brought American beat and Black Mountain poetry in a direct way to British writers and readers.

The break-up of the slightly complacent consensuality of an earlier generation came violently and vividly at the end of the 1960s and both in Britain and across the world was exacerbated in the 1970s. The most memorable poetry of this decade and the next is a commentary upon that exacerbation.

See also: poetry; poetry anthologies; poetry in the 1980s; poetry in the 1990s

Further reading

Jones, P. and Schmidt, M. (eds) (1980) *British Poetry Since 1970: A Critical Survey*, Manchester: Carcanet.

JIM MALONEY

poetry in the 1980s

In Britain the 1980s began in 1979, when the long national political domination of the Conservatives in national government began, and the 1980s became synonymous with the jingoistic nationalism of post-Falkphalism triumphalism and the celebration of greed. One of the most interesting of 1980s' poetic productions was Caryl Churchill's *Serious Money*, a play that used a subtle and sprightly verse form for a sardonic anatomy and an angry celebration of that greed.

The subjects that engaged poets were as various as the poets themselves, but the decade reinforced the emergence of a variety of voices that celebrated a burgeoning diversity in their lives. There is the sense of the poets writing out of their lives and their sometimes painful contexts: Tony Harrison's 'V' (1985), a poem broadcast on television in 1987, meditated upon violence and the impoverishment of contemporary speech following the vandalising of the Leeds cemetery where his parents were buried. It incorporated commentary on the year-long National Union of Mineworkers strike in its vivid narrative. The Mrs Grundys only heard the street crudity of some of the language and chose not to understand its contextualization within the poem. The 1989 Bloodaxe edition of the poem contained critical and documentary material which gives a clear sense of the poem's reception.

A characteristic and illustrative cause célèbre of 1980s poetry was the proposal that the black performance poet, Benjamin Zephaniah, should be awarded a fellowship at Cambridge University. The refusal had a subtext of denial that he was not a poet since his work was political, aware of its blackness, often racially angry as well as funny, and meant to be delivered in a driving, rhythmically powerful way that owed much to black music from jazz to rap. The city and University of Liverpool offered him a fellowship and in return received a year's work of powerful, admonitory and sometimes wryly celebratory poetry.

In the 1980s the emergence of 'difference' in poetry could be embodied in the exemplary figure, Eavan Boland, even though her first collection dates back to 1967. In the 1980s her great strength was that she was a woman born in Ireland and writing as one living in that country during a time of unending conflict. She creates a language of awareness and meditative power that can serve as a reference for all else that goes on both in writing and the real world.

See also: poetry; poetry anthologies; poetry in the 1970s; poetry in the 1990s

Further reading

Kennedy, D. (1996) *New Relations: The Refashioning of British Poetry 1980–94*, Glamorgan: Seren.

JIM MALONEY

poetry in the 1990s

In the middle of the decade, Neil Astley, one of British poetry's most powerful publishers and poets, asked the question, 'Is poetry the new rock 'n' roll?' Someone is always asking, 'is X the new rock 'n' roll?'; but it is instructive that poetry could make it, even putatively, into that litany. What is true is that more poetry books are being sold than ever before. Though the reason might be that the compilation of anthologies, using all kinds of thematic focuses – bereavement and political resistance anthologies give an indication of the range – has become an effective marketing device. They have become the recipe books of poetry publishing, but they remind us that the recognition of resonant topics and themes do attract readers.

Poetry in the 1990s is a cultural activity that is promoted and marketed professionally and even ruthlessly: the London Underground publishes poems on poster sites on its network. There is an annual national Poetry Day. Poetry reading has spilled over from **Radio 3** to **Radio 4** to **Radio 2** and even **Radio 1**. Large public companies have employed 'poets in residence' in their corporate headquarters' offices. The **Internet** offers the possibility of a kind of vanity publishing of poetry at much lower cost.

The most worthwhile part of this phenomenon is that poets who might otherwise not find a public outlet for their writing do have the opportunity to take their work out of their notebooks and off their floppy discs. The means of propagation are very often the real competitions run by regional arts bodies, poetry magazines, national newspapers, colleges and universities. This route has brought some poets to prominence and to publishing contracts. Those in the *Observer* and *Stand* are the outstanding national competitions.

While it is worth acknowledging the success of such means of discovering new voices, it is important to recognize that many of the poets writing so variously and powerfully in the 1990s have been writing for many years: Alan Brownjohn, Edith Scovell, Anne Stevenson, Anthony Thwaite and Derek Walcott have all been publishing for at least the last thirty years. All their work is characterized by a determination to celebrate what it means to be an individual separate from but held within a world that changes; in the world in which they must live, the subjective experiences they record seek to impact upon that much larger mass of the world's objectivity, and make it seem different and surprising.

In the 1990s British poetry has caught up a little with its peers, articulating a quickness and vividness of response seen for much longer, more vigorously and more variously in American and European poetry (particularly Eastern European). The 1990s, ironically and tragically, provide themes for poetry that break out of the precious and academic and speak powerfully and directly. At the beginning of the decade the Gulf War provoked in Britain meditative pieces on the televised horror of that war. Tony Harrison's 'Cold Coming' was printed beneath the burned black rictus grin of a dead Iraqi soldier's head; the soldier had been caught in the firestorm bombing by US aircraft as he fled from Kuwait. The poem's title and subject commented on US male fighting forces in the Gulf having ensured a store of their frozen semen would be available back home to fertilize their partners' ovum, should they fail to return. As a topical extension of the anthologizing principle that has been so powerful a publicization of poetry, editors have given space to writing on the particular horrors of the war in Bosnia in the middle of the decade. Against this kind of occasional writing, the work of Alastair Elliott can stand as a reminder that the reworking of autobiography into meditative, narrative lyric produces from the personal and private a wider significance.

Although poets in this new dispensation are still concerned to signal their particular position, the element of posturing and establishing falsely oppositional stances seems to have passed. Good publishers are concerned not to tokenize the lists of those published but to selection for variety and true quality, and to encourage experimentation in form: Craig Raine's *History: The Home Movie* (1994) is a good example of such experimentalism, a single-handed attempt to revive the long poem.

At the same time, there is a clear sense that poetry's most persistent, post-romantic form of meditative, very often autobiographically based lyric is, if not beset, then certainly being reworked with an emphasis upon the requirements of form, to the point where the term 'New Formalism' has acquired capital letters. A characteristic example would be the work of Glyn Maxwell; his poetry displays elaborately formal qualities, and he has produced versions of Ovid's poetry acknowledging imitatively its formal regularity and complexity. Ted Hughes has produced an equally formally elaborate version of Ovid's *Metamorphoses*, entitled *Tales from Ovid*, as well as *Birthday Letters*, about his relationship with Sylvia Plath.

What is best in 1990s poetry is variety. New poetic forms, in each manifestation, appear certain of their rightness and of their difference. Helen Dunmore has noted that women made hardly any appearances in poetry texts in the earlier years of postwar Britain's cultural life, and characterized this as being created by ' . . . mainstream publishers [building] up their lists [by] "discovering" bright young men from Oxford and Cambridge who would keep British poetry ticking over'. Her sharply perceptive comment, that 'this photocopying process led to a lack of excitement', sums up the deadening quality of some poetry, out of which there has been a slow break-out into the newness that remains the talismanic badge of success and worth so proudly displayed whether it is won or merely claimed. The Barthesian claim that every reading is a new writing throws the challenge back upon the reader, asking all who read to reflect upon the strategies of reading they use, so that in all the uncertainties of reading there is a gently guiding awareness of how it is being carried out and of the very real pleasures to be taken from it.

See also: performance poetry; poetry anthologies; poetry in the 1970s; poetry in the 1980s

Further reading

Day, G. and Docherty, B. (eds) (1997) *British Poetry from the 1950s to the 1990s: Politics and Art*, London: St Martin's Press/Macmillan.

JIM MALONEY

poetry slams

These are open-floor events in which poets compete by performing their poetry for prizes such as cash or theatre tickets. Each competitor reads three minutes of poetry to an audience that includes a panel of five judges with score cards. The scores are added up as the 'slam' develops, and usually first, second and third prizes are awarded. Some events are sponsored by book shops or literary festivals, and book tokens or festival tickets may be given to all entrants. 'Hungry' poets often arrive early to ensure they make the list of readers. At the UK National Poetry Slam in London there are both individual and team competitions (in the latter, a group of poets read a combination of their work on a particular theme).

See also: black performance poets; Johnson, Linton Kwesi; performance poetry

EUGENE LANGE

police

The tactics of the police for controlling public disorders, such as the 1981 city riots, industrial disputes (such as at Orgreave in 1984) and the environmental protests of the mid-1990s, have been criticized as over-violent and militaristic. The persistence of sexism and racism in the ranks has also been identified as a reason why sections of the population distrust the police. Notoriously, the over-policing of ethnic minorities in the inner cities prompted widespread disturbances in the 1980s. In the last twenty years, the police have adapted to financial hardship in a period of reduced public spending, in three ways. First, there has been a 'civilianization' of non-essential services so as to free up police officers. Second, in some areas the police have relied on closed circuit television cameras. Last, private agencies have been contracted to provide police services.

There has therefore been a reduction in police services, which have been taken over by private security companies (in 1994 there were for the first time more private security officers than police officers). This has led some to conclude that the experiment in public policing is now ending, and police services will return to the traditional private organization of law and order. Despite this, the police enjoy the popular support of the general public, who approved of organizational initiatives such as community policing and campaigns against property crime such as 'Operation Bumble Bee', which was launched against domestic burglary in 1995. Television **crime drama** programmes such as *The Bill* and *Inspector Morse* have also demonstrated the popularity of 'England's finest'.

See also: armed forces and police

Further reading

Reiner, R. (1992) *The Politics of the Police*, 2nd edn, Hemel Hempstead: Harvester Wheatsheaf.

BARRY GODFREY

political consumerism

As society becomes increasingly consumption-centred, so the power of the consumer replaces other forms of political power. Boycotts of companies, products of particular countries and individual products represent a successful strategy of protest, causing financial damage and adverse publicity. Campaigning groups such as Third World First advocate avoidance of firms trading unethically in developing countries, and boycotts centred on **environmentalism** (often grouped under the banner of **green consumerism**), **animal rights** and human rights abuses, employment conditions and other ethical issues are a common feature of contemporary life. By shopping ethically and politically, consumers believe they can put significant pressure on the economies of nations and the profits of corporations, and thus effect change.

DAVID BELL

political correctness

Although having a distinguished ancestry in the race relations and equal opportunities acts of the 1970s, the concern with political correctness can be traced to the American academic community of the mid-1980s. Its advocates argue that language, being value-laden, is a site of power relations. Thus terms and symbols loaded with discriminatory nuances of sex, race, sexuality, body image, age and disability should be subject to democratic redress. Attributed in the UK to the Left's powerlessness during the **Conservative Party**'s administration of the 1980s and early 1990s, it became a source of derision in the popular media, mostly through wilful misinterpretation. The state meanwhile tries to ignore semantic disagreements in pursuing the promotion of equal opportunities in a multicultural society.

See also: libel, defamation and privacy; prejudice; Race Relations Acts

Further reading

Feldstein, R. (1998) *Political Correctness*, Minneapolis, MN: University of Minnesota Press.

GORDON URQUHART

political publications

Daily newspapers are often associated with general political standpoints, which can be manifested, particularly at election times, in more specific party views. Election day in 1992 was notable for the *Sun*'s denunciation of Neil Kinnock's Labour Party. Interestingly, the *Sun*, which claimed that it had won that election for John Major, switched its alliance to the **Labour Party** in 1997. More specifically, there are a number of weekly and monthly political publications, some of which are independent of party politics but which may have a broad perspective, and others that are more closely aligned to a party or a narrower political view. A good example of the former is *Socialist Worker*, a well-produced weekly paper (also available as a monthly review) linked directly to the Socialist Workers Party and generally sold directly by party members and activists. Similarly, there is the glossy *Living Marxism*, the product of another far left group. The fragmentation of the Left in the 1960s allowed for a plethora of these types of publications (of varying quality) to appear, with some militant groups with as few as fifty members preparing and producing their own publication to sell at rallies, events and street corners. Also, there are a number of more broadly based political publications such as, on the Left, *New Statesman and Society* and *Red Pepper*, and on the centre right, the *Spectator*. While some of these are broadly based and others espouse a particular ideological line, some have broadened their ambit to cover more cultural issues in an attempt to capture more of the burgeoning publishing market and as a response to the changing political environment.

A prominent and influential publication, *Marxism Today* emerged from the divisions within the Communist Party and represented an attempt to reposition a more traditional Marxist analysis within a contemporary society. At its heart was an acknowledgement that newer generations of political philosophers were becoming increasingly influential, for example, Antonio Gramsci's writings on the function of areas of society (such as culture) within the political process. *Marxism Today* was an indication of not only the past history of the Left and the splits surrounding the legitimacy of the Soviet Union but also the changing political analysis which sought to embrace new elements of civil society such as popular culture.

See also: fringe parties; Marxism

GUY OSBORN
STEVE GREENFIELD

politics

Politics has been described as 'who gets what, when, where and how', 'the art of the possible', and in less polite terms as anything to do with people scheming, manipulating or otherwise abusing or seeking power or influence over others. For feminists, 'the personal is political'; for the ancient Greeks humans were 'zoon politikon' (political animals), while for others, politics refers to the activities and processes associated with government.

A common misunderstanding is the equation of politics and **democracy**. While opinions differ on this, is it more correct to view democracy as a particular form of politics and political systems. Political systems can take different forms ranging from liberal democracies in the West to authoritarian, non-democratic systems found in the former communist states or the fascist states of Franco's Spain or Hitler's Germany.

Politics can be seen as an activity as opposed to a set of rules, the aim of which is to solve collective problems and make decisions without resorting to violence or force. It presumes plurality, disagreement and is a continuous process, rather than a finished product. Winston Churchill expressed a common view of politics when he said that 'jaw-jaw is better than war-war', a view echoed in Bernard Crick's famous *In Defence of Politics*, where he notes that 'Politics, then, is a way of ruling in divided societies without undue violence' (1962: 141).

Many people have a cynical assessment of politicians, political parties and other aspects of politics, seeing them as at best 'necessary evils' and politics at worst a corrupt, ignoble, deceitful activity only engaged in for personal rewards. A more positive account can be found in Crick, who holds politics, in keeping with the ancient Greeks, to be 'a type of moral activity; it is free activity, and it is inventive, flexible, enjoyable and human' (1962: 141). This view of politics sees it as a noble calling, one which engages some of the highest aspirations of humanity, a desire to better one's community through public service, pursue and work for the public good.

However, even if we accept the spirit of Crick's positive assessment of politics, there remains the problem, associated with Niccolo Machiavelli, that politics and political activity often require one to engage in less than moral action for some 'greater good'. For Machiavelli, 'realpolitik', that is the real-world context of political necessity and decision making, sometimes requires extremely difficult decisions the nature of which are departures from normal moral standards.

See also: Marxism; philosophy

Further reading

Crick, B. (1962) *In Defence of Politics*, Harmondsworth: Penguin.

Machiavelli, N. (1513) *The Prince*, Harmondsworth: Penguin, 1981.

JOHN BARRY

poll tax

A poll tax is a tax levied upon individuals at a flat rate per capita within a given geographical area. The community charge, which was to become known as the poll tax, was introduced initially in Scotland, with the first bills due for payment in April 1989. In England and Wales, registration began in 1989 and payments became due one year later.

The poll tax was introduced with a number of objectives in mind. The primary justification for a reform of local government taxation was the issue of accountability. Due to the unpopularity of the 'rates' (the taxation system the poll tax was to replace), successive governments had given grants to local authorities to enable them to maintain expenditure levels without increasing rates proportionally. Therefore, an increasing amount of local authority expenditure was financed by central government. Local electors could vote for increased services knowing they would only have to pay a small proportion of the cost. The Thatcher administration, faced with this situation of limited accountability, introduced poll tax to establish accountability and curb spending.

Criticism of the poll tax was varied and widespread. Most notably, due to the flat rate nature of the tax, it was criticized for its regressive nature (which is to say, the incidence fell disproportionately on lower income groups), despite some exemptions. Animadversion of this nature was not limited to the Left; within the **Conservative Party**, MPs Sir George Young and Michael Mates both put forward amendments in the House of Commons which sought to vary the incidence of the tax in relation to income. These amendments were defeated. The regressive nature of the tax had also been noted outside **parliament**, where popular opposition grew.

As the tax was based upon the electoral register, it was also claimed that the poll tax had an undemocratic element. Because some of the poorer sections of society may have remained off the register, the Conservative Party secured a larger victory at the 1992 election than would otherwise have been the case.

It was the widespread unpopularity of the tax which resulted in its downfall. Organized campaigns of non-payment and rioting in Trafalgar Square are the most public examples of popular resistance. After the change of leadership in November 1990, the 'Tory Titanic', as MP John Biffen had labelled it, sank.

See also: Conservative   governments; Thatcherism

Further reading

Esam, P. and Oppenheim, C. (eds) (1989) *A Charge On The Community The Poll Tax, Benefits and The Poor*, London: CPAG Limited.

ALASTAIR LINDSLEY

pop and rock

Defining what does and does not constitute pop and rock (or more simply 'popular music') is difficult. The criteria could be ethnic, generic or geographical, or relate to ownership, modes of production or consumption, or factors such as age or class. The mythical 'birth of rock 'n' roll' – the first successful 'youth' style to achieve global impact – is usually located around 1955; there are conjunctural factors – demographic, economic, generic and technological – that reinforce this particular date. Often overlooked is the shift in status between the live performance and the recording that also takes place during the 1950s. In this decade, pop's audience increasingly consumed the music via processes of mediation. Elvis Presley was the first major figure to tip the balance decisively in favour of recordings, television and film. Popular music from this period on was an essentially commercially mediated form, as distinct from previously successful idioms and styles such as **jazz**, **folk music**, **blues** and 'tin pan alley'.

1950s rock 'n' roll was mainly a teen phenomenon. As the 1960s progressed, and in the wake of the unprecedented global impact of The Beatles, the audience for pop rapidly broadened. The 1960s saw the first attempts in Britain to validate pop as an art form in ways similar to the incorporation of film into a high-culture canon some years earlier. Many view 1967 as the highwater mark of pop as a unified artistic and cultural movement, 'the year it all came together', in theorist Simon Frith's terms. Following this specific moment, the beginnings of fragmentations based on factors such as race, age, sex, class and genre began to surface, and these have since become more pronounced. The construction of 'rock' with its connotations of authenticity, profundity and virtuosity, as opposed to 'pop', characterized by many as ephemeral, commercially standardized and immature, that begins to gain a hold in Britain during the late 1960s sets the tone for many subsequent binary distinctions: white rock versus black soul, art versus entertainment, and underground versus commercial. There is often a barely concealed class-based agenda at work in drawing upon such distinctions.

Progressive rock, fusing elements of blues, jazz, avant-garde and **classical music** idioms, was the dominant form for the bourgeois audience for pop from the late 1960s to the mid-1970s. By 1975 the distinctions between this form (and others such as **heavy metal**), as opposed to those styles aimed more at the **disco** or 'commercial' market, were at their widest.

The impact of **punk rock** and roots **reggae**, the emergence of a European sensibility which largely dispensed with the dominant values of 'soul' and 'warmth', and the increasing availabilities of new technologies all combined to reshape music, and audiences, in the late 1970s. More importantly, by the mid-1980s the rock mainstream's hostility to dance music (and 'pop' in general) had diminished, and important styles based upon the fusion of elements, cultures and genres such as **new romantic**, electro, **house** and **hip hop** made an impact. Since this period dance styles have proliferated, and the emphasis on rhythmic repetition, stable tempo and time signatures coupled with the widespread use of digital technologies has,

to some extent, filtered into almost all forms of popular music.

Since 1964, Britain has been a hugely influential force in global popular music. Being a small country with a centralized **music press** and the tendency to experiment and innovate in the areas of youth interest (particularly music and fashion) has resulted in a large number of subcultural developments of a specifically British nature achieving widespread attention. These range from Merseybeat and mod, through to **skinheads**, punk, **rave** and **Britpop**. Scenes based on one specific area have also made an impact, from the days of 'swinging London' through to the 'Madchester' club scene (see **clubs**) in the late 1980s and the Bristol-based 'trip hop' culture of the early 1990s.

With the proliferation of media outlets for popular music that is a feature of the contemporary era, we now have the impetus of advertisers seeking to target specific niche markets through 'narrowcasting' and ever more distinct formatting, particularly on radio. In the 1990s, under the broad umbrella of 'dance', there were at any one time dozens of identifiable sub-divisions all servicing the lifestyle needs of disparate audiences. Despite the important musical crossovers achieved during the post-punk era, other factors contrive to reinforce cultural fragmentation, and the trend seems likely to continue.

The post-rock 'n' roll era has witnessed the gradual shift away from ensemble playing of acoustic and amplified 'traditional' instruments towards studio-based styles utilizing electronic and digital instrumentation, thus allowing for performance removed from the constraints of dexterity, real time and established notions of artistry. By the early 1980s complete albums were being programmed rather than played using early digital microcomposers, sequencers and drum machines, a successful example being the Human League's *Dare*, in 1981. In very broad terms this has benefited musical styles based upon notions of groove, cyclical repetition and 'cut and paste' collage. Music composition has in many cases come to resemble architecture, manifested visibly as bits and bytes on a computer screen.

More organic genres drawing upon traditional methods, such as grunge and Britpop, have continued to surface, but most of the major musical trends since the punk era have been groove or dance-based. With the exception of hip hop, lyrics have receded in prominence within popular music as a whole, with the human voice being used increasingly as a form of punctuation or for its percussive qualities rather than as the bearer of a linear narrative. Melody, harmony and 'nice tunes' have not been dispensed with in contemporary popular music, but their significance within certain key styles of dance and **rap** has certainly diminished. In addition, the percentage of music that is broadly or completely vocal-free has been one of the most significant yet overlooked trends of the past decade. Within many contemporary styles there have also been considerable shifts in timbre, tempo and song structure, with the classic historical models based around verse, chorus, bridge, key change and instrumental breaks being decisively challenged.

Music making has always relied to some degree upon technology, but the pop era has seen the distinctions between human and technological output become increasingly blurred. Multi-track tape recording, with its inherent implications for composition, musicianship and artistic status, progressed rapidly between the early 1960s and the mid-1970s. During this period, capabilities in British studios stretched from two- and three-track to sixteen- and twenty-four-track. In the 1980s this analogue process was augmented, and often superseded by digital recording drawing upon computer technology. During this decade, a standardized interface linking computers to musical instruments (Musical Instrument Digital Interface, or MIDI) became widely available. This system has further distanced the composer from the constraints of real-time playing, and has had a huge impact upon musical styles, timbres and wider ethical issues relating to authorship and ownership.

Another crucial technological development is the sampler (see **sampling**), which allows for the digital recording and manipulation of any sound source. Many contemporary musical styles rely heavily upon such technologies as part of the writing and performing process.

The history of mixed-media recorded texts has a long lineage, and many major bands made 'promo' films during the 1960s, but the pop video as creative work and marketing tool only came to world prominence in the early 1980s. Music video, and devoted media outlets such as **MTV**, have exerted a profound influence upon all elements of popular music.

The recording and promotional budget of an act now has to be spread more thinly. This has resulted in a conservatism on the part of major record companies regarding the sort of performers being signed and subsequently actively promoted. Leading on from this scenario, much of the 1980s has seen the global sales dominance of a few performers with the image and resources to meet the demand for audio-visual material: Madonna, Prince and Michael Jackson are the most prominent examples of the new sort of global pop star.

Video has also foregrounded the importance of pop's iconic elements: sexuality, dress, movement and physical gesture. In the early 1980s, many of the British wave of 'new pop' performers (Duran Duran, Culture Club, Wham and so on) made their world breakthrough via video and MTV. The proliferation of data made possible by mixed-media formats like video ties in with many elements associated with the condition of postmodernity: pastiche, irony, depthlessness and hybridity. And although many critics claim that the form has already exhausted itself, under its impact pop can no longer be thought of as a primarily aural from.

During the 1990s the **Internet** began to exert an influence on many aspects of popular music. As well as allowing for the downloading of musical data using MIDI, the Internet can, to an extent, subvert the ownership and control of popular music by the global corporations. Music can be distributed by groups or individuals without the need to have a recording contract. Although the more utopian claims on behalf of the Internet must be treated with some scepticism, the long-term impact upon the world of popular music may well prove to be considerable.

The commercial marketplace has long been dominated in terms of ownership and distribution by a few large record companies – usually referred to as 'the majors'. The last forty years has seen these majors develop into total entertainment companies with ownership of every stage of the production process (including studios, manufacture of instruments, technology, publishing, distribution and retail and entertainment outlets). More recently, the majors have become pan-global operators. The chief source of income is often not from sales of records but the ownership and exploitation of rights, principally concerning publishing and licensing.

Research into the workings of the global record industry suggests that organizations such as Time Warner, Sony or EMI are so huge that a fair amount of autonomy is by necessity granted to national, regional or local branches. A typical 'independent' label will often preserve a degree of autonomy and enter into a fairly flexible relationship with the 'parent' major to ensure distribution and promotion of its acts. Such relationships can allow for options to continue or cancel, based usually upon financial considerations.

This major/indie relationship does allow for the counter-argument to the many more pessimistic scenarios of domination and cultural imperialism that have been forwarded, wherein indigenous ethnic and 'non-commercial' music are strangled in the global grip of the majors. However, while diversity and a richly hybridized world of popular music now exist, and are disseminated to ever greater numbers, the inevitable inequalities of economic and cultural capital do apply. It remains difficult for any act to 'cross over' without considerable concessions being made to the business strategies of the global corporations.

Almost every year sees an 'obituary' of pop being written by a cultural analyst. In the 1990s, these arguments have taken on a new dimension. It is said that for a variety of reasons, today's youth are 'post-pop'. As well as the perceived 'decline' in the quality of songs and artistry many see the major rivals to pop as the new computer-based forms of entertainment, such as video games, CD-Roms and the Internet. Research shows that popular music is now merely one component struggling to be heard in this information overload, and is no longer central.

Popular music, for some critics, no longer defines the experience of growing up, and the projection that follows posits a situation wherein popular music will be intrinsically linked to a precise historical period. Whether such observations will come to pass, or whether they are the opinions of critics unable or unwilling to come to terms with the huge musical and cultural shifts that have taken place over the last few decades, remains to be seen.

See also: alternative music; glam rock; psychedelic rock

Further reading

Frith, S. (1983) *Sound Effects: Youth, Leisure, And The Politics Of Rock*, London: Constable.
Jones, S. (1992) *Rock Formation: Music, Technology And Mass Communication*, Newbury Park, CA: Sage.
Negus, K. (1992) *Producing Pop: Culture And Conflict in The Popular Music Industry*, London: Edward Arnold.

RON MOY

pop art

Pop art is a term dating from the 1950s coined by Lawrence Alloway, a British art critic. It came to be broadly used to refer to fine art which draws from popular culture, epitomized by work by Peter Blake and Richard Hamilton. British pop artists of the 1960s included Clive Barker, Derek Boshier, Pauline Boty, Patrick Caulfield, David **Hockney**, Allen Jones, and R.B. Kitaj (the US-born but London-based artist who in fact refuses the term). Though the quintessential pop artist was Andy Warhol, the general ethic of a removed, detached, disinterestedly cool and analytical approach to the importing of 'low' cultural images and styles into 'high' culture was extremely widespread. Pop art drew its chief influences from the mass media, advertising, graphic styles, comic strips and celebrity icons. In later decades it has been attacked as reactionary and as pandering to a consumerist society which values both mass-produced commodities and the least demanding art form – realism. The term neo-pop is used to refer to younger, pop-influenced artists such as Jeff Koons.

See also: painting

Further reading

Lippard, L.R. (1970) *Pop Art*, London: Thames & Hudson.

PETER CHILDS

pop television

The watershed in pop music programming was *Six-Five Special* with Pete Murray and Josephine Douglas in the early 1950s. Broadcast at teatime on Saturdays, the programme aimed simultaneously to cater generally for a family audience and specifically for teenagers. This BBC show was soon rivalled by ITV's *Oh Boy!* From the beginning, these programmes believed in fast pacing and quick cutting, giving the (assumed to be restless) audience the feel of a dynamic show on the move, in keeping with both the upbeat music and the desire to dance. Even at their inception, following the postwar birth/recognition of the teenager, music programmes challenged studio formats and also television's technology. The 1960s (and much of the 1970s) was then divided between seminal pop shows like *Ready Steady Go* and formula family programmes hosted by the more insipid pop stars: Lulu, Cilla Black or Cliff Richard.

The early 1970s was dominated by two stalwarts: *Top of the Pops* for those interested in singles and *The Old Grey Whistle Test* for the album market. The first is one of the longest running shows on television and has regular facelifts (it still gets over 8 million viewers in the late 1990s). The latter has been eclipsed by more lively music shows with more dynamic presenters than the seated hippie, 'whispering' Bob Harris. The late 1970s, alongside the challenges of **punk rock**, saw the redefinition of the genre by exciting but often short-lived programmes such as *Something Else* and *Revolver.*

In the 1980s, **Channel 4**'s *The Tube* was noted for its technology as much as anything, bending and mixing the picture frame before the audience's eyes. Hosted by Jools Holland and Paula Yates, the programme was beamed live from Newcastle and built a large following not just for its music but also for its irreverent attitude – which backfired when Holland recommended the show to 'groovy fuckers' and was taken off the air. The rise of the promotional video also radically changed music programme formats, allowing a blend of live performances, based on the concert, and videos, which aimed at creating more mysterious associations and repackaged the band's tour image.

Consequently, with the emergence of the music video and VJs, in the last decade music programming has been dominated by the rise of **MTV** (launched in the USA in 1981), followed by other all-music stations like VH1 and The Box. However, for those without **cable and satellite**, innovative programmes like Jools Holland's *Later* have been considered exemplary because they assemble a musical and ethnic range of performers who take it in turns to perform live in the studio. In the late 1990s, *Top of the Pops* also finally allowed its performers to dispense with miming.

See also: youth television

Further reading

Goodwin, A. (1995) 'Popular Music and Postmodern Theory', in N. Wheale (ed.), *The Postmodern Arts*, London: Routledge (this chapter offers an incisive comment on the intersection of popular music with postmodern theory).

PETER CHILDS

Popper, Karl

b. 1902, Vienna (Austria); d. 1994

Philosopher

Karl Popper was chiefly a philosopher of science. His works include *The Logic of Scientific Discovery* (1935), *The Open Society and Its Enemies* (1945), *The Poverty of Historicism* (1957), *Conjectures and Refutations* (1963) and *Objective Knowledge* (1972). Popper distinguishes between genuine science and 'pseudo-science'. Whereas genuine scientific propositions are falsifiable in that they explicitly or implicitly specify the evidence which would refute them, pseudo-scientific propositions (such as many of those expounded in Marxism and Freudianism) are unfalsifiable in that no conceivable evidence constitutes their disconfirmation. Science develops in an evolutionary manner. While no theory can be proved, the 'fittest' survive rigorous attempts to falsify them. In his social and political philosophy, Popper provides a penetrating critique of totalitarianism and a stalwart defence of democracy.

See also: philosophy; science

ROD PATERSON

popular fiction

Popular literature is no longer considered inherently lowbrow or intrinsically inferior to a 'high' culture. Accordingly, a text such as Frederick Forsyth's *The Day of the Jackal* now appears on A-level English syllabuses, and best-selling authors from Agatha Christie to Daphne Du Maurier and Stephen King are studied at university. Popular fiction could be said to cover at least the following categories: adventure stories, rural and local fiction, detective stories, fantasy, romance, historical novels, horror, police dramas, comic novels, sagas, science fiction, sea stories, thrillers, spy novels, war novels and, though not many are written outside the USA, westerns. Other popular authors do not fall easily into any of these categories, and possible new forms are always appearing (for example, the politician's novel as written by Jeffrey Archer, Roy Hattersley or Edwina Currie, or the celebrity's novel as produced by Hugh Laurie, Adrian Edmondson, Naomi Campbell, Michael Palin or Ben Elton). Several of the genres also now have their own prizes, such as the Crime Writers Association Awards or Boots Romantic Novel of the Year, the Historical Novel of the Year in Memory of Georgette Heyer, or the Hugo awards (for science fiction). It is worth saying a little in description of each of the major genres (see also **thrillers**; **science fiction**).

Macho adventure stories have been the making of some enormously successful postwar figures such as Alistair Maclean, Wilbur Smith, Desmond Bagley and Hammond Innes. A new generation including Ken Follett and Craig Thomas appear to lean more heavily on research and rounded characters. Meanwhile, Dick Francis, an ex-jockey, has created a unique niche for himself writing hugely popular novels set in the world of horse racing, which almost invariably go straight to the top of the lists of bestsellers.

'**Romance**' has also now to cover less coy kinds of writing aimed at women, from contemporary glamour to 'sex and shopping' novels. Often these 'bonkbusters' revolve around the worlds of big business and movie stars, and, like the more innocent Mills and Boon shelf-fillers, are written to a formula. They require a considerable amount of marketing and are promoted by specialist publishers such as Bantam Press and MacDonald. The style is exemplified by Jackie Collins, sister of the actress Joan Collins, and Judith Krantz; more recent arrivals at the airport bookstores (where 25 percent of all books are sold in the UK) are Pat Booth, Shirley Conran and Vera Cowie. Detective stories are still associated with the canonical writers such as Agatha Christie, Dorothy L. Sayers and Ngaio Marsh, and the leading contemporary practitioners, Ruth Rendell and P.D. James, are also women; both specialize in intricate, crafted plots, not unlike those found in Roald Dahl's much-admired 'twist in the tale' short stories. Younger writers are Simon Brett, Lesley Grant-Adamson and Emma Page. In terms of police novels, Colin Dexter's Inspector Morse series and its television offshoot (like Rendell's Wexford and James's Dalgleish) have created staple British provincial identities.

The most famously successful British popular authors are probably Catherine Cookson, Barbara Taylor Bradford and Barbara Cartland, who write absorbing, undemanding romantic family stories and interminable sagas. Others in a similar mould are Marie Joseph, Audrey Howard and Pamela Haines (who has an English MA from Cambridge).

Fantasy writing has its roots in folk tales and mythology as well as gothic horror (most popularly continued in the novels of Clive Barker, Anne Rice and Stephen King in the USA) and science fiction. The classic exponent is J.R.R. Tolkein, whose *The Lord of the Rings* has repeatedly been voted the best or most popular novel of the century. Terry Pratchett's more light-hearted Discworld series has probably been the most successful descendant, although Nancy Springer, Peter Morwood, Robert Holdstock, Piers Anthony and especially Michael Moorcock are also widely read. Humorous novels by Douglas Adams, Tom Sharpe, Peter Tinniswood and David Nobbs owe a lot to the style of Keith Waterhouse, and illustrate how the comic novel remains a largely male genre, notwithstanding the enormous sales in 1997 of Helen Fielding's *Bridget Jones's Diary*, a success only rivalled by the confessional, male-identity-crisis books of Nick Hornby. Lastly, historical novels by Jean Plaidy/ Victoria Holt/Eleanor Hibbert, Edith Pargeter/ Ellis Peters, and Joanna Potter/Joanna Trollope exemplify the pleasurable, escapist indulgence of the genre, and their authors' penchant for pseudonyms illustrates how many writers opt for pen names which add mystery or anonymity, protect the reputation of an author known in another field, or, on occasion, change the writer's sex.

In the 1990s, popular fiction is enormously diffuse and the distinction between serious and popular literature is problematic to say the least, with authors as disparate as Mary Wesley, Irvine Welsh and Stephen Fry appealing to myriad and wide-ranging tastes.

See also: novel; romance; science fiction; thrillers, detective and spy writing

Further reading

Hicken, M. and Pryterch, R. (1990) *Now Read On A Guide to Contemporary Popular Fiction*, Aldershot: Gower.

PETER CHILDS

pornography

Pornography is defined by US anti-porn activist Andrea Dworkin as: 'the graphic depiction of whores' (Dworkin, 1981). Most pornography does indeed feature women posing in sexually revealing positions for money. However, in the light of the recent influx of gay and lesbian produced porno- graphy, pornography for women – and the dark underside of the industry, pornography featuring children – another definition seems necessary. This has been hard to come by however, with over a decade of feminist, legal and political debate coming no nearer an agreed definition.

In legal terms, Britain's Obscene Publications Act defines pornographic material as that which may be deemed to 'deprave and corrupt'. That this leaves the definition open to interpretation by a politically conservative state has resulted in some notorious historical cases, such as the banning of

lesbian classic *The Well of Loneliness* in the 1920s and D.H. Lawrence's *Lady Chatterley's Lover* in the 1960s.

The public face of the anti-porn movement in Britain is the Campaign Against Pornography (CAP), which over the last decade, and following the example of US groups Campaign Against Pornography and Women Against Violence in the Media, has launched a series of offensives against the stars, publishers and readers of mainstream porn. In 1986, Labour MP Clare Short took up the baton with her campaign to ban the *Sun* news- paper's page 3 nudes. Her bill failed to get a second reading in **parliament**, but did much to expose the schoolboy sexism of most male MPs, while Off the Shelf campaigns through the late 1980s demanded the removal of pornography from the top shelf of newsagents such as W.H. Smith (see **newsstands and newsagents**).

In the mid-1980s, however, the seemingly uni- form face of feminist anti-porn rhetoric began to be addressed by Feminists Against Censorship (FAC), worried about the effect that wide liberal support of CAP policy might have on subcultural artifacts such as the newly burgeoning vogue in lesbian-produced literary and filmic porn. Arguing that lesbian and gay material, often deemed pornographic by definition, is more likely to be the subject of state censorship than the mainstream porn industry with its big business backing, FAC called for, and continues to call for, a readdressing of the law on obscenity and a re-evaluation of the arguments for censorship.

See also: censorship; top-shelf magazines

Further reading

Dworkin, A. (1981) *Pornography: Men Possessing Wo- men*, London: The Women's Press.
Norden, B. (1990) 'Campaign Against Pornogra- phy', *Feminist Review* 35: 1–8.

CLARE WHATLING

post-colonial writing

As a starting-point, post-colonial studies is about the critique of and the resistance to colonialism. Post-colonial literature is a term which has come to replace the older labels 'world literature written in English', 'Third World literature' or 'Commonwealth literature'. Though 'post-colonial' has its detractors, the latter three have been objected to because of their tendency to ghettoize and to suggest the centrality of Britain or the West. The meaning of the term 'post-colonial' is open to debate. It can refer just to previously colonized countries, which are now independent: this makes it simply a historical phase after colonialism. Expanding from this, some critics say that colonizing and ex-colonizing countries should also be included: Britain is a post-colonial country as much as Nigeria, because Britain is also greatly affected and even defined by its heritage of colonialism – and this will be as much reflected in the writing of Martin Amis or Angela Carter as Derek Walcott or Anita Desai. (On the other hand, Britain is still a colonizing country: Northern Ireland is one example, and many Pacific islands could offer others.) The problem with this definition is it elides the difference between colonized and colonizer. On the other hand, this is also its strength: it does not duplicate the colonial binary through designating the West on the one hand and 'Third World' countries on the other.

A third argument is that post-colonialism is a term that should apply from the start of colonization, not the end. This is the argument of Ashcroft *et al.* in *The Empire Writes Back*. This construction is needed because, they argue, there is a continuity of preoccupations from the moment of European imperial aggression onwards. To create a break at the moment of independence, they argue, creates a false idea of the way culture develops: it is the inception of colonialism that crucially alters writing and identity, while independence just complicates it. However, this is not widely accepted, partly because it seems reductive of the importance and effects of independence, and partly because it becomes such a blanket term that it loses almost all specificity.

Most commonly, however, 'post-colonial' refers to an approach rather than a historical period. Some critics use the absence or the presence of the hyphen to signal the two meanings. In terms of an approach, it is one that is consciously aware of and positioned against the ideology of colonialism and neo-colonialism. By neo-colonialism, it is generally

meant the way in which the West continues to maintain maximum indirect control over ex-colonies through economic, cultural, and political mechanisms.

The term 'post-colonial' has other difficulties because it stresses the importance of European influence in a country's development and in the contemporary World. Some critics resent the term 'post-colonial' in the same way that they reject 'Third World': because it defines the world in terms of the major colonial powers. To say that Pakistan is a post-colonial country implicitly defines it in terms of Britain. Lastly, the term 'post-colonial' seems to lump together widely varying experiences: if India, Rhodesia, Australia and Brazil are all post-colonial countries, their differences are lost in this blanket term.

Additionally, the second half of the twentieth century has been marked by huge demographic shifts. The dismantling of the European empires is one major reason for this, together with the economic, military, nationalist and cultural pressures that have followed on from colonialism. Collective identities along lines of nation or ethnicity are both more forcefully asserted and more complex: dual or multiple affiliations are common and terms such as black British and Indian English are needed to express many people's self-identifications. Many contemporary 'British' writers are displaced or repatriated, born in one country and now living in another: Salman Rushdie (Bombay), Caryl Phillips (St Kitts), Lauretta Ngcobo (South Africa), Grace Nichols (Guyana) and so on. Other prominent writers have far more complex histories: the novelist and playwright Nuruddin Farah was born in Somalia, educated in Ogaden, the Punjab, London and Essex, lived in Somalia until 1973 and has since migrated between Nigeria, Gambia, Sudan, France, Germany, Italy, the USA and Uganda. Again, the national and ethnic make-up of V.S. Naipaul is complex as he was born in Trinidad to parents of Indian descent but lived most of his life in England. His novels and essays repeatedly probe Indian (*An Area of Darkness*), Caribbean (*Miguel Street*) and British (*The Enigma of Arrival*) identity, just as Salman Rushdie's novels dissect Indian (*Midnight's Children*), Pakistani (*Shame*) and multicultural British (*The Satanic Verses*) colonial legacies. As Elleke

Boehmer (1995: 233) has argued, cultural expatriation is also a key theme in novels like V.S. Naipaul's *Guerillas* (1975), Amitav Ghosh's *The Shadow-Lines* (1988) and Chinua Achebe's *Anthills of the Savannah* (1987).

The importance of post-colonial issues to contemporary British writing can be gauged by the Booker Prize. Novels set in India, and linked with the Raj, won the Booker in 1973 (J.G. Farrell's *The Siege of Krishnapur*), 1975 (Ruth Prawer Jhabvala's *Heat and Dust*), 1977 (Paul Scott's *Staying On*) and 1981 (Rushdie's *Midnight's Children*). Other winners often discussed in post-colonial studies have been Keri Hulme, Ben Okri, Kazuo Ishiguro, Michael Ondaatje, Arundhati Roy and J.M. Coetzee. Indeed, there is hardly a winner who could easily fall outside the limits of post-colonial writing, a fact which emphasizes both its power as a discursive category and its in some ways disabling pervasiveness.

See also: literature, African; literature, Caribbean; literature, Indian

Further reading

Ashcroft, B., Griffiths, G. and Tiffin, H. (1989) *The Empire Writes Back*, London: Routledge.

Boehmer, E. (1995) *Colonial and Postcolonial Literature*, Oxford: Opus.

Childs, P. (ed.) (1999) *Post-Colonial Theory and English Literature*, Edinburgh: Edinburgh University Press.

PETER CHILDS

postmodernism

The use of the term 'postmodernism' in connection with architecture was not common until the critic Charles Jencks began publishing on the subject in 1975. Jencks described postmodernism as primarily a matter of 'double coding', by which he meant the simultaneous appeal to different publics. The new architecture owed everything, structurally, to the modern movement (see **modernism**), but at the same time its concern for the facade challenged modernist ideology about form and function. Meanwhile the facades themselves could be doubly

coded, appealing to an 'interested minority', such as architects and critics, as well as the general public. In practice, postmodern architecture made use of modern building techniques – steel or concrete frames, curtain walling, lifts, mechanical servicing and so on – but allowed decoration to return to the facade. Above all, the playful use of the facade allowed postmodern buildings to respond to the styles in their immediate surroundings.

Postmodernist treatment of the façade was ironic. Gothic, classical, or other forms were appropriated playfully, an approach quite distinct from the nineteenth century battle of styles, in which what was being contested though the style of public buildings was nothing less than national identity. Irony separates postmodern architecture not only from these earlier appropriations of style, but from the modern movement which was itself formally varied, and also late modern architecture, represented in Britain by architects such as Norman Foster (see **Foster Associates**) and Richard **Rogers**.

Postmodernism was the dominant architectural mode during the 1980s, but there is little doubt that it has now been superseded. Before 1981, nearly all building described as postmodern had been American, for good reason: before 1981, nearly all building in Britain had taken place in the public sector, and all areas of this had been subject to strict ideological controls. Public sector architects brought up with the belief that architecture could be socially improving had no time for the exuberant facadism associated with the postmodern. There was, it should also be noted, relatively little demand for commercial architecture until the financial boom of the mid-1980s. Postmodernism in Britain is therefore closely associated with the changes of the first two periods of Conservative government after 1979, and as a result has tended to be described unfavourably by left-wing critics.

Regarding postmodern buildings in Britain, it should be remarked first that some of the most significant projects (Canary Wharf, The Sainsbury Wing to the National Gallery, the Broadgate development in the City of London) were designed by American architects, or had substantial American involvement in the planning stages. Second, true postmodern architecture as defined by Jencks is generally only found in London. The economic boom of the 1980s benefited London and the South East much more than other parts of the country, and consequently the opportunities (or the will) to build exuberant architecture were much more limited.

The Clore Gallery extension to the Tate Gallery, built by James **Stirling**, was probably the first major public example of the style to appear. Built 1982–6, it comprises an L-shaped extension built around a small garden. Its complex facade relates to the elements of the older buildings immediately adjacent, so it continues, but quickly modifies, the classicism of the main gallery building. There are a number of characteristic jokes, too: the bright green colour of the window frames is deliberately provocative, while a stone is deliberately left 'missing' at the junction of the old building and the new, as if to pretend that the building is not quite complete.

A similarly chameleon-like building was the Sainsbury Wing extension to the National Gallery, built 1987–91 and designed by the American architect Robert Venturi and partners. Its five facades each relate to a different part of the surrounding environment. The Corinthian columns of the Trafalgar Square side continue, but modify, the main facade of the original building; the second facade, adjacent to this, relates to the more sober Canada House and the gentlemens' clubs beyond.

Terry Farrell's vast office schemes at Vauxhall Cross (1989–92), now occupied by MI6, and Embankment Place (1991) are among the best-known postmodern buildings, because of their size and their prominent sites along the Thames. The latter, which makes use of air-rights above Charing Cross station, is closely related in a number of ways to the surrounding environment. The scheme was linked to environmental improvements such as the pedestrianization of Villiers Street and the establishment of a direct link from the station to Hungerford Bridge. But more significant are the historical references the building makes: its main form is a giant arched roof, from which are suspended the office floors. Facing the river is a giant glazed front, punctuated by a round bay faced in stone. The effect recalls a Victorian railway station, yet this is deceptive; the arches

do not contain the expected open space, but conventional offices. There are nautical references too, connecting with the ships moored nearby on the Embankment: the bay at the front of the building suggests the bridge of a battleship.

Perhaps the most bizarre postmodern office projects was Minster Court (1988–91), built by GMW Partnership in the City of London The scheme is designed to look like a medieval cathedral, and is on the same scale; its central atrium is effectively a nave.

Other British architects associated with post-modernism are Jeremy Dixon, for housing in Docklands and elsewhere; John **Outram** for a storm water pumping station in Docklands; and Campbell Zoglowitch Wilkinson Gough for housing in Docklands (including 'Cascades', a twenty-storey tower on a nautical theme). Outram has continued to design buildings with highly decorated, allegorical facades, but most major post-modernist architects have moved on: the later work of Farrell and Stirling is better described as a reconfigured modernism, and most younger architects seem to prefer this mode. The quotation of historical styles is still common, but Outram apart, this tends to be done much more soberly than before.

Further reading

Jencks, C. (1977) *The Language of Postmodern Architecture*, London: Academy Editions.

RICHARD J. WILLIAMS

postmodernist theory

'Postmodern' is a contested term for various social and cultural phenomena arising in capitalist societies of the late twentieth century: expansion of multinational companies and decline of nation-states, growth of commodification and consumerism, extension of electronic media and the Internet, weakening of traditional and communal forms of social legitimation and undermining of all claims to universal truth. Where theorists differ is in their naming, analysis and estimation of these phenomena. For some, they are the intensification of processes already begun in the modern period, and are effects of 'high' or 'late' modernity; for others, they mark a break with what has gone before and are properly named postmodern. More philosophical uses of 'modern' and 'postmodern' point to changing sensibilities or ways of understanding the nature of the human person, of knowledge and belief, and of claims to truth and meaning. Many theorists combine a mixture of these concerns and interests, and greet the postmodern with varying degrees of enthusiasm.

Postmodernism – as the advocacy of the postmodern – trades on its distinction from the modern and its cult, modernism. But the meaning and reference of the latter is as varied and contested as that of the former. For some it is a historical period, while for others it is a mode of thought and sensibility. But since the latter is always named after its typical appearance in the former – as with Descartes's self-authenticating 'I' in the seventeenth century – one can think the modern that period in which a certain mode of self-understanding, scientific practice and social order came into being. It is when these are questioned and lose their credibility that the postmodern arrives; at least, this is the story told by Jean-François Lyotard.

Religions once provided societies with master stories or grand narratives, 'sacred canopies' (Peter Berger) that offered meaning and security. Modernity replaced God with Man or some other explanatory force: natural (Darwin), social (Marx) or psychological (Freud). Lyotard's favoured example is the old communist meta-narrative of emancipation and socialist utopia, which was defeated in the Soviet bloc by the telling of many mini-narratives (*petit récits*). The postmodern condition is then one in which social and personal life is no longer ordered by a metanarrative, but where each individual has to take responsibility for his or her own story.

This can be read as an intensification of modern autonomy, but it differs from the project of modernity in disavowing any utopic trajectory. There is no hope of a better tomorrow because tomorrow has arrived today. This is caught in the oxymoronic nature of the term 'postmodern', which suggests a time or condition after the 'now', as if we were living ahead of ourselves.

The postmodern is the 'future now', and so the end of history. From now on, the future can mean only more of the same. At the same time, this condition is one of intense disorientation and confusion.

The postmodern would be but a new name for the old avant-garde – for objects and practices that exist ahead of, or before the habits and rules that (will) make them comprehensible – if it were not that it is now held to be ubiquitous. The old avant-garde was an elite, a scandal to the generality, from which nevertheless it took its bearings. But once everything is avant-garde, all of culture is ahead of itself, and thus without orientation and direction. Most theorists of the postmodern are concerned with giving an account of this condition.

Fredric Jameson finds an analogue for the postmodern in the 'hyperspace' of John Portman's Westin Bonaventure hotel in Los Angeles (the quintessential postmodern city). The hermetic, complex and (initially) unsigned spaces of the hotel simulates those of the larger city, depriving its inhabitants of any sense of location, either in the larger city or in the hotel itself. It thus becomes a symbol of that wider sense of disorientation which is life in the 'great global multinational and decentred communicational network' that is late capitalism (Jameson 1991: 44).

Jean Baudrillard is similarly concerned with the unsettling effects (social and moral) of rampant commodification and consumerism, when all objects become signs, and reality gives way to **hyperreality**, as with the Gulf War (1991), when the military-media staged 'bloodless' missile attacks for home consumption on television news programmes. Baudrillard's account of postmodern culture as a sea of signs without depth, in which we can never touch bottom, is paralleled by deconstructionist theories (associated with Jacques Derrida), which find all cultural life textual. Reality no longer founds meaning (and truth) but is itself an effect of textuality, the economy of signs which produces our sense of the 'real'.

Zygmunt Bauman characterizes postmodernity as the radical privatizing of the fear of the Void, once held at bay by the modern metanarrative of scientific rationality and human progress, epitomized by the panoptic prison, where all are seen and all are happy. Postmodernity trades in such security for freedom; but in so doing, the Void returns, and now to each alone. Now each individual has to provide his or her own shelter. This raises the problem of legitimation. We need someone (God) or something (science) to confirm our story, to tell us that we have got it right. In postmodernity this is provided by imaginary communities which, unlike real ones, do not restrict individual freedoms. However, to convince they must be seen, and therefore compete for public attention through spectacular displays, whether acts of terrorism or public grief at the death of glamour icons (Princess Diana). With ethics founded on private whim, Bauman anticipates growing tribalism and intolerance, yet also espies a world re-enchanted. To discern which, we must await what comes after the postmodern.

See also: postmodernism; postmodernist writing

Further reading

Bauman, Z. (1992) *Intimations of Postmodernity*, London: Routledge.

Jameson, F. (1991) *Postmodernism, or, the Cultural Logic of Late Capitalism*, London: Verso.

Lyotard, J.-F. (1984) *The Postmodern Condition: A Report on Knowledge*, trans. G. Bennington and B. Massumi, Manchester: Manchester University Press.

GERARD LOUGHLIN

postmodernist writing

The foremost difficulty in characterizing postmodernist writing is distinguishing it from the traits of high modernist texts such as Woolf's *Orlando*, Eliot's *The Waste Land* and Joyce's *Ulysses*. Because the texts of both periods are associated with a focus on stylization that highlights fragmentary organization and intertextual echoes, identifying distinguishing features other than date of composition has been a primary task of attempts to describe what is truly postmodernist about contemporary writing and not merely retreaded modernism.

David Lodge, in one of the first attempts to evaluate postmodernist writing, argues that postmodernism deploys devices such as contradiction, permutation of narrative line, discontinuity, randomness, excessive figural substitution and short-circuiting of the 'gap between text and world'. Such strategies are employed in an attempt to avoid choosing between the metaphoric and metonymic patterns that had characterized modernist and anti-modernist writing, respectively. Linda Hutcheon similarly emphasizes the tendency of postmodernist writing towards a self-unravelling. She argues that contemporary texts, such as those of Salman Rushdie, Angela Carter and Julian Barnes, emphasize a strategy of irony, a trope achieved by a self-conscious awareness of the text's own fabricated nature, an awareness that knowingly undermines its own textual features. A particularly important mode of the practice of this self-deconstruction is intertextuality, the echoes and allusions to previous texts stressing the fact that a contemporary piece of writing is itself a fabricated document, a move that allows the postmodernist text to problematize our understanding of its 'sources.'

In contrast, the shift from modernism to postmodernism is primarily a philosophical one for Brian McHale, one characterized by a switch in focus from epistemological to ontological problems. Postmodernist writing no longer questions what can be known through the use of competing accounts and stream of consciousness narratives, but instead questions the unity and harmony of a single reality by highlighting the fragmentary and multiplicit natures of textuality and subjectivity. Pastiche (as seen in a writer such as Angela Carter or John Fowles) is the dominant feature of postmodernism according to Fredric Jameson in a formulation that likewise stresses the allusive and disjunctive nature of current writing. Because master narratives of history no longer seem sustainable, it has become impossible to order individual events, moments and texts into an account that is able to offer a coherent narrative of how they relate to one another. Without this stabilizing metanarrative, postmodernism is thus in this account condemned emptily to echo texts of the past, regurgitating them without being able to offer a consistent explanation of their relevance or importance.

See also: novel; postmodernist theory

Further reading

Hutcheon, L. (1988) *A Poetics of Postmodernism*, New York: Routledge.

RYAN S. TRIMM

post-structuralism

Post-structuralism is a term applied to a range of positions and approaches in critical and cultural theory, developed in and from the work of Jacques Derrida, Michel Foucault, Jacques Lacan, Julia Kristeva and Louis Althusser among others. Post-structuralist theory has been increasingly influential in Britain since the 1960s, particularly in literary and cultural studies. It is a term which marks a connection with, and departure from, an earlier theoretical stance, namely **structuralism**. Both 'post-structuralism' and 'structuralism' describe theoretical approaches developed within a diversity of fields of enquiry, ranging from anthropology and psychoanalysis to linguistics, literary or textual, and cultural studies. After, and in some instances before, Derrida's inauguration of 'deconstruction', a reading strategy that does not 'interpret' a text but expose its workings and reveal its hierarchical assumptions, post-structuralists in such fields as psychoanalysis (Jacques Lacan and Julia Kristeva) and history (Michel Foucault and Hayden White) have decentred the principles and precepts of many traditional disciplines. Most important, since post-structuralist interventions, the human subject is now seen as without an 'essence', 'nature', or capacity for 'self-determination', and is instead seen as being inserted in language and discourse. The subject is therefore not considered the centre of history, and such categories as 'meaning' and 'experience' are also no longer authenticated by appeals to the individual consciousness.

The most widely influential work in both structuralism and post-structuralism has been concerned with articulating alternative models of language and subjectivity to those deployed by the empiricist-idealist philosophy which underpins 'common sense' ideas. The most influential theorists of language within structuralism and post-structuralism were, respectively, the Swiss linguist Ferdinand de Saussure and the French philosopher Jacques Derrida. Among structuralism's most important premises was that meanings do not precede language but are constructed by it. Its model of language as a structure in which meaning is produced through the differential relationship of arbitrary signs, each consisting of a signifier (sound image or written shape) and signified (concept), challenged the idea that language reflects reality and that words are labels for things or thoughts.

Post-structuralism built on this work but made a number of significant challenges to structuralism, which was seen as only partly escaping the constraints of traditional Western thought, notably of its scientific and formalist claims and of its limited acknowledgement of historical context. Jacques Derrida endorsed the structuralist model of language but argued that it still privileged concepts or signifieds. His own analysis of 'logocentrism', forms of thought which are grounded in belief in an external reference point such as God or truth, suggested that traditional Western philosophy and metaphysics has maintained a hierarchy in which ideas or thought are primary and writing is a secondary vehicle. In his deconstructive reading of key texts of Western thought, Derrida observed that this hierarchical division was often sustained by what he termed 'phonocentrism', the privileging of speech over writing, based on the assumption that speech directly expresses thought in a way that writing cannot. In contrast Derrida argued that language is a kind of writing and employed the term 'différance', a compound of two French words meaning to differ and defer, to describe and exemplify the way in which meaning is contextual and never absolute.

In British post-structuralist analysis, this model of the production of meaning was combined with ideas from Althusser's reformulation of the Marxist concept of ideology which posited a new understanding of the human subject. Although the analysis of texts and various types of signification is a key strand of post-structuralist work, it is matched by attention to the subject addressed by, and produced by, signifying practices. As Saussure and Derrida's analyses of language overturned conventional idealist–empiricist models, so post-structuralist theories of subjectivity have challenged traditional Western ideas about the status of the subject.

Post-structuralism's challenge to the idea of the human subject as the autonomous source of meaning was developed from work on language and in the work of the psychoanalytic theorist Jacques Lacan, of feminists like Hélène Cixous and Julia Kristeva, and in the cultural and historical analysis of Michel Foucault. In adopting and deploying this work, British critics have explored a wide range of issues of power, knowledge and discourse.

As post-structuralist theories have been adopted and adapted within academic institutions, certain forms, notably deconstruction as practised by some academics in the United States, have been criticized for being either too playful and ignoring the harsh realities of capitalism or for being easily recuperated by a conservative academy. In Britain, where many of its practitioners had or have occupied a Marxist or socialist position, post-structuralism is marked by a more clearly radical theoretical and political engagement and an understanding that criticism is a form of intervention in political and cultural debates and struggles to change existing power relations.

Post-structuralism in Britain has been an important force in changing the content, form and relationships between various academic disciplines which address, as the stress on analysing a diversity of signifying practices necessitates a reappraisal of conventional divisions of knowledge. Among the best-known exponents of post-structuralist theory and analysis in Britain are Colin MacCabe and Stephen Heath, whose contributions to the journal *Screen* were extremely influential in the 1970s, and also Catherine Belsey, Antony Easthope and Christopher Norris.

See also: literary theory

Further reading

Easthope, A. (1988) *British Post-structuralism since 1968*, London: Routledge (a wide-ranging, knowledgeable and critical review across the social sciences and humanities).

TAMSIN SPARGO

Potter, Dennis

b. 1935, Forest of Dean; d. 1994

Playwright

Dennis Potter is the outstanding 'author' of serious television drama (see **drama on television**), with over forty works to his credit. From the early *Stand Up, Nigel Barton* (1965) to plays of his maturity such as *Pennies From Heaven* (1978) and *Blue Remembered Hills* (1979), Potter arrested attention with his individualistic world view and experimentation with form. Continually dramatising aspects of his own predicament, Potter drew the key themes of sexuality, spirituality, vocation and nostalgia together most successfully in *The Singing Detective* (1985), endowing the protagonist with the crippling skin disease that had handicapped his own career. From this time until his much publicized death from cancer, his writing becomes increasingly self-referential and arguably produced more interesting television events than successful drama.

See also: playwrights

Further reading

Cook, J. (1995) *Dennis Potter: A Life on Screen*, Manchester: Manchester University Press.

BOB MILLINGTON

Potter, Sally

b. 1947

Film-maker

Sally Potter is something of a controversial figure in British independent cinema and a champion of feminist issues. Her 1979 short 'thriller' is now regarded as a 'classic' feminist deconstruction of sexual politics in its re-working of 'La Boheme.' Her feature debut *The Gold Diggers* (1983) pursued similar themes, challenging the 'oedipal trajectory' of contemporary narratives and their inherent misrepresentation of general issues. Working in television towards the late 1980s she made several programmes including *Women in Soviet Cinema* and *Tears, Laughter, Fear and Rage*, a discourse examining the representation of emotion. In 1992 she achieved international recognition with her exuberant adaptation of Virginia Woolf's *Orlando*, blending visual flare with a more conventional narrative structure but still remaining true to her concerns regarding the corruption of sexuality. In *Tango* (1977), she further explored her long-time affair with the dance (and with her tutor), but the film received mixed responses owing to its rather claustrophobic self-indulgence.

See also: film, feminist

ROB FILLINGHAM

poverty

Popular representations of poverty have included references to 'scroungers' on the 'Costa del Dole', 'aggressive beggars', the 'dependency culture' and the 'underclass'. Although closer to home, the impact of images of 'cardboard city' has paled in comparison with depictions of the abject poverty of overseas refugee camps.

'Poverty' is a contested concept. Proponents of definitions of 'absolute poverty' which stress biological needs have vied with supporters of the notion of 'relative deprivation', which emphasizes cultural needs. Using the former conception, Lord Joseph claimed in 1976 that, since starvation is the essential characteristic of the condition, poverty was almost non-existent in Britain. Employing the latter notion, whereby people are poor if they cannot afford to engage in customary social behaviour (buying one's grandchild a Christmas present without thereby suffering hypothermia through scrimping on fuel, for instance), researchers such as Townsend have repudiated the myth that poverty had been abolished in an affluent, postwar British society.

While no official 'poverty line' exists in Britain, the unofficial benchmark of half the national average income is often cited. From 1979, depressed lower wages, more regressive taxation and welfare cuts led to massive increases in those beneath this line. Those most vulnerable to poverty include the long-term unemployed, the low-waged, the elderly dependent on state pensions, the disabled and chronically sick, the welfare-dependent one-parent families and, more generally, children and ethnic minorities.

Homelessness has received much media attention. The charity Shelter has observed that the 'official homeless' (those accepted as such by local authorities) nearly trebled between 1978 and 1991. In addition, it estimated that there were some 1.7 million 'unofficial homeless' in 1991.

Increasingly, the term 'underclass' has been used in both journalistic and academic discussion of poverty. The notion has been profitably peddled by Charles Murray. In 1989, he claimed to discern a nascent, British underclass. Characteristics of this putative stratum include high rates of illegitimacy, criminality and self-chosen unemployment. Murray's view that the underclass is marked not so much by its deprivation as by the 'deplorable behaviour' of its members has been widely castigated as crass and victim-blaming. Versions of the underclass thesis which emphasize structural inequality rather than cultural aberration have been more acceptable to most British academics, but for many the term is seen as so confused and stigmatic as to warrant erasure from social scientific vocabulary.

See also: single parents

Further reading

Oppenheim, C. (1993) *Poverty: The Facts*, London: CPAG (a comprehensive, accessible analysis).

ROD PATERSON

poverty, families and

Single-parent families (see **single parents**) tend to be financially worse off than two-parent ones. Ninety-one percent of single parents are women. Women's wages (for mothers who are able to work) average £301 per week, versus £414 for men. Thus families living in one-carer homes are doubly financially disadvantaged and frequently live below the poverty line. Although they are eligible for state benefits such as income support and housing benefit, families at the bottom of the economic pile fall into the trap of not having time or skills to apply for them. The Labour government's proposal to bring in a minimum wage may not help them. Underfunded support organizations such as Shelter and Child Poverty Action Group are their best hope.

See also: homelessness

MIKE STORRY

Powell, Michael

b. 1905, Bekebourne, Kent; d. 1990

Film-maker

Michael Powell is perhaps best known for his partnership with the Hungarian writer Emeric Pressburger. Their independent production company, The Archers, was responsible for the production of some of the finest films of the 1940s and 1950s, including *The Life and Death of Colonel Blimp*, *A Matter of Life and Death*, *The Red Shoes* and *Black Narcissus*. Powell himself wrote, directed and produced along with Pressburger, and his work is held up by many contemporary directors as being amongst the finest ever made. Powell's films have a rich, colourful feel, something uncommon in other British directors, and he used his medium to create work that blurred the divisions between fantasy and real life.

SAM JOHNSTONE

Powell and Moya

In 1946, two years after graduating from the **Architectural Association** School in London, Arnold J.P. Powell and John Hidalgo Moya founded their partnership to carry out the Pimlico Housing Scheme (now Churchill Gardens, 1946–62), which they had won in open competition. Positioned amongst the surrounding fine nineteenth-century terraces and squares, the development was widely acknowledged as one of the first significant postwar comprehensive redevelopment schemes in London. Influential both in attempting to establish a postwar vernacular, and in suggesting a radically new form of urban life based on Le Corbusier's Ville Radieuse, 634 flats of varying size were provided in thirty-six slab blocks of two, four, seven and nine storeys, built in four sections parallel and at right angles to the river. Considered to be exemplary from the outset, Pevsner commented in the early 1980s that: 'The aesthetic significance of Churchill Gardens is that even now, after twenty-five years, it has remained one of the best estates in London'. At first thought elegant and generating well-scaled spaces between them, the slab blocks are now believed to convey an image of overcrowding which fell short of the idealism of their continental inspiration. Now considered megalithic, desolate and cheerless, the scheme is accused, together with the Gospel Oak Estate (1954–80), where Powell and Moya designed a row of houses, of belonging to those well-intentioned architectural crimes committed by the welfare state. Problems have been excused on the grounds of high-density building, but this popular myth is exploded when numbers are compared with those housed in neighbouring Dolphin Square, designed in 1937.

Other work includes the 'skylon' at the Festival of Britain, London 1951; Mayfield Comprehensive School, Putney (1956) described by Ian Nairn as 'subtle, elegant, humane'; the addition to Brasenose College, Oxford (1959), recognizably modern but at the same time respectful of its historical context in its use of stone and lead; the innovative hexagonal theatre with arena stage, Chichester (1961); Cripps Buildings, St John's College, Cambridge (1964), large and linear in form, employing Portland stone and concrete; Princess Margaret Hospital, Swindon (1972), and the Museum of London, in the Barbican redevelopment (1976). Approached at an upper level by bridges, the latter's rather bland and utilitarian exterior belies the extraordinary richness of material relating to the social and cultural development of London housed within.

HILARY GRAINGER

power dressing

A repercussion of the rise in numbers of women entering the workforce, power dressing evolved in the late 1970s as an appropriate form of dress for the office. Power dressers wore sharp, tailored suits with padded shoulders, crisp shirts and court shoes creating a sharp silhouette. This look attempted to address the problem of an appropriate mode of dress for working women, as by the nineteenth-century the male suit had become the metonymic signifier of the world of work, materialism and power. Consequently, the dress of the working woman was problematical as traditionally a woman dressed in expensive clothes was not making a statement about herself but about a man. Power dressers were working women whose dress signified status.

See also: women in business

CAROLINE COX

prejudice

Legally meaning 'damage', prejudice more commonly implies an irrational pre-conceived opinion. The eighteenth-century essayist Joseph Addison's reference to 'natural prejudices' would now be thought odd, as it has been socially outrageous to admit prejudice since the late 1960s. The law forbids bias on grounds of race, gender or marital status (but not age), and some employers voluntarily add sexual orientation and **disability**. There are contested exceptions for the armed forces. Demands by the disabled for access have been made with increasing vigour. All these issues have been championed by supporters of **political correctness** who hope to change attitudes by abolishing certain ideas or words, believing that a rose by any other name would smell completely different.

The effectiveness of this approach is debatable since prejudice is not easy to quantify when most prejudice is secret. Some people bemoan what they call 'the race relations industry', resentfully accusing it of giving unfair advantages to minorities. In reality, its influence is also doubtful and new prejudices evolve unexpectedly. In 1997 there were incidents of anti-white Asian violence in west London, where violence between Sikhs and Muslims had been developing for several years. The **Nation of Islam** movement in New York, which is black, anti-Jewish, anti-white and preaches apartheid for blacks, established itself in London in 1995 but has yet to gain many converts.

Prejudices not generally discussed seem to be subject to different criteria to those against groups more usually seen as having grievances. Men are abused by feminists and this is apparently acceptable, but a men's movement grew up in the early 1990s to fight back. The movement has not been taken very seriously, except inasmuch as there are those who are prepared to weep for their fathers or childhoods. Years of unemployment and rising crime in Liverpool have made Scousers a target. Islamic fundamentalist terrorism and the Salman **Rushdie Affair** have provoked anti-Islamic prejudice.

Some prejudices are acceptable. Hostility to the aristocracy, **monarchy**, big business, or even estate agents is explicable, if possibly unfair. Similarly, the 1988 anti-apartheid song 'I've never met a nice South African' would have been banned if it attacked almost any other nation. **Hippies**, trainspotters and collectors of obscure facts known since 1988 as 'anoraks' are also targets. Why these largely harmless people attract so much venom, unless it is their cultural isolationism, remains mysterious in the face of supreme viciousness and pomposity on display elsewhere. Society and social relations appear to foster prejudices, even if only against our neighbours.

Further reading

Bohm, D. (1996) *On Dialogue*, London: Routledge (leading physicist and thinker explains how to examine prejudices and assumptions).

STEPHEN KERENSKY

Presbyterianism

Presbyterianism is an important Protestant strand within the Christian tradition. As indicated by its name, derived form a Greek word meaning 'old', its distinguishing feature is the system by which individual churches are regulated by its senior members, its so-called 'elders' (who need not in fact be the most aged). Though it emerged as a force during the Reformation, Presbyterianism does not see itself as an innovation, but rather as the restoration of a form of church governance inherited from the synagogues that was characteristic of Christianity in its earliest days, before authoritarian centralization by bishops under the pope. Theologically, Presbyterianism looks to the doctrines advanced by the Genevan reformer John Calvin (1509–64), with their stress on the helplessness of the individual, who is necessarily sinful as a consequence of original sin unless aided by the free gift of divine grace, and on strict ethical standards in personal life and business. In worship, which generally follows accepted patterns though there is no fixed liturgy, the accent is on dignified simplicity without ritualism. Main features are Bible readings and sermons in which the minister expounds scripture, often drawing out practical moral lessons. Though respected, communion is not a central concern as in Catholicism; it is celebrated at varying intervals – sometimes just twice a year – in the different Presbyterian churches.

Strong in Scotland since the time of the formidable reformer John Knox (c.1513–72), Presbyterianism is the doctrine of the Church of Scotland. As well as standing out against the claims of the Episcopal Church of Scotland, it suffered over the centuries from internal feuding. In England, Congregationalism, as it was called, emerged at the time of the Reformation. Breaking away from the Church of England its adherents, under the designation 'Independents', won Cromwell's favour during the Civil War, and though they were attacked for non-conformity at the Restoration, they continued in their own way. In 1832 they amalgamated with the Congregational Church of Wales, and in 1972 the Congregationalists joined with the English Presbyterians, with whom they had marked affinities despite certain differences on organization, to form the United Reformed Church. The Presbyterian and Congregational churches founded across the Empire and beyond, to provide for expatriates and carry out missionary work, have since the War also generally combined in pioneering successful ecumenical experiments.

See also: Anglican Church; Protestant churches

Further reading

Bulloch, J. (1977) *The Church of Scotland*, Exeter: Religious Education Press.
Slack, K. (1978) *The United Reformed Church*, Exeter: Religious Education Press.

CHRISTOPHER SMITH

Press Association

The Press Association (PA) is a widely respected news provider based in London. All regional newspaper groups own PA shares, including the **Mirror Group**, Pearson-Longman and Associated Newspapers. Founded when the British Parliament acquired two telephone companies in 1868, by 1925 the PA had 100 London journalists and 1,500 provincial stringers. Today, the PA provides an extensive news service, a library with research services, feature interviews with leading politicians, live sports coverage and, since 1996, a regional advertising service on the Internet with News International. The PA's dominance of its market has recently been challenged by the Leicester-based UK News Group, and this may affect the PA's plans to become a public company on the London Stock Exchange in the year 2000.

See also: Associated Press; Express Group; News International; Telegraph plc

ANDREW QUICKE

Press Council

A voluntary Press Council was established in 1953 with avowed aims of maintaining high ethical standards within journalism and promoting freedom of the Press. During the 1980s, the efficacy of the Press Council was questioned in lieu of a number of instances of tabloid excess. An ensuing report (the Calcutt Report) recommended the setting up of a new Press Complaints Commission (PCC), which occurred in 1991 against the backdrop of the introduction of a statutory complaints tribunal if the revamped voluntary body failed to be effective. The PCC consists of both representatives of the press and lay members, and it seeks to enforce a Code of Conduct which includes issues such as **privacy**, harassment, accuracy or reporting and chequebook journalism.

See also: Express Group; Mirror Group; News International; Telegraph plc

GUY OSBORN
STEVE GREENFIELD

pressure groups

Pressure groups are organizations whose members act collectively to affect public policy in order to promote a common interest. They are usually distinguishable from political parties in that they do not wish to govern. They may be divided into interest groups, which represent the concerns of their members – examples include **trade unions** and professional bodies – and cause groups, whose members share common attitudes towards a specific issue which will generally benefit society or a section of the community. These are divided between insider groups, which are viewed as legitimate by government and are consulted on a regular basis, and outsider groups who are excluded from access to the decision-making process. NIMBY (Not In My Back Yard) groups also exist to tackle local issues.

Pressure groups now adopt a professional approach, often employing former politicians or civil servants with knowledge of the corridors of power. The most successful groups influence policy through the executive, and the concentration of power in the hands of the executive under the Thatcher administration has made this even more important. Pressure groups also work through **parliament**. Trade unions achieve this by sponsoring Labour MPs and select committees are also lobbied. Large pressure groups are also increasingly lobbying at European level. Some pressure groups use public campaigns, but this is usually interpreted as a last resort for outsider groups such as CND. Nevertheless, this approach can occasionally succeed, as with the Anti Poll Tax Federation whose well-supported demonstrations contributed to the community charge being scrapped (see **poll tax**).

Until the 1980s, government would consult pressure groups before legislation and the trade unions and the **CBI** enjoyed a special relationship with the executive on corporatist bodies. Conflict increased with the unions in the 1970s, but the Thatcher governments were explicitly hostile to pressure groups. Yet pressure group activity continued to rise, especially in groups concerned with issues not traditionally dealt with by the main political parties. Consultation was very limited with the advent of conviction politics, even when important reforms were to be introduced. The New Right consider pressure groups to be undemocratic organizations which undermine legitimate government. This attitude contrasts with the one-nation Conservative view of **democracy**, which stresses governing by consent, and with pluralists who contend that pressure groups are at the heart of the democratic process as they encourage participation in politics.

See also: Friends of the Earth and Greenpeace; lobby groups

Further reading

Baggott, R. (1995) *Pressure Groups Today*, Manchester: Manchester University Press.

COLIN WILLIAMS

Price, Antony

b. 1945

Fashion designer

Born in 1945, Price was at the forefront of British glamrock culture and style in the early 1970s. After studying at Bradford College of Art and working as a designer for Stirling Cooper and Plaza, he founded his own label in 1979. Price designed fashions for the stars of **glam rock**, notably Bryan Ferry and his band Roxy Music. His glamorous, impeccably cut designs in luxurious fabrics drew attention to themselves and to the wearer's body, offering a combination of sophistication and sex appeal which flirted with but was never quite reduced to the fetishistic.

TAMSIN SPARGO

Prince of Wales's Institute

In architecture, as in farming and countryside management, Prince Charles is essentially a traditionalist worried about a headlong dash for modernity that may cause irreparable harm to the environment and the people inhabiting it. Though experts who insist they 'know best' are generally outraged, his opinions are often shared by the public at large. As well as airing his views at speaking engagements, writing *A Vision of England* (1989) and developing Poundbury near Dorchester as a model village to express his ideals in practice, he founded in 1992 the Prince of Wales's Institute in London to train architects and planners in blending traditional values with modern styles and techniques.

See also: Architectural Association; RIBA

Further reading

Jencks, C. (1988), *The Prince, the Architects*, London: Academy (though published before the Institute's foundation, it provides valuable background).

CHRISTOPHER SMITH

privacy

The issue of privacy centres around the notion that a person's individual and family life should be free from unwanted intrusion, whether from institutions of state or the media. However, there is no right to privacy enshrined in English law. In the 1990s, concern centred on the weakness of the **Press Council** in preventing media intrusion into the personal lives of public figures. The royal family were subjected to the most intense scrutiny, details of Princess Diana's telephone conversations and the 'Camillagate' tapes being published, while telephoto lenses and electronic bugs were used to reveal their marital difficulties. The **Conservative Party** also suffered through a string of lurid revelations concerning the sex lives of MPs.

See also: monarchy; sex scandals

COLIN WILLIAMS

privatization

Privatization is the act of returning to private ownership a company or concern that is owned by the state, while nationalization is conversely the opposite. In the postwar period up to the Thatcher administration, nationalization remained prevalent. The Thatcher era changed this.

The validity of nationalization can be explained from the perspective of market failures. Markets are not perfect, because monopoly conditions, externalities and imperfect information can all cause them to be inefficient. Neither do markets distribute in an equitable manner. It was believed that the government had a role to play both in the redistribution of wealth and countering inefficiency. Nationalized industries are also a useful political tool for managing the economy as a whole, especially if using Keynesian demand management economics. It was thought that by investing in public sector projects the government could also stimulate the private sector. Because the nationalized industries in Britain were used as economic tools and many decisions were taken on a political as opposed to an economic level, they were not as commercially viable as they otherwise might have been.

The Thatcher administration in essence supported this view believing in the primacy of the market, postulating that government intervention would itself distort the market to the detriment of the industries involved. The market would, if left free of regulation, result in the optimum allocation of resources to the benefit of the industry and the economy as a whole. By merely regulating industries, let alone owning them, governments exacerbate rather than eradicate inefficiency. Thus it was that the Thatcher administration embarked upon a programme of privatization. British Telecom was one of the earliest and most significant as it held a dominant market position and as a private concern would be open to exploit its monopoly position. The privatization of British Telecom led to regulatory legislation and a body to monitor the industry. This set the pattern for subsequent privatizations such as British Gas (1986), the water authorities (1989) and the electricity companies. The commitment of the Thatcher administration to the market, to privatization and liberalization (as significant as privatization) has permanently altered the British perception of nationalized industries to the extent that they are unlikely to be a dominant feature of the British economy again.

See also: Conservative governments; Labour Party

Further reading

Artis, M.J. (ed.) (1992) *The UK Economy*, London: Weidenfeld & Nicolson.

Veljanovski, C. (1991) 'The Political Economy of Regulation', in G. Dunleavey, B. Gamble and J. Peele (eds), *Developments in British Politics 3*, London: Macmillan.

ALASTAIR LINDSLEY

producers

Often cited as being an extra member of a band, the role of the record producer has changed dramatically over the past few decades, particularly during the 1960s and 1990s. Early producers ran artists' careers, signing them to record labels, choosing songs and arranging and producing the finished product. Producers built small rosters of artists, and became known as starmakers, especially in the first era of rock 'n' roll. Significant names during this period include Joe Meek, Denis Preston and George Martin, all of whom shaped British popular music in some way. Meek in particular followed the American format of becoming a Svengali-like producer, assembling a stable of British stars who competed with American artists during the mid-to-late 1950s. Ironically, it was the production and arrangements of Martin that put an end to Meek's career in the early 1960s, as the global phenomenon of the Beatles (and of the many similar sounding bands of the era) swept aside the rock 'n' roll that Meek was so found of. Unable to cope with the changes in production, Meek committed suicide in 1967.

Martin himself changed the way producers were employed during the 1960s, as most were tied down to long contracts with record companies and had to fulfil the needs of both the artist and the record label (although Meek especially was known as a maverick, independent producer). Martin's involvement and input into the work of the Beatles led to a reassessment of the producer's role, and also brought the idea of the freelancer into being. The studio role of the producer had not changed to a great extent, but the new creative power of artists in the 1960s led to a lessening of the producer's input in terms of song choice and arrangement. Many artists became producers of their own work themselves, leading to problems within the hierarchical structures of the music industry. The 1970s saw the 'producer for hire' phenomenon reach its height, as many record companies refused to keep studio staff on contracts.

Producers as performers became the byword during the late 1980s and 1990s, with many studio staff becoming as famous as their protégés, notably Pete Waterman, Nelle Hooper and Norman Cook. The role of producer had turned full circle, with, at one point in 1994, six of the top ten selling singles in the UK being created and performed by producers.

See also: music industry

SAM JOHNSTONE

product placement

Product placement forms part of a marketing strategy where manufacturers identify and target an audience of consumers and prepare them for products which they then release on to the market in tandem with, for example, the premiere of a film. The screening of *Star Wars* was accompanied by a range of toys and clothes for children. Products can also be 'placed' in a film, because, for example, seeing Superman drink Coke can boost sales.

In Britain, television has been used much more to create the kind of receptive environment for goods which advertisers wish to sell. For example the children's series *Teletubbies* has a range of products to accompany it. Stores selling these capitalize on the fact that the goods are from the television series and peer pressure among toddlers and television advertising convinces parents to buy.

The arena in which product placement is probably most evident in Britain however, is sport. For example, Manchester United football club gets roughly 40 percent of its annual £90m revenue from souvenir and clothing merchandising, whereas Continental clubs' merchandise contributes on average 14 percent of their total revenue. Clubs are well aware of the power of the identification that supporters make with 'their' players, and so purchasers can buy shirts with the number and name of their favourite. They have been attacked for changing their players' strip (football kit) too often, because this places pressure on parents (often single women on welfare) to buy the latest strip for their boys. Football kit, minus boots, for an eight-year-old boy can cost £80. Hence clubs have been accused of abusing their powerful position.

Another contentious issue with regard to product placement is marketing to children. On Saturday mornings in particular, a stream of advertisements for toys is beamed directly at children. This also increases pressure on parents.

Television and publishers have teamed up to complement each other's marketing efforts. It is now commonplace for the book of a television series to be simultaneously available in the shops. James Herriot's Yorkshire veterinary series is a case in point. Publishers time reprints of classic works which are being televised (*Brideshead Revisited*, *Middlemarch* or works of Jane Austen). This often leads to a huge increase in readership, paradoxically so because viewers have less 'need' to read the book than hitherto.

See also: corporate identity

MIKE STORRY

progressive rock

Progressive rock emerged from psychedelia and refers to the trend towards increased technical and textural presentational complexity while retaining thematic links with the 'counterculture' of the 1960s. Progressive rock's ascendant period therefore runs roughly from 1969 to late 1976 when **punk rock** emerged to challenge its hegemonic position. As a cultural and musical phenomenon,

progressive rock was dominated by British bands who, after the Beatles, were more prepared to experiment with diverse musical forms. Enormous success followed this willingness to combine diverse elements, and bands such as Yes, Genesis, ELO, Jethro Tull, Led Zeppelin, The Who and Pink Floyd where transformed into 'stadium bands' with international audiences numbering millions.

Musically, the term covers an eclectic range. While bands such as Yes, Genesis, Pink Floyd and Jethro Tull turned to classical and other forms of music to enhance the texture of their own, they nonetheless remained musically diverse as a result of other non-shared influences (such as Pink Floyd's use of **soul** elements and Jethro Tulle's concern with **folk music** forms). Again, Led Zeppelin (and others such as Uriah Heep) retained more of the form of rock but experimented with more complex instrumentation including the use of mandolins, acoustic and electric guitars and synthesizers.

During the 1970s the popularity of these groups, orchestrated by sophisticated marketing and promotional techniques, placed them at the top of the rock hierarchy. At the same time they retained enough of the values (towards personal freedom) of the counterculture of the 1960s to appeal to a generation (in its non-aspirational form sometimes identified as Generation X) which was itself increasingly diverse. As a result, the audience remained loyal despite the difference in wealth and lifestyles. Permissiveness and the liberty to experiment (with lifestyles, soft and hard drugs, sexuality, sex and so on) remained central themes of the progressive rock lyric, while at the same time adopting a more accepting stance towards the commercialization and materialism of society helped to define the seventies as a period of individualized experiment accommodated within the 'system'. The rock lyric also, with its continued experimental and subversive use of language, maintained the sense of shared values without limiting itself to precise definition. Often (notably with Pink Floyd and Frank Zappa) a more pessimistic and satiric note was struck, but largely the 'system' was seen as too powerful to challenge, thus allowing newer bands to foreground hedonism rather than commentary or critique.

As success raised the most gifted of the bands to

the status of 'supergroup', some critics (mainly rock journalists) began to argue that they were too 'remote' from the lives and concerns of their audience. This became a fully-fledged onslaught with the appearance of punk, which defined itself by its opposition to the supergroups, who were now flaccid 'dinosaurs' bloated by the corrupting influence of success and the corporate values of the music industry. Similarly, their audiences were written off as 'boring old farts'. During the 1980s, the most popular bands retained a large audience including increased popularity among the working class and underclass. In the 1990s, their status has to an extent been reappraised with the arrival of 'retro-bands' such as Oasis and others and the re-emergence of the rock festival, although as yet there has been little to match the technical and formal complexity of the music.

See also: pop and rock; psychedelic rock

Further reading

Heylin, C. (ed.) (1993) *The Penguin Book of Rock & Roll Writing*, London: Penguin.

NEIL ANKERS

promotions

Air Miles, a fully-owned subsidiary of British Airways, was the first successful promotions programme. Initiated in 1988, in 1998 it had a registered database of over 3.6 million collectors and involved nearly 360 companies in Britain and the Channel Islands. Air Miles can be inherited and have been included in divorce settlements. Professor Steve Worthington, an expert on loyalty schemes at Staffordshire University, has suggested that 'with all the different ways of collecting and spending, Air Miles have become a quasi-currency'.

In the mid-1990s leading supermarkets, such as Sainsbury and Tesco, also developed similar loyalty schemes in order to identify and stimulate brand awareness. Database marketing and loyalty programmes, the ultimate promotion strategies for the retailer, are powerful, highly segmented customer-oriented forms of promotion, encouraging custo-

mer retention and purchase activation. From the perspective of the customer, they can be seen as invasive and a loss of privacy, thanks to the indiscriminate use of personal information about the individual.

Further reading

Rossiter, J.R. and Percy, L. (1997) *Advertising Communications and Promotion Management*, New York: McGraw-Hill.

FATIMA FERNANDES

prostitution

In the UK, the Sexual Offences Act (1956) defined prostitution (i.e. exchanging sexual services for money) as a matter of 'private morality' and so not subject to criminal law, although it criminalized most associated activities (such as loitering, soliciting and brothel-keeping). Hence, it is legally possible to sell sex in the UK but all the avenues through which the exchange might take place are, to a lesser or greater extent, illegal.

Explanations for women's involvement in prostitution have included pathologizing explanations, economic explanations, and explanations which focus on male power and male violence. Pathologizing explanations constitute involvement in prostitution as a result of some social or psychological deficiency. Economic explanations focus on the dynamic provided by gender-segregated labour markets which, consequently, constitutes prostitution as a form of economic activity offering women a way out of their poverty relative to men. Male violence and male power explanatory models understand prostitution as a manifestation of men's power over and control of women's sexuality and the acceptability of male sexual violence (linked to **pornography**).

Discussion on prostitution from the 1960s onwards has focused on the issues of increasing punitive sanctions, decriminalization or legalization. A growth in neighbourhood vigilantism towards prostitution was noted in the mid-1990s, when members of local communities that were effected by street prostitution took it upon themselves to 'drive prostitution out' of their area by various high-profile strategies (such as using video cameras to record both the women working and their clients). These groups were concerned with the 'nuisance' prostitution causes such as the 'kerb-crawling' of local women not involved in prostitution, noise and associated criminal activity (such as drug dealing).

In contrast, groups such as the English Collective of Prostitutes have argued for decriminalization wherein any and all legal proscriptions against prostitution are removed. With this, it is claimed that the stigma against prostitutes will eventually disappear and women involved in prostitution will be afforded legal recourse to the violences they may suffer and protection against exploitation.

Against these two positions, various police forces and interested agencies have suggested legalizing prostitution. Women involved in prostitution would work within registered, inspected and regulated brothels, parlours, zones of tolerance and so on. It is argued that this will provide the women and clients with a healthy working environment and reduce the level of financial exploitation of prostitutes.

See also: censorship

Further reading

McLeod, E. (1982) *Women Working: Prostitution Now*, London, Croom Helm.

JO PHOENIX

Protestant churches

Of the world's 1.7 billion Christians (around 25 percent of world population), about a quarter are, at least nominally, Protestants (more than twice as many are Roman Catholics). Historically, 'Protestant' was the nickname for those who at the Diet of Speyer in 1529 rejected the majority decision that would have banned Lutheranism in the Catholic parts of Germany. Though originally applied to churches adhering to the teachings of Martin Luther (1483–1546) or the Genevan reformer John Calvin (1509–64), 'Protestant' became one of the terms used to denote the various churches, sects

and denominations – their very number and diversity provoking further criticism from Catholics – that sprang up during the Reformation in the sixteenth century.

Characteristics of Protestantism are the conviction that the source of revealed truth is the Bible, which is to be read in the congregation's native tongue rather than Latin, and the doctrine of the universal priesthood of believers, which means that the clergy have a less crucial role than in Roman **Catholicism**. While Protestant churches respect the sacraments, with some (such as the Baptists) placing great emphasis on certain of them, they are generally less important than for Roman Catholics. A common factor amid bewildering variations in organization, church discipline and liturgical practice is a distrust of the authoritarianism and centralization considered characteristic of Roman Catholicism. The preference for self-government in individual congregations, which generally have to be financially self-sufficient, is marked, though episcopal structures or something similar often serve a unifying function.

Protestantism accepts as a fundamental in theology the doctrine that mankind is separated from God by sin and cannot be redeemed through any individual's effort, but only by the divine will. Nevertheless, great stress has always been laid on the obligations of examining one's own conscience and following a strict moral code. It has been argued that a consequence has been the development of self-reliance and high standards in personal and public life, translated sometimes into the 'Protestant work ethic' and 'Protestant thrift', thought by some commentators to be, along with individualism, formative and progressive influences in Protestant societies. In a multicultural, multi-faith Britain where Christianity has declined, recent years have seen the gradual replacement of antagonism, not only between the various Protestant churches but also between Protestantism and Roman Catholicism, by tolerance and mutual respect as witnessing, albeit in differing ways, to the same faith.

See also: Anglican Church

CHRISTOPHER SMITH

psychedelic rock

Psychedelic rock was a brief but important strand of British popular music. It emerged in 1967 and its heyday lasted until early 1969, when it was superseded by **progressive rock**. Musically, it was characterized by playfulness and an exploration of varied styles and instrumentation, along with a tendency to use studio techniques (such as tape reversal) to a larger extent than before.

Unlike its American cousin, British psychedelia coupled this with lyrics which were concerned with more than simply flowers and peace. Recurrent themes included an escape into childish fantasy, an interest in eastern mysticism and a use of Victorian imagery. All of these motifs are present on what many claim to be the definitive psychedelic album, the Beatles' *Sergeant Pepper's Lonely Hearts Club Band*, in the songs 'Lucy In The Sky With Diamonds', 'Within You Without You' and 'Being For The Benefit Of Mr Kite', respectively.

Another important element of psychedelic rock was that it attempted to link a visual experience with the auditory one, as witnessed in the light shows of bands such as Pink Floyd and Dantalion's Chariot. To a lesser extent, this can also be seen in the tendency of psychedelic albums to have intricate, multi-coloured covers, a fine example here being the inner gatefold sleeve of the Rolling Stones' attempt at psychedelia, *Their Satanic Majesties Request*.

Psychedelic rock also gave rise to an attempt to change the traditional format of the rock concert. Events such as 1967's 14-Hour Technicolour Dream, along with other 'love-ins', stretched the live performance into an all-night event, and as such were precursors of the rock festival. Songs also grew lengthier, although tracks such as Pink Floyd's ten-minute 'Interstellar Overdrive' are short in comparison to what would follow in the **progressive rock** era. An offshoot of this lengthening was the idea of a linked series of songs, or the 'concept album'. Again, although this idea would be taken to its limits within the progressive rock format, albums such as The Pretty Things' *S.F. Sorrow* and (side two of) The Small Faces' *Ogden's Nut Gone Flake* both have a coherent story running through them.

Psychedelic rock allowed popular music to accept influences from styles of music not directly related to its own history, and so prevented it from becoming overly insular and repetitive. That, perhaps, is its greatest legacy.

See also: pop and rock

SIMON BOTTOM

pub rock

A specifically English minor music genre, pub rock was based in the London music scene of the 1970s and received its name from the lucrative pub venue circuit, which consisted of small bands playing in pub back rooms. Seen as a welcome reaction against the **progressive rock** and stadium rock of this period, it presaged **punk rock** as the antithesis of the overblown clichéd rock scene, although punk would later infiltrate and ultimately take over the circuit. Based in venues such as the Hope and Anchor, the Greyhound and the Falcon, it had no real stylistic features musically but, like punk, it gave bands the opportunity to play live during a period when it was becoming increasingly difficult to be heard. Notable pub rockers include Nick Lowe (and his band Brinsley Schwarz), Ian Dury (Kilburn and the Highroads) and two-tone/ska band Madness, all of whom began their careers on the pub circuit and went on to achieve major chart successes. Other acts, such as Dr Feelgood and The Jam, built up major followings on the circuit but were loath to be a part of the pub rock 'scene'. The opening up of new venues following the punk explosion of the late 1970s ended the dominance of the pub circuit.

See also: pop and rock

SAM JOHNSTONE

public schools

About 6 percent of British children attend 'independent schools'. Though officially inspected to ensure standards, they are largely independent of both the state and the local education authority. Their funding comes from endowments and, for the most part, the fees they charge. Only the most prestigious independent secondary schools are called 'public schools', an imprecise and increasingly discarded term. Some are ancient foundations which were radically reformed in Victorian times, when several more were set up; others followed in the first half of the twentieth century.

The heads of most of these schools form the Headmasters' and Headmistresses' Conference (hence 'HMC schools'). Changing the name to include headmistresses reflected both the status of many girls' schools and trends towards co-education in schools originally admitting only boys. Qualifications for HMC membership include a large sixth form and independence from the state education system, although pupils take GCSEs and A levels. Boards of governors control public schools, acting as trustees, overseeing finances and working with the head for excellent teaching and pastoral care.

While much is made of tradition, modernization is evident in a marked decline in classics in favour of a wide range of A levels. Though less emphasis is now placed on religion, sport is still taken very seriously. Cadet corps, intended as preparation for military careers or the Territorial Army, now exist alongside other leisure activities, from Duke of Edinburgh Awards to bird-watching. Music is highly regarded. Though many public schools cater exclusively or largely for boarders, others – among them some of the best – are day schools; many of them were originally town grammar schools.

In 1997 the government announced the phasing out of the 'assisted places scheme' which met, fully or in part, public school fees for a certain number of pupils from less affluent families. Seeing public schools as bastions of privilege, critics decry them as socially divisive. The more knowledgeable among them admit, however, that intensive, well-resourced teaching to carefully selected small groups regularly leads to impressive results and that, as state secondary education improves and more people go on to university, the 'old school tie' is less of a factor in career prospects than hitherto. 'Old boys' (and girls) are themselves rarely indifferent about their public school; they usually regard it either with loyalty or loathing.

See also: class system; schools system

Further reading

Rae, J. (1981) *The Public School Revolution*, London: Faber.

CHRISTOPHER SMITH

publishing trends

The most significant trend in the publishing industry in recent years has been its increasing concentration in the hands of international media conglomerates. In the 1980s and 1990s, a series of traditional London publishers have been bought out by major parent companies, most notably the simultaneous buyout of three independent houses – Jonathan Cape, Chatto & Windus and The Bodley Head – by the American firm Newhouse in 1987. Many of the subsidiary developments in British publishing – the use of increasingly aggressive forms of book publicity, the growing size of advances for a small number of big name authors, the new importance of literary agents who can broker huge deals for their clients, the vigorous attempts to sell British authors in other English-language markets in the USA and Commonwealth – can be accounted for in part by the more commercial instincts of these large publishers. Similarly, the increasing conglomeration of the industry contributed to the ending of the Net Book Agreement (NBA) in September 1995, which was caused by the withdrawal from the agreement of large international publishers like Random House, HarperCollins and Penguin. In fact, although it was predicted that the collapse of the NBA would lead to price-cutting which would benefit the large publishers and the most commercially successful authors, its effects have so far been minimal. In general, the commercialization of publishing since the 1980s has been offset by other developments, not least the survival of editors committed to less obviously commercial works even within corporate-owned houses.

A second major development in publishing in the 1990s has been the growing importance of interactive multimedia, particularly CD-Roms and pay-to-view on-line computer networks, as another way for publishers to sell text to readers. Although these new technologies are frequently said to be producing a 'post-book' age, it is too soon to say how comprehensively they will alter the nature of publishing. The books most affected have so far been children's, reference and educational texts, and virtually no inroads have been made into the fiction market. In the area of fiction, the huge expansion in audio books, abbreviated works recorded on cassette by the author or an actor, has been more significant.

See also: black literature press; feminist publishing houses

Further reading

Owen, P. (ed.) (1993) *Publishing Now*, London: Peter Owen (includes short chapters by editors, publishers and agents, and is a useful insider's look at developments in publishing in the 1980s and 1990s).

JOE MORAN

punk rock

Punk rock is primarily a British musical genre that reached its creative and popular peak during 1977 and 1978. The precursors of punk rock were those American and British groups of the late 1960s and early 1970s who played rock music with an aggressive feel, with loud distorted guitars and nihilistic lyrics. In particular, many of the original punk rock groups formed in 1976 and 1977 were influenced by bands such as MC5, the New York Dolls, The Stooges, The Who and The Velvet Underground. While most punk rock groups drew influence from some earlier bands, they were specific about rejecting the majority of music produced in the early 1970s; in particular, punk rock musicians were disdainful of what they termed the hippie music of **progressive rock**.

Central to any discussion of punk is the band The Sex Pistols. Not the first punk rock group but certainly the most influential, The Sex Pistols formed in late 1975. Shortly after this the band started touring on the **pub rock** and college gig circuits. Early songs such as 'Submission' and 'Anarchy In The UK' lyrically mocked what the band perceived to be the conformist and drab

nature of British society, against a backdrop of rambunctious guitars and drums. It was not long before The Sex Pistols attracted a fanatical following of punks equally disillusioned with British society and culture.

The media furore that surrounded early Sex Pistol's gigs was nothing in comparison to the outrage that followed their actions in December 1976 when, following the cancellation of an appearance by the group Queen, The Sex Pistols were invited to appear on the early evening London television show *Today*. After drinking heavily before the show, the band verbally insulted interviewer Bill Grundy, and caused a tabloid storm with their explicit language. This set the stage for the release of their 'God Save The Queen' single, a week before the Queen's Jubilee weekend in June 1977. Again tabloid newspapers and the public in general were outraged by the band's forthright attacks upon an institution central to British society, the monarchy. In particular the record cover, created by the band's 'Art Director' Jamie Reid, created a sensation with its image of the Queen with a safety pin through her nose.

'God Save The Queen' was The Sex Pistol's high point. Later in 1977 the band released their one and only official album, *Never Mind The Bollocks*. Like all the band's releases it came in a trademark Jamie Reid cover that mimicked the style of a ransom note, and contained direct attacks on central facets of British culture. The Sex Pistols found that they were unable to obtain gigs in Britain because promoters and venues showed an unwillingness to allow them to perform. Band tensions reached a head following the band's tour of the USA, and they split in early 1978. The band's lead singer Johnny Rotten reverted to his real name John Lydon, formed Public Image Limited, and left the punk rock genre. The band struggled on in his absence, but the drug-related death of bass player Sid Vicious led to their inevitable demise.

At the same time as The Sex Pistols were attracting media attention, a whole wave of other punk rock bands were forming, notably The Damned and The Clash in London and The Buzzcocks in Manchester. Although none received the same mixture of notoriety and fame as The Sex Pistols, many considered them to be musically more interesting. Although shunned by other punk rock groups, The Damned's album *Damned Damned Damned* (1977) was critically acclaimed at the time, and The Damned continue to perform in the late 1990s. The Clash also achieved critical and commercial success with sixteen chart hits in the five years following 1977. Musically and lyrically more sophisticated than The Sex Pistols, The Clash combined the noise and aggression of punk rock with **reggae** and other Caribbean musics. The Buzzcocks developed a different musical agenda and were influential amongst the indie bands that developed in the aftermath of punk (see **indie pop**).

In the wake of the successes of punk rock's first wave, many young people began to form their own bands in 1977 and 1978. In particular these bands developed a 'DIY' attitude to making music. Bands such as Siouxsie and the Banshees, X-Ray Specs, The Adverts and Sham 69 developed different styles of punk, but maintained a central ethos of opposition to mainstream British society. Either implicitly or explicitly, this political ethos was central to punk.

The degree to which punk rock has influenced subsequent musical styles is hotly debated. Throughout the 1980s, new bands formed and drew inspiration from the events of 1976 and 1977. In particular, indie bands' faith in the seven-inch single and suspicion of the LP has been interpreted as directly related to punk's 'DIY' approach. Musically, punk rock has been particularly influential upon American bands, with Nirvana, Hole and Mudhoney all having had chart successes in Britain. These 'post-punk' bands developed a similar sound to the stripped-down aggression of the first generation of punk rock bands. Some British rock groups, such as The Wildhearts, Therapy and the Manic Street Preachers also have their musical roots in punk.

However, some commentators claim that the 'spirit of punk' is not to be found in those groups who sound like their 1970s counterparts, but in the **house**, **techno** and **jungle** acts who make music for reasons other than commercial gain. For many of the first generation of punk rock groups, making music was about 'making do' with the available technology, and they were therefore opposed to the kind of learned musicianship of previous rock genres. It is understandable that house, jungle and techno acts, with their cheap sampling equipment and their own production technology, consider themselves to be the direct descendants of the first punk rock bands.

See also: alternative music; new wave

Further reading

Savage, J. (1991) *England's Dreaming: Sex Pistols and Punk Rock*, London: Faber & Faber (the definitive account of the social, cultural and musical significance of punk rock).

STUART BORTHWICK

Puttnam, David

b. 1941

Film producer

Formerly in advertising, commercial producer Puttnam's first project was the Alan **Parker** scripted *Melody* (1970). Puttnam gradually assembled an ex-advertising film-making coterie, producing Ridley **Scott**'s *The Duellists* (1977), Parker's *Midnight Express* (1978), Adrian Lyne's *Foxes* (1979) and Hugh Hudson's *Chariots of Fire* (1981). Roland **Joffe**'s *The Killing Fields* (1984) and *The Mission* (1986) were among other noteworthy achievements. Puttnam's films have predominantly charted male histories, revelling in the triumph of the human spirit in adversity with well-meaning but sometimes emotionally exploitative intent. Associated with the early 1980s resurgence in British film, Puttnam has campaigned tirelessly on the industry's behalf. A standard bearer of British arts liberalism, he was made a Labour peer in the House of Lords in 1997.

Further reading

Kipps, C. (1988) *Out of Focus*, New York: Silver Arrow Books.

SATINDER CHOHAN

Q

Quant, Mary

b. 1934, London

Fashion designer

Mary Quant was one of the most influential British designers in the 'Swinging Sixties'. Born in 1934 and trained at Goldsmith's College, Quant opened her Kings Road boutique Bazaar in 1955. Her innovative, youthful fashions were an immediate success and led to Quant opening other stores as well as designing for J.C. Penney in New York in 1962. Quant launched her own wholesale company, Ginger, in 1963 and cosmetics and accessories bearing her daisy logo soon joined her hugely successful fashion range. Quant is associated above all with cheeky mini-skirts and dresses which provided the main fashion image of the mid-1960s.

TAMSIN SPARGO

R

Race Relations Acts

Acts of Parliament concerning race relations have been passed in 1965, 1968 and 1976. The most recent Act, which also established the **Commission for Racial Equality**, prohibits discrimination on the basis of colour, race, nationality or ethnic origin, and also outlaws indirect discrimination in the provision of goods, services, facilities, accommodation, advertisements and, most importantly, employment.

See also: British Citizenship Acts

PETER CHILDS

RADA

The Royal Academy of Dramatic Art (RADA) is a school for aspiring actors in London's Gower Street. It was founded by Beerbohm Tree in 1904, over forty years after the oldest theatre school, the London Academy of Music and Dramatic Art (LAMDA). RADA, which benefits from one-third of the Royalties from all George Bernard Shaw's plays, stages performances for the public in its Vanbrugh Theatre, which opened in 1954. British actors trained at RADA include Alan Bates, Glenda **Jackson**, Richard **Attenborough** and Margaret Lockwood.

See also: actors (female); actors (male)

PETER CHILDS

Radio 1

Radio 1 is the **BBC**'s main popular music station for younger audiences, continuously influential and much talked about. The station was launched by the BBC in 1967, following a period of intensive activity by **pirate radio** stations broadcasting pop music from off-shore. The popularity of these stations and the BBC's resistance caused renewed debate (echoing the introduction of commercial television) about standards, tastes and consumers' rights. The Labour government outlawed the stations under the Marine Offences Act of that year and encouraged the BBC, against its institutional traditions and instincts, to establish a specialist youth pop music station alongside Radios 2, 3 and 4.

Radio 1 quickly won a large audience share and a generation grew up with its music and presenters, often listening in bedrooms or workplaces on the new, cheaper portable radios. The weekend top 20 chart countdown became a national institution. Many of the station's disc jockeys established fame in their own right, achieving a relaxed, informal relationship (casual, chatty and cheeky, though until recently mainly masculine) with their listeners. Others, of whom John Peel has been the most enduring and distinctive, developed their own eclectic musical tastes on air. Radio 1's **DJs** have often gone on to appear on the other BBC radio stations (such as Tony Blackburn on Radio 2, Paul Gambaccini on Radio 3 and Andy Kershaw on Radio 4).

In the 1980s, during discussion about the restructuring of broadcasting, Radio 1 faced possible privatization. Subsequently, in the 1990s new commercial stations have developed in keen competition, with continuous press coverage of the varying audience shares obtained by Radio 1 and its main rivals such as Virgin 1215. Controversy has been fostered by the main breakfast time presenters, with some switching between stations.

Radio 1 makes considerable use of computer-generated playlists tracking successful chart records, but at other times presenters' musical choices are more ambitious. A significant amount of live music and pre-release new music is broadcast, including music by new bands.

Despite competition and a certain loss of listeners to Radio 2 and elsewhere as they grow older and find the station's music and style too young for them, Radio 1 covers a wider range of contemporary music, playing more titles each week than other stations. It attracts weekly almost half the population in the 15–24 age range, and retains a key place in British culture and musical life.

See also: commercial radio, national; local radio; Radio 2; Radio 3; Radio 4; Radio 5; radio DJs

Further reading

Barnard, S. (1989) *On the Radio: Music Radio in Britain*, Milton Keynes: Open University Press.
—— (1997) 'Postscript', in T. O'Sullivan and Y. Jewkes (eds), *The Media Studies Reader*, London: Edward Arnold.

MICHAEL GREEN

Radio 2

Radio 2 was established by the **BBC** as a development from its Light Programme. This in turn, after the Second World War, had replaced the General Forces Programme which broadcast in an accessible style to the armed services. The Light Programme in the postwar decades was the BBC's most widely appealing radio service, very different in character to the authoritative public service ambitions of the Home Service or the specialist tastes in the arts and classical music addressed by the Third Programme. The decision in 1967 to establish four very distinctive 'streamed' stations repositioned the new Radio 2 next to a younger sibling, **Radio 1**.

For many years the contrast in style, musical preferences and ways of talking to the listener between these stations has been very great. Radio 2 has attracted a mainly much older audience, offering musical styles from earlier in the century, presented in a consciously relaxed, soothing, sometimes nostalgic way. The station retained a loyal core audience, but was little noticed or discussed. Instead, it was subject to some routine derision, perhaps connected with prejudices about age, though the station also seemed to lack clarity of aim and to be merely undemanding. It became a rumoured target for privatization (fulfilling no obvious public service remit) during the 1980s.

As the BBC developed audience strategies and mission statements in the 1990s, the functions of radio services were closely analysed. There were already signs that Radio 1 had become too youthful for some, while Radio 2 was rethought until, in a development mostly unforeseen, its audience share began to match and at times exceed that of Radio 1.

The BBC describes the station, somewhat ambiguously, as reflecting the 'heritage of popular music and culture' (1997: 9). In practice it now offers considerable variety, anchored around a recognizable address to listeners: a very wide range of music; comedy, quiz and magazine programmes; documentaries, book readings, coverage of the arts, religion and several other areas. Its distinctive voices include those of Terry Wogan, a brilliant improviser and raconteur; Steve Wright, formerly a Radio 1 disc jockey; and several previously associated with other stations. Still not much noticed or discussed, Radio 2 describes itself as 'the most listened-to radio station in Britain' and its future development, including what kind of audience it attracts, will be of considerable cultural interest.

See also: local radio; Radio 3; Radio 4; Radio 5; radio comedy

Further reading

BBC (1997) *Our Commitment to You*, London: BBC Books.

MICHAEL GREEN

Radio 3

The main current function of Radio 3, now broadcast twenty-four hours a day, is to carry a very wide range of live and recorded classical music. Radio 3 emerged when **BBC** radio was reorganized in 1967, but its origins lie in the celebrated, often controversial, Third Programme established in 1946 and described by then Director General William Haley as the apex of a cultural pyramid, above the Home Service and still more the Light Programme. The Third Programme was dedicated to the full range of the arts, including music but also drama, features, discussions of science and much else, though with a distinctive style of presentation leading to much praise for, and mockery of, the station as demanding, intellectual and 'highbrow'.

Since in its early years the Third Programme was sometimes hard to receive and attracted only a small (at times almost invisible) audience share, it has over a long period been seen as public service broadcasting at its most dedicated or, alternatively, its most costly, off-putting, even absurd. However it has been continuously central to British cultural life, and especially **classical music**, particularly as a musical patron. Half its output at present is live or specially recorded, while the BBC's own and other **orchestras**, and many smaller groups and soloists, gain from its dedication to a wide classical repertoire. This reaches a climax in the summer BBC Promenade concerts ('the Proms'), which have become increasingly adventurous and are carried live on Radio 3.

The station still has critics since, despite some airtime for **jazz** and other forms, Radio 3's version of cultural value is confined mainly to music within the western classical tradition (with an important commitment to living British composers). Speech programmes have largely migrated to Radio 4, while drama, **science** and discussion of other arts have become much scarcer in the schedule.

On its central territory Radio 3 faced a particular challenge with the appearance of Classic FM in 1991, a commercial station broadcasting CD extracts in a new, populist format with approachable presenters. The station's success and the debate about Radio 3 elitism led to some uneasy but still evolving attempts to extend its core

audience beyond typically older and (to some extent) more educated and professional listeners.

See also: commercial radio, national; Radio 1; Radio 2; Radio 4; Radio 5; radio drama

Further reading

Carpenter, H. (1996) *The Envy of the World*, London: Weidenfeld & Nicholson.

MICHAEL GREEN

Radio 4

Radio 4 is the **BBC**'s most prestigious, best-resourced radio channel, offering a wide range of speech programmes and a regular focus of political and public attention. It is seen by the BBC, and widely accepted, as an importantly national station with only intermittent attention to 'regional' output.

Radio 4 evolved from the former Home Service (launched 1939), giving considerable time to news and current affairs but also to magazine and discussion programmes, drama, comedy, quizzes and much else including vital (and for some, evocative) shipping forecasts. The popular teatime *Children's Hour* ended in 1961 but *Woman's Hour* has run continuously since 1946. Originally introduced by men, offering advice for housewives at home, it now gives voice to women on air over a huge variety of issues through its journalists and presenters, and is virtually the only dedicated women's space in British broadcasting. Similar specialist programmes designed for a general citizens' audience concern finance, food, gardening, disability issues and much else. Celebrity guests feature in the widely known *Desert Island Discs* or more recently *In the Psychiatrist's Chair.*

Radio 4 (so named since 1967) aims to give intelligent, at times demanding speech coverage to many areas of life, using skilled and at times high-profile presenters. Its breakfast current affairs programme *Today,* though sometimes criticized for its focus on politics as what happens in Westminster, has established itself as compulsory listening; some of its interviewers (such as Brian Redhead and John Humphreys) have been celebrated for their rigorous, at times combative, grillings of politicians and experts.

The station's perception of itself as distinctive, challenging and invaluable radio has been accepted by much of its influential, predominantly higher status and south of England audience. Possible threats to BBC radio in the 1980s drew strong resistance and organized lobbying from groups such as Voice of the Listener and Viewer, while the prolonged cricket coverage on long wave has been resented by listeners missing regular programmes carried on other frequencies. Attempts to restructure Radio 4's schedule, given a mainly older audience and huge drops in listening after breakfast current affairs coverage and the long-running early evening farming soap opera *The Archers*, have given rise to intense press and public discussion. The BBC is committed to developing Radio 4 as its core public service radio channel offering a particular version of quality speech output.

See also: Radio 1; Radio 2; Radio 3; Radio 5; radio comedy; radio drama

Further reading

Crisell, A. (1997) *An Introductory History of British Broadcasting*, London: Routledge.

MICHAEL GREEN

Radio 5

Radio 5 is the **BBC**'s fifth and youngest radio channel, carrying a twenty-four hour mixture of news and sports. Radio 5 joined the network in 1990 with an uneasy mixture of material lacking space elsewhere, including **adult education** and schools broadcasts, sport, stories and magazine programmes. It once seemed that Radio 5 would become home to a planned continuous rolling news service, but in 1994 was instead relaunched as Radio 5 Live, seeking by comparison with **Radio 4** to offer news and current affairs in a format which would gain a younger and broader range of listeners, alongside a wide range of sports commentary. Radio 5 seems to be attracting its

intended audience, which is predominantly male (though too simply stereotyped as 'radio bloke').

See also: phone-ins and chat shows; Radio 1; Radio 2; Radio 3; Radio 4

MICHAEL GREEN

radio comedy

Comedy on radio is inevitably associated with the networks run by the **BBC**, even though it is clear that comedy is essential to most radio, whether national or local, BBC or independent. While the term 'radio comedy' is usually used to refer to a variety of situation comedies, panel games and sketch shows, it can be seen that virtually all radio presenters and disc jockeys use comedy, irrespective of the format of the actual programme. The careers of disc jockeys such as Chris Evans, for example, rely very heavily on their ability to make people laugh. It can be seen that this trend has become more apparent in the 1990s, with **Radio 1** spawning a number of significant comedies, such as *The Mary Whitehouse Experience* and Chris Morris's *Blue Jam*, signalling the increasing importance of comedy to the medium of radio overall.

Despite this, the majority of specific comedy programmes appear on **Radio 4**, which has a lengthy tradition of producing such programming. Panel games such as *I'm Sorry I Haven't a Clue* and *Just a Minute* have been running for decades, as has *The News Huddlines* on **Radio 2**. Radio 4 has broadcast hundreds of sitcoms, the most famous earlier examples probably being *It's That Man Again*, *The Goon Show* and *Hancock's Half-Hour*. However, the format continues to be reinvented on radio in such programmes as *On the Hour* and *People Like Us*, both sophisticated parodies of Radio 4 and its journalistic excesses. The Asian-based sketch show *Goodness Gracious Me!* was seen to be a significant breakthrough for ethnic minorities.

While radio comedy achieves significantly smaller audience ratings than its television counterpart, its future is assured not least because it often serves as a breeding ground for new comedy talent before the lure of television rears its head. A number of television sitcoms began on radio (such as *After Henry* and *Second Thoughts*), while *Goodness*

Gracious Me! transferred to BBC2, Radio 4's *The News Quiz* became *Have I Got News For You* and *On the Hour* moved on to satirize television journalism as *The Day Today*. Many in the radio industry bemoan the low standing the medium occupies compared to television, particularly when it is probable that much television comedy would not exist without radio serving as an apprenticeship.

See also: comedy on television; situation comedy

Further reading

Took, B. (1976) *Laughter in the Air*, London: Robson (affectionate but outdated history of radio comedy).

BRETT MILLS

radio DJs

The cult of the disc jockey, or DJ (see **DJs**), grew up out of the transformation of radio stations in the years 1948–58 in America. Prior to these years, radio was a domestic medium, developed in the 1920s and aimed primarily at housewives. Radio programmes had previously been in-house productions by the major networks, which, because of its large-scale organization, involved a high percentage of specialized departments and job-specification. The initial role of the disc jockey was purely functional. His (as it invariably was a man) job was to cue the records, and ensure the smooth continuity of the show. DJs had no influence over playlists. When radio stations became more localized in the 1950s, career patterns within the industry changed dramatically, the most significant of these being the transformation of the functional radio announcer to personality disc jockey. This reshaping of radio was a key factor in the advent of rock 'n' roll and through this, the disc jockey emerged as a star figure. On American radio, Alan Freed was the epitome of the showman entrepreneur disc jockey, but his downfall was guaranteed when he was exposed for succumbing to the practice of the 'pay-to-play' payola system, whereby disc jockeys would accept financial rewards in return for the promotion of a particular record or artist.

Record companies rely heavily on radio to introduce and promote its products, and disc jockeys are regarded as the 'regulators' or 'gate-keepers' of the industry. Disc jockeys now have the power not only to influence playlists but to make or break a star, playing a crucial part in determining chart success. Disc jockeys have played a crucial part in defining new genres and discovering new markets. Pirate radio, with the pioneering Radio Caroline in 1964, inspired a new brand of 'pop' radio in the UK, with such personalities as Tony Blackburn, John Peel and Kenny Everett. They eventually went mainstream, but John Peel continues to work towards the discovery and promotion of new talent.

Disc jockeys played a major role in the emergence of the twelve-inch single in the 1970s, by mixing the seven-inch single for prolonged playing time. By the late 1970s this became an industry standard, and by the 1990s it comprised 45 percent of sales. Due to the success of club culture, the disc jockey is now the key figure here as well, and can earn as much if not more than musicians.

See also: pirate radio; Radio 1

ALICE BENNETT

radio drama

Most radio drama is broadcast on **Radio 3**, **Radio 4** and the **World Service**, although Radio 3's output was halved in 1994–5 after competition from Classic FM. There is a scattering of drama on **local radio** at Liverpool, Manchester and Newcastle. Radio suits multiple genres and styles including book adaptations, **situation comedy**, detective stories, science fiction, classical works, mainstream British and European plays and modern writing, some of it commissioned. In the early days of radio it was widely regarded as the most avant-garde medium, and work by MacNeice and Dylan Thomas provided an experimental springboard for Beckett and Stoppard, Caryl Phillips and Anthony Minghella because the medium, while imposing strict disciplines of explication in plot and character, allows unlimited freedom of location, action and style. Adaptations of works like Gogol's *Diary of a Madman* which would be impossible on television or on stage can be produced on radio very successfully.

In the nature of contemporary media culture, success is measured in terms of mass audiences and highly-paid stars. Journalists and pundits are unwilling to make qualitative judgements for fear of being thought elitist or politically incorrect by contrasting popular television drama with any other sort of work. To a limited extent this favours radio, as many writers have used the relative freedom and obscurity of radio to develop their careers before going on to wider audiences and closer critical attention. Most notably, Douglas Adams had a huge popular hit with *The Hitch-Hiker's Guide to the Galaxy*. The transfer to television was not so successful because the density of the material failed to register on the screen.

Although radio drama does not maintain a high cultural profile or attract large audiences, its listenership is dedicated, highly articulate and prone to campaign should anything disturb the general tenor of radio output. When allied to the high quality of radio writing, this produces a disproportionately influential effect on the rest of media output. Cultural power has shifted even further away from creative people during the 1990s, as it did from film during the 1970s and television during the 1980s, because of changes in management style introduced for the ostensible purpose of saving (or making more) money. It has been widely suggested that managers simply do not want allegedly wayward creative talents interfering with the smooth running of the organization. However, radio continues to foster talented writers and performers in the production of marginal work other media reject.

See also: radio comedy

Further reading

Kirkpatrick, D. (ed.) (1978–) *Best Radio Plays*, London: Methuen/BBC.

STEPHEN KERENSKY

rambling

Rambling has been a popular activity throughout this century, although numbers have risen significantly as leisure time and car ownership have increased. The Rambler's Association, which was formed in 1931, represents the rights of walkers, protecting rights of way and campaigning for the freedom to roam over uncultivated open country. Successful campaigns have led to the passing of the National Parks and Access to the Countryside Act 1949 and the inclusion of rights of way on popular Ordnance Survey maps. Several rambling 'personalities' have developed over more recent years; perhaps most famously Alfred Wainwright, who first started producing guide books covering walks in the Lake District in the 1950s and 1960s.

HELEN COOKE

Rank

Now the Rank Group, Rank has interests in many areas as one of the world's biggest leisure groups. Its holdings include over 300 Odeon cinemas, **Pinewood Studios**, theme parks, bingo halls, Butlins holiday villages and franchises of the Hard Rock Cafe. Overseas, this extends to ownership of Universal Studios and a theme park in Orlando. The prime mover within the embryonic organization was J. Arthur Rank (1888–1972), a Methodist millionaire businessman who switched from the family flour company to became one of the most important figures in British cinema. Originally J. Arthur Rank had founded a film company, British National, whose aim was to promote **Methodism** through documentaries. This floundered due to lack of distribution, and he later allied with General Film distributors, which became Rank Film Distributors. The powerful position of the Rank organization led to a reference to the Monopoly Commission, which reported in 1943 that the extent of the company's control (over 50 percent of studios and 10 percent of cinemas) was acceptable. The film distribution arm was sold to Carlton for £65 million in 1997.

While Rank produced bawdy films such as *Doctor in the House* (Thomas 1954) and the **Carry**

On films, the Methodist roots of the organization began to show through with attempts to ban X-rated films, now classed as 18 Certificate, from showing in their Odeon chain. Later, having financed Nick **Roeg**'s 1980 film *Bad Timing* with its necrophiliac story line, executives echoed earlier conservatism in condemning it. While Rank's sole commitment to film is fast receding, it is important to appreciate the crucial importance the organization once had and the role J. Arthur Rank enjoyed as its catalyst:

> Rank managed to tie all the discrete strands of British film culture together. In his bid to set the industry on its feet, he intervened on every level. He pioneered technical research and developed equipment. He invested in 'B' pictures. He started a 'charm school' to generate stars. ... For a brief moment in the mid-1940s, it seemed as if he had managed to introduce a measure of harmonious sanity to the schizophrenic organism which the British film industry has traditionally been.
>
> (Macnab 1993: xi)

See also: British film industry

Further reading

Macnab, G. (1993) *J. Arthur Rank and the British Film Industry*, London: Routledge (a thorough, engaging account of both the Rank organization and J. Arthur Rank).

GUY OSBORN
STEVE GREENFIELD

rap

Rap music began as an integral part of New York's burgeoning **hip hop** culture in the mid-1970s. From the beginning, its sound was quite unique, with the music being created collage-style by DJs combining elements from pre-existing records, rather than live musicians. One of rap's early innovators, Kool DJ Herc, is credited with originating the process of taking the instrumental breaks from songs such as James Brown's 'Give It Up Or Turnit A Loose' and extending them by playing two copies of the record on separate turntables, using a crossfader (a simple mixing device) to 'cut' between the two records, manually 'rewinding' the record to the start of the break on one turntable while the other plays. To encourage people to dance at parties where they played, DJs began to have live MCs (originally standing for Masters of Ceremonies) on hand, to throw phrases like 'yes, yes, y'all, and you don't stop,' or 'throw your hands in the air, and wave 'em like you just don't care' into the mix. It was not long, however, before MCs began to expand their repertoire, moving from simple phrases of crowd encouragement to ever longer and more complex spoken rhymes. These rhymes were known as raps, and the music became known as rap music.

The idea of spoken vocals on songs was, of course, not new. In the early 1970s, Isaac Hayes had performed a song entitled 'Ike's Rap', and Millie Jackson included a track on her *Caught Up* album called simply 'The Rap'. What was innovative about rap music was the combination of the spoken vocal of the MC with the recycled beats of the DJ. By 1979, rap music had become a recorded genre itself, although early records, such as The Sugarhill Gang's 'Rapper's Delight' used live musicians to recreate the sound produced by DJs. 'Rapper's Delight' was an international hit, and opened the door for groups such as Grandmaster Flash and the Furious Five to produce records with a DJ rather than a live band.

By around 1983, the sound of rap music was changing, with the prevalent 'disco-funk' giving way to a more stripped down style, with the distinctive tones of the Roland TR-808 drum machine coming to the fore, while DJs played shorter extracts from records, often 'scratching' the record to further alter its sound. At around the same time, social commentary raps such as the Furious Five's 'The Message' and Run DMC's 'It's Like That' began appearing. This trend was taken further in what is often considered a golden age for rap music, the years 1987 and 1988, by one of the leading acts of the time, Public Enemy.

Public Enemy's sound was an intense combination of 808 drum beats, looped samples (the sampler, an instrument for digitally reproducing any sound fed into it had been added to the tools of the DJ, allowing ever smaller extracts of records to be used) and the ferocious rhymes of Chuck D. Along with the likes of Boogie Down Productions, Eric B and Rakim and EPMD, Public Enemy took rap music to new heights of popularity in the late 1980s.

By this time rap was well established in the UK, and although commercial success has always evaded British rap acts (the exceptions being Slick Rick and Monie Love, both of whom relocated to the USA before establishing themselves), fans of the music are fiercely loyal to it. Indeed, it was British rap fans whose cheers and whistles were used for the live segments of Public Enemy's seminal *It Takes A Nation Of Millions To Hold Us Back* album. Rap's popularity in Britain was probably only further increased by a media backlash, with the Beastie Boys coming in for particular press disapproval during their 1987 tour of the UK.

Meanwhile, in the USA, rap music was being attacked in the press for being both violent – the 'gangsta' rap of groups such as NWA (Niggaz With Attitude) and Compton's Most Wanted – and misogynist – the 2-Live Crew's *As Nasty As They Wanna Be* album was eventually banned on grounds of obscenity, and became part of a larger debate over freedom of speech. 'Gangsta' rap became the next major wave of rap music, although it provided few hits in the UK. Whereas earlier rap acts had achieved crossover success (Run DMC and Aerosmith hit the top ten with 'Walk This Way' in 1986), gangsta rap appealed more to the small, solid fanbase.

Throughout much of the 1990s, rap music remained a largely underground form. While there were occasional rap hits (A Tribe Called Quest's 'Can I Kick It?', for example), it was not until the mid-1990s that a resurgence of rap's popularity occurred. While groups such as the Wu-Tang Clan created a sound that renewed the faith of rap followers, commercial success was coming for 'poppier' rap acts like Coolio, whose 'Gangster's Paradise' (the title hints at the content: watered-down gangsta rap) became, in 1995, the first rap song to reach number one in the UK.

Subsequently, rap reached a much wider audience, with rap records and records that incorporated elements of rap music being heard with increased frequency on daytime radio. Although the deaths of Tupac Shakur and the Notorious B.I.G. meant that the shadow of violence was never far from rap music, producers such as Puff Daddy made slick, commercial rap records that were hugely successful. Many long-term rap fans, however, decried this commercialization, preferring to return to the sounds of the 'old school'. By 1998, this more traditional rap sound was making a comeback, as evidenced in groups such as the Jurassic 5. The old school also seemed to be returning with Jason Nevins's house remix of Run DMC's 'It's Like That' (although the lyrical content of the song was less foregrounded in this version) and the related rise in popularity of related hip hop artforms, such as breakdancing.

See also: disco

Further reading

Fernando, S.H., Jr (1995) *The New Beats,* Edinburgh: Payback Press.

Toop, D. (1984, 1991) *Rap Attack 2: African Rap to Global Hip Hop,* London: Serpent's Tail.

SIMON BOTTOM

Rastafarianism

Rastafarians (colloquially 'Rastas') are followers of a cult which enjoyed popularity from about 1930 to 1960 in Jamaica and subsequently abroad, where its main influence became cultural. The movement has a male emphasis, aimed at least in part at repudiating the matrifocal ethos produced by nineteenth-century slavery's dislocation of the family. It also has seen feminism as a manifestation of the moral decline of the West. The Rasta look is very distinctive. Men have long matted plaits of hair, dreadlocks, which replaced the pre-1970s 'afro' cut, and were first worn in a closed community in Jamaica (Pinnacle) in the early 1950s to indicate African warrior status. Rastafarians also wear distinctive clothing, including 'tams' (crocheted or fabric hats) and army-surplus camouflage wear. Women wear their hair in tightly braided arabesques. Clothes are often in the traditional Rasta colours, red, gold and green, taken from the national flag of Ethiopia. Rastafarianism has had considerable cultural significance in

Britain, largely through its offering of an identity to alienated urban black youth, but also through its influence on disaffected white youth culture.

Rastafarians' philosophy of life was originally based on their adaptation of the Christianity they experienced in the colonial West Indies. A religion which countenanced slavery offered them no comfort. However, the Bible gave them hope because they found in it the promise of a return to Africa. They understood as a prophecy Revelation 19:16 'And he hath on his vesture and on his thigh a name written, 'KING OF KINGS, AND LORD OF LORDS'. They identified as their 'saviour' (and hence deified) the Emperor Haile Selassie of Ethiopia (1892–1975). He was known variously as Lion of Judah, and Ras (Prince) Tafari (Selassie's family name, meaning 'Might of the Trinity'), and was believed to be the messiah who was going to lead black people, who were one of the lost tribes of Israel, back to Ethiopia. Rastafarians see themselves as Israelites displaced from their homeland, and Babylon is the collective name for all countries of exile outside Africa.

The authorities in Jamaica, North America and Britain have been hostile or at least unsympathetic to Rastafarianism. Perhaps the person most responsible for offering leadership for Rastafarians was Marcus Garvey (1887–1940), a mercurial black Jamaican with maroon (fugitive slave) ancestors. Garvey was educated briefly at London's Birkbeck College, and founded the Universal Negro Improvement Association on his return to Jamaica in 1914. He advocated a return to Africa for black people, and his followers held firmly to this idea, despite their dispersal throughout such areas as America, Britain and France. Neither Garvey nor Haile Selassie claimed divinity for the latter: Garvey only made a link between a 'black king' and 'the day of deliverance'; Selassie told Jamaicans on a visit in 1966 to liberate themselves before focusing on Africa.

The movement started at a time of adverse social and employment conditions in twentieth-century Jamaica and expressed the aspirations of those who were disaffected and disillusioned with their prospects. From being initially a movement which offered an explanation of blacks' economic plight under white exploitation and promised a heavenly reward to poor people, Rastafarianism moved on in Britain and America to become a focus for alienated, black, urban youth. One of the tenets of the religion is that adherents should make sacramental use of marijuana (ganja). This cultural dimension was misunderstood in Britain and the USA, and became the only widely known aspect of a whole way of life. This also led to the demonizing of Rastafarianism as a subculture and made Rastas even less likely to participate in a society which held travestied notions of their religious beliefs.

Rastafarians have been influential in many cultural ways in Britain. Their hairstyle is shared by some new age travellers or **crusties**. They were probably influential in promoting a climate of tolerance towards soft drugs in the 1980s. For example, they staked out their territory in urban areas of cities like Liverpool with graffiti such as: 'Toxteth Not Croxteth', meaning that marijuana was welcome in Toxteth, but not the heroin which was available in another district of the city. They also marked their area of urban influence by painting the streets and pavements in red, green and gold.

Though the religious group is small, millions appreciate the characteristic Rastafarian music **reggae**, with its development of a slow 'African' rhythm, often with lyrics that remind West Indians in Britain of their roots and recommending a coherent black cultural identity. Its principal exponents were Bob Marley and the Wailers. Marley's music uses a vibrant and compulsive rhythm based on a loud electric bass guitar, accompanied by organ, piano and drums. Marley's music has been enormously influential, for example with many British white **punk rock** bands (such as The Clash, Stiff Little Fingers and The Ruts), plus more mainstream pop groups like Culture Club and UB40. Among other black British groups displaying Rasta influence are Aswad, Misty in Roots, and Steel Pulse. Also, the Rastafarian poets Benjamin Zephaniah and Levi Tafari have published widely and speak for large numbers of people in expressing a spirit of both anomie and resistance.

Today there is less emphasis on the repatriation aspect of the cult and more on its rules. Its 'official' wish to be repatriated to Africa was demoted to the status of an 'ideal' after an 'immigration mission', suggested by a 1959 University of the West Indies commission, visited Africa. Rastafarians practise vegetarianism and aim to consume 'I-tal' or 'unprocessed' food. Their reworkings of English include 'I and I' not 'we' (an assertion of individual identity against the dehumanization of slavery as well as an expression of the speaker's relationship with Jah/God). They continue to reject 'white' Christianity which counsels forbearance and acceptance of one's lot, but for many the movement is now much more about contemporary style than about its original religious meanings.

See also: Afro-Caribbean communities

Further reading

Barrett, L.E. (1977) *Rastafarians: The Dreadlocks of Jamaica*, London: Heinemann (a solid, accessible introduction).
Cashmore, E. (1979) *Rastaman: The Rastafarian Movement in England*, London: Allen & Unwin (a dated but definitive and widely available review of British Rastafarianism).

MIKE STORRY

rave

The word 'rave' (possibly from the Old French *rêve*, to dream or to be delirious) is associated with frenzy, and the term 'raver' has been in use in British slang since the 1960s for a reveller or partygoer. Buddy Holly's song 'Rave On' may also have given rise to the coinage. Raves have been supported by youth subcultural groups spanning a wide range of social, ethnic and income divisions, and have a pan-European youth cultural influence. Raves started in Britain in the mid-1980s. They are usually in rural locations but the concept probably derives from urban acid house parties. Rave organizers rent a hall or farmer's field and sell tickets for this undisclosed location. On the night only, partygoers will be given directions to the event and large convoys of cars will travel, often hundreds of miles, to the all-night party.

The original music of raves was **disco**, but it later changed to **techno** and **indie pop**. Detractors accuse rave music of being just a variant of 'head-banging', and suggest that the experience of

raves is more to do with non-stop, uninhibited, vigorous dancing, enabled by drugs, than with an appreciation of the music. Ravers often adopt uniform clothing styles: for example many female ravers, 'rave grannies', wear long black 'granny' dresses over **Dr Martens** boots.

Police objections to these mass happenings are based on the fact that they create traffic problems, are unlicensed and are places where drugs, particularly ecstasy or 'E', are taken. Rave supporters attribute police hostility to a distrust of any manifestation of youth popular culture which they cannot control. Raves, among other forms of spontaneous gathering, led to government giving the police special powers of arrest under the Criminal Justice Act (1994), whose provisions were so 'catch all' in terms of their curtailment of rights of population movement and assembly that even the staid Ramblers' Association felt threatened.

Debate surrounding raves has centred on whether they indicate a loss of values, are just an aspect of **drug culture**, or offer a form of carnivalesque freedom. This would make them a cultural practice where there is no distinction between actors and spectators, a space to which the hedonistic and marginalized retreat and where rules are temporarily suspended.

See also: clubs; rave culture

Further reading

Redhead, S. (1990) *The End of the Century Party: Youth and Pop Towards 2000*, Manchester: Manchester University Press (short and often sweeping, but still a punchy cultural politics review of rap, rave and youth culture).

MIKE STORRY

rave culture

Rave culture has its origin in the 'second summer of love' in 1988. Initially held in the North of England in disused Victorian mills and warehouses, and on greenfield sites within the M25 motorway surrounding London, raves were all-night parties at which was played a mixture of **house**, acid house, **techno**, **disco** and **hip hop**. Early raves were characterized by the easygoing nature of those who attended. However, the use of the drug ecstasy at these parties meant that they attracted the attention of both drug dealers and the police. In order to prevent a rave being shut down, organizers opened up special telephone lines for ravers to ring on the night of an event for information as to the time and location of the rave. Often convoys of ravers would form on the M25 and on roads heading towards towns in Lancashire and Cheshire.

Police objections to raves initially led to mass arrests, and in 1990 to the Entertainments (Increased Penalties) Act. This legislation meant that 'unofficial' raves and parties were outlawed. As a consequence of this, rave organizers hired nightclubs and outdoor venues for raves. **Clubs** such as Quadrant Park in Liverpool, The Hacienda in Manchester, and Shelly's in Stoke-on-Trent were at the forefront of these developments. While the music of early raves was an eclectic mix of styles, the early 1990s saw the arrival of 'hardcore' rave music, a more aggressive form of **dance music** characterized by high-pitched female vocals, fast beats and 'hoover' noises. Some more commercially orientated rave records reached the official top 40, for instance N-Joi's 'Anthem' and The Prodigy's 'Charly'.

The rave scene of the mid-1990s is a very different one from that of the late 1980s. Outdoor raves are now extremely lucrative events that attract a younger crowd than the 'semi-legal' events of the 1980s. Organizers such as United Dance, Evolution and Dreamscape hold all-night events attended by up to 25,000 ravers, who are often prepared to travel hundreds of miles to attend such events. The music played at the raves of the mid-1990s is gabba (a form of rave music from Holland), 'happy hardcore' and **jungle**.

Ravers often wear fluorescent clothing, white gloves and carry luminous 'glow sticks' that are waved while dancing. The rave scene appears to be more popular in Scotland than in the rest of the UK, with organizers such as Rezerection frequently selling out massive venues. The clubs at the forefront of English rave culture include The Drome in Merseyside and Kinetic in Stoke-on-Trent. While there has been some concern about the growing **drug culture** associated with raves,

drug usage at raves appears to be no greater than at **discos** and other clubs.

Despite the commercialization of rave in the early 1990s, some promoters continue to organize illegal raves. 'Sound systems' such as Desert Storm, Sativa, Exodus and DIY organize secret parties at secluded country locations. Information about such parties is usually spread by word of mouth, or occasionally through the Internet. People who attend such events are usually older than those at legal raves, and often include a sizeable contingent of **crusties** and 'new-age travellers'.

STUART BORTHWICK

Rawls, John

b. 1921, Baltimore, Maryland

Philosopher

John Rawls has become the most important postwar liberal political theorist through his neo-Kantian reformulation of the social contract model. *A Theory of Justice* (1971), emphasizing justice as fairness in an anti-utilitarian argument rooted in rational self-interest, has had great appeal in Europe and the USA. He posits a hypothetical, non-historical situation in which the 'parties' to the contract are placed behind a 'veil of ignorance' of their particular status in society and so would choose that 'all social primary goods – liberty and opportunity, income and wealth, and the bases of self-respect – are to be distributed equally unless an unequal distribution of any or all of these goods is to the advantage of the least favoured.' Non-violent civil disobedience to bring changes in law or government policy is sanctioned. *Political Liberalism* (1993) reaffirms his original stance while attempting to answer critics.

See also: philosophy

DAVID MELLETT

readership

Until the 1970s, literary criticism was content to limit itself to romantic considerations of the writer and historical context. It regularly stretched to aesthetic valuations of the text but remained resolutely uninterested in what it might do for its readers or in the possibility that, without the reader's intervention, the text remained no more than a latency. The idea of readership became central to structuralist and post-structuralist criticism as a consequence of the work of Roland Barthes, especially with regard to his notion of the writerly or productive text, and to phenomenological, reader-oriented theories of literature (see **structuralism; post-structuralism**).

Reader-oriented theory proposes that the literary text can have no meaning, indeed no existence as literature, until it is read. Meaning materializes through the act of reading. It is a response by and to the reader, and hence any assessment of literary meaning must derive not from some hypothetical intention on the part of the writer, nor indeed from a typographic composition on the page, but on a potentially unlimited number of possible acts of reading. Readers actualize, and produce meaning from, literary works by applying a series of codes or conventions to them. That knowledge allows the reader to span the gaps and elisions of the text to produce an intelligible whole, and since those codes are the product of previous reading, each reader will necessarily arrive at a unique and inevitably provisional interpretation of the text with every reading. Every reader's experience will be different and every reading will produce new nuances of meaning. There can be no definitive reading of any text.

The idea of readership thus insists upon the possibility of gendered, class and ethnic inflections in the production of meaning. Interpretation depends on the disposition and competence not only of the individual reader but of their 'reading community'. Reading is culturally and historically determined, and since it is so implicated in the social there will clearly exist common strategies to produce meaning. Reading is doubly transformational in that it not only actualizes the text but changes the position of the reader. Any reading of a given text can never be repeated. Subsequent readings and their precursors are inevitably differently informed.

Readership thus seems to imply that its defining act narrativizes, structures, (re)frames or makes

manifest a range of possibilities that are not located in, but are rather triggered by, the text. Reading achieves its end through a kind of writing.

See also: book marketing; literary theory; popular fiction; publishing trends

JIM HALL

received pronunciation

Received pronunciation is the name given to the Southern pronunciation of English identified early in the twentieth century as the usage of the public schools and the professions and promoted as 'correct'. It became the norm to which educated people were expected to conform, and was taught to foreigners learning English. Though it did not displace such strong regional accents as Scots, which retained prestige, English dialectal variants tended to be despised. The BBC's use of received pronunciation did much to establish it countrywide, as did the stage and the talkies. Over the decades since the Second World War, using received pronunciation has been increasingly seen as artificial and socially divisive.

See also: class system; dialect; Estuary English

Further reading

Honey, J. (1989) *Does Accent Matter?* London: Faber.

CHRISTOPHER SMITH

recession

A recession is a period during which a country's economic output falls below its potential, producing less goods and services than the country has capacity for. Recessions are characterized by negative levels of economic growth and corresponding unemployment. High levels of unemployment alone do not mean recession, as the late 1980s illustrate. The British economy has experienced three recessions since the 1970s. The first came at the end of the Heath government's (1970–4) brief economic experiment. The second was at the beginning of the 1980s following Thatcher's deflationary budgets. The third was at the beginning of the 1990s as the Lawson boom collapsed. In 1998 it was feared that the country was slipping into a fourth recession.

See also: financial crises; monetarism

Further reading

Artis, M.J. (ed.) (1992) *The UK Economy*, London: Weidenfeld & Nicholson.

ALASTAIR LINDSLEY

Red or Dead

Founded in 1982 by Wayne and Geraldine Hemmingway, Red or Dead specialize in footwear and customized second-hand clothing. An internationally known design label, they have shops in England and abroad as well as a mail-order service, The Hemmingway's streetwise anti-fashion stance has been to make clothes that do not endure but which make an immediate statement. A speed for interpreting trends and an idiosyncratic nature has made Red or Dead consistently successful.

See also: Dr Martens; rave culture

PETER CHILDS

Redgrave family

Michael Redgrave (1908–85) forged a distinguished career in films, which included *The Lady Vanishes* (1938), *The Browning Version* (1951) and *The Dam Busters* (1955), despite a preference for the stage. Married to actress Rachel Kempson, their children, daughters Vanessa (1937–) and Lynn (1943–) and son Corin (1939–) also became actors. Vanessa achieved particular popularity in the 1960s in *Blow Up*, *A Man For All Seasons* and *Camelot*, and sustained her career through the 1970s despite political notoriety with diverse leading roles such as *Mary, Queen of Scots* and *Julia*. *Prick Up Your Ears* (1987), *Howard's End* (1992) and *Mission Impossible* (1996) offered her strong supporting roles. Lynn is best known for her 'Swinging

London' performances, especially as *Georgy Girl* (1966). Vanessa's daughters Natasha and Joely Richardson are also actresses, as is Corin's daughter Jemma.

ALICE E. SANGER

Reger, Janet

Fashion designer

Janet Reger is Britain's most famous **lingerie** designer. Her luxurious designs in silk, satin and lace offered a flattering and indulgent alternative to the extremes of utility or sleaze which had characterized lingerie design. Reger's fortunes declined during the 1980s and she sold her company to Berlei in 1983. She bought the company back in 1986, and has since regained a position in a market in which she now competes with many other companies and designers for whom she was undoubtedly a role model.

TAMSIN SPARGO

reggae

Reggae first appeared in Britain in the sometimes illegal drinking and social clubs, known as the 'blues-dance', following the Irish tradition for drinking dens or 'shebeens'. It is in these early blues-dances that the first reggae sound systems – early mobile discos specializing in black music – sprang up. Much of the music was imported from the Caribbean: labels like Melodisc, Bluebeat, and Sonny Roberts's Planitone emerged, before evolving into Orbitone. In 1962, Chris Blackwell travelled to England to expand his Island label, which was launched with Millie Small's pop-ska hit 'My Boy Lollipop'. By 1968 Trojan records was established.

The first British independent labels soon grasped the financial implications of releasing their own local productions, as opposed to merely distributing Jamaican records. London was the imperial capital where many early reggae artists came to break into the international market. Artists like Jimmy Cliff, Peter Tosh, Bunny Livingstone and Bob Marley (the original Wailers), Desmond Dekker, Sharon Forrester, The Aces, Errol Dunkley, Gene Rondo and many more followed this route.

The first British-based reggae band to emerge was Matumbi, founded in 1972. This was the start of a new-wave of homegrown reggae artists. Because most were born in the UK, the socio-cultural background of this new wave was informed as much by British life as by Jamaican. Soon British reggae started to define itself independently from that of Jamaica. This engendered a sense of pride and independence that gave birth to dozens of homegrown reggae bands during the early to mid-1970s. Names like London's Matumbi, Aswad and Misty in Roots, Bristol's Talisman and Black Roots, Nottingham's Naturalites, Liverpool's Cross Section and The Players of Instruments, Birmingham's Steel Pulse and other bands like Black Slate, Dambala, I Jahman Levi, Natrus Roots, Jahdeanko and The Blackstones all became synonymous with a homegrown British 'roots rock reggae' sound.

The group Aswad were formed in Ladbroke Grove, West London, in 1975. Aswad were at the time one of the youngest homegrown bands to have emerged from the mid-1970s school in terms of age. Aswad's success also came from their rebelliousness, and records like *Concrete Slaveship* drew heavily on the experience of life on Britain's housing estates, while songs like 'Three Babylon' were related to the 'SUS' (stop on suspicion) laws that plagued the lives of many black youths in Britain. Rebellious at first, by 1980 Aswad had crossed over to the mainstream pop arena by becoming the first British reggae band to have a number one hit in the UK charts.

Black Slate have been cited as the most overtly British of these bands. Their 1976 hit single 'Stix Man' (since released at least four times in Britain alone), was one of the first profound expressions of the black British experience. Steel Pulse, whose record *Handsworth Revolution* clearly identified them with their Birmingham home, became the most successful on an international level.

Dennis Bovel, co-founder of Matumbi in 1972, left in the early 1980s and went solo as a producer of dub music. His first album *Brain Damage*, a double album, featured Bovel as writer, producer, singer and player of most of the music. Bovel always felt hampered by straightforward reggae, and since his break with Matumbi he has become notorious for his eclectic mixes. Bovel invented Britain's longest standing reggae innovation, 'lovers rock', by mixing **soul** and reggae. Where 'roots rock reggae' was primarily a 'rebel' music and very male-oriented, the sweeter sounding 'lovers rock' was pioneered notably by females. The 1977 carnival in Notting Hill, which was marked by clashes with the police, was also marked by Louisa Mark whose 'lovers rock' anthem, 'Caught You in a Lie', produced by Bovel, placed 'lovers rock' on a par with any of the 'rebel rock' music around at that time. It was not long before a host of solo artists and harmony groups emerged: Cassandra, Black Harmony, Marie Pierre, Carol Kalphat, Janet Kay, Caroll Thompson, Jean Adebambo and Mellow Rose, all selling quantities of records unprecedented in black British history.

People like the Mad Professor and the Scientist followed Bovel by using the mixing desk as an instrument and a means of expression to create something new and distinctly British in origin. After working on sound systems for most of the 1970s, the Mad Professor started his own label Ariwa in 1979, from which he released some of Britain's finest **dub**. Bass player George Oban left the more traditional British reggae scene after five years with Aswad, to create an eclectic mix of a more subtler type than Bovel's. Oban's music avoided the head-on collision of style favoured by Bovel, and emerged as a multi-layered fusion of reggae using the paradigms of **jazz**, Latin and **funk**. Oban was born in Britain, and claims that his musical roots were primarily people like the Beatles and the Beach Boys.

With the experimentation of people like Dennis Bovell and George Oban, by the mid-1980s British reggae was becoming an entity in its own right. After the crash of Trojan in 1975, Virgin, an English rock label, attempted to fill the gap. Other labels that sprung up at the time of the Trojan crash were Groove Music, Hawkeye, D-Roy, Klik, Ballistic, Burning Sounds and Greensleeves. British reggae was up and running.

The reggae sound system played a major role in the development of British reggae because they promoted the music at dances. Most black communities in most major cities had a champion sound: Manchester had President Hi Fi, Liverpool had Jah Crasher (later to become King Struggla Sound), Birmingham had Jungleman, Quaker City and Jah Wasifa, London had Jah Shaka Spiritual Dub Warrior, Frontline from Brixton, Sir Coxsone Outer National and Saxon Sound System. Each 'sound' had its own entourage of singers, toasters and DJs, and as their DJs and toasters moved into pirate radio and the recording industry, so did the music. Macka B, a Rasta from Birmingham's Jah Wasifa Sound, made his name by adding his lyrics and voice to The Mad Professor's London brand of Reggae. Saxon Sound gave birth to such stars as Tippa Irey, who had a big hit with 'Hello Darling', and Smiley Culture's 'Cockney Translation' was another UK chart success that identified itself as both black and cockney. Jah Shaka recorded as a musician-producer in much the same way that Bovel had, but specialized in 'roots Dub'. His 1990 album *Dub Symphony* uses a string section, and creates a reference point where dub meets the Reggae Philharmonic Orchestra. In the 1990s, the raggamuffin style has appropriated the use of hi-tech adding yet another dimension to the ever-changing face of British reggae.

See also: Afro-Caribbean communities; Rastafarianism; ska; two-tone

Further reading

Broughton, S., Ellingham, M., Muddyman, D. and Trillo, R. (eds) (1994) *The Rough Guide to World Music* (contains a useful section on British reggae by Gregory Salter).

Davis, S. and Simon, P. (1983) *Reggae International*, London: Thames & Hudson (a comprehensive account of reggae up to a point, but has a useful bibliography, and an impressive list of contributors).

EUGENE LANGE

Rego, Paula

b. 1935, Lisbon (Portugal)

Painter

For Paula Rego, there is a potential threat, a sinister unease that prevails in fairy tales. Born in Portugal, she settled permanently in London in 1976. In the 1950s she discovered Dubuffet and began to draw on childhood experiences, movies and fairy tales such as *Fantasia*, *Snow White* and *Pinocchio* for inspiration. At this moment her narratives began to function as moral fables. In the early 1980s, animals were used to express the contradictory nature of human emotions and behaviour, such as in her *Girl and Dog* series (1985). The sense of unease that her paintings impart is strengthened by her use of harsh lighting, heavy outlines and sparse settings. She creates large figurative paintings in acrylic or pastel, or smaller etchings reminiscent of storybook illustration.

See also: painting

NATALIE GALE

regulation

The principle of regulation in Britain combines constitutionalism and **privatization**. The constitutional principle, that of the rule of law, is at its weakest in institutions in civil society and in state institutions based on the power of royal prerogative. Formal institutions of regulation have been designed to cover some cases. These are generally monopolistic state utilities transferred to the private sector. Regulators covering gas, telecommunications and numerous others now control both the practice and pricing of monopolistic utilities.

The transparency that such regulation has engendered is leading to a regulation regime that has begun to feed back into all areas of public life. Once regulation and transparency have been invoked, it is unclear that any private or public body, including parliament, should be considered exempt. The Nolan Committee on Standards in Public Life, and the appointment of a parliamentary commissioner to oversee such standards, are parts of a massive sea-change in the way in which institutions are increasingly held accountable to transparent principles. This is a 'quiet' revolution, but a revolution it is nonetheless.

See also: regulatory bodies

PAUL BARRY CLARKE

regulatory bodies

Regulatory bodies are agencies that oversee particular industrial areas or activities where some economic, political or socio-cultural concern exists (for example, over industrial concentration or public interest requirements). Usually they are appointed by government, though self-appointed semi-official regulatory bodies do also exist, such as the Press Complaints Commission. While following a general remit laid down by government (or the industry if an industry-appointed body), the regulatory body has a degree of autonomy in its day-to-day undertakings. Regulatory bodies come in a number of forms, such as those that oversee all industries in terms of a theme, for example the Monopolies and Mergers Commission (MMC), and those that focus on specific activities, such as the Independent Television Commission (ITC).

Historically, broadcasting has been the one area of the media that has had its own specific government regulators: the ITC for the commercial sector and the governors of the **BBC** for the BBC. The reason regulation has been viewed as necessary for broadcasting is because of the nature of the medium: the scarcity of channels, the possible abuse of monopoly power and the perceived influence and power of radio and television in the life of the nation. Therefore, a regulator has been needed to control access to the limited airwaves and to oversee the service and content actually provided on behalf of the public. Other forms of media – cinema and the press – have escaped official regulation by creating their own industry appointed bodies such as the British Board of Film Censors (BBFC) and the Press Complaints Commission. Specific government regulation did not seem warranted in these areas because of the openness of such markets to competition and because of worries about government censorship and control.

With technological developments now providing an abundance of television and radio channels, the role of the regulator is changing. It is argued that, with huge numbers of channels now coming on stream, broadcasting is becoming more like the press in that anyone can now enter the market. Therefore, regulation should concentrate less on the specific working and content of broadcasting and more on the fair and open operation of the market. With the convergence of telecommunications and broadcast technologies and services, the question of whether OFTEL, the telecommunications regulator, and the broadcasting regulators, ITC and the BBC governors, should merge to create one large regulator – OFCOM – has been raised.

See also: democracy; lobby groups

Further reading

Murroni, C. and Collins, R. (1996) *New Media, New Policies: Media and Communications Strategies for the Future*, London: Polity Press.

PAUL RIXON

Reisz, Karel

b. 1926

Film director

Reisz belonged to the late 1950s social realist Free Cinema Movement, collaborating with Lindsay **Anderson** on the film journal *Sequence* and Tony **Richardson** on the shorts *Momma Don't Allow* (1956) and *We Are The Lambeth Boys* (1959). Reisz's *Saturday Night and Sunday Morning* (1960) is a definitive example of the Free Cinema, capturing the 1960s zeitgeist of male working-class defiance. Like other British new wave directors, he worked in the USA directing film adaptations of *Who'll Stop The Rain* (1978), *The French Lieutenant's Women* (1981) and *Everybody Wins* (1990). Reisz translated his mastery of direction, dramatic pace and structure to the theatre during the 1990s with a series of critically acclaimed plays at the Almeida in London.

Further reading

Gaston, G. (1980) *Karel Reisz*, Boston: Thayne.

SATINDER CHOHAN

restaurants and bars

Alternative places to eat and drink have appeared in Britain over the last twenty years. The changes in licensing laws, the appetite for international foods, the increase in numbers of professional women workers, the delay in getting married or having children, and the general increase in spending power and sophistication have all made the traditional British pub and cafe outmoded. British cities have consequently broken out in a rash of theme bars and continental cafes. Many of these are open plan and feature long bars, thus different from the usual pub design which aims to give drinkers privacy rather than public display (the trend to visibility is exemplified in Tchaik Chassay's Groucho Club in Soho (1984)). Following Julyan Wickham's Zanzibar (1976), restaurants and bars are now designed by architects almost as often as interior designers. Typical examples are Eva Jiricna's Le Caprice near the Ritz (1981) and Rick **Mather**'s Zen in Hampstead (1985). Most of these have been influenced by architecture in other countries, particularly New York high-tech chic (for example, Jiricna's Joe's Cafe in Brompton (1985)) and Japanese minimalism (Nigel **Coates**'s industrial baroque style developed in Tokyo).

See also: office buildings; shops

Further reading

Glancey, J. (1989) *New British Architecture*, London: Thames & Hudson.

PETER CHILDS

retro

'Retro' is a 1970s term made current by French writers commenting upon the postmodernist fashion for artists, designers and film-makers to revive and recycle past styles, often very recent ones. A shop called Retro duly opened on the Tottenham Court Road in 1975, and by 1979 the backlash had started with feminist art critic Lucy Lippard coining the term 'retrochic' to denote 'a reactionary wolf in counter-cultural clothing'. Much retro involves the uncritical and gratuitous appropriation of traditions and styles from other ethnic groups under the often spurious name of art.

PETER CHILDS

Reuters

The biggest news agency in the world, Reuters had a turnover of £2,914m in 1995. The largest part of Reuters' earnings comes from the sale of financial information, which reflects the entrepreneurial genius of its founder Paul Julius Reuter who used carrier pigeons to fly stock prices between Aachen and Brussels in 1849. Reuters' huge growth dates from the 1974 introduction of computer-based displays of real-time foreign exchange, and the 1981 birth of the Reuters Monitor Dealing Service. By 1997 Reuters had become a financial services giant, and a leading source of international news for the world's media. Though a public company traded in London and New York, Reuters has elaborate provisions to safeguard its independence.

See also: IRN; news, television

ANDREW QUICKE

Rhodes, Zandra

b. 1940, Chatham

Fashion designer

One of the most colourful and idiosyncratic figures in British design, Zandra Rhodes studied textiles at the Royal College of Art in the 1960s and launched her first solo collection in 1969. She developed a distinctive style, specializing in special occasion clothing such as ethereal dresses in unusual shapes, fabrics and colours with an emphasis on brightly coloured screen-printed textiles and hand finishing and decoration. Her own flamboyant image complemented her designs, and while her clothing is no longer at the cutting edge of fashion, Rhodes is still a popular figure in the British media.

TAMSIN SPARGO

rhyming slang

Witty and often inventively reflecting contemporary persons and events, rhyming slang turns 'use your head' first into 'your loaf of bread', then truncates it to 'your loaf', now an everyday idiom. News from the Afghan frontier prompted 'Khyber' for 'arse', adding a giggle to the film *Carry On Up The Khyber*. A speech habit of Cockneys, in fact all East Enders, and Australians, rhyming slang was identified in the mid-nineteenth century as impenetrable thieves' cant. Today it serves less for communication within the group than as a linguistic means of displaying group identity to bemused outsiders, as much in comedy and chat shows as in real-life situations.

See also: Cockney

Further reading

Franklin, J. (1953) *The Cockney: A Survey of London Life and Language*, London: Deutsch.

CHRISTOPHER SMITH

RIBA

The Royal Institute of British Architects (RIBA) dates from 1834, one of a number of similar institutions founded in London in the first half of the nineteenth century when the **Royal Academy** was not felt to be providing adequately for the study of architecture or, equally important, for the regulation of the architectural profession. The twin focus has remained to this day, with town planning emerging to become one of the Institute's major concerns, and RIBA has played an important role in improving standards. Other bodies control the registration of architects, but RIBA is still a force in British architecture.

See also: Architectural Association

CHRISTOPHER SMITH

Richardson, Tony

b. 1928; d. 1991

Film director

Like Free Cinema collaborator Karel **Reisz**, Richardson was an Oxbridge educated member (arguably, instigator) of the British new wave in both theatre (with his 1958 production of John Osborne's *Look Back in Anger*) and cinema (with his 1959 adaptation for Woodfall Productions, formed with Osborne in 1958). A formidable, nonconformist character who worked simultaneously in television, film and theatre, Richardson's numerous film adaptations included *A Taste of Honey* (1961), *Tom Jones* (1963), *Hamlet* (1969), *Joseph Andrews* (1976) and *The Hotel New Hampshire* (1984), alongside the epic *The Charge of the Light Brigade* (1968). Richardson moved to California during the 1970s, directing his final film *Blue Sky* in 1990.

Further reading

Hill, J. (1986) *Sex, Class and Realism: British Cinema: 1956–63*, London: BFI.

SATINDER CHOHAN

Riley, Bridget

b. 1931

Painter

A leading exponent of op art, Bridget Riley gained recognition during the early 1960s with her abstract black and white paintings, whose patterns created visual sensations such as movement or vibrations. In 1965 she achieved international recognition when her work was included in *The Responsive Eye* exhibition held in New York, and in 1968 she won the International Painting Prize at the Venice Biennale. Towards the end of the 1960s Riley introduced colour to her work, using contrasts which increased the optical effects produced by the image. In the 1980s the artist continued to use the vertical structure which appeared in her stripe paintings, offsetting this with diagonally placed rhomboids to produce a sense of overall rhythm.

See also: painting

LUCINDA TOWLER

riots and civil disobedience

Civil disobedience occurs when a person or group feels morally compelled to publicly break the law, usually without using violence, and is prepared to face the full consequences of the legal system. It is considered justifiable if the law is unjust and there is no other effective means of opposition. Conservatives view civil disobedience as going against the need to maintain law and order, as it encourages selective acceptance of laws and is against the sovereignty of a democratically elected **parliament**. It is contended that civil disobedients act according to the highest ideals of the law and are not above the law.

Civil disobedience has occasionally proved successful, as when London dockers went on an illegal wildcat strike and suffered imprisonment to defeat the Industrial Relations Act of 1971. Civil disobedience defeated government in the 1980s when rallies organized by the Anti Poll Tax Federation and their campaign of public non-payment resulted in the scrapping of the community charge (see **poll tax**).

The dividing line between civil disobedience and rioting is indistinct, as civil disobedience can coerce violent reprisals which may be responded to in the same manner. Organized protests are sometimes aimed to precipitate **violence**, as with the **National Front** demonstrations of the 1970s against coloured immigration and counter-demonstrations by the radical left.

Riots occurred in twenty-seven urban areas in the summer of 1981. Race was a factor in all the riots. The first riot was in Brixton, an area with a high concentration of immigrants and 55 percent unemployment amongst 16–18-year-old blacks. Street crime was high, so police had instigated a stop-and-search policy which antagonized local people. The riot lasted for two days, with firebombs and looting. In Toxteth, Liverpool, deprivation was worse and riots lasted for six days, with white youths joining and eventually outnumbering the blacks. The other 'copycat riots' had the common characteristics of occurring in deprived urban areas characterized by high unemployment, immigrant settlement and aggressive and racist policing.

Government response to riots has been to give the **police** power to ban potentially violent demonstrations, to arrest protesters for the offence of disorderly conduct under the Public Order Act 1985, and to encourage more community policing. These measures have not been entirely successful, as riots have continued to occur in the inner cities in the 1980s and 1990s.

See also: direct action

Further reading

Harris, P. (1989) *Civil Disobedience*, Washington, DC: University Press of America.

COLIN WILLIAMS

Ritchie, Ian

b. 1947

Architect

Ian Ritchie trained first at the Liverpool School of Architecture (1965–8) and then at the Polytechnic of Central London (1970–2), after which he worked for **Foster Associates** until 1976. With Foster Associates, he worked on the design of the Willis, Faber and Dumas office in Ipswich and the Sainsbury Centre for the Visual Arts at the University of East Anglia. He then worked in Paris (he is also a registered architect in France) before establishing Chrysalis Architects (with Michael Dowd and Alan Stanton). This was up to 1981, after which he was a director of Rice, Francis and Ritchie in Paris up to 1986 (he also taught at the **Architectural Association** at this time, from 1979 to 1982). Additionally, he set up a private practice in London from 1981 as Ian Ritchie Architects.

His most noticeable design style is a combination of architecture and engineering, as in the Meccano-kit Eagle Rock House at Sussex (1983) and in his work on Fiat vehicles, cranes and high tensile fabric roofs. In the late 1980s he worked on apartment **housing** in Docklands. Overall, Ritchie is better known in France than the UK, because of his work with Martin Francis and Peter Rice which contributed to the Louvre pyramid. Since his return to Britain, and move to Wapping, he has become a leading UK architectural light and is a Royal Fine Art Commissioner. Despite his technical expertise (he is known for his structural uses of glass), his approach to architecture is holistic. In his book *Well Connected Architects* he says 'to understand the quality of our environmental fabric it requires inspiration, ideas and expertise', from artists, poets, economists and members of the public. He is commissioned to design the new Crystal Palace.

PETER CHILDS

Robert Maguire and Partners

Maguire and Company was founded in 1988, and specializes in student accommodation, other university buildings and church design. The firm has worked on large-scale projects such as the al-Gassim campus of King Saud University in Saudia Arabia, and small-scale conversions such as that of the Old Congregation House at Oxford, the oldest university building in England. Maguire's first enterprise, St Paul's church, London E3, is now a Grade II* listed building. The company sees its work in terms of craft as well as high art, and has skills in the fields of urban design, landscape, product design and graphics.

See also: university building

PETER CHILDS

Robert Matthew Johnson-Marshall and Partners

Robert Matthew and Stirrat Johnson-Marshall established RMJM as an architectural practice in Edinburgh and London in 1956. A prolific output of small-scale and larger commissions reflects RMJM's multidisciplinary nature and stylistic diversity, commencing with Turnhouse Airport, Edinburgh (1956) and including the Common-

wealth Institute (1962), the Universities of York (1966), Stirling (1974) and Lincolnshire and Humberside (completion 1999), Cockenzie Power Station, East Lothian (1968), Royal Commonwealth Pool, Edinburgh (1969) and Hillingdon Civic Centre (1976). New Zealand House (1963) is an early example of the postwar modern movement. RMJM's founding commitment to social architecture has developed by combining dynamic aesthetic and technological considerations with a conservationist conscience, as with Glaxo Wellcome HQ, Greenford (1997).

See also: town planning

Further reading

Knewitt, C. (1997) 'RMJM's 40th Anniversary', *Architect's Journal* 205(23): 30–47.

SATINDER CHOHAN

Robinson, Bruce

b. 1946

Film-maker

First an actor, then a screenwriter and then a director, Bruce Robinson first came to prominence with his Oscar-nominated screenplay for David **Puttnam**'s *The Killing Fields* (1984), but then achieved cult status with his directorial debut, *Withnail and I* (1987), a comedy about two drunken, world-weary but comical actors living out the last days of the 1960s with the sense of doom and disillusionment that Hamlet feels in Elsinore. This was followed by *How to Get Ahead in Advertising* (1989), again with Richard E. Grant, *The Shadow-Makers* (1989) and *Jennifer 8* (1992). He published his first novel, *The Peculiar Memories of Thomas Penman*, in 1998.

PETER CHILDS

rock festivals

Taking their cue from both the major US rock festivals of the late 1960s (Woodstock, Monterey and so on), and from the existing **jazz** and blues festivals that began in the 1950s, the British rock festival circuit has grown in size and become the most prestigious of its kind in the world. The first major British festival was held on the Isle of Wight in 1970, attracting artists such as Bob Dylan, The Band and Jimi Hendrix. Originally intended as a commercial venture, it fell prey to the same problems encountered at the earlier Woodstock festival, most notably lack of security. The festival became free to all-comers, and attracted a crowd of around 150,000.

Also in 1970, a Somerset farmer decided to put on a low-key free festival with mostly unknown acts (including T-Rex and David Bowie), headlined by folk singer Donovan. The Glastonbury Festival (actually based at Pilton, Somerset, some miles away) quickly became a semi-permanent feature during the summer months, and is still the most important rock festival of the season. The numbers that gather at Glastonbury confirm the enduring popularity of outdoor rock events, with over 100,000 paying customers each year. True to the hippie ideal of festivals, most of the proceeds go to good causes, both global and local. Going from strength to strength, the importance of the festival in promoting and resurrecting careers is clear to many artists. Following appearances at Glastonbury during the 1990s, the careers of Tom Jones, Tony Bennett and Lou Reed had massive resurgence, opening up their music to a new, younger audience.

The main rival to Glastonbury is the Reading Rock Festival, a descendant of the Reading Blues and Jazz festival. The rising popularity of the festival is shown in the huge commercial possibilities opened up by having a captive audience of tens of thousands for a three-day period. This potential was quickly seized upon by promoters, particularly during the early 1990s, when many smaller festivals began to be promoted. The Phoenix festival, V96 (-97, -98, etc.), T in the Park (based in Scotland), and other smaller one-day events quickly became an integral part of the summer festival scene, as did genre based events (Monsters of Rock, Futurama) and artist-led outdoor concerts (Knebworth and Crystal Palace, for example). The commercial bubble appeared to have burst, however, in 1998, when many of the smaller events, and notably the large Phoenix festival, failed to sell a sufficient amount of tickets to be financially viable and so were cancelled.

See also: concert promoters; hippies; WOMAD

Further reading

Clarke, M.J. (1982) *The Politics of Pop Festivals*, London: Junction Books.

SAM JOHNSTONE

rockers

Rockers were a male youth subculture of the early 1960s. They wore black leather jackets and biker boots, rode powerful motorcycles and had a reputation for **violence**. In particular, the style of the rocker drew influences from Elvis Presley and Marlon Brando. Rockers hit newspaper headlines in 1964 when they held running street fights at British seaside resorts with their sworn enemies the **mods**, who referred to rockers as 'greasers'. Rockers usually had low-paid manual jobs, and their violence was interpreted as a rebellion against the drab nature of postwar British society. Many rockers became **Hell's Angels**, a closed subculture of motorcycle gangs known for their extreme violence.

STUART BORTHWICK

Roeg, Nicholas

b. 1928, London

Film-maker

Nicholas Roeg started out in British cinema in 1947 as an editing apprentice, becoming a cinematographer in the 1960s (with credits including *The Masque of the Red Death*, *Fahrenheit 451* and *Far from the Madding Crowd*) before directing his first film *Performance* in 1968 (with Donald Cammell). This was followed by *Walkabout*, *Don't Look Now* and *The Man Who Fell To Earth* (1976). In these early works, Roeg displays a virtuoso command of the film medium, particularly in his use of associative montage sequences, disrupting and resisting conventional narrative methods. Since the mid-1980s Roeg has produced more commercial work in *Castaway* (1987) and *The Witches* (1990), and several films for television including *Sweet Bird of Youth* (1989) and *Heart of Darkness* (1994).

STEPHEN C. KENNY

Rogers, Richard

b. 1933

Architect

Richard Rogers studied at London's **Architectural Association** and at Yale University in the USA, where he met Norman Foster (see **Foster Associates**). Rogers and Foster returned to London and established Team 4 Architects, with Su Rogers and Wendy Cheesman. Their defining commission was Creek Vean House in Cornwall (1966), which owes its organic conception to the influence of American architect Frank Lloyd Wright. Team 4 was dissolved in 1968 and Rogers subsequently entered a partnership with Italian architect Renzo Piano. In 1971, Piano and Rogers won the commission to design the Centre Georges Pompidou in Paris. The Pompidou Centre, opened in 1977, is envisaged as 'a people's place … a cross between an information-oriented, computerized Times Square and the British Museum'. Reinterpreting futurist and constructivist aesthetic aims, this flexible and rhythmic structure of steel and glass is recognized as an outstanding achievement in postwar European architecture.

Rogers' international reputation was augmented when he and new associates John Young, Marco Goldschmied and Michael Davies were commissioned to redevelop the Lloyd's of London headquarters in 1977. Richard Rogers Partnership designed a complexly layered futuristic building: its six serrated steel towers, opaque glass walls and central glazed atrium are perceived in dynamic vertical and horizontal sections from street level and as a visually integrated totality from the riverside. The design of the Lloyd's Building, like the Pompidou Centre, allows for the controlled redistribution of internal space to suit changing needs. Since the completion of Lloyd's in 1986, RRP has completed other prestigious projects, notably the European Court of Human Rights in Strasbourg (1994). Major commissions in the late 1990s include Law Courts in Bordeaux, a new terminal at Madrid Airport and the Millennium Dome in Greenwich, London.

Rogers is a trenchant critic of the intensively capitalized imperatives of **postmodernism** in contemporary architecture. Castigating postmodernism as an aesthetic determined by the principle 'form follows profit', Rogers has called for a 'new cultural enlightenment' in which architecture and urban planning would play key roles in the democratic restructuring of public space. He combines this vision of a revivified urban culture with an ecologically sustainable and holistic approach to the built environment. In 1996, Rogers was made a Labour peer and introduced to the House of Lords as Lord Rogers of Riverside.

See also: high-tech

Further reading

Rogers, R. (1990) *Architecture: A Modern View*, London: Thames & Hudson (Rogers's lucid examination of contemporary urban space).

MARK DOUGLAS

romance

British romance writing has witnessed an astonishing profusion of popular novels since 1960, as well as successful commercial earnings. Modern trends towards greater realism, action and simplicity in plot have strengthened the genre, despite negative critiques from academics and disdainful prophecies of imminent demise. The Harlequin publishers imprint has had a phenomenal effect; the novels of British gothic-style romance writers are marketed in abundance in North America, most particularly on the popular reading shelves of supermarkets and shopping centre malls. Carole Mortimer (*A Lost Love, Wildest Dreams*) is a very popular romance novelist because of her glamorous London settings and her sophisticated heroines.

This success reflects, in great part, the fact that

the British romance genre responds to the need for sheer escapism of stressed, often jobless female suburbanite woman. Barbara Cartland (the Queen of Hearts) is a primary example of writers whose novels and television adaptations contrive to focus unapologetically on romantic melodramatic character types such as Regency 'rakes' and crafty 'belles'. Their adventures are situated in an idealized age of a less industrialized England, on an isle of fantasy. These fantasized stories arguably respond to a deeply-rooted desire for nostalgia and hope in the modern age.

However, Cartland's supporters and other believers in escapism exaggerate the lack of psychological realism in the traditional Gothic romance novel, whether in Mary Shelley's *Franken-stein* or in Jane Austen's *Northanger Abbey*, both of which are equally nightmarish and sexually suggestive. It is no accident that, in our times, Gothic romance has returned to its own dreamy, more disturbing introspective realism to express the individual endeavours of people seeking to resolve personal difficulties in the society of post-1960s Britain. The story is sometimes resolved tragically or punitively for the character of the protagonist at the expense of women's personas in the novel. The genre suffers as well from a too-confident belief in the total perfectibility of rationalized gender and childcare relationships, felt to be deeply personal matters by most more conservative Britons.

Northerner Catherine Cookson (*The Black Candle, The Black Gown Woman*) shared Cartland's insistence on a predominantly historical setting. Cookson had written and published nearly 100 novels by the time of her death in 1998, by which time she had reached millionaire status. But she was particularly successful, paradoxically, with contemporary twentieth-century romances. Cookson's romances captured the era of her own youth and harsh upbringing in the early twentieth century, portrayed as a more meritocratic, less ruthless time than the present. Realism also has been the cultivated hallmark of the equally successful Barbara Taylor Bradford's (*A Woman of Substance*) romance fiction, in her characters, in her visually powerful global portrayal of society, and in her panoramic landscape descriptions.

Furthermore, the more feminist novelists of the last four decades who were once considered threats to the values of romantic fantasy fiction have in fact skillfully blended their intuitive concerns for the realistic existential victimized heroine with recognizably Gothic and Romantic themes. Irish-born Edna O'Brien's lead characters (*The Country Girls, The High Road*) are modern but bittersweet British heroines. But these women characters, born in the 1950s, notably react against the still abiding rural repression and religious conformity dating from that period. Traditional expectations of them as 'girls' are still not uncommon on both sides of the channel and do impede character development in a changing social context. In addition, Beryl Bainbridge portrays in her works (such as *Sweet William*) the mistreatment of complex modern heroines; yet her philandering male characters are often gothically eliminated as they receive their 'just' punishment. Old-fashioned justice often takes the form of revenge imposed by women as the plot evolves.

See also: popular fiction; readership

Further reading

Rowbotham, S. (1997) *A Century of Women*, London: Viking-Penguin (although far to the feminist left herself, Rowbotham demonstrates generous and fair understanding of avowed conservatives such as Dame Barbara Cartland).

LAWRENCE IRVINE ILES
BETTY McLANE-ILES

rowing

In rowing (unlike canoe paddling) the human effort of arms and legs, maximized by a sliding seat, is complemented by mechanical advantage as oars pivot in rowlocks fixed on the boat's side or, better still, on outriggers. A sculler pulling a pair of blades can compete alone or in a crew with one or three more other scullers; a rower, with a single oar, always teams up with one, three or seven more. Fours may have a cox; eights always do.

Rowing as a sport emerged from competitions between Thames watermen, who provided an important transport service in London. After the institution of Thomas Doggett's 'Coat and Badge' prize race for Thames watermen in 1715, the gentry started wagering on oarsmen who made their living from rowing. The nineteenth-century decline in commercial rowing was paralleled by the rise of rowing as one of the sports adopted by the middle classes, particularly at the public schools and universities, as a recreation leading to both moral and physical well-being. The founding of the Leander Club on the Thames in about 1818, the first Oxford and Cambridge **University Boat Race** in 1829 and the inauguration of the annual **Henley Regatta** ten years later had counterparts in further developments in Britain and abroad. The establishment of amateurism was crucial; gentlemen rowers shunned competition (and social contact) not only with those who made their living by rowing but also with tradesmen who might have developed muscle power at work. In recent decades, with rowing virtually disappearing as a trade and work generally involving less physical toil, amateur/professional distinctions have been set aside. As rowing has evolved as an international sport, with women's rowing as a vital sector, the norm has become racing over distances up to 2,000 meters in straight lanes in still water. Modern facilities have been provided, for example, at Sutton Valence, because it is felt that the Oxford and Cambridge Boat Race (four and one-quarter miles on the tideway), Henley (1 mile 550 yards upstream on the Thames) and other traditional events are not ideal influences on British rowing. Though recreational rowing on rivers has declined since the Second World War, Steve Redgrave's triumphs in four successive Olympics have given the sport a higher profile, and competitive rowing of all sorts, such as on inshore salt water, has steadily gained popularity.

See also: angling; sailing

Further reading

Wigglesworth, N. (1992) *The Social History of Rowing*, London: Cass.

CHRISTOPHER SMITH

Royal Academy

Founded in 1768 as a society of artists, the Royal Academy (RA) is the oldest visual arts institution in Britain. It sought to raise the status of the artist through the provision of professional training, providing grants for impoverished artists and their families and exhibitions of work by living artists. Although in the eighteenth century there were other societies, the RA enjoyed royal patronage which conferred status and authority, enabling the RA to establish itself as the standard-bearing institution for the practice and teaching of art.

The RA has played an important role in improving the professional conditions for artists historically by providing a system for professional recognition. However, as the arbiter of taste the RA has been criticized by artists and professionals whose own interests do not correspond with its own. In particular, a tendency to conservatism has meant that the RA has often excluded, or publicly attacked, innovative artists, and this reactionary image has damaged its reputation.

When the RA was founded there were few opportunities for artists to exhibit, and therefore sell, their work, and the RA Schools was the first art school in Britain. However, at the beginning of the twentieth century the establishment of municipal arts schools, growing internationalism in art and increased professional and commercial opportunities for artists contributed to the erosion of the importance of the RA and a widening gap between the work exhibited at the RA and the work which is considered to be historically significant. During the Presidency of W.T. Monnington (1966–76), the RA became more sympathetic to progress and its influence and reputation, particularly for its world-famous programme of 'block-buster' loan exhibitions, was partly restored.

The RA comprises eighty members (or Academicians), all of whom are artists or architects. It is governed by an elected President and a Council on which Members serve in turn. There are two main kinds of membership: associated (ARA), and full (RA). Membership is divided into five categories: painting, sculpture, draughtsmanship, architecture and engraving. Each new Academician is required by the Instrument of Foundation to provide 'a

Picture, Bas-relief, or other specimen of his abilities'; these are known as 'Diploma Works'.

Academicians such as John Bellany, Peter Blake, Tony Cragg, Richard Deacon, David **Hockney**, Sir Richard **Rogers** and John Ward may not be fashionable artists by the time of their appointment (normally at an advanced stage of their careers), but are not usually reactionary. For example, R.B. Kitaj's work includes painting, drawing and screen-printing. Kitaj (1932–) has remained committed to drawing from life and the human figure is the basis of his work. Phillip King (1934–) was appointed Professor of Sculpture at the RA Schools in 1990. *Rosebud* (1962, MoMA, New York) combines new materials such as plastics and fibreglass with colourful, abstract forms.

Professorial chairs are appointed from the members to teach in the RA Schools, under the direction of the Keeper. Teaching includes drawing from life, draughtsmanship, carving, engraving, lithography and graphic arts.

The *RA Magazine*, which profiles the RA's exhibitions and the work of Academicians, is one of the highest circulation art periodicals in Britain. The Library was founded to support the teaching of the Schools and is the oldest fine art library in Britain. The RA also administers over sixty trust and award funds for students, artists and their families.

The RA does not receive public funds (although during the 1970s it applied unsuccessfully to the Arts Council for revenue support) and raises its own income through trading activities, donations, sponsorship, the Friends organization, corporate membership and exhibition receipts. 1977 saw the launch of the Friends, entitling free entry to exhibitions on payment of a subscription. By 1980 there were over 25,000 Friends, and this success has encouraged other arts institutions to follow suit.

The annual Summer Exhibition began in 1769. It represents an opportunity for Academicians to sell their work. Around ten times as many entries are received as selected. An open competition, the Exhibition allows members to submit six works and non-members three. Works are selected by a Hanging Committee. Many other open competitions, for example at the Whitechapel Gallery, have been established and are a testament to the importance of this model of exhibition for revealing new talent.

Loan exhibitions began in 1870, when they provided an important opportunity to see work, as public and municipal galleries were rare and art publishing was still in its infancy. The Loan Exhibitions Advisory Committee, consisting of historians and curators, was established during the late 1950s to assist with the exhibitions programme, functioning in a similar way to the Art Advisory Panel of the Arts Council.

There are around six loan exhibitions per annum. Many are originated, although shows often tour to other venues within Britain or abroad, and many are organized in collaboration with other institutions. Exhibitions range from *The Age of Chivalry: Art in Plantagenet England 1200–1400* (1987) to *Cézanne: the Early Years 1859–1872* (1988). Often accompanied by weighty catalogues, these exhibitions provide an opportunity for publishing new scholarship.

Norman Rosenthal was appointed Exhibitions Secretary in 1977, and under his supervision the loan exhibitions have re-established the RA as an important force in contemporary art. With Nicholas Serota and Christos Joachimides, he curated *Post Impressionism: A New Spirit in Painting* in 1979. The exhibition's success in predicting the trends of the next decade focused attention once more on the RA's ability to shape opinion about contemporary art.

Major survey shows of international art have included *German Art in the 20th Century* (1985) and *American Art in the Twentieth Century* (1993). *Sensation: Young British Artists from the Saatchi Collection* (1997) characterized the RA's exhibitions in its attempt to provide a definitive survey of a period, its high media profile and box office success. By exhibiting the work of artists who had in the preceding decade been presented as controversial, the RA revealed its continuing ability to institutionalize the innovative.

See also: painting

Further reading

Hutchison, S.C. (1986) *The History of the Royal Academy 1768–1986*, London: Robert Royce.

CLAIRE GLOSSOP

Royal Ballet

Founded in 1931 as the Vic-Wells Ballet (because it performed at both the Old Vic and Sadler's Wells theatres), and awarded its name by Royal Charter in October 1956, this is Britain's national **ballet** company. The organization is descended from the Academy of Choreographic Art, which was formed in London in 1926. Its centre is now the Royal Opera House in London's Covent Garden, and there is also a Royal Ballet School at White Lodge in Richmond Park. From 1962, Margot Fonteyn and Rudolf Nureyev, a newly defected 'permanent guest' from the Kirov Ballet, were its famous leading partnership. Other notable dancers have been Robert Helpmann, Lynn Seymour, Merle Park and Wayne Sleep. Leading British principal dancers in the 1990s are Darcey Bussell, Jonathan Cope and Viviana Durante. The company was started by Ninette de Valois (born 1898), who was also founder of the Birmingham Royal Ballet and the Royal Ballet School. It was her vision to create a national ballet centre to match the national institutions in other arts, and the formidable de Valois, known to all simply as 'Madam', was herself a major choreographer, director, and teacher who kept a hand in the company up to her recent one hundredth birthday. De Valois resigned as Director in 1963 to be replaced by Frederick Ashton, then by Kenneth Macmillan in 1970, Norman Morrice in 1977 and dancer Anthony Dowell in 1986. Since 1975 the pattern has been to have two large troupes, one of about eighty dancers at Covent Garden, who also do some major tours, and another of about fifty dancers who would mostly be on tour but also hold a London season at Sadlers Wells.

See also: English National Ballet

Further reading

Bland, A. (1981) *The Royal Ballet – The First 50 Years*, London: Macmillan

PETER CHILDS

Royal College of Art

A postgraduate art college in London which took its present name in 1896. With its origins in the early nineteenth century, the College's premises beside the Albert Hall were developed in 1853 with money from the Great Exhibition. Prestigious students over the last few decades have included Bridget **Riley**, Peter Blake and David **Hockney**.

See also: painting; sculpture

PETER CHILDS

Royal Court

Started as a new writing theatre by George Devine, the Royal Court is the site of several theatrical *causes célèbres* including *Look Back in Anger* (1956), *Saved* (1965), *Masterpieces* (1984) and *Blasted* (1995). **Directors** such as Gaskill (1965–72) and Stafford-Clark (1972–93) developed a style of uncluttered staging, based on a belief that acting, direction and design should serve the text, which has had a strong influence on alternative theatre. This theatre's commitment to new writing has been emphatic: many major playwrights had their early work staged here (Brenton, Churchill, Wertenbaker). The Court provides a unique link between the classical and unconventional, and is renowned for inspiring passionate responses from within and without, having as many critics as supporters.

See also: playwrights; theatre

DYMPHNA CALLERY

Royal National Theatre

The National Theatre was established by Parliament in 1949, although the company's opening performance was delayed until 1963 when Lawrence Olivier directed Peter O'Toole in *Hamlet*. The company lacked a permanent home until the **GLC** donated the present South Bank site. The 'brutalist' concrete and glass structure of the National Theatre was designed by **Denys Lasdun and Partners** and opened in 1976 under the directorship of Peter Hall. The National Theatre building houses three theatres: the Olivier, an open stage amphitheatre; the Lyttelton, a proscenium arch stage; and the Cottesloe studio theatre. To celebrate its silver anniversary in 1988, the National was granted the title 'Royal'.

See also: Barbican Centre; Royal Court

Further reading

Callow, S. (1997) *The National: The Theatre and its Work*, London: Nick Hern Books.

MARK DOUGLAS

Royal Shakespeare Company

The modern Royal Shakespeare Company (RSC) was established at Stratford-on-Avon in 1961 under the artistic directorship of Peter Hall. Hall committed the company to a repertoire of classical, modern and new works. In 1962 the RSC established a London home at the Aldwych Theatre, and initiated the continuing practice of touring at home and abroad. In 1982 the RSC moved its London base to the Barbican Theatre. The RSC staged spectacular and popularly acclaimed musical productions during the 1980s and 1990s, including *Les Misérables*. The ambition of the current artistic director, Adrian Noble, is to make the RSC 'the best classical theatre company in the English-speaking world'.

See also: Barbican Centre; directors; theatre

Further reading

Beauman, S. (1982) *The Royal Shakespeare Company*, Oxford: Oxford University Press.

MARK DOUGLAS

rugby league

Rugby League is a northern sport. It was first organized at the George Hotel, Huddersfield in 1895 as a breakaway from **rugby union**. An attempt to introduce it into southern England twenty years ago failed, though it is popular in Australia and New Zealand and touring sides from these countries come to Britain. There is major rivalry between Lancashire (especially Wigan and St Helens) and Yorkshire (Castleford/Halifax) clubs, which is heightened when the Challenge Cup takes place each year at Wembley. The League has been dominated since 1986 by Wigan.

There are a number of significant differences between rugby league and rugby union. League has thirteen as opposed to union's fifteen players on each side. There are no lineouts or loose scrums; each time there is a tackle, the player in possession must back heel the ball to a team mate. This makes possession (rather like American football, where an interception is a major upset) much more important in rugby league than in rugby union. Again like the US game, rugby league has a series of plays (four), although it does not define the amount of ground that must be advanced; a ten-yard gain does not allow the process to start again. After these four plays, the other side gains possession, usually through a kick ahead.

Rugby union, the amateur game, has always been played by the middle classes, but rugby league has working-class roots and remains working class in all its aspects. Its tough, hard-drinking ethos was captured in David Storey's novel *This Sporting Life*, which was made into a successful film by Lindsay **Anderson** (1963) starring Richard Harris and Rachel Roberts. Players have always been paid (one reason for the original breakaway was that working-class players, who had to take time off to play, were tired of being looked down on for expecting compensation) and has attracted some players from rugby union, such as the Welsh international Jonathan Davis. One result of the rivalry between league and union for such players is the 'baptism of fire' they have had to endure when making the transition. They are always seen as 'soft' entrants to a hard sport, and are dished out extra tough treatment until they prove themselves.

A feature of rugby league has been the recruitment of players from Australia and New Zealand. Such 'exotic' immigrants into an economically poor northern environment have integrated well, through working-class solidarity, according to some commentators.

Further reading

Collins, T. (1998) *Rugby's Great Split: Class, Culture and the Origins of Rugby League Football*, London: Frank Cass.

Gate, R. (1986) *Gone North: Welshmen in Rugby League*, Sowerby Bridge: Gate.

MIKE STORRY

rugby union

The Rugby Football Union was founded in 1871 with headquarters at Twickenham, England. There are currently a number of competitions. International championships were instituted in 1884 and are competed for by the five 'home' nations: England, Ireland, Scotland, Wales and France. (The World Cup was instituted in 1987, and won by New Zealand in that year). The Pilkington Cup (formerly the John Player Special Cup) is the English Club knockout tournament, and was first held in 1971–2.

The Rugby League was organized (in 1885) because players needed pay when taking time off work. (One club was fined because its players did not work on the morning of a Cup Final). Rugby union's players, organizers and spectators, on the other hand, have always been quintessentially middle class. This fact is cited as an explanation of the 'Troubles' in Ireland, for example, where there are separate national soccer teams for the North and the South, but both parts of Ireland cooperate in a single national Irish rugby union team. Hence the North's problems are claimed by some to be working class in origin. Spectators at Twickenham, Murrayfield, Cardiff Arms Park and Landsdowne Road (the national English, Scottish, Welsh and Irish grounds), which become the focus for nationalistic fervour during the annual Five Nations Championships, do indeed tend to be middle class, well-behaved and tolerant despite partisan national rivalries.

UK rugby union is in a state of flux because of poor performance, professionalization and politics. Overseas tours in 1998 were particularly depressing. Wales suffered the worst defeat ever of any of the eight rugby playing nations, in South Africa, beaten 96–13 with Wales conceding fifteen tries.

Meanwhile, England was celebrating the fact that it was defeated by the All Blacks in New Zealand by 'only' twenty points. England conceded fifty points or more in four out of five matches, and was beaten 76–0 by Australia, their worst defeat ever.

In 1995, rugby union officially became a professional sport. This major change led to an undignified scramble by top clubs to sign up players, offering money they often did not have. The Rugby Football Union was criticized by international bodies for not controlling the clubs, who even signed up players from overseas, which had ramifications in other countries. A bitter and divisive row between the clubs and their 'governing body' was officially resolved in 1998 and was binding for seven years.

See also: rugby league

Further reading

Rugby Football Union (1994) *Rugby Union*, London: Black.

MIKE STORRY

Rushdie Affair, the

The 1988 publication of Salman Rushdie's novel *The Satanic Verses* precipitated the most dramatic reception ever experienced by a literary text. The intellectual debate and violent protestation associated with this work, crossing boundaries of literature, religion, cultural identity and international politics, have come to be known as 'the Rushdie Affair'.

Muslim opponents of *The Satanic Verses* point to its allegedly blasphemous representation of the Prophet Mohammed, claiming that Rushdie seeks to question the validity of the Qur'an as a holy book. For its critics, the text appears to undermine the very foundations upon which the Muslim faith rests: that the Prophet Mohammed's source for the Qur'an was divinely inspired by God through the Archangel Gabriel. Consequently, charges of apostasy were levelled against Rushdie, followed by the declaration of a *fatwa*, or religious ruling, by the Ayatollah Khomeini. This *fatwa* was based on the view that Rushdie had blasphemed and consequently merited a death sentence. Calls to ban the book in Britain were supported by public demonstrations against Rushdie. Suspected racist attacks against Muslim offices soon followed. However, the Al Azhar Seminary of Cairo, the Muslim religious ruling body, has not passed any decree on *The Satanic Verses*.

Much debate has centred upon the protection against blasphemy afforded by British law to the Christian faith, yet denied to other religions. In 1976, for example, successful action was taken against the magazine *Gay News* for publishing a poem depicting Christ within a homosexual context. Recourse to similar legal redress is denied those of a Muslim faith. Calls to extend the blasphemy laws have so far been unsuccessful. Such debate suggests a tension between Britain as a constitutionally Christian state, and as a multi-cultural society encompassing a variety of religious faiths. However, this view is complicated by Christian leaders' support for Muslim protest.

Defenders of *The Satanic Verses* prefer to direct debate towards issues of freedom of expression. Such debate questions the accountability of literature, as fiction, to non-fictional realms of discourse. Rushdie himself has repeatedly pointed to *The Satanic Verses* as a work of literature, as a product of the imagination, but one that engages with the world. Supporters of the text direct us to Rushdie's use of the imagination, not as an attack upon the Muslim faith but as an attempt to explore and express the nature of cultural identity and religious faith in a post colonial and increasingly secular world.

In 1998, ten years after the first publication of *The Satanic Verses*, the UK authorities negotiated an official 'end' to the *fatwa* with the government of Iran.

See also: literature, Indian; Islam; post-colonial writing; violence

Further reading

Appignanesi, L. and Maitland, S. (eds) (1989) *The Rushdie File*, London: Fourth Estate.

DAVID SMALE

Russell, Bertrand

b. 1872, Trellick, Monmouthshire; d. 1970

Philosopher

Bertrand Russell profoundly influenced British culture in political and philosophical circles. His contributions to **philosophy** are outstanding in conceptual rigour, range and plenitude. His *Principia Mathematica* (with A.N. Whitehead, 1910–13) unsuccessfully attempted to describe meta-language, yet raised puzzles about logical class that still exercise analytic philosophy. Russell increasingly turned from analytic philosophy to political concerns. He stood for parliament, unsuccessfully, before becoming a major public figure from the 1930s onward. He wrote and campaigned for civil rights and pacifist movements (for which he spent six months in prison) and was heavily involved in the Campaign for Nuclear Disarmament (CND). Latterly he came to represent the conscience of a troubled nation. He was rehabilitated with the award of the OM and a Nobel Prize.

Further reading

Pears, D. (1950) *Bertrand Russell and the British Tradition in Philosophy*, 2nd edn, London: Fontana.

PAUL BARRY CLARKE
EMMA R. NORMAN

Russell, Ken

b. 1927, Southampton

Film-maker

Ken Russell directed numerous television documentaries before *Women in Love* (1969) catapulted him into the cinematic mainstream. *The Rainbow* (1989) and television's *Lady Chatterley's Lover* (1993) later concluded his trilogy adapted from D.H. Lawrence. Russell's Tchaikovsky biopic *The Music Lovers* (1970) set the sensationalist tone of much ensuing work, including the overwrought icono-clasm of *The Devils* (1971) and other biopics *Mahler* (1974), *Lisztomania* (1975) and *Valentino* (1977), which preceded a brief Hollywood excursion. From the early romanticism of his pioneering anti-realist documentaries, Russell's work has degenerated into increasingly dark, sexually disturbed, often misogynistic terrain, with *Gothic* (1986), *The Lair of the White Worm* (1988) and *Whore* (1991) demonstrating an exhausted intentional power to shock.

Further reading

Grant, B.K. (1993) 'The Body Politic', in L. Friedman (ed.), *British Cinema and Thatcherism*, London: UCL Press.

SATINDER CHOHAN

Ryle, Gilbert

b. 1900, Brighton; d. 1976

Philosopher

Gilbert Ryle was an exponent of analytic behaviourism, the theory that statements about mind can be translated, without loss of meaning, into statements about actual or possible behaviours. He held that many philosophical misconceptions have their basis in 'category mistakes', whereby objects and attributes relating to one logical category are misrepresented as belonging to another. In his most influential work, *The Concept of Mind* (1949), Ryle delivered an assault on Cartesian dualism. Descartes's view that mind and body are absolutely distinct (disparagingly described by Ryle as the doctrine of 'the ghost in the machine') constitutes a classic example of a category mistake. Attributes such as consciousness, which are subsumed erroneously under the category of mind, are, on analysis, reducible to behaviour.

See also: philosophy

ROD PATERSON

S

sadomasochism

The term 'sadism' originates with the writings of eighteenth-century French noble the Marquis de Sade, whose *120 Days of Sodom* remains a key text. The term 'masochism' comes from a nineteenth-century exponent of the practice, Leopold von Sacher-Masoch; his *Venus in Furs* was made famous by the rock band Velvet Underground, who named a song after it. The two terms coined together have come to represent a side to British culture exposed in titillating commentaries such as the film *Personal Services* (Terry Jones, 1987), an account of London madam Cynthia Payne's 'house of sin'. Indeed, the popular conception of sadomasochism has become inseparable from the notion of political or social satire, conjuring up images of judges in suspenders straddled by a whipcracking dominatrix.

In 1992, the issue of consensual sadomasochism – of whether an individual might willingly consent to being harmed by another person in the pursuit of sensual gratification – was put in full public view by the case of a group of men involved in a consensual sadomasochism ring. Consent, in such a case, was argued to be unlawful and the men were found guilty of, variously, assault, malicious wounding and the publication of obscene material. Operation Spanner spawned much sensationalist media debate and untenably long prison sentences for those convicted. Though appeals against the case were lost, a campaign was instigated which continues to work to change the law around consensual activity.

In Britain in the mid-1980s, the practice of consensual sadomasochism between women rocked the feminist press as it became clear that it was not confined to judges and Tory MPs. The publication in the early 1980s of US West Coast consensual sadomasochist group, Samois's *Coming to Power* precipitated a vigorous, some would say vicious, debate within the London Lesbian and Gay Centre and in provincial centres around the country. Many independent bookshops still refuse to stock the work of feminists and consensual sadomasochist proponents such as Pat Califia, a censoriousness which is reflected in the situation in Canada and the USA where feminist and other sadomasochist publications are often seized at state and national borders.

See also: age of consent; censorship; pornography

Further reading

Samois (1981) *Coming to Power: Writings and Graphics on Lesbian S/M*, Boston: Alyson.

CLARE WHATLING

sailing

There has always been a strong interest in sailing in the British Isles, where there are 1,605 sailing clubs. The south coast of England, the west coast of Scotland and the lochs of Northern Ireland are popular cruising grounds, but throughout Britain's often hostile environments, recreational sailing has always taken place. The television series *Howards Way* and media coverage of the Observer

Single-Handed Transatlantic Race (OSTAR), which started in 1960 and is held every four years, have catered to such interest.

From the 1950s on, plywood (later GRP) sailing dinghies such as the 'Firefly', 'GP14' and 'Merlin Rocket' became popular and opened sailing up to a mass market. 'GP's (General Purpose) and Mirror dinghies (started by the *Daily Mirror*) have sold many thousands. But sailing is more often a low-key pastime, practised locally by people uninfluenced by national or international trends. So, for example, of the seven sailing classes used in the Olympic Games – Soling (three crew), Flying Dutchman, Star, Finn (single-handed), Tornado, 470 and windsurfer (single-handed) – only the last named is popular in Britain.

Dinghy sailing has given way to windsurfing, which is largely restricted to the younger generation. Cruising/racing boat owners are older and now have a wide range of GRP boats available to them: Westerly & Hunter supply this market, and the French manufacturer Beneteau caters for racing enthusiasts.

Due to conservatism (and conservation), numerous local one-design classes (where each boat is identical) remain throughout the UK. There are Rhyl 'Jewels', Hoylake 'Operas', Salcombe 'Yawls' and Solent 'X's. The Howth '17's, built at Carrickfergus in 1898, are believed to be the oldest class still sailing. There has been a revival of interest in wooden boats and boat building. Lancashire Nobbies, Bristol Channel Pilot Cutters and Falmouth Quay Punts are examples of working boats, now called 'classics', which have been converted to purely recreational and racing use.

Public interest in sailing has been fostered by visits to Britain by participants in the Tall Ships race (when they visited Liverpool in 1994 there were fifteen-mile traffic jams and two million visitors, in addition to the 2,000 crew members enlivening the port). The ships saluted the visiting Royal Yacht *Britannia* as they left the Mersey. Organizations such as the Ocean Youth Club run large yachts like the *Malcolm Miller* and the *Winston Churchill* and accept people for specific trips around Britain. Participation in these events has become part of the culture.

See also: angling; rowing; yachting

MIKE STORRY

SAINSBURY CENTRE, NORWICH *see* Foster Associates

sales

Reflecting consumers' invincible conviction that they can buy what they want at bargain prices, and also shop owners' readiness, to cut profit margins in order to increase turnover and improve liquidity by shifting stocks that have not yet found buyers, sales are a feature of British shopping. Traditionally they are seasonal, in mid-summer and at New Year, and Harrod's sale features almost like **Henley Regatta** on the social calendar. But when retailing is slow, sales tend to come earlier and earlier, and some shops appear to have virtually continuous sales. All this encourages 'cherrypicking', the habit of shoppers to defer all but the most urgent purchases until they can buy what they want at reduced price in a sale.

Shoppers at sales are entitled to the same protection as at any other time. Descriptions of materials used in manufacturing must be accurate, and the quality and suitability for purpose of goods should be comparable with that of similar ones, having regard to what may reasonably be expected at a given price level. If these standards are not met, the dissatisfied customer has a just complaint against the supplier. At sale time retailers generally offer a range of specially brought in cheap goods, but customers' attention fixes particularly on stock previously available only at full price and now offered more cheaply. All statements about reductions are subject to a code agreed by retail associations under the 1987 Consumer Protection Act. A retailer is allowed to attract purchasers by announcing that the price of, say, £25 for an item represents a reduction (or 'saving') of £10 only if identical items have been on sale in the shop or (as it is sometimes interpreted) in a branch of the same chain at the higher price for twenty-eight days at some time in the previous six months (though there is no requirement to show that anyone actually paid so much during that period). If a sale is held when a new shop opens or a 'cheap offer' is made to introduce a fresh product, there is a requirement to announce when in the future the full price will be restored. The code covers prices, but not statements purporting to convey ideas of worth or value. These, like advertisements declaring, for example, that 'everything must be cleared regardless of price', are considered advertising hype that consumers should take with a pinch of salt.

See also: discount stores; promotions

Further reading

Silberstein, S. (1994) *Consumer Law*, London: Sweet & Maxwell.

CHRISTOPHER SMITH

Salvation Army

William Booth, a former Methodist preacher, founded the Christian Mission to preach evangelical revivalism and offer material help to down-and-outs in the slums of Whitechapel in 1861. He changed its name to the Salvation Army, giving the movement its present form and character, with quasi-military ranks, uniforms and brass bands that march with banners flying. In hymn-singing, preaching and the *War Cry*, the Salvation Army newspaper, emphasis is laid on the Gospels and on Jesus as a personal redeemer. The Salvation Army, now an international force, always adds a practical dimension to religion by trying to relieve poverty and suffering, maintaining hostels, undertaking youth work and running a missing persons bureau. In the late 1990s the organization tried to update its image, shifting from a traditional profile to a look that might have more in common with the laid-back guitar-based appeal of street-buskers.

See also: evangelism

Further reading

The Salvation Army Yearbook, London: International HQ of the Salvation Army, published annually.

CHRISTOPHER SMITH

sampling

The advent of digital recording technology made possible the extraction of small segments of pre-existing records, which could then be added to new songs. The technique is widely used in **dance music**, with some samples becoming more widely known than either their original source or the records which subsequently use them – as, for example, in the case of the drum break from James Brown's 'Funky Drummer'. The rise of sampling caused widespread debate over the authorship of songs, which resulted in most samples being treated as 'quotations' from the original, for which credit is usually given. A later development, 'timestretching' – changing the tempo of a sample without altering the pitch – was instrumental in the inception of **jungle**.

See also: DJs

SIMON BOTTOM

Sanger, Frederick

b. 1918, Rendcombe, Gloucestershire

Biologist

Frederick Sanger is one of the foremost British scientists of the century. A molecular biologist, he won the Nobel Prize for chemistry in 1958 after working out the structure of insulin. Sanger spent his life at Cambridge, where he attempted to ascertain the nature of several substances vital for biological functioning, including enzymes, antibodies and hormones. In 1980 he won a second Nobel Prize for chemistry, with Walter Gilbert and Paul Berg, for determining the base sequences of nucleic acids. His work has been crucial for biologists attempting to manufacture genetic materials in the laboratory.

See also: science

PETER CHILDS

Savile Row

Traditionally, the best suits for men have been tailored in Savile Row, London. Austin Reed, Dunn's, Gieves and Hawkes and Moss Bros are names of tailors whose work has become the basis for nationwide retail outlets, though the most sought-after suit makers are the smaller Savile Row tailors. However, in recent years, fashion houses in Italy (particularly Armani) and elsewhere have challenged Savile Row's hegemony. Savile Row has also been hit by trends towards casualwear (including denim) and particularly sportswear. Computerized manufacture in the Far East has also undermined Savile Row's position, which was based on traditional tailoring skills and exclusive British cloths which have now been copied extensively abroad.

See also: Knightsbridge; Smith, Paul

MIKE STORRY

Schlesinger, John

b. 1926, London

Film-maker

John Schlesinger began his career as a director in television before moving to feature films. His earliest work seems to typify fashionable 1960s British cinema: the social realism of *A Kind of Loving* and the superficiality of *Billy Liar* and *Darling*. The arresting style and epic qualities of *Far From the Madding Crowd* (1967) effectively demonstrated wider possibilities. An interest in troubled and complicated human relationships which marked Schlesinger's British films was given greater resonance in his US movies, including the intense and poignant *Midnight Cowboy* (1967), and the thrillers *Marathon Man* (1976), *The Falcon and the Snowman* (1985) and the less convincing *Pacific Heights* (1990). In the 1980s and 1990s Schlesinger returned to directing for British television, with *An Englishman Abroad* and *Cold Comfort Farm*.

ALICE E. SANGER

school examinations

Since the nineteenth century, school examinations with syllabuses by outside bodies and question papers, set and marked by examiners unconnected with the candidates or their schools, have served several functions. They have offered **parliament** some assurance that education funding has been well spent; they have reinforced efforts (first in the civil service, but later more generally) to replace appointment by patronage and nepotism by selection based on merit and qualifications; and they have helped raise standards by bringing into all schools the practice of the best and stimulating staff and pupils to greater efforts. Although criticisms that school examinations are educational strait-jackets appear exaggerated, difficulties have arisen both from frequent, underfunded change and also from a persistent tendency to assume that the prime purpose of examinations is discovering who 'comes top' when the emphasis ought to be on assessing candidates' abilities and attainments with the object of determining the most appropriate form of education for them at the next stage and subsequently giving career advice. Similarly, the records of results achieved by schools published annually by the Department for Education and Employment (DEE) are too frequently taken as '**school league tables**' for determining which institutions are 'best' when it is more helpful to use them diagnostically, so that individual schools can regularly appraise their performance by comparison with others with, for instance, a similar intake of pupils.

Doubts about school standards have led the DEE to institute a **National Curriculum** and examinations in such core subjects as English and mathematics, and in a range of options for all state school pupils at three 'Key Stages' at the ages of 7, 11 and 14. At Key Stage 4, when aged 16, candidates sit **GCSE** or various vocational examinations, such as Foundation or Intermediate General National Vocational Qualifications (GNVQs). Advanced Level (A Level) examinations are taken two years later; for university entrance, candidates usually need good A Level passes in three subjects (though some offer one or two Advanced Subsidiary (AS) passes either in lieu of one A Level or in addition). The International

Baccalaureate, demanding competence in a range of subjects, is also a qualification for university entrance. Advanced GNVQs correspond to two A Levels. Scotland has a somewhat different range of examinations serving similar purposes.

See also: GCSEs; schools system

Further reading

The National Curriculum and Its Assessment: Final Report (1993), London: HMSO.
Review of 16–19 Qualifications: The Issues for Consideration (1995), London: HMSO.

CHRISTOPHER SMITH

school league tables

Introduced in 1992, performance tables show the examination results and basic statistics of schools in England and Wales, with primary schools included in 1997. Part of the Citizen's Charter, they are designed to inform the public and act as an incentive to increase national standards to meet government targets and to be used in conduction with prospectuses, governors' reports and inspection reports. Criticism has decreased since their introduction, but many argue that the data is misleading, placing too much emphasis on exam results and not enough on the all-round education a school provides in terms of extra-curricular activities and moral education. Although available elsewhere, important details such as quality of intake and socio-economic conditions are not shown in the league tables.

See also: public schools; school examinations

CHRISTOPHER COLBY

School of London

Michael Andrews, Frank Auerbach, Francis **Bacon**, Lucian **Freud**, R.B. Kitaj and Leon Kossoff constitute the core of artists that were dubbed a 'School of London'. The idea of the emergence of a School is firmly down to the American-born artist R.B. Kitaj, although the term has been adopted by various critics and artists since the term was first used. It was Kitaj, as early as 1976, in the catalogue preface to a group exhibition of figurative works *The Human Clay*, who ruminated over the possibilities of an emergent group. After a discussion with the Paris-based critic Michael Peppiatt a decade later, it was Kitaj again who instigated a touring exhibition under the banner of *A School of London: Six Figurative Painters*. The exhibition toured Europe in 1987–8.

At first, the idea of a School seems improbable when considering six artists whose work is fiercely protective over notions of individuality and is therefore fundamentally opposed to considering the finer points of artistic fashion. It also seems paradoxical that Kossoff is in fact the only one of the six artists who could be considered a Londoner by birth, though the others have formed an attachment to the city through study or long periods of living and working in the capital. The mood of the disinherited city, however, pervades the work of all six artists. A recurring sense of guilt and human vulnerability recalls the atmosphere of such existentialist mentors as Sartre and the works of Giacometti, who was of particular significance to the artistic development of Andrews and Bacon. The most deeply-rooted connection between the six artists, however, centres on an obsessive fascination with the figure, notably throughout the heyday of abstraction. A comprehensive disdain for artistic vogues may also have gone towards drawing the private, even at times reclusive, group more tightly together socially. Akin to the Impressionists, their lives and work have been closely interrelated since early in their painting careers. In-depth discussions and arguments have inevitably added to the way each individual has shaped his work. Although the artists have shared galleries and have appeared in many group shows together, it was not until 1995 that the six artists were shown together in Britain for the first time.

See also: painting

Further reading

The British Council, in association with the Scottish National Gallery of Modern Art (1995–6) *From*

London, London: The British Council (a catalogue containing informative essays).

NICKY COUTTS

schools system

The 1944 Education Act in England and Wales enshrined the principle of balanced responsibilities for the structure and content of education. One of the corollaries of the system of checks and balances was individuals' perception that power seemed to reside anywhere but where they happened to be working in the school system. Lines of accountability and responsibility were unclear, but this was not necessarily a problem because central and local government and teachers had influence in their own domain at a time when what was regarded as their proper domain was relatively unproblematic. This kind of arrangement suited a stable environment, where change was incremental and conceived as largely a professional matter.

Central government's role was restricted mainly to approving the local structure of provision, planning the supply of teachers and attempting to influence the content of education through advice and guidance issued by Her Majesty's Inspectorate for Education. Teachers, largely through the influence of their professional associations, had considerable flexibility in curriculum development. Local Education Authorities (**LEAs**) were, in theory, the managers of the system, responsible for allocating resources, planning the numbers of school places and shaping the local pattern of educational provision, which often owed as much to demographic factors as to any coherent educational philosophy. LEAs also exerted influence on teaching methods, curriculum development, the promotion of teachers and the selection of headteachers through the activities of their advisory services. Until the early 1970s, the conduct of the school system was seen as a professional matter to be determined largely at the local level, with national debates confined most to structural issues, most notably the issue of selection and the replacement of grammar and secondary modern schools with comprehensive schools.

During this period, dominant explanations of patterns of educational achievement shifted from a focus on the individual intelligence of children to the identification of a succession of structural and cultural barriers that located failure in factors such as the inefficiency of the eleven-plus examination, the iniquities of provision between different areas of the country, the nature of society itself, the failings of parents and the cultural mismatch between home and school. The internal workings of schools were left largely unexamined except for a focus on the grouping of pupils and the lowly expectations that teachers had of children from disadvantaged backgrounds.

The critical scrutiny of schools was not an issue, since schools were assumed to be doing their best with the particular children they were working with. Although social class was seen as a major influence on achievement, once most of the country had abolished selection and introduced comprehensive schools, it was generic features of schooling that were held to be the problem rather than the particular school a child attended.

The debate on a wider range of issues, for example, reforming the 'secret garden' of the curriculum, was begun in the early 1970s. Inappropriate teaching styles, the dilution of the curriculum in the interests of 'relevance', perceptions of declining standards of literacy and numeracy and the lack of effective preparation for the world of work were all held up as examples of an educational 'crisis', compounded by the limited powers of central government to act. It was not until the 1980s that the dominant mode of government influence based on advice and guidance gave way to an approach based on legislation to achieve policy objectives.

The 1980s saw the start of a root-and-branch reform of school education that marked a long march through the educational institutions aimed at introducing greater accountability and reducing the influence of the providers as opposed to the consumers of education. At the same time, central government acquired new powers for itself to give it greater leverage over educational policy and practice. 'Blame society' and 'blame the home' gave way to 'blame the school in general and teachers in particular'. This was bolstered by research that demonstrated the differential achievements of schools with children from similar backgrounds.

Although there were numerous Education Acts passed during the Conservative government's period of office, the 1988 Education Act introduced the local management of schools and the **National Curriculum**; it extended the scope of school 'choice' through open enrolment, and enabled schools to opt out of the LEA system through the creation of grant-maintained (GM) schools. It was the most significant piece of legislation since 1944, and altered decisively the balance of power and responsibility between central and local government and individual schools and introduced clearer lines of accountability. Subsequent to that legislation, the introduction of independent school inspections and the publication of league tables of examination results and truancy rates contributed to the development of a competitive quasi market for schools. The key themes of the Conservative approach to education were diversity, choice, accountability and quality.

Diversity was promoted through the establishment of GM schools, city technology colleges and a network of technology, language, arts and sports colleges. They were allowed to select a percentage of their intake based on aptitude in the respective curriculum areas. Choice was to be furthered through enabling parents to express a preference for which school their child should attend and the creation of an assisted places scheme for attendance at independent schools. Accountability was intended to be achieved through the reform of governing bodies that placed 'lay' interests in the majority and the publication of a variety of information about school provision and performance including school inspection reports; the introduction of the National Curriculum also meant that schools could be compared on the basis of tackling a similar curriculum.

The government's approach to 'quality' rested largely on the introduction of the National Curriculum, examination and assessment reform and raising achievement through inspection; the public identification of failing schools and the use of its powers to send in a team of people to take over a school, leading ultimately to its closure, were rarely used. The introduction of teacher appraisal was also intended to improve the quality of teaching, and at the same time reforms, of teacher education were pursued including the introduction of national curriculum for teacher education. Increasingly, ministers and the Chief Inspector for the Office for Standards in Education were vocal about a range of issues that had hitherto been regarded as the preserve of the profession. The quality of teachers, methods of teaching and the organization of classes were all the subject of adverse comment. LEAs had an ambiguous relation to these developments; they provided many of the personnel that undertook 'independent' school inspections and offered pre- and post-inspection advice to their schools. Some LEAs also intervened when schools were deemed as failing to offer an acceptable standard of education, but ultimately a governing body that did not want the advice of its LEA could reject it.

It is inevitable that reforms driven primarily by legislation and centrally imposed with limited consultation tend to be blunt instruments. The National Curriculum quickly ran into difficulty because of overloading and the unrealistic demands made of teachers, leading to a review that reduced its complexity. From work undertaken by the Audit Commission, it has been shown that open enrolment still leaves 20 percent of parents unable to realize their preference, and in some urban areas the figures are much higher. Teacher appraisal is regarded universally as a failure in most respects, and the evidence that inspection leads to improvement is mixed. There are a number of examples of schools identified as requiring special measures improving sufficiently to be taken off the list, but there are other examples of schools who remain on the list following a critical inspection report. The reform of school governance has done little to increase parental involvement, and governing bodies are often either unwilling or unable to monitor educational provision in their schools and reluctant to take action when problems arise.

Examination reform at 16-plus shifted the emphasis away from norm to criterion-referenced assessment where pupils need to demonstrate what they know, understand and can do. There has been an increase in the number of entries and the proportion of candidates achieving grades A to C, but there is a debate about the extent to which this represents a genuine improvement or whether examinations are now easier than they have been in the past. International comparisons appear to show that British pupils achieve relatively well in science but less well in numeracy, although the murky waters of comparative statistical analysis make international comparisons difficult.

The debate about provision for the 16-plus age range centres on the appropriateness or otherwise of the 'A' level examination, the need for breadth as well as depth of study, the amount of specialization and the desirability of combining vocational and academic elements in individual's programmes. However, a preoccupation with educational high performers has given way to a more inclusive emphasis driven largely by changes in the occupational structure and an overall reduction in the numbers of unskilled jobs. Poor educational attainment and the prospect of social exclusion for young people lacking in 'employability' skills is one of the driving forces behind the 'Welfare to Work' scheme introduced by the Labour government.

The creation of a single body, the Qualifications and Curriculum Authority (QCA) to oversee vocational and academic qualifications, will facilitate the development of a single framework enabling equivalencies between different approaches to be worked out, as well as pathways through and bridges between academic and vocational routes. In recent years, the 14–19 age group has emerged as a phase of education that needs to be looked at as a whole, and it is likely that more vocational options will be introduced and collaboration encouraged between schools and further education colleges.

The past few years can be characterized as having had a number of distinctive shifts in thinking about the nature of education. Some of the old philosophical debates about, for example, equality of opportunity and how it should be measured and the purpose of education are more muted, but equity is now a much more widely used term, as is the debate on how to ensure it. A political consensus has emerged about the primary instrumental purpose for education, which is to master the basics as a foundation for lifelong learning in a global economy; there is also a consensus that schools do make a difference to pupils' achievements.

While there is much debate about what else education should strive to achieve, there is at least a widely shared view that without the basic foundations, children cannot easily access whatever else is on offer in the school curriculum. The underachievement of boys has emerged as a concern in recent years, now that they are outperformed by girls, and the ethnic minority experience of education, particularly racial harassment, is beginning to be taken more seriously. Gender issues continue to be a focus for academics and researchers, but have rarely found their way on to national policy-makers' agendas.

Structural questions are now of relatively minor concern; few people believe that independent schools or grammar schools will be abolished. Although grant-maintained schools will be able to call themselves foundation schools, it is only minor differences in governing body representation that will distinguish them from community or LEA schools. Gone are the days when the jibe about the National Union of Teachers making Labour Party education policy had the ring of truth about it. Gone also are the days when standards and quality were regarded as part of the exclusive discourse of the **Conservative Party** and right-wing reactionaries. The **Labour Party** learned some lessons from the 'Educashun isn't Working' campaign run by the Conservatives in 1979. There is now a basis for an emerging political and professional consensus around educational issues and priorities, and it is likely that teachers, although not necessarily their representative bodies, will have a greater involvement in and be consulted about educational change. The creation of a General Teaching Council similar to that which has existed for a long time in Scotland will also contribute to raising the image of the teaching profession.

While the school system in England and Wales can be characterized as the site of much political and professional conflict in recent years, the situation in Scotland has been rather different. Professionals have not had their judgements or capability questioned in the same way, and the reforms that have been introduced have been accommodated without seeming to threaten the professional status of teachers. Devolved management and the creation of school boards has been a low key affair, and teachers have been fully involved in the development of the school curriculum.

In Northern **Ireland**, the 'Troubles' give the school system a particular character, and it is noteworthy that the government reserved the category of grant-maintained status exclusively for previously segregated schools that wanted to become integrated. Not only is the school system divided along religious lines, but the 11-plus examination and an extensive selective secondary education system have been in existence for a long time. The assessment of the 11-plus examination also leaves 55 percent of the cohort with a 'D' grade.

See also: school examinations

JOHN WILLIAMS

science

Science is a process by which evidence, obtained by systematic experiment or observation, is used to verify or negate hypotheses about any aspect of the universe leading to an accumulation of a body of knowledge and principles. Popular usage of the word 'science', however, tends to refer to the actual knowledge and to any technology which derives from its application, rather than to the process itself. The process of science is international and is prosecuted by many thousands of experimental scientists who work in universities, government or commercial laboratories. The information gathered from these activities is promulgated internationally through the publication of specialist journals (of which there are several hundred), which report regularly the data obtained by experimental scientists throughout the world. The quality of science published is regulated by peer review. Eventually, and necessarily in sanitized form, this information finds its way into teaching textbooks, thus establishing a body of consensual knowledge. Much of this body of knowledge, however, is provisional pending the appearance of new, clarifying or even contradictory data and so cannot be considered to be 'truth', except in certain simple circumstances. However, the majority of scientific information forms an empirical knowledge base of sufficient accuracy and validity

to allow very sophisticated technological and medical achievements. Science itself is simply a process which is driven by a combination of philosophical inquisitiveness, commercial considerations and the personal aspirations of individual scientists. Most basic research is funded by tax revenue.

It is generally agreed that physics (with the aid of mathematics) is the core science, since although complex and difficult for non-specialists, it deals with the fundamental properties of matter and energy which give rise to all the more complex phenomena of cosmology and astrophysics, chemistry, geology and biology. These fundamental particles and their energies of interaction can usually be studied on earth only in the high-energy conditions available in particle accelerators, since their association into the more familiar guises of atoms and molecules are extremely stable under normal earth conditions of temperature and pressure. Chemistry is the study and exploitation of the behaviour and interactions of atoms to form molecules, whose interactions occur readily under earth conditions. The highest levels of complexity arise in the biosphere, where extremely complex chemical systems which have evolved over the last 3–4 billion years are present as cells and living organisms, and these organisms interact with each other and the environment to form ecosystems and the entire interactive system of the entirety of the living world known as the biosphere.

Science (in its pure form) differs from pure philosophy in that it is based on evidence. While **philosophy** may have sharpened the use of logic and symbolic analysis, only science can yield new knowledge about the universe and provide the raw material for philosophical debate. The beginnings of the accumulation of knowledge about ourselves and our environment were necessarily conducted in the absence of much real information, in a situation where sets of beliefs, arguably manipulated for social and political advantage, formed the context of such understanding. Because the implications of the real information which became available to refine knowledge through the efforts of systematic observation and investigation often contradicted the original beliefs, there has been continuous conflict between the belief systems and the knowledge system of science. This conflict will probably always remain even if its centre of gravity shifts into the scientific sphere (which has its own set of belief systems), partly for simple reasons of conservatism, prejudice and lack of enthusiasm of those in power to relinquish it, and partly because some aspects of human activity and even the behaviour of aspects of the physical universe may never be amenable to a cogent knowledge-based explanation. The conflict is still clearly visible in the often futile debates between 'science' and 'religion'. It has been an interesting feature of British culture in particular and that of the western world in general that even basic scientific knowledge is not considered a necessary ingredient for 'intellectual' activity. The unexpected success of books in which the scientific arguments underlying current knowledge of some of the fundamental aspects our universe are discussed suggest that there is a previously unexploited enthusiasm for this knowledge which may lead to a reappraisal of such ignorance.

PETE SHETERLINE

science fiction

In the early 1960s the science fiction market was dominated by America. British exponents of the genre were often first published by American companies and thus tended to reflect American preoccupations. There was a void to be filled; an opportunity existed to develop a new national style and to re-affirm traditional British science fiction themes. In 1964, Michael Moorcock became editor of the science fiction magazine *New Worlds*. Inspired by the existing works of J.G. Ballard, *The Four Dimensional Nightmare* (1963) and *The Terminal Beach* (1964), he began to promote the cause of a science fiction 'avant-garde'. Moorcock's own experimental works – the Jerry Cornelius series of novels among others – encouraged science fiction authors to experiment with style and method, notably Brian Aldiss, who produced *Report on Probability* (1968) and *Barefoot in the Head* (1969). Stories which originally appeared in *New Worlds* and its sister magazine *Science Fantasy* also contributed to several important science fiction collections, including J.G. Ballard's *The Atrocity Exhibition* (1970) and Keith

Robert's *Pavane* (1968). This emergent literature largely ignored American postwar science fiction concerns – typically the conquest of the galaxy and the discovery of strange alien cultures – concentrating instead upon essentially British themes: the catastrophic vision of a dim but not necessarily distant future, the condition or transcendence of the human spirit trapped in a technological wasteland. These are themes which might reasonably be traced back as far as the pages of *Gulliver's Travels*.

In the mid-1970s the recession hit the British science fiction market hard. New writers found it increasingly difficult to get published. Major success, it seemed, could only be guaranteed through established notoriety. Stanley Kubrick's film of Arthur C. Clarke's *2001: A Space Odyssey* (1968) assured the author a worldwide reputation still enjoyed to this day. Douglas Adams's radio series *A Hitchhiker's Guide to the Galaxy* spawned a television serial and a succession of best-selling novels, their appeal being broadened by a strong comedic element. Similarly, market conditions encouraged the production of the novel series, with leading examples being Brian Aldiss's *Hellico-nia Trilogy* (1982–5), and Ian Watson's trilogy *The Book of the River*, *The Book of the Star* and *The Book of Being* (1983–5).

By the late 1980s British science fiction was once again a relatively unhealthy genre, the popularity of heroic fantasy largely displacing its function. However, writers such as Terry Pratchett (*Discworld*, 1983 to the present), Robert Rankin (*Armageddon Trilogy*, 1990–2) and Iain M. Banks (*The Player of Games*, 1988; *Use of Weapons*, 1990) continue to flourish in the 1990s using proven formulas, comedy and or serialization.

See also: fantasy and science fiction

Further reading

Greenland, C. (1983) *The Entropy Exhibition*, London: Routledge & Kegan Paul.

MICK TURNER

Scottish language

Scots is the Lowland Scottish dialect of English, with a tradition going back to at least the fifteenth century. It is derived from the Northumbrian dialect of Old English, and is usually readily comprehensible with English. Famous examples are the terms 'kirk' for 'church' and 'bairn' for 'baby'. The royal union of Scotland and England in 1603 and the Act of Union in 1707 have probably kept the two languages close and prevented Scots from developing a markedly separate vocabulary, keeping standard English as the common mode of written communication.

Lallans is Scottish for 'Lowlands', and was a term used by Robert Burns for Scots (in the central Lowlands and up the northeast coast to Aberdeen). There was an attempt to revive it as a literary language by Hugh MacDiarmid's renaissance of the 1920s; this movement has had many inheritors who use both Scots and English, including the poetry of George Mackay Brown, Sorley Maclean, Iain Crichton Smith, Robert Garioch, Norman MacCaig, Gael Turnbull and Edwin Morgan, who has influenced Robert Crawford and W.N. Herbert. More recently, alongside Jackie Kay, Frank Kuppner and Kathleen Jamie, there is the demotic Scots of Tom Leonard and Liz Lochhead. The use of Scots is often associated with a sense of political independence. For example, with no Conservative candidates elected to represent Scottish seats at Westminster, Lochhead's apposite 'Bagpipe Muzak, Glasgow, 1990' superbly parodies Glasgow's marketing as European City of Culture and also echoes MacNeice's earlier similarly-named poem in its rhythm and in the refrain, 'It's all go'. The poem concludes by denouncing a Tory government that Scotland did not elect: 'So – watch out Margaret Thatcher, and tak' tent Neil Kinnock / Or we'll tak' the United Kingdom and brekk it like a bannock.' This threat seemed partially to come true when Scotland enthusiastically voted for parliamentary devolution in September 1997.

See also: literature, Scottish; Welsh language

PETER CHILDS

Scottish press

The distinction between regional and national newspapers has become blurred, as newspapers have moved their editorial and printing facilities from Fleet Street to other parts of London or of Britain. For example, the *Independent* is printed in Bradford, Northampton and Portsmouth, and Scottish editions of the *Sun*, the *News of the World* and the *Sunday Times* are printed in Glasgow.

Scotland, however, is the home of a newspaper circulating throughout Britain, the *Daily Record*, sister paper of the *Daily Mirror* and the *Sunday Mail*, and many other papers including six morning, five evening, three Sunday and 118 local weekly newspapers.

Scotland's newspaper industry has recently become much more competitive, partly because of the fallout from political upheavals including the demise of the Conservative party and the prospect of a Scottish parliament, and partly because consolidation in the media business has thrown up commercial opportunities. So, for example, the Scottish comedian Billy Connolly has buried his famous dislike for the Scottish press (he once appeared on the front page of the *Sunday Mail* for hitting one of its photographers) to join the consortium The Edge with the *Daily Record* to bid for Scotland's largest radio licence, a commercial licence with the potential to reach 2.8 million people, or around half of the country's population.

The Barclay twins, David and Frederick bought Scotsman Publications Ltd from the International Thomson Organisation three years ago, and have spent large sums of money on the *Scotsman* and its sister title, *Scotland on Sunday*. The latter has expanded its readership by introducing several new sections and being repositioned slightly down-market.

Papers north of the border are becoming more nationalistically oriented. The Scottish *Sun* under its English editor Bob Bird famously swung behind the Scottish National Party during the 1997 election, and the Scottish *Mirror* is also slated to become more Scottish. For many years the *Observer* and the *Sunday Times* have carried Scottish supplements, but many other national titles have recently been 'tartanized'. The *Daily Mail*'s Scottish edition now has a much more Scottish focus than it had, and the *Daily Record* is being revamped to reflect its Scottish roots and to shake off a perceived macho image. Despite the fact that it has dominated the Scottish tabloid scene for decades with sales of over 600,000, the *Daily Record* had been looking vulnerable after a failed drive for more advertising revenue.

See also: Northern Irish press; Welsh press

MIKE STORRY

Scott, Ridley

b. 1939

Film director

An art graduate, Scott worked as an award-winning director of television advertisements before embarking on television and then film work with *The Duellists* (1977). He achieved commercial success with his Hollywood vehicles, the science fiction-horror *Alien* (1979) and the futuristic film noir *Blade Runner* (1982). Scott employs *mise en scène* techniques in films with meticulously observed sets, often sacrificing narrative content for a visually spectacular style, for example in *Legend* (1985) and *1492: Conquest of Paradise* (1992). A later proclivity for strong female characters (as in the female road movie *Thelma and Louise* (1991) and *G.I. Jane* (1997)) is undermined by simplistically subverted gendered stereotypes, yet Scott's revisionism of conventional film genres and indeterminate symbolism render his work ideal for feminist and postmodernist analysis.

SATINDER CHOHAN

Scott, Tony

b. 1944, Stockton-on-Tees

Film-maker

Tony Scott is one of a number of British directors who have achieved high-profile Hollywood careers. After leaving the Royal College of Art, he joined his brother Ridley **Scott** in directing commercials and television movies. His first Hollywood film was the vampire movie *The Hunger* (1983), a box office failure which nevertheless bore the hallmarks – a slick visual style – of later mainstream success. In *Top Gun* and *Beverly Hills Cop II*, Scott made the top-grossing films in 1986 and 1987, respectively. With *The Last Boy Scout* (1991) and *Crimson Tide* (1995) he failed to repeat the same level of commercial success, despite working with some of Hollywood's most bankable stars. In 1993 he made the acclaimed *True Romance*, a violent noirish thriller scripted by Quentin Tarantino.

MATTHEW GRICE

scouse

'Scouse' is an eighteenth-century word from 'lobscouse', a sailors' meal of meat and vegetables similar to Irish stew. Hence, 'lobscouser' was the name used for a sailor and 'scouser' became the term for a person from Liverpool, a major port where the stew was popular. 'Scouse' has come to refer fairly recently (probably since the Second World War) to the flat, adenoidal working-class speech of the city, which combines elements of Lancashire with English dialects from Ireland and, to a lesser extent, Wales. Probably the most famous users of scouse were the Beatles, though the **Mersey Poets** used it to literary effect.

See also: Cockney; Geordies

PETER CHILDS

scouts and guides

Robert Baden-Powell, born in 1857, won great popular fame, if not much of a reputation with the military authorities, as commander of Mafeking during its 217-day siege in the Boer War. Returning to Britain, he responded to anxieties about the physical condition and moral fibre of the nation's youth. His initial impulse was to help develop such youth organizations as the Boys' Brigade, founded in 1883 by William A. Smith, a Glasgow Sunday-school teacher. But after an experimental camp on Brownsea Island, near Poole, in the summer of 1907 and publishing *Scouting for Boys* the year after, scouting emerged as something rather different. Criticized by some for jingoism or militarism, it reflected in fact its founder's scepticism about regimentation. Scouts took to wearing uniform, but there was, by Edwardian standards, not much smartness in dress more suitable for cross-country hiking than parade grounds.

Baden-Powell's prime concerns were with health and fitness, promoted by open-air activities, comradeship, loyalty within 'troops' (structured groups) and social responsibility. Such qualities would, it is true, be of value to future soldiers. But Baden-Powell was not the man to turn scouting into a cadet movement. Instead, as became clearer with time, the emphasis was on the development of the individual in the company of others. There was a good deal of moral exhortation, but no more than was common in education generally at the time, and the non-denominational nature of the movement allowed it to be adopted, for instance, by churches of different denominations. The pace at which scouting expanded shows that it matched a need, as was recognized by the grant of a Royal Charter as early as 1912. Girls insisted on being part of the movement, which led to the formation of the Guides. Spreading to other countries, scouting had a million members by 1922 (and 25 million by 1995). Small boys were catered for by Wolf Cub packs, and Brownies appealed even more to little girls. The Duke of Edinburgh Awards represent a modern development of some aspects of scouting, but Baden-Powell's movement, if less significant than formerly, remains an important part of Britain's provision for young people.

Further reading

Rosenthal, M. (1984) *The Character Factory*, New York: Pantheon (informative, though sharply critical).

Springhall, J. (1977) *Youth, Empire and Society: British Youth Movements, 1883-1940*, London: Croom Helm (though concerned with events up to 1940, invaluable for the perspective it provides).

CHRISTOPHER SMITH

scratching

Most commonly heard in **rap** and **hip hop** songs, the technique of scratching involves manually moving a record back and forth, so that one small section – usually only one sound – is heard backwards and forwards, repeatedly. Essentially, the resulting sound is used to provide an extra rhythmic texture to the track. The rise of trip hop music (jazz-influenced, largely instrumental hip hop) has moved scratching to the forefront, with songs such as The Herbalizer's 'Scratchy Noise' employing the technique to great effect. For the most part, though, scratching remains a tool for creative DJing, with Coldcut's *1995 Journeys By DJ* mix album containing many fine examples of the technique in use.

See also: sampling

SIMON BOTTOM

Screen and screen theory

Screen was the most influential journal of British cinema studies in the 1970s and 1980s. Under the editorship of Sam Rohdie, *Screen* developed a theoretical practice of cinematic analysis which investigated the structure of cinema and the positioning of the cinematic spectator. Screen theorists including Colin MacCabe, Laura Mulvey and Stephen Heath were distinguished by their theoretical investigation of the dominant codes of narrative cinema, as well as by their collective attempt to establish theoretical film analysis as a legitimate field of higher education. The internal development of screen theory can be traced through its self-reflexive encounters with Saussurian semiotics, Althusserian Marxism and Lacanian psychoanalysis.

Screen theorists drew upon semiotics to investigate how the cinematic 'language' as a system of signs, images and codes is structurally organized by the conventions of narrative. MacCabe argues that the classic realist text does not reflect reality but instead produces the narrative illusion of the reproduction of reality. Realist cinema establishes a formal hierarchy of film discourses in which narrative functions as the privileged code. It fixes the spectator in a unified position of 'pure specularity' or a point of view from which 'everything becomes obvious'. Heath deploys the concept of 'suture' to define this structural positioning of the spectator. MacCabe critiques the classic realist text as ideologically conservative because it elides the contradictory character of the 'real', and he calls for the production of a progressive, non-narrative cinema.

Extending and critiquing MacCabe's position, Mulvey's 'Visual Pleasure and Narrative Cinema' has become foundational for feminist film analysis. Mulvey uses Lacanian psychoanalysis to argue that the subject is not only produced but decentred by language. According to Mulvey, the cinematic 'gaze' is structured by gendered regimes of power and desire which dichotomize visual pleasure into active/male/subject versus passive/female/object. Cinematic pleasure, then, is voyeuristically encoded as male. Mulvey calls for an attitude of 'passionate detachment' disruptive of the visual pleasures of narrative cinema and, like MacCabe, she calls for a non-narrative avant-garde cinematic practice.

Despite its influence, screen theory has been systematically critiqued for its theoreticism and elitism. Nevertheless, contemporary debate about spectatorship and pleasure continues to engage questions that were central to the *Screen* project.

See also: media and cultural studies

Further reading

Bennett, T. *et al.* (1981) Popular Television and Film, London: BFI Publishing (a useful reader, including essays by MacCabe, Mulvey and Heath).

Mast, G. and Cohen, M. (1992) *Film Theory and Criticism*, New York: Oxford University Press (a useful anthology, including the essays by Mac-Cabe, Mulvey and Heath).

MARK DOUGLAS

Scruton, Roger

b. 1944

Philosopher

A prolific writer, critic and broadcaster, Roger Scruton is also a professional philosopher who has commented widely on political theory and aesthetics. Educated at Cambridge, he has taught at the Universities of Bordeaux, where he witnessed the student upheavals of the 1960s, Birkbeck College in London and Boston. Founding *The Salisbury Review* in the early 1980s, a journal dedicated to conservative thought, his essentially right-wing views have led him to a position of notoriety within academic circles in Britain, though less so in the USA. His essentially Burkean conservatism (*The Meaning of Conservatism*), his view of sex as that which is permissible only within marriage (*Sexual Desire*), and his assertion that animals should not be accorded rights (*Animal Rights and Wrongs*) have done nothing to modify the controversial standing of Britain's only fox-hunting philosopher.

See also: philosophy

PAUL BARRY CLARKE
LAWRENCE QUILL

sculpture

Contemporary British sculpture is informed by two major ideas: the response to the work of the 'new generation' of the early 1960s, and the dominance of a handful of London art schools, including St Martins, the Royal College of Art and Goldsmiths College. Very little contemporary production can be isolated from the fact that almost all recent work is in some way informed by the sculptural debates that began in the 1960s, and nearly all of the current generation of sculptors went to the three schools mentioned above. In common with many other aspects of British life, the production of sculpture is highly centralized, and few sculptors working outside of the London institutions have had success. But these qualifications aside, sculpture is one area in which British artists have made an international reputation.

In 1965, the Whitechapel Art Gallery in London presented *The New Generation*, an exhibition of new British sculpture by artists born mainly in the 1930s, including Philip King, William Tucker and Tim Scott, all of whom were then working at St Martins College of Art. The materials in the show marked a break with traditional sculpture, and included painted steel, polythene, plywood, glass hardboard and wood. But there was little doubt that the most important figure in the show was Anthony Caro, also teaching at St Martins, whose work had been exhibited internationally and had been well-received in the United States. Caro's career began as a studio assistant to Henry **Moore**, and his early work resembled Moore's figurative sculpture. However, after meeting the modernist David Smith on a visit to the United States in 1960, Caro began to make welded steel sculpture, improvising forms with a variety of disparate elements. Two other facts marked a sharp break with the artist's earlier practice: there was no plinth or base in the new work, causing the sculpture to rest directly on the floor; and the sculptures were coloured, using bright, commercially-available colours that had nothing to do with those found in nature. One of the largest and best-known examples of this work is *Early One Morning* (1962).

Caro went on to teach at Bennington College, Vermont in 1963–4 and again the following year, and his acceptance by the American avant-garde was such that his inclusion in the massive survey show *American Sculpture of the Sixties* (Los Angeles County Museum of Art, 1967) went more or less unremarked. Caro's career in the United States was particularly helped by the critical support of Michael Fried, and Caro's work came to represent Modernist sculpture internationally.

Meanwhile, various former students of the Royal College of Art were making work informed by **pop art**. They included Allen Jones, who produced life-size female figures in fibreglass, dressed in fetishistic leather clothing, posed to make furniture; Mark Boyle and family, who made exact replicas in fibreglass of small areas of London streets, selected at random; and John Lacey, whose *Boy oh Boy Am I Living* (1964) was an absurd robot assembled from a Belisha Beacon and artificial limbs.

By the late 1960s, modernist sculpture as practised by Caro and his disciples at St Martins was under attack both from minimalism in the United States and from a new generation of St Martins sculptors in Britain. The new work was extremely diverse, involving the use of soft and flexible materials, the incursion of performance and photography into sculpture, and in some cases the disappearance of any recognizable object altogether. Barry Flanagan's work is a good example: it consisted of cloth or hessian bags stuffed with soft materials and casually arranged, often subject to considerations of gravity or chance. Superficially it resembled so-called 'anti form' sculpture which had recently emerged in New York, and during the late 1960s Flanagan was often shown alongside Americans such as Robert Morris and Eva Hesse.

If Flanagan continued to make sculptural objects, albeit ones which were subject to some new considerations, his contemporaries at St Martins showed ways in which sculpture was no longer necessarily contingent on an object produced for the specific viewing conditions of the gallery. During his time at the College, Richard **Long** began to exhibit his 'walks' as sculpture. Hence, *A Line Made by Walking, England, 1967* was photographic documentation of a straight line made by the artist in a field by the simple process of walking. The line itself was not exhibited, but the photograph was: the material presence of the sculpture all but dissolved, and what was left was a conceptual trace.

The work of Gilbert and George provides a different example of the way sculpture began to lose some of its material aspects. The duo – who met at St Martins in 1967, and have been working together ever since – presented themselves as 'living sculptures' in performances between 1969 and 1977. In *Balls: The Evening Before The Morning After – Drinking Sculpture*, the artists performed an evening's drinking at Ball's, a favourite establishment in Bethnal Green (although Penelope Curtis reports that no alcohol was actually consumed) and the results were photographed and displayed. The final form of *Balls* was, in some respects, functionally equivalent to Richard Long's records of his walks in the country.

An early conceptually-oriented work was *Still*

and Chew (1966) by John Latham, then a part-time lecturer at St Martins, constituted as a direct (and extremely funny) attack on the then-dominant modernist criticism of Clement Greenberg. The piece was in the first instance an event, in which a copy of Greenberg's *Art and Culture* (removed from the St Martins library) was chewed by Latham and assorted colleagues – he reported that there was some selection of pages – and the results were spat into a flask. To this was added an 'Alien Culture', a yeast, and the mixture was left to ferment, and eventually distilled. When the librarian finally recalled the book, Latham took the distillate to the College, and after some argument was able to persuade the librarian that this was indeed the remains of Greenberg's text; the following day a letter arrived stating that his services would no longer be required at the College. *Still and Chew* is displayed in the form of a flask of the distillate, plus assorted documentation, all contained in a case.

If the work of the post-Caro generation of St Martins sculptors opened up a field of epistemological enquiry, the avant-garde of the 1980s evidenced something of a return to earlier concerns. Generally speaking, the work of the so-called 'New British Sculptors' such as Tony Cragg, Richard Deacon, Anthony Gormley, Anish Kapoor, Richard Wentworth and Alison Wilding, acknowledged the formal possibilities opened up by the sculpture of the late 1960s and early 1970s, but deliberately encouraged metaphysical readings. The work was in general poetic, literary and oriented towards the creation of objects. As such, it evidenced a shift away from the previous interest in the means of production.

Examples of this new tendency include Cragg's *Britain Seen From the North* in which a giant silhouette of Britain, rotated ninety degrees and accompanied by a riot policeman, is generated via an assemblage of assorted broken bits of plastic, most of which have recognizable sources. The technique and scale of the work would appear to derive from the horizontal sculptures of artists such as Richard Long, but the piece is wall-mounted, and makes a recognizable image, which at the time of its production was legibly political, a statement of an unequal Britain, regionally divided and beset by social unrest. Wentworth's *Shower* (1984) comprises a kitchen table (with a propeller set, surrealistically,

into the rim) balanced on one leg; the assemblage is anchored, literally it seems, by a heavy iron plate and chain. The ordinariness of the sculpture's materials and their simple juxtaposition again refer back to work produced internationally at the end of the 1960s, but the precise result here is a fantastic spectacle in which the table is only prevented from flying away by means of its tether. A further point of interest is Wentworth's frequent use of anecdote to explain the work; in this case, the sculpture is said to have been inspired by the sight of a café owner rushing outside during a storm to upend the outdoor tables.

The rather literary sculpture produced during the 1980s had obvious equivalents in the field of painting. Since the 1980s there has been something of a retreat from this mode and a renewed engagement with the theme of the body. In many ways this recalls minimalism in its initial phase, with its critical grounding in phenomenology, and a particular interest in the perception of bodies in space. What has appeared to occur in British sculpture in the late 1980s and early 1990s is a re-engagement with this idea, but with a specifically female focus. Two artists best represent this tendency, Helen Chadwick, who died in 1966, and Rachel Whiteread. Chadwick is generally regarded as a sculptor, although her primary medium could be said to be **photography**: her work tends to comprise photographs of arrangements of matter, often configured to generate explicitly sexual readings. Materials in these cases have included meat, lambs' tongues, fur and vegetable matter. There have however been a number of large sculptures, many of which achieved some notoriety on their first showing. *Piss Flowers*, a series comprised a series of plaster casts of holes made by urinating in snow. The results were often both surprising and beautiful.

Whiteread's mature work comprises casts of the interior of domestic objects, furniture and, most famously an entire terraced house. Her materials are extremely varied, ranging from concrete to plaster to rubber and various kinds of resins, and the work has much tactile appeal. The work is often made, and displayed in serial arrangement, which tends to encourage comparison with minimalism, a suggestion that the artists does not dispute. *House*, a huge project in the East End of London, resulted in the making of an inside-out house; commissioned by Artangel, it was created over some months in 1993, and then famously destroyed despite a campaign that it should stay. The controversy over this work has been compared to the destruction of Richard Serra's *Tilted Arc* in New York in 1984.

Both Chadwick and Whiteread evidence a reading of 1960s art which shows its concerns reconfigured to represent a more specific idea of the body; Whiteread's more architectural work shows minimalism reconfigured to specifically English ends; her materials, with their faded colours and decayed appearance, are resonant with decline and nostalgia, which gives her works a specifically English accent.

Of all contemporary British artists, none has attracted so much media attention as Damien Hirst. This is as much to do with the manner in which he has courted attention, which recalls Andy Warhol, as with his startling materials, which include dead farm animals preserved in formaldehyde, cigarette butts, medical instruments and maggots. Precedents for Hirst's cool arrangements can be found in the conceptual art of the 1960s, and Goldsmiths College where Hirst was a student during the mid-1980s has vigorously promoted the investigation of the art of this period. The technical ambitiousness of Hirst's work is nevertheless a departure. In common with other recent British art, it is not an intellectual project, and it remains to be seen whether Hirst's creations have the persistence of the work from which they clearly derive.

It also remains to be seen whether sculpture reasserts itself again as a discrete practice. Much of the interesting or notorious British sculpture of the 1990s has been made by artists who might equally be at home making installation art, photographs or videos; the category 'sculpture' once again seems to have dissolved.

See also: Hepworth, Barbara; Nicholson, Ben

Further reading

Arts Council of Great Britain (1995) *The British Art Show 4*, London: Arts Council.

Curtis, P. (1988) *Modern British Sculpture From the Collection*, Liverpool: Tate Gallery Publications.

Royal Academy of Arts (1987) *British Art in the Twentieth Century*, Munich: Prestel.

RICHARD J. WILLIAMS

SDP

On 25 January 1981, four former **Labour Party** cabinet ministers – David Owen, Shirley Williams, Bill Rodgers and Roy Jenkins, known collectively as the Gang of Four – launched the Council for Social Democracy, which became the Social Democratic Party (SDP) in March. The Gang of Four left Labour because of that party's drift to the far left and changes in the party rules designed to further increase left-wing influence. The SDP was the first political party to be formed since 1900, and by December 1981 it had caused a major stir, attracting 70,000 members and going ahead in the opinion polls with 50 percent of national support. Twenty-seven Labour MPs and one Conservative MP also defected to the new party.

For the first year of its existence the SDP enjoyed a honeymoon period with the media and the public, and it achieved its biggest by-election successes at this time. Yet when the SDP unveiled its policies they were not particularly innovative, despite its attempts to portray itself as a new, radical alternative of the centre left. In June 1982, the SDP and the Liberals emphasized the common ground between them and announced that they would form an alliance for electoral purposes.

In the 1983 general election, the SDP/Liberal Alliance with its dual leadership of Roy Jenkins and David Steel gained 25.4 percent of the vote compared to Labour's 27.6 percent, the best performance by a third party since 1923. Nevertheless, Labour took 209 seats to the Alliance's 23 (of which only six were held by SDP candidates), due to the first-past-the-post electoral system. David Owen replaced Roy Jenkins as SDP leader, and with Steel led the Alliance into the 1987 election. Here the Alliance's share of the vote fell and they held only 22 seats. This failure resulted in widespread calls for merger of the SDP and Liberal Party, to which Owen responded by reiterating the 'need for a fourth party'. Owen was isolated when the SDP membership voted by 57.4 percent to 42.6 percent to join a merged party, which eventually became the Liberal Democrats (see **Liberal Party**). Subsequently there was an acrimonious split, with the Owenites or 'continuing SDP' breaking away. This undertaking was a failure, and the party was wound up in May 1990.

See also: fringe parties

Further reading

Crewe, I. and King, A. (1995) *SDP: The Birth, Life and Death of the Social Democratic Party,* Oxford: Oxford University Press (a definitive guide).

COLIN WILLIAMS

secret services

Founded in 1909, the British secret intelligence service revolves around two major departments of military intelligence with several adjunct executive branches. MI5 is concerned with state security and counter-intelligence. Its responsibilities cover counter-espionage and the investigation of other internal security threats such as political dissenters and subversives. MI5 also prevents the dissemination of classified information and is heavily involved in counter-terrorist activities in the UK. MI6, which, until recently, the government claimed had no official existence in peacetime, deals with obtaining knowledge and with espionage concerning British interests on an international scale.

Other major aspects of the secret services include the Special Branch of the British **police**. While originally centralized in Scotland Yard from 1883, the Special Branch was recently extended in localized form to all forty-two of Britain's police forces.

Army Intelligence and Special Air Service (SAS) are allied with the secret services in several areas, particularly regarding counter-terrorist operations affecting state security. The activities of the IRA have been a main area of responsibility for MI5, especially since the end of the Cold War. However, even within the secret services the tensions between the efficiency of openness and the protective shield

of secrecy are evident. This secretiveness in MI5 has been ameliorated slightly by Stella Rimmington, who was until recently head of MI5 and who gave press briefings. The value of these briefings is limited.

Until the late 1970s, the clandestine nature of the individual agencies ensured that each was reticent about sharing information with the others. They consequently operated on a largely separate basis, which caused a degree of inefficiency in handling the increased IRA activity in Northern Ireland. In 1978, MI5, the Special Branch of the Royal Ulster Constabulary (RUC), Army Intelligence and the SAS coordinated intelligence gathering and set up the first Tasking and Coordination Group (TCG) in Belfast. The resulting success in ambushing IRA activity led to the extension of the TCG throughout Northern Ireland.

The various arms of the secret services are still somewhat jealous of their 'patch'. Set against that, however, is the need to redefine their role after the Cold War and to ensure better coordination of information. The Joint Intelligence Committee (JIC) now handles coordination, and role redefinition has occurred in a number of areas. The most successful redefinition has been the shift of MI5 from generalized mainland security to dealing with the IRA in particular. The effect of this is not to be underestimated. Underlying the current drive to peace in Northern Ireland are many factors, but included in those factors lies a redefinition of the working role of the secret services following the end of the Cold War. More latterly, there is clear evidence that the secret services (widely understood) have been involved in the identification, serving of indictments and arrest of criminals charged with war crimes in Bosnia. This betokens both a shift in the mandate of these organizations and, more significantly, a clear indication that they are now regarded as responsible directly to Downing Street rather than to the Ministry of Defence. The shift is significant, and unprecedented, in that the secret services may turn out to be an arm of the prime minister in particular rather than the government in general. This indicates a shift from parliamentary and cabinet government to a more presidential style of government. The way in which the secret services are being commanded and held accountable indicates a fundamental and unprecedented shift in the way in which Britain is governed.

See also: MI5 and MI6

Further reading

Pincher, C. (1987) *A Web of Deception*, London: Sidgwick & Jackson.

PAUL BARRY CLARKE

EMMA R. NORMAN

self-service

Historically, the human element of the shopping experience was paramount, with shops as an important feature of communities and the shop-keeper as a central figure (even Napoleon in-famously remarked that 'England is a nation of shopkeepers'). However, shifts in lifestyles and the introduction of larger retail units led to new ways being developed to maximize turnover. The growth of supermarkets and the use of shelves stocked with groceries and foodstuffs removed the need for human intermediaries and allowed a more cost-effective way of supplying goods. This shift also created a number of legal problems centring upon when the contract of sale was concluded, as this had consequences for the sale of goods such as intoxicating liquor to minors. A similar experience was seen in the case of garages supplying petrol. Historically, an attendant would have enquired as to how much petrol was required by the motorist and delivered the petrol into the vehicle. However, for similar reasons to the supermarket shift, it became more cost-efficient to permit motorists to supply the petrol themselves and pay the amount due to a central point. This shift also created legal problems when it was discovered that the law of theft did not initially cover situations where the motorist filled up and then decided not to pay, although this problem was later rectified. It is now possible for the whole transaction for petrol to be automated through payment by debit or credit card at the pump itself, completely removing all human contact from the transaction.

Further developments have occurred both with the onset of **mail order** and so-called 'e-commerce'. Mail-order facilities were adopted by many companies such as Littlewoods and Sears Roebuck, as a response to the need for a more convenient mode of shopping for rural or busy consumers with the convenience of shopping via catalogue and having products delivered directly to the home. Coupled with credit schemes that allowed the spreading of costs and outlay (**hire purchase** agreements) this proved a viable and popular means of home shopping. With the advent of the World Wide Web, further opportunities for home shopping have presented themselves, and after some initial scepticism these have been seized upon by many corporations wise to the advantages this might bring. With government figures showing that over 10 percent of the UK population are now online, many see this idea of the 'wired catalogue' being the next logical step in self-service/home shopping.

See also: electronic shopping

Further reading

DTI (1998) 'Moving into the information age', http://www.dti.gov.uk

GUY OSBORN

STEVE GREENFIELD

serial killers

After the horror of the Moors Murders in the 1960s, the 1980s was the decade in which the serial killer entered the public consciousness as a descriptive label for mass murderers. The phrase itself was allegedly coined in 1978 by FBI agent Robert Ressler to describe those who kill repeat-edly and obsessively. Prominent examples of killers who have attracted the term include Dennis Neilsen, Peter Sutcliffe, and Fred and Rosemary West. The portrayal and psychology of the serial killer has since become a focus of popular culture; notable cinematic portrayals are *Manhunter* (Mann, 1986) and *The Silence of the Lambs* (Demme, 1991) both based on the novels of Thomas Harris. Brett Easton Ellis's controversial novel *American Psycho* further explored the subjective dimension to the phenomena.

See also: police; violence

GUY OSBORN
STEVE GREENFIELD

set design

Design jobs in the performing arts include theatre designer, stage designer and, increasingly the European term 'scenographer' (with sub-categories of set designer, costume designer, lighting designer and sound designer). Taken together, these describe a relatively unsettled and developing 'profession'.

The development of set design as a specialist **theatre** discipline in the UK (as distinct from the prevailing orthodoxy, established in the 1920s by the design group Motley, of theatre design (or stage design) where the designer's responsibility is for set and costumes), was probably precipitated by the impact of the theatre design work of the architect Sean Kenny in the 1960s (for example, *Oliver* (1960) and *Hamlet* (1963), and by the influence throughout Europe of the innovative Czech designer Josef Svoboda, who first successfully incorporated slide projection into set design. Kenny was trained as an architect (managing a successful architectural practice throughout his career), conforming to the historical model of set design established in England by Inigo Jones in the seventeenth century. Svoboda began as a carpenter's apprentice.

The number of specialist set designers has increased concurrently with the rapid development of the technology of computer controlled stage mechanics, lighting and sound. Research and development of these technologies has been propelled and financed by the demands of extravagant stage presentations of live pop music (for example, the Rolling Stones and Pink Floyd).

Television and film design have always been separated into the two disciplines of set and costume design, with costume designers generally being the poor relations in a rigid hierarchy; witness the credits for any television programme or feature film. Set design in these media, usually credited as production design, has been dominated by practitioners often trained as architects or interior designers, and whose practice naturally focuses on the output of comprehensive technical drawings, rather than the atmospheric, coloured and textured scale model so central to a theatre designer's language.

Most theatre designers still elect to design both settings and costumes to ensure a visually coherent whole for their productions. However, Ralph Koltai, John Napier (*Starlight Express*, *Cats*, *Les Misérables*, *Miss Saigon*) and William Dudley are distinguished British theatre designers regularly confining themselves to set design.

Further reading

Allen, K. and Shaw, P. (eds) (1994) *Make Space!*, Theatre Design Umbrella in association with The Society of Theatre Designers (a copiously illustrated catalogue of British theatre design between 1990 and 1994, including 135 designers' biographies; each design is accompanied by a brief text describing the underpinning ideas).

DAVID BURROWS

Sex Discrimination Acts

Most feminists have argued women's position in the labour market is a source of female disadvantage. Functionalists have argued that women get paid less than men as they have less skill and labour market experience than men, due to the time women spend in households. Marxist feminists stress material and economic factors and capital–labour relations. However, it is liberal feminists who have placed most emphasis upon the introduction of equal opportunities in the labour market through new legislation.

In 1970, the Equal Pay Act was passed, followed in 1975 by the Sex Discrimination Act. This act barred discrimination on the grounds of sex in employment, education and the provision of goods, services and premises. In employment, women were to be given equal access to jobs and equal chances for promotion as men. Some types of jobs however, were excluded from the provisions of the Act, where there was considered to be a genuine occupational qualification by sex. The act was broadened in scope in 1986. One of the reasons for these legislative changes was the political pressure from women in **trade unions**.

Whether the Sex Discrimination Act has had a significant effect upon women's employment levels and position in the labour market, relative to that of men, is not immediately obvious. There was a slight closure of the wages gap between men and women immediately after the act was implemented; women's wages as a percentage of men's rose from 63 percent in 1970 to 76 percent in 1977 (Equal Opportunities Commission). There was little further increase until the early 1990s, when in 1993 the figure rose to 79 percent. Whether or not the decrease in the wages gap between men and women can be attributed to the legislation has been questioned. There continue to be considerable differences between the average pay of men and women, and men and women still continue to do different jobs. The legislation has also been criticized for failing to address other problems women face in paid employment, such as domestic care of children, husbands and elderly relatives.

See also: armed forces and discrimination; Race Relations Acts

Further reading

Equal Opportunities Commission (1994) Some Facts About Women, based on New Earnings Survey and Labour Force Survey, London: HMSO.

KALWANT BHOPAL

sex scandals

In London on 2 November 1960, *Lady Chatterley's Lover*, the long-banned novel by D.H. Lawrence, was cleared of a charge of obscenity by an Old Bailey jury. In many ways the trial pitted an old Britain against the new; it was not only a case of what was considered literature but of the direction of national morality. In 1963 John Profumo, the Secretary of State for War, resigned after allegations of a sex scandal involving ministers, prostitutes and Russian spies. The Profumo Affair was the biggest crisis in the Macmillan government; the two key protagonists responsible for this political upheaval were Christine Keeler and Mandy Rice-Davies. In 1976 Jeremy Thorpe resigned as Liberal leader, after weeks of Westminster gossip about allegations of a homosexual relationship; the following year, the story of the obsession of Joyce McKinney for a young Mormon missionary was the leading story in the British press, and during the final months of 1977 it was impossible to buy a newspaper or turn on the radio or television and not read or hear about McKinney. She was granted bail and escaped to America, dressed as a nun.

In October 1983, Cecil Parkinson, chairman and architect of the Conservative election victory in June, resigned from the Cabinet following revelations of an affair with his secretary, Sara Keays. Unlike Macmillan with Profumo, Prime Minister Margaret Thatcher supported Parkinson and appointed him Trade and Industry Secretary, thus demonstrating the vastly different attitude to issues of morality. Conservatives in the mid-1980s were prepared to handle the Parkinson sex scandal, through a renunciation of Miss Keays and the saving of the marriage of the disgraced minister. Thus, the party which put the family first kept its conscience clear. Unfortunately, when the news became public knowledge, Parkinson was unable to continue in government.

The major scandal of the 1980s and 1990s involved members of the British royal family. The publication of *Diana – Her True Story* by Andrew Morton in 1992 ended a century and a half of Royal reserve on personal matters, replacing it with indulgent exhibitionism. By 1993 the book had sold nearly five million copies worldwide.

See also: monarchy

Further reading

Cassell, D. (1998) *The Book of Modern Scandal – from Byron to the Present Day*, London: Orion.

FATIMA FERNANDES

S4C

S4C (Sianel Pedwar Cymru, or Channel 4 Wales) is a television station which has broadcast since 1982.

A Welsh-language channel, S4C was the direct result of political lobbying. The Welsh national party, Plaid Cymru, had argued for such a medium to stimulate and protect Welsh in the country. The argument found favour with the incoming Conservative Party in 1979, though the Tories later backed down the following year and it took a hunger strike (by Plaid Cymru's leader Gwynfor Evans) and many demonstrations to reconvince them. The station broadcasts over twenty hours a week, primarily in peak evening times.

See also: Channel 4; nationalist parties; Welsh language

PETER CHILDS

shoplifting

'All property is theft', Proudhon's slogan of the French Revolution, became popular in the late 1960s. Until then, shoplifting was largely seen as a children's activity. Suddenly those owning shops were designated enemies of 'the people', and it was a particularly bad time for bookshops in university towns. Even university libraries now need very costly security systems. This attitude to capitalism and private property is best illustrated by Jerry Rubin, leader of the Yippie movement (the paramilitary wing of the **hippies**) which arose after **police** rioted at the Democratic Party Convention in Chicago in 1968. He wrote *Steal This Book*, on the basis that all commercial operations are a form of theft. Most shops were then vulnerable to a bold approach, and what was known as liberating goods became a popular pastime for under-30s and has remained so. By 1972, gangs of mainly Australian shoplifters specialized in taking large items from big stores in London's Oxford Street.

A culture of making criminals into anti-heroes in the French existential tradition of Sartre and Camus evolved through a long series of American movies from *Butch Cassidy and the Sundance Kid* to *Thelma and Louise* or *Reservoir Dogs* in which shoplifting, bank robbery or murder are admired. This development has been assisted by police actions in which innocent parties have been jailed, as in various anti-IRA operations, or shot, as in numerous US police raids. There is also an increased reliance since the 1970s on **violence** or torture as part of police interrogations, especially in the Third World. These elements have effected the legitimization of criminal activity in the eyes of the young and underprivileged, or in the case of so-called champagne socialists, the overprivileged.

In 1997 a vicar, the Rev. Papworth, attracted hostile attention in the press for suggesting that the poor should not be condemned for stealing from supermarkets. Six months later Jimmy McGovern, writer of the widely-praised television series *Cracker*, about a police psychologist, announced that shoplifting was one of his habitual activities. Security in shops is more intense as open counters and counter assistants have been replaced by detectives, cameras and expensive alarm systems set off by tags at electronic checkouts. No doubt shoplifting will continue until attitudes change, both from industrialists towards their customers and from young people towards society, which sanctions a psychologically insidious and yet voracious materialism to be cultivated by the subtle water torture of television advertising.

See also: advertising, influence of

Further reading

Hoffman, A. (1969) *Woodstock Nation*, New York: Random House (seminal exposition of underground philosophy).

STEPHEN KERENSKY

shopping, recreational

The term 'recreational shopping' refers to the experience of shopping as a leisure activity, and implies the satisfaction of personal and social as well as material needs. The rise of recreational shopping is seen by some as a victory for capitalism, whereby sophisticated marketing techniques have established a 'culture of consumerism' which will ensure its own reproduction. For others, however, recreational shopping is a characteristically postmodern phenomenon, in which the boundaries between work and leisure are blurred, and the locations for social interaction and 'identity work' become fragmented and dispersed.

Recreational shopping is seen to be most clearly demonstrated in the phenomenon of shopping malls, which combine leisure facilities such as **cinemas** and restaurants with more conventional consumption outlets such as supermarkets and chain stores. In such spaces, shopping is rarely a purely functional experience; visitors drift from one shop to the next, browsing in many shops but often only making small purchases, and interspersing their shopping activity with eating a meal or going to see a film.

Recreational shopping is assumed by many to be more common among women than men. Falk and Campbell (1997) suggest that women are more positive about a wider range of shopping activities than men, and are more likely to cite shopping as preferable to other leisure activities. Indeed they suggest that for women, shopping may have intrinsic recreational value, whereas men are likely to see it as comparable to work. It is important to add, however, that most people distinguish between different kinds of shopping (such as food or non-food), and that women in particular often draw a distinction between 'doing the shopping' and 'going shopping', seeing one as a chore and the other as akin to an outing.

Retailers are increasingly keen to exploit the concept of shopping as a recreational or leisure activity. Supermarkets in particular are attempting to find ways to make mundane grocery shopping more attractive, thereby extending the length of time that customers spend in stores; hence the development of 'food courts' in supermarkets, where customers can sit and rest or eat and drink, and the increase in 'luxury' and 'exotic' foods in supermarkets. The overall effect is that supermarkets may become more like malls, and the concept of recreational shopping may be extended to incorporate even the most mundane forms of consumption.

See also: electronic shopping; supermarkets and malls

Further reading

Falk, P. and Campbell, C. (eds) (1997) *The Shopping Experience*, London: Sage.

LIZ MOOR
PETER LUNT

shops

There have been many exciting innovations in shop design in recent decades, aided by the rise in designer fashions and consumer culture, especially in the 1980s, and also by the fast turnaround in businesses as new shops come and go quickly. Japanese style has been an enormous influence, and the use of natural materials, open spaces, light effects and above all simplicity (polished floors, glass and steel) has become a familiar feature of hundreds of clothes shops; early examples of this style were for Japanese clients in London, such as Issey Miyake (by David **Chipperfield** and Ken Armstrong) and Yohji Yamamoto (by Munkenbeck and Marshall). Earlier styles were variously **high-tech**, postmodernist (see **postmodernism**) or experiments in 'creative salvage', such as in the case of several of the shops in London's Covent Garden.

Several of the best examples of architects working to showcase fashion are the remaking of Harrods fashion floor by Jiricna Kerr in 1985, and **Foster Associates**' stark warehouse, complete with access by a steel bridge, for Katharine **Hamnett**. Supermarkets have appeared in ever-increasing numbers in the last two decades, and several have been to experimental designs (though always within corporate lines), such as **Nicholas Grimshaw and Partners**' 1989 Sainsbury's store in Camden Town (Grimshaw has since moved on to designing a north London store for Homebase, the DIY arm of Sainsbury). Malls have also become commonplace; one excellent example is the enormous Ealing Centre (1985) by the Building Design Partnership, which resembles a walled castle.

See also: housing; office buildings

Further reading

Glancey, J. (1989) *New British Architecture*, London: Thames & Hudson.

PETER CHILDS

showjumping

From antiquity, horse owners have rarely been able to resist the temptation to demonstrate their steed's superiority in speed or agility and their own prowess as riders or trainers. Vienna's Spanish Riding School, founded in 1572, is testimony to long-lived international traditions in horsemanship. Apart from horse racing, now largely (though not entirely) a professional sport, equestrianism attracts many amateurs, although a professional upper tier sets the standard. Emerging at nineteenth-century shows designed to foster general agricultural improvement, showjumping had developed to something very like its present form by the time of the second Olympic Games at Paris in 1900 and the first London International Horse Show seven years later. Showjumping courses, which are all basically similar, are designed to confront horses and riders with a variety of obstacles reflecting the challenges that might be encountered in hunting or cross-country riding. Accordingly, some jumps resemble a fence, gate or wall, while others involve negotiating a water-filled ditch or two or three obstacles in rapid succession. Though primarily a test of jumping, with points deducted (for example, when a horse fails to clear an obstacle cleanly or refuses to jump) penalties are also imposed for

exceeding a given time limit. At every level from international events to local pony club gymkhanas, teams or individuals, whether male or female, amateur or professional, compete on a knockout basis, with later rounds often requiring fewer but more difficult jumps in a shorter time.

Puissance competitions, which test to the limit a horse's ability to negotiate high obstacles, are less popular in the UK than elsewhere. Showjumping also constitutes the final discipline in three-day eventing. This sport, which developed from exercises for gauging cavalry officers' efficiency, is well described by its French name as a 'complete test of horsemanship'. The first day is devoted to a 'dressage' competition that assesses the training of horses and riders in a prescribed range of movements. A gruelling cross-country ride over a variety of obstacles, against the clock within strict time limits, occupies the second of the three days. Three-day events and showjumping competitions draw large crowds and are popular on television. Enjoyment of the sport is enhanced by attractive venues (such as Gatcombe Park and Hickstead), the riders' smart traditional turnout and the horses' physical grace.

See also: Grand National; horse racing

Further reading

The Manual of Horsemanship (1993) Kenilworth: Pony Club.

CHRISTOPHER SMITH

Sikhism

A monotheistic religion originating from the Indian Punjab (annexed by the British) in the late fifteenth and early sixteenth centuries by Nanak, a Hindu influenced by the Islamic Sufi teachings. Nanak believed that both Hinduism and Islam expressed truths about God, *sat nam* (the 'true name'). From Hinduism, Nanak took a belief in reincarnation, but he rejected caste, pilgrimages, idols and ritual prayers. Nanak appointed one of his followers to become guru of the Sikh community on his death, instigating a line of ten developers who, among other things, collected Sikh sacred scripture and built the Harmandir (Golden Temple) at Amritsar, which, ironically, has become a major pilgrimage centre. The last Guru, Gobind Singh, created the *Khalsa* to allow followers to demonstrate their commitment to the faith, including the distinctive five K marks of a full Sikh (*sikhi* means disciple). Sikhs have no particular holy day, but keep some festivals of Hindu origin, and celebrate Gurpurbs in honour of the ten gurus. There are 16 million Sikhs worldwide; as it is not a proselytizing faith, nearly all of these descend from Punjabi migrants. Many Sikhs came to Britain in the 1950s seeking employment (often in response to British entreaties) in the cities, and this was followed by another smaller wave in the early 1970s. In Britain, Sikh identity has been typified by the wearing of a turban, for which many were discriminated against at work and school until legislation in the 1970s outlawed such actions.

See also: Hinduism; Indian communities

Further reading

Nesbitt, E.M. (1988) 'Sikhism', in R. Zaehner (ed.), *Encyclopedia of Living Faiths*, 4th edn, London: Hutchinson.

PETER CHILDS

single parents

Single-parent families are also known as 'lone-parent' or 'one-parent' families. There are about 1.5 million such families in the UK. Approximately one in five children live with one parent, of whom 9 percent are fathers. Just over four in ten black British families are headed by a single parent.

Over 60 percent of mothers have been separated, divorced or widowed. More than half have a weekly income under £150, compared with seven percent of two-parent families. Despite the **Child Support Agency** (CSA), only about one-third receive maintenance.

In 1988, the Labour government set up the New Deal for Lone Parents, to encourage them to return to work. Ninety percent want jobs, but are thwarted by lack of affordable childcare and the 'benefits trap', whereby additional costs such as fares reduce income to below the level of state benefits. Over 40 percent of lone mothers are in paid work, with about one million single-parent families relying on Income Support. They are often portrayed in the tabloid press as scroungers, with, for example, girls getting pregnant to obtain council houses. Yet fewer than three percent are teenagers, and single parents are usually offered smaller properties than two-parent families, with mother and child often required to share a bedroom.

The main disadvantages for children are parental absence, economic hardship and spousal conflict. Reports suggest that poor relationships with parents (whether in one-or two-parent families) leads to lower self-esteem; more young people from lower conflict homes enter tertiary education. Thus where stress is concerned, family life could have a more direct effect on health than either material factors or cultural influences.

The National Council for One Parent Families (NCOPF) works for the prosperity and independence of single parents and challenges negative stereotypes about their children. This organization was set up in 1918 as The National Council for the Unmarried Mother and Her Child, to rescue them from starvation on the streets. In 1970, the support group Gingerbread was established when social services would not help Raga Woods unless her family had nowhere to go. She named it after a café, The Golden House of Gingerbread, which had provided her with refreshments on the house.

Over 70 percent of divorces are initiated by women, and one-parent families may be regarded as one of the results of the women's liberation movement. The increasing number of single-parent families is a cause of much social anxiety.

See also: divorce law; marriage; social welfare

Further reading

Macaskill, H. (1993) *From the Workhouse to the Workplace*, London: NCOPF.

CAROLE BALDOCK

Sinn Féin

'Sinn Féin' (Gaelic for 'Ourselves Alone') was founded in 1905 in pre-independence Ireland by Arthur Griffith, as a revolutionary Irish nationalist movement. It was a small movement made up of enthusiasts of the 'Celtic Revival' (Irish language and cultural revivalists) and Irish nationalists committed to the violent overthrow of British rule in Ireland. However, it was not until the Easter Rising in 1916 that it gained popular support as the dominant political force of Irish nationalism.

In the Westminster parliamentary elections of 1918, Sinn Féin won the majority of Irish seats and refused to take them, opting instead to set up an independent Irish parliament (The Dáil). Following the Irish War of Independence (1921–2) and the partition of Ireland, Sinn Féin as the voice of revolutionary, violent Irish nationalism, became a minor party in Irish politics. However as a result of the eruption of the troubles in Northern Ireland in 1968, Sinn Féin became the political wing of the Provisional IRA, with the aim of achieving a united thirty-two-county Ireland by armed insurrection. The 'hunger strikes' by jailed IRA members of 1980–1 was a turning point in popular support for Sinn Féin when it succeeded in getting one of the hunger strikers, Bobby Sands, elected as an MP. After ten hunger strikers died, the nationalist community's distrust in and hostility towards the British government of Margaret Thatcher resulted in a rapid increase in support for Sinn Féin both North and South of the border. Throughout the 1980s, Sinn Féin/IRA adopted a 'ballot box and Armalite' strategy to advance their cause of Irish unity. While Sinn Féin deny it is linked to the IRA, this denial has never been convincing, and there is evidence that Sinn Féin representatives have been IRA members and sit on the latter's Army Council. Indeed, while its democratic mandate has increased in the past decade (in terms of electoral support), its inclusion in the peace process was premised on its link to the IRA and the latter's declaration of ceasefires in 1994 and 1996.

The 'political' turn to Sinn Féin strategy was further strengthened in 1986 when at its annual conference, it recognized the Irish parliament (Dáil) for the first time. This led to some members leaving and founding Republican Sinn Féin.

Support for Sinn Féin has increased in the past decade both in Northern Ireland and in the Republic of Ireland, and it continues to be the only major political party to organize on both sides of the border. In the 1997 Irish general election, Sinn Féin won its first seat, while in the 1997 British general election its two leading spokespersons, Gerry Adams and Martin McGuinness, were elected as MPs, though they refused to take their seats. As a result of the IRA ceasefires of 1994 and 1997, Sinn Féin has been closely involved in the 'peace process' and multi-party talks which led to the 'Good Friday Agreement' of 10 April 1998. In the recent elections to the new Northern Ireland Assembly in May 1998, Sinn Féin won 15 seats out of a total of 110, firmly establishing itself as the second nationalist party after the moderate SDLP (Social Democratic and Labour Party).

See also: Ireland; Irish communities; Ulster Unionists

Further reading

Coogan, T.P. (1980) *The IRA*, London: Fontana.
Patterson, H. (1989) *The Politics of Illusion: Republicanism and Socialism in Modern Ireland*, London: Hutchinson Radius.

JOHN BARRY

situation comedy

Situation comedies, or sitcoms, focus on a comic situation which is returned to by a small cast of actors in successive episodes. Much of the humour in these shows derives from character, and 'straight' actors appear in them more frequently than comedians. Although there have been notable exceptions, such as *On The Buses*, *Dad's Army*, *Yes, Minister* and its Whitehall location, or *Fawlty Towers* with its seaside hotel setting, a domestic environment has been the most common location for the sitcom since shows of the 1960s like *Steptoe and Son*. This characteristic has meant that sitcoms often feature more female characters than many other television genres, and indeed from the 1970s onwards numerous sitcoms have centred on women, including *The Liver Birds*, *Solo*, *Butterflies*,

Girls on Top, Birds of a Feather and, most recently, *Absolutely Fabulous*. Making humour out of the domestic scenarios of sitcoms has equally made them vehicles for 'unusual' domestic arrangements, in attempts to represent shifts in gender and family relations. *A Man About the House* and *The Good Life* were premised, respectively, on the 'swinging' and 'hippie' reputation of the 1970s. *Men Behaving Badly, Home to Roost* and *Fresh Fields* are more contemporary examples of this theme.

Poverty and class differences have been a common theme in sitcoms since the 1960s, in shows like *To the Manor Born, Porridge* and its sequel *Going Straight, Man About the House*'s spin-off *George and Mildred, Rab C. Nesbitt* and *Rising Damp*. In contrast, issues of race and ethnicity have rarely been explicitly a focus in British sitcom. *Desmond's* and its spin-off *Porkpie* starred black actors, as did *Love Thy Neighbour, The Fosters, Empire Road* and *Tandoori Nights* in the 1970s and 1980s. Famously, Alf Garnett's performance as a bigot in *'Til Death Do Us Part* was intended to parody racism but was open to misinterpretation.

Comedy drama was one hybrid of the sitcom, which emerged in Britain from the 1970s, which incorporated straight dramatic acting. One such series, about an idiosyncratic barrister, played by Leo McKern, was *Rumpole of the Bailey. Auf Wiedersehen, Pet* is a more recently broadcast example. The sitcom has also spawned parodies, notably *The Young Ones*, which inserted four 'alternative' comics into the domestic scenario of the sitcom using special effects and visual jokes, like the earlier show *The Goodies*. *Blackadder* might also be considered a programme that spoofs sitcom's conventional situation, since its characters return in various incarnations across the centuries to the same situations and relationships.

See also: comedy on television; radio comedy

Further reading

Crowther, B. and Pinfold, M. (1987) *Bring Me Laughter: Four Decades of Television Comedy*, London: Columbus.

Neale S. and Krutnik, F. (1990) *Popular Film and Television Comedy*, London: Routledge.

NICOLE MATTHEWS

ska

The first precursor of **reggae**, ska originated in Jamaica in the early 1960s. Its sound, which began as a development of American rhythm and blues, is characterized by a steady up-tempo rhythm, with strongly accented off beats. Repeated tuneful basslines and insistent, catchy brass parts are also important, and the main melody is often carried by an organ.

Ska quickly reached Britain, and its first peak of popularity came as early as 1964, with Millie's 'My Boy Lollipop' reaching number two in the charts. This record was seen as something of a novelty hit, however, and for the remainder of the 1960s, ska in Britain remained the preserve of the West Indian community. Many of the records at this time were instrumental, save for wordless vocalizations which added to the general rhythmic feel of the songs, but several of those which did contain lyrics formed an important sub-group: 'rude' songs, packed with sexual innuendo. A classic example of this subgenre was Lloydie and the Lowbites' 'Birth Control'. Songs such as this helped promote the concept of the 'rude boy', a macho young follower of the ska sound.

Around 1969–70, ska found a new audience amongst the urban, white working class in the form of **skinheads**, who embraced it as their music of choice. It seems likely that the macho image of the rude boys played a role in this adoption. Whatever the cause, however, the result was a resurgence in the popularity of ska, with artists such as the Upsetters and the Pioneers releasing singles that reached the charts, and Desmond Dekker's 'Israelites' became the first ska record to reach number one (although by this time the sound was growing less urgent, and the change to reggae was underway).

Ska was now recognized as more than a musical novelty, but with the growth of reggae it all but disappeared until a new generation of urban youth rediscovered the sound around 1979–80. This latest resurgence of ska proved to be its most successful to date. Groups such as the Specials, the Selecter and Madness reached levels of popularity which far outstripped that of the acts which had influenced them. Central to this revival was the Coventry-based record label **Two-Tone**. After this boom was over, ska once again took a back seat to **reggae** and **dub**, but its legacy as a groundbreaking force for West Indian music in Britain is assured.

SIMON BOTTOM

skinheads

The skinhead style is a direct descendant from the **mods** of the early 1960s. In the early 1960s the mod movement split in two ways. Some mods were attracted to the scene that became known as 'swinging London', and their dress became more outlandish and camp. Some of these mods also became involved in the **psychedelic rock** scene. Many working-class mods, known as 'hard mods', rejected what they saw as the effeminacy of the 'art-school' mods and became skinheads.

These skinheads dressed in an aggressive style based upon the clothing of the traditional British working man, namely jeans, checked shirts, boots and braces. The music favoured by this embryonic skinhead movement was **ska**, **reggae**, bluebeat and **soul**. Some skinheads developed a style of clothing that was based upon **Afro-Caribbean youth styles**, and wore sunglasses and wide brim hats.

Towards the end of the 1960s, skinheads began to develop a fearsome reputation for **violence**, and were dubbed 'bovver boys' or 'boot boys' by the media. This name was derived from the skinhead tendency to wear **Dr Martens** boots, particularly those boots that extended to just below the knee and had steel toecaps.

Skinheads were often fanatical **football** fans, and this often led to fights between skinhead gangs and rival football fans. This violence was seen to be the traditional manner of solving disagreements, and fitted into the skinheads' peculiarly conservative ethos, based around patriotism and masculinity. Skinheads were opposed to the hippie movement and to homosexuality, which often led to groups of skinheads going 'queer bashing' and attacking **hippies**, or any group perceived to be either an easy target or willing to fight.

As **punk rock** gathered steam, some skinheads became involved in this movement. Towards the end of the 1970s, in the wake of punk, skinheads developed their own music in the form of **oi**. By the 1980s, skinheads had grown so far from their mod origins that they perceived the mod revivalists of the time to be their enemies, and promptly attacked them. Running gang fights between skinheads and mods occurred during bank holidays at seaside resorts such as Hastings.

Although the skinhead movement has decreased in size since the early 1980s, it is still in existence today. The rivalry between skinheads and mod revivalists appears to have lessened, and skinheads are often seen at scooter rallies alongside mods. A rift has developed between those skinheads who are racist and have fascist sympathies, and non-racist skinheads. The latter are often known as SHARP skins; SHARP being an acronym for Skinheads Against Racial Prejudice. These skinheads emphasize the Caribbean roots of the skinhead movement. The majority of British skinheads are either anti-fascist or apolitical, with membership of SHARP far exceeding the membership and votes for right-wing groups. Some elements of the skinhead style have entered into the clothing vocabulary of British youth in general, in particular the Dr Martens boot and brogue shoe, the Fred Perry t-shirt, and the Ben Sherman shirt with buttoned-down collar.

STUART BORTHWICK

Sloane Rangers

A term invented by the style commentator Peter York to describe a set of upper middle-class women based in moneyed areas of London such as Sloane Square and who were daughters of colonels, admirals and gentleman farmers. Also described as the horsey set or the Headscarf Brigade, the typical Sloane Ranger could be recognized by her safe, scrubbed appearance, traditionalist attitudes and ritualistic behaviour, which were catalogued in *The Official Sloane Ranger Handbook* in 1982. Dressed in a Hermes headscarf and pearls, the typical Sloane Ranger supposedly worked at top auction houses, merchant banks or Bond Street galleries before entering into marriage, which was their real career. Princess Diana was seen as a successful example of the type.

See also: fashion (1980s)

CAROLINE COX

small ads

Shopping, in a mass culture, is sometimes perceived as the only means of restoring identity, because it involves making choices. Responding to, or better, placing an advertisement in a newspaper is a better form of 'individuation'. Such ads (for cars, household goods or services) and are performed 'parallel' to regular shopping transactions. There are numerous **freesheets** plus *Daltons Weekly*, *Loot* and *Exchange & Mart*, but small ads are also found in most newspapers. In 'lonely heart' ads (for example, as in *Private Eye*), advertisers target potential partners as 'tall, non-smoking, London based' or '20s playmate sought by 1950s professional man'; these tend to be more romantic than, and lack the specificity of, American abbreviations such as 'dwf' (divorced white female).

See also: car boot sales; mail order

MIKE STORRY

Smith, Maggie

b. 1934, Ilford

Actress

Maggie Smith is a film actress (though with a commitment to the theatre), who has offered a range of interesting performances in her diverse screen appearances. A supporting role in the star-studded *The VIPs* (1963) established her screen potential, and in 1969 Smith won the Best Actress Oscar for her forceful portrayal of the deluded girls' school teacher in *The Prime of Miss Jean Brodie*. Smith's distinctive balance of intensity and humour in her performances secured scene-stealing roles in her later movies such as *California Suite* (1978) – for which she won a further Oscar – and *Sister Act* (1992), as well as British films *A Private Function* (1984) and *A Room With a View* (1985). Her screen

work beyond comedy includes *The Lonely Passion of Judith Hearne* (1988) and *Richard III* (1995).

See also: actors (female)

ALICE E. SANGER

Smith, Paul

b. 1946

Fashion designer

Paul Smith made his name by revamping classic and traditional styles. He has a distinctive menswear fashion philosophy but no formal design training. Now with over 200 outlets for his R Newbold label in Japan alone, Smith opened his first shop in Nottingham in 1970 when he was unable to find the clothes he wanted on the current market. He mainly worked in wool, tweed and fine cottons, fashioning garments that appealed in the 1980s to both city gents and yuppies. He has been tirelessly copied by retailers such as Next, and he is responsible for reintroducing Filofaxes and boxer shorts in the **accessories** boom of the 1980s. In 1998, Smith launched his first women's wear collection at the **London Fashion Week**; like the men's suits, with which they have much in common, Smith's new clothes were again characterized by external confidence and hidden luxury.

PETER CHILDS

Smithson, Alison and Peter

The Smithsons opened an office in London in 1950, after graduating from the University of Durham. The significance of their contribution to postwar architecture resides both in their architecture and in their exposition of the theoretical principles of **new brutalism**. Both members of the Independent Group and of the radical Team X within CIAM, they were supported by the critic Reyner Banham and other members of the '20th Century Group' in London, in their united desire to convey the realities of modern urban life by means of a new art.

The years 1951–4 were crucial to the formulation of the sensibility of Brutalism, and the Smithsons followed their early success with a sequence of highly original competition entries which, as Banham remarked, can only be seen as attempts to invent a totally 'other' kind of architecture. The building which immediately associated with this movement was the Hunstanton School in Norfolk (1949–54), invoking the elegant steel-frame vocabulary of Mies van der Rohe and reflecting his honest use of materials and explicit display of structure. Their unbuilt design for a town house in Soho (1952) displays an oxymoronic confluence of utility and luxury. Their design for the Sugden House, Watford (1956) was described by Banham as being 'recognized by timid souls as a subtly subversive building', with its mixture of formality and basic utility. Their Golden Lane housing proposal for London (1952), a flatted development, drew on notions of identity and association which developed out of their first hand knowledge of Bethnal Green. 'Street decks' were designed to foster social exchange and somehow to invoke and nurture the traditional working-class domestic environment.

Other significant buildings by the Smithsons include the Economist Group of Buildings in London (1962), whose spatial composition can be located within the urban theories of 'Team X' and also drew from their competition entry for the Haupstadt district of Berlin. The design for St Hilda's College, Oxford (1970) differed dramatically in its social and physical context from Robin Hood Gardens housing estate in London (1972). In designing the estate in two serpentine rows with corridor streets above ground level, they posited an alternative to the slab block. By including two-storey dwellings, they remained faithful to their commitment to a modern equivalent of the East End environment.

See also: housing

Further reading

McKean, John M., 'The Smithsons: A Profile', *Building Design*, May 1977.

HILARY GRAINGER

soap operas

Soap operas were first developed by American detergent companies as radio promotional tools. Their lack of narrative closure and cliffhanger endings rewarded the sponsors with a devoted audience eager for the next (advertisement interspersed) instalment. The modern soap opera still maintains the original structure of varied conflicts and resolutions amidst an indefinitely ongoing whole. Its most successful examples balance escapist fantasy with identifiable everyday events timed at a rate that will maintain the interest of its viewers. Daytime soaps are traditionally cosier and slower in pace, while prime-time broadcasts are more action packed.

The first British soap, *The Robinsons*, appeared on the radio in 1942. It was devised for listeners of the **BBC**'s North American Service, but became popular with British audiences as well.

Britain's longest running soap opera, *The Archers*, has been broadcast on **Radio 4** since 1950. Its nearest television equivalent in longevity, *Coronation Street*, began in 1960. Unlike its grittier rivals *Brookside* and *EastEnders*, *Coronation Street* aims to be more light-hearted and amusing.

British soaps have centred on both working and middle-class people. Their locations vary from rural, urban and suburban environments of the north and south of England, Scotland (*Take the High Road*) and Wales (the Welsh language *Pobol y Cwm* (People of the Valley)).

In the 1970s and 1980s, glitzy American imports such as *Dallas* and *Dynasty* became popular in Britain. In comparison with their homely British counterparts, their storylines were distinctly more fantastical. Australian daytime soaps have also drawn large audiences, particularly *Neighbours* and *Home and Away*.

The habitual degradation of soaps, often provoked by cheap production values, hastily devised scripts, ill-rehearsed acting and lowly women's genre' status, frequently induces viewer guilt. Although soap's traditional targeting of housewives often entails a stereotypical melodramatic treatment, it also offers its women viewers an unqualified range of well-developed female characters.

Soap opera increasingly invites multitudinous

viewing practices. From intense involvement to detached mockery, its audience comes to regard its regularity as an enjoyable habit. Sustained contact can provide a comforting sense of intimacy and community that is not available from other programmes. Soap operas have become valued focal points for discussion and social interaction. By airing common (and normally considered private) problems, they encourage their viewers to voice their own opinions on these issues. The impact of soap characters' actions on those of viewers is also a recurrent issue in forums concerned with media ethics.

See also: daytime television; drama on television

Further reading

Kilborn, R. (1992) *Television Soaps*, London: B.T. Batsford.

KAY DICKINSON

social welfare

'Social welfare' is sometimes a synonym for **welfare state**, but here it is taken to refer to ideas about what the objectives of a welfare state are and by what mechanisms and processes they might best be achieved.

The principle of less eligibility, classically expressed in the Poor Law Report of 1834, has shaped all subsequent discussion and its shadow dogs contemporary social security provisions such as income support. The principle declared that relief to the indigent should be given in such a form that the recipient's condition was rendered 'less eligible' (i.e. less desirable) than that of the lowest-paid independent labourer. This principle could be implemented if relief was made subject to entry to a workhouse, with concomitant loss of freedom. The principle was not officially discarded until 1948, although it was enormously modified, even in the early practice of the 'new poor law' established in 1834. While the truly needy would receive assistance, the thrust of the principle was to give every incentive to being in work; thus, it was believed, benefiting the wealth and welfare of all.

Later, the voluntary body the Charity Organisa-

tion Society (COS) developed 'social work' to enhance an individual's efforts at independence in difficult times, forestalling resort to the poor law. The COS saw 'social welfare' as its distinctive province. This reflected the close ties with 'idealist' thinkers such as Helen and Bernard Bosanquet, who saw charity as a channel of social development, since personal charitable work enhanced the character of both giver and recipient. In their own attempts to meet urgent needs, voluntary organizations such as the **Salvation Army** were less concerned about questions of personal character. Social thinkers such as Herbert Spencer rejected any positive role for the state.

Both the poor law and the COS saw **poverty** and unemployment as caused by personal failing rather than circumstances beyond an individual's ability to control. Around 1900, evidence mounted that such circumstances were significant, particularly low pay at work. The poor law/COS view of how to achieve social welfare famously collided with the 'social causes' view of need in the Royal Commission on the Poor Laws: two Reports were issued in 1909, reflecting the disagreement. The Fabian socialists Beatrice and Sydney Webb, through Beatrice's membership of the Royal Commission, argued in the minority report for the abolition of the poor law as embodying an inappropriate understanding of social problems. Instead, the state should guarantee a 'national minimum' of civilized life in health and education through specialist services staffed by experts, with unemployment tackled nationally. Neither model won the day: Lloyd George, learning from Germany, introduced limited compulsory and contributory insurance schemes for health and unemployment (with state funding as well) as a *via media*, although a reduced poor law was retained.

Between the wars, the Webbs and others were influenced by **Marxism**, believing that capitalism was unstable and decaying, with social welfare only possible in a post-capitalist society. J.M. Keynes's economic analysis suggested a centrally planned economy was possible and desirable, with social welfare provision being a vital component.

In introducing the 'welfare state' in 1948, the government acknowledged that a market economy required the state to provide social welfare for all people on a comprehensive basis. R.M. Titmuss emerged as an influential analyst of social welfare in *Essays on 'the Welfare State'* (1958), *Commitment to Welfare* (1968) and *The Gift Relationship* (1971). Marrying idealism and socialism, he viewed social welfare as fostering equality, social integration and altruistic sentiments, but he criticized remaining selective or means-tested benefits as stigmatizing and inefficient in reaching those eligible; services without a test of means (universal services) were the ideal. Voluntary organizations and private providers had inappropriate 'social' objectives. Titmuss also argued that poverty and inequality were inadequately addressed by the welfare state, and that social welfare services needed integration with fiscal welfare (tax allowances) and occupational welfare (pensions from work).

In criticizing social welfare services, the work of John **Rawls** on social justice and the idea of **citizenship** and associated rights were explored (for example R.A. Pinker, *Social Theory and Social Policy*, 1971). Marxist criticisms too were voiced in the 1970s. However, interest in the voluntary sector's potential contribution also developed (the Wolfenden report of 1978); and less bureaucracy, and more decentralization and participation was urged (see R. Hadley and S. Hatch, *Social Welfare and the Failure of the State*, 1981). Populist, as opposed to socialist, meanings of social welfare were prominent in Pinker's *The Idea of Welfare* (1979). Informal 'social welfare', welfare provided by neighbours, friends and family, and its neglect by statutory and voluntary social welfare services, became major topics. Ideological glosses on such ideas contrary to 'orthodox' social welfare thinking came from the New Right, including the Social Affairs Unit, the Institute of Economic Affairs and Roger **Scruton**.

Social welfare has also been analysed from postmodernist and feminist viewpoints (see Gillian Pascall, *Social Policy: A New Feminist Analysis*, 1997). New demands on social welfare services include tackling **domestic violence**, **drug culture**, **single parents** and issues raised by **environmentalism**.

Conservative governments since 1979 have been sceptical as to the role played by 'social causes' or the **class system** in explaining poverty and illness. Personal responsibility has been emphasized once again, and 'workfare' in America

has been influential. Popular support for social welfare services meant they were transformed, not dismantled. Consumerism has to an extent been encouraged in schools and in reform of the **NHS** and social care which, in reducing the direct responsibilities of government and dividing the purchasing and providing roles, has reduced the power of professionals. Diversity in the NHS may have helped, for example, **aromatherapy** and alternative medicine generally. The achievements of **Thatcherism** in social welfare are to have rehabilitated private markets and the voluntary sector as providers (particularly in social care) and elevated consumer choice over social engineering as an objective, at least in principle.

Further reading

George, V. and Wilding, P. (1993) *Ideology and Social Welfare*, Hemel Hempstead: Harvester Wheatsheaf.

McCarthy, M. (ed.) (1989) *The New Politics of Welfare*, London: Macmillan.

JOHN OFFER

sociology

Sociology sets out to 'describe, understand and explain' (Abercrombie *et al.* 1986) the social world that we inhabit. Far from being a 'new' discipline, it has its roots in the early nineteenth century, with Auguste Comte (1798–1857) first coining the phrase in 1824. By the 1880s, Émile Durkheim (1858–1917) was teaching courses in sociology at the University of Bordeaux; in Germany, Ferdinand Tonnies (1855–1936) was writing *Gemeinschaft und Gesellschaft* (1889) and Max Weber (1864–1920) was moving towards a historical sociology and a comparative analysis of capitalist societies. A serious attempt was being made by sociologists such as Weber, Durkheim, Georg Simmel (1858–1918) and Herbert Spencer (1820–1895) to establish the parameters and concerns of sociology, as wide as social reality itself.

European sociology owes in part its theoretical heritage to the philosophy of Hegel and the work of Karl Marx. **Marxism** has informed a great deal of sociological theory and debate, focusing its perspective on the form and nature of capitalist society, the relations of work and production, and the structure and nature of class and power. In turn, post-Marxist sociology, best characterized by The Frankfurt School (1923–50) and the works of Max Horkheimer, Theodor Adorno (1903–69) Herbert Marcuse (1898–1979) and Georg Lukacs (1885–1971) has provided a valuable critique of Marxist theory in the twentieth century. The postwar period has seen a renewed interest in the work of European philosophers, such as Nietszche, Heidegger and Foucault, sparking a debate within contemporary sociology about the future direction and nature of the discipline, whether towards a more empirical, scientific base or a continuing expansion of the theoretical/ideological tradition (see **philosophy**). Ultimately, the status of sociology as an independent practice in its own right has come into question.

By way of contrast, in the 1950s, sociology in America was dominated by the positivism of Talcott Parsons (1902–79), a functionalist view of society which aimed at a synthesis of individual action and the larger social structures. This was essentially a conservative movement which dissolved the analysis of power and conflict that had characterized sociological theory so far, and gave rise in reaction to a resurgence of 'conflict theory', especially in Britain, in the 1960s and 1970s.

During the 1960s, sociology became firmly established within British **universities**, but has continually come under attack for alleged political leanings (generally to the left), and a failure to separate itself from philosophy or economics and establish a unified approach. On the contrary, the nature of sociology itself denies such an approach, and holds within its boundaries contrasting and competing views and theoretical standpoints. Contemporary debates have centred on issues of ideology, class and power, race and ethnicity, and gender; beginning from a largely structuralist standpoint, with analyses of the larger social structures such as the state and systems of dominance and the public and private institutions of education and family. This is epitomized by the works of such prominent British sociologists as A.H. Halsey (b. 1923) and Anthony Giddens (b. 1938).

The re-emergence of the women's liberation movement in the 1970s brought a whole new area of critique to sociology (although Friedrich Engel's *The Origin of the Family* (1884) had gone some way to addressing the oppressive nature of women's position in society). The tools established for looking at and understanding the nature of power and the structures of human interaction proved valuable to early second-wave feminist attempts at creating a theoretical and historical picture of patriarchy and male dominance. The subjective, everyday experience of women came under scrutiny with such works as Ann Oakley's *The Sociology of Housework* (1974), and *Subject Women* (1981) exploring the nature and details of women's lives within a theorised framework of patriarchy. There have developed three main branches of feminist sociological thought: radical feminism, more recently influenced by the arguably 'essentialist' French feminism of Helene Cixous and Luce Irigaray, which seeks to reclaim the body and name of woman and establish a woman-centred society with the radical overthrow of patriarchy; Marxist feminism, which, as the name suggests, aligns itself with Marxist and post-Marxist critiques, viewing women's oppression as essentially based in the exploitative class nature of society and the means and relations of production; and liberal feminism, grounded in the ideas of equal opportunities and legislative reform.

Most recently, some branches of sociology have shifted into debates around postmodernism (see **postmodernist theory**); indeed, some sociologists argue that sociology has been heralding the postmodern era since the works of Georg Simmel and his conceptualization of the fragmented self within the fragmented society. The decline of industrialism and the encroachment of the post-industrial society has been mapped since the 1960s (for example, D. Bell, *The Coming of Post-Industrial Society*, 1974). Postmodernism has attempted to formulate a poststructuralist idea (see **post-structuralism**) of a society no longer bound by the 'grand ideologies' such as Marxism or Christianity, but a populist cultural free-for-all where anything goes and no one system of thought holds sway. Sociology has responded by, on the one hand, claiming its inherently postmodernist nature, its endemic plurality of content and viewpoint, and, on the other, restating the importance of an understanding of the structures of our society that continue, increasingly, to inform and control our lives. Feminist sociologists have become particularly influenced by postmodern theories, finding renewed impetus in the seeming vastness of cultural and personal/political space it has created, bringing to the forefront of contemporary debate the issues around sexuality, the body, individual identity and the shifting perplexities of power relations.

Sociology, therefore, continues to redress the balance of its own agenda, responding to both economic and cultural pressures, and tensions from within its ranks to questions about its nature and future. Sociology is most often criticized for being contradictory and conflictual. However, the discipline aims to remain diverse and fluid, providing a critical vehicle for the observation and understanding of the society in which we live.

See also: media and cultural studies

Further reading

Abercrombie, N., Hill, S. and Turner, B. (1984) *Dictionary of Sociology*, London: Penguin.

Giddens, A. (1982) *Sociology: A Brief But Critical Introduction*, London: Macmillan.

SARAH CORBETT

Soho

The Soho district in the **West End** of London occupies an almost mythological position in the capital's geography. Most widely renowned today as the heart of London's sex industry, it is also embedded in the showbusiness hub of the city, carries connotations of bohemia, has a thriving lesbian and gay scene, is ethnically diverse, and is home to much of Britain's media, advertising and PR business. By the nineteenth century, Soho had developed a unique reputation within London as avant-garde, chic, cosmopolitan and multicultural, and this reputation remains in its iconography. With its slick offices, artists' and actors' drinking dens, ethnic restaurants, strip clubs and plush gay bars, Soho remains one of the most distinctive areas of London.

See also: pornography; restaurants and bars; top-shelf magazines

DAVID BELL

Solar School, Wallasey

The architect Elmslie Morgan used direct gain passive solar heating in this building in 1961. The entire southern facade is double glazed to collect the solar energy falling upon it. Thick concrete floors store the heat, good insulation reduces the rate of heat loss, and solar control blinds prevent overheating. It was the first school in the United Kingdom to be solar heated. When energy costs escalated, its fuel bills were just half those of similar conventionally heated schools. Its ideology stimulated the later more widespread construction of low energy-consuming buildings having a minimum environmental impact.

See also: environmentalism

ROY WORMALD

soul

Although soul music has played an important role in British popular culture since the 1960s, its impetus has always come mainly from America. Its contribution has been as a sound which has influenced British music, despite rarely being produced in this country.

Early soul music developed as a combination of rhythm and blues, gospel and popular ballads. Its sound was made for dancing, with strong emphasis placed on the rhythmical elements of the music. By the early 1960s it was beginning to be heard in Britain, with bands such as the Rolling Stones drawing heavily on the soul sound on their early records.

In the years that followed, soul came to be dominated by the 'Motown sound', strongly melodic songs, often written to a formula, with performers having little or no artistic control. One offshoot of this sound was **Northern Soul**, a particularly frenetic form of soul which became popular in the north of England.

In the late 1960s and early 1970s, a political element developed in soul music with songs beginning to comment on issues such as racial inequality and **poverty**. At around the same time, **funk** grew out of the soul sound. Over the next few years the sound of soul changed dramatically, with songs becoming slower, more in a ballad style, and lush orchestration being introduced, particularly in the style known as Philly (or Philadelphia) soul. Throughout the remainder of the 1970s and the 1980s soul became more and more commercial, becoming typified by slick production values and precise instrumentation which robbed the music of much of its emotional appeal, although its popularity remained unaffected.

In the 1990s, however, soul has been influenced by **hip hop** (which had, in turn, drawn much of its sound from earlier soul), and the resulting style, know as swingbeat (or simply swing) has brought some passion back to the music. Swing is characterized by fairly stripped down instrumentation, strong melodies (often sung in close harmony) and a seemingly endless lyrical interest in sex.

Soul music has influenced many different styles of popular music in Britain, from the bluesey soul of bands such as the Spencer Davis Group in the 1960s through to the pop soul of artists like Gabrielle and Eternal in the 1990s, and has proved itself to be a lasting and versatile musical force.

See also: blues; reggae

SIMON BOTTOM

SOUTH BANK *see* Martin, Leslie; Denys Lasdun and Partners

special interest magazines

A visit to any large newsagent's in Britain (such as W.H. Smith or John Menzies) will show the amount of material available for Britain's voracious reading public. The following magazines (with their circulations) give an indication of the range of interests of the population at large: *Yachting Monthly* (32,306); *Practical Woodworking* (22,729); *BBC Garden-er's World* (314,759); *What Hi Fi?* (64,460); *Motorcycle News* (135,031); *Autocar* (73,921); *Practical Photography* (64,680); *Horse and Hound* (68,738); *Golf Monthly* (72,629); *The Face* (71,007); and *TV and Satellite Week* (184,750). These magazines are usually arrayed along a single wall and displayed under headings such as DIY, Gardening, Health, Home Computing, Photography, Sport, Pop Music, Television and Satellite and so on. The profusion and variety are persuasive; people stand and browse before purchase.

Special interest magazines may be divided into those which are for a targeted range of trades or professions (*Accountancy Age*, *Campaign*, *The Grocer*), those under the classification of general interest but which are mainly for the professional classes (*The Economist*, *Spectator*, *Investor's Chronicle*, *Newsweek*, *Time*), and the rest which are specialized in terms of their sport or leisure interest (*Shoot*, *Golf Monthly*, *PC Review*).

Because they are essential reading for practitioners in their fields, many trade and professional magazines tend to be expensive and are taken on subscription by, for example, architectural or law practices. News reports on television and radio are occasionally abstracted from journals such as *Nature* or the *Lancet*, but by and large this group of magazines is not read outside its narrow milieu, although the cult television programme *Have I Got News For You* spoofs this type of magazine, by reading it out of context.

General interest magazines are used by busy professionals to replace rather than supplement television and radio news. Their content is topical, and they are designed to supply in shorthand form an informed briefing on current affairs, politics and business.

The third category above contains the magazines read with most enthusiasm. Statistics on job satisfaction in Britain show a disgruntled workforce, who get along by focusing on their interests outside work. They fantasize about fishing or model railways, and these magazines supply them with a means of both following their hobby, and escaping from their work.

See also: newsstands and newsagents; top-shelf magazines

Further reading

McCracken, E. (1993) *Decoding Women's Magazines: From Mademoiselle to Ms*, London: Macmillan.

Ohmann, R. (1996) *Selling Culture: Magazines, Markets, and Class at the Turn of the Century*, London: Verso.

MIKE STORRY

Spence, Basil

b. 1907, Bombay (India)

Sir Basil Spence studied architecture in Edinburgh and London, working under Edward Lutyens and Rowland Anderson, before forming a partnership with Partner and Kinnenmouth in Edinburgh. Moving to London, Sir Basil Spence and Partners established their reputation with the Sea and Ships Pavilion at the Festival of Britain in 1951. Best known for the controversial rebuilding of Coventry Cathedral (1954–62), won in competition in 1950, his subsequent highly successful practice centred around **housing** and university buildings, including Edinburgh, Southampton, Nottingham, Liverpool and Sussex. His later work, such as the British Embassy in Rome (1971), the Knightsbridge Barracks (1970) and government offices in Petty France, London, all modern and employing concrete, always resonated monumentality.

See also: university building

HILARY GRAINGER

spiritual leaders

In a secular age, the role of spiritual leaders has changed and adapted to meet the needs of an increasingly individualistic society. In the 1890s, Freud remarked that the only thing one could be sure of about the next century is that one would die in it. The end of a century has traditionally brought with it a dread of Armageddon; perhaps the approaching end of a millennium spawned such cults as those led by Jim Jones, who persuaded 900 people to commit collective suicide at the People's Temple in Guyana. Freud's remark was also pre-empted by 86 people, including British citizens, when they followed their leader David Koresh to Waco, Texas and death by fire in 1993. In Britain, the Korean Sun Myung Moon found a willing congregation for his **Unification Church** in British youth.

The authority of leaders of the traditional religious institutions of the country was increasingly eroded by a general disenchantment with establishment figures. The Nobel Laureate Mother Theresa of Calcutta became a spiritual icon, but her position was put in doubt when she was dubbed 'Hell's Angel' by a television documentary which questioned her association with dictators. During the 1990s, Roman Catholic clergy fell from grace as news of their sexual indiscretions appeared in the press. The Church of England alienated sections of society with its stance on homosexuality and the opposition of a number of its leaders to the ordination of women. Evangelical Christianity found favour with many people; hundreds flocked to hear preachers such as Billy Graham speak.

'New age' mysticism brought with it spiritual leaders from other cultures and disciplines with its fusion of spirituality and personal growth. Perhaps the New Age godfather was the psychologist C.G. Jung. His teachings appealed to the society of the 1960s, for whom the pursuit of religious experience had become fashionable. His use of the mandala image, used in Eastern meditation techniques, found a popular appeal amongst a population becoming familiar with gurus such as the Maharishi Mahesh Yogi. It was the mix of Western psychology and Eastern mysticism which brought to prominence the Indian mystic Osho Rajneesh, with centres devoted to his teachings established in most countries. The universally respected leader of Tibetan **Buddhism**, the Dalai Lama, also acquired a large following amongst a wide section of British society. It seems today that East has overtaken West in spiritual leadership.

See also: evangelism

JAN EVANS

sport, racism in

Sport in Britain has long suffered from racism, and despite progress over the last few decades, it remains tainted by the problem in the 1990s. The most obvious racism has appeared in football, partly as it is the sport most covered by the media. Apart from the casual abuse, football has also been targeted by hard-core fascist groups, such as the **National Front** and Combat-18. The history of football in the 1970s and 1980s is littered with spectator abuse of players and other fans in this fashion. Players were abused on the pitch by opponents and even by team-mates.

Black supporters were obviously put off attending football matches by such behaviour, but in the 1990s research has shifted from the Afro-Caribbean population to Asian fans, who are clearly interested in football but very rarely attend matches. The Criminal Justice Act of 1996 (though poorly framed) offers some protection from racist chanting, and anti-racist campaigns by sports fans are spreading rapidly across **football**.

Other sports have suffered too; **rugby league** and **cricket** have seen spectator abuse of minority players and confrontations between sets of fans. Test matches between England, India and Pakistan have seen fans squaring up to each other for this reason. Even in the mid-1990s it remained possible for a journalist to publicly question black players' loyalty to the England test cricket team, on the basis of their background.

Racism also operates institutionally: black people might successfully perform in most sports, but they have yet to take the next step and become administrators and managers. There have been very few black Football League managers, and virtually no black administrators; some club chairmen still hold highly suspect views. For British Asians there is the bigger problem of becoming competitors at all. Too many coaches in a number of sports hold racist assumptions: research by Jas Bains in 1996 found that many football officials thought Asian players' religion and language would cause problems, and many felt the Asian physique was not strong enough for the game. The first Asian rugby league player to play for England, Ikram Butt, noted how such assumptions were simply wrong and how they made later success all the sweeter.

The situation is improving, and when a head-bandaged Paul Ince defiantly led the English football team to victory in the run-up to the 1998 World Cup finals, he became an icon of Englishness. However, much work remains to be done and many people are still unconvinced that a minority background is no impediment to a successful sporting career.

See also: black sportsmen and women

Further reading

Jamie, G. (1991) *Sport, Racism and Ethnicity*, London: Falmer.

SAM JOHNSTONE

sport on television

From slow beginnings in the 1950s, sport has become crucial to all television stations, costs millions of pounds and can attract huge ratings. The 1950s saw the **BBC** establish a format for sport that has endured. Wednesday evenings, Saturday afternoons and evenings became the norm, with programmes like *TV Sport Magazine* (later *Sportsnight*) and *Sports Special* aimed at the dedicated fan (assumed to be male). The flagship, *Grandstand*, began in 1958 and covered a range of sports linked by a personality presenter. Once ITV came into existence, it responded with *World of Sport*, but it often suffered both from having to show more minority sports and from comparisons with the BBC.

By the 1970s and 1980s the competition for rights was becoming increasingly fraught, with accusations of bad faith in 1978 over the sale of rights to league **football** for instance, while the economic pressures on the BBC saw commercial television snap up numerous events. Increasingly, however, the significance of television to a number of sports could be seen, particularly in tournaments invented solely for coverage, such as the football Screen Sport Cup, and new tournaments in **athletics**, **tennis** and many smaller sports. The 1990s saw the rise of **BSkyB** and the globalization of television sport, with **Channel 4** showing Italian football, Gaelic football, kabbadi, sumo, gridiron and Australian rules football.

Television sport portrays itself as apolitical, but many theorists have shown how politicized it actually is. The vast majority is male sport; women rarely get shown, and when they do, the coverage reinforces concepts of femininity and elegance, while women spectators are usually categorized as casual viewers more interested in the personalities than the game. Football, rugby and cricket coverage has also been shown to pander to dubious concepts of racial and national identity. Equally, when it suits the national interest, broadcasters forget that they are apolitical, as at the 1980 Moscow Olympics. Usually, overtly political messages are ignored, as when black footballer Paul Ince was racially abused by West Ham fans in 1995. BBC commentary on the game simply redefined this as abuse towards an ex-player.

Sports authorities have recognized that millions of pounds are available from television coverage, directly and indirectly, so getting coverage has become the top priority, while television concedes sport is the best way of securing ratings.

See also: sport, racism in; women in sport

Further reading

Whannel, G. (1992) *Fields in Vision*, London: Routledge.

SAM JOHNSTONE

sports stadia

The design and location of sports stadia has been an active political, sporting and planning issue in Britain since the late 1980s, since when the landscape of stadia has changed beyond all recognition. The catalyst was the Hillsborough disaster of April 1989, in which ninety-six Liverpool **football** fans died. Following Lord Justice Taylor's Reports into Hillsborough in 1990, the government banned terraces at football in the top two English divisions, starting a process of redevelopment that continues today across a range of sports. Many football grounds have been completely redesigned, with Blackburn Rovers rebuilding all four sides of Ewood Park, Manchester United making Old Trafford a 55,000 all-seater venue and Liverpool demolishing their world famous Kop terrace. Other clubs relocated rather than redevelop existing facilities, like Northampton Town, Middlesbrough, Millwall, and Huddersfield, while Newcastle, Sunderland, Bolton and Southampton all intend moving before the year 2000.

These events also highlighted the state of the 'national stadium', Wembley. Used for football, rugby league and pop concerts, it has long needed substantial work, and this coincided with the plan to build another national stadium. Financed by the **National Lottery** and supervised by the Sports Council, this new venue will host both domestic sports and international events (bids for the Olympics, World Cup or Commonwealth Games need new facilities to stand any chance of success). Manchester was expected to get the vote over Wembley (Birmingham, Bradford and Sheffield also bid), but Wembley ultimately won the backing of the Football Association and so is almost sure to win, after announcing reconstruction plans costing £120m. This involves turning the stadium round, installing undulating seats (to create 'Mexican waves' without spectators having to stand up), placing video screens on the armrests of most of the seats, and building retractable seats over the track to give both football and athletics fans a better view.

Football has seen most of this redevelopment, but cricket and rugby have been affected too. Hampshire County Cricket Club will move to a new site around 2000, and Lord's, home of English cricket, recently built an impressive new structure, the Mound Stand. The most successful British **rugby league** side, Wigan, hope to share a site with local football club Wigan Athletic, while new stadia are planned by a number of rugby union clubs near London.

The idea of sharing is also increasingly common, though not as Taylor envisaged: he wanted rival clubs to start sharing a new site, but that has not happened. Instead, sharing a stadium between sports became a cheap alternative to building a new ground: Wasps rugby club was bought by the owner of QPR football club in 1996 and now share

QPR's ground, while Huddersfield's award-winning Kirklees stadium also features rugby league (and hosts pop concerts to pay for itself). Both football and **rugby union** are played at Bristol rugby club and at Cardiff Arms Park, while Murrayfield in Edinburgh is used for rugby union and American football.

There was never much chance of local rivals sharing a ground, since each stadium carries too much emotional importance for fans: the directors of Liverpool might have been happy to discuss sharing a proposed £50m ground near Aintree with local rivals Everton, but the two sets of fans opposed the plan. This hostility often also extended to the concept of all-seater stadia, which has caused higher prices and a loss of atmosphere at football matches.

While most commentators praise the new stadia, there has of course been a price to pay: redevelopment at football alone has cost around £500m, and the need to rebuild stadia jeopardized the existence of some clubs. The future of Brighton football club, for one, will hang in the balance until they can get permission for a new ground, which appears some way off (the issue led to Brighton fans invading the pitch during home games in 1996). Inevitably, obtaining planning permission has proved hard, since clubs often wanted to move to green belt sites. Financial and planning help from local authorities has been slow in coming, and has been ultimately limited in most cases.

British stadia are now seen as amongst the safest in Europe; to host world and European competitions regularly, new facilities were required, and it is even thought that the improved stadia in British sport in the 1990s are helping attract more female and black people to grounds. Certainly the concrete fenced boxes common from the 1960s to the 1980s needed redesign: in those decades, the political and public emphasis was on controlling the fans, with the **police**, the State, the football authorities and the clubs locked into a mindset that saw all supporters as hooligans. This led to the construction of the perimeter fences and pens in the mid-1960s that proved so lethal at Hillsborough. Most clubs were not very interested in providing safe facilities, and standards were often neglected. The 1985 Bradford disaster showed how failures to address basic safety issues could prove

fatal, when uncleared litter beneath a wooden stand was accidentally set alight, causing an inferno that killed fifty-six people.

But whether all the changes that followed Taylor were actually necessary is debatable, and the report has clearly been used by many clubs to charge more for admission, increasingly affecting who can afford to attend sports and how regularly. Certainly much of the old individuality of stadia has gone, replaced by uniform and unimaginative designs (with notable exceptions, like Huddersfield). Some of the cultural aspects of all-seater stadia are undoubtedly negative, with much of the interaction between fans and their sports increasingly lost, and the element of participation reduced. Nonetheless, stadia remain a significant issue in British sport, and the changes are not over yet, for better or worse.

Further reading

Inglis, S. (1996) *The Football Grounds of Britain*, London: CollinsWillow.

Taylor, Lord Justice (1990) *Final Report into the Hillsborough Stadium Disaster 15th April 1989*, London: HMSO.

REX NASH

sportswear

An interesting commercial phenomenon of recent years is the way in which clothing apparel has copied sportswear. Hitherto, the wearing of tracksuits or jogging suits was confined to those practising sports. However partly because of the higher profile accorded to athletes and sports people via television, consumers began themselves to buy sports clothes for leisure wear. Research and investment by shoe companies, particularly Nike and Adidas, undoubtedly improved the quality of athletes' footwear and introduced the running shoe or 'trainer'. The companies used various new materials and technology to, for example, correct pronation and supination and to protect joints. They also pruned their production costs by building factories in Asia and spent fortunes on sponsorship and advertising. As these shoes were both lightweight and comfortable, they became popular with consumers in general. This has meant that the sale of conventional leather shoes has declined, as that of sports shoes has risen.

Sports clothing tends to be bought more by young males (47.8 percent); however, 27.9 percent of all adults bought trainers and 17.7 percent bought track suits in 1994. Even in the age group 55–64, 14.1 percent bought tracksuits (cloned briefly as 'shell suits'). A feature of Britain's supermarkets is the number of overweight people in trainers and jogging suits pushing shopping trolleys around the store as quickly as they can so they can get outside for a cigarette.

Formerly British clothes were discreet in terms of colours and attribution (a small label inside the collar at the rear). Clothes with logos displayed on the breast pocket of, shirts and pullovers then became popular. These included those of Fred Perry (**tennis**), Pringle (**golf**), Ron Hill (running). A striking feature of the high street now is that much of the clothing that people wear is bright and has got large writing on it. That applies to general designer-wear such as Tommy Hilfiger or Helly Hansen, but this trend has come from sportswear where purchasers are practically walking advertising hoardings for: Nike, Umbro, Adidas, Asics, Fila and so on. The baseball cap is also becoming as universal in Britain as it is in the USA, though the influence here is partly sport, partly homage to America.

See also: fashions, youth; military clothing; rap

Further reading

Hebdidge, D. (1979) *Subculture: The Meaning of Style*, London: Routledge (seminal text about the signification of clothes and youth cultural practices).

MIKE STORRY

sprinters

Sprinting – from 100 to 400 metres – is a chequered section of British **athletics**. Lack of money for training and facilities in Britain is contrasted with the USA, where there are specialist

programmes in Los Angeles and other locations. However, between 1987 and 1993 British sprinting did very well.

During these years Britain's 100 metre hopes were pinned on Linford Christie. He won silver medals at the 1988 Olympics, gold at the 1992 Olympics; and, in 1993, he won the world championship. His British 100 metre record of 9.87 seconds (at Stuttgart in 1993) is only just outside the world record held by Donovan Bailey of Canada. Christie captained the British Athletics team from 1992 onwards and led the team to gain twenty-three major championship medals. Disqualification at the Atlanta Olympics and withdrawal from the World Championships in Gothenburg (1996) with a hamstring injury marked his decline.

Among the best known women sprinters is Sally Gunnell. She won the 100 metres at Zurich in 1988 with a time of 12.82, and the 400 metre hurdles at Stuttgart in 1993 in a time of 52.74. She won a gold medal in the 1992 Barcelona Olympic Games. Both Linford Christie and Sally Gunnell announced their retirements at the 1997 Athens Olympics and in June 1998, having both previously been awarded MBEs, they were also awarded OBEs for their services to athletics. It is generally felt that they represent a 'golden age' of sprinting which will be very hard to recreate.

Some, including Malcolm Arnold, Britain's chief coach, insist that things will not improve until the arrival of the £2.6m (of the £4.3m bid for) promised through the **National Lottery** to set up a national coaching and athletes' services scheme. However there are some optimistic straws in the wind. Through the ex-hurdler and multi-millionaire Alan Pascoe, Nivea in 1998 offered £100,000 annual sponsorship for three years. This covers a series of three races for 100 metres runners (the British Sprint Challenge). It takes place at Bedford, Gateshead and Sheffield. The final carries £25,000 in prize money, including £10,000 for the winner.

There are also hopes for the future in the performances of, among others, heptathlon athlete Denise Lewis, Allison Curbishley and Dwain Chambers, who holds the world 100 metres junior record. Roger Black, Mark Richardson, Jamie Baulch and Iwan Thomas formed the relay quartet who won silver medals behind the Americans at the world championships, although Black has since retired.

See also: long-distance runners; marathons; middle-distance runners

MIKE STORRY

Stirling, James

b. 1926, Glasgow; d. 1992, London

Architect

James Stirling, internationally recognized and awarded many design commissions abroad, was arguably the leading British architect of his generation. Born in Glasgow, he moved with his family to Liverpool at an early age. After serving in the army during the Second World War, he studied architecture at Liverpool University.

On graduation, he worked in the office of Lyons, Israel and Ellis, Architects in London, from 1953–56. In 1956 Stirling teamed up with James Gowan to form the Stirling & Gowan Partnership. Notable early buildings were blocks of flats at Ham Common and various small-scale housing projects. The reputation of the practice was established with the design of the Leicester University Engineering Building (1959–63). This building utilized an uncompromising industrial aesthetic, with the various functions of the programme split up and separately expressed.

During these years, Stirling evolved a style heavily indebted to Le Corbusier, but incorporating elements inspired by the northern industrial aesthetic of the nineteenth century. The Stirling Gowan Partnership was dissolved in 1963. In 1971, Stirling took into partnership Michael Wilford, a former assistant, and the practice continued under the title of James Stirling, Michael Wilford and Associates.

Stirling's work first attracted controversy with his design for the History Faculty, Cambridge, 1967. The building's users were soon complaining about roof leaks and excessive solar heat gain through the dramatically 'cascading' glass roof. In 1977, Stirling designed the Staatsgalerie and Workshop Theatre in Stuttgart, possibly his best-known work. This building, in an urban setting, shows the full range of Stirling's ability to re-invent a traditional building type, melding a collection of eclectic elements into a harmonious whole. Stirling's 'Turner Museum' extension to the Tate Gallery, London in 1980 continues the playful eclectic approach to composition, subtly complementing the existing Gallery and its surroundings (see **Tate(s)**).

Stirling's work attracted further controversy with his design for low-cost housing at Southgate, Runcorn New Town (1967–77). Houses were grouped to form blocks around landscaped open spaces, emulating the scale of the English Georgian square. The project was greatly admired in the architectural press, but the tenants were not so happy. Unfortunately, the combination of deck access planning and low-income families with social problems led to insoluble management problems. The scheme was eventually demolished and replaced by more conventional low-rise housing, as preferred by the tenants.

Stirling's later work was marked by the incorporation of robust forms and shapes derived from traditional building. His work was thereby rendered more accessible to the lay public. In 1980, Stirling was awarded the **RIBA**'s Royal Gold Medal for Architecture, and in 1981 he received the Pritzker Architecture Prize. He was also knighted for his services to architecture.

See also: modernism; new brutalism; Smithson, Alison and Peter

Further reading

Arnell, P. and Bickford, E. (1993) *James Stirling: Buildings and Projects*, London: Rizzoli International Publications (Whitaker UK).

JIM HUNTER

St Ives

When the Tate Gallery opened in St Ives, Cornwall, in 1993, it focused attention on the important role that the area had played in the development of modern art in Britain during the twentieth century, as well as renewing interest in the artistic community which still flourishes there. The architects

Eldred Evans and David Shalev were the winners of a nationwide competition to design the new gallery, which is situated on the site of the old gas works, and the cylindrical loggia at the entrance of the building recalls the shape of the gas holder which once stood in its place. This is juxtaposed with the rectangular form which comprises the main body of the gallery, and is reminiscent of other, earlier buildings which existed in the Porthmeor area. The building, while being in a modernist style, manages to suggest a sense of continuity with the location and its past, something which can also be said of the art which helped to establish the area's reputation.

Evans and Shalev wanted the progression through the interior of the building to reflect something of the experience of visiting the town itself. The various gallery spaces, and the way in which natural light is used within them, is reminiscent of a walk around St Ives, particularly the Downalong area in which the building is situated, with its small, narrow back streets which open unexpectedly into larger, brighter areas, with a glimpse of the sea never far away. Many of the artists whose work is displayed in the Tate lived and worked in the immediate area; Ben **Nicholson**, for example, had a studio in close proximity to where the gallery now stands, and the gallery's roof is clearly visible from the cottage which was once occupied by Alfred Wallis. The paintings and sculptures which are exhibited can be seen in direct relation to the environment in which they were executed. This is particularly apparent in the upper and lower terraces of Gallery Two, where there is an impressive view on to Porthmeor Beach through a large, concave window which runs along the length of the gallery. The works which are displayed here can be appreciated in direct relation to the natural landscape which inspired them, while the high quality of light which attracted artists to the West coast of Cornwall is used as natural lighting for the exhibits.

Changing its displays annually, the gallery shows the work of those artists who helped to establish St Ives as a place of international, artistic importance. While artists had been drawn to the area, and nearby Newlyn, during the nineteenth century, and a St Ives Art Club had been established in 1888, it was the discovery of Alfred Wallis by Ben Nicholson and Christopher Wood in 1928, which had far-reaching effects on the direction that abstract art took in Britain. Impressed by Wallis's naive renditions of the town as he perceived it, the artists felt that this retired sailor had captured much in his 'crude' style that they were also striving for, namely a sense of artistic simplicity which was formed by personal experience and freed from the adherence to accepted pictorial devices, such as perspective. However, it was not until the start of the Second World War in 1939 that Nicholson, along with his second wife Barbara **Hepworth**, and the Russian artist, Naum Gabo, moved to the area from London. Nicholson's paintings, and Hepworth's sculptures showed their interest in abstract forms which were derived from the local landscape.

In 1948, the Penwith Society of Artists was formed in opposition to the more traditional work which was being exhibited by the St Ives Society of Artists. Members included Peter Lanyon, Wilhelmina Barns-Graham and Bryan Wynter alongside the influential figures of Nicholson and Hepworth. It is the work of these artists, and that of others including Terry Frost, Denis Mitchell and John Wells, that the Tate gallery in St Ives features in its exhibition programme. Patrick Heron, one of the original members of the Penwith Society, also designed one of the building's main features, a large, abstract stained glass window, which illustrates his interest in colour and light. The work of the potter Bernard Leach, who settled in the area in the 1920s, is also well represented in the gallery.

While the Tate provides something of a focal point for art produced in, or inspired by, the coastline of west Cornwall, other artistic activities which take place outside of the gallery form an important part of its programme. In 1993 *Air, Land & Sea*, the first project with which the gallery was involved, was based upon the work of Peter Lanyon. In this joint venture with the Newlyn art gallery, children from local schools examined the way in which Lanyon's abstract paintings were inspired by his feelings for the Cornish landscape, and they were encouraged to produce work which captured their reactions to, and perceptions of, the local environment. In 1997, St Ives International, a group whose main objective was to manage collaborative arts initiatives in Cornwall, was formed. Their first project, *A Quality of Light*, involved fourteen contemporary artists from Britain and abroad, and took the area's distinctive quality of light as the theme for a variety of works. These included pieces which were exhibited in the St Ives Tate Gallery and a number of other venues in the town, including the parish church and the fisherman's chapel, as well as using one of the historic artist's studios. The work ranged from paintings to installations and video. The artists also exhibited throughout the region of west Cornwall, including the railway station at Penzance, the Geevor Tin Mine at Pendeen and Land's End.

While interest in the area seemed to fade with Hepworth's death in 1975, St Ives has continued to have an established artistic community, and the opening of the Tate Gallery has helped to re-establish the area as a centre of international artistic importance.

See also: painting; Tate(s)

Further reading

Cross, T. (1984) *Painting the Warmth of the Sun: St Ives Artists 1939–1975*, Penzance: Alison Hodge.

Tooby, M. (1993) *Tate St Ives*, London: Tate Gallery Publications.

LUCINDA TOWLER

Stone, Lawrence

b. 1919, Epsom

Historian

Lawrence Stone is the foremost contemporary British historian of the family and society in the early modern period. Now an American professor of history, Stone went to school at Charterhouse, and then studied at the Sorbonne and Christ Church, Oxford. His publications include *Social Change and Revolution in England, 1540–1642* (1965), *The Family, Sex and Marriage in England 1500–1800* (1977), *The Past and Present* (1981), and *Broken Lines: Separation and Divorce in England 1660–1857* (1993). Stone is a historian whose work has been cited in support of feminist revisions of history. For example, he argues that in the nineteenth century

a married woman 'was the nearest approximation in free society to a slave'. Her husband 'could use her sexually as and when he wished, and beat her (within reason) or confine her for disobedience to any orders'. His work shows how from the Hardwicke Marriage Act (1753) onwards, the law aimed to regulate the passage of property and guard against 'spurious issue', men's perennial fear that their sons and heirs are not their own. He refuses to join in the lament for the decline of the family, partly because he sees divorce as simply replacing earlier deaths.

See also: history

PETER CHILDS

Strawson, Peter Frederick

b. 1919, London

Philosopher

Peter Frederick Strawson is a major philosopher, who has taught at Oxford since 1948. He became Waynflete Professor of Metaphysical Philosophy in 1968. Strawson has published numerous articles and books principally in the areas of metaphysics, logic, epistemology and freedom.

His broad approach has been to suggest that certain traits in 'ordinary language' provide better ways of understanding phenomena than those offered by formal philosophical logic. Early criticism of Russell's theory of 'descriptions' through this approach led to his 'solution' of the mind–body problem in *Individuals: An Essay in Descriptive Metaphysics*. The 'descriptive' rather than 'speculative' metaphysics which he developed in this work led him to later reappraise Kant's epistemology in *The Bounds of Sense*. More recently, he has argued against scepticism and reductive naturalism and has published an introduction to philosophy, *Analysis and Metaphysics*, that attempts to understand philosophy as an analysis of the relation between concepts. Peter Strawson can fairly be regarded as one of the most technically sophisticated imaginative and inspiring philosophers of his time. His work combines a high degree of technical analysis with an imaginative grasp of the wider issues involved; an unusual if not unparalleled gift, leading to an unusual if not unparalleled contribution to that combination of technical rigour and wide imagination so necessary to a rapidly shifting philosophical outlook.

See also: philosophy

PAUL BARRY CLARKE
LAWRENCE QUILL

Street-Porter, Janet

b. 1946

Television producer and executive

Janet Street-Porter was educated at Lady Margaret Grammar School, Fulham, and the Architectural Association. After journalism on *Petticoat* and the *Evening Standard*, she emerged in the 1980s, as both presenter and executive, as one of the most prominent women in British television. Tall, bespectacled and strikingly dressed, with prominent teeth and uninhibited **Estuary English**, she revels in stirring controversy by forthrightness. Nine years at the BBC ended with acrimony; in her 1995 Edinburgh Festival lecture she described the Corporation as male, middle-class, middle-aged and mediocre. Winner of a BAFTA originality award (1988) and the Prix Italia (1993), and a Fellow of the Royal Television Society (1994), she has expressed another of her interests as president of the Ramblers' Association.

See also: youth television

CHRISTOPHER SMITH

street selling

There are a number of current examples of street selling, some of which may be traced to the entrepreneurial ethos of Thatcher's Britain. While the market was taken out on to the street and on to the pavements and beyond (a phenomena celebrated in the feted **BBC** television series *Only Fools and Horses*) at the same time the economic and social policies that were pursued created a large swathe of people who might broadly be deemed to constitute part of an economic underclass. Such economic and social policies led to an increase in the emergence of street begging and homelessness on the part of the dispossessed and disenfranchised.

While begging on the streets had always been a feature of city life and in particular the daily life of London (which has always attracted itinerant groups seeking work) the 'problem' became so great in the late 1980s that John Bird launched a publishing venture, **The Big Issue**, in 1991 to give homeless people the opportunity to make a fresh start. *The Big Issue* is a magazine sold directly on the street by badged vendors who are generally homeless or vulnerably accommodated; they buy the magazine for 40p and sell it on for £1. In addition *The Big Issue* 'campaigns on behalf of homeless people and highlights the major social issues of the day. It allows homeless people to voice their views and opinions'.

Busking in many ways is a cultural art form, and there is a long history of buskers in major city centres; the move towards pedestrianized areas within cities and towns has provided further opportunities for street entertainers to ply their trade. For example, the paved area within Covent Garden attracts a variety of street entertainers and the wider area features numerous buskers and other performers. Buskers may fall foul of both the civil and criminal law, although local authorities may operate a scheme of licensing. One problem area is the London Underground, which for obvious reasons actively discourages buskers from performing within stations; the attraction of a huge amount of passing trade inevitably draws performers.

See also: homelessness; poverty

GUY OSBORN
STEVE GREENFIELD

structuralism

Structuralism has made an impact in several disciplines, particularly linguistics, anthropology, psychology and literature. The key initial theorist was the Swiss linguist Ferdinand de Saussure (1857–1913). Saussure argued that language was a system of differences with no positive terms, meaning that no 'word' could be understood in isolation from other words – words did not, in fact, refer to 'objects' in the world but to other words. Saussure also initiated the synchronic study of language, whereas previously forms of speech had been analysed in terms of their change over time, or diachronically. By contrast, Saussure recommended the analysis of speech usages within communities, to reveal not their grammar but their patterns or structures, and that each utterance (*parole*) had to be understood within its system of language (*langue*).

Structural anthropology derives from the work of Claude Lévi-Strauss (1908–) which analysed the structures of culture – its kinship and taboo rules, its eating and story-telling practices and so on – while structural psychology offers an analysis of mental reasoning on the basis of components of thought and feeling.

In literary studies, after the work early in the century of the Russian formalists (for example, Vladimir Propp, who took a structuralist approach to relatively simple narratives in his 1928 work *Morphology of the Folktale*), the most influential practitioner of a structuralist reading practice was Roland Barthes. Perhaps most importantly, Barthes's *S/Z* painstakingly assesses and details the several codes at work in a short story by Balzac (other important texts are Gèrard Genette's *Figures of Literary Discourse* and Tzvetan Todorov's *The Fantastic* and *The Poetics of Prose*) but a better introduction is provided by his *Mythologies*. Here, in a series of bravura performances, Barthes offers a number of cultural readings from a structuralist perspective on such wide-ranging subjects as wrestling and haircuts in films.

Structuralism influenced numerous British literary critics in the 1960s and 1970s, and in some ways initiated the interest in continental **literary theory** that has dominated literary studies over the last thirty years. One other important coinage was made by the Welsh literary and cultural critic Raymond **Williams**, who invented the term 'structure of feeling' (most fully discussed in his *The Long Revolution*) to describe the way in which individuals become aware of how they resemble and differ from each other within a common culture. For example, he says that one generation's shared responses to a cultural phenomenon will have much in common with those of the previous generation, but that they will also have significant differences.

Perhaps most important of all structuralism's contributions is the belief that nothing in human activity is 'natural'; it is all 'constructed' and is therefore open to analysis and critique. This idea is developed much further by the various strands of **post-structuralism**.

See also: literary theory

Further reading

Hawkes, T. (1977) *Structuralism and Semiotics*, London: Methuen.

PETER CHILDS

supermarkets and malls

Supermarkets, defined as large **self-service** stores offering a variety of food and household goods under one roof, have changed the face of British retailing since their emergence in the 1960s. Prior to that date, shopping was an activity mainly associated with small retail outlets and street markets in town centre locations. The abolition of resale price maintenance in 1964 provided the impetus for chain stores such as Kwik Save and Tesco to establish larger premises so that they could offer a wider range of goods at discounted prices. Initially, these retailers sought to adapt and expand existing premises in the city centre, including disused cinemas and car showrooms, although growing development pressures led them to seek purpose-built premises, often in off-centre or suburban locations. In the 1980s, the economic reforms associated with **Thatcherism**, coupled with the relaxation of planning laws, led to a dramatic growth in the number of supermarkets in Britain, with the four biggest grocery chains (Tesco, Sainsbury, Safeway and Asda) particularly targeting out-of-town sites where extensive parking for customers could be provided alongside stores which often exceeded 25,000 square feet. Architecturally, most supermarkets (often referred to as superstores) were undistinguished, designed by in-house teams in bland variants of **postmodernism** and **neo-classicism**, yet were extremely popular, especially with affluent car-owning consumers.

The expansion of **out-of-town shopping** in the 1980s was similarly evident in the development of regional shopping centres, malls of over one million square feet offering a mixture of convenience and comparison shopping. Although British malls (such as Merry Hill, Dudley and Meadowhall, Sheffield) rarely approached the size of their North American counterparts, cultural commentators begun to argue that these malls offered new opportunities for recreational shopping (see **shopping, recreational**), with their careful internal design encouraging new forms of consumerism. To these ends, some malls attempted to recreate 'traditional' retail environments, immersing shoppers into a setting characterized by **hyperreality** and simulation.

Although fears about the impacts of out-of-town shopping on town centre retailing resulted in stricter planning controls on retail development in the 1990s, supermarkets and malls were already established as significant features of the contemporary urban landscape, changing long-established patterns of consumer behaviour in the process. However, while supermarkets and malls perform a number of important social functions in British society (especially if they have extra features like creches and cafés) questions remain as to whether they cater adequately for poorer groups.

See also: corporate identity

Further reading.

Miller, D., Jackson, P., Thrift, N., Holbrook, B. and Rowlands, M. (1998) *Shopping, Place and Identity*, London: Routledge.

PHIL HUBBARD

supermodels

The term 'supermodels', coined in the 1980s, exemplified the changing status of the model from mere clothes horse to a woman with international status and business acumen. Even in the 1960s and 1970s, despite stars like Twiggy and Jean Shrimpton (see **models, 1960s**), the names of models were largely unknown outside of the fashion business unless they married celebrities (as with Jerry Hall, marrying Mick Jagger). By the 1980s models had become household names, often better known than the designers of the clothes they wore on the catwalk. Each supermodel had a particular look which concurred with the fashion moment and epitomized the dominant characteristics of the contemporary western feminine ideal. Accordingly, the influence of the supermodel in the formation of gender identity was fiercely debated, never more so in the 1990s with the introduction of the waif look through the new realist fashion photography of Corinne Day and the appearance on the catwalk of supermodels Kate Moss and Jodie Kidd. Their undernourished, underdeveloped look led to much debate over the link between fashion imagery and eating disorders in young women, and some were dubbed 'vocational anorexics', whose body shape was directly related, like ballerinas, to the demands of the job.

Once a transient and thus well-paid job, from the 1980s on the shelf-life of the supermodel was considerably lengthened through product endorsement, particularly exclusive contracts with cosmetics companies and glamour shoots for personal calendar work. In the 1980s and 1990s the distinctions between runway and catwalk models began to disappear, with the profitability of the fashion image becoming more dependent on the marketable look of each model who had become a personality in the spirit of the film star or pop star rather than a body which displayed clothes. In the volatile business of fashion, the supermodel was seen as a safe marketing tool. The success and status of the supermodel by the end of the 1980s was best expressed by supermodel Linda Evangelista, who was reputed to have boasted she didn't get out of bed for less than $10,000.

Naomi Campbell, a black model from Streatham, South London, became one of the first in Britain to be given the title of supermodel. Campbell went on to appear on the cover of British **Vogue** and was the first black cover girl for the French edition. However, the wholehearted acceptance of black models is debatable, as non-white models have yet to receive major product endorsements or be awarded the more lucrative cosmetics contracts.

See also: models, 1960s

CAROLINE COX

surveillance

The balance of surveillance has shifted markedly in recent years from state to civil society. With the decline of the 'cold war', state surveillance has declined somewhat and is now lawfully restricted only to activities that have a subversive intent. In civil society, surveillance's prime objectives are to build credit and consumer profiles on individuals. It does this in primarily a passive way, assuming credit is good unless there are recorded defaults.

Computerized means of payment, together with 'loyalty cards', have made active surveillance of consumption patterns readily available. A means of surveillance that falls between the active and the passive is provided in the video record, found in places such as shopping centres. Normally this record becomes active only if a crime has been committed.

An increase in surveillance is probably unavoidable. It is, however, striking that such an increase has occurred largely without public debate and without clear mechanisms in place to inhibit 'leakage' from one area of surveillance to another. An increase in **police** surveillance is planned through an increased use of hidden cameras and scanning mechanisms. Initially these mechanisms will be capable of reporting car registration problems and alerting officers within four seconds. It is reasonable to assume that the system will be extended from car profiles to individual profiles. What is at issue here is the extent to which security is traded off against civil liberty. This debate has not yet been fully addressed.

See also: libel, defamation and privacy; riots and civil disobedience; secret services

Further reading

Campbell, D. and Connor, S. (1986) *On the Record: Surveillance, Computers and Privacy*, London: Michael Joseph.

PAUL BARRY CLARKE

swimming

Despite the British weather, swimming is a popular leisure activity enjoyed by people of all ages, backgrounds and cultures. This popularity is maintained by the relatively low cost to participants and the numerous swimming pools throughout the country, both publicly and privately owned. Many 'leisure' pools are now open. These pools are often creatively shaped, relatively shallow and incorporate wave machines and flumes to increase the appeal and excitement for recreational swimmers.

Most people are aware that they should engage in some form of exercise or physical activity as part of a healthy lifestyle. Swimming is ideal because it uses most major muscle groups and can develop, maintain and enhance aerobic endurance and overall mobility. The support provided by the water and the non weight-bearing character of swimming makes it preferable to high-impact activities such as jogging and aerobics, as the risk of injury is greatly reduced. For this reason, swimming is good for sufferers of back pain and arthritis, as well as being a comfortable mode of exercising during pregnancy.

Learning to swim is not exclusive to children, although many schools provide swimming lessons within their physical education curriculum. Most public pools offer lessons for all ages and for different levels of competency. For those who wish to improve their swimming performance and possibly compete, there are a large number of swimming clubs that provide tuition, coaching and training. These clubs train most the UK's competitive swimmers of all age groups. Masters clubs provide training and competition for swimmers over twenty-five. Swimming training is very demanding, especially for the young, as pools can only be given over to clubs when the public are not admitted. This usually means training from 5.30 a.m. and often again in the evening. Not only is this demanding for the swimmers, but it also requires a very high level of commitment from their supporters (parents, family, partners).

There are few British swimmers who are household names. There are exceptions, however, including David Wilkie, Duncan Goodhew, Nick Gillingham and Sharron Davies (though the latter is possibly better known in her role as a television 'Gladiator'). Nonetheless, a number of British swimmers regularly qualify for international and Olympic competition. Others, despite their early promise, never make it to this level. This may reflect a relatively high drop-out rate of young swimmers, as they realize that going out, relationships and parties are increasingly less compatible with the commitment and intensity that swimming traditionally demands, coupled with the unsociable hours.

Pool swimming is only one option. Swimming ability and water confidence provide for a broad spectrum of alternatives. Among these are life-saving, diving, open water or sea swimming, synchronized swimming, scuba diving and many related activities such as water-skiing, sailing, surfing, windsurfing and triathlon. Swimming brings with it benefits such as enhanced self-confidence, greater socialization, improved health and, most importantly, enjoyment.

Further reading

Gorton, E. (1982) *Swimming*, London: Batsford.

JEANETTE WARDROP

T

table tennis

Table tennis has never been a huge spectator sport in Britain, and the professional game faces clear problems in the late 1990s in terms of financial viability and performances. The men's national team were relegated from the top division of the European SuperLeague in 1996 (for the first time since 1984), although the women did far better. The 1997 World Championships, held in Britain, rekindled some public interest.

1996 also saw the formation of a World Grand Prix circuit, including the English Open, but despite featuring the world's top players, lack of television interest remained the central problem. Previous attempts to get television coverage have largely failed: for the showcase 1977 World Championships, held in Britain, the English Table Tennis Association obtained commercial sponsorship and BBC coverage, but the forty hours of play the BBC broadcast failed to attract large ratings. By the mid-1980s, the sport was getting on average just two hours coverage a year, a situation not helped by stars like Desmond Douglas leaving to play in Germany. When he returned in 1987 the sport again tried to generate television interest, by adding extra colour and glitz to proceedings, but this failed once more, leading to the view that table tennis is simply too fast a sport to be successfully televised. It is a measure of the difficulties that table tennis faces that the ETTA did not expect to secure any television coverage for the 1996 English Open, because it clashed with the **University Boat Race**. That said, the sport remains professional, with a British club league (though some top British players have moved to play in Europe), but the warning signs are clear; the top club, Grove, lost its remaining three professional players in September 1996 when it could not pay their wages.

As a participant sport, table tennis is popular in the UK, since it is cheap and easy to learn, and participation is particularly strong in higher education. However, this has not been translated into a strong professional circuit or a high media profile, and since it is clear that since particularly the 1980s, all sports need sustained television exposure (and the sponsorship it brings) to generate a mass public appeal, table tennis will remain in this minority position until it is able to interest television in its events.

See also: tennis

Further reading

Myers, H. (1987) *Table Tennis*, London: Faber.

REX NASH

Tait, Margaret

b. Orkneys

Film-maker

Margaret Tait first qualified as a doctor before changing careers and studying film making in Rome. She produced thirty short films from the 1950s onwards, but her first feature was *Blue Black Permanent* (1993), which she both directed and wrote the screenplay for. It has aspects of autobiography, in its Scottish setting and therapy in its protagonist's search for identity as herself, as daughter and granddaughter. It is a subtle film which examines and replicates the processes that lie behind our ways of seeing. Hence, it deals with the nature of creativity itself and maps a series of experiences which serve as reference points for memory and imagination.

MIKE STORRY

talk shows

The original talk shows involved the use of a seasoned presenter interviewing guests before an audience. The guests would promote books, films or music or be otherwise involved in the public eye. Prominent examples included the *Parkinson* show and *Wogan*, the latter occupying a key early evening slot several times a week. While this format has been maintained (when launched, **Channel 5** used comedian Jack Docherty in this role), a new genre has emerged where the guests are no longer celebrities but members of the public who are chaperoned through a controversial subject area. The personal experiences of the contributors are exploited, sometimes in a confrontational fashion such as when victims of burglaries discuss the issue of theft from houses with burglars, and provide the fulcrum of the shows. Examples of such programmes which have occupied the mid-morning slot on both major terrestrial channels include *Kilroy* (hosted by ex-MP Robert Kilroy-Silk) and *The Time and the Place* (hosted by John Stapleton). Contemporaneously, a number of American made programmes have been imported particularly for the satellite and cable channels (with hosts such as Rolonda, Oprah, Geraldo and Tempest).

The most controversial of the American imports has been *The Jerry Springer Show*, which initially appeared on **cable and satellite** but also gained a mainstream terrestrial lunchtime slot on the independent network. The show was said to be television's biggest cash cow, generating more than $40 million in 1997 via advertising and commercial deals (*Guardian*, 2 May 1998) and displacing the *Oprah Winfrey Show* as the most popular show of its type. The aspects of *The Jerry Springer Show* that

generated most concern were the physical confrontations between guests who were involved in relationships. The subject matter, which frequently involves admissions of sexual infidelity, encourages such direct conflict which is then controlled by the intervention of security staff. Ironically, although some of the physical assaults are broadcast, the language of the participants and audience is subject to severe censorship rendering much of the dialogue inaudible.

Springer himself has been seen to question why people come onto national television to bare their souls and to confess their worst sins. In many of these instances, the desire for exposure outweighs any potential humiliation or accusations of washing dirty linen in public. Perhaps more than any other area, this phenomena illustrates the veracity of Andy Warhol's 'famous for fifteen minutes' dictum and hints at a wider voyeuristic fascination.

See also: phone-ins and chat shows

GUY OSBORN
STEVE GREENFIELD

Tate(s)

Henry Tate, son of a Unitarian clergyman, was born at Chorley, Lancashire in 1819 and entered the grocery trade after a limited education. Prospering, he built up a sugar refining business that subsequently combined with a rival concern to form the firm Tate & Lyle. With increasing wealth, he moved to London in 1874, setting up house at Park Hill, Streatham, and buying pictures for the gallery at his home. Though not unerring in taste, he built up a remarkably comprehensive collection of art by late Victorian masters, such as Millais, Alma-Tadema, Landseer and Stanhope Forbes. A philanthropist who had already made generous donations to hospitals and for educational purposes, he offered his pictures to the nation in 1889. After delays and obstructions, Tate made an additional offer: he would pay £80,000 for the construction of a new gallery if the state would provide the land. Finally, in 1892, the Treasury approved a proposal to make available for a Gallery of British Art the site of Jeremy Bentham's early nineteenth-century panopticon penitentiary in Millbank, London.

The location was and remains inconvenient for access by public transport, and, though the views across the river from the classical portico have become more pleasing with passing years, damage to the collections has been caused periodically by flooding from the nearby Thames. The architect was Sidney R.J. Smith, and when the building opened in 1897 it housed, as well as the works given by Tate (who was rewarded with a baronetcy), modern British pictures from the Chantrey and Vernon Collections and from the National Gallery. Officially recognized also as the home of the nation's collection of modern foreign art since 1916, the Gallery was renamed the Tate Gallery in 1932.

Among more significant recent developments has been the opening of the Clore Gallery, where J.M.W. Turner's pictures are on permanent display, and plans are afoot for expansion into the former Bankside Power Station, on the right bank of the Thames. With the name Tate becoming virtually synonymous with modern painting and sculpture, a Tate Gallery Liverpool opened in Albert Dock in 1988, followed in 1993 by the Tate St Ives, whose striking premises, designed by Eldred Evans and David Shalev, look out to sea from Porthmeor Beach.

See also: painting; St Ives

Further reading

Axton, J. (1995) *Gasworks to Gallery: The Story of Tate St Ives*, St Ives: Axten & Orchard.
Wilson, S. (1995) *The Tate Gallery: An Illustrated Companion*, London: Tate.

CHRISTOPHER SMITH

Taylor, A.J.P.

b. 1906, Birkdale, Lancashire; d. 1990

Historian

Alan John Percival Taylor was one of the most prominent and respected historians of the century. An unorthodox Marxist radical who lectured at Manchester and Oxford (1938–63), Taylor had a narrative flair for provocative, intuitive commen-tary and illuminating detail. His reputation was established by the controversial *The Origins of the Second World War* (1961), an original work which argues that Hitler was an opportunist who improvised history rather than planned it (the book is one of a seminal five-volume history of Europe that covers the period 1848–1948). Many of his theories rest upon notions of history occurring not through progress and human determination but through chance and mistake. He was considered a maverick historian for his irony and commitment, and became a national figure through his appearances in the early 1950s on the BBC's *In the News* and then on ITV's *Free Speech*. His autobiography, *A Personal History*, appeared in 1983.

See also: history; Hobsbawm, Eric

PETER CHILDS

techno

Techno is a form of electronic music that has its origins in **house** music. While the gay club scene of Chicago developed the distinctive 4/4 beat of house music, it was in Detroit that this blueprint was taken further, developing into a harder more electronic music that became known as techno. It was the development of 'MIDI', a way of connecting synthesizers, samplers and computers, that enabled the genre of techno to be developed. In particular, contemporary techno frequently involves the usage of the Roland TR909 drum machine and the Roland TB303 bass sequencer.

The musicians Juan Atkins, Derrick May and Kevin Saunderson are credited with developing the techno sound, although bands such as Tangerine Dream, Parliament, Depeche Mode, Can and, in particular, Kraftwerk are said to be central influences. Techno eschews the melody and vocals of house music, while emphasizing synthesized artificial sounds. While house music continues to draw influence from genres such as **soul**, **funk** and **jazz**, techno is perceived to be more of a 'pure' genre based around a strict technological aesthetic. Connected to this aesthetic are develop-ments in computer graphics and the computer network known as the **Internet**. Many techno acts incorporate these new technologies into their live performances, with, for instance, bands such as The Grid using sound-generated computer graphics as a visual accompaniment to their music.

The music played in British techno **clubs** is particularly diverse, although British DJs often become known for playing one particular style of techno. At one end of the spectrum is 'hardcore', an aggressive techno subgenre that reaches the improbable tempo of 220 beats per minute. This form of techno is particularly popular at raves (see **rave**). At the other end of the spectrum is a techno more akin to **ambient music**, with slow beats and gentle harmonies. In-between these two extremes lie a bewildering array of subgenres that often originate from a particular city, region or country. Within the American techno that is popular in Britain, the Chicago sound is based on a heavily rhythmic percussion, while Detroit techno has a raw, minimal feel. Dutch techno, or Gabba, is popular in Scotland, and is renowned for its speed and the violent imagery of its lyrics. Techno from Germany, Israel and Goa is particularly popular in London **trance** clubs such as Return to the Source. British-produced techno appears to draw influence from a variety of global sources. Artists such as Dave Clarke appear to be highly influenced by the original Detroit sound, while bands such as Orbital and Underworld have an affinity with European trance.

In Britain at the moment, techno is generally played at either large outdoor raves or in small specialist clubs. Those clubs at the forefront of the British techno scene include Voodoo in Liverpool, Bugged Out in Manchester, Beyond The Final Frontier in London and Pure in Edinburgh. While **jungle** appears to be gaining critical acclaim as the logical progression from house and techno, these latter two genres continue to be the dominant sound of the contemporary dancefloor.

STUART BORTHWICK

teds

Teds, or teddy boys, were a youth subculture of the mid-1950s. Teds were working-class young men who adapted the clothes of the Edwardian dandy,

hence their collective name. Ted clothing included drape jackets, 'drainpipe' trousers and crêpe-soled shoes known as brothel creepers. Teddy boys were criticized for their overtly macho behaviour, for their love of rock 'n' roll, and for their tendency to form violent gangs which were prone to vandalism. Teds saw this behaviour as a way of relieving the boredom of their work, which was invariably unskilled labour. Many Teds rode motorcycles, and many became **rockers** in the early 1960s.

See also: mods

STUART BORTHWICK

teen magazines

Teenage or 'teen' magazines have consistently been associated with a feminine market, and more specifically with girl readers between the ages of 11–14. This section of the publishing industry is notoriously unstable, not least perhaps because it tends to be carried along by playground crazes and the most ephemeral of high street trends. Consequently, scores of different titles have been, come and gone, or merged, over the last thirty years, from *Boyfriend*, launched in 1959 (only to cease publication in 1965) to *Sugar*, a 'baby glossy' of the 1990s. For teenage boys, on the other hand, there has been no equivalent range of titles, the assumption being that young male readers are more likely to buy either specific 'hobby' titles or music papers such as the *NME*.

D.C. Thomson's *Jackie* magazine, which first appeared in the mid-1960s, dominated the teenage market for nearly twenty years, and achieved an almost iconic status in British culture because of its associations with 'Cathy and Claire's problem page', pin-ups and comic strip romance. The demise of *Jackie* began with the launch of *Just 17* (owned by **EMAP Maclaren** publications) in 1983, and it finally disappeared altogether in 1993. *Just 17* was set up by the editor (David Hepworth) of *Smash Hits*, and signalled a crucial shift in the teenage magazine market during the 1980s towards formats centred more on music, 'gossip' and fashion than conventional romance. Perhaps the most significant trend in teenage magazines, from the 1970s onwards, was the move from 'romance' to 'real life'. Early teenage magazines consisted mainly of illustrated romantic stories, which were in turn largely superseded by photo-love stories (i.e. narratives acted out by 'real people') in the 1970s. By the late 1980s, however, magazines such as *Just 17* featured almost no fiction, focusing instead upon narratives of readers' 'true-life' experiences.

Teenage titles are strongly influenced by aspirational patterns of consumption, the overriding concern apparently being to identify with an older age group (hence the apparent anomaly that *Just 17* is predominately bought by readers under the age of fifteen). It follows, therefore, that with the ascendancy in the 1990s of more sexually explicit magazines such as *More!* (with its infamous '(sexual) position of the week') aimed at young women in their late teens and early twenties, teenage magazines such as *Just 17* have continued to evolve. For example, in 1997, *Just 17* changed to a monthly 'glossy' format, more overtly modelling itself on adult magazines.

See also: women's press

JO CROFT

teenage and youth programming

The 1950s saw the need for broadcasters to programme specific shows to cater for the burgeoning teenage market. Shows like *Oh Boy!* and *Thank Your Lucky Stars* gave mainstream popular music its first real television exposure. Recording artists would appear weekly, promoting their latest record. The zenith of these shows came with the introduction of the BBC's *Top of the Pops* in 1964, that became both a byword for pop music television, and the longest running show of its kind in the world. Other markets were catered for with programmes like *The Old Grey Whistle Test* (for rock and progressive music), and a British version of the US show *Soul Train*, dedicated to the promotion of black music in the UK. Channel 4's *The Tube*, which began broadcasting on the station's inaugural night, is seen as the high-point of the genre. Featuring both live performances and pop videos, the show was shambolically produced and presented and frequently had technical problems, all adding to the excitement of a live pop music experience.

Channel 4's brief for youth programming extended the boundaries of what was required for young (16–25) audiences. No longer would plain pop music suffice for what was now a highly educated, demanding audience. The introduction of a Sunday lunchtime show on the station turned the notion of youth programming on its head, and created what is now termed 'yoof' television. Produced by Janet Street-Porter, *Network 7* was the first current affairs and entertainment news programme aimed at the youth market. Its quirky camera angles, young reporters, no-nonsense interviewing style and rough production created a style that dominated the genre for the next decade. Street-Porter then moved to the BBC (whose previous efforts at programming had proved both critically and commercially inadequate), creating programmes including *Reportage*, *Rough Guide* and *Standing Room Only*, all of which dealt with issues crucial to the youth market.

Street-Porter's appointment gave the BBC a range of classy, intelligent and popular programmes with which Channel 4 found difficult to compete. With media accusations of 'dumbing down', Channel 4 commissioned new programmes to vie with the BBC, the most (in)famous being *The Word*. The antithesis of the pseudo-serious BBC, *The Word* was accused of many crimes, including bad taste, blasphemy, sexism and perversity. Catering for the post-pub Friday night audience, the show drew viewing figures in the millions and became the most discussed television programme in decades. Following its demise, there have been efforts to create a new format for youth programming, none quite as successful as the previous incarnations.

See also: pop television; youth television

Further reading

Lury, K.E. (1997) 'Cynicism and Enchantment: British Youth Television in the 1980s and 1990s', Liverpool University, unpublished Ph.D. thesis.

SAM JOHNSTONE

teenyboppers

Since the advent of Elvis Presley, teenagers have comprised the most important element of the pop music audience, but it was not until the 1970s that the term 'teenybopper' was coined. The term was applied derisively to fans of Marc Bolan, Donny Osmond, David Cassidy, the Bay City Rollers and, in the 1990s, Boyzone, with the unjustified implication that these artists had nothing to offer musically and only appealed through their image. Arguably, however, teenyboppers have always been more discerning than more 'sophisticated' music fans. Whereas 'intellectual' listeners have fallen for the emperor's new clothes, from the Doors to Radiohead, teenyboppers have always had an ear for a good tune and unpretentiously discarded their idols at the first hint of a drop in quality.

See also: fanzines; pop and rock

CRAIG GERRARD

Telegraph plc

The *Daily Telegraph* is Britain's best-selling 'quality' daily newspaper. At the end of 1997 its circulation was nearly 1.1 million copies a day, challenged only, at some remove, by *The Times* with a figure that had only recently risen above three-quarters of a million, while the *Guardian* totalled fewer than 400,000 and the *Independent* only a quarter of a million. Commanding not far short of 40 percent of the 'quality' newspaper market, and more than 8 percent of total sales nationally, the *Daily Telegraph* appears, even if its figures are not rising, to be in a strong position. Though criticism of the Conservative Party is not precluded, the *Daily Telegraph* is generally regarded, particularly by those preferring other papers, to be firmly oriented towards the right in politics, an aspect reflected more in its comment columns than in its news reporting. Its readers, male and female, tend to be conformist, middle-class and middle-aged or older. Such a readership commands considerable spending power, a factor reflected not only in the fine quality of its business pages but also in the advertising that the paper attracts. The sports pages are good, the arts reporting, especially of musical events, is serious and respected, and the design and layout of its 'broad sheet' pages, characteristic of the quality papers, have improved in recent years.

Founded in 1855, taking advantage of the repeal of the Newspaper Duty, the *Daily Telegraph* encountered varying fortunes before gaining something like its present position just before the Second World War under William Berry (Lord Camrose). It was acquired in 1985 by Conrad Black's Hollinger, a Canadian company. Formerly published from Peterborough Court – hence the pseudonym of one of its regular columnists – the *Daily Telegraph*, like most of the rest of national press, deserted Fleet Street for the Isle of Dogs in 1987. The *Sunday Telegraph* was not established until 1961, with a *Sunday Telegraph Magazine* offered as an extra in 1995. Though there are signs of growth, sales of the *Sunday Telegraph*, at 860,000, are markedly lower than for the daily paper, amounting to only some 30 percent of the 'quality' Sunday market (as opposed to 45 percent for the *Sunday Times*) and to a 6 percent overall share. Apparently a sizeable proportion of *Daily Telegraph* readers opt for a newspaper from a different stable on Sundays, most likely the *Sunday Times*.

See also: Express Group; Guardian Group; Mirror Group; News International

Further reading

Hart-Davis, D. (1990) *The House the Berrys Built: Inside The Telegraph*, London: Hodder & Stoughton.

CHRISTOPHER SMITH

teletext

Teletext is a system of carrying data, graphic and textual information on top of the normal television broadcast signal. With an appropriately equipped television set in 40 percent of households in Britain (in 1992), many viewers are able to access this service. The IBA licensed Oracle in 1973, and the BBC started its service, Ceefax, in 1974. Both provide a mix of news, sports information, recipes, weather reports, travel information and so forth, laid out in indexed pages. Though the information provided is limited and one-way, compared to the more interactive telecommunication's equivalent Prestel, it is free at the point of use and is constantly updated. Teletext is also the means by which broadcasters provide their captioning of programmes for the deaf.

See also: Internet; news, television

PAUL RIXON

television, children's

Both ITV and BBC1 run children's programmes after school hours from 3 p.m. to 5 p.m. every weekday, and also at lunchtime and on Saturday mornings. The midday programmes are designed for pre-school children, as are the earliest afternoon shows. Despite the existence of separate educational programming, an emotive debate on television's educative role has pervaded children's television since its inception in 1946 (with the BBC's *For The Children*). The longest running children's programme is *Blue Peter* (1958–). Consistently endorsing a duty to inform, its presenters suggest socially useful hobbies for children and reward the achievements of the programme's viewers. For younger children, *Play School* (1964) and others achieved a televised version of good nursery education. Cartoons and puppet characters are widely used, asking the naive questions that young viewers wish explained and helping to avoid the alienating didacticism of a pontificating adult.

However charismatic facilitators have frequently made overtly factual and instructive programmes popular, such as Johnny Morris (*Animal Magic*, 1962), Johnny Ball (*Think of a Number*, 1972) and John Craven (*Newsround*, 1972). Entertainment is an equally strong priority in this field. *Tiswas* (1977) created a genre wherein adults behaved like children, exploiting children's innate appreciation of the anarchic within a safe structure. Quiz shows and trials of progress such as *Record Breakers* (1972–) have always been popular with children. Most afternoon shows are shorter than half an hour to account for the short concentration span of the child and to provide a representative range of programmes.

Jackanory (1965–), a children's story read to camera, and serializations of novels such as *The Box of Delights* (1989) prove that powerful narrative is still gripping. Drama featuring magical characters and unusually proactive children are satisfying to the socially powerless child, which accounts for the popularity of fantastic, comedic series such as *Rentaghost* (1983) *Woof!* (1996) and the long-running *Dr Who* (1963–). The activities of fictional children in realistic settings are increasingly favoured. The soap operatic *Grange Hill* (1978–) has been joined by *Byker Grove* (1989) and *The Biz* (1996). Jimmy Savile bridged the intriguing gaps between fantasy, reality, entertainment and documentary by granting the wishes of his young audience on *Jim'll Fix It* (1980), which was enjoyed by both adults and children. For slightly older viewers, children's broadcasters were initially responsible for programmes such as *Top Of The Pops* (1965–).

See also: film, children's; literature, children's and teenage

Further reading

Hartley, I. (1983) *Goodnight Children ... Everywhere*, Kent: Midas.

SARAH CASTELL

television exports

Television exports are the sale of programmes by producers in one national market to broadcasters in another; although, with the increased internationalization of television in terms of production and broadcasting, a clear cut definition is no longer possible. Individual programme exports take a number of forms: there are the straightforward sales of programmes made for a specific national market; pre-sales of programmes not yet made, the joint production of programmes as co-productions, and the selling of formats or programme concepts. The selling of formats usually occurs when the original programme appears too culturally specific for export but, by remaking the programme, it can be tailored for a different national audience (for example, *Cracker*, originally made for the ITV network, has been remade for ABC in America).

By the 1960s, a flourishing international market in programmes appeared, stimulated both by the need to fill more broadcast hours and the supply of popular and cheaply sold American programmes. British broadcasters, keen to derive income from programme sales, soon established themselves as the second largest exporter of programmes after the Americans. A notable early success was the ITV company, Associated Television (ATV). By tailoring productions more to the needs of the American market they were able to sell a number of series to the major US networks, including *The Avengers*, *The Saint* and *Dangerman*. While ATV's success was initially rewarded, gaining the Queen's Awards for Export, the loss of its franchise in 1980 was partly attributed to this export led policy that neglected the needs of its domestic audience.

By the 1970s, Britain had established a reputation for producing quality programmes including historical dramas (*Brideshead Revisited*, *Upstairs, Downstairs*) and factual programmes (*Civilisation*, *The World at War*). The main market for this product was, at this time, the USA, though programmes were almost always sold to the Public Broadcasting System (PBS) rather than to the main US networks. Increasingly, Europe has overtaken the USA as the major market for British programmes. With increasing costs and a squeeze on revenues, the importance of exports, at least for some genres of programming, looks to be on the increase. While some worries are voiced about the possible consequence in terms of an internationalization of domestic programmes for export requirements, it must be noted that the national market is still the most important in terms of revenue.

See also: imported television

Further reading

Collins, R. (1990) *Television: Policy and Culture*, London: Unwin Hyman.

PAUL RIXON

television licence

The television licence, introduced in 1947, is a flat fee payable annually by all those using a television set. Two rates, set by the government, are currently payable, one for black and white television sets and the other for colour television sets. For many years the licence fee has been accepted as the best means of funding the **BBC**, a public service broadcaster, protecting it from both direct governmental interference and commercial pressure. However, the continuation of this licence fee has recently come under attack with the proliferation of new channels and the drop in BBC's audiences. The BBC is now under pressure to develop new forms of income either to supplement or, at some stage, to replace the licence fee.

PAUL RIXON

television unions

The television unions in the UK represent workers active in three main areas: talent, craft and studio support. These unions initially grew out of distinct media areas, such as radio, cinema, theatre and other forms of entertainment, and the different craft and skill divides that existed within such activities. However, as the industry has changed, so the number of different unions has been consolidated. Currently, the main television union is the Broadcasting Entertainment Cinematograph and Theatre Union (BECTU). Alongside this are the talent unions Equity, the Musicians' Union and the Writers' Guild of Great Britain. Journalists have their own specific union, the National Union of Journalists (NUJ). Unions, working alone or together in bodies such as the Federation of Entertainment Unions (FEU), look after the interests of their members, including pay, conditions, employment rights and contracts with employers, and negotiate and lobby on their members' behalf with broadcasters, producers, national governments, regulators and European bodies.

BECTU was created from the amalgamation of the ACTT and BETA in 1990. BETA was itself the result of the merger of the Association of

Broadcasting and Allied Staff (ABS) and the National Association of Theatrical Television and Kine Employees (NATTKE) in 1984. ACTT incorporated the medium of television when, in 1956, commercial television came on stream. From the 1950s, employment in the broadcasting industry came to be linked to belonging to one of the accepted unions, such as the ACTT, and was considered by many to be a closed shop. In many ways this 'closed shop' had been an aim of the unions because of their desire to protect their members from the casualization of labour that had afflicted the film industry for some time. This was accepted by the broadcasters while the industry was healthy and profits made; recently, however, with increased competition, shifts towards more filmed productions, and the appearance of different types of organization with greater reliance on independent productions and the emergence of publisher-commissioner broadcasters, more labour is becoming casualized. It is in reaction to this that unions that once represented the old industrial and craft divides have begun to merge and amalgamate to reflect the new industrial situation.

See also: trade unions

Further reading

Macdonald, B. (1993) *Broadcasting in the United Kingdom: A Guide to Information Sources*, London: Mansell.

PAUL RIXON

Temple, Julian

Film-maker

Julian Temple's first film, *The Great Rock 'n' roll Swindle* (1980), was a cynical parody of the creation of the Sex Pistols. It was characterized by its portrayal of Malcolm McLaren's thesis to manufacture a pop sensation in ten easy steps, including the memorable 'cultivate hatred'. This was followed by Amnesty international fundraiser *The Secret Policeman's Other Ball* (1982) and *Absolute Beginners* (1986), a musical based on Colin MacIn-

nes's novel celebrating teenage culture in 1950s Soho with a soundtrack boasting luminaries such as Paul Weller (himself a MacInnes aficionado) and David Bowie. Other films directed by Temple include his contribution to *Aria* (1987) and *Earth Girls are Easy* (1988), a farcical reflection of the lifestyle and values of Los Angeles culture.

See also: punk rock

GUY OSBORN
STEVE GREENFIELD

tennis

Far more British people watch than play tennis, and the fact that Britain hosts **Wimbledon** makes tennis appear an annual national two-week love affair. Yet while tens of millions of people watch the tournament globally, the millions of pounds it raises for the Lawn Tennis Association (LTA) has generated very little British success. Since 1977, when Virginia Wade won the Wimbledon singles title, no British player has come close to winning a major event, and the standard of the women's game declined so much in the early 1990s that the traditional Federation Cup (between the USA and the UK) was dropped, due to the scale of the American victories. The outlook for the playing standards in the women's game in the 1990s is bleak, with the highest ranked UK player well outside the world top 100 at the end of 1996. Some inside tennis see this as the result of the declining numbers of young girls playing tennis (and sport in general), with three times more boys than girls taking up the junior game every year between 1991 and 1996.

The men saw some improvement in the mid-1990s, with players of true potential appearing (notably Tim Henman and Greg Rusedski), and clearly the LTA's investment in the 1980s had improved the standard of junior tennis, but perhaps real success should not be expected in a country without a genuine grassroots tennis base. There have always been many clubs, but until the mid-1980s most were privately run and expensive. In the 1980s the LTA began building inexpensive facilities for young players from all social classes. More generally, tennis in schools has declined, as has all school sport. The LTA (with an annual budget of £40m by the mid-1990s) has tried to fill this gap, increasing the number of indoor courts from 150 in 1986 to 800 in 1996, and setting up training centres in twenty-six different cities, but these are essentially attempts to shift the culture of the game from its middle-class roots.

Tennis in the UK is as much a social occasion as a sporting one. While this is not necessarily a bad thing, it accordingly reduces the chances of Britain producing world-class players. Until a real popular interest in tennis is generated, the UK cannot really expect to seriously compete in the world game.

See also: table tennis

Further reading

Evans, R. (1988) *Open Tennis: The First Twenty Years*, London, Bloomsbury.

REX NASH

Terry Farrell Partnership

Terry Farrell was born in Cheshire in 1938 and trained at Durham University (1956–61) and the University of Pennsylvania (1962–4). He then worked in partnership with Nicholas Grimshaw up to 1980 before establishing the Terry Farrell Partnership. The practice has contributed greatly to London's cityscape (Farrell has been chair of the Urban Design Group) and has expanded greatly over its first twenty years. Major projects have been the redevelopment of Charing Cross station, the **TV-am** headquarters, the Henley Regatta HQ, Limehouse TV studios and the postmodern Alban Gate office block at London Wall. Farrell is probably Britain's most outspoken postmodernist, influenced by Michael Graves and Charles Jencks, and his modern art deco style is noted for a striking use of colour and decoration.

See also: postmodernism

PETER CHILDS

Thames TV

Thames TV was formed in 1967 with the merger of ABC Television and Associated-Rediffusion, two ITV franchise holders, to create a new company to run the London weekday franchise. Until it lost its franchise to Carlton in 1993, Thames TV was the largest and wealthiest of the big five network broadcasters in the ITV system. With the loss of its franchise, Thames became the largest independent producer in Britain. It has also diversified into satellite broadcasting (for example, UK Gold). Thames, under its own name and subsidiaries, namely Euston films and Compton Hall, has a reputation for making quality historical dramas (*Edward and Mrs Simpson*), documentaries (*The World at War* series), action adventure series (*The Sweeney*) and comedy (*The Benny Hill Show*).

See also: Granada; Mersey Television; TV-am

PAUL RIXON

Thatcherism

Thatcherism is the collective term for the political policies of Margaret Thatcher, Prime Minister from 1979–90. Although Thatcher's policies were not homogeneous, they were consistent with a general policy line. Thatcher sought to liberalize the economy, stressing the importance of the market, deregulation and **privatization**. She sought to minimize state intervention, and to create an enterprise culture in which private industry led the economy. Self-help, the individual accumulation of wealth and independence were all strong themes. Coalescing with these neo-liberal beliefs was an authoritarian social policy, with an emphasis upon increased **police** power and harsher penalties for offenders. Thatcher was ousted in 1990, largely due to her narrow views on **Europe** and the unpopularity of the **poll tax**.

See also: Conservative   governments; Conservative Party

ALASTAIR LINDSLEY

theatre

In the 1950s and 1960s a new wave of angry young playwrights (such as Osborne, Wesker and Delaney) re-established theatre as a vibrant arena of socio-political debate with plays emphasizing a social naturalism focused on working-class culture. George Devine established the **Royal Court** as a theatre devoted to new writing, and the instant success of John Osborne's *Look Back in Anger* in 1956 ushered in a new era of writers concerned with probing the limits of their craft (Orton, Storey, Stoppard). Joan Littlewood's Theatre Workshop took up residence at Theatre Royal, Stratford East, and attempted to create an audience for popular theatre with plays that frequently upset the critics but also transferred to the **West End** (such as *Fings Ain't What They Used To Be* and *Oh What A Lovely War*). Both these **directors** not only promoted new writing talent but also evolved theatrical styles closer to poetic realism than the conventional cluttered naturalism. This return to the 'bare boards' had a major impact on the aesthetics of theatre throughout the postwar period. Additional influences during 1956–68 came from the European absurdists (Beckett's *Waiting for Godot* was first staged in London in 1955), and international visits from Brecht's Berliner Ensemble (1956), Open Theatre and La Mama from New York (1965) and Jerzy Grotowski from Poland (1968).

The 1960s were characterized by new writing and experimental approaches. Individualistic writers like Harold Pinter and Samuel Beckett forged reputations as great stylists of twentieth-century theatre; other playwrights emerged whose concerns were more social and political (Bond, Brenton, Edgar). Practitioners began to embrace innovative approaches focused on the physical and visual priorities of theatre, such as Brook's profoundly influential productions of *A Midsummer Night's Dream* and Weiss's *Marat/Sade*.

The impact of 1968 manifested itself in an explosion of alternative theatre and fringe venues. By the mid-1970s there were two kinds of theatre, official and unofficial: the first was characterized by endorsement of the establishment, the second by a rediscovery of the essential nature of theatre as an encounter between stage and spectator through which new understandings about the human condition might be reached. The notion that theatre had to occur in buildings designated for that activity was overturned, and new venues promoted new styles of presentation and a renewed fervour for 'theatre-as-event', as a spreading network of arts centres, pubs and clubs became sites for theatrical activity. This was the era of 'instant theatre', with performances springing up on any issue in any style at any time. A new generation of performers arrived, often self-taught rather than formally trained; workshops and collectives replaced the old hierarchical ways of working, and no subject was taboo. Theatre became radicalized and politicized.

The spirit of 1968 was ensconced in the abolition of censorship that year. Even commercial theatre availed itself of the new libertarianism with nudity on stage (*Hair* in 1969), although the West End mostly continued to stage well-made thrillers and farces which reinforced the status quo, like *The Mousetrap* and *No Sex Please, We're British*. This kind of theatre, dubbed 'deadly' by Peter Brook in his seminal book *The Empty Space*, has been termed 'theatre of comfort' in contradistinction to 'theatre of commitment' (Edgar, McGrath, Griffiths), which is seen as offering more challenging perspectives on society.

The years 1968–78 produced a tide of radical energy which placed theatre at the heart of cultural transformation. Theatre of commitment flourished in tandem with the growing awareness of cultural issues and oppressions. Women's theatre (for example, Monstrous Regiment), **gay theatre** and lesbian theatre (Gay Sweatshop), **black theatre** (Black Theatre Co-operative, Talawa Theatre) groups toured extensively on the alternative circuit. Text-based playwriting 'driven by a belief in socialism in general and sometimes Marxism in particular' (Shank 1994: 15), from avowed political idealists such as Edward Bond, Howard Brenton and David Hare, was produced at the newly opened National Theatre in addition to the more conservative talents of Tom Stoppard and Alan Ayckbourn. The ICA and Ed Berman's Interaction supplied risqué experimental work which tested the boundaries of theatre and performance; iconoclast Steven Berkoff presented himself in his own highly charged **physical theatre** productions.

The Royal Court continued to stage radical work illustrating the oppressions of race (Fugard's *Sizwe Bansi's Dead*) and homosexuality (Martin Sherman's *Bent*). Women playwrights had work staged in London, again primarily through the Royal Court (Churchill, Page, Gems), in addition to their growing presence on the fringe and alternative scene, although attempts to close the 'gender gap' in theatre (where most directors and decision makers are white, middle-class males) met with little success. Despite the feminist slogan 'the personal is political', the assumption persists that men write 'public' plays suitable for a general audience and while women write 'private' plays focused on personal issues: plays by women have been relegated to studio spaces (for example, Daniels's *Neaptide*, Churchill's *The Skriker* in the National's Cottesloe) while male 'state-of-the-nation' plays take the main stage (Edgar's *Maydays* in the Olivier).

Away from the metropolis, the concept of theatre was changing as local councils embarked on building theatres which embodied notions of civic pride and community. Bolton's Octagon and Sheffield's Crucible were purpose-built places for social gathering, including exhibition spaces, bars and restaurants, alongside modern thrust stages with advanced technical capabilities, signalling an end to 'proscenium arch' naturalism. The number of repertory companies increased from 20 to over 100 by the end of the 1970s, frequently with TIE companies attached to undertake outreach work, and youth theatres with the task of encouraging new generations of theatre-literate audiences.

State support for the arts has had a significant effect on the development of postwar theatre, in both positive and negative ways. The growth of alternative and **community theatre** in the 1970s owes much to the enlightened funding policies of the Arts Council. After four years of Labour government (1975–9), which included the first Minister for the Arts (Jennie Lee), the Thatcher government took office and in 1984 the White Paper *The Glory of the Garden* laid plans for the reduction of public funding in favour of private sponsorship. In the early 1980s, many repertory theatres opened up studio spaces to accommodate more new and experimental work and small-scale touring, only to close them within the decade as they succumbed to the recession and the invidious vagaries of arts funding.

Most repertory companies were disbanded by the mid-1990s, leaving provincial theatres to play host to touring productions while perhaps mounting the annual pantomime. Issue-based radical theatre dwindled, and when the Conservatives were re-elected for the fourth time in 1992, the limitations of theatre dogged by political ideology were exposed. The beginning of the 1990s saw a resurgence of interest in aesthetics and many groups emerged whose aim was to search for new forms of theatrical expression rather than take on ideological battles.

The legacy of mainstream theatre in the 1980s is the musical, a form imported from the USA but reinvented in Britain by Andrew Lloyd Webber, whose string of successful shows (*Cats, Starlight Express, Phantom of the Opera*) make a substantial contribution to the economy. These shows rely on the spectacle of huge casts and technical wizardry, and their emphasis on escapist entertainment places them in the category of 'populist culture'. Webber's directing associate Trevor Nunn put the National back on its financial feet with *Les Misérables* in 1985, a musical adaptation of Hugo's novel, which continues touring internationally. Adaptation has become a significant growth area in theatre as well as film and television, in an attempt to woo back audiences to the theatre.

New writing became much more difficult to fund and revivals, old masterpieces and adaptations burgeoned in the 1980s, spawning a fresh breed of directors whose ethos was to reinvent the classics or rediscover old plays in modern cultural and aesthetic contexts. David Edgar expressed his concern about the fall in the production of new writing in the *Independent* in May 1991, pointing out that 'there has been a shift of writerly energy from theatre to the novel and film' (Wandor 1993: 4), and subsequently a campaign was launched to draw attention to the funding problems in theatre. The problem was not merely funding but attitudinal, as evidenced by statistics: only 6 percent of the population attended theatre in 1988–9. Those who had espoused a 'popular theatre' rooted in working-class concerns had never managed to reach the working class. Theatre is still an elitist art. Yet, despite its minority status, its impact is felt beyond the stage door. When Sarah Kane's *Blasted* premiered at the Royal Court in 1995, it made front-page headlines and generated a debate about tabloid mentality and the 'grotesquerie' of Bosnia that ran in the papers for weeks.

Theatre has had to compete with cinema and television since the 1950s. One of the consequences has been in a new generation of theatre-makers reassessing the live nature of theatre and moving away from the concept of 'literary theatre' to one which privileges its visceral qualities. Experimental theatre has slowly taken hold, particularly in the regions, notably Glasgow, which hosted Peter Brook's *Mahabharata* in 1988, and through the Cardiff Centre for Performance Research, which fostered companies such as Moving Being and Volcano. The impetus to redefine British theatre in relation to its global counterparts has been fuelled by the influx of international touring and the increase in cross-cultural exchanges through workshops, courses and theatre scholarship. The biennial London International Festival of Theatre (LIFT), for example, which was founded by two young women arts graduates in 1981, has acted as an important and provocative influence on contemporary theatre, importing and commissioning a diverse range of experimental work, from the Peking Opera to Peter Badejo's *Kufena*, a dance theatre drawing on disparate traditions, and the Canadian Robert Lepage's *Dragon's Trilogy*.

British theatre in the 1990s demonstrates significant examples of hybridization with other art forms, especially dance, and companies such as DV8 and Motionhouse use text with movement, while others show evidence of cinematic influences (Lip Service, Kaboodle). There is also a noticeable shift away from hierarchical modes of production, informed by new ventures in collaboration and companies who operate on an egalitarian footing. **Improvisation** has been rediscovered as a means of producing texts as well as interpreting them, and the concept of the 'actor-as-creator' is re-emerging. Groups, such as Forced Entertainment, Told By An Idiot, often comprise self-sufficient young artists who develop and perform their own 'texts'; frequently they are more concerned with the performative dynamics of theatre than language, and often they are influenced by European practitioners like Artaud, Grotowski and Lecoq, and contemporary movements in performance art, visual art and **circus**. Many young performers take courses with specialist practitioners abroad, in **mime**, dance or mask work, where they learn new ways to exploit their creative autonomy. Often these schools are multicultural, taking students of various nationalities, and sometimes companies spring from students meeting there, such as Theatre de Complicité, whose members trained with Jacques Lecoq in Paris.

Theatre still has its 'official' and 'unofficial' branches, although these are being constantly infiltrated by a younger generation of performers and playwrights who have different backgrounds and aspirations from their predecessors. A surge of new writing in the 1990s has been dominated by playwrights who reject the moralistic tone of the 'social-issue' play (Gregory Motton, Sarah Kane), and search for the 'unknown' rather than any notion of 'truth' (Shank 1994: 16). The 'issue play' continues to serve a purpose in TIE and community theatre (and several pioneering political troupes from the 1970s are still in business, such as Red Ladder and Welfare State International), although the political play, once so prevalent, has given way to explorations of individuality and postmodern preoccupations with gender and identity. Perhaps the one issue that remains central to much contemporary playwriting is sexuality, as evidenced by the success of Jonathan Harvey's *Beautiful Thing*.

See also: actors (female); actors (male); playwrights

Further reading

Chambers, C. and Prior, M. (1987) *Playwright's Progress: Patterns of Postwar British Drama*, Oxford: Amber Lane Press.

Shank, T. (ed.) (1994) *Contemporary British Theatre*, London: Macmillan.

Wandor, M. (1993) *Drama Today: A Critical Guide to British Drama 1970–1990*, London: Longman.

DYMPHNA CALLERY

theatre, regional

Regional theatre has had a difficult time in recent years. It has had to compete with shifts in the pattern of people's leisure towards home entertainment such as television, videos or music. When people go out, it is more often to cinema than to theatre. There have also been cutbacks in funding. Consequently, many theatres have closed down and those which have survived are struggling.

Loss of theatres is important because traditionally actors have come up through the repertory route, travelling around Britain's regional theatres to learn and practise their craft, and because students in particular, who are notoriously difficult to attract into theatres, need to be exposed to a culture of theatre if it is to be sustained in future years. Historically, much of the original television drama came from the provinces, not least from the many civic theatres (the Belgrade in Coventry, the Leicester Haymarket, the Nottingham Playhouse and so on) which, in the 1960s, nurtured new playwrights.

The picture is not uniformly gloomy, however. For example, in Liverpool both The Royal Court (which was mainly given over to pop concerts) and the Playhouse have closed down, but other theatres continue to thrive, such as the Everyman, the Unity and the Neptune. Also, several regional repertory companies have secured strong local followings for themselves and their theatres. These include the Royal Exchange, Manchester and the Nottingham Playhouse.

Norwich has been fortunate to have a brand new repertory theatre, the Playhouse. Supported by Arthur Miller and Timothy West, it has, like the civic theatres of the 1960s, a deliberate policy of initiating new plays. Malcolm Bradbury's first play for the theatre for thirty years, *Inside Trading*, opened there.

A further gratifying development for regional theatre has been the advent of the **National Lottery**. In 1996, its grants enabled an entirely rebuilt Cambridge Arts Theatre to open, at a total cost of £8.5m. The theatre had been closed for three years. Similarly the Oxford Playhouse, closed for four years, reopened in 1995, radically modernized after a £4m refurbishment. The absence of functional theatres in such influential towns was particularly regrettable. Both theatres, like many others, are however known as 'receiving houses', which is to say they do not sustain their own repertory company but largely buy in existing productions.

See also: fringe theatre; West End

Further reading

Rowell, G. and Jackson, A. (1984) *The Repertory Movement: A History of Regional Theatre in Britain*, Cambridge: Cambridge University Press.

MIKE STORRY

theatre critics

Theatre criticism in national newspapers is largely confined to the daily and Sunday broadsheets and middle-market tabloids. Specialist listing magazines such as London's *Time Out* have given opportunities to new critics, although the profession still tends to be dominated by white males whose aesthetic preferences broadly follow those of their papers, and have ensured that more shows are seen and recorded, albeit briefly (often in about 100 words). Since many productions receive only the most cursory notices, national newspaper critics exert a significant influence in their choice of what they review as well as in what they say about it.

Theatrical managements maintain an uneasy symbiotic relationships with critics: critical acclaim can bolster reputations but critical condemnation can help to close shows. Although the power of critics in Britain is not as great as it is in New York, where a bad notice from the New York *Times* can still kill a play overnight, Harold Hobson and Kenneth Tynan exerted a massive influence into the 1960s, so much so that Laurence Olivier is reputed to have asked Tynan to join him at the new National Theatre partly because he wanted to neutralize him as a critic.

Critics can perform an important mediating function between productions and potential audiences, but are always under pressure from the often conflicting demands of newspaper editors and theatre managements. Theatre criticism may be regarded either as news reporting or as feature writing: the overnight review places a premium on the critic's ability as a reporter able to give an account of a hot news event for the next morning's newspaper. Sunday reviews and those for specialist monthly magazines tend to be more reflective but may lose the eyewitness authenticity that the best overnight criticism can sometime achieve. Theatre criticism demands that its practitioners spend much of their time every week seeing productions of very limited achievement and then writing about them. Sometimes this can lead to an eccentricity borne from a limited knowledge of the world outside the theatre; sometimes it can produce a kind of critical battle fatigue; sometimes it can lead to an eccentric championing of minor talents. However, the newspaper review is a vital source for anyone interested in theatre, not only as a guide to the present but often as the only accessible trace of a past production.

See also: film reviews; theatre

Further reading

Wardle, I. (1992) *Theatre Criticism*, London: Faber (a contemporary journalist's analysis of the trade).

TREVOR R. GRIFFITHS

theatre in education

The first theatre in education (TIE) company was established at the Belgrade Theatre, Coventry, in 1965, as part of that theatre's project of developing its links with the community. TIE is not a theatrical form as such but is rather a movement, characterized by its aims and by its working methods. Whereas the primary aims of children's theatre are to entertain and to make theatre accessible to young people, TIE uses theatre as part of an educational process, focusing on contemporary social and political issues.

Collaborative working practices are at the heart of the TIE movement. Where writers (such as Lisa Evans, Noel Greig, David Holman and Mike Kenny) work with companies, they tend to work collaboratively with other company members. Plays are rarely self-contained, stand-alone entities: interactive workshops are an important part of the educational process. The 'performance' of a programme is thus no less collaborative than the **devising** process. At its best, TIE is challenging, provocative and radical; in many ways it is a development of Brechtian practice, in that the emphasis of the programmes is on making an audience active and reflexive.

In its heyday, funding for TIE companies came from a variety of sources, but predominantly from Local Education Authorities (**LEAs**), Regional Arts Associations and the **Arts Council** of Great Britain. Some companies received support 'in kind' (for example the use of space in schools and access to local authority infrastructures), while some were closely tied to the development of regional theatres' community programmes.

By the early 1980s, LEA financial cutbacks had already begun to result in the closure of some of the less well-established TIE companies. After the 1988 Education Act, which introduced local management of schools (demanding the devolution of budgets away from local education authorities to individual schools), most LEAs cut off their financial support to TIE companies, many of which had prided themselves on being able to develop and tour programmes without charging individual schools, seeing their work as an essential part of the educational process (and a necessary counterbalance to the institutionalization of education). There are now only very few companies operating; none of them are as securely funded as they were in the heyday, and the idealistic impetus of the movement seems (perhaps temporarily) to have been stifled by lack of finance and the increasing demands of the National Curriculum within schools.

See also: community theatre

Further reading

Redington, C. (1983) *Can Theatre Teach?*, Oxford: Pergamon Press.

BRIAN WOOLLAND

Thompson, Edward Palmer

b. 1924; d. 1993, Upper Wick,
  Worcestershire

Historian

E.P. Thompson was the leading Marxist social
historian of the postwar period. Identified with the
New Left, Thompson founded the *New Reasoner* and
published numerous studies and essays. He is best
known for his second book, *The Making of the English
Working Class* (1963). The cultural emphasis of
Thompson's 'history from below' represented a
paradigm shift in social and labour history, and was
theoretically foundational for the practice of British
cultural studies. In the late 1970s and 1980s,
Thompson, increasingly involved with peace activism, was elected vice-president of Campaign for
Nuclear Disarmament and founded European
Nuclear Disarmament.

See also: Hobsbawm, Eric; Marxism; Taylor,
A.J.P.

Further reading

Kaye, H. and McCelland, K. (eds) (1990) *E.P.
  Thompson: Critical Perspectives*, Cambridge: Polity
  Press.

MARK DOUGLAS

Thompson, Emma

b. 1959, London

Actress

Emma Thompson graduated straight from the
Cambridge Footlights to the West End (*Me and My
Girl*) and television, in *Tutti Frutti* (1987) and
Thompson (1988), starring and written by herself.
The BBC's *Fortunes of War* brought her together
with Kenneth **Branagh**, with whom she subse-
quently starred in Renaissance Films' *Henry V, Dead
Again, Peter's Friends* and *Much Ado About Nothing*. Her
other films include *The Tall Guy, Howard's End*, for
which she won the 1991 Academy Award for best
actress, *The Remains of the Day, In the Name of the
Father, Junior* and *Carrington*. In 1996 she adapted

Jane Austen's *Sense and Sensibility*, in which she
starred and for which she won another Oscar, this
time for Best Adapted Screenplay.

See also: actors (female)

ALISON BOMBER

Thomson

D.C. Thomson publishes 145 magazine and newspaper titles including *Beano, Dandy, The Peoples'
Friend, Sunday Post, Weekly News* and *My Weekly*. With
contents emphasizing family values, readers are
mostly aged forty-five or more. Sales of titles have
slumped since the 1950s. By adopting new
promotion strategies, D.C. Thomson is attempting
to increase circulation in British and foreign
markets.

Popular in Scotland, the *Sunday Post* has
approximately 2.5 million readers per week. The
Guinness Book of Records (1990) listed the *Sunday Post*
as the newspaper closest to saturation circulation,
with an audience of 57 percent of Scottish people
aged fifteen or more in 1988.

Beano and *Dandy* **comics** have become institutions of British childhood, achieving acceptance by
parents and children. Each issue contains slapstick
stories of characters such as Dennis the Menace
and Desperate Dan. The largest circulation in any
region is Southeast England, where 29 percent of
children, mainly boys aged 7–15, form the readership. *Dandy* and *Beano* stories have changed little
since their conception in the 1950s by Leo
Baxendale (Bash Street Kids, Minnie the Minx)
and David Law (Dennis the Menace, Beryl the
Peril). Dudley Watkins invented Desperate Dan for
the *Dandy* in the 1930s. In 1994 letters were written
to *The Times* when it was rumoured that the Bash
Street Kids teacher was to be replaced by a robot;
however, this turned out to be a marketing ploy.

Despite their popularity, the *Beano* and *Dandy*
audience has declined from two million in the 1950s
to 250,000 in the 1990s (audience figures for *Beano*
and *Dandy* are combined). This decline is attributed
to the rising popularity of computer games,
television and globally marketed texts. *Dandy* and
Beano also compete against comics with internationally promoted characters such as *Tom and Jerry*.

By means of animated series produced for television and video, D.C. Thomson aims to increase interest in *Dandy* and *Beano* characters abroad. Licences for characters such as Dennis the Menace, Desperate Dan and Bash Street Kids began in 1988. They are featured in 70–80 product ranges including stationery, chewy bars, burger promotions and most successfully clothing for children and adults. Licensing nets approximately £75–£200 million per annum.

Beano and *Dandy* have a mature cult following, which may explain the popularity of adult merchandise. However, to date there are no statistics available. The magazine *Viz*, a comic for adults, is influenced by and pastiches the anarchic humour of the *Beano* and *Dandy*.

See also: teen magazines; women's press

Further reading

Barker, M. (1989) *Comics: Ideology, Power and the Critics*, Manchester: Manchester University Press.

JOAN STEWART ORMROD

thrillers

The thematic conventions of the contemporary thriller – suspenseful and exciting drama, a narrative which locates criminality as its focus – offer a framework perhaps more readily associated with the genre-based US film industry. The British thriller is not always easy to define, its forms shifting at times between and beyond the crime, melodrama, horror, espionage and action categories.

Suspense and intrigue as durable characteristics of the thriller are significantly identified in the prewar films of British-born director Alfred Hitchcock. *The Thirty-Nine Steps* (1935) and *The Lady Vanishes* (1938) are tightly paced, if improbable, spy adventures featuring charming, upper-class protagonists. After the war, the seedy realism of John Boulting's *Brighton Rock* (1947) introduced an altogether different set of players, and its horrifyingly dark portrayal of vicious criminal ambition amongst small-time gangsters offered a more

sustainable model for the contemporary thriller film. However, in the immediate postwar era, crime dramas such as Basil **Dearden**'s *The Blue Lamp* (1949) commanded wide audience appeal and established the conventions of the 1950s crime vehicle. Prosaic crime themes investigated by worthy and uncomplicated police protagonists characterized the typical thriller.

By the end of the 1950s, the reassuringly formulaic narratives were increasingly challenged by crime dramas with plotlines which sought to confront social issues, dramas which can be considered stylistically and thematically suggestive of the social realist tendency that marked 1960s British cinema. Val Guest's *Hell is a City* (1959) offers gritty Manchester locations to reveal the city's seedy underworld as an embittered detective tracks down a brutal escaped convict. In the problematic thriller *Sapphire* (1959), the search for the killer of a black woman uncovers disturbing undercurrents of racial and class tension amongst suspects and their investigators. Joseph Losey's complex story of incarceration and gangsterism, *The Criminal* (1960), presented the prison environment and underworld with new authenticity; the film, however, encountered a poor critical reception in Britain.

While the traditional values of the police drama were maintained in 1960s B movies, main feature crime films diversified. The stylish James Bond action thrillers, which began in 1962 with *Dr No*, followed by *From Russia with Love* in 1963, revitalized the British spy genre and opened the way for the similarly US-funded Harry Palmer trilogy: *The Ipcress File* (1965), *Funeral in Berlin* (1966) and *Billion Dollar Brain* (1967), adapted from novels by Len Deighton. Of these, the most significant, *The Ipcress File*, while lacking the glamour, extravagant plot and budget of its Bond counterparts, offers realism and style in a credible spy drama which speaks with a dry and off-beat humour of Cold War cynicism and disillusion. Michael **Caine** as Palmer supplied a matter-of-fact, civil service secret agent, in deep contrast to the playboy spy Bond. However, the Bond character has proved more sustainable, with Pierce Brosnan introduced in *Goldeneye* to represent the 1990s version of this long-running series.

While Michael **Powell**'s controversial British film *Peeping Tom* (1959) – which explicitly addresses themes of voyeurism and violence – had been greeted with outrage by reviewers on release, in the 1960s the emerging sub-genre of the psychological thriller was popularized by the international success of Hitchcock's US film *Psycho* (1960). The psychological thriller of the 1960s and 1970s allowed film-makers room to deviate on the cinematic possibilities of the crime film in a variety of ways. In the mainstream, Hammer Films (see **Hammer Horror**) made a series of taut melodramas, which began promisingly with *Taste of Fear* (1961). Beyond Hammer, the US–British co-production *The Collector* (1965), a haunting study of cruelty and obsession, and *Sleuth* (1972), an elegantly theatrical mystery, were built on strong and suspenseful plots. Experimental responses to the category include *Blow Up* (1967), in which Italian director Michelangelo Antonioni bound a mysterious and fragmentary plot within a pastiche of Swinging London images and contexts. Similarly, Nicholas **Roeg** used his evocative visual style to disclose a violent and decadent underworld in *Performance* (1969), and to reveal the hidden malevolence of an atmospheric Venetian setting in the supernatural thriller *Don't Look Now* (1973).

Big-budget thrillers of the 1970s offered an unusual internationalism. Lavish Agatha Christie adaptations *Murder on the Orient Express* (1974) and *Death on the Nile* (1978) revamped the British whodunit tradition with glamorous settings and all star casts. Tightly-paced conspiracy stories *The Day of the Jackal* (1973) and *The Odessa File* (1974) – made with British–European funding – combined journalistic plots (from bestsellers by Frederick Forsyth) with international casting and a distinctive use of European locations. Conversely, lower budgets produced a range of British-based crime films: the hard-edged revenge drama *Get Carter* and Stephen **Frears**'s grimly ironic *Gumshoe* (both 1971) are introspective thrillers which make effective use of their North of England locations. Further significant studies of modern gangsterism, *Villain* (1971) and *The Long Good Friday* (1979), are, like Roeg's *Performance*, London-centred.

For the most part the modern British crime film is not immediately identifiable as a thriller; while preserving themes of violence or the underworld, it tends to deal more with characterization than action. Neil **Jordan**'s *Mona Lisa* (1986), a poignant study of the relationship between a prostitute and her minder, *The Krays* (1990), the compelling story of 1960s underworld bosses Ronnie and Reggie Kray, and Jordan's provocative IRA drama *The Crying Game* (1990) represent new responses to the category.

While *Shallow Grave* (1994), a chilling story of greed and duplicity, proved that the thriller could still be made in Britain, the decline of the British film industry and the identification of a marketable national film type in historical drama are factors which have severely diminished the production of crime films in this country. British stars remain visible, however, due to the Hollywood trend of the late 1980s and 1990s to cast British actors, including Terence Stamp, Charles Dance and Jeremy Irons, as villains in big-budget US crime movies. At home, the fragmentary forms of the contemporary thriller, coupled with the precarious state of the nation's film industry, have meant that television can be seen to offer a more stable context for the sophisticated crime drama with the making of feature-length and serialized thrillers, such as *Prime Suspect*, scripted by Lynda La Plante, and Jimmy McGovern's *Cracker*.

See also: crime drama; thrillers, detective and spy writing

Further reading

Merry, B. (1977) *Anatomy of the Spy Thriller*, Dublin: Gill & MacMillan.

Murphy, R. (1992) *Sixties British Cinema*, London: BFI Publishing.

ALICE E. SANGER

thrillers, detective and spy writing

British mystery writing has undergone a significant series of changes over the past three decades. The detective mystery story, highly restrictive, narrowly defined and dominated by the Queens of Mystery – Agatha Christie, Dorothy Sayers and Ngaio

Marsh – reflected an image of England at odds with the realities of life in Britain during the 1970s, 1980s and 1990s. A backlash against the highly restrictive, conservative format of 'genteel puzzle' fiction began in the 1950s and challenged the homogeneity of that format in which suspense and atmosphere, action and characterization were generally sacrificed for the purity of the puzzle itself. There is now a recognition of the existence of 'evil' and a shift in emphasis to a greater interest in psychology. Thrillers, suspense and crime novels, including the psychological thriller and spy stories, have attracted a wider reading public at the expense of the 'pure' detective novel. Although the pure detective story is still continuing to attract new readers and has had some revival during the 1990s in a wave of nostalgia for the manor house settings, upper-class characters and a comedy of manners tone, it is no longer the dominant force in British detective fiction.

As many new writers of mysteries in England reacted against the limitations of the genre itself, they also moved away from the 'well-made' plot format, the artifices that had their field of play in the puzzle, the near distinction between good and evil, and the insistence that the values of societal norms be upheld, particularly in plot resolutions. These crime novels have moved closer to investigating real sociological problems in contemporary Britain, and although they often have the familiar elements of humour and horror, more often they provide new insights into human behaviour and social conditions.

The genre, in effect, has become far more domesticated, as in the novels of Colin Dexter and his creation, Inspector Morse, and in many instances the family conditions of the police official/detective parallels those of the victims and suspects, so that plot situations are intricate and charged with dramatic irony. In addition, complex and perverse sexual relationships are part of the interpersonal complications both inside and surrounding the crimes; homosexuality and even incest are important subjects in crime fiction, as psychologically determined characterization has become a major emphasis. Ruth Rendell, a major force in modern detective fiction explores the criminal mind, homosexuality, misogyny in her psychological novels as well as an optimistic view of

friendship, and village life in her Inspector Wexford novels. Since the 1960s, some of the strongest reputations in British detective literature belong to women writers, particularly P.D. James, the aforementioned Ruth Rendell and, latterly, Lynda la Plante.

In apparent contrast to detectives whose professional and personal problems are determinedly contemporary, there are 'historically-distanced' detectives, such as Ellis Peters's medieval monk-detective, M.J. Trow's Victorian inspector and Peter Lovesey's Victorian police sergeant. Yet they too are observed with minutely scrupulous attention to realistic detail. These new thrillers were actively in competition with – and often indistinguishable from – serious works of literary fiction. In particular, a strong sociological perspective, at times even quite political, influenced crime literature, describing and analysing an England caught between traditional and progressive modes of behaviour, the changes wrought by the advent of the welfare state, the new permissiveness, the disruption of conventional family life and, most recently, such problems as unemployment, drugs and racism.

Espionage fiction, which had burgeoned with the first Eric Ambler novels, persisted through the cold war years and on into the 1970s and 1980s through the works of John Le Carré, Ian Fleming and Len Deighton. Ian Fleming, the creator of James Bond, Agent 007, began writing in the 1950s with a realistic approach to the spy story. In the character of Bond, he expressed reaction against the sobriety of the 1960s. His use of details and brand names, real and fantasy worlds became intertwined. Bond's sexual confidence made him into a hero of the more sexually open world of this time. Fleming's heroines (his 'Bond women') had their own agendas, independent but often tragic figures in his books. His works left a legacy for John le Carré and Len Deighton to follow.

Action and adventure dominate the novels of John le Carré. Since his first publication *Call for the Dead*, he has returned again and again to the same subject matter, the affairs of the British Intelligence Service, and to the same character, George Smiley. His writings reflect his disillusionment with society in the second half of the twentieth century, and his books analyse an individual's relationship with that society. Cynicism and pessimism pervade his ten novels in which George Smiley became his seeker after humanity, epitomized in *Tinker Tailor, Soldier, Spy, The Honourable Schoolboy* and *Smiley's People.*

Len Deighton, on the other hand, portrayed a more rebellious reflection of the cultural tendencies of the 1960s. In later books, the hero opts out. His contributions were to style and the depiction of the anti-hero. Harry in *The Ipcress File* typifies the maverick individualist that Deighton uses as a vehicle for his anti-establishment sentiments. He shifted pragmatically in later works to make a more topical series of responses to political, social and cultural climate of postwar England.

Literary conservatism in detective fiction is well established, with conventions that are consistent and recognizable. The overwhelming majority of published detective novels provide the safe view of the world in which a single hero can both know and correct an important problem, usually as serious as deliberately caused death. This is exemplified in the fictions of such authors as Dick Francis, Cynthia Harriet-Eagles, Ian Rankin, Peter Hill, Derek Raymond, Nicholas Blincoe, Victor Canning, Ted Lewis, Philip Kerr, John Milne, Clark Smith, William McIlvanney and so on. The economic consequences of a conservative posture are equally clear.

The enormous and ever-increasing popularity of the genre, as registered by published titles, sales figures, bestseller lists, and library circulation numbers, could not have occurred unless detective fiction were successfully meeting a wide variety of social needs and expectations. Authors and publishers might rightly conclude that there would be no advantage in tampering with a proven success. The predictable formula of detective fiction is based on a world whose sex/gender valuations reinforce male hegemony. Taking male behaviour as the norm, the genre defines its parameters to exclude female characters, confidently rejecting them as inadequate women or inadequate detectives. A detective novel with a professional woman detective is, then, a contradiction in terms. The existence of one effectively eliminates the other.

Recently, a number of woman writers have emerged to challenge this stereotype, such as Minette Walters, Stella Duffy, Patricia Cornwall, Martha Lawrence, Sharon McCrumb and Patricia

Routledge. The widespread popularity of detective fiction whose readers cross economic, social educational and gender lines suggests that it makes an important political statement about how the culture works; when women are involved, that statement is traditional, stereotyped and restrictive. When detectives are amateurs, they can be ignored and their behaviour seen as a momentary intrusion into public life; the changes in social organization which would arise from women's active participation in public life, disruption of economic activity and involvement in the political process are thus seen as short-lived and inconsequential. The difficulty which authors have in affecting the conventions is paralleled by the problems of their characters, caught between the inside and outside in adopting a traditionally male profession. The challenge to contemporary authors is to take on the genre, to fashion it, and to deconstruct the structures of the patriarchy.

See also: crime drama; popular fiction; thrillers

Further reading

Bloom, C. (1990) *Twentieth-Century Suspense*, Basingstoke: Macmillan.

JIM SINCLAIR

time shares

Time shares became popular in the 1980s but resulted in bankruptcy, court proceedings or simple disappointment and frustration for many people. 'Time share' refers to the selling and buying of the right to occupy a flat or house, usually for holidaying abroad, for specified weeks of each year. Time shares continue to be marketed heavily and promoted by aggressive selling techniques, in which a holiday or similar free gift is offered to any invited person who attends the hardsell pitches; these can last for several hours.

See also: tourism

PETER CHILDS

tobacco industry

Since the 1950s, the tobacco industry has been fighting a rearguard action against consumer protection agencies, the medical profession and the ethical investment industry. Advertising on television was stopped many years ago. Sponsorship of sport by tobacco companies is no longer acceptable. Cigarette packets and other advertising media have long had to carry government health warnings. Despite these efforts, young females continue to take up smoking: 39 percent of the 20–24-year-old age group smokes. Tobacco companies such as BAT have diversified into financial services, and some companies target, as new consumers, people in the Third World, where constraints on advertising and legal redress are much more limited.

See also: newsstands and newsagents

MIKE STORRY

top-shelf magazines

Top-shelf magazines are soft-core pornographic magazines, so called because they are displayed on the top shelves of shops, too high for children to reach them. Readily available in Britain in newsagents and petrol station shops, and generally priced at £2–£3, they are sold as an aid to sexual fantasy and masturbation. The top ten titles have combined UK sales estimated at 2 million.

The social role of top-shelf magazines sheds insights into British attitudes to sex, and the contrast between private and socially acceptable behaviour. Despite their popularity for private use, generally, outside of all-male environments, use of these magazines remains socially taboo. In a recent legal case a secretary tried to have her manager fired after she found top-shelf magazines in his office. The manager was retained but referred for counselling by his employers, and the secretary resigned in protest. The revelation that the late poet Philip Larkin used pornographic magazines caused a storm of disapproval in intellectual circles.

Soft-core is defined as photographs of nude, or more commonly semi-clad women, precluding display of inner genital areas or sexual acts between men and women. Hard-core magazines, often originating in Scandinavia or Holland, which may explicitly portray heterosexual and homosexual acts, along with scenes of female domination, fetishes and corporal punishment, may legally only be acquired through licensed sex shops. In recent years, in the context of an increasingly competitive market, there has been a steady drift towards harder material within top-shelf magazines: for example, the introduction of women in the process of shaving, or shaved of, body hair, posed lesbian scenes with two women, or models clad in fetish or bondage gear.

Some magazines, for example *Mayfair* and *Club*, feature models of Page Three girls or the stars of pornographic video series. Magazines such as *Penthouse* feature professional models in glamorous locations. (One hugely popular issue in the 1980s, which included a photoshoot with a Princess Diana lookalike in apparently royal surroundings, sold out in days.) Other titles, such as *Escort* and *Fiesta*, trade heavily on 'readers wives': polaroid photographs of 'ordinary' women usually submitted by their partners, and on letters purported to be from readers detailing their sexual experiences. Some invite contact (via box numbers) with the 'wives' in question. This is matched by a general trend towards more explicit captions, and exhortation to masturbation ostensibly urged by the models themselves.

The market also supports a growing number of specialist magazines whose titles indicate their contents: *40 Plus*, *Fat and 40*, *Asian Babes*, *Skinny and Wriggly* and *Leg Love*. An attempt to open up the market to women in the early 1990s was largely a failure, perhaps due to British obscenity laws which forbid the display of an erect penis. *For Women* is one exception, which remains in widespread circulation.

The magazine market is closely linked to premium-rate phone sex lines. Up to a quarter of the page length of some titles may be devoted to advertising such services, which provide a vital element of the revenue. Several titles have associated websites. By the late 1990s the pornography market had shifted from its main ground to three relatively new areas: 'lads' magazines like *Loaded* and *FHM* (for softcore), video and the Internet (for hardcore).

See also: pornography; special interest magazines

EDMUND CUSICK

tourism

Demand for holidays, which increased in the 1950s, was stagnant in the early to mid-1960s. Towards the end of the 1960s, rising standards in Britain, coupled with the increasingly competitive position of foreign package tours, led to a rapid rise in the number of holidays taken abroad. Thus, while domestic holiday expenditure rose by 78 percent (from £320 million in 1951 to £570 million in 1968), British tourist spending abroad rose from £60 million in 1951 to £320 million in 1968. Whereas holidays abroad in 1951 accounted for only 16 percent of total expenditure; in 1968 they represented 36 percent. However, it is important to stress that foreign travel in the 1960s was predominantly enjoyed by the higher socio-economic groups and the young.

In the 1970s, the demand for holidays became more geographically diffused, further undermining the established resorts. Also, foreign holidays dramatically reduced the rate of domestic holidays, resulting in a rapid expansion in short-stay holidays along the British coastline. These new types of holidays fell into three main categories: caravans, holiday cottages and day trips. The 1970s was the decade when caravanning became extremely popular, but as package holidays increased, the consumer exchanged the caravan for the beaches of Costa Brava in Spain. Furthermore, the 1970s were the first time that holidays were financially available to people in the lower socio-economic groups. Therefore, it is important to place holidays and tourism in an economic context because of the symbiotic relationship between social and economic change; holidays and tourism must be seen as standard features of consumer society lifestyles, in that they tend to be occasions of extravagance and conspicuous consumption. Further, as David Chaney suggests, 'the practice of holidaying has become a display of citizenship and the tourist is expected to conform to a script of orderly consumption' (Chaney 1993: 165).

The amount of leisure per person within Britain has grown significantly. Key factors have been the reductions in working time, longer periods of retirement, and the rise of forced leisure in the form of unemployment. Until the 1950s paid holiday entitlements were very limited, particularly among manual workers. Between 1950 and 1975 such entitlements were much extended, and by 1980 a majority of manual workers had four or more weeks of paid holidays, secured by the relevant trade unions. This extension of holiday, coupled with the rise in personal incomes, enabled growing numbers to take vacations away from home. In 1980 62 percent of British residents took holidays abroad in comparison with 56 percent in 1966. Tourism in the 1990s was an extremely sophisticated machine, making full use of all information technology strategies, thus securing efficient and effective communications.

Since their formation in 1969, the statutory Tourist Boards have sought to spread the benefits of tourism throughout Britain and to assist the tourist industry to become and remain competitive. In the 1980s, tourism was widely promoted as a coherent entity rather than a multi-product sector, for political and economic reasons. Labelling tourism an industry was a method of unifying a heterogeneous and diverse number of different businesses which individually had very little lobbying power than the more homogeneous industries like transport and agriculture. Thus, they were able to achieve greater visibility with the government and the public.

See also: cross-Channel shopping; heritage

Further reading

Chaney, D. (1993) *Fictions of Collective Life: Public Drama in Late Modern Culture*, London: Routledge.

Holloway, J.C. (1989) *The Business of Tourism*, London: Pitman.

Voase, R. (1995) *Tourism: The Human Perspective*, London: Hodder & Stoughton.

FATIMA FERNANDES

town planning

In retrospect, the 1960s and 1970s seem marked by poor town planning, based on tower blocks, corrupt politics, aggressive property development and bypasses. The 1980s, by contrast, were characterized by a renewed interest in urbanism, in conservation and in historical styles. Buildings are now more likely to be built into a context rather than designed individually or after massive demolition (often of historically important buildings) has made way for their arrival. These new 'infill' buildings of course vary in quality and attractiveness, and many suffer from imitation rather than inspiration, missing the value of contrast in a rush to conformity. However, there are excellent examples of blending and grafting, such as Harper Mackay's Gaemester Kenyon in Southwark, London. Large new sites have also provided great opportunities, notably at Spitalfields Market (Leon Krier), Canary Wharf (Skidmore, Owings and Merrill), Horselydown Square, Southwark (Wickham Associates) and Richmond riverside (Erith and Terry).

See also: city redevelopment

Further reading

Glancey, J. (1989) *New British Architecture*, London: Thames & Hudson.

PETER CHILDS

trade unions

Trade unions are associations of workers who combine to safeguard their collective interest and to maintain or improve their working conditions and wage levels. Union aims can be industrial, social or political. They are either closed organizations, concentrating on the interests of defined groups of workers, or open, seeking to increase the range of their membership. The trend since the 1970s has been towards openness through conglomerates of distinct organizations or through mergers. Closed unions have suffered a drastic fall in membership and many unions have united to survive. Nonetheless, British society is still characterized by multi-unionism.

Eighty percent of union members are affiliated to the coordinating centre of British politics, the Trade Union Congress (TUC). The TUC meets annually when collective policies and strategies are outlined, with voting strength related to union size. The TUC also elects the General Council which carries out policy between congresses. Its current General Secretary is John Monks, who succeeded Norman Willis in 1993. The 1990s have seen the growth of business unionism, with Monks attempting to update the TUC's image, offering affiliates technical and legal advice and financial services. Eight of the ten largest unions also maintain links with the **Labour Party** by paying political levies and having a strong, though diminished, influence at the Labour conference and within the party's National Executive.

In the postwar years, trade unions enjoyed good relations with government. In the era of the postwar consensus, governments joined with trade unions and business in economic planning, and unions were consulted before legislation as a matter of course. However at the end of the 1960s, union militancy began to increase, reflecting public dissatisfaction with Britain's relative economic decline. This was manifested in the increased number of political strikes, work-ins, occupations and demands for greater worker participation in industrial decision making.

Edward Heath and the Conservatives came to power in 1970, committed to the Selsdon Programme which advocated right-wing economic reforms and curbs on trade union power. The latter was attempted with the Industrial Relations Act 1971, which would prevent industrial action harmful to the economy, prohibit unofficial strikes and limit the powers of the closed shop, the practice whereby individuals must join the relevant union as a condition of employment at a specific workplace. Union opposition to this Act was universal, and widespread strikes, originally in sympathy with London dockers who were imprisoned for withholding their labour, rendered the legislation unworkable. Union strength in this period is demonstrated by the National Union of Mineworkers (NUM), whose members received a 27 percent pay rise after a strike in 1972 and then objected to Heath's statutory incomes policy. Heath went to the country in 1974 asking whether the unions or the government ran the country; Labour was elected.

Labour overturned the preceding administration's trade union legislation in return for wage restraint in a voluntary incomes policy in a deal known as the Social Contract. However, this agreement resulted in real cuts in living standards, especially in the public sector, and the TUC was unable to prevent increased industrial unrest. This culminated in the **Winter of Discontent** and electoral success for the Conservatives in 1979.

Mrs Thatcher was ideologically opposed to **corporatism**; following the New Right economic theories of F.A. von Hayek and Milton Friedman, she believed that the market works better unimpeded by the state. The unions were blamed for the nation's economic ills, and their power was systematically reduced through legislation. Secondary picketing was outlawed in 1980, but 1982 saw the most radical changes with the Employment Act, which limited strikes to those concerning pay or conditions, tightened procedures on the closed shop, made occupations and sit-ins illegal and reduced trade union immunities. Further legislation in the 1980s and 1990s made requirements for strike ballots more stringent, restricted rights for union officials and forced unions to give seven days notice for industrial action. The basic right to be in a union was also threatened, with workers at GCHQ from 1984 no longer allowed union membership.

The defeat of the NUM in the 1984–5 miners' strike was a watershed, after which the trade unions were forced to come to a new realism in their dealings with government. The miners were tackled when coal stocks were high, after a general election and when the **police** were ready to deal with mass picketing. The strike was a disaster for the NUM itself, with the breakaway of the Union of Democratic Mineworkers, and its consequent inability to combat the 1992 pit closures programme. NUM membership fell from 250,000 in 1979 to 8,000 in 1993.

The Conservatives succeeded in curbing union strength, with media backing and some public support as unions were perceived to be too powerful and undemocratic. They were aided by the changing face of industry, the erosion of Britain's manufacturing base and the increase in de-unionized service industries. In addition, recessions in the early 1980s and 1990s, the ineffective opposition of the Labour Party and the embourgeoisement of the working class weakened union strength and solidarity within the labour movement.

Trade unions are now considerably weaker than in the 1970s. Militancy has been replaced with business unionism, and the strike rate is low. The unions are consistently denied access to the corridors of power, and consultation is limited, corporatist bodies having been abandoned. Union membership has fallen from thirteen million in 1979 to nine million in 1994, and is a public sector preserve. Nevertheless, unions are still active and seeking to recruit members outside of their traditional areas of influence. They now look to increase their influence at European level, particularly in the light of developments according them a positive role such as the Social Chapter. Some trade unions outside of the TUC have grown in the 1980s and 1990s, and collective bargaining still covers about half of the workforce, suggesting that trade unions will continue to be prominent in British politics for the conceivable future.

See also: Labour Party; New Labour; NUJ

Further reading

Kessler, S. and Bayliss, F. (1995) *Contemporary British Industrial Relations*, London: Macmillan.

McIlroy, J. (1995) *Trade Unions in Britain Today*, 2nd edn, Manchester: Manchester University Press.

COLIN WILLIAMS

tragedies

While there have always been mass tragedies, since the development of radio and particularly television, our perceptions of such tragedies have taken on a more 'national' and intimate perspective. The immediacy of coverage, which in some cases has been contemporaneous, also allows the viewer a voyeuristic position of an unfolding tragedy. An early example that touched the public's conscience was the Aberfan disaster in 1966, where the mid-Glamorgan town's coal waste heap collapsed onto a school and houses, killing 144 people including 116 children. There have been a number of other events that have taken on the mantle of national tragedy and have been the subject of mass grieving, and in some cases, moral panics. Such tragedies have not been confined to any one area of life but have encompassed travel, community life and sites of recreation. Examples of the first include the 1988 fire at Kings Cross station and the aircraft crash onto the town of Lockerbie following an onboard explosion. The Aberfan disaster is an example of the second, as are the mass shootings by a lone gunman at Hungerford in the 1980s and Dunblane in the 1990s. The latter event attracted widespread national and international attention as all but one of the victims were primary schoolchildren. Both these events led to a tightening of gun control, though after the tragic incident at Dunblane the government was criticized for not learning the original lessons of Hungerford.

Prominent examples of tragedies relating to leisure activities have occurred at football grounds. On 15 May 1985, a fire at Bradford City's Valley Parade ground claimed fifty-six lives, and a riot described as 'being like the battle of Agincourt' at Birmingham City's ground killed one fan. These were overshadowed by two further events both involving Liverpool supporters. First, at the 1985 European Cup final in the Heysel stadium in Belgium, thirty-nine Juventus fans were killed when terracing collapsed following disturbances between the opposing fans. The second incident took place at Hillsborough, the ground of Sheffield Wednesday Football Club, on 15 April 1989 at an FA Cup semi-final between Liverpool and Nottingham Forest. Overcrowding at one part of the Liverpool end coupled with perimeter fencing, itself a product of the hooliganism of the 1980s, led to the crushing to death of ninety-six supporters. This tragic event spawned massive media coverage and some of the issues remain largely unresolved.

See also: football; government inquiries

GUY OSBORN
STEVE GREENFIELD

trance

Trance music belongs to the genre of electronically produced sound. Its immediate predecessors include **techno** (*circa* 1990), ambient wave (*circa* 1990), breakbeat (comprising **jungle** and drum 'n' bass, 1991–7) and initially acid **house**. The latter broke onto the dance scene in the UK in 1988 and fundamentally altered club culture; indeed it was the beginnings of a major cultural explosion, giving rise to raves and wild house mutations. By the end of 1990, a fusion of American and European house and techno styles was innovated, forming new sub-styles which included trance and ambient under the general heading of global house nation.

Trance music gained ground around 1994 and provided an alternative to the rawer beats of house and extremities of techno where tracks can exceed 1,000 bpm. Trance music thus probably originated as a counteraction to hardcore techno and identified itself more with ambient, the latter being an atmospheric sound with softer rhythms and restrained noise levels. Hardcore trance and techno are related by the bass beat, with trance having a more moderate melodic sound. From 1994 onwards a new type of sound appeared, known as tribal music: it was the sound between hardcore techno and ambient.

Trance also produced its own sub-genres. Hardtrance, with a faster rhythm, is the popular version played on the club scene; Café Del Mar, for example, is a highly popular trance club in Ibiza. Trancecore is a mixture of trance and hardcore. Goa trance, also known as psychedelic trance, is a more dynamic, deeper and ethno-based version which gained popularity in 1996–7. The name originates from the holiday resort in India, where DJs initially began producing and playing this more ethno-based variant. It involves a complex intermixing of synthetic and kaleidoscopic sound, with a steady 4/4 beat underlying a whirling assembly of analog sounds. A more popular division of trance music has been that of dreamhouse, which incorporates swelling piano arrangements inducing a more peaceful state of mind in the listener: the artist Robert Miles's track 'Children', which reached number one in most European countries, is an example of dreamhouse.

Since the dawn and increasing popularity of

electronic music, coupled with widespread psychoactive experimentation, the age of the dance 'bands' with instruments in the traditional sense has given way to the new age of the sampler and technology in the production of sound. However, trance music in particular has seen a revival in the ideologies of the late 1960s and early 1970s, but this time with an incorporation of a distinctly technological agenda. Trance music is more than merely intertwined arpeggiated sixteenth-notes and one-note chords as is often perceived: hardtrance is arguably small nuances in the arrangements around a repeating rhythm, and thus seems to be designed to induce the listener/dancer into a 'trance' due to its repetitive nature. Yet, the softer, ambient trance is a more contemplative, meditative mix using musical structures with sounds from the electronic wavestation as well as Aztec flutes, bells and African drums. Although this more sombient sound is also electronically derived, its hypnotic sound would more aptly be described as mood-seducing music enhancing an altered state of consciousness. If ambient trance is perceived as music for the 'mind and soul', the club version is its counterpart for 'mind, body and soul'.

As trance music is an abstract construct rather than actual instruments, it has been able to be simultaneously energetic yet sedate, either using an insistent rhythmic pulse to hypnotize into a 'trance' or a free-floating languidity to 'en-trance': either way the music gives expression to a sound which crosses listening genre boundaries and provides a blend of cross-cultural fusions.

See also: hip hop; rave culture

MIRIAM MOKAL

transcendental meditation

Transcendental meditation (TM) has become widely popular in the West since the 1960s. Those who practise do not necessarily have any religious belief, although in some US states TM has the status of a religion itself. Of Hindu and Buddhist origin, TM was first popularized in the West by Maharishi Mahesh Yogi, who had spent thirteen years in seclusion with Guru Dev, the man who had rediscovered the technique this century. The

Mahirishi converted the Beatles and other influential people to the twice-daily twenty-minute stress-reducing and relaxing exercise, which is believed to lead towards self-understanding. There are meditation centres in many British cities; an example is the Liverpool Meditation Centre, established in 1994 by the Friends of the Western Buddhist Order, a registered charity.

See also: spiritual leaders

PETER CHILDS

transmission technologies

Transmission technologies are the electronic means by which communications are sent and received. Historically, communication transmission technologies in Britain have been developed and used in two specific ways: for telecommunication or point-to-point communication, and for broadcasting or one-to-many communication. British Telecom, as it is now known, developed transmission technologies to allow interactive two-way voice communication between any part of its network. The broadcast media developed transmission technologies that allowed a similar service to be delivered to many, over a large geographic area; it was thus non-interactive and one-way. However, current developments in transmission technologies, both software and hardware, are blurring this divide.

For most of the twentieth century, transmission technologies have been of the analogue type. This form of technology creates and transmits signals that are analogous or similar to the original source. Hence, for example, music, which exists as sound waves is picked up and then converted into radio waves for transmission; once received it is converted back into sound waves. Currently, analogue technologies are being replaced by digital technologies which, for some, signal a revolutionary jump in communication technology. By digitalizing data – converting data, voice, text, graphics and video into a binary form – intelligent software can process, manipulate, compress and prepare the signal for transmission. At the receiving end this processes is reversed, turning the digital signal back into an analogue form that can be viewed, read or heard. Digital technologies will allow a huge increase in the number of channels that can be offered, an improvement in the technical quality of these services and the forms that they take will increase. For example, **BSkyB** will be offering hundreds of satellite delivered broadcast, narrowcast and interactive digital television channels after the millennium.

Alongside digitalisation there have been developments in the hardware used: fibre optic, satellite, cable, cellular radio and microwave. While initially such developments reinforced the dichotomy of telecommunication and broadcasting, they are currently helping to redefine the boundaries. For example, as the power of satellites has grown, so their original use for point-to-point communications has been supplemented with the development of direct to home broadcasting (DTH). Thus in Britain, telecommunication bodies are starting to offer various new information and media-styled services, while the media is beginning to be involved in interactive two-way services (for example, cable systems are also providing telecommunication services).

See also: cable and satellite

Further reading

Negrine, R. (1994) *Politics and the Mass Media in Britain*, London: Routledge.

PAUL RIXON

transsexuals

A term coined by Dr D.O. Cauldwell in the early 1950s to describe the case of a girl who desperately desired to be a boy, transsexualism first came to public consciousness in 1953 with the case of male-to-female transsexual Christine Jorgensen. Despite advancements in hormonal and surgical techniques, sex changes, as they are commonly known, are still prohibitively expensive, rarely available on the National Health and emotionally and physically painful processes for those who undergo them. In addition, the British state continues to disregard change of sex with reference to birth certificates, job protection and adoption, a fact that has led to a number of cases (currently under review) being taken to the European Court of Human Rights.

See also: 'gender benders'

CLARE WHATLING

travel writing

For centuries, the genre of travel writing was unchanged. There was very little difference in approach between Richard Hakluyt's *The Principal Navigations, Voyages, Traffiques and Discoveries of the English Nation* (1598–1600) and George Borrow's *Wild Wales* (1862). Travel books contained a truthful account of an actual journey. Travellers went to faraway places and recounted their 'adventures' to the armchair reader. Books which challenged these generic conventions included Jonathan Swift's *Gulliver's Travels* (1726) and Voltaire's *Candide* (1759), but these did not affect the tradition.

The maximum 'deviation' until recent times was the inclusion of 'tall tales'. Joshua Slocum alleged that he sprinkled the deck of his yacht *Spray* with tin tacks to deter marauding Indians in *Sailing Alone Around the World* (1900). Tristan Jones claimed to have pushed his eye back into its socket when it was knocked out by his mast in *Ice* (1979). This increased tendency towards the picaresque and emphasis on the eccentricity of the authors is evident in Dervla Murphy's account of her bicycle ride to India *Full Tilt* (1965) and Rosie Swales's sailing exploits in *Rosie Darling* (1973). But the focus in these accounts remained the same kind of derring-do that had been practised by such great travellers of the past as Lady Hester Stanhope, Richard Burton or Wilfrid Thesiger, whose account of crossing the Empty Quarter in *Arabian Sands* (1959) or living in Iraq in *The Marsh Arabs* (1964) became popular Penguin titles. Even Eric Newby's cult book *A Short Walk in the Hindu Kush* (1958) and Vikram Seth's *From Heaven Lake* (1983), apparently in the 'understated' tradition where the focus is deliberately shifted from the prowess of the traveller to the interest of the people encountered, were really about their authors.

The recent trend has been from the informative to the impressionistic. Rough Guides and the

American Bill Bryson are largely responsible for this. The former, written for budget travellers and students on their year off, are an iconoclastic alternative to tourist-brochure influenced guides, whose production was often subsidized by the tourist industry. Bryson's approach – acerbic, idiosyncratic, opinionated, at times manic – replaced that of gentler writers like Jonathan Raban (*Hunting Mr Heartbreak*, 1990) and Paul Theroux. (*The Great Railway Bazaar*, 1975). His books do not lay claim to veracity, yet have restored travel to the bestseller lists. They include *The Lost Continent* (1989), *Neither Here Nor There* (1991) and *Notes from a Small Island* (1995),

See also: autobiography

Further reading

Jarvis, R. (1997) *Romantic Writing and Pedestrian Travel*, Basingstoke: Macmillan.

MIKE STORRY

tribalism

The distinction between the tribes of Europe are well known, and have indeed led to wars spilling well beyond the bounds of Europe. The threat of such recurrence has brought Helmut Kohl, the previous Chancellor of Germany, to imply in a controversial statement that without a full European unification backed by economic and monetary union (EMU) tribalism in Europe might yet again lead to war and strife in the next millennium.

Less well known is the phenomenon of tribalism in Britain. This tribalism stretches between the countries of the Union, Scotland, Wales, Ulster and England, for example, or even within such regional groupings. Tribalism in Britain can be explained in several ways. It can be viewed as how the people in Britain are identified by particular terms and categories that feed into their identities. These terms can be geographical, as in, for instance, dividing the British people according to their residency. This can be both general – for example, from south or north – or it may associated with counties or regions. Class can also be a source of

the division unveiled in 'tribalism'. Social status thus creates the 'tribe'.

In practice, tribalism is seen at its barest with football supporters, where supporters of a certain football club can be viewed as a 'tribe' within the wider community. Tribalism can to a lesser extent be connected to other sports, but in all these cases it is connected to a need to belong to some grouping from which identity personal and political can be drawn. Worldwide, there is nothing unusual in this; on the contrary, it is quite basic and quite primitive. If there is a prime question overhanging 'tribalism' in developed societies such as British culture, it centres on the degree to which the freedom espoused as a value in such societies can be squared with tribal attitudes.

See also: football; violence

Further reading

Anderson, B. (1983) *Imagined Communities: Reflections on the Origin and Spread of Nationalism*, London: Verso.

Clarke, P.B. (1996) *Deep Citizenship*, London: Pluto Press, pp. 93–7.

PAUL BARRY CLARKE
SVANBORG SIGMARSDOTTIR

tribute bands

Described by some as a postmodern musical development, the tribute band is a peculiar hybrid of fandom and cabaret culture. Usually taking their name from some aspect of their idol's work, tribute bands tend to perform note-perfect renditions of the band they are imitating. Stage shows and costumes, even accents, are meticulously studied and performed to audiences. Bands such as Bjorn Again (Abba), The Australian Doors and the Australian Pink Floyd all regularly perform sell out gigs. The Bootleg Beatles have achieved recognition by performing at Liverpool's Royal Philharmonic Hall, something their illustrious predecessors failed to do. Some artists are pleased by the 'tribute' paid to them; Oasis copyists No Way Sis have the blessing of their idols.

See also: pop and rock

SAM JOHNSTONE

TV-am

TV-am was an ambitious television start-up, the first television company to offer programmes in the mornings. It drew widespread scepticism for the hype surrounding its launch. It recruited high-profile media figures including David Frost and Anna Ford (who were nicknamed 'dinosaurs') and predicted ITV-style success. In 1983, Ford threw a glass of wine over the Conservative politician Jonathan Aitken because she felt he had 'betrayed' her colleagues at the station. The programmes were innovative and ambitious (Ulrika Jonsson was a weather girl), but TV-am never achieved the ratings it set out to gain and eventually lost its franchise.

See also: breakfast television; daytime television; Granada; Mersey Television; Thames TV

MIKE STORRY

2000 AD

2000AD was essentially a product of its time. After *Warlord* was launched by rivals D.C. **Thomson** in September 1974, IPC magazines realized that it was important to counter with their own new magazine. At the time of the launch of *2000AD*, the market was awash with themed comics such as *Roy of the Rovers* (football) and *Action* (war), while *2000AD*'s own theme was to be broadly science-fiction oriented. As the founder of the magazine explained:

> I didn't want *2000AD* to follow in the same old house style of existing publications like *Eagle* or *TV21*. I actually saw sci-fi as a vehicle for increased action and violence, and, more importantly for myself a chance to explore the difficult idea and concept of the human archetype of the beast. *2000AD* was not a vertical progression from previous comics, more a retreat into a darker world, where you could get away with anything.

This development was in parallel with an increasing intervention by Hollywood into the field of science fiction with notable films such as *Logan's Run* (Anderson, 1976), *Star Wars* (Lucas, 1977 re-released 1997) and cult favourite *Blade Runner* (Scott, 1982), also released as *Blade Runner: The Director's Cut* (Scott, 1991). While all may owe something of a debt to *2001: A Space Odyssey* (Kubrick, 1968), they reflected the move of traditional areas of human conflict into visions of a future society. The most telling contribution of *2000 AD* is undoubtedly the character Judge Dredd, the ultimate law enforcer, judge, jury and executioner who rode the streets of MegaCity One in the twenty-first century dispensing justice as and when he felt necessary. The character was utilized in the Hollywood film *Judge Dredd* (Cannon, 1995) though some purists decried its depiction (and Sylvester Stallone's portrayal) for being not true to the 'original'. It is somewhat curious that while we can be precious about cultural artefacts created in the recent past we are far less concerned with interpretations of work with a longer history such as Shakespearean plays. Judge Dredd himself has emerged as a cultural icon, and *2000AD* to a large degree operates within the shadow of its most famous creation.

See also: comics; comics culture

Further reading

Jarman, C. and Acton, P. (1995) *Judge Dredd: The Mega History*, Leonard Publishing (more concerned with Judge Dredd than *2000 AD* itself, but in the absence of any reference works on *2000AD* it provides some useful early detail and context).

GUY OSBORN
STEVE GREENFIELD

two-tone

At its height in the years between 1979 and 1982, the two-tone movement provided an often damning musical commentary on the most significant rightward ideological shift in modern British political thought. Hailing mainly from the more ethnically diverse, though by no means harmonious, communities of Coventry, Birmingham and East London, the Specials, The Beat, The Selecter and Madness formed the nucleus of the bands signed to the Two-Tone label and produced the self-defined two-tone or **ska** music which dominated the charts in the early Thatcher years. Two-tone by name and two-tone in composition, with black and white group members, these bands preached a positive and provocative message of interracial cooperation and understanding, against a background of bureaucratic and political indifference, neo-Nazi nationalism and the planned structural decay of the inner cities.

This post-punk wave of British popular music had its roots and sought its inspiration in the work of Jamaican musicians, such as Prince Buster, Duke Reid and Coxson Dodd, from some twenty years earlier. Indeed, many of the original ska sounds (such as 'Guns of Navarone' and 'My Boy Lollipop') were covered by British two-tone bands and became huge hits with the movement's many skinhead followers (see **skinheads**). But two-tone music was more than ska; it was ska plus pop, **punk rock** and **soul**. This unique cocktail of musical influences created a new dance craze (the title of a 1981 film documenting the British two-tone phenomenon) and a new strain of youth-culture. Rudeboys and rudegirls, or gender-neutral rudies, were a fashion-conscious crowd prone to wearing smart suits, 'pork pie' hats, white socks and slip-on, tasselled brogues. Unlike some extreme nationalist elements of the mod (see **mods**) and skinhead cohort, from which they drew inspiration for their dress code, rudies evidenced an enlightened outlook on issues of race.

Having released a string of hits which dealt with unemployment, foppery in higher education, racial violence and the futilities of the urban nightclub lifestyle, it seems fair to say that the most incisive political commentary from within this musical movement came from the Two-Tone label's founders, The Specials (officially named the Special AKA). But their most prescient and haunting song was 'Ghost Town', a number one in 1981, which coincided with the widespread inner-city rioting of the same year. Furthermore, while recording as the Special AKA in 1987, the band again captured the mood of the moment in contributing to the international campaign effort to secure the release of Nelson Mandela. Their catchy anthem, celebrating the name and plight of the jailed ANC leader, was sung throughout the townships of South Africa.

Several two-tone/ska revivals have occurred since the movement's heyday, while many original two-tone band members have since found success in new group combinations (including the Fine Young Cannibals, General Public and the Fun Boy Three). Meanwhile, perhaps recognizing their obvious influence on younger **Britpop** bands, Madness returned with several sold-out live shows.

Further reading

Marshall, G. (1988) *The Two-Tone Story*, London: Boxtree.

STEPHEN C. KENNY

U

Ulster Unionists

Ulster Unionists support the constitutional status of Northern Ireland tied to state and Crown within the United Kingdom. Popular Protestantism is the traditional link between Unionists and Conservatives, and the former took the Conservative whip until the Stormont Parliament was prorogued in 1972. Unionists oppose sharing power with Ulster's Catholics and any integration with the Irish Republic, hence condemning initiatives such as the 1985 Anglo-Irish Agreement and bilateral London–Dublin talks on the future of the province. In 1998, David Trimble was leader of the official Ulster Unionist Party and Ian Paisley led the more extreme Democratic Unionist Party. Unionist parties have a no-contest electoral agreement whereby sitting MPs are unchallenged, lessening the possibility of the Catholic SDLP gaining more seats.

See also: Ireland; Sinn Féin

COLIN WILLIAMS

underground press and fanzines

The cultural explosions of the 1960s reverberated throughout the publishing world, creating an underground press invigorated by and disseminating ideas synchronously with emerging countercultural movements. Rejecting mainstream publishing conventions, revolutionizing language and visual print with an experimental thrust and unfettered approach which captured the dissenting attitude and mood of the underground, the underground press demonstrated that even those without journalistic, design or publishing experience could produce culturally definitive independent magazines and 'fanzines'.

With localized and international influences ranging from concurrent cultural movements such as the New Left, Beatniks and Situationists International, the 1960s and early 1970s underground press mushroomed with publications including the first British underground magazine *It* (*International Times*, 1966), the satirical *Oz* (1968), the Marxist left *Black Dwarf* (1968) and London listings magazine *Time Out* (1968) alongside a plethora of political manifestos and pamphlets. The early 1970s introduced *7 Days* (1971), *Ink* (1971), feminist publications like *Shrew* and *Spare Rib* (1972) and *Gay News* (1972). The infamous 1970 *Oz* court case for its 'schoolkids' issue featured in a decade of frequent police raids and court action against the transgressive underground press.

All manner of independent publications were to energize the publishing arena in subsequent years. Punk signalled the proliferation of the cheaply produced, xeroxed or photocopied fanzine, with Mark Perry's *Sniffin' Glue* (lauded as the first contemporary music fanzine) and others such as the Glaswegian *Ripped and Torn* and *More-On* demonstrating the punk 'do-it-yourself', working-class ethos with their haphazard, anarchic typography and graphic arrangement indicative of punk music and attitude.

The early 1990s trans-Atlantic Riot Grrrl movement drew upon punk subculture to challenge received gender roles and representations, riot grrrls forming their own bands and producing fanzines such as *Ablaze* and *Fast Connection* which fused music with forthright feminist opinions.

As 1980s underground magazines like *ID* and *The Face* went overground with their stylistic fusion of music, fashion, art and culture, they partly triggered the early 1990s publishing revolution, creating an underground press replete with titles like *Dazed and Confused*, satirical fashion magazine *Blow*, *The Idler*, *aBeSea*, *G-Spot*, *Herb Garden*, *Jockey Slut* and *Zine* which benefited from cheap and accessible desktop publishing and printing methods and a burgeoning creative spirit among aspirant photographers, writers and designers. Other magazines like the ragga *Skank*, second-hand fashion *Cheap Date* and Charlotte Cooper's thematic zines have followed.

Independently published and distributed on smaller budgets and with smaller circulation figures than its mainstream counterparts, the underground press is aimed at specific audiences and irreverently covers all aspects of culture. It resists dominant trends by creating them instead through a risk-taking approach without the marketing, advertising and orthodox constraints of larger publications.

Further reading

Fountain, N. (1988) *Underground: The London Alternative Press 1966–74*, London: Routledge (fascinating, revealing appraisal of the nascent contemporary London underground press).

SATINDER CHOHAN

Unification Church

A North Korean electrical engineering graduate, Sun Myung Moon (1920–) founded his church as God's new religious vehicle in 1954. His followers are known derogatively as 'Moonies' because they believe their leader is the Second Coming. Moon chooses members' marriage partners, who are usually unknown to one another. His mass marriage of 30,000 couples in 1992 is in *The Guinness Book Of World Records*. The religion is unpopular because its adherents are allowed to lie to raise money. The group uses 'front' names, such

as 'The Kensington Garden Arts Society', 'The New World Singers' and 'The International Conference on the Unity of the Sciences'.

See also: evangelism; Jehovah's Witnesses

MIKE STORRY

universities

During the postwar period, universities underwent a series of significant and revolutionary changes. Up until the Robbins Report (1963), chaired by Lionel (later Lord) Robbins, universities were relatively autonomous academic republics receiving a quinquennial recurrent grant from central government via the University Grants Committee (UGC). The latter, established in 1919, advised government on the distribution of funds to universities and acted, as Hugh Dalton noted, 'as a buffer or shock absorber between the government and the universities'.

That role, and indeed the system of university finance, management and autonomy, changed radically following the Robbins Report, which outlined details recommending a move from elite to mass higher education. This involved a projected tripling of student numbers by 1980 and a higher education system dominated by the universities. The demands placed on universities by growing numbers of eligible students, together with an overall projected increase in population size, prompted Robbins to recommend expanding the number of universities.

Robbins introduced the principle, sacrosanct until recently, that all students capable of benefiting from higher education be permitted, if they so wished, to proceed to such education. A significant correlative to this was that education should be free at the point of delivery. The underlying justification for this was that as the benefit was not just to an individual but to society in general, the cost could reasonably be borne by the community.

What followed the Robbins principle was the building of a number of new 'plate glass' universities, or as Harold Wilson somewhat disparagingly called them 'Baedeker' universities, in towns such as Canterbury and Colchester. The UGC had promptly followed Macmillan's commission of

Robbins in 1959 with a proposal to build seven new universities, and by 1974 the number of universities had doubled from its pre-Robbins total to forty-four. Ultimately, the final number was determined by bids that were able to meet the deadline set by the Treasury. Such bids conformed to the UGC's guidelines: that a site of at least 200 acres be made available, and that there was evidence of local financial support, an ability to accommodate students and an attractive location for staff.

Although the funding of higher education was a popular political move at the time for the Conservative Party, the speed with which the Robbins Report was adopted almost *in toto*, without even the briefest of discussions in the House of Lords, was exceptional. The proposals reflected the popularity of, and demand for, higher education at the time. The manner in which higher education was presented was also clearly an attempt by an ailing Conservative Party to appear populist rather than elitist. This was particularly evident after Macmillan stepped down, leaving Alec Douglas-Home as leader and Prime Minister. Ironically, however, while Robbins envisaged an expanding university sector that remained beyond the direct control of central government, the degree of planned university expansion came at the turning point of Britain's economic fortunes. This left the incoming Labour government of Harold Wilson with no choice but to become more actively involved in the organization of the universities. For the first but not for the last time, government began to undercut the autonomy of universities. To his great credit, Wilson forced through the institution of the Open University, a primarily home, local and distance learning form of education that expanded the opportunities of higher education beyond anything previously imagined. On some accounts, this was his greatest political legacy.

The Robbins Report had already outlined the costs of the university system from its 1937–8 figure of £26 million to its 1962–3 figure of £129 million. The plans for university expansion saw that figure climbing much higher, leaving Tony Crosland, the Labour Secretary of State for Education in 1964, with no other option but to take the first of a series of steps towards increasing

government control and further undermining traditional university autonomy.

The degree-awarding institutions, a right previously confined to universities holding Royal Charters, were expanded through the creation of the CNAA. This was a nationally and centrally accredited authority that was able to validate degrees in institutions outside the traditional and autonomous universities. In addition, there was a transfer of direct responsibility for the UGC from the Treasury to the Department of Education and Science (DES). Consequently, universities were made subject to inspection by the Comptroller and Auditor General, and the Permanent Secretary of the DES became the Accounting Officer for the universities. In addition, responsibility for academic salaries was transferred from the UGC to a National Incomes Commission. In an unprecedented use of state influence, the DES intervened directly to control university fees. In 1967 the raising of overseas students' fees to a sum £200 in excess of home fees was recommended, and, while this was resisted strongly at the time, the raising of overseas student fees as a reasonable economic export was an argument used repeatedly by successive **Conservative governments**.

A worsening economic crisis meant that by the early 1970s the DES continued to exert ever-greater control over universities. The UGC, a body that had protected universities from government interference, now became an arm of government interference. In 1974, the quinquennial funding system, which had stretched back to the creation of contemporary universities, was abolished in favour of an uneven and irregular annual allocation of funds. The effect of such action was to tie universities ever more closely to the economic policy of a particular government and to alter the role of the UGC such that it became an interventionist agent of government. Thus the autonomy of universities as organizations established under direct authority of the crown as 'bodies politick' (bodies embodying the highest ideal of faith and trust) was, at a stroke, ended by a convenient political fiat.

The return of a Conservative government under the leadership of Margaret Thatcher in 1979 laid the Robbins principle to rest. One of the government's first actions was to remove the subsidy on overseas student fees altogether, requiring universities to charge the full amount; a decision which led to universities needing to 'market' themselves overseas. Furthermore, the home student fee payable to universities was halved. This was a blatant attempt to encourage universities to adhere to the student number targets defined by the UGC (a failure to comply led the UGC to fine institutions that exceeded these limits).

In 1979–83, £100 million was withdrawn from the university system through a series of different stringency measures. In 1980, a reduction of £30 million (3.5 percent) of the recurrent grant for the following year was announced, prompting the UGC to issue a directive requiring the universities to plan for three scenarios: a projected zero increase in funding, a 2 percent increase, and a 5 percent reduction. The actual variation in grant allocation varied widely, and following the recommendations from its sub-committees, three universities (Aston, Bradford and Salford) received a reduced grant in the order of 30 percent.

The differential squeeze placed upon institutions by the UGC marked the beginning of a process of selectivity between and within the universities, altering radically the shape and composition of British higher education. The chairman of the UGC, Sir Peter Swinnerton Dyer, announced in the publication of *A Strategy for Higher Education into the 1990s* (1984) that the Robbins principles were to be revised. The principle that higher education be available to all who could benefit from it, was, therefore, replaced by offering such education only to those qualified by ability and attainment. The report also mentioned that the amount of recurrent grant available from central government would be based on an institution's effectiveness in research.

This principle introduced the Research Assessment Exercise, a method of determining the quality of research in a university and a means of differentially allocating funds to universities. The first round of research assessment exercises in 1985–6 rated departments based on their research record. Gradings such as 'starred', 'above average', 'average', or 'below average' were translated into funds via a resource allocation model. Even those that were 'successful' were still required by the UGC to submit formal plans annually detailing

how an institution was allocating resources earmarked for particular departments.

The next round of research assessments in 1988–9 saw a number of changes. First, by the time of its publication in 1990 the UGC had been eliminated and replaced by the Universities Funding Council, a body composed of a considerably smaller number of people with far fewer academics present. Second, the publication of *A Strategy for the Science Base* by the Advisory Board for the Research Councils (ABRC) in 1987 paved the way for a stratified university system with institutions falling into three broad categories: first, those with excellent research capabilities across a wide range of disciplines; second, those engaged in research of high calibre within particular fields; and third, those without the provision of advanced research facilities.

While Robbins recommended that all universities should have a significant research capability as well as a teaching function, the adoption of research as the definitive criteria of institutional excellence seemed to push the universities away from this principle and towards a tiered university system. This tendency was reinforced by the presentation of numerical listings, with each department listed from 1 (below average) to 5 (excellent) and in the latest round (1996) to 1–5*. The differential funding more or less removed research monies from grade 1 departments and quite markedly concentrated research funding in 5* departments.

The effects of the research exercises have on the one hand meant that more research has been produced, some of which is of extremely high quality. On the other hand, it has also meant that the need for universities to discriminate in favour of those departments with a good research rating has resulted in a shift away from teaching towards research.

The idea of a university is now less the body politic as stated in its statutes and charters, and more an institution with managers. The Education Reform Act of 1988 abolished academic tenure. That institution which had ensured freedom of speech replaced it with a system that permitted enforced redundancies, enforced early retirement and dismissals for academics who expressed dissatisfaction with the way in which their institutions were managed. While most institutions have retained their quality, their standing and the basic trust on which all sound institutions must be based, it is clear that some institutions have destroyed quality, standing, openness and trust while also severely curtailing academic freedom.

In the course of the early 1990s, reclassifying polytechnics as 'autonomous' universities increased the number of universities. In consequence, there are now 100 or so universities. The UGC, and its successor the UFC, have been replaced by the Funding Councils, established by the Further and Higher Education Act of 1992.

Student fees have been dramatically reduced and maintenance awards have been frozen for ten years, falling 36 percent against inflation. This has led to a serious reduction in university income. It is now quite usual for student income and public funding combined to be less than 50 percent of a university's total income. The effect of this, together with the Research Assessment Exercise, has been to divide universities into primarily teaching or research institutions.

In either case, the shortfall in student fees is so serious that universities have considered breaching the Robbins principle and charging students 'top-up' fees. In the light of this, a bipartisan committee under Ron Dearing was established to re-examine the fee structure of universities, their function, their wider purpose and their place in the community.

The Dearing report ended the Robbins' principle of free university education at the point of delivery and recommended that students be required to pay for a substantial part of their fees. The government's response has been to accept this and to simultaneously eliminate the maintenance grant replacing the cumulative total (approx. £10,000) with a twenty-year payback scheme that will come into effect once earnings have passed a certain level. In practice, the costs of such payback are likely to be relatively small, but the principle of higher education free at the point of delivery has formally been breached. It is also regrettable that there are no guarantees that the money so recouped has been 'ring-fenced'; that is to say there is no guarantee that it will be fed directly back into higher education. In consequence, students could find themselves paying more towards a better service that cannot be provided because the money they pay does not find its way back into education.

It will be some years before the effect of all these proposed changes are known, whatever the detailed outcome it will result in the biggest shake-up in universities since the Robbins report. It will regard the student as a consumer with a consequent duty to pay for the advantage obtained from higher education, and will regard the universities as providers with clear duties and standards. In many cases this will lead to vast improvements. How widespread those improvements turn out to be, only time will tell.

See also: adult education; schools system

Further reading

Clarke, P.B. (1986) 'Exporting Education: Risks and Benefits', *The Australian*, 22 January.

Higher Education in the Learning Society: Report of the National Committee of Inquiry into Higher Education (The Dearing Report) (1997), London: HMSO.

Shattock, M. (1994) *The UGC and the Management of British Universities*, London: The Society for Research into Higher Education and Open University Press.

PAUL BARRY CLARKE
LAWRENCE QUILL

University Boat Race

The Boat Race is an annual rowing race between Oxford and Cambridge Universities along the Thames, first rowed at Henley in 1829. The race became an annual event in 1839, and moved to its present course from Putney to Mortlake (four and one-quarter miles) in 1845. Cambridge recorded the longest straight run of wins from 1924 to 1936, and there has been one dead-heat in 1877. The event is televised by the BBC, bet on by thousands of punters, and deemed to sit alongside such once-a-year television regulars as the Grand National and the London Marathon as a quintessential British armchair spectacle. Most people arbitrarily support one or other of the two 'blues', and the elevation of a parochial Oxbridge novelty to a national occasion is arguably one of the chief sporting definitions, like Royal Ascot or the Henley Regatta, of a continuing class society.

See also: rowing

PETER CHILDS

university building

The 1950s in Britain witnessed an unprecedented period of school building, partly as a result of the 1944 Education Act. During the 1960s attention turned to university building. The social climate favoured an expansion of the university system which had fallen behind other countries in Europe, notably Italy, France and Germany. The Robbins Commission, established in 1959, contended that appropriately qualified individuals ought to be entitled to a university place. These ideas happily coincided with the recognition that modern architecture could be socially adaptable and could serve the wide range of challenges presented by both old and new universities.

This potential was fully exploited in the British universities founded and partly built in the 1960s, including Sussex (1961), East Anglia (1963), York (1963), Lancaster (1964), Essex (1964), Warwick (1965) and Kent (1965). All built in parkland, well outside the towns, they adhered to the brief that each university required about 200 acres to accommodate sports facilities and playing fields. This principle, while denying the many advantages offered by bringing together 'town and gown', allowed for expansive and individual planning. The seven examples cited differ considerably. Four are unitary, with communal buildings arranged variously towards the centre and with student residences placed on the periphery. Sussex, located in Stanmer Park just outside Brighton, was planned by Sir Basil **Spence**, together with most of the principal buildings. The style adopted was a variant of **new brutalism**, with red brick and concrete lintels creating a certain monumentality even though no building rises above three storeys, with the exceptions of the Meeting House and the Gardner Arts Centre.

East Anglia, by **Denys Lasdun and Partners**, places science buildings in a continuous east–west spine with others, including the stepped, eight-storey student residences, arranged to the north and south. Essex, near Colchester, takes advantage of the contours of the site. Principal buildings forming long parallel, linked blocks, with courtyards and walkways at upper levels connecting also to the fifteen-storey student residences. Warwick, outside Coventry, by Arthur Ling and Alan Goodman with contributions from **Yorke, Rosenburg and Mardall** and Grey, Goodman and Partners, provides another variant. The collegiate Universities of York, Kent and Lancaster offered the opportunity for architectural variety amongst the colleges. Surrey, in Guildford (1966) sited on the hill below the cathedral, integrates more successfully with the city.

Further reading

Birks, T. (1972) *Building The New Universities*, Exeter: David and Charles.

HILARY GRAINGER

V

Vadim, Jean

b. 1966

Film-maker

Jean Vadim has directed three movies: *Leon the Pigfarmer* (1992), *Beyond Bedlam* (1994) and *Clockwork Mice* (1995). As screenwriter and director, his films have been characterized by gentle comedy and social observation. His debut effort is a parable about race and identity that tells the story of a Jewish London twenty-something who finds out that his true parents are Yorkshire farmers. Though the film, which degenerates into farce, did comparatively well at the box office as 'the first Jewish comedy to come out of Britain', his later films treat psycho-social situations more seriously, such as *Clockwork Mice*, about the relationship between a delinquent pupil and the special needs teacher who tries to develop in him a sense of ambition and achievement through cross-country running.

PETER CHILDS

video art

The term 'video art' refers to recordings by fine artists on videotape plus sculptures and installations. In its early days in the late 1960s and early 1970s, video art explored its own construction and toyed with the medium itself. In Britain, artists' video only appeared on television arts programmes in the 1980s. Video's capacity to time-shift and to mirror spectators led to a range of innovative installations in galleries as well as the arrays of monitors that eventually became standard backdrops on television programmes like *Clive James on TV*. Artists such as Gilbert and George, Mick Harvey, Susan Hiller and Catherine Elwes have used the medium. The term also covers television art, video sculpture, street video or guerrilla television.

PETER CHILDS

Video Recordings Act

This 1984 Act controls the classification system and the distribution of video recordings. The British Board of Film Censors provides classification certificates for all legal video recordings and it is illegal to supply any video without one, or without meeting the stipulated labelling requirements. The aim of the Act, which provides for powers of confiscation, is to control the depiction of sexual, violent, genital, urinary and defecatory acts.

See also: censorship

PETER CHILDS

viewing technologies

Watching television has traditionally been thought of as a passive activity. The viewer would watch television for several hours, only occasionally getting up to change channels. Television scheduling and advertising was built round this premise.

The viewer would absorb advertisements between programmes while waiting for another programme segment. The true significance of the television experience was one of viewing programmes. However, with the development of video, the introduction of television sets with remote controls and with more channels being provided, questions have been raised about the way audiences view and use television. With new technologies of viewing, it would seem that the viewer is gaining new pleasures from watching and using television and is indeed more active than previously thought. It is now recognized that the tyranny of the schedule and the programme timetables, is no more: the viewer now has the freedom to watch when, what and how he or she likes.

With the increased use of VHS video people are able to watch programmes at different times than originally shown. Thus they are able to re-schedule or 'time-shift'. No longer are they restricted to the carefully controlled and constructed television schedules, but can watch programmes hours, days or months after they were shown. Video technology has also introduced the ability for viewers to fast-forward through advertisement breaks. This has become known as zipping, and is a practise that worries the advertising industry as more and more people time-shift and are increasingly able to 'miss out' the advertisements.

Video helped to introduce the remote control, since by using the video handset people could change video channels from the comfort of their seats. Most television sets now also come with their own remote control. This technology has also given the viewer the power to change channels quickly. So, for example, when an advertisement break comes on, viewers can switch to another channel for the duration of the break. This is referred to as zapping. Where the remote control is used to flick through many channels, increasingly possible in the multi-channel environment, a form of 'channel surfing' or 'grazing' occurs. Here, part of the pleasure is the experience of creating one's own collage or programme experience divorced from that offered by the programmers of a particular channel.

See also: cable and satellite; transmission technologies

Further reading

Silverstone, R. and Hirsch, E. (eds) (1994) *Consuming Technologies: Media and Information in Domestic Spaces*, London: Routledge.

PAUL RIXON

violence

Violence is a pervasive and enduring aspect of all societies and takes many forms from politically motivated violence (terrorism) to 'common' assault or rape, and can be directed against the person or property. In Britain, political violence has taken and takes different forms, from the bombing campaigns of the Provisional IRA and the street violence of the fascist British National Party to the violent clashes between strikers and police during the miners' strike of 1984–5. Other forms of violence include collective forms such as football hooliganism or riots, and individual ones such as muggings, rape and murder and the violence associated with 'gang culture' and the illegal drugs trade. A less commonly acknowledged form of violence is the legitimate institutionalized organization of violence by the state in the form of the police and the armed forces. In common with all states, the British state claims, in the words of Max Weber, a monopoly on the legitimate use of violence, and it is the latter which constitutes the ultimate authority of the state and its agencies.

A simple way of analysing violence, useful for distinguishing 'political' from 'ordinary' violence, is to determine who or what is the perpetrator, who or what is the victim and what is the reason for the violence. However, the distinction between political and ordinary violence is extremely porous; for example, many feminists have claimed that rape is a form of political violence since it is the ultimate means by which women are exploited and subjugated in a sexist, patriarchal society. A similar argument is often used to explain racial violence on ethnic minorities and the past violent reaction of black and Asian communities to perceived police racism and harassment in the inner city riots of Brixton and Liverpool in the early 1980s.

Violent crimes have been on the increase in Britain over the past decade, and recently there has been a good deal of support for the argument that socio-economic inequality, unemployment and deprivation are the major cause of crime and violence. However, the strict regulation of personal firearms makes Britain a less violent society than others, such as the USA.

Just as important as violence itself is the threat of violence, and on this measure many people feel that Britain is a more violent society. For some, this is due to a 'culture of risk' in which people in advanced societies feel increasingly insecure, unsafe and fearful, as a result of the decline in community and solidarity and the rise of a materialistic and individualistic culture which, in the context of an absence of sufficient means to take part in this consumerist lifestyle (without enough jobs or money to go round), explains the rise in violence.

See also: armed forces and police; domestic violence; Ireland; police; WAVAW

Further reading

Burton, J.W. (1997) *Violence Explained: The Sources of Conflict, Violence and Crime and their Prevention*, Manchester: Manchester University Press.
Honderich, T. (1977) *Three Essays on Political Violence*, Oxford: Blackwell.

JOHN BARRY

Vogue

British *Vogue* is part of the Condé Nast International Magazines Group, and *Vogue* is one of the nine magazines published in Britain by this highly influential company. Its award-winning British magazines have a readership of over five million adults, accessing a combined household income in excess of £88.4 billion. *Vogue* was launched in Britain in 1916 and is commonly regarded as the British fashion bible. British *Vogue* is aimed at affluent, brand-literate and brand-conscious readers. It thus influences purchasing habits and greatly impacts upon the editorial direction of other media. (The average *Vogue* woman reader spends circa £2000 per annum on clothes, whereas a typical middle-class woman generally spends less than a third of that figure). The combination of beauty and fashion is central to *Vogue*'s enduring success. Its influence in these related fields is unparalleled among retailers and readers alike. It is read by nearly two million adults every month, building and shifting specific products, and directing the spending power of affluent Britain.

FATIMA FERNANDES

W

Ward, Barbara

b. 1914, York; d. 1981

Economist

Barbara Ward (later Baroness Jackson of Lods-
worth) was an economist who influenced thinking
on aid to underdeveloped countries, the global
environment and the plight of the world's poor.
*Only One Earth: The Care and Maintenance of a Small
Planet* (1972) (co-authored with René Dubos) and
Progress for a Small Planet (1979) are her best-known
works. Her first book, *The West at Bay*, was
published in 1948. In *Progress for a Small Planet*,
she identified three principal threats to the global
environment: pollution, affluent nations' consumption of limited resources, and consequent growing
tensions between rich and poor. She offered
practical strategies for recycling waste, more
efficient use of energy and meeting the basic needs
of the disadvantaged.

See also: environmentalism

MIKE STORRY

Warnock, Mary

b. 1924

Philosopher

Baroness Warnock has contributed to contemporary British culture in both academic philosophy
and public services concerning education and
bioethics. A former headmistress of Oxford High

School, Fellow and Tutor at St Hugh's College,
Oxford and Mistress of Girton College, Cambridge
from 1985–91, Warnock was made a life peer in
1985. She is married to the philosopher Sir
Geoffrey Warnock.

Mary Warnock is well known for her work in
moral **philosophy**, particularly concerning existentialist ethics, J.S. Mills's utilitarianism and the
concept of moral sense in Hume and in contemporary bioethics. Her short but extremely
respected book *On Ethics Since 1900* presents a
lucid and accessible account of the major transformations occurring in English and continental
moral philosophy in the twentieth century. She
has also devoted an interesting volume to women
philosophers. Her most recent research has centred
around the philosophy of mind, to which she has
contributed substantial works, *Imagination* (1976)
and *Memory* (1987).

Warnock's reputation as a moral philosopher led
her to chair two government inquiries that have
exerted considerable influence on British public
awareness and legislation. The first inquiry in the
mid-1970s concerned education, particularly special education needs. The second, and most
famous, was the Committee of Inquiry into
Human Fertilisation and Embryology, established
in 1982.

In July 1978, the first test-tube baby was
successfully delivered in Britain. The social, ethical,
theological and legal implications of this scientific
breakthrough and its potential developments were
enormous. For the first time, human life could be
created and/or assisted artificially. This offered
great hope in alleviating the infertility problems

experienced by many British couples. However, it generated deep anxieties from different sections of British society concerning where the limits to practices such as artificial insemination by donor (AID), in vitro fertilization (IVF), human egg/embryo donation and surrogate motherhood should be drawn. Arguments against some or all of these practices mainly rested on the deviation from the natural process of fertilization and the separation of unitive and procreative aspects of marital sexual intercourse. Other arguments against concern the introduction of a third party into the procreative process, possibly for financial gain, and the likelihood that IVF would create a surplus of embryos, some of which would not have the chance of reintroduction into the mothers uterus.

The possibility of IVF raised a number of serious ethical dilemmas never before experienced. For the first time, the existence of embryos outside the mother's uterus had to be considered, and their moral status had to be defined and protected. This required a reassessment of where the boundaries of personhood, and the respect of rights that go with it, should now be placed. The deepest anxieties revolved around the ethical sustainability of the use of human embryos for the scientific research necessary to improve human assisted reproduction techniques.

The new techniques and practices clearly required careful examination and protracted discussion, from which an adequate ethical and legal framework could be drawn and implemented. In consequence, the committee chaired by Mary Warnock deliberated upon many of the issues and implications involved in recent and potential developments in human assisted reproduction. It took evidence from all interested parties and attempted to reach conclusions that were both philosophically well-based and consensually satisfactory. Its findings and recommendations were published as *The Warnock Report on Human Fertilisation and Embryology* in 1984.

Warnock stressed that the methods of deliberation undertaken by the Inquiry could not be based on obedience to established moral rules alone. The creation of human life in laboratory conditions constituted such a radical departure from former practices that established codes of moral conduct could not be expected to govern all the principles behind the new techniques and their implications. To some extent, therefore, new principles governing moral conduct would be required. As such principles were not altogether forthcoming or clear, some decisions were based less on clearcut moral criteria than on the need to 'allay public anxiety'.

The report separated out certain issues. In a free society, it was felt that assisted reproduction could not be regulated and/or policed without encroaching on some basic individual liberties. However, the report advocated that AID, gamete/embryo donation, surrogacy and IVF should always be practised non-commercially and that involved medical practitioners must be licensed to, and subject to the regulations of, a proposed authority. The most difficult problem the report had to deal with was the limits that should be placed on embryo research. Some representations to the Committee were based on the principle that human embryos should be afforded some protection in law. Hitherto, the human embryo *per se* did not have direct legal protection.

It was felt that the report attempted to ameliorate the opinions such dissension represented by restricting the period over which embryo research could be undertaken. They recommended that research might be carried out on an in vitro embryo until the end of the fourteenth day after fertilization, after which any further research/handling of the embryo would be a criminal offence. The fourteen-day distinction was based on some scientific evidence, primarily the appearance of the primitive streak within the embryo when the beginnings of the spinal cord develop, thus leading to distinct cellular division and even to the possibility of feeling pain. Nonetheless, it was admitted that there was no clear scientific grounds at which point a respected rather than an unrespected embryo occurred: 'However we agreed that this was an area in which some precise decision must be taken, in order to allay public anxiety'. The report made it clear that a new, independent statutory licensing authority was essential to regulate Britain's infertility services and embryo research, to inquire into and license current practice(s) and to technically and ethically scrutinize any future proposals for their ethical significance.

The Warnock report was sent out for consultation under white papers in 1986 and 1987, and after submission was enshrined in the 1990 Human Fertilisation and Embryology Act, which also set up an authority to license procedures, police the act and take a broad legal and ethical view on actions and proposed actions falling under its general remit. Broadly speaking, there is a wide consensus that the Act has worked fairly well and that, within its fairly narrowly defined remit, the licensing authority has worked moderately well. There is some concern that membership of the licensing authority has been drawn fairly narrowly and might overly represent vested interests. This seems to be a general weakness in the appointments that have been made to such bodies: on the whole, they tend to take a narrow view of their remit. A recent, highly publicized case has been that of Diane Blood, who sought permission to utilize the sperm of her dead husband taken from him while he was comatose and on life support. While it was widely agreed that he had previously given verbal consent to such a procedure, the Embryology Authority refused permission on the narrow if formal grounds of lack of written consent. In the event, after appeal she was permitted to take the sperm to another European country. In respect of this case, Mary Warnock publicly said that this was exactly the difficult kind of case that the Committee had not foreseen and that it indicated the need for flexibility in this area. This indicates that the Embryology Authority needs a degree of philosophically and consensually based common sense rather than merely strict legal definitions in guiding its decisions. The latter alone will never do: the situation is far too fast-moving for the law to lead. It must, therefore, be philosophically acute, legally aware and publicly acute individuals that form part of such bodies. Warnock, it seems, established the broad principles, but the combination of flexibility of practice and clear limits has yet to be met.

See also: Abortion Acts; euthanasia

PAUL BARRY CLARKE
EMMA R. NORMAN

WATERLOO TERMINAL *see* Nicholas Grimshaw and Partners

Watkins, Peter

b. 1935

Film-maker

A RADA graduate and pioneering drama-documentarist, Watkins introduced his documentary reconstruction technique in *Culloden* (1964). He began working for BBC documentaries in 1963, but resigned following their international suppression of his nuclear film *The War Game* (1965). He emigrated abroad after his first feature *Privilege* (1967). Against charges of hysterical paranoia, Watkins reconstitutes official truth and freedom narratives by questioning existing orthodoxies and repressive ideologies. His uniquely experimental style is invested with performative, realist and expressionistic elements in documentaries like *Punishment Park* (1971), *The Journey* (1987), *The Media Project* (1991) and the epic biographies *Edvard Munch* (1976) and *The Freethinker* (1994), about August Strindberg. Despite his continued marginalization by the film-making community, Watkins' contribution remains pivotal.

Further reading

Macdonald, S. (1993) *Avant-Garde Film Motion Studies*, Cambridge, Cambridge University Press.

SATINDER CHOHAN

Watts, Alan

b. 1915; d. 1973

Writer

Watts was known as one of the high priests of the counterculture which burgeoned in the USA and Britain during the 1960s and early 1970s, and his writings on Zen Buddhism and Taoism were widely read by its participants. The recipient of an English public school education, by the age of twenty Watts had written and published his first book on Zen. He had already studied the

Orientalists extensively and been greatly influenced by the Japanese scholar D.T. Suzuki. He left his native England for America in 1938, and although he became an Episcopal priest for a period of some five years, it was his individualistic interpretation of Zen which earned him lasting recognition.

See also: Buddhism; transcendental meditation

JAN EVANS

WAVAW

The first Women Against Violence Against Women (WAVAW) conference took place in London in November 1981. Papers from this and two further conferences were published in 1985 by Onlywomen Press under the conference title. The view that **violence** against women should be understood as an expression of patriarchy reinforced by economic, familial and cultural arrangements first gained popularity in the 1970s. Among others, WAVAW argued that violence was fundamental to male biology and also that it had a spectrum of symptoms including murder, battery, rape, reproductive technologies, psychiatry, pornography, and even make-up and fashion. For WAVAW, a radical feminist organization, even when individual men did not actually participate in any of these acts, men as a group still benefited since brutal and physically coercive acts served to keep all women oppressed by placing the threat of violence over all heterosexual relationships.

See also: domestic violence; violence

PETER CHILDS

welfare state

By 1950, it was unremarkable to describe Britain as a 'welfare state'. Mostly this term referred to the new legislation to promote **social welfare**, but sometimes it stood for a more general view of social and political culture. References could be either positive or negative. Other countries were also so described. The more specific sense is the one discussed here.

Social provision in the 1930s faced problems with high unemployment, leading the wartime government to ask William Beveridge to report on social insurance. In his Report of 1942, Beveridge recommended that employers and employees should contribute to a unified, comprehensive and compulsory insurance scheme, which would pay subsistence level benefits in sickness, old age and unemployment, irrespective of income. For those excluded from 'National Insurance', 'National Assistance' provided a means-tested 'safety net' benefit. Family allowances (not means-tested), full employment policies and a health service for all were 'assumptions' made by Beveridge.

In 1948, under Attlee's Labour government, most of Beveridge's recommendations became reality. Alongside National Insurance and National Assistance was a National Health Service (free at point of use), family allowances and a children's service (for children deprived of a normal home life; providing too career opportunities for qualified women). High standards of service were intended. The health service was aimed at the whole population, even though private practice continued. Abolishing apparently many sources of insecurity and social division, these provisions creating 'the British welfare state' were popular.

The precise significance of the welfare state remains controversial. Its radical and egalitarian aims and the unpopularity of previous provisions, even including the Poor Law, may have been overemphasized. The new state provision was rarely integrated with voluntary or private provision. If the form of the 'welfare state' owed much to populist idealism, it owed little less to consensus politics and the lobbying of **pressure groups** for the professions.

By the early 1960s, the optimism expressed in Rowntree and Laver's *Poverty and The Welfare State* (1951) that poverty was virtually eliminated was evaporating. Following new research, in 1965 the pressure group Child Poverty Action Group (CPAG) was formed to lobby for families in poverty. The 'rediscovery' of 'child poverty' embodied a still-controversial new definition of '**poverty**', in relativist terms, where poverty was defined not as a minimum and essentially fixed living standard but according to the changing nature of needs and standards in a more affluent Britain. Abuse in long-stay institutions for old people and people mentally ill or with a learning disability also became widely publicized, assisted by the popular **sociology** of Erving Goffman's *Asylums* and *Stigma*. Ken **Loach**'s television film *Cathy Come Home* highlighted **homelessness**.

The response of Harold Wilson's Labour government was low key. Deinstitutionalization and the development of community care proceeded slowly, and a promised grand reform of social security ended in a renaming of National Assistance to Supplementary Benefit in 1966. However, comprehensive schools increased rapidly between 1965 and 1970, and it was the Labour Social Services Act of 1970 that introduced almost a new social service (social work), although implementation was left to Edward Heath's Conservative government of that year. In Britain, social work services for families and communities in which children, chronically sick, disabled and elderly people needed care were developed by local authorities separate from the NHS. In Northern Ireland the two were the responsibility of one administrative body (the welfare state is thus shown as taking different forms in different parts of the United Kingdom, a point often overlooked).

Heath's government also introduced Family Income Supplement in 1971 (known as Family Credit since 1986, and under review) to tackle child poverty. This was a means-tested benefit, related to family size, for families with low income from employment. While the Institute of Economic Affairs supported such 'targeting' of resources, the CPAG opposed means-testing as stigmatizing 'the poor', producing 'inefficient' 'low take-up' requiring corrective 'welfare rights' work, and constructing a 'poverty trap' whereby extra money earned resulted in more lost through diminished eligibility for benefits.

Electorally vulnerable and dogged by inflation, oil price increases and eventually the **Winter of Discontent**, Labour governments from 1974 to 1979 managed to modify state funding and provision for **pensioners** to take account of the trend of relatively fewer people of working age and more of pensionable age. In 1975, Child Benefit superseded Family Allowances, being neither means-tested nor taxed. The abolition of tax allowances accompanied extending benefit to cover the first child.

By contrast, Margaret Thatcher's victory in 1979 brought big changes in the 'welfare state', which were continued by John Major from 1990 to 1997. The Conservatives, supported by new thinking about social welfare and committed to improving choice and quality of service, **privatization** where practicable and value-for-money and market disciplines, encouraged tenants to buy council houses, and reduced **corporatism** by introducing splits between purchasers and providers in health and social care (whereby voluntary agencies and the private sector competed with the state to be providers). A new factor in the expansion of social care was acknowledging the preferences of informal carers (usually family members). However, charges for care might result in the need for the patient to sell their home.

To reinforce incentives to work or train, Supplementary Benefit was replaced by Income Support in 1986, with a loan-based Social Fund for 'special needs'. The Conservatives also modified the **schools system**, empowering schools to opt out of the control of local education authorities, and introducing the **National Curriculum**. Preventative health measures were encouraged and an emphasis was placed on personal responsibility for health. 'Scroungers' on benefits remained a bogey, as did **single parents**, and a 'dependency culture' and an 'underclass' created by the 'welfare state' drew attention. Child abuse was established as a problem. Feminist theory and research questioned women's employment patterns in the 'welfare state' and inequalities of provision. Similar questions were raised respecting ethnic minorities. **Thatcherism**'s changes look safe with the new Blair government. However, the 'welfare state' will be changing again as European Union policies filter through and if devolution takes place.

See also: class system

Further reading

Hill, M. (1993) *The Welfare State in Britain*, Aldershot: Edward Elgar.

Hills, J. (ed.) (1990) *The State of Welfare*, Oxford: Clarendon Press.

JOHN OFFER

Welsh language

Welsh is acknowledged as the strongest surviving Celtic language, partly thanks to the Welsh Language Act and the setting up of the Welsh Language Board, which insist, among other things, that the language appears on road signs, is taught in schools and is a requirement for certain jobs. Also, the University of Wales's Board of Celtic Studies is working on a historical dictionary of the Welsh language and major surveys of place names and dialects at its Aberystwyth Centre for Advanced Welsh and Celtic Studies.

Known as *Cymraeg*, Welsh comes from a Celtic branch of the Indo-European language family. It is spoken more in the north than the south. After a period of decline, the trend is now towards more Welsh being spoken, especially by young people. A 1981 census showed that 18.9 percent of the Welsh population used it. A Bangor University report showed that figure had risen to 22.8 percent by 1996. The advent of the television station **S4C** has obviously enhanced the survival of Welsh. The popular Welsh-language sitcom *Pobol y Cwm* (People of the Valley), for example, reflects daily Welsh-speaking lives, and the Welsh news programme *Newydd* mediates everyday events through the Welsh language.

Outside Wales, the forty-year-old Welsh School, housed in a Welsh chapel in Willesden in northwest London, is more popular than ever. The Canadian astronaut Dr Dafydd Rhys Williams learned Welsh so that he could send messages from the space shuttle *Columbia* to the BBC Wales television programme *Wales Today*.

Immigrants to Wales face difficulty with the education of their children, which is often solely through the medium of Welsh. This practice is also questioned locally by people who fear it will narrow job prospects for their children. Litigation has even been initiated by non Welsh-speaking people from South Wales to outlaw the compulsory learning of Welsh.

See also: literature, Welsh; Scottish language

MIKE STORRY

Welsh press

A total of eighty-three newspapers are published in Wales. Because of the relatively small size of the population, the readerships of individual titles tend to be smaller than those of English papers. For example, the readership of the Cardiff *South Wales Echo*, 79,189, is a fraction of that of the *Liverpool Echo* at 191,000, or even of the *Leicester Mercury* at 118,594. In addition to the major commercial titles, there are many Welsh community newspapers. This large number is partly because they receive an annual grant as a result of the government's wider financial support for the **Welsh language**, which has undergone a resurgence in recent years.

Most of the newspapers are locally owned and run, and none seems to be 'a licence to print money' – quite the reverse – even though they have reasonable circulations. For example the tabloid Swansea *South Wales Evening Post* has a circulation of 68,935. Smaller papers like the Newport-based evening broadsheet *South Wales Argus* and the tabloid *Wrexham Evening Leader*, with circulations of 35,644 and 31,598 respectively, are much less viable.

In Welsh newspapers there is a substantial difference in advertising rates per page. The *South Wales Evening Post* charges £1,763 where the Cardiff morning broadsheet *Western Mail* charges £7,728. The circulation figures for these two papers, in the mid-60,000s, are more or less the same. This price difference is in line with a British national trend, that broadsheets charge more than tabloids, but nowhere else is the discrepancy so extreme. Against another national trend is the fact that of two Cardiff-based newspapers, the Sunday paper *Wales on Sunday* charges half as much for advertising as the tabloid evening *South Wales Echo*. Normally, Sundays are slightly more expensive. The Welsh edition of the *Liverpool Daily Post*, owned by Trinity Holdings and with a circulation of 73,436, also sells significant numbers of papers in North Wales.

Under the Broadcasting Act (1990) no proprietor of a national or local newspaper is allowed more than a 20 percent interest in direct broadcasting by satellite channels, independent television Channels 3 and 5 and national and local radio within its circulation area. Partly because of the financial constraints referred to above, this limit does not look like being breached by any of the local owners in Wales.

See also: literature, Welsh

MIKE STORRY

West End

Until the appearance of television in the 1960s, the West End was the epicentre of British entertainment, including everything from music hall acts at the London Palladium to *Oedipus Rex* the Old Vic. During the 1970s the West End lost this place, for several reasons. First, there were the costs of finally paying a living wage for actors and stage crew combined with London rents. West End theatre became expensive and shows now attract mainly tourists. This in turn means that serious drama, which gave the West End its kudos, was replaced by musicals. The National Theatre, **Royal Shakespeare Company** and Young Vic came to London during the 1960s and their subsidized prices accessed everything from Stoppard to Shakespeare, taking risks no commercial management could justify. Everything interesting then seemed to be in the subsidized sector, even though that is unfair to managements responsible for *Brief Lives*, plays by Simon Gray and Peter Shaffer or *Beyond the Fringe*. Nevertheless, the growth of **fringe theatre** at the Hampstead Theatre Club, the King's Head in Islington and the Bush Theatre directed the artistic focus away from the West End. Additionally, the national companies and regional repertory theatres developed ensemble styles of acting that quite simply produced better results. The 'star system', more of a payscale than a style of acting, tended to militate against good performances in all but the smallest casts. Productions at the National and the RSC concentrated on the play as opposed to the way, for example, Noel Coward's plays were vehicles for him and Gertrude Laurence. West End acting was a hangover from those days of the great actor-managers who did not always give fellow actors a full script.

See also: Royal National Theatre; theatre

STEPHEN KERENSKY

Westland Affair

At the close of 1985, the UK military helicopter supplier Westland needed financial support. Two interested parties emerged, Sikorsky of the USA, supported by the Trade and Industry Secretary Leon Brittan, and a European consortium favoured by the Defence Secretary, Michael Heseltine. The Cabinet agreed to take a neutral line. However, officials from the DTI promoted the Sikorsky offer to MPs and, with Downing Street's approval, leaked a letter from the Solicitor General questioning Heseltine's assertion that Sikorsky would have difficulty finding European outlets. Heseltine resigned and Brittan soon followed, admitting his knowledge of the leak. The Defence Select Committee investigating Westland was denied access to several key witnesses including Mrs Thatcher, and complained about obstruction from senior civil servants and Brittan.

See also: government inquiries

COLIN WILLIAMS

Westwood, Vivienne

b. 1941, Derbyshire

Fashion designer

Vivienne Westwood began her career as a designer in 1971. She partnered Malcolm McLaren in running a boutique which has had various names (most famously, Sex, in 1974) and came to prominence in the mid-1970s as the fashion designer who accompanied McLaren's launching of punk in London. Noted for revival gear and anti-fashion, she began with 1950s **retro** teddy boy styles, and moved through new brutalism and punk bondage to a new romantic look (see **new romantics**), with pirates, highwaymen and then hobos. She first showed under her own name in

1982 and started a menswear collection in 1990. By 1998 Westwood's collections were variously marked by tweeds, strapless mini-crinolines, corsets, twinsets and Regency costumes. She won the British Fashion Industry Designer of the Year Award in 1990 and 1991.

See also: punk rock

PETER CHILDS

Wilkinson, Chris

Architect

Wilkinson has worked for Norman Foster (see **Foster Associates**) and Richard **Rogers**, whose architectural styles he greatly admires and to a degree emulates, and has practised in London since 1983 with his partner James Eyre. Wilkinson's Jubilee Line Maintenance Depot work (plus Stratford Market Station on the same line) brought him attention in 1995, and he has had rapid success since (while Wilkinson Architects designed the concourse for the new Stratford Station on the Jubilee line, Troughton McAslan is the chief architect on the line's platforms and station accommodation). Other major new and recent work has been Liverpool Street Station arcade, an £8 million Science World Building Millennium project for Bristol, and a £120 million sports and university complex on Teesside. Wilkinson's firm have gained much attention in the last few years and have become sought-after architects for their English **high-tech** image.

PETER CHILDS

Williams, Raymond

b. 1921, Wales; d. 1988, Cambridge

Literary critic

The son of a Welsh miner, Raymond Williams became a Cambridge professor, seminal British cultural historian and a leading Marxist (literary) critic, as well as a media commentator as widely regarded as E.P. **Thompson**, Richard Hoggart or Stuart **Hall**. Key early works were the enormously influential pair of books *Culture and Society 1780–1950* (1958) and *The Long Revolution* (1961). Williams argued for a materialist reading of the production of culture, the inception of the social studies of communication, and the recognition of mass popular culture's usurpation of (the value placed on) high art. Other notable books were *The Country and the City* (1973) and *Keywords* (1976), an extensive glossary of the main terms of the new cultural studies. Later work, pervaded by a stoical pessimism about Britain's social and economic decline, ranged over the novel, drama, television, film and left-wing politics.

See also: Marxism; media and cultural studies

PETER CHILDS

WILLIS FABER OFFICES, IPSWICH *see* Foster Associates

Wilson, Colin St John

Architect

Colin St John Wilson heads up an architectural practice which has worked abroad (particularly Hong Kong) and in Britain. It has designed many school buildings, and in Britain specializes in designing public buildings, particularly libraries. The partnership designed London's new British Library, which has a six-story glass tower housing the entrance lobby, and the King's Library. Incorporated in the partnership's philosophy is the idea that libraries are as much about recreation as about scholarship, and thus must be made congenial places for casual browsers as well as for serious academics. Hence the new British Library has an informal and asymmetrical layout with 'student-friendly' galleries, exhibition rooms and recreational facilities.

PETER CHILDS

Wimbledon

Wimbledon is the most famous tennis tournament in the world, hosted on the grass courts of the All England Club in Wimbledon, London. Lasting for a fortnight from the last week of June, it is one of the four grand slam tournaments, along with the Australian, French and US Opens. The tournament has had to adapt to the pressures of the commercial era, while striving to maintain its traditional character. It offers increasing levels of prize money and has invested strongly in facilities, such as the building of a new Number One Court. The tournament attracts global interest and has become a summer tradition in Britain, despite the lack of British success in recent years. The Club celebrated its centenary in 1977.

See also: tennis

CHRISTOPHER COLBY

Winner, Michael

b. 1935, London

Film-maker

With a background in BBC documentary and nudie films, Winner's early films like *Play It Cool* (1962), *West Eleven* (1963), *The Jokers* (1967) and *I'll Never Forget What's 'is Name* (1967) variously captured the ambience, enterprising attitudes and fashionable settings of 1960s swinging London. A Hollywood phase of brutally violent movies commenced with the Western *Lawman* (1970), through thrillers such as *The Mechanic* (1972) and *The Stone Killer* (1973) to the box office success of *Death Wish* (1974) and its sequels (1981, 1985). Later British comedies *A Chorus of Disapproval* (1988) and *Bullseye!* (1990) merely accentuated Winner's ponderous style, with *Dirty Weekend* (1992) signalling a return to the monotonous sex and violence of his earlier films in a largely undistinguished film career.

SATINDER CHOHAN

Winter of Discontent

Shakespeare's metaphor (from *Richard III*) was used in the press to refer to the troubled state of British industrial relations during the winter of 1978–9, when a wave of strikes across a range of industries resulted in the loss of more working days at any time since the General Strike of 1926. The tabloid media denounced trade union militancy and relayed increasingly grotesque images of closed hospitals, uncollected rubbish and even unburied bodies. The opposition **Conservative Party** under Margaret Thatcher strategically represented itself as embodying the national against the sectional interest of the unions and, mobilizing anti-union rhetoric, won the May 1979 general election with the slogan 'Labour isn't Working'.

See also: Conservative governments; trade unions

MARK DOUGLAS

WOMAD

WOMAD stands for World of Music, Arts and Dance. The aim of the WOMAD festival, as stated by its founder Peter Gabriel, is simply to bring together and celebrate as many diverse forms of music and dance as possible, from cultures and countries worldwide. Since the first festival in the UK in 1982, WOMAD has presented sixty-nine festival events in seventeen countries across the globe, including Australia, the USA, Japan, Spain, Denmark, Canada and several countries throughout Europe. A typical WOMAD weekend also offers particpatory workshops which include special events for children, and these family-oriented activities introduce the audience to many of the visiting artists.

See also: Notting Hill Carnival; rock festivals

EUGENE LANGE

women, employment patterns

There have been significant increases in the proportion of women who work. Data from the

Labour Force Survey indicates that, in 1961, women made up 32.3 percent of the labour force; in 1981 they made up 39.5 percent, and in 1993 they made up 44.4 percent. This significant rise in women working has been mainly due to the increasing numbers of married women in employment. However, women are also overrepresented in part-time work. In 1970, women working full-time earned 63 percent of the average male full-time wage. This figure increased to 76 percent in 1977. There was little further increase until the early 1990s when this figure rose to 79 percent (Equal Opportunities Commission 1994). Whether the legislation of the 1970s (Equal Pay Act and Sex Discrimination Act) has had any significant impact on women's position in the labour market has been questioned, as there are still considerable differences between the average pay of men and women.

Although women do make up an increasing proportion of the labour force, they are not equally represented throughout the occupational structure. This is due in part to horizontal segregation (men and women doing different types of jobs) but also in part to vertical segregation (men having higher paid jobs, in more advanced positions than women). The Labour Force Survey data (1993) indicates women are considerably more likely than men to work in hotels and catering, education and the health service. Men are more likely to work in agriculture, forestry and fishing, as well as in construction and transport. Employment in banking and finance is more evenly balanced. Men are more likely to dominate most areas of management and higher status professions such as medicine, whereas women are more likely to be in lower paid, lower status professions such as teaching and nursing. Clerical and secretarial work is overwhelmingly carried out by women. Furthermore, few women occupy high positions in society; in 1988 women made up only 6 percent of government ministers and the number of **women in parliament** amounted to only 6 percent of MPs.

See also: women in business

Further reading

Equal Opportunities Commission (1994) *Some Facts*

About Women, based on New Earnings Survey and Labour Force Survey.
Labour Force Survey (1993, 1994), Department of Employment.

KALWANT BHOPAL

women in the arts and media

Women have reached many influential positions in the Arts and Media over the last twenty years. Although they have a long way to go to achieve parity of representation with men, they hold top administrative positions in broadcasting organizations like the BBC and ITV, and are very visible in print media.

In performing arts, Britain displays a stunning range of talent. Emma **Thompson** and Helena Bonham Carter are well known actors, but numerous other versatile women take on roles beyond those called for by the 'Merchant-Ivory' version of Britain. These include Marianne Jean-Baptiste (Mike **Leigh**'s *Secrets and Lies*) and Kathy Burke (Gary Oldman's *Nil by Mouth*). Among Britain's many women directors are Margaret **Tait** and Beeban **Kidron**, and the concerns of both actors and directors goes well beyond 'women's agendas'.

Examples of influential younger journalists are Julie Burchill, who writes for the *Sunday Times*, and Cristina Odone, the deputy editor of the *New Statesman*. Radio has offered opportunities to women far beyond their traditional toehold of *Woman's Hour*. Radio 4's respected *Analysis* programme is often presented by eminent women, as have been the Reith Lectures. Libby Purvis presents *Mid Week* on Radio 4. Anna Ford co-presents the *Today* programme. However, television is probably where women are most in evidence and most successful. News presenters like Julia Somerville and Katie Derham receive six-figure salaries. The ex-BBC presenter Kirsty Young, Channel 5's news presenter, at age twenty-nine earns £750,000. Television's first woman presenter, Angela Rippon, earned little more than a teacher. In 'serious' television, current regulars on the *Late Show* include Sarah Dunant and Germaine Greer. An older generation of women from Mavis Nicholson to

Esther Rantzen secured the television bridgehead, but arguably American imports, such as Oprah Winfrey's chat show and alternative women comedians like Penny Arcade and (UK resident) Ruby Wax have supplied powerful role models for women in British television. Relatively young female presenters on television include Magenta De Vine on BBC2's *Rough Guide* travel programme and Caroline Hook with her popular chat show *Mrs Merton*. Gaby Roslin, who used to present *The Big Breakfast* with Chris Evans, has her own show.

People complain that many of the women who have succeeded on television have done so because of their looks. Ulrika Jonsson (*Gladiators*) and Anna Ford (newsreader) are cited in this context; but television stations deny it is a determining factor.

See also: women in business; women in rock

MIKE STORRY

women in business

In the late 1990s, women are still grossly underrepresented in business. In 1997, only 5 percent of directors and 15 percent of managers were women. Although these figures are low, they represent a significant increase on previous years; but even a limited increase in numbers has to be treated with caution. Research from the Equal Opportunities Commission has shown that new managerial jobs for women are predominantly in new grades which are often inferior in pay and status to the jobs previously occupied by men (Coyle 1995). This is echoed by the fact that women managers and directors continue to be paid substantially less than their male counterparts: in 1995 the average woman director earned £56,446, as against average earnings for all directors of £78,692. Even when women are let into the boardroom, they occupy certain posts which are seen as being more appropriate for women, namely personnel, marketing and company secretary.

Change may come in the form of new management styles which are associated with women. Considerable emphasis is being given to so-called female management skills such as teamworking, negotiating, consensus management, the ability to handle several projects at one time, less hierarch-ical styles and interpersonal skills. Organizations such as the Institute of Management claim that these are the skills which women managers can bring to business, and moreover that these are the skills that are now in demand. There are difficulties, however, with such changes. For example, an emphasis on non-hierarchical management affords less opportunities for career advancement for women. Further, an emphasis on 'women's skills' essentializes all women and may in fact have a damaging effect on those women who do not conform to the stereotype. In addition, when such skills are no longer in vogue, women will again be sidelined.

However, it is cultural change which is required, and an emphasis on the development of new skills and new ways of working by women and men is an appropriate way to proceed. Such change must be managed and promoted in a way that is inclusive of all women and men, and will result in lasting change.

See also: women, employment patterns; women in parliament

Further reading

Coyle, A. (1995) *Women and Organisational Change*, Manchester: EOC.
Marshall, J. (1995) *Women Managers Moving On*, London: Routledge.

CLARE McGLYNN

women in parliament

The female suffrage struggle before the First World War led to important reforms in 1918. Among the provisions of the Representation of the People Act was the grant of the vote in Parliamentary elections to all women over thirty (the franchise was not extended to women aged twenty-one and upwards for another ten years). Under the Parliament (Qualification of Women) Act, women became eligible as MPs for the first time. Countess Markiewicz (née Constance Gore-Booth) contested Dublin St Patrick's in the 1918 election and gained a majority, but as she was imprisoned in Holloway at the time for Republican activities, she did not take her seat in the Commons. The first woman to do so was Lady Nancy Astor. A Virginian by birth, she won Plymouth Sutton for the Unionist Coalition on 28 November 1919 in a by-election called when her husband, MP for the constituency in 1911, entered the Lords on inheriting a viscountcy at his father's death. An irrepressible character who quickly put paid to suggestions that women might, literally or figuratively, be unable to make their voice heard in the Commons, Lady Astor was soon followed by a handful of other women MPs, mostly earnest intellectual politicians, with opinions tending left of centre. Though doubts about their capacity for the job were soon proved mistaken, the number of women MPs increased only gradually. From the time of Margaret Bondfield's appointment as Minister of Labour 1929, however, it became customary to include a woman in the government, generally with departmental duties perceived as involving a caring role.

Such typecasting has been abandoned in the post-Thatcher era. In 1992, Betty Boothroyd became the first female Speaker of the House of Commons. Discontent in the mid-1990s over the low proportion of women MPs led Labour to oblige certain constituency parties to select a candidate from an all-women short list. In the 1997 election, the number of women in Parliament doubled, to 119 (18 percent of the members, 24 percent of Labour MPs). Possibly distorted by the landslide, these figures, though the highest yet, are still far from reflecting the male/female balance in the population. Under the Life Peerages Act (1958), women became eligible for nomination to the House of Lords just like men, and the Peerage Act (1963) allowed hereditary peeresses in their own right to take their seats there as well.

See also: women, employment patterns; women in business

Further reading

Vallance, E. (1979) *Women in the House: A Study of Women Members of Parliament*. London: Athlone Press.

CHRISTOPHER SMITH

women in rock

A traditional aspect of the music industry is the emphasis on its masculinity. Sexism has always pervaded, from the organization of its workforce down to the lyrics of its songs. It means a struggle for nearly every woman working at all levels of the industry. Women are the exception to the rule: an addition to, rather than an integral part of, the music-making process. There continues to be fewer women than men working in the management, engineering and production aspects of the industry. Music is a way of expressing a social or political statement, and most pop and rock music is often a vehicle for the objectification of women, classing them as secondary and static. Women who make inroads into the industry often have to comply with these values, casting aside notions of individuality to become a part of the process of 'otherness' so readily set out for them, becoming 'female' musicians or 'all-girl' bands. They had their established roles as lead singers, backing vocalists or groupies. The 1960s saw a host of successful British performers, including Lulu, Sandie Shaw, Petula Clark, Dusty Springfield and Marianne Faithful, none of whom achieved full artistic control.

The video, now established as a crucial accompaniment to the song, with institutions such as MTV dedicating their whole airtime to music, means the image of the performer is as essential as the song itself. It is of cultural, social and economic significance that how a person looks can determine their income and status; hence the birth of the 'rock chick' and 'babe', manufactured acts such as Louise and the Spice Girls, Eternal and All Saints relying on their looks rather than on any specific talent to gain chart success. Innovative women are often assigned dual roles, or signified as unnatural. Kate Bush is the English eccentric, or just plain weird. Annie Lennox, Sharleen Spitieri from Texas and Justine Frischmann of Elastica all adopt the androgynous look. Cerys Matthews from Catatonia is largely defined in terms of her sex appeal. An A&R man at a major UK record company, when recently asked whether he was interested in signing an all-girl band replied 'No thank you, we already have one of those.' The industry is nevertheless having to readjust itself to female power, because, as Kurt Cobain so succinctly argued shortly before his suicide in 1994 'the future of rock belongs to women'.

See also: women in the arts and media

Further reading

O'Brien, L. (1995) *She Bop: The Definitive History of Women in Rock, Pop and Soul*, London: Penguin.

ALICE BENNETT

women in sport

Historically, women have struggled to be allowed to compete, attract television and sponsor interest, and bring their sporting excellence to public attention. But in the 1990s, the picture changed and, crucially, television and sponsors became interested.

Women's professional golf took a long time to develop in Britain (longer than the US or Europe), but tournaments were covered live by both BBC television and BBC **Radio 5** in 1996, and the quality newspapers devote considerable space to women's events. The first British female golfer to become a popular icon, Laura Davies (also once the world number one), is both talented and successful, and was mentioned in 1996 as a possible BBC Sports Personality of the Year. These advances have seen women golfers commentate for television and radio on men's tournaments, and over 12,000 spectators watched one day's play at the 1996 British Open.

Women's tennis has the jewel of the **Wimbledon** tournament televised each year, but the British game has had no success or genuine stars since Virginia Wade won Wimbledon in 1977; prize money remains about 75 percent of that of the men. British athletes have a better record: Sally Gunnell has won world and Olympic 400m hurdles medals, and is Britain's richest ever female athlete (from her numerous sponsorships), while Tessa Sanderson and Fatima Whitbread both won Olympic javelin medals in the 1980s, and Ashia Hansen took bronze in the 1996 Olympic long jump.

In other sports, British women do not fare badly: the hockey team were rather unlucky to only finish fourth at the 1996 Olympics, and the women's England cricket team have been world champions, although British swimming declined in performance and public profile after Sharron Davies retired. The football team has always struggled (mainly because so many other nations have full-time professional leagues), but women's matches were televised on **Channel 4** in the early 1990s, and international fixtures played at professional clubs (like Luton and Walsall). Women's football started developing its grassroots in the early 1990s, and many clubs in the national league linked up with men's teams; Liverpool Ladies take their name from Liverpool FC, who advertise the women's fixtures and results. A small breakthrough is the £250,000 invested by UK Living in the women's FA Cup over two years from 1996. That the tide has turned was equally clear in the £100,000 two-year sponsorship agreed for women's rugby in 1996.

However, the media depiction of sportswomen has remained problematic, and despite the women's ample professionalism and high performance, many commentators still repeatedly refer to the femininity of competitors rather than their performance. There have often been blunt remarks about the figure of female shotputters, about the women's family circumstances or the birth of a child, or women are simply called 'girls'. This regularly causes controversy, and suggests that male commentators have not accepted women as valid competitors. This is also evident in the general tendency for newspapers to just tag the women's results on the end of an article about the men. Feminist theorists call this 'symbolic annihilation', which is even more insidious than traditional stereotyping of masculinity and femininity, since it damages the mass interest and appeal that would allow women's sport to develop, and destroys the level of seriousness with which it is taken.

The fact that the BBC have broadcast women's golf live offers some hope, since without television sponsors will not become involved, and this gives governing bodies a good excuse to offer women less prize money (as at Wimbledon). But sponsors remain less interested in women's sports since they have lower profiles, and so women generally earn a good deal less from their career. They also have to make more financial and personal sacrifices, juggling the competing demands of their sport and their job or family. This of course assumes they are allowed to compete at all, with a predictable and rather sexist storm greeting the decision in 1996 to allow British women to box professionally for the first time.

As for spectating, there were signs in the mid-1990s that more women were watching professional sport, and clearly many sports became more accessible to women. But theories about the 'feminization' of crowds probably underestimate how many attended in the 1970s and 1980s, and the concept rests on rather dated notions of female passivity and gentleness.

Women as journalists however still face bigger problems: their numbers started increasing in the late 1980s, and women in the 1990s got bigger and more important events to cover, but no woman has yet presented the top sports programmes, like the Olympics, the **FA Cup** Final or Match of the Day. Female reporters had to endure considerable hostility and disbelief from male counterparts for years before they became accepted as serious journalists, notably in football, and certain sports appear off limits, with few female reporters at rugby or cricket. Radio has a better story to tell in this sense, with BBC Radio 5 Live featuring a number of female reporters at games (particularly from the early 1990s), and women regularly presenting the station's high-profile football and general sports programmes. Indeed, women have started producing such programmes as well.

As simple participants, women have been a target group for decades, with the Sports Council and others trying to entice more women, particularly from working-class and minority backgrounds, to become active in sport and leisure. But all these campaigns have failed to increase attendance rates amongst women (and especially from these specific target backgrounds), and it seems that family demands, considerations of money and time, and dominant cultural norms about 'femininity' and appropriate gender roles remain too pressing or strong for many women to feel able to participate. By the mid-1990s, it was suggested that the increased numbers of women

entering the workforce was affecting the numbers of female participants in sport and leisure.

See also: sport, racism in

Further reading

Birrell, A. and Cole, J. (eds) (1994) *Women, Sport and Culture*, Chicago: Human Kinetics.

REX NASH

women priests

The ordination of women received royal assent in November 1993, and the Church of England General Synod gave its approval in February of the following year. The first women priests were ordained in March 1994 amid both protests and celebrations; many male priests switched to the Catholic Church, while many feminists saw the move as the first positive improvement the Establishment had made in the rights of women since the Conservatives had come to office in 1979. The debate over whether women should be priests extends as far back as Thomas Aquinas's thirteenth-century view that, though ordination concerns the soul and not the body, women must not represent authority. After 1994, Catholic, Orthodox and some Anglican churches continue to deny women the right to become priests. The Vatican continues to hold by its 1976 encyclical, which maintained that only men can represent Christ.

See also: Anglican Church; Catholicism

PETER CHILDS

Women's Institute

Catering particularly for country women, the Women's Institute (WI) network in England and Wales (the Women's Rural Institutes are an equivalent in Scotland) offers social and educational facilities. Noted for its middle-class, middle-aged image, the organization moved to Britain from Canada in 1915. Still flourishing, and visible selling homemade produce and handicrafts at fairs and village halls, the WI has around 9,000 branches in Britain.

PETER CHILDS

women's press

Over the last forty years, women's magazines have changed from offering advice to wives and mothers about their families and homes, through the single-girl sexual revolution of the 1970s, to catering for diverse consumer markets in the 1990s.

The 1960s saw many more changes in the magazine world than the previous two decades. Many magazines folded, even more merged (because of various takeovers, particularly by the **Mirror Group**), and over a dozen new titles were launched (including *Honey, FAB, 19, Petticoat* and the best-selling *Nova,* 'the new magazine for the new kind of woman' of the 1960s). The launch of *Family Circle* in 1964 began the trend for selling magazines at supermarket checkouts; it became the top-selling women's monthly and even achieved the unheard of figure of a million sales. *Fashion* was (unsuccessfully) launched to challenge the hegemony of *Vogue, Queen* and *Harper's* (the latter two soon to merge as **Harpers and Queen**), and a new kind of magazine was created when a husband and wife team brought out *Slimming and Family Nutrition.*

The 1970s saw still more intense activity. Most notable was the new launch of *Cosmopolitan* in 1972 (incredibly, it was first sold in the USA in 1886). The principle behind the magazine, to encourage and enable liberated career girls to succeed for themselves and not through men, was forged by its first editor Helen Gurley Brown, author of *Sex and the Single Girl.* The frankness and intimate discussions that informed every topic were an instant success, and have of course been imitated countless times in magazines (*Company* was the most important in the 1970s) which have the same set of concerns: careers, relationships, body maintenance, fashion, health, food and most of all, sex. The previously cardinal subjects of the home and babies were discarded. When *Cosmopolitan* was launched in Britain, following unprecedented success in the USA, the first issue sold out on its first day (the second, which increased its print run

by one-half to 450,000, sold out in two days). In the same year the radical, unglossy, political and uncommercial *Spare Rib* was launched, describing itself as a 'women's liberation magazine'. The magazine folded in 1993, but its remit is still fulfilled by *Everywoman* and *Women's Review.* Other new magazines were *Look Now* (for the 18–24s), *Candida* (an upmarket weekly), *Personal* (on readers' sexual problems), *Good Life* (cashing in on the image of the television programme), *Womancraft* (promoting and catering for multiple hobbies) and numerous **teen magazines**.

In the 1980s, *Options* tried to catch the 'Cosmo Girl' before she turned to *Good Housekeeping;* **EMAP Maclaren** launched *Just Seventeen,* followed by *Looks; Working Woman* tried to cater for the professional 'realist'; *Chic* and *Candace* were aimed at black women; *In Store* focused on furnishings and shopping; *Cachet* was for women size 16 and above; *Essentials* was a compendium of practicality from index cards to cut-outs; *House Beautiful* in 1989 was stuffed with detail about the modern home for the millions who did not own the houses that appeared in *House & Garden;* and Rupert Murdoch launched *Elle* in the UK in 1985. Perhaps the big launch of the 1980s was the Spanish *Hello!,* which followed on from the success of *Prima, Bella, Best* and other German imports. By 1993 *Hello!* was selling nearly a half a million copies a week (the European invasion of the 1980s was completed by the UK launch of the French *Marie Claire*).

The 1990s has seen further fragmentation, specialization and proliferation. The latest kid on the block is the competitions and puzzles magazine *Take A Break* which, at 1.4 million copies, became the biggest selling women's weekly magazine in the 1990s. Sex became more pictorially explicit in *For Women, Women on Top* and *Bite.* Supermarkets began to produce their own checkout magazines, and *OK!* arrived to rival *Hello!.*

See also: feminist publishing houses; women in business

Further reading

Braithwaite, B. (1995) *Women's Magazines,* London: Peter Owen.

PETER CHILDS

Working Title

Working Title was formed in 1985 by Tim Bevan as a minor independent production company in the midst of Goldcrest, Palace and Zenith. The company financed such movies as **Frears**'s *My Beautiful Laundrette*. In 1992 Bevan was joined by Eric Fellner from Initial film and Television. Polygram bought up Working Title in the same year and input enough money to make nearly 100 new movies, from several of the Coen brothers films to *Four Weddings and A Funeral, Bean, Trainspotting* and *Notting Hill*. In 1998 Bevan and Fellner were honoured alongside nine others at Cannes in a new category of 'the world's best-respected producers'.

See also: Channel 4 Films

PETER CHILDS

Workshop Declaration

An agreement between the ACTT (Association of Cinematograph, Television and Allied Technicians) union, the British Film Institute (**BFI**) and **Channel 4**. The Declaration recognized a number of 'franchised workshops' for the production of work commissioned by Channel 4 at sub-normal rates with smaller crews. The aim of the Declaration was to stimulate the creation of community workshops based on race and gender as well as region. Partly as a consequence, black workshops such as Sankofa, Ceddo and **Black Audio Film Collective** were established in the mid-1980s. Women's workshops in Leeds and Sheffield were also franchised, as well as regional ones in Cardiff, Birmingham and the East Midlands.

PETER CHILDS

World Service

The World Service is the **BBC**'s globally broadcast radio station, with a distinguished history and formidable reputation (though now also working alongside a world channel for television news). An Empire Service in English was established in 1932, with broadcasting in Arabic starting in 1938 and then rapid expansion during the Second World War. The Service may now be heard throughout most of the world in one or more of over forty languages. It employs specialist staff including journalists, experts and translators.

There is evidence that the World Service is the most listened to international radio station, despite strong competition from Voice of America and Chinese and other broadcasters, and also the most trusted. The BBC's news coverage during the war was widely perceived as authoritative, balanced and reliable in depth, free from propaganda or national bias. Some of its war correspondents and their live coverage became widely known. Later, during the Cold War, listeners in Eastern Europe and elsewhere often turned where possible to the BBC for news about both the world and their own country, despite persistent attempts by some governments to prevent the reception of BBC broadcasts.

For many, the core of the World Service has been its broadcasters' close knowledge of and affection for the countries to which they broadcast and on which they report. Some correspondents have eloquently defended the Service as the core of the public service broadcasting ideal and objected to management changes and 'rationalization' in the BBC of the 1990s.

In addition to its wide range of news and current affairs, the Service carries English language teaching, and also many other kinds of programmes concerned with business, science, the arts, religion and sport. It can now be heard in Britain (though not straightforwardly) while a major development through digital technology is planned and the World Service has its own website, which may grow in importance. An associated monitoring service obtains and analyses information (available commercially) from a large range of foreign media sources.

The World Service has always been funded through the **Foreign Office** (which has offered advice on how much broadcasting time should be given in what languages to what countries) but has remained a successful example of 'arm's length' autonomy from government. A proposed major restructuring of the BBC was seen by many of its most famous and internationally recognized journalists and others as threatening the Service's quality and independence. After considerable parliamentary and press discussion, a BBC/ Foreign Office steering group was set up in 1996 to safeguard the World Service's quality and character.

See also: Radio 3; Radio 4

Further reading

Mansell, G. (1982) *Let Truth be Told: 50 Years of BBC External Broadcasting*, London: Weidenfeld & Nicholson.

MICHAEL GREEN

wrestling

Wrestling, a one-to-one unarmed combat sport in which the participant grapples with his opponent on a mat delimiting the field of play in an endeavour to defeat him by winning points for gaining various advantages or by scoring a 'fall' (that is, overcome him by forcing him to the ground), has a worldwide recorded history stretching back beyond antiquity. Sumo is a form of wrestling that makes much of its place within Japanese tradition; various rituals certainly add an air of solemnity, but not many Western spectators get beyond marvelling at the huge bulk of the fighters who clash only for very brief bouts in the course of championships that take place over a fortnight.

From the outset, the Olympic movement recognized two styles of wrestling, and in both combatants compete in a range of weight divisions, as in boxing, so that physical differences are to some degree evened out. Graeco-Roman wrestling, which is practised particularly in Scandinavia and Eastern Europe, observes rules that are based on those attributed to the legendary Theseus and observed in contests described in Homer's epics. The basic rule is that only the arms (and not the legs) may be used in an attempt to score a fall, and holds below the waist are not allowed. Freestyle wrestling involves no such prohibition, though kicking, biting, punching and dangerous holds are banned. Freestyle wrestling evolved from Lancastrian catch-as-can, which, like the Cumberland and Westmoreland and the Devon and Cornwall styles that still survive, was popular as both a participation and a spectator sport at country fairs.

Professional wrestling also follows the freestyle code. In the nineteenth century it had a status among sporting events similar to that of professional boxing nowadays, but standards were not maintained. The bouts, which are presented in the halls and on television with glitzy razz-ma-tazz, are ostensibly contested with savage ferocity and a total disregard for referee and rules as if reflecting unbridled rage and boundless personal animosity. But, in the eyes of many who note how rarely the fighters' seemingly unbridled ferocity results in serious injury, these bouts, like those of women's professional wrestling, appear not as genuine sporting encounters but rather more or less choreographed display combats designed to thrill fans whose noisy partisanship is all part of the entertainment.

See also: boxing

Further reading

Kent, G. (1968) *A Pictorial History of Wrestling*, London: Feltham.

CHRISTOPHER SMITH

Y

yachting

Yachting used to be known as 'the sport of kings' (possibly from Charles II's having been presented with a 'jacht' by the Dutch East India Company in 1660). Prince Philip continued the royal tradition into the 1960s by sailing a Dragon class yacht at Cowes on the Isle of Wight with Uffa Fox (the designer of the GP14). Today, UK yachting lacks the royal patronage it enjoyed, but Cowes week is still the premier annual yachting venue in Britain and, in 1990, attracted 661 boats in 19 classes. In the prewar period, local fishermen in ports around Britain were taken on by rich owners as 'paid hands' to race in prestige races. This reflected the money and class divide between owners and professional crew. Nowadays the sport has become more 'democratic' in that it is no longer only open to the rich, though amateur participants still have to contribute up to £25,000 for a passage in the major races listed below.

British yachting will always be associated with the America's Cup. In 1851 the schooner *America* beat all-comers in a race around the Isle of Wight. Thomas Lipton was the last British individual rich enough to mount a challenge for the return of this cup, in the 1930s. In recent years commercially sponsored syndicates led by businessmen, notably Peter de Savary, have unsuccessfully attempted to regain it.

The *Observer* Single-Handed Transatlantic Race (OSTAR) began in 1960, but arguably yachting did not impinge on the national consciousness, until the solo circumnavigations of Sir Francis Chichester and Sir Alec Rose in 1966–7. Television coverage obviously contributed to this. Since then, commercial sponsorship has made a huge difference in yachting. Each of the major international races is sponsored by a commercial organization, and each boat carries the advertising slogans of its sponsor. This has led to a proliferation of races such as the BT Global Challenge 2000/2001, the Whitbread Round the World Race (sponsored by Volvo for 2000/2001). The website for the 1998 Whitbread Round The World Race was visited by one million people per day.

Yachting in Britain is still dominated by its exclusive traditional clubs such as the Royal Ocean Racing Club, which holds the Admiral's Cup, and the Royal Yacht Squadron at Cowes which was founded in 1812. To earn the 'Royal' title, clubs' members must own yachts over a certain tonnage.

See also: sailing

MIKE STORRY

Yates, Peter

b. 1929, Aldershot

Film-maker

Peter Yates is a versatile director who has covered numerous subjects utilizing different styles. Two of his early British films, *Summer Holiday* (1963) and *Robbery* (1967), reflect different aspects of English cultural life in the 1960s. The former, a musical starring Cliff Richard, romanticized teenagers' newfound freedom, while the latter, based on the Great Train Robbery, aimed to uncover the world of British organized crime. The car chase in *Robbery* led to Yates directing the thriller *Bullitt* (1968), which starred Steve McQueen. Numerous films followed in the 1970s including an Oscar nomination as Best Director for his cycling movie *Breaking Away* (1979), a story depicting class conflict in America. He received a similar nomination for *The Dresser* (1983).

GUY OSBORN
STEVE GREENFIELD

Yiddish

With about 4 million speakers worldwide, Yiddish is the language of Eastern and Central European Jews and their descendants. Jewish English, in its most common variety, has elements of Yiddish and Hebrew, introducing neologisms such as *nosh* and *shlep*. Jewish English has been important to many English and American writers such as Dan Jacobson, Israel Zingwill, Joseph Heller, Saul Bellow and Philip Roth.

See also: Jewish communities

PETER CHILDS

Yorke, Rosenberg and Mardall

The YRM partnership was founded in 1944 by F.R.S. Yorke (a pioneer of modernism in Britain), Eugene Rosenberg and Cyril Mardall. An early routine European modern style gave way to an espousal of the Chicago style. Their rebuilding of St Thomas's Hospital (1963) proposed an open 'campus' layout of rectangular buildings arranged at right angles. A 'house style' emerged here, with the white tiles used in the cubic ward block and linear nurses' home being employed extensively in YRM's buildings of the late 1960s, for example, at Warwick University. Their airport oeuvre ranges from the black, steel-framed Cargo Agents' building and offices at Heathrow, to Gatwick, where the elegant, patrician architecture serves contemporary society perfectly.

HILARY GRAINGER

youth television

The arrival of satellite and cable technology, combined with broadcasting deregulation, meant that in the 1980s, British broadcasters were searching for new markets to exploit. Youth television was designed to attract 16–25 year-olds, a socio-economic group perceived to have a relatively high disposable income. Youth television programmes such as *Network 7*, *The Tube*, *Snub TV* and *The Word* contained information on youth culture, pop music and show business gossip, and were distinctive in their use of fast editing, unconventional camera angles and computer graphics. While some have praised youth television for its lively style, it has been criticized for amateurism and for patronising young people.

See also: MTV; pop television; teenage and youth programming; television, children's

STUART BORTHWICK

youth theatre

Groups and organizations whose aim is to engage young people in theatre-related activities outside formal education. The National Youth Theatre was established in 1956 by Michael Croft, whose former pupils wanted him to continue staging Shakespearean productions. Its popularity led to the formation of other youth theatres, with the aim of classical drama professionally produced in conventional theatre spaces.

In 1959, actor Ewen Hooper founded the Greenwich Young Peoples' Theatre (GYPT), bringing together community theatre companies, youth theatre, professional repertory theatre and theatre in education. The County Youth Theatre, founded by drama adviser Silas Harvey in 1963, took a more experimental approach, comprising devised work and productions by modern writers.

The popularity and success of youth arts saw a dramatic growth in the 1970s and 1980s. Initiated or supported by the youth service and youth-orientated community arts/theatre groups, their philosophy hinges on an approach to working practices centred on young people. As for the inclusion of amateur groups (i.e. the junior sections of amateur dramatic societies or groups developed from private stage schools), this is still disputed, largely due to definitions of financial status, working practices and approaches, social and personal education, and, indeed, the actual term 'amateur'.

Most participants in youth theatre are aged twelve to twenty-four, are predominately white European (about 90 percent), and around two-thirds are female. The next largest group, African/Caribbean, accounts for approximately 5 per cent); the lowest (about 1.5 per cent) is Asian Other, while the number of participants with a disability has increased.

An estimated 700 youth theatres cater for more than 50,000 participants. Since 1991, funding has been reduced by approximately 20 per cent as a result of cuts in local authority education and youth service budgets. Former members of youth theatre have gone on to jobs as workshop leaders, to take performing arts courses and become involved in film, television and theatre work. The National Association of Youth Theatres, an educational charity formed in 1982, sums it up thus: '[Youth Theatre offers] the opportunity for young people to gain invaluable practical, vocational and social skills, to explore themselves and the society in which they live.'

See also: community theatre; devising

Further reading

Ripley, N. and Canning, P. (eds) (1996) *Strategies for Success*, Birmingham: National Association of Youth Theatres (a comprehensive publication, useful to all those involved, whether as members or organizers, workers in education or funding).

CAROLE BALDOCK

Index

Page numbers in **bold** indicate references to the main entry.